LONDON - WORLD CITY
1800-1840

The exhibition is presented under the patronage of
Her Majesty Queen Elizabeth II
and the President of the Federal Republic of Germany,
Dr. Richard von Weizsäcker.

LONDON – WORLD CITY
1800–1840

Edited by Celina Fox

1992
YALE UNIVERSITY PRESS
NEW HAVEN & LONDON

in association with

THE MUSEUM OF LONDON

Editor's acknowledgements:

In the preparation of this catalogue the editor would like to thank the working party and all the writers of the essays and catalogue entries who generously contributed their time and expertise. She would also like to thank Aurel Bongers of Verlag Aurel Bongers and John Nicoll of Yale University Press for their patience in seeing this work to fruition. The following were crucial to the editorial and photographic production: Mary Carruthers, Edwina Ehrman, Lorraine Germain, Penny Lane, Caroline Lucas, Maria Reitinger and Shirley Waller. At the Museum of London, the conservation and photographic departments made a substantial visual contribution. Finally, the editor wishes to thank Jürgen Schultze, Valerie Cumming and Chris Ellmers for their unstinted support and understanding over many months.

The exhibition is mounted by and the catalogue published with the assistance of Kulturstiftung Ruhr, Essen

Exhibition dates: 6 June-8 November 1992, Villa Hügel, Essen

Front and endpapers: G. Scharf, *A View of High Street Southwark*, 1830. Cat. No. 151

Set in Linotron Garamond by SX Composing Ltd, Rayleigh, Essex
Printed in Germany by Graphische Kunstanstalt Bongers, Recklinghausen

Library of Congress Catalog Card Number: 92-50447
ISBN 0-300-05284-7

The Kulturstiftung Ruhr is grateful to the photographers, especially those of The Museum of London, for their invaluable help and support.

© Copyright by:
Her Majesty Queen Elizabeth II; Ackermann & Johnson, London; Bank of England (Fotos Raymond Fortt Studios), London; Birmingham Museums and Art Gallery; H. Blairman & Sons, West Lothian; The Bridgeman Art Library Ltd, London; The Royal Pavilion, Art Gallery and Museums, Brighton; City of Bristol Museum & Art Gallery; British Architectural Library/RIBA, London; British Museum, London; Geremy Butler Photography, London; Richard Caspole, Yale Center for British Art; The Institution of Civil Engineers, Westminster; A. C. Cooper Ltd., London; Courtauld Institute of Art, Maidstone, Kent; Fotos Prudence Cuming Associates Ltd., London; Derby Museums and Art Gallery; Royal Crown Derby Museum (Fotos Northern Counties Photographers), Stoke-on-Trent; Courtesy of the Dyson Perrins Museum, Worcester, England; Master and Fellows of Emmanuel College, Cambridge; e.t. archive, London; Fitzwilliam Museum, Cambridge; P. J. Gates (Photography) Ltd., London; Mark Gudgeon, London; Guildhall Art Gallery, London; Guildhall Library, London; Jonathan Harris, Works of Art, London (Foto John Hammond, London); Lloyd's of London; Don Manning, Cambridge; Paul Mellon Centre, Photo Archive, London; John Murray Ltd., London; Museum of London; National Maritime Museum, Greenwich, London; National Portrait Gallery, London; City of Newcastle upon Tyne, City Repro Photo Unit; Philadelphia Museum of Art, The John H. McFadden Collection; Photographic Records Ltd., London; Public Record Office, London; Mandy Reynolds A.B.I.P.P.-Intec, Bath u. Hattingen; Royal Academy of Arts, London; Royal Astronomical Society, London; The Royal Institution, London; Royal Ontario Museum, Toronto; Board of Trustees of the Science Museum, London; Graham Snape, Winsford; The Trustees of Sir John Soane's Museum, London; Society of Antiquaries of London; Spode Museum Trust Collection; City Museums, Stoke-on-Trent; The Tate Gallery, London; The Marquess of Tavistock and the Trustees of the Bedford Estates; Thorvaldsens Museum, Copenhagen; United Grand Lodge of England; University of Bristol, Arts Faculty Photographic Unit, Bristol; University College, London; Vestry House Museum, London; The Board of Trustees of the Victoria & Albert Museum, London; Elke Walford, Hamburg; John Waterman, Fox-Waterman Photography Ltd., London; Josiah Wedgwood & Sons Ltd., Barlaston/Stoke-on-Trent; Dean & Chapter of Westminster; Ronald White, Maidstone, Kent; The Woodbridge Company, Toronto; Wordsworth Trust, Grasmere, Cumbria; Yale Center for British Art, New Haven

CONTENTS

Exhibition Organisation ... 6

Preface ... 7

Working Party ... 8

Essay Writers ... 8

Catalogue Entry Writers ... 9

Lenders ... 10

Celina Fox
INTRODUCTION: A VISITOR'S GUIDE TO
LONDON WORLD CITY, 1800-40 ... 11

Martin Daunton
LONDON AND THE WORLD ... 21

Valerie Cumming
PANTOMIME AND PAGEANTRY:
THE CORONATION OF GEORGE IV ... 39

Andrew Saint
THE BUILDING ART OF THE FIRST INDUSTRIAL
METROPOLIS ... 51

J. Mordaunt Crook
METROPOLITAN IMPROVEMENTS
JOHN NASH AND THE PICTURESQUE ... 77

Simon Jervis
RUDOLPH ACKERMANN ... 97

Clive Wainwright
PATRONAGE AND THE APPLIED ARTS IN
EARLY NINETEENTH-CENTURY LONDON ... 111

*Iwan Morus, Simon Schaffer
and Jim Secord*
SCIENTIFIC LONDON ... 129

Ian Jenkins
'ATHENS RISING NEAR THE POLE':
LONDON, ATHENS AND THE IDEA OF
FREEDOM ... 143

Peter Funnell
THE LONDON ART WORLD ... 155

Andrew Wilton
PAINTING IN LONDON IN THE EARLY
NINETEENTH CENTURY ... 167

Marilyn Butler
HIDDEN METROPOLIS ... 187

Iain Mackintosh
DEPARTING GLORIES OF THE BRITISH
THEATRE ... 199

H. T. Dickinson
RADICAL CULTURE ... 209

EXHIBITION CATALOGUE

London World City ... 226

Urban Infrastructure ... 290

Ackermann's Repository of Arts ... 328

Science and Technology ... 342

Watercolours ... 353

Household Furniture and Interior Decoration ... 382

The Shows of London ... 418

Painting and Sculpture ... 447

Literary London ... 477

Silver and Jewellery, Porcelain, Watches and Scientific
Instruments ... 494

Silver ... 494

Porcelain ... 504

Watch and Clock Making ... 524

Scientific Instruments ... 539

Theatre and Music ... 544

The Culture of Reform ... 556

Clubland ... 588

The New Age ... 606

Bibliography ... 616

Exhibitions ... 623

PREFACE

The previous exhibitions held by the Kulturstiftung Ruhr featured three major European cities – Dresden, Prague and St. Petersburg – whose names today still evoke vivid images of a resplendent courtly tradition.

This year's exhibition is devoted to a world city of different character and prestige. It documents four decisive decades between 1800 and 1840 in the history of London, Europe's first modern trading, financial and industrial centre. London was to set standards for all emerging major European cities, not just in this commercial context but also as a focus of fundamental political change in the reorientation of aspirations, substance and power between the nobility and the confident middle classes. With the concentration of industrial, economic and military power came a blossoming of art and culture which demonstrated a new confidence commensurate with the country's imperial role beyond European boundaries.

To represent such an important epoch, however sketchily, is a demanding challenge. An additional dimension is provided by the venue, Villa Hügel in Essen, the former residence of one of Germany's great industrial dynasties whose rise in the nineteenth century was connected, albeit marginally, with that flourishing period in Britain's economic history.

The decades in which London developed into Europe's first industrial metropolis also marked the beginnings of the industrialisation of the Ruhr. In November 1811 Friedrich Krupp and two partners established a factory in Essen 'for the making of English cast steel and all products therefrom'. Alfred Krupp, who on the death of his father was put in charge of the small firm, travelled to England in 1838/39 in order primarily to expand his knowledge of the manufacture of English cast steel, which at that time could not be matched for quality. His visits to London, Birmingham, Liverpool and Manchester were not without consequences for the emergence of Krupp as an international enterprise and Essen as a major industrial city.

Such an exhibition as this would not have been possible without the close cooperation of many institutes and scholars and the generosity of numerous private and public lenders. My thanks therefore go to the ladies and gentlemen of the working party, who had to take the expert decisions, and the staff members in Britain and Germany on whose assistance we could always rely. Without the committed endeavours of our closest partner, the Museum of London, and their friendly cooperation, it would hardly have been possible to translate the idea of this exhibition into reality. The Director of the Museum Max Hebditch, his deputy Valerie Cumming, and in particular the Curator Dr. Celina Fox, who was charged with the task of preparing and organising the exhibition at the London end and had the heaviest load to bear, spared no effort to ensure that the common objective was reached. I also express thanks to the British Council in London and Cologne, especially Director of the Fine Arts Department, Henry Meyric Hughes, for having vigorously supported the plans of the Kulturstiftung Ruhr right from the outset.

Very special thanks are expressed by the Kulturstiftung Ruhr to the numerous lenders, including the Royal Collection, the public and private museums, institutes and institutions and the private owners whose kind cooperation has made it possible to organise this unique exhibition. Thanks to their generosity numerous valuable items can be put on public display for the first time in Essen.

May I express my very deep personal gratitude to Her Majesty Queen Elizabeth II of Great Britain and Northern Ireland and Dr Richard von Weizsäcker, President of the Federal Republic of Germany, for acting as joint patrons of the exhibition.

The Executive Committee and Advisory Council of the Kulturstiftung Ruhr hope that on this occasion too the endeavours of all concerned will be rewarded by the public's response.

Prof. Dr. H. C. Berthold Beitz

WORKING PARTY

CELINA FOX (Chairman), The Museum of London

CHRIS ELLMERS, The Museum of London

RALPH HYDE, Guildhall Library, Corporation of London

LINDSAY STAINTON, British Museum

CLIVE WAINWRIGHT, Victoria and Albert Museum

ANDREW WILTON, Tate Gallery

CATALOGUE ESSAY WRITERS

CELINA FOX, Keeper, Paintings, Prints and Drawings, The Museum of London

MARTIN DAUNTON, Astor Professor of British History, University College London

VALERIE CUMMING, Deputy Director, The Museum of London

ANDREW SAINT, Historian, London Division, English Heritage

J. MORDAUNT CROOK, Professor of Architectural History, Bedford and Royal Holloway College, University of London

SIMON JERVIS, Director, Fitzwilliam Museum, Cambridge

CLIVE WAINWRIGHT, Research Department, Victoria and Albert Museum

IWAN MORUS, SIMON SCHAFFER AND JIM SECORD, Lecturers in the History and Philosophy of Science, University of Cambridge

IAN JENKINS, Assistant Keeper, Greek and Roman Antiquities, British Museum

PETER FUNNELL, Curator of the Nineteenth-Century Collection, National Portrait Gallery

ANDREW WILTON, Keeper of the British Collection, Tate Gallery

MARILYN BUTLER, King Edward VII Professor of English Literature, University of Cambridge

IAIN MACKINTOSH, Theatre Designer and Historian

H. T. DICKINSON, Richard Lodge Professor of British History, University of Edinburgh

CATALOGUE ENTRY WRITERS

DANIEL ABRAMSON (DA)
Department of Fine Arts, Harvard
University

ANNEKE BAMBERY (AB)
Derby Museum and Art Gallery

MALCOLM BEASLEY (MB)
Natural History Museum

J. A. BENNET (JB)
Whipple Museum of the History of
Science, Cambridge University

JONATHAN BETTS (JDB)
National Maritime Museum

GAYE BLAKE ROBERTS (GBR)
Wedgwood Museum

CYPRIAN PETER BLAMIRES (CPB)
University College London

DAVID BLAYNEY BROWN (DBB)
Tate Gallery

BRIAN BOWERS (BB)
Science Museum

ROGER BRIDGMAN (RB)
Science Museum

NEIL BURTON (NB)
English Heritage

MICHAEL CHRIMES (MC)
Institution of Civil Engineers

ROBERT COPELAND (RC)
Spode Museum

MATTHEW CRASKE (MJC)
University College London

JOHN CULME (JC)
Sotheby's

VALERIE CUMMING (VC)
The Museum of London

ANNA DATTA (AD)
Natural History Museum

NICK DAWTON (ND)
University College London

RICHARD DURACK (RD)
Science Museum

ANN EATWELL (AE)
Victoria and Albert Museum

RICHARD EDGCUMBE (RE)
Victoria and Albert Museum

EDWINA EHRMAN (EE)
The Museum of London

CHRIS ELLMERS (CE)
The Museum of London

WENDY EVANS (WE)
The Museum of London

JOHN FORD (JF)

JILL FORD (MF)

CELINA FOX (CF)
The Museum of London

HARRY FROST (HF)
Dyson Perrins Museum

BEN GAMMON (BG)
Science Museum

RICHARD GODFREY (RG)
Sotheby's

ROSEMARY HARDEN (RJH)
Bath Museum Service

TIMOTHY HAYES (TH)
The Museum of London

PETER HINGLEY (PH)
Royal Astronomical Society

RALPH HYDE (RH)
Guildhall Library

SALLY JEFFERY (SJ)
Corporation of London

IAN JENKINS (IJ)
British Museum

PETER KAELLGREN (PK)
Royal Ontario Museum

JOHN KEYWORTH (JK)
Bank of England

KRISTEN LIPPINCOTT (KL)
National Maritime Museum

GHISLAINE LAWRENCE (GL)
Science Museum

IAIN MACKINTOSH (IM)

PETER MANN (PM)
Science Museum

JOANNA MARSCHNER (JM)
Court Dress Collection

RICHARD MAUDE (RM)

I. C. MCILWAINE (ICM)
University College London

JAMES MOSLEY (JMM)
St Bride Printing Library

TESSA MURDOCH (TM)
Victoria and Albert Museum

ANTHONY NORTH (AN)
Victoria and Albert Museum

M. J. ORBELL (MJO)
Baring Brothers and Co Ltd

MICHAEL RHODES (MR)
The Museum of London

MARGARET RICHARDSON (MAR)
Sir John Soane's Museum

JOHN ROBINSON (JR)
Science Museum

ANDREW SAINT (AS)
English Heritage

PHILIP SAUNDERS (PS)
Corporation of London

SIMON SCHAFFER (SS)
Department of the History and
Philosophy of Science, Cambridge
University

JANET SEMPLE (JES)
University College London

WENDY SHERIDAN (WS)
Science Museum

DEBORAH SKINNER (DS)
City Museum and Art Gallery, Stoke-on-
Trent

LINDSAY STAINTON (LS)
British Museum

DORON SWADE (DDS)
Science Museum

DAVID THOMPSON (DRT)
British Museum

ERIC TURNER (ET)
Victoria and Albert Museum

JOHN TWITCHETT (JT)
Royal Crown Derby Museum

ROBERT UPSTONE (RU)
Tate Gallery

JONATHAN VOACK (JV)
Wellington Museum

CLIVE WAINWRIGHT (CW)
Victoria and Albert Museum

IAN WARRELL (IW)
Tate Gallery

ALEXANDRA WEDGWOOD (AW)
Palace of Westminster

ALEX WERNER (APW)
The Museum of London

JANE WESS (JW)
Science Museum

STEPHEN WILDMAN (SGW)
Birmingham Museums and Art Gallery

ROBERT WOOF (RW)
Wordsworth Trust

MICHAEL WRIGHT (MW)
Science Museum

HILARY YOUNG (HY)
Victoria and Albert Museum

LENDERS

The Kulturstiftung Ruhr would like to express deep gratitude to the following lenders to the Exhibition:

Her Majesty Queen Elizabeth II

The Abbotsford Collection

Arthur Ackermann and Son Ltd

Dr David Alexander

The Athenaeum

The Governor and Company of the Bank of England

Barclays Bank plc

Baring Brothers and Co Ltd

Mr Bob Bates

Bath Museums Service

Birmingham Museums and Art Gallery

The Trustees of the Bowood Collection

The Royal Pavilion, Art Gallery and Museums, Brighton

Bristol City Museum and Art Gallery

British Architectural Library, Royal Institute of British Architects

The Trustees of the British Museum

The Burghley House Collection

The Institution of Civil Engineers

The Worshipful Company of Clockmakers

The Court Dress Collection

Coutts and Co

The Crown Estate and Institute of Directors

Derby Museums and Art Gallery

The Dickens House Museum

The Diocese of London

Alfred Dunhill and Son Ltd

The Dyson Perrins Museum Trust

Lord Egremont

The Master and Fellows of Emmanuel College, Cambridge

The Faringdon Collection Trust

The Syndics of the Fitzwilliam Museum, Cambridge

Mr John Ford

The Garrick Club

Mr Jonathan Gestetner

Christopher Gibbs Ltd

Mr Richard Godfrey

Guildhall Art Gallery, Corporation of London

Guildhall Library, Corporation of London

Gunnersbury Park Museum

Hamburg Kunsthalle

Mr John Hardy

Jonathan Harris Works of Art

Mr Laurence Harvey

The Principal, Fellows and Scholars of Jesus College, Oxford

Laing Art Gallery

Lloyd's of London

The Lord Major of London

Mr Iain Mackintosh

Maidstone Museum and Art Gallery

The Raymond Mander and Joe Mitchenson Theatre Collection

Mr Richard Maude

Mr Christopher Mendez

John Murray

The Museum of London

The National Maritime Museum

The National Portrait Gallery

National Railway Museum

The National Trust

The Natural History Museum

His Grace The Duke of Northumberland and the Northumberland Estates Trustees

Philadelphia Museum of Art: McFadden Collection

The Worshipful Company of Makers of Playing Cards

Public Record Office

Mr Robin Reilly

The Earl of Rosebery

Royal Academy of Arts

Royal Astronomical Society

The Royal Crown Derby Museum

Royal Institution of Great Britain

Royal National Theatre

Royal Ontario Museum

The Governors of the Royal Shakespeare Company

Sadler's Wells Trust Ltd

The Board of Trustees of the Science Museum

The Trustees of Sir John Soane's Museum

Society of Antiquaries of London

The Spoke Museum Trust Collection

Dr Gavin Stamp

Stoke-on-Trent City Museum and Art Gallery

The President and Council of the Royal College of Surgeons of England

Board of Hunterian Trustees, the Royal College of Surgeons of England

Tate Gallery

The Marquess of Tavistock and the Trustees of the Bedford Estates

The Times

Theatre Royal, Drury Lane Archives

Thorvaldsens Museum

Library and Museum of the United Grand Lodge of England

University College, London

University of London Library

Vestry House Museum

Trustees of the Victoria and Albert Museum

Victoria University of Manchester, Tabley House Collection

The Trustees of the Wedgwood Museum

The Wellington Museum

The Dean and Chapter of Westminster

His Grace the Duke of Westminster

Palace of Westminster

Whipple Museum of the History of Science

Mr Humphrey Whitbread

Dr Williams's Library

The Wordsworth Trust

Yale Center for British Art

Young and Co's Brewery plc

and Private Owners who wish to remain anonymous

INTRODUCTION

A VISITOR'S GUIDE TO LONDON WORLD CITY, 1800–40

Celina Fox

In his first major popular success, *The Pickwick Papers* (1836–37) Charles Dickens introduced the character of 'Count Smorltork . . . the famous foreigner – gathering material for his great work on England' to an affable Mr Pickwick:

> 'Have you been long in England?'
> 'Long – ver long time – fortnight – more.'
> 'Do you stay here long?'
> 'One week.'
> 'You will have enough to do,' said Mr Pickwick, smiling, 'to gather all the material you want, in that time.'
> 'Eh, they are gathered,' said the Count.
> 'Indeed!' said Mr Pickwick.
> 'They are here,' added the Count, tapping his forehead, significantly. 'Large book at home – full of notes – music, picture, science, potry, poltic; all tings.'
> 'The word politics, sir,' said Mr Pickwick, 'comprises, in itself, a difficult study of no inconsiderable magnitude.'
> 'Ah!' said the Count, drawing out the tables again, 'ver good – fine words to begin a chapter. Chapter forty-seven. Poltics. The word poltic surprises by himself –' . . . And down went Mr Pickwick's remark, in Count Smorltork's tablets, with such variations and additions as the Count's exuberant fancy suggested, or his imperfect knowledge of the language, occasioned.[1]

Our attempt here to present an exhibition on London in the first decades of the nineteenth century, to distil its complexity into a series of galleries, is perhaps as foolhardy an endeavour today as Count Smorltork's was then to reduce the whole country to a series of chapters. There is the same potential for misunderstanding across different languages and different cultures, and a relative shortage of time and space to do justice to the subject. But equally, the exhibition has been embarked upon in a similar spirit of enthusiastic inquiry. Smorltork was Dickens's wicked parody of a stream of foreigners who came to Britain, and above all to London, between 1800 and 1840, and who felt inspired to write about their experiences both for a home audience and even in translation for the indigenous population. Why did they feel this need? What was so different, so novel, so curious about their adventures that persuaded them to set pen to paper? The organisation of this exhibition seeks to answer these questions by following those paths which the visitor trod and remarked upon, and resurrecting those sights which astonished, impressed or depressed him. It groups together the products of the age in a way which we hope suggests how they were first seen, and in the context they were first understood. Overall, it is an attempt to comprehend London during its most rapid period of change, when in its size and internationalism it set the pace for all other world cities to come. It is a means, we hope, towards an increased appreciation of London, both then and now, for its identity today is most profoundly influenced by its development in this period.

The themes in the exhibition have emerged not only, of course, from such immediate sources but from the subsequent accumulation of layers of historical scholarship. We started from the assumption that as all artefacts are historical phenomena – the product of human intention – historical knowledge is not only needed to understand and appreciate them, but even in order to *see* them properly. We did not want to present the exhibits as a set of disembodied products and achievements for deracinated contemplation, devoid of any sense of the structure and process that produced them. Both the essay writers and the working party responsible for the selection of exhibits endeavoured to make connections between, for instance, on the broadest level, taste and economics, politics and culture. We have tried to clarify the historical analysis that underlay our judgements, to explain our criteria for selection, the significance of the choice, and the intellectual justification for the decisions we made.

Thanks to the extraordinary generosity of the Kulturstiftung Ruhr, it has been possible to bring the multifarious strands together on a scale as never before, and we hope the questions we raise and ideas we present will open up long-term benefits for scholarship throughout Europe and further afield. Some may criticise the breadth of our choice, encompassing as it does the fine and decorative arts, social display, the theatre and literature, architecture, technology and science, economics and politics. But we wanted to reflect the age in which the divisions – at their crudest, between art and science – were

---

1 Dickens 1836-37, chapter 15.

still not clear, where culture had not yet been removed to a ghetto independent of the rest of life. Art (*Kunst*) in the early nineteenth century still meant something like technology or trade. The notion that literature, the visual arts and music had something in common which set them apart from mere technical crafts, and that their products were in some way self-contained, was being developed in eighteenth-century German thought but it would not have been widely recognised in London, the most pragmatic of capitals, devoted principally to the pursuit of money, to lining the pocket rather than embellishing the soul.

Let us first admit, however, that there are certain aspects of the city that we cannot hope to project, for they concern subjective atmospheric impressions and feelings half submerged. Undoubtedly, what struck the foreign visitor most forcefully was the size of London and concomitantly, the alienating effect this had on the individual – that sudden panic over the loss of identity that occurs on first arriving in a great city. It was the biggest city anybody had ever seen. Despite willing himself not to be impressed, Heinrich Heine wrote to Friedrich Merckel on 23 April 1827: 'London has surpassed all my expectations in respect of its vastness; but I have lost myself.'[2] The artist Johann David Passavant wrote of his visit in 1831, 'London itself seems a vast desert of men and houses, where a foreigner may feel himself most truly alone.'[3]

And almost as quickly, visitors remarked upon the horrible climate (something almost impossible to recreate) – the smoke, the dirt, the damp, the fog, which accentuated the dissociation of one man from another. For the French-born American Louis Simond, who visited England in 1810–11, a 'uniform dinginess seemed to pervade everything'.[4] The anonymous German author of *Letters from Albion* written in the years 1810–13 advised his friend not to look upwards, 'for there you see nothing but the naked brick fronts of the houses all blackened by the smoke of coal'.[5] The Danish traveller, J. A. Andersen, found that the 'gloomy solemnity' of the houses in London presented a 'very ungrateful contrast' to the chequered gaiety of Copenhagen.[6] Heine was more precise: the 'barrack-like' blocks of houses were a brown olive-green colour, on account of the damp and coal smoke.[7] The feeling of living in a twilight zone was experienced by all those who passed the winter and spring in the capital. Simond noted that the smoke 'terminates the length of every street with a fixed grey mist, receding as you advance'.[8] On 5 November 1827, Prince Pückler Muskau reported to his wife that such a fog covered the whole town that he could not see to breakfast without candles.[9] According to Richard Rush, who had just arrived in

London as American ambassador, on New Year's Eve 1817 the fog was so thick that the shops in Bond Street had their lights on by noon. He could not see people in the street from his windows, 'I am tempted to ask, how the English became great with so little daylight?'.[10] On 15 May 1835 Professor Frederick von Raumer recorded:

> Thick fog, rain; everything cold, wet, grey, miserable. On my complaining of this in company, a gentleman maintained that there had not been a fog in London for the last two months; that nobody thought of calling it foggy, so long as he could see the houses of the other side of the street by day, or the lamps burning by night. Another added, that last winter, out of a party of two-and-twenty invited to dine in the Regent's Park, only four arrived; all the others were afraid of losing their way.[11]

Such impressions did not obscure for long the city's underlying character of financial and commercial might. For Heine, London was the place for a philosopher, not a poet – a sentiment with which, as Marilyn Butler makes clear, the English Romantic poets would have concurred. If a philosopher were to stand on Cheapside in the heart of the City, he asserted, as waves of humanity dashed around him, he would hear the pulse-beat of the world, for London was the 'active, mighty, right hand' of the world. But the experience was not for the poet: 'This bare reality of all things, this colossal uniformity, this mechanical movement, this sour-visagedness of joy itself, this over-worked London oppresses the fancy and rends asunder the heart.'[12] For von Raumer, the noise and bustle of the streets had a totally distinct character: 'in London it is always the tumult and clamour of business' (compared with the 'obtrusiveness and petulance of vanity' in Paris).[13] On a brief escape to historic Windsor in search of the poetical, he reflected,

> In the rich, busy, hurrying London, I have often longed for the quiet of decaying Venice – often looked

2   Heine, quoted in Stigand 1875, vol. 1, p.276.
3   Passavant 1836, vol. 1, p.13.
4   Simond 1817, vol. 1, p.22.
5   *Letters from Albion* 1814, vol. 1, p.79.
6   Andersen 1809, vol. 1, p.7.
7   Heine, *English Fragments* quoted in Stigand 1875, vol. 1, p.289.
8   Simond 1817, vol. 1, p.48.
9   Pückler Muskau 1832, vol. 4, p.231.
10   Rush 1833, p.29.
11   Raumer 1836, vol. 1, pp.238-39.
12   Heine, *English Fragments* quote in Stigand 1875, vol. 1, p.287.
13   Raumer 1836, vol. 1, p.10 (24 March 1835).

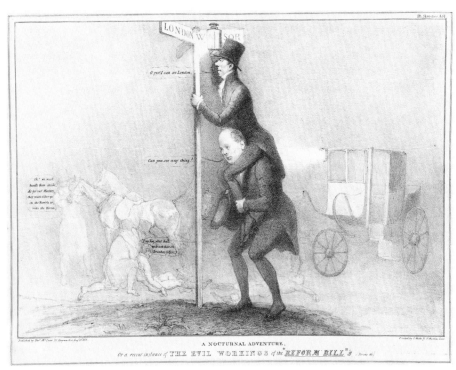

G. Hunt after M. Egerton, *A Thoroughbred November & London Particular*, aquatint, 1825. British Museum Satires No.15004. The Museum of London

H. B. (John Doyle), *A Nocturnal Adventure*, lithograph 1831. British Museum Satires No.16763. Lords Brougham and Plunket try to get back to London in the fog, after too much drink at Windsor. The Museum of London

for a tinge of poetic melancholy, or of fantastic originality. In vain; no trace was to be found even in society. Always the sharp outline of reality; the mathematics of life; the arts of calculating, of gaining, of governing.[14]

Few found this hard-nosed business capital without soul immediately attractive. On a visit to the Royal Exchange on 10 October 1826, Pückler Muskau reported that it 'and the whole City, have a repulsive sinister aspect, which almost reminds one of the restless and comfortless throng of the spirits of the damned'. The celebrated Lloyd's Coffee House on the upper storey of the Exchange, home of maritime insurance, he found to be 'the dirtiest place of its kind in London, which exhibits few traces of the millions daily exchanged in it'. Yet even he could not fail to be impressed by the vastness of the West India docks and warehouses which helped to fuel this activity: 'an immeasurable work; one of those at the sight of which the most cold-blooded spectator must feel astonishment, and a sort of awe at the greatness and might of England.' In the boundless warehouses, he maintained, there was sugar enough to sweeten the whole adjoining basin, and rum enough to make half England drunk. He admired the

number of well-contrived tools and machines, 'I looked on, with great pleasure while blocks of mahogany and other foreign woods, many larger than the largest oak, were lifted up like feathers, and deposited on drays or waggons as carefully as if they had been the most brittle ware.'[16] We introduce the exhibition with this city, whose financial workings are described by Martin Daunton and whose great commercial building projects are explained by Andrew Saint; it provided the basis from which all other advantages accrued.

Commerce was king in London. If there is a single major point to emphasise, unlike the other cities in this series of exhibitions so far – Dresden, Prague, St. Petersburg – London was not a court culture and the trappings of state power were rarely in evidence. Many visitors remarked upon the splendour of the equipages in the street, particularly on the days of court drawing rooms, but as von Raumer perceptively noted, in 1835 at least, 'Nothing is perhaps more striking to a Berliner than the almost total

14 Raumer 1836, vol. 2, p.97 (5 June 1835).
15 Pückler Muskau 1832, vol. 3, pp.59-60.
16 Pückler Muskau 1832, vol. 4, pp.107-09 (28 July 1827).

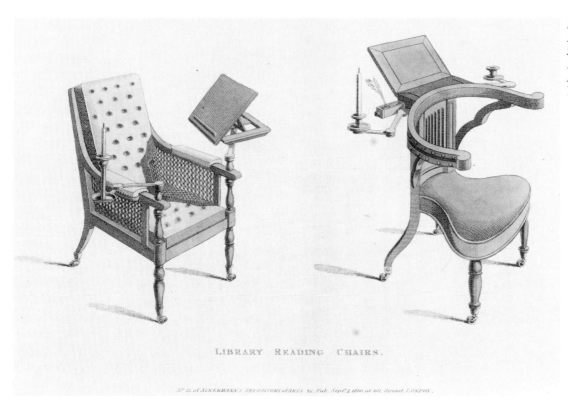

Library Reading Chairs by Messrs. Morgan and Saunders, engraving from Ackermann's *Repository of Arts*, 1810. The Museum of London

LIBRARY READING CHAIRS.

absence of uniforms and orders in England.'[17] Not surprisingly, Pückler Muskau could comment on the lounging habits espoused by Englishmen, encouraged by the comfort of their furniture and carpeted floors:

> It is a positive pleasure even to see an Englishman sit, or rather lie, in one of these couch-like chairs by the fire-side. A contrivance like a reading desk attached to the arm, and furnished with a candlestick, is so placed before him, that with the slightest touch he can bring it nearer or further, push it to the right or the left, at pleasure. A curious machine, several of which stand around the large fire-place, receives one or both of his feet; and the hat on his head completes this enchanting picture of superlative comfort ... The practice of half lying instead of sitting; sometimes of lying at full length on the carpet at the feet of ladies; or crossing one leg over the other in such a manner as to hold the foot in the hand; or putting the hands in the arm-holes of the waistcoat, and so on – are all things which have obtained in the best company and the most exclusive circles.[18]

By such subtle nuances of behaviour, a society reveals its casual disregard of the rigid hierarchies of authority and codes of manners which circumscribe traditional cultures.

It is true that George IV, as Valerie Cumming so clearly demonstrates, was deeply preoccupied with his personal appearance and with ceremonial magnificence, never more so than on the day of his coronation. But as such, he was maintaining the values of the *ancien régime*, not the London which surrounded him and which was acquainted with him principally through *lèse-majesté* caricatures and the public cavortings of a wronged wife.

Nevertheless, in attempting to place himself on the same footing as the autocratic rulers of St. Petersburg, Berlin and Paris, George IV did do London one inestimable service. He supported any effort to make it *look* more like a capital city by the grandiose standards of his peers. Hitherto, the city had exhibited few external signs of wealth. On first arriving in 1817, Richard Rush was disappointed in the general exterior of the houses, 'I had anticipated something better at the west end of the town; more symmetry, buildings more by themselves, denoting the residences of the richest people in the richest city in

17 Raumer 1836, vol. 2, pp.120-21 (11 June 1835).
18 Pückler Muskau 1832, vol. 3, pp.105-08 (20 November 1826).

INTRODUCTION

Europe.' Instead shops were mixed up with residences, 'This may be necessary, or convenient, for the supplies of a capital too large to admit of one or more concentrated markets.'[19] But when he visited again in 1829, he was impressed by the improvements, singling out Regent's Park and Carlton Terrace for special praise. Pückler Muskau was similarly complimentary about improvements made by John Nash in the ten-year gap between his visits and documented in J. Mordaunt Crook's essay:

> Now for the first time, it [London] has the air of a seat of Government, and not of an immeasurable metropolis of 'shop-keepers', to use Napoleon's expression. Although poor Mr Nash ... has fared so ill at the hands of connoisseurs, – and it cannot be denied that his buildings are a jumble of every sort of style, the result of which is rather 'baroque' than original, – yet the country is, in my opinion, much indebted to him for conceiving and executing such gigantic designs for the improvement of the metropolis. The greater part too is still 'in peto', but will doubtless soon be called into existence by English opulence and the universal rage for building.[20]

H.B. (John Doyle), *Repose*, lithograph, 1829. British Museum Satires No.15833. The Duke of Wellington as Prime Minister rests from dealing with state papers. The Museum of London

Not all of Nash's efforts were praised. All Saints, Langham Place, was the target of particular ridicule, Pückler Muskau dubbing it a 'strange architectural monster',[21] and the improvements made to Buckingham Palace were universally condemned. For Passavant: 'every one will join in regretting that so much money should have been expended in converting a fine old palace into one, which, from the insignificance of its proportions, and unimposing exterior, does little credit to the taste of the English nation.'[22] For von Raumer, viewing the interior, 'I never saw anything that might be pronounced a more total failure, in every respect'.[23]

At the root of the problem were the incoherent revisions and economies brought about by the lack of control the king had over the purse-strings and the lack of will on the part of parliament to loosen them. After sixty years of supporting him, the government had good grounds for suspicion regarding their monarch's spending plans. His bills are scattered like confetti throughout this catalogue – from unpaid tailors' accounts for £30,000 in the 1790s to the astonishing £200,000 owed to Seddon, the cabinet makers in 1830. Nor was George IV alone; others emulated his domestic largesse. If London had little to offer on the outside it certainly, as Clive Wainwright reveals, had plenty to boast about in its plutocratic interiors. Passavant somewhat primly commented apropos York (now Lancaster) House, the Duke of Sutherland's London residence:

> Generally speaking, in all matters where display of wealth is concerned, no Englishman is content with moderate measures ... the word 'rich' comprises the highest encomium he can bestow on any object ... It is owing to this, viz. that whatever is most rich is most desirable, that we find the English in their gilt balustrades, chandeliers, brackets, &c. so closely imitating the taste of Louis XIV, in whose reign this mannered style of ornaments was most in vogue. There is something in these wreaths of curling leaves and twisted ends, especially when covered with the most gorgeous gilding, which attract the eye more than the simple forms of a purer taste; and even furniture of this kind, inlaid with a profusion of tortoiseshell, or brass, and groaning beneath the weight of numberless little knick-knacks, no less grotesque than itself, is everywhere to be met with in the houses of the wealthy.[24]

His views echo those of Pückler Muskau, who condemned the gambling establishment Crockford's, designed

19 Rush 1833, p.28.
20 Pückler Muskau 1832, vol. 3, p.45 (5 October 1826).
21 Ibid.
22 Passavant 1836, vol. 1, p.119.
23 Raumer 1836, vol. 2, p.252 (20 June 1835).
24 Passavant 1836, vol. 1, pp.136-40.

on the plan of the 'salons' at Paris, but with a truly Asiatic splendor almost surpassing that of royalty. Everything is in the now revived taste of the time of Louis the Fourteenth; decorated with tasteless excrescences, excess of gilding, confused mixture of stucco paintings, &c., – a turn of fashion very consistent in a country where the nobility grows more and more like that of the time of Louis the Fourteenth.[25]

There is more than a whiff of philistinism accompanying such *mise-en-scènes*. Carl Maria von Weber was asked to play at a 'rout' at Lord Hertford's on 12 March 1826:

> Heavens, what a vast assembly! A magnificent room, 500–600 people there, all of the greatest brilliance. Almost the entire Italian opera company ... Some finales were sung, etc., but not a soul listened. The shrieking and jabbering of this throng of humanity was atrocious. While I played they tried to get a little quiet, and *c.* 100 people gathered round, displaying the greatest interest. But what they can have heard, God only knows, for I myself heard very little of it. Meanwhile I thought hard about my 30 guineas, and so was perfectly patient. At last, about 2 o'clock, they went into supper, whereupon I took my leave.[26]

But in more modest accommodation, visitors had nothing but praise for their comfort. According to the anonymous author of *Letters from Albion*, 'Enter the meanest-looking house; carpets on the stairs, in lobbies, and rooms, pier and swing-glasses, mahogany furniture, China and Staffordshire ware, and the highest cleanliness in the world, strike and gladden your sight.'[27] Even Pückler Muskau was impressed, reporting on his lodgings to his wife:

> What would delight you here is the extreme cleanliness of the houses, the great convenience of the furniture, and the good manners and civility of all serving people. It is true that one pays for all that appertains to luxury ... six times as high, but then one has six times as much comfort.[28]

And while von Raumer found the new houses small and narrow, the English preferring – he believed – vertical-living to inhabiting a large suite of apartments and enduring strange occupants above and below them, 'On the other hand, the hall and staircase of these houses are far more elegant than in ours. The stairs and floors are usually covered with handsome carpets, and even my lodging is not without this luxury.'[29] Perhaps it was on this middle-class level of society that the 'schönen Englischen simplicität', so admired in Germany and pro-

moted, as Simon Jervis suggests, by Rudolph Ackermann's publications, could be experienced.

The streets themselves had other material attractions. Even a visitor as sophisticated as Pückler Muskau was impressed by the shops and bazaars. 'The convenient walking on the excellent "trottoirs", the gay and ever-changing groups, and the numerous splendid shops, make the streets of London, especially in the evening, a very agreeable walk to a foreigner'.[30] For the author of *Letters from Albion*:

> here you discover wealth and magnificence that you would in vain look elsewhere for. All that Peru and the mines of Golconda can afford, all that refinement and luxury can invent, all treasures that the four quarters of the globe possess, – are here heaped up. It is impossible not to be astonished in seeing these riches displayed. Here the costly shawls from the East Indies, there brocades and silk-tissues from China, now a world of gold and silver plate, then pearls and gems shedding their dazzling lustre, home manufactures of the most exquisite taste, an ocean of rings, watches, chains, bracelets, and aigrettes, ready-dresses, ribbons, lace, bonnets, and fruits from all the zones of the habitable world – attract, tempt, astonish, and distract your eyes. You are carried along by the current; otherwise you would stop at every pace, to gaze, to admire, and to covet.[31]

As Martin Daunton points out, London was crucial to the process of creating markets for commodities, for spreading fashion and emulation. London was the largest manufacturing centre in Britain, as the range of goods in this exhibition indicates. Moreover, London was enmeshed in the industrial cycle of the whole country. Provincial manufacturers had to open London showrooms to present their products to the richest sector of society, to make sales and receive commissions; their London managers reported back to the factories on the latest trends. To supply the London market, some canny metropolitan wholesalers even moved into production in the cheaper provinces. This is why we decided to include works manufactured outside London, notably in the pot-

25 Pückler Muskau 1832, vol. 4, pp.338-39 (29 April 1828).
26 Weber 1886.
27 *Letters from Albion* 1814, vol. 1, p.81.
28 Pückler Muskau 1832, vol. 3, pp.48-50 (7 October 1826).
29 Raumer 1836, vol. 1, p.99 (12 April 1835).
30 Pückler Muskau 1832, vol. 3, p.50 (7 October 1826).
31 *Letters from Albion* 1814, vol. 1, pp.79-81.

Shops in the Strand, anonymous watercolour, *c*.1830. The Museum of London

teries of Staffordshire, Worcester and Derby, which could barely have survived without their London warehouses. Similarly, in the furniture trade, nearly all the best work was designed in London, most of it manufactured and all retailed in the capital, even if it ended up in Scotland or St. Helena.

Besides the shops, what were the other sights, the novelties, the extraordinary curiosities that visitors marvelled at in London? For the more sober, there was a range of genteel scientific institutions and heavily promoted technical feats. Simond visited the Royal Institution lectures, where he found that more than one half of the audience was female, 'and it is the most attentive portion. I often observe these fair disciples of science taking notes timidly, and as by stealth, on small bits of paper; no man does that, – they know already the things taught, or care little about them!'[32] Prince Pückler Muskau took himself off twice to visit the Thames Tunnel, soon after it had flooded, 'It is a gigantic work, practicable nowhere but here, where people don't know what to do with their money.'[33] Von Raumer visited Thomas Babbage and his calculating machine and

very soon perceived that an hour's explanation in a language with which I was little familiar would not make a mathematician of me: yet thus much I understood, that the machine accomplished such extraordinary and marvellous things by the mere motion of its relative parts, that most certainly Mr. Babbage would have been burned for a conjuror a few centuries ago.[34]

Two months later he heard Faraday lecture at the Royal Institution on zinc, which he found highly interesting even for the ignorant and uninitiated: 'Mr Faraday is not only a man of profound chemical and physical science, (which all Europe knows,) but is a very remarkable lecturer . . . he delivers himself with clearness, precision, and ability.'[35]

32 Simond 1817, pp.41-43.
33 Pückler Muskau 1832, vol. 4, p.97 (19 July 1827); p.130 (20 August 1827).
34 Raumer 1836, vol. 1, p.36 (31 March 1835).
35 Raumer 1836, vol. 2, pp.60-61 (31 May 1835).

High on everyone's cultural itinerary was the British Museum. Nevertheless, it must be admitted it scarcely lived up to its subsequent reputation. For the author of *Letters from Albion*, 'If you are desirous of seeing the motley habit of his Otaheitean majesty, or the horrid hawks-bill mask of a Sandwich-island warrior, you must come hither. But more interesting is the collection of minerals and birds, though the latter are for the most part badly preserved.'[36] When Louis Simond visited the museum, conducted round in a group under the charge of a German cicerone, the rooms were full of stuffed birds and animals, 'many of them seemingly in a state of decay'.[37] Passavant, on his tour some twenty years later, did see the Hamilton, Townley and Elgin collections of antiquities but was deeply disappointed by their display:

Those who remember the apartments which were first allotted to the collection of sculpture, will sufficiently understand and sympathise with my indignation at seeing those magnificent specimens of the purest antique, which had adorned the Parthenon, and glistened beneath the sunny skies of Greece, here crowded into a dirty, dark apartment, and loaded with the defiling accumulations of London soot and dirt.

He did however mention that preparations were being undertaken for the new museum to Smirke's design.[38]

The annual exhibitions of contemporary painting at the Royal Academy and British Institution did not elicit much praise either. When Louis Simond visited Somerset House in 1810–11, 'I own I did not expect so much mediocrity . . . Portraits swarm, – and this uninteresting branch of the art is the best here.'[39] Passavant with his artist's eye was more drawn to the collections of Old Masters than to modern British art. He did note Wilkie's *Blind Fiddler* as 'one of Wilkie's best pictures' in the National Gallery, favourably mentioned the Lawrence Waterloo Chamber portraits, commended Callcott's *View on the Thames* at Bowood as a 'large and beautiful picture, of transparent and luminous tone', but thought that Wilkie's *Waterloo Dispatch* in Apsley House, 'though rich in design, has rather a scattered effect'.[40]

Many visited the Colosseum panorama of London and the Diorama in Regent's Park and were greatly impressed. Pückler Muskau, who was more diverse in his interests than most, went to the Exeter 'Change, before it finally closed down, where he saw

the representatives of the colonies, – the wild beasts. The variety is great, and the price moderate . . . The ambassador of the late King of Würtemburg had, as I well remember, more occupation here than in St. James's and Downing Street; and, indeed, I know that he was for a considerable time in fear of losing his post on account of a strange enormous dead tortoise.[41]

By the time von Raumer came to London in 1835, the Zoological Gardens had opened in Regent's Park, with over 200,000 visitors and total receipts the preceding year of £18,458: 'Such an income affords ample means of embellishing the gardens, and enriching the collection of animals. The Society gave £1,050 for a rhinoceros.'[42]

Pückler Muskau also attended the theatre, though he commented, 'The most striking thing to a foreigner in English theatres is the unheard-of coarseness and brutality of the audiences.'[43] Nevertheless, this social mix which was, as Iain Mackintosh points out, such a feature of early nineteenth-century London theatre audiences, did not inhibit him from seeing the 'glorious acting' of Edmund Kean in *Othello*, nor visiting the pantomimes after Christmas, 'the strange extravagance of which was sustained by such admirable scenery and machinery, that you could think yourself in fairy-land, without any great effort. Such pretty nonsense is delightful.'[44]

It is only with hindsight that we can fully appreciate the immense energy that these seemingly disparate activities – lectures, experiments, societies, exhibitions, soirées and entertainments – represented, and the underlying forces that were bringing London nearer to the city we recognise today. It would have taken a very acute visitor to have sensed the deeper currents of change behind the whirl of constant movement and ever-extending physical fabric of bricks and mortar, of stucco, iron and concrete. But there is no doubt that the period 1800–40 witnessed a general broadening of the base of society, and a greater articulacy of involvement that heralded reform, and not simply political reform.

Some common trends emerge from the essay writers' multi-faceted interpretation of London. We can detect the development of a new breadth of confidence and regeneration on the part of those involved in urban cultural life, which manifests itself physically in new institutional

36 *Letters from Albion* 1814, vol. 1, pp.116-17.
37 Simond 1817, vol. 1, pp.106-09.
38 Passavant 1836, vol. 1, pp.13-22.
39 Simond 1817, vol. 1, p.164.
40 Passavant 1836, vol. 1, pp.54, 120-21, 200-01, 313.
41 Pückler Muskau 1832, vol. 3, pp.64-65 (10 October 1826); p.143 (28 August 1827).
42 Raumer 1836, vol. 2, p.134 (13 June 1835).
43 Pückler Muskau 1832, vol. 3, pp.126-27 (23 November 1826).
44 Pückler Muskau 1832, vol. 4, pp.284-85 (16 January 1828); pp.324-25 (13 March 1828).

forms. It arose in some measure as a result of the country seeing itself as the saviour of Europe during the Napoleonic Wars. This potent national myth reverberated to the extent that, as Ian Jenkins shows, when the Elgin marbles were for sale, an implicit parallel was drawn between England and the freedom-loving Athens of antiquity, not to mention the 'genius and energy of her citizens', and used to justify their purchase. It was in the spirit of providing an 'honourable asylum' rather as a symbol of tyrannical (Napoleonic) *force majeure* that the new British Museum was constructed, designed in the pure Greek Revival style appropriate to the enhanced status of the classical collections. The growth of these collections was assured by British diplomatic and naval pre-eminence in the Mediterranean, with cartographers from the Admiralty mapping out the sites of future excavations and acquisitions.

The same confident cultural imperialism can be discerned in the natural sciences, sponsored principally by Sir Joseph Banks and the Royal Society, and enriching not only the British Museum but the splendid new College of Surgeons, the Zoological Gardens and Kew. Besides the prestigious Royal Institution and its imitators, a host of specialist societies was founded devoted to different branches of the sciences – Geology, Astronomy, Statistics and Meteorology – along the lines of the new Pall Mall clubs to which both Pückler Muskau and von Raumer were given temporary membership. It must surely have been in this period the hoary joke was coined that whenever two Englishmen get together, they form a club. Yet in such a vast and expanding capital, it was probably the most sensible way of ensuring that like minds met with a reasonable degree of frequency.

In the fine arts no scheme was more eloquently expressive of national confidence than the Prince Regent's commission of Thomas Lawrence, with a knighthood thrown in, to paint all the allied kings and princes, statesmen and commanders in London in 1814, and at Aix-la-Chapelle, Vienna and Rome in subsequent years. Besides the enhanced professional status such a commission conferred, the artists of Lawrence's generation and younger, as Andrew Wilton points out, were far better versed in the skills of draughtsmanship, composition and use of materials, more expert in technique and adventurous in subject matter than their predecessors had been. George IV and the King of Bavaria competed over a painting by David Wilkie. John Constable was presented with a gold medal by Charles X at the Paris Salon in 1824. The reputation of British watercolourists was second to none; British engravers were in demand throughout Europe. If the Royal Academy failed to capitalise on this position

and promote the national school as part of a trans-European network of academies, then there were other institutions ready to take up the slack: the societies formed by the engravers and watercolour artists, the British Institution administered by connoisseurs and the belated founding of the National Gallery.

There was a sting in the tail of all this activity. The windows of opportunity let light and air into the stuffy, closed, cultural corporations run by privileged elites left over from a previous era. Their authority and reputation were no longer safe from scrutiny nor insulated from change. Their opponents had many weapons at their disposal, not least a degree of their own institutional cohesion through common meeting places and societies, backed up by a radical press and the threat of appeal to an even wider public. Moreover, within the constituency of those advocating change there was considerable interchange. Reform was an attitude of mind rather than a narrowly defined goal. As Ian Jenkins shows, the London Greek Committee, which exported the concept of freedom and civilisation back to the Greeks as a political movement to overthrow Turkish rule, was largely composed of reforming Whigs and radicals, with Jeremy Bentham as its leading light, and financed by City money. The same nexus operated in the founding of London University as an 'emporium for the supply of intellectual goods'. Iwan Morus, Simon Schaffer and Jim Secord cogently demonstrate how it aimed to create a new generation of professionals – lawyers, medical men, engineers, civil servants – who would run the country, its government, trade and empire on sound utilitarian principles, not privilege and vested interest. Similarly, although lip service had been paid for decades to the concept of the utility of the arts, it was the radicals backed by industrial and commercial interests who lobbied most effectively for state intervention to ensure that the country's undoubted technological pre-eminence would be matched by an equal supremacy in the field of design. They were conspicuously well represented on the government select committee established in 1835 to investigate the state of arts and manufacturers; not surprisingly, as Peter Funnell points out, witnesses used the opportunity to attack the corruption and privilege of the Royal Academy.

Far from being secluded in academic cloisters, these reformers were charged with the capital's potent spirit. The presence of that one-man Valhalla, Jeremy Bentham, is all pervasive, although the precise degree of his influence is under dispute. Certainly by the 1830s his disciples had made their way into the heart of government and the legislature. In 1827 Pückler Muskau reported that Lord Brougham delivered a six-hour speech on the defects and abuses of English law. 'The most stupendous of these seemed to be, that there is now in "the Court of Chancery" the enormous sum of fifty millions sterling, which has no actual determined owner. A suit in this Court is become proverbial for something interminable.'[45] Three years later Brougham was in a position to do something about the state of affairs as Lord Chancellor in Grey's administration.

Brougham was in the forefront of the movement to harness popular agitation and the political aspirations of the lower classes, as described by H. T. Dickinson, with the palliative of 'useful knowledge'. The Old Price riots and the Queen Caroline affair showed that the London crowd could still be relied upon to make its presence felt in the cause of justice; penny publications and caricatures could still deflate aristocratic pretensions. Even during the Napoleonic Wars, Simond realised that, 'The freedom of the press is considered in England as the palladium of national liberty; on the other hand, the abuse of it is undoubtedly its curse.'[46] Pückler Muskau noted a 'strange custom in England is the continual intrusion of the newspapers into the affairs of private life' and that 'Politics are here a main ingredient of social intercourse; as they begin to be in Paris, and will in time become in our sleepy Germany.'[47] In the post-Reform Act era of von Raumer's visit, the power of the press was readily conceded. Visiting Lambeth to see the twenty steam printing-presses which could produce 200,000 copies of the *Penny Magazine* (the principal organ of the Society for the Diffusion of Useful Knowledge, founded by Brougham) in ten hours, the Professor concluded, 'A steam printing-press like this would strike terror into an army of censors . . . All the censors in the world could not stop the movement of the steam-press, but would be hurried along, or torn in pieces by its resistless force.'[48]

Even from his elevated stance, Pückler Muskau was aware that by the late 1820s all was not well with the old order, a political system that depended on rotten boroughs and bribery at elections, though he was sceptical about the benefits reform might bring:

We must not forget that an approach to perfection is all that can be expected from human beings; and therefore reformers ought carefully to keep in mind 'que le mieux est l'ennemi du bien'. Nevertheless, I think I see many indications that England is advancing towards a reform; and indeed, that it is, from various causes, quite inevitable. Whether it will end advantageously for her, or not, is another question. Perhaps the very necessity is a proof that she has outlived her highest greatness, and is already declining.[49]

We must leave others to be the judge of that, but we end with a London radically different from the city in 1800, one which had doubled in size and which was more sober, solid, respectable, weighty – with more bread, less circuses; more elevation, less diversion; more integrity, less corruption; more queen and (about to be) family, less king and mistresses. It is in our period that this journey of transition took place.

45 Pückler Muskau 1832, vol. 4, pp. 305-06 (28 February 1828).
46 Simond 1817, vol. 1, pp.46, 78.
47 Pückler Muskau 1832, vol. 3, p.123 (23 November 1826); p.178 (10 December 1826).
48 Raumer 1836, vol. 1, pp.191-93 (24 April 1835).
49 Pückler Muskau 1832, vol. 4, pp.306-07 (28 February 1828).

LONDON AND THE WORLD

Martin Daunton

Some years ago, in pulling down the French church in Threadneedle Street, there was exposed to view a tesselated pavement, which, at least fourteen centuries ago, had borne the actual tread of Roman feet; and the immediate neighbourhood was probably the most opulent part of Roman London. A greater power than the Roman, a power of which the masters of the old world had no conception, now reigns supreme on this very spot.

Knight's Cyclopaedia of London, 1851, p. 640

Threadneedle Street, the home of the Bank of England, formed the heart of the financial world of the City of London: clustered in the immediate vicinity were the Stock Exchange, Royal Exchange, the Baltic and Lloyd's coffee houses, the offices of bill brokers, merchant bankers and private bankers. Here was the hub of a new empire of commercial influence, financial power, and territorial authority, as impressive as Rome. The crown had lost the American colonies, yet the Barings retained an immense commercial role in the independent United States, and the East India Company from its offices in Leadenhall Street ruled an empire of formidable extent. The sinews of power of the British empire in its worldwide tussle with the French, which reached a triumphant conclusion at Waterloo, rested upon the ability of the government to raise finance to pay for the war, without provoking a serious political crisis such as drove France to revolution.

British government finance rested upon a 'funded' national debt, the issue of loans backed by specific taxes which made the payment of dividends secure. It proved possible to raise taxes at three times the level of France, in large part because the power to raise taxes was in the hands of a representative parliament, so that the debate over which goods to tax was played out in the public arena, and the actions of the government were accountable and legitimised. Peers and the church were not exempted, offices were not sold, and private tax farmers were not utilised. The British state did not spawn the sprawling and ineffective system of France: the land tax was collected by unpaid local commissioners and a small,

Fragment of Roman tesselated pavement discovered at the depth of 14 feet under the French Protestant Church in Threadneedle Street, April 1814, lithograph from C. Roach Smith, *Illustrations of Roman London*, 1859. The Museum of London

effective bureaucracy of excise officers dealt with a limited range of goods produced in centralised plants, such as breweries. Although the British state was apparently more constrained than were European absolutist monarchies, it was in fact able to tap a larger proportion of the national income. Constraint meant legitimacy.[1]

The taxes were used to support the sale of government loans. Here was the vital role of the City of London, the Bank of England and Stock Exchange. In 1694, the Bank lent £1.2m to the government in return for a royal charter giving it a monopoly of joint-stock banking which was retained until legislation in 1826 and 1836 allowed joint-stock banks respectively outside and within a sixty-five-mile radius of London. The Bank of England kept the records of changes in the ownership of government stock and paid the dividends. The issue of loans was in the

---

1 Brewer 1989; Mathias and O'Brien 1976; O'Brien, 'Political Economy' 1985.

J.C. Stadler after T. Rowlandson and A.C. Pugin, *New Stock Exchange*, aquatint from Ackermann's *Microcosm of London*, 1809. The Museum of London

The funded national debt was at the heart of political debate, and at no time more so than around 1820. Here, it was argued by its supporters, was a guarantee of Protestant liberty against tyranny, whether in the form of Catholicism and French absolutism, or Jacobinism and Napoleonic ambition. Yet the national debt and the Bank of England could also be seen as a threat by 'country' critics. They viewed the Bank of England as the symbol of a shift of power from national, landed virtue to monied corruption and cosmopolitanism, and the Stock Exchange as a form of gambling which threatened legitimate trade. An individual who possessed real property had, so it was argued, the leisure and liberty to engage in public affairs, and was independent of narrow vested interests; monied wealth was seen as a self-interested, corrupt, cosmopolitan clique incompatible with citizenship. The monied interest of the City, so it was claimed, created harmful 'luxury' which sapped the nation and generated a malign political pressure group, supporting a flourishing system of patronage and corruption. Loans financed a bloated navy and army, which offered places for the favoured men of the ruling oligarchy, and provided opportunities for lucrative contracts in supplying munitions, stores, and transports. The monopoly granted by the government to the East India Company, the protection of West Indian planters offered by the system of mercantilism, the special status granted to the Bank of England, all seemed to be part of this world of favour and privilege. There was, contended the critics of the system, a corrupt vicious circle: wealth was created by political privilege, and wealth could then buy power through borough mongering. The defence of Protestant liberty was, on such a view, secured at a high cost, threatening to create the very thing which was abhorred.[3]

This 'country' ideology appealed not only to gentry families who felt excluded from the charmed circle of spoils and privileges comprising the monied oligarchy and the great landowners. It was shared by 'legitimate' commerce within the City, the middling merchants, traders and shopkeepers who dominated in numbers if not wealth. They were critical of what they saw as the depredations of a corrupt oligarchy. The financiers who disposed of the loans, and the rentiers who lived on the interest, were battening on the productive classes. The taxes which were required to fund the loans were diverting funds from land and 'real' commerce and production,

hands of underwriters, a small group of great City financiers who made a contract to take up a loan at a discount, guaranteeing to pay the government, say, £85 on every £100 of stock. The underwriters then placed the stock with the investing public, in the hope that they would get more than the £85 which they had paid. The stock promised the payment of a fixed dividend in perpetuity, and stock holders who wished to get back their money needed a market where stock could be bought and sold. Dealers in stock congregated at Jonathan's Coffee House, and in 1773 a number of brokers left to found the Stock Exchange, which was rebuilt in 1802 to handle the increased volume of business during the Revolutionary and Napoleonic Wars. Taxation and the national debt were the pillars both of the British state in its struggle with France, and of the financial power of the City of London.[2]

2   Clapham 1944.
3   Hoppit 1990; Pocock 1985; Sekora 1977.

creating a credit shortage and driving up the cost of money for useful ventures. The burden of taxes and high interest rates, it was claimed, limited employment, increased costs, held down domestic consumption, and priced British goods out of markets. The result, according to such an analysis, was economic instability and a desperate search for overseas markets. Here was the basis for the revival of radicalism within the City in the early nineteenth century, epitomised by the election of three radicals for the four parliamentary seats of the City in 1818. Robert Waithman, a retail linen draper, had attacked the national debt in 1800 as a device 'to enrich the few by impoverishing the many'. His colleague, the druggist Matthew Wood, gained notoriety as the champion of Queen Caroline in 1820–21, a convenient cause around which critics of an extravagant court and sinecurists could rally.[4]

The greatest loan contractors of the Revolutionary and Napoleonic Wars were the Goldsmids. Aaron Goldsmid, was a Dutch Jew who settled in London in the mid-eighteenth century. George went into his father's firm which dealt in drafts and remittances with Amsterdam, Hamburg and other German towns; Asher went into partnership with Abraham de Mottos Mocatta as bullion broker to the Bank of England and East India Company; Benjamin and Abraham became bill brokers. The great advantage of the Goldsmids was their close family and religious ties with Amsterdam, which was still the major European money market. Benjamin, who secured a dowry of £100,000 on his merger with Israel Solomons, a prosperous East India merchant, became one of the greatest figures on the Stock Exchange, a financial adviser to William Pitt, and a major loan contractor. Both brothers committed suicide, Benjamin in 1808 and Abraham in 1810. Abraham was driven to desperation by financial ruin, for he had underwritten a loan of £14m in 1810 in association with Francis Baring, who died shortly afterwards. The market fell, and Goldsmid was unable to sell the bonds for the price he had guaranteed to pay the government. The business was rescued by Asher's son, Isaac Lyon Goldsmid (1778–1859), a partner in Mocatta and Goldsmid and a member of the Stock Exchange who became a contractor for foreign loans after the war. He was amongst the wealthiest men in the City, actively involved in the campaign for the emancipation of slaves and the extension of civil rights to Jews, and a founding benefactor of University College London.[5]

Baring Brothers had a similarly cosmopolitan background, embedded in a web of connections linking Europe, Britain and the United States. The firm was founded by Francis (1736–1810), the grandson of a Luth-

R. Dighton, *Stock-jobbers Extraordinary*, watercolour, *c.*1795. Guildhall Art Gallery

eran minister from Bremen who became pastor to the German community in London. His father was a cloth merchant in the west of England, who sent Francis to London to train with a German merchant. He was to become 'the first merchant in Europe', and was reputed to be worth £7m. In 1810, the headship of the firm passed to his son Alexander (1774–1848) who had been a partner in the leading merchant house of Amsterdam, Hope and Company. War in Europe brought him back to London, and in 1798 he travelled to the United States to obtain commercial knowledge and, less expectedly, a rich American wife. Alexander was a key figure in the City, a director of the Bank of England, a cabinet minister, a

4 Prothero 1979; Dinwiddy 1973; Hoppit 1990.
5 Picciotto 1875, pp.249-56; Alexander 1808; Cope 1942; *Bankers' Magazine*, vol. 19, 1859, pp. 375-82 and vol. 20, 1860, pp.200-04.

writer on financial issues, a trustee of the British Museum and National Gallery, and a supporter of University College.[6] However, the immediate gap in underwriting British loans which was left by the demise of the Goldsmid brothers was filled by Nathan Rothschild, who was related to them. Nathan was to become the greatest financial power in Europe after Waterloo, a symbol of the power of the cosmopolitan financier which so alarmed the 'country' critics and the middling men of the City.[7]

The world of chartered monopoly and government favour was symbolised by Robert Wigram (1744–1830), who trained as a doctor and in 1764 sailed to India as a ship's surgeon. When ill-health forced him to retire, he turned his knowledge of medicine and the East to good effect, trading in drugs in London and supplying the Dutch and German market. In 1787, he married the daughter of the head of the Navy Victualling Office, and in 1788 he became a 'ship's husband'. The East India Company, which had a monopoly of trade to the East, did not itself own ships, but chartered armed merchant vessels from private owners. Wigram was one of the greatest owners; he was also a partner in the Blackwall shipyard which constructed East Indiamen, and in 1803 became a member of the East India Dock Company which constructed the East India Docks. In 1795, he fitted four ships as troop transports and organised the merchants' declaration of loyalty in favour of William Pitt.[8] Or there was William Manning (1763–1835), the owner of considerable slave plantations in the West Indies, a leader of the West Indian interest in parliament, a Commissioner of Exchequer Bills, and a director of the Bank of England.[9] Wigram and Manning were typical of many City men who did well from the war, building fortunes on the back of government contracts and monopolies supported by royal charters and mercantilist legislation.

The extent to which 'country' criticism of luxury and monied corruption was justified continues to puzzle historians, who focus upon two issues. Could the national debt and war finance 'crowd out' investment in industrialisation, and could the tax regime distort the market for industrial goods in a way which hampered growth? There is a consensus amongst historians that Britain had a low rate of economic growth until the 1820s, and that the industrial revolution consisted of a significant shift of workers from agriculture into an industrial sector which continued to use labour-intensive technology with limited opportunities for productivity gains. One possible explanation is that City loan contractors absorbed funds until the 1820s, when a reduction in the national debt released investment and permitted more rapid growth.[10] Such an argument is not altogether convincing, for the

national debt could 'crowd in' investment by attracting idle balances which would help to finance productive enterprise. The rise of public borrowing created a range of securities which gave merchants, brokers, insurance offices and banks a more varied outlet for funds than land, encouraging the development of a complex structure of financial services by the mid-eighteenth century which increased liquidity and flexibility. London was able to develop as the fulcrum of the English credit network.

In the late nineteenth century, a commonplace in the debate on the City of London and the banking system was its failure to provide capital for domestic industry, in comparison with German industrial banks which were seen as agents in the creation of a dynamic industrial economy. Such an analysis obscures the genuine role of London bankers in the industrial revolution, when industrial concerns required little fixed capital and considerable amounts of circulating capital and credit. An important source was the bill of exchange: a merchant or manufacturer who sold goods worth, say, £100 on three months' credit sent a bill to the purchaser requesting payment in three months; the purchaser accepted the bill and returned it to the issuer, who then had three options. He could retain it until it fell due; he could pass it to one of his own creditors; or he could obtain cash by 'discounting' it at a bank, obtaining an immediate payment of, say £95 for the bill. This was an attractive investment for the bank, and bills became a major part of their holdings. Bills were issued in large numbers in areas of capital shortage such as Lancashire, and were transferred to City bankers in London who supplied country bankers in areas of capital surplus such as East Anglia. The wealth of one locality and social class was fed to another locality and social class, not through investment in fixed capital but through the provision of credit.

The crucial role of coordination was undertaken by the private bankers in the City, a group which was distinct both from the West End bankers who catered for the aristocracy and the evolving merchant bankers who were concerned with financing international trade.[11] The City

6   Fox Bourne 1886, pp.447-59; *Dictionary of National Biography*, vol. 1, pp.1110-12; Hidy 1949.
7   Chapman, 'Foundation' 1977.
8   Green and Wigram 1881, pp.29, 45-54; Thorne, *Commons 1790-1820*, vol. 5, 1986, pp.554-56.
9   Purcell 1896, pp.6-7; Thorne, *Commons 1790-1820*, vol. 4, 1986, pp.540-43.
10   Wrigley 1988; Williamson 1984; Black and Gilmore 1990; O'Brien, 'Political Economy' 1985.
11   Black 1989; Pressnell 1956; Ashton 1945; Hudson 1986.

bankers had diverse origins, emerging from the business world of London as well as migrating from the provinces, and had varied attitudes, including both supporters and critics of the world of monopoly and privilege among their number. William Curtis (1752–1829), manufacturer of ships' biscuits at Wapping, founded the bank of Robarts, Curtis and Company in 1792. He was involved in East Indies shipping and government contracting; he underwrote the loan of 1801 with Goldsmid; and he served as a diehard Tory M.P. for the City between 1798 and 1818 and 1820 to 1826. He was the antithesis of Waithman and Wood, defending the war, supporting the East India Company's monopoly, and opposing both parliamentary reform and revision of the Corn Laws. Wood was the protector of Queen Caroline; Curtis, a 'bottle-nosed *bon vivant* and unconscious buffoon', was admirably suited to be an intimate of George IV.[12]

By contrast, Smith, Payne and Smith emerged from a provincial base. The country bank of Smith and Company developed from the hosiery trade in Nottingham to become a leading country banking concern in the Midlands and the major port of Hull. In 1758, Abel Smith II of Nottingham entered into a partnership with John Payne of London, and the City bank of Smith, Payne and Smith was to be the London agent for the Smiths and other country banks. Although Abel Smith IV (1788–1859) became a major landowner in Sussex and a staunch Conservative M.P., other members of the firm took a different line. His uncle, John Smith II, was a founding benefactor of University College London, purchasing the site with Isaac Lyon Goldsmid. Thomas Perronet Thompson (1783–1869), a partner in the bank, was co-founder of the radical *Westminster Review* with Jeremy Bentham.[13] Another leading utilitarian was George Grote, the grandson of Andreas Grote of Bremen who settled in London in 1731, and who was a reluctant partner in the family bank of Prescott and Grote. He preferred to devote himself to scholarship and politics: he was a disciple of James Mill and Jeremy Bentham, a leading radical in the City and supporter of University College.[14] Such men are indicative of the deep fissure in the City's politics between the supporters of traditional values and reform.

The City of London tapped the resources of areas such as East Anglia and channelled them to Lancashire, which suggests that it was helping to 'crowd in' investment: industrial districts were more able to use their available funds for fixed investment in machinery and factories. The 'crowding out' hypothesis is, in fact, flawed because it assumes that there was a single capital market, in which funds were mobile between government loans and industry. In reality, the capital market was segmented, and

an industrialist who was building up a firm was not attracted by government bonds. He tapped local supplies of capital from family and friends, and retained profits within the firm. Government loans appealed to a different type of investor disinclined to put money into domestic industry. The government loans during the war were not necessarily at the expense of industry, and some of the funds were in any case attracted into London from Europe. Men such as the Huguenot banker, Peter Isaac Thelluson, were well placed to receive the funds of the French aristocracy through a family network which linked Geneva, Paris and London. Other firms relocated in London as a result of the disruptions of war, such as the great Anglo-Dutch merchant banker Henry Hope, who left Amsterdam for London in 1794 and was soon joined by his partners Pierre Labouchere and Alexander Baring. The disruption of the trade of Hamburg led a number of firms to shift to London, such as Schroders in 1802, E. H. Brandt in 1805, Frederick Huth in 1809, and Fruhling and Goschen in 1814. The war against France was, in part, financed by mobilising the resources of the Continent through the London capital market. Napoleon's Continental System hampered British exports to Europe, which threatened the remittance of funds to the allies. Although British goods did find new markets outside Europe, the ability to continue financing the armies of Europe arose from capital movements as continental merchants and aristocrats invested in British funds. War finance was consequently not entirely at the expense of domestic investment, and when the demand for British government loans declined after the war, these funds were not released into British provincial industry so much as into foreign government loans.[15]

Although the financing of the war probably did not 'crowd out' the industrial revolution, the contention of the radicals that it distorted the market for industry is more plausible. London reappears in a new guise, less as a financial centre starving industry of funds, than as a playground where the aristocracy squandered its wealth in an orgy of conspicuous consumption. The land tax provided a declining share of government finance during the eighteenth century, and an increasing role was played by

12 Thorne, *Commons 1790-1820*, vol. 3, 1986, pp.545-48; *Dictionary of National Biography*, vol. 5, pp.349-50.
13 Leighton-Boyce 1958; *Bankers' Magazine*, vol. 19, 1859, pp.205-08, 352.
14 Grote 1873; Clarke 1962.
15 Heim and Mirowski 1987; Hudson 1986; Neal 1990; Chapman, 'International Houses' 1977; Cope 1983; Thorne, *Commons 1790-1820*, vol. 5, 1986, pp.362-64.

excise duties, which fell on domestic consumption and production. By 1798, there was a crisis in government finance as the costs of the war mounted, and Pitt's solution was to replace the land tax with an income tax which tapped the income of all sectors. Although the income tax was accepted as a temporary wartime measure, parliament was not willing to sanction it in peace and the government's desire to retain the income tax in order to maintain a degree of equity was firmly rejected in 1816. Although the income tax was removed, the land tax was not restored, with the consequence that the tax system lurched in a regressive direction. The rich were relieved of taxation, which fell increasingly upon indirect taxes on industrial production and working-class consumption.[16] The radicals at the end of the war developed a perceptive critique of the consequences of such a pattern of taxation which contained a considerable element of truth. Income was redistributed to the rich, who were more likely to save than the poor. Although a higher savings ratio could in theory encourage growth by removing the constraints on investment in industry, the segmented nature of the capital market does not make this a likely outcome. It is much more plausible that these savings went to fuel the speculation in foreign loans in the early 1820s, much of which was highly dubious. A more significant constraint on economic growth was the level of demand. Here the redistribution of income had a serious effect, for the level of domestic demand was depressed and producers were forced to seek foreign markets which were more uncertain. Growth was directed towards a limited range of staple exports rather than a diversified domestic economy. The war and postwar policy, by boosting the income of the landed elite, produced a particular type of demand, encouraging London-based expenditure on 'luxury' and conspicuous consumption. Here was the basis for the show of Regency London: a landed aristocracy which had done well from the war and was self-confident and assertive in its blatant parading of wealth.[17]

Rents were recycled from provincial estates for consumption in the West End, to which the landed aristocracy and gentry migrated for the season between April and August. The private bankers of the West End specialised in the accounts of landed families, transferring income from the country to London and lending money to landowners on the security of their estates in order to finance expensive building programmes or to release capital to pay dowries. Such was the role of Thomas Coutts (1735–1822), who was banker to the royal family and many leading landed families. Private bankers could themselves move into the landed elite, either by purchase of estates, or by marriage.[18]

The Prince Regent, in his improvement of the West End and his lavish coronation as George IV, had 'the extravagance of a Renaissance Pope', as Valerie Cumming shows. He was not alone. The wealthiest landed families had 'private palaces' which rivalled or surpassed in opulence their country seats. Devonshire House on Piccadilly was the urban counterpart of Chatsworth, and in 1798 they were valued at respectively £29,286 and £22,322. At Spencer House on Green Park, or Norfolk House on St. James's Square, society met in a glittering round of balls and receptions. Not all houses were so grand, but even the modest country gentleman might aspire to rent a house in town. During the Revolutionary and Napoleonic Wars, the British aristocrats waxed rich as their continental counterparts faced crisis; here, as Clive Wainwright demonstrates, was the opportunity for dealers to supply works of art from straitened families in Europe to an eager British market. And a new spate of building started, 'the extravagance of which came close to eclipsing all that had gone before it'. The Prince Regent set the tone with his lavish transformation of Carlton House, and he was followed by the Earl of Grosvenor in 1808 and the 6th Duke of Devonshire in 1811. The level of expenditure was staggering. The 3rd Duke of Northumberland was thought to have spent £160,000 on refurbishing his town house around 1820. He paid the upholsterers Morrell and Hughes £34,000 between 1821 and 1823, and in 1823 the glass enameller and manufacturer William Collins of the Strand supplied '4 superb chandeliers executed in Grecian metal' for £2,700 and two large candelabra for £2,000. Such luxury trades were an important part of the industrial economy of London, creating a demand for highly skilled artisans, for cabinet makers, milliners, gilders, coachmakers, tailors, jewellers. One consequence was a high degree of seasonality, as dressmakers toiled to produce lavish gowns for balls and routs during the Season, and faced a slack period when the aristocracy departed for the country.[19]

Nevertheless, it would be wrong to exaggerate the limits to the market. London consisted not only of private palaces but also of the town houses of merchants, tradesmen and professionals. The market was wider than in other European capital cities, and production was not

16 O'Brien, 'Political Economy' 1985; Hilton 1977; Prothero 1979.
17 O'Brien, 'Political Economy' 1985; Beckett and Turner 1990; Prothero 1979.
18 Davidoff 1973; Robinson 1929; Cassis 1984, chapter 6.
19 Sheppard 1971, p.xviii; Sykes 1985, pp.103, 228, 238; Summerson 1945; Smout 1969, chapters 12 and 14; Borsay 1977.

constrained by the regulations of guilds, nor the privileged position of 'court artisans'. Astute provincial entrepreneurs could exploit the luxury market as a means of penetrating further down the social scale. Matthew Boulton is perhaps best known for his partnership with James Watt in producing steam engines, but his business rested upon the manufacture of ormolu decoration and all sorts of metal 'toys' at his works in Birmingham. He opened a showroom in London, and sought the widest market, criticising his London agent for concentrating on the more exclusive outlets.

> We think it of far more consequence to supply the People than the nobility only; and though you speak contemptuously of hawkers, Pedlars and those who supply *Petty shops*, yet we must own that we think they will do more towards supporting a great Manufactory, than all the Lords in the nation.

Boulton was such an innovative capitalist that he even contracted with the Royal Mint to provide copper coins during the great currency shortage of 1797. The Staffordshire potter Josiah Wedgwood adopted a different strategy, creating an air of exclusivity. Rather than cutting prices like his competitors, he sought to differentiate his goods by capturing the world of fashion. Once he had the support of the court and aristocracy, he exploited it by advertising, exhibitions, salesrooms and travelling salesmen. London was crucial to the process of creating markets for commodities, spreading fashion and emulation.

Not only did provincial producers open London showrooms; metropolitan wholesalers moved into production to cater for the fashionable market. For example, Miles Mason, a china and glass merchant in London, became one of the greatest potters in Staffordshire.[20]

The City of London was, however, more than the home of banks, for there were many textile warehouses clustered around Wood Street. London merchants had imported cotton cloth from India, and the metropolis was a major centre both of silk weaving in Spitalfields and of textile printing. Even when textile printing shifted to the North, there were close ties with London merchants who had knowledge of fashionable markets.[21] A firm of hosiery manufacturers such as the Wards of Derbyshire felt that a link with London was essential, and in 1803 they entered into a partnership with George Brettle in London. The manufacturing business was effectively run from their warehouse in Wood Street, and the financial commitment to the London end of the business was much greater, above all in the provision of large amounts of trade credit which was essential to the success of the enterprise.[22] James Morrison (1789–1857), whose fortune

20 Sturmer 1979; Kellet 1957-58; McKendrick, Brewer, Plumb 1982; Crouzet 1985; Eatwell and Werner 1991.
21 Unwin 1924; Edwards 1967, chapter 8; Chapman 1974 and 1979; Fitton 1969.
22 Harte 1977.

Messrs. Harding, Howell & Co., 89 Pall Mall, from Ackermann's *Repository of Arts*, vol.1, 1809. The Museum of London

rivalled even the Rothschilds', made his money from the London textile district. He was the son of an innkeeper, moving to London in 1809 where he worked for Todd and Company, a firm of retail and wholesale haberdashers in Cheapside which supplied street hawkers and small retailers. Morrison was Todd's partner by 1814 and he was soon his son-in-law. He was 'the Napoleon of shopkeepers', building up a colossal business through high volume, low value turnover of Manchester cotton goods. By the early 1820s, he was a rich man and part of the circle around Bentham, associated with radicals such as Waithman, standing as a radical parliamentary candidate, and supporting University College. By the 1830s, he was moving in the direction of banking, at first providing mortgages to aristocrats and in 1836 forming a merchant bank with particular interests in the United States. The transition into a merchant bank failed, and the family retreated into a more passive rentier role of landowners and investors.[23]

The role of London in the marketing of provincial industrial goods, and its provision of trade credit through the banking system and textile warehouses, modify the impression that the metropolis was a parasite, sucking the wealth of producers through taxes, loans and rents. The emergence of the British national debt was one reason for the financial revolution of the eighteenth century, and the

crises of the Revolutionary and Napoleonic Wars gave a fillip to the transfer of financial power to London, by disrupting Amsterdam, Hamburg and Frankfurt and encouraging continental capital to shift to London. However, the settlement of European merchants in London was part of a larger process which was motivated by factors other than government finance and war. The emergence of the British textile industry to pre-eminence contributed to London's rise to dominance. The arrival of Nathan Rothschild in England in 1798 was not simply the result of a flight from continental disruption and a desire to participate in lucrative loan contracts. His father, Mayer, was certainly involved in royal finances and government loans in Frankfurt, yet the motive for sending Nathan to England arose from his business importing calicoes woven in Lancashire and printed in London. Rothschild was related to Jewish families in Amsterdam who were involved in both finance and printed textiles, and London was emerging as a rival of Amsterdam in both branches of business. Here was the motivation for Levi Barent Cohen (1740–1808), the son of an Amsterdam linen merchant, to settle in London in 1763. Nathan

23   Gatty 1976; Rubinstein 1981, pp.44-45.

LONDON AND THE WORLD

T.H. Shepherd, *East India House, Leadenhall Street*, watercolour, 1817. The Museum of London

gained experience in London with Cohen, before moving to Manchester where he purchased textiles for the continental market, arranging their dyeing and printing for European tastes and securing credit through London. Nathan was not so much fleeing the armies of Napoleon as seeking the textiles of Lancashire. In 1806, he married Cohen's daughter, entering a web of family connections which included the Goldsmids. In 1808 he moved to London, and by 1811 he had wound up the textile business and moved into loan contracting. The Jewish merchants and financiers, like the Huguenots before them, came from a minority group with strong internal affiliations, and family members located in cities such as Frankfurt and Amsterdam. These networks gave them a competitive edge in securing commercial information, and a greater security at a time when business was so dependent upon trust.[24]

Textiles formed one vital component in international trade, which made a base in Britain essential. Another was the increasing trade between Britain and its colonies in North America and the East and West Indies. Military and naval success and imperial power meant not only a buoyant market in government loans; it also created import trades from the empire which made a London base

essential. The proprietors of the East India Company met at East India House on Leadenhall Street, which they rebuilt between 1796 and 1799, in order to administer their expanding empire of trade and territory, and to auction the goods imported from the East which were stored in the fortress-like warehouses at Cutler Street. Buyers were attracted from the whole of Europe, and in the nearby streets of Mincing Lane there were brokers and merchants specialising in the colonial goods of sugar, coffee, tea, spices and dyes.[25] Colonial trade still operated within the system of 'mercantilism', designed to limit the colonial trade to British built and owned ships, and to require that goods be brought to Britain whatever their final destination. During the Napoleonic Wars, the entrepôt trade was fostered by Pitt's Warehouse Act of 1803. Previously, imports paid duty as soon as they were landed and merchants subsequently claimed a 'drawback' when re-exporting. Now merchants could place goods in a warehouse for fifteen months free of duty; the merchant paid duty when they were released for the domestic mar-

24   Chapman, 'Foundation' 1977; 'International Houses' 1977.
25   Beckett and Turner 1990.

J.C. Stadler after T. Rowlandson and A. C. Pugin, *Interior of Sale Room, East India House*, aquatint from Ackermann's *Microcosm of London*, 1808. The Museum of London

ket, but not when re-exported. The owner of the warehouse paid a bond, providing security that duty would be paid. The aim was to create stock-piles in response to Napoleon's Continental System, but there was also a desire to foster the entrepôt function of London. The Foreign Trade Committee of 1820 was convinced that the emergence of London as the warehouse of the world produced 'pure profit': warehousemen secured rents, merchants received commissions and the balance of trade was benefited. There was, however, a potential conflict of interest. Thomas Wallace, chairman of the Committee, explained in 1821 that

> he wished to give to the commerce of foreign nations the freest possible access for the purpose of exportation from England. In short, he was desirous of making this country the general depot, the great emporium of the commerce of the world.

Yet a policy of open access might threaten British shipowners, undermining their protected position in the longhaul trades. The conflict of interests led to a complex battle within parliament, and the legislation which emerged in 1822 was a timid compromise.[26]

The emergence of a merchant navy protected by the mercantilist system led to the development of a market for marine insurance in London, which soon rivalled and surpassed Amsterdam, encouraged by the uncertainties of shipping during the war. The market was in the hands of private underwriters meeting at Lloyd's Coffee House, which was taken over by the members in 1771 as a specialist market. The number of underwriters increased from 79 in 1771 to about 1,500 in 1810. Ironically, the underwriters at Lloyd's were the unwitting beneficiaries of the world of corporate monopolies which dominated the eighteenth century. An act of 1720 restricted corporate marine insurance to two companies, the London Assurance and Royal Exchange Assurance, and also banned underwriting by partnerships. The effect was to strengthen the hands of the private underwriters of Lloyd's. The status quo was challenged in 1824 when Nathan Rothschild and Moses Montefiore, with the backing of the Barings and others, formed the Alliance British and Foreign Fire and Life In-

---

26 Hilton 1977, chapter 6; Palmer 1990, chapter 5; Jackson 1983, pp.58-59.

J.C. Stadler after A.C. Pugin and T. Rowlandson, *Lloyd's Subscription Room*, aquatint from Ackermann's *Microcosm of London*, 1809. The Museum of London

surance Company. The opposition of Lloyd's and the privileged companies, which had seen off earlier challenges in 1806 and 1810, was defeated. In fact, Lloyd's was able to maintain its position because it was more flexible than the cautious companies which concentrated upon fire and life insurance.[27]

The development of the overseas trade, as Andrew Saint shows, led to the construction of enclosed docks in London. Despite the war with France, which resulted both in competition for funds and inflation, the new dock companies became an instant focus of investment for London's merchant class. The West India Dock Company had an initial capital of £500,000, and the London Dock Company £1,200,000. Unrivalled as examples of civil engineering and entrepreneurship, the large investment in these docks – together with the East India Dock – was protected by the government granting twenty-one-year monopolies on the handling of all dutiable goods from different parts of the globe. The Warehouse Act of 1803 gave the new dock companies a further boost. The proposed extension of these monopolies came under

attack from Thomas Tooke in 1820. His challenge succeeded, and in 1823 the St. Katharine's Dock Company, with Tooke as chairman, obtained an act of parliament to build a new dock beside the Tower of London 'established on the principle of free competition in trade, and without any exclusive privileges and immunities'. Here was another strand in the freeing of the City from privileges, a process full of ironies and based on special pleading as much as ideological commitment to a free market. Tooke's criticism of monopolies was not confined to the dock companies, for in 1820 he also organised a petition for free trade. London, it would seem, was divided between the defenders and critics of mercantilism and monopoly. The lines were by no means simple and unambiguous. Certainly, there was not a majority for free trade in 1820, and the London merchants' petition was in reality part of a campaign by one set of vested interests

27   Supple 1970, chapter 9; Martin 1876, chapters 15 and 16.

against another. North European merchants who traded in Baltic timber disliked colonial preferences for timber from Canada; the East India Company wanted free trade in sugar as a ploy against the West Indies, while defending its own monopoly in tea from China.[28] The City of London was not a driving force in the campaign for free trade, which was orchestrated in the industrial North. Certainly, the dismantling of mercantilism did spell disaster for some leading figures within the City, such as William Manning who was driven into bankruptcy in 1831 or the Wigrams who were unable to maintain their dominant position in the Eastern shipping industry. The shift in economic policy meant a significant change in the personnel and interests of the City.

The financiers who built up their wealth on the basis of war loans faced the need to adjust at the end of the war, when retrenchment curtailed the loan market and the government was eager to free itself of the trammels of the London money market. The government of Lord Liverpool accepted part of the 'country' critique of the power of the monied oligarchy, drawing a distinction between 'real' and 'artificial' trade and credit. The concern was to maintain balance in society during a period of readjustment at the end of the war, which was one reason for the introduction of the Corn Laws in 1815 in order to allow a transitional period during which agriculture could adjust to lower postwar prices. The government also had to grapple with the restoration of the gold standard, which had been suspended in 1797. The Bank of England had issued bank notes without the backing of bullion during the period of suspension, which was due to end six months after the war. The consequence would be a tighter monetary policy and deflation, which would cause serious difficulties for debtors struggling to repay loans from falling incomes, and for farmers who had moved on to marginal land during the war which was only profitable when prices were high. Liverpool decided to delay the resumption of the gold standard, in order to provide a transitional period of gradual adjustment to lower prices. Resumption was finally accepted in 1819, to come into effect in 1821. The policy generated bitter debate, in which the lines of division were far from simple. In the eyes of some landholders, resumption was a plot to undermine their position, for holders of the funds would continue to receive fixed dividends and would be better off in real terms, while the taxes needed to pay the dividends would fall ever more heavily upon producers. More plausible was the contention of some industrialists that they were paying higher taxes to support fundholders, labouring under the burden of agricultural protection, suffering from falling prices, and challenged by the increase in the

real burden of debts. Resumption could therefore be interpreted as a policy designed to benefit parasitical financiers and creditors of the City against landowning and industrial interests.

Reality was more complicated. Many, perhaps most, landowners defended resumption and there was a considerable element of opposition within the City. The reason for this apparently paradoxical position was that easy credit and soft money were assumed to stimulate speculation and easy fortunes, which subverted the social order. Paper money implied social dislocation, a class of *nouveaux riches* adventurers who had been permitted to speculate; a sound money policy based on gold would act as a sieve to separate unsound speculation from reputable traders, fictitious from real trade and credit, killing off 'improvident and unreasonable speculations'. Resumption also appealed to the government as a means of regaining independence from the Bank of England and financiers such as Rothschild whose power had been increased by the need to manage the currency in the absence of the automatic adjustments of the gold standard, and by the imperative of large loans. The danger, however, was that the policy of 'hard' money would harm those it hoped to benefit, threatening the productive class who had borrowed money. The result, argued Alexander Baring, would be to redistribute income from useful to less useful members of society, so that 'the industrious were obliged to labour under difficulties, that the drones might live in the greater affluence'. It was a moot point whether a tight monetary policy could differentiate between 'real' and 'fictitious' capital and credit. Industrialists, merchants and the banking system were highly dependent upon bills of exchange and trade credit, and their concern for liquidity led more than 400 City merchants and bankers to protest against resumption.

The government's belief that 'real' bills for legitimate trade were clearly distinguishable was a delusion which shaped policy in the financial crisis of 1825–26. The government refused to intervene, arguing that cyclical failure was the responsibility of individuals who should bear the consequences of their own actions. Government assistance, argued William Huskisson in 1826, would only make matters worse, for it would be 'as much calculated to encourage speculation as the poor-laws were calculated to encourage vagrancy, and to discourage honest industry'. The crisis of 1825-26 was welcomed by the government as a corrective to the pretensions of the *nouveaux*

28   Hilton 1977, pp.173-76.

riches and over-trading, and the policy pursued after the crisis was indeed to increase monetary stringency, tying the volume of paper money more firmly to the gold supply. Although the gold standard was to become a shibboleth of the City in the later nineteenth century, it was introduced, like free trade, against the wishes of many elements in the City.[29]

The curtailment of new loan issues for the British government at the end of the war turned the attention of City financiers in a new direction. The occupation and reconstruction of Europe provided one opportunity for profit, which London was better placed to meet than its erstwhile rivals in Amsterdam. In 1817, the Barings floated the first of several loans to finance French war reparations and the costs of the army of occupation. In 1818, Nathan Rothschild raised a loan for Prussia, which was soon followed by loans for Austria, Russia and Spain. Loan contractors to the British government transformed themselves into loan contractors to foreign governments, a trend which was encouraged in 1822 by the conversion of the national debt to a lower interest rate. Investors were eager to find higher interest rates elsewhere, and the newly independent states of Latin America provided a ready solution.

The Latin American loan bubble was an episode compounded of idealism and speculation, altruism and avarice, cunning and ignorance, which were sometimes not easily distinguishable. General Sir Gregor MacGregor was the most notorious swindler, a soldier who had served in the Peninsular campaign before joining Simon Bolívar in the Latin American struggle for independence. His bungling led to his ignominious dismissal, but in 1820 the 'king' of the Mosquito Indians of Honduras granted him 8m acres. He duly styled himself Gregor I, Cazique of Poyais and raised a loan of £200,000 in 1822 to finance his imaginary kingdom. With fraudsters such as MacGregor able to secure backers, it is no surprise that South American governments were able to float loans with remarkable ease. An emissary would arrive and contact a City bank or merchant house, who was offered a commission and agreed to take bonds at a discount. The bonds were then sold to the public, the insiders often creating an illusion of an active and buoyant market by buying and selling from each other, until they could tempt the public to take up the offer, when they would pull out and take a profit. The bonds for the Columbian loan of 1822 were produced by Rudolph Ackermann, and he was himself swept along by the vision of a prosperous, independent Latin America. He translated *Ivanhoe* into Spanish and started a magazine for the new market; he purchased Mexican, Columbian and Brazilian bonds, and

shares in the Chilean Mining Association and Tlapuxahua Mining Association. The mines were usually no better than the government loans. Between 1822 and 1825, seven Latin American countries issued bonds for over £20m and over £19m was in default in 1829. Perhaps Huskisson had a point, and the speculators needed a fall.[30]

The participants in the loans of the early 1820s were not all scoundrels such as MacGregor. Although there were failures, others prospered. Barings issued a loan for the province of Buenos Ayres, and survived as one of the great merchant banks of the nineteenth century, continuing to lend to Argentina and playing a major role in the trade of the United States.[31] There were even some merchants who prospered from trade with Latin America, such as the firm of Antony Gibbs and Son which shifted its focus from Spain to its former colonies.[32] Mercantile firms such as Barings and Gibbs moved in the second quarter of the nineteenth century from a direct involvement in trade to become merchant bankers, abandoning direct trade on their own account and instead providing commercial credit, dealing in foreign exchange, and seizing any opportunities offered by foreign loans.

In 1820, the separation of function between trade and finance was still not complete, and the City was in many ways a mixture of the practices of the eighteenth century and the new order which was to dominate the later nineteenth century. Merchants trading with China, India and Australia still congregated at the Jerusalem Coffee House; those interested in tallow, hemp and oil gathered at the Baltic Coffee House. The trend from coffee houses to specialist exchanges with formalised rules started with the Stock Exchange and Lloyd's in the 1770s, but was still not complete. In 1823, regular attenders of the Baltic called a meeting in order to close ranks against speculators in tallow, limiting their numbers to thirty of whom only six could be members of the Stock Exchange. They continued to meet in a private room at the coffee house, and it was only in 1857 that they acquired a separate building. The physical reconstruction of the City, the decline of a resident population of traders and artisans, had not yet proceeded very far; specialised office buildings had still not yet replaced the counting houses.[33]

29 Hilton 1977, chapters 2 and 7; Checkland 1948 and 1954; Fetter 1965; Horsefield 1949.
30 Dawson 1990; Gilbart 1834, p.59.
31 Hidy 1949.
32 Matthew 1981.
33 Montefiore 1803, 'Royal Exchange'; Evans 1852, chapters 6-8; Lillywhite 1963; Findlay 1927, pp.14-16; Barty-King 1977, pp.62-128.

D. Havell after T.H. Shepherd, *A View of the Royal Exchange, Cornhill*, aquatint, published by R. Ackermann, 1815. The Museum of London

Metaphorically, the 'country' critics saw London as a devourer of population, a centre of conspicuous consumption by a bloated aristocracy and of gambling by dubious speculators. Their case was doubtless exaggerated, but in a literal sense they did have a point: in the eighteenth century more people died in London than were born, with an annual average of 20,800 burials and 14,800 baptisms in the 1750s. By the nineteenth century, London had ceased to destroy people and the annual averages of burials and baptisms in the 1820s stood at 20,700 and 27,700 respectively. London, said Samuel Leigh in 1818, was freed from 'the unhealthiness and liability to epidemic and other disorders which usually prevail among crowded populations'. The explanation is possibly that social segregation and improved housing reduced the pathways along which infectious disease was conducted. Segregation was becoming a reality by the end of the eighteenth century as a result of new estates built in the West End, and it was noted in 1801 that merchants 'make a part of their well-being consist in living in a different quarter of the town from that in which they work'. Ground landlords such as the Duke of Bedford, with their covenants, squares, gates and beadles could at least hold the slums at bay. The metropolis lacked an overall political authority, and beyond the well organised City Corporation were some 200 parish vestries. Their failings were many, yet the absence of a London-wide responsibility was not disastrous until the coming of cholera in the 1830s. There was improvement: local Paving and Lighting Acts marked a shift from a medieval system of control, permitting the appointment of commissioners to pave and repair the streets.[34]

The building of Georgian London, as Andrew Saint demonstrates, took place in a number of frantic bursts of activity, which resulted in a speculative over-building of houses followed by a flurry of bankruptcies, until demand caught up with the glut and the process was repeated. The development of London was not restricted by city walls; on the contrary, most landowners were eager to participate in development, often making sites available ahead of demand to speculators and builders. Even small

34 Landers 1987; Olsen 1986, p.23 and 1964 Part III; Schwarz 1982 pp.172, 179; George 1930, p.96, 99-100.

builders were willing to take their chance in erecting a few properties, drawing on the abundant credit which boom periods generated. The diffusion of modest wealth amongst the shopkeepers and artisans of London allowed the purchase of leases on a few houses as an investment and to provide security. The growth of London was the result of the drive for profit by landowners and speculative builders, rather than the aggrandisement of the crown or state. London had fewer vistas and grand boulevards than Paris; it also had a lower death rate and better housing conditions.[35]

The growth of London was more than a matter of reducing the curse of mortality which hung over all large cities. It was also a matter of supplying food and fuel, which were inescapable constraints on the size of any city. A large urban population could generate economic development, its massive market stimulating agricultural specialisation, and creating a virtuous circle of growth as commercialised farmers bought urban goods and services. The cattle driven into Smithfield, or the barley brought to the huge breweries of Truman and Whitbread were cases in point. Yet there was also the danger that the virtuous circle could turn vicious, for decreasing marginal returns in agriculture could lead to price increases, allowing landowners to demand higher rents, reducing wages to subsistence level, and squeezing profits. Adam Smith (1723–90) was conscious of this threat, but it was David Ricardo (1772–1823), the stock broker and loan contractor turned political economist, who made it the heart of his analysis in the early nineteenth century. He suggested that growth would grind to a halt in a 'stationary state' as a result of the burden of rent.[36] It was a vision which had some substance, with a stickiness of agricultural productivity and a redistribution of income towards landowners since the publication of Smith's *Wealth of Nations* (1776).

The constraints on growth could restrict an economy which relied heavily upon organic sources of energy, whether food for men and horses, or timber for heating and building. The crucial point about London is that these constraints were slackened by the availability of seaborne coal from the north-east of England and home produced and imported foodstuffs. London continued to produce a virtuous circle of growth, escaping the shift from positive to negative feedback which occurred in such European capital cities as Madrid and even Paris, where the demands for food created serious problems, forcing the government to intervene to prevent unrest. London, a larger city in a smaller country, avoided these problems.[37]

Everything which has so far been said about London contributed to one inescapable fact: the metropolis was the greatest centre of industrial production in Britain and Europe, before, during and after the industrial revolution. London was the centre of the luxury trades for the wealthy. The lawyers, doctors, bankers and merchants who serviced the City and the government emulated their social superiors, increasing the social depth of demand from the milliners, tailors and saddlers of the West End, the coach builders of Long Acre, the cabinet makers of Tottenham Court Road, the jewellers and watchmakers of Clerkenwell. The demand was not simply to adorn their persons and homes. Doctors bought specialist surgical tools, ships' captains needed chronometers and telescopes, and men of science commissioned instruments from London tradesmen. The law, commerce and parliament had an insatiable appetite for stationery and printing, and London newspapers and publishers catered to a literate public in search of information and entertainment. London was more than a simple playground of the rich, for such demands generated a very specialised engineering industry, able to produce high-value goods such as printing presses, machine tools and steam engines. The huge size of London meant that it was also the largest single market for basic consumer goods, which stimulated the production of shoes, clothing, furniture, bread, beer and the other necessities of life. London breweries were amongst the most capital intensive concerns in the land. The cattle driven to the market at Smithfield supplied hides for the tanners at Bermondsey who produced leather to be used in shoes, saddles, coaches, book bindings. Bones were used to make glue for the furniture trades. The port generated a host of industries. London still produced naval vessels at the royal dockyards at Deptford and Woolwich, as well as the best merchant ships in a host of private yards. Vessels were repaired and refitted in London, and there was a huge demand for iron, copper, cables, pumps, masts, spars, ropes, sails and anchors. Imported goods were processed: sugar from the West Indies was refined and tallow from Russia was turned into soap and candles. Coopers toiled to produce barrels to hold these and many other commodities. The construction of London was another source of demand for industrial goods – bricks, tiles, lead pipes and cast-iron kitchen ranges. London was the centre of the transport network on land as well as sea. Every night, fast mail coaches left St. Martin's-le-Grand for the provinces, and they were built and serviced at extensive works at Mill-

35 Summerson 1945; Olsen 1964 and 1986.
36 Wrigley 1987, chapter 2, and 1988.
37 Wrigley 1987, and 1990.

bank. The coal brought down the coast kept vats, furnaces and boilers steaming in a myriad of tall chimneyed factories along the banks of the Thames. The scale of the larger industrial concerns in London could rival anything in northern towns, where the mills were simply more visible. 'The densely packed masses of building forming the eastern districts of the metropolis, on both sides of the river', commented George Dodd in 1841–42, 'include individual establishments which, although they would appear like little towns if isolated, scarcely meet the eye of a passenger through the crowded streets'. London's industry, unlike that of provincial centres, was highly diversified which made it a dynamic generator of new products and firms.

The experience of London's trades in the early nineteenth century was much more varied than the later stereotype of 'sweatshops' and casual labour would suggest. Breweries and distilleries were enormous enterprises, and their workforce consisted of reasonably well-paid labourers with a fair degree of regularity of employment, under the control of skilled foremen. Those in the specialised engineering workshops were skilled artisans, who were more likely to have constant employment than their counterparts in the shipyards and engineering works of the north, which were more susceptible to cyclical fluctuations in export markets. On the other hand, trades which were dependent upon society or affected by the seasonal variations of the port, had a high degree of insecurity.[38] Many London trades – particularly watch-making, gunmaking and cutlery – had a symbiotic relationship with provincial makers, whose semi-finished products they were dependent upon. Even these, however, like many other London trades, came increasingly to face competition from finished goods produced in the provinces and Europe, both of which benefited from lower labour costs than London. London manufacturers, as H.T. Dickinson demonstrates, often responded by attempting to become more competitive through intensifying the division of labour and weakening the hold of the traditional seven-year appenticeship system. With regard to the latter, events came to a head in 1813 when a group of leading London engineers – who had a vested interest in destroying the power of organised skilled labour – confronted the defenders of the apprenticeship system, per-

38 Hall, *Industries* 1962 and 'East London Footwear' 1962; Pollard 1950-51; Stedman Jones 1971, Part I; Goodway 1982, Part IV; Bedarida 1975; Prothero 1979; Booth 1903, p.84; Southall 1988; Schwarz 1985.

J.C. Nattes, *Bone Boilers, Willow Walk, Chelsea*, pen and wash, 1811. The British Museum

sonified by the Clockmakers' Company.[39] The engineers won, which meant that the survival of controls was left to the action of individual groups of artisans.

The artisan radicals sought to protect the honourable trades against the threats of a competitive market economy and capitalist relations. In 1820–21, the artisan radicals mobilised behind Queen Caroline, as a symbol of the attack upon the forces of corruption represented by George IV, and they could form an alliance with the shopkeeper radicalism of Matthew Wood and Robert Waithman. The critics of 'old corruption' were agreed that they wanted to overturn the placemen, loan contractors and monopolists; they differed on what should be substituted. The ambition of John Gast, the leader of the shipwrights and the spokesman of the radical artisans, was to return to an artisan commonwealth of the 'honourable' trades, which was hostile to an unfettered free market as well as political privilege. On the other hand, Francis Place saw the solution as the acceptance of political economy and free competition, creating a world in which respectability was defined as upward mobility through capitalist entrepreneurship. Here was the ideology of Thomas Tooke or Nathan Rothschild, whose attacks on the monopolies of the dock and insurance companies were couched in terms of free competition

which was anathema to the artisans. Perhaps Gast had more in common than he realised with men such as Wigram and Manning, who stood to lose from the rejection of mercantilism and the introduction of free competition.[40]

These different conceptions of London were being debated in the years around 1820, seizing upon the plight of Queen Caroline, informing the dry technicalities of monetary policy, and appearing in the struggle between privileged dock and insurance companies and their opponents. They reflected a sea change that was taking place in the economy, society and politics of London. The world of the artisan was being undermined by the challenge of provincial competition and subdivision of labour. The extravagance of London society, the dissipation of the court of George IV, gave way to a greater decorum. Patricians ceased to frequent the public pleasure gardens at Vauxhall and Ranelagh, retreating into a private world which was more strictly regulated by hostesses and the rituals of presentation at court. Evangelicals had ex-

39   Prothero 1979, pp.51-61.
40   Prothero 1979; Behagg 1990.

pressed grave unease about public morality since the late eighteenth century, stressing the need for self-discipline, and the moral contamination of public entertainments. The coronation of 1821 was a last fling before more rigid conventions were imposed. Consumption became less conspicuous, and much more private.[41] The privileges of the chartered companies and mercantilism were slowly yielding to a more competitive world. Financial retrenchment at home turned the City towards foreign loans, creating snares for the gullible yet also developing the expertise which was to make London the capital market of the world up to the First World War. The City had emerged to dominance on the basis of government loans to finance the military and naval battles of the eighteenth century; the construction of a powerful empire brought valuable cargoes to London. The power of the City was in part the product of national policy, a result of the struggle for commercial dominance over the Dutch and the strategic containment of the French. It was, however, also the product of merchants from Europe, men such as Nathan Rothschild or Alexander Baring who could provide crucial links with wider European networks of trade and finance. London in 1820 depended upon its pivotal role between Europe and the empire, a position which was to change in the following quarter century. The Latin American loan bubble was a sign of a wider involvement in international finance, and Britain's exports turned away from Europe to the newer markets of Latin America and Asia. One pattern of growth had reached its climax; another was about to begin.

41   Olsen 1986; Davidoff 1973; Malcolmson 1973.

PANTOMIME AND PAGEANTRY: THE CORONATION OF GEORGE IV

George, Prince of Wales born 1762; Prince Regent 1811; King 1820; died 1830.

Valerie Cumming

On 1 December 1826 King George IV attended the opening of parliament in the House of Lords, Westminster and was observed by a German visitor, Prince Pückler Muskau. Such public sightings of the monarch were infrequent as, by the late 1820s, he was almost a recluse with a marked sensitivity to adverse comment on his gross appearance and unwieldy movements. The prince observed 'He looked pale and bloated, and was obliged to sit on the throne for a considerable time before he could get breath enough to read his speech.' He went on

> it excited in me a strong feeling of the comic, to see how the most powerful monarch of the earth was obliged to present himself, as chief actor in a pantomime, before an audience he deems so infinitely beneath him. In fact, the whole pageant, including the King's costume, reminded me strikingly of one of those historical plays which are here got up so well; nothing was wanting but the 'flourish of trumpets' which accompanies the entrance and exit of one of Shakespeare's Kings, to make the illusion complete.[1]

It was a sad irony that a king who had, throughout his adult life, cared more deeply than any other before or since, about personal elegance, ceremonial magnificence and the good opinions of others, should be reduced in old age to a figure of fun.

Writing later in his letters, in 1828, Pückler Muskau tried to analyse the social stratification of British society at this period. He hypothesised, from his own experiences in Great Britain, that 'fashion' was more important than wealth, birth, or ability. He uses the term in its widest sense, and stated,

> it sounds ludicrous to say, (but yet it is true) that the present King, for instance, is a very fashionable man; that his father was not in the least so and that none of his brothers have any pretension to fashion; – which is unquestionably highly to their honour; for no man who has any personal claims to distinction, would be

frivolous enough to have either the power or the will to maintain himself in that category.

He compared such fashionable Englishmen with the dissolute roués of the court of Louis XV of France condemning their 'selfishness, levity, boundless vanity' and 'utter want of heart'.[2] Such harsh strictures ensured that the prince was unpopular in Great Britain after the publication of his letters in 1832 but his specific and general descriptions of British society captured something of the character and preoccupations of George IV without acknowledging the king's charm and graciousness which were recorded elsewhere.

Born in 1762, George IV was the child of King George III and Queen Charlotte (a princess of Mecklenburg-Strelitz). He was the eldest of a family of fifteen children, thirteen of whom grew to maturity, and was his mother's favourite. His relations with his father were less than easy; the Hanoverian monarchs all showed an unfortunate tendency to distrust the heir to the throne. He was created Prince of Wales at the age of one week, and shortly afterwards was displayed, in his cradle, to admiring courtiers.[3] He quickly became accustomed to public appearances, sometimes in exotic or ceremonial dress. The artist Johann Zoffany painted a portrait of Queen Charlotte in 1764/5 in which the prince and one of his younger brothers were dressed as Telemachus and a Turk respectively. On his fourth birthday he 'danced a hornpipe in a sailor's dress'; aged eight he was in a group painted by Zoffany of the royal family in 'Vandyck' costume, and the following year, 1771, saw the first painting of him in garter robes.[4]

By the time he reached his majority in 1780 he was used to public admiration and had developed into a charming but precociously sophisticated young man, whose early romance with the actress Mary Robinson had provoked comment and caricatures likening them to Prince Florizel and Perdita in Shakespeare's *The Winter's Tale*. There were to be many more caricatures throughout his life, but increasingly critical and hostile ones which attacked everything about him, from his appearance to his dis-

I am particularly indebted to Joanna Marschner of The Court Dress Collection, Kensington Palace, who allowed me unrestricted access to her unpublished research on the costume worn at George IV's coronation.

1 Pückler Muskau, ed. Butler 1957, pp.88-89.
2 Ibid., pp.334-35.
3 Brooke 1972, p.264.
4 Ibid.; Walker 1985, vol. 1, pp.206-13.

solute manner of life. Perhaps his father recognised the prince's susceptibility to the flattery and snares of fashionable society for he wrote detailed instructions about the manner of life and behaviour that the prince was to follow once he had been given his own establishment. Amongst this plethora of advice was the firm admonition 'I shall not permit the going to balls or assemblies at private houses ... As to masquerades you already know my disapprobation of them in this country, and I cannot by any means agree to any of my children going to them.'[5] The Prince of Wales ignored his father and swiftly espoused all the pleasures, including masquerades and private parties, and vices of fashionable society.

His friend, Georgiana, Duchess of Devonshire, wrote a short character sketch of him in 1782. Even then he was a contradictory man: extravagant, overly susceptible to wine, women and gambling, given to meddling in opposition politics, too fond of pleasure but also good natured, loyal to his closest friends, with an 'ease and grace of ... manner' which was unusual in his family. She described him as 'rather tall' with

> a figure which tho' striking is not perfect. He is inclined to be too fat and looks too much like a woman in men's cloaths, but the gracefulness of his manner and his height certainly make him a pleasing figure. His face is handsome and he is fond of dress even to a tawdry degree, which young as he is, will soon wear off. His person, his dress and the admiration he has met, and thinks still more than he meets, from women take up his thoughts chiefly.[6]

The duchess was wrong only in her opinion that the Prince of Wales would grow bored with clothes as he matured. It was one of the abiding interests of his adult life, despite a life-long battle against corpulence; in his teens he had noted in himself 'rather too great a penchant to grow fat', but never strong-willed he dieted fiercely, but briefly, before succumbing once more to the pleasures of good food and wine.[7]

Remembered today as the most informed royal connoisseur and patron of the fine and applied arts since Charles I, concentrating his energies on the glorification and improvement of royal residences and collections, he was ridiculed in his lifetime as 'The Prince of Whales'; his real and perceived excesses epitomising the supposedly rackety society of late eighteenth and early nineteenth century London. However, a short essay such as this can only hint at the complexities of George IV's character and interests. It is intended as an introduction to his fascination with the ephemeral concerns of personal appearance, in private and in public, formally planned and recorded for posterity (e.g. in portraits, official publications and, most notably, at his coronation), or trivialised and lampooned by caricaturists.

His father, George III disliked London, abhorred fashionable society and its concerns, and preferred the country, but George IV was a thoroughly metropolitan prince and monarch. His maturity coincided with the international recognition of the excellence of men's tailoring in London. There was widespread admiration for and adoption of the sober but well-cut men's tailcoats, made of the finest cloth and seen to advantage when worn with linen shirts, exquisitely ordered cravats and closely fitting knee breeches, or (after c.1800) pantaloons and then from c.1825 trousers. The Prince of Wales and his friend George 'Beau' Brummell vied with each other for recognition as the most elegant men in Europe at the turn of the century. Brummell was perhaps more single-minded in his obsession with clothing than the prince, but both personified a style which was expensively understated and closely copied.

Tailors such as Schweitzer and Davidson, in Cork Street, Joseph Weston in Old Bond Street, and John Meyer in Conduit Street, were concentrated on the Burlington Estate in the West End close to the modern Savile Row. Meyer started his career in Germany as a military tailor. His skills in cutting uniforms made of woollen cloth were obviously applicable to the requirements of men's fashionable clothes in the late eighteenth and early nineteenth centuries when the change from silk to cloth took place.[8] The Prince of Wales also patronised these firms and in the early 1790s had unpaid tailors' bills of over £30,000.[9] He was a prodigious customer and immensely knowledgeable about the details of menswear. His wife, Princess Caroline of Brunswick, with whom he briefly cohabited before they separated in the late 1790s, commented on his shortcomings and suggested that they might have been better matched if she had been the man and the prince 'the woman to wear the petticoats ... He understands how a shoe should be made or a coat cut ... and would make an excellent tailor, or shoemaker or hairdresser but nothing else.'[10] The princess had been adept,

5   Hibbert 1972, pp.20-21. This is by far the most complete and balanced biography of George IV and an essential source for everyone who works on any aspect of the king's interests.
6   Bessborough ed. 1955, p.289.
7   Ibid.
8   Walker 1988, pp.21-22; Hibbert 1972, pp.174-77
9   Hibbert 1972.
10 Ibid., p.218.

from the outset of their short-lived alliance, at wounding her husband's vanity. When she saw him for the first time she said, with her usual tactlessness, 'I think he's very fat and nothing like as handsome as his portrait.'[11] His weight fluctuated, but he was rarely less than plump, often obese. He controlled this by wearing a corset or 'body belt' as it was euphemistically called. A surviving pattern of one made for him in 1824, indicating a waist measurement of 50 inches, is included in the exhibition.[12]

Portraits of the prince recorded him in fashionable dress, military uniform and ceremonial robes. In the first category the excellence of his tailors and other suppliers is evident, as the Honourable George Keppel recalled, 'His clothes fitted him like a glove; his coat was single-breasted and buttoned up to the chin . . . Round his throat was a huge white neck-cloth of many folds out of which his chin seemed to be always struggling to emerge.'[13] Portraiture, however, can flatter and he was often depicted in

profile or three-quarters stance to the viewer, thus suggesting a more heroic, less corpulent figure. The heroic qualities are especially evident when he was portrayed wearing uniform. From his father and great-grandfather (George II) he inherited a fascination for military uniform, and like them he took a personal interest in the design of new uniforms. His daughter, Princess Charlotte of Wales, with whom he had an uneasy relationship, found him at his most genial when discussing uniforms. Shortly after her marriage to Prince Leopold of Saxe Coburg Gotha in 1816, the Prince Regent visited his daughter and she wrote of a conversation

11   Ibid., p.242.
12   Museum of London, A27042; donated by A.T. Barber in 1924.
13   Hibbert 1972, p.242.

being fully occupied with discanting and discouraging upon the merits and demerits of such and such a uniform, the cut of such a coat, cape, sleeve, small clothes etc. In short for two hours and more I think we had a most learned dissertation upon every regt. under the sun wh. is a *great mark* of the *most perfect good humour*.[14]

In the same year, a decree was issued in his name, supposedly to support British manufactured textiles, which required 'all his state and household officers to wear costly dresses of home fabrication . . . to be made in three classes of uniforms, according to the respective ranks of these officers.'[15] This was unpopular with those concerned well into the 1820s but eventually the categorisation of public officials into ranks of civil uniform became so acceptable that by the 1830s four classes were required and, by the 1840s, five classes. The imposition of uniform is, of course, one method by which groups in society can be regulated and identified. It suppressed individuality but enhanced the idea of a structured and coherent society in which outward appearance communicated social status.

By the time George IV became King of Great Britain and Hanover on 29 January 1820 he was fifty-seven and in poor health. The succeeding eighteen months between his accession and the coronation on 19 July 1821 were a severe test of his physical and mental well-being. The coronation, originally planned for 1 August 1820 was postponed and was replaced by the spectacle of his estranged wife Queen Caroline, who had returned from Italy on 5 June, appearing before an enquiry in the House of Lords. This was the first stage in the process of a parliamentary bill to effect a divorce between king and queen, on the grounds of her adulterous relationships. London and the country at large were split unevenly in its support, with the queen evoking much popular sympathy. Many satirists, caricaturists and artists supported the queen and there was an unprecedented number of unfavourable prints and pamphlets lampooning the king.[16] For much of his adult life George IV had been the butt of caricature but his sensitivity to them did not decrease. Throughout his life, which coincided with the golden age of British portrait painting, he had chosen the finest artists to convey an elegant and heroic image. Gainsborough, Stubbs, Beechey, Hoppner, Lawrence and Wilkie all contributed to this visual iconography, but undoubtedly the majority of his subjects were more familiar with him through the caricatures of Rowlandson, Gillray, Cruikshank and others. Their image of him as an obese, dissolute spendthrift ensured that his faults were more in public view than his undoubted but less well-known assets.

Fortunately plans for the coronation provided the type of diversion which he relished. The interest in detail and the pursuit of perfection which had characterised his major building and interior decoration projects at Carlton House and Brighton Pavilion were brought to bear on the arrangements for his coronation. The coronation of his parents had taken place on 22 September 1761 and details of the ceremonies enacted then were readily available but the new king also consulted Francis Sandford's *Coronation of James II*, a lavishly illustrated and detailed volume published in 1687. Although the Divorce Bill was abandoned in November 1820, it was not George IV's intention to share his coronation with his estranged queen and he ordered that on no account was she to be admitted to Westminster Abbey as participant or spectator. Undoubtedly the king perceived the coronation as an opportunity both to win back some degree of public popularity and also to impress upon foreign ambassadors and dignitaries that, since the defeat of Napoleon at Waterloo in 1815, Great Britain, personified by the British monarch, was the most powerful country in Europe. Naturally this was all going to cost a great deal of money and the published Treasury account of 1823 gave a total expenditure on the coronation of £238,238.0s.2d. Significantly this was broken down into two funds. Parliament voted £100,000 in the 1820 session but the larger share of £138,238.0s.2d. was paid 'out of Money received from France on Account of pecuniary Indemnity, under Treaty, Anno 1815'.[17] The French nation therefore had, directly and indirectly, paid for the two most lavish coronations celebrated in the period 1800 to 1840; the Emperor Napoleon I's on 2 December 1804 and King George IV's. Napoleon died on 5 May 1821 in exile on St. Helena, but the spectacular nature of his coronation undoubtedly inspired George IV to attempt an event of even greater magnificence.

The major ceremonial events which comprised the coronation were well established. Firstly, there was an assembly in Westminster Hall of those who formed part of the coronation procession and spectators who would also be present later in the Abbey; followed by the procession on foot from Westminster Hall to Westminster Abbey. Then the coronation of the king with its specified order of service was enacted. The return procession to Westminster Hall was followed by the coronation ban-

14 Aspinall ed. 1949, p.242.
15 *Annual Register 1817*, p.100.
16 Hibbert 1973, p.157.
17 Tanner 1952, p.67.

quet at which a series of feudal offerings and services were performed, the most dramatic of which was the appearance of the King's Champion on horseback. This all took a great deal of planning and organisation and was the responsibility of the Earl Marshal of England (nominally the Duke of Norfolk, but his duties were performed by his deputy, Lord Howard of Effingham). Fortunately the postponement of the coronation from August 1820 until July 1821 allowed a considerable amount of extra time to be spent on the arrangements. The Treasury account of expenses listed fifteen categories of expenditure, the smallest of which was £118.18s.6d. paid to the Master of the Horse for organising 'the Charger for the Champion'; a trained and docile beast used to crowds was hired from Astley's circus for the occasion. However, of the total expenditure, four categories account for a sum of £211,428.17s.5d. most of which was spent on ephemeral show, marking this coronation out as the most extravagant in English history. These categories are, in the order given in the account,

Lord Steward . . . Expenses attending the Banquet	£25,184.9s.8d
Lord Chamberlain . . . for the Furniture and Decorations of Westminster Abbey, and Westminster Hall; for providing the Regalia; for Dresses etc of the Persons attending and performing various Duties	£111,172.9s.10d
Master of the Robes . . . for His Majesty's Robes etc	£24,704.8s.10d
Surveyor General of Works . . . for fitting up Westminster Abbey and Westminster Hall, Platforms etc	£50,367.9s.1d[18]

According to the *Annual Register* for 1821 the proclamation of 6 May 1820 which had appointed 1 August 1820 as the original date for the coronation had led to works commencing in Westminster Hall, Westminster Abbey and the vicinity. These were suspended once Queen Caroline had arrived in England and re-established herself in London. The works started again in May 1821 and on the 9 June a proclamation announced that Thursday 19 July 1820 would be coronation day. In fact, as early as March 1820 the Surveyor-General, Colonel Stephenson and his two principal architects had started 'to consult a great number of ancient authorities', mainly being guided by the *Coronation of James II* but adopting 'such improvements as might seem advisable'.[19] The works were ex-

M. Dubourg after C. Wild, detail from the *Procession of the Dean and Prebendaries of Westminster carrying the Regalia into Westminster Hall*, aquatint published in Nayler's *Coronation of George IV*, 1824. The Museum of London

tensive for Westminster Hall had to be prepared for both the pre-coronation assembly and post-coronation banquet. A raised wooden floor was installed; tiers of galleries projected upwards and outwards at each side; boxes for the royal family and other dignitaries were constructed, sideboards, dining tables, platforms, a triumphal arch, and stables for the Champion's Horse were prepared. There was much use of crimson and scarlet cloth, fringing and ornamental ropes and the overall design inclined heavily to the Gothic. Imitation Gothic panelling, Gothic arches, Gothic fretwork, Gothic pillars, Gothic-style chairs must have suggested a pseudo-medieval pageantry in keeping with the period of the building. Temporary structures were also installed in the Abbey where the organ was given 'a new gothic front'. The finest

18 Ibid.
19 *Annual Register 1821*, Appendix to Chronicle, pp.324-25, 328.

Detail from the *Coronation Procession, showing the Canopy held aloft over the King, guarded on either side by the Honourable Band of Gentlemen Pensioners,* aquatint published by G. Humphrey, 1821. The Museum of London

textiles were used in the Abbey: blue and gold brocade for the altar, garter-blue and gold Wilton carpet on the altar steps and sacrarium floor, crimson velvet and sarsenet for the royal box and a good deal of crimson cloth for the boxes and benches inside the western aisle. The last area had been 'let for a large sum to a person by the name of Glanville' by the dean and chapter, a profitable undertaking for both parties. Access was carefully regulated along all routes leading to the Abbey and Westminster Hall and, on the Wednesday evening the 1,500 feet-long platform, raised 3 feet above the ground which connected both buildings was completed. Earlier that day a rehearsal had taken place 'of all the duties to be performed by the state officers' according to a printed plan issued to each of them. Throughout all the preparations, the needs of the press were borne in mind and they were given seats from which 'they could command an excellent view of all the ceremonies'.[20]

Such comprehensive structural and decorative effects account for the Surveyor-General's expenditure of over £50,000 and for a portion of the Lord Chamberlain's £111,000 spent on furniture and decorations for both buildings. It is also not difficult, examining the list of food and wine consumed at the banquet to understand how easily £25,000 might be spent by the Lord Steward. Twenty-three kitchens, supervised by Jean-Baptiste Watier, produced 160 tureens of soup, a similar amount of fish dishes, roast joints of venison, beef, mutton and veal, vegetables and appropriate gravies etc presented in 480 sauce boats. Cold dishes, including ham, pastries, seafood and jellies number 3,271. All this was washed down with 9,840 bottles of various wines and 100 gallons of iced punch.[21]

Such munificence would, undoubtedly, have rendered the coronation memorable as an example of regal extravagance. There was, however, an additional element which rendered it wholly exceptional in the history of English coronations. This became apparent when participants in the procession began arriving wearing 'splendid, and in some instances grotesque dresses . . . Of the latter description were the dresses of the pursuivants, gentlemen pen-

20 Ibid., pp.328-38, 344.
21 Tanner 1952, p.67; *Annual Register 1821*, pp.111-12, 381.

sioners, the attendants of the lords spiritual, and many others, which were fashioned after the model of the earliest times.'[22] George IV's delight in the unusual and exotic, his interest in the visual coherence imposed by uniform, and his pleasure in masquerades and fancy dress should perhaps have prepared the world for an unexpected style of coronation dress. In earlier centuries peers and royal officials wore formal versions of fashionable dress under the robes, but this allowed unpredictability to mar an overall visual image. In the dedication to George IV by Sir George Nayler, Garter King of Arms, of the volume in which he recorded the coronation in much the same manner as Sandford had recorded James II's, a justification is given for the unusual style of dress. Nayler wrote of

> the superb Habiliments which Your Majesty, not less regardful of the Prosperity of Your People than of the Splendour of Your Throne, was pleased to enjoin should be worn upon the occasion, thereby affording employment to Thousands of Your industrious and loyal Subjects, and rendering the solemn Ceremony the most magnificent which this Country ever beheld.

These are the words of a consummate and ambitious courtier, who had received £3,000 'towards the Publication of the Account of the Ceremony', a work which had been issued in part but was unfinished at his death in 1831.[23]

The inspiration for the 'grotesque dresses' came from a number of sources. It was, after all, a period in which there was considerable interest in a romanticised view of the sixteenth and seventeenth centuries. As had been mentioned, George IV had been painted on more than one occasion as a young man in 'Vandyck dress', that perennially favourite form of fancy dress for eighteenth-century aristocrats. It was loosely based on the style worn at Charles I's court in the 1630s. He had also, on several occasions, been depicted in garter robes, essential elements of which were an underdress of silver doublet and matching trunk-hose; these quasi-historical garments blended sixteenth-century and early 1660s' styles into a stylish whole. One of the most successful portraits of him in garter dress had been painted by Sir Thomas Lawrence in 1818. Although flattering, it was generally well received by the British press, attracting such comments as 'dignified and graceful' and 'very magnificent'.[24] Lawrence also painted George IV in coronation robes and the similarities between the two depictions are evident, not merely in pose but in the fanciful details of the costume. George also professed respect for the French King Henri IV 'whom I admire almost to the point of extravagance'.[25]

Henri was assassinated in 1610 and formal portraits of him depict the early seventeenth-century fashions which, in pastiche form, were used for garter dress, and remained a stock-in-trade for certain types of theatre costume (c.f. catalogue entry for Edmund Kean's costume for Richard III). Their influence was also found in the types of dress devised for post-revolutionary French officials and published in Jacques Grosset de Saint-Sauveur's *Costumes des Représentans du Peuple Français* in 1795.

George IV was not a monarch who would have expressed interest in or admiration for the achievements of either the revolutionary rulers of France or their successor, the Emperor Napoleon I. It cannot be doubted, however, that the experiments with quasi-classical and historical forms of official dress during the 1790s in France, which culminated in the 'most elaborate system of court and official dress ever put into practice' under Napoleon, had a widespread and lasting effect throughout Europe.[26] By expressing admiration for Henri IV, and re-working seventeenth-century English styles, it may be supposed that George IV and his advisers were distancing themselves from pre-1815 France. However, it is impossible to understand the 1821 coronation without briefly considering the magnificent pageantry of Napoleon I's coronation in 1804. It set a standard in organisational detail and visual splendour and was so well recorded that its influence was felt long after the event.

Napoleon I's coronation costume was pishly described by an observer as resembling 'a walking dish of ice-cream', consisted of a *grand costume* and a *petit costume*. Both had been designed by Jean-Baptiste Isabey, who with his fellow artist Jacques-Louis David was responsible for all aspects of the pageantry and dress for the participants at the coronation. The distinction between the *grand costume* of imperial mantle of crimson velvet and ermine worn over an ankle-length, white satin tunic, both heavily embroidered with gold emblems, and the *petit costume* of crimson velvet, knee-length mantle, matching coat and white embroidered knee breeches and stockings was that the former was worn for the religious service of

22 *Annual Register 1821*, p.346.
23 Nayler 1837, dedication, publisher's advertisement; Tanner 1952, p.67.
24 Levey, 1979, p.67.
25 Halls 1973, p.12.
26 Ribeiro 1988, pp.104-05, 140. Dr. Ribeiro's analysis of the development of official and court uniform is essential reading for all who are interested in this subject. See also Delpierre, No. 2 1958 and No. 1 1978, for articles on Napoleonic and Revolutionary costume.

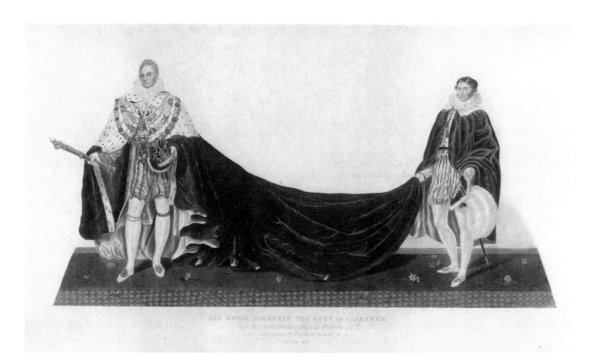

The Duke of Clarence, brother and heir to George IV in procession to the Abbey; the extravagance of this coronation prompted the duke, when William IV, to resist all but the simplest coronation ceremonial, engraving published in Whittaker's *Coronation of George IV*, 1823. The Museum of London

coronation. The *petit costume* was worn before and after and for later ceremonial occasions. It was similar to the styles designed for the officials and courtiers who accompanied the emperor at his coronation. Their costumes were categorised by colour and scale of decoration and were the originals of all later official styles worn during the first empire in France. The cost of all this was prodigious; gold embroidery for the emperor's costumes alone cost over 29,000 francs. The overall effect, as David's painting of the coronation conveys, was magnificent, with every participant literally designed to form part of a colourful, glittering masterpiece of state pageantry.[27]

As a connoisseur of paintings, interior decoration and tailoring, and with his sympathy for the Gothic and fancifully historic, it was inevitable that George IV would wish the participants in his coronation to be as visually coherent and as memorable as possible. This was achieved by means of a carefully prepared set of designs for all those who formed part of the procession. These were either prepared or adjusted at the College of Arms in the City of London. From the College a notice was issued on 17 June 1820 requesting the attendance of peers of the realm and other senior dignitaries to view 'under habits and dresses' to be worn at the coronation. The postponement of the coronation meant that a second notice about the viewing of styles to be worn by those below the rank of peer, pages, train-bearers etc was not issued until 22 June 1821, less than a month before the coronation.[28] Given the number of participants it was, however, likely that work

on the various garments had taken place throughout the period of postponement. The Lord Chamberlain's department had a large number of suppliers working on coronation preparations. These included 2 silk mercers, 6 gold lacemen, one silk laceman, 3 embroiderers, one robemaker, 28 tailors, one button maker, one cap maker, 2 hatters, one 'plumasoier', 2 sword cutlers, one herald painter and 2 goldsmiths, all with substantial workshops or establishments.[29] An example of their work can be provided by considering the robemaker William Webb's involvement. He received £2,044.4s.0d. for mantles and other garments worn by members and officers of orders of chivalry, kings of arms, heralds and so forth: well over 150 were provided. His invoice for the complete set of garments ordered by Lord Braybrook, including gloves, shoes and a cedarwood storage chest came to £250. On the day of the coronation Webb took twenty men to assist with the robing and unrobing of peers, his account for this service and 'Expenses for Provisions and Boats to and from Westminster' came to £43.10s.6d.[30]

All the complex preparations finally came to fruition on the evening of 18 July 1821 when George IV arrived to spend the night before his coronation at the Speaker of

27 le Bourhis ed. 1989, pp.86-89, 93, 209-11, 205.
28 Nayler 1837, pp.59, 97.
29 Public Record Office, LC2/50.
30 Campbell 1989, pp.36-37, 19.

E. Scriven after J.P. Stephanoff, *The King attended by the Eight Eldest Sons of Peers who held the Train of his Crimson Mantle as he processed to the Abbey*, engraving published in Whittaker's *Coronation of George IV*, 1823. The Museum of London

the House of Commons' residence at Westminster. It cannot have been a peaceful night as the noise of continued preparations and clamour of the crowds were heard outside. Adding extra tension, early on coronation morning Queen Caroline drove to Westminster Abbey and demanded entry, attracting widespread attention. The *Annual Register* recorded that a number of the curious were ready for the day ahead: 'The grotesqueness of their dresses, as they appeared on the leads of the committee rooms of the House of Commons, had a most singular appearance'. As the participants and spectators assembled, 'the splendour and singularity of the costumes produced much amusement among the ladies'.[31] Then at 10 a.m. the king arrived in Westminster Hall 'most splendidly attired' and the formal proceedings began with the presentation of the regalia. At 10.25 the procession commenced its serpentine route, along a blue cloth covered platform to the Abbey, with every sort of response from hisses to applause emanating from the watching crowds. The king, dressed in a cloth of silver doublet and trunk-hose, a crimson velvet surcoat and fur-lined, crimson velvet mantle of great weight and length, a hat decorated with plumes of feathers on his head, walked beneath a canopy of cloth of gold carried by sixteen barons of the Cinque Ports. His robe was so massive that it took eight rather than the usual six eldest sons of peers to carry it. The robe was akin to that worn by Kings of France, it was heavily embroidered in gold thread and as he moved forward he exhorted his pages to 'Hold it wider'.[32] In the

Abbey he 'appeared distressed, almost to fainting', due in part to the heat, the weight of his state robe which 'might have overpowered a man in the most vigorous bodily health' and his vanity: he had corsetted himself more tightly than usual.[33] The coronation service then began; it took several hours, the procession did not return to Westminster Hall for the banquet until 4 p.m., the king now robed in purple velvet.

Undoubtedly, George IV succeeded in his intention of creating a spectacular and memorable day of pageantry. Even the lapse into melodrama caused by Queen Caroline's attempts to participate added to the general excitement. The sceptics derided the absurdities but the majority were impressed by the dignity and grandeur of the occasion. A Westminster schoolboy thought the king 'looked too large for effect, indeed he was more like an Elephant than a man' but Sir Walter Scott thought him 'every inch a King'.[34] Both the Earl of Denbigh who was closely involved as a participant and Benjamin Haydon, a spectator, were united in their view that this was a personal triumph for the king, and a day of almost magical enchantment. Haydon had a ticket for Westmin-

31 *Annual Register 1821*, pp.348, 352.
32 Ibid., pp.353-63; Halls 1973, p.48; Hibbert 1973, p.192.
33 *Annual Register 1821*, p.365.
34 Tanner 1952, p.64.

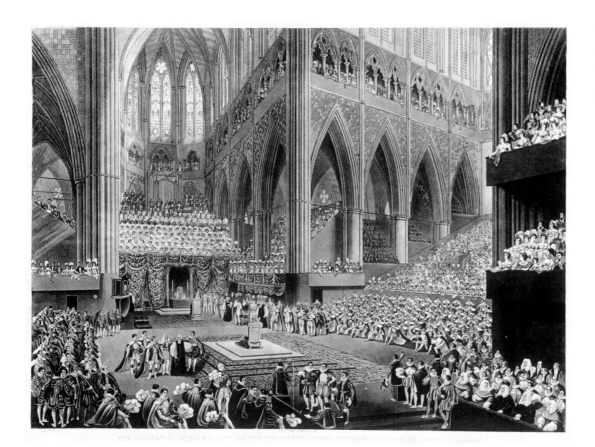

M. Dubourg after J.P. Stephanoff, *The Coronation Ceremony in Westminster Abbey*, aquatint published by R. Bowyer, 1822. The Museum of London

ster Hall, but not the Abbey, so he observed the pre-coronation events and the post-coronation banquet. The arrival of George IV in the morning caused the spectators to rise 'with a sort of feathered silken thunder! Plumes wave, eyes sparkle, glasses are out, mouths smile. The way in which The King bowed was really monarchic! As he looked towards the Peeresses and Foreign Ambassadors,he looked like some gorgeous bird of the East.'[35] In the Abbey Scott thought 'the effect of the scene . . . was beyond measure magnificent', although he had reservations about the unusual style of dress: 'Separately so gay a garb had an odd effect on the persons of elderly or ill-made men'.[36] The king being one of these elderly men, he looked, according to Lady Cowper 'more like the victim than the hero of the fête', but after recourse to sal volatile he revived.[37] He returned, triumphantly to Westminster Hall for the banquet, and Lord Denbigh confided to his mother, 'Of the splendour of the whole spectacle it is impossible for me to give you the *slightest* idea. It exceeded all imagination and conception.' He described the participants, the 'most magnificent dresses' and the 'blaze of diamonds', with Prince Esterhazy 'said to have had jewels on his person estimated at *eighty thousand* pounds'.[38]

Haydon was much taken by the King's Champion 'a man in dark shadowed armour' who, attended by the Duke of Wellington and Lord Howard, 'was certainly the finest sight of the day. The herald read the challenge; the glove was thrown down; they all then proceeded to the throne. My imagination got so intoxicated that I came out with a great contempt for the plebs . . .' In summarising his impressions of the day he provided a description which would surely have endeared him to the king:

It combined all the gorgeous splendour of ancient chivalry with the intense heroic interest of modern times; – every thing that could effect or excite, either in beauty, heroism, genius, grace, elegance, or taste; all that was rich in colour, gorgeous in effect, touching in association, English in character or Asiatic in magnifi-

35 Haydon ed. Joliffe 1990, p.78.
36 Quoted in *The Sun* newspaper's coronation supplement, 28 June 1838, p.4.
37 Hibbert 1973, p.192.
38 Ibid., p.193; cf. *The Sun* 28 June 1838, p.4.

THE CORONATION OF GEORGE IV

G. Scharf, *The Procession after the Coronation Ceremony to Westminster Hall*, lithograph published by G. Humphrey, 1821. The Museum of London

cence was crowded into this golden and enchanted hall![39]

This view passed into popular mythology very rapidly, for by 1838, the year of Queen Victoria's coronation it was being recalled as 'the most splendid [coronation] ever celebrated in England'.[40]

Other successes followed before the king withdrew into semi-seclusion. He visited Ireland in 1821, undertook a tour of France and Belgium en route to Hanover in the same year and, in 1822, visited Scotland. This provided an opportunity for him to add a range of Scottish items to his wardrobe, which included royal tartan in satin, velvet and cashmere. As a Scotsman he did not look altogether convincing, although he was painted in kilt, plaid and bonnet by David Wilkie. His appearance suggested an actor in a part, an aspect of his public persona which Prince Pückler Muskau noted in 1826. However, to the end of his life he did not lose interest in clothing which, like all of his more substantial and long-lasting interests and achievements, combined a keen visual sense with a desire for novelty and amusement. He was, essentially, a figure of the *ancien régime*, out of step with the changes of the post-1800

period; as Talleyrand indicated, after his death 'King George IV was *un roi grand seigneur*. There are no others left.'[41]

His legacy is found in his inspired patronage of artists, craftsmen, architects. Of his most personal effects little survived. At his death he was deeply in debt, a victim, as his brother William IV succinctly described it, of 'damned expensive taste'. His clothes and other personal items were auctioned over three days in December 1830 and ran to 438 lots. The range was enormous as the catalogue of 'the expensive wardrobe, military jackets and splendid silk and velvet robes, plumes of ostrich feathers and mis-

39 Haydon ed. Joliffe 1990, pp.77, 78. Haydon's comparisons with oriental splendour may, in part, reflect the king's interest in Indian and Chinese decoration which found principal expression in the works at Brighton Pavilion. Lord Byron's verse drama *Sardanapalus*, published in 1821, suggested analogies between George IV and the Assyrian monarch, as Professor Marilyn Butler's essay in this volume demonstrates.
40 *The Sun,* 28 June 1838, p.4.
41 Hibbert 1973, p.345.

cellanous items' demonstrated.[42] A further sale took place in June 1831 when the *Annual Register* recorded the details of items connected with his coronation, namely the lace ruff, the crimson coronation mantle, the matching surcoat, the 'silver tissue' doublet and trunkhose, and the purple velvet mantle worn on that occasion; sold for £133.7s.0d.[43] It is fortunate that the families of those who attended the coronation and whose ancestors' garments are displayed in this exhibition, cared more for posterity's interest in this extraordinary occasion than did George IV's brother. Perhaps, however, it is more appropriate that he is represented in this exhibition as portrayed by Lawrence, in the pristine glamour of his glittering ensemble. It would not have pleased the 'first gentleman of Europe' to be remembered by worn and repaired shells of those garments he wore in the greatest pageant of this period.[44]

42 The auction was conducted by Mr. Phillips at his Bond Street sale rooms on 15, 16 and 17 December 1830; items described are taken from the catalogue of the second and third days, MoL 38.294/1.

43 *Annual Register,* Chronicle section 1831, pp.81-82. These garments were acquired by Madame Tussaud's waxworks and exhibited to the public. Robert Elliston, actor-manager and lessee of the Theatre Royal, Drury Lane had tried to borrow them in July 1821 for theatrical use. He was unsuccessful, see de Marly, 1982, p.35.

44 George IV's coronation mantle survives in the collection of Tussauds but is fragile. The surcoat, silver tissue doublet and trunk-hose etc. once associated with him, and owned by the Earl of Ancaster (see Halls 1973, p.48) may be contemporary copies, made for George IV but not worn by him. I am indebted for this information to Joanna Marschner.

G. Scharf, detail from *The Procession after the Coronation Ceremony to Westminster Hall with the King shown wearing the Crown*, lithograph published by G. Humphrey, 1821. The Museum of London

THE BUILDING ART OF THE FIRST INDUSTRIAL METROPOLIS

Andrew Saint

'London is at the same time the metropolis of the empire, the centre of England's home trade and the centre of its foreign trade. The concurrence of these three factors is what makes it the richest, the largest and the most populous among all the cities of the old world.'[1] The writer of these words belonged to a new breed of visitor to London in the years after Waterloo. Charles Dupin (1784–1873) was a patriotic young French engineer from the prestigious École Polytechnique. Caught up in the drama of the Napoleonic years, he had helped build the flotilla of barges assembled at Boulogne in 1804 for the invasion of England that never happened, and then to reconstruct his country's fleet after the crushing defeat of Trafalgar. When peace came, one issue preoccupied Dupin. Why had less populous, ill-trained and incoherently administered Britain managed to outwit and outlast almighty France? What were the practical keys to British power?

To find the answers, Dupin made lengthy visits to Britain – above all, London – from 1816 to 1819 and published a sequence of writings in the hope that France might profit from his analysis. They are different from the piquant travel memoirs of earlier visitors to England. Dupin is obsessed with technology and infrastructure: with machines, docks, arsenals, bridges, factories, ships and commerce. These, rather than its ceremonial or private architecture, had made London distinctive and Britain dominant over the short twenty years of the Revolutionary and Napoleonic Wars.

Similar aims underlay the Prussian bureaucrat Peter Beuth and architect Karl Friedrich Schinkel's British visit of 1826. Beuth had been to England before as part of his campaign to invigorate Prussian trades and manufactures. He knew what to show his friend: again, docks, factories, warehouses and bridges. Compared to these, the conventional major London public works by the major London architects made scant impact on Schinkel, though he did not ignore them. If we wish to grasp what was unique about London between 1800 and 1840 it is with infrastructure, manufactures and commerce we must start: above all, with the docks.

THE DOCKS

London owes its existence to the Thames. Its position, close to the open sea but protected by a stretch of easily navigable river, made it a port of world importance almost from the instant of its Roman foundation. Trade always came before elegance as a priority for London's city fathers. That is why the ideal plans of Wren and others for rebuilding the city after the Great Fire of 1666 came to nothing. It is also why London has been slower to embank and ornament its river frontages than cities like Paris, where rapid access from quays to ships was less vital to its prosperity.

For centuries nearly all international shipping still used quays in the heart of the City of London, downstream of the ancient, many-arched London Bridge. But the system had reached the point of suffocation by 1800. London at that date handled something like 70 per cent of Britain's imports and 56 per cent of its exports, and had enjoyed a three-fold leap in the value of its international trade in the previous thirty years.[2] All this passed either through the 'Legal Quays', less than 500 yards of open river frontage between the Tower of London and London Bridge, presided over by the Custom House, or through a number of extra 'sufferance wharves' which had been added piecemeal. The total available quay space was no larger than that of the much smaller port of Bristol, and lacked security. Pilfering was endemic, delay chronic and labour chaotic.

The answer lay in retrenchment and reorganisation downstream in a massive system of enclosed wet docks – an idea first put forward by an insurance broker, William Vaughan, in 1793. The Port of London had been seeping eastwards for three centuries. The great naval dockyards at Deptford and Woolwich, founded by Henry VIII, were still operating at full stretch in the Napoleonic Wars. But they were declining in importance compared with Chatham, Portsmouth and Plymouth because modern 'ships of the line' needed a deeper draft than the Thames could offer.[3] Merchant-shipbuilding, one of London's great industries until 1900, centred upon Blackwall on the Isle of Dogs peninsula, whence the founders of Virginia set out in 1606. Two basins away from the river already existed, but these were for shipbuilding, repair or 'park-

---

1 Dupin 1824, pp.2-3. See also Bradley and Perrin 1991, pp.47-68.
2 Bird 1957, pp.28-51.
3 Morriss 1983, pp.39-45.

N. Pocock, *Woolwich Naval Dockyard*, oil on canvas, 1790. Though overtaken in importance during the Napoleonic Wars by Chatham, Portsmouth and Plymouth, Woolwich and the smaller dockyard up-river at Deptford remained major naval establishments and were very large employers. National Maritime Museum

London and the Thames in 1830, showing the position of the bridges, docks, canals and military-industrial institutions.

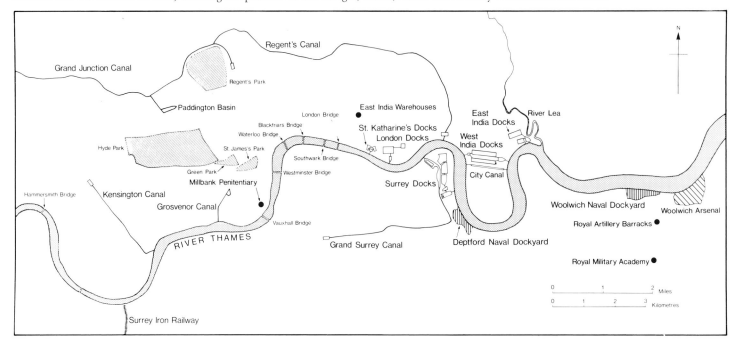

THE BUILDING ART OF THE FIRST INDUSTRIAL METROPOLIS

ing', not for loading or unloading (whale oil being an exception).

As crucial as better docking was safe storage in modern warehouses away from the river. Here the powerful East India Company, flush with the produce of British conquests in India, was the first to break away from the chaos of the Legal Quays. In 1792–99 its directors raised huge 'stacks' of brick warehouses close to their City headquarters – the earliest of London's great 'bonded warehouse' systems, still extant in carcase.[4] The precious East India cargoes were conveyed hither under guard from the river and stored under a bond that duty would be paid at the time of sale. The scale of this establishment forced others to reconsider. To the forefront were the West India merchants who dealt in bulkier produce such as rum, sugar, molasses and mahogany and had long been suing for better port facilities. Vaughan's proposal was the next step of building secure, enclosed wet docks which could combine better arrangements for handling cargoes with bonded warehouses on the quayside. Some other ports, notably Liverpool and Le Havre, had already begun to move in this direction. But London's docks were to be on a scale never before envisaged and constructed with astonishing speed, under the impetus of the war with France.

From the plethora of dock plans put forward in the 1790s, two parallel schemes of Roman immensity emerged. One was the West India Docks, laid out on the northern portion of the Isle of Dogs between 1800 and 1806 by the engineers William Jessop and Ralph Walker. It boasted two long dock basins and a range of warehouses over half a mile long fringing the import dock. Less than one-third of the length of these inexorable 'stacks' survives today. To the south of the basins ran Jessop's short-lived City canal, built for the Corporation of the City of London and intended as a bypass for the loop round the Isle of Dogs. At Wapping, another group of merchants – who included William Vaughan – built the London Docks (1800–05), also with separate basins for export and import. Here the engineer was John Rennie and the architect Daniel Alexander. The latter's stacks, more rhythmic and architectonic than those of the West India Docks, have all been wantonly destroyed apart from the tobacco warehouse, an afterthought of 1811.[5]

The West India and the London Docks were soon supplemented by others. The East India Company saw the virtue of unloading down river and in 1803–06 the East India Dock Company took over one of the old shipbuilding basins at Blackwall. They built no storage space, bringing in their cargoes by road to their City warehouses instead. On the south or Surrey side of the Thames, on

Tobacco Warehouse, London Dock, branching iron support. Daniel Alexander, architect, 1811. An example of the radical use of iron in London warehouse construction during the last phase of the Napoleonic Wars. Greater London Record Office

the Rotherhithe peninsula, a further system of docks grew up (1807–11), connected by canal to the hinterland and much used by the coal, timber and building trades. Later came St. Katharine's Docks next to the Tower (1825–29), the sole London work of the great engineer Thomas Telford. This complex boasted the first set of stacks that allowed unloading directly from ship to warehouse, rather than the quayside or transit sheds as at other docks.

To link all these East End docks with England's busy canal system was the aim of the Regent's Canal (1812–20). This fine canal still snakes round the outskirts of north

4   Hunting 1984, pp.58-68.
5   Hadfield and Skempton 1979, pp.184-221; *Dockland* 1986, pp.21-39, 196-212; Cruickshank 1989, pp.56-61.

THE BUILDING ART OF THE FIRST INDUSTRIAL METROPOLIS

London from Paddington in the west, to reach the Thames at a strategic point between the London and the West India Docks. With the help of unloading basins at regular intervals, industry sprang up along its length, helping to galvanise the growth of north London. It also spawned smaller imitations like the Grosvenor Canal (1824–26) and the Kensington Canal (1824–28), sponsored by landowners seeking to open up their property for development.[6] Similar in aim but different in type was the horse-drawn Surrey Iron Railway (1801–03), which ran from a small dock off the Thames at Wandsworth to Croydon. Though based on a technology familiar from private colliery railways, it was backed by a joint-stock company and therefore ranks as 'the world's first independent public railway'. William Jessop, its engineer, preferred it to a canal because the latter would draw off water from factories on the Wandle tributary, 'the works on which are perhaps more valuable than any others within an equal compass in the kingdom'.[7] But few of these smaller transport enterprises enjoyed the financial success of the great dock companies.

RIVER CROSSINGS

Inseparable from the docks and canals are the Thames crossings. Because of the river's width, London was never a true, two-bank city until the late eighteenth century. Then the new bridges at Westminster (1750) and Blackfriars (1769) and the widening of London Bridge (1758–62) began to create growth beyond the southern nucleus of Southwark and the fringes of the river.

For a while, little except ribbon development along the approach roads to the new bridges materialised. But by 1810 the pressure for further crossings was irresistible. It began with the debate of the 1790s about the Port of London. One idea, not in the end adopted, was to rebuild London Bridge so as to make the Thames frontages further upstream available to ocean-going vessels. It was with this purpose in mind that Telford devised his breathtaking scheme for leaping the river with a single-arched bridge of cast iron, some 200 yards in span. This design was rejected along with many others. But the arguments for rebuilding London Bridge remained. It was eventually done in 1823–31. The main reason for the delay was the colossal value of City property, then as now, and therefore the cost of new approaches.[8]

In the interim no less than three further toll bridges, all major feats of engineering, were smartly built during the 1810s: Southwark Bridge, Waterloo Bridge and, further upstream, Vauxhall Bridge. Something yet more remarkable was in the offing – the world's first major underwater tunnel. Twin-bore and nearly 400 yards in length, the Thames Tunnel was started optimistically on a line from Rotherhithe to Wapping in 1825. It underwent many setbacks and was abandoned for years at a time. When Schinkel saw the tunnel in 1826 (it was one of the few sites he visited twice),[9] the works were in full spate again under the direction of Marc Isambard Brunel, using a tunnelling shield he had patented. But further mishaps delayed completion until 1843.

The new crossings opened up south London at last to more than ribbon development. The district of St. George's Fields, where roads from Blackfriars, Waterloo and Westminster Bridges converged, began to take shape with a medley of housing and institutions, foremost among them the rebuilt Bethlehem Hospital or 'Bedlam' (1812–15). Wealthy commuters looked increasingly to outlying southern villages for places to live. A necklace of factories transformed the south bank into the industrial powerhouse of post-Napoleonic London. Here were located the most go-ahead London engineers (Maudslay, Bramah, Rennie), brewers (Barclay and Perkins' Anchor Brewery, Goding's Lion Brewery), and printers (Clowes). Here, too, could be found the London building world's chief concentration of wharves, depots and factories like Coade's Lambeth Pottery, which produced a cast ceramic 'stone' of miraculous durability, much in demand for architectural ornament. These were the giant London employers of their day, outfacing the crafts-scale manufacturers of the north bank, who put up with poky shops, back yards and alleys. In size, structure and looks, their premises increasingly resembled the dock warehouses, but with steam power annexed. It was on the south bank indeed that the prototype of the very large multi-storey London factory or warehouse had first appeared. This was Samuel Wyatt's massive Albion Mill, built at the southern foot of Blackfriars Bridge as a corn-grinding plant in 1783–86.[10] It did not last long, falling victim to fire in 1791. But its impact was immediate.

If one hero is sought for the transformation of London's commercial infrastructure between 1800 and 1830, it must be John Rennie (1761–1821). This empirical, Scottish-born engineer had a hand in almost every major riparian project of these years. A millwright by trade,

6   *Survey of London* 1986, vol. 42, pp.322-24.
7   Hadfield and Skempton 1979, pp.175-81.
8   Rennie 1875, pp.183-95.
9   Riemann 1986, pp.119, 274.
10 Skempton 1971, pp.53-57.

Thomas Telford's design for a single-arched London Bridge in cast iron, 1800. One of several suggested proposals for narrowing the Thames and building new quays and warehouses upstream of London Bridge instead of the East End docks. Guildhall Library

Millers dance on Blackfriars Bridge because of the burning of the Albion Mills, 1791. The scale of operations of this first great purpose-built London factory made it deeply unpopular with its competitors. British Museum.

Rennie first came to London in 1785–86 to design and install the machinery supplied by the great Birmingham firm of Boulton and Watt for the Albion Mill. After it burnt down, he set up his own workshop and office nearby. He remained Boulton and Watt's London representative, contriving that firm's precision machinery for the new Royal Mint at Tower Hill (1805–14) and for the Grand Junction Waterworks Company (1812).[11] His steam-powered smithy at Woolwich Dockyard is described by Samuel Smiles as 'the most splendid piece of machinery in its day'.[12] But Rennie's mechanical works are overshadowed by his feats as a constructor of canals, docks, harbours and bridges. Not content with the vast labour of laying out the London Docks and the later phases of the West India Docks, he reconstructed the old Legal Quays in front of the Custom House and made schemes for recasting the Thames naval bases.[13] As engineer to the Grand Junction Canal Company, Rennie set out the original line for the Regent's Canal.[14] He also

11   Crook and Port 1973, pp.453-56; Dickinson 1954, pp.98-99.
12   Smiles 1861, vol. 2, p.265.
13   Ibid., pp.93-284; Morriss 1983, pp.53-57.
14   Spencer 1976, pp.16-19.

tried to bore a tunnel for the Great North Road out of London through Highgate Hill – one of his rare failures. Charles Dupin regarded him as the outstanding British engineer of the age: broad-minded, informed on developments abroad (he made visits to French docks and harbours in 1816 and 1819) and 'friendly and welcoming to all foreign engineers who came to England to study his works and profit from his genius'.[15]

Rennie's masterpieces were his Thames bridges: two if you count only those built during his lifetime, Waterloo and Southwark Bridges, four if you include the work he did on Vauxhall Bridge before it fell into other hands, and on London Bridge before his death and its execution by his sons. Waterloo and Southwark, arched in masonry and iron respectively, sum up the state of the urban bridge-building art in their day.[16] Both were paid for not by government but by private joint-stock companies. This fact never ceased to amaze foreign commentators; they would have been less impressed had they known that both turned out to make heavy losses and that Southwark Bridge caused the bankruptcy of its ironwork suppliers. Both bridges were built at breakneck speed by Jolliffe and Banks, the first great firm of London engineering contractors.

Canova is supposed to have said (doubtless with irony) that it was worth coming to England, if only to see Waterloo Bridge (1811–17). Its rhythm of rusticated granite arches in low profile with twin Doric columns against the piers gave it an Augustan assurance possessed by no other Thames bridge. Its loss in the 1930s is still regretted. It was the biggest multi-arched bridge then built, with long approaches and no awkward rise to the centre. It also introduced granite into London's architecture. Blackfriars and Westminster Bridges had been built of Portland stone, the standard stone for major London buildings between 1666 and 1815. By this time they were decaying rapidly. Rennie therefore opted for granite, hitherto untried in London, for its endurance and monumentality. This innovation had a rapid impact. Bases of public and other London buildings where hard wear from carts or hobnail boots was expected began to be constructed in granite; the scale of masonry blocks, too, increased, to the great gain of monumental architecture. For the superstructures of stone-faced buildings architects continued to specify Portland or orange-brown Bath stone – the fashionable stone of the 1820s, newly available via the canal system.

Southwark Bridge (1814–19) was London's most visible early symbol of the so-called 'iron revolution'. It stood upstream of London Bridge, but in an area still much used by shipping. Rennie therefore built three great uneven iron arches with a modest rise to the crown, resting on abutments of huge granite blocks. Though less graceful than Telford's contemporary suspension bridges in iron (London's first suspension bridge was well upstream at suburban Hammersmith, of 1824–27), it was admired almost as much as Waterloo Bridge.

TECHNOLOGY AND ITS TROUBLES

The use of iron was a feature of British architecture and engineering upon which visitors particularly remarked. Yet leaving aside a few building-types such as conservatories and hothouses, iron in London buildings before the 1830s was mostly used in subordination to other materials. Timber and brickwork predominate in the series of factories and warehouses from Albion Mills onwards. The factories and warehouses of 1790–1805 have supports, floors and roofs of timber. A shift to iron supports, most spectacular in Daniel Alexander's Tobacco Dock, comes in the decade 1805–15. It is crystal-clear who was responsible: Napoleon. Timber had long cost more in Britain than in continental Europe, though London, the centre of the timber trade, had some advantages. Big price rises in timber occurred because of war in 1801–04. Then came the French occupation of Germany, the Treaty of Tilsit (1807) and the 'Continental System', intended to starve Britain of Baltic timber for its navy.[17] Its effect was felt straight away in building. At just this time, London terrace houses began to lose their high, 'M-shaped' roofs in favour of lower, less visible roof-frames which saved on large pieces of wood and could be tucked behind parapets. In the commercial and industrial sphere, ironfounders stepped into the breach. By the time peace came, the use of iron for supports, girders and single-storey roofs was established, while London water companies were using cast-iron main pipes (or, briefly, stone ones) instead of timber ones.[18]

Even then, traditional materials were not supplanted. At the fine Hungerford and Covent Garden Markets of the 1830s, for instance, Charles Fowler, a bold but solid constructor, used granite, Portland stone and brick in combination with concealed iron.[19] Only a single-storey afterthought to protect the fish-traders at Hungerford

15 Dupin 1821, p.6.
16 Ruddock 1979, pp.166-69, 178-83.
17 Albion 1926, pp.316-413; Morriss 1983, pp.73ff.
18 Dickinson 1954, pp.100, 118-19.
19 Stamp 1986.

THE BUILDING ART OF THE FIRST INDUSTRIAL METROPOLIS

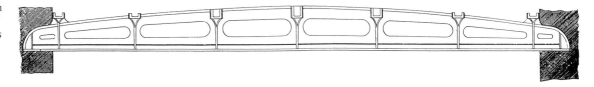

The King's Library, British Museum, with a section of one of the cast-iron girders used to span the room. Robert Smirke, architect, John Raìstrick, engineer. 1823-6. Robert Thorne

Market was of naked ironwork, prophetic of railway-platform roofing. In covering up his ironwork, Fowler was following the practice of two prominent architects, John Nash and Robert Smirke, who took up iron in the building boom of the 1820s as a way of getting greater spans. The celebrated instance is the King's Library in the British Museum by Smirke, where iron beams help to achieve broad trabeation and are covered by Greek plasterwork. Schinkel felt wary about this when he saw it going up in 1826 ('Constructionen sind nicht zu loben').[20] Nash's liberality with hidden iron at Buckingham Palace met with outright hostility. Yet by freeing up internal structure and planning, the ironwork of these buildings did as much to develop architecture as the more conspicuous warehouses, hothouses and bridges.

If London was slow to develop an explicit iron architecture, that is partly because it lay some distance away from the iron foundries of the Midlands and North. By contrast, its proximity to the septarian deposits of the Thames and Medway estuaries made it central to another great change in building methods, the cement-and-concrete revolution.[21] This first made itself felt on the outsides of London buildings. Stucco or cement, often known as 'plaister' and long common as a substitute for stone dressings on basements or round windows, began to take over the face of London houses during the age of the Adams and the Wyatts (1775–1810), in part to combat the dirty dullness of brickwork. The material was not reliable, however, before 'Parker's Roman Cement', a water-based compound, was patented in 1796. When the Parker

20   Riemann 1986, pp.158, 274.
21   Francis 1977, pp.19-75; Preston 1977, pp.68-71.

Blackheath New Proprietary School, Lee. George Ledwell Taylor, architect, 1836. Modelled on the Propylaea at Athens but built of concrete blocks. Lewisham Library Services

patent lapsed in 1810, an explosion of stucco ensued. All-over stucco fronts, usually off-white in tone, keyed to give a hint of stonework and regularly repainted to offset the filth deposited from chimneys (and in due course gaslight), were a commonplace of London estate development between about 1820 and 1840. The idiom dominated in many but not all of the new suburbs: in Regent's Park and its outlier of St. John's Wood, in Belgravia, Pimlico and the seemingly infinite acres of Kensington, where stucco fronting was not cast off until the 1860s. The suburban stucco villa, too, fast became a sentimental cliché. Not everyone liked stucco. 'This tasteless innovation in the art of building, will entirely supersede the ancient art of brickwork, which we so much admire in our more ancient domestic structures', lamented Kensington's historian, Thomas Faulkner.[22]

Along with stucco went, as with iron, an invisible but equally historic development: that of early concrete construction. Since about 1750 primitive 'concrete' foundations mixing gravel, rubble and lime had been tried now and then in French and British harbour and bridge works, including the London docks. The first studied use of concrete foundations seems to have taken place in 1816. In that year Robert Smirke was called in to rescue the sinking walls of the half-built Millbank Penitentiary – a huge, Thames-side prison inspired by Jeremy Bentham as a model institution, but a source of endless trouble since construction had begun. On Rennie's suggestion, Smirke and his brother-in-law, Samuel Baker, rescued the penitentiary by underpinning it with a deep concrete raft. They did likewise in 1825–26 at the Custom House, when part of David Laing's beautiful but negligently built riverside *palazzo* – a kind of administrative coping stone to the new docks – suffered ignominious collapse.[23] By 1830 Portland cement, essential for good concrete, was available from the Medway and Thames estuaries, and in the following decade the material made modest headway. The Brunels built experimental concrete arches in connection with the Thames Tunnel.[24] Several methods of building with concrete blocks were patented and enjoyed brief currency. A little school in suburban Lee designed of such blocks by George Ledwell Taylor (1836), was perhaps the first British building of architectural interest to be constructed entirely of concrete.[25] To all appearances it looked like the Propylaea at Athens.

22 *Survey of London* 1986, vol. 42, p.112.
23 Crook 1965-66, pp.5-22.
24 Francis 1977, pp.47-49.
25 Taylor 1870, vol. 1, p.171.

Changes in building technology go hand in hand with building failures. The Victorians reviled what they saw as the slapdash craftsmanship of Regency London. Nash earned a reputation as a risky constructor. James Burton, the foremost London speculative builder of the period 1800–25 with interests in Bloomsbury, Regent's Park and the new Regent Street, was not above questionable construction. His contemporary Charles Mayor, who started to build Nash's Park Crescent but then went spectacularly bankrupt, was no more reliable. David Ricardo moved into an expensive Mayor-built town house in 1812. 'I hear strange tidings of your house in Brook Street tumbling about your ears,' wrote a friend soon afterwards. The great economist fulminated back: 'that Mayor of whom I bought the house was a complete knave, and from the holes in the chimnies, and the communication between them and the beams, he perhaps intended that it should be destroyed by fire, so that no one might ever find out the total insufficiency of the materials to support the house.'[26]

Cases of this kind do less to prove the guilt or incompetence of individuals than to expose the instability of the whole London building world between 1800 and 1830. Where professional roles are in flux, responsibilities become vague. Engineers, architects, surveyors, 'builders' (never an easy concept to define) and craftsmen were all jockeying for position in a market in which the volume and the nature of building work were changing out of recognition. Processes of specialisation and fragmentation conflicted with attempts to coordinate each building or development under a single control. No wonder there was confusion, haste, risk-taking and the occasional disaster.

Much has been written about the relation between the building professions in London in these years, and in particular about the rise of the engineer and the 'general contractor' at the expense of the architect and the craftsman.[27] This certainly was part of the pattern. Engineers formed an effective professional body before architects, in 1818 as opposed to 1834. Wedded as they were to the entrepreneurial spirit of the times, by the end of our period they had assumed technical control over works affecting London's infrastructure – roads, railways, canals, bridges and docks. Builders too were beginning to acquire a

FEET 10 5 0 5 10
METRES 3 2 1 0 1 2 3
Scale for elevation

FEET 10 0 10 20 30
METRES 3 0 3 6 9
Scale for plan

Flat roof

Library

Dining-room

Hall

GROUND FLOOR PLAN

David Ricardo's house, Upper Brook Street, Mayfair. S. P. Cockerell, architect, Charles Mayor, builder, 1811-2. Elevation and plan by John Sambrook from *The Survey of London*, Vol. 40

26 *Survey of London* 1977, vol. 39, p.126; 1980, vol. 40, p.221.
27 Cooney 1955-56; Port 1967; Hobhouse 1971, pp.7-18.

Monument to the contractor Sir Edward Banks (1769-1835), Chipstead Church, Surrey, with reliefs of Waterloo, Southwark and London Bridges, all built by his firm. National Buildings Record

respectable and powerful identity. The outstanding figure in London building between 1820 and 1840 was Thomas Cubitt, who rose from the rank of carpenter to preside over much the biggest and safest construction firm that London had seen.[28] Though geared mainly to speculative building and management, Cubitt's enterprise also offered a complete 'design-and-build' service that Queen Victoria and Prince Albert were not ashamed to patronise.

The success of figures like Cubitt was partly due to a shift for large buildings from the 'contract for prices', whereby each trade tendered a schedule of prices to the architect or surveyor in charge, to the 'contract in gross', whereby 'builders' estimated a complete sum for the whole works and agreed to procure and supervise the different trades themselves. The contract in prices led to better-constructed buildings, the contract in gross to quicker completions. The new system first made itself felt in wartime, when the invasion scare of 1803–04 induced the government to build no less than forty-seven barracks in a hurry.[29] But the novelty of building firms like Cubitt's and the effects of the contract in gross can be exaggerated. There had been large 'design-and-build' concerns in eighteenth-century London. The celebrated Adam brothers ran one (it survived to build the West India Dock warehouses), their rivals the Hollands another. Several big civil engineering contractors grew out of the English canal mania of the 1790s. Jolliffe and Banks, the builders of Rennie's bridges, for instance, came into being from an alliance between Edward Banks, the contractor for Jessop's Surrey Iron Railway and an experienced canal builder, with Colonel Hylton Jolliffe and the Reverend William Jolliffe, landowners on the railway's route.[30] In such an arrangement one partner was the chief investor and risk-taker, while the other supplied the technical skills.

One reason for the dynamism of building activity in London after 1800 was precisely the lack of clear-cut professional demarcations. If individuals had business ability and enjoyed their client's confidence, they could go beyond the limits of their particular skills and run whole projects, irrespective of whether they were themselves architects (Nash, Smirke), surveyors (Burton, Banks), engineers (Rennie) or craftsmen (Cubitt). Speculating architects, builders employing their own draughtsmen, or

28 Hobhouse 1971.
29 Dupin, 1822, vol. 1, p.221.
30 Dickinson 1933, pp.1-8.

THE BUILDING ART OF THE FIRST INDUSTRIAL METROPOLIS

C.R. Cockerell's design for the Royal Exchange. An ebullient, eye-catching drawing made for a bungled architectural competition, 1839. Not built. British Architectural Library

lawyers running building contracts raised no eyebrows. Not that this led to orderly or clear arrangements. Investigations into the Office of Works in 1828–29 were soon sidetracked into the chaos of the London building industry. It might just work during booms, but there were savage slumps to contend with as well.

Architects, the most articulate of the building professionals, were often bemoaning their lot. At the top of the tree, old Sir John Soane and young Augustus Welby Northmore Pugin both believed that competition and lack of clear responsibilities were destroying the artistic quality of architecture, though they would have disputed what that quality consisted in. Lower down the scale, there was a glut of impoverished young architects. Few independent men in London practice could survive merely by designing buildings; extra employment, preferably a surveyorship to an estate or a department of government but often just bits and pieces of all sorts, was required. Typical of the middle rank of architects and tolerably successful was J.B. Papworth. His well-documented *oeuvre* reads as a litany of executed trifles and far-flung improbabilities: shopfronts for City merchants, minor additions to their suburban villas, an *Essay on the Causes of Dry Rot in Timber*, a sherbet service for the Pasha of Egypt, a figurehead and decorations for the Thames paddle-steamer *London Engineer* a hypothetical palace at Cannstatt for Wilhelm I of Württemberg (who was briefly taken by a whim to 'anglicize some of the Royal Domains'), a utopian town to be called Hygeia on the banks of the River Ohio.[31]

George Wightwick's reminiscences describe how he unavailingly took one approach for the architectural tiro in London, that of soliciting custom from his solitary, single-room office. He issued a book of travel sketches, produced as many ideal designs as he could ('an "Academy of the Arts", a "Hall of Science", a "Theatre", and a "Temple to Shakespeare, and the Dramatists of the Antique and Middle Ages"'), and entered every conceivable architectural competition.[32] Competitions were a new bugbear of 1820s and 1830s London. They were fuelled by the ethos of enterprise and of dissatisfaction with official 'placemen', above all in the Office of Works. Government officials came to look on them as a way of getting cheaper public buildings. They could take many forms, limited or open. They were rarely well regulated, and almost always led to ridicule, bitterness, disappointment – and poor architecture. Money was at the root of most of the arguments: the extravagance or meanness of the winning design, or the lack of reward for participants. Very occasionally a masterpiece resulted, as in the greatest competition of all, for the Palace of Westminster in 1835. As a result the system seemed justified and was perpetuated. But almost never did a competition lead to fame and fortune for one of the Wightwicks of the London building world.

31   Colvin 1978, pp.615-19.
32   Wightwick 1853, pp.541-48.

Another budding architect, Charles James Mathews, was advised by a friend to get a start in life by becoming a district surveyor, the official responsible for ensuring that the London building acts were obeyed:

'A district surveyorship!' I exclaimed. 'What's that? Measuring chimney pots and cleaning out gully holes? What has an architect to do with that?' 'Everything,' said he. 'You must study the Act of Parliament, superintend the erection of all the dwellings in the district, regulate all the party walls and flues, and show yourself master of the practical part of the science as well as the ornamental. Bow and Bethnal Green are both vacant. Start at once.' Bow and Bethnal Green! Here was a bathos! From Rome and Venice to Bow and Bethnal Green. However it was to be done, and at it I went . . . I was successful, and found myself staggering under the honour of being publicly recognised as Surveyor of Bow. Down I went on the top of the omnibus, with the Building Act in my hand, to take possession of my new kingdom. A charming mission it turned out; and for three years – on the top of the same omnibus, with the same Building Act in my hand, and which I never succeeded in understanding to the last – I journeyed to perform the pleasing duties that devolved upon me.[33]

The 'Building Act' which Mathews affected not to grasp (he became a comedian in later life instead of an architect) is the key to understanding such urban discipline as London then possessed. This discipline derived not from any active lead given by king, parliament or City in metropolitan development, but from the passive framework of the London building regulations. Such a framework was perhaps the only one possible in a mercantile, property-conscious, proto-democratic city. It had various advantages. It made London for all its immensity a structurally safe city by the standards of the time; it inhibited the spread of fires; it applied to all types of building; and it led to that distinctive language of street-architecture and minimal aesthetic conformity which so fascinated foreign visitors.

London's 'building acts' had been born from the trauma of the Great Fire of 1666. They stressed brick construction, discouraged external woodwork and insisted upon high, unbroken party walls. Early nineteenth-century development relied upon a meticulously drafted consolidating Act of 1774.[34] In this there had been two main innovations, both inducements to uniformity. One was to distinguish between four 'rates' of ordinary terrace houses according to their size and value and to lay out how each rate should be constructed. The other change was that the regulations were enforced after 1774 by district surveyors, to whom builders had to pay fees upon starting construction. Such was the post, lucrative in good neighbourhoods, vexatious in bad ones, that Charles James Mathews obtained.

It is a tribute to Sir Robert Taylor and George Dance the elder, drafters of the 1774 Act, that throughout the technological upheavals and building booms of 1805–25 no clamour for a new act seems to have been heard. The dock warehouses and public works of the period were built to regulations framed with far smaller buildings in mind. In estate development, their influence upon architectural form was so strong that Regency London owed its appearance more to them than to any architect or architectural style. The dry texts of the London Building Act embody a philosophy of planning and of the city as real and as form-giving as any visionary scheme of metropolitan improvement.

PUBLIC BUILDING

Against the disciplinary success of the London building regulations must be set the failure of any creative, urban vision. As the richest city in the world, the London of George IV might have given birth to a public architecture of unrivalled splendour. There was certainly no shortage of metropolitan ambition during the period. Buckingham Palace, the residence of the sovereign, was amply reconstructed. Soane, the most original European architect of the generation before Schinkel, added toplit Law Courts to the Palace of Westminster and built offices for the Board of Trade in Whitehall. A new Royal Mint and a new Custom House were erected – the latter an aesthetic masterpiece but a technical disaster.[35] A formidable prison for 'offenders of secondary turpitude' arose at Millbank;[36] remoter still, by the side of the Grand Junction Canal near Hanwell, the Middlesex County Justices in 1827 provided an asylum for London's pauper lunatics. At Woolwich, artillery barracks commanded a frontage of

33 Dickens 1879, vol. 2, pp.58-60.
34 Summerson 1978, pp.125-29.
35 Crook and Port 1973, pp.423-30.
36 Elmes 1827-29, vol. 2, p.150.

The Long Room at the Custom House as originally built to designs by David Laing, 1813-17. After the Custom House's partial collapse, the room was recast by Smirke, 1825-27. Guildhall Library

czarist proportions, James Wyatt raised a Gothic military academy, and the dockyard and arsenal were updated to meet the Napoleonic challenge. To the sphere of the arts belong Smirke's well-funded British Museum and Wilkins' hapless National Gallery, the latter dating from William IV's reign after the masters of the public purse had turned niggardly. For exercise, diversion and parade, Regent's Park was laid out in the period, while St. James's Park and Hyde Park were radically recast.

This is a selection of public works in the strict sense. If you add the semi-public works, in other words buildings more or less in the public domain but not funded by royal revenues or taxation, the list becomes more impressive: the great enclosed docks, the Rennies' three bridges, the Regent's Canal, Soane's reconstruction of the Bank of England, University College and King's College, the rebuilding of the Theatres Royal at Covent Garden and Drury Lane by Smirke and Benjamin Wyatt respectively, the clubs of Pall Mall and, above all, the 3 miles or so of improvements masterminded by Nash. At the end of the period, Philip Hardwick's stupendous Euston Arch of 1838 for the London and Birmingham Railway heralds the monumentality of the railway age.

Yet over the sum of these efforts hangs a question mark. Nearly all are marred by economy or by urban incoherence. The best London public buildings of the period, the Bank of England or the British Museum, for instance, rank among the finest in Europe. But they have to be read as self-sufficient and enclosed. Their relation to the city and street-pattern around them is, by and large, accidental. Where a public space of potential grandeur is laid out, as at Trafalgar Square, parsimony and changes of mind prevent London from achieving the formal ensembles that other states and cities take pride in. Developments on the outskirts offer architects the chance to be more coherent. But there the subtlest ensemble of street, square and crescent is rarely crowned by anything grander than a district church or private mansion. Nor can the creators of these new neighbourhoods be persuaded to rise above brick and stucco fronts, or to erect houses that will endure more than three generations.

The root of these shortcomings, as Professor Crook's essay on the Nash improvements shows, lies in the fact that power and administration in London were so delicately balanced that any but the most pragmatic approach to planning was doomed to failure. Visions of an improved London were constantly put forward by underemployed architects, painters, arch-royalists or utopians. Parliament itself was the crucial forum. Here, Colonel F. W. Trench persistently advocated grandiose schemes: a victory pyramid in the future Trafalgar Square, a fresh palace in Hyde Park, a Thames Quay beside Waterloo

Bridge.[37] But parliament saw its role in regard to buildings as a regulator of royal and other extravagance, not as a facilitator of fine things; these, it usually believed, should be left to private individuals and institutions.

Tory administrations might be more generous than Whig-Liberal ones, but were not always so. After long debate about a monument to the victory of 1815, the only outcome was that Rennie's great bridge, to which Lord Liverpool's government had paid not a penny, was opened by the Prince Regent and had its name changed from the Strand Bridge to Waterloo Bridge. Later, William Wilkins contended that the Duke of Wellington 'exercised an influence less beneficial to the arts and science than that of any of his predecessors'.[38] But the change to the Whig-Liberal regime of the 1830s helped him not at all. His National Gallery project had now to contend with the argument that parliament 'should not be called upon to erect palaces for the exhibition of works of the Fine Arts, when a famishing population was crying for bread'.[39]

The debacle of Buckingham Palace points up the difficulty caused for grand London projects by the British habit of balancing power and 'muddling through'. The embarrassments caused by Nash's reconstruction of the palace are usually put down to royal extravagance and slapdash architecture.[40] The evidence for this comes from parliamentary enquiries. But parliament was *parti pris*. That George IV, sovereign of the greatest power in the world, should on his accession have wanted a finer palace than incoherent Carlton House was not intolerable; he did, in fact, abjure a totally new building. The difficulty was that no English king had built on this scale since the 1690s. No one had the courage to come to grips with what a modern British palace was to be – a place to rule from, or merely somewhere extra-large to live in. To do so would have required clearer constitutional ground rules between king and parliament than then existed. This lack of lucidity soon led to revisions, overspending, aesthetic mistakes, fury over costs, and parliamentary lust for revenge upon George IV and his architect-favourite. Charges of structural incompetence were levelled against Nash but never proved. As for the quality of the work, the front was an admitted failure, largely because of the revisions; Nash's elastic, extemporary brilliance could not

37 Barker and Hyde 1982, pp.57-59, 82-89.
38 Liscombe 1980, p.186.
39 Ibid., p.183.
40 Crook and Port 1973, pp.263-77.

stretch to palace scale. The back, which survives, is a creditable design.

CHURCHES

In just one sphere did the government under the Regency actively promote and subsidise urban development – by helping to build Anglican churches. The two decades after Waterloo were a silver age of London church architecture which paved the way for the lavish and passionate 'ecclesiology' of the Victorian church-builders.

Then as now, Anglicanism was England's official creed. The Church of England's cumbersome administration was bound up with that of the state. But in the mid-Georgian years its bishops, appointed by politicians, had grown lethargic. Church accommodation lagged behind the spurt in population of British cities, while migration and industrialisation undermined patterns of parochial life. The effects were worst in London. Nonconformists and Catholics were many (though never dominant in any part of London) and tolerated *faute de mieux*; in enlightened circles, radicalism and even atheism gained ground. Many people, as today, went to church only for functional and official reasons – birth, marriage, baptism and death. Fees for such services and charges for seats discouraged the poor from attendance. Nevertheless, by 1800 the influence of John Wesley and others had done much to dissipate apathy in England and renew the idea of a personal religion. The events of 1789–94 in France, too, shocked conservatives everywhere, notably in England and Austria, into revitalising national compacts between church and state. Church-building was one means of achieving this.

Churches were more than symbols of religious and moral authority. They were also the focus of any major extension of the city. Shrewd London landowners would give a good site for a church or a cheaper 'chapel-of-ease' when they began to develop their land, knowing it would increase the district's respectability and their property's value. Further, the parish remained until the 1830s the basic unit of English local administration, in which local secular and religious affairs were jumbled up together. In theory the 'Vestry', which might be elected in various ways, met in the parish church. In the larger London parishes, secular local government had grown quite elaborate in scope. But its ties with the church seemed permanent until the post-Napoleonic rise of the radicals. Then a series of epoch-making reforms, beginning with Catholic

The New Synagogue, Great St. Helen's, interior. John Davies, architect, 1837-38. An example of the more ambitious places of worship built by non-Anglicans after 1830. English Heritage

Emancipation in 1829, unpicked the system and half-disestablished the Church of England. Thereafter, church affairs and church building in London were run and paid for on a more or less voluntary basis and the parish church ceased to be the local 'town hall' or seat of administration.

While the old system lasted, some parishes built or rebuilt churches as symbols of local pride and independence – always a strong factor in London's history. But they were often frustrated by faction and the creaking institutional mechanisms of the Church of England. St. Marylebone, richest of the West End suburbs, is a case in point. Its ancient village church was already bursting at the seams with residents from new streets in 1770. There were then no less than eight privately owned Anglican chapels-of-ease in the parish, built to boost different estate developments. Yet it took over forty years of effort, four acts of parliament and sundry changes of site and intention before the old church could be replaced by Thomas Hardwick's church of 1813–17. The outcome was a fine porticoed building and a worthy civic forum for an ambitious parish. But its extravagant cost of over £60,000 brought down the invective of local taxpayers on the Vestry's heads.[41]

The rival parish of St. Pancras spent an unheard-of £80,000 in order to erect the *dernier cri* of Greek Revivalism. St. Pancras New Church (1819–22) was designed by William and Henry Inwood, son and grandson of parish bigwig Lord Mansfield's bailiff. Dispatched to Athens at Mansfield's expense, Henry Inwood came back with drawings of the Erechtheum and Tower of the Winds. The result was showily Hellenic. Most flagrant of the adapted details are Rossi's terracotta caryatids flanking the entrance to the burial vaults. These were among the last such vaults attached to a London church. For after the cemetery movement, slow to catch on in England compared to France, Germany and the United States, began to spread, London churches were built without burial grounds. The melodrama of funerary art then shifted from the cluttered urban churchyard to the liberally landscaped, company-run suburban cemetery. Kensal Green of 1831–33, modelled on Paris's Père Lachaise but with a greener and more tranquil layout, is the first of London's 'joint-stock', non-denominational cemeteries. Others followed at Highgate, Brompton and Norwood.[42]

The exceptional sums which the St. Marylebone or St. Pancras Vestry could command reflected the status and functions of these 'town halls'. But what London needed most was district churches within existing administrative parishes to serve the swelling population. Here it was that the government intervened, after a campaign of lobbying by a cabal of influential London churchmen.

The early nineteenth-century revival of Anglicanism owed much of its force to two pressure-groups consisting of rich men resident in amenable London suburbs: the so-called Clapham Sect and Hackney Phalanx. It is no accident that the parish churches of both these former villages had been rebuilt, Clapham's in 1774–76, Hackney's with a fine church by the architect James Spiller in 1792–97. The Clapham Sect belonged to the Protestant wing of the Church of England. Its leaders such as Henry Thornton and William Wilberforce stressed personal salvation, belief and liberty. They were not deeply interested in the administration of the Church of England. But they welcomed the building of churches in areas where none existed before. Wilberforce, the anti-slavery campaigner, indeed promoted an abortive parliamentary bill for more churches in 1800.[43]

The Hackney Phalanx was different. High Churchmen and conservatives who held the links between church and state to be inviolable, they saw the church as a social organism rather than a conduit for individual salvation. Organised religion was for them a national, moral and public responsibility and a means of combatting nonconformity and radicalism. Their informal leader, Joshua Watson (1771–1855), retired from business in 1814 to devote his life to committee work and the reform of the church's administrative structure.[44]

The Phalanx's first target was education. In 1811 Watson and his friends set up the National Society, aimed (with the help of government grants) at funding Anglican parish schools so as to keep up with the plethora of new proprietary schools and the revolution in teaching methods for poor children set on foot in London by Joseph Lancaster, Samuel Wilderspin and other nonconformists, utilitarians and radicals.[45] 100,000 children were in National Schools by 1815.[46] Rural or suburban parish schools tended to be small and humble, but in London proper they could be quite grand (Clerkenwell Schools, Tudor-Gothic by W. C. Mylne, 1828; St. Martin-in-the-Fields Schools with a classical front by Nash, *c.*1830). The Phalanx and their friends then moved on to grapple with higher education, lamentably deficient in London. To counter the 'godless' and Greek-looking University College, founded in 1827–28 on the model of the reformed University of Bonn, they set up King's College (1829–31), conducted on Anglican principles and housed by Robert Smirke in a tactful extension of Somerset House on the Strand. These were the original – and opposing – colleges of the present University of London.

But the great prize was church building. Here the Hackney Phalanx's links with Lord Liverpool, Tory prime minister between 1812 and 1827, bore fruit. Watson and his allies began lobbying the government immediately after Waterloo. Acts of 1818 and 1819 ensued, establishing a commission and earmarking over a million pounds for new churches, aimed especially at accommodating the poor in free seats. In tandem, a body called the Incorporated Church-Building Society gave grants for restoring or enlarging existing churches on condition that a proportion of the seats should be free. These were national

41   Sheppard 1958, pp.245-74.
42   Brooks 1989, pp.8-11.
43   Webster 1954, pp.60-61.
44   Ibid., pp.58-77.
45   Seaborne 1971, pp.131-97.
46   Webster 1954, p.36.

St. Martin's-in-the-Fields National School. John Nash, architect, perhaps assisted by George Ledwell Taylor, c.1829. Built in conjunction with a new vestry hall and vicarage as part of Nash's West Strand improvements. English Heritage

measures, aimed at northern industrial towns as well as Londoners. But London was in the forefront of the promoters' minds. The capital acquired thirty-five of the 214 new churches built by 1829, after which government funding was wound down.[47]

Architecturally the 'Commissioners Churches' (sometimes known as the 'Waterloo Churches') were a mixed bunch. The aim was to cram in as many seats as possible – not a recipe for distinguished design. £20,000, the maximum subsidy for any one church, could not match the sums lavished by St. Marylebone and St. Pancras on their civic symbols. Soane, Nash and Smirke, consulted as the official government architects, were none of them deeply interested in church-building. But they did help to draw up the simple ground rules for the new churches (square or rectangular plans with a deep recess for the altar, galleries on iron or stone supports, towers, and elevations in brick or stone – not stucco).[48] Each of them also built two London examples: a district church apiece in prestigious and populous St. Marylebone and three in other suburbs. Soane's Holy Trinity, Marylebone Road and St. Peter's, Walworth are among his weaker creations. Nash's All Souls, Langham Place is a typically dashing piece of urban scenery. Smirke, more sedulous than his older colleagues, built two solid and similar churches, St. Anne's, Wandsworth and St. Mary's, Wyndham Place.

All these were in the classical style which, against an overwhelming national trend towards Gothic for the Commissioners Churches, obtained for most churches built in London during the 1820s. To build in Gothic in that decade was still residually felt to be anti-urban. Edward Blore's enlargement in scholarly Tudor-Gothic of Lambeth Palace, London seat of the archbishops of Canterbury (1829–30), did much to confirm the Church of England's official conversion to the Gothic Revival. Almshouses, among which there was an upsurge at just this time as part of the renewal of civic and religious responsibility, were also usually in a Tudor-Gothic style. But it was the Palace of Westminster competition of 1835 that finally sanctioned Gothic for major London buildings. Here, after protracted pamphleteering, it was agreed for reasons of history and context that only Gothic or Tudor entries would be permitted.

St. Peter's, Eaton Square (by Henry Hakewill) and St. Luke's, Chelsea (by James Savage) well represent the tenor of architecture found in the better Commissioners Churches. If they are above the average in quality, that is because their budgets were less mean than usual. Like many of the London churches, St. Peter's, Eaton Square

47 Port 1961; Carr 1979.
48 Port 1961, pp.38-40.

Lambeth Palace, watercolour for Edward Blore showing his new residential wing for Archbishop Howley, 1829-30. British Architectural Library

recapitulates in Greek dress the cliché of classical portico with tower and steeple in the roof behind, first introduced at St. Martin-in-the-Fields a century before. More prophetic is St. Luke's, Chelsea, the most accomplished Gothic church built in England during the 1820s. Here Savage advances the cause of a scholarly Gothic Revivalism with an authentic stone vault, thick stone walls and well-detailed tracery. Only the slenderness caused by the Commissioners' insistence upon side galleries to cram in the poor could have offended the growing band of medieval purists. St. Luke's comes close to the ideals of Pugin and Victorian ecclesiology. Neither of these buildings, however, rivalled the European sophistication of the very best Commissioners Church. This was C. R. Cockerell's twin-towered Hanover Chapel, once an incident of condensed subtlety and reproach amidst the gimcrack classicism of Regent Street. It vanished as long ago as 1896.[49]

49   Watkin 1974, pp.136-45.

St. Peter's Church, Eaton Square. Perspective by J. H. Hakewill of his father Henry Hakewill's design nearing completion, 1827. A typical Commissioners' church in Greek Revival dress. Fischer Fine Art Ltd

THE LONDON HOUSE

Houses and housing are at once the pride and the peculiarity of English architecture. Every visitor to London in the early nineteenth century was struck by the city's boundless acreage of 'terrace houses': confined between narrow 'party walls', lightly built of brick and timber, bare outside, boxy and cramped inside, yet neat, convenient and tolerably private. All classes of society seemed content to put up with such houses. In the right hands their interiors – those of Thomas Hope in Duchess Street or John Soane in Lincoln's Inn Fields, for instance – could occasionally reach the highest level of elegance or genius. Every kind of activity might be carried on within them. Crafts-industry, storage, shops, museums, schools, pubs, coffee houses, smart hotels, fetid lodging-houses, brothels, banks and offices all operated within the same basic framework of front rooms and back rooms on different levels off a simple set of stairs. The London terrace house was most commonly built with the middle-class family in mind. But over the centuries it had been honed down to an instrument of infinite flexibility. It could vary in size from the inflated scale of Belgrave Square to tiny infill developments on a 10 feet frontage in back courts and alleys. Taken as a whole, London in 1800 consisted of little else. The proliferation of specialised urban building-types which we take for granted is the outcome of the last two centuries.

European visitors mixed respect for the simple comfort of the London terrace house with sarcasm over its pokiness and scant pretension. Count Pecchio, friend and biographer of the poet Ugo Foscolo, writing in the 1820s, is a specially vivid commentator:

The houses are small and fragile. The first night I spent in a lodging- house, I seemed to myself still on board the vessel; the walls were equally slender, and, in great part, of wood, the chambers small, and the staircase like a companion ladder; the walls are generally so thin, that they allow the passage of sound without interruption. The lodgers would hear one another talking, but that they are accustomed to speak in an under tone . . . I distinguished, at intervals, the words, 'Very fine weather, – indeed – very fine – comfort – comfortable – great comfort' – words which occur as often in their conversation, as stops and commas in a book . . . In a three-storey house, there are three bedrooms, one over the other, and three parlours in the same situation, so that the population is as it were warehoused in layers like merchandise – like the cheese in the storehouses at Lodi and Codogno. The English have not chosen without design this (I will venture to call it) *naval* architecture. The advantages they derive from living in houses of small size and little durability are these: in general, a house is only built for 99 years, if it outlive this term, it belongs to the proprietor of the ground on which it is built. It seldom happens, therefore, that they attain to any great longevity; on the contrary, they sometimes tumble to pieces before the natural period of their existence. The English, who are better arithmeticians than architects, have discovered, that, by building in

this slippery manner, they consume less capital, and that consequently the annual interest and the annual loss of the principal are proportionately less. There is another advantage: by this method, posterity is not hampered or tyrannised over. Every generation can choose and build its own houses, according to its own caprices, and its own necessities; and, although in a great measure composed of wood, all the houses are as it were incombustible, by means of the insurance companies, which guarantees the value of the house, the furniture and everything else . . . To an Englishman, his house is his Gibraltar; he must not only be inviolable, but absolutely without dispute or *fuss*. He prefers living in a shell like an oyster, to living in a palace with all the annoyance of a hen-roost. Independence is the vital air of the Englishman. Hence as soon as a son is married, he leaves home, and like the polypi, which when cut in pieces make so many polypi more, goes to *evolve* elsewhere another family . . . [50]

Evidently the count lodged in one of London's older quarters. His remarks about the smallness and weakness of metropolitan houses might have been disputed by a resident of the new, palazzo-sized terraces of the 1820s. But they could well apply to modern, middle-class development. House-hunting in 1834, the Scottish essayist and sage, Thomas Carlyle, came upon a property in Edwardes Square, Kensington, a suburban development then only twenty years old with 'a beautiful grass-square in the centre; houses small but neat'. Investigation proved disenchanting:

rent £35 [per annum] fixtures included; four stories of the smallest dimensions (which I have measured since): two kitchens, *six-feet three inches* (!) in height; dining-room with folding doors . . . perhaps 14 feet by 22 (taken together), drawing-room above, 17 feet by eleven; back room (divided by a wall from this), where our big Bed might by possibility stand, for the height is 9 feet 7½; upper story 8 feet 1 inch high, which seems the despicable universal height of such houses here . . . Finally there is a garden (*ach Gott!*) of perhaps 12 feet broad in front of the house, with iron railing, and a brick-walled one . . . of 21 yards long. [51]

Faced with these 'sorryish prospects', the Carlyles aban

50   Pecchio 1833, pp.29-32.
51   *Survey of London* 1986, vol. 42, p.257.

doned thought of Edwardes Square and took a house, no bigger, in Cheyne Row, Chelsea.

The meanness of houses like these derived, as Pecchio remarked, from the leasehold building system. Very few London householders lived upon ground that they owned, and not many more occupied houses that they or their families had commissioned or built. There was a minor exception to this rule: a set of aristocratic town houses, never more than two dozen in number, scattered along the Strand and Piccadilly and the sectors of Mayfair and St. James's close to the royal parks, the focus of fashionable promenade. Mostly cased in stone and preceded by ample forecourts, these were the nearest London ever came to the aristocratic Paris *hôtel* or Italian palazzo, though they rarely matched such mansions in scale. Several were built in the heady years of conservative rule after Waterloo. The outstanding survivor is the Duke of Wellington's Apsley House at Hyde Park Corner, originally of brick but aggrandised in Bath stone for the Iron Duke by Benjamin Wyatt in 1828–29.

Everyone else, including most of the peerage, expected to inhabit property on a short tenancy or long lease of anything from a few months to ninety-nine years. Whatever its drawbacks, the system encouraged mobility and economic vitality. Almost all domestic building in London and its immediate outskirts, that is to say perhaps 90 per cent of all building activity, took place on the speculative leasehold method, involving an intricate chain of relationships between landowners, their representatives, developers, architects, builders, craftsmen, lawyers, mortgagees, house-agents, leaseholders and tenants.

London in these years took housing further than any other city in the world towards the status of a pure commodity. The structure, servicing and even the style of its houses depended more upon the way in which they were produced, bought and sold than it did upon tenants' demands or habits of life. The terrace house might be built in unprecedented numbers, dressed up with stucco and other stylistic novelties and cleverly grouped. But it remained at heart conservative in arrangement and equipment. This despite London's dynamism and innovation in other types of building during the period. That is because speculative house-building was, as it still is, acutely sensitive to marginal economic change. London houses were built mostly by modest operators without much capital. There was no proven economic incentive to make structural or technical improvements – to experiment with flats, for instance, or central heating, or better construction.

Changes there certainly were between 1800 and 1838 to the way in which London houses were produced. On grander estate developments, big developer-builders like James Burton (Bloomsbury and Regent's Park) and Thomas Cubitt (Bloomsbury, Belgravia and Pimlico) began to upstage the small combinations of master-craftsmen who erected houses in twos or threes at a time. That tended to make house building in these districts a less risky business for all concerned. It also meant that a landowner's architect could begin to group houses together in a uniform design for a terrace or an entire square in reasonable expectation that his design might be accurately completed. Before 1800 this had been hard to achieve. The first successful instance of the uniform London square is Bedford Square of the 1770s, still intact.[52] Fitzroy Square, the Adams' last London venture, is more typical: though started in 1792, two of its sides date from the 1820s and are correspondingly debased. An unprecedented outburst of squares, crescents and balanced terraces took place in almost every suburban quarter during the great London building boom of the 1820s – in Belgravia, Kensington, Bayswater, St. Marylebone, Bloomsbury, Clerkenwell, Islington, Hackney, Mile End, Greenwich, Walworth and Camberwell alike. This was due to more than an improvement in urban taste; the ideal of symmetry and uniformity had at last become achievable. Very often it was not achieved, because most builders were still small and the risk of bankruptcy remained high. But the prospect was there.

The link between London speculative building and economic cycles may sound academic. For developers and builders it was brutally real. The pattern can be read in almost every major London project of the period. Despite (perhaps because of) the war with France, building in London proceeded apace in the decade after 1800. In the Somers Town district of St. Pancras, 'every person who could obtain the means became builders: carpenters, retired publicans, persons working in leather, haymakers and even the keepers of private houses for the reception of

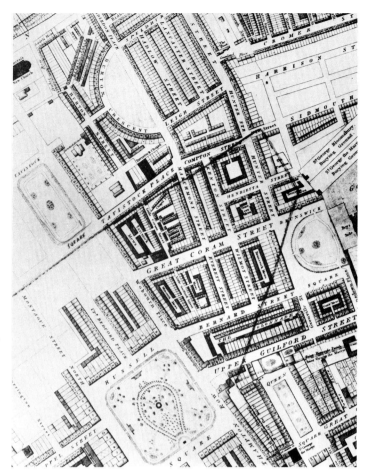

Part of Bloomsbury in the 1816-19 edition of Horwood's map of London, showing streets and squares of varying formality. On the Bedford Estate, Russell Square is complete but Tavistock Square is scarcely begun. East and north are the new, three-sided Brunswick Square, and the sweep of Burton Crescent (now Cartwright Gardens). Guildhall Library

Lloyd Square, Clerkenwell, in 1937. J. and W. J. Booth, architects, c.1825-30. Linked semi-detached houses impart a note of informality to the London square. Greater London Record Office

52   Byrne 1990.
53   Sheppard, Belcher and Cotterell 1979, p.193.

lunatics, each contrived to raise his house or houses and every street was lengthened in its turn'.[53] Then came a severe crash in 1811–12, as the war grew in intensity and cost, government borrowed more money, and interest rates spiralled. Many builders collapsed, among them the original entrepreneur of Carlyle's Edwardes Square. The fate of Regent's Park hung in the balance for years with Nash's grand circus (now Park Crescent) in carcase, half-started. It was never to be completed.

The recovery after Waterloo was gradual. It gathered pace in the early 1820s to reach a peak in the *annus mirabilis* of 1825, when over ten thousand property deeds were registered in Middlesex.[54] A credit crisis in the autumn of that year led to a crushing wave of bankruptcies and the scaling-down of building all over London. Soon afterwards came an abrupt halt to the development of Regent's Park. Traces of this hiatus can still be seen all over London in the shape of a few far-flung suburban terraces or villas of 1825 surrounded by houses added much later, when the speculative appetite had recovered. The 1830s were a quiet time for building, picking up only after Victoria's accession.

THE GROWTH OF THE SUBURBS

A striking feature of London's history is the urge of its citizens to live far from their work, in the hope of securing a better and quieter home. Urban economists gloss this as a preference for spending more on 'carriage' and less on 'rent' – a helpful formulation, because it points to the link between suburban transport and suburban living.

Why and when commuting became commoner in London than in other cities is hard to gauge. The hapless sequence of plague in 1665 and fire in 1666 had something to do with it. In the hundred years that followed, the City of London lost much of its population, the court many of its economic functions. So it was a short step for those without formalised social obligations (mainly the merchant class) to move further away from the centre.

Hatred of the city was a component of early romanticism and radicalism. Already in the 1820s the radical journalist William Cobbett was calling for the 'dispersion of the wen' as the only way of 'settling the affairs of the nation and restoring it to a happy state'.[55] Cobbett himself opted to live on a smallholding at the edge of London. But the chief incentive for moving out was more basic: noise and pollution, exacerbated by London's unstoppable growth and industrialisation. Worst of all was the smoke from dirty Newcastle coal, London's universal fuel. Count Rumford, the reformer of the fireplace, put the issue trenchantly in 1796:

> The enormous waste of fuel may be estimated by the vast dark cloud which continually hangs over this great metropolis, and frequently overshadows the whole country, far and wide; for this dense cloud is certainly composed almost entirely of *unconsumed coal*, which having stolen wings from the innumerable fires of this great city has escaped by the Chimneys, and continues to sail about in the air, till having lost its volatility, it falls in a dry shower of extremely fine black dust to the ground, obscuring the atmosphere in its descent, and frequently changing the brightest day into more than Stygian darkness.[56]

With the advent of gas lighting, conditions deteriorated further. Not until the age of electricity did they improve.

Faced with such sentiments and conditions, those that could do so opted to live as far out of town as they could. As John Thompson, 'eminent as a valuer of effects in the brewery line', expressed it when defending his eccentric neo-Gothic home in Hampstead against a threat of encroachment: 'To any person whose professional engagements place him in that part of the day usually devoted to business in situations of bustle and noise, the relief which must be experienced on returning to a house retired and undisturbed must be highly valued.'[57]

The minor architect George Ledwell Taylor's domestic evolution is typical. As a young man Taylor lived with his mother at amenable Earl's Terrace, Kensington, walking 3 full miles to work by nine o'clock, and back again 'along the dull wall from Knightsbridge to Kensington' in time for dinner. In 1820 he married and took a town house in Bedford Square, using the rooms at the back for offices. But he disliked the neighbourhood 'by reason of the great smoke of the adjoining brewery' and the heavy taxes. By 1830 Taylor had enough money to buy 10 acres at Lee, some 8 miles south-east of London. Here he built a villa for himself on the highest part of the land, with kitchen gardens, gravel walks and a pond below the house.[58]

The pattern is common enough for the London professional classes or, to use the preciser term of the time, 'carriage folk'. Once you could afford a conveyance

54 Ibid., pp.188, 193-95.
55 Cobbett 1912, vol. 1, p.43.
56 Brown 1979, p.167.
57 Thompson 1974, p.121.
58 Taylor 1870, vol. 1, p.162.

and space to house it in at both ends of your journey, the commuting limit imposed by the time and energy required for walking was vastly enlarged. But better-administered and better-surfaced main roads were needed for this wider dispersal. The banker and philanthropist Henry Thornton, travelling up to London the short distance from Clapham in the Napoleonic years, thought it 'cruel to drive even to town with only a pair' when the roads were heavy, so would take a coach and four.[59] Before the 1820s, the roads in and out of London were managed partly by parish vestries, partly by 'turnpike trusts'. Revenue was collected at frequent tollgates, the 'continual stoppage' at which caused greater grievance than their expense. The solution was consolidation of management, plus the transfer of road maintenance costs from tolls to local taxation. In 1826 all the turnpike roads north of the Thames were brought under a single commission. Twenty-seven gates disappeared in a day, and the efficient Scottish road surveyor, James McAdam, was brought in to preside over a six-year programme of 'macadamisation' (redraining and resurfacing the roads with layers of small granite chips, well rammed). Many of London's smarter streets, too, had been 'macadamised' by 1830.[60]

Suburban villas like Taylor's, or cottages as they were often pretentiously called, proliferated after 1800. Advocated by medical men on grounds of health, encouraged, too, by the growing craze for gardens and garden design, they were puffed by young architects in seductively pictorial books of designs. Charles Busby was early in the field with *A Series of Designs for Villas and Country Houses adapted with economy to the Comforts and Elegances of Modern Life* (1807). 'The true impressions of cheerfulness, elegance, and refinement are so well understood and so happily united in our modern domestic dwellings,' Busby told his readers, 'that I hesitate not to say we are rapidly advancing to a state of perfection.' Busby built three villas in Clapham, so his creations are not all imaginary, which is more than can be said for some of his fellow authors. One, Nightingale Cottage, a plain box of a storey and a half, shows that such houses might be as small as the terraced houses to which they were preferred. Its architect's response: 'it is a fact I am allowed to state, that the numerous accommodations in this house have, on inspection, surprised most persons who judged it

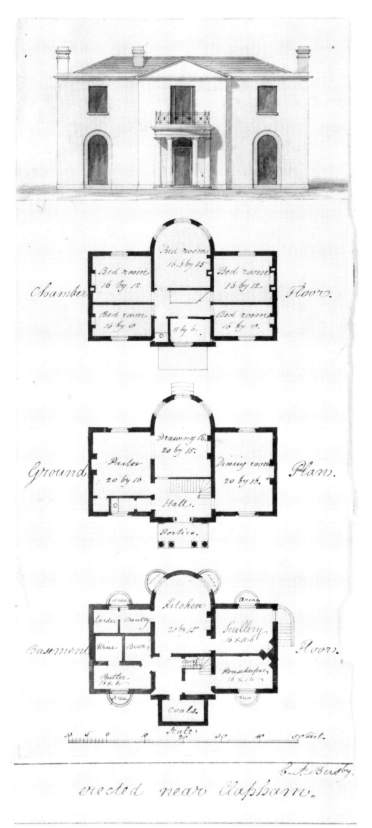

Clapham Common South Side, plans and elevation of small suburban villa by Charles Busby, *c.*1808. British Architectural Library

59 Forster 1956, p.34.
60 Reader 1980, pp.165-71.

Clapham Common South Side, Busby's villa as it appeared in 1971. Greater London Record Office

only by its external appearance'. The plausible Busby went bankrupt in 1814.[61]

To escape London, however, many middle-class people had to await the advent of proper public transport. Until about 1810 'short-stage' coaches coming into London were few in number, expensive, small and cramped. They gradually became more frequent. Yet a proper omnibus service – the so-called 'box on wheels' – was licensed only in 1829, just seven years before the first section of the pioneering London and Greenwich Railway opened.[62] So it is not far wrong to think of public commuting in London as coincident with the railway age, even if more people at first went to work by horse-bus than by train. Once commuting habits were established and fares began to drop, the havens of suburban bliss carved out by the likes of Thompson, Taylor and Busby soon became less exclusive.

Apart from those able to create their own little villa-estates, early residents of the outer suburbs tended to huddle together in 'ribbon-development' terraces with long gardens on the fringes of main roads, or in squares at the edges of established villages like Camberwell, Greenwich or Kensington. Many such communities took on a lease of life as a result. Kentish Town, once a shabby northern hamlet on the route to Highgate, was swollen out of recognition by cottages and short rows along or just off the main street. To add to its existing chapel-of-

ease, between 1807 and 1821 it also gained two nonconformist chapels, a dispensary, a National School, a watch for winter nights, and various voluntary societies dedicated to the 'melioration' of the neighbourhood.[63]

It took time for an authentic and coherent mode of London suburban development to appear. When it did so, it became one of the great English innovations in architecture. Experimental suburban layouts, taking their cue from the open space at hand, had to await the maturing of the Picturesque movement. Their harbinger was a handful of south London developments by Michael Searles. To this little-known architect and entrepreneur is due most credit for the phenomenon of the semi-detached house – a peculiarly English compromise between rustic independence and urban companionship which has yet to exhaust its appeal.[64] In the exquisite crescent of The Paragon at Blackheath (1794–1805), Searles's consummate essay in the genre, the separate pairs of houses face the void of open country but still hold on to one another reassuringly by means of short colonnades. Free-standing semi-detached houses ('double detached houses' in the terminology of the Picturesque architect and journalist J. C. Loudon, who built a well-publicised pair for himself and his mother in Bayswater,[65] or 'two having the appearance of one' as they are sometimes termed[66]) start to penetrate the suburbs soon afterwards. The stuccoed villa, too, shrinks to suit the budget of the short-stage commuter. By the 1820s these types, minimally Gothic or Greek according to taste, begin to alternate along the roads of ampler suburbs such as St. John's Wood, Clapham Park and Blackheath Park. But it is Nash, in his miniature Park Villages on the edge of Regent's Park (1824–28), who takes the creative leap of fostering the semi-independent relationship between small suburban houses by means of curving road layout, asymmetrical siting and landscape. Here, in Sir John Summerson's words, 'Nash the cottage architect came back to his favourite employment and left behind him a model – slight, hasty as ever and gently humorous – for a suburbia of the future.'[67]

Promoters might present the London suburbs in idyllic terms, but they were far from uniformly attractive. Cobbett shuddered at the 'cockney-like appearance' of the

61 Bingham 1991, pp.30-32.
62 Barker and Robbins 1975, pp.3-21.
63 Tindall 1977, pp.117-20.
64 Bonwitt 1987.
65 Loudon 1838.
66 Thompson 1974, p.87.
67 Summerson 1980, p.129.

THE BUILDING ART OF THE FIRST INDUSTRIAL METROPOLIS

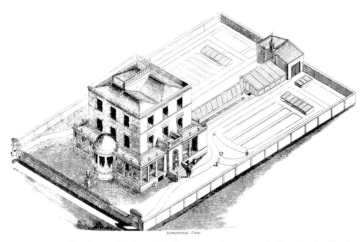

Axonometric view of John Claudius Loudon's semi-detached villa for himself and his mother, Porchester Terrace, Bayswater, 1823-24. From Loudon's *The Suburban Gardener*. Guildhall Library

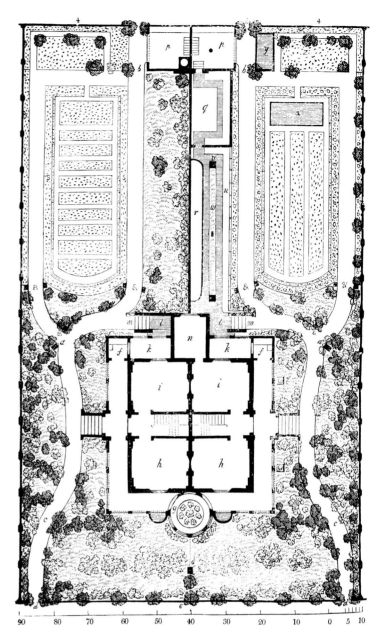

Plan showing layout of houses and garden at Loudon's Bayswater villa. Guildhall Library

countryside around London with its 'houses, gardens, grass plats and other matters to accommodate the Jews and jobbers, and the mistresses and bastards that are put out a-keeping'.[68] Northern and western districts boasted prosperous orchards and market gardens, but eastern and southern ones were less fertile and often scruffy. The few non-domestic buildings to be found could be ornaments to the neighbourhood, like Soane's exceptional Dulwich College Picture Gallery. But they might also be reminders of the grimmer side of metropolitan life like the Middlesex County Lunatic Asylum at Hanwell, or the secret silk-weaving mill equipped with the first British jacquard looms erected by Stephen Wilson in the outlying village of Streatham during the early 1820s in an attempt to break the high wage rates and restrictive practices of the Spitalfields weavers. Wilson's experiment – a rare example of an effort to extend the factory system of the Midlands and North of England to London – failed. Even on the periphery of London, the degree of control of the workforce practised by industrialists in smaller communities was just not possible. His mill, recently rediscovered, is now a supermarket.[69]

Another curse of the suburbs was the small brick-kiln – pervasive in times of building boom, since until the 1830s most London bricks were still made from London clay, extracted as close to the site of building operations as possible. Louis Simond, a French-American visitor, describes a drive out of town in 1811:

London extends its great polypus-arms over the country around. The population is not increased by any means in proportion to these appearances, – only

68   Cobbett 1912, vol. 1, pp.213, 256.
69   Harwood and Saint 1991, pp.223-24.

transferred from the centre to the extremities ... People live in the outskirts of the town in better air, – larger houses, – and at a smaller rent, – and stages passing every half hour facilitate communications. Certain parts of the extremities of the town are, however, exposed to a great nuisance; the air is poisoned by the emanation from brick-kilns, exactly like carrion, to such a degree, as to excite nausea, and the utmost disgust, till the cause of the smell is known ... As soon as we got beyond the sight and the smell of bricks the country appeared to great advantage.[70]

In sum, pollution was not confined to the city centre. Often the urge to escape London proved vain.

The perfect spectacle of contradiction between suburban aspiration and reality in George IV's London is offered by another foreigner, the Italian poet-in-exile, Ugo Foscolo. Penniless but resourceful, Foscolo contrived in the 1820s to build a stucco villa on the banks of the Regent's Canal, which he christened Digamma Cottage to commemorate a pamphleteering triumph on the subject of an archaic letter in the Greek alphabet. Attended by two maidens in Grecian attire, Foscolo relished his riparian prospect. But the great romantic was pained to observe dirty coal barges and bargees plying past his garden rather than the ancient craft of his imagination. He enjoyed Digamma Cottage all too briefly before his creditors caught up with him.[71]

70 Simond 1817, vol. 1, p.260.
71 Franzero 1977, pp.79-83.

METROPOLITAN IMPROVEMENTS: JOHN NASH AND THE PICTURESQUE

J. Mordaunt Crook

Once, and only once, has a great plan for London, affecting the development of the capital as a whole, been projected and carried to completion. This was the plan which constituted the 'metropolitan improvements' of the Regency, the plan which embraced the Regent's Park layout in the north, St. James's Park in the south, the Regent Street artery connecting the two, the formation of Trafalgar Square and the construction of the West End of the Strand, and the Suffolk Street area; as well as the cutting of the Regent's Canal, with its branch and basin to serve Regent's Park. The whole of this immense plan, which gave a 'spine' to London's inchoate West End and had a far-reaching effect on subsequent northward and southward expansion, was carried out under the presiding genius of John Nash.

Sir John Summerson, *Georgian London*

Any study of Regency architecture has to begin with Summerson's image of John Nash as London's master-planner.[1] But the more closely we examine the story of these metropolitan improvements, the less coherent they appear. Episodic, protracted, fragmented, inconclusive – the rebirth of Regency London cannot reasonably be described in terms of principled town planning. It was much more a matter of instinct and luck: a classic case of 'muddling through'.

The muddle was, in origin, constitutional. The metropolitan improvements of the early nineteenth century were the product of an alliance between the public and private sectors: public in the form of three government departments; private in the shape of individual builders and developers. The link between the two was indeed John Nash. But he arrived late on the scene. The genesis of these improvements lay with those three departments: the Office of Works, the Land Revenue Office and the Office of Woods and Forests.

The Office of Works had been purged and professionalised in 1782. It dealt with royal palaces and public buildings in so far as they were a charge on the taxpayer. Its impact on the face of Regency London was considerable: the British Museum, the General Post Office, the Mint, the Custom House, Somerset House, the National Gallery, Buckingham Palace – all these were, in different ways, Office of Works projects. But the involvement of the Office of Works with metropolitan improvement – that is with the programme of development in the Regent's Park, Regent Street, Trafalgar Square and St. James's Park areas – was at most tangential. What of the other two departments? The Land Revenue Office dealt with the leasing, sale and redevelopment of crown property; the duties of the Office of Woods, Forests, Parks and Chaces were implicit in its comprehensive title. By amalgamating both of these in 1810, the government centred in one department responsibilities which are today allocated to at least five: urban renewal (Department of the Environment), road improvement (Ministry of Transport), aforestation (Ministry of Agriculture), military and naval provision (Ministry of Defence), and the management of the crown estate (Crown Estates Commissioners). In 1815 one section of this multiple role – that relating to building in royal parks – was transferred to a reconstituted Office of Works. But in 1832 all three departments were united under the umbrella title of Woods, Forests, Land Revenues, Works and Buildings. Twenty years later it was clear that the operation of that triple department was as cumbersome as its nomenclature, and public buildings were once again separated from royal lands in the year of the Great Exhibition.

The idea of redeveloping crown land in London grew out of the need to maximise revenue at a time of royal extravagance and unprecedented wartime expenditure.[2] In 1786 William Pitt set in motion a series of statutory inquiries. Seventeen reports were produced between 1786 and 1793;[3] four between 1797 and 1809;[4] and seven more between 1812 and 1830.[5] The heroes of this prolonged bout of investigation and reform were two busy Scottish civil servants: John Fordyce[6] and Sylvester Douglas,

1 Summerson 1962, p.177; see also Summerson 1935; Summerson 1980.
2 Pugh 1960.
3 *Commons Journals,* vol. 42, p.310; vol. 43, pp.145, 559; vol. 44, pp.126, 552; vol. 45, p.120; vol. 46, p.97; vol. 47, pp.141, 883, 1031; vol. 48, p.267; Binney 1959.
4 1797, 1802, 1806, 1809: reprinted *Parliamentary Papers* 1812, vol. 12.
5 Triennial Reports: *Parliamentary Papers* 1812, vol. 12; 1816, vol. 15; 1819, vol. 19; 1823, vol. 11; 1826, vol. 14; 1829, vol. 14; 1830, vol. 16.
6 Fordyce was one of several Scottish administrators promoted under Viscount Melville. PRO, WORK 16/40/3, 158: 27 June 1796; *Gentleman's Magazine* 1809, pt 2, pp.658, 780.

Baron Glenbervie.[7] Between them they transformed the administration of crown lands into something like a modern government department.[8] Each replaced a prime example of Hanoverian corruption. In 1782 Fordyce succeeded George Augustus Selwyn, wit, rake, gambler and multiple sinecurist.[9] In 1783 Glenbervie succeeded 'Rat-catcher' Robinson, ring-master to the King's Friends.[10] Both changes – and still more the arrival of Glenbervie's successor William Huskisson in 1815 – tell us a good deal about the shift in public life from Georgian to Victorian codes of conduct. When the metropolitan improvements came – and they were half-a-century in gestation – they would at least be conducted with integrity.

Integrity, rather than efficiency or consistency. Between Fordyce's first enunciation of the crown estate's grand strategy in 1793 and the suspension of operations forty years later, in a flurry of royal scandal and extravagance, there were innumerable changes of plan, nearly always dictated by accident rather than design.

The first accident was the death of William Pitt in January 1806. That brought in the coalition Ministry of All Talents. Their nominee as 'chief woodman' was an old gambling crony of Charles James Fox, Lord Robert Spencer, 'comical Bob'.[11] Spencer brought with him two figures of key significance in the history of the Picturesque: John Nash and Uvedale Price. Nash was called in to investigate the incompetence of the current architect at Woods and Forests, John Harvey.[12] This task he performed so thoroughly that he was immediately rewarded with Harvey's job.[13] The circumstances of Price's appointment are rather more obscure. Technically, at least, he was the first and last Superintendent to the Deputy Surveyor of the Forest of Dean.[14] But clearly, Spencer was simply looking after his Whig friends. And those friends happened to be devotees of the Picturesque. It was Price who first explained to Nash the principles of that philosophy: during the planning of his triangular castle at Aberystwyth in 1795 he had expounded the optical benefits of linking architecture and landscape. Nash apparently 'never thought of [it] before in the slightest degree'.[15] Now, ten years later, Nash and Price were in the same government department, no doubt still talking the language of the Picturesque.

The second accident was a quite extraordinary co-incidence. In April 1811 the leases on Marylebone Park fell in and reverted to the crown. Two months before, in February 1811, George III had been finally declared insane, and the Regency formally began. Within weeks – in March 1811 – Nash's first scheme for Regent's Park was ready, and soon after that the Prince Regent was boasting that he would 'quite eclipse Napoleon'.[16]

The third accident was the sudden death of James Wyatt in a road crash in September 1813. Wyatt had been Surveyor General in the Office of Works, and a very negligent one too. At his death the responsibilities of that office were therefore divided. In effect, Nash received the royal palaces, Soane Whitehall and Westminster, and Smirke the British Museum, Post Office, Royal Mint and London prisons. 'I [am] the King', Nash told Soane, 'you are the Lords, and *your* friend Smirke the Commons.'[17] The result, as regards metropolitan improvement, was this. From October 1813 onwards – formally from April 1815 – Nash had a triple authority: for the Office of Woods, Forests and Land Revenues he dealt with the development of the crown estate; for the Office of Works he dealt with royal palaces paid for out of the public purse; for palaces covered by the privy purse (Brighton Pavilion

7   For Glenbervie's departmental reforms, see PRO, CRES 8/1 (1803), 8/2 (1805-06), 8/5 (1810), 8/7 (1812).

8   Despite ceremonial sinecurists; e.g. the Hereditary Lord Wardens, Rangers or Keepers of Forests, (PRO, CRES 8/2, 142, 146, 421).

9   Pitt had presented Selwyn with the Surveyor Generalship of Land Revenues in 1783 as compensation for the loss of his profitable paymastership in the unreformed Office of Works (*Gentleman's Magazine* 1791, pt. 1, p.94).

10 Robinson won the favour of Farmer George by planting 20,000 oak trees and millions of acorns at Windsor (*Dictionary of National Biography*).

11 Thorne ed. 1986, vol. 5, pp. 241-43.

12 This was a post with a history of incompetence. Surveyors to the Land Revenue Office – John Marquand, Thomas Leverton, Thomas Chawner, Henry Rhodes – were departmental appointees, concerned only with mundane duties of house valuation, measurement and cartography; but architects to the Office of Woods – Charles Cole, John Soane, James Wyatt, John Nash, James Morgan – were Treasury appointees, subject to shifts of political patronage and responsible for potentially contentious works in royal parks. Soane resigned, Cole and Wyatt were dismissed, and Nash and Morgan were made redundant by the reorganisation of 1815.

13 PRO, CRES 8/2, 505; 8/3, 11, 18, 35. Nash and Morgan were temporarily appointed on 23 October 1806 (PRO, CRES 8/2, 515), and their position was confirmed on 23 March 1807 (PRO, CRES 8/3, 147). See also *Parliamentary Papers* 1813, vol. 5, pp.499, 501.

14 His duties were to strengthen the Deputy's hand in eliminating abuse of Forest land by yeomen and miners, while encouraging the growth of timber (PRO, CRES 8/2, 386, 400, 405). His post disappeared in the reorganisation of 1810 (PRO, CRES 8/5, 19).

15 Price to Sir George Beaumont, 18 March 1798, quoted in Summerson 1980, p.21. For Castle House see Mansbridge 1991, no. 38.

16 Thomas Moore to James Corry, 24 October 1811 (Russell ed. 1856, vol. 8, p.97).

17 Bolton 1927, p.352.

for example) he was already responsible as personal architect to the Regent. When it came to Buckingham Palace, all three aspects of his duties collided, with results which were – financially and administratively speaking – fatal.[18]

To recapitulate, Nash arrived late on the scene of metropolitan improvement, thanks to a series of accidents. He inherited a financial strategy for exploiting the crown estate. With that strategy came a major programme of urban renewal and road building. It was his job to give both strategy and programme architectural form. By the time he began work, in 1811, there was a body of thinking on the subject dating back thirty years. In 1795, for example, the Earl of Lonsdale had suggested to the Prince of Wales a novel way to liquidate old debts: simply redevelop the periphery of Hyde Park.[19] Nothing came of that particular proposal. But when the prince became Prince Regent – and decided to 'eclipse Napoleon' – Lonsdale's advice was no doubt remembered.

That the Prince Regent and his architect should eventually think in Parisian terms was quite understandable. Here was a chance to set up permanent symbols of victory, as well as urban promenades which would rival the Rue de Rivoli. Nash was not a learned architect. Whether he actually read Ledoux's great folio of 1804, with its plan for a utopian *ville sociale*, must remain unproven.[20] What we do know is that in October 1814 Nash was in France, celebrating peace with a visit to the architectural delights of Paris.[21] And he was there again in November 1815.[22] When in 1825 he came to redesign Buckingham Palace, the Tuileries cannot have been far from his mind. Certainly Marble Arch owes something to the Arc du Carrousel. And when in the same year he was at last in a position to finalise one of Regent's Park's most conspicuous monuments – Chester Terrace – he noted with satisfaction that it would indeed be 'nearly as long as the Tuileries'.[23] As for Carlton House Terrace, he set out in 1827 to make it a significant improvement on Gabriel's Place de la Concorde.[24]

There was, however, another tradition. In a striking passage in his thirteenth *Discourse*, Sir Joshua Reynolds had suggested that:

The forms and turnings of the streets of London, and other old towns, are produced by accident, without any original plan or design; but they are not always the less pleasant to the walker or spectator, on that account. On the contrary, if the city had been built on the regular plan of Sir Christopher Wren, the effect might have been, as we know it is in some new parts of the town, rather unpleasing: the uniformity might have produced weariness, and a slight degree of disgust.[25]

When it came to designing Regent Street, the High Street at Oxford would turn out to be a more useful precedent than the Palais Royale.[26]

In the absence of any official metropolitan planning authority, the administrators of the crown estate became *faute de mieux* coordinators of London's town-planning; ancestors, in that respect, of the Metropolitan Board of Works, the London County Council, and the Greater London Council. The grandest redevelopment scheme in London's history thus fell into the hands of an unelected group of civil servants, whose only official responsibility was to maximise the revenues of the crown.[27] That they did so without neglecting public amenity, tells us much about that political generation's sense of civic virtue, to say nothing of its aesthetic sensibility. Anyway, it was Fordyce's reports to the Treasury – primarily those of 1793[28] and 1809[29] – which sketched out the parameters that one day Nash would follow: a redeveloped Marylebone Park, with housing, sewerage, lighting, servicing and transportation; roads, canals, markets, hostelries, churches, shops and monuments, even perhaps a Valhalla; at all events an urban precinct of north London linked to the centres of power and fashion – Mayfair, Charing Cross, Whitehall, Westminster – by a bold network of new thoroughfares.

Fordyce, of course, produced no designs; but he did sponsor a survey,[30] and an abortive competition.[31] And from that stemmed the first plan for metropolitan im-

18 The Treasury stipulated that Buckingham Palace 'was to be considered as... entirely detached from the service of the Office of Works, both in respect to salary, and to the superintendance of new works' (PRO, WORK 1/17, 129: 1 June 1828). Financially, the distinction proved impossible to maintain, and Nash was suspended from the Office of Works by a Treasury order dated 2 October 1830 (PRO, WORK 1/18, 332), though in fact he had waived his salary as Attached Architect since 1826 (Ibid.; Noble 1836, pp.33-35).
19 Aspinall ed. 1965, vol. 3, p.120; no. 1055: 1795.
20 Summerson 1960, p. 14.
21 Ruch 1968, p.46, note 20.
22 PRO, CRES 8/10, 358: 23 May 1816.
23 PRO, CRES 2/1737.
24 Reynolds ed. Wark 1959.
25 Ibid., p.243.
26 *Parliamentary Papers* 1812, vol. 12, Appendix 12B: 1st Report.
27 *Parliamentary Papers* 1816, vol. 15, pp.122-24: 31 March 1813.
28 *Parliamentary Papers* 1812, vol. 12, pp.517, 530-31: 1st Report, Surveyor General of Land Revenues, Appendix 3A, 27 June 1793.
29 *Parliamentary Papers* 1812, vol. 12, pp.718, 763-4: 4th Report... 6 April 1809.
30 By George Richardson (1794): PRO, MR 324 [LRRO 1/479]; MR 1103 (2) [LRRO 1/1042 (2)].
31 *Parliamentary Papers* 1812, vol. 12, pp.517, 530-31: 27 June 1793. Only John White submitted plans (Ibid., pp.355-56).

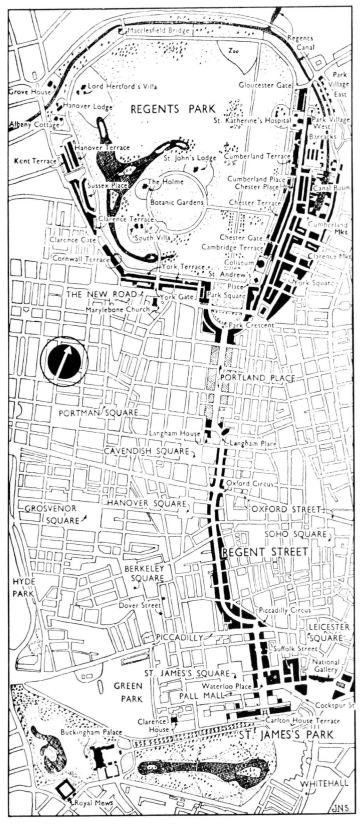

Map of Nash's improvements. Sir John Summerson

provement: John White's proposal of 1809.[32] In White's scheme were several features which – in modified form – recur in future plans: a 'grand crescent' near the head of Portland Place with a major church at its centre; an 'Ornamental Water' sinuously laid out on Picturesque principles to follow the contours of the land; and, around the park, a cordon of villas, accessible from a peripheral highway forming the boundary of the entire estate. Fordyce's ideas were clearly still in the air: in 1810, a few months after Fordyce's death, they formed the basis of a set of draft instructions prepared by the newly amalgamated departments. These guidelines were then sent out to the respective departmental architects: Thomas Leverton and Thomas Chawner (for the Land Revenue Office) and Nash and James Morgan (for the Office of Woods and Forests). Both teams were directed to study Edinburgh and Bath as possible models; accordingly, both produced schemes which contained only hints of Picturesque planning.

Leverton and Chawner began with the kind of reticulated layout familiar from London's Georgian estates – Bedford, Portland, Southampton, Portman – and then combined it with the crescent (now reversed) and peripheral highway envisaged by White.[33] Following Fordyce's directional axes, they also proposed to link Marylebone to Westminster by means of a route – first proposed in 1808 – somewhat to the east of what was to become Regent Street.[34] It was a good scheme, in effect a new Bloomsbury. But it fell short as regards two features upon which Fordyce and his successors had clearly set their hearts: civic dignity and public amenity.

Nash's plan – his first for Regent's Park, dated March 1811[35] – proved, in terms of density, almost equally urban; a metropolitan annexe, laid out on geometrical lines, dominated by a circus and a double circus, with squares, avenues and crescents, plus a sinuous lake and a scattering of villas within its interstices: just enough to create an illusion of rurality. All this was speciously illustrated by two giant panoramas, probably prepared by A.C. Pugin and George Repton, designed to emphasise the Picturesqueness of the scene.[36]

32 PRO, MPE 918 (1)-(3) [LRRO 1/1062 (1)-(3)]; published in White 1813.
33 PRO, MR 1108 (1) [LRRO 1/1042 (1)]. Published in *Parliamentary Papers* 1812, vol. 12, p.429: 1st Report.
34 Ibid., p.419.
35 PRO, MPEE 58 [LRRO 1/1000]. Summerson 1977, pp.56-62 and, 1980, pl. 22
36 *Parliamentary Papers* 1812, vol. 12, p.435: 1st Report.

The Treasury was not deceived. Spencer Perceval, Prime Minister and Chancellor of the Exchequer, summoned Nash to Downing Street and told him firmly to reduce the housing density: amenity was just as important as profit.[37] Now this was a matter on which the Tory government may well have felt vulnerable. Even after the balance had been shifted towards accessibility, Lord Brougham was able to protest vehemently against the crown's virtual enclosure of Marylebone Park: a building programme like this was 'trenching on the comfort of the poor for the accommodation of the rich'.[38] After all, this whole episode – the re-drawing of the map of London's West End – could be interpreted as an exercise in social manipulation. Perceval set out to draw the teeth of such criticism by increasing the percentage of accessible park space. The result was Nash's second scheme, prepared in the autumn of 1811 and published in 1812.[39]

In this second layout, Nash switched – belatedly – to the principles of 'picturesque beauty'.[40] Leverton and Chawner's plan, as James Elmes explained, had been 'more *urban* and builder like'.[41] Nash's first design had been a compromise between urbanity and rurality. His second 'embraced', in Elmes's words, 'those beauties of landscape gardening which his friend Humphry Repton so successfully introduced'.[42] In this scheme there are fewer villas, perhaps no more than fifty; fewer terraces too, and all tucked away around the circumference. The circus and double circus are still there, with monumental buildings – a church and a Valhalla – at their centres; so is the royal pavilion, or *guinguette*, with its formal water garden; so are the crescents, though now they have been moved up to the northern boundary. But the tentacles of the Ornamental Water have been extended, and the serried plantations have given way to informal clumps and shrubberies. This is certainly Picturesque, but it is an urban Picturesque. 'The leading object', Nash explained, is 'that of presenting from without one entire Park complex in unity of character and not an assemblage of Villas and Shrubberies like Hampstead, Highgate, Clapham Common . . . [But above all] the buildings and even the Villas should be considered as Town residences and not Country Houses.'[43] These terraces might be occupied by City magnates and professional people of middle rank; but they must *look* like metropolitan palaces.

One further change: the Regent's Canal has now been discreetly shifted to the north-west corner of the park. Not that Nash was totally averse to canals: 'many Persons', he noted, 'would consider . . . Boats and Barges passing along the Canal as enlivening the Scenery, provided the Bargemen . . . were prevented from landing in the Parks . . . by fencing out the Towing Path on one side,

and by stakes in the Water on the other.'[44] Clearly the Picturesque could not tolerate too much reality.

Here, then, was a plan designed to maximise crown revenue while increasing 'the beauty and salubrity of the metropolis'.[45] 'Open space, free air, and the scenery of nature', Nash explains, will prove irresistible to 'the wealthy part of the Public'.[46] And Repton's principle of 'apparent extent' will guarantee an illusion of space: 'no Villa should see any other,' Nash asserts, 'but each should appear to possess the whole of the Park'; and the 'Streets of Houses which overlook the Park should not see the Villas, nor the Streets of Houses overlook those of another street.'[47] By foregoing the majority of his 'Streets, Squares, Circuses and Villas', he had – inadvertently – secured 'a greater variety of beautiful scenery' as well as a higher level of leasehold value.[48] And by tying this new park to an elegant New Street, the worth of all these properties would be multiplied by ease of communication.

Nash had now satisfied his ministerial masters.[49] He had yet to satisfy the market. The postwar property slump made new building unprofitable. 'The disposition to building', he explained, 'suddenly became paralyzed' by 'the sudden stoppage . . . of credit'.[50] By 1819 only three sets of villas had been let. By 1823, the planned number had been reduced to twenty-six.[51] By 1826 the twenty-six had again been cut back, this time to a mere

37 Ibid., pp.357, 463, 467.
38 *Parliamentary Debates* 1812, vol. 23, p.72.
39 PRO, MPE 902 (6) [LRRO 1/1047 (6)]; *Parliamentary Papers* 1812, vol. 12, 465: 1st Report.
40 Ibid., p.417.
41 Elmes 1827, p.11.
42 Ibid.
43 PRO, CRES 2/742.
44 *Parliamentary Papers* 1812, vol. 12, p.435: 1st Report.
45 Ibid., p.463.
46 Ibid., p.433.
47 Ibid., p.434.
48 Ibid., p.463.
49 Glenbervie told Col. McMahan: 'Mr. Nash . . . has estimated that the value of Marylebone Park will be increased to the amount of at least £15,000 a year if the [new] street shall be made. I believe much more, but as his estimate is to be sworn to he does right to keep within bounds' (Royal Archives, Windsor Castle 19999-20000: 31 August 1812).
50 'For the last five years the great interest which the public Funds have offered has diverted the capital formerly employed in [building] speculations; [but] as the Funds rise in price the floating capital in the country will flow into other Channels, and should those of building not be damned up, a part of that capital will certainly find its way into Mary-le-Bone Park' (*Parliamentary Papers* 1816, vol. 15, pp.113-14: 4 February 1816, 2nd Report).
51 *Parliamentary Papers* 1823, vol. 11, pp.26, 127, Appendix 24, plan: 7 March 1823, 4th Report.

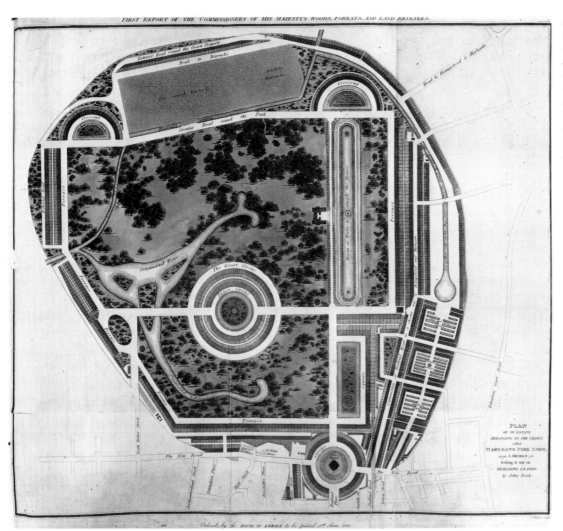

Plan of an Estate belonging to the Crown called Marybone Park Farm, upon a Design for letting it out on Building Leases, by John Nash, engraving from *The First Report of the Commissioners of Woods, Forests and Land Revenues,* 1812. The Museum of London

eight.[52] The Valhalla had been quietly shelved. The number of terraces was reduced as well. St. Andrew's Terrace and Kent Terrace did not appear in their intended form. Carrick Terrace and Munster Terrace never even reached the drawing board; they – and the projected barracks – were replaced, on the northern side, by a novel entertainment: the Zoological Gardens (Decimus Burton, 1826–41).[53] The barracks were relocated to the eastern perimeter. The circus at the head of Portland Place became Park Crescent (1812–22) and Park Square (1823–25) after its initial contractor, Charles Mayor, went bankrupt in 1815.[54] The idea of a church at its focus was abandoned.[55] And the central double circus – centrepiece of Nash's plan – was first slimmed down to a single circle and then came near to being turned into the site of King's College, London;[56] it ended up, more popularly, as a Botanical Garden (Decimus Burton, 1840–59).[57] Meanwhile, the

52 *Parliamentary Papers* 1826, vol. 14, p.11: 5th Report; Crook, 1968.

53 Zoological Society prospectus, 15 June 1827. Burton's plan: PRO, MPE 906.

54 *Parliamentary Papers* 1816, vol. 15, pp.17-18, 114: 2nd Report; 1819, vol. 19, p.10: 3rd Report.

55 Soane exhibited a design in 1821 for 'a church proposed to be built in the Regent's Park' (exhib. R.A., 1821, nos. 950, 964, 978).

56 PRO, MPE 912; Summerson 1980, pl. 33B.

57 Burton's report: *Gardeners' Magazine* 1840, vol. 16, pp.514-16.

idea of a Long Walk, or avenue of trees, had been first dropped and then re-introduced as a formal approach to the royal *guingette* or summer pavilion.[58] That too remained a mirage.

To recapitulate: Nash did not at first intend to design a public park; that eventuality was forced on him first by the good sense of his political masters, then by the pressure of market forces. From the start, the profitable urban precinct which he envisaged had a number of suburban features: self-sufficiency, good communications, and an illusion of rurality. Only gradually did it take on the characteristics of a popular recreational facility.

Illusion, of course, was one of the principal ingredients in that cluster of ideas and attitudes which came to be labelled Picturesque. Appropriately, among the delights available in Regent's Park – actually in Park Square East – was a distant ancestor of the modern cinema known as the Diorama.[59] Here, James Elmes explains, is 'a display of architectural and landscape scenery, arranged . . . so as to exhibit changes of light and shade and a variety of natural phenomena in a really wonderful manner'. 'The delusion,' he adds, 'is perfect and almost incredible.'[60] So, too, with Regent's Park. The authors of the Diorama – its 'pictorial enchanters' – were not architects but scene-painters: Messrs. Bouton and Daguerre. But in Regent's Park itself Nash was both architect and scene maker. Like the Diorama, his transformation of Marylebone fields was a compound of 'powerful pictorial illusions';[61] in effect, it was a scenic conjuring trick.

That was certainly Nash's intention. As the drawings came in – from builders: James Burton, W.M. Nurse, Richard Mott, George Thompson, T.M. Aitkens; or from architects: Decimus Burton, James Thomson, J.J. Scoles, Ambrose Poynter – he inserted modifications in pursuit of Picturesque effect. Decimus Burton's first design for Cornwall Terrace (1820–21), for example, was dismissed as altogether too monotonous: like 'a hospital, almshouse, work-house or some such building'. Nash failed to persuade the young architect to sub-divide the facade into several distinct units, 'each assuming the character of a nobleman's villa'; but he did secure a much more broken silhouette, with boldly projecting porticos.[62] And when it came to Chester Terrace, he tolerated no half-

58 *Parliamentary Papers* 1826, vol. 14, p.137: 5th report, plan; Summerson 1980, pl. 33A.
59 Altick 1978, p.163 *et seq*. The building was designed by A.C. Pugin and James Morgan.
60 Elmes 1827, p.23.
61 Ibid.
62 PRO, CRES 2/767.

The Crescent, Portland Place, aquatint from Ackermann's *Repository of Arts*, 1822. The Museum of London

THE CRESCENT, PORTLAND PLACE.

JOHN NASH AND THE PICTURESQUE

J. Tingle after T.H. Shepherd, *Cumberland Terrace, Regent's Park*, engraving from J. Elmes, *Metropolitan Improvements*, 1827. The Museum of London

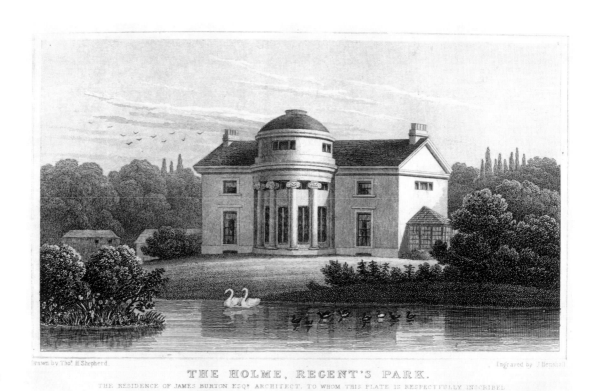

J. Henshall after T.H. Shepherd, *The Holme, Regent's Park*, engraving from J. Elmes, *Metropolitan Improvements*, 1827. The Museum of London

H. Wallis after T.H. Shepherd, *York Gate, Regent's Park, & Mary-le-bone Church*, engraving from J. Elmes *Metropolitan Improvements,* 1827. The Museum of London

measures: we owe those transverse triumphal arches, which multiply the terrace's theatrical effect, to Nash's personal insistence on Picturesque values.[63] These same values made his own designs – notably Sussex Place (1822–23) and Cumberland Terrace (1826; executant James Thomson) – virtuoso performances in scenographic imagery. To the end of his life he saw all these designs as discrete compositions; visually autonomous, like 'so many distinct pictures'.[64]

Nash's Picturesque vision found its perfect expositor in the person of James Elmes, the orotund author of *Metropolitan Improvements* (1827). The architect's conception, Elmes explains, was essentially Reptonian.[65] The choicest views of The Holme (1816–18) – selected for himself by James Burton, and designed by his son Decimus – are framed in trees and reflected in 'the glassy surface of the silver lake', for all the world like sketches from 'the magic pencils of Ruysdael and Claude'.[66] South Villa (1818–19), Albany Cottage (c.1822), Hanover Lodge (1827), Grove House (1822–24) – mostly by Burton under Nash's direction: each acts as focus of a 'picturesque group'; each, to the mobile spectator, is part of a sequence of 'living pictures'.[67] Even St. Marylebone Church (Thomas Hardwick, 1813–17) is transformed by Nash into a piece of theatre – a veritable 'stereotomous scene' - by being placed between York Gate's flanking terraces (1822); lit

from east, west and north, explains Elmes, the result is an 'architectural pictorial symphony of three parts'.[68] Circular roads, winding paths; mazy walks, umbrageous pools: 'See! the sparkling undulating line of beauty.'[69] Cornice and pilaster, bow and pediment; Cumberland Terrace's mighty colonnades, spotlit by sunbeams and shadowed by shifting light: 'see ... how they play in ... sunny coruscations'.[70]

Each terrace of houses appears to be a palace; each villa a country seat. The spectator's progress is a trail of continuous illusion. No urban scars can spoil this sylvan scene: the gardens of Park Crescent and Park Square are even linked by a tunnel beneath the traffic of Marylebone Road. These inner gardens, notes Elmes, are not Picturesque according to the 'Gilpin school'. Even so, they are crammed with Reptonian devices: 'meandering walks',

63 PRO, CRES 2/1737.
64 PRO, CRES 2/742: 1832; *Parliamentary Papers* 1829, vol. 14, p.74: 6th Report.
65 Elmes 1827, p.11.
66 Ibid., pp.28-29.
67 Ibid., pp.30, 46-47, 50.
68 Ibid., pp.29, 36-37.
69 Ibid., p.29.
70 Ibid., p.44.

W. Radcliff after T.H. Shepherd, *Park Village East, Regent's Park,* engraving from J. Elmes, *Metropolitan Improvements,* 1827. The Museum of London

'ambrosial shrubs', 'velvet turf', 'gay flowers', and – of course – 'serpentine walks'.[71]

> As you are rowed [on the lake, sighed Charles Ollier in 1823], the variety of views . . . is admirable; sometimes you are in a narrow stream, closely overhung by branches of trees; presently you open upon a wide sheet of water like a lake, with swans sunning themselves on its bosom; bye and bye your boat floats near the edge of a smooth lawn fronting one of the villas; and then again you catch the perspective on the periphery of a range of superb edifices, the elevation of which is contrived to have the effect of a palace . . . the inhabitant of each [villa] seems, in his own prospect, to be the sole lord of the surrounding scenery. In the centre of the park, there is a circular plantation of immense circumference, and in the interior of this you are in a perfect Arcadia.[72]

In a way, Nash's Picturesque vision was fully realised only in miniature, and at the very end of his metropolitan career, in Park Village East and West. One of the subsidiary streets was even named Serpentine Road. The first design for this canal-side site dates from 1823.[73] Its specimen vignettes sketched out a rustic village of *cottages ornées,* not unlike the thatched arcadia of Blaise Hamlet (1810–11). As built, however, in 1824–28,[74] under James

Pennethorne's direction, these stuccoed miniatures – Gothic, Tudor, Tuscan, Italianate – were intended neither for peasant nor artisan, nor even for ladies of pleasure.[75] They were decidely bourgeois. At 12, Park Village West – note its echo of Cronkhill, Shropshire – lived, for example, Dr James Johnson, physician to the Duke of Clarence, and indeed to John Nash himself. A later occupant was the artist W.P. Frith. In the 1840s, one eminently respectable neighbour was the Reverend Benjamin Webb, editor of the *Ecclesiologist.* Today little of Park Village East survives.[76] But Park Village West has become a textbook classic. In their variety of styles, their irregularity of plan, their coy self-consciousness, both villages seem almost an epitome of Picturesque theory. In their purpose, their setting, even their inhabitants, they turned out to be prototypes of a universal suburbia.

But without Regent Street, Regent's Park would have

71   Ibid., p.88.
72   Ollier 1823.
73   PRO, CRES 911 [LRRO 1/1059].
74   PRO, CRES 2/778; *Survey of London* 1949, vol. 21, pp.653-58, pls. 87-99.
75   For their restoration after bomb-damage, see *Architect and Building News* 14 April 1950, pp.387-95.
76   Plan by Philip Hardwick, 1829 (PRO, MPE 907 [LRRO 1/1055]).

J. Tingle after T.H. Shepherd, *All-Souls Church, Langham Place*, engraving from J. Elmes, *Metropolitan Improvements*, 1827. The Museum of London

arcaded boulevard; a straight-angled thoroughfare punctuated by squares and circuses. Parallel colonnades, on either side of this avenue, were to march all the way from Pall Mall to Portland Place, swivelling on three axes – Picadilly Circus, Oxford Circus and Regent's Circus – with a piazza and a major 'public building' masking that change of direction later performed by the only part of the colonnade which was eventually built – Nash's celebrated Quadrant. Finally, there were to have been civic monuments at each key point.[80] The parallactic effect would have been stupendous. But it would not have been Picturesque.

The first change, made in 1813 in accordance with Treasury preference, involved – in the Commissioner's words – the replacement of piazza and public building by 'a bending street, resembling in that respect the High Street at Oxford'.[81] There were other changes, notably the insertion of All Souls, Langham Place, a Commissioners' church tucked in by Nash in 1822–24 at just the point where a new directional axis was needed to link Portland Place and Regent Street. Later changes, in disposition of buildings rather than route, were made pragmatically, according to the dictates of leasehold finance. As building succeeded building, the street emerged as less formal, more Picturesque. At every point Nash was answerable to the Commissioners of Woods and Forests, and thence to the Treasury ministers in parliament. It was a huge operation: the expenditure at its completion in 1826 had run to more than £1.5m.[82] That was twice the estimate of 1819,[83] and four times the original estimate of 1813; but then – as the First Commissioner of Woods and Forests admitted in 1828 – 'the whole plan' had been 'entirely remodelled', indeed the 'alterations' had been 'numberless'.[84]

Nash's control over the circumstances of this business was clearly never absolute. Nor was his supervision of the buildings which eventually appeared. He explained his methods of work – as architect cum developer in chief – as follows:

> I negotiate the original purchase of the ground, negotiate the letting of the ground, and make the design of

been a rather inaccessible Arcadia. As with the park, so with the street, Nash was a late arrival. Fordyce had dreamed of it; James Wyatt had proposed it; Leverton and Chawner had planned it.[77] And Nash's original scheme for a New Street, published in 1812[78] – it had no name until 1819[79] – had been very different to the Regent Street which was eventually built. In the first place it was envisaged as a processional way from Carlton House to a royal summer pavilion in the park. Alas, Carlton House was demolished and the pavilion never built. In the second place, Nash's New Street was to have been an

77 Summerson 1980, p.76.
78 *Parliamentary Papers* 1812, vol. 12, p.447: 1st Report.
79 The New Street Act of 1813 merely refers to 'a more convenient communication from Marylebone Park. . . to Charing Cross'.
80 Summerson 1980, p.79.
81 *Parliamentary Papers* 1812, vol. 12, Appendix 12B: 1st Report.
82 *Parliamentary Papers* 1826, vol. 14, p.12: 5th Report.
83 *Parliamentary Papers* 1819, vol. 19, p.13: 3rd Report.
84 *Parliamentary Papers* 1828, vol. 4, pp.418-19, 421: 1828 Report. For illustrations of individual buildings, see Elmes 1827, and Tallis 1838-40; also Mansbridge 1991, no. 102.

J. Tingle after T. H. Shepherd, *St. George's Chapel, Regent Street* (Hanover Chapel), engraving from J. Elmes, *Metropolitan Improvements*, 1827. The Museum of London

the elevations; I set out the ground for building, draw up the terms of building, I superintend it in a general way in the execution; I draw the plans on the leases; for all which I receive a fee of one half year's ground rent; ... [For] the Opera House ... and the Haymarket Theatre I made the drawings, and did everything that architects usually do ... [But] the Quadrant was built by myself; I took the ground ... Being a peculiar sort of building, it could not be erected house by house, as in other parts of the street, it was obliged to be erected at once, and the speculation was too great for one person. I therefore entered into it, and took the ground at the price at which it was offered to others. I then furnished the design, and let it to a set of builders, and advanced them a large sum of money, to enable them to build, to the tune of £64,000. I do not think that the Quadrant would ever have been carried into execution but in that way.[85]

Nash's supervisory role as a designer – as regards both builders and consultant architects – is again best explained in his own words:

All the improvements of the new street, speaking of the elevations of the houses, are made by me, and approved by the Office of Woods, and then the builders who built them were obliged to conform to that elevation; I

am sorry to say that they do not do it in every particular ... [Besides] if a person presents a design for the elevation of a building, and I do not see a material defect, it would be invidious of me to find fault with it; I return it as approved by me. Mr. Soane made a design, I could not object ... Mr. Smirke has made designs; to those I could not object, and others have made designs.[86]

One day, when George Dance was strolling down Lower Regent Street, he stopped to admire young Robert Smirke's newly built Junior United Service Club. 'And what do you suppose that building is intended for?', Nash 'sneeringly asked'. Dance replied that it 'appeared to be well built and the work of a sensible man! ... The building opposite', Dance told Farington – that is, Warren's Hotel – 'was designed by Nash in imitation of some Roman building, but not [in] as good [a] taste.'[87] Clearly, in a Picturesque street there was room for disagreement. The taste of individual architects: Robert Smirke, C.R.

85 *Parliamentary Papers* 1828, vol. 4, p.387: 1828 Report.
86 Ibid. PRO, CRES 24/7, 328: 18 March 1813 *et seq.*; CRES 26/1-5 (Quadrant).
87 Farington 1978-84, vol. 14, p.5131 (30 December 1817).

PART OF THE EAST SIDE OF REGENT STREET.

Cockerell, George Repton, Decimus Burton, Robert Abraham, John Soane; the business instincts of individual builders and shopkeepers – all acted and reacted reciprocally under the aegis of the Crown's Commissioners and their metropolitan factotum, John Nash. In Nash's pragmatic aesthetic there was room for Soane's austerity as well as Smirke's rectitude; for Robert Abraham's Fire Office (1819) – a neo-classical variation on a theme by Inigo Jones – as well as C.R. Cockerell's Hanover Chapel (1821–25), an essay in coolest Franco-Greek, with Picturesque – indeed Claudian – overtones.[88]

But it was Nash who must take the credit for the final choice of route, the brilliant stroke which planned Regent Street to mark exactly the frontier between first and third grade property, between Mayfair and Soho. By choosing this route, Nash guaranteed a profit: he was able to build cheap and sell dear. He explained that

> If a straight line, had been continued from Regent's Park to Carlton House, it would have passed through St. Giles, leaving all the bad streets between the new street and the respectable streets at the West end of the town, through which the persons residing in those better streets, the members going to the House of Commons and House of Lords, must pass before they could use the new street. In forming that street, my purpose was, that the new street should cross the East-

ern entrance to all the streets occupied by the higher classes, and to leave out to the East all those bad streets . . . [hence] the line [of] the new street. [However, all was not plain sailing]; I was shoved to the Westwards by the proprietors on the East of [Cavendish] Square; otherwise my intention was to have entered Portland Place in a straight line from Oxford [Street].[89]

Clearly, the sinuous path of Regent Street was not Hogarth's Line of Beauty but the developer's line of maximum profit.

While street and park were being built, accident had intervened once again. The death of George III in 1820 meant that at last the Prince Regent was king. Carlton House was no longer grander enough.[90] Nash had already produced alternative schemes for reconstruction: one a forest of columns facing a *grande place* in Lower Regent Street; the other a Tudor Gothic fantasy, with ogee-capped towers peeping out over St. James's Park.[91] Soane

88 Watkin 1974, pp.136-43. For later plans relating to this chapel, see LRRO 1/2305 and 2522.
89 *Parliamentary Papers* 1828, vol. 4, p.388 (1828 Report).
90 Farington 1978-84, vol. 16, p.5741: 27 October 1821.
91 Windsor Castle, n.d., but possibly 1814, when Philip Hardwick exhibited 'A royal palace designed for the South side of Pall Mall, of which Carlton House is proposed to form the right wing' (R.A. 1814, no. 746).

tried to tempt the king with neo-classical palaces in Hyde Park and Green Park, as well as a triumphal arch at Hyde Park Corner.[92] Nothing came of these: the new Gateway to London fell into the hands of young Decimus Burton, chosen personally by Charles Arbuthnot of the Woods and Forests.[93] Around 1825 Philip Wyatt floated an idea for a palace in Hyde Park.[94] Again, nothing came of it. The king said he was too old to build a palace, but he 'must have a *pied a terre*' – Buckingham House for preference.[95] From 1825, therefore, Nash proceeded to make Buckingham House into a palace. It proved to be his Waterloo.

First the design was unsatisfactory: the wings had to be pulled down and rebuilt. Then the cost turned out to be impossibly high. And then the structure itself – with elaborate use of cast iron girders – proved unsound. Nash's first estimate had been £250,000; by 1829 that had nearly doubled,[96] at a time when – as one critic put it – 'troops were collecting from every part of the kingdom to keep down a starving people'.[97] By 1830 expenditure was clearly out of control. Nash – the king's own architect – was dismissed from his post in the Office of Works,[98] and Buckingham Palace was completed by Edward Blore. But Nash still retained his position in the Office of Woods, Forests and Land Revenues. While parliamentary enquiries rumbled on, he continued to act as impresario to London's metropolitan improvements. His reputation was now under a cloud. In fact his standing as a public servant rose and fell with his royal patron: the Regency in 1811; the accession of George IV in 1820; the king's death in 1830 – these were the turning points in his career. Buckingham Palace pleased nobody but its royal resident. In 1832, the politicians tried again: Woods, Forests *and* Works now became a single, merged department. Nash's position disappeared in the process. His metropolitan career was over.

Meanwhile, what of the New Street to Westminster? By the mid-1820s, Regent Street was at last a splendid thoroughfare. But it had no terminal focus: it was a road with no beginning and no end. It was starting to make sense in terms of profit; it made very little sense in terms of urban grandeur. Lower Regent Street needed a feature, and so did Portland Place.

In 1812 Nash had certainly envisaged monuments at key points along his processional route. The first chance came in 1816. In 1799,[99] and again in 1807,[100] competition designs for military and naval monuments had been produced. In 1815 parliament had sanctioned a Grand National Monument in St James's Park, in commemoration of Waterloo. Nothing came of any of these. But the competition of 1816 did steer a little closer to success.

W. Wilkins and J. M. Gandy, *Commemorative Tower for the north end of Portland Place*, watercolour, Victoria and Albert Museum

92 Soane Museum, Inv. no. 93 (1821), exhibited 1827 as designs 'for a Royal Residence' (R.A. 1827, no. 911, 954). For other palace designs see Soane Museum, Inv. no. 123, 1817; exhib. R.A. 1821, no. 949 and R.A. 1828, nos. 1028, 1035. For entrance designs see R.A. 1796, no. 731 and R.A. 1826, nos. 870, 879, 889.
93 *Parliamentary Papers* 1828, vol. 4, pp.437, 444 *et seq*: 1828 Report; exhib. R.A. 1827, no. 917.
94 Trench 1827, pl. 16.
95 *Parliamentary Papers* 1831, vol. 4, p.271: 1831 Report.
96 *Parliamentary Debates* NS. 1829, vol. 21, col. 1578 *et seq.*: 25 May 1829.
97 John Wood: Ibid., col. 1583.
98 *Parliamentary Papers* 1831, vol. 4, pp.187-92: 1831 Report.
99 Soane exhibited a 'national mausoleum' (R.A. 1799, no. 942). Flaxman designed a giant Britannia for Greenwich (Barker and Hyde 1982, pl. 57; Farington 1978-84, vol. 4, p.1266: 12 August 1799; pp.1331-32: 25 December 1799); Smirke designed a commemorative column (Ibid., p.1326: 17 December 1799).
100 Westmacott designed a monument to Pitt; Flaxman and West designed memorials to Nelson (Ibid., vol. 8, pp.2989-91: 16 March 1807; Taylor ed., 1964-65, pp.68-69).

J. Flaxman, *Proposed Commemorative Arch*. Princeton Art Museum

There were the usual wild cards: J. B. Papworth designed a trophaeum;[101] Philip and Matthew Cotes Wyatt a million-pound pyramid.[102] But the two winners were certainly buildable. From Smirke came a design for a giant obelisk;[103] from Wilkins and Gandy a multicolumned tower.[104] Smirke's Trafalgar obelisk was to have been destined for Greenwich. But the Gandy-Wilkins tower was scheduled for the northern end of Portland Place. There – with its three orders of columns rising from a circular colonnade modelled on the Tivoli Temple of the Sybils – it would indeed have been a mighty focus for Nash's New Street. And, most intriguingly, among the defeated designs there seems to have been one by Nash himself: a Waterloo Column for Waterloo Place.[105] Alas, all these remained dreams, ruled out on grounds of cost.[106] 'The times', Wilkins remarked tartly, 'were considered to be only favourable for the construction of new and the *alteration* of old palaces ... The nation's gratitude [to her heroes] cooled.'[107]

Today Portland Place ends with an anti-climax: Gahhagen's diminutive statue of the Prince Regent's younger brother, the Duke of Kent. John Martin's fantasy – a triumphal overpass traversing the Marylebone Road – might at least have supplied a focus which was suitably vast.[108] On the other side of town events proved equally inconclusive. Hyde Park Corner never became an overture to Buckingham Palace, still less the ceremonial en-

101 Papworth 1879, p.116.
102 *Repository* 1816, pt. 2, p.8.
103 Sketches, R.I.B.A., J11/19-22, n.d. (watermark 1813-16).
104 Perspective, V and A Prints and Drawings, D 1075-1887. A.112. Farington 1978-84, vol. 14, p.5023: 23 May 1817. Payne Knight may have been instrumental in this award.
105 Variant perspectives, coll. J. Harris and Soane Museum, Drawer 17, set 8, item 3; Mansbridge 1991, no. 166.
106 *Gentleman's Magazine* 1817, pt. 1, p.501; 1818, pt. 1, p.624.
107 Wilkins 1831.
108 Barker and Hyde 1982, pl. 54.

trance to London. Flaxman's sculptural rainbow remained a *jeu d'esprit*.[109] Decimus Burton's triumphal arch had to be dismantled soon after its erection: it once led – urbanistically speaking – into a blind alley;[110] now – in the middle of a roundabout – it leads nowhere at all. Nash's Marble Arch had to be removed from the forecourt of Buckingham Palace in 1850:[111] Blore's new entrance made it superfluous; in any case it was too narrow for the outriders of the Coronation Coach. Today it graces a traffic island in Park Lane. London's monument to the heroes of Waterloo ended up as a bridge over the Thames. Today Waterloo Place has to rest content with Florence Nightingale. Most curious of all, the site of Carlton House is marked neither by the National Gallery, nor by the Royal Academy – both of which were possibilities in 1825[112] – but by a monument to the 'grand old Duke of York'.

The empty site of Carlton House had created an urban vacuum. Nash decided to turn it into an extension of Waterloo Place, with the Athenaeum on one side and the United Service Club on the other. The Prince Regent's garden, facing St. James's Park, was developed as Carlton Gardens and Carlton House Terrace. Carlton House Terrace, East and West (1827–33) consisted of a pair of terraces, each dramatically large, with spacious offices overlooking the Mall, all raised on ranks of cast-iron Doric columns. This was originally only part of a much larger scheme involving a third terrace on the site of the garden of Marlborough House, plus a crescent and still more terraces on the site of what is now Wellington Barracks.[113] Carlton House Gardens (1827–30) consisted of a group of smaller houses, again partly delegated by Nash, this time to Smirke and Decimus Burton.[114] The two major blocks – Carlton House Terrace, East and West – consciously echoed Gabriel's Place Louis XV in Paris (today the Place de la Concorde). In compositional terms, they were awkwardly related: as design theorists say, their duality was unresolved.[115] To deal with this, Nash hit upon the idea of linking them by a raised piazza. In the centre he envisaged a peristyle fountain composed of eight columns from Carlton House, with a dome on top and jets of water within rising 35 feet into the air.[116] 'I think', Nash explained, 'everybody coming down [Regent] Street must miss the old portico of Carlton House . . . the Fountain is a necessary substitute.' 'Speaking as a painter', he added – that is, speaking in accordance with Picturesque principles – 'it will improve the view . . . you will see [St. James's] Park between the columns in a most picturesque manner . . . I think it will glitter by the light that falls upon it . . . It was not my original suggestion, [but] I highly approve of it.'[117]

Nash's ministerial employers thought otherwise. Not until 1831–34 was the vacancy filled, and then by the Duke of York's monument. Its architect was not to be Nash but Benjamin Dean Wyatt.[118] Nash's contribution to the Picturesqueness of St. James's Park was confined to the serpentine lake itself (1827).

Meanwhile, the building of the Athenaeum and the United Service Club had also been dogged by vacillation. At first Nash insisted on uniformity. Then this was found to be ruled out by the two clubs' differing sites. The Athenaeum's architect, Decimus Burton, was in any case disinclined to replicate Nash's plan for the United Service. In the end, not only did Nash settle simply for uniformity of bulk, he was even 'persuaded of the bad effect of an attempt at perfect uniformity'.[119] In other words, by 1829 he had come to see the ultimate advantage of Picturesque design: it turned pragmatism into principle. And this glorification of opportunism served him equally well as architect-planner and garden-designer: whether adapting Capability Brown's plan for St. James's Park,[120] or devising a scheme to incorporate Henry Holland's Carlton House staircase within the fabric of the United Service Club.[121]

All this was Woods and Forests work, at the behest of George IV, and authorised by the Treasury. 'The Board of Works', as Nash put it, 'had nothing to do with it . . . I received [my] directions from . . . my patron and protector'.[122] To a certain extent that was also true of the final –

109 Flaxman drawing, Art Museum, Princeton University, 10, 1948-1681.
110 '. . .a beautiful gate. But to what did it lead? To nothing' (*Parliamentary Debates* NS. 1829, vol. 21, col. 1579: 25 May 1829). It had been intended as an entrance to Buckingham Palace; it eventually became a focus for Constitution Hill.
111 Crook and Port 1973, p.297.
112 *Parliamentary Debates* NS. 1825 vol. 13, cols. 1120-21: 9 June 1825.
113 *Parliamentary Papers* 1829, vol. 14, 6th Report, Appendix no. 16: plan, 5 June 1829.
114 PRO, LRRO 60, 118/533.
115 *Parliamentary Papers* 1828, vol. 4, p.381: 1828 Report. 'These two terraces', Nash concluded, 'on account of their uniformity, demand a centre'. (Ibid., p.384).
116 PRO, MPE 891, no. 16; Mansbridge 1991, no. 166.
117 *Parliamentary Papers* 1828, vol. 4, pp.380, 381, 385: 1828 Report. Estimated cost £8,000, including the columns from Carlton House.
118 In 1831 Soane vainly exhibited a design prepared in 1828 for 'a monopteral temple to enshrine a colossal statue of. . . the Duke of York' (R.A. 1831, no. 990).
119 *The Atlas* 18 October 1829, p.685: ill.; *Parliamentary Papers* 1828, vol. 4, pp.447-48: 1828 Report; *Survey of London* 1960, vol. 29, pp.386 *et seq.*
120 Stroud 1975, pl. 54A.
121 Hypothesis suggested in Summerson 1980, p.169.
122 *Parliamentary Papers* 1828, vol. 4, p.385: 1828 Report.

W. Railton, *Second Design for Nelson Monument*, watercolour and gouache, *c.*1838. The Museum of London

and in some ways culminating – phase of Nash's metropolitan improvements: the development of the area now known as Trafalgar Square.

Ever since Fordyce's proposals of 1793, the goal of the great north-south thoroughfare had been Whitehall and Westminster. By extending Pall Mall in the direction of St. Martin-in-the-Fields, and by linking the Strand to Charing Cross, and Charing Cross to Cockspur Street, Nash opened up the grandest urban space in London. But if ever a piece of townscape was created by accident, that townscape was surely Trafalgar Square. Even its name was imposed belatedly on a reluctant William IV by one of Nash's executant architects: George Ledwell Taylor.[123]

As conceived by Nash, this key public space was to have been the nodal point for a sequence of radiating avenues: south to Whitehall, north to the British Museum, west to Regent Street, east to the Strand and

Charing Cross.[124] At its centre was to have been not Nelson's Column but a Doric temple dedicated to the Royal Academy, with equestrian statues of George III and George IV on either side. One side of the square was scheduled for the Union Club and Royal College of Physicians; the opposite side for the Athenaeum; and the head of the square for the National Gallery. Little of this came to fruition. Smirke's Union Club and Physicians' College indeed appeared: their building is now Canada House. But the site destined for the Athenaeum became first Morley's Hotel and then South Africa House. The Royal Academy's Grecian headquarters never left the drawing board. And the diagonal avenue linking Trafalgar Square and Bloomsbury was abandoned even before the stage of preliminary planning. Smirke's British Museum was doomed to remain hidden in a backstreet.[125]

But plans for the periphery of the new square fared rather better. Nash did complete the long delayed re-fronting of the Royal Opera House on the corner of Haymarket and Pall Mall.[126] And he did engineer the parallel redevelopment from 1820 to 1824 of the Haymarket Theatre and Suffolk Street area.[127] But while clearing and developing 'the finest site in Europe', he was forced to wait upon events. In 1813 he was still thinking in terms of a symmetrical network of streets on the site of the crown's Lower Mews. By 1819 he had arrived at the idea of a space in front of the Upper Mews, that is William Kent's Great Stable. But it was the accession of George IV in 1820 which made the square as we know it possible. By moving the Royal Mews to Pimlico, next to a newly magnificent Buckingham Palace, Nash was able at last to achieve his *tabula rasa*.[128] By 1825 the site was empty and he began work on a plan which would extend the space eastwards towards the Strand. In 1826 the powers of the New Street Act were formally extended to 'Charing Cross, the Strand and places adjacent'.[129] By 1835 the new square actually had a name.

123 Taylor 1870-72, pp.177-78 (1830).
124 *Parliamentary Papers* 1826, vol. 14, p.12: 5th Report; PRO LRRO 1/216 (watermark 1825), n.d. but sent to the Office of Works, with Nash's report of 10 May 1830.
125 Nash's plan for a new road from Leicester Square through Holborn to the City was also abandoned. For the abortive attempt to open up the area round St. George's Bloomsbury as part of a new British Library piazza, see Crook 1972.
126 *Survey of London* 1960, vol. 29, pp.237, 241.
127 PRO, CRES 26/5, 222; Britton and Pugin 1828, vol. 1, pp.262-72; Mansbridge 1991, nos. 198-99.
128 Crook and Port 1973, vol. 6, p.303; PRO, MPE 1255-6.
129 *Gentleman's Magazine* 1831, pt. 1, p.201.

Even as late as 1831 the Crown's Commissioners were still toying with the idea of a terrace of houses on the north side of Trafalgar Square.[130] In the following year, however, the Treasury decided to dedicate that space to the National Gallery, and with it to the Royal Academy.[131] Nash's Parthenon was never needed. The central area was therefore set aside for 'some national monument which may reflect honour on the patriotism and taste of the country'.[132] While the government launched a competition, Nash turned to the layout of a series of triangular plots known as the West Strand Improvements.[133] These he delegated to two architect-builders: W. M. Nurse (Chandos Street and William Street)[134] and William Herbert (the 'pepperpot' triangle and Lowther Arcade);[135] and three executant architects: G. L. Taylor (Morley's Hotel), William Tite (Golden Cross Hotel) and Decimus Burton (Charing Cross Hospital) – all 1831–34. Smirke weighed in with the Exeter 'Change, or East Strand Improvements of 1832.[136] Nash himself designed a Vicarage for St. Martin-in-the-Fields (1828–30).[137] In this way, a network of clean-cut stucco replaced the labyrinth of alleys – with names like the Bermudas and Porridge Island – which, until 1829, had constituted the hinterland of St. Martin's Church.[138] Designs for all these new buildings followed the same process of authorisation. Each had first to be submitted to the New Street Commissioners – acting for the Commissioners of Woods and Forests – and thus to the Commissioners' architect, John Nash.

'England expects every architect to do his duty.' That was the motto under which the competition for a national Trafalgar Monument was launched in 1832.[139] The result was a battery of obelisks, urns, pyramids, columns, globes, arches and statues. William Railton's Nelson's Column won the prize. But some of the glory went to the defeated competitors.[140] John Goldicutt, for example, suggested a gargantuan globe poised precariously on sculptural supports; John Britton a Gothic Nelson Cenotaph modelled on the Chapter House of Westminster Abbey. One continental competitor, Alexis de Chateauneuf, would have turned Trafalgar Square into a commemorative grove, with fountains and statuary shaded by trees, a green oasis in a desert of stone. The problem was – and is – that the giant scale of the square makes any conventionally-sized monument look ridiculous; and any monument which is appropriately gigantic wreaks havoc with the view from Whitehall towards the National Gallery. In the end the judges plumped for a giant column, and were then faced with the problem of what to do with the rest of the square. In 1840 Sir Charles Barry was called to the rescue. He attempted to impose some sort of visual order within an architectural grid of balustrades, steps and fountains. In the event, Railton's column was indeed erected, but significantly reduced in height. Sir Robert Peel gravely explained to the House of Commons: 'it would be extremely inconvenient should the monument fall in that crowded part of the metropolis.'[141]

Not surprisingly, there was agitation for a different system of planning, for something less *ad hoc*, more *dirigiste*, more Parisian. In 1842, at the behest of the Metropolitan Improvement Society, Peel set up a metropolitan Improvement Commission.[142] 'Every session', he wrote to Sir Robert Smirke,

> brings forth a motion for a select committee of enquiry into some scheme or other of Metropolitan Improvement . . . without reference to general and comprehensive principles . . . and (what is worse) – is sometimes the offspring of self-interested speculations for the increase of the value of private property . . .[143]

Out of such early Victorian optimism was born, in 1856, the Metropolitan Board of Works.[144] But Peel's confidence was not shared by the architectural profession as a whole: 'jobbing and jobbery', prophesied one journal, 'will be the order of the day . . . We shall watch its proceedings with jealousy.'[145] No doubt John Nash could be

130 PRO, CRES 26/15, 438.
131 Crook and Port 1973, vol. 6, p.463.
132 *Gentleman's Magazine* 1831, pt. 1, p.201.
133 *Survey of London* 1940, vol. 20, pp.56-57, pls. 34-8; Mansbridge 1991, no. 245. It was authorised by the Treasury in 1825 (*Parliamentary Papers* 1828, vol. 4, p.428: 1828 Report).
134 PRO, MPE 786.
135 PRO, MPE 778: 1830; *Gentleman's Magazine* 1831, vol. 101, pp.204-06; Reilly 1922. Witherden Young may also have been involved in the design of the Lowther Arcade (Beresford Chancellor 1913, p.40).
136 PRO, WORK 5/178/1 and 5/179/1: 1831-2; PRO, MR 1046; *Parliamentary Papers* 1826, vol. 14, 5th Report. The builders were Samuel and George Baker.
137 PRO, WORK 1/16, 408-9: 11 July 1828; 1/17, 130: 1 June 1828 and 458: 25 August 1829; CRES 26/32, 59, 268.
138 *British Almanac and Companion* 1830, p.238.
139 *Civil Engineer and Architect's Journal* 1838, vol. 1, p.204. For details, see Mace 1976.
140 Madsen 1965; Barker and Hyde 1982, pls. 45 46-9.
141 *The Builder* 1844, vol. 2, p.369.
142 For details, see *Athenaeum* 1842, pp.114, 712, 790, 1042; *Civil Engineer and Architect's Journal* 1843, vol. 6, p.26. One of its first tasks concerned the new Thames Embankment (*Athenaeum* 1843, p.164). For its early work, see *Illustrated London News* 1843, vol. 2, p.420 and vol. 7 1845, pp.55, 150.
143 BL, Add.MS. 40518, f.258: 10 November 1842.
144 Owen 1982.
145 *Architect, Engineer and Surveyor* 1843. p.23.
144 Owen 1982.
145 *Architect, Engineer and Surveyor* 1843. p.23.

heard murmuring from his grave: *'plus ça change . . .'*

So where does Nash's reputation stand today? He died in public disgrace, pilloried for 'inexcusable irregularity' and 'great negligence';[146] 'a jobber';[147] or at the very least 'a great speculator . . . a most suspicious character'.[148] To his accusers Nash had a simple, and lordly, reply: 'I am not a public accountant'.[149] His trump card was a brand of pragmatic vision which triumphed over the trivialities of finance. As one contemporary M.P. put it: 'if Mr. Nash had not been speculator as well as surveyor, Regent Street would never have been finished . . . .'[150] In 1835 T.L. Donaldson, 'Father of the Architectural Profession', paid his predecessor a handsome tribute:

Mr. Nash has done much . . . for Metropolitan Architecture . . . [he has] rescued it from the dark, heavy cumbrous shapeless brick boxes . . . [And though] the eye . . . must be offended here and there with details that sin against the purer examples of Greek and Roman art . . . for general arrangement, enlarged conception of masses in plan, and the distribution of ornamental grounds, he was unrivalled.[151]

As a neo-classical architect, Nash was neither an archaeologist nor a rationalist. In fact he was a self-confessed eclectic. One critic in 1820 called him 'not so much a designer as a collector of designs . . . he has taken them from all schools, more for their variety than for their beauty'.[152] 'An Ionic is an Ionic', he once told James Elmes, and he 'did not care which one his draughtsmen used'. When an assistant queried the accuracy of drawings for some of the Regent's Park detailing, he replied: 'Never mind, it won't be observed in the execution.'[153] Such a cavalier approach to matters of detail was all part of the Picturesque mentality. And it was this subordination of neo-classicism to the Picturesque which particularly provoked a thoroughbred classicist like C.R. Cockerell. Regent Street he condemned for its superficiality: 'all . . . done hastily . . . hastily thought, hastily executed'. As for All Souls, Langham Place, he thought it only 'very good for those who know nothing about it'.[154]

Nash's Regent's Park terraces certainly epitomise the precarious balance between neo-classical archaeology and Picturesque theory.[155] Their details are vestiginally Grecian; their composition is posthumously Palladian; and their dramatic impact is largely dependent on scenic conjuring tricks. Cockerell saw through the illusion: 'The architecture of Regent's Park', he noted in 1825, 'may be compared to the poetry of an *improvisatore* . . . But if as many were versed in the Grecian rules of this science as there are in those of Homer and Vergil this trumpery would be less popular.' Even so, Cockerell in old age lived happily enough in Chester Terrace. 'Nash', he grudgingly admitted, 'always has original ideas.'[156]

Unfinished, decayed, rebuilt; vandalised, bombed, redeveloped – what survives of Nash's London is but a fragment of what was constructed, and a shadow of what might have been. Even so, there is no mistaking the imprint of his vision. The broad space of Trafalgar Square; the sweeping curve of Regent Street; the central focus of Oxford Circus; the glorious panorama of Regent's Park: all testimony to a master pragmatist, a virtuoso of scenographic art. Defying the swings and roundabouts of taste, Nash continues to rank with Wren as a maker of modern London. But his genius was essentially opportunism writ large.

146 *Parliamentary Papers* 1831, vol. 4, p.10: 1831 Report.
147 Alexander Baring: *Parliamentary Debates* NS. 1829, vol. 21, col. 1585: 25 May 1829.
148 Sir Joseph Yorke: Ibid., cols. 1582, 1825, 1826.
149 *Parliamentary Papers* 1828, vol. 4, p.386: 1828 Report. When it came to royal command, he admitted no choice but 'implicit obedience'; at Buckingham Palace he was 'totally independent of the Office of Works', except for 'measuring, moneying, and making out of the accounts' (*Parliamentary Papers* 1831, vol. 4, pp.194, 204: 1831 Report).
150 John Calcraft: *Parliamentary Debates* NS. 1830, vol. 22, col. 1164: 2 March 1830.
151 R.I.B.A. MS. SP.4/1.
152 *Gentleman's Magazine* 1820, pt.1, p.34. Nash admitted that his Marble Arch was 'a plagiarism of the Arch of Constantine' (Crook and Port 1973, p.294 note 7).
153 Crook 1972, p.121.
154 Cockerell Diaries, quoted in Watkin 1974, p.68.
155 Crook 1972 *passim*.
156 Cockerell Diaries, quoted in Watkin 1974, p.69.

RUDOLPH ACKERMANN

Simon Jervis

'A perpetual exhibition of whatever is curious in nature or art, exquisite in workmanship, or singular in costume; and the display is perpetually varying as the ingenuity of trade, and the absurdity of Fashion are ever producing something new.' Thus Robert Southey, adopting the guise of a Spanish traveller, characterised the shops of London in his *Letters from England* of 1807.[1] He could equally have been describing *The Repository of Arts, Literature, Commerce, Manufactures, Fashions and Politics*, a new magazine of which the first issue appeared in January 1809, bearing a dedication, by permission, to the Prince of Wales from its proprietor, Rudolph Ackermann, who was born in Saxony in 1764.[2]

It is sometimes easy to overlook the extent to which English culture was already in the eighteenth century part of a European continuum and that this continuum extended to Germany. The inscription which Frederick the Great dedicated to his friend, the Venetian scientific and artistic pundit Count Francesco Algarotti, an admirer of Lord Burlington as the restorer of true architecture, 'ALGAROTTI OVIDII AEMULO. NEWTONIS DISCIPULO. FRIDERICUS MAGNUS', reflects the conspicuous position of Newton and by extension England in international enlightenment hagiography.[3] But the English presence is also felt in small things: in 1760 Johann Wilhelm Meil, who illustrated the Berlin editions of Algarotti's works, designed a title page of Pope's early poems,[4] and about the same date illustrations to the 1750 French translation of Fielding's *Tom Jones*, published in London, entered the collection of prints assembled as models by the Berlin porcelain factory.[5] These illustrations were designed by Gravelot, a Frenchman settled in London. Chodowiecki, the great Berlin *Kleinmeister* of the late eighteenth century, illustrated not only Shakespeare but also Goldsmith, Lady Mary Wortley Montague, Sterne, Richardson and Smollett, as well as less celebrated English writers.[6] Many of Chodowiecki's illustrations were from 1777 destined for the 'Königl. Grossbrit. Churf. Braunschw. Genealogischen KALENDER',[7] a reminder of the dynastic position of the electors of Hanover as, since 1714, kings of England. In the same year, 1777, Chodowiecki engraved twelve plates on the progress of vice and virtue for the 'Goettinger Taschen CALENDER',[8] which were accompanied by texts written by the great Hogarth interpreter, Lichtenberg, who was the publisher of the CALENDER, and who offered Chodowiecki the loan of Hogarth prints to serve as models. Later instances of the pervasive presence of English prints include the decision taken in 1797 by Albert von Sachsen-Techsen to purchase a complete set of the works of Bartolozzi, a Florentine settled in London,[9] and Philipp Otto Runge's excited response to his father in 1800 on receiving Flaxman's outlines to the *Iliad* and Aeschylus: 'The Flaxman outlines . . . My God, I have never in my life seen anything like them; the outlines after the Etruscan vases [i.e. d'Hancarville's catalogue of the Hamilton collection] are nothing in comparison.'[10]

In the late 1730s Abraham Roentgen worked for the London cabinet maker, William Gomm. He could thus call himself an 'englische Kabinettmacher,' a title claimed by his son David Roentgen, the greatest cabinet maker of the epoch. Both Abraham and David imitated English models,[11] the latter several times working directly after designs in Chippendale's *Director*.[12] Chippendale's influence is also visible on chairs produced from about 1770 in Altona.[13] Later Altona chairs are influenced by Hepplewhite,[14] and in 1794 an edition of Sheraton's *Modell- unde Zeichnungsbuch für Ebenisten, Tishler, Tapezierer und Stuhlmacher* was published in Leipzig.[15] In the following year the Leipzig cabinet maker Friedrich Gottlob Hoffmann published a catalogue of his wares entitled *Neues Verzeichnis und Muster-Charte des Meubles-Magazin*, which includes many direct borrowings from Hepplewhite.[16] Among such German instances of London influence it is worth interpolating the example of the Marquis de Marigny who acquired mahogany furniture from London in substantial quantities from the late 1760s until 1780.[17]

On the tomb in Dessau of Friedrich Wilhelm von Erdmannsdorff, it is recorded that he travelled to Britain

---

1 Southey 1951, p.78.
2 *Repository* 1809, title; Tedder 1885, p.58.
3 Miracco 1978, fig. p.22.
4 Wirth 1970, p.11; p.18.
5 Baer 1986, p.308.
6 Wormsbächer 1988, pp.45-31; p.82; p.99; p.114; p.116.
7 Ibid., p.38.
8 Ibid., p.39; Märker 1978, p.106.
9 Sandner 1968, p.41.
10 Betthausen 1983, p.46.
11 Austen 1986, p.349; Thornton 1966, pp.137-47.
12 Gilbert 1978, p.65.
13 Kratz 1988, p.274; p.275.
14 Ibid., p.276; p.277.
15 Himmelheber 1974, p.51; fig. 3.
16 Hoffmann 1981, pls. 2, 3; White 1990, pp.86, 87, 105.
17 Gordon 1989, pp.86-108.

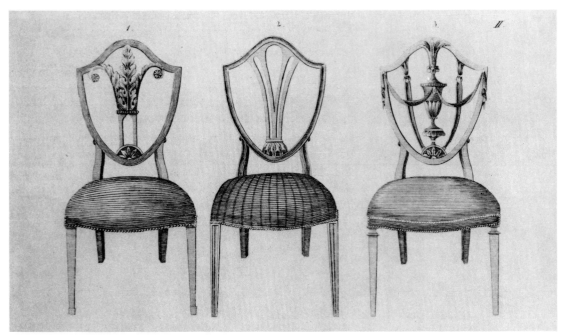

Design for chairs after Hepplewhite, engraving from F. G. Hoffmann, *Neues Verzeichnis und Muster-Charte des Meubles-Magazin*, 1795

three times, to Italy four.[18] In Erdmannsdorff's varied works for his great patron and friend, Fürst Franz von Anhalt-Dessau, English influence and connections are ubiquitous. The most piquant example, perhaps, is the miniature copy of the iron bridge of 1778 at Coalbrookdale, built in 1791 in the garden of Schloss Wörlitz.[19] The Schloss itself is furnished with chairs in the Chippendale style designed by Erdmannsdorff and made by Johann Andreas Wimmer, and decorated with Wedgwood vases and reliefs; upstairs the prince's dressing room has wall paintings depicting West Wycombe and Windsor.[20] In 1775, during a visit to London, the Fürst and his party met Reinold and Georg Forster, naturalists on Captain Cook's second voyage; the Forsters presented the Fürst with a collection of artefacts from Tahiti and the South Seas, and Georg Forster subsequently wrote a catalogue on a visit to Wörlitz in 1779.[21] The Tahitian taste, which crops up in the lantern room of Schloss Wörlitz, and in a cabinet in the 1790s Gothic folly on the Pfaueninsel in Berlin, was thus channelled through London.[22]

Fürst Franz and Erdmannsdorff had many schemes for the advancement of education and art in Dessau. These included from 1796 to 1803 the Chalcographische Gesellschaft zu Dessau, an institute for the encouragement of engraving, designed to overcome the English monopoly in prints and to raise the level of German taste.[23] Its business manager was Friedrich Justin Bertuch. Translator, journalist, businessman, private secretary to Herzog Carl August in Weimar, Bertuch had a finger in numerous pies.[24] His first independent journalistic venture, the *Allgemeiner Literatur-Zeitung*, a literary daily, first

appeared in 1785.[25] It was followed in 1786 by the *Journal des Luxus und der Moden*, of which he was co-editor with his friend George Melchior Kraus, who had been Goethe's drawing master in Frankfurt.[26] In 1791 the *Journal* was taken over by Bertuch's newly founded Landes Industrie Comptoir, 'a charitable public or private institution whose aim it is to seek out the natural wealth of their province and to promote their culture as well as to guide and improve upon the artistic skills of their inhabitants.'[27] The Comptoir produced artificial flowers and fruit (a collection of Bertuch's wax fruit survives at Wörlitz), games and educational material, prints and playing cards, tiles, stoves and art pottery, and optical and physical instruments.[28] The publishing activities came to dominate and in 1825 Bertuch was employing about 280 workers, and had 6 printing presses, as well as his own copperplate and lithographic workshops.[29]

Among the other periodicals published by Bertuch was, from 1798, *London und Paris*. Political realities and

18 Speler 1986, p.27.
19 Boettiger 1982, p.87.
20 Alex 1986, p.90; pp.79-81; Speler 1986, p.36.
21 Alex 1988, p.119.
22 Börsch-Supan 1977, fig. 10.
23 Hirsch 1986, p.22-24.
24 Kaiser 1980, p.10.
25 Ibid., p.21.
26 Ibid., pp.21-24, p.51.
27 Ibid., p.23, pp.34-35.
28 Ibid., p.35, 38; Alex 1988, p.135.
29 Kaiser 1980, p.460.

the increasing prominence of Vienna are reflected in successive changes of title to *Paris, Wien und London* (1811), *Paris und Wien* (1812), and, finally, *London, Paris und Wien* (1815). The apposition of London and Paris is clearly set out in the first volume of the *Journal der Moden* (*Luxus* added to the title in 1787), published in 1786: France owed its commercial superiority to the encouragement of luxury trades, but England has become a dangerous competitor; furnishings are a test case of modern progress in industry:

> English furniture almost always has this character: it is solid and practical. French furniture is lighter in proportion, more composed and seductive to the eye. The English by thoroughly studying the works of art of their old craftsmen and by incorporating their tasteful application in all branches of technology actually have improved the furnishings, enhancing their beauty as well as their suitability. Everyone knows how important and profitable this was, and still is, to their factories and artists. However, France and Germany, Holland, Sweden and Denmark have learned from England to train skilled craftsmen and thereby noticeably improve their own furnishings. But there is no doubt that England will remain the leader in this field throughout Europe for some time to come because of the coordination amongst their factories and the necessary support they give to each other. Furthermore, their equipment being of the highest standard, they already are in full swing, their materials are of the best quality and, last but not least, they pay their workmen far better than anyone else, by any criterion.[30]

This comparison between London and Paris, or England and France, was a constant theme at this date. It is interesting to compare Thomas Hope's remarks in the preface to his *Household Furniture* (1807) on the superiority of foreign taste, and in particular that of his friend Percier, with the tribute paid by Charles Moreau in the preface to his *Fragments et Ornements d'Architecture* (1800) to Hamilton's *Vases*, which he saw as an encouragement to English industry to the detriment of France.[31] The *Journal des Luxus und der Moden* described the difference in more concrete terms in 1787: England had 'carpets in rooms and on the stairs, dainty objects of various sorts carved in mahogany, superb works in steel, objects from East India, precious fire places, vases, busts and medallions'; and France, 'parquet floors, magnificent panelling, lacquerwork, gilding, etc.'[32] The mention of vases and medallions as typical English products may be a reflection of the appearance in the 1787 and 1788 *Journal* of an article on Coade stone, as well as the firm's complete price list.[33] Other English products mentioned by

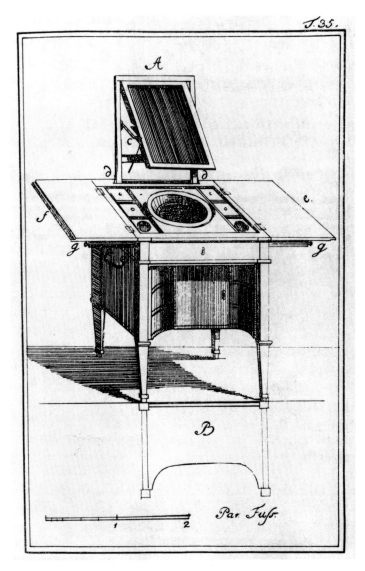

Design for an English shaving table after Chippendale, engraving from F.J. Bertuch, *Journal des Luxus und der Moden*, 1788

the *Journal* are various indeed: pianos and fire-irons (1786), a washing machine (1791) and a cucumber cutter (1800), a shaving table (1788) directly borrowed from Chippendale's *Director*,[34] and one of Flaxman's *Iliad* outlines (1802). The unifying themes would appear to be practicality and what was called in 1789 'schönen Englischen Simplicität.'[35]

The *Journal des Luxus und der Moden*, which survived until 1827, was concerned with fashion, with design and

30 *Journal der Moden* 1786, pp.28-9.
31 Jervis 1987, p.6.
32 *Journal des Luxus und der Moden* 1787, p.135.
33 *Journal des Luxus und der Moden* 1787, pp.171-73, Intelligenz-Blatt 1788, pp.lxix, lxxxvi, xcvii, cxiii, and cxxviii.
34 Kaiser 1980, p.25; White 1990, p.256.
35 *Journal des Luxus und der Moden* 1789, p.361.

manufacturers, with trade and literature, with art and manners, with gardening and music. It was not without competitors: for example a *Journal für Fabrik, Manufaktur und Handlung*, which later added *Kunst und Mode* to its title, was published in Leipzig from 1792 to 1810, and it was followed by further Leipzig titles: *Magazin der neuesten Englischen und deutschen Moden* (1793), *Magazin für Freunde des Guten Geschmacks* (1794), *Taschenbuch für Garten Freunde* (1795), *Ideenmagazin für Leibhaber von Gärten, englischen Anlagen und für Besitzer von Landgütern* (1796), *Allgemeines Journal für Handlung, Schiffahrt, Manufaktur* (1800), *Zeitung für die elegante Welt* (1801), *Miscellen für Gartenfreunde, Botaniker und Gartner* (1802), *Magazin aller neuen Erfindungen, Entdeckungen und Verbesserungen* (1802). Such magazines were part of an unparalleled explosion of periodical publishing which took place in Leipzig and other German cities such as Dresden and Weimar from the late eighteenth century onwards, one of whose central purposes was to encourage German emulation of the example set by England in trade, manufacturing and taste, and particularly gardening.

Rudolph Ackermann, as was noted earlier, was born in 1764 at Stolberg in the Harz mountains, roughly at the centre of a triangle comprised by Hanover, Leipzig and Weimar.[36] In 1775 his father, a successful saddler, moved to Schneeberg, south of Leipzig and equidistant between Weimar to the west and Dresden to the east.[37] Ackermann was destined to follow his father's trade, but, having

shown talent for drawing, trained as a designer of coaches. Spells in Dresden and Leipzig were followed by a three-year apprenticeship near Basel, whence Ackermann moved to Paris, where he worked for Antoine Cavassi, a leading coach-maker.[38] At some point in the mid to late 1780s, Ackermann moved from Paris to London, where his talents were soon recognised; in 1790 he designed a coach for the Lord Lieutenant of Ireland and in 1791 another for the Lord Mayor of Dublin. In the latter year J. C. Stadler published *Imitations of Drawings of Fashionable Carriages* by Ackermann, the first of a long series of which the *Thirteenth Book*, the last, was published on 1 August 1819.[39] From the *Third* of 1794 onwards they were published by Ackermann himself.[40] His continued interest in coach design is reflected in his responsibility for Nelson's funeral car (and coffin), and in his patenting a moveable axle invented by Max Lankensperger, coach builder to Ludwig I of Bavaria.[41] In order to publicise this invention Ackermann published *Observations on Ackermann's Patent Moveable Axles* (1819) and his Munich connection is further evidenced by his retailing the first volume, published in 1818, of the great

36 Tedder 1885, p.58.
37 Ibid., p.58.
38 Ford 1983, p.15.
39 Ibid., pp.15, 16; Berlin 1986, No. 1437.
40 Ford 1983, p.16.
41 Ibid., pp.23, 30-31, 65-66.

RUDOLPH ACKERMANN

Ackermann's Repository of Arts, aquatint from Ackermann's *Repository of Arts*, 1809. The Museum of London

history of coach building by Johann Christian Ginzrot, the royal coach designer, who had been summoned from Strasbourg by Maximilian I.[42] An interest in coaches had its specialised technical aspects, but coach design was not a world apart: the Crace dynasty of interior decorators started as coach designers and painters,[43] while in 1760 John Linnell, the most accomplished and versatile English designer to work in the rococo style, submitted a design for the Royal State Coach in collaboration with his uncle, the coach builder Samuel Butler, who later built the successful design by Sir William Chambers.[44]

In 1794 Ackermann married Martha Massey, from Cambridge, and in the following year he purchased premises at 96 Strand, whence he conducted a business as 'Printseller & Draftsman', and set up a drawing school, an enterprise reflected in his *Lessons for Beginners in the Fine Arts* (1796).[45] Expansion led to a move in 1797 to 101 Strand. The school, having expanded to eighty pupils, was closed in 1806, because the space was needed for the expanding retail business, which Ackermann had in 1798 christened 'The Repository of Arts'.[46] This incorporated a 'Gallery of Ancient and Modern Paintings and Drawings'.[47] Although Ackermann gave up his school in 1806, he continued to be a prolific publisher of drawing manuals. Landscape manuals included *Ackermann's New Drawing Book of Light and Shadow, in Imitation of Indian Ink* (1809–12), with plates by David Cox, numerous works by Samuel Prout, commencing with his *Rudiments of Landscape: In Progressive Studies* (1813),

George Harley's *The First Principles of Landscape Drawings* (1829) and several works by George Pyne, including *Groups of Figures for Decorating Landscapes* (1798). But Ackermann also published manuals on flower painting such as J. Sillett's undated *Grammar of Flower Painting*, or B. Hunter's *Six Progressive Lessons for Flower Painting* (1810), on miniatures – Leon Mansiori's *Letters upon the Art of Miniature Painting* (1822), on anatomy – Minasi's undated *Fifteen Academical Studies in Chalk*, and, with Le Brun's evergreen *A Series of Studies of the Passions*, on the representation of the emotions. Richard Brown's *Principles of Practical Perspective* (1815) was aimed at the architect and dedicated to Sir John Soane, while *An Essay on Mechanical Drawing* by Charles Blunt, who seems to have been responsible for some of Ackermann's later carriage designs, was for the mechanic.[48]

Ackermann not only published and retailed drawing manuals, he also published *A Treatise on Ackermann's Superfine Watercolours* (1801), and the title of Harley's *First Principles* (1829) noted that it incorporated 'coloured specimens of R. Ackermann's colours'.[49] In 1810 Acker-

42 Ackermann, 1818, p.242; Petzet, Wackernagel 1967, p.10.
43 Snodin 1990, pp.33 ff.
44 Hayward, Kirkham 1980, pp.58-59.
45 Ford 1983, pp.11, 16, 21.
46 Ibid., pp.17, 31, 18.
47 Ibid., p.17.
48 Ibid., pp.220-30; Bicknell, Munro, 1987; Berlin 1986, No. 1437; Jervis 1984, p.86.
49 Bicknell, Munro, p.48.

mann stated that his paints were on sale 'at all Book-sellers, Printsellers and Stationers in Great Britain'.[50] Other aids to the artist included special papers and, for use in connection with Pyne's *On Rustic Figures* (1813), models of the figures 'as a further aid to drawing'; furthermore Ackermann assembled a circulating library of prints and drawings to serve as models for imitation, and in 1815 he was offering for sale watercolours by the most distinguished painters of the day, including Turner, Girtin, De Wint, Cox, Cristall and the Varleys.[51]

Among the remaining stock-in-trade of the Repository of the Arts were prints, transparencies, medallions, borders, Tunbridge ware, plaster-casts, needlework patterns, games, writing instruments and a whole variety of knick-knackery.[52] Its character may be illustrated by verses advertising a rival establishment, S. and J. Fullers' The Temple of Fancy, in Rathbone Place:

There the Ladies will beautiful *Work Tables* find,
Bedeck'd with Medallions, or finish'd with *Borders*
And varnish'd and polish'd according to orders;
Writing Desks, Netting Boxes, Tunbridge Tea Caddies,
For the Beaux pretty *Housewives*, and *Screens* for the
   Ladies.[53]

Ackermann's account of the production of these articles is worth citing:

During the period when the French emigrants were so numerous in this country, Mr. A. was among the first to strike out a liberal and easy mode of employing them, and he had seldom less than fifty nobles, priests and ladies of distinction, at work upon screens, card-racks, flower-stands and other ornamental fancy-works of a similar nature. Since the decree permitting the return of the emigrants to France, this manufacture has been continued by native artists, who execute the work in a very superior style.[54]

Ackermann's publishing activities were extremely various, ranging from lithographs after Dürer, Géricault and James Ward, to Accum's works on *Gaslight* (1815) and *Cookery* (1821). There was frequently an accent on the foreign or exotic, as in *Views of Switzerland* (1822),

50 Ford 1983, p.25.
51 Ibid., pp.25-26, 28; Bicknell, Munro, p.102.
52 Ford 1983, pp.45-46.
53 Bicknell, Munro, p.101.
54 *Repository* 1809, p.54.

T. Rowlandson, *Death and Bonaparte*, aquatint from Ackermann's *Repository of Arts*, 1813. The Museum of London

DEATH and BONAPARTE.

the undated *Five Views of the Great Falls of Niagara*, M. Titsingh's *Illustrations of Japan* (1822), Captain Smith's *Asiatic Costumes* (1828), Emeric Essex Vidal's *Picturesque Illustrations of Buenos Ayres and Monte Video* (1820), and George Ramus Forrest's *A Picturesque Tour along the River Ganges and Jumna in India* (1824). Sport and natural history crop up, as in Peter Henderson's *Pomona* (1808–09), Sarah Bowdich's *The Fresh-Water Fishes of Great Britain* (1828), William Somerville's *The Rural Sports* (1813) or T. Hughes's *The Sportsman's Companion*. Ackermann's most popular books were the three *Tours of Dr Syntax* in which comic drawings by Rowlandson were accompanied by verses by William Combe. The first tour *. . . in search of the Picturesque* (1812) was based on Rowlandson drawings originally published in *The Poetical Magazine* (1809–10), one of Ackermann's less successful ventures. The second *. . . in Search of a Wife* (1820–21) was produced to exploit the popularity of the first. Rowlandson and Combe also collaborated on *The English Dance of Death* (1816). A more serious note is struck by Rowlandson's brilliantly mordant transparency celebrating Napoleon's defeat at Leipzig, exhibited at the Repository of Arts in 1813 and recorded in an aquatint of 1814.[55]

However, Ackermann's greatest fame as a publisher is due to an outstanding series of topographical books, illustrated with aquatints. The first, *The Microcosm of London* (1808–10), contained 104 plates with architecture drawn by Augustus Charles Pugin, who had arrived in London as a young emigré in about 1792, and lively figures by Rowlandson. It was followed by *The History of the Abbey Church of St. Peter's Westminster* (1811–12), *A History of the University of Oxford* (1813–14), *A History of the University of Cambridge* (1814–15), and *The History of the Colleges of Winchester, Eton and Westminster* (1816). The series involved the printing of no less than 372,000 aquatints.[56]

It was while this prodigious venture was in progress that Ackermann launched a new magazine, entitled *The Repository of Arts, Literature, Commerce, Manufactures, Fashions and Politics*, to which allusion has already been made at the beginning of this essay. The *Repository*, a monthly, survived until December 1828, by which date

55   Ford 1983, pp.220-30, 52-60.
56   Ibid., p.36.

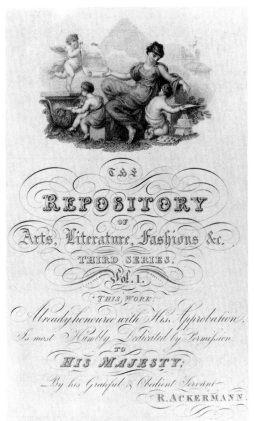

Ackermann's *Repository of Arts*, engraved frontispiece, 1823. The Museum of London

Allegorical Woodcut, with Patterns of British Manufacture: (1) fret-work striped muslin (2) Arabian jubilee silk (3) imperial green shawl print (4) chintz kerseymere for gentlemen's waistcoats, Ackermann's *Repository of Arts*, 1809. The Museum of London

Ball Dress and Promenade Dresses, engravings from Ackermann's *Repository of Arts*, 1810. The Museum of London

RUDOLPH ACKERMANN

some 1,400 plates, the majority in colour, had been published. There were usually six plates to an issue, two of fashion, one miscellaneous, one of manufactures, one a view, and the last an 'Allegorical Woodcut' with three or four cloth patterns affixed, although the latter were replaced by black-and-white ornaments or muslin patterns in later issues. The text always included commentaries on the plates, but there was at first much else besides – politics, agriculture, medicine, inventions, anecdotes, sport, poetry, music, exhibitions, the theatre, books, natural history and the weather. From around 1816, however, the magazine was directed with ever increasing exclusivity at the female reader, and light fiction and the arts took over from heavier matter. In 1815 arrangements were in place for the export of the *Repository* to New York, Halifax, Quebec, the West Indies, Hamburg, Lisbon, Cadiz, Gibraltar, Malta, or any part of the Mediterranean, the Cape of Good Hope and the East Indies.[57]

Many but by no means all of the plates from the *Repository* were gathered together and republished as a series of books. They included *Select Views of London* (1816), seventy-six plates all but one published in the *Repository* from 1809 to 1816, and *Rural Residences consisting of a series of designs for cottages, decorated cottages, small villas, and other ornamental buildings*, [18] twenty-seven plates published in 1816 and 1817, both of which were credited to J.B. Papworth, the *Upholsterer's and Cabinet Maker's Repository* (1816), seventy-six plates published from 1809 to 1815, *Engravings of Fashionable Furniture* (1823) forty-four plates from 1816 to 1822, *Gothic Furniture* (1829) twenty-seven plates of 1825 to 1827 designed by A. C. Pugin, and *Views of Country Seats* (1830), 146 plates from 1823 to 1828.

The first volume of the *Repository* included five plates, which were not reprinted, of prominent retailing showrooms in London.[58] The first, inevitably, was Ackermann's own shop at 101 Strand; next came the Wedgwood & Byerley showroom in York Street, St. James's Square; then Harding, Howell and Company's 'Grand Fashionable Magazine' at 89 Pall Mall, selling furs, fans, haberdashery, jewellery, ormolu, French clocks, perfumery, millinery and dress; then Messrs. Lackington Allen and Company's 'Temple of the Muses' in Finsbury Square, a bookshop on the grand scale built by James Lackington in 1794, which may have helped to inspire Ackermann's own Repository; and finally the show room of Messrs. Pellatt and Green, glass makers to the king, in St. Paul's Churchyard. Another plate, published in late 1809, depicted the upstairs ware-room of Morgan & Sanders,[59] whose furniture formed the subject of no less than nineteen plates in the *Repository*, from 1809 to 1815, often catering for a

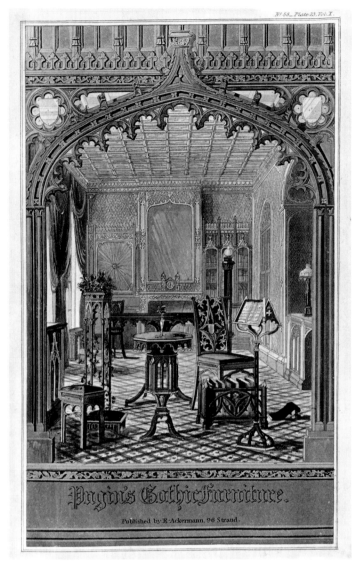

Gothic Furniture designed by A. C. Pugin, aquatint from Ackermann's *Repository of Arts*, 1827. The Museum of London

taste for novelty and invention with such innovations as Pitt's Cabinet Globe Writing Table (1810), the Metamorphic Library Chair (1811) and Merlin's Mechanical Chair (1811).[60] Ackermann also published two plates (1810 and 1815) of the museum or Egyptian Hall in Piccadilly created by William Bullock, and from 1816, when a chimneypiece of 'Mona' marble was illustrated, numerous plates of furniture and furnishings by his equally entre-

57 *Repository* 1815, title-page.
58 Ibid., 1809, pls. 3, 8, 16, 22, 28 (plate numbers from Abbey 1953, pp.155-86).
59 Ibid., pl. 53.
60 Ibid., 1810, pl. 90; 1811, pls 206, 223.

Messrs. Morgan and Sanders's Ware-Room, Catherine Street, Strand, engraving from Ackermann's *Repository of Arts*, 1809. The Museum of London

Drawing room Window-Curtain and Cabinet designed by G. Bullock, aquatint from Ackermann's *Repository of Arts*, 1816. The Museum of London

Merlin's Mechanical Chair, engraving from Ackermann's *Repository of Arts*, 1811. The Museum of London

'Gothic', Tedeschi or old German Furniture, engraving from Ackermann's *Repository of Arts*, 1819. The Museum of London

preneurial brother, George Bullock.[61] Ackermann also had provincial contacts: in 1819 and 1820 he published twelve plates of window draperies taken from an unknown pattern-book of about 1815 entitled *Interior Decorations* by John Stafford, a Bath upholsterer.[62]

The *Repository* was by no means the exclusive focus of Ackermann's activities. Much earlier, in 1801, he had shared in a patent for waterproofing cloth and paper; a factory was set up in Chelsea, but the venture seems to have fizzled out. In 1807 he successfully tested a scheme to scatter anti-Napoleonic propaganda from balloons. And from about 1823 to 1828 Ackermann was heavily involved in publishing for, and investing in the market opened up by the liberation of South America; this venture proved disastrous and caused heavy losses. More successful was the introduction in 1822 of an illustrated annual, the *Forget-Me-Not*, based on German models; it survived until 1857 and sometimes sold 20,000 copies a year. The *Forget-Me-Not* used steel plates from 1825. Ackermann had shown an early interest in Alois Sene-

felder's process and in 1816 he set up his own lithographic press; in 1819 he published Senefelder's *A Complete Course of Lithography* and in 1824 *The Art of Drawing on Stone* by Charles Hullmandel, whose press Ackermann was using by late 1823. It is tantalising that a relationship with Nicéphore Niépce, the pioneer of photography, initiated in 1828, did not bear fruit.[63]

Although Ackermann was naturalised as a citizen of the United Kingdom in 1809 he seems never to have ceased regarding himself as a Saxon. He chose as editor for the *Repository* and, later, the *Forget-Me-Not*, Frederick Schoberl, a Moravian, like Abraham and David Roentgen, of German ancestry.[64] And the *Repository* included in

61 Ibid., pl. 118; 1815, pl. 522; 1816, pl. 551.
62 Ibid., 1819, pls. 782, 795, 812, 819, 825, 838; 1820, pls, 848, 856, 868, 874, 880, 892; Jervis 1984, p.459.
63 Ford 1983, p.20, 31-32, 84-88, 64-65, 92.
64 Boase 1897, p.147.

1819 a plate, misleadingly entitled 'Gothic Furniture', directly borrowed from Joseph Friedrich von Racknitz's extraordinary *Geschichte und Darstelling des Geschmacks*, published in Leipzig in 1796 to 1799, a book which can hardly have been common in England, although, remarkably, Sir John Soane possessed two copies.[65] There are many other references to German matters in the *Repository*, but Ackermann's most active and positive contributions to his native country lay in his secret work to relieve the sufferings which resulted from Napoleon's victories at Jena and Auerstadt in 1806, and in his very public contribution, as joint secretary of the Westminster Association, in raising £100,000, which the government matched, for those who had suffered after the battle of Leipzig in 1814.[66] As a reward for his prodigious exertions Ackermann was awarded the Order of Civil Merit by the King of Saxony, and received a present of Meissen porcelain. It is interesting to find that the small committee formed to distribute money from London in Weimar included Friedrich Justin Bertuch, the founder of the *Journal des Luxus und der Moden*.[67]

There seems little reason to doubt that the *Journal des Luxus und der Moden*, which incidentally mentioned the *Repository* in 1816, was its direct prototype. There were a few London fashion magazines before the *Repository* appeared in 1809, themselves influenced by continental models, such as *Le Beau Monde, or Literary and Fashionable Magazine, Heideloff's Gallery of Fashion*, and *La Belle Assemblée*, and some of them included a variety of incidental information in their texts: *Records of Fashion* (1808) even had a colour plate of a Gothic piano made for the Prince of Wales by Mr Jones of Golden Square.[68] But none approaches the *Repository*'s formula as closely as the *Journal des Luxus und der Moden*. Ackermann must have been well aware of its existence. He was an exhibitor at the Leipzig book fair, and maintained an extensive correspondence with Karl August Böttiger who served as editor of the *Journal* from 1795 to 1803.[69] Böttiger, whom Goethe dubbed 'Magister Ubique', was then director of the Gymnasium in Weimar.[70] He later, in 1814, became director of the Dresden collection of antiquities and was a prodigiously fertile writer and publisher. In the *Artistisches Notizenblatt*, a supplement to the *Dresden Abend-Zeitung* which he edited from 1822 to 1835, Böttiger recommended Ackermann's wares.[71] Reciprocating, the *Repository* (1828) puffed Retzch, a protegé of Böttiger, and Ackermann published editions of Retzch's outlines to Shakespeare and Faust.[72] The evidence is circumstantial but convincing. It also seems plausible to suggest that Bertuch's Landes Industrie Comptoir, founded in 1791, was the prototype for Ackermann's *Repository of Arts*, so

titled in 1798. Of course, London offered vastly greater and more extensive commercial opportunities than Weimar, but the idea of an enterprise with an educational bias, based on painting and fancy wares, is remarkably similar. It may even be that the foundation of the Chalcographische Gesellschaft zu Dessau in 1796 filtered through to Ackermann and contributed to the evolution of his ideas: Böttiger visited Wörlitz in 1797 and was well aware of developments there.[73]

From 1825 to 1830 the covers of Ackermann's *Forget-Me-Not* annual were designed by John Buonarotti Papworth. In 1812 Papworth designed a new library for the Repository of Arts at 101 Strand, and at about the same date he planned a picture gallery as an addition to Ackermann's house in Camberwell. And in 1827, when Ackermann finally moved back to rebuilt premises at 96 Strand, Papworth was his architect.[74] Papworth's very extensive contributions to the *Repository of Arts*, and the books which resulted, have already been noted. The *Repository* in 1823 published a view of the showroom designed by Papworth for the glass manufacturer, James Blades, who made a glass throne for the Shah of Persia also designed by Papworth, whose versatility extended to furniture, silver, stained glass, lighting, textiles, and, for Ackermann again, a transparency commemorating the peace in 1814.[75] Between 1817 and 1820 Papworth prepared designs for a palace for Wilhelm I, King of Württenberg. Only some garden designs were executed, but nonetheless he was given the title of Architect to the King.[76] Perhaps this was a connection which owed something to Ackermann. Papworth and he must have had much in common, and it seems plausible to suggest that Papworth's illustrations to *The Social Day*, a poem by Peter Coxe published by Ackermann in 1823, may have expressed their mutual taste as regards both design and domesticity. Comfort, informality, solidity and a mild classicism seem to constitute an English equivalent of Biedermeier, and to echo that 'schönen Englischen simplicität' praised by the *Journal des Luxus und der Moden* in 1789.

65 *Repository* 1819, pl. 789; Jervis 1984, p.401-02.
66 Ford 1983, pp.48-50; Webster 1954, p.49-57.
67 Kaiser 1980, p.70.
68 *Records of Fashion* 1808, p.103.
69 Vaughan 1979, pp.24-25.
70 Boettiger 1982, pp.3, 72.
71 Vaughan 1979, p.24.
72 Ibid., pp.24-25; Ford 1983, p.228.
73 Boettiger 1982, p.71.
74 Colvin 1978, pp.616, 619; Ford 1983, p.61.
75 *Repository* 1823, pl. 1082; Jervis 1984, pp.369-70; Ford 1983, p.50.
76 Colvin 1978, p.616.

Pl. 21. Vol. I.

J. Gendall del.ᵗ

Mr BLADES' UPPER SHOW ROOM.

J. Gendall, *Mr. Blades' Upper Show Room of Ornamental Glass, Ludgate-Hill*, aquatint from Ackermann's *Repository of Arts*, 1823. The Museum of London

The images of early nineteenth-century London, and indeed England, created under Ackermann's aegis have indelibly coloured the perceptions of posterity. As a product of the German enlightenment and an heir to its published traditions, including in particular didactic illustrated periodicals, which promulgated the achievements of England, Ackermann was no neutral mirror. His *Repository* was not replaced after ceasing publication in 1828. The *Journal of Design and Manufactures*, which expressed the reforming views of Henry Cole and his circle in 1849 to 1852, was a more earnest version of those segments of the *Repository* concerned with design: it also incorporated fabric samples, and also reflected strong German influence. The 1830s interim was filled, to an extent, by the manifold and very worthy publications of John Claudius Loudon, a Scotsman settled in London. But, whereas the keepsake industry which he had founded with the *Forget-Me-Not* prospered, the aims expressed in Ackermann's prospectus for the *Repository* 'to convey useful information in a pleasing and popular form – to

beguile the unlearned into an acquaintance with the arts and sciences – and occasionally to assist even the man of letters in cultivating a taste for both' were after 1828 too catholic for any one magazine.[77]

Ackermann's brief will lists various presents from the Kings of Saxony and Prussia, and a parrot painted in enamel by Joseph Nigg in Vienna, from 'his Imperial Highness John Arch Duke of Austria'.[78] Although an exile by choice and a naturalised citizen of Britain, these marks of esteem from his native Saxony and from Prussia and Austria, must have been particularly precious. However, Ackermann's public memorial consists in the great series of aquatints published under his aegis which provide such a permanently fixed image of the London and England of his age. It is an achievement of entrepreneurial patronage without parallel.

77 Ford 1983, p.79.
78 Ibid., p.97.

Interior of the Sir John Soane's Museum from Sir John Soane *Description of the House & Museum*, 1835

PATRONAGE AND THE APPLIED ARTS

PATRONAGE AND THE APPLIED ARTS IN EARLY NINETEENTH-CENTURY LONDON

Clive Wainwright

The first decades of the nineteenth century saw that unprecedented growth of London so graphically described in Chapters 2 and 4. Whilst many of the buildings newly built or adapted to modern use were banks, shops, warehouses, factories and churches there were also of course many domestic houses. This essay is concerned only with houses and most particularly with their interiors: how they were furnished and decorated, as well as the market for both the new and the old objects which their creators and owners purchased to furnish them. Inevitably the discussion will not be confined to houses built in the period covered by this exhibition for it is in the nature of London houses and indeed, those in continental cities also that whilst the exterior could remain unchanged the interiors were constantly being refurbished and rearranged.

Two problems immediately arise for so many and various were the interiors created at this time and so patchy the documentation that only a representative few can be considered here. Some of these are well known, but this is often only because full documentation in the form of illustrations, bills, inventories and perhaps actual furnishings happen to survive. Others, however, though celebrated in their day remain difficult to study because such documentation simply does not exist. It is thus impossible to arrive at an objective assessment of the whole range of types and styles of interior from the simplest to the richest and most elaborate. As might be expected the survival of documentation – though to some extent dictated by historical accident compounded by ignorance, fire and flood – has tended to favour the grander examples. Adequate descriptions or illustrations of middle-class interiors are rare and as we move down the social scale these cease all together. Sadly in England that vigorous continental tradition of paintings and watercolours depicting domestic life so widespread particularly in Biedermeier Germany and Austria, had no parallel. A glance at any well-illustrated work on the subject of historic interiors will confirm this, but Peter Thornton's seminal work on the subject with its wide international coverage demonstrates very clearly the sparseness of the English urban material.[1]

The case with the manufacturers and suppliers is far worse, for even the records of the largest firms of cabinet makers, carpet or wallpaper makers or the shops selling silver or ceramics very rarely survive. With those vital individuals the brokers in ancient furniture, armour, ceramics or old master paintings, the archival material is even rarer. These at best were just as secretive as our modern antique dealers and at worst seem to have kept no records of their operations at all. In some cases bills and correspondence concerning the furnishing and decoration of London houses still survive with the family papers in the muniment rooms of country houses and once one has the name of a stained-glass broker or a silversmith in one's mind, whenever documentation appears this can be pieced together to create a composite biography of such a person.

'Country house' archives introduce a further problem. Most aristocratic, and a considerable number of other families who had a country seat, also had a London house in the eighteenth and nineteenth centuries. Such houses – especially the aristocratic ones – were a more important feature of London social and cultural life by the early nineteenth century than ever before. But since the 1920s virtually all of these London houses, large and small, have been given up or demolished. This was beginning to happen even in the later nineteenth century when the Duke of Northumberland sold Northumberland House in Trafalgar Square for demolition to create Northumberland Avenue. He retreated to his great Adam house of Syon to the west of London and at much the same time the Duke of Devonshire gave up Burlington House in Piccadilly to the Royal Academy and moved to Chiswick House near Syon. By the 1930s, when the Duke of Norfolk sold to the demolishers Norfolk House in St. James's Square, which had been the focus for Roman Catholic society in the 1820s and 1830s, and moved to Arundel Castle in Sussex, all the great London houses were going. Some were demolished like the Duke of Westminster's Grosvenor House to make way for a hotel of the same name, others like Bridgewater House and Lancaster House were sold and some like Spencer House were let to business tenants.

This move by the rich and powerful families led to the preservation of the country houses which are still such a feature of our national life. Indeed, many were enhanced by the arrival of the furnishings and works of art which had been created or collected specifically for the London houses. Families had naturally often kept their best old master paintings in their London houses for the delight of

1   Thornton 1984.

The Monk's Parlour of Sir John Soane's Museum from *Sir John Soane Description of the House & Museum*, 1835

their guests: it was always the tradition to entertain more grandly and lavishly in London than in the depths of the country. Thus, it is in the muniment rooms of country houses that the documentary evidence for their appearance and the processes gone through in building and furnishing them often survives. Similarly, when the family gave up the London house the silver, furniture, sculpture and paintings were integrated into the collection already existing in their country houses. Were I writing about country house interiors rather than those in London, I could illustrate and discuss many surviving examples of every stylistic type of early nineteenth-century interior, whereas only the Soane Museum and Apsley House survive intact in London to represent metropolitan town houses of the period.

To give some idea of the splendour of the major houses it is perhaps appropriate to describe a number of them. The grandest of all was Carlton House transformed be-

tween 1783 and 1820 by the Prince of Wales into what was in all but name a royal palace. The whole story of this fascinating building and the splendid collection which it contained is currently being told in an exhibition at the Queen's Gallery at Buckingham Palace. The scholarly catalogue which accompanies the exhibition contains more information than has ever before been gathered together.[2] A number of the objects which furnished it are also on display here and demonstrate to a small degree how splendid the interiors must have been. The house stood between Pall Mall and the Mall overlooking St. James's Park. The entrance front faced north and was in Pall Mall, divided from it by a stone screen, while the view from the principal rooms was south over the gardens and the park. The names which appear in the building and furnishing accounts read like a roll-call of the most celebrated names in their fields in both Britain and France. The architects were Sir William Chambers, James Wyatt, Henry Holland, Thomas Hopper and John Nash. The London cabinet makers included Morel and Hughes, Marsh and Tatham, Thomas Parker, Edward Bailey and François Hervé. The suppliers of silver, jewellery and metalwork, Rundell, Bridge and Rundell and the Vulliamys. But these were in almost every field outclassed by their Parisian counterparts: the *marchand merciers* Dominique Daguerre and Martin Lignereux, the *ébénistes* Etienne Levasseur and Adam Weisweiler, the *ciseleur doreurs* Pierre Gouthière and Pierre Delafontaine and the *fondeur ciseleur* P-P. Thomire.

These modern products – though the best that almost unlimited money could buy - were supplemented and frequently overshadowed by vast royal purchases of antique French eighteenth-century furniture, bronzes and Sèvres porcelain. The discerning visitor to Carlton House would have had his eye drawn away from the modern objects to the pre-revolutionary furniture by A-C. Boulle, J-P. Latz and Bernard van Risemburgh or the superb bronze of *Prometheus Chained* by F. Dumont and that of *Louis XV* by Lemoyne. The vast collection of Sèvres displayed throughout the rooms would have been one of the most notable features. It was, however, the old master paintings that would have demanded the most attention; some of these like the Rubens self-portrait from the collection of Charles I had been inherited whilst others like the celebrated Rembrandt *The Shipbuilder and his Wife* had been recently acquired.

As is clear from the watercolours of the interiors

2 *Carlton House* 1991.

The exterior of Apsley
House today

painted just before 1820, Carlton House followed that Regency innovation in furnishing which considerably changed the appearance of interiors; this consisted in clothing the walls with dwarf cabinets rather than the tall cabinet pieces fashionable in the eighteenth century. The tops were often marble and they provided an ideal surface for the display of small bronzes, marble busts, porcelain or other small *objets d'art*. Then the upper part of each wall was available for the display of paintings so that at Carlton House there was no need for a room to be set aside as a formal paintings gallery.

At Carlton House we see all the stylistic trends of the period at their grandest and most sophisticated. The exterior was severely neo-classical and closely modelled upon late eighteenth-century French prototypes and this style was widely used inside as well. There were far more exotic interiors: as early as 1790 a Chinese Room was created when an elaborate pier table in this style by Weisweiler was imported and further furniture made in Britain to go with it. The oriental character of some of the interiors was captured by Lady Elizabeth Fielding in 1813 'I am afraid that all my powers of description would fail to give you an idea of the oriental glitter of spangles and finery, of dress and furniture ... '[3] George, of course, used his experience with this style when he created his seaside oriental extravaganza at Brighton.

Far more significant were the several Gothic Revival interiors, for by 1800 this was quickly becoming the highly fashionable style which was to be so important by the

1840s. In 1807–09 the spectacular conservatory designed by Thomas Hopper was finished. The fan vaulting inspired by Edward VII's chapel at Westminster Abbey was of iron but with a wonderfully theatrical touch Hopper filled the spaces between the ribs with coloured glass. This glass, the stained-glass windows in the walls and the lanterns of stained glass hanging from the vaulting ensured that the interior was bathed in coloured light both night and day. More conventional lighting was provided at night by oil lamps standing upon Coade stone candelabra decorated with suitably Gothic bats and dragons. In 1814 the Gothic dining room was completed to Nash's designs for the vast sum of £8,866 4s.9d. There were other Gothic interiors including a library and possibly a bedroom, but quite where the amazing Gothic piano stood is not known. The armchair, also in the exhibition, may well have been designed for one of these rooms.

As soon as George became king in 1820 he began to lose interest in Carlton House; in 1826 it was abandoned and in 1827 demolished. It had been one of the wonders of London and had influenced lesser buildings and their interiors throughout Britain. It had also been the venue for spectacular banquets, celebrations and firework displays, notably in December 1813 for the allied victory at Leipzig,

3   Ibid., p.40.

J. Nash, *The Waterloo Gallery at Apsley House set for a Banquet*, watercolour, 1852

and in June 1814 for the visit of the Emperor of Russia and the King of Prussia.

On his accession George inherited all the royal residences including Buckingham Palace and Windsor Castle and immediately set about refurbishing them. George III had already initiated the creation of a series of Gothic Revival interiors at Windsor under the control of James Wyatt, the most important architect working in this style at the time. Wyatt, however, was killed in an accident in 1813 and the work at Windsor was taken on by his nephew, Jeffry Wyatville.

In 1827 the king employed the fifteen-year-old A.W.N. Pugin to design a whole range of Gothic Revival furniture for the Wyatville interiors.[4] Whilst most pieces are in the flashy, polished, parcel gilt wood so typical of the un-archaeological approach of many designers at this time, some, however, have a more truly medieval appearance. All this furniture was made by the famous London firm of Morel and Seddon who had worked at Carlton House. In 1829 just before the king died, Pugin set up in a loft in Covent Garden his own firm producing more archaeologically correct Gothic furniture and wood- and stone-carved details.[5] From this time on Pugin was to become

increasingly established until by the 1840s he was the most celebrated Gothic Revival architect and designer in Britain – indeed he also had considerable influence in Germany. His scholarly approach combined with his brilliance as a designer led not only to the creation of remarkable applied arts and buildings but to the writing and publishing of polemical works on the nature of architecture and design.

Virtually all of the highest quality objects were *designed* in London, many manufactured and nearly all retailed in the capital. They were then sent all over the country or to the empire, as well as being exported to Europe and America. Many of these objects were designed in the London offices of the architects building the house as a natural part of the design process. London and its environs were a major manufacturing centre, so most of the plant needed to make any object was close at hand. Also, if the design process is to work efficiently the de-

4 De Bellaigue and Kirkham 1972, pp.1-34.
5 Wainwright 1976, pp.3-11.

signer needs to be in constant touch with the person actually making the object so that necessary small changes can be made. However, most of the crafts which concern us here do not require vast industrial resources: a silversmith could operate as well in Dean Street, Soho as anywhere. In some specialised cases, as with Wedgwood's pottery in Staffordshire, manufacture went on outside London though many of the new designs originated in London and some historicist ones were taken straight from Greek vases in the British Museum. With textiles as with pottery, the Midlands were an important manufacturing centre but a considerable number of textiles were being woven in London, notably Spitalfields silks.

The way in which large industrial enterprises could and did operate for many years in the midst of London is nowhere better illustrated than by the example of the firm of Seddon, the celebrated cabinet makers. They operated from premises in Aldersgate Street close to the northern boundary of the City of London from 1753 to 1830, when they moved to a larger site outside the City near King's Cross. As early as 1783 they were employing three hundred men and in 1827 they went into temporary partnership with Nicholas Morel to make the furniture for Windsor Castle. The scale of this commission, which was carried on alongside other work, can be judged by the debt to them of £200,000 when George IV died in 1830. Two years later they were eventually paid £179,300 18s.6d. by the Treasury, thus making a considerable loss on the venture.

Another important workshop, but this time in the West End of London, was set up in 1814 by the sculptor turned cabinet maker George Bullock (1782–1818). He was relatively unknown but the information concerning his career, which has only recently been pieced together, has established him as one of the most important and innovatory figures amongst the designers and craftsmen of his age.[6] Fortunately, we now know more about his operations and the character of his workshop and its practice than for any of his contemporaries. This is thanks largely to the discovery by Martin Levy of the sale catalogue of the contents of his workship after his premature death in 1818.[7] His career throws a great deal of light upon the whole world of Regency interior design.

He started as a sculptor before setting up as a cabinet maker in Liverpool where his brother William had established a museum. William was to move to London first in 1809 and there he established his celebrated Egyptian Hall. George was unusual in that not only did his workshops produce the furniture, but he himself also designed much of it, though he did employ other designers like the talented Richard Bridgens. Most cabinet makers, in this

The Waterloo Gallery at Apsley House today

period – as had always been the case – merely executed the designs of architects. Bullock's firm also acted – like many cabinet makers – as complete house furnishers supplying carpets, light fittings, wallpapers and ceramics besides the furniture. Bullock designed in all these media and probably designed silver as well.

There was another side to his business, for when he set up in London he described himself as 'Sculptor, 4, Tenterden Street, Hanover Square, Mona Marble & Furniture Works, Oxford Street'. He established himself in a grand neo-classical house in a street off the fashionable Hanover Square between Regent Street and Oxford Street. He furnished the house with the most elaborate pieces of furni-

6 *Bullock* 1988.
7 Ibid., Levy, pp.84-50. Levy 1989, pp.145-213.

ture and other products from his own workshops. Sadly we only have one illustration of the interior[8] which shows a grand staircase hung in a very baronial manner with arms and armour and Bullock himself leaning languidly on the bannister. Higher up the staircase were hung modern paintings and in 1817 these were by Benjamin Robert Haydon: 'The Macbeth, Judgement of Solomon, and the Death of Denatus by the same historical painter, are again assembled in London, being hung on the magnificent staircase of Mr. G. Bullock, in Tenterden Street, who with great liberality, permits amateurs and others to view them'.[9]

Bullock certainly entertained both friends and potential clients at his house. Other cabinet makers did not have sufficient social standing or self-confidence to behave in this way, but Bullock seems to have charmed everyone he met. There was also a shrewd commercial mind at work, for at the bottom of his garden fronting on to Oxford Street were his workshops. Any potential clients being entertained in his house could easily be taken to the workshops to see actual pieces under construction. Just as important as the cabinet making side were the marble

workshops which manufactured tops for cabinets and tables and also produced whole chimneypieces. Here again we see Bullock the entrepreneur, for even before he came to London he had leased a marble quarry on the Isle of Anglesea in North Wales. It was impossible during the Napoleonic Wars to import marble from Italy so Bullock promoted his 'British' marble on patriotic grounds calling it 'Mona' marble after the ancient British name from Anglesea.

Indeed, he took this patriotic theme further by advocating the use of British woods for furniture rather than exotic foreign ones like the universally fashionable mahogany. He then exploited the fashion which had spread from France for the revival of metal inlay inspired by the newly emergent taste of collectors for the early eighteenth-century furniture by A. C. Boulle. He designed and manufactured elaborate marquetry pieces

8   Ibid., p.25.
9   *Annals of the Fine Arts* 1819, pp.106-07.

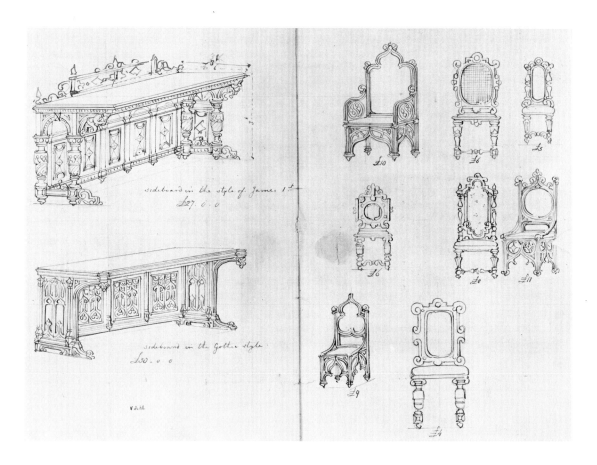

using combinations of metal or wood. But he suggested the replacement of foreign plant ornament with wholly British plants. On the neo-classical table he designed, in the exhibition, the brass Roman *Thyrsus* on the pedestal, instead of being encircled with the usual grapes, has a hop plant instead. Many of these pieces also had British Mona marble tops like that on his table for Sir Walter Scott.

In 1816, he received the commission to furnish New Longwood the pre-fabricated house which the British government shipped to St. Helena to house the exiled Napoleon. Bullock supplied all the furniture and furnishings and far from giving Napoleon furniture made from his favourite mahogany, only the very best British oak was used and other pieces had Mona tops. He even designed neo-classical ceramics for Napoleon's use, but sadly these were never sent because the Minister of War objected. He believed that the 'laurels of victory' were portrayed too prominently on these objects to be used every day by someone Britain had vanquished. The St. Helena commission was perhaps an atypical example of London as the source of supply for the far reaches of the British empire.

Bullock also worked in the Gothic and Elizabethan style and designed and supplied an elaborate, gilded brass,

Gothic lantern for Napoleon. With the neo-classical style British designers followed behind the Continent, but with the Gothic Revival many French and German designers sought inspiration here. A fascinating example of this influence is the lantern very similar to that supplied for Napoleon, imported to Germany from England presumably in the 1820s. It formed part of the furnishings of the medieval castle of Rheinstein restored by Schinkel. Though Bullock was dead when Schinkel visited England in 1826, many of his designs were still in production – did he buy the lantern in London? Schinkel was certainly looking carefully at the British contemporary Gothic Revival buildings. The fact that Bullock had supplied so many of the furnishings for Sir Walter Scott's Abbotsford, the model for many continental Gothic Revival buildings, would have appealed not only to Schinkel but to his literate patron. I have dwelt upon Bullock at some length for, quite apart from the fact that he is important as a designer and entrepreneur, by studying him one gains a clearer idea of how the luxury trades functioned in the capital.

Let us now consider the most radical suite of Greek Revival interiors in London not this time in a royal or even aristocratic house but in that of the banker, Thomas Hope

A dwarf cabinet with marquetry of various woods designed and made by George Bullock in about 1817

Ceramics designed by George Bullock in 1816 for Napoleon's use at New Longwood House on St. Helena

PATRONAGE AND THE APPLIED ARTS

(1769–1831). The Hope family came originally from Scotland but during the eighteenth century built up a highly successful bank in Amsterdam; in 1794, due to the Revolutionary Wars they moved to London. After an abnormally long Grand Tour, which as well as the usual countries included Egypt, Turkey, Syria, Greece, Prussia and Spain, Hope in 1799 bought a house in Duchess Street near Oxford Circus. He soon set about transforming it internally to his own remarkable designs. It was a large but dull house designed by Robert Adam in the early 1770s and was unchanged externally as noted by the German artist J.D. Passavant when he visited in 1833 soon after Hope's death:

> Being furnished with the necessary card of admission, we turned our steps towards the mansion of the late Thos. Hope, Esq., for the purpose of inspecting his celebrated gallery. What to our astonishment on finding ourselves before a heavy gloomy building, almost devoid of windows, blackened with accumulations of soot, and to all outward appearance conveying rather the idea of a large brewery, than an opulent banker's town house. The threshold, however, once passed the interior proved worthy of its possessor; the numerous small apartments being luxuriantly adorned in the usual style of the present century, when a taste for the antique, however imperfectly understood prevailed. One of the most attractive features on first entering the rooms, is the collection of ancient etruscan vases . . . [10]

How Passavant obtained a ticket he does not say, but the tradition started by Thomas Hope still continued and tickets were issued after 'An application signed by some persons of known character and taste'.[11]

Two years later that acute German observer of British artistic life Gustav Waagen visited the collection:

> I find ever fresh causes for astonishment at the abundance of works of art in this country; thus I have lately become acquainted with a real museum in the house of Henry Thomas Hope, Esq. Here you are alternately surrounded by ancient and modern marble statues, Greek vases, Italian and Dutch pictures . . . The pictures of the Italian school, which with some historical paintings of the Flemish school, are hung in a spacious gallery lighted from above . . . [12]

Both give a long description of the paintings and classical antiquities but do not mention the remarkable modern furniture and the elaborate and highly wrought interiors which it furnished.

In 1826 another German visitor, Prince Pückler Muskau, though impressed by the man whom he rightly

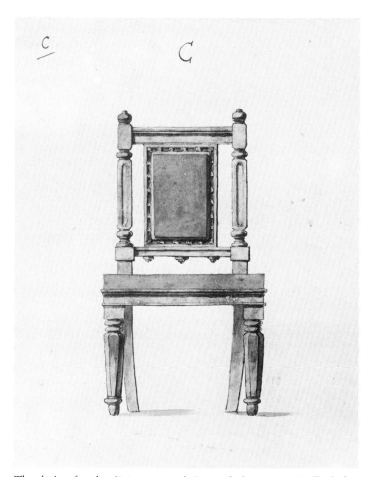

The design for the dining room chairs made by George Bullock for Abbotsford

divined as the author of the exotic oriental novel *Anastasius*, was scathing about his furniture:

> I made acquaintance with Mr. Morier the clever and very agreeable author of Hadji baba, and of Mr Hope, the imputed author of Anastasius, a work of far higher genius. This book is worthy of Byron; many maintain that Mr. Hope, who is rather remarkable for his reserve than for anything poetical in his appearance, cannot possibly have written it. This doubt derives a considerable force from a work which Mr. Hope published on furniture, the style and contents of which certainly contrast strangely with the glowing impassioned Anastasius, overflowing with thought and feeling. An acquaintance of mine said to me: 'One thing or the

10   Passavant 1836, vol. 1, pp.223-24.
11   Watkin 1968, p.100.
12   Waagen 1838, vol. 2, pp.324-25.

other: either Anastasius is not by him or the work on furniture'. But matter so different brings with it as different a style; and as I observed, Mr. Hope, perhaps with involuntary prepossession, appeared to me no ordinary man. He is very rich and his house full of treasures of art and luxuries which I shall describe hereafter. His furniture theory, which is fashioned on the antique, I cannot praise in practice:-the chairs are ungovernable, other trophy-like structures look ridiculous and the sophas have such sharp salient points in all directions that an incautious sitter might hurt himself seriously.[13]

It would seem likely that Pückler Muskau's own taste inclined more towards the Renaissance Revival than to the Grecian. In 1822 he commissioned from the English architect, John Adey Repton, a scheme rather in the Jacobean manner to remodel his family castle at Muskau in Silesia.[14] After starting work Repton was ousted by Schinkel whose scheme was also never executed.

It must be admitted that whilst some of Hope's furniture is of the utmost elegance and refinement, other pieces are singular to say the least. His book *Household Furniture and Interior Decoration* of 1807, seminal though it was for the Greek Revival in the applied arts, must to many like Pückler Muskau have looked rather dull. This was because rather than rendering the pieces illustrated in perspective or even in colour as with many contemporary pattern books, he chose to emulate the dry linear style advocated by Flaxman and used in Percier & Fontaine's *Recueil des Décorations Intérieures* published in Paris in 1801. The designs would have been remarkable even had Hope been an architect, but without formal training he was able to combine the best forms of French neo-classicism with his observations of classical antiquities from his grand tour. He changed the whole direction of British furniture and interior design so that a purely commercial pattern book like George Smith's *A Collection of Designs for Household Furniture and Interior Decoration*, published in 1808, was even down to the title largely plagiarised from Hope.

Hope had returned from the Continent with a taste for the highly sophisticated continental version of neo-classicism and indeed some of the furniture at Duchess Street was purchased in Paris.[15] After trying to obtain suitable objects in London, he was driven to design and commission them himself as he described:

Under the general denomination of Household furniture are comprised an infinite variety of different productions of human industry, wrought in wood, in stone, in metal, in composition of various descriptions, in silk, in wool, in cotton . . . Almost every one of these various articles however, abandoned, till very lately, in this country, to the taste of the sole upholder, entirely ignorant of the most familiar principles of visible beauty, wholly uninstructed in the simplest rudiments of drawing . . . [16]

The upholder was the upholsterer or cabinet maker; indeed George Smith on the title page of his book describes himself as 'Upholder extraordinary to his Royal Highness the Prince of Wales'.

Hope genuinely wished others to continue the revolution that he had started rather than merely copy his designs and urged 'the young artist' particularly to

consider it as published rather with a view to give a vague idea of what has, hitherto, with imperfect means, been restrictedly and hastily effected, in a new line of industry and taste, than with the intention of offering specific models of what should in the future, by greater study and application, be in this new line, more extensively and more permanently executed; still should I have warned him most earnestly against confining his exertions to a mere servile copying of the contents of this volume.[17]

It is worth noting that all the objects illustrated had actually been made to Hope's designs and existed at Duchess Street for all the visitors to see. This very much added to the impact of the book on other designers for by contrast many of the objects illustrated in applied art pattern books like Smith's had never actually been made.

The major rooms at Duchess Street were also illustrated and described in detail. The Egyptian antiquities had a room to themselves furnished with the two dramatic Egyptian sofas with sphinxes as arms and four armchairs in the same style. This room was painted pale yellow, bluish green, gold and black. The linear engravings give no clue to the brilliantly polychromatic character of the interiors. The Aurora Room was devoted to the marble by Flaxman of *Aurora visiting Cephalus on Mount Ida*. The curtains around most of the room were yellowish orange satin – an appropriate colour for Aurora – drawn back in places to reveal mirrors and edged in black velvet

---

13 Pückler Muskau 1940, p.60.
14 Maddison 1991, p.110, fig. 39.
15 Thornton and Watkin 1987, p.168.
16 Hope 1807, p.1.
17 Ibid., p.17.

which matched the black marble chimneypiece. The ceiling was sky-blue, the frieze was polychromatic and most of the furniture gilded. There is no doubt that though not as large as some of the aristocratic London houses, Duchess Street set standards of quality and sophistication in the application of Grecian and Egyptian forms to interior design in England that had lasting influence.

The best known aristocratic house of the 1830s and one around which much social life revolved was York House, later called Stafford House and today known as Lancaster House. It was designed by Benjamin Dean Wyatt who also enlarged Apsley House. In 1833, Passavant naturally visited it to see the remarkable collection of old master paintings but as well as devoting a number of pages to these he makes some interesting observations about the character of the interiors:

> This most splendid of all modern mansions is situated near the venerable palace of St. James . . . It was destined for the residence of the Duke of York, and consequently bears his name; but the death of the Duke intervening, it was purchased, and the building carried on by the Duke of Sutherland . . . the hall and the staircase present a coup d'oeil of which nothing can exceed the magnificence; they occupy a square of fifty by seventy . . . The walls of this magnificent hall, are entirely lined with the finest sorts of marble, and a gallery leading to the principal apartments . . . the rooms are appropriately filled with every variety of chair, settee and table, with which it is so much the fashion to crowd the floors: these being loaded in their turn with the costliest specimens of art and literature and with those thousand other fragile and nameless ornaments which render the navigation of an English drawing room a task of danger . . . we find the English in their gilt balustrades, chandeliers, brackets, &c. so closely imitating the taste of Louis XIV in whose reign these mannered style of ornaments was most in vogue.[18]

Wyatt was in the 1820s one of the pioneers of what was rather inaccurately known as the Louis XIV style for it actually included forms from the reigns of Louis XIV, XV and XVI. York House was an early example of this style, which, when applied to the furniture and all the other furnishings gave rise, as Passavant describes it, to that over-elaboration which is more usually associated with the mid-Victorian interior. It was a great contrast to the chaste Grecian character of Duchess Street; indeed Hope himself attacked the style in his last book published posthumously in 1835:

> Finally as if in utter despair, some have relapsed into an

The Aurora Room at Duchess Street as illustrated in Hope's *Household Furniture and Interior Decoration*, 1807

admiration of the old scroll-work – the old French style – of which the French had become ashamed, and which they had rejected, and greedily bought it up. Not content with ransacking every pawnbroker's shop in London and in Paris, for old buhl, old porcelain, old plate, old tapestry, and old frames, they even set every manufacturer at work, and corrupted the taste of every modern artist by the renovation of this wretched style.[19]

Despite these attacks this style became widely fashionable during the later 1820s and 1830s. In the hands of a talented designer like Wyatt it could be elegant and sophisticated. This was especially the case when, as Hope describes mixed in with the modern work were genuine eighteenth-century objects like Sèvres porcelain, Gobelins tapestries, Boulle furniture or old master paintings of high quality. The Waterloo Gallery at Apsley House designed by

18   Passavant 1836, vol. 1 pp.136-40.
19   Hope 1835, pp.560-61.

Wyatt for the Duke of Wellington in 1828 still survives intact and represents the style at its best. As with York House the rigorously neo-classical exterior gives no clue to the elaboration of the Louis XIV interiors within. The problem was as Hope noted when mentioning, 'manufacturers', that the gilded scroll work could cheaply and easily be produced in papier mâché or stamped out of brass and applied indiscriminately to low-quality furnishings and interiors.

For those small-time upholsterers and their clients who were too mean or unimaginative to employ an architect there were pattern books to guide them. We have met George Smith already. On the subject of furnishing the main rooms he advised: 'In Drawing Rooms, Boudoirs, Anti Rooms, or other dressed apartments, east or west indian satin-woods, rose-wood, tulip-wood, and the other varieties of woods brought from the East, may be used: with satin and light-coloured woods the decorations may be ebony or rose-wood: with rose-wood let the decorations be *or-molu*, and the inlay brass.'[20] One of the most widely used books of this type was by Thomas Sheraton, who drew particular attention to the drawing room and stressed that all the furnishings should be devised to encourage a social atmosphere:

The Drawing-Room is to concentrate the elegance of the whole house, and is the highest display of richness of furniture. It being appropriated to the formal visits of the highest rank, and nothing of a scientific nature should be introduced to take up the attention of any individual, from the general conversation that takes place on such occasions. Hence, the walls should be free of pictures, tables not lined with books, nor the angles of the room filled with globes; as the design of such meetings are not that each visitant should turn towards his favourite study, but contribute to the amusement of the whole company.[21]

By contrast such social engineering could be applied in other rooms. 'The tea-room or breakfast room, may abound with beaufets, painted chairs, flower-pot stands, hanging bookshelves or moving libraries, and the walls may be adorned with landscapes, and pieces of drawings, &c. and all the little things which are engaging . . .'[22]

One group of interiors which though not domestic are closely allied to the more formal house interiors, are the London clubs. Waagen observed that:

Amongst the most stately buildings at the west end of town are the club-houses. Each of these houses has the finest saloons for reading-rooms, for a library, and also a complete culinary establishment. The whole arrangement is so extremely elegant and they are such agreeable places of resort, that the ladies have reason on their side, when they vehemently declaim against these establishments, as taking the men away from their family circle. These splendid societies would not be possible without the astonishing wealth in England; for each member pays, for instance, in the Athenaeum, twenty guineas, entrance and an annual subscription of six guineas; and yet I hear of many persons who are members of three or four such clubs.[23]

A number of celebrated clubs such as Boodle's and Brooks's had existed since the eighteenth century, but the Athenaeum was set up in 1824. The founders included the sculptor Francis Chantrey, the painter Thomas Lawrence, the architect Robert Smirke and the scientist Humphry Davy. In 1830, they moved into a grand neo-classical club house to the designs of Decimus Burton built on the site of the recently demolished Carlton House in Pall Mall. Fortunately all the original furniture and furnishings remain *in situ:* these were supplied by the firm of Taprell and Holland and are very well documented.[29] The Athenaeum chose well for the firm would soon become Holland and Sons and by the 1840s they had established themselves as the largest and most important cabinet makers to have ever existed in Britain. In the late 1840s they furnished Osborne House for the Queen and supplied furniture to Pugin's design for the new Palace of Westminster. They dominated the London cabinet making world for the rest of the century.

The Athenaeum furniture is rigorously Grecian and masculine in character as is usual with club furniture and is executed in mahogany or rosewood. In 1841 shortly after Waagen would have first visited the club the furniture was described thus: 'it is the grand, massive, chaste, and severely simple outline, the unity and the harmony of the design that give form and character.'[25] By this time, alongside the Athenaeum had been built Charles Barry's Renaissance style Travellers' Club and the Reform Club both furnished in a similar fashion to the Athenaeum. As a prominent curator and scholar, Waagen singled out the club libraries for mention and indeed the three clubs I

20   Smith 1808, p.xiv.
21   Sheraton 1803, vol. 2, p.218.
22   Ibid., p.219.
23   Waagen 1838, vol. 1, p.22.
24   Jervis 1970, pp.43-61.
25   Ibid., p.50.

have mentioned have elegant and well-stocked libraries. Sadly, however, many members neglected to use them as that inveterate clubman and novelist Thackeray observed of his club library:

> What a calm and pleasant seclusion the library presents after the brawl and bustle of the newspaper room? There is never anyone here. The English gentlemen get up such a prodigious quantity of knowledge in their early life, that they leave off reading as soon as they begin to shave, or never look at anything but a newspaper. How pleasant this room is, – isn't it? With its sober draperies, and long calm lines of peaceful volumes – nothing to interrupt the quiet – only the melody of Horner's nose, as he lies asleep upon one of the sofas.[26]

I have largely confined myself to interiors furnished with modern objects though as at Duchess Street ancient ones played a key role in the whole scheme of furnishing. By 1800, however, there was a whole species of interior throughout England whose character was wholly dependent upon the collections of ancient objects which they contained. These may be defined as 'Romantic Interiors'[27] and the only surviving London example is Sir John Soane's Museum. Though most of the interiors are dominated by classical antiquities mixed with neo-classical objects in the basement is the Monk's Parlour which is Gothic in character. Soane the architect, though usually thought of as a classicist, did in fact design some Gothic Revival buildings, most notably the extensions to the Palace of Westminster. For the Gothic library at Stowe, a country house in Buckinghamshire, he designed the elaborate Gothic table in the exhibition. Interestingly, the modern furniture for his own house was largely rather dull standard neo-classical pieces bought from various London upholsterers. For instance, in 1816 he ordered from John Robins of Warwick Street in Soho 'Six lyre backed chairs, neatly japanned bamboo cane seats, 14s. each'.[28] It was, however, the ancient furniture which Soane had collected which contributed much more to these interiors than the functional modern pieces: for instance, the black-painted William Kent table in the Monk's parlour and the ivory chairs and table captured from the tent of Tippoo Sultan at the battle of Seringapatam. Such interiors are so much the personal creation of their owners that they are far less easy to analyse than say a neo-classical room. They have a dense and highly wrought nature, with the collector's treasured objects often collected over a lifetime arranged in a way that is logical only to himself. Waagen had difficulty in seeing

the point of Soane's house though he admired the 'praiseworthy intention of the owner to bequeath it to the English nation'. He felt that:

> The principal part has the appearance of a mine with many veins, in which instead of metallic ores, you find works of art. Thus in most of the apartments a broken light falls from above, which heightens the feeling of the subterranean and mysterious . . . the whole, notwithstanding the picturesque, fantastic charm, which cannot be denied, has, in consequence of this arbitary mixture of heterogeneous objects, something of the unpleasant effect of a feverish dream. As a splendid example of English whimsicalness which can be realized only by the union of colossal English wealth, and the English way of thinking it is very remarkable . . .[29]

Many such interiors existed in the early nineteenth century in London and throughout the country. As with the other early nineteenth-century interiors which I have discussed, the survival rate is far higher in the country than in London. One of the most important at this date was Abbotsford, Sir Walter Scott's house.[30] This fortunately still survives intact. Not more than 15 miles from the Soane Museum on the River Thames at Twickenham, Strawberry Hill still existed complete with its collection until 1842. It was the most celebrated early example of this movement in interior design: Horace Walpole had started to collect the furnishings of Strawberry Hill as early as 1742; he died in 1797. Walpole promoted the fame of the collection by issuing tickets to visitors and had even written a guide book to the house. It was an easy day trip from London and visitors from all over Europe came to see it during Walpole's lifetime and continued to do so through the early decades of the nineteenth century.

Strawberry Hill was a Gothic Revival building purposely created for the largely medieval and early Renaissance collection of its creator. In London itself as we saw with Hope's Duchess Street the houses themselves were usually rather dull and anonymous externally – only when inside was the character of the collection obvious. Certainly the very grand examples like Apsley House or York House were purpose built in the classical style and

26 Thackeray 1989, p.32. Thackeray first published these essays as a series of articles from 1844-50.
27 Wainwright 1989.
28 Bolton 1924, p.135.
29 Waagen 1838, vol. 1, pp.180-81.
30 Wainwright 1989, chapters 6 and 7.

An equestrian armour from the Meyrick Collection as shown at the Manchester Art Treasures exhibition of 1857

ancient sculpture and old master paintings formed the bulk of their collections rather than the medieval armour, stained glass and Tudor furniture which filled most of the 'Romantic Interiors'. There was, however, no grand Gothic Revival house built in London in the early years of the nineteenth century. Even the Gothic interiors at Carlton House were not obvious from the outside. It was not that aristocratic collectors did not dabble in the style, for the Duke of Westminster was building his vast Gothic Eaton Hall in Cheshire; yet in London he occupied the neo-classical Grosvenor House. The Duke of Buckingham had created his Gothic library at Stowe by 1810 but did not use the style in London. The Duke of Northumberland had his vast medieval Alnwick Castle in Northumberland with its elegant Gothic Revival interiors by Robert Adam yet he refurbished his Jacobean Northumberland House in London in the Louis XIV style. Whilst in town the Duke of Norfolk lived at Norfolk House in St. James's Square with its elaborate genuine

eighteenth-century rococo interiors. In the country in Sussex he was busy until 1815 Gothicising his real medieval castle of Arundel.

Yet lurking behind bland and anonymous soot-encrusted facades of many London terraces houses were many fascinating suites of 'Romantic Interiors'. In just such a dull-looking house in Upper Cadogan Place in Chelsea, Sir Samuel Rush Meyrick (1783–1848) displayed his collection of armour and medieval works of art. By the mid-1820s he had 'a very large collection of armour which not only filled the garrets, the staircase, and the back drawing-room, but even encroached upon the bedrooms'.[31] Meyrick was not only an avid collector, but he was Europe's first modern armour scholar, publishing widely on the subject. He wrote in 1834 an introductory essay to the first book ever published in English on ancient furniture. He encouraged all who bought the book to collect ancient furniture: 'The fact is, that modern furniture is too poor . . . A feeling has now arisen for the ancient decorative style, which it is hoped the present work will materially assist; for however beautiful the elegant simplicity of Grecian forms, these are not in themselves sufficient to produce that effect that should be given to an English residence'.[32]

Meyrick encouraged visitors many of whom were the leading artists of the Romantic movement wishing to sketch documented pieces of armour for their paintings of medieval subjects. In July 1825 Delacroix and his friend Richard Bonington came over from Paris and sketched details of the armour at Meyrick's house. They both portrayed Meyrick's armour in paintings inspired by Walter Scott's *Quentin Durward*. Delacroix was later perceptively to remark that Meyrick 'had the finest collection of armour there has ever been'. In the late 1820s the size of the collection drove Meyrick to emulate the aristocratic collectors and he built his splendidly Gothic Goodrich Court on the River Wye on the edge of Wales. Sadly, whilst we have illustrations of the interiors at Goodrich[33] none survive of the London house.

In Gower Street in Bloomsbury in a nondescript late Georgian terrace lived a close friend of Meyrick's, the omnivorous collector Francis Douce (1757–1834). He was at one stage Keeper of Manuscripts at the British Museum and knew everyone including Flaxman who was a near neighbour. By the time he died, Douce had packed in his

31 *Gentleman's Magazine,* 1848, vol. 184, p.92.
32 Shaw 1836, p.26.
33 Wainwright 1989, pls. 216, 221-23. Chapter 9 is devoted to the Meyrick collection.

house 13,000 books, 400 manuscripts and many remarkable prints and drawings as well as medieval stained glass, enamels, ivories and metalwork. Douce bequeathed the books, manuscripts and prints to the Bodleian Library in Oxford and the rest of the collection to Meyrick who integrated it into the interiors at Goodrich. Again there are no illustrations of the Douce collection *in situ* nor any reliable contemporary descriptions.

Though the existence of a number of other similar collections of medieval and Renaissance objects used to create suites of 'Romantic Interiors' in early nineteenth-century London are known, again illustrations rarely exist. Fortunately, I recently identified a watercolour of one that hitherto was only documented through a few engravings of objects and written and printed material. This house was Pryor's Bank in Fulham in west London the importance of which was rediscovered by Simon Jervis some years ago.[34] Often all we have is the sale catalogue of when the collection was auctioned.

Just as the cabinet makers, silversmiths, weavers and

potters were vital to the furnishing of modern interiors, the brokers in ancient objects were equally important to the creation of 'Romantic Interiors'. Even the modern Louis style interiors at York House needed the services of the dealers in old masters to clothe the walls with the very pictures to which both Waagen and Passavant devote several pages. Due to the arrival of the flood of objects 'liberated' from the churches, monasteries and castles of the Continent during the Napoleonic Wars, London became the centre of the world trade in art and antiquities. Some of the objects were imported by enterprising individual brokers, but the bulk trade was through public auctions. Christie's sold in June 1808 a *Unique Collection of Ancient Stained Glass ... for Churches, Collegiate Buildings and Gothic Country Residences*. They and other auctioneers held similar auctions of a wide range of

34 Jervis 1974, pp.87-99.

objects, some of which could stand free like armour, tapestries and furniture, whilst stained glass, carved stone chimneypieces or carved panelling were actually built into houses. In November 1825, Christie's held a sale of *Ancient and very curious carvings in wood many of which may be found suitable for fitting up of private chapels, and many of them applicable for the furniture of gothic mansions . . . the whole of which has lately been imported from the continent.*

This world of the trade in ancient objects is a complex and ill-documented one, especially the activities of the brokers who were beginning by the 1820s to establish themselves in and around Wardour Street in Soho.[35] I can do no more here than stress their vital role in that rich mix of individuals and firms which made up the luxury trades in London at this time. They took far more risks than conventional craftsmen but the potential for profit was greater, as Waagen wryly commented 'scarcely was a country overrun by the French, when Englishmen skilled in the arts were at hand with their guineas'.[36] As with the trade in the modern applied arts, houses throughout Britain were supplied by the London brokers. Indeed, numbers of English churches also gained better medieval stained glass or carved oak pews from the Continent than they had ever had when built in the middle ages.

One object which illustrates the central role played by the London antiquities trade is an elaborate ivory cup and cover now in the Royal Collection.[37] The carved ivory and part of the mounts are probably German and date from the late seventeenth century. Nothing is known of its history until it was purchased by William Beckford.[38] Beckford fits the category described above of the collector who created 'Romantic Interiors' in the country but whose house was classical in town. In 1813 when he bought the cup, his London house was a dull Georgian one at 6 Upper Harley Street – a short walk from Thomas Hope's house. In the depths of the country in Wiltshire he had, however, been engaged since 1796 in creating Fonthill Abbey, his immense Gothic Revival house.

He furnished Fonthill with one of the greatest collections of ancient works of fine and applied art ever to have been assembled in England. Though he bought widely in

Carved ivory cup and cover, German, late seventeenth century with jewelled mounts made in London. H.M. Queen Elizabeth II

35 Ibid.; Wainwright 1989, chapters 3 and 4.
36 Waagen 1838, vol. 1, p.50.
37 *Carlton House* 1991, p.186.
38 I would be very interested to know more about the early history and provenance of this object; any information would be welcome.

PATRONAGE AND THE APPLIED ARTS

A group of objects from William Beckford's collection including a blood-stone tazza mounted by Paul Storr

King Edward's Gallery at Fonthill Abbey in 1823

Europe, much of the collection passed through the hands of London brokers. All the modern furnishings including the elaborate modern historicist metalwork were also made in London. For instance, the more traditionally neo-classical bloodstone tazza supported on silver-gilt dolphins standing amongst some of Beckford's prized objects was made in London by Paul Storr.

Beckford bought the ivory cup from R. Davies, a goldsmith and jeweller of York Street, Portman Square believing it to have been carved by 'Magnus Berg Medallist to the Emperor of Germany'. Though the Berg attribution has been questioned, it is still thought to be German. It was taken down to Fonthill and given pride of place in King Edward's Gallery where it stood on the immense Italian Renaissance *pietre dure* table which had been looted by Napoleon from Italy and purchased by Beckford in Paris.

Beckford's immense wealth came from the rum and sugar which his slaves produced on his West Indian plantations but when these began to fail he was forced to sell Fonthill; an auction of its contents was held in 1823. At this sale a broker acting for King George IV bought the cup for 90 guineas and it was taken back to London for Carlton House. Even though it already had silver-gilt mounts the king sent it to the goldsmith John Bridge to have an additional jewelled silver-gilt foot and rim added at a cost of £148. 10s., more than the cup had cost at auction. Thus, we see both the London brokers and the London craftsmen involved in handling this object for two of the most celebrated Regency collectors twice within a decade.

One further example of the trade in action is the elaborate ebony, boulle and *pietre dure* cabinet from the Royal Collection. One of Beckford's neighbours in Wiltshire was George Watson Taylor, M.P., who like Beckford derived his great wealth from the West Indies and was also affected by the slump in rum and sugar prices in the 1820s. Taylor's large country house, Erlestoke Mansion, with its superb collection – some purchased at the Fonthill Sale – was auctioned in 1832. Earlier however in an effort to raise money he auctioned the major contents of his large London house in Cavendish Square at Christie's in May 1825. At the sale the Soho broker Robert Fogg purchased for George IV several remarkable cabinets including the present example. Before it was taken to Windsor it was sent to Morel and Seddon where it was repaired, the mounts regilded and the mirrors resilvered.[39]

Taylor had been influenced by Beckford's taste even though Beckford despised him, and he emulated Beckford by having several pieces of furniture for both his houses made-up from imported Italian *pietre dure* panels, as Beckford had done for Fonthill. It is likely that Taylor even used Robert Hume of Berners Street to make the cabinets. Hume worked almost exclusively for Beckford at this time as a cabinet maker and broker. To complete another strand in this complex web of trade and collector contacts, Beckford frequently bought from Fogg. For instance, he wrote in July 1814, 'This morning I fell right into Fogg's net. Alas, I was seduced by a little Saxon tazza, certain sea green bottles incredibly decorated with bronze, gilded in hell fire – so bright and strong their colours.'[40] Thus, as part of the web of which this cabinet is the centre we have Taylor, George IV, Beckford, Hume, Fogg, Christie's and Morel and Seddon and even though it has – until its visit to Essen – not left Windsor since 1826, its early history is a London one.

This essay has attempted to give an impression of the central role that London played in the design and manufacture of modern English applied arts in the early nineteenth century and to discuss the important role played by the London art and antiquities trade. During the period 1790–1820 there were more important objects available to the trade than has ever been the case before or since. The most perceptive collectors made the most of this unique situation when furnishing their London houses. This was a rich, complex and rapidly changing period about which a considerable amount has been written, but many questions still remain to be answered. The quality of its artefacts you can judge for yourselves in the exhibition.

39 I would like to thank Hugh Roberts for giving me the history of this cabinet and finding the Morel and Seddon accounts.
40 Alexander 1957, p.152.

SCIENTIFIC LONDON

Iwan Morus, Simon Schaffer and Jim Secord

INTRODUCTION: SIGNS OF THE TIMES

Early nineteenth-century London witnessed a revolution in the sciences. Most of the institutions associated with modern science, teaching laboratories and national scientific rallies, new disciplines such as geology and biology, electromagnetism and stellar astronomy, were established in the period. An unprecedented number of new scientific objects and devices were offered to a fascinated public: powerful oxyhydrogen microscopes and monster reflecting telescopes, galvanic batteries, electromagnets and telegraphs, exotic animals and extinct reptiles. The very term 'scientist' was coined in 1833. London's role was crucial. Its enormous wealth, population and technical skill were magnets for ambitious men of science. When Charles Darwin returned from his voyage round the world he spent a few months back in donnish Cambridge before moving to comfortable London lodgings at Great Marlborough Street in early 1837. 'It is a sorrowful, but I fear too certain truth,' he reflected, 'that no place is at all equal, for aiding one in Natural History pursuits, to this odious dirty smokey town, where one can never get a glimpse, at all, that is best worth seeing in nature.'[1] Londoners might not be able to see the sights of bucolic nature through their gaslit smog, but they helped make natural knowledge. Darwin recognised that London mattered not simply because it was a place where natural knowledge could be consumed, in lectures, clubs, museums and theatres, but also because science was produced there in the highly artificial milieux of basement laboratories and backroom workshops, gentlemanly debates and filthy surgical wards.

New maps of the sciences matched the capital's social geography. Shut off by urban gloom from the starlit heavens, and, as many held, from future heavenly salvation, Londoners were, for example, nevertheless presented with a remarkable range of rival astronomies. On the edges of the city were the Royal Observatory at Greenwich, home of state-sponsored nautical measurement, and wealthy suburban private observatories such as James South's fine refractors on the hill above Holland House. Beyond, up river, was the giant 40-feet reflector

J. Stow after E.F. Burney, *Walker's Exhibition of the Eidouranion at the English Opera House*, 1817, engraving from Wilkinson's *Theatrum Illustrata*, 1825. The Museum of London

of William Herschel at Slough, the most powerful instrument in the world, whence unimaginably distant, and ancient, nebular and stellar objects were seen by the favoured few. His telescope graced the seal of the new Astronomical Society, managed from rented rooms in Lincoln's Inn Fields by his son John Herschel and the energetic stockbroker Francis Baily in a struggle for their science's autonomy, resources and social status. Nearby in Fleet Street, world-class instrument-makers, led by the Astronomical Society's co-founder Edward Troughton, designed amazingly accurate measurement devices and transit circles. Less specialist audiences could glimpse Herschel's discoveries at the English Opera House on the Strand, where William and Deane Walker, the heirs of a famous lecturing family, showed their Eidouranion, a moving, and musical, planetarium 20 feet high and 27 feet in diameter: 'every planet and satellite seems suspended in space, without any support; performing their annual and diurnal revolutions without any apparent cause'. Young

1   Darwin 1986, p.11.

Michael Faraday, a bookbinder's apprentice in Blandford Street, thought Walker's lectures the best in London.[2] But he had many competitors, including the very popular John Wallis, who earned a good living from astronomical shows at the London Mechanics' Institution in Finsbury. Public demand required repeat performances on successive nights. Others were much more concerned with causes than was Walker. During Passion Week, lectures at the Italian Opera House and the King's Theatre drew the appropriate scriptural messages from stars, eclipses and other heavenly signs. From 1830, at Richard Carlile's headquarters at the Rotunda in Blackfriars, home of the National Union of Working Classes, Robert Taylor, the 'Devil's Chaplain', hammered home a materialist and universalist cosmology from a pulpit emblazoned with the signs of the socialist zodiac.[3]

Londoners were by no means passive consumers of others' science. The city helped produce high-class machines, techniques and natural philosophies. Struggles about the content and management of knowledge also helped define what science meant. And by defining the proper place of science in public culture, and the appropriate places where these sciences should be made, the political geography of the capital became a vital factor in the intellectual geography of the learned world. To explore the contrasted scientific worlds of London gentlemen, reformers, artisans and radicals, it is necessary to map the places where they worked and fought.

THE IMPERIAL CENTRE

One of the best ways to approach scientific London was along the Thames, for the principal societies concerned with natural knowledge met behind the imposing classical facade of Somerset House on the Strand. The location recognised the close ties of organised science to the political, social and religious establishment. The best known and most traditional society was the Royal, also known as the 'Old Lady'. Throughout the Regency, conflict over the meaning and aim of science dominated its affairs, as in the metropolis more generally. An older faction favoured natural history, agricultural improvement and the study of antiquities – the 'learned empire' of Sir Joseph Banks, president until 1820. He coordinated agricultural, economic and imperial institutions such as the Board of Longitude, the Board of Agriculture and the gardens at Kew – an entrepôt for invaluable seeds and specimens collected worldwide by British expeditions – the Linnaean Society

which Banks helped found in Soho Square in 1788, and the Horticultural Society, which from 1804 met every fortnight in Regent Street. Robert Brown, prince of botanists, stewarded Banks' own collections as the Soho Square librarian and agent. Banks willed Brown the use of his massive collections, indicating that they should then be given over to the British Museum, run for the gentry at Montagu House by a board under the patronage of the Archbishop of Canterbury and the Speaker of the House of Commons.[4]

Under Banks' patronage, the Society for Bettering the Condition of the Poor, a coterie of Tory landowners, launched the Royal Institution from his rooms in 1799. As wartime rents and food prices rose, their aim was to back agricultural improvement through rational chemistry, and to disseminate knowledge of the useful arts throughout society. During the next two decades the Royal Institution, based in fashionable Mayfair, weathered hard financial storms to become the premier venue for the production and dissemination of science in Regency London.[5] In their Albemarle Street rooms the dashing Cornish chemist Humphry Davy and then his erstwhile assistant Michael Faraday lectured on natural philosophy to large and wealthy audiences. They could draw on the prestigious Institution's resources and support staff (including an in-house instrument maker) to produce knowledge tailored to the requirements of fashionable London society. The Institution had been initially conceived as a place where both the upper and lower echelons of society could receive instruction. The original plans included a staircase from the street so that mechanics could enter the lecture theatre directly without offending their betters' sensibilities as they congregated in the lobby; this staircase was never built. The architecture and location of the Royal Institution were, in fact, designed to emphasise its exclusive nature and the Institution's Friday evening discourses, inaugurated by Faraday in 1825, were emblematic of its activities. Here the social and intellectual elite of London society gathered to hear lectures by Faraday or an invited speaker. Geological and natural historical specimens, electrical experiments or new mechanical contrivances were put on display here in a safe and sanitised setting and explained to the gathering.

Financial pressure and political clamour prompted a

2 Dreyer and Turner 1923, pp.1-36; King and Millburn 1978, pp.312-17; Faraday 1971, p.56.
3 Hays 1983, p.99; Prothero 1979, p.277; Thompson 1968, pp.843-44, 892.
4 Miller 1981.
5 Berman 1978.

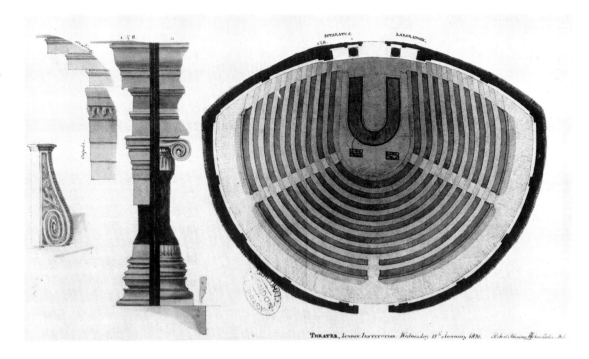

THEATRE, London Institution, Wednesday 12th January 1820. Robert Blemm Schnebbelie del.

progressive specialisation of the scope of lectures and of the boundaries of the sciences. Aping the Royal Institution's success were the London Institution (f.1805), which moved to Moorfields in 1819 and possessed a laboratory costing several thousand pounds designed by the chemist William Pepys; the Surrey Institution (f.1808) at Blackfriars Bridge, which provided aspiring experimenters with 'an excellent Library and still more a decent Laboratory', and the Russell Institution (f.1808) in Bloomsbury. Smaller groupings, such as the City Philosophical Society in Dorset Street (f.1809), sponsored natural philosophical discussions and lectures by members. They found it hard to compete in the rapidly expanding world of London scientific popularisation. After learning much from his friends at the City Philosophical Society and the Surrey Institution when still a bookbinder's apprentice in the 1810s, Professor Faraday came to view his competitors across town with some contempt: 'to the world an hour's existence of our Institution is worth a year's of the London', he exclaimed in 1826. Competition for scarce resources prompted the lectures' managers to shorten courses to drive up custom. Programmes of up to 100 lectures offered by the Royal Institution's early speakers such as Thomas Young were displaced, from the 1820s, by brief surveys of focussed topics: entomology, galvanism or mineralogy rather than the traditional divisions of natural philosophy and natural history.[6]

By the 1830s the territory of natural knowledge had been carved up in a new and decisive way. There was a startling proliferation of scientific societies, from the Geological (f.1807) and the Astronomical (f.1820) to the Statistical (f.1834) and the Meteorological (f.1839).[7] These groups were dominated by an elite coterie, strongly defined not only by their specialist knowledge and commitment to a vocation of scientific discovery, but also by class and gender. In effect, these societies were gentlemen's clubs, extensions of the cosy world of the Athenaeum, the Reform and other retreats for wealthy males. No women were admitted – although a bust of Mary Somerville, the celebrated interpreter of Laplace, was eventually allowed inside the Royal Society.[8] London was a crucial instrument for forging new specialist disciplines. For, with a few exceptions, it was only in the metropolis that a sufficient combination of gentlemen with the appropriate interests and commitments could be brought together to form a self-validating consensus. At weekly scientific meetings during the season, at dinner parties and at *conversazioni*, agreement about the proper ways of producing knowledge could be forged. By contrast, the provincial elites who had dominated British cultural life during the final decades of the eighteenth century had to be given carefully circumscribed roles, often as humble collectors for an enterprise dominated from the centre.

6 Inkster 1977; Faraday 1971, pp.71, 165; Hays 1983, pp.96-105.
7 Morrell 1976, pp.132-37.
8 Benjamin 1991.

STUDIO FALLENTE LABOREM.

London Institution
1820.

NOTICE
OF

A SERIES OF LECTURES

TO BE DELIVERED IN

The Theatre of the London Institution.

COURSE I.—On NATURAL PHILOSOPHY, *viz.* ASTRONOMY, OPTICS, HYDROSTATICS, and MECHANICS; to be illustrated by Experiments. By GEORGE BIRKBECK, M.D. &c. (Late Professor of Natural Philosophy to the Anderson Institution of Glasgow) to commence on WEDNESDAY the 19th of January, at *One* o'Clock in the Afternoon; and to be continued each succeeding WEDNESDAY until the Course shall be completed. (*The Proprietors and Subscribers are informed that Dr. Birkbeck has very handsomely undertaken to deliver this Course of Lectures gratuitously.*)

COURSE II.—On EXPERIMEMTAL PHILOSOPHY; or the useful Application of Natural Philosophy to Society, by HYDRAULICS, MECHANICS, OPTICS, and the use of STEAM ENGINES and other Machines. By JOHN MILLINGTON, Esq. to commence on THURSDAY the 20th of January, at *Seven* o'Clock in the Evening; and to be continued each succeeding THURSDAY until the Course shall be completed.

COURSE III.—On the ELEMENTS of CHEMISTRY, and its Connection with the ARTS and MANUFACTURES. By RICHARD PHILLIPS, Esq. F.L.S. to commence on MONDAY the 24th of January, at *Seven* o'Clock in the Evening; and to be continued each succeeding MONDAY until the Course be completed.

COURSE IV.—On BOTANY. By Sir JAMES EDWARD SMITH, P.L.S., F.R.S., HONORARY MEMBER OF THE LONDON INSTITUTION, &c. &c. &c.; who has obligingly offered to give two Lectures on a novel subject connected with this science, in the month of JUNE next.

ROBERT STEVENS,
Secretary.

Otherwise there was always a danger that other approaches, such as Scriptural literalism in the case of geology, might be given scientific sanction.[9]

By the third decade of the century, London had also moved to the centre of scientific education in medicine, occupying a place in Europe second only to Paris. An extraordinary variety of educational establishments confronted prospective students. Within the space of a few hundred yards, lecturers offered sharply contrasting concepts of the role of medicine, of medical practice and of the body politic. Teachers at the older institutions, especially the Royal College of Surgeons at Lincoln's Inn Fields, emphasised clinical practice, bedside skills and classical learning for an aristocratic clientele. Closely linked by patronage to church and state, this was a vision of medicine for the wealthy. The founders of the secular London University in 1826 demanded that these traditional skills be replaced with science. The aim was to train solicitors and professional medics, engineers and civil servants in the assured lessons of utility and practice. Faraday was told in 1828 that the aim was to teach 'knowledge of even the leading chemical manufactures' such as acid works, brewing and metallurgy. But cash flow was always a problem – professors were supposed to give profit making lectures, and student numbers were way below target. Ideological splits inside the college tore the professoriate apart. The Tory and Anglican King's College, founded on the Strand in 1829, was a more establishment response to the challenge from Gower Street.[10]

The disciplinary sciences, and specifically Parisian comparative anatomy, would serve as the mark of a new middle-class professional elite. The Edinburgh anatomist and newly hired London University professor, Robert Grant, argued that human anatomy was to be studied 'philosophically' through comparisons with other animals. Morphology, the study of animal form, could be reduced to regular predictable laws. Reforms of this kind went beyond anything that the coteries in Somerset House were typically willing to contemplate. Specialist expertise would hound the jobbing aristocrats out of their corporation citadels, and keep superficial speculators, midwives and other 'humbugs' in check. The key journal of the medical reformers was the cheap weekly *Lancet*, founded in 1823 and edited by Thomas Wakley, radical M.P. for Finsbury. Wakley was a brilliant crusader, unsparing in his denunciation of medical privilege. In its place, he demanded power for a new corps of scientifically trained professionals. London, as a counter to Oxford and Cambridge, had a key place in his strategy.[11]

The utilitarian campaign also extended to other sciences, including geology and botany. Henry De la Beche, an independently wealthy geologist whose slave estates in Jamaica had fallen on hard times, turned his position as geologist to the Ordnance Survey into the basis for a national survey of the strata. His position allowed him to coordinate geological knowledge for

9   Morrell and Thackray 1981; Rudwick 1985.
10 Desmond 1989, pp.33-41, 94-99; Faraday 1971, p.172.
11 Desmond 1989.

W. Deeble after T.H. Shepherd, *The London Institution, Finsbury Circus*, engraving from J. Elmes, *Metropolitan Improvements*, 1827. The Museum of London

urban planning, as when in late 1838 he consulted Faraday on the stone to be used in Charles Barry's new parliament building. Like Wakley and Grant, De la Beche hoped to model London institutions on Parisian ones. The Geological Survey (f.1835), the Museum of Economic Geology (f.1839) and the Royal School of Mines (f.1851) closely imitated their French counterparts. Maps of strata, tides and magnetism could serve as tools for central administration and social control.[12] In this way, reforms in geology, zoology and medicine could become part of Whig initiatives in the wake of the 1832 Reform Act, including the great sanitary surveys, the Anatomy Act and debates about education.

At the time of the Reform Bill there were seventeen private medical schools in the capital, eager to open medical learning to a less exclusive clientele. Their proprietors, men like George Dermott, John Epps and Richard Grainger, were typically sons of men in trade and middle-class medical practice. Joshua Brookes, whose private anatomical museum in Blenheim Street rivalled that of the Royal College of Surgeons, was 'not a gentleman, and very dirty'.[13] Such 'vulgar' purveyors of medical knowledge advocated developmental materialist anatomies, drawing on the classic works of the late French Enlightenment. They ranged living creatures in a continuous developmental series from monad upwards, a move that potentially threatened the special status of man. Many –

long before Charles Darwin's *Origin of Species* – believed in evolution. These were dangerous doctrines in the 1830s, for they undermined a social order based on a static hierarchy of place and position. London, with its filthy dissecting rooms and temptations for the unwary, threatened to corrupt the country into unbelief.

The Royal College of Surgeons responded with vigour. In 1836 they hired the brilliant young anatomist Richard Owen as Hunterian professor. Owen had studied at Edinburgh, but like most of the new generation he made his mark in London. He catalogued the collections at the Hunterian Museum, and showed that science could meet the highest standards of Berlin and Paris without serving utilitarian or materialist ends. In his first lectures in 1837, he tailored the embryological work of the Prussian Karl Ernst von Baer to a purposive, idealist vision of animal structure – thereby taking the initiative from radical anatomists. A year later the Royal College opened a splendid new library and museum, with spectacular anatomical displays like the Irish giant and the fossils that Darwin had brought back from South America.[14]

12 Secord 1986, pp.223-34, 246-47; Faraday 1971, p.321.
13 Desmond 1989, p.161.
14 Ibid., pp.236-75.

(See also following illustration) G. Scharf, *Building the new College of Surgeons, Lincoln's Inn Fields*, watercolour, 1834. The Royal College of Surgeons of England

It was this period that also saw the foundation established for London's position as an imperial city of science. Institutions like the Museum of Economic Geology, the Zoological Gardens, the Royal College of Surgeons, Kew Gardens and the British Museum, were markers of London's status as the nexus of a new scientific empire. As early as the 1830s, the natural sciences had emerged as the leading edge of imperial expansion. As penny publisher Charles Knight said of the museum of the Royal College of Surgeons, 'the whole earth has been ransacked to enrich its stores'.[15] Fashionable visitors marvelled at the exotic beasts brought to the Zoological Gardens in Regent's Park (f.1828). Such costly displays, not open to the public at large, were opposed by reformers who thought imperial, commercial and middle-class interests would be better served by specialist museums and support for research. They argued that such spectacular 'raree shows' ventured too close to popular entertainments like Exeter 'Change and William Bullock's Egyptian Hall.[16] For a few fortunate researchers, though, the zoo provided a seemingly inexhaustible supply of exotic cadavers – from rhinos, baby giraffes and rare great apes, to the wombat, duck-billed platypus and other anomalous marsupials. The results appeared in the expensive quarto transactions of the Zoological Society, illustrated by George Scharf, who earned much of his day-to-day income this way. Dissecting these bizarre beasts gave an authority unrivalled in European science to Richard Owen, who used them to bolster both his reputation and his particular brand of conservative anatomy.[17]

In a similar way, the Tory geographer Roderick Murchison conducted a campaign to map the ancient strata of the globe. From his handsome mansion in Belgrave Square, he coordinated his own field researches with dozens of correspondents. His friend George Greenough advised travellers from Grove Lodge, the villa in Regent's Park he had purpose-built for natural history research.

15 Ibid., p.251.
16 Ibid., pp.134-39.
17 Desmond 1985.

Later in life, Greenough mapped India geographically without ever having to leave the metropolis.[18] Energies of empire, concentrated by the metropolis and carefully manipulated by an individual, could fuel discovery in the natural sciences on a heroic scale. Men like Owen, Murchison, and Greenough were seen in the popular press as the 'great guns' or 'big wigs', celebrities whose opinion vouchsafed natural truth. Artists painted their portraits and had them engraved for widespread distribution; editors printed their speeches at length in the newspaper press; men of state sought out their opinions.

REFORMERS AND ENGINEERS

Forging the institutions of a new imperial scientific capital demanded the management of these relations between men of science and the state. Where Banksians exploited, and reinforced, relations of genteel patronage and obligation, London reformers from the law schools around Lincoln's Inn and the military schools at Woolwich and Addiscombe were keen to change the politics of science

and, if necessary, redesign the state on what they reckoned were scientific lines. They found some inspiration in the work of the visionary Westminster lawyer, Jeremy Bentham, whose utopian 'Panopticon' scheme, a 'laboratory for men' and a scheme for national scientific management, foundered after three decades of agitation in 1812. Bentham used the state money paid in compensation to start a campaigning *Westminster Review* which propagandised his attack on the Banksian model of authority. Against the evils of power, opulence and reputation stood the virtues of science: 'at the top of the scale of trustworthiness stands that mass of authority which is constituted by scientific or professional opinion ... By having the motives which tend to correctness of information, the professional man has the means likewise.' Experts managing the military budget, cleaning up the metropolis and fighting plebeian protest should use knowledge of the natural laws of matter and mind, and the careful collection of statistical data, rather than the

18   Secord 1982; Stafford 1989; Golden 1981.

natural history of bugs and ferns, and the careful amassing of aristocratic patrons.[19]

Reformist London was a home of engineers, administrators and statisticians eager to remake the polity in their own image. They saw the city as a potentially universal centre of calculation whence trade and machinery would link worldwide networks of British power. Thus, the new London University was advertised as an 'Emporium for the supply of intellectual goods' to the 'Queen of Cities – Empress of the commercial world'. The emerging imperial capital also hosted other centres of scientific expertise, including those devoted to the militarily crucial disciplines of nautical science, engineering and surveying. The East India Company, which through the Benthamite James Mill and his allies was strongly represented on the board of London University, also sponsored major scientific surveys and commissioned important new batteries of instrumentation from metropolitan craftsmen. Down the Thames were the Royal Observatory at Greenwich, which under successive Astronomers Royal Nevil Maskelyne, John Pond and, from 1835, the Cambridge mathematician George Airy, became a centre of precision measurement and world-class nautical astronomy; and the Royal Military Academy where the mathematics professor Charles Hutton trained successive generations of teachers and surveyors after being sacked from the Royal Society's secretaryship by Banks' clique in 1784.[20]

Mathematical practitioners also clashed with the Society's managers at the Board of Longitude, whose dealings with London's clockmakers were widely seen as scandalous. Admiralty-sponsored voyages helped evaluate the performance of rival longitude schemes: these evaluations were fought out in the institutions under Banksian control.[21] One victim was the High Holborn clockmaker Thomas Earnshaw, whose clocks went on Vancouver's Pacific voyage in 1791 and who won Maskelyne's backing. Between 1791 and 1805 Banks denied Earnshaw's clocks' virtues, preferring his own candidate John Arnold. Earnshaw alleged that Arnold had plagiarised him. Banks hit back in a pamphlet of 1804. These conflicts directly involved the Royal Society. In 1812, Banks was accused of using the Society's *Philosophical Transactions* to blacken the reputation of William Mudge, director of the Ordnance Survey and Hutton's prize student. By 1818, Banks had drawn the Board of Longitude under direct Society control. Mudge got eloquent backing from Olinthus Gregory, Hutton's Woolwich colleague, who published a scurrilous mock-eulogy at Banks' death in 1820. In contrast, conservative divines such as the Bishop of Carlisle mourned the passing of the 'quiet scientific dinners' which Banks had hosted for so long.[22]

The lobby of mathematical practitioners found staunch allies in young Cambridge mathematics graduates such as John Herschel, Augustus de Morgan and Charles Babbage, who reached London just after the end of the Napoleonic Wars. Babbage's London lifestyle linked tavern rallies with engineering workshops and fashionable salons. Banks and the powerful Admiralty Secretary, John Croker, kept him out of the Board of Longitude. Babbage joined Herschel and disaffected practitioners such as Gregory and Troughton in setting up the Astronomical Society in 1820 at the Freemasons' Tavern in Great Queen Street. Banks damned the new group as a threat to the Royal Society. Davy succeeded him as president later that year.[23] The new Somerset House regime made some concessions to the reformers, linking the Royal Society with the capital's politics through the establishment of a set of prestigious committees to advise the Admiralty on ship design and London administrators on stone for the new London Bridge and on the capital's gas-works, and plans to change the British Museum into a more specialist institution. But Davy's project did not match that of the Benthamites and the mathematicians.[24] He resigned in 1827, engineered the election of the reliable Tory M.P. Davies Gilbert, and coolly ignored reform recommendations from a committee including Babbage, Herschel and their friend the astronomer James South. De Morgan, an energetic supporter of Henry Brougham's Society for the Diffusion of Useful Knowledge and author of more than 800 articles for the populist *Penny Cyclopaedia*, recalled that 'the great epidemic which produced the French Revolution, and what is yet the English Reform Bill, showed its effect on the scientific world.'[25]

Babbage made himself a carrier of the epidemic. He used the Astronomical Society to launch his plan to 'calculate by steam', the celebrated Difference Engine. Technical resources were drawn from the best of London's precision engineers, especially Joseph Clement, a former employee of the master of precision design Henry Maudslay, whose 'Lord Chancellor' micrometer was so-named for its role as the tribunal of machine accuracy and whose work on steamship engines transformed the means of transport on the Thames and in the colonies. Maudslay and Clement had crucial links with another of Babbage's

19 Bentham 1962, pp.19-20; Halevy 1972; Finer 1972.
20 Desmond 1989, p.36; Forbes 1975, pp.131-56.
21 Mackay 1985, pp.3-27.
22 Miller 1983, pp.10-12, 26.
23 Gilbert 1955; Dreyer and Turner 1923, pp.1-10.
24 Miller 1983, pp.33-34; Desmond 1989, pp.145-51.
25 Siegfried 1980, p.195; Macleod 1983 p.62; De Morgan 1882, p.4.

engineering allies, Marc Brunel, whose joint work for the Thames Tunnel started in 1825, stopped after funding and design problems, and resumed a decade later. In the 1830s Babbage acted as advisor for the Great Western Railway, using his analytical engine team to design a remarkable chart-recorder system for assaying carriage stability. He successfully urged the virtues of wide gauge rails against the engineering journalist and University College natural philosophy professor, Dionysius Lardner, at a stormy meeting at the London Tavern in early 1839. He coordinated advice from Faraday on railway lubrication and railway-clock designs from the celebrated maker Edward Dent. Engine work became a vital centre of design for new precision tool devices and a source of major industrial innovation in the metropolis. Reform of calculation helped make London's huge skilled workforce into a visible engine of political change.[26]

During the political crises of machine-breaking and reform in the late 1820s and early 1830s, scientific activists began to link their expertise with institutional change. 'How much better it is to be a bastard than a philosopher in England at present', Babbage thundered. 'But a mighty change is at hand.' In 1830, both he and South tried to back Herschel's unsuccessful campaign for the Royal Society's presidency with incendiary pamphlets on the corruption of the old scientific regime. The *Athenaeum* judged that Society reformers were debating 'what is, or is not, science'.[27] In summer 1832, Babbage launched his best selling *Economy of Machinery and Manufactures* through Charles Knight, chief purveyor of Useful Knowledge for Brougham, and deposited copies in the London Mechanics' Institute. The work aimed to reveal the sources of Britain's industrial strength to the metropolitan elite. The following autumn it won him the endorsement of the patent agent J. C. Robertson's *Mechanics' Magazine* when Babbage unsuccessfully stood for parliament alongside Wakley at Finsbury and debated science and political economy in the Canonbury Tavern with the socialist Ricardian Thomas Hodgskin.[28] The aim was to carry the issues of machinery and rational planning on to the London hustings.

After the Reform Act, reformist and Benthamite interests began the establishment of London-based centres for scientific administration and data-gathering. Crucial amongst these were the Statistical Department at the Board of Trade run by George Porter from 1832; the London Statistical Society which Babbage helped found at the Horticultural Hall in 1834, in collaboration with medics such as the University College graduate William Farr; the General Register Office started two years later, where Farr based his medical statistical work; and in-

struction projects such as Brougham's Society for the Diffusion of Useful Knowledge and Thomas Wyse's Central Education Society. In alliance with reformist and radical politicians such as the London M.P.s Joseph Hume, Thomas Wakley and George Grote, the aim, as Porter put it in 1836, was to 'point out the progress of the whole social system in all its various departments and as affecting all its various interests'.[29]

The reformers used this 'science of progress' to make their politically partisan knowledge look apolitical and universal. New London science institutions were supposed to exemplify this form of expertise, and to provide the means to extend its grip from the capital throughout the nation and the empire. In cash-starved reformist institutions and ideologically fraught metropolitan society this was a hard trick to pull off. Intellectual fissures opened into publicly visible chasms under the political pressure of London debate. Brougham launched his Useful Knowledge campaign in 1826 as a means of teaching the truths of divinely designed nature to the dangerous classes. With his ally the Edinburgh medic George Birkbeck he helped patronise a dozen new Mechanics' Institutions around London to propagate this creed. Birkbeck became founder-president of the London Mechanics' Institute in Chancery Lane in 1824, established in response to a mass campaign by Hodgskin, Robertson and the autodidact reformer for artisan education, Francis Place. But plebeian radicals judged this knowledge to be useless; Tories regarded it as incendiary. Robertson turned his *Mechanics' Magazine* against the moralising lectures in Chancery Lane. The Institutes eventually catered rather more to the polite bourgeois than to the lower orders at whom Brougham and his publisher Knight had aimed. Hodgskin lost to Brougham in his fight for socialist political economy classes at the institutes. Richard Carlile, who tried to make the London Institute into a home for radical science, had 'the idea that every school-master ought to be a Man of Science, and not a parish priest, as Mr Brougham would have'.[30]

The Benthamites were no more successful at representing their statistical and educational campaigns of the 1830s as disinterested and scientific, even though they staged

26 Hyman 1982, pp.47-58, 146-49, 156-63; Babbage 1864, pp.68-96, 313-36.
27 Hyman 1982, pp.76, 82, 88-99, 130; Hoskin 1989, pp.177-78.
28 Hyman 1982, pp.82-87, 103-22; Babbage 1864, pp.259-92.
29 Hilts 1978; Johnson 1977.
30 Shapin and Barnes 1977; Hays 1964; Prothero 1979, pp. 191-203; Berg 1980, pp.145-73; Carlile 1972, p.96.

R. Seymour, 'Have You read the Leader in this paper, Mr. Brisket?'
'No, I never touch a newspaper, they are all so wery wenal and woid of
sentiment', etching, c.1830, illustrating the competing claims of
science, politics and literature for a London carpenter and coalman

powerful performances to hammer home the messages of
materialism and law-like nature. Utilitarian science made
good theatre. During the campaign for an Anatomy Act,
Bentham's physician, the Unitarian reformer Southwood
Smith, performed a public dissection of his corpse, promulgated the appropriate utilitarian lessons, then ceremo-
nially shifted the embalmed body to London University's
Council Room. Supplies for public anatomies were
secured: their source, however, was the new workhouses
set up by the Whigs' Poor Law of 1834. The reformers'
concerns with 'what is science and what is not' helped
dramatise the political burden which all practical expertise
carried, and enhanced the need for an apparently con-
sensual, secure form of natural knowledge.[31] Reformers of
every stripe helped promulgate a tense message about the
cultural place of the sciences. On the one hand, they
publicly demonstrated that the ideal of science should

transcend political interest. Herschel influentially propagandised for this message in 1830 in a *Discourse* prefaced
to Lardner's best-selling series, the *Cabinet Cyclopaedia*.
When Herschel returned from surveying the southern
skies at the Cape in 1838, a dinner in his honour at the
Freemasons' Tavern attracted the queen, Lord Melbourne, and a host of scientific notables. The *Athenaeum*
reported on the message of scientific consensus and compared this with the sectarianism of London political life:
'the interest excited in the literary and scientific world resembled that which stirred the political on the occasion of
the Grey and Peel festivals – only that this united all interests and had the good wishes of all parties.'[32]

But this did not mean that reformist science was politically irrelevant. In 1838, the leading geologist and King's
College professor Charles Lyell told Darwin, also just
back from a long voyage, that Britain was a country
where 'a most exaggerated importance is attached to the
faculty of thinking on your legs, and where, as Dan
O'Connell well knows, nothing is to be got in the way of
homage or influence, or even a fair share of power, without agitation'. In fact, scientific reform helped define the
meaning of political agitation and the metropolitan constituencies for change.[33] Herschel's *Discourse* insisted that
through scientific progress 'legislation and politics
become gradually regarded as experimental sciences'.
Babbage also tried this balancing act: quantative analysis
and precision engineering were at once above politics and
politically vital. He used the metropolitan scene to dramatise this lesson. Lyell told Darwin 'that Babbage's
parties are the best in the way of literary people in
London – and that there is a good mixture of pretty
women'. Babbage's house became a stage for the display
of London machines and London lobbying. In 1834, he
bought a remarkable dancing automaton from Weekes'
mechanical exhibition in Cockspur Street and showed it
at home in the next room to his 'difference engine'. All his
guests save two overseas visitors preferred the dancer to
the calculator. 'In that room – England. Look again at this
– two foreigners'. Babbage angrily diagnosed the endemic
metropolitan disease of hostility to, and ignorance of, the
machines and machinists on which he reckoned their
wealth relied.[34]

31 Richardson 1987; Desmond 1989, pp.132, 200-03.
32 Schweber 1985, pp.15-20, 33.
33 Darwin 1986, p.101; Morrell and Thackray 1981.
34 Schweber 1985, p.21; Darwin 1986, p.8; Babbage 1864, pp.365,
    427.

The metropolis' instrument makers inhabited a different social sphere from that of self-assured gentility and polite reform. During the eighteenth century, they were the foremost in the world. Family ties and inheritance of workshops were crucial means of acquiring skill and equipment. Firms such as those of the clockmaker Benjamin Vulliamy, based in Pall Mall, and of John Addison, the premier globe-makers in London, sold elegant devices which commanded very high prices. Vulliamy's regulators, time standards for astronomical observatories such as those supplied to the monarch's private station at Kew, had helped make London one of the world centres of celestial measurement. Addison's globes cost up to sixty guineas for a pair. His orreries, based on designs inherited from the prestigious William Jones, also advertised their maker's work for the Crown. Georgian instrument making was a respectable profession and a route to a fellowship of the Royal Society. Practitioners were regarded as legitimate producers of knowledge, as well as of mechanical artefacts. John Russell, a Royal Academician, combined accurate micrometric lunar surveys with clever engineering in a table device, his 'Selenographia', patented in 1796 to display the three different librations of the moon as it orbited the earth. Walker incorporated a large-scale version of Russell's device in his London shows.[35] Few reached the status of Troughton, a fellow of the Royal Society who, according to the *Philosophical Magazine*, 'does and always will hold that rank among makers of astronomical instruments that Sir Isaac Newton does among philosophers'. Troughton equipped most of the surveying expeditions of the period. His shop at 'The Orrery' in Fleet Street inherited a century of instrument-making expertise. His instruments defined astronomical precision – hence the vigour with which the London public followed his risible, if violent, fight with Babbage and South in 1834–39, which culminated in South's destruction, and public auction, of the equatorial which Troughton had mounted at Campden Hill Observatory.[36]

Significantly, however, South's criticism of Troughton was that his incompetence had ruined an astonishing Cauchoix refracting lens from Paris costing over £1,000. In an 1842 poster advertising the sale of the metal left from the Troughton device, South mocked this '*souvenir piquant* of the state of the Art of Astronomical Instrument Making in England during the 19th century'. London makers were losing out to French and German competitors. The intellectual status of artisan practitioners and instrument makers changed as the spaces where they plied

their trade were transformed. Their trade was no longer an easy route to the Royal Society's prestigious fellowships. Their work was not likely to appear in the august pages of the Society's *Philosophical Transactions*. They were not to be found among the Royal Institution's well-heeled clientele, though their output was on show there: Friday evening discussions featured the steam press and the best new microscopes, the telegraph and Babbage's engines. Some, like the clockmaker Edward Dent, gave well-attended lectures at the Mechanics' Institutes.[37] Their shops and workshops were gathered around the west end of the Strand, Haymarket and Regent Street. John Newman, the Royal Institution's instrument maker, was at 122 Regent Street. Edward Clarke, philosophical instrument maker and specialist in electromagnetic apparatus, had his 'Laboratory of Science' in the Lowther Arcade between the Strand and Adelaide Street. William Cary, a designer of excellent mathematical instruments and famous for his oxyhydrogen microscope, worked at 272 Strand: his microscope was used throughout the London lecturing empire, notably from 1833 at Joseph Kahn's anatomical museum. From the 1820s, Cary's nephews George and John kept his business going while designing fine globes at 86 St. James's.[38]

The kinds of instruments produced by the different makers varied considerably. John Newman made specialist apparatus on commission for Faraday, as well as off-the-shelf instruments, his chief source of income. Items such as voltaic batteries, electrical and magneto-electric machines, telescopes and globes, were widely advertised in makers' catalogues and in the popular press. Watkins and Hill, based at 5 Charing Cross, sold electrical machines with attachments for £6.16s.6d. Batteries cost between six and sixteen shillings. For the more popular market they also advertised an 'artificial spider', which moved by electrical attraction and repulsion. This cost a mere two shillings. Electrical discharge through evacuated glasses provided an appealing, and lucrative, means of illumination. Artisan instrument makers provided a vital, if largely invisible, resource for professors such as Faraday or John Frederic Daniell, the chemistry chair at King's College. The makers possessed the technical skills and experience required to guarantee that popular lecture demonstrations upon which many scientific reputations

35 King and Millburn 1978, p.314; Bennett 1985.
36 Hoskin 1989.
37 Bennett 1985; Hoskin 1989, p.199; Hays 1983, p.109.
38 Taylor 1966, pp.306, 385, 400; Hays 1983, p.106.

were based went smoothly. When the Royal Military Academy tried successfully to woo Faraday as chemistry lecturer for the cadets' science course in 1829, he explained the importance of 'possessing a perfect laboratory with an assistant in constant occupation, and of having the command of an instrument maker and his men'. In compensation for the lack of such facilities at Woolwich, he demanded and got at least £200 for the course, an income which supplemented his small regular stipend at the Royal Institution and the extra £8.15s. he got for each well-staged lecture there. When the Academy agreed to hire the instrument maker James Marsh to help him, Faraday estimated that on past experience Marsh would need to work for up to two days in preparing the experimental demonstrations for each lecture. Marsh was paid thirty shillings a week – despite his plea that he should be accorded the status of an annual salary, not a weekly wage.[39] Instrument makers employed as laboratory or lecture assistants were wage labourers not professionals.

During the 1830s, however, venues were developed where instrument makers could appear before the public as men of science. When the National Gallery of Practical Science in Adelaide Street opened in June 1832, it was hailed in the press as a great advance for the mechanical arts. Its aim was to exhibit the latest developments in machines and scientific instruments to the paying public.[40] Its greatest attraction was Perkins' steam gun, advertised as firing seventy rounds in four seconds. It also featured the magneto-electric machine invented by the American instrument maker Joseph Saxton, then living in London. The Adelaide Street gallery also featured scientific lectures, on chemistry by William Maugham and on electricity by William Sturgeon. Sturgeon had been a private in the Royal Artillery until 1820, then a bootmaker in Woolwich. In 1824 he became science lecturer at the East India Company's Royal Military College at Addiscombe. The next year he came to public attention as an instrument maker after his improved electromagnetic apparatus won the Society of Arts' silver medal, and thirty guineas. Sturgeon made his living by instrument making and popular lectures. Clarke's 'Laboratory of Science', round the corner at the Lowther Arcade, provided him with another venue. By the late 1830s the Adelaide faced competition from the Royal Polytechnic Institution on Regent Street, famous for its diving bell, where Georg Bachhoffner lectured on chemistry and natural philosophy. The Coliseum in Regent's Park also opened a Department of Natural Magic, featuring London's biggest electrical machine under the direction of William Leithead, formerly an operative chemist based in Compton Street, off Brunswick Street.

The existence of such venues fostered the development of a popular culture of electricity which was soon institutionalised by the foundation of the London Electrical Society in 1837. The Society's active members were artisans, makers and popular lecturers such as Sturgeon, Leithead, Henry Noad and Charles Vincent Walker. More elite members of the London scientific community, such as Faraday or Daniell, never joined.[41] The natural philosophy disseminated by members of the Society was also very different from that of the Royal Institution. For them, experiment was the province of the skilled mechanic whose understanding of the workings of machinery allowed him to master the workings of the universe. Electricity was the all-embracing force which powered the cosmos. According to one member, the Somerset gentleman Andrew Crosse, expert in the production of insects from electrified Vesuvian rock, electricity was 'the right arm of God'. Conveying to their audiences a detailed understanding of the working of their apparatus was part and parcel of their task of disseminating knowledge. Spectacular displays of sparks and shocks were more than just rational entertainment. When Sturgeon submitted his electromagnetic apparatus to the Society of Arts, one of the virtues he claimed for it was that it let the audience see exactly what was going on in the equipment and how it worked. But at the Royal Institution, experimental apparatus was regarded as a means to an end. Faraday did not see his job as teaching his audience about the instrumentation. His audience wanted a gentlemanly, not a mechanic, understanding of the production of natural phenomena.

This mechanics' culture was transient. By 1845, the Adelaide Street gallery had been converted into a casino. The London Electrical Society had been disbanded. When the American Joseph Henry visited London and Paris in 1837 to buy instruments most of his purchases were French.[42] The London makers' market dominance was over. However, 1837 also saw the first British patent for an electromagnetic telegraph, by the King's College professor, Charles Wheatstone, and his pugnacious partner, William Fothergill Cooke. Interactions with Paddington railway engineers and Clerkenwell instrument makers were crucial for their project. Many of the techniques and instruments which made the telegraph possible had been developed by London makers and artisan experimenters

39   Faraday 1971, p.176; Faraday 1991, p.502.
40   Altick 1978, pp.377-89.
41   Morus 1992.
42   Gee 1990.

such as Sturgeon, inventor of the first electromagnet, and Clarke, one of the first enthusiastically to approve Cooke's design. As Chartist protest grew, Cooke canvassed his device as a means by which the government could transmit its orders: 'all dangerous excitement of the public might be avoided'. This short-lived culture of artisan experiment and display helped spawn one of the British empire's most potent instruments of long-range control.[43]

CONCLUSION: THE LABORATORY AND THE CITY

In the face of protest and turmoil, control and authority were difficult to maintain. The wider political culture could inform the most technical disputes. London was central to the making of science because it provided a flashpoint for controversy. Beneath the calm tone of quarto scientific transactions, issued under the imprint of respectable publishers like William Nicol and John Murray, were fears of competing approaches to knowledge from other sources and other presses. Were the last days approaching, as the fiery preacher Edward Irving claimed, and should physical truth come from literal words of the Bible? Should science be an instrument of state power, under the control of trained professionals? Or – as the pauper press proclaimed – should it be used as an instrument of popular emancipation and democratic reform? In the wake of the reaction to the French Revolution and the rise of an expanded reading public, the boundaries of knowledge were being redrawn, with constant battles over the definition and limits of the bounds of 'science'. Who was to have control over the making of natural knowledge and what was knowledge for?

The visitor to London could find one answer by listening to Davy at the Royal Institution. He viewed cultivation of chemistry and natural philosophy as the proper object of the 'sons of genius', intellects elevated above the mass audience. Work of this kind led to true faith, away from politics. In this way, Davy wrote, 'perceiving in all the phenomena of the universe the designs of a perfect intelligence', the man of science 'will be averse to the turbulence and passion of hasty innovations, and will uniformly appear as the friend of tranquility and order'. The advantages of science were most striking of all in the metropolis. Chemistry could offer 'men collected in great cities' an escape from the artificial complexities of urban life. At least one of Davy's more attentive contemporary

readers, Mary Shelley, drew the appropriate lesson from his lectures, and, in response, invented the lonely figure of Victor Frankenstein in her best-selling fantasy of 1818. *Frankenstein* displayed the costs of isolation and scientific power; Davy celebrated their virtues. The laboratory was a place of withdrawal and solitude, in the city but not belonging to it.[44]

A very different view could be obtained from Richard Carlile, a leader in the fight for removing restrictions on the press and imprisoned for six years for selling works that used Enlightenment natural philosophy to attack 'priestcraft' and 'kingcraft'.[45] He composed his manifesto from Dorchester Gaol in 1821, *An Address to Men of Science*:

> Then come forward, ye Men of Science, it is reserved for you to give the death blow, or the last blow to superstition and idolatry. Now is the time – you are safe even from momentary persecution, if you stand forward numerously and boldly. You will have a people, an all mighty people, with you, a circumstance which no philosopher could ever heretofore calculate upon. You have nothing to fear, and nothing to lose, but every thing to gain, even that which is most dear to you, the kind reception of your institutions, the adoption of your principles, founded in truth and the nature of things.[46]

Carlile had Davy in mind when he penned his shilling prison tract, although (not surprisingly) the 'revolutionary' chemist ignored it. Carlile defined 'science' by reference to materialist cosmologies from the previous century, works like Baron d'Holbach's *System of Nature*, Thomas Paine's *Age of Reason* and Elihu Palmer's *Principles of Nature*. Original discovery, the core of Davy's heroic vocation, had little place in the radical vision of the use of science. In fact, Carlile had never witnessed an experiment and had probably never been in a laboratory. But from inside gaol in 1823 he was able to organise the pirating and distribution of an edition of the London hospital surgeon William Lawrence's materialist *Lectures on Comparative Anatomy*. Carlile helped make esoteric, if controversial, talks to the College of Surgeons into widely available political subversion. His sponsorship of the Rotunda lectures from 1830 was but another example of

---

43 Hubbard 1965, pp.31-36; Morus 1991.
44 Davy 1802, pp.25-28; Lawrence 1990; Golinski 1990; Mellor 1987.
45 Hollis 1970.
46 Carlile 1972, p.108.

his marketing of radical science. From his perspective, if the Laboratory at the Royal Institution had any purpose, it would have been a centre for political action. His *Address* severely condemned those who believed that 'the Man of Science had much better pursue his studies and experiments in silence and private'.[47] The laboratory, like the printing shop with its presses and pamphlets, should be an organ for communication and a place for mobilising the people to revolution. Science was politics and belonged in the city.

47 Carlile 1972, pp.95, 111; Desmond 1987; Goodfield 1969, pp.307-08.

'ATHENS RISING NEAR THE POLE': LONDON, ATHENS AND THE IDEA OF FREEDOM

Ian Jenkins

H.W. and W. Inwood, St. Pancras Church, Caryatid Porch

Around 1820 the Greek Revival in art and architecture reached its peak. The piles of Grecian masonry raised up in St. Pancras and Bloomsbury alone leave us in no doubt that Greek had become the dominant style of the day: H.W. Inwood's remarkable pastiche of the Erechtheum rose between 1819 and 1822; Robert Smirke's new British Museum was begun in 1823, and University College was built to a design by William Wilkins and J.P. Gandy-Deering around 1827–28.[1] Further afield we might mention Decimus Burton's Gate at Hyde Park Corner (1825) and his Athenaeum Club (1827–30), both of which carry friezes adapted from that of the Parthenon by the sculptor and modeller John Henning.[2] The newly designed British Museum had recently amassed such a body of original Greek sculpture as had not been seen since the fall of Constantinople. The Parthenon sculptures, long admired from a distance by travellers who saw them still on the building, were brought down to earth by Lord Elgin's agents at the beginning of the nineteenth century and purchased for the museum in 1816.[3] They were there installed in a temporary apartment shared with another important set of Greek sculpture, the frieze from the temple of Apollo Epicurius at Bassae, said by Pausanias to have been designed by Ictinus, one of the architects of the Parthenon. This frieze had been unearthed by some of the same travellers, including the British architect Charles Cockerell, who had also recovered the pedimental sculpture of the late-archaic temple of Aphaia on the island of Aegina. Owing to a bungling of the British attempt to purchase them, the Aegina marbles went to Bavaria where they would become the centrepiece of Ludwig I's Glyptothek at Munich designed by Leo von Klenze and completed in 1830. It was better so, lest through *hubris* England should provoke the avenging spirit of those same gods whose protection she now sought as the *genius* of

1 Crook 1972, p.98.
2 Malden 1977, *passim*.
3 Rothenberg 1977, *passim*.

her endeavours to establish Arcadia in Albion.[4] Already the poet Byron had attempted to set the Curse of Minerva on Elgin's tail.

The arrival of the Elgin Marbles in Britain and the publicity surrounding them caused a stir. From 1807 the collection went on show in a makeshift museum in Park Lane. Here for all to see in the very heart of London was the living link with the lost art of the Greeks. Ancient authority assigned the major public works of Pericles' building programme to the supervision of Pheidias, and these were sculptures, if not from his own hand, then from his workshop. What immediately struck all those who saw the Parthenon sculptures for the first time was their likeness to nature. The painter Benjamin Robert Haydon took this as cause to abandon the 'false beau-ideal' of traditional art theory based upon the repertoire of Greco-Roman models, such as the Laocoon, the Venus de' Medici and the Apollo Belvedere. He hailed the Elgin Marbles as marking the commencement of real art, taking its inspiration from the twin exemplars of the Parthenon sculptures and Nature. In so doing he flew full in the face of the academic tradition of Joshua Reynolds and the Royal Academy, which placed ideal above actual form. Another critic who saw here an opportunity for promoting the professed beauty of particular as against generalised nature was William Hazlitt, essayist and biographer of Bonaparte, who described the Elgin Marbles as 'the best answer to Sir Joshua Reynolds' discourses'.[5]

Far from being overthrown by the Elgin Marbles, as Haydon had hoped, the Establishment received new life from their arrival and, with some necessary adjustment, ensured its own survival by attaching itself to these new gods. Official acknowledgment of the supremacy of the Elgin Marbles, however, was largely an academic affair, since for practical art-training the Academy professors continued to insist upon young artists drawing from plaster casts of the old canon, or from the Greco-Roman Townley Marbles at the British Museum.[6] Haydon, in professing a revolution in taste, had overacted his part appallingly, but, for all that, his drawings are one of only two genuinely inspired artistic responses to the Marbles, the other being the poet Keats' *Ode on a Grecian Urn*, which captures so movingly the timeless melancholy of the Parthenon Frieze.[7]

Elgin was by no means the first to 'transport old Greece into England', for such, according to Henry Peacham, had been Lord Arundel's intent in the seventeenth century when he commissioned Sir Thomas Roe, a forerunner of Elgin in office at the Sublime Porte, to gather antiquities for him along the coast of Asia Minor.[8] The posthumous dispersal of Arundel's and other seven-teenth-century collections meant that the endeavour fell into abeyance. In the eighteenth century private collections of antiquities were amassed mainly in Rome and, although from around 1750, there was a revival of interest in Greece, it was not until the beginning of the nineteenth century that the opportunity arose for large-scale acquisitions. The Napoleonic Wars provided the occasion, while the supremacy of British diplomacy, combined with the strength of the Mediterranean fleet, afforded the means for enlarging the collections of the British Museum: Napoleon's invasion of Egypt was an assault on the stability of the Ottoman empire and Lord Elgin's embassy to Constantinople coincided with Britain's military role as the saviour of the Sultan's north African dominions. The firman authorising the removal of sculpture from the Athenian Acropolis reached Elgin only weeks after the capitulation of French forces in Egypt.[9]

Although the British Museum had been founded in 1753, by the end of the century the antiquities collection was still neither numerous nor very important. The purchase of Sir William Hamilton's first collection of vases and other antiquities had certainly added some lustre, but at a time when classical sculpture was valued above all, the museum had as yet very little. The first fruits of victory over the French were not Greek, however, but ancient Egyptian antiquities, the proceeds of Napoleon's abortive Egyptian campaign. These, including the now famous Rosetta stone, reached England in 1802. Their acquisition prompted the museum to take urgent measures to alleviate what had long been a serious want of adequate accommodation in the old mansion of Montagu House that then housed the national collection. The architect George Saunders was instructed accordingly to draw up plans for a new gallery, which was to be tacked on to the old building, providing space for the Egyptian sculptures on the ground floor and room for Hamilton's vases in the upper storey. A hurried revision of these plans was soon necessitated, however, by the opportunity occasioned by the death of the celebrated eighteenth-century antiquary Charles Townley, to acquire his collection of Roman sculptures. These were mostly imported from Rome in

4 Stoneman 1987, pp.179 ff; Potts 1980, pp.258-83.
5 Liscombe 1976, pp.34-39; Cummings 1963, pp.367-80; Cummings 1964, pp.323-28; Rothenberg 1977, pp.230-53; Postle 1991, pp.23-24.
6 Jenkins 1992, chapter two: 'The Museum as a Drawing School'.
7 Ashmole 1964, p.44.
8 Michaelis 1882, pp.6-27; Howarth 1986, *passim*; Stoneman 1987, pp.42-50.
9 St. Clair 1983, p.88.

G. Scharf, *The Townley Gallery . . .* (left) *and partially completed Western Wing of Smirke's new British Museum* (right), watercolour, 1828. The British Museum.

the latter part of the eighteenth century. The eventual building was opened to the public in 1808 and became known as the Townley Gallery; it was later demolished to make room for Robert Smirke's new museum.[10]

Townley's house-museum at Park Street, Westminster was one of a number that grew up in London around

1800. His collection of marbles was rivalled by that of the Marquess of Lansdowne, purchased in Italy to adorn his newly built house in Berkeley Square.[11] Other house-museums included the architect Sir John Soane's eclectic fantasy at Lincoln's Inn Fields where, as in the Townley ménage, visitors were admitted by appointment. The Sir John Soane Museum is happily preserved to this day by the mandate of his will (he died in 1837).[12] The financier Thomas Hope issued tickets at the beginning of 1804 for admission to his Duchess Street mansion.[13] This was no less eclectic than Soane's, with Egyptian and oriental elements, but it is best remembered as an epitome of the Greek Revival he made so much his own. Among his imitators was the banker and poet Samuel Rogers, who laid out his house in Thomas Hope style at St. James's Place, overlooking Green Park.[14]

A prominent feature of these collections was Greek vases; Byron describes Hope in *The Curse of Minerva* as a 'victim sad of vase-collecting spleen'. Sir William

The First Vase Room, Duchess Street, engraving from T. Hope, *Household Furniture and Interior Decoration*, 1807

10 Cook 1977, *passim*.
11 Michaelis 1882, pp.435 ff.
12 Feinberg Millenson 1987, *passim*.
13 Watkin 1968, p.96.
14 Clayden 1887, pp.448-49.

Hamilton had done much to promote vases and the recognition of their Greek origin: because they had been found in large quantity in Italy, they were thought to be Etruscan.[15] The taste for vases reached its peak in the first two decades of the nineteenth century when a number of private collections were built up and exchanged hands in a flurry of London sales. In 1801 Thomas Hope bought Hamilton's second collection of vases, and sold off or gave away those he did not wish to keep. Some were acquired by the artist Henry Tresham who, in turn, sold a number on to Samuel Rogers. Tresham had also acquired vases in Italy during his sojourn in Rome in the company of John Campbell, later first Baron Cawdor. He too

brought vases back with him, among them the so-called Cawdor Vase. This handsome south-Italian volute-krater was purchased at the Cawdor sale by John Soane.[16]

Soane, like Hope, arranged his vases in arched niches or columbaria signifying the original context of such vessels which, since they were found in tombs, was thought to be funerary and religious. There is no more telling a document of the eschatological and sacred, even mystical, function attributed to Greek vases than Adam Buck's re-

15 Vickers 1987, *passim*.
16 Jenkins 1988, pp.452-55.

markable portrait of himself and his family.[17] Executed in 1813, it shows a fashionable Regency group arranged as a frieze against a background of columbarium niches set with vases. In analysing the subject matter of the painted vases we find, from left to right, Herakles resting in the paradise garden of the Hesperides; the release of Orestes from the wrath of the Furies; a scene of bacchic revelry; the apotheosis of Homer; and, finally, Triptolemos entrusted during his life with Demeter's life-giving grain and, after his death, judge of the dead. 'Vases', wrote Thomas Hope, 'relate chiefly to Bacchanalian rites . . . connected with the representations of mystic death and regeneration'.[18] There is a subtle symbolism in Buck's family portrait, the meaning of which is to be found in the terminal figure of the deceased child linking the lively scene of the foreground to the sombre setting behind. It is, moreover, curious to note that this Irish-born Catholic appears to have taken the mother and child and, indeed, something of the overall composition, from Poussin's *Divine Family*.

The vogue for vases reached its peak at a time when British collectors were prevented by Napoleon's occupation of Europe from collecting in Italy; the competition in the salerooms at home, therefore, was all the more intense. Nor was the growth of the classical collections at the British Museum unrelated to events abroad: in 1802 the Peace of Amiens brought a brief respite in Anglo-French hostilities, and a number of British visitors took this opportuniy to cross the Channel and see for themselves the great works of classical sculpture plundered from Italy by Napoleon and displayed in the Louvre.[19] There in the Galérie des Antiquités was the Laocoon, the Venus de' Medici and the Apollo Belvedere. Townley's marbles were not in the same class as these, but their purchase for the British Museum in 1805 went some way towards making up an obvious deficiency. The French were, moreover, soon to be deprived of their trophies: when in 1815 the Battle of Waterloo finally defeated Napoleon, Lord Elgin's former secretary W.R. Hamilton was put to work assisting in the dismantlement of the Louvre and the restitution of its artworks.[20]

In 1816 the Italian marbles reached Rome and in that same year a parliamentary enquiry recommended the acquisition of Lord Elgin's Marbles for the nation. Under her conquering tyrant, Napoleonic France had declared itself the new Rome; now with the Elgin Marbles in London, England – the saviour of Europe – likened herself to freedom-loving Athens after the Persian Wars. The parallel is made explicit in a remarkable passage in the published findings of the Select Committee who sat to determine the fate of the Elgin Marbles.

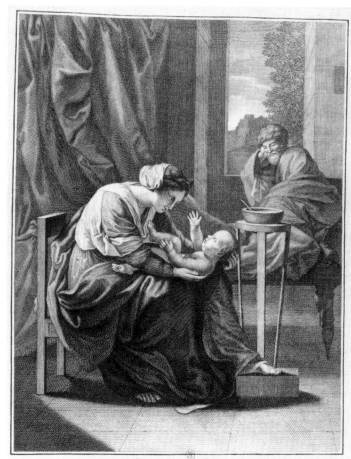

La Sainte Famille.

DÉDIÉ À MONSIEUR LE COMTE DE CAYLUS

Gravée d'après le tableau original de Nicolas Poussin de 25 pouces de haut sur 20. pouces 6 lignes de large qui est au Cabinet de S.E. M. Le Bailly De Breteuil Ambassadeur De Malte à Rome.

C. Faucci after N. Poussin, *The Divine Family*, Bibliothèque Nationale, Paris

In contemplating the importance and splendour to which so small a republic as Athens rose, by the genius and energy of her citizens . . . it is impossible to overlook how transient the memory and fame of extended empires and of mighty conquerors are, in comparison of those who have rendered inconsiderable States eminent, and who have immortalized their own names by these pursuits. But if it be true, as we learn from history and experience, that free governments afford a soil most suitable to the production of native talent . . . no

17 Ibid., pp.448-51.
18 Hope 1807, p.23.
19 Larrabee 1943, pp.257 ff.
20 Smith 1916, pp.331-32; Haskell and Penny 1981, p.115.

B. Pistrucci, The Waterloo Medal, 1819-47. British Museum, Coins and Medals

country can be better adapted than our own to offer an honourable asylum to these monuments of the school of Phidias . . .[21]

The Elgin Marbles were not a trophy of conquest but what a contributor to the popular *Gentleman's Magazine* described as a 'Triumph of Excellence'.[22] An eloquent expression of the manner in which the Elgin Marbles were seen to commemorate the Battle of Waterloo can be found in a comparison of two medals designed by Benedetto Pistrucci, one modelled between 1817 and 1820, the other around 1819.[23] Waterloo was Britain's Battle of Marathon and, like ancient Athens, London needed a Periclean-style programme of artistic and architectural regeneration to commemorate both the victory and the new age of greatness it was supposed to have engendered. The poet William Wordsworth's *Thanksgiving Ode* of 1816 holds up a Grecian mirror to contemporary events:

Victorious England! bid the silent Art
Reflect, in glowing hues that shall not fade,
Those high achievements; even as she arrayed
With second life the deed of Marathon
Upon Athenians walls;
So may she labour for thy civic halls:
And be the guardian spaces
Of consecrated places
As nobly graced by Sculpture's patient toil;
And let imperishable Columns rise
Fixed in the depths of this courageous soil;
Expressive signals of a glorious strife,
And competent to shed a spark divine
Into the torpid breast of daily life.

This is not the poet at his best, but the verse highlights a notion, at the heart of Hellenist sensibility, that freedom and the arts rise and fall together. Winckelmann, by far the most influential Hellenist of the later eighteenth century, had attributed the greatness of Greek art to the liberty of the Greek people, by which he had principally in mind the democracy-loving Athenians.[24] Earlier in the century we find Alexander Pope expressing the hope that Britain might take over from ancient Athens the guardianship of liberty and the arts:[25]

When Athens sinks by fates unjust,
When wild barbarians spurn her dust;
Perhaps even Britain's utmost shore
Shall cease to blush with strangers' gore
See arts her savage sons control,
And Athens rising near the pole!

Pope gives voice to two related themes: the one we have already touched upon, namely the idea of Britain and, ultimately, London as the new Athens; the other concerns the plight of Athens itself and the Greek people conquered by the Ottomans. In Pope's day Philhellenism, the love of modern Greece and its people – as distinct

21 *Parliamentary Papers: Report from the Select Committee on the Earl of Elgin's Collection* etc. 1816, pp.26-27.
22 *Gentleman's Magazine*, vol. 86, 1816, p.39.
23 Pirzio Biroli Stefanelli 1989, vol. 1, pp.92-100, cat. nos 30-41, pls. 17-18, vol. 2, pls. 30-39; Vermeule 1964, pp.150-52, pls. 126-27.
24 Podro 1982, p.8. Howard 1990, pp.172-73.
25 Alexander Pope, 'Two Choruses to the Tragedy of Brutus: Chorus of the Athenians', strophe 2.

B. Pistrucci,
Model for
an Elgin
Marbles
Medal,
1817-20
Museo delle
Zecca,
Rome

from Hellenism, a reverence for ancient Greece – had hardly been conceived. In London around 1820, however, the idea of independence for a modern Greek state became one of the great issues of the age. The radical movement of Philhellenism lay rooted in the pre-existing tradition of enlightened Hellenism.

At the height of the Italian Renaissance, when scholars were reviving the classical tradition that brought western Europe into renewed contact with the genius of ancient Greece, contemporary or 'modern' Greece had been allowed to fall into Asiatic oblivion. As a remnant of the old Byzantine empire, she had long ceased to be identified with the classical land; if antiquarian minds gave the matter any thought at all, it was to explain this event as the inevitable revenge of the Turks for the loss of Troy to the ancient Greeks; by this reasoning *Turks* were supposed descendants of the ancient Trojans, or *Teucri*, as the Latin poets had called them.[26] Besides, the Italian Renaissance focussed naturally upon the culture of its Roman ancestors: Ovid and Vergil were more obvious classical sources than Homer and Aeschylus. Through the accounts of Latin authors such as Pliny and Cicero, scholars were certainly aware of Roman admiration for Greek art; the immediate inspiration, however, for Renaissance classicism was not ancient Greece but old Rome.

Latin was the language of the Roman Church, while Greek represented the outlandish liturgy of eastern Orthodoxy. The old Byzantine heresy alienated modern Greeks still further from the sympathies of western Europe. Indeed, in Shakespeare's day the term Greek was a byword for a 'voluptuary' and, according to the travel literature of the day, Greeks were wanton, frivolous, drunken and deceitful.[27] There were, however, a few who in their admiration for ancient Greece came close to expressing what might be considered Philhellene sentiments. Fynes Moryson spent the years 1591–97 travelling through Europe, with a grant from Peterhouse College, Cambridge and his journal sows an early seed of pro-Greek feeling:

> The Empire and kingdom of the Greeks from all antiquity famous (and continuing of great power till the Turks invaded Europe and took Constantinople), from that time have been utterly abolished, and the people have been trodden underfeet. Of them some live as in exile (at Naples, in Apulia, in Calabria, at Rome, and in the City of Venice) having neither land nor coin of their own.[28]

Moryson equates the 'modern' Greek, living in exile, with the ancient inhabitants of Greece and wipes out at a stroke the Byzantine interval. This was typical of later Hellenism which found the Christian era of Greece's history distasteful.

Athenocentricity was to be another feature of Hellenist writing. The fame of Athens had been handed down through the testimony of the Roman authors. The infatuation of Rome with Greece is treated as a love affair in the poetry of Propertius, the pain of which will not subside until the longing has been sated:

26   Spencer 1974, pp.9-12.
27   Ibid., p.40.
28   Ibid., p.61.

To break this hard passion
I must make the great journey
Take the long road
To erudite Athens.[29]

Ancient Athens was to Rome what, in the eighteenth century, Rome became for the cultured elite of the European Grand Tour. The sons of noble Romans, like Hellenistic princes before them, were sent to university in Athens. One emperor after another courted the city, endowing her with monuments, while Cicero had exercised his eloquence in praise of the famous walks outside the city walls. We hear an unmistakable echo of this in one of the greatest of all the praise-hymns of ancient Athens, a much quoted passage of Milton's *Paradise Regained*:

> Behold
> Where on the Aegean shore a city stands
> Built nobly, pure the air and light the soil,
> Athens, the eye of Greece, Mother of Arts
> And Eloquence, native to famous wits
> Or hospitable, in her sweet recess,
> City or Suburban, studious walks and shades . . .[30]

Milton was another proto-Hellenist whose regard for ancient Greece, coupled with his own republican sympathies, inclined him to advocate the freedom of its modern inhabitants. In his day British merchants expanding their interest through the Levant Trading Company greatly increased the number of reports of Greek manners and customs. Curiosity at home increased and gradually fostered a sympathetic image of modern Greece as a picturesque Arcadian landscape peopled by exotic figures in ornamental costume, dwelling among the ruins of their ancestors. Ruins real or imaginary became the vogue: antiquities and British love for them, in particular, would act as a vehicle for promoting Hellenist sentiment.

Here, then, we have something of the prelude to the great Greek Revival that occurred in Europe from around 1750 and reached its zenith in London around 1820. During that period the attention of cultivated Europe was increasingly focussed upon the beauty of the modern Greek landscape; but what of its people? As reverence for the glorious past increased, so the modern Greek seemed in the eyes of many Hellenists to have degenerated all the more from the noble race of his ancestors. Let Edward Gibbon's summing up of modern Athens in the forty-second chapter of his *Decline and Fall of the Roman Empire* stand *pars pro toto*.

The Athenians are still distinguished by the subtlety and acuteness of their understandings; but these qualities, unless ennobled by freedom and enlightened by study, will degenerate into a low and selfish cunning . . . The Athenians walk with supine indifference among the glorious ruins of antiquity; and such is the debasement of their character that they are incapable of admiring the genius of their predecessors.[31]

In spite of a disconcerting obloquy heaped upon the modern Greeks, there is a practical message of hope here that was to have far-reaching consequences. Winckelmann, with the democracy-loving Athenians in mind, had attributed the greatness of the ancient Greeks to their political freedom. It was this that set them apart from other ancient peoples, who lived under the rule of a tyrant. Freedom, therefore, was the necessary prerequisite for the elevation of the Greek spirit: remove the Turkish yoke and the modern Greek's intrinsic intelligence would flower into a human condition worthy of his ancestry. This idea of freedom attributed to the ancient Greeks took on a new immediacy in the minds of supporters of political and social reform in the heady years following the French Revolution. That event, with its cry of *liberté* and remarkable declaration of human rights, had promoted the idea of political freedom everywhere to an unprecedented degree. Radical causes abounded in the early decades of the nineteenth century and the campaign for Greek independence became a *cause célèbre* for progressive Hellenists.[32] Napoleon's occupation of Europe had prevented British travellers from visiting the traditional haunts of the Grand Tour; the determined went instead to Greece with a consequent increase in the number of reports on the prospect of a free Greece. Speculation on the likeness or otherwise of the modern to the ancient Greek and an opinion upon his fitness for self-rule became a set piece in travel literature of the day. F.S.N. Douglas travelled in Greece for two years between 1810 and 1812, and in 1813 published *An Essay on Certain Points of Resemblance between the Ancient and Modern Greeks*.[33]

In it he concluded that although the moderns were an altogether disappointing relic of the ancient Greeks, there were nonetheless vestiges of the ancient Greek temper. In short, like the ruins of the Greek landscape, the people were treated as a monument broken and misshapen, yet still suggestive of a former grandeur. Douglas considered

---

29 Propertius III. 21, translated by J.P. McCulloch, quoted by Stoneman 1984, p.124.
30 John Milton, *Paradise Regained*, Book IV. pp.237-43.
31 Gibbon 1898, vol. 6, chapter 62, p.486.
32 Woodhouse 1971, *passim*.
33 Spencer 1974, pp.242-46.

the Greeks not yet ready for liberty but urged they be led further along the path of enlightenment through education.

Douglas's cousin Frederic North was less begrudging. He was the third son of the second Earl of Guilford and would himself later accede to the earldom. In 1788 at the age of twenty-one he arrived in the Ionian islands and went wholeheartedly native.[34] He learned modern Greek, affected ancient Greek dress and had himself baptised into the Orthodox religion. More importantly he recognised the importance of championing education in Greece and began to give money to a school in Preveza on the mainland opposite Corfu. His family became alarmed and called him home. Guilford returned to Corfu, however, when in 1815 at the end of the Napoleonic Wars the Ionian islands became a British protectorate and Corfu was chosen for the seat of the newly appointed High Commissioner, Sir Thomas Maitland. The latter was firmly opposed to any suggestion of Greek independence, but Guilford succeeded, in spite of official censure, in founding and financing from his own pocket a university on Corfu. Guilford is remembered fondly today as one of the most devoted of the Philhellenes. No one, however, can eclipse the fame of the greatest of them all.

Lord Byron departed on his Greek adventure from Falmouth on 2 July 1809. He had already established his notorious reputation for being, in the words of Lady Caroline Lamb, 'mad, bad and dangerous to know'. Socially he was an outsider, politically a radical. His political friends were reformists and the disciples of Jeremy Bentham. He appears to have made only three speeches in the House of Lords, all in support of liberal causes. Byron's travelling companion was another conscientious radical, John Cam Hobhouse. Touching at Lisbon, Cadiz, Gibraltar and Malta, the two friends finally landed at Preveza and from there travelled to Patras and so on to Athens. Byron, being contemptuous of Elgin's 'Pheidian freaks', did not share his companion's fascination for ruins; his libertine temperament found other distraction in the beauty of the famed 'Maid of Athens'. Like Frederic North he took the trouble to learn modern Greek and, in order to demonstrate to his fellow countrymen that the Muses had not forsaken Greece, he translated modern Greek poets into English. Byron gave his life to the Greek cause for independence, dying from a fever at Missolonghi on the shores of western Greece at Easter 1824. More importantly, through the genius of his poetry he had raised the status of modern Greeks in the eyes of western Europeans, and his lasting gift to Greece was his eloquence in support of the call for independence. *Childe Harold*, Byron's semi-autobiographical account of his travels, went into at least twelve editions between 1812 and 1821 and was read in several European languages. Byron was a true Philhellene, genuinely fond of the living Greece, and he made the cause of Greek independence famous as it had never been before. There was something about the country and its inhabitants that appealed to his poetic instinct and the place became his spiritual home. Byron's call for the freedom of modern Greece served as a rallying cry for other Philhellenes who would take up arms and fight against the Turk.

Percy Bysshe Shelley, who died in 1822, did not have first-hand experience of Greece but found the cause was conducive to the revolutionary politics he poured out in a stream of vitriol in *The Mask of Anarchy* of 1819. This was followed in 1820 by the *Ode to Liberty*, composed in the year before the revolution broke out:

> . . . Athens diviner yet
> Gleamed with its crest of columns, on the will
> Of man as on a mount of diamond set;
> For thou [Liberty] wert, and thine all creative skill
> Peopled, with forms that mock the eternal dead
> In marble immortality, that hill
> Which was thine earliest throne and latest oracle.

In the autumn of 1821 Shelley composed *Hellas*, his great hymn to Greek independence, which he viewed 'as a portion of the cause of civilization and social improvement'. Athens' ancient fame is resung, and the final chorus expresses the hope of a resurrection no longer remote:

> 'Let there be light!' said Liberty;
> And, like sunrise from the sea,
> Athens arose! . . .

Another voice that had begun to make itself heard as part of the growing clamour for Greek independence was that of educated and often wealthy Greeks living outside Greece. It was they who first developed a nationalist movement for the establishment of a Greek state in Europe. In 1814 a group of them living mainly in Russia formed a secret society with the aim of promoting a revolution in the Ottoman empire.[35] Their society became part of a general conspiracy that spread throughout Europe. The expatriate Greeks adopted Western notions of Hellas and promoted the archaising of their culture. They urged the purification of the Romaic form of Greek and a return to the classical language. They sent money

---

34 Woodhouse 1971, p.19.
35 Finlay 1971, pp.96-99.

and books to Greece in order to advance the kind of education they considered appropriate for the would-be sons of ancient heroes. It became customary for boys to be given names of distinguished ancient Greeks in place of the usual names of the saints.[36] The uprising itself when it came was a confused and somewhat unedifying affair, and the catalogue of atrocity and counter-atrocity need not detain us here. Nor can we reiterate the somewhat depressing narrative of the events by which, often more by accident than design, Greece fumbled its way to independence. More important for our theme is the impact these events abroad had on Hellenist sympathies in Britain.

In March 1823 a group calling itself the London Greek Committee issued a paper signed by John Bowring listing the names of some twenty-six founding members, whose company had grown to eighty-five by the end of the year. Among them were nearly forty M.P.s, mostly Whigs and radicals, who had joined with an assortment of 'lawyers and parliamentarians, poets and antiquarians, merchants and reformers, Scots and Irish and other vicarious nationalists'.[37] They provided financial support for the Greek cause through a loan negotiated by Bowring in the City of London. This was one of the grander follies of Hellenomania, since what was presented to the investors as a loan turned out in reality to be no more than a gift, prompting George Finlay, the Philhellene historian of modern Greece, to sardonic reflection upon how 'Homer, Plato and Co. became creditors for a large capital and an enormous accumulation of unpaid interest'.[38] For most members of the London Greek Committee, however, the motive was not commerce but politics. In an age of progressive reform the struggle for Greek independence was seen as one more radical cause in a growing catalogue of such movements as that for the freedom of the press, the campaign against the exploitation of children, opposition to the slave trade and Catholic emancipation. The London Committee were not Philhellenes; they did not see their role as a passionate and self-sacrificing commitment to the Greek cause; rather, they subscribed to it as one in a number of ways of undermining the Tory establishment whose official policy was support for Turkey against the threat of Russian incursion in the Balkans. No one exemplifies this kind of abstract liberalism better than Jeremy Bentham, the presiding genius of the Committee. When he was not declaring the freedom of the Greeks, addressing them as 'My Dear Children', he was writing patronising letters to Mohammed Ali, Pasha of Egypt – whose troops were engaged against the Greek rebels – exhorting him in his own struggle for independence against the Sultan in Constantinople.[39]

Conspicuously absent from the London Committee's list of subscribers was Bentham's sympathiser, the City banker turned historian, George Grote. This progressive Hellenist bypassed the modern Greek cause to direct his offensive at the British constitution itself. He became heavily involved in the campaign for parliamentary reform, entering the newly reformed parliament in 1833, where he became a leader of the 'philosophic radicals' before his eventual disillusion with reformist politics and retreat into private life. He turned instead to completing a new history of Greece that he had begun some years before.[40] Despairing of the modern age Grote set about elevating the status of the ancient Athenian constitution to an ideal form of government, worthy as a model for right-minded Englishmen. In F.M. Turner's words: 'after the appearance of Grote's *History of Greece* Englishmen looked at the Athenians and saw in large measure the reflection of their own best selves'.[41] Grote's *History* was brought out in twelve volumes between 1846 and 1856, but he was already putting together notes for it in the 1820s, and in 1826 had published a review of William Mitford's *History of Greece*. Printed in ten volumes between 1784 and 1810 this was the standard history of the day and, moreover, essentially hostile to what Mitford regarded as the evils of republican democracy as exemplified in the Greek experience. We could not find two better examples for proof of the principle that history is written in response to the historian's own age than Mitford's, composed against the background of the French Revolution, and Grote's belonging to the years of reform.

The outcome of the Greek uprising was determined by October 1827, when at the Battle of Navarino a Turko-Egyptian Fleet was destroyed by Admiral Sir Edward Codrington and his French and Russian allies. The official British government response was to describe this as an 'untoward event', and it was to be another five years before the principal European powers recognised the freedom of Greece. French, British and German Philhellene volunteers had fought for the cause on Greek soil, and the leading military commands had been held by their nationals. And yet their governments remained aloof and refused to give official sanction to such activities. Greek independence was a radical cause fought by extremists,

36   St. Clair 1972, p.20.
37   Woodhouse 1971, pp.80-81; St. Clair 1972, pp.145-49.
38   Finlay 1971, p.328; St. Clair 1972, p.223.
39   Woodhouse 1971, pp.90-91.
40   Momigliano 1952, *passim*.
41   Turner 1981, p.213.

many of them refugees from the fight for freedom in their own country. Greece was not the only country to see rebellion at this time; in 1820 a revolution had been proclaimed in Spain in favour of a constitutional government; shortly afterwards a similar insurrection took place in Portugal. In July 1820 the Kingdom of Naples rebelled, and this uprising was followed by revolutions in Piedmont and Sicily. 'I have grown old in the search for freedom', one veteran of Napoleon's armies is reported to have said to his Philhellene comrade as they joined the Greek revolution.[42]

Many who first heeded the rallying call were quickly disillusioned as they succumbed to famine and disease, some even murdered by the very Greeks they had gone to defend. As in other wars, those who stayed at home had little inkling of the sufferings of the ones doing the fighting. When at last the dust began to settle over the revolution, and it became clear that free Greece would tear itself apart in civil war, if left to its own devices, a Bavarian prince assumed a throne, while the interested European powers carried on a war of intrigue. The radical movement in British politics moved on, meanwhile, to other causes, leaving traditional Hellenism to the utopian idyll of timeless Arcadia it had enjoyed before the age of reform, when Byron and his following had introduced a note of dissonance. A few Philhellenes like General Sir Richard Church and George Finlay made their home in Athens and Finlay went on to write a history of Greece ancient and modern. Although frequently critical of the Greeks he remained loyal throughout his life to the Philhellenic cause. Like Byron, he was suspicious of Hellenists and upheld the poet's censure of Elgin by becoming signatory to one of the earliest Greek demands for the return of the Elgin Marbles.[43] The arrival of the Marbles in London, however, was the culmination of a Hellenist tradition reaching back to the seventeenth century which, as we have seen, was the necessary prelude to the resurgence of a modern Greek state. Philhellenism's refusal to acknowledge the role of enlightened Hellenism, in raising European consciousness about Greece, was a child's denial of its parent.

42 Elster 1854, p.319, quoted by St. Clair 1972, p.32.
43 Jenkins 1990, p.106.

T.H. Shepherd, *Somerset House from the Strand*, pen and ink and watercolour, 1818. The Museum of London

THE LONDON ART WORLD AND ITS INSTITUTIONS

Peter Funnell

For Prince Hoare, Secretary for Foreign Correspondence at the Royal Academy, the new century promised much for the position of Britain within the international art world. Appointed in 1799, Hoare had immediately set to work according to the title of his new post. 'I forwarded several letters', he writes grandly in 1802, 'two of which had the honour of being presented to the Presidents of the respective Academies, by the hands of His Majesty's Ambassadors, Lord Minto at Vienna, and Lord St. Helens at St. Petersburg.'[1] The replies he received from the Viennese and Russian academies – including details of their respective constitutions, a history of the visual arts in Austria and lists of practising artists in St. Petersburg – were published by Hoare in 1802 in the first of four slim volumes. Over the following years, Vienna and St. Petersburg prove the mainstays in his plan for, as he says, 'a regular communication between various Academies on the subject of Art'.[2] Further letters and information from them appear in the next volume of 1803 as well as some account by Hoare of artistic affairs in London. In a year or two, Hoare predicts, he would be able to collect sufficient material in order to put together no less than 'an authentic record' of the state of the arts 'in most of the countries in Europe'.[3] Certainly, by the third volume of 1805, he has added the academies of Milan and Madrid and we are presented with accounts of their institutional activities as well as further news from Austria and Russia. Clearly, however, Hoare's enterprise was beginning to falter. It is not until four years later that his final volume appears, prefaced by the announcement that although 'no efforts have been wanting' and 'letters have been repeatedly forwarded . . . these letters either have never reached their destination or . . . have been confounded in the general mass of prohibited intercourse'.[4] The 1809 volume is thus given over entirely to events in the London art world.

Whatever its failings, the ambition of Hoare's project cannot be denied. It is an attempt to produce a survey of the international art scene during the Napoleonic period, a survey which would be published and printed by Hoare in London and which would act as a sort of cosmopolitan digest to be circulated around his network of contacts.

His activities, Hoare genuinely seems to feel, might transcend the war and provide common ground in a period of hostility.[5] But alongside this apparently pacific intent runs a strong vein of patriotism. As the progress of his scheme demonstrates, his object was not only to gather material from abroad but also to spread the word about British accomplishments. He was attempting to create a map of the international art world but, equally, he was trying to shift London from a peripheral to a central place in that world. As a contemporary journal expressed it, Hoare's efforts show that Britain 'desires to be regarded not only as a medium by which trade and commerce diffuse their benefits through the world but as a *central point* of information also in other matters, which regard intellectual cultivation'.[6] Moreover, for Hoare, and other writers at the time, the particular circumstances required for London's emergence as the cultural centre of Europe seemed propitious. Just as he believed Britain would eventually triumph in the war by virtue of its constitution, its commercial supremacy, and its supposed social cohesion, so it could also lead in the fine arts. Elsewhere in his writings of this period, Hoare finds encouragement for his ambitions in what he regards as the unusual degree of patriotism and social union occasioned by the war with France. Thus he speaks of a people who 'have so conspicuously displayed' every 'noble sentiment' in 'the present most interesting moment of our political state'.[7]

Yet however imminent Hoare felt Britain's artistic supremacy to be, however propitious the circumstances, he was equally convinced of the need for major reforms to the way the London art world was organised. A further point to his campaign of academic correspondence was, he writes in 1802, to have the effect of exciting 'competition' and 'emulation' at home. And it is not by chance, I think, that the two institutions which receive most attention in Hoare's aborted survey – the academies of Vienna and St. Petersburg – were among the largest, and most institutionally rigorous, of their time. The Viennese Academy occupied very extensive premises, while St. Petersburg combined sheer scale with a very high degree of state involvement. Its elaborate regulations, and its

1 Hoare 1802, p.vi.
2 Ibid., p.v.
3 Hoare 1804, p.v.
4 Hoare 1809, p.vi.
5 See Hoare 1804, p.vi.
6 *The Cabinet or Monthly Report of Polite Literature*, July 1807, p.294.
7 Hoare 1806, p.56.

unique combination of 'secondary school, trade school, and art academy',[8] to quote Pevsner, draw forth Hoare's warmest enthusiasm. And in introducing this material, Hoare is at pains to emphasise examples of public works proposed or carried out under the auspices of foreign governments. These vary from a public gallery of art at St. Petersburg to the more technical matter of casting a giant equestrian statue of Joseph II in Vienna.

Like most writers on the fine arts in this period, Hoare's activities were based upon a firm belief in those theoretical precepts of which, in London, the Royal Academy was the principal bearer. The *Discourses* of its founding president, Sir Joshua Reynolds, had provided a body of art theory which naturalised continental orthodoxies, orthodoxies which held history painting to be the highest form of the art within a rigid hierarchy of genres. To paint history subjects, works informed by a learned and elevated intelligence and conveying matter for moral instruction, was advanced as the height of artistic ambition and achievement. Although this essay will not examine these theoretical questions too closely, as they are discussed by Andrew Wilton, it is important to recognise the hold which these ideas had on artistic debate in early nineteenth-century Britain. For the aspiration to paint history subjects informed, and often destroyed, many artists' careers during this period and served as the mainspring for countless institutional initiatives in the London art world. Yet however forcefully these precepts were advanced, and whatever the conviction in their theoretical correctness, it was equally clear that Britain had not produced a substantial body of work in this genre. Attempts to pursue this line of art had usually ended in professional disaster. Thus James Barry, whose large and ambitious cycle of paintings decorated the Society of Arts at the Adelphi, died in 1806 in a state of wretched indigence only to head a long, and frequently cited, roll call of disappointed genius. The isolated example of success in the field – that of Reynolds' successor as president, Benjamin West – was due largely to the king's patronage. Those who were not extended this privilege were unable, realistically, to support their careers through the production of history alone and the predominant genre on view at the Academy's annual exhibitions remained portraiture. The first decade of the period is dominated by demands that some means should be found to redress the situation and, as we shall see, the call most frequently heard was that funding and encouragement was required from the state. Government was showing at least a modest interest in the arts by commissioning, through a body called the 'Committee of Taste', monumental statues. But, as Hoare and a number of other commentators argued, some more com-

prehensive intervention was required if a British school of history painting was to succeed: this truly public art form could only be supported by public funding.

To return briefly to his activities as Secretary for Foreign Correspondence, we can see how wide the gulf was between those foreign art worlds, funded and regulated by the state, and the institutional structure prevailing in London. In institutional terms, the London art world at the beginning of the nineteenth century was the Academy. Its exhibitions provided the only formal means for the display of works, and it supplied a rudimentary training from the antique and the life under the supervision of a senior member. Given his theoretical position, and his fascination with institutional protocol, it is not surprising that Hoare regarded the Academy's foundation in 1768 as an act little short of heroic importance. Thus, in an extraordinary flight of fancy, Hoare quotes from the Seventh Book of the *Aeneid*, comparing Reynolds and his colleagues to Aeneas and his persecuted followers at that moment when 'they reached the shores destined to be the seat of their future greatness'.[9] But as constituted in 1768, the Academy fell far short of that institutional rigor which Hoare finds so attractive in his continental models and which he believed necessary to fulfil its theoretical mission. Under the patronage of the king, but effectively governed by the forty, self-elected, full Academicians, the Academy retained many of the characteristics of the mid-eighteenth century artists' societies which it had supplanted. It was in effect, as Hoare observes, little more than 'a friendly professional society', 'private' and 'not in any degree connected with the great civil institutions of England'.[10] And, although Hoare never lost faith in the Academy's central place in London's artistic life, and never lowered his Olympian notions of its potential, it is equally clear that his own projects as Secretary for Foreign Correspondence were severely undercut by the Academicians. Discussions of his plan reveal, at best, a wearied tolerance of his scheme and, as it progresses, there is clearly resistance to his wider aims. They are especially alarmed, for instance, by a proposal of Hoare's to publish minutes of their proceedings: in effect to make the Academy more publicly accountable.

Given the temper of the Academy in the early years of the nineteenth century, this is hardly surprising. For in the very period when Hoare was attempting to advance his schemes the Academy underwent an unprecedented

8   Pevsner 1940, p.182.
9   Hoare 1806, p.115.
10 Ibid., pp.123-24.

degree of internal division and disruption. As Joseph Farington, one of the Academy's most influential members, vividly records in his *Diary*, between 1803 and 1805 the Academicians behaved in a manner which hardly measures up to the heroic notions Hoare entertained of the institution and its proceedings. Remarkably, although he constantly insinuated himself into the Academy's meetings, Hoare seems to have been quite blind to its true disposition at this time, nor to have seen quite how near it was, as Farington feared, to breaking up completely. Thus, after an especially stormy meeting on 24 December 1803, Farington records with some astonishment how Hoare had remarked that 'He never attended a public society where the business was conducted with so much good manners'. But as he goes on to relate, 'in private there had been the reverse', the evening witnessing an altercation between Turner and his fellow Academician Sir Francis Bourgeois which had ended with Bourgeois calling Turner '*a little reptile*, which the other replied to by calling Him *a Great Reptile* with *ill manners*.'[11] Although somewhat extreme, the incident does nevertheless illustrate the degree of antagonism in the art world during these years and the highly personalised nature in which disputes about the Academy's rules and procedures were conducted.

On the face of it, the disputes were procedural and are worth briefly recording. Thus 1803 was dominated by a lengthy confrontation concerning the respective powers of the executive committee, or council, and the general assembly of all Academicians, a confrontation which led to the temporary suspension of five members. The wrangles of this year were also compounded by accusations that the president, Benjamin West, had broken the rules by attempting to exhibit a picture of *Hagar and Ishmael* which he had previously shown in 1776. Factional antipathy towards West expressed itself again in 1804 when at the annual elections of 10 December a group – including several of those who had been expelled the previous year – attempted to unseat him and vote in the architect James Wyatt as president. West survived this attempt to depose him but in the following year was led to resign just prior to the elections, giving way – for a year at least – to Wyatt. Again, 1805 proved to be especially disputatious, factional antagonisms revolving around the decision to admit a portrait by James Northcote of the celebrated boy-actor Master Betty to the exhibition after the closing date for admissions. Such was the in-fighting in the Academy by this time, that this apparently trivial breach in the rules led to a further constitutional crisis and calls for reforms from younger members like the Irish born painter, Martin Archer Shee.

The significance of the Academy disputes should not be underestimated since they tell us much about its institutional make up and had important repercussions. They are disputes which are stamped by professional jealousies, and which perhaps could only happen in a body which was as small, and as essentially self-regulating, as the Academy. As one might expect, apart from the odd passage which was expunged, the Academy minutes of these years are as discreet as official minutes usually are. But although these battles were conducted privately, in the heated atmosphere of Somerset House, they became public knowledge through the press. Indeed, anonymous paragraphs appearing in the press served as the means whereby factions could conduct their side of these disagreements. As the *Herald* commented on 3 May 1803, 'those who cannot *paint a picture*, can at least *pen a paragraph*'.[12] And Farington himself passed several months in 1805 in a state of intense agitation as the result of one such 'paragraph' which appeared in the *Morning Post*, concerning his role in the affair of Northcote's *Master Betty*. Moreover, such public feuding, conducted over such an extended period, considerably weakened the Academy's position during the negotiations which led to the most significant development of the period, the founding of the British Institution for Promoting the Fine Arts.

During the first five years of the century attempts had already been made to establish alternative exhibition spaces to the Academy. Thus, groups of practitioners in media which were accorded a lower status by the Academy – engravers and watercolourists – formed exhibiting societies in 1802 and 1804 respectively. These societies succeeded as viable organisations, representing distinct sections of the profession, and in many ways complementing the Academy. But a body which had formed itself on a more ambitious plan, the British School, had failed after just one exhibition held in 1802 at its premises in Berners Street. The British Institution was to be another matter, and its success can be traced back to the impressive way in which the art world activated itself between March and May of 1805. Again Farington, closely involved in the negotiations, provides a detailed record of events. The original idea for the Institution was that of the philanthropist, Thomas Bernard. On 18 March a meeting was held at West's house when Bernard presented his plan to West and Farington, and the connoisseurs Sir George Beaumont, Richard Payne Knight and

---

11 Farington 1978-84, vol. 6, p.2202.
12 Royal Academy, volume of press cuttings and letters, mostly relating to 1803 disputes, RAA F3, 30.

William Smith. During the following weeks, almost daily meetings were held, Bernard's prospectus revised and redrawn, and the original group increased in membership. The latter was a process of individual communication by word of mouth or letter, until by 14 May a list could be compiled of almost thirty names, including London's leading collectors and connoisseurs and a healthy clutch of the nobility. To succeed fully, however, and to encourage yet further membership and subscription, it was essential to secure the patronage of the king. Accordingly the proposal, and list of those supporting it, was presented to him through the offices of Lord Dartmouth who was able to write to Beaumont on 27 May 1805 that the king had given his assent. There was, however, one major condition which was to alter the relationship between artists and connoisseurs, and cast a shadow over the Institution's success, in the years that followed. During the negotiations Farington had been concerned as to the king's likely opinion of the Academy's involvement in the new body and the danger of the 'peevishness & jealousies of Artists'[13] preventing the good effects of the scheme. Indeed the scheme did go ahead but only under the king's proviso 'that *Artists* should not have any concern with the management of the British Institution'.[14]

I shall return to the way in which the British Institution served to divide artists and connoisseurs shortly. But let us look at how it quickly succeeded, and the men who took the lead in its establishment and subsequent management. The Institution's principal aim, according to a prospectus full of patriotic rhetoric similar to Hoare's was to promote history painting and redress the neglect from which it suffered. Funded by subscription, it had already established a sound financial base before the end of 1805, with no less than £7,100 raised.[15] In December a set of rooms at 52 Pall Mall was acquired and in February the Institution's first exhibition was opened. This proved an extraordinary crowd-puller, some ten thousand tickets being sold, and was the most important way in which the Institution was to fulfil its role of fostering contemporary art. It was, in effect, a second chance for artists to display and sell their works after the Academy exhibition. Another way in which the Institution sought to encourage art, and history painting in particular, was by the distribution of annual prizes or 'premiums' for the most promising works. In addition, the Institution also served at least a modest training function, those among its leading members lending Old Master paintings from their collections for students to copy from. Within a few years, then, the Institution firmly established itself and remained an important feature on the institutional map of the London art world throughout this period.

Those connoisseurs who became its leading figures, styling themselves The Directors, emerge as an interestingly heterogeneous group. Indeed, it seems probable that its initial success in attracting subscribers was due partly to the fact that its originators represented a cross-section of moneyed London society, a broad base of potential appeal and influence. Of those who were in at the very start, Bernard and Smith stand for a philanthropic and Evangelical strand, something which is significant in the emergence of the many provincial institutions which soon imitated the London organisation. Smith was closely associated with Wilberforce's anti-slavery campaign and Bernard, after his retirement as a City lawyer, dedicated himself to a life of tireless philanthropy. He had taken a leading role in establishing the Royal Institution and, according to one calculation, was a member of twenty-six societies, vice-president of seven, on the committee of two and governor of four.[16] Other Directors provide a different profile, prominent among them being old money Tories like Beaumont and Lord Mulgrave but also the Foxite Whig, and the connoisseur who was to take the most aggressive position in the disputes which soon encircled the Institution, Richard Payne Knight. Representing quite a different constituency were figures drawn from the City, most especially one of the wealthiest collectors of the period, John Julius Angerstein. Like Bernard, Angerstein was involved in numerous charitable committees and, significantly, took a leading role in the Patriotic Funds established during the Napoleonic Wars. But Farington's assessment of Angerstein, with its clear mapping of his social aspirations, testifies to the extent that Angerstein must have been seen in certain circles as something of an outsider. 'Mr. Angerstein', he writes in 1803,

is much respected for his good heart & intentions but is considered defficient in Education, & very embarassed on all occasions when He is required to express himself . . . [he] might have been at the head of popularity *in the City*, but has chosen to associate chiefly at the west end of town.[17]

As lobbying for the Institution clearly shows – and this added an especial intensity to the disputes which followed

13 Farington 1978-84, vol. 7, p.2559.
14 Ibid., p.2564.
15 For further details see Fullerton 1982, p.63.
16 See Brown 1961, p.356.
17 Farington 1978-84, vol. 6, p.2059.

P.C. Wonder, *Patrons and Lovers of Art*, oil on canvas, 1830. An imaginary gallery hung with pictures from famous collections in England, and leading collectors discussing the works. Private collection (photograph National Portrait Gallery)

– relations between artists and connoisseurs could often be close and assume at least a degree of social parity. Senior Academicians could move with relative ease through the drawing rooms of the great and wealthy and, again, the Academy played an important function in elevating the social status of artists. Both its theoretical doctrines, rendering the practice of painting a 'liberal' pursuit, but also its outwards ceremonials, served to enhance the prestige of the profession. In the latter sense the annual dinners preceding the exhibition, to which the Academy invited the social leaders of the day, assumed considerable symbolic importance. Thus Farington's fussy preparations for these events, his worries as to who was invited and how they were placed – preparations which can at first seem absurdly scrupulous – in fact underline the significance attached to the occasion.

But it would be wrong to suggest that relations between artists and patrons, the former often drawn from humble backgrounds, were not without an element of social ambiguity and this is especially so in the case of young painters. This can be briefly illustrated by the patronage given by Mulgrave and Beaumont to three young artists who entered the London art world in 1804-05: John Jackson, David Wilkie, and Benjamin

Robert Haydon.[18] These painters unquestionably benefited from Mulgrave and Beaumont's patronage, both through direct commissions and through the wider influence they were able to wield. But the story of their relationships was not always a happy one. Mulgrave's patronage of Jackson was fairly straightforward, with Jackson, the son of a Yorkshire tailor, being treated much as a paid member of Mulgrave's entourage down to continued complaints of his idleness. But the impression of clientage, and of social divisions kept firmly in place, becomes blurred in the case of Beaumont's treatment of Wilkie and Haydon. Both artists make frequent appearances at his dinner table, both spend time at his country house of Coleorton and both receive the fatherly advice of Beaumont, himself an amateur artist. But social divisions there were, as is clear from an episode, reported to Farington by Beaumont, when Wilkie was invited to dine at Mulgrave's house in Putney. 'It was the first time Wilkie had been in high company', Farington writes, 'but Sir George said such was His attention and observation of

18   For a full account see Owen and Brown 1988, pp.156 ff.

P.C. Wonder, *Sir Robert Peel, David Wilkie and the 3rd Earl of Egremont* (seated), oil on canvas, c.1830. Study for *Patrons and Lovers of Art*. National Portrait Gallery

ing facilities for copying, and in adjudging the merits of works through prize-giving, gave the appearance of outright rivalry. Thus Thomas Lawrence was expressing a widely felt opinion when he complained of the 'arrogant pretensions'[21] of the Directors and of their becoming 'Preceptors of Artists; & thereby acting in direct rivalship or opposition to the Royal Academy as a Seminary'.[22] Moreover, in setting themselves the task of fostering a British school of history painting, the Directors instead became the focus for all the dissatisfaction and frustration which that question provoked. For Haydon, most notably, the Institution had expanded the influence of men like Beaumont and Knight to such a degree as to present an insurmountable obstacle to his ambitions. 'The great objects I oppose, Payne Knight & Sir George Beaumont, are men no doubt of fortune & taste', he writes in his *Diary* in 1812, but

> these are the men on whom the Nobility pin their faith – with a detestation in fact of great works . . . these are the men who rule Patrons and patronise Artists, and if such be the Patrons, what chance, what prospects for historic art?[23]

'Great works, and great works only',[24] he protests in a letter to the *Examiner* newspaper of the same year, will establish British painting in the rank it deserves. But Haydon was only the most vociferous of a number of young artists, of similar aspirations, who saw their ambitions thwarted when they directed their appeals for further patronage to the connoisseurs who ran the Institution.

'Gentlemen artists', a correspondent complained to the short-lived *Review of Publications of Art* were behaving more like 'highwaymen'.[25] And, in turn, the connoisseurs themselves reacted against these insistent demands. The formidable Lady Beaumont, for example, referring to a lengthy poem by Shee on the need for greater encouragement to artists, 'spoke with irritation of *Shee's poem and remarks*; and said the public were not to be *bullied* into patronage of the arts'.[26] But the most forthright of the connoisseurs in responding to this barrage of demands

what was done by others *at the table* that by the time dinner was over He was as well bred a man as any in England.'[19] Wilkie was sufficiently level-headed to survive the pressures which this sort of relationship brought with it. But the misunderstandings between painter and patron which these approaches to friendship engendered led to serious disagreements between Beaumont and the volatile young history painter, Haydon. Their protracted dispute over the intended size of a painting from *Macbeth* – Beaumont preferring a 'pretty furniture picture'[20] as opposed to the grandiose masterpiece which Haydon's inflated ambitions projected – left a degree of mistrust on Haydon's part which was permanently to embitter the artist.

Returning to the Institution, we can see how tensions between artists and connoisseurs in the early years of the nineteenth century were only reinforced by its successful emergence. Dominated by connoisseurs, it seems to become a powerbase from which they can impose their interest and prejudices. To the Academicians, so conscious of their hard-won status, the role the Directors assumed in mounting their annual exhibitions, in supply-

19 Farington 1978-84, vol. 7, p.2716.
20 Haydon 1960-63, vol. 1, p.138.
21 Royal Academy, Lawrence Papers, LAW/2/19, Lawrence to Farington, 12 June 1812.
22 Farington 1978-84, vol. 14, p.4921.
23 Haydon 1960-63, vol. 1, p.266.
24 Reprinted in *Annals of the Fine Arts*, vol. 1, no. ii, 1817, p.170.
25 *Review of Publications of Art* 1808, vol. 1, p.15.
26 Farington 1978-84, vol. 7, p.2556.

was Knight. In two vigorous articles in the *Edinburgh Review*, Knight sought not only to undercut the theoretical basis of history painting, but to challenge head on the ambitions of those like Haydon who sought to practise it. 'Let us hear no more' he thunders in 1810, 'of these clamours of misguided and disappointed vanity'. 'Not only more money, but more wealth', he asserts,

> has been expended, by private individuals, upon living artists, within these last forty years, than ever was expended in any country during any period of equal length; and if men of taste and skill do not overrate their talents, nor measure their hopes of future renown by the size, rather than the excellence, of their works, they will not want due encouragement.[27]

These tensions between artists and connoisseurs reached a climax in 1815, when the Institution arranged the first of a series of exhibitions of old master paintings. In retrospect the exhibition can be seen as a further innovation on the part of the Directors, but to the artists it was evidence that they were neglecting their prime duty of fostering contemporary British art. This was the principal charge of what proved one of most violent, and talked about, attacks on connoisseurs of the period, a spoof *Catalogue Raisonee* (sic) of the exhibition, published anonymously, and condemning the Institution in the strongest terms. The *Catalogue Raisonee* mainly consists of an ironic rubbishing of the pictures in the exhibition and of the taste and knowledge of the Directors, Beaumont and Knight in particular. But it builds in its last pages to a pitch of abuse, such that Beaumont felt both printer and author would be liable to prosecution. No printer's name is given, however, and its authorship remains open to question. Beaumont and Knight could only read of their 'proud insolence', the 'meanesses into which it leads them', their 'paltry feelings', their being 'folded up in arrogance and conceit' and, more generally, of how they had hijacked the Institution to the destruction of contemporary British art.[28]

The publication of the *Catalogue Raisonee* marks something of a watershed in these battles between artists and connoisseurs, battles which dominate the early part of our period. They are, as I have suggested, disputes which concern the artists' conception of their social status and which focus on the question of which sector of the art world should hold control over the future course of British painting. But more sober expressions of doubt as to the possible effectiveness of the Institution raise those broader issues of institutional scale, and the need for state involvement, which we have seen Hoare addressing in the first years of the century. In a publication of 1813, Hoare openly questions whether 'a thousand galleries and schools'[29] would have the effect of promoting history painting and renews his assertion that support must be secured from the state. 'From the state', he writes, 'from the state alone, it can be sought'.[30] As I have mentioned, Hoare's calls for state intervention are far from unusual during this period and are arguments which can be found in countless books, pamphlets, letters and periodical articles. Thus Haydon is consistent throughout his life in expressing the need for 'public assistance', for 'Parliament to vote Pictures as well as Statues to the heroes or the legislators of the Country'.[31] A figure who operated more at the margins of London's artistic life, William Paulet Carey, makes the same point repeatedly in pamphlets printed at his own expense. As he writes in 1825, 'the whole frame of government is the *only competent* source and support for the *public* or *historical style*.'[32] That active reformer Martin Archer Shee is equally insistent 'that liberal protection from the government is the only effectual stimulus which can now be applied to the powers of taste in this country'.[33] The patronage of individuals, or even of individuals grouped collectively as in the case of the British Institution, would not be sufficient in the view of these writers. For this was merely extending existing forms of private patronage and, at best, through the exhibition of works for sale, providing a further market outlet. It was, as Shee writes, false to assume that it was possible 'to regulate the powers of genius, by the principles of trade, and cultivate the arts like a common manufacture'.[34] It is a point also taken up by a reader of Shee's early work *Rhymes on Art*, the political philosopher and administrator Sir James Mackintosh. It is incomprehensible, Mackintosh writes in a letter of 1808, 'that there are people dull enough to excuse the public discouragement of English art, upon the principles of liberty of trade' and he too goes on to insist on the need for wholesale government intervention.[35]

These appeals for state support – reasoned in tone, appealing to patriotic feeling, and stressing the reciprocal benefits which the state might receive – clearly gained

27 [Knight] 1810, p.310.
28 *Catalogue Raisonee,* quoted variously, pp.67 ff.
29 Hoare 1813, p.281.
30 Ibid., p.279.
31 Haydon 1960-63, vol. 1, p.265.
32 [Carey] 1825, p.7.
33 Shee 1809, p.17.
34 Ibid., p.8.
35 Mackintosh 1835, vol. 1, p.372, Mackintosh to John Hoppner, 19 February 1808.

currency outside the narrow bounds of London's artistic circles. Yet, as we shall see, it is not until the very end of our period that parliament seriously begins to interest itself in the affairs of the art world, and this takes a form which in many ways is quite different to what these earlier writers had in mind. Appeals in the early decades of the century fall on deaf ears. Even a very carefully worked out scheme advanced by Shee in 1809, which envisaged an elaborate system of prizes, using the British Institution as an agency but funded by £5,000 from government, seems to have got nowhere. Bernard again was involved, drafting a letter which stressed the patriotic advantages of Shee's project, and the commercial benefits which pre-eminence in the fine arts would have, by a filter down effect, in improving the decorative arts. But as Farington records on 26 June 1810 the application presented by Lord Dartmouth to Spencer Perceval, Prime Minister and Chancellor of the Exchequer, had been declined.[36] This direct approach to government is constantly cited until as late as 1840 as a missed opportunity.[37] In this instance, one senses again a lack of commitment in those who mattered. Senior Academicians were clearly concerned by the Institution's involvement and, in private, Bernard's fellow Directors, such as Beaumont, voiced their scepticism.

Yet, in more general terms, this rejection of quite a modest appeal conforms to a pattern of governmental diffidence with regard to supporting the arts. The reasons for this are complex. The administrative limitations of government in the early nineteenth century have been advanced as a factor[38], as, of course, has a sheer tightness of funds, especially during the Napoleonic period. But, as we have seen, the patriotic, and indeed propagandist, value of large scale works was vigorously argued as a reciprocal benefit to a fairly modest degree of expenditure. As Linda Colley has suggested, however, this in itself may well have proved a further disincentive to government.[39] Government showed itself to be distinctly wary of such patriotic sentiment, of the possible consequences of a growing national consciousness, and it may be that this actively discouraged it from playing the role in the arts which was so frequently demanded. Patriotic fervour was left to voluntary organisations such as the Patriotic Funds in which Angerstein was so active. And so was the responsibility of promoting the fine arts. As I have mentioned, the British Institution formed the model for similar organisations, based on subscription and adopting its aims and protocol, in many of the large provincial centres. 'Hardly a town exists', as Lawrence remarked in 1829, 'where the liberality of some individuals' had not formed itself into exhibiting societies, and societies for the pro-

motion of art.[40] As such, these organisations find their institutional analogies in the mass of voluntary and charitable organisations of the period. But in this sense, they fall far short of those institutional ambitions, and the demands for state involvement, advanced by Hoare, Shee, Carey and the like. They are effectively private bodies, composed of private individuals, much in the same way that Hoare had found the Academy's institutional equivalent to be the 'friendly professional society'.

I have dwelt on disputes between artists and connoisseurs in the early part of our period, since they gave the London art world its very distinct character and since, as will be clear, the relationship of painter to patron was far from being a simple transaction between producer and consumer. There were, however, ways in which artists attempted to reach the public directly, without the mediation of either the Academy or the Institution. A large number of painters during these years exhibited their works independently, either on a permanent basis at their own premises or through one-off exhibitions. But the expense of this could easily outweigh the benefits of public and critical attention. Thus, for instance, the highly regarded painter of subject and history pictures, Richard Westall, clearly over extended himself, and compounded his already ruinous financial position, when he took rooms next to the Institution in the summer of 1814. Nevertheless, for a figure like Haydon, suspicious of the Institution and, after 1809, increasingly estranged from the Academy, independent exhibitions proved the principal means by which he could pursue his dogged insistence to paint history. Haydon's exhibition of his enormous canvas, *Christ's Entry into Jerusalem*, at the Egyptian Hall in 1820 was a considerable public and critical success. But receipts for admission and catalogues, though amounting to £1,760,[41] did not offset the debts he had built up during the six years that he had laboured away on the work. 1823, the year of his next exhibition at the Egyptian Hall, saw these debts finally catch up on Haydon, leading to his first bankruptcy and imprisonment. This also caused the effective dissolution of Haydon's highly innovative 'school' for young artists. Organised according to a regime which emulated the workshop method of training of the Italian High Renaissance and

36   See Farington 1978-84, vol. 10, p.3676.
37   See Edwards 1840, pp.191 ff.
38   See Minihan 1977, p.28.
39   See Colley 1986.
40   Royal Academy, Lawrence Papers, LAW/6, *Address*, vol. 5, p.9.
41   See George 1948, p.133.

inculcating in his students the highest principles of art – even down to their assuming a Raphaelesque manner of dressing their hair – Haydon's school was another way in which he sought to operate outside London's established art institutions.[42]

The degree of popular interest in exhibitions such as Haydon's, the numbers who were willing to pay their shilling admission, suggests the extent to which, by the 1820s, painting could appeal to a sizeable art public. The most significant institutional development of the 1820s – the formation of the Society of British Artists in 1823 – was in many ways a response to this phenomenon. The Society acquired elegant rooms designed by John Nash in Suffolk Street, Pall Mall and opened its first exhibition there in April 1824. In spite of financial difficulties in its early years, largely due to structural problems with the roof of Nash's building, the Suffolk Street exhibitions, like those at the Academy and the Institution, became a regular part of the London season. Again the Society was based on subscription, with contributions invited on a sliding scale, conferring different privileges, from as little as one guinea to one hundred guineas. Support was solicited from titled patrons, with an elaborate dinner presided over by the Duke of Sussex inaugurating the first exhibition. But the Society was essentially an artist's affair, its members taking a financial interest and managing its business. Like Haydon, who exhibited at the first exhibition, the artists who formed the Society were convinced of the professional need to establish an alternative to the Academy and the Institution. And although they constantly insisted that they had no wish to rival any other institution, there was a pointed emphasis on the way in which the Society was conducted on 'liberal principles',[43] its exhibitions open to all 'without any exclusive privileges or distinctions'.[44] In a significant way, too, the aims of the Society differed from those of the Academy or, for that matter, Haydon. As he pointed out, it was largely run by, and adapted to the needs, of 'modern landscape painters'.[45] History paintings were included in the exhibitions, but they consisted predominantly of landscape and genre pictures. In short, the project was not informed by those theoretical aspirations which lay at the heart of the Academy, which drove Haydon's career, and which had prompted the founding of the Institution. The Suffolk Street exhibitions were conceived far more as being simply a means of access to the buying public: a point of sale. And as such, the Society was almost immediately censured in the *European Magazine*, for having 'no grand animating first principle, and no aim at any nobler purpose than may be supposed to govern an assembly of ware-shewing money-getters, of narrow views, met for a selfish and present purpose merely'.[46] Yet in other quarters, the Society's exhibitions appeared to offer a refreshing openness, not only to artists but also to the art public. As the *Literary Chronicle* reported, the works at its first exhibition were not bought by 'the higher and more polished orders of society' nor 'by a nest of picture dealers', but 'by the middle and respectable classes of an opulent and well-educated British public'.[47]

One should, perhaps, be cautious of overestimating the degree to which picture-buying became a 'middle-class' habit in the later years of our period. But certainly, as Edward Bulwer-Lytton observed in 1833, the desire to own paintings, if not perhaps of the more elevated type on which Haydon would insist, was strong and widespread. 'With us they are a necessary part of the furniture', he writes, and tells a story of 'a house-agent taking a friend of mine over a London house the other day, and praising it to the skies', concluding: ' "And when, sir, the dining-room is completely furnished – handsome red curtains, sir – and twelve good 'furniture pictures' – it will be a perfect nonpareil". The pictures were as necessary as the red curtains'.[48]

In the 1830s, the perception of a larger and socially more diverse art public, and of an expanded body of practising artists, comes to bear on these questions of how the art world was organised, and whether its institutional structure was adequate, which have been the main concern of this essay. Finally also, in this decade, these issues are debated at the highest level, and the condition of the art world receives thorough examination in parliament. It becomes matter for debate on the floor of the House of Commons, and is accorded the most intense scrutiny by a Select Committee on Arts and Manufactures, hearing evidence over two sessions in 1835 and 1836. At last, it seems, the state of the art world is given the political interest which had so frequently been called for in the preceding decades. Indeed much that is said during these years is strikingly familiar. But, as we shall also see, the debate absorbs the political temper of the 1830s and the demands of those advocating reform are in many ways dissimilar to those of earlier commentators I have discussed.

42 On Haydon's school, see Cummings 1963.
43 *Exhibition of the Society of British Artists* 1824, p.3.
44 Whitley 1933, p.24, quoting letter of invitation to artists from W. Linton.
45 Quoted ibid., p.27.
46 *European Magazine*, April 1824, p.371.
47 *The Literary Chronicle*, 21 August 1824, quoted by Hubbard 1937.
48 Lytton 1833, p.380.

The Academy remained the focus of attention and, in the 1830s, underwent the most formidable barrage of opposition in its history. The immediate cause for agitation was the proposal that the Academy should move from its old home at Somerset House and occupy rooms at the new National Gallery building in Trafalgar Square for which parliament had voted funds in 1832. By the time the Select Committee turned its full attention to the Academy in June 1836, this move was imminent and in fact was more or less complete by the following year's exhibition. But the move again raised questions as to the Academy's role in the art world, as well as stirring up old grievances from those, including Haydon again, who were excluded from its proceedings. For a month in 1836, the Select Committee under the chairmanship William Ewart, the reforming M.P. for Liverpool, heard witness after witness issue the severest indictments as to the Academy's cancerous influence within the London art world and its position as a bastion of corruption and privilege. Old sores are revisited, artists recounting incidents, often dating back many years, when their pictures were poorly hung at the exhibition or when, as non-members, they were denied the right to varnish, or properly prepare their works for public view. This, it is explained to Ewart, was a privilege accorded to Academicians alone and on which outsiders felt especially 'sensitive'.[49] But it forms only part of a long catalogue of ways in which the forty full Academicians are charged with using the Institution for their exclusive professional advantages. It is this note of privilege and exclusivity which is most constantly sounded, the 'putting power', as Haydon says, 'into forty men's hands and making them royal'.[50] The Academy exhibition, it was argued, remained the principal place where artists were able to display their works, but the hanging is controlled by just a few Academicians and all proceeds from the exhibition return to the Academy's ample coffers. The R.A. dinners are likewise advanced as a mechanism where the forty steal a professional lead since 'the other artists, being entirely excluded, have not an opportunity of showing themselves or their works to the same advantage'.[51] Moreover, as Frederick Hurlstone, President of the Society of

49 *Parliamentary Papers: Report from the Select Committee on Arts and Manufactures* 1836, p.59.
50 Ibid., p.96.
51 Ibid., p.60.

THE NATIONAL GALLERY — CHARING CROSS.

British Artists, protests, the Academy is also 'the channel for which all the honours of the profession flow', its members assuming the title 'esquire', its President being elevated to a knighthood.[52]

The evidence of Hurlstone, and his fellow member of the Society, Thomas Christopher Hofland, is among the most condemnatory and shatters the notion of the Society, by this time at least, enjoying an harmonious relationship with the Academy. Yet the Committee's proceedings reveal more than simply the expression, however potent, of an artistic 'out of doors'. The evidence also raises questions, very reminiscent of Prince Hoare's observations thirty years earlier, as to whether the Academy can be considered a private or a public organisation. It is a point which the sculptor George Rennie, whose evidence of 21 June initiated the full scale assault on the Academy, constantly returns to. 'I conceive the Royal Academy', he says, 'should either have laws and regulations framed such as are suited to a public body, or they should be strictly private; at present I consider it quite an anomaly'. The Academy 'stands in an undefined position', Rennie asserts, 'it receives its apartments from the public, its members have the royal patronage and diplomas, but its internal regulations are such as ought to belong to an entirely private institution'.[53] And, of course, the transfer of the Academy to a building erected from government funds suggested that it was, almost by default, being given public status. As Hurlstone asserts, this would be 'in some degree a positive recognition of it as a national institution'.[54]

The extent to which the quasi-public status of the Academy should make it accountable to parliament was taken up with vigour in the last years of the decade by the radical M.P., Joseph Hume. Supported by his fellow radicals, Hume pursued the matter in the House, eventually bringing it to a full debate on 24 July 1839. Hume's ostensible point on that occasion was that, if the Academy was a truly public body, it should submit its financial returns to parliament. Hume failed to win the motion, but it was only the final act in a campaign aimed at undermining the Academy's position in the most comprehensive way. As such it formed part of a broader battle in which the radicals, with Hume taking a position in the most leading role, sought out and challenged instances of institutional privilege and corruption in every area of national life. Outside the Commons, Hume fought his case in a paper war with the artist who had by now risen to the position, and honours, of the Academy Presidency, Sir Martin Archer Shee. Hume's demands for reforms, his arguments that the Academy exhibition should admit visitors from all classes of society, free of charge, pushed Shee into an increasingly conservative position. And although Hume eventually failed in 1839, he was nevertheless able to relish the experience of reading to his fellow M.P.s highly re-

52 Ibid., p.69.
53 Ibid., p.57.
54 Ibid., p.65.

form-minded passages from Shee's publications of the first decade of the century.

As I have suggested, the assaults on the Academy of the 1830s were conditioned by a feeling that the artistic profession had outgrown existing institutions and by a new sense of the existence of a broader art public. Haydon, in his evidence to the Select Committee, estimated that there were two thousand professional artists in London in 1836,[55] far too many to sanction the dominant position of the forty Academicians. And in terms of who had access to the arts, the whole thrust of the Committee's wider concerns, advanced for reasons of commercial advantage, was that fine art should be made available to all ranks of society. Like Hume, witnesses constantly insist on the need to make exhibitions freely available to the broad mass of the public. But, again, what role was government, in terms of direct funding, to play in all this? Certainly, the Committee's proceedings did result in one positive initiative funded by the state, the establishment of a School of Design in the Academy's old rooms at Somerset House. It was not long, however, before this came to be seen as an Academy 'job' and state patronage of history painting had to wait until the following decade. But then the beliefs of those advocating reforms in the 1830s were hardly conducive to state intervention, aside from examining and reporting on the condition of the art world. Ewart, when advocating his Committee in 1835, had made his position clear. He was uncertain, he admitted, of the best mode of fostering knowledge of the arts but was, nevertheless, 'of the opinion, that arts, like commerce, ought to be essentially free'.[56] And, encouraged by Ewart, a number of the artists giving evidence to the Committee – Haydon being the obvious exception – concur in this view, couched as it is in a rhetoric of free trade. Thus Rennie warmly agrees when Ewart puts it to him that 'where Government interferes too much by academic institutions with the progress of art, it gives a false stimulus'[57] and that 'if Government interpose at all in matters of art, they should interpose on the principle of free competition'.[58] Likewise Hofland, representing the Society of Artists, states that he would strongly 'prefer free trade in art' as opposed to government intervention, and goes on to concur with Ewart's assertion that 'free competition' was 'the principle that prevailed in the time when the Italian schools obtained their greatest celebrity'.[59] For a moment, at least, the initiative lay with those who felt that the art world, when rid of its institutional corruption, would be best served by a lack of regulation, and that artists should enjoy an unfettered approach to their public.

55 Ibid., p.93.
56 *Parliamentary Debates (Commons)*, 3rd. ser., 14 July 1835: 554
57 *Parliamentary Papers: Report from the Select Committee on Arts and Manufactures* 1836, p.56.
58 Ibid., p.62.
59 Ibid., p.107.

PAINTING IN LONDON IN THE EARLY NINETEENTH CENTURY

Andrew Wilton

By the beginning of the nineteenth century London had boasted a Royal Academy of Arts for more than thirty years. The spring exhibitions regularly held there were the arena in which two generations of painters had proved themselves. Its prestige acted as a magnet to artists from all over Britain, who were in any case attracted to the metropolis as the natural centre of patronage. Through its schools, the Academy was also the only systematic disseminator in England of technical and theoretical training. Its first president, Sir Joshua Reynolds, had laid down, in the series of Discourses that he presented at the annual prize-giving, laws of art that were received by almost every practising painter as immutable truths.[1]

These laws took as their premise a combination of practicality and idealism which set the tone for all discussion of the fine arts. Reynolds acknowledged that 'Our elements are laid in gross common nature, – an exact imitation of what is before us'; but he immediately added: 'when we advance to the higher state, we consider this power of imitation, though first in the order of acquisition, as by no means the highest in the scale of perfection.' He compared 'a view of nature represented with all the truth of the *camera obscura* and the same scene represented by a great Artist', and was decisive in his judgement: 'how little and mean will the one appear in comparison of the other'. The principal task of the artist – the 'great Artist' – was to raise 'common nature' to a higher plane of significance.[2]

Reynolds sought generalised, not specific, reference. He advocated, as the vehicle for this, heroic subject-matter taken from history or myth, and a bold style of designing with a system of colouring that was subordinate to the intellectual principles embodied in the Florentine ideal of *disegno*. He himself relied heavily on the more sensuous art of the Venetians, whose sumptuous colouring provided an almost equally authoritative model, as well as learned justification for his own less academically respectable practice, portraiture. This judicious alliance of intellect and instinct earned him a pre-eminent position as a portrait painter; well into the next century he continued to be considered a master on a par with the Ancients. As the Earl of Aberdeen said in 1813, although Reynolds's works 'might differ in appearance' from those of the Greeks and the Italians, they 'were to be ranked with them, their aim being essentially the same – *the attainment of nature with simplicity and truth*'.[3] But already it might have been possible for some of Aberdeen's auditors to interpret those two important words, nature and truth, in ways that he did not intend.

Reynolds's teachings had enshrined an aristocratic view of art entirely appropriate to his own *métier* as chief portrait painter to the nobility and gentry. He spoke, more generally, for an age in which the formal prescriptions of past epochs carried immense weight. When Henry Howard was appointed Professor of Painting to the Academy, as late as 1833, he began his lecture series by referring to the 'mass of sound doctrine' enunciated by his predecessors which made it 'scarcely possible to add any thing very novel or important'.[4] Yet, perhaps imperceptibly to someone working, like Howard, within the conventions of history painting, great changes were occurring. Writing much later in the nineteenth century, the journalist and art critic Tom Taylor could recall of the first decade or so, 'The fashion of the day in art was classical. "The Antique," "the Nude," "High Art," and "Michael Angelo," were dinned into the ears of the student.' That student believed implicitly in 'the orthodoxy of these doctrines'; Taylor, from a vantage-point in 1860, could contrast them with the notion that 'a painter's style and subject must be determined by the painter's own bent and capacity'.[5] By that date it was possible to look back on the old Academic orthodoxy with detachment.

But Victorian painters had not freed themselves from theoretical restrictions. A new pundit had replaced Reynolds: John Ruskin. Ruskin, whose encyclopaedic *Modern Painters* began to appear in 1843, taught that matters like 'the Antique' and 'High Art' were much less important than the close observation of detailed nature, and the diligent rendering of what was observed. It has been supposed, on this account, that he subordinated meaning to description – a complete reversal of Reynolds's principle. That is not so; his real difference from Reynolds was in his willingness to find meaning in concatenations of details that would have seemed to Reynolds vulgar and trivial. He could describe an early success of Edwin Land-

---

1 Hutchison 1968, chapters 4 and 5.
2 Reynolds ed. Malone 1801, vol. 2, pp.122-23 (13th Discourse, 1786).
3 Leslie ed. Mayne 1951, p.41.
4 Holland 1848, p.1.
5 Leslie ed. Taylor, 1860, vol. 2, p.18.

seer's, *The Old Shepherd's Chief Mourner* (1837) as an assemblage of details which by their juxtaposition create a pattern of ideas: they are

> all thoughts – thoughts by which the picture is separated at once from hundreds of equal merit, as far as mere painting goes, by which it ranks as a work of high art, and stamps its author, not as the neat imitator of the texture of a skin, or the fold of a drapery, but as the Man of Mind.[6]

Ruskin's 'Man of Mind' is the mid nineteenth-century successor to Reynolds's 'great Artist'; yet the details with which Landseer's picture is crammed would surely have struck Reynolds as far too mundane, and the whole sentiment of the work, centring as it does on the grief of a dog, unworthy of genius. It is not simply that classicism seems to have been thrown out of the window. It is not just that generalisation has been replaced by an almost obsessive interest in the local and specific. The very nature of seriousness has apparently been redefined. The first decades of the century saw the high idealism of Reynolds steadily stripped away and an art apparently much more prosaic, more closely dependent on the data of everyday experience, established in its place. We may well ask what social and ethical forces were at work to produce such a radical shift of emphasis.

The move from the classical, the generalised and the grand to the informal, the intimate and the natural is paralleled by the increase of arts patronage in the same period among the mercantile and professional class. It is plausible to conclude that art became more 'bourgeois' in the years prior to Victoria's accession in 1837: the devaluation of idealism, of nobility, and the elevation of the ordinary in art, seems a metaphor for just such a class shift. But patronage had not ceased to come from the aristocracy and landed gentry; rather was there a general broadening of the social basis of the art market, and all classes were subject during the period to profound changes in taste.

But what do we mean by saying that art is, or becomes, 'bourgeois'? Reynolds and Ruskin had something in common: both were articulate members of the professional classes. But their terms of social reference were very different. If Reynolds was portrait painter to the upper class, Ruskin was the son of a sherry importer who practised drawing as an amateur interested in botany, geology and architecture.[7] These enthusiasms could by matched by the explorations and enquiries of the aristocratic Society of Dilettanti of Reynolds's day, but they derived much of their motivation from Ruskin's parents' Calvinistic Protestantism – a religious impulse unknown to Reynolds or

his circle. The wonders of God's earth, down to the growth of leaves on the ash-tree or the formation of rocks and clouds, were miraculous signs of His creative wisdom; they were susceptible to experiment, description and analysis. That wish to see everything more clearly the better to understand God's purposes was not confined to the Ruskin household: it was an integral part of the middle-class outlook when John was growing up (he was born in 1819). His writings, therefore, are the summary and culmination of a new attitude to visual experience, and it was this that qualified them to become the philosophical basis for the art of the next generation – that of the Pre-Raphaelites.

Changes in religious attitudes are, then, as fundamental as economic progress to the shifts observable in aesthetics during the early nineteenth century, and they were still capable of carrying with them the equally important advances being made in the scientific description of the universe. They can partly explain why the public projects of painters of the decades immediately before 1800 – Benjamin West's designs for the audience chamber at Windsor Castle, for instance[8] – are different from the designs submitted to the competition for the decoration of the new Houses of Parliament in the 1840s. These designs are in the direct line of descent from West, but are influenced by a much more specific sense of the interrelationship of history, religion and public life. That sense expressed itself in a new feeling for medieval art, as exemplified in Pugin's reverence for Gothic as the 'true' Christian idiom.[9] The movement in taste is summed up in the contrast between Soane's classical Bank of England (begun in 1795) and the gothicised Houses of Parliament that Charles Barry and A.W.N. Pugin built in the 1840s. We shall return to this point.

In so far as the Westminster frescoes were quite explicitly about a shared national experience they followed the eighteenth-century model for history painting. James Barry's paintings of 1777-84 for the Great Room of the Society of Arts celebrated the progress of civilisation in ancient Greece and suggested that London, and the Society in particular, represented the modern equivalent of that development. Alderman John Boydell's Shakspeare Gallery, initiated in 1786, did honour both to the national school of painters by then well-established and

---

6 Ruskin 1888, vol. 1, p.8 (Part I, Sect. I, Chapter 3.)
7 Ruskin gave his own account of his family and upbringing in *Praeterita* 1885. Although his parents were strongly Evangelical, he at one time contemplated taking holy orders in the Church of England.
8 Von Erffa and Staley, 1986, pp.192 ff.
9 Pugin 1836, pp.2-7.

J. Bluck after A.C. Pugin and T. Rowlandson, *Society for the Encouragement of Arts*, aquatint from Ackermann's *Microcosm of London*, 1809. Barry's painting cycle decorates the walls of the Great Room. The Museum of London

institutionalised in the Academy – and to England's greatest poet. Both were intended to be viewed by the public at large, and to inculcate appropriate moral lessons.[10] But both were privately-funded projects which never attracted universal attention (indeed the Shakspeare Gallery was a financial disaster), while the rebuilt Houses of Parliament were a state enterprise, the embodiment of a new democracy that came into existence with the passing of the Reform Bill in 1832. This was the focal moment of a long-drawn-out process of political change that embodies, or symbolises, the subtler alterations, including those of aesthetics, that were taking place in British society during the reigns of George IV and William IV.

The first stage in the process whereby the grand generalisations of Reynolds's epoch were tamed, as it were, for more popular consumption was, paradoxically perhaps, the spread of high neo-classicism. The taste for the 'classical' of which Tom Taylor spoke had undergone important modifications in the last decade or so of the eighteenth century. They can be summarised as a change of preference from spurious to genuine Greek antiquity. This was simply the consequence of increased knowledge. The classicism of Reynolds was substantially that of the

seventeenth century: a taste for the well-known examples of 'Grecian' sculpture to be found, above all, in the Papal collections in the Vatican, and exemplified in works like the Medici Venus, the Apollo Belvedere and the Laocoon. The exploration of Greece and Asia Minor in the 1750s and '60s, and the gradual publication of findings, sharpened an understanding of true Greek art. James 'Athenian' Stuart's *Antiquities of Athens* began to appear in 1762, acquainting London for the first time with the achievements of Pericles' Greece.[11] The Parthenon marbles were not published until 1788, and first-hand experience of them was delayed until 1803 when Lord Elgin brought important fragments to London. That experience refined sensibilities still further. Although the older generation of connoisseurs, exemplified by Richard Payne Knight, were unable to see the superiority of the Athenian marbles, they provided a heady stimulus for the next generation of artists like Benjamin Robert Haydon who

10 See Pressly 1981, chapter 4; and Santanello 1968.
11 Pevsner 1940, chapter 5; Irwin 1966.

J.M.W. Turner, *The Lake, Petworth: Sunset, Fighting Bucks*, oil on canvas, 1827-28. The National Trust, Petworth House

were dedicated, as Barry had been, to high seriousness.[12]

Another key publication was d'Hancarville's sumptuous catalogue of the Greek ('Etruscan') vases in the collection of Sir William Hamilton, the first part of which appeared in 1766–67.[13] It was the true Grecian aesthetic of these even more than the works of art that he saw in Rome that enabled John Flaxman to redefine the notion of 'Greek'. He did this not only in his sculpture but even more influentially in his outline illustrations to Homer, Aeschylus and Dante, which appeared in the 1790s and were quickly disseminated all over Europe.[14] The importance of these outlines cannot be overstressed. They established on an international basis the fundamental neoclassical principle of pure expressive outline – the outline, as George Cumberland defined it, that is yielded in infinite variety by every statue as it is revolved before one.[15] This was both a logical extension of Reynolds's doctrine of generalisation and a reaffirmation of his belief in *disegno* as the vital ingredient of all great art. At the same time in the archaeological precision and refinement of their draughtsmanship Flaxman's drawings were a departure from Reynolds. Both their reduction of scale, in which Flaxman was perhaps encouraged by d'Hancarville's vases, and their literary bias are central strands in the evolution of the nineteenth-century aesthetic.

This development had an unlikely parallel in the sphere of watercolour painting. The landscape artists of the eighteenth century, especially those who specialised in watercolour, tended to concentrate on topographical view-making; but they all acknowledged the theoretical superiority of the idealised landscape manner evolved by Claude in the seventeenth century and, as many thought, perfected by Richard Wilson in the eighteenth. Wilson, it was felt, achieved a universality, a lack of petty detail, that

had eluded even Claude himself.[16] Such breadth of vision was not, at first sight, especially appropriate to the recording of specific places mainly interesting for their architecture. But Wilson's landscape style had a range, paralleling that of Reynolds in portraiture, which was applicable equally to mythology or local record-taking. In the hands of watercolourists like John Robert Cozens and Thomas Girtin, who had learned the lessons of Wilson, topography found its consummation as the pure, generalised art form that it surely ought to be. Girtin's extraordinarily bold, broad washes of rich colour, orchestrated within a limited range of deep greens, greys and browns, showed what the newly enfranchised medium could do. In 1804, within two years of his early death, a Society of Painters in Water-Colours was established to rival the Academy itself.[17]

No sooner had Girtin formed his style of sublime topography, as we may call it, than its implicit simplicity of structure began to be analysed and developed by another master: John Sell Cotman. For Cotman, who might be termed the Flaxman of landscape, the pure, expressive outline was essential to composition, and it was upon the basis of a finely conceived structure of outline

12 See for instance Haydon ed. Blunden, 1927, p.85.
13 D'Hancarville (P.F. Hughes) 1766-67.
14 See Irwin 1979, especially chapters 3 and 5; Bindman ed., 1979.
15 Cumberland 1794, pp.9, 33: 'A statue is *all* outline . . . there are statues in the world which, if turned round on a pivot before a lamp, would produce, on a wall, some hundreds of fine Outlines'.
16 See for example *Dayes*, 1805, pp.357-58.
17 Roget 1891, vol. 1, Book I, chapter 6, Book II, chapters 1, 2, 3. See also Sloan 1986, and Girtin and Loshak 1954.

forms that he built his subtle harmonies of subdued colour. Later in his career that gamut of colour became much brighter; indeed, his use of outline as a means of composition in its own right seems to have led him by a kind of logical necessity to liberate colour and endow it with an existence of its own, with a saturated strength unprecedented in the medium.[18] This functional interrelationship between line and colour is one of the key preoccupations of the decades covered by this exhibition; so that Cotman's development as a watercolourist serves as a paradigm for the aesthetic progress of the whole period.

The link between line and colour was not merely theoretical. The practical relationship between the two elements was borne out in the economics of early nineteenth-century art. The practice of painting, in whatever medium, was closely allied to the reproductive processes of engraving. During the eighteenth century artists had fostered ever more intimate and profitable relationships with printmakers; Reynolds had controlled a large school of mezzotinters copying and distributing his works. The art of line engraving, too, reached new heights of subtlety and accuracy of interpretation.[19] Aquatint, introduced in the 1770s, provided a means of achieving surprisingly accurate facsimiles of wash drawings and watercolours of the old topographical type; but mezzotint and line engraving proved to be better suited to the complex images that watercolourists began to create in the wake of Girtin, and were exploited by artists and print publishers throughout the first half of the nineteenth century.

One of the purposes of the newly-formed Water-Colour Society was to demonstrate that its chosen medium was suitable for works of art as significant as those in oil. Girtin had been influenced by the ideas of Reynolds and Wilson; his colleague and exact contemporary J.M.W. Turner, who survived him by fifty years, all his life professed devotion to those two masters. He gave practical expression to the principle by giving as much weight in his own output to oil as to watercolour.[20] At a very early stage his work provided ample evidence of this, and its success was another spur to the watercolourists to incorporate themselves in an academy of their own. Their work, now regularly conceived for public exhibition rather than for inclusion in private portfolios or as designs for engraved illustrations to antiquarian tours, grew in size proportionately to its increased seriousness, and was often presented in gilt frames as elaborate as those chosen for oil paintings. Instead of being used almost exclusively for landscape views or quasi-ephemeral subject-matter such as social satire and caricature, watercolour was expected to tackle also the human figure on a large scale in historical and mythological subjects, or domestic and rustic genre. In landscape, it was as likely to be the vehicle for an essay in the 'elevated' manner of Claude or Poussin as a simple topographical view.[21]

But watercolour had not abandoned its traditional concern with the immediate, the informal and the evanescent. It remained the medium *par excellence* for outdoor studies of natural phenomena, for rapid observation of passing effects. In the new fervour for experiment that arose under the stimulus of Girtin's achievement and the current example of the prolific Turner, many young artists began to make a habit of sketching aspects of the world around them that had before been dealt with according to formulas. The grandiose ambitions of the members of the Water-Colour Society demanded of them an evolved academic discipline in the accumulation of careful studies from life. Accordingly a more broadly-based representationalism entered their work. And as watercolour expanded to embrace the grand style, so oil enlarged its boundaries to address the intimacies of nature that had previously been the province of the draughtsman and watercolour sketcher. Informal *plein-air* sketching in oil had, of course, been occasionally practised by artists in the past, especially by artists studying in Italy. The Welsh amateur Thomas Jones had experimented in this way, in Naples in the 1780s, with oil studies of bits of wall and glimpses of domes against the blue sky. He pursued the practice in Wales on his return and so is a forerunner of the more thoroughgoing efforts of the artists of the next generation. Of these, John Constable elevated the activity into a veritable system for studying nature. By the first years of the century, he was regularly taking small canvases or sheets of paper out of doors to jot down with oil paints in a notably free style the effects of light, of cloud, of massed foliage, of recession and reflection, that he observed in the skies, lanes and valleys of his native Suffolk. Others, like John Linnell and William Mulready, were based in London and chose old buildings or gravel pits or stretches of the Thames as subjects for their studies, using oil or watercolour according to their mood or temperament.[22]

Another vital consequence of the enhanced standing of watercolour was that artists were more likely as a matter of course to learn its lessons, to translate its techniques and approaches into the language of oil – to think, in fact,

18   Kitson 1937, and Rajnai ed., 1982.
19   Alexander and Godfrey 1980.
20   See for instance Wilton 1979, chapter 2, and Gage 1987.
21   See Roget 1891. A recent study of the subject is Bayard 1981.
22   See Gage 1969; and Brown 1991.

more flexibly about the potential of the medium. Thanks to the new status of watercolour there is throughout the early nineteenth century in England an undercurrent – at times an explicit movement – towards the free, broad handling of freshly observed data in the immediately experienced world that is effectively what we should now call impressionism. It manifests itself particularly in the work of the group of artists who followed Girtin, notably David Cox and Peter de Wint (both of whom worked in oil as well as watercolour), and so can be seen emerging from the Reynoldsian tradition of breadth and 'generalisation' as well as from the anti-Reynoldsian interest in *plein-air* naturalism.[23]

On the other hand, the 'exhibition' watercolour became in the same period increasingly formal and academic. The interplay between the two strands of development is a primary symptom of the new independence of the artist, of his freedom to express his sense (also a relatively new phenomenon) of a personal and unique relationship with the natural world, and of his entitlement to present that personal feeling as a public statement, as High Art. The Romantic period is often characterised as the first age in which artists spoke as individual and personal voices, rather than as mouthpieces for a religious or political establishment. In social terms this was important too: men who had formerly been mere mechanics or artisans were joining the articulate professional classes; the Academy conferred status on its members (its presidents even acquired knighthoods), and dignified the profession as a whole. Their art inevitably became a channel through which the ideals and aspirations of those classes could be expressed.

At the same time, artists became more articulate in airing their professional point of view. There emerged, therefore, a more clearly-focussed idea of an audience, on whom exhibitions act as a kind of propaganda, and for whom a properly-instituted national gallery of painting, including the British School, should necessarily be established. In 1805 the portrait painter Martin Archer Shee issued some *Rhymes on Art*, subtitled *The Remonstrance of a Painter*, in which he voiced these ideas, and ruminated on the relationship of the Academy to its public, especially as that relationship was defined by the critics:

Dolts from the ranks of useful service chas'd
Pass muster in the lumber troop of Taste;
Soon learn to goad with critic shot, and play
Their pop-guns on the genius of the day.[24]

On the other hand, Academicians were enjoined to take criticism seriously and profit from it. In 1825 C.M. Westmacott, a sculptor as well as a journalist, who came from a large family of artists, wrote the versified report of an imaginary Academy council meeting in which the 'courtly' president, Thomas Lawrence, urges:

Sirs, the great enemy of all R.A.'s
Is the dull dog of indiscriminate praise . . .
That writer serves us best – who'er he be
That praises justly, and that censures free –
Led by no party, by no titles caught,
Yields commendation, justified by thought –
. . .
If just the censure, all the world agree,
And if unjust, have they not eyes to see?[25]

These exchanges imply corresponding developments in the attitudes of the viewing and collecting public, who now had enlarged opportunities to study contemporary art. The British Institution, which was founded largely with the intention of publicising the national school, devoted one large exhibition each year to submissions by living artists. Several private individuals took up the cause. Early in the century Sir John Fleming Leicester opened his London house to visitors, who were invited to inspect a distinguished group of British works, from the time of Reynolds to the present day. The 3rd Earl of Egremont also patronised contemporary painters and sculptors, building a gallery to house his acquisitions, which were shown alongside his old masters and antique sculpture. A retired coach builder, Benjamin Godfrey Windus, was one of several successful businessmen who formed collections of watercolours in the period: he held a weekly open day at his suburban villa, where the library full of Turners was a particular attraction. Robert Vernon, a horse dealer, amassed a comprehensive representation of British art up to 1840; he gave it to the nation in 1847. These men are representative of the changes in taste that took place; the social positions of Leicester and Egremont on the one hand, and of Windus and Vernon on the other, exemplify the perpetuation of aristocratic collecting in the period and the advance of middle-class patronage alongside it. Although it was obvious that size might determine a collector's choice of works, no distinctions

23 For Cox see Wildman 1983, and Wilcox 1984; for de Wint see Scrase 1979.
24 Shee 1805, p.99. See Venning 1982, no. 1, pp.36-46 and no. 2, pp.40-49. See also Wilton 1990, pp.23-28.
25 Westmacott, 'Minutes of Council. A Pindaric', *The British Press*, reprinted in *The Spirit of the Public Journals for the Year 1825*, 1826, pp.279-300.

J.M.W. Turner, *The North Gallery at Night, Petworth House*, pen and ink, watercolour and bodycolour, 1827. Flaxman's *St. Michael overcoming Satan* (1822) commissioned by the 3rd Earl of Egremont dominates the scene. Tate Gallery

based on class governed preferences for particular types of picture.[26]

The debate on the desirability of a national gallery, to which Shee had contributed, became increasingly urgent, and in 1824 the kernel of such a gallery was formed when parliament authorised the purchase of an important group of pictures belonging to the financier John Julius Angerstein; to these were added later in the decade several works from the collection of Sir George Beaumont, and three masterpieces by Titian, Poussin and Annibale Carracci owned by the goldsmith Thomas Hamlet.[27] These new facilities for studying at close quarters examples of the greatest masters ancient and modern, together with the training provided by the Academy's schools, created an unprecedentedly stimulating environment in which the younger generation of painters could develop. Technical skill, in design, drawing and colouring became much more a matter of course than it had been in the eighteenth century. Reynolds was notorious for his lack of draughtsmanly ability (his 'generalisation' could be interpreted unkindly as a rationalisation of his failure in this respect). Thomas Lawrence, who became president of the Academy in 1820, was as impressive when wielding a

pencil or chalks as he was with a brush, a virtuoso in all departments. The same can be said of many of his contemporaries, including the Scot David Wilkie, the Irishmen Mulready and Maclise, and the Yorkshireman William Etty, all of whom gravitated inevitably to London and became members of the Academy.

The technical proficiency of the generation trained by the Academy gave a new impetus to the national school, and immensely increased its self-confidence. It was already apparent in the second half of the eighteenth century that the splendours of the great Italians were not what the British public most required of its own artists. Londoners preferred a more matter-of-fact art, one that served them specifically, and recorded the world they

26 See Whittingham 1986, no. 2, pp.24-36, (this issue contains articles on other collectors of the period); Butlin, Luther and Warrell 1989, contains information on Egremont as a collector of contemporary art; for Vernon see Hamlyn (forthcoming, 1993).
27 See Whitley 1930, pp.65-76, 103.

J. Ward, *Bulls fighting with a view of St. Donatt's Castle, Glamorgan*, oil on panel, 1804. Victoria and Albert Museum

recognised. One might say that a tacit pact was now cemented between the Academy and the public, which, by means of the perpetual give-and-take of the annual exhibitions and the criticism they engendered, created a *modus vivendi* for both, and fostered a generation of painters more confident than their predecessors had been of their right to entertain rather than to instruct. The painters who emerged as pre-eminent were those who could suggest grandeur and seriousness while effectively providing visual excitement of an order previously undreamed of. Lawrence, working in what was still the most lucrative branch of the profession, portraiture, achieved supreme success with his suave, bravura likenesses of the grandees not only of Britain but of all Europe. He was indeed un-British in his flair for presenting his sitters as both glamorous and dignified, perhaps the most completely Van Dyckian of all British portrait painters in his technical and psychological mastery.[28] There is, though, something inimitably English about his penchant for Reynoldsian compromise in what he called 'half-history'

portraits of the actor John Philip Kemble, in such tragic roles as Hamlet, Coriolanus and Addison's Cato.

Lawrence's ability effortlessly to evoke and, in a highly personal and original way, to continue the achievements of the past exemplifies the change which, by the 1820s, had come over Reynolds's notion of taking ideas from the old masters. Instead of being limited to an academic use of Renaissance and Baroque motifs in subject pictures, it became a living impulse behind much of the best work of the time. Baroque artists who had remained in relative obscurity in the eighteenth century – Velasquez, for instance, who is not referred to by Reynolds (Spain had not been on the Grand Tour, but after the Napoleonic Wars became a popular destination for travellers) – began to exert their influence, notably on the work of Wilkie. Etty,

28   See Garlick 1989; and West 1991, pp.226-49.

J.M.W. Turner, *Dort or Dortecht: The Dort Packet-boat from Rotterdam becalmed*, oil on canvas, 1818. Yale Center for British Art, Paul Mellon Collection

who became famous as a student of the nude, and for his virtuoso handling of sensuous paint, showed that the splendours of Renaissance Venice could be recreated in modern London, and that the human figure could be made the vehicle for serious ideas without being deprived of its sensuality. He gave a fresh validity, not to say appeal, to themes rendered austere and cold by neo-classicism. He was, of course, admonished for impropriety; but his successful invocation of Titian and Rubens – and of course of the doctrines of Reynolds – ensured his place on the Academy walls. Etty is thought of as an exception among Protestant English artists for his concentration on nakedness. But his links with sculpture and with neo-classicism are obvious: throughout the period it remained perfectly normal to present the human body naked in stone.[29]

The same principle held good even in landscape paint-ing. James Ward, supreme as an animal painter at a time when the demand for sporting art bred many distinguished exponents in that department, applied his great admiration of Rubens to many grandly-conceived landscapes inspired by *The Château de Steen*. This immensely influential picture had been acquired by Sir George Beaumont in 1803; it entered the National Gallery with his gift in 1828. Ward's animal pictures were produced equally under Rubens's spell. His heroic horse-portraits are among the great romantic images, and he translated them into a series of lithographs that deserve wider attention as pre-eminent among the prints of their period.[30] Another

29 Farr, 1958.
30 See Ward 1960; Fussell 1974; Nygren 1982.

devotee of Rubens and the 'dewy light and freshness' of his panoramic landscapes was Constable, who succeeded in importing that quality into his own work and making it the *leit-motif* of much of his art.[31] Despite the debt to Rubens, Constable's was so intensely personal a vision of nature, his handling of paint so radically innovative, that he was many years finding favour. Although Beaumont championed him from the start of his career, he did not become an Academician until nearly the end of his life.

Unlike Constable, Turner attained instant fame and managed to retain his standing as the leading landscape painter of his time throughout a long career, in spite of providing the critics with some of the most fertile material for satire that they ever enjoyed. His success was perhaps owing to the fact that he operated over such a wide gamut of types of work. His highly theatrical historical landscapes, intended explicitly to demonstrate that a serious landscape art was possible, gained the approval of the Academy while his topographical watercolours, engraved and published in many places, brought him a plentiful income.[32] His experiments were undertaken in the context of a highly academic and essentially retrograde view of art – of all the great painters of his time Turner is the most reliant on the example of the old masters. If Lawrence drew inspiration from Van Dyck, Etty from Titian and Ward from Rubens, Turner was prepared not merely to acknowledge a debt but to paint elaborate pastiches of Cuyp, Rembrandt, Watteau or Canaletto. These pastiches epitomise the art-historical preoccupation of the age, though they are far more than mere imitations, embodying as they do an entirely personal vision. But they go much further than Turner's contemporaries in paying art-historical homage. He was almost invariably provoked to it by the example of some modern master, a professional colleague or rival. Thus his greatest essay in the style of Cuyp, the *Dort* of 1818, was prompted by Augustus Callcott's *Pool of London* of two years earlier; while in the 1820s he became a Watteau imitator through the example of Stothard, and a Rembrandt follower via his friend George Jones.[33] His early love of Wilson matured into a passionate admiration for Claude which he indulged almost obsessively throughout his life. Claude became the starting point for innumerable compositions, including the last he ever exhibited. It is one of the most piquant ironies of art history that Beaumont, the arch traditionalist in matters of art criticism, always championed Constable and heartily loathed Turner.[34]

The lessons to be drawn from Beaumont's perversity are that the connoisseur does not possess any absolute powers of judgement, and originality takes unexpected forms. It was Beaumont who recommended that a landscape should have the brown colour of a Cremona fiddle, eliciting from Constable his famous response – placing a violin on the grass in front of Beaumont's house. Constable too admired and copied Claude, though he never imitated him in his original work as Turner did. The Claude he copied was one 'which warms and cheers, but which does not inflame or irritate'.[35] Turner's academicism was the forcing-house of a mass of innovatory ideas both technical and aesthetic, and they must have seemed all the more shocking on that account. The Academy was already creating – as all academies must – the terms of reference (or self-reference) which were to make true innovation increasingly difficult. With both oil and watercolour institutionalised in this way, it might have proved hard for the practitioners in either medium to break new ground; yet, because of the constant interchange of ideas between the two media, development could and did occur. Turner's extraordinary originality was certainly in part attributable to his concurrent use of both.

One artist who saw himself as a great original genius was significantly at loggerheads with the Academy throughout his career. This was Benjamin Robert Haydon, who (like Turner) admired the equally farouche and eccentric James Barry, venerated the old masters and based his most important works closely on their example. He deplored the debasement of art that seemed inevitably to accompany its popularisation. His large historical subjects were carefully studied and diligently worked out; they dealt with the most sublime of human dramas – the Judgement of Solomon, Christ entering Jerusalem, Macbeth about to murder Duncan – but they met with precisely the same fate that had befallen Barry's similarly ambitious works. Haydon was not slow to infer that the British were incapable of higher feelings when it came to art.[36] He scored more success with his smaller scenes from contemporary life, in which he stooped to ally himself with the genre painters.

By the standards of the eighteenth century this was indeed a condescension. Reynolds occasionally painted a

31 Leslie ed. Mayne 1951, p.315.
32 For Turner's life and career in general see Finberg 1939, rev. edn. 1961. For recent discussions of the prints after his work see Lyles and Perkins 1989 and Herrmann 1990.
33 For Callcott see Brown 1981. Brown deals at length there with the relationship between Callcott and Turner.
34 See Leslie ed. Mayne 1951, and Owen and Brown 1988, p.87 and chapter 11.
35 Leslie ed. Mayne 1951, pp.109, 114.
36 Haydon's attitudes are perfectly clear from his *Autobiography* (see note 12 above) and *Diary*, ed. Pope, 5 vols., 1960-63.

landscape – even, in his younger days, caricature; but domestic genre was hardly to be countenanced. He nevertheless admired the great social satires of Hogarth (who had died in 1764).[37] But these were followed by works whose satirical edge was severely blunted by the sentimental movement that prevailed in the 1780s and '90s. Francis Wheatley's rustic scenes reflected the influence of Greuze, and are charming rather than mordant; George Morland's peasants grouped at the doors of stables or taverns are painted with a gusto that imbues the best of them with a convincingly bucolic life. His work, like the many prints after it, and like the artist himself, was easygoing; it made few demands and asked to be appreciated simply as fluent painting of simple subjects. Much of it is denuded even of the kind of sentimental moralising that was normal at the time.[38]

Within a year or two of Morland's early death the whole field of the genre was transformed by a reinterpretation of its typical subject-matter in terms that, like Flaxman's neo-classicism and Girtin's watercolour, both developed and rejected the Reynoldsian position. Just as Turner was advancing topographical landscape by presenting it in the guise of Claudean idyll or Poussinesque drama, the young Wilkie made explicit the art-historical credentials of peasant genre by depicting contemporary low-life scenes in a way deliberately reminiscent of Ostade, Steen and the seventeenth-century Dutch masters. This was a self-conscious and deceptively intellectual approach. At the same time, Wilkie's figures are characterised with virtuoso clarity and their settings observed with a novelist's awareness of place so that his subjects have an authority, a sense of reality, that rises above both satire and sentiment. They are humorous, but not merely humorous; some are not humorous at all. His first success in London, *Village Politicians* of 1805, was conceived as a comic piece with clear Hogarthian resonances; *The Blind Fiddler* of 1806 is an advance in sophistication in using Dutch prototypes. Subsequent pictures are more personal and assured, subtly designed to present their material objectively (as it were), leaving comedy or poignancy to emerge incidentally. *The Penny Wedding* (1818) and *Reading the Will* (1820) do not patronise or condescend to rustic simplicities, and *Distraining for Rent* of 1815 is a domestic tragedy of the economic depression that accompanied the Napoleonic Wars, analysed with insight and compassion.[39]

This new, more intelligent type of genre had an immense impact. It was as influential as Flaxman's outlines in shaping European aesthetics in the early nineteenth century. *Reading the Will* was actually painted for Ludwig I of Bavaria. Wilkie introduced a new 'branch' of art

C.R. Leslie, *My Uncle Toby and the Widow Wadman from Sterne's 'Tristram Shandy'*, oil on canvas, c.1831. Victoria and Albert Museum

37 Reynolds ed. Malone 1801, vol. 3, p.163.
38 Morland has been subjected to modern analysis in Barrell's influential *The Dark Side of the Landscape* 1980, but it is difficult to find any corroborative evidence in the pictures themselves for the elaborate socio-political ideas expounded there.
39 For an interesting recent interpretation of Wilkie's subject-matter see Errington 1985.

into the canon of respectability, while at the same time blurring the distinctions between other branches. This had a highly subversive effect on the old hierarchy of subject types. The new subject-matter involved several, often many, figures in psychological interaction, but on a small scale, so that it offered much of the creative challenge of history painting, but in a form more palatable to buyers (especially those living in modest houses) and with terms of reference less recondite.

So the depiction of modern manners flourished, as did anecdotal history painting: twin ramifications of the same branch of art. The unheroic moments, the intimacies of celebrated lives, or the incidents of ordinary life in distant epochs – these now figured more frequently in the Academy catalogues, and the grandiose performances of Haydon and Howard began to look old fashioned. The Shakespeare subjects promulgated by Boydell were looked at again, and the comedies taken up with a fresh delight in the opportunities they offered for showing period costume, psychological analysis and humour. The American C.R. Leslie had progressed from *Timon of Athens* and *Macbeth* in 1812 and 1813 to an unexhibited scene from *The Merry Wives of Windsor* in 1818. In 1819 he submitted *Sir Roger de Coverley going to Church accompanied by the Spectator*, and gave a further fillip to the progress of the genre.[40] It was now possible to plunder for subjects all the popular classics of the last two hundred years, and Addison's *Spectator*, in which the character of Sir Roger appeared, was quickly joined by *Tristram Shandy, Gil Blas, The Vicar of Wakefield, The Deserted Village* and innumerable others. Many of these works were classics of the sentimental period, and much early nineteenth-century genre harks back nostalgically to the atmosphere of the eighteenth. But the emotional and dramatic range is greatly increased in comparison with that of Wheatley and his contemporaries, and the degree of careful archaeological reconstruction remarkable when we consider that this phenomenon predates Ruskin by twenty years and the Pre-Raphaelites by almost thirty.

What had happened can perhaps be explained by a comparison with developments in the late twentieth century. Just as the grandiose and sometimes sublime abstractions of the New York School gave way to the sharp immediacy of Pop Art and Photorealism, so the generalisation of the Reynoldsian grand manner was followed by a reaction in favour of more local and specific themes, more realistic treatment. The national school was beginning to evolve its own dialectic, and it was natural to look back to great indigenous precursors. Hogarth was invoked, not merely as a founding father of the British School, but as the progenitor of a branch of art whose im-

portance was newly recognised as seminal. By 1831 it was possible for Henry Crabb Robinson to assert that 'Were Reynolds's works taken from the world by a miracle they would not be missed, but the loss of Hogarth would leave a chasm, if not in fine art strictly speaking, but in pictorial wisdom. He was the greatest of moral painters that ever lived.'[41]

Genre painting was, then, seen as a tradition of morality which could assume some of the intellectual responsibility of history painting. It even invaded the territory of portraiture. In the 1820s there arose a fashion for painting single figures as 'historical' portraits – usually heroines from Shakespeare or Byron – which occupy the ground somewhere between genre and portrait. These often highly decorative works availed themselves of the popularity of subjects taken from serious or sentimental fiction, while continuing the eighteenth-century tradition (practised by Reynolds) of the fancy picture, which also frequently had erotic appeal. Hence the type was not eschewed by the high-minded: Charles Lock Eastlake, one of the most earnest of his generation, exhibited works of this kind at the Academy, and allowed them to be engraved for publication in the Annuals.

These Annuals were presentation volumes which came out each year under names like *The Gem, The Keepsake* and *Friendship's Offering*, and were much in vogue in the twenties and thirties. Anthologies combining snatches of literature with engravings after contemporary works of art, they aimed at being light, agreeable and entertaining. Yet the most serious artists did not scorn to appear in their pages, and their subject-matter ranged from the solemn to the ludicrous. The illustrator Thomas Stothard was to be found there, with his elegant variations on themes after Watteau; George Jones might contribute a historical subject or one of his continental townscapes; the learned Eastlake and the comic Robert Smirke were equally likely to be encountered. Several of Turner's watercolour views were engraved for the Annuals, and his curious picture of *Jessica*, purporting to illustrate a scene from *The Merchant of Venice* and exhibited in 1830 (*The Times* called it 'an incomprehensible daub'), was almost certainly conceived with publication of this sort in mind.[42] Engraving was a natural outlet for his ideas, and over the course of his career he had trained a substantial

---

40 Leslie ed. Taylor 1860, pp.72-74.
41 Crabb Robinson *Diary*, 4 December 1831.
42 Wilton 1989, pp.14-33.

J.M.W. Turner, *Music in the White Library, Petworth House*, watercolour and bodycolour, 1827. Tate Gallery

school to reproduce his designs in watercolour with consummate skill. In this too he was the heir of Reynolds.

Given the predominantly literary and anecdotal nature of the Annuals, an unexpected contributor to them is Richard Parkes Bonington, whose small-scale landscapes and interiors were first seen in London at the British Institution in 1826. Bonington, only twenty-four and destined to die within three years, had spent his adult life in France, and has come to epitomise the links between England and France in the period. His modest scenes from the family life of the Valois kings and little watercolour imitations of Dutch domestic interiors with figures constitute an extraordinarily dispassionate commentary on the fashion for anecdote. Figures, fabrics and objects, light and shade, are composed into rich tableaux almost devoid of moral or even narrative purpose – they have evidently been painted for the sake of painting.[43] The Grand Manner tradition and the sentimental historical content of the French Troubadour painters are both equally subverted. Even the slight narrative excuses usual in Dutch art are forgotten. The existence of these pictures is then something of an anomaly among the determinedly anecdotal work that proliferated in London in the 1820s. They were admired simply for their technical qualities,

and it is clear that moral content was no more an absolutely necessary ingredient in painting then than it was to be a hundred years later. The aesthetic merits of the object *qua* object were understood as capable of being sufficient in themselves.

About the time that Bonington made his first impact on London, some indigenous artists seem to have been moving in a similar direction. Turner's colour, for instance, had become much clearer and brighter since a visit to Italy in 1819, and from the twenties onwards he worked in oil almost invariably on a white ground, exploiting brilliant new pigments like chrome yellow and the recently invented emerald green. These advances were evidently made possible by his knowledge of watercolour. In the small gouache designs that he made in the 1830s showing domestic scenes at Petworth he seems to have had Bonington specifically in mind; those illustrating tours of European rivers employ a spectrum of saturated hues without parallel before the twentieth century, and have an equally twentieth-century lack of concern for natural-

43   Noon 1991.

J.M.W. Turner, *The Billiard Players, Petworth House*, watercolour and bodycolour, 1827. Tate Gallery

ism.[44] Although they are much more elaborate, the intricately detailed watercolours of John Frederick Lewis also have much in common with Bonington's jewel-like world: they have the lazy, unimportant figural subject-matter, and the chromatic brilliance of a Turkey carpet. Indeed, much of Lewis's work was inspired by the patterns of Moorish interiors. Cotman's later watercolours make use of an even brighter palette, and this, combined with his astringently linear compositions, achieves a clarity and boldness that is entirely at one with the new departures that characterise painting in the 1830s.[45]

Bonington, on the other hand, when he was painting landscape or marine views tended towards a very cool palette and replaced the warm clutter of his interiors with empty expanses of pure atmosphere that anticipate those of Whistler. That joy in the medium for its own sake is the underlying assumption behind much of what was achieved in watercolour, a medium in which Bonington also excelled. Unknown as he was then to the London public, he was recognised as the painter of

pictures which would grace the foremost name in landscape art. Sunshine, perspective, vigour; a fine sense of beauty in disposing of colour, whether in masses or

mere bits ... Few pictures have more skilfully expressed the character of open, sunny daylight ... and we have seldom seen an artist make more of the simple materials which the subject afforded.[46]

This catalogue of abstractions is a recognition that modern landscape painting could as legitimately concern itself with intangible effects of light and air as with topographical facts.

It was, of course, a development from the treatment of light and atmosphere in traditional watercolour topography – the source of far more radical innovation than it has been given credit for. Bonington's teacher in France, F.L.T. Francia, had studied with Girtin, but Bonington's handling of paint was uniquely his own. His work was making its impression on his French colleagues at just the time when Constable's revolutionary landscape style,

44   Powell 1991.
45   For Lewis see [Green] 1971. Cotman's later work has been neglected; but see note 18 above.
46   The *Literary Gazette*, quoted in Whitley 1930, pp.99-100.

J. Constable, *The Hay Wain*, oil on canvas, 1823. National Gallery

with its awareness of the value of the brushstroke in its own right, was seen at the Paris Salon in pictures like *The Hay Wain*, which won a medal there in 1824. Constable too, as we have already noticed, was concerned to relate the physical features of English scenery to the more fleeting effects of atmosphere, as he made explicit in his publication *Various Subjects of Landscape, Characteristic of English Scenery*, which appeared in parts between 1830 and 1832.[47] It consisted of a series of mezzotint plates by David Lucas after compositions – mostly oil studies – that Constable chose to demonstrate the range and chief preoccupations of his work. Its conception no doubt owed something to Turner's more ambitious survey of his own achievement, the *Liber Studiorum*, also executed in mezzotint, which had been issued in instalments between 1807 and 1819.[48] In the letterpress that Constable wrote for *English Landscape Scenery* he composed a kind of mani-

festo of his purposes as a landscape painter, chief among which was the desire 'to mark the Phenomena of the Chiar'Oscuro of Nature', as the subtitle to the second edition of 1833 put it. This was a goal that Turner had also been pursuing from an early stage. But in fact his aims were very different from Constable's. He retained a Haydonesque regard for significant content, and continued all his life to paint historical subjects. His intention in bathing them in a vividly realised atmosphere of sunlight or mist was to endow them with a greater sublimity: for Turner Romantic naturalism was the servant of the tradi-

47 See Parris and Fleming-Williams 1991, pp.319-57.
48 Finberg 1924.

J.M.W. Turner, *The Burning of the Houses of Parliament*, oil on canvas, 1835. The Cleveland Museum of Art, Bequest of John L. Severance

tional grand manner. Thus it was possible for one of the greatest of Reynolds's adherents to be the idol of Ruskin.

Turner's thematically loaded historical landscapes are then a pivot of the see-saw of aesthetics in our period. They embody the grand literary ideas of Reynolds and the freedom and close observation of the progressive watercolourists. Turner could, moreover, embrace modern subjects. His two canvases of *The Burning of the Houses of Lords and Commons* (1835) present a contemporary Day of Judgement with a cast of thousands of ordinary Londoners. The pictures are journalism, topography and grand opera rolled into one.

But Turner was not the only practitioner in this genre. The two extremes of grandeur and immediacy are more clearly separated out in the work of Francis Danby, who alternated scenes of apocalyptic drama with intimate rural life. As the recorder of crisply-observed scenes of middle-class relaxation in the woods of the Avon Gorge near Bristol he belongs with the landscape painters, like Cotman, William Havell and Joshua Cristall, who practised more in watercolour than in oil and betrayed in their work the extent to which the neo-classical aesthetic could affect even the naturalists of their generation. There is a simple dignity, a sense of order, in their scenes of full-leaved groves and gentle rivers that harks back to Poussin. That mood played an important role in defining the common style of the old Water-Colour Society after its foundation, and remained a dominant factor throughout the

F. Danby, *The Upas, or Poison Tree in the island of Java*, oil on canvas, 1819. Victoria and Albert Museum

period in the watercolours of men like William Turner of Oxford and George Fennel Robson.[49]

But the moral overtones of decay and decline that are inherent in true classical landscape sometimes become more urgent, and create a world that totters on the brink of violence. That violence is usually suppressed in Danby's work, though on certain memorable occasions it becomes his dominant subject-matter. His Avon views, with their almost Biedermeier tidiness, are very far removed from the stark grandeur of the visionary subjects he painted not for local patrons but for showing in London at the Academy. The first appeared in 1820: *The Upas Tree* is one of the bleakest images of the whole period, a nightmare glimpse of a lonely and miserable death in an impossible, lunar landscape blighted by the mephitic Upas. More usually his visions concerned the fate of crowds generally; *The Crossing of the Red Sea* and *The Opening of the Sixth Seal* are about the fate of humanity as a whole.[50] They embody apocalyptic ideas that were widely entertained in these years, and which motivated several new movements in the non-conformist church. A sense of impending doom was common, millenarianism a popular creed among working people in London and elsewhere; the preaching of radical self-appointed prophets like Richard Brothers called forth an art to illustrate it. Their ideas were anti-establishment and

49 Roget 1891, and Taylor 1973; also *William Turner of Oxford*, 1984-85.
50 Greenacre 1988-89.

much of the painting that illustrates them has a provincial, anti-academic quality that lends it great vigour. The doyen of these apocalypse-merchants was the Northumberland-born John Martin, whose work was regularly exhibited at the Academy and the British Institution and widely disseminated in the form of mezzotints which he executed himself. They are among the most powerful of Romantic prints. His visions of the end of the world, of the Deluge, of Pandemonium, remain definitive images, sensational as Hollywood epics, devastating, thrilling and absurd.[51] Martin, indeed, belongs more to the sphere of entertainment than art strictly defined. His comprehensive sensationalism is allied to that of the panorama, which flourished throughout these decades but was understandably felt by some connoisseurs to lack seriousness. It is interesting that they should have thought fit to judge it by the standards of academic art. There was, in fact, a cultural continuum from the walls of the Academy to the incidental and occasional street-shows of the metropolis which is characteristic of the interrelationship between painting and public in this period.[52] 'Sir George Beaumont', Leslie records, 'was of the opinion, and perhaps with some reason, that the effect of panorama painting has been injurious to the taste, both of the artists and the public, in landscape.' In Constable's view, such painting exhibited more imagination than nature, and was therefore at fault: he called Martin's work 'pantomime' and, talking of both Danby and Martin, said 'The art is now filled with *Phantasmagoria*'.[53]

The true, if unacknowledged, leader of the non-conformist enthusiasts was William Blake. Like Turner's his mind was formed on a diet of promiscuous and often recondite reading. Unlike Turner, though, he used his art as a means of expressing an immensely complex philosophy that is hardly comprehensible without reference to his extensive writings – his Prophetic Books, the product of the frequent visions that he claimed inspired all his work, and his wayward, highly idiosyncratic criticism. The lyric verse of his *Songs of Innocence and Experience* is by far the most accessible of his poetry, and the decorative designs that accompany the *Songs* on small, characteristically integrated pages, printed by means of a process that Blake also claimed was revealed in a vision, are some of his most attractive images. They betray an early awareness of medieval illumination which anticipates a lifelong oscillation between the classical and the Gothic in his own art. Towards the end of his career he paid his most extensive tribute to the middle ages in a series of watercolour designs (never finished) illustrating Dante's *Inferno*, *Purgatorio* and *Paradiso* which embody his profoundest ideas concerning the use of watercolour as a

pure technique, very different in almost every way from his contemporaries. In them the freshness of eighteenth-century methods is combined with an exploitation of the expressive potential of the medium to evoke a shimmering and iridescent envelope of light which imbues them with an unearthly – one might well say visionary – atmosphere.[54]

On a much smaller scale are the woodcuts that he made, also late in life, to illustrate a volume of verse edited for schools by a Dr Robert Thornton. These are tiny epitomes of rustic life, of the discourse of shepherd swains in an arcadia perpetually illuminated by a chilly yet consoling moon. They constituted a revelation to a group of younger artists who found Blake's visionary, miniature landscapes congenial to their own passionate feeling for a fecund natural world lovingly cultivated by man under the inspiration of a benign and immanent God. Of these, John Linnell was already confirmed in his patient study of the details of landscape, as we have seen. A younger friend, Samuel Palmer, attempted in his own work to give a more personal and mystical account of the spirituality he felt to be inherent in nature. This was a more explicitly religious version of the ordered neo-classical landscapes of the Water-Colour Society, though one that expressed a very different religious sense from that of the millenarians.[55]

The religious tendency that can be perceived in so much of the art of the 1820s and '30s contrasts strongly with the formalised and largely nominal religious art of the Reynoldsian period. It has the ring of personal conviction about it, rather than the cachet of intellectual respectability. While Pugin was developing his notions of a serious religious architecture, collectors were beginning to discover the paintings of the early Italians, the gold-ground altarpieces of Duccio and Giotto and Fra Angelico that Reynolds had regarded as crude and primitive. Already in the early 1800s on the Continent painters were imitating the clear colours and simple designs of art before the High Renaissance, and doing so with a devotional fervour which they believed to be a sincere replica of medieval faith. The German Nazarenes, in particular, adopted a pure quattrocento style which epitomises the movement.[56] In its aesthetic purity it was, at bottom, not

51   Feaver 1975.
52   Hyde 1988.
53   Leslie ed. Mayne 1951, pp.17, note 79, 178.
54   Gilchrist 1863; Keynes, ed. 1966, and Bindman 1977. For a recent bibliography see Butlin 1981.
55   Grigson 1947; Lister ed., 2 vols, 1974.
56   Vaughan 1979.

so much Gothic as a version of neo-classicism, and the religious sculpture of Flaxman has much in common with it. It would be unthinkable without the influential Flaxman outlines we have already noticed. Indeed, Flaxman himself copied Gothic sculpture and discussed it in his lectures as Professor of Sculpture at the Academy. In its turn, Nazarene art adopted his outlines and converted them from classical to Gothic. The interplay between the two aesthetic tendencies, ostensibly opposed to one another, lies behind much of the energy of the Romantic period.

One of the first collectors of pre-Renaissance art in London was a German merchant, Charles Aders (1780-1846). Aders was married to the daughter of an artist, the pastellist and mezzotinter John Raphael Smith; she herself was a painter. The couple were friendly with some of the principal literary figures of the time, including Coleridge and Wordsworth, and were close to the diarist Henry Crabb Robinson, who was interested in both German art and the work of Blake. The Aders themselves owned drawings by Blake and frequently entertained him. In their house in Euston Square the walls were 'closely covered' with early Italian pictures and an important group of works by or after Van Eyck, Memling and Matsys. Crabb Robinson reported Blake as saying that 'in my youth I was always studying that class of paintings'. This would have been very advanced taste for the 1770s when Blake was an apprentice. Aders also knew a number of contemporary German artists, at least one of whom, Gotzenberger, met Blake at Aders's house.[57] Another contact of Aders's was the Keeper of the British Museum's Print Room, William Young Ottley, whose own forceful pen drawings after early Italian pictures and sculptures are a kind of halfway house between Flaxman's Grecian outlines and the Gothicised German designs of Schnorr von Carolsfeld and Moritz von Retsch. Ottley was instrumental in fostering a new understanding of the engravings and woodcuts of Dürer, and his engraved facsimiles of works of the Italian quattrocento constitute a landmark in the development of the 'Pre-Raphaelite' taste.[58]

It would be wrong, then, to ascribe the resurgence of Gothic simply to the intensification of religious feeling in Britain during these decades. The Ruskins' puritanism and Samuel Palmer's rather high Anglicanism flowered simultaneously with a fresh departure on the part of connoisseurs and artists, who took up medieval art as an extension of their existing enthusiasm for the Antique. This again signals a general broadening of the foundations of understanding. The common denominator, however, remains the concern with line as a vehicle for expression. As

we have seen with Cotman, the renewed sense of the importance of line went hand in hand with a completely new approach to colour. The Nazarenes had demonstrated the possibility of using clear, saturated colour without chiaroscuro as it was found in the frescoes of the quattrocento, and they were an obvious source of inspiration when plans were in hand for the decoration of the new Houses of Parliament, which, significantly, it was proposed should be in fresco. Charles Lock Eastlake, who had known many of the Nazarenes in Rome, but had worked in a high-mindedly neo-classical style in the 1820s, was put in charge of the project. He organised a nationwide competition, to which almost every painter of ambition submitted a design.[59]

A substantial proportion of the winning designs were by the Scotsman William Dyce, whose work relates closely to that of the Germans in style and preoccupations. Dyce too had known some of the Nazarenes as a young man in Rome, and his entire output reflects that experience. Although he disclaimed the direct influence of Nazarene art on his work at Westminster, the medievalising themes, the simplified, rhythmic designs betray his community of interest with them. He was to be joined in his work at Westminster by Maclise, who also embodied many of the new tendencies in his work. His painting, enormously successful in its day, is more full-blooded, more sensual, in a word more vulgar than Dyce's; his style is characterised by a glossy finish, strong, bright colours and a plethora of crisply indicated detail. He is theatrical and brash where Dyce is measured and cerebral. But both Dyce and Maclise differ from West and his contemporaries in giving primary importance to carefully defined form – to outline as the boundary of clear, pure colour. The two men represent well the state of painting in London after Prince Albert's arrival from Germany in 1840.

Needless to say, Haydon disapproved. He traced a downward curve in the graph of British achievements since the end of the Napoleonic Wars which made England vulnerable to all manner of dubious foreign influences.

We escaped the contagion of David's brickdust . . . the

---

57   Vaughan 1979, pp.20 ff., and Gilchrist 1863, p.333.
58   Vaughan 1979, pp.22, 29.
59   For Eastlake see the Memoir of him by Lady Eastlake, in Eastlake, 2nd ser., 1870. A brief but informative summary of the commissions for paintings in the Palace of Westminster is given by Boase in Port ed. 1976; chapter 12 (5).

frescoes are but a branch of the same Upas root grafted on Albert Durer's hardness, Cimabue's gothicism, and the gilt ground inanity of the middle ages. All the vast comprehensiveness of Velasquez, Rubens and Titian, are now to be set aside, and we are not to go on where they left off, but to begin where their predecessors began.[60]

Alas for Haydon, he was flying in the face of history. On 22 June 1846, he cut his own throat and shot himself in the head. It was a sad conclusion to a heroic, if misguided, attempt to continue applying the old principles of painting in a world that had changed for ever.

The teutonic flavour of English painting in the 1840s is unmistakable. The Prince Consort's presence as a new personality in the art world quickly began to make itself felt. He was known to be actively interested in aesthetic matters – more so than Victoria and far more so than her predecessor William. It was to be expected that artists would attune their output to a different mood. The Germanic sharpness and cleanness of finish now became the norm; it is hardly surprising that the late masterpieces of Turner, still harking back to Burkean sublimity and Reynoldsian generalisation, looked old fashioned and 'indistinct'.[61] He was an old man and, in his own way, like Haydon thoroughly out of date.

Bright colour, smooth finish, multitudinous detail: these are the preponderant qualities of the new art, the painting of the age following the Reform Bill. It required a Ruskin to assess them in relation to the older order, and it is highly ironic that he used as his yardstick and touchstone the work of Turner, who, of all Romantics, lived most wholeheartedly in the Reynoldsian world of the classic sublime. And it is not surprising that Ruskin found much of the new art wanting, for it sprang, not out of any pious philosophy of aesthetics, as did the painting of Reynolds's immediate successors, but in response to a lively new public, more active as collectors of both original works and reproductive prints, as exhibition-goers, and as critics, than the public of the eighteenth century. It is undoubtedly an art that records a more popular experience of the world than Reynolds's or Barry's – an art, in short, altogether closer to twentieth-century democratic ideas of what a relevant visual culture should be about.

60 Leslie 1860, vol. 1, p.228.
61 For the famous story of Turner accusing himself of 'indistinctness' in connection with his *Staffa*, see Holcomb 1972, pp.557-58.

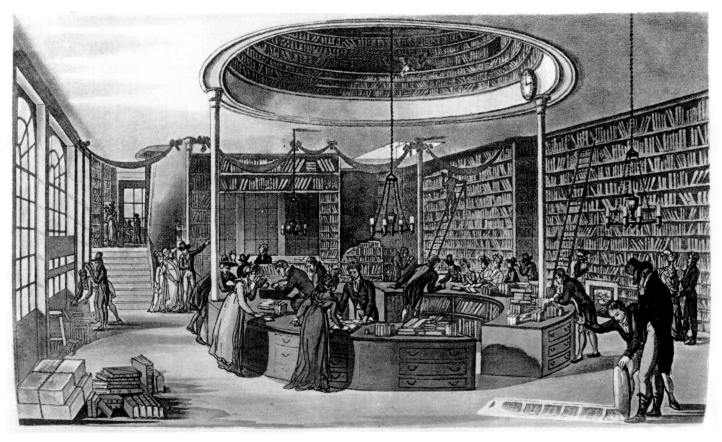

Lackington's Temple of the Muses, Finsbury Square, the largest bookshop in London, aquatint from Ackermann's *Repository of Arts*, 1809. The Museum of London

HIDDEN METROPOLIS: LONDON IN SENTIMENTAL AND ROMANTIC WRITING

Marilyn Butler

Metropolis. 1535. [μητρσ mother + πσλις city]
1. The see of a metropolitan bishop
2. The chief town of a country; a capital, 1590
3. The parent-state of a colony; mother country, 1806

In 1800 London remained what it had been since the early middle ages, the literary capital of England. The removal of state regulation and of censorship of the printing trade in 1694 contributed to a boom in books and journals. The same act legalised printing in English provincial cities and towns. In the course of the eighteenth century many provincial newspapers emerged, and the Scottish and Irish capitals, Edinburgh and Dublin, produced a range of books from theology and topography to polemical tracts and poetry. Even so, the numbers, wealth and enterprise of London publishers, and the size of London's reading public, easily enabled the Londoners to dominate the trade in general books for leisure reading. Travels, memoirs, histories, novels, plays and poetry poured out in steadily rising numbers, along with the general journals and specialised literary reviews (invariably owned and edited by publishers) which created and maintained the vogue for new books in English at home and overseas.

British writers experienced less surveillance than their opposite numbers in pre-Revolution France or in the absolutist German states. Though dependent on commercial publishers and on the market, by the middle of the eighteenth century they were virtually free of the aristocratic patron. Writing was establishing itself as a profession open to talent rather than to family influence or money; this distinguished it from the church, the armed

I.R. and G. Cruikshank, *An Introduction. – Gay Moments of Logic, Jerry, Tom and Corinthian Kate*, aquatint from Pierce Egan's *Life in London*, 1821. The Museum of London

services, and to a lesser extent medicine and law. Just as the mid-century reviews waged a campaign to make reading fashionable, so writers began to promote writing. Samuel Johnson and his friends Goldsmith, Garrick, Boswell and Burke, the publisher John Nichols, Isaac D'Israeli, the Romantic men of letters Hazlitt, Lamb, Hunt, Moore and De Quincey, gossiped about and memorialised one another alongside statesmen, war heroes and royalty.[1] Though a high percentage of successful British writers and publishers at this time began life in the provinces, as a virtual condition of advancement they became Londoners, and if lucky the celebrities of a sphere known as 'literary London'.

It seems puzzling that London as an environment, a society, an idea, received so little written attention at a time when the London printing industry and those who lived by it were fashioning themselves so successfully. A question of comparable interest is why, after so long in an imaginative void, the metropolis emerges, reinvented, in 1820. In the troubled and scandal-racked first year of the reign of George IV journals and journalists turned the content and style of literary culture. The *London Magazine* emerged, lively, readable, cosmopolitan, metropolitan, and thus a deliberate challenge to the prestigious *Edinburgh Review* (f. 1802) and its offshoot the *Quarterly Review* (f. 1809), both specialising in long

semi-academic reviews, and to *Blackwood's Edinburgh Magazine* (f. 1817), written in a vigorous homely idiom attuned to a Scottish middle-class readership. Thomas De Quincey's *Confessions of an English Opium Eater* (first serialised in the *London Magazine* from 1820), Hazlitt's *Table Talk (New Monthly Magazine*, from 1821), and Lamb's *Essays of Elia (London Magazine*, from 1821) were the literary sensations of George IV's first years, short informal prose pieces set in the present or remembered past, and mostly located in London. As though gracefully going with the tide, Byron's last instalment of *Don Juan*, Cantos X – XVI (written 1822–23), brings the hero from the Mediterranean, the Turkish empire and Catherine the Great's Russia to London.

Another work symptomatic of these years enjoyed a runaway popular success. Written by an Irish-born

---

1 Ground-breaking literary biographies include Johnson *Lives of the Poets* 1779-81; Boswell *Life of Johnson* 1791; D'Israeli *Curiosities of Literature* 1791 and *Calamities of Authors* 1812-13; Nichols *Literary Anecdotes of the Eighteenth Century* 1812-15; Hazlitt, 'On my first acquaintance with poets' 1823; and *The Spirit of the Age* 1825; Moore *Letters and Journals of Lord Byron, with notices of his life*, 2 vols 1830; De Quincey *Reminiscences of the Lake Poets* 1837.

I.R. and G. Cruikshank,
*Lowest 'Life in London' –
Tom, Jerry and Logic among
the Unsophisticated Sons and
Daughters of Nature at 'All
Max' in the East*, aquatint
from Pierce Egan's *Life in
London*, 1821. The Museum
of London

London printer and sporting journalist, Pierce Egan, and illustrated in Hogarthian style by the brothers Robert and George Cruikshank, *Life in London; or The Day and Night Scenes of Jerry Hawthorn Esq and his elegant friend Corinthian Tom, in their Rambles and Sprees through the Metropolis* is hard to categorise. A guidebook, novel, sequence of caricatures, collection of comic songs, and eventually a stage drama and musical comedy, it first appeared from September 1820 in monthly parts (a cheap sales-technique not previously thought suitable for fiction), and as a book only in July 1821. As tourists, voyeurs, nascent anthropologists and recorders of slang, its well-born heroes Tom and Jerry became household names, and familiarised the public with the capital as a world of many sub-cultures. At home in the West End, scanning crowded Hyde Park, the exclusive salon Almack's, the racehorse saleroom Tattersall's, they take much more pleasure from low-life scenes at dog and cock fights, or from the gin-parlours or 'sluiceries' of the slums, where they meet whores, pickpockets, con-men and drop-outs.

In mapping the literature published between 1800 and 1840, we are faced with a sharp contrast. From 1820 the metropolis itself – topographical London, fashionable London, literary London, slum London – becomes a topic of interest and admiration. After the essayists in the mid-1820s came a group of novelists of high life known as the 'Silver Fork school', including Edward Bulwer Lytton and Benjamin Disraeli, who long afterwards became Queen Victoria's favourite prime minister. By the 1830s the journalist Charles Dickens was evoking low-life London with a familiarity reminiscent of Egan's, though in far better fiction – *Sketches by Boz* (begun in the *Monthly Magazine*, December 1833), *Oliver Twist* (1837-38) and *Nicholas Nickleby* (1838–39).[2]

The decades 1820–40 are often thought of as a mediocre transitional phase before the High Victorian age of Tennyson, Browning and the great nineteenth-century novelists. The prosewriters, journalists and versifiers of this era, many of them plainly scaling down their work to the needs of a rapidly growing, ill-educated readership, stand in equally sharp contrast to the period of English 'High Romanticism' they supersede. Six major poets (at least) were publishing in London between 1789 and 1824, and the period is rich in prose, including fiction. Especially where poetry is concerned, what we now most value from the years 1800 to 1840 belongs disproportionately to the

2 Reid 1971, pp.197-220, makes a case for Egan's cultural importance, particularly his influence on Dickens.

first two decades, when it expresses attitudes to London which are equivocal or hostile.

The six leading English Romantic poets divide conveniently into two generations: the three who had accomplished most of their significant work in poetry before 1810, and the three whose professional careers began after 1810. Blake (1757–1827), Wordsworth (1770–1850) and Coleridge (1775–1834) are the long-lived 'older Romantics' (along with their friends and acquaintances Southey, Lamb and Hazlitt; George Crabbe, Maria Edgeworth, Walter Scott and Jane Austen also belong to this generation). Blake's most innovative and prolific period is 1789–95, when his *Songs of Innocence* (1789) was followed by more illuminated and prophetic books in a rapid series, including *America* (1793), *Europe* (1794), *The Marriage of Heaven and Hell* (1794), *The Songs of Experience* (1794) and *The First Book of Urizen* (1794). As poets Wordsworth and Coleridge shared a 'Great Decade', 1797–1807, in which most of their poems now deemed memorable were written. From 1807 until the 1830s they and their circles exercised a considerable and growing influence over middle-class opinion as advocates of distinctive conservative philosophies.

The so-called 'younger Romantics', principally Byron (b.1788), Shelley (b.1792), and Keats (b. 1795), have much shorter active lives. All three began their careers in London. Byron woke to find himself famous with the two first books of *Childe Harold* (1812), Shelley's name first appeared on a volume of poetry in 1816, Keats's in 1818. While in the capital these poets moved in separate social strata, but shared significant literary acquaintances such as the leading journalists Hazlitt and Leigh Hunt, and the philosopher and novelist William Godwin. Byron lived mainly in Italy from 1816, as did his friend Shelley from 1818, and all three died abroad, Keats in Rome of tuberculosis in February 1821, Shelley by drowning in the Gulf of Spezia in May 1822, and Byron of fever at Missolonghi in Greece in April 1824.

Should we expect to find consistency between the two generations of English Romantic poets, or between the English and their continental contemporaries? The two generations of writers came from varied regional and class backgrounds; they often considered themselves in disagreement on substantial points, ideological and artistic, and every attempt thus far to produce a coherent movement sufficiently capacious to include all six has come to grief. But on one matter – London – the six poets have an instinct in common, the need to keep a distance. Just as the best work of the younger Romantics shows a strong Mediterranean influence, a debt to classical and Italian Renaissance models, so the older Romantic generation is

rooted in the English provinces – the Bristol region (Southey, Coleridge), the Lake District (Wordsworth, Coleridge, Southey), the Scottish borders (Scott) and rural eastern England (Crabbe). With the exception of two important works by the inveterate Londoner Blake, *The Marriage of Heaven and Hell* and *Jerusalem* (1820), not one located most of a major poem in contemporary London.

The long absence of London from good novels as well as good poetry received surprisingly little comment at the time, except from Charles Lamb (1775–1834), an enthusiastic Londoner. Lamb contributed a series of essays on London life to Leigh Hunt's literary journal *The Reflector* (1810), but these attracted far less notice than his *Essays of Elia* (1821), for which the time was ripe. Yet Lamb's belated success rests on a paradox, that he uses public London only slightly: his gentle, humorous sketches are equally often set in small-town or outer-suburban interiors, and populated with eccentrics real and imaginary, who share Lamb's love of food and drink, collect china, play whist, and tolerate one another's foibles.

Lamb is a belated sentimentalist, deeply indebted to Sterne and Goldsmith, both of whom belonged to his grandfather's generation, and his literary genealogy should classify him among provincial artists. For Sterne (*Tristram Shandy*, 1760–67, *A Sentimental Journey*, 1768), Goldsmith (*The Vicar of Wakefield*, 1766, 'The Deserted Village', 1773), Henry Mackenzie (*The Man of Feeling*, 1771, *The Man of the World*, 1773, *Julia de Roubigné*, 1777) are all convinced provincialists; they use an idealised countryside as a counter in an anti-metropolitan rhetoric. In sentimental plots intuitive, innocent characters are made to suffer because of old institutions – Law, Church, Aristocracy, the mercantilism or accumulated capital based in the City of London. Plutocrats, bishops and men of the (London) world are seldom good news; merchants, country squires and pastors step in with the alternative ideology – middle-class benevolence, or solidarity with mankind in general. The most shining examples of virtue or the best parables involve humble creatures arrived at by inverting the normal social hierarchy – wronged peasant girls, perhaps driven mad by their lover's desertion, maimed sailors and soldiers, small vulnerable creatures such as Sterne's ass and sparrow in *Sentimental Journey* and his fly in *Tristram Shandy*.

The extremes to which pathos can go have become easy to ridicule, and tend to distract us from their function. Increasingly reliant on commercial publishers for royalties and advances, English writing had become distinctly commercial in its ethos by the time of the death of Pope in 1744. In the late eighteenth century the real wealth of the country could be seen to shift decade by decade from the south-east or London region to the western industrialising corridor, from Bristol through Birmingham to Liverpool; the journals, with their tables of crops, commodities and prices, chart what is among other things a shift in the consumers of culture. Insofar as prosperous provincials represented a lobby, they often stood for proto-nationalist or 'patriot' sentiments, and demanded active government support in their fight for overseas markets against French and Spanish competitors (the 'foreigners' with whom the cosmopolitan upper classes were thought to sympathise). But in the arts, which aim to please educated readers generally, a gentler middle-class programme, humanitarianism, seems more definitive of the period. Adam Smith's *Theory of Moral Sentiments* (1754) speaks for an ideology of common interests and goodwill, bonding the middle classes to the poor and needy, and incidentally displacing the hereditary responsibility of aristocratic paternalists to watch over the poor. Smith's *Wealth of Nations* (1776) identifies the 'landed and the moneyed interest' as essentially selfish: great landed proprietors, who virtually monopolise power at Westminster, and the merchants and bankers who run the City of London are rich themselves but stand in the way of the wealth of the nation. The idealised provincial businessmen in Thomas Amory's *Life of John Buncle* (1756-66) or Henry Brooke's *The Fool of Quality* (1766–70) or Robert Bage's *Mount Henneth* (1781) are alternative heroes championing the sentimental novel's alternative and utopian sociology, its group-portrait of the nation *without London* as whole, healthy and happy. As a culture independent of court influences, English middle-class journal-writing and fiction produced a much-idealised and tendentious group-identification which served the causes of constitutional reform and practical power-sharing in the decades before 1832.

But the French Revolution made sentiment's cult of shared simplicity and mutual kindness begin to look critical of the entire propertied class, and brought about a counter-revolution in taste as well as politics. Late in the 1790s Wordsworth and Coleridge move away from the directly political themes each uses between 1793 and 1796; they 'return to nature' (as if writers of the 1770s and 1780s were not already wedded to naturalism) and pointedly excise what is tendentious and implicitly confrontational in the sentimental style of handling (say) the poor and their benefactors. Though Wordsworth continues to use beggars in his poems, they cease to seem socially confrontational, as they certainly are in *Salisbury Plain*, a political poem written in 1794 but withheld from publication till 1834. The Old Cumberland Beggar in the poem of that

Robert Hancock, *William Wordsworth*, pencil and wash, 1798. National Portrait Gallery

name (1798) is a benign figure who contributes to social harmony by prompting his humble neighbours to acts of kindness and charity. Elsewhere in Wordsworth's lyric poetry sympathy within a class or between the classes breaks down: Harry Gill fails to help Goody Blake (*Lyrical Ballads*, 1798), the educated adult in 'We Are Seven' unperceptively tries to correct the reasoning of the peasant child (ibid.), the poet out walking cannot understand the song of the solitary Highland Reaper (*Poems in Two Volumes*, 1807), and, in the great ode called 'Resolution and Independence', he strangely fails to hear the old leech-gatherer he questions on the moor.

In fact, Wordsworth's shorter poems of 1797–1807 nervously re-examine those successful class relationships of which sentimentalism boasted, and show them to be too mysterious for the would-be philosopher, 'Rational Man', to grasp. Though Wordsworth's famous Preface (1802) to the *Lyrical Ballads* was read by its opponents as a manifesto for poetry in the language of the common people, his practice as the writer of *lyrical* ballads signals his remoteness from the spirit of folk art. By foregrounding the viewpoint of the sophisticated onlooker, he inverts the social message encoded in the democratising modes of the later Enlightenment, producing instead a poetry which is individualistic rather than communitarian, meditative rather than active. Increasingly Wordsworth becomes known (by opponents again) as an 'egotist': these critics are registering not so much that in his poems he keeps the *poor* at a distance (which would be nothing new), but that he has detached himself from the middle-class ideology of social harmony to which the style of assumed simplicity belongs.

Coleridge, a clergyman's son and a moralist, argues strenuously in poetry and journalism for social relatedness and humanitarian causes, but at his best, as in 'The Ancient Mariner' (1798) and 'Dejection: an Ode' (1802), he writes heartrendingly of loneliness. When in 1797–98 Bonaparte's victories and domestic high prices produced unrest and destabilisation in Britain, he sought themes suggestive of security, and typically found them by imagining hiding-places, closely and almost myopically observed. In 'This Lime-tree bower my prison', he lurks alone, imagining the dark, ferny place his friends have walked to; in 'Fears in Solitude' (1798), where the 'fears' in question are of a French invasion, he has apparently taken cover in a field:

> the dell
> Bath'd by the mist, is fresh and delicate
> As vernal cornfield, or the unripe flax,
> When through its half-transparent stalks, at eve,
> The level sunshine glimmers with green light

[11.7–11]

The role of public leadership towards which Coleridge gestures in his poetry as well as his journalism is betrayed by language; an obsessive particularity of observation speaks instead of his restlessness, anxiety and longing to hide from public issues, public criticism and decision-making.

As the vogue for simplicity became ideologically overcharged between 1797 and 1800, the short philosophical tale, modelled on French work by La Fontaine, Voltaire and Marmontel, finally gave way to the long, discursive, non-didactic novel, domestic or Gothic. Lyrics modelled on ballads soon enjoyed less prestige than long verse romances, for which the models are the poets of the Italian Renaissance, Ariosto, Pulci and Tasso, and their English follower Spenser. Narrative prevails in the nineteenth century, and at first sight it has a convenient neutrality, accessible but not brazenly democratic. Historically it pre-dates French hegemony and the most

familiar old regime court culture, that of Louis XIV at Versailles; the English, like the Germans at this time, are looking for non-French styles. A number of long poems by Rogers, Campbell and Landor succeeded in the 1790s, but the most influential proved to be Robert Southey's Arabian romance *Thalaba the Destroyer* (1801). An eclectic adventure story drawn from middle-eastern and European folk materials, *Thalaba* is arranged in twelve books like *The Aeneid* and many Renaissance epics, but written in an experimental loose metre and stanza-form borrowed from Robert Sayers' 1791 volume of poems translated from Old Norse.

Southey's longer poems have not been adequately reprinted in the twentieth century, and there is still no extended criticism of them. Yet his romances, for some of which he supplied scholarly annotations, plainly provide the basis for the long narrative poems of Scott, Byron, Shelley, Moore and Keats – the series, stretching across the first two decades of the century, that for the first time brought poetry a mass readership. Southey followed *Thalaba* with *Madoc* (1805), set in Wales and Mexico in the twelfth century, and with *The Curse of Kehama* (1810), set at an unspecified date in a Delhi ruled by a Hindu rajah. While Friedrich Schlegel and Friedrich Majer in Germany are showing India as a paradisal homeland, the original site of a synthesising mythology and religion, the formative English Romantic treatments represent the pagan world (by this time typically India) as an unregenerate polity governed by malign religious institutions. Southey's three epics are political poems, confrontations between individual citizens or settlers and cruel tyrants in league with priests; he began work on *Madoc* in 1794, the year in which he and Coleridge planned to emigrate to Pennsylvania to set up a utopian community, and utopianism remains the key to his concept of romance.

Like his friends Wordsworth and Coleridge, Southey was a conservative polemicist by the end of the Napoleonic Wars, but until 1810 his romances advocate revolution, cleansed of any likeness to the French style. In the Mexican scenes of *Madoc* and in *The Curse of Kehama* it seems to be a moral revolution or the reformation of a degenerate religion that he is calling for. As his letters confirm, he detested Bonaparte as a military opportunist and a tyrant, the restorer of slavery and the destroyer of revolution; but he still harboured hopes that there might be internal revolution in both the Austrian and French empires. Southey thought that self-governing colonies in the New World (like the United States and Brazil) would save the old world; his romances never promote, indeed never represent, an empire ruled from metropolitan Britain. A highly significant omission from

Henry Edridge, *Robert Southey*, pencil and wash, 1804. National Portrait Gallery

Don Juan Canto VI, illustrate how the forcefulness of Byron's manner and the compelling interest of his autobiographical subtext combine to deflect our attention from geopolitics to the personal – the harem as a land of fantasy draws us to contemplate male sexuality, especially Byron's own.

Of the other leading Eastern romancers, Shelley in *Laon and Cythna*, reissued with some prudent cuts as *The Revolt of Islam* (1818), sets out to generalise the issue of revolution and empire with some success, yet again without clearly bringing it home to the British themselves. The most directly political and hard-hitting of these long narrative poems is probably Moore's underrated *Lalla Rookh* (1817), which consists of four verse novellas embedded in a frame borrowed from Chaucer's *Canterbury Tales*. An embassy from the Moghul emperor in Delhi is escorting his daughter Lalla Rookh to Kashmir, where she is supposed to meet her future husband, the King of Bokhara. But the king, disguised as a strolling poet, woos her each evening on the journey with romantic and libertarian tales, which are furiously criticised by Fadladeen, an ultra-conservative vizier. Moore wittily bestows on Fadladeen some of the unfavourable English notices of his own nationalist *Irish Melodies* (1807–34). Since Britain occupied Delhi in 1807, its vizier is an apt spokesman for the stream of British orthodoxies which he delivers. In fact Moore's unusually explicit references to Ireland's political and religious oppressions and to the comparable case of the Indian sub-continent make politically overt what elsewhere remains latent. *Lalla Rookh* continued to be read as a poem valorising small-nation independence against metropolitan government; tableaux from it were acted in Richmond, Virginia, the Confederate capital, during the American civil war.

The 'folk'-derived lyrics of the late eighteenth century and the revamped archaic romances of the early nineteenth century have in common their reluctance to represent the metropolis and their preoccupation with it. Directly concerned with war and despotism, and released by their exotic 'otherworld' setting to dwell on the illicit topic of sexuality, the oriental romances were unorthodox and political in what seemed a risky new way. But, paradoxically, they seem to have done much less to shape public attitudes than the sentimental movement of 1760–90, when journals and novels especially not only promoted liberal, humanitarian causes, but provided the middle classes with a flattering group identity. By the early 1800s sentiment's dialoguic and potentially confrontational relationship to London as the seat of government was revised from within the movement, out of all recognition. The paradigmatic English Romantic poem for

Southey's oriental epics is then 'metropolis' in its third sense, newly fashionable in English at this time, to signify the mother country of a world empire.

As a Scottish patriot, Scott in his poems and novels sets up a specifically Anglo-Scottish dialogue which masks the nineteenth-century realities of power, whereby Britain and other European powers took possession of the greater part of the non-European world. Byron's eastern poems pose a stranger problem. Contemporary reviewers quickly sensed that they contained modern political references, but found these hard to tease out. The Turkish narrative poems of 1812–16 contained a weight of documentary detail about the eastern Mediterranean that prevented their being easily read as an allegory about Britain's empire or empires generally. Even then the seat of authority, Constantinople, tends to be masked or localised; Byron likes to substitute a harem as a metaphor for enslavement, exploitation and emasculation under Turkish rule. The most brilliant of his harem scenes, in

many modern critics, Wordsworth's *The Prelude*, gives the topic of country-and-city a very different ideological significance, by treating the city as the home of demos, the monstrous crowd.

In 1802 Wordsworth, accompanied by Lamb the enthusiastic Londoner, visited St. Bartholomew's Fair, the great annual London street-fair held at this date in early September. Two years later he introduced a set-piece description of the fair into his great project of a verse autobiography, which he completed in a thirteen-book version in 1805, though it was finally published in a revised form in fourteen books after his death in 1850. *The Prelude* has interesting relations, quizzical and often negative, with Rousseau's brilliant self-betraying autobiographical writings, the *Confessions* and the *Reveries of a Solitary Walker*, both of which reached the height of their reputation and influence in England in the early 1790s, though modern American Wordsworthians such as M.H. Abrams and Geoffrey Hartman see a profounder likeness to Augustine's *Confessions*, that classic conversion-narrative.[3] Certainly Wordsworth casts his life into a narrative not unlike Augustine's – a careless though relatively innocent youth, early adult worldliness (represented by belief in the French Revolution, which he saw at first hand in 1790 and 1792), followed by his spiritual awakening and retreat from the world.

Other debts are discernible in the 1805 *Prelude*. In 1803 Southey became a neighbour of Wordsworth in Lakeland, and it seems probable that his twelve-book format in *Thalaba the Destroyer* (1801), derived from classical and Renaissance epic, influenced Wordsworth when in the following year he set out to extend an autobiographical blank-verse poem in two books (1799) on his boyhood in the Lakes. In *Thalaba*, the hero comes from a false Paradise, created and ruled by a wicked enchanter (Books VI and VII); he destroys it, and in Book VIII is visited by a vampire from Hell who tempts him by masquerading as his wife. In *The Prelude*, Wordsworth organises the narrative of his 1790 visit to France as a series of promises betrayed, a false Paradise (Book VI), and for the visit to the Fair (Book VII) he draws on descriptive conventions long applied to Hell:

> What a hell
> For eyes and ears! what anarchy and din
> Barbarian and infernal, – 'tis a dream,
> Monstrous in colour, motion, shape, sight, sound!
> Below, the open space, through every nook
> Of the wide area, twinkles, is alive
> With heads; the midway region, and above,
> Is thronged with staring pictures and huge scrolls,

> Dumb proclamations of the Prodigies . . .
>> – him who grinds
> The hurdy-gurdy, at the fiddle weaves,
> Rattles the salt-box, thumps the kettle-drum,
> And him who at the trumpet puffs his cheeks,
> The silver-collared Negro with his timbrel,
> Equestrians, tumblers, women, girls, and boys,
> Blue-breeched, pink-vested, and with towering
>> plumes.
> All moveables of wonder, from all parts,
> Are here – Albinos, painted Indians, Dwarfs,
> The Horse of knowledge, and the learned Pig,
> The Stone-eater, the man that swallows fire,
> Giants, Ventriloquists, the Invisible Girl,
> The Bust that speaks and moves its goggling eyes,
> The Wax-work, Clock-work, all the marvellous craft
> Of modern Merlins, Wild Beasts, Puppet-shows,
> All out-o'-the-way, far-fetched, perverted things,
> All freaks of nature, all Promethean thoughts
> Of man; his dulness, madness, and their feats
> All jumbled up together to make up
> This Parliament of Monsters. . . .

> [VII. 658–66, 670–91]

Despite the specificity of the contemporary detail, with its allusions to sideshows like the ventriloquists and the learned pig, well-read readers would notice the literariness: the reminders, for instance, of Flemish paintings of Hell and of Milton's *Paradise Lost*, with its great set-pieces of fallen worlds 'alive with heads', like some infestation of lice. Wordsworth's Fair also reads like a late-medieval or Renaissance enactment of Folly or Gluttony, most familiarly Ben Jonson's play *Bartholomew Fair* (1614), that re-enactment of carnival which easily shrugs off the attempts of its two Puritan moralists, Zeal-of-the-Land Busy and Adam Overdo, to close its pleasures down. A Puritan himself at heart, Wordsworth mentions with distaste that the fair is 'Holden where martyrs suffered in past time' (VII.650) – at Smithfield, where in 1555–58 the Catholic Queen Mary I, wife of Philip II of Spain, burnt scores of her Protestant subjects.

Self-consciously positioned and worded in the grand manner, Wordsworth's renunciation of the metropolis is not just the turning-point of his greatest poem but

---

3 See for example Hartman 1964; Abrams 1971.

for some twentieth-century commentators an exemplary passage in which Romantic/modern culture rejects the Enlightenment, with its goal of material progress.[4] Suggestively, the phrase 'parliament of monsters' echoes Burke's imagery in his *Reflections on the Revolution in France* (1790). Then, ignoring actual chronology, Wordsworth uses his London experiences of the crowd as a stage in his mental odyssey, following it with Books IX-XI, where he describes another urban nightmare, the Paris of the Terror.

Long before the public had an opportunity to read Wordsworth's poetic self-portrait, other work by members of Wordsworth's circle (some of whom had read *The Prelude*) established the genre of Romantic autobiography in English: Coleridge's wayward, congested but intellectually rich *Biographia Literaria* (1817), Lamb's humorous *Essays of Elia*, Thomas de Quincey's extravagant *Confessions of an English Opium Eater*. These books are self-conscious and interactive: De Quincey's *Confessions* can, for example, be interpreted as a low-life version, initially set among the prostitutes and drop-outs of London's Oxford Street, of Coleridge's unremittingly academic *Biographia* and Wordsworth's idealised 'Portrait of the Artist'. Partly in imitation of De Quincey, and again as a corrective to Wordsworthian and Coleridgean idealism, Hazlitt in 1823 issued his own fictionalised autobiography, the *Liber Amoris*, based on love-letters which Hazlitt at forty-four sent his London landlord's nineteen-year-old daughter.

Sharing the stance and street vernacular of the new literary journals, their normal vehicle, Lamb, Hazlitt and De Quincey made no visible bid for social leadership, political influence, or the moral high ground – as journals and writers had been doing for more than half a century, in the interests of the middle classes or themselves. The new styles were changeable, surprising, appetising: they meant to stimulate the commercial market, not to exhort the general public. Omitting large issues and theories, the essayists bring an identifiable everyday London to life, in prose far more sinewy and rich than any yet produced in the period. De Quincey is the period's prose-poet, an admirer of the long, early seventeenth-century sentence, which he uses to orchestral effect in his descriptions of 'the pains of opium'. Partly for his style, partly for his bold trope of opium as a metaphor for the imagination, partly for his topography of the unconscious, he has a long line of literary descendants who include Charlotte Bronte, Poe, Dickens and Baudelaire. The tense, self-lacerating Hazlitt had been a fine theatre critic and political polemicist; after 1820 he does his best work, vigorous spontaneous-seeming occasional essays ('On Going a Walk', 'The Fight', 'The Indian Jugglers') and his sketch-book of his leading contemporaries, *The Spirit of the Age* (1825), which remains one of the most quoted works of the period.

Did the entrepreneurial journals and a handful of middle-aged journalists of genius elbow the poets out of the way, even before their deaths? English 'High Romanticism' reached an impressively large readership, Byron's in its totality probably even outstripping Tom Paine's.[5] But their very success in reaching a 'half-educated' (or non-classically educated) readership created a backlash hostile to difficult language and ideas, political challenges, learned allusions and social exclusivity. The most successful 'High Victorian' poet, Tennyson (1809–92), the only Briton raised to the peerage for writing poetry, took fifteen years from his first published volume before the success of *Poems* (1842) enabled him to rebuild a public for lofty serious verse. Between the late 1830s and the late 1840s the Romantic poets Wordsworth, Coleridge, Scott, Byron, Shelley and Keats also became installed as English classics, deserving of veneration along with Chaucer, Shakespeare and Milton. In spite of the real tensions and divisions within the national community betrayed in their work, they became part of an official literary culture habitually praised for its role in upholding national continuity and cohesion.

It often happens that a clash between two tendencies, in this case the grand style and the vernacular, produces very interesting work. Two of the best Romantic poems emerge in 1820 and 1821, and they are grand-style representations of London – though, typically for this topic, they appear at first sight to be about something else. Blake's longest, most difficult and ambitious prophecy, *Jerusalem* (1820), sounds as if it could be another Middle-Eastern poem. Byron's verse drama *Sardanapalus* (1821) is similarly displaced temporally and spatially, to the era of the Fall of Nineveh in the reign of the last Assyrian monarch descended from Nimrod. But each of these books ironically portrays London as a modern metropolis.

Byron's Nineveh is a richly-imagined other world and at the same time the familiar Western and modern world

4 See Abrams 1971; Bloom 1961 and 1970; Frye 1968.
5 The readership of Paine's *Rights of Man*, Pts I and II (1791-92) is a much-disputed question, but modern scholars agree that it must exceed 100,000 in all. St. Clair estimates the sales of Byron's *Don Juan* alone, complete or in part, in official and pirated editions, at 150,000 at least. 'The impact of Byron's Writings: an Evidential Approach', ed. Rutherford 1990, pp.1-25.

turned upside-down. In the first scene King Sardanapalus enters dressed as a woman and decked with flowers. Brushing off the warnings of his soldier brother-in-law Salamenes, who tells him that his lifestyle has brought together a powerful opposition, Sardanapalus also rejects his ancestors' favourite solution to domestic difficulties, a war of conquest in India. His court is a place of perpetual party-giving, a world which revolves round women and slaves, one of whom is Myrrha, the king's mistress, a Greek patriot. Despite Byron's denial that the play is intended to be read politically,[6] 'the Assyrian king's marital troubles, extra-marital affairs, and lavish oriental pavilion for entertaining in must have reminded any British reader in 1821 of Britain's new King George IV. The stage-king is extravagantly effeminate; George's subjects used the word to complain of his fondness for the arts and the company of women. The self-confidence generated by victory in the Napoleonic Wars had recently helped to convince the British of their historical destiny to rule others; it was an opinion hard to reconcile with the scandalous private lives of the king, his brothers, and much of the aristocracy, Byron included.

Byron's plays were acted in the nineteenth century but generally neglected in the twentieth century. They fall into two types: fairly conventional neo-classical tragedies centred on aristocratic republican heroes, and modelled on Alfieri; and the less naturalistic, more experimental *Manfred* (1817), *Cain* (1821), *Heaven and Earth* (1823) and *The Deformed Transformed* (1824). *Sardanapalus* manages to belong to both kinds; its membership of the second group perhaps explains why Byron dedicated it to Goethe. It has a regular five-act structure, observes the unities, and presents the hero as an eighteenth-century republican gentleman – dissipated but tolerant and progressive, a man living by the promptings of a humane conscience in a post-religious world. Yet the play's language and its many allusions to primitive religion create a world at the beginning of historical time, just emerging from myth. The king nominally worships the Sun, but toasts Bacchus, the Greek god of wine; he is likened to Hercules and more pervasively to Lucifer, 'Son of the Morning' – a Biblical phrase which suggests, according to Shelley, that the Lucifer myth was based on the fall of a historical Assyrian king.[7] Other terms used to describe him, 'the prince of flowers' and 'king of peace', must bring Jesus to mind. The play does not belong among Byron's *tragedies*, then, for these larger resonances mark it out as an intellectual comedy which looks satirically at the ethics and idealisms invoked in modern as well as ancient public life. Ancient Nineveh is being mapped on to the London of 1821, Assyria on to Britain. As the

metropolis of an Eastern empire, each is a world split open by its mental and moral contradictions; a world maintained by a public ethic of 'manliness', that is of war, aggrandisement, domination, while its private pleasures are 'effeminate' and its most civilised aspirations those of peace and love.

Blake's great poem *Jerusalem*, a mythologised history of the British people, also challenges Britain's flattering present-day self-image. Blake's main model is the Bible, which he interprets (in the Enlightenment manner of Lowth, Michaelis and Herder) as among other things the national historical chronicle of the Jewish people. The 'action' tells how the giant Albion fell into the sickness of disunity, followed by a long sleep, from which he eventually awakens to a triumphant apocalypse. It is a plot nowadays commonly interpreted subjectively, as an allegory of the spiritual experiences of an exemplary individual, or perhaps of mankind in time. But in eighteenth-century writing there is often particular significance in the use of the poetic word 'Albion' for the nation, in preference to either England or Britain. It originates in the Roman period – that is, it pre-dates the arrival of the English, and brings to mind the older Celtic population. After a millenium the Welsh and Irish still suffered the fate of most conquered peoples: the English did not think of either as a nation, but as a low-status group within the population. After the Union of Scotland with England (1707), poets sensitive to these social nuances, including Thomas Gray and the Scotsman James Thomson, preferred to write of Britain or Albion. Meanwhile the English practice of continuing to use the familiar 'England' slighted approximately half of the amalgamated nation created by the parliamentary Union of Britain and Ireland in 1800.

When in 1804 Blake began his huge *Jerusalem* (in its final form engraved on a hundred plates), he was, like Southey and Coleridge, actively interested in a massive new work, an anthology of the entire surviving corpus of Welsh literature up to the twelfth century.[8] His interest in Welsh primitive art and history over the next few years is a matter of record, but most modern accounts of its basis are unsatisfactory: while in no sense a Welsh nationalist

---

6 Cf. Byron to John Murray, 14 July 1821: 'I trust that *Sardanapalus* will not be mistaken for a *political* play ... I thought of nothing but Asiatic history ... in these times one can neither speak of kings or Queens without suspicion of politics or personalities.' *Byron's Letters and Journals*, ed. Marchand 1978, vol. 8, p.152.
7 See Shelley, 'On the Devil and Devils' (written 1819-20), ed. Clark 1972, p.274.
8 Owen Pughe and Williams 1801-07.

(as his Welsh scholarly mentors were), the Englishman Blake clearly responds imaginatively to the antiquity of this culture and sees that its fate of long burial represents the experience of the mass of the population. He portrays the British as a patriarchal people, senior even to the Jews – 'All things Begin & End in Albions Ancient Druid rocky shore' (Plate 27). *Jerusalem* is partly then a poem of national origins, a not uncommon exercise in the era following the French Revolution; it exalts but more significantly it democratises and 'mongrelises' the concept of British nationhood which wartime rhetoric was centering too simply on the present state and thus on London. The figure of Albion signifies not merely all the people of the British Isles but its topography. The poem's preoccupation with the naming of places leads to litanies evoking hilltops on the western Celtic fringes, Mam Tor in Devon or Penmaenmawr in Wales. Erin, Gaelic name for Ireland, appears as a character. Albion's awakening from sleep is a signal for the divided peoples to come together:

> What do I see? The Briton, Saxon, Roman, Norman
>   amalgamating
> In my furnaces into one nation, the English; &
>   taking refuge
> In the loins of Albion . . .
> The sinful nation created in our loins & furnaces is
>   Albion!

> [Plate 92, 1–3, 6]

London is omnipresent, 'for Cities/ Are men, fathers of multitudes' [Plate 38.46–47]. The title *Jerusalem* is sly and ironic; this is as much a poem about London as Joyce's *Ulysses* is a novel about Dublin. But London figures largely as streets and suburbs, most memorably the villages to the north (Paddington, Marylebone, St. Pancras and Islington) which the aristocratic developments of the West End and Regent's Park had reached and were starting to engorge. Blake's astonishing imagination transfigures them into the unspoilt pastoral playground of his childhood memories, merged with the millenarian perfection to come:

> The fields from Islington to Marybone, [sic]
> To Primrose Hill and Saint John's Wood:
> Were builded over with pillars of gold,
> And there Jerusalem's pillars stood . . .

> Pancrass [sic] & Kentish town repose
> Among her golden pillars high;
> Among her golden arches which
> Shine upon the starry sky.

Thomas Phillips, *William Blake*, oil on canvas, 1807. National Portrait Gallery

> The Jews-harp-house & the Green Man;
> The Ponds where boys to bathe delight:
> The fields of Cows by Willans farm:
> Shine in Jerusalem's pleasant sight.

> [Plate 27, 1–4, 9–16]

Blake avoids mentioning royal and political London – the court at St James's, the administrative offices in and around Whitehall, and parliament at the Westminster end of the road. He also omits the financial City of London to the east. As so often in eighteenth-century writing, England and London each have an absent centre, here filled symbolically in a most sinister fashion, by Tyburn tree, the capital's gallows at the western end of Tyburn way (modern Oxford Street). Tyburn is often replaced by its historical equivalent, the stone of human sacrifice at ancient Stonehenge. Blake's reimagining of London without its centre is a part of his consistent refusal to order national life hierarchically or to include among its many names its kings, heroes and leaders. The British become instead a mass, an amalgam of tribes and races, none distinguished, no name or place superior to the rest. Albion himself is not merely Everyman but everything, down to the rivers and rocks. He and his alter ego, the Blakean artificer called Los, are always on the point of dissolving into their elements, among the caverns and underground tubular veins which weave among the words of the text.

Blake was becoming a cult figure to a small group of re-ligious artists, and his name was recognised by collectors and literary enthusiasts. Yet he seems to have sold only six copies of the long-awaited *Jerusalem*, and in some of these cases reduced the price of three of the four chapters. The 'book of London' which caught on during that year of George IV's coronation was neither radical nor trans-figurative, though it too could claim to be democratic – Egan's *Life in London*, the low-cost, comic-strip serial introduction to metropolitan pleasures.

DEPARTING GLORIES OF THE BRITISH THEATRE: SETTING SUNS OVER A NEO-CLASSICAL LANDSCAPE

Iain Mackintosh

'I have in Mr. Garrick's acting studied the manners of all men and I have made more discoveries about the human heart than if I had gone over the whole of Europe' wrote Suzanne Necker, wife to Louis XVI's Minister of Finance after witnessing the farewell season of David Garrick in the summer of 1776.[1] Garrick (1717–79) had been actor-manager at the Theatre Royal, Drury Lane since 1747 during which time he had never performed outside London let alone Britain and yet when he made the Grand Tour in 1763–64 he was fêted from Paris to Rome.

For the intelligentsia of Europe in the latter part of the eighteenth century the name of Garrick was synonymous with that of Shakespeare.[2] In Britain he casts an even longer shadow: all the great actors of the next century were to be measured against Garrick – John Philip Kemble (1757–1823), Edmund Kean (1787–1833), William Charles Macready (1793–1873) and even Henry Irving (1838–1905). It was not only a question of the actor's own genius but the fact that theatre in Britain at the end of the eighteenth century had become largely Garrick's creation. In his eulogy, the statesman Edmund Burke (1729–97) recorded that Garrick 'raised the character of his profession to that of a liberal art, not only by his talents, but by the regularity and probity of his life and the elegance of his manners'. Garrick made theatre respectable and placed it at the centre of society, a position it had once before occupied briefly in Elizabethan and Jacobean London but one that it would retain after Garrick until the 1830s. He also made the theatre popular.

That popularity is measurable. In 1709 there was only one regular company of players in all Britain. In the first decade of the nineteenth century James Winston, one time manager of Drury Lane and 'theatric tourist', researched the existence of over 300 theatres in the British Isles. This popularity was spread socially as well as geographically. In the century that followed the restoration of the Stuart monarchy in 1660 theatre was of interest to a minority only, as in most cities of Europe, but in 1771 a commentator wrote: 'As it was in Athens the playhouse in London is for all classes of the nation. The peer of the realm, the gentleman, the merchant, the citizen, the clergyman, the tradesman and their wives equally resort thither to take places, and the crowd is great'.[3] This could have been written at any time between 1760 and 1830.

It was a golden age, not because of the wealth of dramatic literature – on the contrary very few plays of the period have survived as stageworthy – but because of the cohesive quality of the Georgian playhouse. To the Theatres Royal of Drury Lane and Covent Garden came every stratum of society. Even if they were seated separately in four shilling boxes and sixpenny gallery they breathed the same air; on entering, peer rubbed shoulders with prostitute, clerk with poet. In Georgian London this was as natural as it would have been unthinkable in Victorian times.

A contributory cause of this concentration was the fact that until the opening of such 'minor theatres' as the Royal Coburg (the Old Vic) in 1818 there were only three theatres in London licensed to present spoken drama. These were the Theatre Royal, Drury Lane, first opened in 1663 which operated under the royal 'Patent' granted to Thomas Killigrew by King Charles II in 1662; the Theatre Royal, Covent Garden of 1732 which operated under the royal 'Patent' granted to Sir William Davenant also in 1662; and the Theatre Royal in the Haymarket, a much smaller and less significant theatre which is not to be confused with the opera house opposite, on the site of the present Her Majesty's Theatre, that had its own opera 'Patent'. The Theatre Royal, Haymarket, received its summer-only 'Patent' as late as 1766 as recompense to its manager, the comedian Samuel Foote (1720–77), following the amputation of a leg made necessary by his being thrown by an unmanageable horse on which he had been amusingly mounted by 'friends' who included the Duke of York.

The royal 'Patent' system concealed the fact that the British royal family, almost alone amongst the crowned heads of Europe, did not support the theatre financially in any way. They built no playhouses, no opera houses despite the titles 'Theatre Royal', etc., and, except for the short-lived Royal Academy of Music, which presented

---

1 Hannah More when writing to the Reverend James Stanhouse, a mutual friend, described David Garrick in his farewell performances as 'one of those summer suns, which shine brightest at their setting'. Roberts 1834, vol. 1, pp.73-75.
2 The inscription on the monument to Garrick in Poet's Corner at Westminster Abbey concludes:
    'Shakespeare and Garrick like twin stars shall shine,
    An earth irradiate will a beam divine'.
3 Talbot, *The Oxford Magazine*, 1771.

The Theatre Royal, Drury Lane, designed by Henry Holland, opened 1794. Reconstruction drawing by Richard Leacroft

annual seasons of opera at the King's Theatre (the opera house in the Haymarket) from 1720 to 1726 under the direction of Handel, paid for no players, actors or musicians. Nor did the nobility keep companies of players under their patronage as they had in Elizabethan England. In contrast to all Europe the theatre of the Georgian golden age was totally commercial, run by actors and managers for their benefit and occasionally for the benefit of investors and shareholders who often lost their money. The royal involvement was limited to the useful device of reducing competition by limiting the number of theatres licensed by royal 'Patent', rather as commercial television stations are limited today by the granting of franchises.

The exclusive 'patent' system was abolished by Act of Parliament in 1843. This transferred the licensing of theatres in London to the local authorities, a power possessed by local parties outside London since 1788. But the 1843 Act merely legitimised what had become practice following the success of 'minor theatres' such as Sadler's Wells and the Royal Coburg.

London's expansion at the end of the eighteenth century is discussed elsewhere in this catalogue. Until such time as the demand for theatre could be legitimately satisfied by adding new theatres, or at least anticipated as it was in the early 'minor theatres', there was only one way in which the increased demand could be satisfied. The old small playhouses of Drury Lane and Covent Garden were demolished and replaced with much larger buildings. This happened twice at both Theatres Royal within a span of twenty years.

In 1792 Henry Holland (1754–1806) was hired by manager Thomas Harris to replace John Inigo Richards' modest auditorium of 1782 with a much larger one. Nothing changed on the outside, the theatre being still almost invisible from either the piazza or Bow Street, which accounts for this significant enlargement of Covent Garden being omitted from many of the histories. It was Holland's Covent Garden which burnt on 20 September 1808 and which was replaced by a magnificent new theatre designed by Sir Robert Smirke (1780–1867). Smirke's theatre was a free-standing structure occupying a site 218 feet by 166 feet, hitherto shared with older houses and taverns which had also burnt. At the time it was one of the largest and finest theatres in Europe. It held 2,800 people plus some private boxes in the third tier with full

T. Luny, *The Burning of Drury Lane Theatre seen from Westminster Bridge*, oil on canvas, 1809. The Museum of London

height partitions, an anti-social device introduced from Europe for the first time. It also cost a great deal of money: £150,000 which was three times what the proprietors had decided to raise only a year earlier. The managers, Thomas Harris and actor John Philip Kemble, could do only one thing: raise the price of admission. The new theatre opened on 18 September 1809, and the riots that ensued, the O.P. (Old Price) riots, continued until December when Kemble gave way, reinstated the one shilling gallery and reduced prices elsewhere. The theatre may have had to operate commercially but it did so as much by permission of the populace as by 'Patent'.

The Smirke theatre endured with only small though significant alterations, such as the removal of the proscenium arch doors in 1819, until 1846 when the neo-classical interior was gutted and a horseshoe opera house auditorium substituted with six levels of closed boxes designed by Italian engineer Benedict Albano. This was when Covent Garden ceased to be a playhouse and became primarily an opera house.

Meanwhile at Drury Lane a similar sequence of rebuilding, fire and further rebuilding took place. The playwright and politician Richard Brinsley Sheridan (1751–1816) had bought the majority share in the Theatre Royal, Drury Lane in 1776 from David Garrick who was to write

a prologue and help to stage Sheridan's *The School for Scandal* in 1777. In 1791 he engaged Henry Holland to rebuild Drury Lane and, later that year, demolished the entire theatre which had retained much of Christopher Wren's original structure of 1674. The architect Holland was therefore engaged on redesigning both of the major 'Patent' theatres in the autumn of 1791 at a time when he was also busy transforming Carlton House for the Prince Regent. Of the two theatres the plans for Drury Lane were much more ambitious, Sheridan having envisaged a new street to the south which would have created an island site for the new theatre.

Holland's Drury Lane did not open until March 1794 and even then it lacked the surrounding taverns, coffee houses and shops arranged behind the classical colonnade modelled on Victor Louis's Grand Théâtre in Bordeaux of 1780. Nevertheless, the new theatre was enormous and when it burnt to the ground on the night of 24 February 1809,[4] barely five months after the fire at Covent Garden,

---

4   Sheridan hurried from the House of Commons where he had been debating but there was nothing he could do. Seated at a nearby tavern he brushed aside commiserations with 'Cannot a man take a glass of wine by his own fireside?'

the blaze could be seen from the terrace of the House of Commons at Westminster. Holland's Drury Lane had been the first secular building to break the uniform four storey building line of London.

Once again it took three times as long to rebuild Drury Lane as Covent Garden. In May 1811 an architectural competition was finally held. In October the winner was announced, Benjamin Dean Wyatt (1775–c.1855) who had beaten his brother George Wyatt and William Wilkins, architect of the National Gallery and of many theatres of the Norwich circuit including the surviving one in Bury St. Edmunds.

The sheer size of both the rebuilt Drury Lanes had a profound effect on all the arts of the theatre. There was a new emphasis on spectacular scenic effects, on Romantic pictorial illusion, created by artists such as Clarkson Stanfield, David Roberts and the Grieve family. In 1806 playwright Richard Cumberland (1732–1811) compared the new Drury Lane of Henry Holland with Garrick's theatre:

> Since the stages of Drury Lane and Covent Garden had been so enlarged in their dimensions as to be henceforward theatres for spectators rather than playhouses for hearers, it is hardly to be wondered at if managers and directors encourage those representations, to which their structure is best adapted. The splendor of the scene, the ingenuity of the machinist and the rich display of dresses, aided by the captivating charms of music, now in a great degree supersede the labours of the poet. There can be nothing very gratifying in watching the movement of an actor's lips when we cannot hear the words that proceed from them, but when the animating march strikes up, and the stage lays open its recesses to the depth of a hundred feet for the procession to advance, even the most distant spectator can enjoy his shilling's worth of show . . . On the stage of the old Drury in the days of Garrick, the moving brow and penetrating eye of that matchless actor came home to the spectator. As the passions shifted and were by turns reflected from the mirror of his expressive countenance, nothing was lost; upon the scale of modern Drury many of the finest touches of his act would of necessity fall short. The distant audience might chance to catch the text, but would not see the comment.

Holland's 'new Drury' needed to have its proscenium narrowed and the old proscenium arch doors reinstated in 1797. Wyatt's Drury Lane of 1812 also failed in its original form to connect audience to actor. Proscenium arch doors and stage boxes were reintroduced as early as 1814. In 1822 the auditorium was removed and replaced with a

highly successful auditorium by Samuel Beazley (1786–1851), who also added the cast-iron colonnade in Russell Street. The present Drury Lane auditorium, which dates from 1922, bears no resemblance to either Wyatt's or Beazley's although it sits well with the original, still surviving, grand salon, rotunda and principal staircase of 1812.

Mention of the removal, reinstatement and final abolition of the proscenium and doors in the two major 'Patent' theatres between 1794 and 1822 introduces the second great change in theatre architecture, other than an increase in sheer size, at the beginning of the nineteenth century. Hitherto, the English actor had performed on an acting stage in front not only of the scenery but of the proscenium arch. The audience was on three sides, the side stage boxes being highly valued in the age of oil and candle lighting, not because one could be seen by other less fashionable theatregoers (that came later), but because there one had a much better view of the acting. Most of the entrances by actors on to the acting forestage were by proscenium arch doors beside and below stage boxes occupied by audience. These were treated architecturally as part of the auditorium.

In addition much of the drama, tragedy as well as comedy, was performed in 'modern dress' or pastiches of a 'Tudorbethan' variety which suggested the distant past. There was little scenic illusion; the audience were constantly aware that the actor was a fellow human being who represented a stage character[5] rather than a larger than life character occupying another world which the audience viewed, through an imaginary picture frame, as was usually the case from the mid-nineteenth century to the mid-twentieth century.

However, fashions were changing at the outset of the Romantic age. In the vanguard were the theoreticians. In 1790 George Saunders published his *Treatise on Theatres* proposing 'model' theatre designs that were a major influence on Wyatt. Saunders quoted with approval the pronouncements of Count Algarotti, whose English edition of *An Essay on Opera* had been dedicated to William Pitt in 1767:

> the great advance of the floor of some stages into the body of the theatre is too absurd I imagine ever to be again considered. In particular a division is necessary

---

5   See Guthrie 1960, p.277 for the re-establishment of the acting area with audience on three sides at the Assembly Hall, Edinburgh in 1948 for *The Three Estates*.

between the theatre and the stage and so characterised as to assist the idea of these two being separate and distinct.

Proscenium arch doors were aesthetically untidy and blurred the new conventions of the romantic theatre of pictorial illusion. When they finally vanished from the major London theatres, if not the minor and provincial theatres where they survived for a generation, *The Sunday Times* of 20 October 1822 congratulated architect Samuel Beazley:

Nor blame him for transporting from his floors
The old offenders here, the two stage doors,
Doors which oft with burnish'd panels stood,
And golden knockers glittering in a wood . . .
That served for palace, cottage, street or hall,
Used for each place, and out of place in all . . .
So much for visual sense; what follows next,
Is chiefly on the histrionic text . . .

At the same time, certain pioneering work, undertaken by Kemble introduced audiences to new styles of stage costume and, in collaboration with William Capon (1757–1827), some suggestion of historical sets for plays, such as 'The tower of London, restored to its earlier state, for the play of King Richard III'. Absolute accuracy was not necessarily to Kemble's taste, and in horrified response to the notion that he should follow the correct republican styles for Shakespeare's Roman plays (he preferred the grander imperial models) he said 'Why, if I did, sir, they would call me an antiquary'. It was the great tragedian's much younger brother Charles Kemble (1775–1854) who drew together the emergent antiquarian ideas on historically accurate sets and costumes when he managed Covent Garden in the 1820s. His tame 'antiquarian' was James Robinson Planché (1796–1880) who designed and supervised costumes based on historical research for such plays as *King John* (1823) and *Henry IV* (1824). The actors were suspicious but the audiences acclaimed this innovation.

Planché is more than an interesting footnote to theatrical history in this period. Practical, hard-working and multi-faceted, he was fascinated by the theatre from his youth. He progressed from amateur performer to writer of burlesques and pantomimes; he was musical director of Vauxhall (1826–27) and adviser to the Mme Vestris-Charles Mathews management at the Lyceum Theatre in the 1830s. He designed costumes, penned opera librettos, agitated for the reform of the copyright laws, becoming the first major British costume historian, scholar and Somerset Herald. His innovations drew upon the developing taste for antiquarianism and translated it into a theatre tradition which was more than a fashion of the 1820s, although it did not reach its pinnacle until the second half of the century.

The histrionic King and Queen of the early nineteenth century were undoubtedly John Philip Kemble and his sister Sarah Siddons. The first was called 'the last of all the Romans'; the latter was painted by Sir Joshua Reynolds as the Tragic Muse, and described by critic William Hazlitt as 'Tragedy personified. She was the stateliest ornament of the public mind.'

Kemble and Siddons occupied a loftier plane of existence than the mere mortals that Garrick had striven to represent. The author, Henry Fielding (1704–54) had had the simple countryman Mr Partridge compare Garrick's Hamlet with the actor playing Claudius in the same production:

He the best player? Why I could act as well as he myself. I am sure if I had seen a ghost, I should have looked in the very same manner, and done just as he did . . . the King for my money speaks all his words distinctly, half as loud again as the other. Anybody may see he is an actor.

In 1749 Fielding was comparing the ponderous style of a Quin or Betterton to the naturalistic Garrick. But style in theatre is ever cyclical and at the beginning of the nineteenth century the taste of the new Romantic age, coupled with the huge scale of the new pictorial theatres, brought back to the fore those very qualities which had been derided half a century earlier. Foremost was Kemble, who ruled the London stage at Drury Lane and Covent Garden from 1788 to 1819, as acting manager if not majority shareholder, assisted much of the time by his sister.

The new classical landscape, on which the actor's theatre of Georgian London was to set and the Romantic age dawn, was not as all pervasive in Britain as it was in imperial France. Nevertheless, the commentators on Kemble, both complimentary and critical, tended to use classical language. Hazlitt was equivocal: 'Mr. Kemble is compared to the ruin of a magnificent temple in which the divinity still resides. This is not the case. The temple is unimpaired; but the divinity is sometime from home.'

Coriolanus, which Kemble first played in 1789 and in which character he was painted by Sir Thomas Lawrence (1769–1830) in 1798, was the perfect role at a time when Britain stood almost alone against the continental mob. Coriolanus's words in Act Three, Scene One had a particular meaning for audiences who had endured news of revolutionary excess in both America and France:

T. Lawrence, *J. P. Kemble as Hamlet*, oil on canvas, 1801. Tate Gallery

T. Lawrence, *J. P. Kemble as Cato*, oil on canvas, 1810. The Garrick Club

In soothing them, we nourish 'gainst our senate
The cockle of rebellion, insolence, sedition,
Which we ourselves have ploughed for, sow'd and
    scatter'd,
By mingling them with us.

Ironically it was the same audience who had cheered the patrician disdain of Kemble the actor, who rioted when Kemble the manager had to raise prices to pay for the new Covent Garden in 1809.

The grandeur of Kemble was preserved for posterity as a result of the concerted experiment in 'half-history' painting undertaken by Sir Thomas Lawrence between

1798 and 1812.[6] Garrick had set a pattern for theatrical portraiture: play and scene chosen by patron and actor in consultation, with Garrick ever aware of what would now be called the 'reproduction rights', the oil followed by the publication of limited editions of engravings or mezzotints. These were generally advertised after the painting had been shown at the annual exhibitions of the Society of Artists or, from 1768, of the Royal Academy. In addition, artists such as Johann Zoffany (1734–1810) painted more

6 West 1991, pp.226-49.

DEPARTING GLORIES OF THE BRITISH THEATRE

than one version of a scene, one of which would hang on the walls of Garrick's villa.

Kemble and his sister Sarah Siddons did not need to connive to employ leading artists to promote their careers in this way; the artists came to them. In 1797 Lawrence had shown *Satan Summoning the Angels* at the Royal Academy. Its reception encouraged Lawrence to embark on the series of 'half-history' paintings of Kemble, to succeed where Reynolds thought he had failed[7] and where the painters of Josiah Boydell's ill-fated Shakspeare Gallery of 1789 to 1805 undoubtedly did fail. Some mezzotints of the four paintings of John Philip Kemble did sell but the pictures themselves were unsold and remained in Lawrence's house and studio at his death, although the Duke of Wellington did try and ship *Kemble as Rolla* to Paris as a centrepiece of the reoccupied British Embassy.

These four paintings with their dates of exhibitions at the Royal Academy are: as Coriolanus, 1798; as Rolla in *Pizarro*, 1800; as Hamlet, 1801 and as Cato, 1810. Kemble was a willing accomplice even to the extent of allowing his body as Rolla to be modelled by a professional boxer named Jackson. The play *Pizarro* was a strange adaptation from the original by German dramatist August Friedrich Ferdinand Kotzebue (1761–1819), recreated by Sheridan for Kemble with the scene depicted by Lawrence inserted as a rallying cry for a nation at war. The London audiences found no difficulty in equating the Spaniards with mighty Napoleon and the oppressed but proud Peruvians with brave England.

Kemble retired in 1817, Sarah Siddons five years earlier. She did return briefly in 1816 for a Royal Command Performance in her most famous role as Lady Macbeth, recorded by George Henry Harlow (1789–1819). She had chosen it for her first farewell, on which occasion the audience would not allow the play to continue after the sleepwalking scene. This was scarcely surprising since Siddons here inserted an epilogue, written in the third person, which ended:

> Herself subdued, resigns the melting spell
> And breathes, with swelling heart, her long
> Her last farewell.

Hazlitt spoke for the nation:

> She was not only the idol of the people, she not only hushed the tumultuous shouts of the pit in breathless expectation, and quenched the blaze of surrounding beauty in silent tears, but to the retired and lonely student, through long years of solitude, her face has shone as if an eye had appeared from heaven . . . To have seen Mrs. Siddons was an event in everyone's life . . .

G. Clint, *E. Kean as Sir Giles Overreach in 'A New Way to Pay Old Debts'*, oil study *c.*1820. Victoria and Albert Museum

As the careers of Kemble and Siddons waned theatregoers sought a new idol. Their choice was Edmund Kean, 'the sun's bright child', who was the opposite to Kemble. Kemble had grappled with the responsibilities of the actor manager, his private life beyond reproach, with all his energies devoted to the noble art of the theatre. Kean drank and womanised; he even had to flee England for America in 1825 when the scandals of his relationships were reported in every newspaper. But on stage Kean was incomparable, the greatest villain in theatre history. Kean lacked the range of David Garrick or of Laurence Olivier

7 In 1790 when Sir Joshua Reynolds saw Lawrence's portrait of Mrs Farren hung close to his *Mrs. Billington as St. Cecilia* he is reported to have said to the younger painter, 'In you, sir, the world will expect to see accomplished what I have failed to achieve'. Ashton and Mackintosh 1982-83, p.79.

D. Maclise, *Macready as Werner*, oil on canvas, 1849-50. Victoria and Albert Museum

again. His pride, his meticulous professionalism, his disdain for actors and the social side of theatre marked him out as the first of the Victorian actor managers. While standards slipped, audiences fragmented and the sell-out to spectacle was all pervasive, Macready alone was guardian of the theatre's conscience. This he managed to keep alive until Henry Irving went into management in 1878 and started a resurrection of the English theatre which had been intellectually and emotionally impoverished since the 1830s.

There were, of course, many other actors working in the London theatre of 1800 to 1840. That we recognise them and many lesser jobbing actors is largely due to Samuel de Wilde (*c*.1751–1832) whose studio was conveniently placed in Tavistock Street, a hundred yards from the stage doors of both Covent Garden and Drury Lane. Nearly 400 of his portraits survive: quickly painted, in watercolour, at £2.12s.6d., or in oil £12.12s. as his account book show.

Neither Thomas Collins (1775–1806) nor Charles Farley (1771–1859) were important actors but they survive vividly in de Wilde's paintings, the one Watteauesque as Slender, the other an early essay in Gothic. Farley was more important as a producer of Covent Garden pantomimes until his retirement in 1834, an early success being *Harlequin and Mother Goose* in which Joseph Grimaldi (1778–1837) made his Covent Garden debut in 1806. Other actors, including even the infant phenomenon Master Betty (1791–1874), made their names first outside London. Grimaldi, though Genoese by descent, was a real Londoner, brought up back stage at Drury Lane and apprenticed as a dwarf or an elf from an early age. His next step, before becoming the most famous clown ever to play both the major theatres was at a 'minor theatre', at Sadler's Wells.

Sadler's Wells had, as the name suggests, an aquatic reputation, first as a well-watered rural retreat for London audiences on a summer's evening, and, from 1804 under the management of Charles Dibdin the elder (1745–1814), as The Aquatic Theatre. Augustus Charles Pugin (1762–1832) and Thomas Rowlandson (1756–1827) recorded the Sadler's Wells auditorium complete with an aquatic spectacle on stage in a plate prepared for publisher Rudolph Ackermann's *Microcosm of London* in 1809. In addition there is a watercolour by Pugin in the exhibition probably prepared to give atmospheric colouring to the engraver. At the Art Institute of Chicago are two earlier stages in the process: a watercolour sketch by Pugin and a pencil drawing, the architecture by Pugin and the figures by Rowlandson. The four provide a complete record of an Ackermann illustration.

(1907–90) but few have rivalled his Macbeth or his Sir Giles Overreach, the performance of which, on the first night of a new production of *A New Way to Pay Old Debts* in 1816, had Drury Lane in hysterics. Byron swooned. And nobody has ever equalled his Richard of Gloucester in *Richard III*, the Everest of moral turpitude for every English actor.

When Kean died in 1833 an era ended. William Charles Macready was his successor. Although his career (1816 to 1851) overlapped with Kean's, Macready was different yet

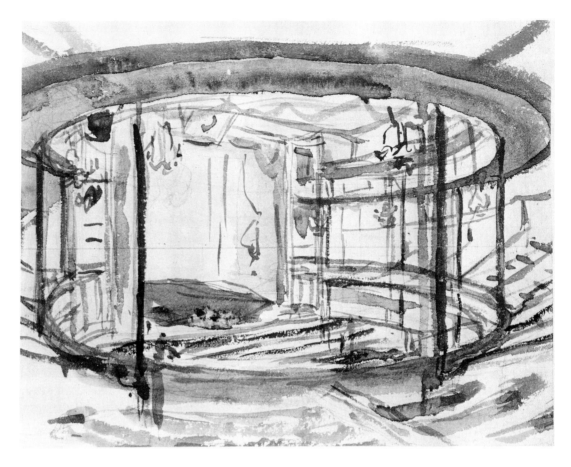

A.C. Pugin, *Sadler's Wells Theatre*, watercolour wash, *c*.1809. The Art Institute of Chicago

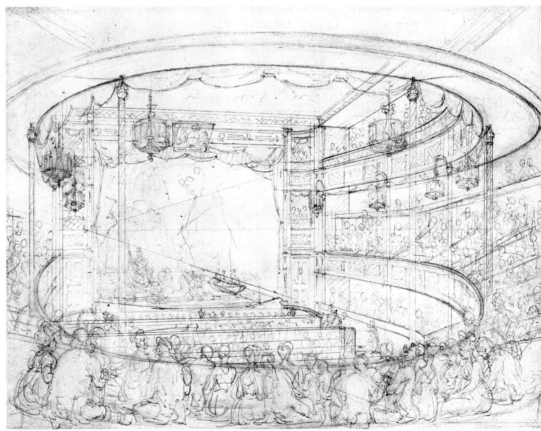

A.C. Pugin and T. Rowlandson, *Sadler's Wells Theatre*, pencil *c*.1809. The Art Institute of Chicago

DEPARTING GLORIES OF THE BRITISH THEATRE

It is significant that of the hundred separate views in the *Microcosm* nine are of theatres: Holland's Drury Lane; the Covent Gardens of both Holland and Smirke; the King's Theatre or Opera House in the Haymarket; Sadler's Wells; Richardson's travelling theatre and both popular equestrian theatres, Astley's and the Royal Circus, subsequently the Royal Surrey, which were south of the Thames. The balance of aquatic and equestrian entertainment, drama, opera, dance and, in one instance, sacred oratorio indicates the good cross section of what was on offer in the first decade of the nineteenth century in London. The only significant absentee is the Theatre Royal in the Haymarket where John Liston, comedian (1776–1846), made his famous debut in 1825 as Paul Pry with the catchphrase 'hope I don't intrude'.

In 1809 the same London audience might have patronised all of these auditoriums. But by the 1830s the London audience had ceased to be that 'great amalgam' as it had been from Garrick to Kean. The more respectable audience, including the young Princess Victoria might be tempted to visit Macready's Covent Garden or later Charles Kean's respectable Princess Theatre, so named with Victoria's permission.

Symphony and choral concerts were always respectable. But until 1847 London lacked any concert halls larger than Hanover Square and the concert room at the King's Theatre, both of which held less than 1,000 even at the tight densities of the period. For concerts there were few alternatives: the short-lived (1819–30) Argyll Concert Rooms in Regent Street, the acoustically unsuitable but popular indoor and outdoor venues at Vauxhall and Ranelagh Gardens, or the Theatres Royal of Covent Garden and Drury Lane. These were in regular use as concert halls for oratorios in Lent. Handel's organ was still being wheeled centre stage at Covent Garden in 1807 shortly before the fire of 1808.

The large theatres whose capacity had been increased for economic reasons struggled financially throughout the period; it was ever thus, the bigger the theatre the bigger the loss. What started to flourish in London in the 1820s and 1830s were the 'minor theatres'. These were as much community centres as theatres. They were not very different from the smaller country houses to be found outside London. The audience depicted by George Cruikshank (1792–1878) in 1836 in *Pit, Boxes and Gallery* might have been the very audience that Charles Dickens' Nicholas Nickleby joined at a 'minor theatre' for 'positively the last appearance of Mr. Vincent Crummles of Provincial Celebrity!!!'[8] Whatever the problems in the West End, theatre further down the social scale was very much alive if of little artistic merit.

Theatre always flourished in Britain in wartime. The end of the Napoleonic Wars and the accompanying social and economic dislocation combined to devalue the significance of a now fragmented theatre. In Britain, until 1792, the theatre had been small and focussed on the actor in contrast to the Continent where playhouses and opera houses had generally been conceived for spectacle. After 1792 the theatre was a victim of its own success. It grew too big, cutting the actor down to size, which encouraged a new broad style for the new broad stages.

By 1840 London was no more the theatrical centre of Europe. The Romantic age was to find its theatrical apotheosis in Romantic opera while theatre sank for half a century until Irving led its revival and helped it regain its self respect. But before this decline the period of 1800–30 saw many careers rise and fall. How fortunate they and we are that they and their theatres were captured, so vividly, by artists such as Lawrence, de Wilde, Harlow, Drummond, Andrews, Pugin, Rowlandson, Cruikshank and Schnebbelie.

8 Dickens 1838, chapter 47. See also chapter 24, for an account of the occupants of a family box, 'Six, Pa and Ma eight, and nine, governess ten, grandfather and grandmother twelve. They, there's the footman, who stands outside, with a bag of oranges and a jug of toast and water, and sees the play for nothing through the little pane of glass in the box-door'.

RADICAL CULTURE

H.T. Dickinson

From the late eighteenth century onwards major social and economic developments within Britain were combining to create a growing body of opinion critical of the power and the policies of the aristocratic landed elite who dominated the formal political institutions of the country. Initially, these changes had their greatest effect on the political consciousness of the middling orders, especially those who lived in the larger urban areas, but economic crisis and social dislocation produced by population growth, industrialisation, urbanisation and prolonged warfare, from the 1790s onwards, did much to recruit many skilled craftsmen and artisans into the long campaign for radical political reform. From the tumultuous Wilkite demonstrations of the late 1760s to the astonishing public reaction to the Queen Caroline affair in 1820-21, London set the pace and established the tone for the widespread popular agitation and the radical demands that sought the reform of parliament and many other institutions in Britain. The metropolis gave a lead in the production of plans to redress the grievances of the people and in the development of intellectual justifications for radical change. London also promoted many of the most important radical organisations and activities, including political clubs and societies, the popular press, and mass public meetings, that did so much to keep radical demands at the forefront of public attention. The political lead given to the radical cause by London reached a peak during the Queen Caroline affair. Thereafter, however, London ceased to give a political lead to the radical movement in Britain as a whole. For a variety of reasons the centre of radical agitation shifted to the industrial towns of the North and the Midlands.

ORIGINS AND INFLUENCES

There are a great many reasons why London should have been the leading centre of popular radicalism in the early nineteenth century. The metropolitan area of London was by far the largest conurbation in Britain, indeed in Europe. By 1800 the population had already topped one million inhabitants and by 1821 this had risen to about 1,600,000. The City of London was the centre of the monied interest and of the financial life of the whole nation. The port of London was easily the greatest centre of trading activity in the country, and in Europe. London was also, of course, the political capital of the nation and the seat of the royal court, the houses of parliament and the government bureaucracy. The inhabitants of London were more politically conscious than those elsewhere partly because London was by far the most important centre for the activities of the political press. It also had the highest literacy rates of any major urban centre in the country and it possessed hundreds of coffee houses and taverns, where men from all ranks of society could rub shoulders with each other and read about and freely discuss the political issues of the day.

The City of London itself was one of the largest parliamentary constituencies in Britain, returning four M.P.s to parliament. Westminster and Southwark also elected two M.P.s each while voters in the metropolis had a considerable influence over the M.P.s returned by the counties of Middlesex and Surrey. The City certainly possessed the most open and vibrant civic institutions in the whole country and these had long jealously guarded the privileges of its citizens. The citizens of London formed the largest, most sophisticated, most articulate and most active urban community in Britain. The City's elaborate infrastructure of 26 wards and 242 precincts, and the existence of many large and influential livery companies, ensured that many citizens gained experience of limited self-government and had some opportunity to participate in civic affairs. About 15,000 resident freemen ratepayers elected the 236 members of the Common Council each year and they also chose the 26 aldermen who served for life. Most of the common councilmen were small merchants, shopkeepers and master craftsmen, who closely identified with the interests of those who elected them. In addition to these elections, some 8,000 or so liverymen also met in Common Hall to elect the City's four M.P.s and also to choose the chamberlain, the sheriffs and the two candidates from which the aldermen chose the lord mayor. Even the 'mere' inhabitants of the City, who were not freemen but who did pay rates, could elect the petty officers in their own wards and precincts. Humble citizens were also involved in the activities of the parish vestries which operated the poor law and other local amenities.[1]

1 Rudé 1971, pp.118-23.

About 90 per cent of the population of the metropolis lived outside the boundaries of the City proper and so they could play no formal role in these civic institutions. There was no authority concerned with the administration of the metropolis as a whole. Nonetheless the inhabitants outside the City could still play a role in the affairs of well over a hundred parish vestries which were still 'open' and where all the local ratepayers could still elect the parish officers. Westminster, which did not have an elected corporation like London, was, however, the most open parliamentary constituency in the country. Nearly 18,000 inhabitants were qualified to vote and parliamentary elections in Westminster were probably the most exciting and turbulent in the whole land.[2]

Although London was not at the forefront of the new industries and the technological innovations that were doing so much to transform Britain's economy in the early nineteenth century, she was still by far the largest manufacturing centre in the country and the chief source of goods and services for much of the nation. London was primarily a centre of highly-skilled, but unmechanised, handicraft trades producing a great range of quality goods. By 1815 there were over 150 different trades practised in London and over 30,000 separate businesses, most of which were run by small masters. The most important trades were those practised by tailors, shoemakers, hatters, silk weavers, coach makers, furniture makers, coopers, carpenters, engineers, shipwrights, metal and leather workers, printers, bookbinders, masons, smiths, builders, plasterers, brewers and those engaged in processing sugar, tobacco, coffee and a wide variety of foodstuffs. Although large numbers of men were employed in many of these trades, very few of these businesses were on a large scale. The main large-scale businesses were those engaged in coopering, shipbuilding, printing and engineering. Most work in the building industry was done by domestic out-workers. The vast majority of skilled artisans worked in small workshops with a handful of other craftsmen. Very few businesses employed over fifty men and there were no factories in London employing hundreds or thousands of unskilled or semi-skilled workers as was the case in the industrial towns of the North and Midlands.[3]

The economic structure and the social composition of London helped it to become the leading centre of radical agitation in the early nineteenth century. It was a more heterogeneous and socially complex society than those in any of the other large towns in Britain. About 15 to 20 per cent of the adult male inhabitants were small merchants, shopkeepers, craftsmen and professional men. Of the 75 per cent or so adult males who worked for others, about one-third were skilled artisans and tradesmen, while the rest were unskilled or semi-skilled.[4] Many of the middling men were proud of their independence and respectability and they were conscious of being free men. They could fairly easily be drawn into political activities to preserve their rights and privileges and to challenge the abuse of authority by the ruling class. Many of the skilled artisans shared the same values, assumptions and aspirations of the lower middle class of small shopkeepers and employers rather than those of the mass of the labouring poor. Indeed, they hoped to become small masters or property owners themselves. Working mainly in small workshops, and using traditional handicraft techniques, these artisans possessed considerable autonomy, knew each other on a face to face basis, and related to each other outside working hours. They often owned their own tools, had some control over their hours and conditions of work, and were usually on good terms with their masters. They were proud of their skills and of their ability to sell their products and not just their labour, and they were usually better paid and had more secure employment than less skilled workers. Not surprisingly they were determined to preserve their advantages. Fearing a growing gap between themselves and their employers, and conscious of being distinguished from the poor by their 'respectability', they defended both their relative independence and their skills as a 'right' or 'property'. They were the least deferential and the best organised of working men. Under pressure from adverse circumstances, they were prepared to engage in collective action, whether in trade unions, cooperative and educational ventures, or in radical political agitation in a determined effort to safeguard their status.[5]

The early nineteenth century found many small masters and skilled artisans in London facing severe social and economic pressures. During the long wars with France they suffered from high taxes, inflation, financial instability and an economy distorted by wartime demands and occasionally dislocated by commercial warfare. Soon after the end of the war in 1815 the economy went into recession and stayed depressed until the early 1820s. The country was burdened by an enormous national debt, the labour market was flooded by 300,000 men released from the army and the navy, and the government no longer

2 Sheppard 1971, pp.22-23.
3 Prothero 1979, pp.22-25.
4 Schwarz 1979, pp.250-59.
5 Prothero 1979, pp.26-40.

gave contracts for a wide variety of military and naval supplies. With foreign countries raising tariff barriers to protect their own domestic industries from British competition, the export of British goods slumped rapidly after 1815. Most of these problems were beyond the government's control and the government can even be credited with avoiding unnecessary extravagance and with abolishing many sinecures and useless offices. Nonetheless, the government could be blamed for passing the Corn Laws which prevented the importation of cheap grain and kept food prices unnecessarily high. The government also unwisely abandoned the wartime income tax, a direct tax on the rich, and relied instead on a wide range of indirect taxes which fell more heavily on the middling and lower orders. The tax burden as a whole was reduced, but this only served to deflate the economy further. The economic depression of 1816–21 was undoubtedly a major factor in producing social unrest and in creating political demands for radical reforms in London and elsewhere.[6]

In addition to these unfavourable economic circumstances the artisans of London faced particular threats to their privileged status that drove many of them into radical political activity. They feared the growth of capitalism and the free play of market forces in general, but they also resented the weakening of apprenticeship regulations and the dilution of their skills by a flood of new and semi-skilled entrants to their trade and, sometimes, by the introduction of new machinery. Some skilled artisans, such as the tailors, shoemakers, carpenters and furniture makers, saw a considerable increase in their numbers, while others, such as the shipwrights, experienced severe competition from machines and from workers in other countries. Some artisans, especially the cloth workers, faced threats on all fronts.

The most skilled artisans and those under least pressure such as the printers, bookbinders, coopers and hatters, defended their status by developing effective friendly societies and trade societies. The less skilled artisans, including the tailors, handloom weavers, shoemakers, plasterers and carpenters, saw their skills degraded and were more readily drawn into political agitation as a means of preserving their independence and their status. The least secure artisans in London were those most likely to be attracted to radicalism.[7]

AIMS AND IDEOLOGIES

Those Londoners who were most aggrieved about their circumstances and who most resented the government's failure to redress their grievances, sought a wide variety of reforms and justified their demands by appealing to different ideologies. They were often led into a whole range of self-help activities and into moral crusades, but their most popular objective was to secure a radical reform of parliament which would give them much greater influence over the membership and the decisions of the House of Commons. In justifying these aims they appealed to a number of ideologies which were being propagated in London in the early nineteenth century.

The more highly skilled artisans of London had long formed friendly or benefit societies to guard themselves against the calamities arising out of accident, sickness, premature death or old age. By paying regular small subscriptions to such societies they could seek compensation when hard times befell them. These benefit societies were often a cover for trade union activity, which was in fact illegal until 1824. Through unity, solidarity and joint activity, some groups of skilled artisans were able to wage small-scale industrial disputes and could even organise effective strikes in order to protect their wages and conditions of work, but they could not prevent parliament repealing the traditional apprenticeship regulations in 1814 and they could rarely make significant improvements to their circumstances.

Some of the radical activists in London engaged in a number of moral and religious crusades designed to make poor men fit for liberty or to offer greater freedom to groups in society who were regarded by the elite as being unfit to be full citizens. Francis Place, Thomas Evans, John Richter and other radicals worked hard to provide education for the children of the poor and to establish the London Mechanics' Institute to educate working men.[8] Many radicals were also engaged in the revived campaign to abolish slavery in the British empire. They helped to organise a prolonged and eventually successful campaign based in London between 1823 and 1833. Many radicals also supported the campaigns to secure greater religious equality; campaigns which led to the repeal of the Test and Corporation Acts in 1828 and to Roman Catholic Emancipation in 1829. Some went further than these demands and campaigned against church rates, tithes and the privileged position of the Church of England. Anticlericalism was widespread in reforming circles and among the ultra-radicals, there were a number of Deists,

6 Gash 1978, pp.145-57.
7 Prothero 1979, pp.51-70.
8 Prochaska 1977, pp.102-16.

G. Cruikshank, *A Peep into the City of London Tavern* engraving, 1817. Robert Owen addresses a meeting with his cooperative schemes. British Museum Satires, No.12891

freethinkers and atheists. Some leading London radicals, including Richard Carlile, Thomas Evans, William Hone and George Cannon, argued that all religious restraints must be thrown aside so that the people could enjoy full political and personal liberty. A number of infidel chapels and Zetetic societies were established in London, mainly in 1818-19. According to Jeremy Bentham and some of his disciples, religion bolstered authoritarian regimes, crippled freedom of thought and divorced obedience from reason.[9]

Some London radicals believed that the advance of capitalism, industrialisation and urbanisation were so threatening that an entirely new social and economic order needed to be created. As early as 1817 Robert Owen proposed in London that small self-supporting communities should be set up where there was a collective management of the means of production and exchange. In 1821 a small cooperative community was set up in Spa Fields and it survived for three years. In the 1820s a number of cooperative societies, cooperative magazines and labour exchanges were established in London.[10] The radical disciples of Thomas Spence (who died in 1814) propagated an even more extreme social programme in the London Society of Spencean Philanthropists in the years after 1815. They opposed private property and they wished to see the land and natural resources of each parish taken over by parochial corporations made up of every man, woman and child in the parish. The land and natural resources would be rented out to the highest bidder and the income used to provide a range of public amenities, while the rest would be shared out every four months among all the inhabitants of the parish.[11]

Most London radicals, however, sought a political solution even to their social and economic problems because they made a political diagnosis of the causes of these problems. They were convinced that political power produced wealth, rather than that wealth produced power. They were critical of the ruling elite because they believed that these men used their power to advance their own economic interests while impoverishing the rest of the population. This conviction led them to conclude that parliamentary reform was necessary not only because all men had a right to political liberty and to an active role in the decision-making processes of the state, but because it would be the first step towards empowering the poor to redress their social and economic grievances. If the people as a whole were fairly represented in parliament, then government economy, lower taxes, an improved poor law, the proper regulation of relations between employers and workers, even higher wages and a variety of welfare reforms, might well follow. While some reformers advocated only a moderate reform of parliament, in an effort to enfranchise the urban middle classes, the radical reformers proposed a much more extensive reform. They were particularly keen to achieve universal adult male suffrage, equal electoral constituencies, annual general elections and the secret ballot. Most of these radicals were convinced that the right to vote should be attached to the person and not to the property of a man. To deny any man the franchise was to cast a slur on his moral character and to assert that he was less than a man. The possession of wealth was no proof of moral worth or civic virtue, and nor was poverty any evidence of the lack of these qualities.

In seeking to justify the various reforms which they

9   McCalmam 1988, pp.73-94; Hole 1989, pp.202-08.
10   Sheppard 1971, pp.311-12.
11   Dickinson ed. 1982, pp.vii-xvii.

G. Cruikshank, *A Free Born Englishman! – The Pride of the World! and the Envy of Surrounding Nations!!!*, engraving, 1813. A ragged John Bull in shackled and made homeless by repressive legislation and taxation. British Museum Satires, No.12037

G. Cruikshank, *Universal Suffrage. or – the Scum Uppermost – !!!!!*, engraving, 1819. Cruikshank attacks extreme radical demands. British Museum Satires, No.13248

advocated, the London radicals appealed to a number of ideologies, both old and new. Relatively few radicals of the early nineteenth century based their demands on the doctrine of universal, inalienable and equal natural rights that Thomas Paine had done so much to propagate and popularise in the 1790s. Recognising that the weight of historical evidence supported the conservative claim that there had always been a propertied franchise, Paine had preferred to demand political rights on the grounds of man's natural equality and common humanity. In his *Rights of Man* (1791–92), Paine had advocated a democratic republic in which all men enjoyed equal civil liberties and full political rights. Such radical views had been made very unpopular in Britain because of their association with the violence and instability of the French Revolution and so few London radicals proclaimed such opinions in the early nineteenth century. One of the exceptions was Richard Carlile, who republished Paine's works and who announced his support for natural rights and for a republican democracy in the pages of *The Republican*, particularly in the years 1817–18.[12]

Much more common than the appeal to natural rights was the demand for a restoration of the historic rights of Englishmen. Many of the leading radicals, including John Cartwright, John Horne Tooke, Francis Burdett, William Cobbett and Henry Hunt, revived notions of England's

12   Thompson 1968, pp.838-43.

C. Williams, *The British Atlas, or John Bull supporting the Peace Establishment*, engraving, 1816. John Bull is weighed down by the military at the end of the Napoleonic Wars. British Museum Satires, No.12786

been voiced for more than a century, but the consequences of the recent long wars with France had led to a renewed concern for the executive's ability to exploit its vast patronage in order to undermine the independence of parliament and the liberties of the subject. This growing alarm about a government conspiracy against liberty in turn fuelled demands for economic and parliamentary reform. It was frequently argued that urgent measures needed to be taken to reduce taxation, the national debt, the size of the civil and military establishments, and the number of government sinecurists, placemen and pensioners who sat in parliament. Only by legislative action to reduce the government's ability to reward its political followers in and out of parliament, and by reforms to increase the accountability of the House of Commons to the people at large, could the old harmonious relations between King, Lords and Commons be restored.[14]

The most active critic of 'old corruption' was William Cobbett, the most prolific, influential and widely-read journalist of the early nineteenth century. Cobbett believed in a prior and better state that had been undermined by a corrupt aristocratic elite, by monied men, and by the advance of industrialisation. In his weekly *Political Register*, he regularly launched into bitter denunciations of the executive's vast patronage system, with its extensive and ever-growing distribution of jobs, honours, contracts, promotions, pensions and bribes. He condemned ministers for presiding over a system which corrupted politicians, financiers, contractors, civil servants, officers in the armed services, and even clergymen of the Church of England. Horrified by the size of the national debt and by the burden of taxation on the poor in particular, Cobbett maintained that this system of 'old corruption' enriched the few while impoverishing the many. If the process was not curtailed, it would destroy the constitution and erode the liberties of the subject.[15]

Opposition to 'old corruption' was probably the greatest influence operating on the London radicals of the early nineteenth century, but it ignored the inconvenient fact that the government had reduced some of its sources of patronage since 1815 and it offered a rather weak and defensive analysis of the problems facing the British people. Unfortunately, only relatively few radicals were prepared to adopt the new utilitarian justification for par-

ancient constitution and claimed that the Anglo-Saxons had operated an essentially democratic system of representation. They insisted that they were not seeking innovation, but were endeavouring to renovate the old constitution. They wanted to restore the constitution to its original purity and to recover the lost rights of Englishmen. They did not seek to abolish the monarchy or the House of Lords, but to make the House of Commons representative of the people as a whole.[13]

Even more significant than these renewed appeals for a restoration of England's ancient constitution was the revival of the old 'country' ideology that opposed the growth of executive tyranny and the expansion of government patronage. Arguments expressing such fears had

13 Dickinson 1985, pp.69-70.
14 Ibid., p.70.
15 Ibid., pp.70-71; Thompson 1968, pp.820-37; Spater 1982, pp.347-49.

RADICAL CULTURE

liamentary reform or were able to grope towards a sophisticated labour theory of value which would justify improved financial rewards for the labouring classes. The utilitarian justification for parliamentary reform was developed by Jeremy Bentham as early as 1809, but his views were not made public until the appearance of his *Plan for Parliamentary Reform* in London in 1817. Bentham explicitly rejected the doctrine of natural rights and he made no appeal to the notion of the ancient constitution. Instead his utilitarian philosophy led him to assert that every man prefers his own interest above that of others and that each man is the best judge of his own interests. Since every individual is the best judge of what will bring him pleasure or pain, then all individuals collectively are the best judges of what will produce the greatest happiness of the greatest number. Unfortunately, by the same argument, all governments were more inclined to serve the interests of the governors than those of the governed. To prevent this abuse of power, the governors must be made accountable to the people and, in order to serve the interests of the people, they must have an active political role in society. These ends could be most easily achieved by a democratic system of representation.[16]

Bentham's complex argument and his laboured and tortuous prose prevented his ideas reaching a wide public, but his ideas were popularised by a number of disciples. In his essay on 'Government', published in the fifth edition of the *Encyclopaedia Britannica* in 1820, James Mill put forward an essentially utilitarian defence of representative democracy. In Mill's view, human selfishness could not be cured, but, if all men possessed the vote and the middle classes gave the common people a clear moral lead, then the reformed political system would come nearer than any other to creating a harmony of interests among creatures who naturally seek to promote their own personal interest. Few of the popular radicals were attracted to the austere logical reasoning of Bentham, but his views did have some influence on Francis Place and Francis Burdett, and a few of his ideas did appear in T. J. Wooler's *Black Dwarf* and in John Wade's *The Gorgon* in 1818–19.[17]

A few radicals moved towards a realisation that the long-standing aristocratic oppression of the commoners was being replaced by the growing capitalist exploitation of the workers. Thomas Paine and Thomas Spence had both recognised in the late eighteenth century that the poor had been cheated of their claim to the land, but they justified this claim by an appeal to natural rights. Paine had wanted to offer the poor some monetary compensation for their loss, whereas Spence wanted them to regain control of the land. Neither, however, developed an effec-

William Cobbett by an unknown artist, oil on canvas, c.1831. National Portrait Gallery

tive labour theory of value. In the early nineteenth century a number of utopian or proto-socialists in London began to contemplate how to respond to the economic oppression and the gross inequalities produced by rapid industrialisation and unrestrained capitalism.[18] In the opinion of such men as Charles Hall, William Thompson, Thomas Hodgskin and John Gray the new industrial society was giving the largest rewards to those who possessed property and controlled capital, whereas pitifully small rewards were given to the labouring masses whose work made the greatest contribution to the production of wealth. This unjust and unequal society was

16 Dickinson 1985, p.72.
17 Dinwiddy 1986. pp.15, 31-32.
18 Thompson 1984, pp.47-51.

J. Gillray, *True Reform of Parliament, i.e., Patriots Lighting a Revolutionary-Bonfire in New Palace Yard*, engraving, 1809. Sir Francis Burdett incites a mob to destroy parliament and overthrow the constitution. British Museum Satires No.11338

wasteful, blindly competitive and oppressive. Political reforms alone would not suffice to improve the lives of the labouring masses. The economy should be controlled and labour organised so that industrialisation would bring greater benefits to the working classes. Labour must be freed from the oppressive control of capital and from an unjust government which existed precisely in order to preserve private property, exploitation and inequality. Although these writers strove to explain the exploitation of labour in an industrial society, they did not produce a very sophisticated labour theory of value and their ideas had limited appeal for the artisans who so dominated the radical movement in London.[19]

METHODS AND ACTIVITIES

There were many signs of political disenchantment among the lower middling orders and the artisans of London in the early nineteenth century, but the entrenched conservatism of the propertied elite and the divisions within the ranks of the radicals made it difficult to

agree on the best political strategy to pursue in order to achieve political success.

As we shall see, some reformers were content to pursue change through the established and traditional channels of elections, petitions and printed propaganda. Others recognised the need for extra-parliamentary organisations and strategies that would demonstrate the extent of popular support for radical reforms. They established a variety of political clubs, held mass open-air public meetings, and organised street processions and crowd demonstrations. A minority of ultra-radicals were prepared to go further still and were ready to provoke riots and even to plot insurrection. Although these different strategies were sometimes pursued by different radical groups, there was, in fact, no clear demarcation between those who favoured constitutional action and employed moral force, and those who contemplated unconstitutional action and were prepared to use physical force. And yet divisions between moderate reformers, popular radicals and the ultra-radicals certainly existed. Only very occasionally, as during the Queen Caroline affair of 1820–21, were virtually all elements of the reform movement allied together and almost all political strategies pursued at the same time.

RADICAL CULTURE

For much of the period before 1830 the Whig opposition in parliament, despite their own vociferous complaints about executive tyranny and the abuse of patronage, were generally timid and cautious about supporting parliamentary reform. Although they opposed the repressive legislation of 1817 and 1819 and they occasionally expressed some support for very moderate measures of parliamentary reform, they often condemned the London radicals as mischievous, misguided and even dangerous men, who would create social disorder if they were not restrained. Nonetheless, the Whigs did have to recognise the small body of radical or progressive M.P.s who were more whole-hearted in their support of parliamentary reform. This group of parliamentary radicals only numbered two dozen or so M.P.s; the most prominent among them, such as Francis Burdett, Samuel Romilly, Lord Cochrane, Robert Waithman and John Cam Hobhouse, representing constituencies in the metropolitan area. They stood for some of the most open constituencies in the country, they owed their seats to their willingness to support parliamentary reform, and they sometimes depended for their electoral success on the efforts of radical activists who campaigned on their behalf.[20]

In 1807 a group of about twenty radical activists, including Francis Place, John Richter, Paul Lemaitre and William Adams, formed the Westminster Committee to secure the election of Francis Burdett as an independent candidate. Burdett, who had spent heavily in an unsuccessful attempt to win and retain one of the seats for Middlesex, agreed to contest the Westminster seat, provided he contributed none of his own money, did not personally canvass for votes, and did not appear on the hustings. As a wealthy patrician, Burdett wished to remain aloof from the humble shopkeepers and master craftsmen who proposed to manage his election campaign. With about 18,000 ratepayers eligible to vote, the Westminster electorate was too large to be bribed or placed under secure aristocratic influence. The members of the Westminster Committee, although they had no formal organisation, were determined to wage an effective struggle on behalf of the smaller men of property against the propertied elite. Resentful of the social and economic barriers between the aristocratic elite of Westminster and the shopkeepers and tradesmen who supplied their needs, they urged the voters to demonstrate their independence from their supposed superiors. The Westminster Committee campaigned assiduously for Burdett. Although they had only limited funds to fight the election, they made up for this with unflagging energy and impressive efficiency as they canvassed a high proportion of the qualified voters. With the aid of Cobbett's *Political Register*,

they propagated their radical views throughout the constituency. The result was a remarkable electoral success, with Burdett topping the poll and another radical Lord Cochrane, winning the second seat. This was an important breakthrough and the Westminster Committee remained active in succeeding elections, keeping Burdett as their main champion, but returning other reformers for the other Westminster seat. The Committee also held annual celebration dinners and helped to rally Westminster opinion on a number of issues of public concern to radicals.[21]

The London radicals used other formal and traditional channels to pursue their campaign for parliamentary reform. The Common Council of the City of London, for example, protested about several government scandals in 1808–09, passed resolutions in favour of parliamentary reform in 1812 and 1816, and protested against the repressive legislation of 1817 and 1819. The London radicals, mainly through the efforts of John Cartwright, also gave a lead to the nation in the presentation of petitions in favour of parliamentary reform. On several occasions between 1812 and 1816 Cartwright went on prolonged and extensive evangelising tours of the country, leaving printed petitions among radical sympathisers wherever he visited, and then collecting them after they had been signed, for submission to parliament. In 1813 he claimed to have obtained over 130,000 signatures, while in 1817 he was instrumental in the campaign which resulted in over 700 petitions, signed by over 1,500,000 people in over 350 different towns, being presented to parliament. In 1818 there were even more petitions, though with appreciably fewer signatures.[22]

The most effective ways of bringing radical ideas and demands to the people, however, was not by means of petitions, but through the efforts of the London press to reach a mass readership of hitherto unheard of proportions. The total annual sales of newspapers in this period increased from 16 million in 1801 to 30 million in 1832. The majority of these were produced in London and the provincial press was heavily influenced by the contents and tone of the London newspapers. In addition, there were many London magazines and periodicals, a huge number of political pamphlets published in London every year, and a host of savagely polemical caricatures and

19 Dickinson 1987, pp.84-87; Beales 1933.
20 Dinwiddy 1986, pp.1-10.
21 Dickinson 1985, pp.74-75; Main 1966, pp.186-204.
22 Miller 1968, pp.705-28.

THE

MAN IN THE MOON

&c. &c. &c.

" If Cæsar can hide the Sun with a blanket, or put the Moon in his pocket,
we will pay him tribute for light."—*Cymbeline.*

WITH FIFTEEN CUTS.

LONDON:
PRINTED BY AND FOR WILLIAM HONE,
45, LUDGATE HILL.

1820.

ONE SHILLING.

G. Cruikshank, *The Man in the Moon,* woodcut titlepage of verse satire published by William Hone, 1820. The Prince Regent attempts to put out the sun which encloses a printing-press with a blanket on the point of his sword. British Museum Satires No.13508

other graphic prints. The years after 1815, in particular, saw a vast outpouring of political propaganda from the London press. Since 1806 William Cobbett's weekly *Political Register* had carried comments harshly critical of the existing political system, but, because of its relatively high price, its readership was largely middle class. In November 1816 Cobbett decided to extract the main political essay from each issue of the *Political Register* in order to publish it as a single folded-sheet which would evade the stamp duty on newspapers and thus retail at a mere twopence. This new publication was an immediate and an astonishing success. Cobbett's style appealed to the ordinary reader and he built up an extremely effective distribution system so that he sold copies across the whole country. Sales almost immediately reached 44,000 copies per week and a few issues sold 60-70,000 copies. It was only after Cobbett had fled to the United States in 1817, to avoid prosecution, that sales fell away.

Cobbett's initial success, however, inspired a number of other radical London journalists to follow his example. T.J. Wooler started the *Black Dwarf,* selling at fourpence, on 29 January 1817. Even bolder than Cobbett, he specialised in biting sarcasm and vicious personal attacks. By 1819 he was claiming weekly sales of over 12,000 copies. In April 1817 Richard Carlile started *The Republican,* a very radical journal which preached Painite ideas and reached weekly sales of 15,000 copies by 1819. In 1818-19 a number of ultra-radical, though short-lived, newspapers flourished in London, including *The Medusa,* the *Cap of Liberty* and the *White Hat.*[23] Some individual political works reached even more readers than these radical newspapers. William Hone and George Cruikshank combined their talents to produce several immensely successful illustrated works, including *The Political House that Jack Built, The Queen's Matrimonial Ladder,* and *The Divine Right to Govern Wrong.* In 1820 Cobbett claimed that some 100,000 copies had been sold of Hone's *Peek at the Peers,* exposing aristocratic corruption and dedicated to Queen Caroline, while a truly amazing two million copies of the queen's *Answer to the King* were distributed from London alone in 1820.[24] It was widely reprinted elsewhere. In years of intense political excitement, including 1819-21 and 1830–32, several hundred different graphic satires were also produced in London, most of them selling hundreds of copies each.

Although it was the radical London press, particularly

23 Cranfield 1978, pp.92-119.
24 Stevenson 1977, p.129; Lacqueur 1982, p.429.

S. de Wilde, *The Robbing Hood Society*, aquatint, 1809. A conservative satire on radical London debating societies. British Museum Satires No.11211

The ROBBING Hood Debating Society.
Published for the Satirist Jan.ʸ 1809. by S. Tipper 37 Leadenhall Street

in the years 1817–20, that kept a vast public politically informed, and often entertained, it was the political clubs and societies that catered most for the much smaller number of radical activists, who needed the stimulus of organised debate and who believed that only formal institutions of this kind could give a lead to the people in their struggle for political liberty. Political clubs and societies had flourished in London in the later eighteenth century, but their activities had ceased in the late 1790s because of government repression and a powerful conservative reaction. It was not until 1811–12 that a few of the leading metropolitan radicals established new political societies. In 1811 Thomas Northmore suggested the establishment of the Hampden Club to campaign exclusively for moderate parliamentary reform. Northmore stressed the need to recruit men of property, but John Cartwright urged a less exclusive membership and a more radical programme of reform. It was not until 1814 that Cartwright won over the Hampden Club to his views, but only at the cost of a sharp reduction in membership. Meanwhile, Cartwright had laboured to establish an alternative radical society in London. In June 1812 he set up the Union for Parliamentary Reform according to the Constitution or, more simply, the Union Society. This society favoured a more radical political programme than the Hampden Club, but it still did not commit itself to universal adult male suffrage. Moreover, its annual subscription rate of three guineas effectively excluded the lower orders from membership. Although William Cobbett and Henry Hunt

agreed to join it, the Union Society soon languished. Cartwright had more success in encouraging the spread of radical societies in the provinces during his evangelising tours of 1812 and 1813. It was not until London experienced the widespread distress of 1816 that Cartwright, with the assistance of Thomas Cleary, was able to revive the Hampden Club and the Union Society in London.[25] Cartwright was also able to organise a convention of about seventy radical delegates from the provinces to attend a convention at the Crown and Anchor Tavern in London on 22 January 1817. This meeting planned the nationwide petitioning campaign of 1817 and, inspired by Henry Hunt, it adopted the demand for universal manhood suffrage.[26]

The London Hampden Club has always attracted the attention of the historians of radicalism, but, in more recent years, it has become clear that the most lively and interesting radical societies in London were the more informal debating clubs and the 'free and easy' societies meeting weekly in London taverns. It was these which attracted the London artisans and the ultra-radical activists who so alarmed the ruling authorities in these years. John Gale Jones opened his debating society, the British

25 Miller 1974, pp.615-19.
26 Hone 1982, pp.268-69.

C. Williams, *The Smithfield Parliament*, engraving, 1819. Henry Hunt, with the head of an ass, addresses an audience of cows, pigs, sheep and horses in London's principal cattle market. British Museum Satires, No.13252

Forum, as early as 1806, but in its initial respectable form it did not survive long. It was not until 1815, when it opened five times every week for readings, debates, singing and revelry, that it made an impact. Meanwhile, other informal debating clubs had spring up in London, including the Athenian Lyceum, the new Robin Hood Debating Society, the London Institute, the Socratic Society and the Polemic Club. The ultra-radical disciples of Thomas Spence, the Spencean Philanthropists, set up four to six federated societies in London taverns, such as the George in East Harding Street and the Mulberry Tree in Moorfields, in order to debate Spence's Land Plan, discuss political reform and entertain their members with political songs and ridicule hurled at the ruling elite. In 1817 Thomas Evans and the mulatto, Robert Wedderburn, took out a joint license to run a Dissenting chapel of 'Christian Philanthropists' in a basement in Archer Street. Neither was genuinely religious and it was a political message that they preached to their congregation. By 1819 Wedderburn was operating another Dissenting chapel in Hopkins Street, where he used the Bible to justify his extreme political demands. The ultra-radicals in these London taverns and chapels mixed serious political discussion with conviviality, amusement, ritual, singing and hard drinking. They sought to undermine and lampoon the roles, distinctions and ceremonies of the ruling elite and they resorted less to a discussion of printed propaganda than to songs, obscene parody, scurrility, shocking toasts and blasphemous oaths. When they did debate politics in a serious vein, they were combative, theatrical, polemical and even profane. The men who ran them were often drawn from the less skilled trades or they were men who had not succeeded in middle-class occupations. Frequently failing to make a secure living, they often depended on charity, begging, prostitution, crime or even informing on fellow radicals.[27]

Radical clubs and societies attracted only the minority of activists. Large numbers of ordinary Londoners could, however, be attracted to lively processions and street demonstrations, or to huge open-air public meetings where charismatic orators, such as Henry Hunt, could instruct, inspire and entertain. Hunt made a triumphal entry into London in September 1819, after his famous

27 McCalman 1987, pp.309-33; McCalman 1988, pp.89-90, 113-27.

G. Cruikshank, *Poor John Bull – The Free Born Englishman – Deprived of his Seven Senses by the Six New Acts*, engraving, 1819. Cruikshank attacks the Six Acts which repressed freedom of speech and restricted public meetings. British Museum Satires, No.13504

clash with the authorities at 'Peterloo' in Manchester, while the Queen Caroline affair generated many large processions through the streets of London in 1820–21. Even more significant were the mass public meetings in London, many of them addressed by Henry Hunt. He was the main speaker at the famous Spa Fields meetings in London on 15 November and 2 December 1816, and on 10 February 1817, and at the political rallies held in Palace Yard on 7 September 1818 and at Smithfield on 21 July 1819. Although he took these occasions as an opportunity to reject violence and unconstitutional protests, Hunt did hope that the appearance of huge crowds in the centre of London would demonstrate the popularity of parliamentary reform and might even intimidate the ruling elite. On the mass platform he adopted an independent, uncompromising and resolutely democratic tone. The master of the rhetorical question and of audience participation, he was an exciting and dramatic performer who would denounce the more faint-hearted radicals and urge such confrontational strategies as advising his listeners not to pay their taxes.[28]

A small number of ultra-radicals in London, many of them influenced to some extent by Spencean ideas, sought to take advantage of Hunt's ability to draw large crowds together in order to provoke the people into violent confrontations with the authorities and even into armed insurrection. At the Spa Fields meeting on 15 November 1816, when Hunt led a procession with a reform petition to the Prince Regent's residence at Carlton House, some of the crowd rioted and smashed the windows of food shops. At the Spa Fields meeting of 2 December 1816 Dr. James Watson addressed the crowd on Spence's Land Plan before Hunt had arrived, and then Watson's son and Thomas Preston led a breakaway group which ran riot for several hours and even considered launching at attack on the Tower of London. It was this action which provoked the government into presenting repressive legislation before parliament in 1817. Even before this, however, the windows of the Prince Regent's coach had been smashed

28   Belchem 1985, pp.42-70.

on 28 January 1817 in the so-called 'pop-gun plot'. In September 1817 the Spenceans planned a rising, but this failed to materialise and, in May 1818, one of their number, Arthur Thistlewood, was imprisoned for a year for challenging Lord Sidmouth, the Home Secretary, to a duel. In September 1819 the ultra-radicals in London urged simultaneous risings all over Britain. A few small groups in London did gather arms, but only a few hundred turned up at an armed rally called by Dr. Watson at Finsbury Market Place on 1 November 1819. Under pressure from the repressive Six Acts of 1819 the organisation of the violent radicals disintegrated, but this collapse did not prevent Arthur Thistlewood and a small band of extremists plotting to murder the whole cabinet. Government informers soon penetrated this conspiracy and the ringleaders were arrested in Cato Street in February 1820. Thistlewood and a few others were later executed.[29]

The Cato Street conspiracy was a disaster for the radical cause and this episode has often been seen as marking the end of the heroic age of postwar London radicalism. In fact, however, 1820–21 saw the greatest manifestation of radical activity in London in the early nineteenth century. The surprising cause of this massive demonstration of popular protest was the effort made by the Prince Regent, who succeeded his father as King George IV in 1820, to divorce his wife, Queen Caroline. Although barely deserving of any respect or even much sympathy, the queen was placed at the centre of a popular protest movement of such impressive dimensions that it brought the long and deeply-entrenched Tory administration close to resignation or dismissal. The whole affair seems an aberration from mainstream radical activity, but it does, in fact, offer some fascinating insights into the development of radicalism in general and of London radicalism in particular. It sparked off the most massive display of outraged public opinion seen in London since the days of John Wilkes in the late 1760s and it marked the high-water mark of the postwar political agitation.

In 1820 the new king, George IV, was determined to divorce and even degrade his queen, and to prevent her from being crowned with him. Although they had long lived apart, and the queen had been abroad since 1814, public opinion regarded her as a wronged and injured woman. Her situation was regarded as analogous to the people at large, who suffered under a weak, immoral and oppressive monarch. Escorted back to Britain by the radical London alderman, Matthew Wood, her entrance into the capital on 6 June 1820 produced not only an immediate sensation, but several months of popular agitation on her behalf, as well as bitter denunciations of the king and his Tory ministers. While the king and his advis-

ers sought legal or legislative means to secure the royal divorce, the parliamentary Whigs, the corporation of the City of London, the metropolitan radicals and tens of thousands of ordinary citizens of London rallied to the queen's cause and gave a lead to the whole nation. William Cobbett danced attendance on the queen and all the radical press rallied to her, even Wooler's *Black Dwarf*, which justifiably regarded the whole affair as a diversion from more serious issues. The amount of press propaganda generated was absolutely staggering. For several months the newspapers were full of little else, and hundreds of individual pamphlets and graphic satires, many of them best-sellers, appeared in support of the queen. Never had a reigning monarch been so savagely and coarsely attacked in the public prints. In addition, over 800 petitions and addresses were presented to the queen by livery companies, trade societies, political clubs, and the 'married ladies of the metropolis'. In London there were numerous popular celebrations, public processions, crowd demonstrations and loyal deputations to the queen. The metropolis revelled in a welter of pageantry, with many activities accompanied by bands, banners, slogans and symbols, and with buildings, streets and even ships on the Thames illuminated. The radicals were able to combine with the Whigs and the moderate reformers more effectively than ever before in a broadly-based liberal alliance. The prestige of the monarchy and the stability of the Tory government were both badly shaken and the radicals were able to restore the freedom of open political agitation during the crisis, despite the repressive legislation of 1819 and the reaction against the Cato Street conspiracy.

When the government abandoned its campaign against the queen in October 1820, there were great popular celebrations, but, once the queen had accepted a pension of £50,000 per annum and had been successfully denied a coronation, the liberal alliance soon began to break up. The parliamentary Whigs and the City leadership again deserted the radicals. The queen once more became the centre of attention after her death in August 1821. The government approved of her wish to be buried in Brunswick, but, rightly fearing a last popular demonstration on her behalf, the authorities ordered the funeral cortège to make its way around the outskirts of London to Har-

29   Parssinen 1972, pp.266-82; Prothero 1979, pp.99-131; McCalman 1988, pp.97-112.

wich. The queen's metropolitan supporters refused to tolerate this subdued send-off. Vast crowds barred the route on 14 August and forced the cortège to go through the centre of London, where huge crowds could pay their last respects. In a clash with troops, two men were killed and this gave the radicals the opportunity for a last great rally when these 'martyrs' were buried on 26 August 1821. Some 70–80,000 people attended their funeral. This finally brought to an end one of the most surprising, remarkable and prolonged popular agitations ever to effect London. It was to be the last significant radical demonstration in London for the rest of the decade.[30]

THE DECLINE OF LONDON RADICALISM?

From the Wilkite demonstrations of the late 1760s to the Queen Caroline affair of 1820–21, London had given the nation a lead in demanding radical political reform and in organising popular protests. The massive agitation of 1820–21, however, marked the last occasion when London gave a clear political lead to popular radicalism in Britain. The radical protests in London reached their greatest breadth of appeal precisely at the point when the whole radical movement went into steep decline. When radicalism did revive very significantly in Britain in the 1830s and 1840s, it undoubtedly reappeared in London, but the capital no longer played the leading and dominant role in popular politics that it had played for so long in the late eighteenth and early nineteenth centuries.

Radicalism declined in London, and indeed everywhere in Britain for most of the 1820s for a number of reasons. The governing elite never lost control of the situation and repressive measures meant the arrest, imprisonment and harassment of most of the leading radical journalists and spokesmen. Although there were very few executions and the authorities usually proceeded in a constitutional way, the political activities of the radical leadership were severely disrupted. Moreover, without a great issue or a major figurehead on which to focus, it was difficult to create an effective liberal alliance or to rally mass support. It is abundantly clear that economic distress had always been a major recruiting agent for the radical cause and so the general improvement in the economy for most of the 1820s weakened the ability of the radical activists to interest the people at large in their demands for political reforms. The radical activists themselves had also displayed many weaknesses and had made many mistakes. Too many of the leading campaigners had been preoccupied with heady rhetoric, emotion and self-dramatisation.

They had been over-confident, ill-disciplined, too interested in their own self-promotion, and too ready to advance their personal solutions to the grievances of the people. They had relied far too much on the appeal of public oratory and the printed word. They had always lacked funds, they had failed to create the formal organisations capable of enduring concerted action, and they had never developed a coherent ideology able to attract and unite mass support.

When popular radicalism revived during the Reform Bill crisis of 1830–32 and during the years of Chartist protest from 1838 to 1848, the lead came principally from the industrial towns of the North and Midlands. London did become an important centre of radical activity in these years, but it never again played the kind of leading role it had previously done. It did remain a major centre for radical publications, but many of the most important radical newspapers and periodicals were now published in the provincial cities; important radical debating societies and political clubs were once more set up in London, but the size of the membership and the leadership role that they played did not match those in the industrial centres such as Birmingham, Manchester and Leeds. Radical petitions, protest marches and demonstrations were also organised once more in London, but, again, not on the scale of those in other cities. Given the fact that London remained by far the largest city in the country, the relative decline of its importance to popular radicalism requires further explanation. It was, in fact, partly due to the sheer size of London. As the metropolis grew, the City itself, which had the most effective civic institutions, became a smaller proportion of the whole. Greater London was cut in half by the River Thames and it was made up of a number of quite distinct urban communities, each with its own social and economic peculiarities. Transport across the metropolis was difficult. The whole conurbation lacked cohesion and the kind of homogeneous communities found in much smaller provincial towns. It was too large and impersonal and too socially and economically diversified to have close-knit communities or particular local grievances. London was little affected by industrial change, there were very few large factories, and there were no large groups of distressed workers facing depressed wages or widespread unemployment. There were still substantial numbers of skilled workers in

30 Stevenson 1977, pp.117-45; Prothero 1979, pp.132-55; Lacqueur 1982, pp.417-66

London, whose wages and employment prospects were often better than those of the industrial factory workers elsewhere. Even in times of economic distress London, relatively speaking, had a smaller proportion of its workforce facing a really grim situation than did some of the industrial towns. London was never a city dominated by a very small number of staple industries and by a very cohesive workforce as was the case in such places as Birmingham, Manchester and Leeds. These and other towns like them were to dominate the new, more class-conscious radicalism of the 1830s and 1840s.

31 Thompson 1968, pp.665-90; Rowe 1968, pp.472-87; Rowe 1977, pp.149-76.

LONDON WORLD CITY

According to the first census of 1801, the population of London was 959,310, almost twice the size of Paris and the largest of any city in the world; by 1841, it had risen to 1,949,277. It was also the richest city in the world, with a globally dominant economy, its commercial might expressed in the construction of the new docks, its financial power accrued through sophisticated banking and insurance systems. After the battle of Trafalgar, the country's maritime pre-eminence was assured; after Waterloo, its military strength confirmed. The coronation of George IV in 1821 provided the occasion for an appropriately lavish display of pageantry and splendour. The metropolitan improvements undertaken by John Nash and the relentless march of 'bricks and mortar' left London a more permanent legacy.

William Daniell, *Perry's Dock Blackwall, c.* 1803. Cat. No. 5

Robert Havell Junior
1793–1878

1

An Aeronautical View of London

Enlarged from the original coloured
aquatint, which measures 27.4×99 cm
Published by R. Havell, 88 Oxford Street
(opposite the Pantheon), 20 April 1831
Literature: Hyde 1981; Hyde 1988, pp.
76–77

Havell's view shows the great sprawling
metropolis from a point 402 feet above the
Thames, mid-way between Bermondsey on
the left and the recently constructed St. Katharine's Dock on the right. Windsor Castle can
be spotted on the horizon. Rennie's New
London Bridge, due to be opened on 1 August
1831, is shown; Old London Bridge, demolished in 1832, is prematurely not. The panorama's title would have been chosen to
capitalise on the intense ballooning interest at
that moment. During the royal opening of the
new bridge, the intrepid aeronaut, Charles
Green, made a ceremonial ascent from the
Southwark end.

Robert Havell junior, though primarily an
engraver and publisher of ornithological
prints (most notably those of J. J. Audubon,
Cat. Nos. 347), published several panoramas
of towns. *An Aeronautical View of London,*
however, must have been his favourite. He included a thumb-nail version of it on one of his
trade cards. The panorama is also to be seen in
an image of his shop (the Zoological Gallery,
Oxford Street), hanging on the wall.

There are four large drawings related to
Havell's print in a private collection in North
America (they are known as the *Rhinebeck
Panorama of London*). The drawings repre-
sent London *c.* 1810. **RH**

Christopher Greenwood and John Greenwood
Gisburn, 1786–1855 London, Gisburn, 1791–
1876 Gisburn, respectively

2

Map of London from Actual Survey Comprehending the Various Improvements to 1835

Line engraving, 122.5×182.5 cm
Published by the Proprietors E. Ruff and
Co., Hind Court, Fleet Street, 2 March 1835
London, Guildhall Library, Corporation of
London
Literature: Harley 1962; Howgego 1978,
No. 309(3)

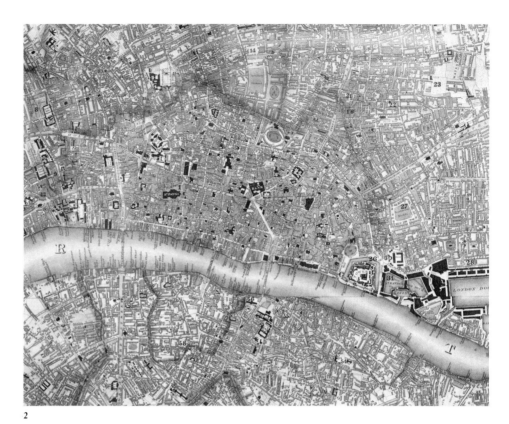

2

Greenwood's six-sheet map of London and its
environs, with its views of St. Peter's (Westminster Abbey) and St. Paul's, represents Regency map making at its finest. It shows the
expanding metropolis, with new docks completed or still being built in the East End; new
roads – King William Street, and the Commercial Road in particular; new bridges including
New London Bridge opened in 1831; the
course of the Thames Tunnel; the New Cattle
Market, Islington; and London's first railways. Ambitious new housing developments
include Bayswater (the Ecclesiastical Commissioners' Paddington estate immediately
north of Hyde Park) and Portland town (in St.
John's Wood, north of St. Marylebone).

Christopher Greenwood, a Yorkshire surveyor, launched his business in 1817 with a
large-scale survey of his own county. In 1818
he moved to London where he had access to
materials, map-engraving and printing expertise, and capital. Besides issuing more large-
scale country maps – he produced thirty-eight
in all – Greenwood embarked on a new survey
of London to a scale of eight inches to one
mile. The very handsome map, dedicated to
George IV, appeared in two editions in 1827.

For the 1830 edition the map was completely redrawn and re-engraved. The area
covered was extended at bottom centre to include Stockwell Park, Camberwell, Denmark
Hill, and Peckham. What accident had befallen the original copper plates is not known.
The new ones were sold off to the map moun-

ters Edward Ruff and Co., who produced an
edition dated 1 January 1835, the edition exhibited here dated 2 March 1835, and further
editions into the 1850s. **RH**

Robert Havell Junior
1793–1878

3

Panorama of London

Coloured aquatint, 7.6×419 cm
Published by Rodwell and Martin, 46 New
Bond Street, 1822
London, The Museum of London
Inv. No. A23741
Literature: Hyde 1985, p. 135, No. 62

Havell's very long view of the Thames begins
at Vauxhall Bridge, opened only six years

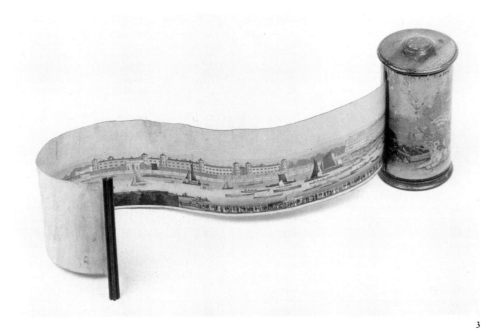

3

Tower of London.

The ninety-gun sailing vessel was designed by Sir William Symonds, cost £90,000, and had a complement of 850 officers and men. In 1854 she served in the Black Sea during the Crimean War and took part in the bombardment of Sebastopol. Converted to steam and fitted with screw propulsion shortly afterwards, she spend her last years as a store ship and headquarters at Zanzibar as part of the naval force involved with the suppression of the slave trade along the coast of East Africa. In 1884 she was sold for breaking.

During the late eighteenth and early nineteenth centuries, the facilities at Royal Naval dockyards on the Thames and Medway were gradually modernised. Sir Samuel Bentham, Inspector-General of Naval Works, designed steam-powered machinery including blockmaking machinery and bucket dredgers, as well as introducing covered slipways. He employed Sir Marc Brunel (Cat. No. 214) to install new sawmills at Chatham. **APW**

William Daniell
Chertsey 1769–1839 London

5
Perry's Dock Blackwall, c. 1803

Oil on canvas, 56×106.5 cm
London, National Maritime Museum
Inv. No. BHC 1867
Provenance: Edward William Green
Bequest, 1951
Literature: Anon. 1799, pp. 46–47;
Skempton 1978–79, pp. 89–90; *Concise Catalogue* 1988, p. 146, reproduced; Werner and Lane 1991, pp. 24–25

John Perry was the grandson of Philip Perry who had been Sir Henry Johnson's dock manager at Blackwall. The painting was probably commissioned by him. The new dock was constructed on land to the east of the famous shipbuilding yard, which comprised slips, dry docks and an old wet dock (Daniell delineated it in his 1808 view of the East India Dock).

London had a monopoly on all British trade with the East, through the operations of the East India Company. This domination applied to the building of all the chartered East India Company ships. A powerful group known as the 'City and Shipping Interest', made up of East India shipowners, husbands and captains as well as those who controlled the building, docking, fitting out and equipping of the Company's ships, helped to perpetuate and consolidate London's central position in this trade. The ships built or repaired at yards nearby were made ready for their voyages in Perry's Dock.

The dock was in fact made up of two linked

---

earlier. Designed by James Walker, it was the first iron bridge over the Thames in London. To the east of it is London's latest and, therefore most modern prison, the Millbank Penitentiary completed in 1821 (Cat. No. 00). Moving down the panorama we pass two more new bridges, Waterloo Bridge (Cat. No. 146) completed in 1817, and Southwark Bridge (Cat. No. 147) completed in 1819. Our journey ends at St. John Wapping.

River traffic is represented in abundance. It includes the Margate Steam Yacht, personal yacht of Alderman Sir William Curtis M.P., the biscuit maker and sailing friend of George IV It also shows a civic procession of City ceremonial barges, six 'four-oared pleasure galleys' taking part in a rowing match, several colliers and hay barges and fishing boats.

The panorama is housed in a lacquered boxwood drum which Havell described as a 'Brighton-ware Box'. The drum incorporates a simple winding mechanism enabling the user to retract the print after inspection. **RH**

4
H.M.S. London figurehead, 1840

Painted wood, H 212 cm
London, National Maritime Museum
Inv. No. FH12/1936
Literature: Fraser 1908, pp. 418–31;
Banbury, pp. 73–107; MacDougall 1982, pp. 123–50; Morris 1983, pp. 53–61

In 1840, H.M.S. *London* was built and launched at the royal naval dockyard at

4

Chatham. One of a long line of famous men-of-war to be named *London* and the last to be built of wood, the ship bore a figurehead said to portray the young Queen Victoria wearing a crown representing the White Tower of the docks. In the larger of the two, the western dock (5 acres), the 500 to 1,250 ton East Indiamen were fitted out, the entrance lock being able to accommodate these large ships. The outstanding feature of the dock was the 117-foot-high mast house. It became the dominant landmark for homeward-bound sailors. Smaller ships such as West Indiamen, Greenland and the South Sea whalers used the eastern dock (3 acres) to lay up away from the dangers of the tidal river. The unloading of cargo was prohibited, the exception being whale oil. Blubber boilers were provided along the east side of the dock.

Even before these new facilities were built, Blackwall Yard was described as the largest and best equipped in the kingdom. After Perry's Dock had opened in 1790, it was spoken of as the most substantial private shipbuilding and repairing yard in the world. **APW**

6

The London Dock series of aquatints 1802-1813

Each print, 48 × 85 cm
Literature: Sutton 1954, pp. 112–13, 162; Stewart 1955, pp. 79–82

William Daniell gained first-hand experience of life on board ship in 1785 when he sailed out to the East Indies with his uncle Thomas Daniell (1749–1840). On their return to London in 1794, they began to work up their watercolours and sketches amassed during their stay in India and China. They produced prints known as 'coloured aquatints' – etchings which resembled watercolours in the subtlety of their shading and colouring. This important topographical work, *Oriental Scenery*, was published in six large folio volumes between 1795 and 1808, with the first volume dedicated to the Honourable Court of Directors of the East India Company.

One of their major patrons was Charles Hampden Turner (1772–1856) who owned over thirty of their oil paintings. He was a director of the East India Dock Company, a partner in the patent rope manufactory of Huddart and Co. at Limehouse as well as a part owner of East Indiamen. It may be that Turner played a part in encouraging William Daniell to undertake these aquatints of London's new docks.

The series consisted of six large coloured aquatints produced separately at £2.12s.6d. each. They were published in the following order: West India Dock (1802), London Dock (1803), Brunswick Dock (1803), East India Dock (1808), London Dock (1808), Commercial Dock (1813).

These were the only contemporary representations which managed to convey the vast extent of London's early nineteenth-century dock undertakings. The print of George Dance's proposal for the improvement of the Port of London was related to this series, showing an imaginative scheme for a double London Bridge and a rebuilding of the Legal Quays and the Sufferance Wharves. **APW**

a) An Elevated View of the New Docks & Warehouses now constructing on the Isle of Dogs

Published by William Daniell, 9 Cleveland Street, Fitzroy Square, 15 October 1802
London, Guildhall Library, Corporation of London
Literature: Stern 1952; Sutton 1954, pp. 112, 162; Hatfield and Skempton 1979, pp. 184–97

As the letters state, this print represents: 'the general appearance, when finished, of that magnificent and truly national work completed in the short space of little more than two years from its commencement in Feb[y]. 1800, in so much that on 27 Aug[st]. 1802 the Thames was permitted to flow into the larger bason, which is 2600 feet in length, containing an Area of thirty Acres; and two Ships, the *Henry Addington & Echo*, being the first Vessels admitted, were received amidst the shouts of an immense concourse of spectators assembled to behold a scene so highly interesting to every well-wisher to the prosperity and glory of this Country.'

During the late 1790s there were two rival proposals for the building of docks in London. Robert Milligan, a West India merchant, favoured the construction of docks on the Isle of Dogs. He argued that West India ships were too large to be safely navigated up the Middle Channel of the river as far as Wapping, the location of the other scheme.

The Pool of London, an area of the River Thames between London Bridge and Limehouse, was known to be the place where most of the plunderage of sugar and rum occurred from the West India ships moored in tiers on either side of the Middle Channel. The distant location of docks on the Isle of Dogs was initially seen as a disadvantage, being well away from the port's traditional cargo-handling area as well as London's sugar refineries. However, such an isolated position, it was argued, would offer better security from theft, profiting both the merchant and the Revenue.

In 1797 the City of London joined with the West India merchants in presenting a bill before parliament for docks on the Isle of Dogs and a canal across it. Their proposal had gained the support of a key figure in terms of the operation of London's port – George Hibbert (1757–1837). He was an immensely wealthy West India merchant, a wharfinger as well as a City alderman. Finally, in 1799, after a number of delays, the West India Dock Company Act was passed and the City of London commenced buying up the land required for the scheme. Excavation work started in the following year, under the supervision of the engineer, Ralph Walker, and with William Jessup as the consulting engineer.

Daniell's representation of the new docks and canal was closely based on John Fairburn's plan published in 1802. He must have sketched the North Quay warehouses, designed by the Gwilts, or seen architectural drawings of them, as they are accurately delineated. The warehouses shown surrounding the Export Dock and the houses along the southern section of the canal were never built. The print, dedicated by Daniell to the Chairman and Directors of the West India Dock Company, proved to be a success; Daniell was reported to have 'cleared two hundred guineas'. **APW**

6a

6b

b) An Elevated View of the New Docks at Wapping

Published by William Daniell, No. 9 Cleveland Street, Fitzroy Square, 1 January 1803
London, Guildhall Library, Corporation of London
Literature: Vaughan 1839; Sutton 1954, pp. 112, 162; Skempton 1978–79, pp. 95–97

William Vaughan (1752–1850) was the most energetic and persuasive of those London merchants and brokers who supported the improvement of the Port of London and the building of docks. In 1793 he published privately the first of a number of tracts on the state of the port. Circulated widely in the City among merchants and financiers and in parliament, it proved to be very influential and led to a meeting of interested parties in 1794 at the Merchant Seamen's Office.

Vaughan explained that the object of his pamphlet was 'to remove prejudices, to quiet claimants, and to unite great leading and commercial interests in an application to Parliament for the creation of Docks, as one of the best securities and encouragements to our commerce, and prosperity to our country.'

He analysed the operations of the port and set out plans for a dock or docks at Wapping, with a canal extending east to the River Thames at Blackwall, thus avoiding the hazardous route for ships around the Isle of Dogs. By 1795, the Merchants' London Dock Scheme was financially secure with a subscription of £800,000 having been raised.

The arrangement of the rival West India and City of London Dock and Canal Scheme resulted in the London merchants dropping the proposed canal to Blackwall. After a series of parliamentary deferrals, an act of parliament was granted in 1800 for the building of docks at Wapping. In 1801 John Rennie was appointed as engineer. He employed a series of iron railways to help speed the removal of the spoil and carry building materials to different parts of the dock. A Boulton and Watt steam-powered piling engine was used for the first time to drive cofferdam piles. Rennie designed the world's first double-leaf iron swing bridge across the Wapping Entrance. In the words of Skempton, the 'London Docks show Rennie at the height of his powers, as an innovator, designer and director of a great undertaking in which excellence ranked as the main criterion.'

Daniell's print, dedicated to the Chairman and Directors of the London Dock Company, was based upon the survey and architectural drawings of Daniel Alexander and the 1802 map of John Fairburn. It accurately portrays the likely appearance of the London Dock. The mooring tiers on either side of the Middle Channel were shown to be densely packed with shipping. The river was to remain very congested, especially with colliers, despite the opening of the new docks. **APW**

c) A View of the East India Docks

Published by William Daniell, 9 Cleveland Street, Fitzroy Square, 1 October 1808
London, Guildhall Library, Corporation of London
Literature: Sutton 1954, pp. 112, 162; Pudney, 1975, pp. 48–52; Skempton, 1978–79, pp. 98–100

In 1803 the East India Dock Company was formed, backed by East India merchants and those involved with East India ships, shipbuilding and ship repairing. It raised sufficient funds to acquire Perry's Dock from the Wells family. John Rennie and Ralph Walker were appointed as joint engineers. Work proceeded rapidly on transforming it into the Export Dock, with a completely new dock being cut to the north, the Import Dock, and both were linked to an entrance basin and a new dock entrance. The East India Docks (26 acres) were constructed very economically, benefiting from the lessons learnt as well as the equipment used in the building of the West India and the London Docks. The lock entrance was the largest in the world (210 feet long, 48 feet wide and with the sills laid 25 feet below Thames High Water).

The dock opened in 1806, with a twenty-one-year monopoly on the handling of all East India produce. Initially, there was no warehouse accommodation provided along the quayside. Instead, 'close covered carriages, or light wagons, each mounted on four wheels and capable of conveying 50 chests of tea each' were employed to carry cargo from the docks to the East India Company's City warehouses. The directors of the East India Dock Company bought twenty copies of Daniell's print for their own use. **APW**

6d

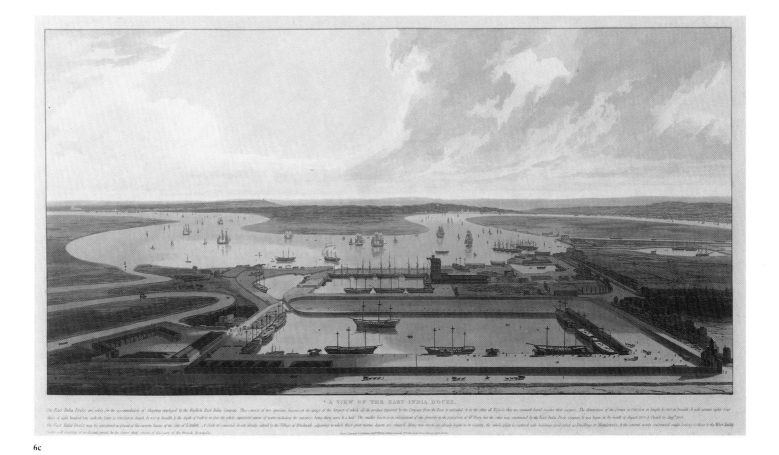

d) A View of the Commercial Docks at Rotherhithe

Published by William Daniell, 9 Cleveland Street, Fitzroy Square, 1 June 1813
London, Port of London Authority
Literature: Gould 1841; Griffin 1877; Sutton 1954, pp. 112, 162; Skempton, 1981–82, pp. 73–77

'These docks are intended chiefly to receive the Shipping employed in the Trade from America and the North of Europe, to land and stow their Cargoes consisting of Timber, Wood Goods, Hemp, Corn, Iron &c. &c. and to extend the Bonding System to those Articles thereby affording accommodation to a numerous Class of Shipping with increased Security to the Revenue and to the Importers. – There are Five Docks in one of which the Greenland Oil Ships are accommodated and their Cargoes expeditiously boiled and Warehoused by the Dock Company in most excellent Cellars properly adapted for the prevention of Waste or Leakage.'

Private docks were built in London during the seventeenth and eighteenth centuries. The largest was the Howland Great Dock (1696–99), later called the Greenland Dock, situated in Rotherhithe. It was not used for the loading and unloading of cargo but for the fitting out and laying up of ships, with facilities provided for extracting oil from whale blubber. In 1807, the Commercial Dock Company acquired the old Greenland Dock and proposed converting it into a dock principally for the handling, bonding and warehousing of timber. It reopened in 1809 after the entrance lock had been widened and deepened. Further land was bought to the north and by 1811 two new docks had been built as well as a large warehouse with iron columns.

This was not the only dock scheme in Rotherhithe. In 1801 an act was passed allowing a canal to be built between Rotherhithe and Epsom with plans to extend to Portsmouth and Southampton. By 1811–12, the works had only reached Camberwell, though at its entrance into the river at Rotherhithe a 10-acre basin had been constructed by widening and deepening a 650-yard stretch of the canal. This was used as a dock, as can be seen in the middle distance of Daniell's aquatint. To the south of the old Greenland Dock, the East Country Dock had opened in 1811 (part of it is just discernible in the lower left-hand corner of the print). With a water area of only 4 acres, it was the smallest cargo-handling dock in the Port of London, specialising like the other two docks on the south side of the river, in the Baltic Trade. **APW**

James Walker
1781–1862

7
Plan of the late IMPROVEMENTS in the PORT of LONDON

Coloured engraving, 43 × 142 cm
Published by Robert Wilkinson, 58 Cornhill, 7 August 1804
London, The Museum of London, P.L.A. Collection

Until the docks were constructed, narrow and poorly maintained roads such as Ratcliff Highway, Cable Street, Fore Street, Limehouse Causeway and Poplar High Street were the only thoroughfares available to carry goods to and from the City. Most cargo was transported by river. However, it could be prey to plunder from river thieves and damage often occurred when it was being loaded and unloaded from barges. In 1802 an act of parliament was granted to the Commercial Road Trust to build a toll road between Aldgate and Limehouse. It cut across existing roads and completely changed the face of east London.

The choice of the name for this road was particularly appropriate as commerce had become one of the catchwords for the propo-

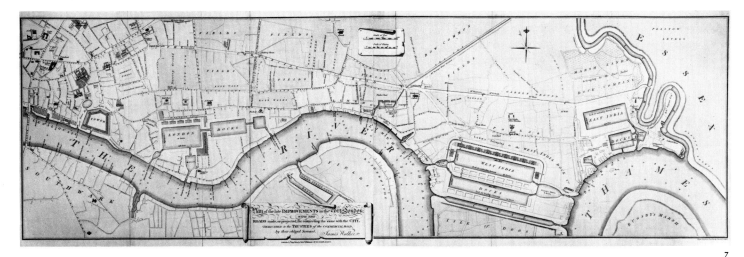

sals and plans drawn during the mid 1790s for dock construction in Wapping and on the Isle of Dogs. Appropriately, the inscription on the foundation stone of the West India Dock ended with the words: 'An Undertaking which, under the Favour of God, shall contribute Stability, Increase and Ornament, to British Commerce.'

James Walker, the nephew of Ralph Walker, was appointed as engineer of the new road. Two eastern branches were built from Limehouse, known as the West India Dock Road and the East India Dock Road, extending right up to the main entrances of the docks. The capital for these new roads came largely from West India and East India merchants. Milestones were set up along the course of the route, showing that the West India Dock was just three miles from the Royal Exchange. It was not long before houses began to be built along the course of the road. **APW**

constructed for the reception of these valuable commodities. Appropriately, the first ship to enter the London Docks, on 30 January 1805, was a brig, called *The London Packet*, laden with wine from Oporto. So great was the trade in wines from Spain and Portugal during the war with France that the vaults were soon completely full. In 1809, 44,000 pipes of wine and brandy were housed in the vaults and sheds, 12,000 casks and barrels were laid out in the open air along the quays and on the gauging ground, and a further 22,000 were stored on board ship in the dock awaiting discharge.

This inadequate arrangement was comparable to the problems faced by the West India Trade in the 1790s, before the West India Dock was built. At that time, the Port of London had storage for only 30,000 hogsheads of sugar, whereas over 100,000 hogsheads arrived in 1793 over a period of only two summer months.

Daniel Alexander drew up plans for vaulted sheds and warehouses along the south quay

and behind the large stacks along the north quay of the dock. The vault and ground floors were specially designed to maximise the number of wine casks that could be easily stored. The vaults were often put into use as soon as they were completed, the upper floors being added later. A tour of the wine vaults at the London Docks was considered one of the treats of a visit to London. **APW**

9
London Docks Castings Tobacco Warehouse Roofings

Pen and watercolour with notes in ink, 56.2×75 cm
Signed bottom left: Office for Works, London Docks, January 4th 1811
London, The Museum of London, P.L.A. Collection
Inv. No. 4620492
Literature: Skempton 1981–82, p. 77; Thorne 1986, pp. 29–38

Daniel Asher Alexander
London 1768–1846 Exeter

8
London Docks, South Quay Stacks, Section from East to West, *c.* 1810

Pen and ink and watercolour, 45.8×92.8 cm
London, Port of London Authority Collection, The Museum of London
Inv. No. 4620116
Literature: Elmes 1838, p. 49; Crouzet 1953; Cruickshank 1989, p. 61, illustrated

The London Docks had extensive storage facilities for wine and brandy. Under the range of warehouses, a series of vaults were specially

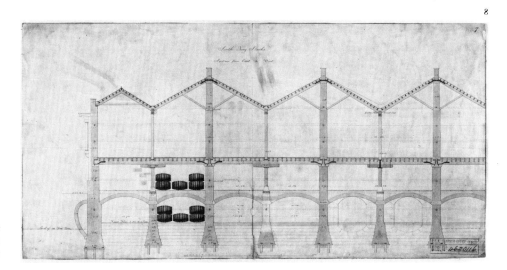

The twenty-one-year monopoly of the London Dock Company included the handling of all tobacco, rice, wine and brandy, except for that carried in ships from the West and East Indies. In 1805, when the dock opened, a special bonded warehouse was provided for the storage of tobacco, located on the southeast quay of the Import Dock. Daniel Asher Alexander, the Company's surveyor between 1796 and 1833, designed and supervised its construction as well as all the main warehouses and sheds in the dock.

By 1811 further accommodation was required for the storage of tobacco. A small dock, designed by John Rennie, was cut to the east of the Western Dock and new warehouses were built around it, linking up with the old range to the south. Alexander's new tobacco warehouse made use of cast-iron stanchions to support the 54-foot span queen-post roof trusses. The method of supporting the roof was completely original. Each stanchion branched out to support a bolster timber on which rested the truss ends. Another two Y-shaped struts sprang from just beneath each branching-point to support their companion struts at circular crown pieces. There were no bolts or rivets in the structure, the joints on the stanchions and crown pieces simply slotted together.

The description of this warehouse in the Dock section of Rees's *Cyclopaedia* (1819, Cat. No. 198) revealed the high regard in which it was held by contemporaries: 'The whole building stands upon an area of near five acres, covering more ground, under one roof, than any public building or undertaking, except the pyramids of Egypt. Its roof is light, airy, and simple, and adds greatly to the beauty and boldness of the design, and stands unrivalled in architectural buildings of its kind.' APW

John Rennie

Phantassie 1761–1821 London

10

Transverse and Longitudinal Section of New Mahogany Shed in East Wood Yard

Pen and watercolour, 47×63 cm
Signed bottom right: Engineers Office, West India Docks, 1 August 1817
London, The Museum of London, P.L.A. Collection
Inv. No. 6620877
Literature: Dupin 1824, pp. 59–60; Sargent 1991, p. 134; Thorne ed. 1990, p. 9

The architectural and engineering features of London's new docks were noted and sketched by foreign visitors such as Schinkel, Dupin and Carlsund. At the West India Docks, they wondered at John Rennie's transit sheds along the north quay of the Import Dock, the rum quay sheds and machinery such as the hydraulic mechanism, based on a Bramah invention, employed to lower rum barrels from the quay into the vaults.

The high cost of timber led dock engineers and architects to experiment with cast iron in the construction of warehouses and sheds. They designed ambitious, sometimes revolutionary structures as they looked for the most cost-effective solution to facilitate the handling or storage of a particular cargo.

Mahogany, an important cargo arriving from the West Indies, had initially been stored in the open along the south quay of the Import Dock. In 1817 John Rennie designed a building specially for the handling of this hardwood. The shed was constructed end-on to the quay, with tall cast-iron columns supplied by the Horseley Ironworks Company supporting elaborate roof trusses.

The roof carried rails for crane-trucks running across the building. The 5-ton logs of mahogany were wheeled up the aisles of the sheds on railway trucks and then stacked up by means of the roof crane-trucks' crabs. This was believed to be the first ever use of an overhead travelling crane. APW

Sir John Rennie

London 1794–1874 Bengeo, Hertfordshire

11

a) Proposed north elevation of No. 1 and 9 warehouses, West India Docks, 1827

Pen and ink, 72×129 cm

b) Section of warehouses No. 1 and 9, showing the proposed mode of raising New Work upon Old Foundations, West India Dock, 1827

Ink and coloured wash, 65×123.5 cm

London, The Museum of London, P.L.A. Collection
Inv. Nos. 6620689 and 6620679 respectively
Literature: Sargent 1991, p.138; Cruickshank 1989, pp. 55–61

Between 1800 and 1804 George Gwilt and his eldest son designed and supervised the building of the run of warehouses along the north quay of the West India Dock. Six six-storey warehouses, 223 feet long in three divisions were constructed, each able to store 8,000 hogsheads of sugar on the four main floors, as well as 2,000 hogsheads of coffee in the attic floor and 2,000 casks of rum in the vault. They were known as No. 2, 3, 4, 6, 7 and 8. One-storey buildings about 74 feet long, with basements, linked them together.

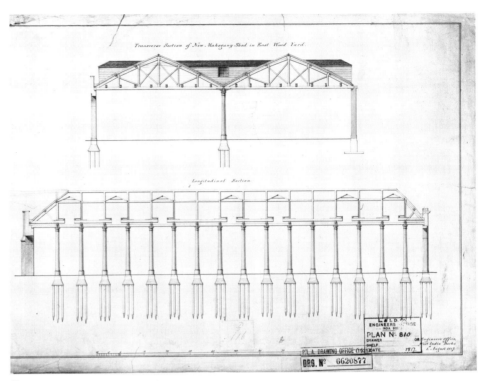

10

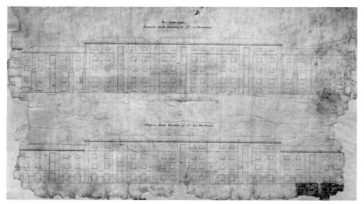

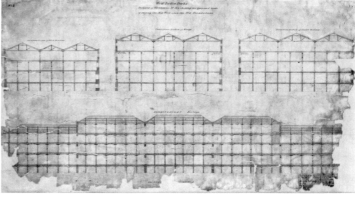

11a

11b

The plan had included a further three 'high' warehouses but the West India Dock Company's capital had been almost expended on other works. Instead, 'low' warehouses were built in the centre and on the ends, No. 1, 5 and 9, with strong foundations and walls to allow upward building at a later date. Just as the Import Dock was to be the world's largest until the 1850s, so the run of warehouses along the north quay could claim to be the longest in Europe. During most of the West India Dock Company's twenty-one-year monopoly (1802–1823) on the handling of West India produce arriving in the Port of London, these warehouses were completely full.

In anticipation of the expiry of East India Dock Company's twenty-one-year mono-poly on the handling of East India produce, the directors of the West India Dock Company decided to provide extra warehouse accommodation for the India trade. Sir John Rennie, who had succeeded his father as principal engineer of the Dock Company, drew up plans for raising the low warehouses at each end of the north quay of the Import Dock. He took care to match the work of the Gwilts, lining up the cornices with those of the existing buildings to give an effect of one continuous line of warehouses. The miscellaneous nature of India produce required a range of ceiling heights, making inappropriate the low 7-foot clearance needed for the storage of hogsheads of sugar. As a result of this No. 1 and 9 warehouses were only five storeys high. **APW**

W. Ranwell

12
St. Katharine's Docks: the works in progress January, 1828

Watercolour, 76 × 91.5 cm
London, Port of London Authority
Inv. No. 59
Literature: Stewart 1955, p. 44; Skempton, 1981–82, pp. 82–87

The prospect of the termination of the twenty-one-year monopolies held by the three major dock companies spurred on a group of City merchants and financiers to set up the St. Katharine Dock Company. They selected a site very close to the City, between the Tower and the London Docks. Strong opposition to the scheme came from the dock companies, especially the London Dock Company, as well as sufferance wharf owners.

Despite their petitions, on 10 June 1825 the St. Katharine Dock Company was granted an act of parliament for 'making and constructing certain Wet Docks, Warehouses, and other Works'. Some 1,250 houses and tenements were pulled down to make way for the dock, including the Royal Hospital and Collegiate Church of St. Katharine-by-the-Tower which had survived the Great Fire of London. Over 11,000 inhabitants were displaced.

Thomas Telford and Philip Hardwicke came up with an imaginative scheme to maximise the limited space (23½ acres) available. The excavations began in May 1826 and the works were completed in eighteenth months. Two docks were dug linked to a basin, with just one entrance lock into the river. Warehouses were built with deep foundations, some with two floors of vaults.

At this period, dock construction was very labour intensive. Excavation was done by hand and the spoil was carried away either in wheelbarrows or in horse-drawn wagons on iron railways. The material not reused on site was hauled up to a special jetty on the river by means of a steam engine and taken away by barges to raise land levels at Pimlico. **APW**

12

13

William John Huggins
1781–1845 London

13
The Opening of St. Katharine Dock, 25 October 1828

Oil on canvas, 30.5×50.8 cm
London, Port of London Authority
Inv. No. 305
Provenance: G. G. Hallam, 1928
Exhibitions: London, The Museum of London, 1989
Literature: Stewart 1955, Plate p. 35

Dock openings, like ship launches on the Thames, were attended by a vast crowd of Londoners. The first ship to enter the St. Katharine Dock was the *Elizabeth*, an East India free trader. She was dressed overall with her yards manned. The next ship, the *Mary*, similarly attired, had fifty Trafalgar veterans in her rigging. The opening ceremony attracted a flotilla of small craft on the river and over 10,000 visitors were admitted to the dock on the day.

The opening of the St. Katharine Dock

Company marked the end of the second period of major dock construction and heralded the start of fierce competition between the rival undertakings. During the 1830s and 1840s dock dues fell generally and dock company dividends were put under pressure. The St. Katharine Dock Company, through the able management of John Hall (later Sir John), its secretary, succeeded in persuading ship owners and merchants to make use of its new facilities.

One of the Company's main attractions was its proximity to the City. High value cargoes, such as tea, silk, carpets, curios and drugs could be conveniently stored and displayed in its extensive warehouses. In 1836 the St. Katharine Dock Company acquired the large Cutler Street warehouses from the East India Company and was able to offer select storage accommodation and show-floors in the heart of the City. **APW**

Thomas Telford
Glendinning 1757–1834 London

14
a) Section through Chamber of Entrance Lock, *c.* 1827

Pen and ink and watercolour, 48.2×64 cm
London, The Museum of London, P.L.A. Collection
Inv. No. 4760077
Literature: Rolt 1958, pp. 142–44; Skempton 1981–82, pp. 82–87

b) Mooring Ring as fixed in Dock Wall, *c.* 1827

Pen and ink and watercolour, 47.7×73.3 cm
London, The Museum of London, P.L.A. Collection
Inv. No. 4700011
Literature: Telford 1838, p. 157

In 1824 Thomas Telford was approached by the directors of the St. Katharine Dock Company to draw up plans for the new dock. He had been involved with many civil-engineer-

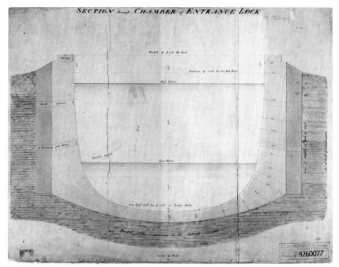

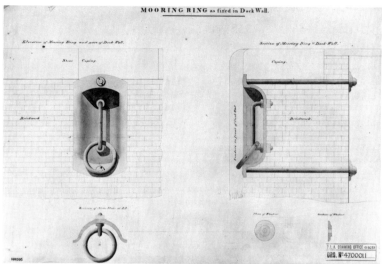

14a

14b

ing works in Britain including canals, bridges, roads and harbours, but strangely he had never undertaken a major contract in London. The awkwardness of the site at St. Katharine, as well as the speed in which the works were carried out, caused him some concern and called upon all his skill and experience. He wrote, 'Seldom, never indeed within my knowledge, has existed any instance of an undertaking of this magnitude, in a very confined situation, having been perfected in so short a time; nor could it have been accomplished in any other place than London, where materials and labour to any extent are always to be procured, as likewise the command of capital in the power of intelligent directors, accustomed to transactions on a large scale.'

Telford's designs were of the highest order with the best quality materials used throughout. Thomas Rhodes, one of Telford's most able assistants, supervised the day-to-day building of the dock. He made sure that the cofferdam was constructed correctly and that the wharf wall foundations were watertight. The mooring rings in the basins and docks allowed for changes in the water level. Telford refers to them in his autobiography, modestly stating them to be 'new, and . . . deserving of attention'.

In the lock entrance, lias-mortar was laid between the grey stock bricks and the finest Yorkshire Bramley Fell stone was chosen for the platforms and copings. Bramah's Pimlico manufactory supplied the dock gates and Boulton and Watt installed the two 80-horse-power steam engines, three boilers and six double-acting pumps. The sills of the lock were set some 28 feet below Thames High Water, at the time the deepest in the Port of London. This allowed ships of up to 600 tons to enter and leave the dock three hours before high water. The lock could be filled rapidly by pumping water from the river and by gravity flow through sluices from the basin. **APW**

Handbill

15
Notice regarding dogs in the St. Katharine Docks, 23rd September 1831

Printed by Marchant, Ingham-Court
21 × 28 cm
London, The Museum of London, P.L.A. Collection

The St. Katharine Dock Company was efficiently managed by John (later Sir John) Hall, its secretary. His administration of the company was authoritarian yet paternalistic. He drew up, published and circulated among his staff a set of very detailed regulations which governed all aspects of their work. There were further rules for owners, pilots and ship captains and others using or visiting the docks. These became a model for the instructions issued by other dock companies regarding the arrangement and operation of their docks.

The permanent staff were divided into two departments – the In-door and the Out-door.

15

NOTICE.

Considerable Injury having at times been done to Goods, particularly those for Export, deposited upon the Quays, by DOGS *belonging to Ships lying in these Docks*; the Captain and Mates of such Vessels are requested to cause DOGS belonging thereto to be tied up on board.

The Constables and Watchmen are instructed to lock or tie up all DOGS found straying about the Quays, and remove them from the Docks, upon the termination of Business, daily.

The Gate-Keepers will prevent the admission of DOGS, unless the Owners shall have them fastened by a Cord or Handkerchief.

St. Katharine Docks, Sept. 23, 1831.   MARCHANT, PRINTER, INGHAM-COURT.

The In-door staff were well paid and benefited from gratuities and superannuation allowances as a reward for loyal long-term service. The Out-door staff were governed by their own 'Codes of Instructions'. The Permanent, Preferable and Extra Labourers were allowed a quarter-hour lunchbreak at twelve noon. The Gatekeepers had to supervise the distribution of their 'beer, bread and cheese, cold meat, and hot potatoes' at the dock gates, which was brought in by authorised personnel. It was specified that only 'one pint of beer, per day' was 'to be allowed to each man'. Sobriety and honesty were stated to be indispensable qualifications for dock workers. The older Permanent Labourers, as a result of 'infirmity or length of service', were employed in departments which did not require great physical exertion. **APW**

E. Duncan after
William John Huggins
1781–1845 London

16
The Launch of the Hon East India Compy's Ship Edinburgh, November 9th 1825

Aquatint, 37.2 × 56.7 cm
Published by W. J. Huggins Marine Painter, 105 Leadenhall Street, 10 August 1826
London, The Museum of London
Inv. No. A14385
Literature: Green and Wigram 1881, p. 57, illustrated; Lubbock 1922, pp. 44–48; Prothero 1979, p. 47

This print shows the ship-building activities at Blackwall with the launch of the *Edinburgh* and her sister ship, the *Abercrombie Robinson*, on the stocks – both 1,325-ton East Indiamen – in the yard of Wigrams and Green.

Sir Robert Wigram (1744–1833) was one of the most prominent East India husbands, with interests in drugs, brewing, rope making and, from 1812, the Blackwall Yard; he became chairman of the East India Company. Blackwall Yard was the largest private yard in the country, employing 600 men, and was essential for the fitting out and repair of ships for the navy during the war. Wigram exemplified the connection between capital and the state, with a seat in parliament and a baronetcy conferred by Pitt. He had twenty-three sons by two wives and in 1819 sold a half share of his interest in the Blackwall dockyard to two of them, and the remaining half to George Green.

By the early nineteenth century the building of East Indiamen was at its zenith, and Wigrams and Green were famous for the high cost, quality, strength and reliability of their passenger-carrying merchant ships, equal to men-of-war with a social status to match, as the production of this print implies. **CE and CF**

16

Franz Thaller
Vienna 1759–1817 Vienna
and Matthias Ranson

17
Vice Admiral Horatio Nelson, Viscount Nelson, 1801

Marble, 71 × 43 cm
Inscribed: FRANZ THALLER/ET/
MATTHIAS RANSON/VIENNA
AUSTR /MDCCCI
London, National Maritime Museum
Inv. No. 48-720/179
Provenance: given by Lady Hamilton to Alderman Smith; purchased from his widow by Thomas Pettigrew, Nelson's biographer; purchased from his daughter, Miss Pettigrew by Herbert Agar; given to the 3rd Earl Nelson; acquired by the Museum, 1948
Exhibitions: London, New Gallery, 1891, No. 1614
Literature: Walker 1980, pp. 324–25; Walker 1985, Vol. 1, p. 362

No victory was as overwhelming as Nelson's almost total destruction of the French fleet in Aboukir Bay on 1 August 1798. He returned to Naples to be welcomed by the queen, whilst the king awarded him the title of Duke of Bronte in Sicily; this was also the moment when his love affair with Lady Hamilton, wife of the British ambassador, commenced. In

17

England he was raised to the peerage as Baron Nelson of the Nile and Burnham-Thorpe (his birthplace in Norfolk); parliament voted him a pension of £2,000 a year and the East India Company awarded him £10,000.

His fame spread throughout Europe and in August and September 1800, he was fêted in Vienna. He gave sittings to Friedrich-Heinrich Füger for an oil and to Thaller for this bust, which was probably based on a life mask.

Nelson wears his Rear Admiral's full-dress uniform, with the Ribbons of the Bath and the Crescent, Stars of the Crescent (above), St. Ferdinand (left), Bath (right), two naval gold medals in front (St. Vincent and the Nile, the Nile in reverse incised NILE/FIRST AUGUST/1798), with another gold medal below the stars fastened with a bow of ribbon, probably intended to represent Davison's Nile Medal. His empty right sleeve (his arm had been amputated when his elbow was shattered by grapeshot off Santa Cruz in 1797) is fastened straight across, the two naval gold buttons at the cuff worn horizontally.

The bust was shipped to England probably in 1801 and was placed in the drawing room at Merton, Surrey, where Nelson lived with Lady Hamilton. As Nelson's status as national hero rose after Copenhagen and finally with Trafalgar, many copies of the bust were made by a variety of sculptors but no acknowledgement was given to Thaller and Ranson for the original. **CF**

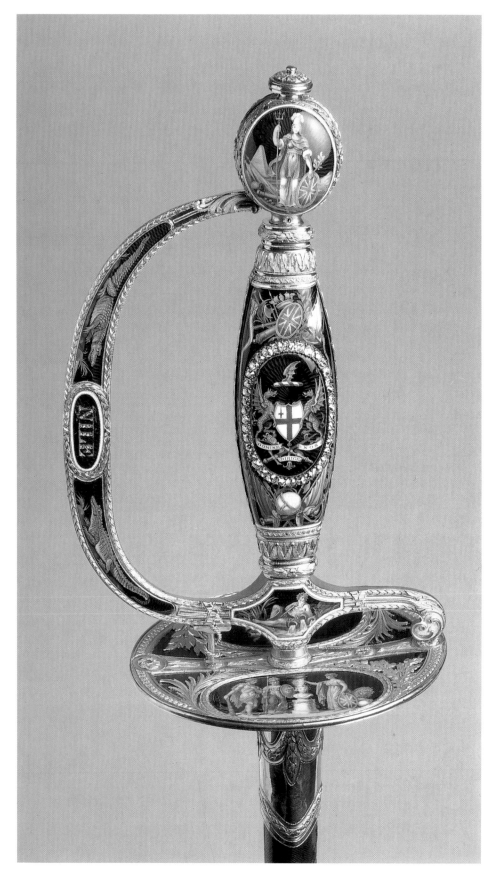

18
Sword of Honour

Gold hilt, enamelled and set with diamonds,
1798
L 101.5 cm
Marks: the scabbard mounts bear the
signature of the retailer, 'Makepeace,
London', and London hallmarks and the
mark 'IM' for James Morisset; the guard
bears the date letter for 1798
London, The Museum of London
Inv. No. 11952
Provenance: by descent from Lord Nelson's
sister; acquired by Lord Wakefield, 1928,
who presented it to the Guildhall Museum
Exhibitions: London, The Museum of
London, 1991, p. 454, Cat. No. 454, Plate 3
Literature: London's Roll 1884, pp. 81–83;
Roe 1928, pp. 355–56; Blair 1972, p. 13;
Southwick 1983, pp. 32–35, Plate 3

This Sword was presented to Lord Nelson
with the Freedom of the City of London by
the Corporation of London in 1800 in re-
cognition of the victory of the Battle of the
Nile in 1798. The following inscription is en-
graved under the shell: 'ANDERSON
MAYOR/A Common council holden in the
Chamber of the GUILDHALL of the CITY
OF LONDON on Tuesday the 16 Day of
October 1798 RESOLVED UNANI-
MOUSLY that a sword of the Value of Two
Hundred Guineas be presented to REAR
ADMIRAL LORD NELSON OF THE
NILE by this COURT as a Testimony of the
HIGH ESTEEM they entertain of his Public
Services and of the eminent advantages he has
RENDERED HIS COUNTRY/RIX'.
(William Rix was the Town Clerk in 1799.)

The sword was presented in response to the
gift Nelson made to the lord mayor of the
sword of the commanding French admiral at
the Nile, Monsieur Blanquet. According to
the City Cash Accounts for 1799 (292), Robert
Makepeace was paid £210 'in full of his Bill for
a rich chased gold sword with painted enamelled Medallions and Ornamented with
Brilliants voted by this Court to be presented
to Rear Admiral Lord Nelson of the Nile'. **TM**

19
Patriotic Fund Sword

Made by Richard Teed, 3 Lancaster Court,
Strand, 1805–06
Angular ormolu hilt; shaped and turned
ivory grip, 12.4 cm
Curved steel blade; single forward convex
cutting edge and blunted back edge, double-
edged point; decorated with etched blue and

18

gilt ornament emblematic of patriotism and mythology; presentation inscription; verso, similar ornament and the initials R. G. (Richard Grindall) in monogram within a star of twenty rays, L 83.8 cm, W 3.4 cm
Scabbard of leather with ormolu outer encasement cast in a single piece; suspension mounts in the shape of sea serpents; ornamented with scenes set in ovals against trophies of arms; pierced and cast panels of ornament comprising naval and classical trophies of arms backed by black velvet, L 85 cm, W 5 cm
Gilt and blue cord and tassel attached to hilt
Mahogany box; circular brass plate with recessed handle on lid engraved with presentation inscription; lined in green baize, 98×19×7 cm
Marks: engraved around throat of scabbard, R. Teed, Sword-Cutler, Lancaster-Court-Strand
London, Lloyd's of London
Provenance: Messrs. Spink and Son, 1909; Williamson Lamplough; presented by E. S. Lamplough to Lloyd's, 1931
Literature: Dawson 1932, pp. 17–19, 400; Southwick 1988, pp. 223–84, 291–311, Plate 82

The national competition for the design of 'badges of distinction' staged by the Management Committee of the Patriotic Fund extended only to a vase (Cat. No. 20) and a medal (won by Edward Edwards), but not to the usual sword of honour. Instead recipients were to be given money to purchase swords of their own choice 'for each of which the Committee will recommend an appropriate inscription, commemorating the action for which they were voted'. But on 17 January 1804 this decision was reversed in favour of the award of swords commissioned by the fund. Richard Teed, who had trained as a jeweller and goldsmith and was one of the leading London suppliers of swords in the Napoleonic period, was given the contract to supply them.

By 1809 some 180 had been officially awarded, in three grades. The £100 type was given mainly to commanders and naval captains; the £50 to naval lieutenants, Royal Marine officers and captains of East Indiamen, and the £30 to midshipmen, lieutenants of the Marines and masters' mates. Twenty-nine special Trafalgar or Ferrol £100 swords were offered to all commanders involved in these two naval actions of 1805, the present example being awarded to Captain Richard Grindall (1750–1820) of H.M.S. *Prince* on 3 December 1805 and received with Grindall's 'best thanks' on 1 September 1806.

Teed's Patriotic Fund sword was distinctive in British terms both in design and decoration. The angular-hilted, curved-bladed sabre, Turkish in origin, was used by elite hussar regiments on the Continent, notably Fred-

19

erick II's officer corps, but had only been adopted by the British army in the late eighteenth century, the Light Cavalry sword 1796 pattern being the closest model to the present example. The elaboration of the ornament in ormolu, making lavish use of mythological and patriotic motifs, was more commonly found on French swords of honour, the use of bold neo-classical decoration and Roman imperial iconography being prevalent in Napoleonic France.

That the maker evidently took particular pride in the work is suggested by his offer of 4 December 1804 to provide the naval swords with a blue and gold cord and 'handsome gold Tassel so as not to obs[cure] any part of the design on the Hilt' at no additional expense, an offer accepted by the fund, as demonstrated in this instance. **CF**

20
Patriotic Fund Vase

Silver gilt, 71 × 28 cm
Marks: London hallmark for 1807; mark of Benjamin Smith
Inscribed on rim: Rundell, Bridge et Rundell, Aurifices Regis et Principis Walliae, Londini Fecerunt
London, National Maritime Museum
Inv. No. 48/720
Provenance: 1st Earl Nelson; by descent to 5th Earl Nelson; purchased 1948
Literature: de Rougement 1914; St. Quintin 1923, p. 50; Wright and Fayle 1928; Berkowitz 1981, pp. 104–05; Southwick 1990, pp. 27–48

Following the failure of the Peace of Amiens, in 1803 the merchants, underwriters and subscribers of Lloyd's decided to inaugurate a national Patriotic Fund to help those wounded or the dependants of those killed in the conflict, and to grant 'pecuniary rewards, or honourable badges of distinction, for successful exertions of valour or merit'.

A nationwide competition instigated by the Committee of Management for the Design of a Presentation Vase was won by John Shaw. The commission to supply it went to the country's leading goldsmiths and jewellers, Rundell, Bridge and Rundell of Ludgate Hill (Cat. No. 463), who called in John Flaxman to undertake some modifications to the winning design. Based on recommendations made by the Admiralty and the War Office, seventy-three vases were awarded between 1803 and 1809, the majority to naval officers of the rank of captain or above, fifteen being given to captains at Trafalgar. In lieu of Lord Nelson, two special £500 vases were voted on 17 December 1805, one to Earl Nelson, the late Admiral's

20

brother (the present example), and the other to Lady Nelson, his widow (now in the collection of H.M. Queen Elizabeth II).

The shape of the vase is based on that of a Greek volute krater, familiar to designers from examples in the Hamilton collection at the British Museum (Cat. No. 358), but with suitably patriotic embellishments. The cover is surmounted by a stalking British lion, much used in anti-Napoleonic imagery. On the neck of the two Nelson vases is an applied wreath of acorn and oak leaves (laurel in the other examples). The body bears the arms of Lord Nelson on one side and a full presentation inscription in Latin on the other, thoughtfully translated into English on Lady Nelson's version. The octagonal pedestal base is embellished at the corners with four tritons sounding conch shells. The antique tablets between them are engraved with four Latin inscriptions, illustrative of Nelson's principal victories at Cape St. Vincent, the Nile, Copenhagen and Trafalgar.

Earl Nelson's vase was finally delivered in May 1810, now costing £649.10s.10d. By this time the committee of management had

decided (24 August 1809) to discontinue the gifts of honour and to use the fund only for the relief of dependants of those killed in war, for the wounded, for aged and infirm British prisoners of war, and to support hospitals. **CF**

Clarkson Stanfield
Sunderland 1793–1867 London

21
The Battle of Trafalgar, 21 October 1805

Oil on canvas, 254 × 457 cm
London, Crown Estate on loan to the Institute of Directors
Provenance: commissioned by the United Services Club, 1833
Exhibitions: London, Royal Academy, 1836, No. 290
Literature: Van der Merwe 1979, pp. 110–11.

By the 1830s Britain's defeat of Napoleon still had the power to stir patriotic pride. The Duke of Wellington, the victorious commander at Waterloo, was a national hero, and later became prime minister. Although dead, Nelson evinced similar feelings, his great naval victory at the Battle of Trafalgar in 1805 remaining a cause of celebration. In 1830 the recently constructed square to the north of Whitehall was christened Trafalgar Square, and in 1839 work began there on the construction of Nelson's column, a prominent monument to the hero and the battle.

In 1833 the United Services Club formed a committee to raise a subscription among its members to commission a pair of paintings, one to commemorate the Battle of Trafalgar, the other Waterloo. The Trafalgar commission was given to Clarkson Stanfield, an artist whose maritime knowledge was strong, and which was put to good use in the picture.

Stanfield shows the *Victory*, Nelson's flagship, at the centre of the battle which took place to the west of Cape Trafalgar. The artist went to great trouble over the accuracy of his portrayal, reportedly interviewing the officers who had taken part in the action, many who had contributed to the subscription for the picture. Stanfield shows the battle at about 2.30pm, an hour and a half after Nelson had fallen, the victim of a sniper's bullet. The *Victory* is the ship to the right of centre of the composition, half turned, with its bows bathed in sunshine.

Trafalgar gave Britain control of the sea for the remainder of the Napoleonic Wars and staved off the very real threat of French invasion. It was the last battle to be fought under sail between European powers. Nelson's reputation had been strong before his death, but after it he was idolised. **RU**

22
Tureen

Silver, parcel gilt, H 30.5 cm
Marks: London hallmark for 1806-07; mark of John Edwards III
The lid bears the collar of the Order of the Bath engraved on each side; the bowl bears the arms of Wellesley within the collar of the Bath; presentation inscription on base
London, Apsley House, Wellington Museum, Trustees of the Victoria and Albert Museum
Inv. No. W.M. 748 & A & B – 1948
Provenance: the 1st Duke of Wellington; by descent to the 7th Duke of Wellington; gift to the nation under the terms of the Wellington Museum Act, 1947
Exhibitions: Sydney, 1964, Cat. No. 62
Literature: Oman 1973, p. 41

22

Colonel the Hon. Arthur Wellesley, later to become the 1st Duke of Wellington, was put in charge of the city of Seringapatam following his part in the expedition against Tippoo Sultan, the legendary ruler of Mysore, which culminated in the capture of Seringapatam in 1799. In 1803 the Second Mahratta War began, a confrontation between Wellesley's troops and a French-supported coalition of Indian rulers. Wellesley inflicted severe defeats on the enemy at Argaum and Gawilghur culminating in his decisive victory at Assaye in September 1803. To the end of his life he regarded Assaye as his finest military achievement. His courage and leadership drew the respect of his officers, prompting the gift of a service of 125 pieces of plate, to become known as the Deccan Service.

The novel design, particularly of the tureens and standing salts, which are supported on elephants, was thoroughly topical. By 1800 the Adam style had lost much of its original vigour and the British campaign in India was welcomed by goldsmiths for the fresh sources of ornament and inspiration which it provided. It is not known which retail firm handled the order but it was divided between four London makers: John Edwards (whose mark is on the tureen), William Fountain, Joseph Preedy and John Moore. Edwards is known for a high standard of design and execution and produced a quantity of domestic plate. **JV**

23
Presentation small-sword

The hilt of gold set with two enamel plaques showing the arms of the City of London and of Hill; the etched blade of hollow triangular section
Marks: quillon stamped with the London hall-mark for 18 carat gold, date letter for

1813–14 and marks of John Ray and James Montague
Presentation inscription on shell-guard
Blade length: 83 cm; hilt length: 18.5 cm
London: Trustees of the Victoria and Albert Museum
Inv. No. M.50-1963
Provenance: Royal United Services Museum Whitehall; transferred to the Victoria and Albert Museum, 1963
Exhibitions: Shrewsbury, 1898

21

Literature: Blair 1972, p. 21; North 1982, No. 81

General Sir Rowland Hill (1772–1842), to whom this sword was presented by the Corporation of the City of London, held senior commands throughout the Peninsular Campaign and commanded the right of the army at the Battle of Vittoria on 21 June 1813 when the French armies, under Jourdan and Joseph Bonaparte, were routed. **AN**

Luke Clennell

Ulgham 1781–1840 Newcastle-on-Tyne

24

Banquet given by the Corporation of London to H.R.H. The Prince Regent, the Emperor of Russia and the King of Prussia, 18 June 1814, *c.* 1814

Oil on canvas, 127 × 177.8 cm
London, Guildhall Art Gallery
Inv. No. 1026
Provenance: Col. Brownlow, Ashridge Park, Hampshire, from whose trustees purchased by Sir William H. Dunn, and presented to the Guildhall Art Gallery, 1923
Exhibitions: London, Victoria and Albert Museum, 1967, Cat. No. 107; Edinburgh, 1969, Cat. No. 129

Following the conclusion of peace with France in 1814, the sovereigns of the other allied nations that had fought with Britain against Napoleon were invited to visit London as the guests of the court. Emperor Alexander I of Russia and King Frederick William III of Prussia arrived in the capital on 7 June 1814, and spent the next three weeks there. On 18 June the Corporation of London entertained them and the Prince Regent to a lavish banquet held in the medieval Guildhall in the City. The royal party, which numbered twenty-one members of the various royal families, were seated at a table on a dais beneath a specially constructed canopy. Protocol proved problematic; the Prince Regent was able to leave at 11.30pm, but more humble guests, who had to

wait until persons of a higher rank than themselves had left, were still there at 3am the following morning. The celebrations of peace proved to be premature; Napoleon's return to France led to a renewal of the war, not to be finally concluded until the Battle of Waterloo in 1815.

The painting, previously attributed to George Clint, has now been firmly ascribed by Vivien Knight to Clennell. The artist was one of the most gifted pupils of the wood engraver Thomas Bewick (1753–1828). His painting of the *The Decisive Charge made by the Life Guards at the Battle of Waterloo* established his reputation and led to this commission. Unfortunately, according to Byran's *Dictionary*, 'The honour was fatal to his health and life. the vexations he had to encounter from vanity, caprice, and supercilious arrogance, affected his mind so much that he lost his reason' in 1817; though he recovered, the illness returned in 1831 and he entered an asylum in Newcastle where he remained until his death. **RU**

25

An Account of the Visit of His Royal Highness The Prince Regent, with their Imperial and Royal Majesties The Emperor of all the Russias and the King of Prussia, to The Corporation of London in June 1814

London: by order of, and for, the Corporation of the City of London, by Nichols, Son, and Bentley, Red Lion

Passage, Fleet Street
The Prince Regent's copy; bound in red morocco, tooled on front and back boards with the prince's arms the royal arms with a label, surrounded by the Garter, surmounted by the Prince of Wales's coronet; the doublures of watered royal-blue silk, bordered with roll-tool work in gold featuring a scroll and cross design; the corners decorated with stylised gold acanthus leaves, 38 × 27.5 × 2.1 cm
Windsor Castle, Royal Library, H.M. Queen Elizabeth II
Inv. No. RCIN 1005093

The label of Hering, Newman Street, on the verso of the flyleaf indicates that this rich binding was executed by Charles Hering senior or his brother John. **CF**

26

Medal

The Battle of Waterloo, 1819–49

Electrotype, D 13.5 cm
Engraved by Benedetto Pistrucci
Obverse: Laureate draped busts of the four allied sovereigns, the Prince Regent, Francis II of Austria, Alexander I of Russian and Frederick William III of Prussia. Reverse: 2 equestrian figures in classical dress with the features of Wellington and Blücher being guided by Victory
London, Trustees of the British Museum
Inv. No. 1945. 1-1-40
Literature: Brown 1980, pp. 208–212, No. 870; Eimer 1987, p. 133, No. 1067, Plate 29

Following the victory at Waterloo in 1815 it was decided to issue a medal struck in gold for presentation to the allied sovereigns, their generals and ministers. The design submitted by Benedetto Pistrucci (1784–1855) was accepted and in 1819 the Treasury authorised the work to begin on the models. Pistrucci's design was complex and required skilled engraving and the unusually large size caused technical problems. Progress was slow; further delays were caused by Pistrucci's nagging dissatisfaction with his position at the Mint and his salary which he raised with each successive master.

Finally, in 1849, the master of the Mint was able to report that the dies were ready. By this time, however, all the sovereigns were dead, and although Pistrucci had solved the problem of making dies of sufficient size, it was decided to issue only soft impressions of the medal in gutta percha and electrotypes. The latter were offered to the public at 2 guineas each, the obverse and reverse being in two separate pieces, mounted in a case or frame. **EE**

George Jones
London 1786–1869 London

27
The Battle of Waterloo: the Height of the Battle, 18 June 1815

Oil on canvas, 208.3 × 447 cm
London, Crown Estate on loan to the
Institute of Directors
Provenance: commissioned by the United
Services Club, 1833
Literature: Hichberger 1983 and 1988

Following the triumph of Waterloo in 1815, attempts by the British Institution to initiate a competitive exhibition, with a premium for the best picture 'illustrative of our recent successes', were largely viewed with disapproval and attracted only fifteen entrants. Many of the reviewers of the exhibition did not consider battle painting to sit naturally with the British characteristic of anti-militarism. Besides which, in the past it had been closely associated with the functional, low-status genre of topographical draughtsmanship.

George Jones was among the group of entrants to the British Institution competition, submitting two sketches for picture of Waterloo, for which he claimed 'on-the-spot' fidelity in the catalogue which accompanied the exhibition. Along with James Ward, he won one of the premiums of a thousand guineas and was required to finish one of his sketches as a large-scale canvas to hang at the Royal Military Hospital, Chelsea, a task he completed single-handed over a period of four years, the picture being installed at Chelsea in 1820.

The Battle of Waterloo was, in many respects, the making of Jones: he received commissions for repetitions of the theme from patrons among the ruling classes, such as those from the Earl of Egremont or the United Services Club, the present picture. The type of patron likely to buy a battle picture sought authenticity as much as aesthetic accomplishment, and Jones, with his background as a serving captain in the army of occupation in Paris following the victory of 1815, was for many a natural choice. He associated himself closely with the traditions of military, in particular, taking tremendous pride in his supposed resemblance to the Duke of Wellington.

Jones's pictures have none of the emotional ambiguity to war that an artist such as Turner was able to invoke in his famous picture of Waterloo (Tate Gallery. See also Cat. No. 243). However, if Jones is in many ways crude in his execution of individual details, he is at least successful in deploying and dramatising the massed forces of the conflict, achieving, as has been observed by Hichberger, an innovative synthesis of the bird's-eye view of the Baroque battle scene with a more panoramic view of the battlefield. **IW**

27

28
Pair of Standard Candelabra

Silver gilt, H 113 cm
Marks: Base, London hallmark for 1816–17; oil adaptors, London hallmark for 1824–25; mark of Benjamin Smith; the base bears the name of the retail goldsmiths GREEN, WARD & GREEN, LONDINI, FECerunt Presented to the 1st Duke of Wellington by the Merchants and Bankers of the City of London
London, Apsley House, Wellington Museum, Trustees of the Victoria and Albert Museum
Inv. No. W.M. 804/805-1948
Provenance: 1st Duke of Wellington; by descent to the 7th Duke of Wellington; gift to the nation under the terms of the Wellington Museum Act, 1947
Literature: Oman 1973, pp. 45–46; Waldron and Culme 1992, pp. 32–36

'. . . the sideboard exhibited a varied collection of gold plate . . . the whole being lighted from the superb candelabra, presented to his grace from the citizens of London' (*Morning Chronicle*, 20 June 1848). The event described is the annual Waterloo Banquet hosted by the 1st Duke of Wellington at his London home, Apsley House, for the officers who served under his command at Waterloo.

The designer of the candelabra is not known. The merchants and bankers of the City intended these monumental pieces of Regency presentation plate to announce Wellington's achievements in India, the Peninsular and at Waterloo and, in particular, their allegiance to the victorious duke.

One candelabrum terminates in the figure of Victory holding a laurel wreath and a palm branch and its pair terminates in the figure of Fame holding a laurel wreath and a trumpet. The two triangular bases adorned with military trophies are each supported by three figures; one by English, Irish and Scottish

Infantrymen and the other by a Sepoy, a Portuguese soldier and a Spanish guerrilla.

The commission was handled by Green, Ward and Green, one of the most fashionable retail goldsmiths and jewellers in London. The costliest plate in the world could be found in the vicinity of St. Paul's Cathedral and it was at 1 Ludgate Street to the east of the Old Bailey that Greens' premises were located. Benjamin Smith first registered his mark, in partnership with Digby Scott, in 1802.

The candelabra were originally made to hold candles but were converted to burn colza oil in 1825–26. The oil adaptors were designed by Lewis Vulliamy (1790–1871), a great exponent of the use of classical ornament. **JV**

28

29
The Wellington Shield

Designed by Thomas Stothard
Silver-gilt, D 103 cm
Marks: London hallmark for 1821-22; mark of Benjamin Smith
Engraved with an inscription recording the name of the retail goldsmiths 'GREEN, WARD & GREEN LOND : FECT'
Presented to the 1st Duke of Wellington by the Merchants and Bankers of the City of London
London, Apsley House, Wellington Museum, Trustees of the Victoria and Albert Museum
Inv. No. W.M. 806-1948
Provenance: 1st Duke of Wellington; by descent to the 7th Duke of Wellington; gift to the nation under the terms of the Wellington Museum Act, 1947
Literature: Bray 1851, pp. 150–161; Oman 1973, pp. 46–47; Yorke 1988, pp. 214–15; Waldron and Culme 1992, pp. 32–36

In 1814 the merchants and bankers of London appointed a committee to raise money by subscription for the design and manufacture of a shield to be presented to the 1st Duke of Wellington. Napoleon had abdicated on 6 April 1814. Wellington was created duke and returned to England in triumph.

The subscription raised over £7,000 and the committee invited both silversmiths and artists to compete for the commission. Designers of plate were frequently artists who had trained as architects, painters and sculptors. The painter Thomas Stothard (1755–1834) was approached by every manufacturer; he gave preference to the fashionable company of Green, Ward and Green of Ludgate Street, with whom he had not worked previously.

The artists were to choose subjects from the career of Wellington and Stothard's design was unanimously selected by the committee. The obvious source for the Wellington Shield is the Shield of Achilles designed by John Flaxman R.A. (Cat. No. 465). It struck Stothard that the arrangement of compartments used by Flaxman would also apply to the Wellington Shield. The events commemorated by the ten border compartments are in chronological sequence, recording Wellington's victories and ending with the Prince Regent conferring a dukedom on him in 1814.

Green, Ward and Green had engaged the firm of Benjamin Smith to cast and chase the shield and Stothard made many journeys from his home at 28 Newman Street to Benjamin Smith's workshop in Camberwell to supervise the chasing, although he was later to criticise the inferior quality of the work and privately thought that bronze would have been a richer and more classical material for his design.

Wellington took great interest in the development of the shield, even calling at Stoth-ard's home with his duchess to examine the artist's drawings. Sadly Stothard was denied due credit for his design, most newspapers describing the shield crediting John Flaxman. In this context, it is hardly surprising that Stothard did not attend the presentation of the shield, only hearing about the occasion afterwards. The shield did, however, take the pride of place at the annual Waterloo banquets held by the duke at his London home, Apsley House, for the officers who served under him at Waterloo. It was displayed on a sideboard at the west end of the Waterloo Gallery flanked by the earlier gift of candelabra. **JV**

30
The Waterloo Vase

Designed by Thomas Stothard
Silver gilt, H 65.4 cm, W of plinth 25.7 cm, W of bowl 45.7 cm
Marks: vase, London hallmark for 1824–25; mark of Benjamin Smith III; plinth, London hallmark for 1825–26; mark of Robert Garrard
Vase engraved with presentation inscription
London, Apsley House, Wellington Museum, Trustees of the Victoria and Albert Museum
Inv. No. W.M. 800-1948
Provenance: 1st Duke of Wellington; by descent to the 7th Duke of Wellington; gift to the nation under the terms of the Wellington Museum Act, 1947
Literature: Bray 1851, p. 162; Oman 1973, pp. 46–47; Waldron and Culme 1992, pp. 32–46

By the 1820s the fashion for presenting monumental pieces of plate to national heroes was widespread. A group of noblemen and gentlemen subscribed to the commission for the Waterloo Vase and their names are inscribed on each side and the top of the plinth. Ninety-four names of individuals, regiments and companies are recorded, from H.R.H. Prince Leopold of Saxe-Coburg and the Bishop of London to the King's Dragoon Guards and Coutts Bank. Unlike the gift of the Wellington Shield and standing candelabra from the mer-

30

chants and bankers of the City of London, the Waterloo Vase seems to have been commissioned by open subscription.

The retail goldsmiths and jewellers Green, Ward, Green and Ward received the order and they engaged Benjamin Smith (1793–1850), eldest son of Benjamin Smith II to make the vase from designs executed by the painter Thomas Stothard R.A. (1755–1834). George Ward became a partner of Green, Ward and Green in 1818, after which the firm became known as Green, Ward, Green and Ward. Benjamin Smith was apprenticed to his father and entered his first mark in 1816. His workshop was at 12 Duke Street, Lincoln's Inn Fields.

Thomas Stothard incorporated handles composed of the figures of Victory and Fame, and the cast and chased plaque on one side with a representation of Wellington at the heart of a British infantry square under attack by French cavalry. The plaque was modelled by the designer's son, Alfred Joseph Stothard (1793–1864), who specialised as a medallist.

The plinth bears the mark of Robert Garrard junior (1793–1881), one of three brothers who inherited an important firm of manufacturing and retail jewellers and silversmiths on their father's death in 1818. The firm became known as R., J. and S. Garrard or Robert Garrard and Brothers and traded from Panton Street, Haymarket. **JV**

Sir Francis Chantrey R.A.
Norton 1781–1841 London

31
Arthur Wellesley, First Duke of Wellington K.G. 1823

Marble, H 78.7 cm
Signed on back: Chantrey SC. 1823
London, Apsley House, Wellington Museum, Trustees of the Victoria and Albert Museum
Inv. No. WM 14441948
Provenance: purchased from the artist by the 1st Duke of Wellington; by descent to the 7th Duke of Wellington; gift to the nation under the terms of the Wellington Museum Act, 1947
Literature: Gunnis 1953, pp. 91–96; Potts 1981, Cat. No. 7; Webb, *Index*

In September 1824 a 'strong packing case' was delivered to Apsley House, the Duke of Wellington's London home at Hyde Park Corner. It contained the replica of a marble bust of the duke which had first been commissioned by the prime minister, the 2nd Earl of Liverpool. It is this replica, ordered by the duke himself in September 1821, which is exhibited here.

31

Liverpool, in 1820, gave the commission to Sir Francis Chantrey, a sculptor who had already established a reputation for accepting only the most interesting and important commissions. As his reputation grew he increased his fee above that charged by fellow artists, believing that only then would the most distinguished sitters be recommended to him. The price agreed for the Wellington bust was 150 guineas for the first version and the same for each of three known replicas (Apsley House, Windsor Castle and Petworth House).

As well as being a sculptor of public heroes, politicians, prominent landlords and royalty, Chantrey was an extraordinarily successful businessman and amassed a considerable fortune. At his death his estate was valued at about £150,000, although he was fearful of bankruptcy throughout his life. Perhaps he was justified as his distinguished customers often did not settle their accounts on time; it was twenty years before Wellington paid for his bust, two months after the artist's death.

At the time that the first bust was commissioned, the duke was serving in Liverpool's Cabinet as Master General of the Ordnance, a post he accepted in 1818. Having earned the respect of the nation for his brilliant campaigns in India, Spain and Portugal and for his part in defeating Napoleon at Waterloo, Wellington launched himself on a political career. **JV**

Print Shop Window

The windows of London's print shops served as democratic picture galleries, providing for the majority of the population their only conscious encounter with art. The works on display ranged from portraits, topography and topical events, as in the selection below, to satires and caricatures on the political and social scene.

M. Merigot after
Augustus Charles Pugin
France 1762–1832 London

32a
Remains of Lord Viscount Nelson laying in State in the Painted Chamber at Greenwich Hospital, 1806
Aquatint, 32×44 cm

I. Hill after
Augustus Charles Pugin

32b
Funeral Procession of the late Lord Viscount Nelson from Greenwich to Whitehall, 8 Janary 1806
Aquatint, 31.6×43.7 cm

Artist unknown

32c
Perspective View of the Grand Funeral Car . . ., 9 January 1806
Broadsheet, 36×24 cm
Published by N. Heideloff, 12 Norfolk Street, 14 January 1806

Artist unknown

32d
Order observed in the public Funeral Procession of the late Vice Admiral Horatio, Viscount Nelson
Engraving, 42×34 cm
Published by John Wallis junior, 72 Fleet Street

M. Merigot after
Augustus Charles Pugin

32e
Funeral Procession of the late Lord Viscount Nelson from the Admiralty to St. Pauls
Aquatint, 34.1×44.4 cm

32a

32c

32b

32d

Frederick Christian Lewis
London 1779–1856 Enfield
after Augustus Charles Pugin

32f
Interment of the Remains of the late Lord Viscount Nelson in St. Pauls
Aquatint, 31.6×43.2 cm

London, The Museum of London
Inv. Nos. A18861, Z6660, A18867, A18863, A18862, A18872 respectively
Literature: Warner 1958, pp. 358–59, Pocock 1987, pp. 334–43

32e

32f

barge of the *Victory* and rowed upstream to Whitehall, watched by thousands, despite a south-west gale. It rested overnight at the Admiralty and the following day was carried in procession to St. Paul's accompanied by royalty, officers of state and representatives of both services including the men from the *Victory*.

For this final stage of the journey, the coffin was placed on the 'quarterdeck' of an elaborate car draped in richly fringed black velvet, designed by Rudolph Ackermann (Cat. Nos. 170ff) in imitation of the hull of the *Victory*. The canopy was formed as a sarcophagus supported by four palm trees, in tribute to Nelson's victory of the Nile. Finally, at the end of the four-hour funeral service in the cathedral, the coffin was lowered into the crypt. CF

Artist unknown

33a

Description of the Grand National Jubilee, held in St. James's, Hyde, and the Green Parks, on Monday the 1st August, 1814
Engraving and letterpress, 44 × 36 cm
Printed and published by John Fairburn, Jun. Fountain Court, Minories

R. W. Smart and I. Jeakes after J. Pain

33b

A Perspective View of the Revolving Temple of Concord, 1814
Coloured aquatint, 37 × 46.3 cm
Published by T. Greenwood, 9 Featherstone Buildings, Holborn and G. Latilla, 70 Charlotte Street, 27 July 1814

Artist unknown

33c

The Chinese Pagoda and Bridge
Coloured engraving, 29.2 × 44 cm
Published by James Whittle and Richard Holmes Laurie, 53 Fleet Street

London, The Museum of London
Inv. Nos. 60.46, A21025 and Z6656

The celebrations which greeted the Peace of 1814 were extensive. The first of August was set aside for a Grand National Jubilee to take place in the three central royal parks, in the presence of Alexander I, Frederick William III and the Prince Regent. The Serpentine in Hyde Park featured a mock battle between the

Nelson's funeral in London was one of the great state occasions of the early nineteenth century. After the Battle of Trafalgar (21 October 1805), Nelson's body was returned to England preserved in a cask of spirits. On 23 December it was carried up the Thames to Greenwich and, having been transferred to a coffin made from the wood of the mainmast of *L'Orient* (the French flagship blown up in the Battle of the Nile in 1798), was conveyed into the Royal Hospital, where it lay in state in the Painted Chamber for three days.

On 8 January 1806, escorted by 500 naval pensioners, the coffin was transferred to the

33a

33b

33c

British and French fleet, followed by fireworks. A 'jubilee balloon' was launched from Green Park where could be found the royal observation booth, a Chinese bridge and, not least, an elaborate 'castle' invented by Sir William Congreve (who had introduced rockets to the British army), made by Messrs. Greenwood and Latilla of the Theatre Royal Drury Lane, with transparencies designed and painted by a number of Royal Academicians; the machinery was by Maudslay and Co.

As it grew dark, the castle was illuminated with Chinese lanterns and transparencies. Rockets discharged themselves from it for two hours and finally it was transformed from 'a fabric designed for the purposes of war into a temple of peace, and an illuminated monument of victory.' In St. James's Park, boat races took place on the canal and in the evening a bridge bearing a pagoda was illuminated and fireworks followed. Unfortunately, these set the pagoda alight and a lamp-lighter employed at the top of the building was killed when, in attempting to throw himself into the water, he hit the bridge; five others were seriously injured. **CF**

Artists unknown

34a
View of the Thames off Three Cranes Wharf, when frozen, 31st January to 5th February 1814
Aquatint, 37.5 × 50 cm
Published by Burkitt and Hudson, 85 Cheapside, 18 February 1814

34b
A View of Frost Fair as it Appeared on the Ice on the River Thames Feby. 3rd 1814
Woodcut, 38.2 × 51.3 cm
Published by J. Pitts, 14 Great St. Andrew Street, Seven Dials, 19 March 1814

London, The Museum of London
Inv. Nos. A23139, A23129 respectively
Literature: Frostiana 1814

The Thames frequently froze over during severe winters before the demolition of old London Bridge, which slowed the flow of the river. The frost fairs that resulted were the subject of paintings, prints and watercolours from 1608 to the winter of 1813–14, when the

last fair was held. A hard frost on 27 December was followed by eight days of thick fog and unusually heavy falls of snow. The cold weather continued throughout January and by the end of the month the river between London and Blackfriars Bridges was packed with ice. On 1 February the watermen began setting up their tolls at the steps leading down to the river, charging for a safe crossing: some made £6 per day. A street of tents called City Road was constructed with booths offering food, drink, souvenirs, sports and entertainment. On 5 February it rained and there was a thaw; by the following afternoon, the tide flowed rapidly in both directions and the river was 'covered with wrecks'.

These two contrasting prints were intended as souvenirs for entirely different markets. The aquatint was published by a respectable City-based print seller; the woodcut by John Pitts, who, together with James Catnach – also based in Seven Dials – virtually monopolised the trade in cheap and frequently luridly illustrated chapbooks and broadsides for the poor. The latter gives a much livelier impression of the fair, depicting the queues that formed for the swings and skittles and to buy souvenirs, and a refreshment tent appropriately named 'The City of Moscow'. **CF**

34a

34b

Martin Arthur Shee after Thomas Lawrence
Dublin 1769–1860 Brighton

35
King George IV, 1821

Oil on canvas, 275×179.1 cm
London, Royal Academy of Arts
Provenance: painted at the request of the
General Assembly of the Royal Academy,
1838
Literature: Millar 1969, p. 61, No. 873;
Garlick 1989, pp. 193–94, No. 325 (e);
London, National Portrait Gallery, 1979, p.
13

In the official portrait to mark his coronation, the king is shown wearing his coronation robes with the collars of the Golden Fleece, the Guelphic Order, the Order of the Bath and the Order of the Garter. Beside him on the Svres 'Table des Grands Capitaines' (commissioned by Napoleon and presented by Louis XVIII to the Prince Regent in 1817) is the Imperial Crown. The prime version was completed by the end of 1821 and hangs in the Throne Room at St. James's Palace.

This copy was commissioned in 1838 from the then President of the Royal Academy, Sir Martin Archer Shee; at the same time he was requested to make a copy of his own full-length portrait of the late king, William IV; furthermore, the Academicians wrote to Queen Victoria requesting a sitting for her portrait, also by Shee. The resolution in the General Assembly Minutes (Vol. 4, p. 293, 6 September 1838) makes clear that Shee was free to select 'any' full-length portrait of George IV as the basis for his work. Shee chose that of his predecessor as president and did full justice to the original. Completed in 1840, it cost £315. **CF**

John Whittaker

36
The Ceremonial of the Coronation of George IV, 1823

Presentation copy on heavy paper, bound in brown morocco with central tool of the Royal Arms (1816–37), rolled tooled border of oak leaves, ferns and flowers, folio atlas, 69.3×65×7 cm
Windsor Castle, Royal Library, H.M. Queen Elizabeth II
Inv. No. RCIN 1005090
Literature: Adams 1983, pp. 516–18, No. 232

This sumptuous publication was initiated by the printer John Whittaker of Queen Street, Westminster and continued under Sir George Nayler, Garter King of Arms, in 1823. Both sponsors died in 1831, leaving it incomplete, but most of the plates were purchased by Henry Bohn, who published the work in an edition of forty-five plates with an accompanying text in 1839, expanding it further two years later with a de luxe edition of seventy-two plates printed on satin and vellum in two elephant folios.

The original drawings of the main participants in the coronation were mostly executed by members of the Stephanoff family and Charles Wilde; the engravings were made by R. Havell junior, William Bennett, William Bond and H. Meyer, and richly embellished by hand in watercolour and body colour. This page illustrates H.R.H. Prince Leopold George Frederick of Saxe-Coburg-Saalfeld (1790–1865), in Garter robes, who married the Prince Regent's only child, Princess Charlotte in 1816. The couple were handsome and popular at a time when esteem for the royal family was generally at a low ebb. When Princess Charlotte died in childbirth the following year, the country was plunged into deep mourning, but Prince Leopold's connections with the British court continued through his sister, who married the Duke of Kent and gave birth to Princess Victoria, over whom he exercised considerable influence after the death of her father in 1820. Ten years later, he accepted the invitation of the Belgian people to be their first king. He was instrumental in arranging the marriage of Queen Victoria to his nephew and her cousin, Albert of Saxe-Coburg and Gotha, in 1840. **CF**

37a

Sarah Ann Walker was one of six 'maids' who attended Miss Fellowes, the King's Herbwoman. All seven were dressed in white, Miss Fellowes in white satin 'with a scarlet mantle trimmed with gold lace' with 'a wreath of laurel and oak around her head' and the 'badge of her office' – a silver-gilt medallion and chain worn around her neck. She carried a small basket and scattered seasonal flowers and was immediately followed by the six maids, walking two abreast carrying larger double-handled baskets containing similar flowers. They led the procession from Westminster Hall to Westminster Abbey and on arrival 'remained at the entrance within the west door' while others in the procession continued until they found their appointed places. Miss Fellowes received a badge and chain in a case which cost £19.14s. and a sum of £20.9s.6d. for her dress and mantle. Each of the maids received 10 guineas for their dresses (PRO LC2/50).

The post of the King's Herbwoman was an hereditary one, first introduced at the coronation of Charles I in 1625 when the sweetening of the air with herbs was thought to ward off contagious and infectious diseases. The maids who accompanied the herbwoman were young: Sarah Ann Walker was seventeen in 1821 and her companions, the Misses Garth, Collier, Ramsbottom, Hill and Daniel would have been her contemporaries. George IV's coronation was the last at which the herbwoman and her maids appeared, for at subsequent coronations, the procession from Westminster Hall to the Abbey was discontinued. **VC**

Costumes for the Coronation of George IV, 1821

The group of costumes described below provides a lively evocation of the fashionable, quasi-historical and traditional forms of dress worn at this spectacular coronation. It was well recorded for posterity in both visual and literary terms; therefore it is possible to follow the order in which individuals processed from Westminster Hall to Westminster Abbey, and reproduce closely how the participants were dressed on this occasion.

In processional order the figures are a herbstrewer, a pursuivant, a privy councillor, a baron, a duke who alone held the post of hereditary grand falconer, an officer of the band of gentlemen pensioners and a gentleman usher. The first five preceded the king, the other two followed him. **VC**

37a
Herbstrewer's Costume, Coronation of George IV
London 1821

Ivory cotton gauze dress with silk underdress and long sleeves, the upper arm overlaid with full, round puffs of fabric; round neckline with detachable Medici-style wired blond lace collar; the lower edge of the skirt decorated with two rows of double-thickness silk gauze arranged in ruched, flower-like swags
Brighton, The Royal Pavilion Art Gallery and Museums
Inv. No. H367
Provenance: Miss Sarah Ann Walker; by descent to Miss Helen Nussey, by whom presented to Brighton Art Gallery and Museums, 1960
Literature: Annual Register 1821, pp. 351, 356, 364; le Lievre 1987; Nayler 1837, pp. 36, 112

37b *(illus. p. 253)*
Pursuivant's Tabard, Coronation of George IV
London after 1816

Silk damask with cloth of silver and silk satin; raised and couched embroidered royal arms of an English pursuivant, with the crowned arms of Hanover centrally positioned at back and front of the tabard and on the hanging sleeves; lined with red silk sarsenet and fastened with red silk ribbons; worn over late eighteenth-century brown wool cloth court suit
London, The Museum of London
Inv. Nos. A13815 (tabard); 77.94/1 (suit)
Provenance: tabard purchased by the London Museum, 1914; court suit purchased by the Museum, 1977
Literature: Annual Register 1821, pp. 358–59; Nayler 1837, p. 60; Halls 1973, p. 49; Marks and Payne 1978, pp. 102–05; Mansfield 1980, p. 194

For the coronation of George IV, new tabards were made for the pursuivants who followed Garter Knights and Knights of the Bath in the coronation procession. The most costly element was the embroidery undertaken by George D'Almaine; the tailors were Baker and Son. The overall cost was around £54. The tabard is traditionally associated with Francis Martin (1767–1841), appointed Windsor Herald 4 April 1819. **VC**

37c *(illus. p.253)*
Privy Councillor's Costume, Coronation of George IV
London 1821

Dark blue silk-satin doublet-style jacket and breeches decorated with rows of gold lace and gimp, with rosettes on each cuff; short cloak of dark blue silk edged with gold lace and lined with crimson silk
London, The Museum of London
Inv. No. 39.67/1-4
Provenance: gift of Viscountess Canning to John Backhouse; by descent to Mrs A. G. C. Sheppard, by whom presented to the London Museum, 1939
Literature: Annual Register 1821, p. 288; Halls 1973, pp. 13, 48; Stevenson and Bennett 1978, p. 67

George Canning (1770–1827) as a privy councillor wore a costume described in the Annual Register as 'Blue dress, laced the same as the peers. Blue satin cloak. White hose. Shoes with rosettes. Sword. Hat with three feathers'. Privy councillors who held other royal office or were members of orders of chivalry wore the designated costume or robes for such office. Canning was not a peer and was one of a group of twenty-seven who walked four abreast behind the Clerks of the Council in Ordinary and ahead of the Register of the Order of the Garter. The makers and cost of Canning's costume are unknown, but the Lord Chamberlain's office accounts for similar outfits indicate a cost of around £90, including hat and sword.

George Canning entered parliament in 1794 and the Tory administration two years later as under-secretary of state for foreign affairs. He became minister for foreign affairs in 1807, but disagreements with his cabinet colleague, Lord Castlereagh, led to his temporary retirement; he returned to office as president of the Board of Control in 1816. At the time of the coronation, he was in some odium with George IV for refusing to support the government during the 'Queen's Trial'. He became foreign minister again in 1822 and prime minister in April 1827. He died in office on 8 August the same year. **VC**

37d
Baron's Robes and Costume, Coronation of George IV
London 1821

Crimson silk-velvet full-length circular robe lined with white silk, edged with white fur; matching knee-length surcoat, open fronted and with hanging sleeves, and sword belt with ornate gilt lion's head buckle; coronet of silver gilt, ermine and crimson velvet with central gold tassel; white silk satin doublet-style jacket and breeches decorated with row of 'richest gold braid, plate lace and Vandyke fringe'
London, The Museum of London
Inv. No. 77.101/1-6
Provenance: by descent through the Fitzherbert family; Christie's South Kensington, 19 August 1976, Lot 135
Literature: Annual Register 1821, p. 359; Nayler 1837, pp. 9, 25, 58, 98, 115; Campbell 1989, pp. 19, 22; Mansfield 1980, pp. 8–9

Alleyne Fitzherbert, Baron St. Helens (1753–1839) belonged to the lowest rank of the peerage in Great Britain. He was one of fifty-two barons who walked four abreast in the coronation procession 'in their Robes of Estate of Crimson Velvet, with their coronets in their hands'.

Alleyne Fitzherbert began a long career in diplomacy in 1777 when he was appointed British minister to Brussels. His interests and circle of friends were wide: he was a regular correspondent of Jeremy Bentham (Cat. No. 00). From 1805 to 1837 he was a trustee of the British Museum. At his death in 1839 he was the longest serving member of the Privy Council. The title became extinct on his death as he had never married. **VC**

37d

37e *(illus. pp. 252-53)*
Costume of the Duke of St. Albans, Hereditary Grand Falconer of England, Coronation of George IV
London 1821

Dark green velvet jacket and breeches with gold and silver metal thread embroidery; the design of acorns and oak leaves on the jacket and breeches is associated with the title and can also be seen on the sword hilt; hat of dark green velvet with gold and silver metal thread embroidery and black ostrich feather; falcon depicted on both the hat and the sword hilt; the costume includes a ceremonial version of a falconer's glove
Provenance: gift of the Hon. Miss Mary Loder, sister of 2nd Baron Wakehurst, 1958
Literature: supplement to the London Gazette, 3 August 1821, p. 1604; Langley Moore 1965

The costume was worn at the coronation of George IV by William, 8th Duke of St. Albans (1768–1825). The title was created in 1670 when Charles II made Charles Beauclerk, a son of Nell Gwynn, the Duke of St. Albans. The honorary title of Hereditary Grand Falconer of England was added in 1684 and all subsequent Dukes of St. Albans have included Hereditary Grand Falconer among their titles. The title denoted no particular role in the proceedings of the coronation of George IV and the 8th Duke took his place along with the other non-royal dukes who walked four abreast in the procession immediately preceded by three kings of arms and followed by a similar number. **RJH**

37f
Costume of the Honourable Band of Gentleman Pensioners. Coronation of George IV
London 1821

From a detailed description of the fabrics and cost in the Public Records Office (LC2/50): doublet-style jacket, breeches and shoulder cape made from '7½ yards of rich scarlet genoa velvet . . . slashed with blue [velvet] and richly laced and covered with gilt diamond cut buttons'; decorated with over 150 yards of gold lace, gold 'gymp',

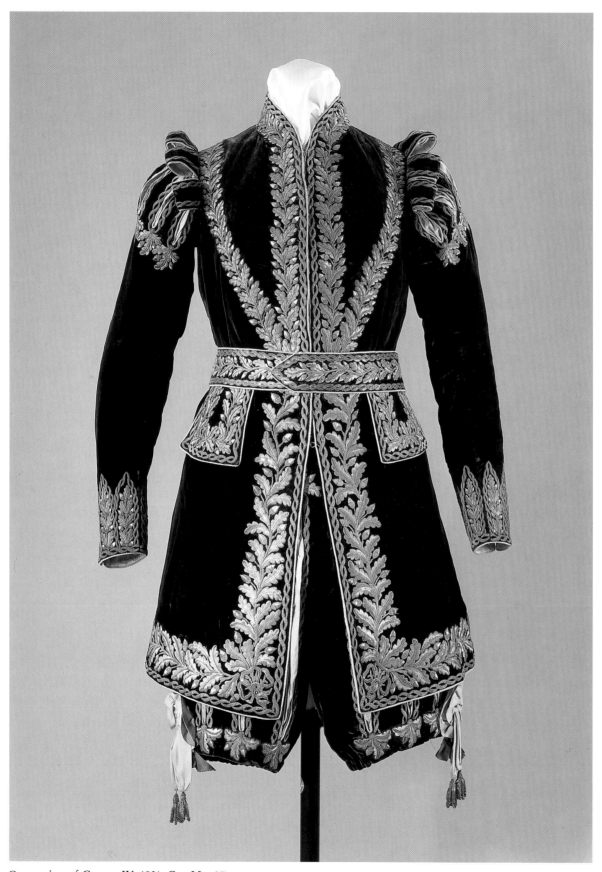

Coronation of George IV, 1821. Cat. No. 37'

(above left) Privy Councillor's Costume, Coronation of
George IV, 1821. Cat. No. 37c
(above right) Pursuivant's Tabard, Coronation of
George IV, 1816. Cat. No. 37b

(right) Accessories of the Costume of the Duke of St.
Albans, Coronation of George IV, 1821. Cat. No. 37e

37f

wide and narrow gold fringe; breeches edged with gilt tags; doublet and breeches studded with twelve gross 'rich gilt diamond cut buttons'; 'white kid shoes with gold gymp and rosettes' supplied by John Meyer of 36 Conduit Street, at a cost of £181.6s.3d.; hat of 'rich black velvet'
London, The Museum of London
Inv. No. 32.214
Provenance: Colonel Samuel Wilson; by descent to the Rev. A. Lea Wilson by whom presented to the London Museum, 1932
Literature: Annual Register 1821, pp. 362–63; Nayler 1837, p. 120; Halls 1973, pp. 48–49; Mansfield 1980, pp. 201–03

The Honourable Band of Gentleman Pensioners was created as a royal bodyguard by Henry VIII around 1540. They attended the monarch on ceremonial occasions but were not a military order. Originally fifty in number, there were forty-four at the time of George IV's coronation. The band included young men awaiting a military career, serving and retired officers.

This costume was worn by Colonel Samuel Wilson who was possibly Lieutenant, Standard Bearer or Clerk of the Cheque for the Band. In the procession to the Abbey, the Lieutenant and twenty of the band were to the right of the king, with the Standard Bearer and a similar number to his left. **VC**

37g
Gentlemen Usher's Costume, Coronation of George IV
London, 1821

Doublet-style jacket and breeches of ivory silk satin piped with red silk satin and decorated with gold lace; white kid shoes with red heels and ivory silk stockings survive with the costume
London, Court Dress Collection, Kensington Palace
Inv. No. 1985.2
Provenance: Sir Thomas Mash, by descent to Mrs. E. C. Wyndham, by whom presented to the Court Dress Collection, 1985
Literature: Annual Register 1821, pp. 363, 380; Nayler 1837, p. 119; Royal Kalendar 1821, p. 119; Thomas 1838, pp. 334–35

37g

Sir Thomas Mash was a First Class Gentleman Usher, Daily Waiter in the Lord Chamberlain's Department. His costume resembled those worn by other royal household officers who worked in the Jewel House or Wardrobe. Their garments were distinguished by the distinctive scarlet satin edgings. In the procession to Westminster Abbey two Gentlemen Ushers Daily Waiters were in the group attendant upon and behind the king to the rear of the procession. John Meyer, the tailor of 36 Conduit Street, supplied the garments at a cost of £56.13s.

Gentlemen Ushers Daily Waiters were next in authority to the Lord Chamberlain and Vice Chamberlain of the royal household. They were in attendance upon the king within the Presence Chamber of the respective royal residences. Whilst all officiated monthly, by turns, the senior gentleman usher undertook, in addition, the office of Usher of the Black Rod in the House of Lords and Usher for the Order of the Garter. **JM**

Denis Dighton
London 1792–1827 St. Servan, Brittany

38
The Third and Last Challenge by the Champion during King George IV's Coronation Banquet in Westminster Hall, 1821

Watercolour, 42.4×55 cm
Signed: Denis Dighton Military Painter to His Majesty
Windsor, Royal Library, H.M. Queen Elizabeth II
Inv. No. 13630
Literature: Annual Register 1821, pp. 385–86; Oppé 1950, p. 50, No. 182, Plate 48

The stage was set in the vast medieval expanse of Westminster Hall for the last coronation banquet ever to take place. The pugilists hired as doorkeepers got drunk; people lost their tickets and squabbled over seats. Yet it was a memorable occasion, never more so than when at twilight, after the first course of the banquet had been served, the King's Champion, Henry Dymoke, entered the Hall on horseback as the central figure in a spectacular ceremony which had medieval origins.

To left and right of him, wearing robes and coronets, despite being mounted on horseback, were the Acting Earl Marshall, Lord Howard of Effingham and the Lord High

Constable, the Duke of Wellington. sat astride his brightly caparisoned horse (a docile creature used to crowds and hired from Astley's Circus).

Trumpets sounded, the challenge was read, and the champion threw down the gauntlet; this ceremony was performed as the party entered, in the centre of the hall, and at the steps of the throne. After the final return of the gauntlet, the king drank a toast to his champion from a gold cup which was passed to the champion who drank a toast to his sovereign; rewarded with his 'fee' of a gold cup and cover, the champion and his party left the hall.

Henry Dymoke (1801–1865) represented his father the Reverend John Dymoke as King's Champion. The office of King's Champion was an hereditary one in the Dymoke family. The earliest record of the champion appearing at the mid point in the coronation banquet was in 1399 when Henry IV was crowned. **VC**

Artist unknown

39 *(illus. p. 256)*
Coronation of His Most Gracious Majesty, King George the Fourth, 19th of July 1821

Coloured aquatint, 37×116 cm
Published by G. Humphrey, 27 St. James's Street, 22 October 1821
London, Guildhall Library, Corporation of London
Literature: Annual Register 1821, pp. 357, 360–62; Adams 1983, pp. 516–17, No. 232/9

The coronation, George decided, would be the most magnificent in British history, though he feared, with justification, that his wife might turn up and spoil things.

On Coronation Day (19 July) the procession made its way from Westminster Hall to Westminster Abbey. The coronation service was due to begin at 11 o'clock. George IV is shown in the centre of the procession. He is preceded by the Bishops of Gloucester, Ely and Chester who carry a paten, Bible and chalice. In front of them are three officers of state with the sceptre, the crown and the orb. (In the following year Messrs. Rundell, Bridge and Rundell would complain that they were still owed £33,000 for this regalia.)

When she arrived at the Abbey, the queen was refused admission by the doorman since she had no ticket. She retreated to Brandenburgh House in tears, the crowd crying, 'Go back to Bergami!' **VC and RH**

40

John Jackson
1778–1831

40
Sir John Soane, 1828

Oil on canvas, 76.1×63 cm
London, National Portrait Gallery
Inv. No. 701
Provenance: commissioned in 1828 for the Governors of the British Institution and presented by them to the National Gallery, 1839; transferred to the National Portrait Gallery, 1883
Exhibitions: London, British Institution, 1829, No. 254; South Kensington, 1868, No. 107
Literature: Summerson 1952; Walker 1985, Vol. 1, p. 465, Vol. 2, Plate 1134; Colvin 1978, pp. 765–72

Sir John Soane (1753–1837) was born the son of a bricklayer at Goring-on-Thames near Reading. In 1768 he entered the office of George Dance junior (1741–1825), the City surveyor, and was admitted to the Royal Academy Schools in 1771. The following year he was taken on as an assistant by Henry Holland (1745–1806), won the gold medal at the Academy with a design for a triumphal bridge in 1776 and two years later, set out for Italy on a King's Travelling Studentship.

He returned to England in 1780 but failed to win any large-scale patronage until 1788 when he was appointed surveyor to the Bank of England. This post provided him with the greatest commission of his life, as well as financial security, professional status and an introduction to wealthy clients.

In 1791 he secured his first government appointment, that of clerk of the works at

Whitehall, Westminster and St. James's and two years later, was made deputy surveyor in the Office of Woods and Forests. In 1814 he was selected as one of the three 'attached architects' to the Board of Works (the others being Nash and Smirke), with special responsibility for the public buildings in Whitehall, Westminster, Richmond Park, Kew Gardens and Hampton Court Palace. Elected a Royal Academician in 1802, he succeeded Dance as the Academy's professor of architecture in 1806.

Passionately dedicated to his profession and concerned with raising the standard of architectural education, he prepared his lectures with care and was an influential teacher. He was a generous benefactor of the Institute of British Architects and the British Institution. He left his house in Lincoln's Inn Fields and his collection to the nation as a museum for 'the study of Architecture and the Allied Arts'. His highly individual architectural style which stemmed from his innovative handling of proportion, light, space and surface ornament, though derived from classical precedent, was affected by his love of the primitive and belief in the 'poetry of architecture'. He was widely admired but little understood during his lifetime (Schinkel was intrigued by Lincoln's Inn Fields but thought the Bank of England contained 'much useless stuff') and had no real followers until the twentieth century. **CF**

Joseph Michael Gandy
London 1771–1843 Devon

41
Architectural visions of early fancy, in the gay morning of youth, and Dreams in the evening of life, 1820

Watercolour, 97 cm×154 cm in frame
London, Trustees of Sir John Soane's Museum
Inv. No. P.81
Exhibitions: London, Royal Academy, 1820, No. 894
Literature: Soane 1835, p. 18; Summerson, Watkin, Mellinghoff 1983, Plate 5; Lukacher 1987, pp. 56–58

This perspective is a retrospective inventory of Soane's unexecuted designs set in a 'sublime' landscape of mountains, rivers, ruins and a cloud-swept sky. The buildings recall the neoclassical projects of his youth: the design for a triumphal bridge, on the left, which won the gold medal at the Royal Academy in 1776, the James King mausoleum on the far left, at the top, with the Earl of Chatham mausoleum placed centrally on the mountain – as well as the numerous professional disappointments of Soane's career: the triumphal arch intended

Coronation of His Most Gracious Majesty, King George The Fourth . . . 1821. Cat. No. 39

J. M. Gandy, *A Selection of parts of buildings . . . 1818. Cat. No. 42*

J. M. Gandy, *View of the Rotunda at the Bank of England*, 1798. Cat. No. 44.

J. M. Gandy, *View of the Court of Chancery*, 1827. Cat. No. 57

J. M. Gandy and H. H. Seward, *View of the Consols Transfer Office at the Bank of England*, 1799. Cat. No. 49

J. M. Gandy, *View of the Privy Council Chamber*, 1827. Cat. No. 58

T. Lawrence, *John Nash*, 1824–27. Cat. No. 75

for Hyde Park Corner in the centre, to the right of which is a version of his 1793 design for the House of Lords. In the centre of the drawing is the design for a British senate house made by Soane in Italy in 1779.

The melancholic strain of dashed expectations is characteristic of the architect's temperament. He described the drawing, which hung (and still hangs) in his picture room in the following way: 'Among the designs above enumerated are also some Dreams in the evening of life, and Architectural Visions of early fancy – wild effusions of a mind glowing with an ardent and enthusiastic desire to attain professional distinction, in the gay morning of youth: Palmyra and Baalbec suggested the idea of the arrangement in this assemblage, which is enriched with the funeral procession of the immortal Nelson.' **MAR**

41

42 (illus. p.256)
A selection of parts of buildings, public and private, erected from the designs of J. Soane, Esq., RA, between 1780 and 1815, 1818

Pen and watercolour, 97 × 152 cm, in frame
London, Trustees of Sir John Soane's Museum
Inv. No. P87
Exhibitions: London, Royal Academy, 1818, No. 915
Literature: The Sun, 25 May 1818; Summerson 1949, passim; Summerson, Watkin, Mellinghoff 1983, Plate 6; Lukacher 1983, p. 45; Lukacher 1987, pp. 54–57

In what must be one of the most elaborate and inventive of all architectural perspectives, Gandy has assembled over one hundred of Soane's buildings, shown either as models, on a giant scale, or in drawings, set in a panoramic chamber distinguished by one of Soane's characteristic canopied domes.

Most conspicuous, in the centre, is the Bank of England, to the right of which is Dulwich Picture Gallery. On the extreme left, in shadow, is 13 Lincoln's Inn Fields, with Mrs. Soane's Tomb, draped in black, to the right of it. On the right, in shadow, is Tyringham House. Many more modest buildings, tombs and monuments are also scattered throughout the composition which is lit by the rays of a circular oil lamp with reflector in alternating bands of light and dark. In the right foreground, sits the draughtsman, who looks like Soane but who could be Gandy himself.

Joseph Michael Gandy found employment in 1798 as a draughtsman in the office of Sir John Soane, to whom he was indebted for financial assistance for the rest of his life. He set up on his own in 1801 and was elected

Associate of the Royal Academy in 1803 but continued to act as Soane's perspectivist on a freelance basis until Soane's death in 1837.

Unusually, this perspective which is such a testimony to Soane's architectural career, was the only one of all the others illustrating Soane's work to be exhibited under Gandy's own name at the R.A. In many ways it did promote Gandy's artistry as the originals of the framed drawings seen in the perspective were mostly in his hand. **MAR**

43
Bird's eye view of the Bank of England, 1830

Pen and watercolour, 84 × 139.5 cm
London, Trustees of Sir John Soane's Museum
Inv. No. P267
Exhibitions: London, Royal Academy 1830, No. 1052
Literature: Bank of England 1928; Bolton 1924, p. 37; Booker 1990, pp. 2–5, 12; Du Prey 1985, pp. 64–69; Lawrence 1991, pp. 1–7, 12–14, 28; Watkin 1978, p. 21; Oechslin 1981, pp. 19–25; Pevsner 1976, pp. 201–02; Royal Academy 1830, p. 42; Schumann-Bacia 1989, illustrated pp. 46–47; Summerson 1986, pp. 143–49, Summerson, Watkin, Mellinghoff 1983, pp. 61–63

Throughout the nineteenth century, the Bank of England's wealth symbolised the City of London's economic dominance over Great Britain, its empire, and the developed world. No less imposing was the Bank's building, which physically dominated the surrounding financial district. In this unusual imaginary view, the building is represented so as to cele-

brate John Soane's architectural achievement while giving expression to the institution's historical character.

The Bank of England, a private corporation, derived power from its function as the government's banker, and from the legal monopoly which guaranteed its position as the country's largest bank. The Bank's original building, erected in 1732 (following its establishment in 1694 it had first leased space), symbolised the new institution's prosperity and stability, and was also the first purpose-built bank building in the country. In the 1760s and 1780s, the architect-politician Robert Taylor erected some additions, but the greatest growth took place in three phases during the forty-five-year tenure of John Soane, which ended in 1833. The Bank had developed institutionally in an *ad hoc* and complex fashion, and this process is reflected in the building's accretive growth and in its highly irregular layout, as clearly shown by this drawing.

By eliminating most of the superstructure, Gandy was able to portray the building in its totality: interior and exterior, construction and decoration, substructure and superstructure, all publicly revealed like a model on a tabletop. Soane's earnest intention expressed itself in the quotation chosen to accompany the picture, taken from a popular novel by the moralist Le Sage: 'I am going to lift off the roof of this magnificent national pile . . . the insides will reveal themselves to you like seeing the insides of a pie whose crust is coming off.' Besides this revelatory, analytical purpose, the mode of representation makes the modern Bank of England appear significantly like a vast Roman ruin, further defining and ennobling Soane's achievement by linking it to prestigious antiquity. **DA**

43

stormed in the Gordon riots of 1780, and later the Bank's directors feared that revolutionary mobs might be tempted to destroy the Bank's invaluable records and steal its gold.

In order to safeguard the rotunda's vulnerable roof, Soane had first to invent a new type of lightweight, incombustible hollow brick, and then find a way to support this new structure on the older walls. This model served to test and demonstrate Soane's solution. Ingeniously divided into fourteen separate pieces, it shows the disposition of the masonry coursings at the crucial level of the niche arches, where the weight of the dome is transferred to the walls.

It seems most likely that Soane first used the model to explain the system to the masons building the rotunda, and later in the 1810s and 1820s as an innovative teaching device for his Royal Academy lectures. He admitted that, 'wherever the Model has been dispensed with, I am afraid the building has suffered in consequence thereof, either in solidity or convenience, and perhaps in both.' **DA**

44 *(illus. p. 257)*
View of the Rotunda at the Bank of England, 1798

Pen and watercolour, 63 × 70 cm
Dated: July 6th 1798
London, Trustees of Sir John Soane's Museum
Inv. No. 9.2.1C
Literature: Summerson, Watkin, Mellinghoff 1983, Fig. 22 on p. 73; Acres 1931, pp. 480–83; Gibson-Jarvie 1979; Evans 1852, p. 23; Binney 1984, p. 73; Bolton 1927, p. 62

Joseph Gandy's luminous watercolour of the rotunda of the Bank of England is deceptively tranquil, for it was in this great domed hall that the traders in Bank of England and government stock conducted daily their rowdy business. The astronomical increase in government borrowing during the Napoleonic Wars had a profound impact on London's financial markets, and at the centre of this historic change was the government's broker, the Bank of England and its public rotunda. It was here, before the Stock Exchange was formalised a few yards away in Capel Court, that a new class of City men first learned to make a living from the trading of stock.

The rotunda had originally been built in the late 1760s by Robert Taylor based on the Pantheon in Rome. In 1794 the rotting wooden roof of Taylor's rotunda had to be rebuilt by John Soane. Gandy's watercolour vividly depicts how Soane's remodelling lightened the room with semi-circular openings around the dome's base and, above, a lantern ringed by classical caryatids, statues of women acting as columns. But while the Roman grandeur of Taylor's hall remained, Soane's sinuous, decorative, surface patterning marked a distinct break. **DA**

Henry Provis

45
Constructional model of a niche in the Rotunda, Bank of England, 1794

Painted wood, 39.5 × 60 × 32.5 cm
London, Trustees of Sir John Soane's Museum
Inv. No. M 606
Literature: Wilton-Ely 1969, p.17, Cat. No. 18, Figs. 16a and b; Bolton 1929, p. 191

When John Soane rebuilt the rotunda of the Bank of England his primary functional objective was to make the structure fireproof. This mahogany model, representing a section of the rotunda's wall, demonstrates the novel structural system that Soane devised to support the new fireproof dome.

The Bank of England, like every other City institution of its time, was haunted by the spectre of fire: not just accidental fires like the Great Fire of 1666, but also deliberate, mob-set conflagrations. The Bank had nearly been

45

Artist unknown

46
Perspective design of Lothbury Court at the Bank of England, 1798

Pen and watercolour, 85 × 65.5 cm
London, Trustees of Sir John Soane's Museum
Inv. No. 12.3.14
Literature: Acres 1931, pp. 381, 395, Plates 47, 50; Bolton 1924, pp. 34–36, 50–52; Du Prey 1982 pp. 148–51; Steele and Yerbury 1930, pp. 13–16, Plates 19-26; Summerson, Watkin, Mellinghoff 1983, pp. 61–63.

The view is of the Lothbury Court, seen from within the Residence Courtyard, so called because it was ringed by large apartments and offices for important Bank functionaries like the secretary, assistant chief cashier and deputy chief accountant. Housing staff within the workplace, usually for security purposes, was typical of traditional London, and was practised at the Bank from its beginnings until, by 1808, some thirty-six people, including families and servants, were living within the Bank's walls. The domestic Residence Courtyard was separated from the more public Lothbury Court by a screen of giant Corinthian columns copied from the first-century Roman Temple of Vesta at Tivoli, a favourite ruin of Soane's which he had visited as a student in 1778.

The screen between the courtyards, as well as the similar columns in the Lothbury Court, created an effect of architectural and spatial complexity consonant with the Bank's functional diversity. They also evoked the ruins of the Roman forum, a symbol of ancient civic life well known to the English from their travels and collections of engraved views. Furthermore, colonnades and screens had recently been deployed by English and French architects to create a distinctly modern urban image for the streets of London and Paris.

Soane tried to create within the confines of the Bank of England a representation of an ideal city, where a crowd of activities could be contained and ennobled by architectural order. But as the hushed scene shows, Soane's vision excluded the chaos of the real city beyond the walls, thus fashioning for the Bank an architectural image of pure self-containment. This identity served the Bank's purposes, for it embodied an ideal of institutional autonomy that to this day helps secure employees' loyalty and awes the public. **DA**

46

Joseph Michael Gandy
London 1771–1843 Devon

47
Section showing the south side of Lothbury Court at the Bank of England, 1799

Pen and watercolour, 67.5 × 124.5 cm
Dated: Octr 2 1799
London, Trustees of Sir John Soane's Museum
Inv.No.12.3.2
Literature: Schumann-Bacia 1989, pp. 91–106; Figs. 76–87; Stroud 1984, pp. 157–60, Figs. 113–115; Summerson 1988, pp. 192, 197

One of the Bank of England's more significant functions was to serve as a storehouse for the nation's gold, which was transported by vans via a narrow passage from Lothbury, through the Lothbury Court, and into the Bullion Yard vaults deep in the heart of the building. Strict security was symbolised architecturally by the Bank's forbidding exterior walls. But within the Lothbury Court itself, John Soane created a triumphal setting that celebrated, rather than secluded, the Bank's treasure.

This section drawing – an imaginary plane cutting through the building – enabled the architect to visualise not just the south side of Lothbury Court, but also the complex spatial relationships of the flanking colonnades, steps, courtyards, walls, stairways and cellars.

The central importance of the archway leading to the Bullion Yard, however, is clearly emphasised by its scale and ornate sculptural decoration.

As a model for this centrepiece, Soane selected the Roman triumphal arch, with its monumental opening flanked by raised pairs of free-standing columns and high attic. Following his model, Soane decorated the walls with allegorical sculpture appropriate to the character of the institution. Between the columns are *caducei:* wing-tipped wands entwined by snakes, emblems of Mercury the god of messengers, travellers, merchants and commerce. This symbol appeared frequently on the Bank's interior walls. Atop the columns stand four figures personifying, in the final built version, the Four Parts of the World – Europe, Asia, Africa and America – emblematic of the Bank's global influence.

Soane achieved for the Bank an atmosphere of self-glorifying power that was probably just as well hidden from potentially critical public view. This kind of imperial triumphalism did not appear publicly in London for nearly thirty years, until after Waterloo, in the late 1820s Hyde Park arches of John Nash and Decimus Burton. **DA**

47

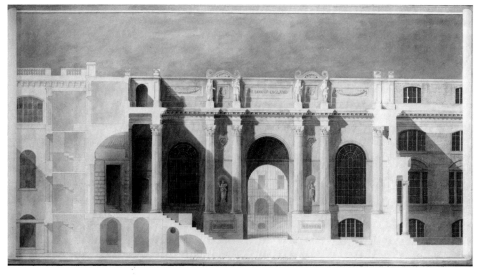

48

Joseph Michael Gandy
London 1771–1843 Devon

and Henry Hake Seward

49 *(illus p. 258)*
View of the Consols Transfer Office at the Bank of England, 1799

Pen and watercolour, 72×101 cm
Dated: 28 April 1799
London, Trustees of Sir John Soane's Museum
Inv. No. 11.6.6
Exhibitions: London, Royal Academy, 1823, No. 987
Literature: Bolton 1929, pp. 179–80, 182–83, 187–88; Colvin 1978, pp. 40–41; Crook 1969, pp. 66–67; Saint 1983, pp. 58–59

This unusual drawing, depicting the Consols Transfer Office before plastering, was used to illustrate an 1815 Royal Academy lecture by John Soane on the subject of 'Construction'.

The particular skill to be learned from this drawing was Soane's innovatory means of building fireproof vaults using various types of brick. But 'Construction' as a concept for Soane embodied not just the use of materials; it signified a general attitude of professional responsibility. As the Bank of England's appointed architect, Soane held a position of trust, like that of a lawyer's. Soane's principal duties over his forty-five-year career, much more so than designing, involved negotiating with suppliers and builders, overseeing work, paying bills and in general ensuring that the Bank received the best results for the best prices. For all of this, Soane was held to close account by the Bank's directors.

The reward for Soane's close attention to 'Construction' at the Bank of England was in part pecuniary. (His total compensation, a 5 per cent commission on building expenses of £860,000, may be estimated at £43,000 – £1.5 million at least in today's terms.) Also important was an elevation in his social status to that of a respected professional man. **DA**

48

View of the Consols Transfer Office at the Bank of England, 1799

Pen and watercolour, 70.5×99 cm
London, Trustees of Sir John Soane's Museum
Inv. No. 11.4.3
Exhibitions: London, Royal Academy, 1800, No. 1036
Literature: Acres 1931, pp. 184, 395–96; Binney 1984, Fig. 16; Schumann-Bacia 1989, pp. 70–74, Sheppard 1971, p. 56; Steele and Yerbury, p. 16; Summerson 1990, pp. 145, 165; Summerson, Watkin, Mellinghoff 1983, pp. 71–72

The Bank of England's most common type of public banking hall is represented here by the Consols Transfer Office. The term consols refers to a number of separate government funds grouped together at a 3 per cent rate of interest and collectively known as the three per cent consolidated annuities, or consols for short. The clerks behind the counters transacted business with the public and kept the books for these annuities, carefully registering the frequent transfers of ownership and arranging the semi-annual dividends. Numerous departments in the Bank were involved in managing the numerous government funds, of which the consols represented just a fraction, and the largest departments gave their names to the half-dozen banking halls of the transfer office type.

Banking as we think of it today, that is having a checking or savings account, pertained to only a very few people during the first half of the nineteenth century, but the class of banking represented by the Consols Transfer Office – private individuals investing in government stocks – was not socially insignificant, for as the historian Francis Sheppard has noted, 'it diversified the social structure of the nation by greatly increasing the number of people able to live on small independent incomes . . . a point of particular significance for London, where many of the people lived.'

Architecturally, the Consols Transfer Office, built as part of the Bank's late 1790s northward extension, represents a variation of Robert Taylor's Reduced Annuity Office (1787) and Soane's own Bank Stock Office of 1792. The practical need for a maximally lit, flexible, open-floor space was met by reducing the number of internal supports to four massive piers, carrying an unusually widespreading circular ring of windows to light the spacious central area, which was then enclosed on three sides by banking counters.

But Soane's innovation lay not in the pragmatism of his design, which was borrowed from Taylor anyway, but in his conscious attempt to recompose with ornament, light, and mass, the monumental qualities of antique Roman interiors. Soane's illustrator, Joseph Gandy, had the same ambitions for the Consols Transfer Office which is why when he made this drawing, perhaps for public exhibition at the Royal Academy, he exaggerated not just the lighting but also the scale, making the link with a monumental Roman bath hall that much more obvious. **DA**

Joseph Michael Gandy
London 1771–1843 Devon

50

Perspective of a design for the Tivoli Corner, Bank of England, 1803

Pen and watercolour, 92×150 cm in frame
London, Trustees of Sir John Soane's Museum
Inv. No. P118
Literature: Acres 1931, pp. 397–402, frontispiece to Vol. 2; Bolton 1924,

illustrated pp. iii, 31; Bolton 1933; Lawrence 1991, p. 7; Schumann-Bacia 1989, pp. 107–23; Steele and Yerbury 1930, p. 20, Plate 5; Stroud 1984, p. 157, illustrated on pp. 162–63; Teysott 1974, Fig. 147

The location and form of the Tivoli Corner represents John Soane's attempt to relate the Bank of England symbolically and physically to a contemporary town-planning scheme in London. Named after its model, the Temple of Vesta at Tivoli, this ornamental porch rivals the main Threadneedle Street entrance (Cat. No. 55) as an architectural symbol of the Bank. The circular composition, erected in 1806–07 as part of the extension along Lothbury (left) and Princes Street (right), wrapped the acute north-west angle and formed the final enclosure of the 3½-acre Bank site.

Curiously, for a composition of the Tivoli Corner's grandeur, its visibility when first built was drastically limited by the cramped, irregular junction of four streets in front of it. In fact, Soane designed the Tivoli Corner not for the intersection as it existed in 1807 but probably as he imagined it would be in the future, after the realisation of an ambitious but unexecuted plan by the City of London's architect, George Dance, to improve the area north of the Bank. **DA**

51

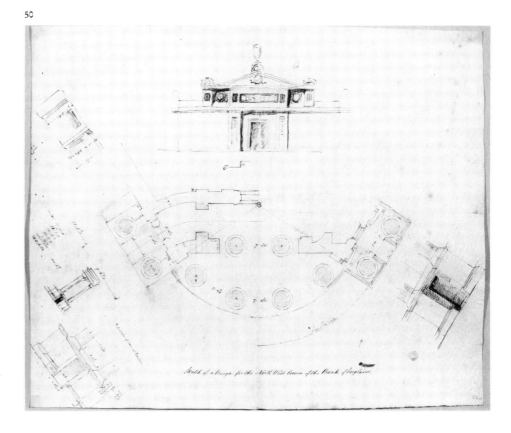

50

Sir John Soane
Goring-on-Thames 1753–1837 London

51
Preliminary design for the Tivoli Corner, Bank of England, 1805

Sepia pen and pencil, 55×68.5 cm
London, Trustees of Sir John Soane's Museum
Inv. No. 1.6.23

In the City of London, because of the irregular street pattern, corners often tend to be the parts of buildings most visible from the greatest distances. The location of the Tivoli Corner presented John Soane with the opportunity of erecting a conspicuous architectural emblem for the Bank of England, but in order to monumentalise the corner Soane had to first heighten the visual impact of the narrow angle, in plan, with the appearance of breadth, recession, and mass. For several months in 1804–05, Soane wrestled with the design. This sheet of working drawings represents one stage of the process.

It was practically predetermined that Soane would employ a colonnade (a screen of columns indicated in the plan by shaded circles) at Tivoli Corner since this had been done already in 1795 at the corner of Lothbury and Bartholomew Lane. As before, Soane placed the convex colonnade in front of the set-back rear wall, the layered planes giving the angle a sense of depth. To further the effect at the Tivoli Corner, Soane inserted a second colonnade behind the first and made the back wall slightly concave at its ends.

The corner was still, however, relatively sharp and Soane now had to broaden the composition. To do this he framed the curved colonnade with pairs of columns projecting from the plane of the flanking walls, thus widening and deepening the frontal elevation. This device had the additional effect of heightening the composition's visibility from the far ends of Lothbury and Princes Street, so that the person passing along the Bank's high boundary walls behind the corner would be able visually to anticipate, in the projecting columns, the full monumental appearance of the Tivoli Corner. **DA**

52

52
Model of the Tivoli Corner at the Bank of England

Painted wood, 52.5 × 56.5 × 26 cm
London, Trustees of Sir John Soane's Museum
Inv. No. MP 225
Literature: Wilton-Ely 1969, pp. 19–20, Cat. Nos. 24 and 27, Figs. 7a, b

The purpose of this model was to enable John Soane to visualise three dimensionally his spatially complex design for the Tivoli Corner. There is even a small panel at the back which can be removed to obtain a view from the inside.

Very likely, this model was also shown, along with an alternative design, to the Committee of Building at the Bank, who lacked the training needed to visualise a building from a plan or elevation. With the help of the models, the eight-member committee could decide which design for the Tivoli Corner was an appropriate symbol for their institution. The presentation of alternative designs to the

directors, then selected or further modified, was typical of the collective process by which Soane and the Bank directors arrived at decisions. Unfortunately, no record of their discussions exists, so it is impossible to know with certainty what the directors wanted their architecture to signify. Nevertheless, a common architectural language existed at the time, which architect and client would most likely have both understood.

There were a number of conspicuous references and meanings in Soane's architecture, the most obvious being the adaptation of the plan and Corinthian order from the round Roman Temple of Vesta at Tivoli. Soane had made references to antique architecture in his interiors, but this was the first complete exterior expression of Roman imperial grandeur and nobility. The Corinthian order signified wealth and opulence (not least because its ornate mouldings were expensive to carve), and for centuries architectural theorists had prescribed its use only for the most distinguished public buildings. **DA**

Artist unknown

53
Perspective design of the Five Per Cent (later Colonial) Office

Pen and watercolour, 71.5 × 96.5 cm
London, Trustees of Sir John Soane's Museum
Inv. No. 11.4.2
Literature: Summerson, Watkin, Mellinghoff 1983, p. 14, Plate 4; Acres 1931, pp. 351–63; Schumann-Bacia 1989, pp. 143–49, p. 147, Plate 122; Steel and Yerbury 1930, p. 24; Plates 58, 62, 65, 68–70.

This watercolour of the Five Per Cent Office at the Bank of England depicts significant changes not just in the evolution of John Soane's architecture but also developments involving the nature of work in the Bank. The hall, erected 1818–23, was the last of Robert Taylor's eighteenth-century transfer halls to be renovated and fireproofed, and one of the very last of Soane's projects at the Bank.

Here the thirty-year-old domed Office prototype received its final refinements. Soane leavened the heavy Romanness of the Consols Transfer Office with a new effect of Gothic lightness and with a conspicuous adoption of Greek ornamentation, as seen in the ring of Greek Ionic columns around the lantern and the prominent Greek fret pattern incised over the front and back arches. This diversification of historic references was characteristic of English public architecture in general in the post-Waterloo era.

There is also a noticeable difference between the figures of the clerks here and those

53

depicted some thirty years earlier. Because of the growth in business occasioned by the war, the staff had increased three-fold, from 300 in 1792 to 900 in 1813. As part of its attempt to rationalise the increased work, the Bank directors after 1800 established special committees to oversee the clerks' conduct both inside and outside the Bank. Attendance was closely regulated; behaviour towards the public monitored; even the number of annual holidays was cut back from forty-two to eighteen in an attempt to increase efficiency. Public drunkenness, frequenting certain taverns, and even theatre-going could get a clerk into trouble at the Bank.

The impact of these changes can be seen in the sobriety of the dark-suited Five Per Cent clerks, bent diligently over their ledgers. Sociologically, the Bank's attempt to discipline its work force was characteristic of transformations taking place in London and elsewhere in England. **DA**

54

54

Model of the Five Per Cent (later Colonial) Office

Painted wood and metal on fixed stand, 72×48.5×35 cm
London, Trustees of Sir John Soane's Museum
Inv. No. MR 16
Literature: Wilton-Ely 1969, p. 23, Cat. No. 36, Fig. 14a, right; Summerson 1983, pp. 500–05; Bolton 1929, pp. 157–58

John Soane's special concerns for interior lighting and façade design during the final period of his tenure as architect to the Bank of England are illustrated in this model. Both matters involved the tricky issue of architectural representation, or how the building was to communicate with its audience, individually and collectively.

Like the earlier model for the rotunda, this one served the purpose of demonstrating the structural system for the hall's fireproof vaulting. But it was also a means of visualising the specific ways that the openings among the vaults would light the interior. For Soane, the illumination of the interior played a key role in his audience's experience of what he called the 'poetry of architecture': an emotional feeling of mystery and sublimity.

The further significance of this model is its revelation of Soane's ambition in the 1810s (not realised until the mid 1820s) to rebuild the southern Threadneedle Street front of the Bank. By juxtaposing a token bay of Taylor's existing east façade with his own proposed design for the south-east angle, Soane demonstrated how he could bring the main south front of the Bank in line with the exteriors he had earlier built along Princes Street and Lothbury. **DA**

55

Model of the central part of the Threadneedle Street façade, Bank of England

Painted wood, 68.5×115×12.5 cm
London, Trustees of Sir John Soane's Museum
Inv. No. SC3
Literature: Acres 1931, pp. 405–06, 409–10, Plate 67; Bolton 1924, pp. 66–68; Olsen 1986, pp. 21–28; Schumann-Bacia 1989, pp. 149–158, 126–34; Steele and Yerbury 1930,

pp. 24–26, Plate 12; Stroud 1984, p. 167; Summerson 1983, p. 369; Summerson 1988, pp. 282–89; Summerson, Watkin, Mellinghoff 1983, p. 63, p. 66; Wilton-Ely 1969, p. 24, Cat. No. 42, Fig. 8b

John Soane had to wait until the very last phase of the building of the Bank of England for the opportunity to redesign the principal façade but, ironically, the apogee of his career was soon followed by a radical devaluation of his reputation. The dilapidated condition of

55

the Portland stone front had concerned Soane since at least 1800, but the Committee of Building would not grant permission to re-build and thicken the walls until 1823. This wooden model, one of two presented to the Committee of Building in February 1825, depicts Soane's final design for refacing the Threadneedle Street central entrance block.

The paramount aesthetic concern, to unify the Threadneedle Street front with the build-ing's other fronts, was achieved by deploying rows of Corinthian columns equivalent in level and height to those used since the 1790s. The functional importance of the entrance was only marginally accentuated, the model shows the colonnade set slightly forward from the wall, as Soane believed that an overall coherent architectural image would better express the institution's character than a single central emphasis. In his words, 'the whole of the Ex-terior of this extensive pile, erected at so many different times and under so many different circumstances, will appear uniform, simple and characteristic.'

It is ironic then that it was over just these criteria of architectural clarification and ex-pression that the next generation judged Soane's Bank a failure. C. R. Cockerell, who succeeded Soane in 1833 as the Bank's archi-tect, criticised the 'domestic' façades, with their doorways and windows, as misrepre-sentations of the Bank's character as a public treasury. Other more typical critics could find absolutely no meaning in Soane's architecture: 'odd vagaries and elaborate curiosities'; 'a costly mass of absurdities', they called it.

Not until another ideology re-evaluated Soane's London as orderly and urbane, in the mid twentieth century, was the Bank's posi-tion resecured in the canon of English archi-tecture. **DA**

Joseph Michael Gandy
London 1771–1843 Devon

56
View of the Scala Regia, leading to the House of Lords, 1823

Pen and watercolour, 132 × 93 cm in frame
London, Trustees of Sir John Soane's Museum
Inv. No. XP16
Exhibitions: London, Royal Academy, 1823, No. 974 or 984
Literature: Bolton 1924, pp. 112–13; Crook and Port 1973, pp. 520–25

For many years Soane wanted to build grand neo-classical architecture at the Houses of Parliament to replace the inefficient jumble that had grown up there, and in the 1790s de-voted much fruitless time to the project. In the 1820s he finally got an opportunity to produce major work there when, from 1813, he was the attached architect at the Office of Works with responsibility for the Westminster area.

Following the influx of Irish members after the Act of Union in 1800, the House of Lords moved from their tiny chamber at the south-ern end of the site into the former Court of Re-quests. As part of this work between 1800 and 1812, James Wyatt made a new royal entrance and offices fronting the Court of Requests in Old Palace Yard. Wyatt's work in a simple Gothic style was much criticised and when George IV came to the throne he insisted that the royal entrance be improved. Soane's plan was submitted in February 1822 and over the next two years he built a new royal entrance and stair. There then followed between 1823 and 1824 a royal gallery, to complete an im-posing route to be taken by the monarch at the state opening of parliament, and a few years later committee rooms and a library.

The royal carriage entrance was in the centre of a curved passageway. It was Perpen-dicular in style with fan vaulting. From this the grand neo-classical staircase (or Scala Re-gia) rose in three flights to the Prince's Chamber. This splendid and ornate domed staircase, which A.T. Bolton considered to be 'perhaps the best of all Soane's designs' is well shown in this watercolour by Gandy. **AW**

56

57
View of the Court of Chancery, Law Courts, Westminster, 1827

Pen and watercolour, 81 × 103.5 cm in frame
London, Trustees of Sir John Soane's Museum
Inv. No. P274
Exhibitions: London, Royal Academy, 1827, No. 968
Literature: Crook and Port 1973, pp. 504–612

Westminster Hall had been home to the courts of justice since medieval times, including Chancery and King's Bench, which were housed in makeshift wooden enclosures at the south end. These enclosures were improved by William Kent in 1739 but remained in-adequate for their purpose. Following rest-oration work on the north front of the medie-val hall in 1819, and the removal of the courts for the coronation of George IV, it was decided to rebuild the law courts outside the west wall of the hall, with Soane as the archi-tect. Between 1821 and 1825, therefore, seven courts and their ancillary offices were inge-niously fitted into this complicated site on which already existed six medieval flying but-tresses and an incomplete mid-eighteenth-century Palladian scheme at its southern end. On the exterior Soane chose to continue the earlier Palladian elevation. This provoked considerable criticism from members of the House of Commons in March 1823, when they saw this style adjacent to the north wall of Westminster Hall, and he was forced to goth-icise the New Palace Yard elevation.

It is, however, the plan and the interiors which reveal the brilliance of the architect. Soane must have greatly enjoyed the challenge of designing the courts themselves, all of which had to be top-lit. He varied the designs with immense skill, reusing many motifs from earlier buildings. The Court of Chancery, one of the largest courts, was the only one to have an oval gallery beneath a square sky-light. **AW**

58
View of the Privy Council Chamber, Board of Trade offices, Whitehall, 1827

Pen and watercolour, 94.5 × 72 cm
London, Trustees of Sir John Soane's Museum
Inv. No. 15.5.1
Exhibitions: London, Royal Academy, 1827, No. 905
Literature: Crook and Port 1973, pp. 551–62

The history of this commission illustrates clearly the difficulties that Soane experienced with his designs for public buildings, which were subject to interfering politicians who felt they understood good architecture but who chiefly reacted to expenses. In April 1823 it was decided to rebuild the Board of Trade on the west side of Whitehall, and in October of that year the project was expanded to include the dilapidated Privy Council Office adjoining to the south, entered from Downing Street.

In 1824 there were several meetings between the architect and ministries regarding the Board of Trade, with many difficulties about the design. In particular, the Chancellor of the Exchequer, Frederick John Robinson, later Viscount Goderich, questioned the form of the columns and the order of the capitals for the continuous colonnade on the façade to Whitehall. There was also considerable controversy about the height of the building, but by November 1924 it was ready for roofing.

Arrangements for the Privy Council Chamber and offices were approved on 1 March 1825, although it was not until December that work began on the foundations. In September 1827, Charles Greville, Clerk of the Privy Council, asked for the removal of the main features of Soane's design: the pairs of Ionic columns in the centre of each wall and the groined elliptical dome suspended between skylights. They were left, but the Treasury, inaccurately, said that they had not been consulted about the plans for them. **AW**

An act of parliament passed in 1798 had allowed the formation of 'Voluntary Associations' for the defence and security of the realm and similar volunteer regiments had been established throughout the country, unsurprisingly many in London, the focus of the strength of the nation's economy. Plans were laid that in the event of a French invasion, the bullion, the presses for printing notes and the Bank's records would be transported to safety in the West of England in wagons escorted by members of the Bank Volunteers. The Bank's architect, John Soane, who held the rank of quartermaster in the Corps, was responsible for the move.

The Bank Volunteers survived as a private defence force financed by the Bank until 1907 when military reforms meant that it could no longer be guaranteed that their duty would solely be the defence of the Bank. It is said that the unofficial motto of the Bank volunteers was 'No Advance without Security'. **JK**

This chair was made in 1809 by David Bruce (at a cost of 4 guineas) to the design of John Soane, the Bank of England's architect from 1788 to 1833. It is one of a set of six specially made for the seat of power in the City – the Governor's room in the Bank of England.

By the end of the eighteenth century, as well as being visited by increasing numbers of people transacting business there, the Bank was regarded as one of the sights of London. In consequence one enterprising clerk had even published (anonymously) a guide to the Threadneedle Street building: it explained to which counter one went to change a note into coin, to buy a Post Bill, to have a note verified and so on. It is understandable, therefore, that one of the leading architects of the period should design the building, specify the colour schemes of the public offices, have a hand in the design of the uniforms of the messengers who guided and assisted the public and propose the furniture for the prestigious offices of the institution. **JK**

Thomas Stothard
London 1755–1834 London

59
Presentation of Colours to the Bank of England Volunteer Corps, 1799

Oil on canvas, 88.9 × 121.9 cm
London, The Governor and Company of the Bank of England
Provenance: purchased June 1800
Exhibitions: London, Piccadilly, 1939; National Army Museum, 1973; Barbican Art Gallery, 1984; M.C.C., 1987

The scene is set at Lord's Cricket Ground on 2 September when the wife of Samuel Thornton, governor of the Bank from 1799 to 1801, presented colours to the Bank of England Volunteer Corps.

The Corps was founded in 1798 from the staff 'for the immediate defence of the Bank'. Officers were drawn from the Court of Directors, the Bank's governing body, and the rank and file from the clerks. Uniforms and arms were provided by the Bank itself. Service was voluntary and unremunerated although it seems clerks had little choice as to whether they served or not.

60

60
Chair

Designed by John Soane; made by John Bruce, 1809
Mahogany and leather, 88.9 × 51.4 × 57.8 cm
London, The Governor and Company of the Bank of England
Literature: Bill Book No. 9, Sir John Soane's Museum

James Gillray
London 1756–1815 London

61 *(illus. p.280)*
Political-Ravishment, or The Old Lady of Threadneedle-Street in Danger!

Coloured etching, 25 × 36 cm
Published by H. Humphrey, St. James's Street, 22 May 1797
London, Guildhall Library, Corporation of London
Literature: George 1942, Vol. 7, pp. 351–52, No. 9016; Hill 1966; Woods 1975

In 1797 legislation was passed leading to the restriction of cash payments by the Bank of England. James Gillray produced this caricature showing the Bank of England as 'The Old Lady of Threadneedle Street'. The Old Lady is dressed in £1 notes, and sits on a treasure chest. She is being ravished by the Tory prime minister, William Pitt the Younger, and cries, 'Murder! – murder! – Rape! – murder!'

James Gillray, Britain's most celebrated caricaturist, was the son of a Scottish ex-soldier, but was born in London. His early ambition was to be a straight portrait painter. He obtained work with the printmaking firms of Matthew and Mary Darly, William Holland and S.W. Fores. Most of his work, however, was for their rival, Hannah Humphrey, whose shop was in Bond Street until 1797, and then 27 St. James's Street, where Gillray also lodged, not far from White's Club (Tories), and Brooks's Club (Whigs). **RH**

62

more proof against forgery led the Bank to invite suggestions from the public as to how its notes might be made inimitable.

The first practical proposal came from Alexander Tilloch, an engraver who, accompanied by Francisco Bartolozzi and James Heath, both engravers to George III, submitted an engraving in May 1797 which Tilloch declared to be inimitable. A memorial endorsing the submission from several other eminent personalities from the art world was also presented. As far as the Bank was concerned, the acid test was whether the in-house engraver was able effectively to copy the proposal. He could and did, and there the matter rested with all the 400 or so ideas received from the public. **JK**

George Cruikshank
London 1792–1878 London

63
Bank Restriction Note

Line engraving, 14 × 21.5 cm
Published by William Hone, 1819
London, Guildhall Library, Corporation of London
Literature: Cohn 1924, No. 45; George 1949, Vol. 4, pp. 878–79, No. 13198; Evans 1978, pp. 35–37

On 26 January 1819 George Cruikshank looked down the Old Bailey from Ludgate Hill and saw bodies hanging from the Newgate gibbet. Two of the bodies were of women. He asked what their crime was and was told they had passed forged £1 notes. Scandalised that people could be hanged for so petty a crime, Cruikshank returned to home and 'forged' his own 'Bank-note not to be imitated'. Shortly after he was visited by William Hone, the Ludgate Hill publisher. Hone saw the engraved note and insisted on publishing it. This is Cruikshank's version of the story. But according to Hone the idea was his. **RH**

62
Book of Specimens of Bank Notes

20.5 × 28.5 × 3 cm
London, The Governor and Company of the Bank of England
Inv. No. B356

Pitt's 1797 declaration through the Privy Council that Bank of England notes should no longer be convertible into gold enabled the government to safeguard the national reserves for the war effort. The £5 note was the lowest denomination note then issued by the Bank and, as was to be expected, the gold in circulation (guineas and sub-divisions thereof) soon

disappeared from circulation. In response the Bank printed £1 and £2 notes to oil the wheels of trade which were in danger of grinding to a halt.

However this seemingly innocent act brought a considerable amount of criticism on the Bank and its directors because the new notes, although quickly produced, were of poor quality and easily forged. The forgery of Bank of England notes remained a capital offence until 1832 and during this period of inconvertibility or 'Restriction' as it was known (which lasted until 1821) upwards of 600 people were capitally convicted and some 300 hanged. The public outcry and pressure on the Bank to improve its notes and make them

64
Sovereign and Half Sovereign

Sovereign, D 2.1 cm; half sovereign, D 1.8 cm
London, The Museum of London
Inv. No. 33.320/64, 66
Provenance: Yates Bequest
Literature: Seaby 1991

1816 saw important changes in coinage. Gold coin, of 22 carats and prescribed weight, was declared the legal standard and for the first

63

time silver coins were produced with an intrinsic value below their face value, thus forming the first official token or subsidiary coinage. A decision was also taken to bring back gold coinage to the unit of 20 shillings, which involved the withdrawal of the guinea and its replacement by the sovereign, the weight of the coins being reduced by one twenty-first part, in accordance with a Mint Indenture dated 6 February 1817. The sovereign was proclaimed legal tender on 1 July 1817 and the half sovereign on 10 October 1817. By the end of the year £4,275,000 of gold coin had been issued.

The reverse of the sovereign is struck with the image of St. George and the Dragon, designed by Benedetto Pistrucci (1784–1855), an Italian carver of gems and cameos. William Wellesley Pole, the master of the Mint, impressed by a ring cameo of St. George by Pistrucci, commissioned him to make models of this and the king's head for the new coinage. These models then had to be adapted for steel dies and Pistrucci was so critical of the resulting quality of the struck coin that he learned to engrave the dies for himself. His Mint commissions for 1817 were expanded to include die work, and he personally cut the steel matrix for the George and Dragon accepted for the sovereign of 1817 in which St. George holds the shaft of a shivered lance. **EE**

65
£1,000 Bank of England Note

No. 7402; Acc. No. 1/828, dated 17 July 1834, 12.7×21 cm
London, The Governor and Company of the Bank of England

By the end of the first quarter of the nineteenth century the note issue of the Bank of England had become pre-eminent. The Bank's notes were widely accepted because of their unquestioned convertibility into gold as well as their convenience. For example the coin equivalent to the £1,000 note one thousand sovereigns weighed a hefty 17 lb. Furthermore, the benefits of paper money were not lost on the public: a note could not be reduced in value if a small piece were torn off but if the weight of a sovereign were diminished in some way the holder would not necessarily receive full value.

In 1833, the year before this note is dated, the Bank's notes were made legal tender for any amount over £5 and this, of course, gave the Bank's paper a distinct advantage over other issues. At that time the Bank's notes ranged in denomination from £5 up to £1,000. To have the equivalent purchasing power today as £1,000 had in 1834 a sum approaching £37,000 would be required. **JK**

Sir Thomas Lawrence
Bristol 1769–1830 London

66 *(illus. p. 279)*
Sir Francis Baring Bt., John Baring and Charles Wall, Partners of Barings, 1806

Oil on canvas, 155×226 cm
London, by arrangement with Baring Brothers and Co. Ltd.
Provenance: commissioned by Sir Francis Baring; by family descent
Exhibitions: London, Royal Academy, 1807, No. 210; British Institution, 1830, No. 31; Royal Academy, 1961, Cat. No. 28; National Portrait Gallery, 1979, Cat. No. 23
Literature: Garlick 1989, No. 62, Plate 29

At his death in 1810 Sir Francis Baring was reckoned by one observer to be 'unquestionably the first merchant in Europe'. A decade or so later, on the conclusion of the raising of French reparation loans in which Baring Brothers had played a major role, the Duc de Richelieu, first minister of France, was quite sure that the six great powers in Europe were Britain, France, Prussia, Russia, Austria and Baring Brothers. Barings' emergence as the leading merchant house in London reflected the rise of London as the major international capital market and hub of world trade, in succession to Amsterdam.

This portrait, one of Sir Thomas Lawrence's finest, conveys the confidence of the senior

67a

partners of Barings as they look outwards from their partners' room. Commissioned in 1806 by Sir Francis Baring from Britain's most fashionable artist, it is a flattering compliment to Sir Francis, to his brother John, and his son-in-law, Charles Wall.

On the table before them is a fat banker's book, opened at the account of Hope and Co., the leading Amsterdam merchants, and a letter to them is held by Sir Francis. It confirms Hopes' standing as Barings' most intimate correspondents, a relationship which had enabled the two houses to undertake huge international transactions, such as the financing of the 1803 Louisiana Purchase, using both the London and Amsterdam capital markets. But it was a watershed and by the end of the Napoleonic Wars London and Barings were in the ascendancy over Amsterdam and Hopes. **MJO**

67
Works relating to the 1824 Barings Loan for the Government of Buenos Aires

a) 500 sterling bearer bond
Paper, 40.8×27.5 cm

b) Ledger account in Barings' books showing transactions in 1824 stock
Bound manuscript volume, 43×65 cm

c) Ballot box used by Barings for selecting, on a random basis, 1824 bonds for redemption
Metal, 46×36×36 cm

London, Baring Brothers and Co. Ltd.
Literature: Ziegler 1988, pp. 100–11; Griffith Dawson 1990

The emergence of London by 1815 as the major international capital market is no more clearly illustrated than by the stream of borrowers from the New World who came to London to raise funds for the first time. The United States led the way and was joined in the 1820s by Latin American borrowers who then raised some £21 million through the issue of long-term sterling bearer bonds. The State of Buenos Aires was among the first when, in 1824, Baring Brothers raised a £1 million loan through the issue of Buenos Aires bonds to London investors.

It marked the beginning of a long and rewarding association between Argentina, the London capital market and Barings. By end of century capital raised from British investors had transformed Argentina's infrastructure, industries and agriculture.

Yet the path to these rewards was not easy. The 1824 loan went into default in 1828 and remained so for thirty years. It tested all concerned – the Buenos Aires government which, at this moment, had little need of foreign funds, London merchant banks such as Barings which were still gaining experience of countries outside Europe and North America, and London investors who were still unfamiliar with the risks of lending their savings overseas. **MJO**

68
The King's Ledger, 1826

Bound manuscript volume, 46×39×5 cm
London, Coutts and Co.

The Prince Regent's extravagance and improvidence which brought hardship to his creditors and exasperated his bankers are well known. The prince originally banked with Coutts, but the huge sums of money he expended on Carlton House and on his personal appearance and pleasures caused an estrangement which forced him to raise money with other banking houses at home and abroad as well as from friends and relatives.

In 1792 Thomas Coutts loaned the prince

£60,000 advising him that unless 'His Royal Highness goes heartily firmly and decidedly into the plan of reform, and will obstinately persevere in it for years to come, he will do himself an injury instead of any good.' Although the prince rebuked Coutts for his tone and signally failed to take his advice, relations were repaired and Coutts and his wife enjoyed the prince's friendship and company.

George IV's extravagance was balanced by his natural generosity which extended not only to official bodies but particularly to individuals, such as the 'poor Pilot's widow' and the 'two poor women in distress' recorded on this page of the Privy Purse Accounts. Some of the more substantial payments were for works of art: £1,000 to Richard Westmacott and £2,100 to David Wilkie. Other payments are to members of the royal household and to the king's surgeon and dentist. The king's health was deteriorating quite rapidly at this time and both his teeth and his sight were a particular concern to him. **EE**

69
Handkerchief

Nathan Mayer Rotschild (sic) on the London Exchange 1836

After an engraving by H. Heath, 29 August 1831
Silk, plate print in brown ink, 88×90 cm
London, The Museum of London
Inv. No. 91.133
Provenance: Miss R. B. Smith

Nathan Mayer Rothschild (1777–1836) founded the English banking house of N. M. Rothschild and Sons in 1810. During the Napoleonic Wars he acted as financial agent for the British government, facilitating payments to Wellington in Spain and arranging substantial subsidies for the government's allies, thereby establishing his personal fortune. His influence continued to grow and he successfully floated major loans for the British government and those overseas.

Heath's image of Rothschild seems to be derived from an earlier engraving, *A Pillar of the Exchange*, by Thomas Jones, published in 1829 by F.V. Webster. This shows Rothschild standing by his favourite column in the Royal Exchange, a position reserved for Jewish brokers and known as Jews' Walk.

The handkerchief was an essential fashion accessory for the well-dressed man of the 1820s and '30s. Fashion plates and satirical drawings show it protruding from a back coat pocket, making it, in view of its value, a lucrative target for pickpockets, a hazard memorably amplified by Charles Dickens in *Oliver Twist* (1837–38).

From the mid eighteenth century the production of such handkerchiefs was considerably increased by improved dyeing techniques and mechanisation and these technological advances were accompanied by new imagery and uses, for instance as teaching aids, expressions of patriotism and vehicles of social comment. However, possibly the most convincing role of the pictorial handkerchief is as a souvenir, to commemorate both personal and public events. **EE**

70

70
Subscription Room Ledger

Lloyds Subscription Rooms, 1799
Bound volume, 52×78.5 cm (open)
London, Lloyd's of London, on deposit
Guildhall Library
Inv. No. MS14, 931, No. 26

These ledgers, which were held in the Subscription Rooms at Lloyd's, contain details of the movements of ships, and any reported loss or damage, together with their masters' names. Included in the shipping list for 19 October 1799 is the following entry 'The Lutine Frigate from Yarmouth to Hambro was wrecked in the night of the 9 Inst off Vlie Island.' When the *Lutine* sank after hitting a sandbank she was carrying a cargo whose value was said to be enormous and has been established as high as £1.4 million. It consisted of bullion and gold and silver coins being transported on behalf of the London banking house of Goldschmidt to Hamburg.

Most of the cargo was insured by Lloyd's, but although the claim was honoured, the underwriters were unable to claim their salvage rights as the Dutch government, at war with England, claimed the wreck as war booty, a claim not revoked until 1828 when Lloyd's were granted 50 per cent rights. Salvage attempts, hampered by the shifting sandbanks, were carried out intermittently throughout the nineteenth century with the estimated eventual recovery of approximately £100,000. Also salvaged were the ship's bell, which now hangs in the Underwriters' Room at Lloyd's and which is rung when an announcement is to be made, once for good news and twice for bad, and the ship's rudder, from which an elaborately carved, and uncomfortable chair was made for the chairman. EE

Marine Insurance Policy

71
Ship and Goods Policy on the *Guipuzcoa*, 1794

39 × 24 cm
London, Lloyd's of London
Literature: Wright and Fayle 1928, p. 148

This rare policy issued by Lloyd's provides insurance for a slave ship, the *Guipuzcoa*, for her voyage from Liverpool to the coast of Africa and on to Cuba. By 1800 Liverpool controlled 90 per cent of the British slave trade and in that year 120 ships, with accommodation for at least 31,844 slaves, left the port for Africa. The trade was triangular, with alcohol, textiles, metalware and firearms for England being traded for slaves in Africa. They in turn were traded in South or Central America for staples such as sugar, cocoa, indigo and ginger.

The second leg of the journey known as the 'middle passage' was the most hazardous but the most lucrative. The value of £45 each placed on the slaves suggests the profits to be made, but the corresponding risk to the insurers is indicated by the high premium demanded. Mutinies were a recognised hazard of the trade and a symptom of its inhumanity. A marginal clause in the policy made it a condition that if, in an insurrection, less than 5 per cent of the slaves were killed, this did not constitute a claim. Insurrections occurred when the ships lay at anchor on the coast; once at sea with no knowledge of navigation, there was no hope of escape and large numbers of slaves suffered and died from disease, starvation, lack of water, despair and suicide. EE

72

72
Ship and Goods Policy on the *Ajax*, 1820

38 × 49 cm
London, Lloyd's of London

The *Ajax* was an East Indiaman sailing out of London for Madras. Her cargo, which was valued at £2,800, consisted mainly of high quality goods probably intended for the European market in India. It included several items almost certainly made in London including mathematical instruments, jewellery and watches, and others such as twenty cases of glasses which were probably supplied through London firms. The 40 hogsheads of pale ale may well come from one of the large London breweries. This particular ale matured on the journey. By contrast the ship also carried soap, perfumery and a quantity of 'wearing apparel' and fabric, including seven cases of printed cotton. The raw cotton would have been imported from the East, then manufactured and printed in the latest fashion before being re-exported to India.

The *Ajax* was built in Newcastle in 1811 and weighed 472 tons. Detailed information on the ship can be ascertained from the Lloyd's register of shipping where she is classified A1, i.e. of the first quality both structurally and materially. She was owned by Somes and Co., one of the most prominent shipping companies in the nineteenth century. **EE**

73
Admission disks

Ivory and stained ivory, D 3.6 cm
London, Lloyd's of London

In 1800 the continuous and severe overcrowding of the Subscribers Rooms at Lloyd's premises in the Royal Exchange prompted the committee to propose regulations concerning both the use of the rooms and those entitled to enter. The rooms were thronged with subscribers and their clerks and substitutes, for whom they paid no extra fee, and others who had paid no subscription, some using their access for information gathering and others for business unconnected with insurance.

Prior to 1800 subscribers paid £15 which entitled then to life membership of Lloyd's, admission to the Subscribers Rooms and the right to vote at general meetings. There were

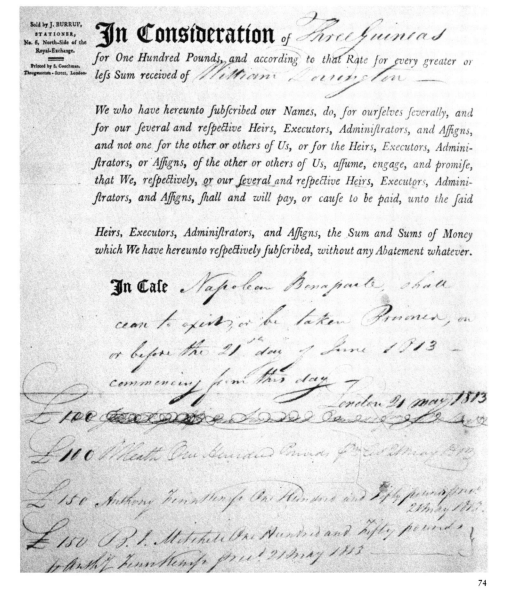

no restrictions on membership. Following the general meeting of 2 April 1800 a resolution was passed that in future only merchants, bankers, underwriters and insurance brokers should be admitted. Furthermore, each applicant had to be recommended in writing by at least six subscribers. Numbers were further reduced by restricting partnerships to one subscriber only and by imposing a separate entrance fee of £15 for each substitute.

These regulations were enforced by issuing admission disks, white for subscribers and red for substitutes, which had to be shown at the door. A list of subscribers was also to be printed annually. The implementation of these regulations points to the more structured and corporate approach Lloyd's wished to adopt. **EE**

74
Policy taken against the life and liberty of Napoleon Bonaparte, 1813

27 × 22.5 cm
London, Lloyd's of London
Literature: Wright and Fayle 1928, Fig. p. 96; Flower and Wynn Jones 1974, Fig. p. 51

On 21 May 1813 one William Dorrington gambled 12 guineas that Napoleon would 'cease to exist, or be taken prisoner on or before the 21st day of June 1813'. He lost his bet which was in fact in contravention of the Life Assurance Act of 1774 which forbade insurance of the life of another where the insurer had no financial interest in the life. Bets made on the life expectancy of ailing men were considered parti-

cularly pernicious and were described by the Committee of New Lloyd's in 1774 as being 'Virtually an Accessary (sic) in a Species of Slow Murder'. **EE**

Thomas Lawrence
Bristol 1769–1830 London

75 *(illus. p. 260)*
John Nash, 1824–27

Oil on canvas, 138.4×110.5 cm
Oxford, The Principal, Fellows and Scholars of Jesus College
Provenance: painted for the College at Nash's request in lieu of payment
Exhibitions: London, Royal Academy, 1890; Oxford, 1906, No. 194; Brighton, 1951, No. 24; London, Royal Academy, 1951, No. 194; National Portrait Gallery, 1979, Cat. No. 47
Literature: Colvin 1978, pp. 579–85; Summerson 1980; Garlick 1989, No. 592

John Nash (1752–1835) designed and executed the greatest schemes of metropolitan improvements in Regency London and for the first time introduced the principles of the Picturesque to an urban setting. Born the son of an engineer and millwright in Lambeth, he was first employed in the office of Sir Robert Taylor (1714–1788), before building up his own practice in Wales. He returned to London in 1796 and went into partnership with the landscape gardener Humphrey Repton. The partnership was dissolved in 1802 and in 1806 Nash was appointed architect to the Office of Woods and Forests. In this capacity he planned the redevelopment of Marylebone Park as the Regent's Park, with a new street, Regent Street, to connect it with the West End. On the death of James Wyatt in 1813, he was one of a triumvirate of architects (with Soane and Smirke) who divided up the responsibilities of surveyor-general in the Office of Works: he held responsibility for Carlton House, Kensington and St. James's Palaces and the royal lodges in Windsor Great Park.

When this portrait was exhibited at the Royal Academy in 1827, Nash was at the summit of his success. The *Examiner* commented 'Nature has amply compensated this gentleman by gifting his mind instead of his face, if it is a portrait of the able architect of that name; and the painter has displayed that refinement of mind.' Nash had given advice to Jesus College in 1815–18 on altering the roofs and battlements of both college quadrangles and later helped in some negotiations over college property at the south end of the proposed London Bridge, hence the commission.

The background shows the gallery in Nash's own house at 14 [Lower] Regent Street, where the architect used to work. **CF**

76a

John Bluck after Thomas Hosmer Shepherd
fl. 1791–1831, France 1793–1864 London respectively

76
a) [Lower] Regent Street from Piccadilly, 1822

Aquatint, 43×53 cm
Published at R. Ackermann's Repository of Arts, 101 Strand, 1 July 1822.
London, The Museum of London
Inv. No. A18138

b) The Quadrant, Regent Street, 1822

Aquatint, 34.5×49.5 cm
Published at R. Ackermann's Repository of Arts in Strand, 1 May 1822
London, The Museum of London
Inv. No. C120
Literature: Adams 1983, pp. 507–09, No. 221/17–18

One of the poles of Nash's Regent Street development was Carlton House, the residence of his patron the Prince Regent, set back behind its screen of columns (Cat. No. 00). From here, Lower Regent Street sloped gently upward in a straight line to Piccadilly Circus. This was the first part of the scheme to be started, partly because much of the land already belonged to the crown, and clearance of old houses began in 1816.

Thanks to the proximity of Carlton House, Lower Regent Street had a smart character which was missing from the centre portion of the Street. Hotels, club-houses and chambers made up most of the frontages, but Nash designed a very grand block containing his own house, whose square projecting bays can be seen on the left of this view, and a picturesque accent was provided by the tower of St. Philip's Chapel. The appearance of Lower Regent Street was drastically changed in 1827 with the demolition of Carlton House, no longer required by the king. In its place came, eventually, the Duke of York's column.

The Quadrant, bending north from Piccadilly Circus, was the key element in Nash's Regent Street development, linking the disparate lines of Lower Regent Street and the central part of the street. To ensure that both sides of the Quadrant were completed together and in a uniform manner, Nash himself acted as developer, taking all the ground and bearing the entire cost.

The ground and first floors behind the cast-iron colonnades were occupied by shops, the three floors above by private houses. Originally Nash had envisaged the colonnade running the whole length of the street, but this grand idea was not realised, and even the Quadrant colonnades were removed in 1848. At the southern end the Quadrant abutted the County Fire Office, whose front, designed by Robert Abraham and based on Inigo Jones's old Somerset House, closed the view from Carlton House up Lower Regent Street.

These aquatints were part of a series of eighteen published by Ackermann between 1811 and 1822. **NB**

76b

George Stanley Repton and John Nash

1786–1858 London, London 1752–1835 East
Cowes, Isle of Wight respectively

77
Design for the Argyll Concert Rooms, Regent Street, *c.* 1819

Watercolour, 22×53.4 cm
New Haven, Yale Center for British Art
Inv. No. B1975.2.369
Provenance: Leo Kersley; John Harris

The Argyll Concert Rooms, also known as the
Royal Harmonic Institution, provided one of
the elegant architectural accents which enlivened the palace-fronted commercial blocks
of Regent Street. The site was formerly occupied by a wing of an eighteenth-century mansion belonging to the Duke of Argyll which
has been converted into a place of public
entertainment.

   The old Argyll Rooms were completely rebuilt in 1819 to Nash's design for Messrs.
Welsh and Hawes. Nash provided the design
free of charge but exploited the full commercial potential of the site, tucking the concert
hall at the back, with shops on the Regent
Street front and a large public room above.
With his usual scenic skill, Nash disguised the
acute angle of the southern corner by treating
it as a columned bow with a small dome. The
façade had terracotta sculptural decoration by
James George Bubb (1782–1853), who also
provided much of the sculpture for the Regent's Park terraces.

The Harmonic Institution was one aspect of
the 'improving' organisations which sprang
up all over England in the late eighteenth
century: every provincial town has its 'Athenaeum', with library and concert rooms. Liszt
(aged twelve), Weber and Mendelssohn all
performed at the Harmonic Institution and
established a musical tradition in Regent
Street, but the building burnt down in 1830, a
common fate for theatres and concert halls,
and was rebuilt as shops and houses. **NB**

Artist unknown

78
Houses fronting Regent Street between Conduit Street and Maddox Street, 1838

Pen and ink, 20×48.5 cm
London, Public Record Office
Inv. No. MPE 1356

Almost all the buildings in the central section
of the new Regent Street were of the same type
– shops with houses above – and there was
little opportunity for the picturesque variation
of Lower Regent Street. Nash could have
attempted a rigidly formal architecture, of
the kind he essayed in the Quadrant, but the
irregular spacing and width of the streets
opening on both sides made this difficult
and would have made speculative letting
more complicated.

   To bestow some coherence and dignity on
this part of his new street, Nash tried to ensure
that between each pair of side streets there was
at least one symmetrical palace front, leaving
the rest of the frontage to smaller buildings. In
this he was consciously following the model of
the High Street at Oxford, where stately college buildings stand alongside houses and
shops.

   The success of this policy depended on the
ability and willingness of speculators and
builders, notably James Burton, to take large
plots of ground. The entire frontage between
Conduit Street and Maddox Street was taken
by Burton in 1828 for shops and houses with a
neo-Greek façade probably designed by
Nash. Behind the pilastered centre was a large
hall housing the Cosmorama – a public show
like the Diorama in Regent's Park. **NB**

78

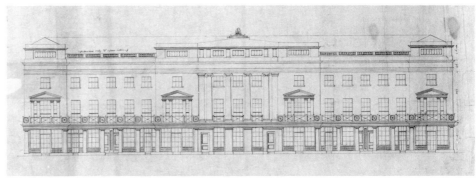

T. Stothard, *Presentation of Colours to the Bank of England Volunteer Corps*, 1799. Cat. No. 59

John Nash

London 1752–1835 East Cowes, Isle of Wight

79
Carlton House Terrace, 1827

Album of drawings, 71×110.5 cm (open)
London, Public Record Office
Inv. No. MPE 891

In 1826 the Commissioners of Woods and Forests were informed at the king's wish that Carlton House, his former residence at the foot of Regent Street, 'should be given up to the Public in order to its being taken down and the site thereof and the gardens attached thereto being laid out as building ground for dwelling houses of the first class'. Demolition

was complete by 1829.

John Nash prepared a scheme which embraced not only the Carlton House site but the whole of St. James's Park, following the principles of his successful Regent's Park development. There would be three long terraces of houses on the park's north and south sides,

flanking the vista from the rebuilt Buckingham Palace. Linking the park with Lower Regent Street, the wide Waterloo Place was laid out on the site of Carlton House itself, with the United Services Club on one side and the Athenaeum club on the other. In the event only two of the three proposed terraces on the

79

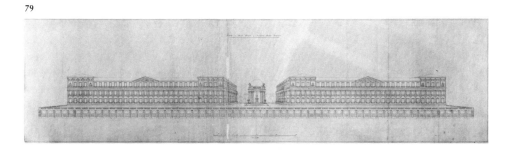

J. Linnell, *Kensington Gravel Pits*, 1811–12. Cat. No. 91

north side were built – Carlton House Terrace East and West; they were designed by Nash and their erection was superintended by James Pennethorne.

Towards the park the fall in the ground enabled Nash to bring forward the basement stories to support a spacious terrace overlooking the park. The cast-iron Greek Doric columns of the basement fronts recall Nash's arcades in the Regent Street Quadrant. For the space between these two massive terraces Nash proposed a domed fountain which would draw the eye down Lower Regent Street and out into St. James's Park beyond, but nothing was built until the Duke of York's column designed by Benjamin Wyatt was erected in 1834. **NB**

Artist unknown

80
West Strand Improvements, c. 1832

a) viewed from the East
Watercolour, 61 × 95 cm

b) viewed from the West
Watercolour, 60 × 96.5 cm

London, Coutts and Co.
Exhibitions: London, Barbican Art Gallery, 1984, Cat. Nos. 36 and 37, illustrated
Literature: Stokes 1974, pp. 119–28; Summerson 1980

The Strand is an ancient street and the principal connection between the cities of London and Westminster. Following the commercial success and popular acclaim of the Regent's Park and Regent Street improvements, the Commissioners of Woods and Forests obtained in 1826 an act of parliament for carrying out

improvements at the Strand's western end.

The development would create more convenient communication between the east and west ends of the town, linking Lower Regent Street, Whitehall and the Strand. It would include public buildings like the new National Gallery and a new public square (to become Trafalgar Square), as well as the usual speculative commercial buildings.

Four years were spent in acquiring the necessary land and in 1830 John Nash submitted his designs for the large block of 'first rate' houses and shops which would form the principal improvement to the West Strand itself. As with the Regent Street blocks, the whole Strand frontage was treated as a single architectural entity. The central section was given columned upper floors and a raised attic and at each extremity of the triangular site, Nash placed 'pepper-pot' turrets which served to camouflage the awkward corner angles. Behind the central section and bisecting the block was a covered arcade – the Lowther Arcade – of the kind which Nash had originated in London with his Royal Opera House Arcade. **NB**

T. Lawrence, *Sir Francis Baring Bt., John Baring and Charles Wall, Partners of Barings*, 1806. Cat. No. 66

80a

80b

An Appropriate Emblem for the Triumphal Arch of the New Palace, 1829. Cat. No. 85

(above left) J. Gillray, *Political Ravishment*, 1797. Cat. No. 61
(left) 'Paul Pry' William Heath, *Monster Soup*, 1828. Cat. No. 103

'Q in the Corner' George Cruikshank
London 1792–1878 London

81
Nashional Taste!!!

Coloured etching, 34.5 × 24.5 cm
Published by G. Humphrey, 24 St. James's Street, 7 April 1824
London, Guildhall Library, Corporation of London

Literature: George 1952, Vol. 10, p. 414, No. 14644; Pückler Muskau 1957, p. 38; Summerson 1980, pp. 156–83

Prince Pückler Muskau felt Britain was much indebted to John Nash, the architect improving the West End of London. Nevertheless, in his opinion, it could not be denied that Nash buildings were 'a jumble of every sort of style' and one ought not 'to look too nicely into details'. 'The church [All Souls Langham Place], for instance, which serves as a *point de vue* to Regent Street, ends in a ridiculous spire . . . There is an admirable caricature in which Mr. Nash, a very small shrivelled man, is represented booted and spurred riding spitted on the point of the spire.'

In parliament H. G. Bennett demanded how much All Souls church 'this mass of deformity' he called it – had cost. He was ready to subscribe to the cost of its demolition. Nash, when he saw 'Q in the Corner's' caricature, exclaimed to his assistants, 'See gentlemen, how criticism has exalted me!' **RH**

Augustus Charles Pugin
France 1762–1833 London

82
Buckingham Palace, the front, 1827

Pen and ink and watercolour with white
heightening, 20.6×40.3 cm
London, The Museum of London
Inv. No. A8087

John Nash's Buckingham Palace was not a
new building but the amplification of Buckingham House, where George III had lived in
modest state since the 1760s. George IV, un-
challenged as the world's most powerful
monarch in the 1820s and the first Hanoverian
king of Great Britain to take an interest in the
arts, wanted something superior to his existing
seat, Carlton House. But he proved unable to
brief his architect with precision, in part
because of his captious personality, in part
because the status of a palace in a parliamentary monarchy was doubtful. Work started in
1825 and was not complete when the king died
in 1830. Its extravagance (£576,353 had been
spent) infuriated parliament and led to several
financial investigations and Nash's disgrace.

Dissatisfaction with the palace's architecture focused on the ceremonial front facing St.
James's Park. It is depicted here by Nash's
occasional assistant and delineator, Augustus
Pugin, in its first form of 1825–28. Its disconcerting staccato quality derives from the artic-
ulation of the Regent's Park terraces. Nash
himself admitted disappointment with the
boxy projecting wings. These were reconstructed in 1828–30 to a uniform height, while
at the entrance to the forecourt Nash added
the grand Marble Arch. This afterthought was
an experimental venture intended to test the
suitability to London's atmosphere of Carrara
marble, as championed by the sculptor
Chantrey.

The watercolour was engraved by Wallis for
the 1828 *Stationers' Almanack*, published by J.
Robins and Sons. **AS**

Thomas Higham
1796–1844

83
Buckingham Palace from the back, 1831

Engraving, hand-coloured, 21.6×40.7 cm
Published by J. Robins, *Stationers'
Almanack*, 1831
London, The Museum of London
Inv. No. 35.97

82

83

Buckingham Palace had virtues to compensate
for its architectural vices. It was planned
round the old Buckingham House with skill as
well as Nash's habitual haste, so as to incorporate processional routes of dignity and
variety. Nash, seventy-three when work
began in 1825, designed all the structures himself, using hidden iron with a freedom that
worried rivals but could not ultimately be
faulted. He also expended effort to create
Greco-Italianate and Louis-Seize interiors of
genuine grandeur. These were an important
testing ground for the development of the
English decorative arts.

The garden side of the palace, faced like the
whole of the building in the fashionable Bath
stone, never attracted the violent attacks reserved for the front. It survives in essentials,
though the central dome has been reduced in
height and the irregularity of the roof-line
muted by a continuous attic. Its stylistic
ancestry lies in pre-Revolutionary France,
Nash and George IV being both knowledgeable admirers of Parisian architecture. **AS**

'Paul Pry' William Heath
1795–1840 London

84
John Bull & the Arch-itect Wot Builds
the Arches – &c – &c – &c – &c

Coloured etching, 23×33 cm
Published by T. McLean, 26 Haymarket, 5
June 1829
London, Guildhall Library, Corporation of
London
Literature: George 1954, Vol. 11, p. 159, No.
15794; Summerson 1980, pp. 156–83

John Nash, wearing a mason's apron and
carrying a trowel, is presented by the caricaturist as an illiterate but cunning artisan. He
stands in the front courtyard of a miniaturised
Buckingham House (later Palace), one wing
on either side and Marble Arch in front (its
position before being moved to Hyde Park).
John Bull on the right scrutinises a long scroll

84

The Duke of Wellington, at this date prime Minister, stands outside his home, Apsley House, looking towards Decimus Burton's triumphal arch, erected here in 1828. Apsley House, refaced with stone in 1828, is covered in scaffolding. In the background is Buckingham Palace, then being rebuilt by John Nash, and Windsor Castle, also being rebuilt by Sir Jeffry Wyatville. Wellington holds a candlestick on which there is a saveall, a device for burning every bit of a candle and wasting nothing. Above it is a ducal coronet and from this protrudes a vice which holds the lighted candle. The duke is about to extinguish it with his hat.

The caricature draws attention to building extravagance and accuses Wellington of meanness. On 20 March 1828 Nash informed Wellington that the king wanted part of Buckingham Palace to be demolished and replaced by a new plan. Wellington refused. **RH**

on which appears many times the word 'Commission'. Quizzing Nash he says, 'Here's a charge for building the Wings.' Nash: 'Yes – that ere's all right.' John Bull: 'Here is also a charge for pulling down wings.' Nash: 'Yes – them ere was all wrong.' John Bull: 'Then there's a charge for building them up again.' Nash: 'Yes that ere's all right.' John Bull: 'But the Bill is more than double the Estimate.' Nash: 'Yes that eres always wrong – we never minds no Estimates.' **RH**

Marble Arch, moved to its present site at Cumberland Gate near Speakers' Corner in 1850, originally formed the east entrance to Buckingham Palace. It is an imitation of the Arch of Constantine in Rome. On top of it Nash planned to erect the statue of George IV by Sir Francis Chantrey which is now to be found in Trafalgar Square. The artist, however, has placed a knock-kneed and destitute John Bull there, dressed in a clown's outfit and with a fool's cap on his head. In the background is the new Buckingham Palace. On the pediment are the figures of Lady Conyngham (the king's mistress), the Duke of Wellington (prime minister), and Robert Peel (home secretary). **RH**

86

Artist unknown

85 *(illus. p. 280)*
An Appropriate Emblem for the Triumphal Arch of the New Palace – Dedicated to the Poor – Pennyless – Priest-Ridden and Paralysed John Bull.

Coloured etching, 34 × 24 cm
Published by S. W. Fores 41 Piccadilly, August 1829
London, Guildhall Library, Corporation of London
Literature: George 1954, Vol. 11, pp. 184–85, No. 15850; Summerson 1980, pp. 156–83

'Paul Pry' William Heath
1795–1840 London

86
The Saveall or Economy

Coloured etching, 35 × 24 cm
Published by T. McLean 26 Haymarket, *c.* 1828
London, Guildhall Library, Corporation of London
Literature: George 1954, Vol. 11, pp. 42–43, No. 15563

Artist unknown

87
Perspective of Hyde Park Corner, Arch and Screen, *c.* 1827

Watercolour, 24 × 40.5 cm
London, British Architectural Library, Drawings Collection, Royal Institute of British Architects
Inv. No. XOS/D/5
Exhibitions: Royal Academy, 1827, No. 917
Literature: Summerson 1945, Plate 50; Richardson ed. 1972, Vol. 'B', p. 147

For some time before 1800 it was generally accepted that the Hyde Park Corner, where the eastern tip of Hyde Park adjoins the western tip of Green Park, formed the most important entry to London. As early as the 1770s distinguished architects like Robert Adam, and subsequently Jeffry Wyatt and John Soane, made designs for a grand entrance archway. The prestige of the area was further enhanced by Nash's transformation of Buckingham House into Buckingham Palace.

In the mid 1820s, when the Office of Woods and Forests decided to embark on a general programme of London improvements, Decimus Burton was employed to enrich the setting of Buckingham Palace with suitable gateways and lodges for Hyde Park. In 1825 he submitted his scheme for Hyde Park Corner. At the principal south-west entrance to Hyde Park and immediately adjoining the Duke of Wellington's Apsley House was to be a long Ionic screen with central and subsidiary arches. On axis across the public road was to be a grand triumphal arch based on the Roman Arch of Titus and leading to the Green Park and Buckingham Palace. Both screen and arch (called at different times the Pimlico Arch, the George IV Arch, the Wellington Arch or the Constitution Arch) were finished by 1827.

Although it boasted a carved Parthenon frieze carved by John Henning junior, the other sculptural ornaments proposed for both the screen and the arch and shown in this perspective were never executed. **NB**

87

Richard Morris
fl. 1820–1840

88
Panoramic View round the Regent's Park

Coloured aquatint, 10×569 cm
Published by R. Ackermann, 96 Strand, 1831
London, Guildhall Library, Corporation of London
Literature: Hyde 1985, pp. 148–49

This 360-degree panoramic view around Regent's Park shows all the Nash terraces, the Colosseum (Cat. Nos. 184), St. Katharine's Hospital and the other buildings situated on the perimeter. Foreground staffage includes a showman with performing dogs, a May Day Jack-in-the-Green, begging sailors pulling a model of their ship, figures on stilts, King William and Queen Adelaide riding in an open carriage, an invalid in a bath chair and Steam

Washing Company vehicle with baskets of washing. (Steam washing had only recently been introduced.)

The panorama was issued, like the example exhibited, folded in a portfolio. It was also issued wound on to a roller in a varnished canister, in which form it is referred to in contemporary advertisements as a 'Tonbridge case'. **RH**

Artist unknown

89
Plan of Regent's Park, 1837

Pen and ink and watercolour, 80×73 cm
London, Public Record Office
Inv. No. MPEE 135

88

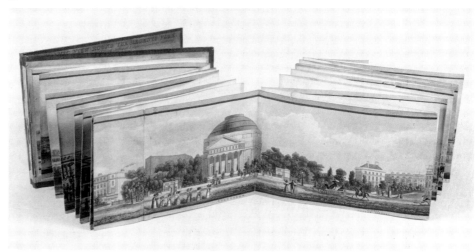

The development of the Regent's Park was guided by twin purposes: to exploit with speculative residential development the vacant land of the old Marylebone Park, and to provide a suitable northern termination for the new Regent Street. The first was the original purpose, articulated by John Fordyce in the 1790s; the second was superimposed by John Nash on behalf of the Prince Regent.

In his first plan for the park made in 1811 Nash proposed the building of a royal pavilion or 'guinguette' fronting a formal basin in the northern part of the park, as well as quite intensive development, with terraces of houses on all sides and much building in the centre.

After a sticky start caused by the postwar slump in building, leases for building the terraces on the east, south and west sides were all taken up. Between 1819 and 1823 these terraces had been completed and a handful of private villas erected inside the park itself. Completed buildings are shown black on the plan. Many

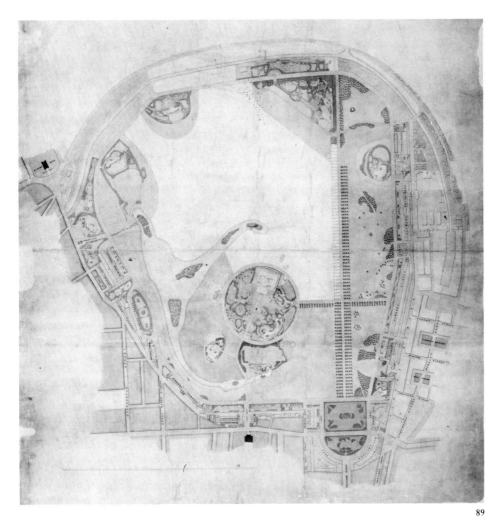

89

more villas, the northern terraces, a double circus in the centre of the park and the royal guingette are shown in red as still to be built, but by this date all momentum had been lost and none of these was ever begun. A lifting flap over the circus shows an alternative proposal for housing the new King's College, but this also proved speculative and the circus became a botanical garden. **NB**

Peter Nicholson
Prestonkirk, 1765–1844 Carlisle

90
New and Improved Practical Builder and Workman's Companion

Vol. 2, 1823, Vols. 1–3, 1837, 28×22 cm
London, British Architectural Library,
Royal Institute of British Architects
Literature: Colvin 1978, pp. 593–94;
Cruickshank and Burton 1990, pp. 105–07,
137, 148–49, 151, 181–85, 266

From the beginning of the eighteenth century a steady stream of books had appeared about architecture and building. Some, like James Gibbs' *Book of Architecture* or Isaac Ware's *Complete Body of Architecture* were by leading architects, but the great majority were 'pattern books' containing basic mechanical information for craftsmen about construction and proportion, with some designs in current styles for copying.

Between 1790 and 1840 there was a huge increase in the number of architectural publications. Most of these new books consisted only of a series of designs for houses and villas. Peter Nicholson was a Scottish carpenter turned architect with an engineering bent. Although his career as an architect was not markedly successful, he is coming to be recognised as one of the leading intellects behind nineteenth-century English building technologies. His books were a development from the older craft tradition.

The first to appear was *The New Carpenter's Guide* of 1792. Nicholson's two-volume *Architectural Dictionary*, which appeared between 1812–19, is the best published summary of contemporary building practice, but weak in those areas like painting and decoration where Nicholson did not have first-hand knowledge. It was eclipsed in popularity by Nicholson's *New and Improved Practical Builder and Workman's Companion*, first published in 1823.

This proved to be the best pattern book of the time, applicable to the four 'rates' of domestic housing, and went through six editions, the last in 1861. **NB**

John Linnell
London 1792–1882 Redhill

91 *(illus. p.278)*
Kensington Gravel Pits, 1811–12

Oil on canvas, 71.1×106 cm
Signed bottom left: J. Linnell
London, Tate Gallery
Inv. No. NO5776
Provenance: purchased at the Liverpool Academy 1813 by Henry Hole . . . Leggatt Brothers, London, from whom purchased by the Tate Gallery, 1947
Exhibitions: London, British Institution, 1813, No. 99 as The Gravel Pits; Liverpool, 1813, No. 75; London, Royal Academy, 1889, Cat. No. 44; Colnaghi, 1973, Cat. No. 18; Tate Gallery, 1973–74, Cat. No. 245
Literature: Story 1892, Vol. 1, pp. 85–86, Vol. 2, p. 160

Linnell grew up in London, and received his artistic training in the capital at the Royal Academy Schools and from John Varley, through whom he came to know Mulready. From 1808 to 1811 Linnell shared lodgings with Mulready at Kensington Gravel Pits, then a village on the site of what is now Notting Hill Gate in London. He made a number of detailed studies on walks in the area.

One of Linnell's most notable pictures from these excursions is this oil which shows the gravel pits themselves, which supplied the London building trade, and the men who worked there. To choose to depict such a scene of labour, and in such minute detail, went against what normally appealed to collectors and when the picture was first shown at the British Institution it failed to attract a buyer, much to Linnell's irritation. Under these circumstances he felt than the Institution itself should have purchased the picture.

Linnell had a long and prosperous career, although he was never to become a Royal Academician despite numerous attempts, a testimony perhaps to his uncompromising character rather than to his artistic prowess. **RU**

George Cruikshank
London 1792–1878 London

92
London Going Out of Town – or – The March of Bricks & Mortar!, 1829

Etching, 21.5×29.2 cm
London, The Museum of London
Inv. No. NN
Literature: Cohn 1924, No. 180; George
1954, Vol. 11, p. 240, No. 15977

Perhaps the most famous satire on the early
nineteenth-century expansion of London is
George Cruikshank's 1829 view of suburban
brickfields, published in the second part of the
artist's *Scraps and Sketches.* Cruikshank lived
in the northern suburb of Islington which was
developing fast in the 1820s, and he doubtless
drew what he saw, but the location is a composite, with the smoke-begrimed dome of St.
Paul's and the rural heights of Hampstead in
symbolic not actual relation.

Leaving satire aside, the drawing gives a
detailed picture of the brickmaking and
house-building processes: earth is being dug
in the foreground and fresh-moulded clay
bricks set to dry out in straw-covered rows;
ash for mixing with the brick earth is being
sifted in the middle ground and the kilns firing
the bricks belch smoke in the background.
The pits formed by brick digging were filled
with domestic rubbish and after a (short)
period rows of houses were erected over this
made-up ground, supported on brick vaults
with the streets between then made up with
yet more rubbish.

This smelly and disruptive process was continuous, except in times of slump. 1829 was a
slump year and the rows of unlet and collaps-
ing houses are a reminder that such sights were
commonplace when the market was flat. **NB**

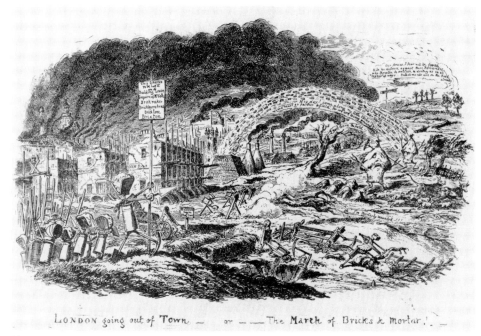

LONDON going out of Town — or — The March of Bricks & Mortar!

92

Michael Searles
1750–1813

93
Elevation and plans for a House for Mr Barton, *c.* 1792

Pen and coloured washes, 25.5×26.5 cm
British Architectural Library, Drawings
Collection, Royal Institute of British
Architects
Inv. No. K6/41 [1]
Literature: Richardson ed. 1976, Vol.S, No.
41 [1]; Worsley 1991, p. 144

Michael Searles followed his father's profession as a surveyor, but by the 1790s he was
regularly calling himself 'architect' and was
evidently an able designer. The great bulk of
his work was middle-class housing, whether
in terraces, individual small houses or villas,
and most of these buildings were in south
London or the southern suburbs. Mr Barton,
for whom Searles designed this house in the
1790s, was a trademan, a size maker. His product, used in house decorating and gilding,
was obtained by boiling down animal bones.
Bone boiling produced unpleasant smells and
was classed as a 'noxious trade', to be excluded
from good residential areas and exiled to the
working suburbs like King's Cross, or Bermondsey south of the Thames. The intended
location of this building – which was to contain a workshop as well as living accommodation – is unknown, but it was probably in Searles' usual south London theatre of operations.
The house conforms to the fourth 'rate' – with
a basement, two principal storeys and garret
rooms in the roof. The plan shows the two
upper floors. Attached to the garret plan is a
cross-section of the timber structure of the tall
'M'-shaped mansard roof, resting on a timber
tie-beam. Placing the main entrance to the side
gave more space on the ground floor by
obviating the front hallway, and this was a
common suburban arrangement; but in
central areas frontage was too valuable to
waste on such things. **NB**

94
a) Elevation of houses in Surrey Square, 1795
Pen and ink and watercolour, 18×62 cm
Signed, dated and inscribed: M Searles
Surrey Square / Built 1795

b) Elevation of central houses in Surrey Square, 1795
Pen and ink and watercolour, 17.5×61.5 cm
Signed, dated and inscribed: M Searles
Surrey Square / Built 1795

British Architectural Library, Drawings
Collection, Royal Institute of British
Architects
Inv. Nos. K6/23 (23)
Literature: Richardson ed. 1976, Vol. S, p.
28, No. [23] 2–3

Surrey Square was a typical London speculative residential development. The land, off
the Old Kent Road, was owned by a family of
nurserymen who were keen to cash in on the
housing boom. They were members of the
Society of Friends and with financial assistance from their co-religionists, they built first
a terrace on the main street front in 1784. In
1792 the development continued, financed this
time by a consortium of building tradesmen,
including Michael Searles himself. Twenty-
nine more were built. They were of good size –
the second 'rate' – and all let quickly. In this
the speculators were lucky, for 1794 saw the
beginning of a major building slump.

Like many architects engaged on speculative house building, Searles tried to articulate
the long façades composed of uniform three-

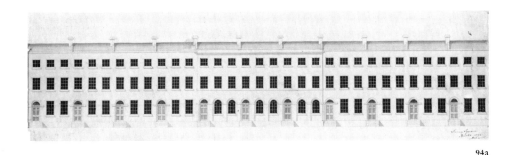

bay houses. In the shorter terraces, he differentiated the three centre houses by giving them round-headed windows and a roof parapet, though these modest gestures hardly outweighed the insistent rhythm of the chimney stacks and part-wall firebreaks rising through the roof, in accordance with the building acts.

For the main range of Surrey Square, Searles proposed a pedimented centre, and by skilful juggling of the component houses ensured that the front door of the central house should be in the centre. But in execution the architecture of the scheme fell victim to private interest. The pediment was built, but the doors and windows were placed to suit the convenience of the tenants with little regard for the niceties of Searles's design. **NB**

94b

95
Elevation of a house, the Paragon, Blackheath

Pen and ink and watercolour, 32 × 51.5 cm
Signed and inscribed: ft. M. Searles For
Paragon / Blackheath
London, British Architectural Library,
Drawings Collection, Royal Institute of
British Architects
Inv. No. K6/16 [4]
Literature: Richardson ed. 1976, Vol. S, p. 27, No. [16] 4

The Blackheath Paragon is a crescent-shaped terrace of fourteen semi-detached houses, linked by single-storey wings behind Doric colonnades. Michael Searles's client here was James Cator, a wealthy Quaker timber merchant who had purchased the Wricklemarsh estate at Blackheath in 1783. Cator approached Searles to provide a handsome suburban development to enhance the northern edge of his estate where it faced the public expanse of the heath.

The Blackheath Paragon was begun in 1794 but stopped after two houses because of the building slump which made Searles bankrupt, and finished piecemeal with the last house finally occupied in 1806. In this case, the owner bought back the leases granted to Searles to ensure that there would be no deviation from the agreed scheme. The houses of the Paragon were very large, with five reception rooms on the ground floor and four bedrooms on each upper floor; they were also provided with water-closets as standard. The original tenants were all wealthy and included a solicitor, tea merchant, Oporto merchant, insurance broker and ship owner. **NB**

95

Artist unknown

96
Houses in Woburn Place, Russell Square, *c.* 1810

Pencil, pen and watercolour, 64×78 cm
London, Trustees of Sir John Soane's
Museum
Inv. No. 76.4.9
Literature: Cruickshank and Burton 1990

In 1800 the Duke of Bedford finally decided to
quit the old family mansion of Bedford House
in Bloomsbury and to develop the site of the
building and its grounds with superior private
houses. The layout was to be a formal grid, relieved by two garden squares. The Bedford
Estate office had gained experience of such developments with the building of Bedford
Square in 1770s and took the same approach
here. House plots were leased singly or in
groups to builders or contractors, who agreed
to follow the elevations and the standards of
construction imposed by the estate.

By far the most important of the contractors
was James Burton (1761–1837). Most of the
terraces had the tall, plain, stock brick fronts
typical of eighteenth-century London terraces, but there is some indication that Burton
himself designed the more elaborate elevations
in Russell Square, and these first 'rate' houses
in Woburn Place were also his work.

This coloured perspective drawing was
made to illustrate Sir John Soane's Royal
Academy lectures on architecture, but never
used. In his lectures Soane vigorously attacked
both leasehold development and speculative
buildings for their degrading effect on public
architecture; perhaps his perspective was intended to accompany one of his attacks. **NB**

96

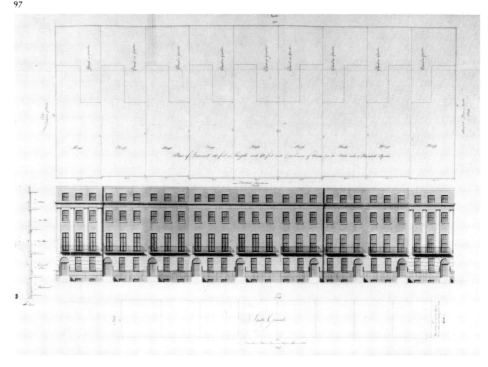

97

97
Contract for building the south side of Tavistock Square, lease and elevation, Mr. Cubitt's part, 30 April 1821

Paper, 57×108 cm
Woburn, The Marquess of Tavistock and the
Trustees of the Bedford Estates
Literature: Hobhouse 1971, pp. 69–70

Tavistock Square was part of the Bedford
Estate redevelopment of Bloomsbury. The
east side of the square was built by James Burton in about 1800, but the deepening slump
after 1805 halted further work. It took fifteen
years for the market to revive and the 1820s
saw a second phase of development in

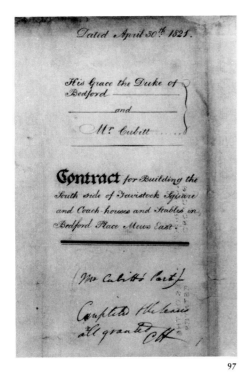

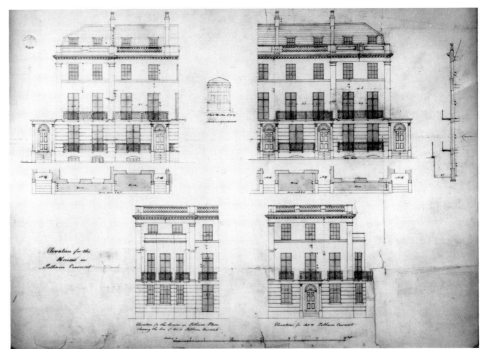

97

98

Bloomsbury. The principal contractor now was Thomas Cubitt (1788–1855), who is generally regarded as the pioneer of the large building firm. Instead of sub-contracting the building of houses to individuals, Cubitt maintained a large permanent staff of all sorts of building tradesmen based at his London yard – a system which gave him direct quality control. His architect brother Lewis provided designs where needed.

In April 1821 Cubitt contracted to build the south side of Tavistock Square. Attached to the lease from the estate stipulating plot sizes and standards of materials, is an elevation of the proposed new house fronts, almost certainly drawn by Lewis Cubitt and complementing the fronts of the square's eastern side built by Burton twenty years earlier. **NB**

George Basevi
1794–1845 Ely

98
Elevations and plans for houses in Pelham Crescent, 1833

Pen and wash, 32 × 96.5 cm
London, British Architectural Library,
Drawings Collection, Royal Institute of
British Architects

Inv. No. E6/12
Provenance: on permanent loan from the Trustees of Smith's Charity Estate, Chelsea
Exhibitions: London, Heinz Gallery, 1991
Literature: Stroud 1959; Richardson ed. 1972, Vol. 'B', p. 60, Fig. 42; Worsley 1991, pp. 136–37

The development in the late 1820s of the Belgravia district on land belonging to the Grosvenor Estate near the new Buckingham Palace sparked off much other development on the west side of London. One of the architects employed in Belgravia was George Basevi who designed the houses in Belgrave Square. Basevi was a favoured pupil of Sir John Soane, and his education in Soane's office had been enriched by three years travelling in Italy, Greece and Turkey.

In 1829 he was appointed as the salaried surveyor to the Smith's Charity Estate, and laid out ground belonging to the charity in Kensington with a considered development including both shops and houses. Basevi was continuing the best tradition of estate development, on the accepted principles set out in 1790 by S. P. Cockerell in a report on the Foundling Estate. The houses had conventional plans, but Basevi articulated the standard London house front with pilasters, cornices, balconies and rustication. In this he may have been influenced by Soane's well-known vilification of bald speculative houses. One noticeable feature is the use of large-paned casements or French windows for the principal rooms, marking the contemporary improvements in glass production. **NB**

Attributed to William Lake Price
1810–1891

99
North-West View of St. Pancras Church, c. 1822

Watercolour, 64 × 84.5 cm
Glasgow, Gavin Stamp
Exhibitions: London, Barbican Art Gallery, 1984, p. 31, Cat. No. 20
Literature: Britton and Brayley 1825, pp. 145–66; Lee 1976, pp. 1922

Sir John Summerson refers to St. Pancras as 'the parish church, *par excellence*, of Regency England'. It was certainly the most expensive. The status symbol of a rich and rapidly expanding parish, it took over from a small worn-out village church. Prominently sited on the important New Road at the edge of the built-up area, it soon attracted good houses around it. Its cost, some £90,000 all told (most of which came from parish rates), could therefore be seen as an investment which would return in the form of high pew rents.

A competition for the church was held in 1818 and won by the local architects William and Henry William Inwood, father and son. The exuberant Greek dress of their design, clothing an orthodox plan-form, came soon after the British government's acquisition of the Phigaleian and Elgin Marbles, and was to be copied in many London churches of the 1820s. In 1819 H. W. Inwood went to Athens 'for the express purpose of making drawings from the Erectheum and the Temple of the Winds to complete the design'. Hence the elaborate Attic archaeology of the church's external detail, as built in 1819–22. Most spectacular were the caryatids bearing the entablature of the projecting vestries, which doubled as entrances to the burial vaults. These were adapted from the Erectheum caryatids, and were made of the sculptor J. C. F. Rossi's patent terracotta on a cast-iron frame.

The splendour of St. Pancras New Church gratified many, but others found it secular and meretricious. The *News* called it 'a very classical, ornamental, Grosvenor-square-like, kind of edifice; with pews well carpeted, pulpits French polished, fanciful green pillars, and windows like those of a conservatory. It is a very elegant sort of place for a very elegant sort of a party: it will do very well to read prayers in; and would be no bad place in summer to sip lemonade or punch *à la romain*; but it has little of the appearance, and nothing of the arrangement, which fitness and (we think) policy should have given to a parish church.'
AS

99

George Scharf
Mainburg 1788–1860 London

100
Design for the Westminster Life and British Fire Office, Strand, by Charles Robert Cockerell (1788-1863), 1831

Pen, pencil and watercolour, 54×39.5cm
British Architectural Library, Drawings Collection, Royal Institute of British Architects
Inv. No. J10/23B
Provenance: presented by the daughters of F. P. Cockerell in 1930–32
Exhibitions: London, Royal Academy, 1832, No. 985; Royal Institute of British Architects, 1984; Heinz Gallery, 1991
Literature: Worthington 1932, p. 270; Young ed. 1934, p. 180; Ferriday ed. 1963, p. 114; Mordaunt Crook 1968, Plate 42; Richardson ed. 1972, Vol. C-F, p. 32; Stamp 1982, Fig. 26; Worsley 1991

One of the new London building types of the early nineteenth century was the purpose-built office block – as opposed to a warehouse – intended for occupation either by a single commercial concern or by several.

Charles Robert Cockerell's building for the combined company was his first commercial work and one whose success led to his appointment in 1833 as architect to the Bank of England in succession to Sir John Soane. The office was built on a rising corner site at the

western extremity of Nash's West Strand improvements. Cockerell's first design was not unlike the rather flat neo-Greek buildings of Nash and Decimus Burton, though faced all in stone and not stucco. In his final revised design the office was given the consequence of a small temple – a synthesis of Greek and Palladian classicism, enlivened by sculptural decoration. The Westminster Life office was widely admired by contemporaries; it was demolished in 1907. **NB**

100

Francis Edwards
London 1784–1857 ?London

101 *(illus. p. 290)*
a) Elevation of the river front of the Storehouse Building at the Lion Brewery, Belvedere Road, Lambeth, 1836

Pen and watercolour, 36×52 cm
Inscribed: notes on details

b) Transverse section, 1836
Pen and watercolour, 36×52 cm
Inscribed: notes on details

London, British Architectural Library, Drawings Collection, Royal Institute of British Architects
Inv. Nos. J8/9 [2-3]
Exhibitions: London, Heinz Gallery, 1991
Literature: Taylor 1968, Plates 12–13; Richardson 1972, Vol. C-F, p. 103, Nos. 23; Worsley 1991, p. 159, Nos. 137–8

The Lion Brewery stood on the south bank of the Thames where now stands the Royal Festival Hall. In 1836 the north bank was occupied by Fowler's Hungerford Market (Cat. No. 116) and the Adam brothers' splendid Adelphi development. Their presence may have caused Edwards to give his brewery storehouse a handsome Palladian front. There was nothing new about giving an ornamental front to a purely commercial building but the Lion Brewery is a good example of the increasing employment of architects for work

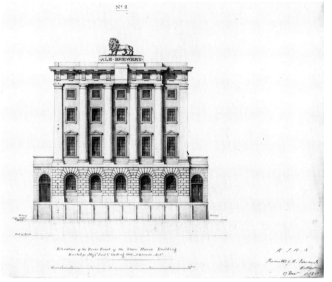

101a

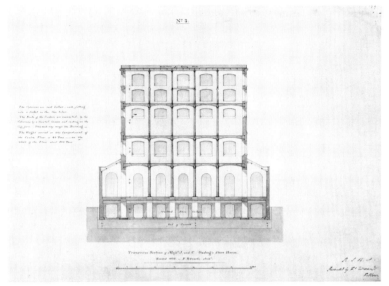

101b

which a generation before would have been entrusted to millwrights or builders.

The principal ornament of Edwards' façade was the great lion on the parapet, made of Coade stone, a patent terracotta-like material produced in a large factory owned by Eleanor Coade only a short distance upstream.

The architect's cross-sectional drawing shows that while the external wall of the store-house were brick (stuccoed), the internal structure of columns and horizontal girders were all of cast iron. London warehouse designers were generally more conservative than the cotton millers of the north-west, where iron-framing was pioneered, and the majority of London warehouses had timber internal frames until the 1860s. In this case, iron might have been used to reduce the weight on the river-bank soil as much as to reduce flammability. As in many breweries, the roof was made to serve as a huge water tank, principally to supply the beer-making process carried on in other buildings, but also to provide further insurance against fire. **NB**

URBAN INFRASTRUCTURE

The ever-growing city strained the traditional servicing patterns to breaking point. The old systems were expanded and new methods explored to provide water, drainage, lighting, heating and food for the population. Transport into, out of and across the city was facilitated by means of road, bridge and canal construction, and by improved horse drawn and patent steam-driven carriages.

George Scharf
Mainburg 1788–1860 London

102 (illus. p. 321)
The Laying of the Water-Main in Tottenham Court Road, 1834

Watercolour over pencil, 25 × 44.3 cm
Signed and dated: G. Scharf del 1834.
Tottenham Ct. Road
London, Trustees of the British Museum
Inv. No. 1862-6-14-308
Provenance: from a collection of the artist's works purchased from his widow, 1862
Exhibitions: London, British Museum, 1985, Cat. No. 148c, Plate 105

From the beginning of the seventeenth century London had enjoyed an excellent water supply. In the early nineteenth century, the capital was supplied by eight private companies of varying size, each having a monopoly in its area. One of the largest was the New River Company which supplied central and north London, including the Tottenham Court Road district, from its reservoirs at Sadler's Wells. The main pipes were laid under principal streets and the owners of adjacent properties paid for a connection, or not, as they chose. There were continual protests about the charges, and many preferred to draw their water from wells, or from public pumps.

In the eighteenth century most main pipes were of wood; they leaked, could not with-stand anything more than negligible water pressure and were only filled intermittently. These leaks caused havoc with roads and pavements and in 1817 the Metropolitan Paving Act ordained that henceforward all new water pipes should be of iron, which dramatically improved the water pressure and supply. In this drawing, a large cast-iron main is being drilled for the connection to a private supply.

Scharf had studied the relatively new art of lithography before leaving Munich and having settled in London in 1816, became well known for his precise illustrations of scientific and antiquarian subjects, although he never made more than a modest living. But his views of London life and topography provide a unique record of a great city. **NB and LS**

'Paul Pry' William Heath
c. 1790–1840

103 *(illus. p. 280)*
Monster Soup commonly called Thames Water, being a correct representation of that precious stuff doled out to Us!!!, 1828

Etching, hand-coloured, 25.5×37 cm
London, Guildhall Library, Corporation of London
Literature: George 1954, Vol. 11, pp. 44–45, No. 15568

In 1827 the social reformer Sir Francis Burdett (Cat. No.) presented a petition to the House of Commons declaring that 'the water taken from the river Thames at Chelsea, for the use of the inhabitants of the western part of the Metropolis [is] charged with the contents of the great common sewers, the draining from dunghills, and laystalls, the refuse of hospitals, slaughter-houses, colour, lead and soap works, drug mills and manufactories, and with all sorts of decomposed animal and vegetable substances, rendering the said water offensive and destructive to health.'

Heath's savage caricature, with its passing reference to the fashionable enthusiasm for the technology of natural science, reflects the distaste of the wider public for the brown and fetid fluids supplied by the Thames-side water companies, to whom the print was sarcastically dedicated. In response to such protests James Simpson, chief engineer of the Chelsea waterworks, constructed in 1828, over about an acre of land, the first large slow sand filter bed. This method of purification was eventually adopted by every water company in Britain. **NB**

George Cruikshank
London 1792–1878 London

104
Salus Populi Suprema Lex, 1832

Etching, 49×24 cm
London, Guildhall Library, Corporation of London
Literature: Reid 1871, No. 1464; Cohn 1924, No. 1952; George 1954, Vol. 11, pp.583–84, No. 16956

The steady improvement in London's water supply from about 1815 put increasing strain on its sewage system. This was under the control of several independent commissions of

A PEEP AT THE GAS LIGHTS IN PALL-MALL.
105

sewers established in the sixteenth century to dispose of surface water, largely by existing watercourses draining into the Thames. Open streams like the Walbrook first became open sewers and were eventually covered in because of the stench. It was expressly forbidden to put solid waste into the sewers, and all liquid waste was meant to pass through an intercepting trap, but plenty of solid filth entered the system. Contaminated water from intercepting traps and cesspools also seeped into the water courses and thus into the river from which several water companies drew their supply. In this satire, John Edwards, owner of the Southwark Waterworks, poses as Britannia or Neptune – 'Sovereign of the Scented streams' – crowned with a chamber-pot, seated on a close stool which stands in turn on a cesspool which doubles as the water-intake for his south London customers.

104

ROYAL ADDRESS

By the 1830s the link between polluted water and poor health had at last been perceived and the need for the reforms advised by the several royal commissions was reinforced by the cholera epidemics of 1832 and 1839, resulting in the Public Health Act of 1848. **NB**

George Moutard Woodward and Thomas Rowlandson
Derby 1760--1809 London, London 1756–1827 London respectively

105
A Peep at the Gas Light in Pall Mall, 1809

Etching, partly coloured, 24.3×34 cm,
Published 22 December 1809
London, Trustees of the British Museum
Inv. No. 1868-8-8-7894
Literature: George 1947, Vol. 8, pp. 882–83, No. 11440

The first public display of gas lighting in London took place in 1807, when Frederick Winsor, a flamboyant Moravian, organised an experimental scheme to light part of Pall Mall, nominally in celebration of the birthday of the Prince of Wales, but more probably to advertise the company he had formed with £50,000 of investors' money, all of which was lost.

Curious spectators are shown examining the newly installed gas lamps directly outside

GAS LAMP-LIGHTERS
POEM.

The Gasometer.

Drawing the Retort.

GAS

WORKS

106

108

Carlton House, the Prince's splendid London residence; the house on the far left has a door plaque inscribed 'Sherry', for Richard Brinsley Sheridan, the playwright and impresario who was one of the Prince's closest friends. Reactions to the gas lamps range between naive appreciation on the part of a country bumpkin, the pious reaction of a Quaker, '. . . what is this to the *inward* light?', and the concern expressed by a prostitute who fears that 'if this light is not put a stop to – we must give up our business. We may as well shut up shop.' As her prospective client comments, 'True my dear not a dark corner to be got for love or money.'

The chief impetus for the introduction of gas lighting in the succeeding ten to fifteen years was in fact to reduce the incidence of street crime; domestic use followed. **LS**

Charles Papendick
d. 1835 London

106
Illustrations of Street Lights, 1819

Pencil and watercolour, 93 × 62.5 cm
Dated: 4 November 1819
London, Trustees of Sir John Soane's Museum
Inv. No. 76.3.13

From the middle of the eighteenth century the streets of central London were lighted by oil lamps erected by the parish authorities and paid for out of the rates. In most districts this public lighting was supplemented by lamps at the entrance to private houses. Oil lamps were self-contained and were often mounted on buildings. But within twenty years of gas lights being first demonstrated in 1807 by Mr

Winsor in Pall Mall, they had displaced oil lamps in most central districts. As gas lights required a piped supply, they were usually mounted on metal posts standing on the pavement.

This page, prepared but not used for Sir John Soane's Royal Academy lectures, contains a miscellany of designs – three gas lampposts and two oil lights. The large suspended oil lamp is probably Parisian; the rest could be found in London's streets. **NB**

Richard Dighton
London 1796–1880 London

107

a) A London Nuisance, Pl[at]e. 3rd.
One of the Advantages of Oil over
Gas

b) A London Nuisance, Pl[at]e. 5th.
One of the Advantages of Gas over
Oil

Etchings, 26×21 cm, 26×22 cm respectively
Published by Thos. McLean, 26 Haymarket,
after 1821
London, Guildhall Library, Corporation of
London
Literature: George 1952, Vol. 10, p. 268,
Nos. 14291, 14293 respectively

These come from a set of six prints dealing
with London nuisances. In plate three, a lamp
lighter carelessly tilts his can and pours oil
over a fashionably dressed pedestrian man. In
plate five, a fashionably dressed lady pedestrian and a small boy are hurled backwards by
the force of a gas explosion in the window of a
chemist's shop. The horrified chemist looks
through the broken panes of the shop door.
The other prints in the series deal with snow,
passing a mud cart, colliding with a porter
who is carrying a chest of drawers, and bump-
ing into the projecting handles of a meat tray
carried on a butcher's boy's shoulder – a pleasant way to lose an eye. **RH**

108
Gas Lamp-Lighter's Poem

Broadside, letterpress and woodcut,
49×37.5 cm
Printed and sold by Quick, 77 Great Saffron
Hill, 1820s
London, Guildhall Library, Corporation of
London
Inv. No. Broadside 1.74

Broadsides and smaller handbills were issued
by some tradesmen before Christmas to re-
mind customers to give them their traditional
gratuities. This example, with its bold woodcuts of the gasometer, drawing the retort, the
gas works and lighting the lamps (as well as
hinting at the dangers thereof) also serves as
propaganda in the cause of gas. The poem expresses the hope that: . . . amidst the merry
cheer/That makes this season of the year,/
You'll not forget the Gasmens' prayer,/That
in your bounty they may share,/Who labour
morning, noon, and night,/To furnish you
with extra light . . . **CF**

107 a

107 b

George Scharf
Mainburg 1788–1860 London

109
Navvies laying a Gas Main, 1834

Pencil, 23×13.9 cm
Signed and dated bottom right: G. Scharf
1834
London, Trustees of the British Museum
Inv. No. 1862-6-1-304*
Provenance: from a collection of the artist's
works purchased from his widow, 1862
Literature: Jackson 1987, pp. 70–71

By 1823, London had four private gas-supply
companies – The London Gas, Light and
Coke Company, the City of London Gas
Light Company, the South London Gas Light
and Coke Company, and the Imperial Gas
Light and Coke Company. Each company
had its own works for producing coal gas,
sited in peripheral areas like Bankside and St.
Pancras where transport (for the coal) was
good, land was cheap and the explosions
which were confidently expected would not
cause undue damage. Together, these four
companies had over 200 miles of gas mains
supplying 7,268 street lights and 61,203 private
lamps. Many of the latter were shop lights and
visitors to London were always impressed by
the brilliant show of the capital's shops.

There was at first a reluctance to use gas for
domestic lighting, either on grounds of the
safety risk or of the high cost. There were
some enthusiastic consumers, but both
candles and oil lamps continued to be the
mainstay of home lighting until the 1830s or
1840s. With the laying of gas mains, London's
principal streets began to assume their modern
character of service arteries with water pipes,
gas pipes and sometimes sewers jostling for
place beneath the road surface. What is surprising in this view is that the gas mains were
laid so near the surface; they must have
suffered constant displacement and leaks as a
result. **NB**

109

111

John Williams

110
An Historical Account of Sub-Ways in the British Metropolis, for the flow of Pure Water and Gas . . .

Published by Carpenter and Son and J.M. Richardson, 1828
Octavo, 21.5×14.5 cm
London, Guildhall Library, Corporation of London
Inv. No. SL 48.12
Provenance: presented by the author
Literature: Harrison 1971, p. 68; Trench and Hillman 1985, pp. 81–82

In dedicating this work to George IV, the author promised that the King's metropolitan improvements 'will be rendered not only complete, but will raise this Metropolis to an elevation of grandeur not attained even by Imperial Rome'. To prevent the disruption caused by the constant digging up of roads to lay and repair pipes, Williams' rational plan was to dig a vast trench in the middle of the roads, some 10 feet deep, and build a large dry tunnel with 5-foot-high walls and an arched roof in which all the gas and water pipes could be placed, with smaller tunnels at 20-foot intervals through which connections to the houses could be made. At the same time drains would be sunk from the tunnel to the sewers below, also for better access.

The scheme would stop the roads having to be dug up, since safe and ready access could now be gained through the tunnels. The companies could quickly stop any leak of water or escape of gas (and cut off the supply of tenants who did not pay); the decay of pipes through the pressure of the earth and damp would be curtailed, while on street level there would be improved water facilities for fire engines, and a reduction in the wear and tear to carriages and the injury of horses.

Williams first took out a patent on his scheme in 1822 and proceeded energetically to adopt the standard lobbying tactics of the day, involving the issue of prospectuses, public meetings and presentation of petitions to parliament. He formed a London Sub-Way Company in 1824, and this book was obviously intended as further propaganda for the cause, comprising mainly various prospectuses and correspondence and being sent to everyone whom Williams thought would be of influence: Thomas Telford's copy is the Institution of Civil Engineers. **CF**

Artist unknown

111
The Adelphi Wharf, c. 1810

Watercolour, 63.5×100 cm
London, The Museum of London
Inv. No. 86.148
Provenance: Anthony Dallas and Sons Ltd., 1986
Exhibitions: London, The Museum of London, 1987
Literature: Fox 1987, pp. 172–73, 262

Coal brought in ships from the north-east to the Thames was unloaded into lighters downstream from London Bridge, whence it could be distributed at wharves further upstream in water too shallow to take the larger boats. The spectacle of coal porters, carters and their teams of horses could be seen at many points along the river. But once the Adam brothers' scheme to use the arches below the Adelphi (constructed to counteract the slope from the Strand to the river) for storing government munitions had fallen through, they were leased to coal, builders' and wine merchants. The coal merchants Findlater and Ellis were, according to the London trade directories, joined by Pugh in 1810. Their wharf was variously described as Salisbury Wharf or Beaufort Coal Wharf, Strand.

Unusually for a topographical watercolour, the figures here are more than a token presence, with heavers breaking up the coal and bagging it on the lighters, before loading it on to carts which were then drawn through the arches into the Strand. Illicit scavengers pick up the loose coal from the foreshore. Labourers are also at work on the adjacent stores of timber, cut stone and cobbles. **CF**

John Augustus Atkinson
London *c.* 1775–*c.* 1833

112
A London Coal Cart, c. 1810

Watercolour, 26×36.9 cm
London, The Museum of London
Inv. No. 83.236
Provenance: Thomas Agnew and Sons Ltd., 1983
Exhibitions: London, Agnew, 1983, Cat. No. 11; The Museum of London, 1987
Literature: Fox 1987, pp. 172–73, 262

Atkinson's watercolour shows the last stage in the chain of coal delivery from the mines of the north-east to the homes of Londoners. The carter backs the horse up so that his cart is as close as possible to the coal hole, while his companion takes some refreshment from a pewter tankard before the work of shooting the coal into the cellar. The coal merchants Johnson and Horner were based – as inscribed on the cart – at the Adelphi Wharf, from around 1808 to 1818 according to the London trade directories.

The artist lived in St. Petersburg from 1784 to 1801 recording Russian life, and although on his return to England he exhibited principally history paintings and landscapes, he also executed a number of attractive genre watercolours of street traders and labourers. **CF**

112

London, Trustees of the British Museum
Inv. Nos. 1862-6-14-120, 122 respectively
Provenance: from a collection of the artist's
works purchased from his widow, 1862
Literature: Jackson 1987, pp. 44–45, illus-
trated

Scharf noted of the watercolour showing the
cow keeper's premises, 'This I drew in Golden
Lane in the City in order to compare it with
the elegant milk shop in the Quadrant, Piccadilly.' Much of the milk supplied in London
came from cows kept not in the country but in
the heart of the city, where the animals were
confined in stalls, exercised in backyards and
fed on hay (a boy here is bringing up a truss
from the cellar), grain and turnips. The milk
was then sold on the premises, as shown here,
together with eggs, butter and cream, or delivered by milkmaids to their customers; a
common complaint, however, was that the
milk was often adulterated by being diluted
with water in order to increase the retailer's
profit, many cow yards having water pumps
especially for this purpose.

The Westminster Dairy, situated in Nash's
Regent Street Quadrant, which had been built
only five years earlier, was an altogether smarter establishment than the City cow keeper's,
but may well have sold milk that was less
fresh, probably being dependent on supplies
from a dairy in the countryside just outside
London. **LS**

George Scharf
Mainburg 1788–1860 London

113
a) Cow Keeper, Golden Lane, 1825

Watercolour over pencil, 14 × 22.5 cm
Signed bottom left: G. Scharf del 1825

b) The Westminster Dairy, Regent Street, 1825

Watercolour over pencil, 22.7 × 13.8 cm
Signed bottom left: G. Scharf del 1825
Quadrant Regent Street and also inscribed
with a scale of measurement

113a

113b

117

A market established itself as an unplanned afterthought in the centre of London's first formal square, the Covent Garden piazza, in about the 1640s. By the late eighteenth century it was 'the greatest market in England for herbs, fruits and flowers', while the once-elegant piazza had turned into 'the great square of Venus' surrounded by 'open houses whose principal employment is to minister incitements to lust'.

In 1828–31 the freeholder, the 6th Duke of Bedford, brought in Charles Fowler (1792–1867) as architect-engineer and William Cubitt (1791–1863) as builder to reorder the overflowing market. Lewis shows their rebuilding half finished. The two arcaded granite and limestone ranges house covered shops for established retailers and wholesalers but the central avenue is still to come. Between the ranges was to be open space where small retailers, still littering the edges of the square in the painting, could pitch their stalls.

Fowler's rugged but technically assured building shows the compatibility of simple Greek Revivalism with the English tradition of industrial construction. It makes a striking counterpoint to the remnants of Inigo Jones's Piazza buildings around it. **AS**

M. Dubourg after
James Pollard
London 1792–1867 London

114 *(illus. p. 298)*
London Markets

Coloured aquatints, each 26 × 32 cm
Published by Edwd. Orme, Bond Street, corner of Brook Street, 10 May 1822
London, Guildhall Library, Corporation of London
Literature: Houfe 1990, pp. 60–61

These prints come from a set of four depicting different shops retailing food; the others show fish and poultry. The fruit and vegetable shop displays an impressive range of summer produce. Strawberries were brought to London from Shropshire and even Wales, and sold in small, distinctively shaped wicker 'pottles'. Most of the rest of the stock would have been grown in the extensive market gardens which surrounded the capital.

The butcher is prepared for Christmas sales. Note the label 'Duke of Bedford GRASS FED'. The 5th Duke of Bedford (1765–1802) was first president of the Smithfield Club, founded in 1798 to improve the breed for meat. He established a model farm at Woburn and was renowned for breeding and fattening cattle, as well as sheep breeding. He started exhibitions at Woburn of sheep shearing, which lasted for days, ended with prizes and ban-

quets, and attracted the whole of the agricultural world.

His brother, the 6th Duke (1766–1839), continued in his footsteps. He, too, was president of the Smithfield Club. He drained his land with the help of Telford and the Rennies and, as an enthusiastic naturalist, made valuable experiments concerning the nutritive effects of grasses. Under his direction George Sinclair (1786–1834) published *Hortus Gramineus Woburniensis* (1816). **CF**

Frederick Christian Lewis
London 1779–1856 Enfield

115
Covent Garden Market, c. 1829

Oil on canvas, 85 × 136 cm
Woburn, The Marquess of Tavistock and the Trustees of the Bedford Estates
Inv. No. 1518
Provenance: probably commissioned by the 6th Duke of Bedford
Exhibitions: London, The Museum of London, 1980
Literature: Scharf 1878, pp. 34–55, No. 41; Survey of London 1970, Vol. 36, pp. 135–37, 147–49

J. Harris after unknown artist

116
A View of the new Hungerford Market taken from the Terrace, 1834

Etching and aquatint, hand-coloured, 37.8 × 57.6 cm
Published by S. W. Fores, 41 Piccadilly, 1 January 1834
London, The Museum of London
Inv. No. A18111
Literature: Stamp 1986, pp. 58–70

Old Hungerford Market was a covered market built in the late seventeenth century near Charing Cross as a rival to Covent Garden. It was rebuilt at a cost of £210,000 by Charles Fowler in 1831–33. Fowler exploited the change in level by dividing the site into three rectangles, planning an upper and lower court on either side of the central market-hall. The lower court, shown here, was arranged on two levels; the lower storey was used for selling fish, the upper for fruit, flowers and vegetables. The open space of the lower court was covered over in 1834 with an innovatory freestanding metal roof of zinc supported on cast-iron columns.

However, the market was not a commercial success and was finally demolished in the early 1860s to make way for Charing Cross railway station. **CF**

115

W. Barnard after Dean Wolstenholme
Yorkshire 1757–1837

117
A Correct View of the Golden Lane Genuine Brewery

Mezzotint, 48×60 cm
Published by Dean Wolstenholme, 4 East Street, Red Lion Square, September 1807
London, The Museum of London
Inv. No. 91.16/2

Brewing was one of London's major industries and called for plant and equipment on such a scale that the breweries became one of the sights of London.

By 1807, the major establishments were producing around 1.3 million barrels (each of 36 gallons) of porter and some 70,000 barrels of ale. Porter – a malted liquor which combined the taste of ale, beer and a strong drink known as 'twopenny' – had become popular with labourers in the 1720s and quickly became the mainstay of London breweries.

The leading brewers were immensely

powerful men, often sitting as M.P.s and having the ability to raise investment funds from wealthy financiers, merchants and manufacturers. The outward show of their wealth was evident from the size of their breweries – of which they commissioned paintings and prints – and the large number of public houses they owned.

The work seen here was dedicated to 'Messrs Brown & Parry, & the patrons, and friends of the Golden Lane Brewery'. The dedication records a remarkable initiative by the brewer, William Brown, to establish a cooperative venture supported by many publicans, rather than a small number of wealthy individuals, as shareholders.

Brown and his supporters deliberately set out to undercut the large porter breweries by producing a beer that could be sold for a half-penny per quart cheaper. Although only of moderate size, Brown's brewery had a very powerful Boulton and Watt beam engine. By 1807 it was producing 125,654 barrels of porter and held fourth place in the league table of London breweries. The success, however, was short-lived and by 1815 output was down to 72,367 barrels. Brown and Co. appear to have ceased brewing at Golden Lane, in 1816. **CE**

Follower of Dean Wolstenholme
Yorkshire 1757–1837

118
Barclay and Perkins's Brewery, Park Street, Southwark, c. 1835

Oil on canvas, 50.3×64.7 cm
London, The Museum of London
Inv. No. A8069
Provenance: purchased from Leggatt brothers, 1912
Literature: Pückler Muskau 1827, pp. 106–07; Hayes 1970, pp. 192–93, No. 111, illustrated

The Anchor Brewery covering a 12-acre site (including that of Shakespeare's Globe Theatre) in Southwark was by the mid-nineteenth century the largest brewery in the world. During the eighteenth century the brewery had been owned by the Thrale family, friends of Dr. Johnson, until 1781 when it was sold to Robert Barclay of the Quaker banking family. Barclay swiftly appointed Thrale's manager, John Perkins, as partner and the business thrived. In his capacity as a beer brewer (courtesy of his being a

M. Dubourg after J. Pollard,
London Markets, 1822. Cat. No.
114

URBAN INFRASTRUCTURE

Meat Dish. Cat. No. 127

Vegetable Dish and Cover. Cat. No. 133

F. Chantrey, *John Rennie*, 1881. Cat. No. 145

Teutonic knight), Prince Pückler Muskau visited the brewery in July 1827 and was duly impressed: 'the vastness of its dimensions renders [it] almost romantic'. Everything was done by machinery set in motion by a single steam engine and an enormous chimney devoured the smoke of the whole establishment; 'a hundred and fifty horses, like elephants . . . are daily employed in carrying out the beer'.

Five years later, the brewery was greatly extended and modernised following a disastrous fire. The present view shows the entrance to the brewery in Park Street with the offices at the rear of the yard, the range housing the fermenting vessels to their right and on the street front, the great brewhouse, with eight arched windows and a suspension bridge that connected it with buildings across the street. **CF**

118

119
Model of a Rumford Stove

Iron, 61×61×30.5 cm
London, Royal Institution of Great Britain

Rumford proposed three separate improvements for domestic fireplaces: that the depth of the hearth should be lessened to bring the fire itself further into the room, that the sides of the chimney opening be splayed to allow heat to radiate sideways as well as forwards, and the chimney throat narrowed both to improve draught and to form a shelf at the base of the chimney flue to check descending currents of cold air. Rumford certainly drew on the ideas of his countryman, Benjamin Franklin, who had also made proposals to cure smoky chimneys, but he can take the credit for producing a thoroughly practical working solution which quickly passed into common use. This model was presumably made expressly for the Royal Institution as a demonstration piece. **NB**

James Gillray
London 1756–1815 London

120
The Comforts of a Rumford Stove, 1800

Etching, coloured, 25.5×20.7 cm (trimmed)
Published by H. Humphrey, 27 St. James's Street, 12 June 1800
London, Trustees of the British Museum
Inv. No. 1851-9-1-1035
Literature: George 1942, Vol. 12, pp. 635–36, No. 9565

Sir Benjamin Thompson, Count Rumford (1753–1814) was an American soldier of fortune, scientist and social improver. As a pro-British Tory he rose rapidly in the British army, but after the American Revolution he prudently moved to Bavaria. Here he undertook the reorganisation of the army and of the workhouse system and founded the English Garden in Munich, for which he was made a count of the Holy Roman Empire.

In 1795, he arrived in London and at once loosed a stream of pamphlets, of which one, *On Chimney Fireplaces*, proposed a remedy to the scourge of smoky and inefficient fireplaces which afflicted London houses. Rumford enjoyed the patronage of Lady Palmerston and his proposed improvements were widely taken up by fashionable English society. Rumford was particularly concerned with the efficient use of heat and light and went on to propose improvements to conventional English cooking arrangements, especially favouring the use of closed stoves over open fires.

Rumford accrued considerable wealth, with which he endowed research awards at both the Royal Society and the American Academy of Arts and Sciences at Boston. More significantly, he was the effective founder of the Royal Institution in Albemarle Street in 1800. The Institution was intended as 'a grand repository of all kinds of useful mechanical inventions' and also contained a lecture theatre and laboratory for 'teaching the applications of science to the useful purposes of Life'. Rumford intended the Institution to be for the educating of artisans and working men; in the event, it became a centre for the promotion of experimental science, with particular emphasis on heat and light (Cat. Nos. 196ff.). **NB**

120

George Scharf
Mainburg 1788 –1860 London

121
Jahrtags Procession der Kupferschmidte – und Messing Verzierung Arbeiter, London, 1831

Watercolour, 27×129 cm
London, Guildhall Library, Corporation of London

The braziers' elaborate and costly procession, with its extravagant costumes and bizarre accoutrements – made up largely of domestic brassware – would seem to have become an annual occasion. **RH**

Frederick Accum
Buckebourg, Westphalia 1769–1838 Berlin

122
Culinary Chemistry

Published by R. Ackermann, 101, Strand, 1821
Octavo, 19×12 cm
London, Guildhall Library, Corporation of London
Inv. No. S641
Provenance: T.H. Staples; presented by Mrs Staples, 1897

Accum published this pioneering work to explain the principles of cookery as a branch of chemical science, stating 'The subject may appear frivolous; but let it be remembered that it is by the application of the principles of philosophy to the ordinary affairs of life, that science diffuses her benefits, and perfects her claim to the gratitude of mankind.'

The book is also full of sound advice on the practice of cookery, containing a wide range of preserving recipes and issuing stern warnings on the dangers of using copper cooking utensils and the adulteration of foods. Accum had published a number of articles on the latter subject which are here appended, one entitled *There is death in the pot*. The illustration on the title page depicts the kitchen range which could be found in most ironmongers shops in London: with a roasting oven in the middle of the grate, the boiler on the right, the baking oven on the left, and a cast iron hearth. Figure (1) on the frontispiece shows a Dutch oven; figure (2) the type of range suitable for larger families with the hearth and boiler separate from the fireplace; figure (3) a steam preserving pan and figure (4) a coffee percolator, deemed by Count Rumford to be the best method for making coffee. **CF**

Copperware

123
a) Double-handled saucepan

Copper, H 15.4×D 31.2 cm
Mark: D W L 4 with coronet
London, The Museum of London
Inv. No. 50/81/134
Provenance: His Grace the Duke of Wellington

b) Boiling Pan

Copper, H 23.5×D 32.5 cm
Mark: D W L 2
London, The Museum of London
Inv. No. 50/81/3
Provenance: His Grace the Duke of Wellington

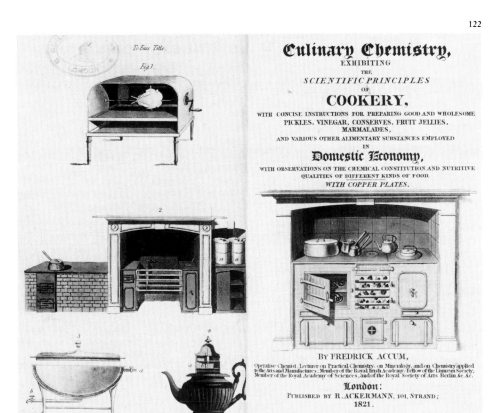

122

123a

123b

c) Jelly Mould

James Williams and Sons, London SW1
Copper, H 12.3 × D 13.7 cm
Mark: Crowned orb and '483'
London, The Museum of London
Provenance: National Domestic Service
Training College

The double-handled saucepan and boiling pan are part of a set of copperware used in the kitchens at Apsley House, the Duke of Wellington's London residence. The pots are engraved with the letter D W L standing for Duke of Wellington London and each pot is numbered so that it could be quickly returned after use to its place in the kitchen, the shelves of the dresser being similarly numbered.

Copperware was widely used for the preparation of food but Frederick Accum in *Culinary Chemistry* graphically highlights its dangers. Unless kept scrupulously clean and regularly tinned the food cooked and served in the vessels was liable to become tainted and the individual exposed to gradual poisoning. He lends support to his recommendations with a quotation from Dr. Kitchiner, a fellow author of cookery books, who warns 'if not kept nicely tinned, all your work will be in vain; the broths and soups will look green and dirty, and taste bitter and poisonous, and will spoiled both for the eye and palate . . . '

It was Dr. Kitchiner who urged James Gunter, the proprietor of Gunter's in Berkeley Square to write the *Confectioner's Oracle* (1830). Gunter's was, and remained throughout the nineteenth century, the fashionable caterer of the day, providing for any occasion from shooting parties and private dinners to balls and wedding feasts. The firm was celebrated for its turtle soup, made from turtles killed in Honduras, but its original shop sign was the Pot and Pineapple, and it was for his sweets and particularly his ices that Gunter was famous. Fashionable society thronged to Berkeley Square in the summer and it was a common sight to see ladies reclining in their carriages parked beneath the trees opposite Gunter's enjoying their ices – the most popular being agras or iced green grape. Jellies, set in elaborate and ornate moulds, were another favourite dessert of the period and in the *Confectioner's Oracle* Gunter gives a number of recipes in the section entitled Diaphanous Jellies. **EE**

George Scharf
Mainburg 1788–1860 London

124
The Artist's Kitchen in Francis Street, 1846

Watercolour over pencil, 24 × 36.7 cm
Signed and dated bottom left: G. Scharf del 1846
London, Trustees of the British Museum
Inv. No. 1862-6-14-80
Provenance: from a collection of the artist's works purchased from his widow, 1862
Literature: Jackson 1987, p. 8, illustrated

124

125

126

Following the demolition of the house in St. Martin's Lane where Scharf had lived since his arrival in England in 1816, the family – George and Elizabeth Scharf, her sister Mary and their two young sons – moved in 1830 to Francis Street on the east side of Tottenham Court Road, very near the British Museum. They were to live here until 1848 in a house built in 1772, with a view from its back windows of an old farmhouse which later became the site of the famous furnishing business of Heal's.

This watercolour was in fact painted 'from recollection whilst at Munich in 1846', according to a note Scharf later added to a preliminary pencil sketch he had made in 1843. The kitchen was a spacious, well-lit and well-equipped room to judge from this record of it, with a stone-flagged floor (there is a rug or perhaps an oil-cloth in the centre) and a capacious dresser, on which is displayed a large blue and white dinner service. This appears to be typical of the products made in vast numbers in the industrial Midlands – the 'Potteries' area around Stoke-on-Trent – in this period.

In 1836 Scharf had been commissioned by a leading Staffordshire potter, John Ridgway, to design a jug decorated with giraffes modelled in relief (the first giraffes in London Zoo had arrived earlier that year), and was offered as payment a tea or dinner service. Scharf wanted money, but perhaps the plates and dishes shown here were indeed from Ridgway's. Spode was another famous manufacturer producing wares of this type for a growing middle-class public, both at home and abroad.

The clock on the wall between the windows may have been German, a reminder of Scharf's homeland. The woman was perhaps Ellen, the family's maidservant for many years. **LS**

Spode

Josiah Spode (1733–1797) established his pottery manufactory in Stoke-upon-Trent in 1770. Just eight years later his son, Josiah II (1755–1827), opened premises in Fore Street, Cripplegate, in the City of London in order to trade in pottery. His business increased substantially after his father's development of the technique of transfer printing designs engraved on copper plates on to biscuit (unglazed) earthenware. This was in 1784, when the principal products were copies of Chinese blue and white landscapes, made to fill the market need for replacements which were increasingly difficult to obtain from Canton in China. The same year, William Copeland went to work for Spode II in London, becoming an equal partner in 1805 and sole administrator in 1812. His son, William Taylor Copeland (Lord Mayor of London 1835–36), became a partner in 1824 and sole owner in 1833 of both the London business and the Spode factory. From 1795 to 1849, the London warehouse was at number 5 Portugal Street, Lincoln's Inn Fields. The firm remained in the Copeland family until 1966. In 1970, in order to commemorate the founder, the name of the company was changed to Spode Limited.

Apart from the development of blue printed earthenware, Spode perfected the production of a bone porcelain (Cat. Nos. 505-09) which, being easier to make and providing a wider range of colours than true porcelain, became the standard English porcelain, now universally known as 'Fine Bone China'. **RC**

125
Cheese Cradle

Pearlware (earthenware with blue-tinted glaze), transfer printed in ultramarine blue with 'Rome' pattern,19.4×30.3 cm
Mark: SPODE printed underglaze in blue (RC 36)
Stoke-on-Trent, The Spode Museum Trust Collection
Inv. No. AGC 344
Exhibitions: Frankfurt, 1965, No. 18 (also Cologne, Osnabrück, Hanover); Royal Academy, London, 1970, No. 9; Stoke-on-Trent, 1983, No. 86
Literature: Williams 1949, pp. 91–93; Whiter 1970, p. 168

The scene is a composite one drawn from aquatint engravings in Merigot's *Views of Rome and its Vicinity* (1796–98). The pattern was incorrectly called 'Tiber'. It was introduced by Spode in 1811. **RC**

126
Meat Dish

Pearlware, transfer printed in ultramarine blue with 'Greek' pattern,42×33 cm
Marks: SPODE/1 impressed (RC 2a); workmen's marks in blue
Stoke-on-Trent, The Spode Museum Trust Collection
Inv. No. SBC 2
Literature: Williams 1949, pp. 184–85; Whiter 1970, p. 170; Drakard and Holdway 1983, pp. 164–65

The main source for the subjects used in this pattern is *Outlines from the Figures and Compositions upon the Greek, Roman and Etruscan vases of the late Sir William Hamilton; with engraved borders, drawn and engraved by the late Mr. Kirk*, published in 1804. The pattern was introduced *c.* 1806. The scene in the centre of this meat dish, however, is derived from Tischbein's *Collection of Engravings from Ancient Vases . . .* (1791–95), Vol. I, Plate 13, and depicts Theseus attacking two centaurs. **RC**

127
Meat Dish *(illus. p. 299)*

Pearlware, transfer printed in ultramarine blue with 'Indian Sporting' pattern, 63.6×51.6 cm
Marks: SPODE/1 impressed (RC 2a); SPODE printed in blue (RC 33); SHOOTING A LEOPARD (RC 66)
Stoke-on-Trent, The Spode Museum Trust Collection
Inv. No. WTC 261
Exhibitions: Royal Academy, London, 1970, No. 55
Literature: Williams 1949, pp. 28–57; Whiter 1970, p. 170; Drakard and Holdway 1983, pp. 152–58

Every piece displays a different scene in the centre, the source being the illustrations in *Oriental Field Sports, Wild Sports of the East*, by Captain Thomas Williamson with coloured aquatints after the watercolours of Samuel Howitt. Prints were offered first in 1805, and Spode's dinnerware was probably marketed a few years later. The present scene represents 'Shooting a Leopard'. The border design is derived from several of the scenes. **RC**

128
Dinner Plate

Pearlware, transfer printed in ultramarine blue with 'Caramanian' pattern, D 25.4 cm
Marks: Spode and 2 impressed (RC 3); ♂ in blue (WMT 1)
Stoke-on-Trent, The Spode Museum Trust Collection
Inv. No. WTC 249
Literature: Williams 1949, pp. 58–87; Whiter 1970, p. 170; Drakard and Holdway 1983, pp. 158–64

128

The scenes are taken from Luigi Mayer's *Views in the Ottoman Empire chiefly in Caramania . . .*, published in 1803 as a three-part work. Caramania is that area of Turkey which extends along the coast from Bodrum to Antalya. The scene on the dinner plate is of Sarcophagi and Sepulchres at the head of the harbour of Cacamo (just west of Finike) from Vol. II. **RC**

129
Dinner Plate

Pearlware, transfer printed in ultramarine blue with 'Italian' pattern, D 25.2 cm
Marks: SPODE/21 impressed (RC 2a); A in blue (WMT 11)
Stoke-on-Trent, The Spode Museum Trust Collection
Inv. No. WTC 270/P-5
Literature: Williams 1949, pp. 118–20; Whiter 1970, p. 168; Drakard and Holdway 1983, p. 138; Copeland 1992, Vol. 2, pp. 138–41

The identity of the view has eluded research, although the scene occurs on Italian maiolica,

and a watercolour drawing, now in the Spode Museum Trust Collection, may be the source of the scene. The border design is a copy of a Chinese porcelain border of the Yung Chêng period (*c.* 1735). The pattern is possibly the next most famous blue and white pattern after the 'Willow' pattern (which was pioneered by Spode). The 'Italian' pattern was introduced by Spode in 1816. **RC**

129

131
Fluted Dessert Dish

Pearlware, transfer printed in royal blue
with 'Willow' pattern, D 22.5 cm
Marks: SPODE (RC 2a); ≏ printed in blue
(WMT 24)
Stoke-on-Trent, The Spode Museum Trust
Collection
Inv. No. AGC 464
Exhibitions: Stoke-on-Trent, 1983, No. 24
Literature: Whiter 1970, pp. 148–49;
Copeland 1980, pp. 33–39

Spode's 'Willow I' pattern was based on a
Chinese porcelain design with the addition of
a bridge with three persons upon it, a pavilion
and a fence. This is the only Chinese landscape
which should be called the 'Willow' pattern.
The legend dates from 1849, whereas the pattern was introduced about 1790. **RC**

132
Soup Tureen and Cover

Pearlware, transfer printed in ultramarine
blue with 'Indian Sporting' pattern,
25.5×35.6 cm (length over handles)
Marks: base SPODE/13 impressed (RC 2a),
SPODE printed in blue (RC 33); cover
SPODE/46 impressed (RC 2a); SPODE (RC
33) and A (WMT 11) in blue
Stoke-on-Trent, The Spode Museum Trust
Collection
Inv. No. SBC 1
Literature: Williams 1949, pp. 28–57; Whiter
1970, p. 170; Drakard and Holdway 1983,
pp. 152–58

The scene on the side of the base depicts 'The
Hog at bay'; that on the cover 'Hunting an old
Buffalo'. **RC**

133
Vegetable Dish and Cover

Pearlware, transfer printed in royal blue
with 'Greek' pattern, 15×26.7 cm
Marks: base SPODE / 56 impressed (RC
2a), ≏ printed in blue (WMT 24); cover
SPODE/6 impressed (RC 2a)
Stoke-on-Trent, The Spode Museum Trust
Collection
Inv. No. SBC 2
Literature: Whiter 1970, p. 170; Williams
1949, pp. 184–85; Drakard and Holdway
1983, pp. 164–65

The scene printed derives from Kirk, Plate 61,
and represents Cassandra and Bellerophon
being conducted to the nuptial couch. **RC**

130
Dessert Plate

Pearlware, transfer printed in ultramarine
blue with 'Tower' pattern, the rim pierced
with continuous arcaded holes, D 19.2 cm
Marks: SPODE impressed (RC 1d), D
impressed; C printed in blue
Stoke-on-Trent, The Spode Museum Trust
Collection
Inv. No. AGC 250
Literature: Williams 1949, pp. 98–115;
Whiter 1970, p. 168

The scene is derived from an aquatint engraving of the Bridge of Salaro, near Porta Salara,
in the environs of Rome, which appeared in
Merigot's *Views of Rome and its Vicinity*
(1796–98). The 'Tower' pattern was introduced by Spode in 1814, and a version continues to be popular today. **RC**

134
Tureen, Cover and Stand

Pearlware, transfer printed in underglaze-blue cobalt with 'Hibiscus' pattern, H overall 26.5 cm, D of stand 29 cm
Mark: WEDGWOOD impressed
Robin Reilly Collection

Pearlware was introduced at the Wedgwood manufactory in 1779. The white body contained a larger proportion of white clay and flint than creamware and the glaze had small quantities of cobalt oxide added further to whiten the appearance of the piece. The introduction of the 'Hibiscus pattern' was probably influenced by the founder's eldest son, John Wedgwood (1766–1844), who became a partner in 1800, taking an active part in the management of the works until February 1812. He was deeply interested in horticulture and botany and was one of the founders of the Royal Horticultural Society in 1804.

Due to the popularity of underglaze-blue printed patterns, the Wedgwood company introduced five floral designs in the early years of the nineteenth century including 'Hibiscus', which was first produced in 1807. The original engraving of this pattern is attributed to William Hales. **GBR**

136 and 137

135
Plate

Pearlware, transfer printed in brown with 'Water Lily' pattern, D 25 cm
Mark: WEDGWOOD impressed, overprinted in orange enamel and gilt
Barlaston, Wedgwood Museum Trust
Inv. No. 3372
Literature: Reilly and Savage 1980, p.358

The 'Water Lily' pattern was produced in brown from 1807. It is possible that a service of this design was ordered by Susannah Darwin on the recommendation of her brother Josiah Wedgwood II. The theory is supported by a letter written by Susannah to Josiah on 25 August 1807. 'We are very much obliged by your kind intention respecting the dinner service which we are in no kind of haste for, as it is not the custom of this town [Shrewsbury] to give dinners in summer – I am therefore well inclined to follow your advice, and wait for the very handsome pattern.'

The 'Water Lily' pattern was originally engraved by Semei Bourne, John Robinson and William Hales. Invoices survive for the engraving of the design on to copper plates dated November 1806, and completed in 1807.

The 'Water Lily' appears to have been the only design being printed in brown at Etruria at this date. Confirmatory evidence occurs in the receipt for brown ceramic colour; 2 ½ lb was ordered in October 1806, 8 lb in January and 89 lb in February 1807, indicating that by January printing was underway.

The 'Water Lily' pattern is composed of three different plants, each with its botanically correct leaves, flowers and fruits. The plants are all members of the family Nymphaeaceae, the species being *Nymphaea stellata*, *Nymphaea lotus* and *Nelumbium speciosum*, also known as *Nelumbo nucifera*. The original drawing of the nelumbo, which forms the centre of the Wedgwood 'Water Lily' design, was made by Sydenham Edwards from flowers growing in the Rt. Hon. Charles Greville's hot-house in Paddington, published as a print in the *Botanical Magazine* on 1 February 1806. **GBR**

136
Jug

Pearlware, transfer printed in underglaze-blue cobalt with 'Water Lily' pattern, H 24.5 cm
Mark: WEDGWOOD impressed
Barlaston, Wedgwood Museum Trust
Inv. No. 3729

The jug decorated with the 'Water Lily' pattern has a 'cut reed' pattern border. Originally the pattern was produced in brown, but Josiah Byerley, manager of the Wedgwood's York Street Showrooms, requested on numerous occasions that the design be executed in blue. He wrote, 'A variety of pattern in blue being necessary, or the Lily being certainly novel . . . I wish you had made it in blue instead of brown.' His wish was granted: on 2 May 1811 when Josiah II sent a memorandum to London saying, 'If you have any Brown Lily in the rooms, turn it all out that you may not take orders for it which we cannot execute but at a loss – we will print some in Blue.' (Mss No. E13-11684) **GBR**

137
Meat Plate, Tureen and Ladle

Meat Plate, L 47.2 cm, tureen, L 37 cm, ladle, L 28.5 cm
Marks: WEDGWOOD 3, impressed; B printed in blue

Earthenware, underglaze-blue transfer-printed harbour scene known as 'Blue Claude' engraved by Thomas Sparkes after Claude
Stoke-on-Trent, City Museum and Art Gallery
Inv. Nos. 3492, 3491 respectively
Literature: Coysh and Henrywood 1982, pp. 45, 396

William and John Turner took over their father's works on his death in 1787. They continued in partnership until their bankruptcy in 1806. Their father, John, was in partnership with Andrew Abbott in a London retail business which, from 1783, traded from 82 Fleet Street, premises later occupied by J. Mist and the Davenports. **DS**

139
Tobacco Jar

? Turner, Lane End, Staffordshire, early nineteenth century
White stoneware, applied relief-moulded sprigs on brown-coloured slip, H 14.3 cm
Mark: J.MIST Pottery Warehouse FLEET STREET, LONDON, impressed
Stoke-on-Trent, City Museum & Art Gallery
Inv. No. 30 P 1933

James Underhill Mist was proprietor of a pottery and glass retail warehouse at 82 Fleet Street from 1802. Initially, he was in partnership, but from 1811 until 1814 worked on his own account. The warehouse traded in goods from a number of Staffordshire potters including the Turners. Most major manufacturers had outlets in London. **DS**

137

Josiah Wedgwood and Sons began production of underglaze-blue transfer-printed earthenware in 1805. This design, 'Blue Claude', was introduced in 1822. Thomas Sparkes (1773–1848) was a specialist engraver to the pottery trade at Hanley, Staffordshire. He supplied designs to Ridgway, Spode, Stevensons and Wedgwood among others. **DS**

138
Wine Cooler

Turner, Lane End, Staffordshire, *c.* 1800
White stoneware, applied relief-moulded decoration depicting Britannia and a classical scene, painted bands of brown slip, H 17.6 cm
Mark: Turner, impressed

138

139

140
Pie Dish

Davenport, Longport, Staffordshire, early
nineteenth century
Caneware (coloured stoneware), relief-
moulded and applied decoration, clear
glazed interior, L 22cm
Mark: Davenport over an anchor, impressed
Stoke-on-Trent, City Museum & Art Gallery
Inv. No. 2329
Literature: Foxley 1831, p. 62

John Davenport had a London showroom for
his Staffordshire ware by 1807 and in 1818 the
company took over the warehouse at 82 Fleet
Street, previously occupied by J. Mist and
Turner and Abbott. After 1822 Davenport became increasingly unhappy with its management in the hands of Henry and Victor Pon-
tigny, writing to his son in January 1831, 'The
trade here [in London] I think may be
mended, but not without a better direction –
Victor like his father, will never get a shilling
in the mug trade.' **DS**

140

Mark: S. Green Lambeth, applied cartouche
London, The Museum of London
Inv. No. 41. 6/5
Provenance: Dr. F. Corner

Stephen Green made moulded jugs representing both Wellington and Napoleon. The
handle of this jug incorporates various military regalia, suggesting that the jug commemorates Wellington's military victories in
the Peninsula War and at Quatre-Bras and
Waterloo rather than his political successes.
EE

141
Jug, the Duke of Wellington

S. Green, c. 1830
Freckled greenish-brown stoneware,
12.8×12.5 cm

George Cruikshank after George Murgatroyd Woodward
London 1792–1878 London,
Derbyshire c. 1760–1809 London

142
The Art of Walking the Streets of London, Plate 1st and Plate 2nd

Coloured etchings, each 25×34 cm
Published by Thos. Tegg, 111 Cheapside, 1
January 1818

141

142

143a

143b

London, Guildhall Library, Corporation of London
Literature: George 1949, Vol. 9, pp. 838-39, Nos. 13049 and 13050

These caricatures must have been drawn before 1809 (the year of Woodward's death), the designs being updated by Cruikshank to mock not only contemporary bad manners but also dandy fashions.

The four images of the first plate deal with accidents that befall umbrella users; collisions at street corners; the fate of those who meet a row of arrogant pedestrians taking up the whole width of the pavement; and the perils of wearing the latest but unsuitable and outlandish fashions.

The four images on the second plate deal with the blocking of the pavement by those with nothing much to do, impeding the work of those who do have work to do; deliberately splashing mud on fellow pedestrians; reading whilst walking (the book being read is one published by Tegg, the publisher of the print); and indulging in the sport of attacking watchmen. **RH**

Heinrich Schutz and Thomas Rowlandson
Frankfurt 1760–1822 and London 1756–1827
London respectively

143
a) View of London, No. 3. Entrance of Tottenham Court Road, with a view of St. James's Chapel

Coloured aquatint, 37 × 46 cm

b) Views of London, No. 6. Entrance from Hackney or Cambridge Heath Turnpike with a Distant View of St. Paul's

Coloured aquatint, 36 × 46 cm

Published at Ackermann's Gallery,101 Strand, 1 August 1809
London, Guildhall Library, Corporation of London
Literature: Searle 1930, pp. 191–92, 238

Originally the upkeep of the roads into London was the responsibility of individual parishes. By the seventeenth century, however, these roads were in such a deplorable condition that an act of parliament was passed establishing Turnpike Trusts.These Trusts were authorised to put up gates and tollbars and to collect tolls from those who needed to pass through them. Ackermann's series of aquatints shows in a light-hearted way the scenes at six of London's busiest turnpikes.
The view of the Tottenham Court Road Turnpike is taken from the Hampstead Road looking south towards London down the Tottenham Court Road. St. James's Chapel, designed by Thomas Hardwick and built in 1791, was a burial chapel, and served the needs of the parish of St. James's Piccadilly. It was demolished in 1964.
People resented the tolls, and the toll keeper was regularly abused for doing his job. At the Hackney turnpike two men in a light cart drove through the gate at such a furious pace the keeper could not catch them. In the evening they returned and tried to get through the gate in the same manner. This time the keeper seized the reins of the horse and stopped them. One of the men then flogged the keeper with his whip until it broke, then stepped down and struck the keeper in the face. **RH**

J. Hill after
Augustus Charles Pugin
France 1762–1832 London

144a
View of the Highgate Archway, 1812

Coloured aquatint, 38.5 × 55.4 cm
Published by the Proprietors by A. Pugin, 39 Keppel Street, Russell Square
Dedicated by permission to H.R.H. the Prince Regent by the Directors of the Highgate Archway Company

G. Hunt after
James Pollard
London 1792–1867

144b
Highgate Tunnel, c. 1812

Coloured aquatint, 44.2 × 56.5 cm
Published by J. Moore at his Picture Frame Manufactory, 1 West Street, Upper St. Martin's Lane
London, The Museum of London
Inv. Nos. 18108, 14384 respectively

For centuries the principal route into London from the north was the Great North Road, passing over Highgate Hill and dropping down towards the town. It was used by all the main coach services and by drovers bringing sheep and cattle into the London markets. The steep hill and a poor road surface were a nuisance for northbound travellers and in 1806 a Cornish engineer named Robert Vaizey proposed a tunnel through the hill. John Rennie

144a

advised that a cutting would be safer, but he was overruled by local landowners. Excavation began in 1812 but in April of that year the tunnel collapsed.

John Nash was then employed to superintend the making of a cutting and to provide a design for a bridge to carry the east-west cross road. In his new bridge, Nash followed the arrangement of Roman aqueducts with two tiers of arches, though with only a single tall arch in the lower tier. This unadventurous solution proved perfectly satisfactory and the Highgate Archway survived until 1897, when it was replaced by the present wider iron bridge. The roadway beneath was improved in 1829 by Thomas Telford, who made an early and experimental use of concrete for the road surface.

The Pugin print issued at the Highgate Archway Company's behest as publicity for the new scheme illustrates the increasingly suburban character of Highgate with its outcrop of picturesque villas. The Pollard print celebrates, like many Pollard subjects, the mail coach. **NB**

Sir Francis Chantrey
Norton, near Sheffield 1781–1841 London

145 *(illus. p. 300)*
John Rennie, 1818

Marble bust, 77.5 cm
Incised: JOHN RENNIE./CHANTREY./ SCULPTOR./1818
London, National Portrait Gallery
Inv. No. 649
Provenance: commissioned by the sitter; by descent; John Keith Rennie by whom donated, 1881
Exhibitions: London, Royal Academy, 1818, No. 1072; Edinburgh, 1822; Manchester, 1857, No. 137; London, National Portrait Gallery, 1981, Cat. No. 18
Literature: Walker 1985, Vol. 1, p. 410; Vol. 2, Plate 989

This forceful bust was commissioned by John Rennie in 1818, the year of the completion of his Waterloo Bridge. It was described by Chantrey's secretary, the poet Allan Cunningham, as one of the sculptor's 'finest busts . . . by many reckoned his masterpiece'.

Rennie (1761–1821) was eminent in the long line of Scottish architects and engineers who have worked with distinction in London. Engines and milling machinery, were always part of his trade, but during the 'canal mania' of the 1790s Rennie achieved an equal reputation as a civil engineer. He had a hand in almost every major scheme for naval and commercial docks, canals and river improvements. The London Docks and the later parts of the West India Docks were laid out to his design. But his reputation rests chiefly on his three great bridges: Waterloo Bridge and Southwark Bridge of the 1810s, and the posthumous London Bridge (1823–31), carried through by his two sons George and John.

Rennie was a reliable, all-round, empirical engineer. He did not have the flair of Telford, but could be bold where circumstances warranted it and often used iron originally. His work was informed by a theoretical understanding, and he was better versed in French techniques and achievements than any other successful British engineer of his time. **AS**

144b

148

meier calm of the scene mutes the technological progress represented.

Waterloo Bridge (1811–17) was the first of three metropolitan bridges built by the Rennie engineering dynasty – John Rennie and his sons George Rennie (1791–1866) and Sir John Rennie (1794–1874). By consensus it was the finest bridge ever built in London. At first called the Strand Bridge, it acquired its new name at the time of its opening by the Prince Regent as a cost-free way of commemorating victory over Napoleon. Waterloo Bridge was promoted entirely by private enterprise and financed on the expectation of tolls. The contract, by far the largest for a British bridge up to that time, was taken by the partnership of Jolliffe and Banks and earned Edward Banks a knighthood.

In the bridge itself, Rennie senior set the seal on the European art of bridge building in masonry as it had developed in the eighteenth century. It represented a qualified act of homage on Rennie's part to Perronet's Pont de Neuilly. The piers, built up within cofferdams excavated with the help of steam power, carried hidden inverted brick arches within the spandrels and supported nine evenly loaded arches. The facing material was Cornish granite, a novelty in London, chosen for its resistance to weather and pollution. The twin Doric columns on the piers were a Rennie trademark, used on his Scottish bridges. They were criticised by cognoscenti, but gave the bridge distinctive magnificence. **AS**

Charles Deane
*fl.*1815–1851

146 *(illus. p. 317)*
Waterloo Bridge and the Lambeth Waterfront from Westminster 1821, 1821

Oil on canvas, 110 × 184.8 cm
Signed and dated bottom left: C. Deane 1821
London, The Museum of London
Inv. No. C355

Provenance: A. Leonard Nicholson; presented through the National Art-Collections Fund, 1928
Exhibitions: London, British Institution, 1822, No. 206; Whitechapel Art Gallery, 1911, No. 129

Charles Deane was a London-based artist, best known for his pictures of the Thames. This painting shows the commanding site occupied by Waterloo Bridge at a slow bend in the Thames. The bridge did much to speed up the industrial development of the South Bank, already manifest on the right, but the Bieder-

147
Wherry seat-back

Painted wood, 127.5 × 39 cm
Inscribed: 6th Annual Prize-Wherry, Given by the Inhabitants of Queenhithe-Ward, August 9th, 1824
London, The Museum of London
Inv. No. Guildhall 23316
Provenance: donated by Mr. Deputy Skilbeck

Before the building of the new bridges, those who could afford to still crossed the river by hiring one of London's 3,000 wherries. The watermen who rowed them were proud of their skills at navigating the river currents and competed annually for various prizes. Winners were normally awarded a 'prize' wherry with splendidly painted seat-backs, as in this example. During the 1830s the competition from the new bridges and the growing number of paddle-steamers – which also endangered wherries with their wash – began to threaten the livelihood of London's watermen.

The race portrayed here is shown finishing near Southwark Bridge (1814–19), the second of the three great London bridges built by the Rennies and London's most conspicuous

149

early monument of the 'iron revolution'. The central span of some 240 feet was the widest ever constructed in cast iron. The side spans were a little shorter. The two piers in the river were built of massive blocks of Peterhead granite.

The bridge, a privately funded venture like the more famous Waterloo Bridge, was never a financial success. Rennie's design, strong, safe but heavy, cost almost three times what was anticipated. Neither the contractors for the approaches and piers, Jolliffe and Banks, nor the suppliers and erectors of the ironwork, the famous Yorkshire firm, Walkers of Rotherham, were ever paid in full. **AS**

148
Laying the Foundation Stone for New London Bridge

Watercolour, 44.5×54.6 cm
London, Guildhall Library, Corporation of London
Provenance: Daniel Shackleton; bought by Guildhall Library with grants from National Art-Collections Fund and MGC/V & A Purchases Grant Fund, 1990
Exhibitions: London, The Museum of London, 1989
Literature: Thomson 1827, p. 663; *National Art-Collections Fund Review* 1990, p. 155

The move to build a new London Bridge began in earnest in 1801 with the publication of the 'Third Report from the Select Committee upon the Improvement of the Port of London'. This carried several interesting schemes for a new bridge. In 1821 a Committee of the House of Commons recommended the adoption of a design by John Rennie senior. The 'Act for the Rebuilding London Bridge and for Improving and making suitable Approaches Thereto' received royal assent on 4 July 1823.

Dighton's drawing depicts the laying of the foundation stone for New London Bridge on 15 June 1825. A cofferdam was erected at the south end of the site of the new bridge, within which an arena was magnificently fitted out in red to receive the Lord Mayor and Corporation. The Duke of York, at this moment keenly interested in London improvement (Cat. No. 154), graced the occasion with his presence. According to the *Morning Chronicle*, 16 June 1825, about 2,000 spectators viewed the ceremony.

The drawing shows the scene at the bottom of the cofferdam (i.e. on the bed of the river, 45 feet below high-water mark), with the Lord Mayor, Alderman John Garratt, holding the golden trowel with which he will tap home the

149

9-ton foundation stone of Hayton granite. To his left stands the Duke of York. The man with a roll of plans under his arm is John Rennie junior, son of the bridge's architect, who had died in 1821. Rennie junior was knighted when the bridge was completed in 1831. **RH**

Sir John Rennie
London 1794–1874 Bengeo, Hertfordshire

149
London Bridge: Plan and section of cofferdam for pier no. 3. Scale 1″:48″

Pen and watercolour, 92×61 cm
London, Institution of Civil Engineers
Inv. No. First Rennie Collection no. 32
Literature: Cresy 1847, Vol. 1, pp. 446–47; Nash 1981, pp. 331–56

The piers of the medieval London Bridge were founded upon starlings (artificial islands) which severely restricted the flow of the river at low water. From the middle of the eighteenth century there was a growing demand for the replacement of the bridge, and a more satisfactory means of founding the piers had to be created if this problem were to be avoided again. Cofferdams offered a method of building the foundations of a bridge in the river whereby an enclosure or dam was made around the site of a pier from which water could be excluded and the area

pumped dry. Although John Rennie had died before work on the bridge began, his son John was a worthy heir in his father's professional practice, and had personally supervised the construction of the foundations of Waterloo Bridge. **MC**

George Scharf
Mainburg 1788–1860 London

150 *(illus. pp. 318–19)*
a) Crooked Lane at the Time of the Construction of New London Bridge

b) Old London Bridge in Course of Demolition

Watercolours, 52×78 cm, 49×67 cm respectively

London, Guildhall Library, Corporation of London
Provenance: bought from Scharf by the London Bridge Committee, February 1835
Literature: Jackson 1987, pp. 110-11

The Act to build New London Bridge also provided for the construction of approach roads. Sadly the Wren church of St. Michael, Crooked Lane, at the eastern end stood in the way and demolition was necessary. The second view is taken from Thomas Street, with Sir Christopher Wren's church of St. Magnus the Martyr on the left and New London Bridge on the right. The City Corporation commissioned Scharf to make these records of their development. **RH**

A VIEW OF HIGH STREET SOUTHWARK being THE ANCIENT ROADWAY leading from OLD LONDON BRIDGE taken July 1830. previous to its Removal for the New Line of Approach.

151

151
A View of High Street Southwark, July, 1830

Lithograph, 56×157 cm
Printed by C. Hullmandel
London, Guildhall Library, Corporation of London
Literature: Jackson 1987, pp. 112–25

The most sensational outcome of the City Corporation's commission were two long views of the works at either end of the new bridge. The watercolour originals were destroyed in World War II. Here we have the lithographic copy of the scene to the south. Extending into the distance is Borough High Street, renowned for its coaching inns. New London Bridge lying a few yards west of the old Bridge meant that Borough High Street had to be widened to meet it. All the buildings on the west side were thus demolished. **RH**

Clarkson Frederick Stanfield
Sunderland 1793–1867 London

152 *(illus. p. 320)*
The Opening of New London Bridge, 1 August 1831, 1831

Oil on canvas, 152.5×208.3 cm
London, H. M. Queen Elizabeth II
Inv. No. BP1234
Provenance: commissioned by William IV
Exhibitions: London, Royal Academy, 1832, No. 313; Royal Academy, 1870, No. 224; Somerset House, 1977, Cat. No. 54; Sunderland, 1979, pp. 109–10, Cat. No. 171

Stanfield was commissioned to make this picture, along with a view of Portsmouth, by William IV, who as a seaman had been much impressed by the painting of St. Michael's Mount that Stanfield had submitted to the Royal Academy in 1830. The choice of Stanfield for the commission caused some controversy, since he was not then a member of the Royal Academy: his application to become an associate was accepted at the third attempt in 1832 after the exhibition of this picture, convincingly demonstrating the advantages of royal favour. However, on 8 January 1832 the *Examiner* expressed the view that of the more suitable candidates for the commission, Turner would have been too unpredictable and Callcott could not match Stanfield's mastery of drama and scenic effect.

Stanfield had already charted the earlier stages of the construction of the bridge in both a scene design for the 1827 pantomime *Harlequin and Cock Robin* at Drury Lane and in watercolours that were engraved in 1834 for the *Views in London and its Vicinity* published by George and E. W. Cooke.

The opening ceremony of the bridge was considered by the Annual Register to be 'the most splendid spectacle that had been witnessed on the Thames for many years'. Stanfield, as official painter, was granted special facilities for sketching the occasion. The king and Queen Adelaide set off in their barge from Somerset House along with many other craft and proceeded down the river towards the new bridge. They are shown in the finished painting approaching the landing stage. The bridge was partially covered by a huge tent in which refreshments were served to the royal party after the opening. The painting reached a wider audience through T. A. Prior's engraving published for the *Art Journal* in 1858.

The bridge was sold in 1968 and reconstructed in Arizona, where it now bestrides the artificial lake at Lake Hawasu City. **IW**

Thomas Hosmer Shepherd
France 1793–London 1864

153
The Regent's Canal, 1822–25

a) Entrance to the Regent's Canal, Limehouse
Watercolour over pencil, 24.6×36.6 cm
Signed and dated lower left: Tho. H. Shepherd 1825

b) The Limehouse Dock
Watercolour over pencil, 24.7×37.1 cm

c) City Basin
Watercolour over pencil, 24.1×36.5 cm
Signed and dated lower left: Tho. H. Shepherd 1825

d) East Entrance to the Double Lock and the Islington Tunnel
Watercolour over pencil, 24.3×36 cm
Signed and dated lower centre left: Tho. H. Shepherd 1822

e) Macclesfield Bridge, Regent's Park
Watercolour, 24.3×35.8 cm

f) Junction of the Regent's Canal, at Paddington
Watercolour over pencil, 24.4×37.4 cm
Signed and dated lower right: Tho. H. Shepherd 1826

London, The Museum of London
Inv. No. 63.68/1-6
Provenance: Arthur Ackermann and Son Ltd.
Exhibitions: London, The Museum of London, 1981, Nos. 91–96

153a

153b

153c

153d

153e

153f

Literature: Elmes 1827–30, pp. 57–58, 157 (quarto), pp. 57, 172, 175 (octavo); Spencer 1961, pp. 21–72, Figs. on pp. 58–64; Adams 1983, pp. 374–77, Nos. 154/12, 23, 24, 58, 59, 78

Shepherd's calm prospects of the Regent's Canal from Limehouse to Paddington reveal nothing of the problems which had beset its construction. The idea of building a canal to connect the Grand Junction Canal – and thence the Midlands – with the ever-expanding trade on the Thames was first projected in 1802 by an entrepreneur Thomas Homer and the engineer, John Rennie. The scheme received new impetus in 1811 with Nash's plans for Regent's Park. Besides recognizing the picturesque possibilities of incorporating a stretch of water into his scheme, Nash was also aware of its practical uses in providing a cheap means of transport for heavy goods and, by encircling the Park's northern perimeter, affording some protection from less salubrious developments.

Despite opposition from wharfingers at the newly prosperous Paddington basin and from landowners along the entire route, the Act for 'making and maintaining' the Canal by means of a Company of Proprietors received the royal assent on 13 July 1812. Neither Nash nor his assistant James Morgan, appointed as engineer, had any experience of canal construction and problems with the water supply, the design of the locks and with property damaged by tunnelling for half a mile under Islington were compounded by financial difficulties. Homer was arrested for embezzlement and sentenced to seven years' transportation. After the initial raising of 254,000 capital, further flotations foundered in the post-war economic climate, leaving Nash himself majority shareholder and the govern-

ment bailing the company out.

The Canal finally opened on 1 August 1820, a tribute to Nash's courage and persistence but at a cost of half a million pounds. Although its presence greatly facilitated the 'March of Bricks and Mortar', it never fully realised the hopes of its investors, soon losing out to competition from the railways. But it has survived with its forty bridges and twelve locks more or less intact. Morgan's Macclesfield Bridge, shown here, was destroyed accidentally in 1874 when the *Tilbury* barge carrying gunpowder blew up beneath it.

The views were engraved by R. Acon, F.J. Havell and S. Lacey for Elmes, *Metropolitan Improvements* (1827–30). **CF**

Artist unknown

154
Portrait of Lt-Col Frederick William Trench MP, c. 1827

Oil on canvas, 75.9×63.8 cm
National Portrait Gallery
Inv. No. 5505
Exhibitions: London, Barbican Art Gallery, 1984, Cat. No. 18
Literature: Trench 1827; Trench 1846; Robinson 1977, pp. 324–31; Barker and Hyde 1982, pp. 8–9, 57–59, 81–91; Walker 1985, Vol. 1, pp. 502–03, Vol. 2, Plate 1244

George IV used John Nash as his tame architect, and his brother, the Duke of York, used Benjamin and Philip Wyatt. The contrast is revealing. Whilst the West End developments of

George IV and Nash are essentially benign, the proposals supported by the Duke of York are militaristic and authoritarian.

The visionary whose schemes these were was the Irish Protestant Tory Member of Parliament for Cambridge, Lt.-Col. F.W. Trench (1775–1859). Trench, who enthused in parliament about flogging in the army, devised his plans in harness with a second visionary and architectural meddler, the beautiful Duchess of Rutland. In the portrait we see Trench working on T. M. Baynes' perspective for the Thames embankment scheme (Cat. No. 155). The bust to the right is of the Duchess of Rutland. Spilling out across the sofa is Trench's plan for the two-mile triumphal way. **RH**

URBAN INFRASTRUCTURE

C. Deane, *Waterloo Bridge and the Lambeth Waterfront from Westminster*, 1821. Cat. No. 146

Thomas Mann Baynes
1794–1854

155
View of the North Bank of the Thames from Westminster Bridge to London Bridge . . .

Lithograph, 19.5 × 544 cm
Published by R. Ackermann, 101 Strand,
January 1825
London, The Museum of London
Inv. No. 66.128/1
Literature: Trench 1827; Robinson 1977;
Barker and Hyde 1982, pp. 8, 80–86, 89–90

In 1824 Lt.-Col. Frederick William Trench
M.P. proposed the construction of an 80-foot-
wide embankment to extend along the north
bank of the Thames from Scotland Yard to
Blackfriars. This carriageway and promenade,
supported on arches, would relieve traffic
congestion in the Strand, besides improving
the appearance of the river. The scheme incorporated a fine terrace of houses, fountains, a
double flight of stairs from the river to St.

Paul's and a large equestrian statue of George
IV.

Trench's scheme aroused fierce controversy. London's high society on the whole
approved of it, but violent opposition came
from the wharfingers, Strand tradesmen
(Rudolph Ackermann, the publisher of the
lithographs excepted), the benchers of the
Temple and Westminster aristocrats whose
town houses bordered the Thames.

To demonstrate his adaptability Trench
provided an alternative Sheet 3 for the panorama, showing the scheme minus the terrace.
The panorama's publication was announced in
The Times on 5 March 1825. This was ten days
before the debate on the Thames Quay in the
House of Commons, at the moment when
protest meetings were being organised and
petitions presented. The purpose of the print
was thus to inform the public and to convince
it of the scheme's viability. Though the detail
for the embankment was designed for Trench
by Benjamin and Philip Wyatt, John Rennie
had been consulted for engineering advice,
and various suggestions made by Trench's col-
laborator, the Duchess of Rutland, were incorporated.

A large painted moving panorama '. . . commencing at Blackfriars Bridge, passing thro'
the other Bridges, & shewing the intended
alterations of the Grand Promenade on the
Banks of the Thames' was announced in a
playbill as part of the programme for the
Theatre Royal, Covent Garden, between 27
December 1824 and 24 February 1825. **RH**

Attributed to George Garrard
1760–1826 London

156 *(illus. p. 322)*
The Surrey Iron Railway, Wandsworth Basin, c. 1803

Oil on canvas, 63.5 × 84 cm
London, Young and Co.'s Brewery plc.
Literature: Lee 1944, pp. 3–37; Townsend
1949–51, pp. 51–68

Parallel iron rails of track were extensively
used by the late eighteenth century for hauling

G. Scharf, *Crooked Lane at the Time of the Construction of New London Bridge*, Cat. No. 150a

wagons in the industrial Midlands and North. But the Surrey Iron Railway which ran from Wandsworth to Croydon was the first railway to be established, in 1801, by act of parliament, independent of a canal.

Laid out by the Derbyshire engineer, William Jessop, it was built by Edward Banks over land owned by the Jolliffe family and opened in 1803. The track started from a small dock basin on the Thames at Wandsworth, north of the Ram Brewery, visible on the right, and ran past it south through Earlsfield, Colliers Wood and Mitcham. The line was operated by horse traction and a variable toll was charged, depending on the type of goods carried.

The initial subscription to pay for it was raised from local industrialists, including Florance Young, a Southwark brewer and philanthropist, whose son, Charles Allen Young, became joint owner of the Ram brewery in 1831; it has belonged to the same family ever since. The line was superseded by steam railways and closed in 1846, but the stone sleepers can still be seen in the brewery wall. **CF**

Richard Trevithick
Illoggan 1771–1833 Dartford

157
Steam Locomotive, 1808

Model, 1:11 scale, steel and brass,
50×20×40 cm
London, Board of Trustees of the Science Museum
Inv. No. 1962-271
Literature: Pendred 1920–21, pp. 34–49; King 1930, pp. 200–02

The steam engines and boilers of Thomas Newcomen and James Watt had required large buildings to house them. By the introduction of the double-acting, high-pressure engine, Trevithick was able to build much smaller and lighter engines, which could be set up to drive almost any machinery, and to build the world's first steam locomotive.

In 1808 Trevithick gave Londoners their

157

318

URBAN INFRASTRUCTURE

G. Scharf, *Old London Bridge in Course of Demolition.* Cat. No. 150b

first glimpse of a steam locomotive when he demonstrated one on a circular track in Bloomsbury. For what should have been an epoch-making event it was scantly reported. All that it is known of this locomotive is that it was built by the Hazledine Foundry at Bridgnorth, weighed 8 tons, was called 'Catch-me-who-can', and that its structure was more like Trevithick's stationary engines than his earlier, gear-driven locomotive of 1803–05 built for Coalbrookdale, Pennydarran and Newcastle.

The model is conjectural and based on the *c.* 1806 Hazledine-built Trevithick stationary engine exhibited in the Science Museum but with the crankshaft and flywheel replaced by road wheels. It was made in 1960–62 by F.G. Kennard and presented to the Science Museum.

A drawing supposedly by Rowlandson shows the locomotive in operation on the site of the present Euston station. However, this cannot be relied upon as it shows buildings which were not erected until some time after the event. According to the London papers it should have commenced operation on Tuesday 19 July 1808, in fields between Euston Road and Torrington Place, where University College now stands, and admission was five shillings. In the event the ground was too soft, the locomotive was derailed, and it was displayed for no more than a day. It was probably moved to a site a few hundred yards further south where Birkbeck College now stands on Mallet Street. **PM**

Denis Johnson

158
Hobby Horse

Iron and ash wood; prop and rest for chest and padding for saddle replaced,
H108 × L171 × W57 cm
Marks: brass plate on handlebars 'JOHNSON 75 Long Ac[re]'; incised into wood under saddle, C (for No. 100)
Knutsford, Victoria University of Manchester, Tabley House Collection
Provenance: Sir John Fleming Leicester, Bart

This machine is one of two purchased by the art collector, Sir John Fleming Leicester, in April and May 1819, for 10 and 8 guineas respectively.

It is thought that the coach builder, Denis Johnson, had seen *draisiennes* probably in

C. F. Stanfield, *The Opening of New London Bridge, 1 August 1831*, 1831. Cat. No. 152

Paris shortly after Baron von Drais started putting his *draisiennes* on show there. Johnson took out a patent for his design on 21 June 1819. The Johnson hobby horse was much lighter and more upright than the *draisienne*, with an adjustable riding position. Taken up as a fashion by dandies, the hobby horse soon became known as the 'Dandy Horse'.

It is not known how many Johnson hobby horses were made, but it appeared to be a profitable business, costing forty or fifty shillings to the patentee. They came in different sizes and colours. Models were made for ladies and youths. They could also be rented by the hour or day by those who could not or did not wish to buy.

London streets were extremely congested and the hobby horses, because of the speed they could attain, were eventually banned by magistrates. Many races were held throughout Europe. A familiar challenge was the road from London to Brighton, and it is reputed that one hobby horse rider beat a four-horse coach to Brighton by half an hour.

Clearly the hobby horse was not the ideal means of transport as the iron clad machine shook and rattled considerably. The road sur-

158

faces of the day were frequently poor. The hobby-horse fashion died out by around 1830 although accounts of their use exist until about 1836. It would appear that the hobby horses in use during this later period were second-hand models which had been bought or acquired by the working classes and children. **PS**

Artist unknown

159
Johnson's Pedestrian Hobbyhorse Riding School, at No. 377, Strand

Coloured aquatint, 26 × 30 cm
Published by R. Ackermann, 1819
London, Guildhall Library, Corporation of London
Literature: Woodforde 1970, pp. 7–12; Goldman 1983

Some copies of this print carry instructions in their bottom margins on how to ride a hobby horse: 'The rider mounts it, and seats himself in a saddle conveniently fixed on the back of the horse (if allowed to be called so), and placed in the middle between the wheels; the feet are placed flat on the ground, so that in the first step to give the Machine motion, the heel should be the part of the foot to touch the ground, and so on with the other foot alternatively, as if walking on the heels, observing always to begin the movement very gently.'
RH

G. Scharf, *The Laying of the Water-Main in Tottenham Court Road*, 1834. Cat. No. 102

G. Scharf, *The Strand from the Corner of Villiers Street*, 1824. Cat. No. 161

Attributed to G. Gerrard, *The Surrey Iron Railway, Wandsworth Basin, c.* 1803. Cat. No. 156

George Cruikshank
London 1792–1878 London

160
a) Royal Hobby's, or The Hertfordshire Cock-horse! 1819
Etching, coloured impression, 23.7 × 33.5 cm
Published by M. Clinch, 20 April 1819

b) Accidents in High Life, or Royal Hobby's broke down! 1819
Etching, coloured impression, 24.5 × 34.9 cm
Published by E. King, 24 April 1819

London, Trustees of the British Museum
Inv. Nos. 1868-8-8-8432, 1868-8-8-8434 respectively
Literature: George 1949, Vol. 9, pp. 834–95, Nos. 13220, 13222 respectively

Print shops in 1819 were full of caricatures inspired by the current sensation. Here the real point of both satires is not the hobby horse as such – though it provided a convenient smokescreen – but the notorious question of the Prince Regent and his long-standing mistress, the Marchioness of Hertford, and the scandals associated with the Duke of York, who had had to resign as Commander in Chief of the Army after it had been revealed that his mistress Mrs. Clarke had accepted bribes for arranging promotions through the influence of her lover (Cat. No. 614). He had, however, received a parliamentary vote of £10,000 per annum to discharge his debts and to establish what was hoped would be a respectable way of life.

In *Royal Hobby's*, the fat and absurdly *décolletée* Lady Hertford bestrides the Prince

Regent, flourishing a knotted whip with a sceptre for a handle; she wears a garter inscribed with the Prince of Wales's motto Ich Dien ('I Serve'), while the jewel of the George (the insignia of the highest order of chivalry) hangs from her neck. At the back of the velocipede three ostrich feathers (part of the Prince of Wales's crest) project from the central pole of the machine, cleverly combining with the silhouette of the Prince and the hobby horse to give the impression of a cock. The Prince expresses his weariness, and at the far left is a signpost 'To the Horns Inn. Hertford', an allusion to the cuckolded Marquess of Hertford.

Accidents in High Life, published only four days later, employs the same iconography. But this time the riders have fallen from their velocipedes. The Duke of York's fall from grace has been cushioned by his £10,000 annual grant. The Prince Regent – 'Royal Roley Poley' – has ass's ears, and terrible gout in one foot. He is complaining (with a good deal of sexual innuendo) about his mistress: '. . . this <u>Hertford</u> road is so d-d <u>rough</u> I'll not <u>drive</u> on it any more – I'll go the <u>Richmond</u> road next time' – the first allusion to his alleged infatuation with the Duchess of Richmond. Lady Hertford, toppled, her coronet falling off, clutches a birch rod and screams '. . . I was a great fool to trust myself with such an <u>Old Stick</u>' – the Prince Regent. The print is dedicated, somewhat tongue in cheek, to 'the society for the Suppression of Vice'. **LS**

159

George Scharf
Mainburg 1788–1860 London

161 *(illus. p. 321)*
The Strand from the Corner of Villiers Street, 1824

Watercolour over pencil, with black ink, 21.8×37.2 cm (the sheet has been made up on either side by about 3.5 cm and at the top by 0.5 cm)
Signed and dated bottom right: G. Scharf del Sept. 1824
London, Trustees of the British Museum Inv. No. 1862-6-14-19
Provenance: from a collection of the artist's works purchased from his widow, 1862
Literature: Jackson 1987, pp. 64–65, illustrated

The Strand, although never so fashionable as Bond Street, Piccadilly or the recently built Regent Street, was one of the busiest thoroughfares of London, with an enormous variety of shops and eating houses. Scharf's watercolour records a fire which broke out on 5 September 1824 in the shop of Mr. Martin, a sausage maker. Many of the houses were timber framed and there was fear that the fire would spread rapidly; in fact it was soon extinguished by the Sun Fire Office's fire engine, shown drawn up in front of the burning house, with its water hose directed into the first-floor window. In the 1830s these houses, at the Trafalgar Square end of the Strand, were demolished and replaced by a neo-classical development planned by John Nash (Cat. No. 80). **LS**

160a

160b

162

The model represents a horse-drawn, manually operated fire engine of a type common in Britain throughout the nineteenth century. W. J. Tilley were building fire engines from 1820 to 1851 and were one of a line of the most prominent manufacturers of fire engines in London. The line began with Samuel Phillips in about 1774, becoming Hopwood in 1798, Tilley in 1820, and Shand Mason in 1851. With very few changes, this type of fire engine became the very successful, standard London Brigade manual.

The pump has two vertical, single-acting cylinders with the valves in separate valve boxes for greater accessibility as patented by Charles Simpkin in 1792. The suction hose is fitted to the back of the machine, and provision is also made for supplying water to the machine by emptying buckets into the trough at the back. Two screwed couplings are provided for the delivery hose, one on each side of the machine.

With wheels made of solid brass, and a body of polished mahogany, the model does not seek accurately to represent a machine in service. It is believed to be a contemporary model and may have been made by Tilley. It was purchased from W. J. Perkins for £30. **PM**

W. J. Tilley

162
Manual Fire Engine, early 19th century

Model, about 1:4 scale, mahogany and brass, 45×44×86 cm
London, Board of Trustees of the Science Museum
Inv. No. 1932-269

163

J. Farey for
Sir Goldsworthy Gurney
Cornwall 1793–1875 Cornwall

163
Apparatus for Propelling Carriages on Common Roads or on Railways, 14 May 1825

Pen and ink and watercolour, 47.5×64 cm
London, Public Record Office
Inv. No. C54/10532 M29

Since the late sixteenth century the crown had granted inventors letters patent protecting for a limited period their exclusive right to manufacture their inventions. Two principal types of document resulted: letters patent, constituting legal protection, and specifications describing the invention in more detail, often with an explanatory drawing. Other subsidiary documents, such as petitions and reports, were also produced.

The inventor began by preparing a petition to the crown. This he took to the Home Office. Then it was endorsed and referred to one of the law officers. Once the inventor had obtained a favourable report from the law officer he took it with his petition back to the Home Office. A warrant was then made out instructing the law officer to prepare a bill which would in its turn – after complex formal procedures had been completed – result in the grant of letters patent. A specification, giving fuller details of the invention, was later enrolled at one of three Chancery offices.

Specifications are the most informative records about inventions; in many cases, as in this instance, they include plans or drawings. Introduced in 1711, they became mandatory from 1734. Sheet one of Gurney's specification drawings for his first patent of 1825 shows a horizontal plan and vertical section of his steam road carriage. **CF**

164

Sir Goldsworthy Gurney
Cornwall 1793–1875 Cornwall

164
Steam Road Carriage, 1827

Model, 1:8 scale, wood and metal,
44×30×86 cm
London, Board of Trustees of the Science Museum
Inv. No. 1958–234
Literature: Fletcher 1891; Smith 1959, pp. 58–62; 'The Gurney Steam Carriage' 1959, pp. 424–25

Gurney began building steam road carriages in Albany Street, Regent's Park, London in 1825. In 1827 he built an improved carriage represented by this model. It ran experimentally for eighteen months around London at speeds up to 20 mph. It also made a journey from London to Bath but broke down on the way. After being repaired, it was able to complete the return journey during which it covered the 84 miles from Melksham to Cranford Bridge in ten hours including stoppages.

Gurney then built a smaller steam drag which pulled a carriage containing passengers. Using three of these vehicles, Sir Charles Dance ran a service four times a day from 21 February to 22 June 1831 between Gloucester and Cheltenham. They averaged 55 minutes for the nine-mile journey, carried nearly 3,000 people and covered 3,564 miles. However, having spent £30,000 developing steam carriages without achieving financial success, Gurney stopped building carriages in 1832.

The model was commissioned by the Science Museum from S. T. Harris and made in 1956–1958. Final finishing and painting were carried out by the workshops of the Science Museum. It was made to the drawings in Gurney's patent number 5554 of 1827. The model is accurately built but uses brass and copper for the body instead of wood. **PM**

George Shillibeer
1797–1866 London

165
Horse Drawn Omnibus, 1829

Model, 1:6 scale, wood and metal,
50×50×94 cm
London, Board of Trustees of the Science Museum
Inv. No. 1930-667
Literature: Lee 1962; Day 1973

On 4 July 1829 George Shillibeer introduced Britain's first regular bus service in which a vehicle operated a route at a fixed fare picking up and setting down passengers at designated points along the route. Shillibeer's first route was over the New Road from Paddington Green to the Bank of England. It catered for people living in the Paddington and Marylebone area who could afford to pay to travel to the City but could not afford to keep their own carriage. The service was immediately popular, but so many other omnibus services sprang up to compete with Shillibeer that he was declared bankrupt two years later. The model was presented to the Science Museum by the London General Omnibus Co. Ltd. to celebrate the Shillibeer centenary in 1929. **PM**

165

166

166
Hackney Coach and Cabriolet Fares, Regulations and Acts of Parliament, 1832-34

Silk, plate print in black ink, 90×93 cm
London, The Museum of London
Inv. No. A10434
Provenance: Charles Davis M.V.O.
Exhibitions: London, The Museum of
London, 1988
Literature: Schoeser 1988, pp. 2-3, Fig. 2

The handkerchief is printed from an engraving attributed to J. Bishop, 79 Charterhouse Lane. Like maps on handkerchiefs, many of which survive and which Charles Dickens refers to in *Dombey and Son* (1848) as 'printed with a view to pleasant and commodious reference', these tables were compact and durable.

The four vehicles depicted show some of the transport available at this time. The horse-drawn omnibus, top right, was introduced to England in 1829 by George Shillibeer (Cat. No. 165). The cabriolet (lower right), a two-wheeled vehicle drawn by a single horse, grew in popularity as the hackney coach declined. The greater speed of the 'cabs' made them popular with a younger clientele. It was not uncommon for passengers to be tossed from the vehicles after a racing collision.

Despite the publication of regulation fares travellers still encountered problems. Writing in 1825, 'Jehu', a correspondent of the *London Magazine*, complained of the filthy state of the hackney coaches and of the extortionate charges made by the coachmen. To rectify this, he suggested an early form of meter. **EE**

168

167
Stage Coach, c. 1830

Model, 1:8 scale, 35×46×27 cm
London, Bob Bates

Stage coaches first provided services to provincial towns and cities in the second half of the seventeenth century. These, however, were very cumbersome compared to the sleek and fast vehicles of the late eighteenth and early nineteenth centuries. Stage coaches were designed to carry more passengers than mail coaches (Cat. No. 168), to which they bore a superficial resemblance, and sometimes carried mail under contract. Whilst mail coaches departed from London at 8pm, most stage coaches left in the early hours of the morning.

The *Tally Ho* was one of nine coaches on the London to Birmingham run. The team of four horses that pulled the *Tally Ho* had to be changed at each of ten stops made between London and Birmingham.

On a normal journey, the *Tally Ho* covered the 109 miles to Birmingham in around 11.5

167

hours (9.5 mph), equal in speed to the fastest mail coaches. During the famous London to Birmingham race on May Day 1830 – when the coaches did not carry passengers – the *Tally Ho* set a record in coaching history by covering the course in 7.5 hours (14.5 mph). Coaching services declined rapidly with the building of railways in the late 1830s and 1840s.

This model was made by Bob Bates in 1977. **CE**

R.G. Reeves after James Pollard

168
The Royal Mails starting from the General Post Office

Coloured aquatint, 50.5×68.6 cm
Published by Thos. McLean, 26 Haymarket, 19 April 1830
London, The Museum of London
Inv. No. A18109

The St. Martin's-le-Grand façade of Smirke's new General Post Office, viewed here from the north, provided an impressive backdrop for the 8pm departure of the mail coaches. Five of the twenty-eight mail coaches operating out of London can be seen in the print – each painted in scarlet, maroon and black livery, and bearing the royal arms, George IV's monogram and their respective numbers. The departure of the mails was one of the sights of London.

The early mail coaches – first introduced on the London to Bristol route in 1784 – were somewhat clumsy top-heavy vehicles. By the early 1800s, however, better body design led to fast journey times of around 9.5–10.5 miles per hour over the much improved turnpike roads that radiated outwards from London.

Mail coaches were built to approved post office designs, by John Vidler and Company of Millbank, and sold to private coaching firms who contracted to carry the mails. Only the mail guard, with his scarlet uniform, was a post office employee and his task was to ensure that the strict regulations relating to the safety of the mails and timekeeping were rigorously adhered to. They were armed with blunderbusses (not really necessary by the nineteenth century) and carried a long horn to announce arrivals in town and to alert toll keepers to open their gates, through which mail coaches could pass free of charge.

The mail coach operators were also able to carry people and packages, but the number of outside passengers was limited to three, compared with up to twelve on the largest stage coaches. Whilst the fares were higher than for stage coaches, the two vehicles were essentially complementary forms of travel and both types were operated by the larger coaching establishments. The Bull and Mouth, opposite the General Post Office, was run by Edward Sherman from 1823. He operated 77 mail and stage coaches and owned 700 horses. **CE**

'Shortshanks' Robert Seymour
Somerset 1798–1836 London

169
Locomotion, Plate 1st and Plate 2nd

Published by Thos. McLean, 26 Haymarket, c. 1830
Coloured etchings, each 25×35 cm
London, Guildhall Library, Corporation of London
Literature: George 1954, Vol. 11, p. 411, No. 16438 (Plate 2nd only)

These caricatures present visions of a steam-driven future. On the left of the first plate a smiling pedestrian, reading a booklet entitled 'New Inv[entions]', has his legs in colossal cylinders attached to a cog-wheel, and a boiler strapped to his back. He is overtaken by two ladies gaily riding on a liveried steam kettle. An aeronaut astride a winged boiler calls down cheerfully from the sky. This happy scene is spoilt by a hint of reality – a steam vehicle exploding discreetly behind a bush in the background.

The second print shows the probable reality of steam travel. An angry pedestrian fears that the fire in his boiler has gone out. A coster-monger in a steam cart overtakes a steam-driven open carriage. The driver of, and the ladies in, the latter react angrily to the smoke from the costermonger's vehicle. Two aeronauts in the sky are experiencing serious trouble with their machines. In the background one steam coach explodes, and another topples over a cliff. A steam packet in the water sinks. **RH**

169a

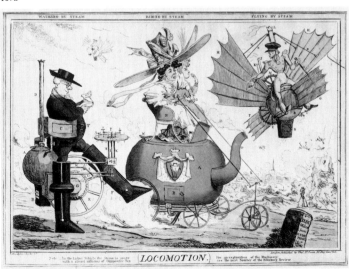

169b

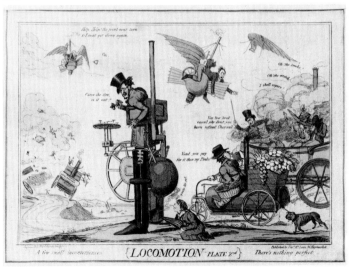

Rudolph Ackermann (1764–1834) was the foremost publisher of colour-plate books and decorative prints in early nineteenth-century London. From his gallery and shop at 101 Strand, he issued works which collectively purvey the most wide-ranging, if not deep-searching, image of the Regency city. Ackermann was also a leading entrepreneur and patron of watercolour artists and scientific inventors. His philanthropic efforts of behalf of his native Saxony won him many civic honours.

170

François Nicolas Mouchet
1750–1814

170
Rudolph Ackermann, 1814

Oil on canvas, 125 cm × 100 cm
London, Throgmorton Trust
Provenance: Rudolph Ackermann 1814 and by descent to Arthur Ackermann and Son Ltd.
Exhibitions: London, Ackermann, 1983, Cat. No. 94
Literature: Ford 1983, p. 237, illustrated facing p. 12

Rudolph Ackermann was born at Stolberg near Leipzig in 1764. He completed an apprenticeship as a carriage designer in Basle, Switzerland, and then worked for the carriage maker Antoine Carassi in Paris. Ackermann arrived in London in 1783. He married an English girl and became a naturalised British subject in 1809. He worked initially as a carriage designer in London and then established a drawing school in the Strand and began to manufacture watercolour paints. He published books of carriage designs and drawing books, and from 1800 became the leading publisher in London of decorative prints and colour-plate books. For thirty years he gave more or less permanent employment to the artist Thomas Rowlandson.

His gallery and shop premises, The Repository of Arts, 101 Strand, London, became the resort of artists, professional and amateur. He patronised *émigrés* from the European wars, providing employment to French, German and Spanish artists and craftsmen in the workshops below the trading areas. He also became a ceaseless promoter of a variety of technical innovations.

The portrait was probably commissioned to celebrate Ackermann's fiftieth birthday in 1814. The two books depicted are likely to be his favourite publication *The History and*

171

Antiquities of . . . St. Peter's Westminster (Cat. No. 179). The gas lamp illuminates Ackermann's pioneering role in the introduction of gas lighting to London. He installed a furnace in the basement of 101 Strand in 1811, supplying gas lighting to his workshops, the gallery and his quarters above. **JF**

172

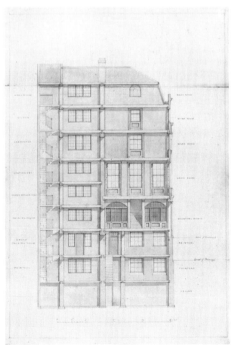

171
Vase, early nineteenth century

Vaso compana in hard-paste porcelain, from the Meissen factory under Count Marcolini, 43 cm high
London, Throgmorton Trust
Provenance: Rudolph Ackermann, 1816, and by descent to Edgar Ackermann 1920; Russell Button, Chicago; Rudi Leuser, Grand Rapids; Arthur Ackermann and Son Ltd., 1986
Literature: Ford 1983, pp. 48–50

This Meissen vase was presented in 1816 to Rudolph Ackermann (a native of Saxony) on behalf of the King of Saxony by the ambassador in London, Baron St. Just, together with a pair of figures.

The King of Saxony had awarded Ackermann the Order of Civil Merit for his work as secretary of the Westminster Association, which raised and distributed the extraordinary sum of £200,000 for the relief of distress in Germany following the Battle of Leipzig in 1813. **JF**

John Buonarotti Papworth
London, 1775–1847 Little Paxton

172
Section of 96 Strand, London, c. 1819

Pencil with watercolour wash, 47.5×33 cm
London, British Architectural Library, Drawings Collection, Royal Institute of British Architects
Inv. No. Pap [95] 23
Provenance: probably Wyatt Papworth by whom presented to the R.I.B.A.
Exhibitions: London, Ackermann, 1983, Cat. No. 103
Literature: McHardy 1977, p. 35, No. 95/23; Ford 1983, pp. 89–90

Papworth, a personal friend of Rudolph Ackermann, designed the premises of the new Repository of Arts at 96 Strand, London. The design featured a cellar and seven storeys, comprising showrooms, library, counting house, packing and store rooms, together with workshops for printers, gilders and carpenters.

Ackermann moved to 96 Strand in 1827 from 101 Strand, a site now occupied by a bank near the Savoy Hotel. Number 96 was occupied by Ackermann's Repository until 1857 and this site is now Simpson's Restaurant. **JF**

173
Broadsheet

Published by R. Ackermann, 101 Strand, 4 May 1802; printed by T. Bensley, Bolt Court, London, 50×35 cm
London, Throgmorton Trust
Provenance: Arthur Ackermann and Son Ltd.

An advertisement for Ackermann's Repository of Arts, 101 Strand, London, featuring an engraving by Maria Cosway and advertising Ackermann's Superfine Watercolour paints. **JF**

174
The Repository of Arts, Literature, Commerce, Manufactures, Fashions and Politics

40 Vols. 1809–28, quarto, 24.2×15.5 cm
London, The Museum of London
Inv. No. E.391.2
Exhibitions: London, Ackermann, 1983, Cat. Nos. 88–93
Literature: Ford 1983, pp. 77–83; Tooley 1973, No. 8

Das ostindische Haus, der große Saal.

The most characteristic of Rudolph Ackermann's publications was *The Repository of Arts*. The 240 monthly parts contain 1,432 coloured plates of ladies' fashions, furniture and furnishings, carriage designs, architecture, portraits, views of London and country houses, samples of cloth and paper. They helped to spread fashion and taste from London to the provinces and they provide an illustrated picture of Regency England over a period of twenty years.

Ackermann's original idea was to publish a magazine of record 'to convey useful information in a pleasing and popular form – to beguile the unlearned into an acquaintance with the arts and sciences – and occasionally to assist even the man of letters in cultivating a taste for both'. However, the *Repository* soon became a magazine aimed principally at female readers. Articles on politics, commercial news and sporting intelligence were omitted, while fashion and furnishing styles with news on the latest bonnets mingled with reviews of books, music and art. This concentration improved the magazine, making it a key publication in the history of fashion and decorative art of the period.

Each monthly issue carried four hand-coloured plates employing most forms of engraving – aquatint, woodcut, line, stipple and lithography. Many of these were published separately in book form. These include: Thomas Rowlandson, *Naples and the Compagna Felice* (1815); J.B. Papworth, *Select Views of London* (1816); *Upholsterer's and Cabinetmaker's Repository* (1816); J.B. Papworth, *Rural Residences* (1818); Thomas Rowlandson, *Journal of Sentimental Travels* (1821); Gabriel Lory, *Picturesque Tour through the Oberland* (1823); *Designs of Household Furniture and Decoration* (1823); Augustus Pugin, *Gothic Furniture* (c. 1828); *Views of Country Seats*, 2 Vols. (1830). **MF**

John Samuel Agar
1775–c. 1820

175 *(illus. p. 339)*
Fashion Plate

Preliminary watercolour drawing and finished aquatint, 23 × 14 cm
London, Throgmorton Trust
Provenance: Arthur Ackermann and Son Ltd., London; Throgmorton Trust, London, 1991

The print was published in Ackermann's *Repository of Fashions* 1829, the short-lived successor to the *Repository of Arts* 1807–28. **JF**

William Henry Pyne and William Combe
London 1769-1843 London,
Bristol 1741-1823 London respectively

176
The Microcosm of London

London, printed for R. Ackermann, Repository of Arts, 101 Strand, by T. Bensley, Bolt Court, Fleet Street, 1808–10
3 volumes, large quarto, 34.2 × 29 cm
London, The Museum of London
Inv. No. Z1014
Exhibitions: London, Ackermann, 1983, Cat. No. 108
Literature: Tooley 1973, No. 7; Ford 1983, p. 39; Adams 1983, pp. 223–28, No. 99

The Microcosm of London provided a picture of the exteriors and interiors of London's major buildings and their inhabitants in the early nineteenth century. It illustrated not only the Establishment and its institutions but the teaming vigour of London life. Places of entertainment are included as well as places of work and worship. The London theatres are particularly well served and views of the River Thames provide much of the background of the city. It was the first of Rudolph Ackermann's major topographical books and became a publishing model for its successors, i.e. all were large quarto size, with hand-coloured aquatint plates, printed on Whatman paper with letterpress printed by Harrison and Leigh, or T. Bensley. All were published in monthly parts in limited editions of one thousand with pre-publication subscriptions.

Originally issued in twenty-six monthly parts, each part of the *Microcosm* contained four coloured plates and was issued at 7s. for subscribers and increased to 10s.6d. for non-subscribers. On completion, the three volumes were sold for £13.13s. The original drawings were by Augustus Pugin and Thomas Rowlandson in collaboration, Pugin providing the architectural setting and Rowlandson adding vitality and interest with figures. The 104 aquatints were printed on the premises at 101 Strand and their consistent high quality is a major feature which sets the work apart from the other views of London of the period.

The accompanying text for the first two volumes was by William Henry Pyne, himself a gifted artist and employed by Ackermann in his gallery. Volume 3 was by William Combe, a versatile hack who was to be the principal author of many of the other topographical books published by Ackermann. **MF**

177
London oder Beschreiburg der merkwärdigsten Gebaude, Denkmäler und Astalten der Haupstadt Gross britanniens, 1812

Bound volume, 33.3×27 cm
London, J. Gestetner Esq.

The publication in Germany of a plagiarism of Ackermann's *Microcosm of London* indicates the wide appeal of the subject matter and German interest in London. It is illustrated with twenty copies of *Microcosm* plates. Those chosen illustrate the commercial and political life of London and some of the well-known historical and contemporary sights of the city.
EE

178a

178a
Thomas Rowlandson
London 1756 – 1827 London

Smithfield Market

Watercolour, 28×43.5 cm
London, Guildhall Library, Corporation of London
Exhibitions: London, The Museum of London, 1981, No. 60
Literature: Fox 1987, pp. 149-50, reproduced

178b
John Bluck after Thomas Rowlandson

A Bird's Eye View of Smithfield Market

Aquatint, 43×53.2 cm
Published at R. Ackermann's Repository of Arts, 101 Strand, 1 January 1811
London, The Museum of London
Inv. No. A18151
Literature: Adams 1983, pp. 502-09, No. 221/2

Smithfield was, and still is, London's largest and busiest meat market. Until 1855 it was a live as well as dead meat market, the sheep and cattle being driven to it (the cattle sometimes stampeded to it) through the streets of London. Thomas Rowlandson, the artist responsible for the Smithfield watercolour, also produced a view of London Bridge showing the effect on pedestrians and traffic of an 'over-drove' ox.

Rowlandson's bird's-eye view shows the live meat market as seen from a public house on the north side called the Bear & Ragged Staff. Bordering the market on the south is St. Bartholomew's Hospital. Giltspur Street is to the right of the Hospital. The dome of St. Paul's looms over the roof-tops.

Rowlandson's Smithfield view is one of a pair of watercolour drawings, the other being a bird's-eye view of Covent Garden, the market for fruit, vegetables, and flowers. Both drawings were engraved by John Bluck and published by Rudolph Ackermann in 1811, to form the first in a series of eighteen large aquatinted views of important London landmarks. The young Thomas Hosmer Shepherd, and John Gendall contributed to the series. The ultimate plate, *Regent Street from Piccadilly*, appeared on 1 July 1822 (Cat. No. 76). **RH**

178b

179

179

179
The History of Antiquities of the Cathedral Church of St. Peter's Westminster

Rudolph Ackermann, 1812
2 volumes, folio, printed on vellum, and illustrated with the original watercolours mounted on vellum, bound in crimson velvet, ornamented richly in gilt and chased ormolu, Vol. 1, 43×32×14 cm, Vol. 2, 43×32×15.2 cm
Inscribed on the clasp of Vol. 1: 'Designed by J.B. Papworth Architect'

London, The Dean and Chapter of Westminster Abbey
Provenance: Rudolph Ackermann 1812; John Allnutt 1815 and by descent; Arthur Ackermann and Son 1926; H.M. King George V by whom presented, 1926
Exhibitions: London, Ackermann, 1983
Literature: Ford 1981, pp. 461–78

This unique copy contains the original eighty-three watercolours from which the aquatint prints were made. The work was originally published in 1811 by subscription in twenty monthly parts each containing text by William

Combe and four hand-coloured aquatints, the principal artists being Augustus Charles Pugin and Frederick Mackenzie.

Ackermann, regarded the publication of the two-volume work as a significant achievement. He commissioned J. B. Papworth to design a special binding in Gothic style with symbols of the Abbey – the rose and the port-cullis – in ormolu on crimson velvet. J. Hering of Newman Street, London, was the binder. The binding of this copy represents a massive technical achievement, the considerable weight being only one of the features. This special work was exhibited in Ackermann's premises, the Repository of Arts, 101 Strand, London, and advertised for sale at £1,500 in 1815, where it was bought by John Allnutt, a London wine merchant and collector of watercolours. **MF**

180

William Combe
Bristol 1741-1823 London

180
A History of the University of Oxford, its Colleges, Halls, and Public Buildings

Printed for R. Ackermann, 101 Strand, by L. Harrison and J.C. Leigh, 373 Strand, 1814
2 volumes, large quarto, 37×30.5 cm
London, J. Gestetner Esq.
Exhibitions: London, Ackermann, 1983, Cat. No. 109
Literature: Ford 1983, p. 42; Tooley 1973, No. 5

Ackermann's *Oxford* contains sixty-four coloured aquatints of views with seventeen coloured plates in line and stipple of the costumes of officials of the University, and thirty-three portraits of the founders also in line and stipple. The principal artists are Augustus Pugin, who provided thirty-one views, Frederick Mackenzie twenty, and Thomas Uwins who provided the seventeen costume drawings.

The working relationship between publisher and artist is revealed in a letter from Pugin to Ackermann. The publisher provided a £238 advance between November 1812 and May 1813 for Pugin to make his drawings in Oxford. On his return to London Pugin paid back £71, thus receiving £14.3.6d for each of the published views.

One thousand were printed, at 12s. per issue for the first five hundred, and 16s. for the second five hundred. On completion, the work was issued in two volumes, at £16 for the ordinary size and £27 for the large paper edition, of which there were fifty copies. Twenty-five copies with the plates on India paper uncoloured were also issued. Ackermann's *Oxford* is a most beautiful example of the art of book making: the typography is elegant and the pages are well designed. **MF**

William Combe

181
A History of the University of Cambridge, its Colleges, Halls, and Public Buildings

Printed for R. Ackermann, 101 Strand, by L. Harrison and J.C. Leigh, 373 Strand, 1815
2 volumes, large quarto, 34.3×29.5 cm
Cambridge, The Graham Watson Collection, The Master and Fellows of Emmanuel College
Exhibitions: London, Ackermann, 1983, Cat. No. 111
Literature: Tooley 1973, No. 4

Ackermann's *Cambridge* was originally issued in twenty monthly parts, along with the histories of Oxford, the Public Schools, Westminster Abbey and *Microcosm of London*. One thousand copies were printed, the first five hundred being sold at 12s., the second five hundred at 16s. a part. The two-volume work was issued in boards for £16, with fifty copies on large paper at £27, and there were twenty-five proof copies on India paper. Each number contained four coloured aquatints after Augustus Pugin, William Westall, Frederick Mackenzie, Thomas Uwins and William Henry Pyne. The engravers are J. C. Stadler, David Havell, John Samuel Agar, John Bluck, J. Hill, and R. G. Reeve. **MF**

182
The History of the Colleges of Winchester, Eton and Westminster; with the Charterhouse, the Schools of St. Paul's, Merchant Taylors, Harrow, and Rugby and the Free-School of Christ's Hospital

Printed for and published by R. Ackermann, 101 Strand, by L. Harrison, Printer, 373 Strand, 1816
Large quarto, 33.7×27.3 cm
Cambridge, The Graham Watson Collection, The Master and Fellows of Emmanuel College
Exhibitions: London, Ackermann, 1983, Cat. No. 112
Literature: Ford 1983, pp. 43–44; Ford 1984

This work is often referred to as Ackermann's *Public Schools* and the famous London schools of Westminster, Charterhouse, Merchant Taylors and Christ's Hospital are featured. The details of the publication are unusually well documented.

Rudolph Ackermann advertised his plans for publishing this work by subscription in twelve monthly parts, each part to contain four coloured engravings with appropriate text. The first five hundred copies were priced at 12s. per number, while the next five hundred were increased to 16s. On completion, it was issued in quarto boards at 7 guineas with fifty large paper copies at 12 guineas. There were also twenty-five copies with uncoloured proof impressions of the plates on India paper.

From the start difficulties were experienced. There were only 337 pre-publication subscribers, much the lowest number for any of Ackermann's major colour-plate books. Ackermann wrote to the headmasters of Winchester, Eton, Westminster and Harrow at the beginning of 1814 for permission for his artists to draw views of the interiors and exteriors of the schools. He then decided to include four more schools – Rugby , St. Paul's, Merchant Taylors and Christ's Hospital – and deferred the advertised publication date of the first part by three months.

His artists were those who had been employed on the histories of the universities of Oxford and Cambridge: Augustus Pugin, William Westall, Frederick Mackenzie and John Gendall. The engravers of the forty-four coloured aquatint views were J.C. Stadler, David Havell, John Bluck, W. Bennett and John Agar, with Thomas Uwins engraving the four coloured line engravings of the costumes.

Changes were made during the course of publication to some of the plates. The view entitled *Charter House School from the Playground*, showing two washerwomen laying out linen on the lawn and eleven figures on the path, was later changed by means of a printed overslip lettered *Charter House from the Playground* (the word school being omitted), and later still the view was changed to show thirteen boys and masters playing cricket, with thirteen figures on the path, the laundry and washerwomen having been entirely removed. The plates were issued separately at various times with specially printed titles.

As well as coordinating the work of the artists, etchers, aquatinters and plate printers in order to produce the illustrations, Ackermann had problems finding authors to write the texts. Each school was treated in the same way, having a history, a description of the buildings, a list of fellows, a list of boys attending the school, with the scholars and a list of famous old boys, giving the total work a cohesion and uniformity. But because Ackermann chose to place the prints opposite the appropriate reference in the text there was an inconsistency in the balance of plates and text. William Combe who wrote Eton, Charterhouse, St. Paul's, Westminster, Merchant Taylors and Christ's Hospital wrote the letterpress 'in such a way as to prevent the plates interfering with each other'; that is he employed a space-filling technique of using extended quotations, which often makes for dull reading. The authors of the remaining three histories did not have Combe's professional experience and as a result the plates do not fall in regular intervals.

The choice of the three additional authors displays the complexity of the whole undertaking, and it clearly taxed Ackermann's noted efficiency. Winchester was the work of a former headmaster, William Stanley Goddard, a prebendary of St. Paul's Cathedral, and Harrow was written by a master there, Henry Drury. Combe complained that Drury persuaded Ackermann 'to let him have it to puff off the school and the inhabitants of it so that it does not bear the least conformity to the rest'.

Combe and Ackermann believed that the text of Rugby was from the pen of the headmaster, Dr. Wooll, but evidence points to the fact that Wooll farmed it out to a country clergyman, Thomas Reynolds. A Rugby schoolboy wrote to his father in October 1816: 'Mr. Reynolds is on a visit to Dr. Wooll, who has prevailed upon him to write an account of Rugby School for Ackermann's Work . . . He is still at Dr. Wooll's house and I have shown him about the building.'

It is indeed extraordinary that the publisher should not know the name of one of his authors, but the history and making of the *Colleges* highlight some of the complexities inherent in the making of a book in the early nineteenth century. **MF**

mann also published an edition in Spanish for the Spanish American market, *Viaje pintoresco a las orillas de los Rios del Rin* in 1826. The English edition was translated by John Black.

The work was designed to be similar to the elegant topographical books with large aquatint plates of the great rivers of the world. The other volumes in this informal series were: Jean-Baptiste-Balthazar Sauvan, *Picturesque Tour of the Seine* (1821); Charles Forrest Ramus, *Picturesque Tour along the river Ganges and Jumna* (1824); William Westall and S. Owen, *Picturesque Tour of the River Thames* (1828).

The 24 drawings were by C. G. Schutz and the coloured aquatints engraved by Thomas Sutherland and David Havell. **MF**

Artist unknown

184
a) Grand Entrance to the Colosseum, Regent's Park

b) The Geometrical Ascent to the Galleries

c) Bird's Eye View from the Stair-Case & the Upper Part of the Pavilion

Published by R. Ackermann and Co., 96 Strand, June 1829
Aquatints, 25 × 33 cm, 32 × 24 cm, 32 × 24 cm respectively
London, Guildhall Library, Corporation of London
Literature: Altick 1978, pp. 141–62; Wilcox 1976, pp. 99–121; Hyde 1982; Hyde 1989, pp. 79–89

The Colosseum, a panorama rotunda designed by Decimus Burton, stood at the south-east corner of Regent's Park. Erected in 1824–26 and demolished in 1875, it resembled the Pantheon in Rome. Within it, suspended from an iron hoop, was a 360-degree panorama of London measuring 24,000 square feet. This had been drawn from an observatory constructed by Thomas Horner above the ball and cross of St. Paul's. The canvas was painted by an ever-changing crew of artists working under the direction of E. T. Parris.

When publishing his five aquatints of the Colosseum in 1829, Rudolph Ackermann gave the Colosseum as well as his Strand premises as his address. It is possible he was a member of the Colosseum's Committee of Management. The title page to the series states that the engravings were after drawings made by

183

Baron Johann Isaac von Gerning

183
A Picturesque Tour along the Rhine, from Mentz to Cologne . . .

Published by R. Ackermann, 101 Strand, 1819-20
a) In monthly parts, 37 × 30.5 cm, box 39.6 × 33 cm
London, J. Gestetner Esq.

b) Large quarto, 42.9 cm × 33.7 cm
Cambridge, The Graham Watson Collection, The Master and Fellows of Emmanuel College
Exhibitions: London, Ackermann 1983, Cat.

No. 119
Literature: Tooley 1973, No. 234; Ford 1983, p. 70

Ackermann's *Rhine* was originally published in six monthly parts at 14s. each for the first 500 subscription copies with the next 250 copies at 16s. and £1.1s. for fifty large paper copies. The complete volumes were sold at £4.4s. each on ordinary paper and £6.6s. each on large paper. There were 584 subscribers with many royal and noble names of Europe in the list headed by King George IV.

Two editions were published in German by Ackermann, the original edition being published in Wiesbaden in 1819 under the title *Die Rheingegenden von Mainz bis Cölln* unillustrated, and another issued in 1820. Acker-

184a

184b

'Gandy, Mackenzie, and other eminent artists'.

Plate I shows the view one had when walking up the drive towards the building's massive portico. The lawn was divided from the Outer Circle of Regent's Park by iron railings painted in imitation of bronze. In front of the columns five American aloes were arranged. The building was tinted in tones of grey, yellow and brown to look like a temple 2,000 years old.

A corridor from the Colosseum's vestibule brought visitors to the Saloon of Arts and to the Ascending Room (London's first passenger lift) and spiral staircases. In Plate IV the Saloon is being fitted with a roof of fluted linen. Around the perimeter the recesses are occupied by settees. When completed the Saloon would serve as an exhibition hall.

In June 1829, when the Ackermann aquatints were published, the Ascending Room was not yet functioning. One therefore took the stairs to arrive at the Lower Gallery. From here the visitor had the most satisfactory view of Thomas Horner's London panorama. At this date, though the Colosseum was open to the public, the panorama and the sky were still being painted. The Lower Galley was balustraded to appear like the Golden Gallery of St. Paul's. Immediately below it was a projecting frame which, when looked at from above, had the appearance of the dome of the Cathedral.

Continuing up the staircase the visitor came to the Upper Gallery. Another flight of stairs brought one to the room which surrounded St. Paul's ball and cross, and a further flight to the Exterior Gallery. From this Exterior Gallery visitors could view the living panorama of west and north London.

Plate V shows the scene within the Colosseum looking down from one of the artists' platforms. It shows the situation as in April 1829 when the scaffolding gallery had been re-moved completely. The artists now use 'sheers' consisting of two poles from which to suspend their cradles. The painting was completed on 29 November 1829.

The print shows the Upper and Lower Galleries, the corridor doubling up as the nave of St. Paul's and the two campanile towers at the west end of the Cathedral. Many thought these towers were modelled, though in fact they were painted on the canvas. On the canvas itself one can see Regent's Park in the distance, and can even pick out the Colosseum. **RH**

184c

Rudolph Ackermann
Stolberg 1764–1834 London

185 *(illus. p.336)*
Design for a private carriage, c. 1791

Watercolour with gouache, 17.8×28 cm
London, Throgmorton Trust
Literature: Ford 1983, p. 16

Rudolph Ackermann executed this design for the carriage makers Huttons of Great Britain Street, Dublin. Ackermann had trained as a carriage designer in Basle, and designed coaches for ceremonial usage in London, Dublin and Paris. These included the funeral carriage of Admiral Lord Nelson (Cat. No. 32c). The Pope was conveyed to the self-coronation of Napoleon Bonaparte in an Ackermann coach. The great majority of Ackermann's designs were for private carriages and between 1791 and 1820 he published a series of thirteen books of carriage designs. **JF**

Artist unknown

186
Patent drawing for Ackermann's Axle, 1818

Pen and ink and wash, 60×35 cm
London, Public Record Office
Inv. No. C54/9748/Membrane 6
Literature: Repository 1819, 2nd Ser. Vol. 8, No. 39, pp. 125–35; No. 43, pp. 16–18; Ford 1983, pp. 65–66

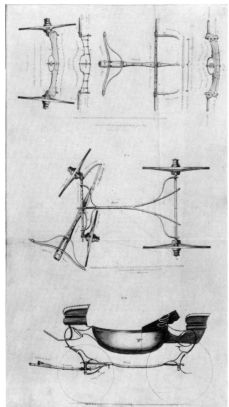

185

In May 1817 George Lankensperger, coach-maker to the king of Bavaria, wrote to Acker-mann explaining his invention of a moveable axle, and sending a working model. In the old system, the whole front axle swivelled on a central 'perch bolt', taking the wheels round with it. In the new system, the front axle stayed parallel to the back, and only the front wheels turned. The new axle was revolution-ary; according to Ackermann, it provided car-riages with a smaller turning circle, enabled them to be built shorter and lighter, with greater stability.

With the agreement of the inventor, Acker-mann applied for a patent to be given in his name and set about exploiting it. The model was advertised as being available for inspec-tion at 101 Strand; plans were printed and a book was published; testimonials were pro-duced from the British envoy to the Court of Bavaria and from the Board of the Master of the Horse to the King of Bavaria, Baron von Kesling. But there was opposition from the London coachmakers who, Ackermann sus-pected, saw their lucrative repair trade being reduced, not to mention adding 20 guineas to the cost for of new carriages and £50 to those already built.

In fact given the comparatively slow speed of carriages there was no real need for the dynamic benefits bestowed by the invention, so it did not get beyond the experimental stage until the arrival of the motor car in 1886.
JF and PM

186

187
Artist's Colours Box, 1810

Mahogany box, containing watercolour cakes, marble mixing dish, brushes etc., with drawer below, 8 × 23 × 20 cm
Inscribed on label inside lid: R. Ackermann London, Throgmorton Trust
Exhibitions: London, Ackermann, 1983, Cat. No. 35

The era of the wooden paint-box began in London around 1780. The first to mass pro-duce them were the Reeve brothers. In 1799 Rudolph Ackermann began to manufacture his own paints. With a sound knowledge of chemistry and with assistance from the chemist Frederick Accum (Cat. No. 197), he developed a number of new colours derived from mineral and vegetable sources and by 1802 there were sixty-nine colours available.

As watercolour painting became an essen-tial accomplishment for young ladies, the mar-ket for wooden paint-boxes increased. Acker-mann led the way, followed by other London-based manufacturers, Reeves, S. and J. Fuller, and Newman. A new and potent competitor appeared in 1832 when Winsor and Newton issued their first catalogue. **JF**

187

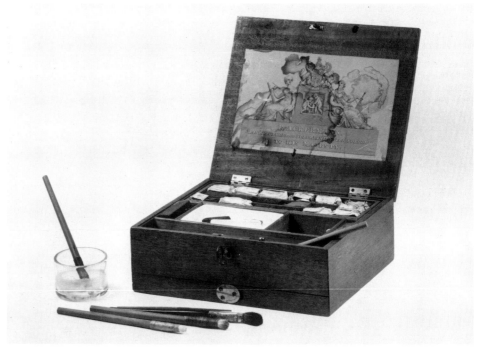

188
Ackermann's New Drawing Book of Light and Shadow, in imitation of Indian Ink

Published by R. Ackermann, Repository of Arts, 101, Strand, 1812
24.4×29.5 cm
London, Trustees of the British Museum
Inv. No. 167*b.13
Literature: Ford 1983, pp. 21, 220

Ackermann published his first drawing book, *Lessons for Beginners in the Fine Arts*, in 1796, and by 1802 he had produced twenty-five. All catered for the amateur, where a proficiency in watercolour painting was an increasingly fashionable accomplishment. In his introduction to this work Ackermann claims that British artists have exhibited to the world the beauty and power of watercolours 'and by their united efforts has this mode of painting been raised to its present unparalleled state of perfection.' After a brief disquisition on the merits of Sandby, Cousins and Girtin, he returns to his true market to flatter 'our lovely countrywomen': 'It is to the cultivation of the study of drawing in water-colours, by the enlightened ladies of our time, that the best artists have owed their encouragement.' The first edition of this work, containing twenty-four aquatints by David Cox, was published in 1809. **CF**

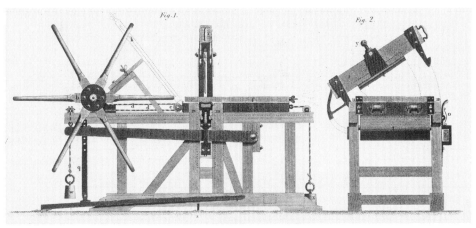

189

In characteristically energetic and practical style, he set about the promotion of lithography. He presented a small lithographic press to the Royal Society of Arts and demonstrated its use; he harangued Members of Parliament to remove the import duty on Bavarian limestone; he sold to America some of the first presses to reach that continent; and he persuaded the Society of Arts to award Senefelder a gold medal for his invention and a silver medal to the young Charles Hullmandel for lithographic drawing.

Ackermann also published in English the two most important manuals by Senefelder and Hullmandel: Senefelder's *A Complete Course of Lithography* (1819) and Hullmandel's *The Art of Drawing on Stone* (1824). **JF**

189
Lithographic Press

Model, approx. 1:5 scale, wood, made by Vic Green, Woodley Models
London, Throgmorton Trust
Provenance: Arthur Ackermann and Son Ltd.
Exhibitions: London, Ackermann, 1983, Cat. No. 77
Literature: Twyman 1970; Ford 1983, pp. 61–64

Rudolph Ackermann played a crucial role in the commercial development of lithography in England. He had followed the experiments of his fellow German Alois Senefelder closely. He had tried to buy the patent in 1803 and he published in London early lithographs (or polyautographs) printed by licensees of Senefelder. After visiting Senefelder in Germany in 1816 Ackermann decided to open his own lithographic press in London in 1817 and published a facsimile edition of Albrecht Dürer's *Designs of the Prayer Book*.

190

'An Artist of Vienna' Matthäus Loder
Vienna 1781–1828 Bad Gastein

190
Transformation Playing Cards – 'Beatrice, The Fracas'

Published by Rudolph Ackermann, Repository of Arts, 101 Strand
Stipple etching, each 9.3×6.5 cm
London, Worshipful Company of Makers of Playing Cards, deposited Guildhall Library
Inv. No. 255
Literature: Berry 1991; Berry 1991; Curl 1991, p. 223

Initially these transformation cards (playing cards in which the suit-signs are incorporated into pictures) were published as a series of plates, four cards to each, in Ackermann's *Repository of Arts*. The first plate appeared in the January 1818 issue, and the final plate in January 1819. As magazine plates the cards would have escaped the duty the government demanded from the makers of playing cards published as packs. Later Ackermann reissued them with plate numbers erased and on stiff card, but still four to a sheet.

Curl has drawn attention to the very Masonic character of some of the designs. Four of the spade cards in fact relate to a Viennese story, *Beatrice, or The Fracas*. A booklet accompanying the Ackermann reissue provides some introductory text and also the Beatrice story. The booklet states that the cards were 'designed by an artist of Vienna'. This artist has been identified as Matthäus Loder.

The prototype of the Ackermann cards is a pack published in Vienna by H.F. Müller, possibly as early as 1809. Ackermann improved the designs slightly by adding background scenes to the attractively coloured court cards and incorporating the suit-signs in the transformation fashion. **RH**

191
Playing cards: Changeable Portraits of Ladies and Gentlemen

Published by R. Ackermann, 1 January 1819
Aquatints, hand-coloured, 8.6×6.3 cm;
wooden case with sliding lid,
10.3×7.2×3.1 cm
New Haven, Yale Center for British Art
Inv. Nos. GVI199 C.42, GV1199 C.4
respectively
Exhibitions: New Haven, 1977, Cat. No. 3
Literature: Ford 1983, p. 72, illustrated

Ackermann produced a variety of card games, usually with a strong didactic flavour, combining 'amusement with instruction'. In these games, the twenty-eight cards are each divided into three interchangeable parts, making it possible to make over 20,000 different faces of each sex. As the cards include portraits of historical figures, Ackermann was perhaps not being serious when he commended the games on the grounds that 'all tastes will find samples for matrimonial choice'. **CF**

191

Thomas Talbot Bury
London 1811–1877 London

192

192
Fantascope or Optical Delusions

Published by Ackermann and Co., 96 Strand, July 1833
Circular cards, D 23.9 cm; wooden and ivory handle; case 25.8×25.8 cm
New Haven, Yale Centre for British Art
Inv. No. GV1199/+BB
Exhibitions: New Haven, 1977, Cat. No. 24, illustrated
Literature: Ford 1983, pp. 148–49, illustrated, p. 222

The psychological belief in the malleability of man widely disseminated through the writings of John Locke resulted, by the second half of the eighteenth century, in an increasing emphasis on the importance of education as a means of forming the future citizen. Improving books, toys and games for children were produced in large quantities. The leading London publishers in this trade were Newbery, Wallis, Darton, Spooner and, by the early nineteenth century, Ackermann.

This scientific toy was a manifestation of the popular enthusiasm for science, and was called a phenakistoscope. It works because the eye retains an image for a split second after seeing it. Therefore images shown in rapid succession seem to merge, and the illusion of movement is possible. **CF**

J. S. Agar, *Fashion Plates.* Cat. No. 175

S. Drummond, *Sir Marc Isambard Brunel, c.* 1835. Cat. No. 214

[William Combe]

Bristol 1741-1823 London

193

The Tour of Doctor Syntax through London, or the Pleasures and Miseries of the Metropolis

Published by J. Johnston, Cheapside, 1820
Octavo, 24×15 cm
London, The Museum of London
Inv. No. 8958
Literature: Abbey 1953, p. 225, No. 265

This work is one of many plagiarisms produced to exploit the popularity of Ackermann's *Dr. Syntax in Search of the Picturesque*, a verse satire written by William Combe with illustrations by Thomas Rowlandson. Issued first in parts in Ackermann's *Poetical Magazine* in 1809 and then in 1812 in book form at the cost of a guinea, it was a phenomenal success, going through four editions the same year, a fifth in 1813, a sixth in 1815, seventh in 1817 and eighth in 1819. A Second and Third Tour of Dr. Syntax were published by Ackermann in 1820-21, with a cheap pocket edition of all three tours in 1823.

The Syntax idea was copied repeatedly, both in England and on the continent (the German version was written by Fred Hempel, under the pseudonym 'Perigrinus Syntax'). But Johnston's plagiarism is of special interest in that it was, like the original, issued first in parts and the verse was written by Combe himself, 'moonlighting' – as is typical of hack writers – from Ackermann. Furthermore, the metropolitan tour undertaken by the albeit ingenue Dr. Syntax anticipates Pierce Egan's more famous *Life in London* published a year later (Cat. No. 671), and the quality of the illustrations, probably by Robert Cruikshank, is high.

Dr Syntax goes to a gaming house, is robbed in St. Giles and falls into the Thames, but he

193

also visits more intellectual sights. He hears a scientific lecture at the London Institution, inspects the Bank of England, listens to a debate in the House of Commons and goes to a Royal Academy exhibition. Combe's poem comments on the actual paintings hung in 1819, including Wilkie's *The Penny Wedding*, Callcott's *Rotterdam* and Turner's *Richmond Hill, on the Prince Regent's Birthday* (Cat. No. 392), as illustrated in the accompanying aquatint: 'She [Mrs Syntax] caught a view of Richmond-hill:/A spot she oft heard prais'd for beauty,/And which she thought 'twas her duty/To see.' The slightly sour footnote adds 'A noble indication of the artist's talent for local nature, which with sweetening and a little more aerial tinting would most certainly be one of his finest prospects.' **CF**

The character of Dr. Syntax, a pious, henpecked clergyman who toured Britain in search of the picturesque, and subsequently in search of a wife, was originally created by William Gilpin, but it was the illustrations of his adventures by Rowlandson that made him a popular subject on nineteenth-century English ceramics.

The scene here is taken from Rowlandson's illustration *Dr. Syntax in the Glass House* (1820), a composition that has an involved pedigree, and which ultimately derives from an illustration to the 1688 edition of Antonio Neri's *L'Arte Vetraria*, probably by way of a print by Gravelot. The scene was also copied on Staffordshire earthenware, and – appropriately enough – enamelled on to English glassware. William Combe's verses describe Dr. Syntax's attempts to make a bottle at a glass-house in Warrington, near Liverpool. The glass-house described was probably that of Perrin Geddes and Co., who made some of the most adventurous glass of Regency Britain.

New Hall made at least two patterns with Syntax subjects, and he occurs on other Staffordshire porcelains; Robert Bloor's Derby factory produced thirteen figures of him, and he appears on both Bloor and Crown Derby tablewares; he was also very popular with Staffordshire manufacturers of blue and white earthenwares, notably James and Ralph Clews of Cobridge, who produced a series of thirty-one Dr. Syntax plates, chiefly for the American market.

The New Hall factory, which had held the patent for the manufacture of hard-paste porcelain, followed other factories in about 1814 and went over to the production of bone china, the characteristic British porcelain body of the nineteenth century and the one used here. **HY**

194

194
Plate *c.* 1830

New Hall; bone china, gilded and enamelled in colours, the central panel painted with 'Dr. Syntax in the Glass House', D 21.2 cm
Mark: Pattern Number 2679 in red enamel
Inscribed: 'Dr. Syntax in the Glass-House'
London, Trustees of the Victoria and Albert Museum
Inv. No. C.41-1987
Literature: Gough 1967; Weedon 1987; Gray 1987, pp. 13 and 16

195
Jug, Dr. Syntax stopd by Highwaymen, *c.* 1820

Unknown factory, probably Staffordshire
Earthenware, printed in red and enamelled,
13×15×9.5 cm
Brighton, The Royal Pavilion, Art Gallery
and Museums
Inv. No. HW1012
Provenance: Henry Willett Collection
Exhibitions: London, Bethnal Green
Museum, 1899, p. 76, No. 1012

The transfer print on the jug is a close copy of
Rowlandson's etching illustrating Canto II of

195

William Combe's poem *The First Tour of
Doctor Syntax . . .* (1812).
 'But ah! how false is human joy!/When least
we think it, ills annoy./For now with fierce
impetuous rush,/Three ruffians issued from a
bush;/One Grizzle stopp'd and seiz'd the
reins,/While they all threat the Doctor's
brains./Poor Syntax, trembling with affright,/
Resists not such superior might,/But yields
him to their savage pleasure,/And gives his
purse, with all its treasure.'
 The unfortunate Dr. Syntax was left not
only robbed and bound securely to a tree but
also without his hat and wig which had fallen
off in the fray, leaving his bald head to be
'eaten alive' by insects until the fortunate
arrival of two comely dames released him
from his misery. **EE**

SCIENCE AND TECHNOLOGY

London was a magnet for ambitious men of science. It had the wealth to invest in new discoveries, the skilled craftsmen to
build machinery and equipment and an increasingly educated public eager to learn of the latest inventions through lectures
and periodicals.

James Gillray
London 1756–1815 London

196
**Scientific Researches! – New
Discoveries in Pneumakicks! – or – An
Experimental Lecture on the Powers
of Air, 1802**

Etching, coloured impression, 25.2×37 cm
Published by H. Humphrey, 23 May 1802
London, Trustees of the British Museum
Inv. No. J3-59
Literature: George 1947, Vol. 8, pp. 112-14,
No. 9923

The Royal Institution was founded in 1799 by
Benjamin Thompson, Count Rumford (Cat.
No. 120), with the intention of 'diffusing the
knowledge and facilitating the general introduction of useful mechanical inventions and
improvements, and for teaching by courses of
philosophical lectures and experiments the
application of science to the common pur-

poses of life'. Lectures and demonstrations
were the chief way in which such ideas were
explained to the public, establishing a tradition which still continues today.
 Two of the most celebrated scientists associated with the history of the Royal Institution
were appointed in the early years of the nineteenth century: Humphry Davy, professor of
chemistry from 1802 until 1823, and Michael
Faraday, who was engaged as Davy's assistant
in 1812, carried out his experiments in electricity in the 1820s and 1830s, and was professor of
chemistry from 1833 until 1867.
 Gillray's *Scientific Researches!* is a satire on
the early lectures held at the Institution, which
appealed chiefly to the fashionable world. The
audience is seated in a semi-circle facing the
lecturer's desk, which is crowded with scientific apparatus, watching with considerable
fascination the experiment being carried out
on one of the leading supporters of the institution, Sir John Coxe Hippisley, whose
nose is grasped by the lecturer, while a tube
from a series of retorts in which a gas has been
made, is applied to his mouth; a violent ex-

plosion of flame and smoke issues from the
victim's breeches. Standing nearby, with a sardonic expression and holding a pair of bellows
with vapour and gas spouting from its nozzle,
is the young Humphry Davy, who had joined
the Institution as assistant lecturer in 1801.
Facing the table from the right is Count Rumford, looking on at the activity. The audience
includes a number of distinguished figures,
among them Isaac D'Israeli, father of the
future prime minister Benjamin Disraeli.
Several ladies are present, including one of the
best-known bluestockings of the day, Mrs.
Locke, who earnestly takes notes; in 1804, the
Institution's lectures were to be ridiculed as fit
only for ladies of fashion.
 Gillray combines satire with realism; in 1801
Humphry Davy gave lectures on 'pneumatical
chemistry', and had administered nitrous
oxide – laughing gas – to several gentlemen.
However, the Institution went through a difficult phase in 1801–02 with internal disputes
and the departure of Rumford, and was thus
particularly vulnerable to spirited and witty
criticism such as Gillray's. **LS**

Thomas Rowlandson

London 1756–1827 London

197

Mr. Accum lecturing at the Surrey Institution, 1809

Pen and ink and watercolour over pencil,
22.4×32.7 cm
Inscribed bottom right: Mr. Acchum
Professor of Chemistry/Lecturing at the
Surrey Institution
London, The Museum of London
Inv. No. A.9269
Provenance: probably W.T.B. Ashley;
Christie's, 12 February 1912, Lot 79
Exhibitions: London, The Museum of
London, 1981, No. 61
Literature: Grego 1880, Vol. 2, pp. 366, 419;
George 1947, Vol. 8, p. 960, No. 11605;
Hayes 1960, p. 18, Plate 11

Friedrich Accum (1769–1838) was born in
Buckebourg, Westphalia, trained as a chemist
and came to London in 1793 where he helped
to promote the popular understanding and
application of science, notably gas, through
lectures and a wide range of publications (Cat.
No. 122). From 1808 he lectured at the Surrey
Institution in Blackfriars Road, Southwark,
which had been founded the same year as the
south London counterpart of the Royal Institution and the London Institution in Finsbury Circus. Accum was briefly employed as
librarian at the Royal Institution, but was
accused of embezzlement and shortly afterwards dismissed. At his trial he was acquitted
but he left for Berlin where, in 1822, he was
given a professorship at the Technical Institute, a post he held until his death. **CF**

Abraham Rees

Llanbryhmair, Montgomeryshire 1743–1825
London

198

The Cylopaedia; or Universal Dictionary of Arts, Sciences, and Literature

Published by Longman, Hurst, Rees, Orme
and Brown, Paternoster Row
1802–20, Vol. 2, 28×42 cm (open)
London, Guildhall Library, Corporation of
London
Inv. No. S.O.32

The *Cyclopaedia* was one of the most ambitious publications in the English language de-

196

signed to meet the increasing thirst for knowledge of the period. Abraham Rees, the son of
a Welsh non-conformist minister, received his
doctorate of divinity from Edinburgh University in 1775, and became patron of
London's Old Jewry Presbyterian Congregation in 1783 – a post he held until his death.

Rees's career as a cyclopaedist began in the
1770s when he produced a new edition of

Ephraim Chambers' *Cyclopaedia*. Its success
led to him becoming a fellow of the Royal
Society (1786), and he was later elected to the
Linnean Society and the American Society.

Work then started on his own *Cyclopaedia*,
issued as forty-five volumes, including six
volumes of plates, between 1802 and 1820. In
1819 and 1820 new title pages were printed for
the text and plate volumes respectively. When

197

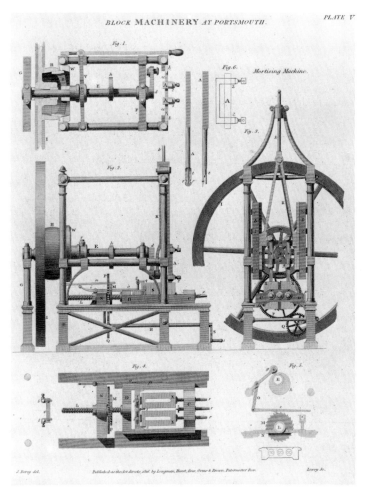

198

199

congratulated on this gargantuan task, Rees simply observed, 'I thank you, but I feel more grateful that I have been able to publish my four volumes of sermons.'

The *Cyclopaedia* has become best known for its treatment of science, industry and technology. The engraving shown here, taken from the second volume of plates, depicts Marc Isambard Brunel's mortising machine (1803) for pulley blocks. **CE**

George Scharf
Mainburg 1788–1860 London

199
The Polytechnic Institution, 1840

Lithograph, 33.7 × 24 cm, published 1840
London, Trustees of the British Museum
Inv. No. 1862-6-14-801
Literature: Jackson 1987, p. 95, illustrated

By the 1830s a much wider public than that addressed by the Royal Institution had begun to take an interest in applied science, stimulated by the publication of popular journals such as the *Penny Magazine*.

Two bodies were established in the 1830s to cater to this new audience, the Gallery of Practical Science, founded in 1832, and its great rival, the Polytechnic Institution of Regent Street, founded in 1838, shown here in Scharf's lithograph published two years later. A regular programme of lectures was organised, and demonstrations of inventors' machines and models were popular attractions for an admission fee of one shilling. The Great Hall shown here was the centrepiece, dominated by a U-shaped miniature canal, holding thousands of gallons of water, complete with lock gates and waterwheels, on which clockwork model boats sailed. The most spectacular exhibit was the diving bell to be seen at the far end of the hall, in which six visitors at a time were submerged in the water tank. The popularity of such displays may be gauged from the large number of visitors of all ages who came to admire the curiosities, both natural and mechanical, in the Institution. **LS**

Thomas Phillips
Dudley 1770–1845 London

200
Sir Humphry Davy, 1821

Oil on canvas, 91.5 × 71 cm
London, National Portrait Gallery
Inv. No. 2546
Provenance: painted for the Earl of Durham, 1821; Lambton Castle sale, 18 April 1932, Lot 61; Leggatt Brothers, from whom purchased, 1932
Exhibitions: Newcastle, 1887 and 1929
Literature: Walker 1985, Vol. 1, p. 148; Vol. 2, Plate 349

As new president of the Royal Society, Sir Humphry Davy was, by 1821, the dominant figure of fashionable London science. After working as an apothecary and trying his poetic skills in Cornwall, he attained fame as assistant to the Pneumatic Institution in Bristol between 1798 and 1801, where his work on the exciting effects of breathing nitrous oxide and of galvanic electricity drew metropolitan

200

Edward Hodges Baily
Bristol 1788–1867

202
Michael Faraday, 1834

Plaster cast after the original marble of 1830,
72 × 42 × 26 cm
Signed and dated: Faraday 1834 on the back
London, The Athenaeum
Exhibitions: the original marble at the Royal
Academy, 1830, No. 1244
Literature: Ward 1926, illustrated opp. p. 26;
Ormond 1973, Vol. 1, p. 169; Pearce
Williams 1965; Gooding and James ed. 1985;
Thomas 1991; Cantor, Gooding and James
1991; Bowers 1991; Lemmerich 1991

Michael Faraday's discoveries in electricity
and magnetism were the most important
scientific research in London in the first half of
the nineteenth century because they provided
the basis for all electrical engineering.

Born in 1791, the son of a blacksmith, Faraday lived all his life in London. He was
apprenticed as a bookbinder to George Rie-
bau, a bookseller and bookbinder, who encouraged his developing scientific interests. In
1812 Faraday was given tickets to hear Sir
Humphry Davy, lecturing at the Royal Institution and eventually he was appointed laboratory assistant at the Royal Institution,
mainly helping Davy with his work.

Faraday soon established a solid reputation
as an analytical chemist, but he leapt to prominence in 1821 for his discovery of electromagnetic rotations, showing how continuous
movement could be created by an electric current and a magnet. Ten years later, in 1831,
Faraday established the converse effect: electricity could be produced from magnetism.

Faraday's later work was concerned with
the fundamental nature of electrical, magnetic
and other forces. He showed that in certain
circumstances magnetism could affect light.
His ideas about the nature of electrical and
magnetic forces inspired James Clerk Maxwell
and others to develop the theory of electro-
magnetism that led eventually to radio. His
discovery of benzine and the laws of electrolysis were crucial to the development of chemistry.

He was a leading member of the Sandemanian church – a very small Christian sect. He
believed firmly that since God had created all
the natural world there must be some connection between the forces of nature, and he
believed, too, that it was possible by observation and experiment to learn of the working of
God's creation. His wife, Sarah, was also a
member of the Sandemanian church. The only
sadness in their marriage was that they had no
children, though they effectively adopted a
niece, Jane Barnard. **BB**

202

Michael Faraday
London 1791–1867 London

203
Notes on Sir Humphry Davy's lectures, 1812

Autograph manuscript, bound by Faraday,
21 × 32.7 cm (open), 386 pp.
London, Royal Institution of Great Britain
Exhibitions: London, National Portrait
Gallery, 1991–92, Cat. No. 9

While still a bookbinder's apprentice, Michael
Faraday was given tickets to hear some of
Humphry Davy's lectures on chemistry at the
Royal Institution in London. The Institution,
situated in Albemarle Street in the West End,
was then the scientific centre of London.
Davy's chemical discoveries had made him
famous, and his scientific lectures were a
fashionable attraction.

Faraday made notes of the lectures, bound
them, and sent the volume to Davy asking for
some scientific work. Davy was impressed,
and when a post became available, offered it to
Faraday. **BB**

attention. Hired to direct the laboratory at the
Royal Institution in 1801, Davy rapidly
attracted large audiences and wealthy patrons.

In 1806–07 he used his command of un-
precedently large electrical batteries of up to
200 plates, to extract new elements such as
potassium, sodium and chlorine. His antipathy to French chemistry and French politics
did not prevent him winning Napoleon's
international prize for galvanism in 1807.

His metropolitan success won him a knighthood from the Prince Regent in 1812 and a
baronetcy in 1818. His marriage to the heiress
Jane Apreece secured Davy a large income;
work for the government on ventilation and
for the coal owners on a miner's safety lamp,
helped propagate the image of scientific genius
and its uses. **SS**

201
Miner's safety lamp, 1815

Invented by Sir Humphry Davy
Experimental model, H 28.5 × D 8.8 cm
London, Royal Institution of Great Britain

Several mining disasters were caused by the
presence of the gas methane, known as 'fire
damp', in coal mines. The gas could form an
explosive mixture with air, and was ignited by
the open lamps used to light the mines. In 1815
Sir Humphry Davy developed the safety
lamp, in which a fine wire gauze around the
flame prevented the transmission of flame
from the lamp to the surrounding atmosphere.
Methane gas, however, could pass through the
gauze whereupon it burned with a dull red
flame, giving warning of its presence. **BB**

205

206

Michael Faraday

204
Experimental notebook, Vol. 1, 1821

Autograph manuscript, 20.7×36.3 cm
(open), 138 pp.
London, Royal Institution of Great Britain
Exhibitions: London, National Portrait
Gallery, Cat. No. 20

One of Faraday's main scientific interests was
electricity which, in the early nineteenth
century, was considered to be a branch of
chemistry. In 1820 the Dane, Hans Christian
Oersted, published his discovery that an electric current in a wire affected a nearby compass needle. This was the first proof that electricity and magnetism were inter-related.

Many people, including Faraday, repeated
Oersted's experiment. Faraday believed that it
should be possible to exploit the effect to produce continuous movement. In September
1821 he devised arrangements, described here
in his laboratory notebook, in which either a
current-carrying wire rotated around a fixed
magnet, or a moveable magnet rotated around
a fixed current-carrying wire. This is the basis
of the electric motor, though Faraday did not
look on the arrangement as a source of power:
his interest was to show the relationship between the electric and magnetic forces. **BB**

205
Induction ring, 1831

Original apparatus, D 18 cm
London, Royal Institution of Great Britain
Exhibitions: London, Science Museum, 1991;
National Portrait Gallery, 1991–92, Cat. No.
23

Oersted had shown that an electric current
could produce magnetic effects. Faraday, who
was convinced that the forces of nature must
be inter-related, sought to produce an electric
current from a magnet.

In August 1831 he made his 'induction ring',
in which two coils of wire are wound on an
iron ring. He showed that when a current
began to flow in one coil there was a brief
pulse of current in the other. When the first
current stopped there was another brief pulse
in the second coil, but in the opposite direction.

This is the basis of the electric transformer
which converts, for example, the high voltage
used in the national grid to lower voltage required for domestic electricity supplies. **BB**

206
Magnet and coil used for electromagnetic induction, 1831

Original apparatus, magnet L 21 cm, D
1.8 cm; coil L 17 cm, D 5 cm
London, Royal Institution of Great Britain
Exhibitions: London, Science Museum, 1991

The 'induction ring' experiment produced
electricity from the magnetism in the ring, but

that magnetism had been produced by another
electric current. A few weeks later Faraday
found that he could produce electricity from a
permanent magnet by moving the magnet near
a coil of wire.

Faraday used several different arrangements, including the coil and magnet shown
here. He found that the essential condition
was that the turns of the coil should cut
through the 'lines of force' of the magnet.

The electric generators in power stations are
mechanised versions of these experiments.
The steam turbine, water turbine, or other
prime mover, rotates large magnets close to
coils in which the electric current is produced.
BB

207
Copper disc, used in Faraday's disc generator, 1831

Original apparatus, D 26.5 cm
London, Royal Institution of Great Britain
Exhibitions: London, Science Museum, 1991

Faraday arranged a copper disc to turn between the poles of a horseshoe magnet. Sliding
contacts pressing on the axis and on the edge
of the disc were connected to a galvanometer.
When the disc turned, a small electric current
was produced in the part which was between
the poles of the magnet. A simple galvanometer connected to the sliding contacts indicated the presence of the current. Although its
output was very small, this was the first electric generator. **BB**

208

209

209
Spherical condenser

Original apparatus, 35.5×30.5×20.2 cm
London, Royal Institution of Great Britain
Exhibitions: London, National Portrait
Gallery, Cat. No. 41f

In studying the electrical properties of insulating materials, Faraday placed shaped test pieces in the gap in this brass spherical condenser. He measured the capacity of the condenser with the different materials inside, and thus drew conclusions about the 'specific inductive capacity' of various materials. **BB**

210
Cruickshank Battery

Invented by William Cruickshank
H 9×L 59.7×W 5 cm
London, Royal Institution of Great Britain
Inv. No. FH9

The first practical source of a continous electric current, Volta's pile, announced in 1800, could produce only a very small current. The 'galvanic trough' devised by William Cruickshank was more powerful and was the main source of electric current until the Daniell cell devised in 1836. **BB**

210

208
Electric egg

Original apparatus, H 64 cm, base D 18 cm
London, Royal Institution of Great Britain
Exhibitions: London, Science Museum, 1991

Faraday made a study of electrical discharges through gases at reduced pressure. This glass vessel was connected to an air pump, and the gap between the brass balls could be changed by sliding the upper rod through the seal at the top. High voltage electricity was then applied from an induction coil. Faraday noted the striations – a light and dark that appear in the discharge – and observed that under certain conditions a dark space (now called 'Faraday's dark space') occurs near one end of the luminous column.

Electrical discharges were not used for lighting until the end of the nineteenth century, but Faraday's work contributed to the understanding of the phenomenon. **BB**

John Isaac Hawkins
Taunton 1772–1855 Elizabeth Town, New Jersey, U.S.A.

213
Report upon two experimental brick cylinders laid down in the river Thames at Rotherhithe, in the year 1811, for . . . a tunnel under the river . . . for the Thames Archway Company

The drawings executed by Thomas Chalmers, 33 pp., 9 plates with adjoining text, pen and watercolour, 31.6×45.8 cm
London, Institution of Civil Engineers
Inv. No. Original Communication (OC) 436
Literature: Repository 1805, pp. 371–73; *Repository* 1809, pp. 397–407, Dickinson and Titley 1934; Lampe 1963; James 1974–76, pp. 161–78

In the eighteenth century the Thames presented a considerable barrier to north-south communications; and navigation interests, combined with the width of the river, made a bridge impractical below London Bridge. As a solution a succession of tunnel schemes were proposed from the 1790s onwards.

The earliest such proposal (*c.* 1798), involved a tunnel between Gravesend and Tilbury. A tunnel shaft was sunk at Gravesend in 1800–02 before work was abandoned. Despite this failure the Thames Archway Project was launched in 1804 for a tunnel between Rotherhithe and Wapping. The driftway was driven

212

211
Prospectus for 'A Course of Six Elementary Lectures on Chemistry . . .' 1827–28

Printed sheet, 14.5×10.5 cm
London, Royal Institution of Great Britain

211

Exhibitions: London, National Portrait Gallery, 1991–92, Cat. No. 34

As director of the Royal Institution, Faraday began several series of lectures designed both to promote public awareness of scientific matters, and to raise funds for the Institution. One such series was the Christmas Lectures for young people in which eminent speakers present a survey of a topic to an audience consisting mainly of older schoolchildren. Faraday gave many of the series himself, his theme being usually a survey either of chemistry or electricity. **BB**

Harriet Moore

212
Faraday's Laboratories, the Royal Institution, *c.* 1850–55

Pencil and watercolour, 41×47.2 cm
London, Royal Institution of Great Britain
Exhibitions: London, National Portrait Gallery, Cat. No. 26

The artist, Harriet Moore, painted several watercolours of scenes inside the Royal Institution in the 1840s, including both the basement laboratories and the upstairs flat where Faraday lived with his wife, Sarah. **BB**

213

within 65 feet of the north bank before work was halted in the face of increasing costs and technical problems.

In 1809 the company invited schemes for completion of the archway. The winning proposal of Charles Wyatt involved making a tunnel by excavating a trench in the bed of the Thames, sinking brick cylinders into the trench and joining them. This was essentially the world's first immersed tunnel project, and Hawkins was brought in by the company to demonstrate the practicability of the scheme and carry out an experiment of sinking two cylinders and joining them.

Experiments began in 1810 in manufacturing the cylinders and testing cements but were curtailed, however, due to their cost and the obstruction they caused to the river. On 27 November 1811 the company suspended operations, and shortage of funds meant work was never resumed. **MC**

Samuel Drummond

London 1765–1844 London

214 *(illus p.340)*
Sir Marc Isambard Brunel, c. 1835

Oil on canvas, 127×101.6 cm
London, National Portrait Gallery
Inv. No. 89
Provenance: the artist's son Julian Drummond; bought by James Roffway, 1846, from whom purchased, 1859
Exhibitions: London, Royal Academy,1836, No. 236; Guildhall Library, 1900–11; Home Office, 1914; Manchester 1968, Cat. No. 18; London, Science Museum, 1969
Literature: Walker 1985, Vol. 1, pp. 70-71; Vol. 2, Plate 151

Marc Isambard Brunel (1769–1849) was one of the leading engineers and inventors of his age. Born into a farming family at Hacqueville, Normandy, he served in the French navy, acquiring hydrographic surveying skills. Lacking sympathy with the Revolution, however, he went to America in 1793, ending up as chief engineer of New York.

In 1799 Brunel came to London, where he patented a pantograph and developed a cotton winding machine. He patented machinery for making ships' rigging blocks (1801), of which Henry Maudslay (Cat. No. 704) constructed eight working models. Between 1802–09 Maudslay produced forty-five machines, of twenty-two different types, for installation at Portsmouth dockyard. They represented the first large scale use of machine tools for mass production. With an output of 150,000 blocks a year, tens of thousands of pounds were saved.

Brunel also developed power-driven log-cutting saws which he installed in his own saw

215

mill at Battersea (1810) and at Chatham dockyard (1811). Machinery for making army boots and shoes was another invention, and he patented an improved form of stereotyping (1819). Financial security, however, eluded Brunel and in 1821 he was imprisoned at the King's Bench for debt. His release was only secured by a government gift of £5,000.

Between 1824–43 Brunel was mostly employed on the Thames tunnel (see below), which forms the backdrop to Samuel Drummond's portrait. Then sixty-five years of age, Brunel is depicted alongside a safety lamp, models of a lighthouse and a cotton-winding machine. He became a fellow of the Royal Society (1814), a member of the Institution of Civil Engineers (1823), and was knighted in 1841. He died in 1849, ten years before his even more famous son, Isambard Kingdom Brunel (Cat. No. 702). **CE**

Artist unknown

215
The Tunnel!!! or another Bubble Burst!

Coloured etching, 24×36 cm
Published by S. Knights, Sweetings Alley Royal Exchange, May 1827
London, Guildhall Library, Corporation of London
Literature: Rolt 1957, pp. 20–42; Pückler Muskau 1957, pp. 232–33, 248; Lampe 1963, Clements 1970, pp. 88–250; Altick 1978, pp. 373–74

The Thames tunnel was designed by Marc Isambard Brunel and constructed between Wapping and Rotherhithe in 1825–43. The first tunnel in the world actually to be built beneath a navigable river, it represented a major triumph for British engineering. Tunnelling was achieved by means of a shield, patented by Brunel in 1823 and built by Henry Maudslay which allowed only a small area of the excavation face to be exposed at any one time. To produce needed income, spectators were encouraged to descend the tunnel and view the works, being charged the standard fee for shows in London at the time – one shilling. On some days there were as many as 700 visitors.

During construction many lives were lost. This was generally due to water pollution rather than drowning. There were five major inundations, nevertheless, the first on 18 May 1827. On 19 July 1827 Prince Pückler Muskau 'exchanged the clear air of heaven for subterranean gloom. I went into the famous tunnel, the wonderful passage under the Thames. You have read in the papers that the water broke in some weeks ago and filled the part that was completed, 540 feet in length. Any event, lucky or unlucky, is sure to give birth to a caricature in a few days. There is one representing the tunnel catastrophe, in which a fat man on all fours, looking like a large toad, is trying to save himself and screaming "Fire!" ... With the aid of a diving bell the hole has been so stopped that it is asserted there is no fear of a recurrence of the accident ... It is a gigantic work, practicable nowhere but here, where people don't know what to do with their money.' **RH**

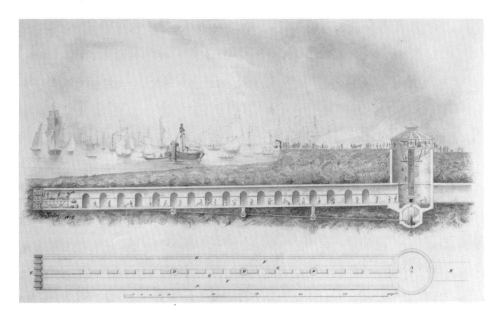

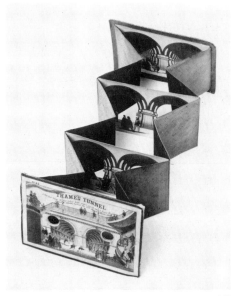

217

Le Chevalier Benjamin Schlick
Copenhagen 1796–1872 Paris

216
Rapport sur le chemin sous la Tamise, dit Tunnel, after 1825

Bound copy, watercolour, pen and ink, 33 × 21 cm
London, Jonathan Gestetner Esq.

Benjamin Schlick was a Danish architect who wrote several reports on the construction of the Thames tunnel. This one, the boards of which are ornamented with the arms of the Russian imperial family, may have been written for presentation to the Czar.

An early report dated 1826, read by Schlick to the Académie des Beaux-Arts de l'Institut de France, makes it clear that he spoke from first-hand experience of the work and suggests that he was possibly a friend and certainly a correspondent of Brunel himself.

The technology employed would have been of considerable interest to civil engineers in Russia. The River Neva in Leningrad is of a similar width (810 feet) and the construction of a satisfactory bridge had long proved problematic. **EE**

217
Thames Tunnel Peep Show, 1843

Lithograph, hand-coloured and varnished, 92 × 12.2 × approx. 26.5 cm (extended)
London, The Museum of London
Inv. No. 69.42

Operations to build the Thames Tunnel began on 16 February 1825 and in 1827 Isambard Kingdom Brunel (1806–59) became resident engineer under his father. Work was delayed by the flooding and by strikes and completely suspended between 1828 and 1835 because of lack of funds. The tunnel was finally opened to the public in March 1843 after work had been completed with a new improved shield and substantial government funding. Although it was intended for vehicles, there was not sufficient money to build the necessary access ramps, and it was only used as a foot tunnel.

In the 1860s the tunnel was converted for use by the East London Railway. It now carries East London line underground trains. **EE**

Henry Maudslay
London 1771–1831 London

218
Screw-cutting lathe, c. 1800

Model, scale of 1:6–1:8, bronze, steel and wood, 20.2 × 33.6 × 17.3 cm
London, Trustees of the Science Museum
Inv. No. 1900-19
Provenance: purchased from W. H. Maudslay Esq.
Literature: Holtzapffel 1846; Gilbert 1971

Henry Maudslay was perhaps the finest mechanic of his generation, setting entirely new standards of excellence in the design and construction of machinery: it was largely the work of his firm that made London work a synonym for the best quality in engineering.

Maudslay was trained at the Woolwich Arsenal, first in the carpenters' shop and then in the smithy. When still only eighteen he had such a reputation as a skilled worker and as an able designer, that he was engaged by Joseph Bramah to solve problems in the production of Bramah's patent lock (Cat. No. 219).

Maudslay's supremacy depended on these traits: his appreciation of first class practical work, his grasp of sound design and his willingness to go to great lengths to improve mechanical detail. Soon after setting up on his own in 1797, he began a long course of work aimed at perfecting screws and the tools for making them. The variations between binding screws, even when made with the same tools, was a nuisance, but the screw had also taken on a new significance as a driving or measuring element, and precision was essential.

Maudslay's first and second screw-cutting lathes are believed to be held in the Science Museum, London, and the Henry Ford Museum, Dearborn, U.S.A. respectively. This model illustrates a third and rather more developed design. All three machines have a slide rest to carry the cutting tool drawn along the bed by a lead screw, connected by gears to the mandrel that turns the screw to be cut. The earlier machines have beds formed of pairs of bars of triangular section, but in this machine we see a flat bed with dovetailed edges formed as a single casting, which later became the standard form; this machine may have been the first so designed. Maudslay was one of the first engineers who regularly resorted to building models of projected machines, either to secure the interest of a potential client (as in the case of the model blockmaking machines executed for Marc Brunel), or to try out an idea (as with certain steam engines, and perhaps this lathe), or purely as a recreation (as with the model of the engines for the P.S. Dee, Cat. No. 704). **MW**

219
Bramah lock and board, *c.* 1801

Made by Henry Maudslay
Lock, brass and steel, 17.8×7.6×17.8 cm
Board, wood, 40.5×30.5×2.54 cm
London, on loan to the Science Museum
since 1972
Inv. No. 1972-290/91
Literature: Price 1856, pp. 268–321, 559–82;
McNeil 1968, pp. 36–55, 190–201

This padlock was manufactured by the engineer Henry Maudslay around 1801 while he was working as a craftsman for the inventor and locksmith Joseph Bramah (1749–1815). It was placed in the window of Bramah and Company's shop at 124 Piccadilly, London, along with the board which translates: 'the artist who can make an instrument that will pick or open this lock shall receive 200 guineas the Moment it is produced'. There it remained, unpicked, until 1851 when it was opened after sixteen days by the famous American locksmith A.C. Hobbs and he was eventually awarded the prize money.

The Bramah lock was originally patented in 1784 and was one of the first high-security locks to be mass produced. It was specifically designed to thwart the lock picker since, unlike earlier designs, it was not possible to construct a skeleton key for this lock. The mechanism consists of a series of metal plates

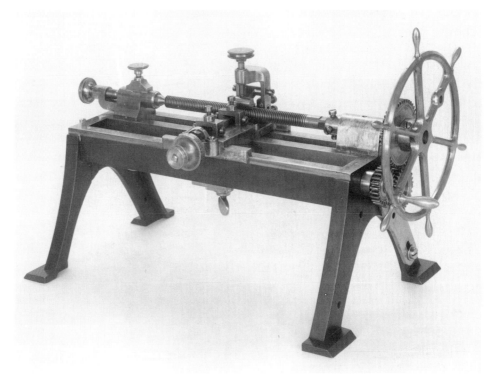

218

or slides, which each carry a notch at some point along their length. The lock can only be rotated and the bolt moved when the correct key has aligned the notches to form a groove in which the lock may turn.

Significantly, the Bramah lock appeared during a period of rising crime and general unrest. **BG**

219

220

220 (illus. p.351)
Charles Babbage's Difference Engine No. 1 – demonstration model

Bronze and steel on wooden base,
30×38×33 cm
London, Science Museum
Inv. No. 1967-70
Provenance: Henry Prevost Babbage;
University College London
Exhibitions: London, Science Museum
1991–92
Literature: Cohen 1988; Swade 1991, pp.
34-36

Charles Babbage (1791–1871) is credited with the design of the first automatic calculating machines. He conceived the Difference Engine No. 1 in 1821 to eliminate the risk of human error in the preparation of mathematical tables. He spent over a decade designing and constructing the machine with help from the engineer, Joseph Clement. The project was abandoned, uncompleted, in 1833.

The model shown was assembled by Charles' son, Henry Prevost Babbage, from unused parts made by Clement for the full-sized engine. It is one of five or six similar models sent by Henry to prominent centres of learning, as objects of historical and educational interest. This model was sent to University College, London; others were sent to Harvard, USA, and Cambridge University. The design of the complete machine called for 25,000 individual parts, of which an estimated 12,000 were made. Most of these were later melted down for scrap. Loose parts and a few partial assemblies are all that remain from the project.

The model demonstrates the basic logical element of the difference engine, an adding device, which is replicated many times in the full machine. The mechanism adds two numbers, takes account of any carry from units to tens, and includes mechanisms for automatically locking the number wheels to prevent derangement. It is operated by setting and turning the shafts from above by hand. The full-sized engine, on the other hand, was automatic: once the initial values were entered, it would not have required the intervention of the operator other than to turn a large handle.

A similar model offered to Harvard in 1896 came to the attention of Howard Aiken, a pioneer of modern electronic computing in the 1930s. He recalls that it was these 'calculating wheels' that drew his attention to Babbage's work and greatly influenced him. The piece represents one of the tenuous links between Babbage's work on automatic calculating machines in the nineteenth century and the modern era of electronic computing. **DS**

221

221
Ornamental turning lathe, No. 620, 1824

Holtzapffel and Deyerlein
Lathe, in mahogany, iron, steel and brass, with tambour top, overhead gear and a range of special cutting frames and chucks, which enable a wide variety of work to be undertaken, 194 × 116 × 68 cm
Marks: headstock signed Holtzapffel and Deyerlein, London, 620
London, Richard Maude
Provenance: sold to H. Wormald on 23 January 1824
Literature: Abell 1950; Ogden, 1987

John Jacob Holtzapffel was born in Strasbourg on 28 July 1768, and George Deyerlein in Mannheim in 1767. Deyerlein, a journeyman locksmith, worked in Strasbourg for thirteen months in 1787–88, where presumably he met the mechanic, Holtzapffel; he then spent

about a year in Paris and arrived in London in 1790.

Holtzapffel also came to London via Paris but did not arrive until 1792, where he was initially employed until 1794 by Jesse Ramsden, the famous instrument maker. He then went into business with Deyerlein as an employee, who was made a partner in 1804, remaining one until 1827 when the partnership was dissolved. Deyerlein died in 1829 and is buried in Sutton. Holtzapffel died in 1835 having become a British citizen, and the business was carried on by his descendants until about 1930.

Lathes manufactured by Holtzapffel date to 1795. Although neither the originator nor the only maker of ornamental turning lathes, Holtzapffel was the most famous and brought them to their zenith in the nineteenth century.

The Holtzapffel and Deyerlein partnership had addresses at 118 Long Acre (1804–11), 10 Cockspur Street (1812–20), and 64 Charing Cross (1821–27), and produced around 1,300 lathes. Lathe 620 was sold in 1824 for £200 – equivalent to four years' wages for an ordinary workman – but its numbering sequence suggests a date of 1807–09. Holtzapffel and Deyerlein (who also made other mechanical and edge tools, as well as dealing in ivory and hardwoods for turners) sold plain lathes and ornamental turning lathes which could reach £400 in price. Whilst a wide variety of London manufacturers were customers, their main market was the wealthy gentry, clergy, aristocrats and heads of state: Queen Victoria gave Archduke Otto von Hapsburg of Austria a lathe by Holtzapffel as a wedding present in 1886; this was a second-hand one but refurbished by Holtzapffel. **RM**

WATERCOLOURS

By 1800 the art of watercolour had evolved into a highly specialised and eagerly collected art form. Many artists chose to work exclusively in the medium, in order to capture fleeting changes in the quality of light and atmosphere. But watercolour was seen as inferior to oil and the Royal Academy relegated watercolours to a small room in its annual exhibition. The Society of Painters in Water-Colours was founded in 1804 to remedy this situation and its annual exhibitions drew thousands of visitors. Counterpointing their public success, William Blake created watercolours whose visionary subject-matter appealed only to a small group of patrons and fellow artists.

Stephen Rigaud
London 1777–1861 London

222
The Genius of Painting Contemplating the Rainbow, 1807

Watercolour, 59.7 × 49.9 cm
Signed lower left: S. Rigaud 1807
London, Trustees of the Royal Watercolour Society
Provenance: presented by the artist, 1807
Exhibitions: Society of Painters in Water-Colours, 1807, No. 294; Birmingham, 1987, No. 9

This watercolour, painted and exhibited in 1807, commemorates the foundation of the Society of Painters in Water-Colours three years earlier; Rigaud was one of the sixteen original members. The Society was the first to be devoted exclusively to the exhibition of watercolours, and was to be of considerable influence in shaping contemporary taste. Here, the Genius of Painting – a watercolourist of course – is shown dipping his brush into the stream flowing from Mount Helicon's Spring of Hippocrene (itself created by Pegasus striking the mountainside with his hoof), while he gazes at a now sadly faded rainbow, and seeks inspiration from nature. **LS**

John Hassell
1767–1825

223
Aqua Pictura, 1813

Second edition, published by Hassell and Co., 11 Clement's Inn, Strand
29.8 × 46.7 cm
London, Trustees of the British Museum
Inv. No. 167*c.15

Aqua Pictura.

ILLUSTRATED BY A

SERIES OF ORIGINAL SPECIMENS

FROM THE WORKS OF

MESSRS.

PAYNE	WHEATLEY	CLENNELL	OWEN
MUNN	YOUNG	COX	GLOVER
FRANCIA	CHRISTAL	PROUT	TURNER
SAMUEL	CARTWRIGHT	HILLS	LOUTHERBOURG,
VARLEY	GIRTIN	DEWINT	&c. &c.

Exhibiting the Works of the

MOST APPROVED MODERN WATER COLOURED DRAFTSMEN,

WITH THEIR STYLE & METHOD OF TOUCH,

ENGRAVED AND FINISHED IN PROGRESSIVE EXAMPLES.

BY J. HASSELL.

SECOND EDITION.

LONDON:

PRINTED FOR THE PROPRIETORS, AND SOLD BY HASSELL & CO. **11,** CLEMENT'S INN, STRAND; AND MESSRS. SHERWOOD, NEELY & CO. **20,** PATERNOSTER-ROW.

W. Wilson, Printer, 4, Greville-Street, Hatton-Garden, London.

223

According to the introduction, this work was intended for those amateur artists who wanted to get beyond the stage of slavish copying of one master: 'when earlier studies are matured and expanded by contemplating exhibitions, respectively, of the various masters, the student then begins to perceive that excellencies may attach to every style, and consequently to every professor. Upon this discovery he bursts the trammels of plagiarism, and selects, in tasteful combination, the perfections of any specimen placed before him.'

Hassell's novel 'teach yourself' proposal was to publish each month originals provided by the 'most approved modern water coloured draftsmen, with their style & method of touch, engraved and finished in progressive examples'. To facilitate copying, Hassell explained the colours used by the draughtsmen 'with a practical and descriptive specimen of every tint that appears in each drawing'. **CF**

George Scharf
Mainburg 1788–1860 London

224
Allen's Colourman's Shop, St. Martin's Lane, 1829

Watercolour over pencil, 13.8 × 22.7 cm
Signed, dated and inscribed bottom right: 1829 G. Scharf del. In St. Martin's Lane
London, Trustees of the British Museum
Inv. No. 1862-6-14-119
Provenance: from a collection of the artist's works purchased from his widow, 1862
Exhibitions: London, British Museum, 1985, Cat. No. 148b, Plate 104
Literature: Jackson 1987, p. 32

The shop shown here had sold artists' materials since the 1790s; in Scharf's day it was

owned by Edward Allen – perhaps the figure visible inside grinding pigments – and as Scharf and his family lived further down St. Martin's Lane until 1830, it is very possible that he depicts himself leaving the shop with his purchases, accompanied by his elder son, George.

Although painters in oil had been able to buy their colours ready-prepared since the mid seventeenth century, it was not until *c.* 1780 that watercolourists were able to do so. The convenience of portable 'Watercolours in cakes', a British innovation successfully developed by Thomas and William Reeves, and Winsor and Newton, made the medium accessible to amateurs, as well as increasing its use among professional artists. **LS**

George Scharf

225 *(illus. p. 359)*
Interior of the Gallery of the New Society of Painters in Water-Colours, Old Bond Street, 1834

Watercolour and bodycolour with scratching-out over pencil, 29.6 × 36.9 cm
Signed and dated bottom right: G. Scharf Pinxt. 1834
London, Trustees of the Victoria and Albert Museum
Inv. No. 2979 – 1876
Provenance: William Smith, by whom bequeathed in 1876
Literature: Hardie, 1966–68, Vol. 3, p. 18, Plate 23; Lambourne and Hamilton 1980, p. 339, reproduced; Bayard 1981, p. 32, Fig. 9

Paintings of picture galleries gained popularity in Britain at the end of the eighteenth century. George Scharf had already painted a smaller watercolour of the 1828 Royal Academy exhibition (Cat. No. 382) before taking on the New Society, of which he was a founding member. Its premises, at 16 Old Bond Street, were quite cramped, although the dense hanging shown in Scharf's watercolour derived as much from fashion as from necessity. In 1835, however, the society moved to 53 Pall Mall, where it remained until taking even larger galleries in Piccadilly in 1880. Retitled the Institute of Painters in Water-Colours in 1863, it still maintains a friendly rivalry with the 'Old Society' (now the Royal Watercolour Society). **SGW**

John Scarlett Davis
Hereford 1804–1845 ?London

226 *(illus. p. 358)*
The Library at Tottenham, the Seat of B.G. Windus, Esq., 1835

Watercolour with gum arabic, 29.9 × 55.7 cm
Signed: SCARLETT DAVIS 1835
London, Trustees of the British Museum
Inv. No. 1984-1-21-9
Provenance: B. G. Windus; . . . Sotheby's, 17 November 1983, Lot 154; Thomas Agnew and Sons Ltd.
Exhibitions: London, British Museum, 1985, Cat. No. 169, Plate 118
Literature: Shanes 1984

This picture records some of the finished watercolours by Turner in one of the most distinguished nineteenth-century collections of British graphic art. Benjamin Godfrey Windus (1790–1867) was a prosperous industrialist, a member of a long-established family of coach builders, who lived in Tottenham Green, on the northern outskirts of London, and began to collect drawings from about 1820. His interest was not in the traditional area of old master collecting, but in contemporary and specifically British art. By 1840, he had amassed some two hundred watercolours by Turner; he also owned Fuseli's *Roman Album* (now in the British Museum), as well as large numbers of drawings by Thomas Stothard and David Wilkie, and was later a patron of the Pre-Raphaelites.

In February 1835 he was commissioned by Windus to paint this picture of his children Mary and Arthur in the library at Tottenham, which was hung exclusively with watercolours by Turner, almost all of which can be identified; in keeping with contemporary taste they were displayed against scarlet walls and close-framed *en suite* in an elaborate gold moulding, in the manner of oil paintings. Scarlett Davis later recorded that Turner himself had seen this drawing 'and spoken in the highest terms of it . . . it now hangs in company with fifty of his best works'. **LS**

William Blake
London 1757–1827 London

227
A Descriptive Catalogue of Pictures, Poetical and Historical Inventions, Painted by William Blake in Water Colours, being the Ancient Method of Fresco Painting Restored, and Drawings, For Public Inspection, and for Sale by Private Contract

Thirty eight leaves bound with original wrappers in blue morocco gilt, 19.5 × 11.8 cm
Printed by D.N. Shury, 7 Berwick Street, Soho for J. Blake, 28 Broad Street, Golden Square, 1809
Inscribed in title page in Blake's hand: At N 28 Corner of Broad Street Golden Square
Cambridge, Syndics of the Fitzwilliam Museum
Provenance: gift of Charles Fairfax Murray, 1912
Exhibitions: Cambridge, 1970, Cat. No. 31
Literature: Keynes 1921, pp. 85–89, copy G; Crabb Robinson 1932, pp. 17–20; Keynes 1957, pp. 560–86; Bentley 1969, pp. 215–20, 225–26; Macmillan 1971–72, pp. 203–06; Bindman 1977, pp. 154–64; Paley 1978, pp. 47–49, 51–53, 66; Butlin 1981, Vol. 1, pp. 472–73

Despite the support of a small number of loyal patrons, notably Thomas Butts, Blake failed to establish himself with the wider public. In desperation, he put on an exhibition of his own work at his brother James's house in Broad Street, Soho. The exhibition opened in the middle of May and was scheduled to close at the end of September; admission was by this catalogue, sold at 2s.6d. Its contents were ambitious, for not only did it give long descriptions of the works on show, but it included the artist's views on the tempera technique he had adopted and called 'fresco', and an attack on those artists who, he believed, sacrificed form or outline to colour.

The exhibition was not a success. No works were sold and the only review was hostile. The exhibition was extended well into 1810, for Henry Crabb Robinson (Cat. No. 431) visited it in April and June that year. His purpose was to write an article on the 'insane poet and painter engraver Blake' for a new German magazine published by Friedrich Perthes of Hamburg, entitled *Vaterländische Annalen*. The article duly appeared in the only number of the second volume of the magazine, which, owing to the vicissitudes of the Napoleonic Wars, then ceased publication; according to Crabb Robinson, Perthes concluded, 'as he had no longer a Vaterland, there could be no *Vaterländische Annalen*'. **CF**

William Blake

228
The Soldiers casting Lots for Christ's Garments, 1800

Pen and watercolour over pencil, 44×33.5 cm
Signed, dated and inscribed: W B inv 1800; John 19, c. 23 and 24 v
Cambridge, Syndics of the Fitzwilliam Museum
Inv. No. PD.30.1949
Provenance: Thomas Butts; Thomas Butts junior; Richard Monckton Milnes, lst Lord Houghton; lst Marquess of Crewe; W. Graham Robertson; given by his executors to the Museum through the National Art-Collections Fund, 1949
Exhibitions: London, 28 Broad Street, 1809, pp. 85–86, Cat. No. 12; Wildenstein, 1986, p. 86, Cat. No. 45, illustrated
Literature: Bindman 1970, pp. 22–23, No. 22, Fig. 10; Butlin 1981, Vol. 1, pp. 359–60, No. 495; Vol. 2, Plate 571

The watercolour was included in Blake's exhibition of 1809–10, according to the catalogue as one of the four drawings 'the artist wishes

228

were in fresco on an enlarged scale to ornament the altars of churches, and to make England, like Italy, respected by respectable men of other countries on account of art.' The prominence of the soldiers and the depiction of the crosses from behind may reflect the influence of Nicolas Poussin's *The Crucifixion* (Wadsworth Athenaeum, Hartford, Connecticut), which was in the Sir Lawrence Dundas sale at Christie's in 1794, and could also have been known to Blake through an engraving. The work was one of a series of small paintings of biblical subjects commissioned in 1799 by Thomas Butts, a government clerk. **CF**

229

William Blake

229
As if an Angel Dropped down from the Clouds, or The Genius of Shakespeare, 1809

Watercolour with pen and ink, 23.1×17.3 cm
Signed bottom right: W. Blake 1809
London, Trustees of the British Museum
Inv. No. 1954-11-13-1 (37)
Provenance: Reverend Joseph Thomas; his widow; their daughter Mrs. John Woodford Chase; Drummond Percy Chase, 1876; Alexander Macmillan, 1870; by descent to W. E. F. Macmillan; presented to the British Museum by his executors, 1954
Exhibitions: London, British Museum, 1957–58; Tate Gallery, 1978, No. 254, illustrated; Tokyo, 1991, No. 64
Literature: Rossetti 1880, p. 217, No. 79; Blunt 1959, p. 19; Butlin 1981, p. 406, No. 547(6)

This work is one of six watercolours painted by Blake for the Reverend Joseph Thomas, to be inserted as illustrations to his copy of the 1632 second folio Shakespeare; thirty watercolours by other artists were included, and the project, begun in 1801, was completed in 1809, the year in which this was drawn.

W. M. Rossetti correctly identified this as an illustration of Act IV, Scene I of *Henry IV*, Part I, where Richard Vernon describes the sight of Prince Henry, in full armour: 'Rise from the ground like feather'd Mercury,/ And vaulted with such ease into his seat,/ As if an angel dropp'd down from the clouds,/ To turn and wind a fiery Pegasus,/ And witch the world with noble horsemanship.' Yet, characteristically, Blake goes far beyond the task of pedantically illustrating a specific text; his visual imagination soars with an energy that matches Shakespeare's own. **LS**

Thomas Girtin
London 1775–1802 London

230 *(illus. p. 357)*
a) Westminster and Lambeth, 1801

Watercolour with pen and ink over pencil, 29.1×52.4 cm
London, Trustees of the British Museum
Inv. No. 1855-2-14-23
Provenance: Chambers Hall, by whom presented to the British Museum, 1855

230b

Exhibitions: Manchester and London, 1975, No. 25; London, British Museum, 1985, No. 82a, Plate 60; Barbican Art Gallery, 1988-89, Cat. No. 34
Literature: Whitley 1924, pp. 13–20, Fig. 2; Whitley 1928, pp. 37–43; Girtin and Loshak 1954, pp. 35–6, 44–45, 58–59, 105, 115, 117–18, 165

b) The Thames from Queenhithe to London Bridge, 1801

Watercolour over pencil, 20.6×44.4 cm
London, Trustees of the British Museum
Inv. No. 1855-2-14-28
Provenance: as above
Exhibitions: Munich, 1950, No. 131; Manchester and London, 1975, No. 28; British Museum, 1985, No. 82e, Plate 63; Barbican Art Gallery, 1988-89, Cat. No. 34
Literature: Whitley 1924, Fig. 6; Girtin and Loshak 1954, pp. 33–36, 164

In the year before his death (which occurred at the early age of twenty-six), Girtin undertook his most important project, a panorama of London, known as the *Eidometropolis*. Hitherto he had worked on the small scale of the watercolourist, but this was painted on an enormous scale – a press announcement described it as 108 feet in circumference and 18 feet in height, a circular panorama within which the spectator stood – and in oil, a rare instance of his use of the medium.

Many previous artists had found the banks of the Thames a rich source of subject matter, but Girtin's immediate inspiration must have been the detailed large scale panorama of London from the Albion Mills, which Robert Barker and his son Henry had exhibited in 1792, and two other panoramas painted by friends of his in 1800. Girtin seems to have recognised that this new and highly popular art form offered him the opportunity of displaying his talents without being dependent on the whims of a private patron. Six studies in the British Museum and a small group of pen and ink drawings (in the British Museum, the Guildhall Library and the Yale Center for British Art) made in preparation for the *Eidometropolis* provide the only reliable surviving information for its appearance; two of these watercolour studies are shown here.

The *Eidometropolis* was exhibited at Spring Gardens from August 1802 until Girtin's death on 9 November, and was subsequently reopened until the end of March 1803, when it was put into storage. To judge from Book VII of *The Prelude* (Cat. No. 428), it may well have been among the sights of London to

which Charles Lamb took the Wordsworths. In later years, the panorama disappeared; according to one source it was sold around 1825 to a Russian nobleman.

Girtin brought to the panorama, hitherto conceived in terms of dry topography, a new understanding of atmosphere, light and distance. The watercolour studies show him developing the atmospheric effects which were so striking. *Westminster and Lambeth* shows the view from his vantage point looking towards Westminster Abbey and St. John Smith Square, with its distinctive pepper pot towers. *The Thames from Queenhithe to London Bridge* is the most dramatic of the series. The spires and towers of the city churches punctuate the horizon, which is further dramatised by the threatening storm clouds. LS

Thomas Girtin and Frederick Christian Lewis
London 1775–1802 London,
London 1779–1856 London respectively

231
The Pont de la Tournelle and Notre Dame from the Arsenal, 1802

Soft ground etching by Thomas Girtin with aquatint by F. C. Lewis, 15.1×44.2 cm
Published by T. Girtin, 17 August 1802
London, Trustees of the British Museum
Inv. No. 1897-11-17-210
Literature: Morris 1986, pp. 25–27

At the beginning of November 1801 Girtin went to Paris for reasons that remain mysterious, partly perhaps, like other artists, taking advantage of the brief Peace of Amiens – a lull in the Napoleonic Wars – to see the city and the astonishing spoils looted by Napoleon in Italy, ranging from Laocoon to Raphael's *Transfiguration*. He also had in mind the possibility of exhibiting his *Eidometropolis* in Paris, although he soon decided that this was not realistic. Girtin seems also to have contemplated a panorama of Paris, of the same type as the *Eidometropolis*, but a rival (though considerably inferior) English artist, J.S. Hayward, had already reached an advanced stage in his preparations for a panorama.

The chief fruit of his visit was the material he assembled for his only prints, *Twenty Views in Paris;* nineteen drawings survive, all of which are in the British Museum. They are taken from viewpoints all over Paris and its immediate environs, most of them combining

231

WATERCOLOURS

T. Girtin, *Westminster and Lambeth*, 1801. Cat. No. 230a

a view of the River Seine with an important monument – medieval or modern. Only two form a continuous view in the manner of his London watercolours.

Shortly after his return from Paris in mid May 1802, Girtin began to make etched outlines for *Twenty Views*. He then washed at least one or two sets of etchings with soft tones of watercolours as guides for the aquatinter (Turner later followed Girtin's method quite closely in his *Liber Studiorum* of 1807–19, Cat. No. 420). The aquatinting was completed after Girtin's early death, in November 1802, and they were published in 1803 by his brother John. Their simple perfection of design and sense of panoramic grandeur made the *Twenty Views* a significant influence on the next generation of artists, notably Samuel Prout and Thomas Shotter Boys, who wrote of the series: 'It is so correct there is not a line out.'
LS

John Sell Cotman
Norwich 1782–1842 London

232
The Scotchman's Stone on the Greta, Yorkshire, c. 1805–08

Watercolour over pencil, 26.7×39.4 cm
London, Trustees of the British Museum
Inv. No. 1902-5-14-12
Provenance: the artist's son, John Joseph Cotman; William Steward; James Reeve, 1861; purchased from him, 1902
Exhibitions: Norwich, 1808, No. 104; Norwich, 1888, No. 16; London, Burlington Fine Arts Club, 1888, No. 19; Manchester, 1961, No. 50; Arts Council, 1982–83, No. 69; London, British Museum, 1985, No. 122, Plate 89
Literature: Kitson 1937, pp. 83, 368; Holcomb 1978, pp. 10–11, Plate 23

Cotman was born in Norfolk. He moved to London in 1798 where he found a job colouring prints for Rudolph Ackermann. He had no formal training as an artist but was taken up by Dr. Thomas Monro, who offered him the same sort of hospitality and encouragement as he had previously to Girtin and Turner. In

1800 he exhibited at the Royal Academy for the first time and in that, or the following year, he became a member of the Sketching Society, a group of young avant-garde landscape artists led originally by Thomas Girtin and, in due course, by Cotman himself. It was at meetings of the society when everyone present drew a subject set by the presiding member that Cotman's distinctive style began to develop; it was to find its fullest expression in the watercolours inspired by his annual visits to Yorkshire between 1803 and 1805.

For around five years Cotman was regarded as one of the most promising landscapists, but in 1806, he took the fatal decision (perhaps prompted by his mysterious failure to be elected a member of the Society of Painters in Water-Colours) to leave London and return to his native city. For the next twenty-seven years he barely exhibited his work in London, and thus forfeited any serious possibility of achieving the wider recognition he merited. He worked chiefly as a drawing master and etcher of antiquarian subjects, and eventually, in 1834, returned to London to teach at King's College. Although the watercolours he made c. 1800–10 are generally regarded as his finest, those from the 1820s and 1830s are increasingly admired.

In July 1805 Cotman was invited to Rokeby

J. S. Davis, *The Library at Tottenham, the Seat of P. G. Windus, Esq.,* 1835. Cat. No. 226.

Park in North Yorkshire, where he stayed for around four weeks, first as the guest of Mr. and Mrs. John Morritt and then at the local inn. Morritt was a classical scholar, had travelled extensively and was a collector of paintings (among them the *Rokeby Venus* by Velasquez now in the National Gallery, London). The park at Rokeby was threaded through by the River Greta, whose wooded banks were to inspire some of Cotman's most remarkable works.

The Scotchman's Stone is a large boulder in the river bed, and Cotman refers in a letter of August 1805 to 'having coloured a sketch of it'. He was certainly familiar with the traditional procedure, then practised by almost all landscape watercolourists, of making pencil sketches in front of the motif and then working them up in the studio into finished watercolours. At the same time, some artists, Cotman included, were beginning to use colour while working outdoors. He wrote to his Norfolk patron, Dawson Turner, from Yorkshire in 1805 that his 'chief study had been colouring from Nature', adding that many of his works were 'close copies of that ficle (sic) Dame', which might suggest that he found the process unfamiliar and difficult. Whether this work is a coloured sketch from nature or a finished watercolour is not resolved.

By 1806 it may be that Cotman's style was perceived as being too quirky, too individualistic; perhaps this accounts for his rejection in London's artistic circles. His delicate observation of isolated natural motifs was hardly calculated to appeal to contemporary taste; as a friend and patron told him: 'Two thirds of mankind, you know, mind more about what is represented than how it is done.' This watercolour, unsold in Cotman's lifetime, was among a large number later pledged to a pawnbroker by one of his sons. **LS**

232

G. Scharf, *Interior of the Gallery of the New Society of Painters in Water-Colours, Old Bond Street*, 1834. Cat. No. 225

John Sell Cotman
Norwich 1782–1842 London

233 *(illus. p. 360)*
Durham Cathedral, 1806

Watercolour over pencil, 43.6×33 cm
London, Trustees of the British Museum
Inv. No. 1859-5-28-119
Provenance: Dawson Turner; Puttick and
Simpson, 16 May 1859, Lot 812; purchased
by the Museum, 1859
Exhibitions: London, Royal Academy, 1806,
No. 461; Norwich Society of Artists, 1807,
No. 18; London, Royal Academy, 1951–52,

No. 488; Norwich, 1955, No. 54; Arts
Council, 1982–83, No. 42; London, British
Museum, 1985, No. 123, Plate 87

This is among the most monumental of Cotman's watercolours. Early in September 1805
he visited Durham after a month spent sketching at Rokeby Park. He had been reluctant,
despite urging from friends, to visit the city,
being preoccupied with his intensive study of
nature. 'But seriously,' he wrote, 'what have I
to do with Durham? Am I to place it on my
studies of trees like a rookery? No, and
besides, I have no time for Durham.'
    In fact the mighty cathedral and its majestic
setting impressed him so much that he made at

least five views, of which this is the finest,
showing the cathedral perched like his 'rookery' high above the trees. It is probably the
watercolour exhibited by Cotman at the
Royal Academy in 1806 and at the Norwich
Society of Artists in the following year. It subsequently belonged to his patron, the banker
Dawson Turner, a considerable antiquarian,
whose passion for medieval architecture
would have predisposed him to find this subject of particular interest. Characteristic of
Cotman, however, is the fact that this is in no
way simply a topographical watercolour; the
overwhelming impression is one of grandeur
and noble simplicity. **LS**

J. S. Cotman, *Durham Cathedral*, 1806. Cat. No. 233

John Varley
London 1778–1842 London

234
The Valley of the Mawddach, 1805

Black chalk and watercolour with
scratching-out, 44.1×62.6 cm
Signed and dated lower left: J. Varley, 1805
Cambridge, Syndics of the Fitzwilliam
Museum
Inv. No. 1607
Provenance: Thomas Agnew and Sons Ltd.;
bought by the Friends of the Fitzwilliam,
1931
Exhibitions: Queensland and Cambridge,
1982–83, p. 43, Cat. No. 52, Plate 27

Born in Hackney, John Varley was a key
figure for the generation of watercolour artists
who matured in London during the early
nineteenth century. He himself trained under
F. L. T. Francia at J. C. Barrow's drawing
school in Holborn, and exhibited at the Royal
Academy for the first time in 1798. By the
early 1800s he was in contact with Dr. Monro
and his sketching circle, and belonged to the
club started by Thomas Girtin and continued
by Cotman.

  With his brother Cornelius, Varley was a
founder member of the Society of Painters in
Water-Colours in 1804 and subsequently, as a
teacher he helped many younger artists, encouraging them to sketch directly from
nature. In this early work, the delicate subtlety
of the atmospheric washes reveals a lingering
debt to Girtin. **CF**

234

Varley was a highly active member of the
Society of Painters in Water-Colours, at the
first exhibition showing over forty works, and
continuing in subsequent years to be the most
numerous exhibitor. Apparently the largest
watercolour Varley ever made, *Suburbs of an
Ancient City* was shown at the 1808 Society

exhibition where he sold it to Thomas Hope
for £42, then one of the highest prices fetched
for a contemporary watercolour. Self-
consciously reminiscent of the landscapes of
Poussin, in this work Varley shows watercolour to be a legitimate vehicle for historical
landscape. **RU**

235

John Varley

235
Suburbs of an Ancient City, 1808

Pencil and watercolour, 72.2×96.5 cm
Signed bottom right: J. Varley
London, Tate Gallery
Inv. No. TO5764
Provenance: purchased in 1808 at the Society
of Painters in Water-Colours exhibition by
Thomas Hope; Hope Collection sale,
Christie's, 20 July 1917, Lot 8; Basil Taylor;
Mrs. Basil Taylor, from whom purchased by
the Patrons of British Art and presented to
the Tate Gallery, 1990
Exhibitions: Society of Painters in Water-
Colours, 1808, No. 163; Society of Painters
in Water-Colours, 1823, No. 196; London,
Spink and Son, 1973, Cat. No. 86; New
Haven, 1981, Cat. No. 36
Literature: Kauffmann 1984, pp. 47–48

236

John Varley

236
Snowdon, 1810–13

Watercolour with scratching-out, 37×48 cm

Signed and dated bottom right: J. VARLEY
1810 (or 1813)
Birmingham, Museums and Art Gallery
Inv. No. 913
Provenance: purchased (Public Picture
Gallery Fund), 1913

Exhibitions: London, Society of Painters in
Water-Colours, 1810, No. 118 or 1813, No.
130; Arts Council, 1980–81, Cat. No. 30,
reproduced p. 35
Literature: Birmingham 1930, p. 200; Lister
1989, No. 38, reproduced in colour

This is a classic example not only of early 'old'
Water-Colour Society painting, but also of
Varley's standardised but highly effective picturesque compositions. Here he practises
what he preached in his influential *Treatise on
the Principles of Landscape Design*, published
in 1816, placing shadowed foreground against
successive receding planes of light and shade,
with 'the subject principally in the distance'.
No opaque bodycolour is used, nor is there
any evidence of pencil under-drawing: an im-
maculate 'pure' watercolour technique en-
hances the simplicity and directness of a view
of the most noble mountain in Wales.

Many Snowdonia subjects number among
Varley's earliest exhibited works, following
his extensive tours in north Wales from 1798 to
1802. The large and impressive *Snowdon from
Moel Hebog* (private collection) was one of his
forty-nine contributions to the society's first
exhibition in 1805; fifteen other views of
Snowdon appeared over the next decade.
SGW

David Cox
Birmingham 1783–1859 Birmingham

237
Old Westminster, 1811

Watercolour over pencil, 33×45.5 cm
Signed and dated, verso: D. Cox May 1811
Newcastle upon Tyne, Laing Art Gallery
Inv. No. JWR 57
Provenance: London, Palser Gallery, 1929;
bequeathed by John Wigham Richardson
Exhibitions: London, Associated Artists in
Water-Colours, 1811; Newcastle upon Tyne,
1962, Cat. No. 25; Birmingham and London,
1983–84, Cat. No. 9
Literature: Newcastle upon Tyne, 1939, p.
36; Newcastle upon Tyne, 1976, Plate 26

Cox was born in Deritend, a manufacturing
quarter of Birmingham, where his father was a
whitesmith. Engaged as a scene painter with
Astley's Theatre (Cat. No. 562), he moved to
London in 1804 and soon met John Varley,
who gave him lessons. His earliest success was
as a drawing master, and he published several
manuals (Cat. No. 188) including *A Series of
Progressive Lessons in Water Colour*, which
ran into nine editions between 1811 and 1845.

Before joining the Society of Painters in
Water-Colours in 1812, Cox was a member of
the short-lived rival Associated Artists in

237

Water-Colours. He showed works in four of its five annual exhibitions from 1808, and was its president in 1810. Cox's earliest work is difficult to identify with certainty, but this watercolour, inscribed on the reverse, can safely be accepted as an Associated Artists exhibit. Behind the ancient houses in the foreground are the towers of St. Margaret, Westminster and Westminster Abbey. **SGW**

John Linnell
London 1792–1882 Redhill

238
Primrose Hill, 1811

Pen and ink and wash, heightened with white chalk, 39.5×67.8 cm
Signed, dated and inscribed: Primrose Hill. J Linnell 1811; part of primrose hill
Cambridge, Syndics of the Fitzwilliam Museum
Inv. No. PD.16.1970
Provenance: by descent to Mrs. J. Lucas, great-great-granddaughter of the artist; Christie's, 3 March 1970, Lot 56; P. and D. Colnaghi and Co. Ltd., 1970
Exhibitions: London, P. and D. Colnaghi and Co. Ltd., 1973, No. 17, Plate 5; Cambridge and New Haven, 1972–73, pp. 5–6, Cat. No. 14; London, Tate Gallery, 1973–74, p. 102, Cat. No. 243, reproduced

Born the son of a carver and gilder of Bloomsbury, Linnell was apprenticed to John Varley in 1804 and the following year entered the Royal Academy schools. Together with

238

William Henry Hunt, he worked in the evenings for Dr. Thomas Monro, copying his collection of drawings and during the day, sketched in oils at Twickenham, where Varley had taken a house, with his friend William Mulready (Cat. No. 410). All three artists concentrated on rendering everyday scenes in the threatened outskirts of London. Primrose Hill, north of the newly planned Regent's Park (Cat. No. 88), was a featureless piece of hillside near Linnell's lodgings in the Hampstead Road, here transformed through the artist's intensity of observation into an abstract study of textures and underlying forms. **CF**

John Linnell

239
a) William Blake, 1820

Pencil, 20.1×15.5 cm
Signed, dated and inscribed: J L Fecit, Portrait of Wm Blake – 1820

b) William Blake in Conversation with John Varley, 1821

Pencil, 11.3×17.6 cm
Signed, dated and inscribed: J.L. Sept.1821, Cirencester Place, Mr Blake/Mr Varley

239a

239b

241

Provenance: the artist; Linnell Trustees;
Christie's, 15 March 1918, Lot 169; T. H.
Riches, by whom bequeathed, 1950
Exhibitions: London, P. and D. Colnaghi
and Co. Ltd., 1973, Nos. 106a and b; Tate
Gallery, 1978, p. 134, Cat. No. 280;
Cambridge and New Haven 1982–83, pp.
29–30, Cat. No. 77
Literature: Keynes 1921, pp. 482–83, Nos.
13, 17; Wilson 1927, Plates 19, 24; Butlin
1969, p. 8; Bindman 1970, p. 55–57, Nos. 46,
50, Figs. 63, 67.

Linnell married Mary Ann Palmer in 1817 and
his home at 6 Cirencester Place, Great Titch-
field Street, became a meeting place for his
friends. He was introduced to William Blake
the following year, and gradually took over
the role of helping the impoverished artist find
a means of support. The two men made study
tours together and Linnell introduced Blake to
his doctor, Robert Thornton (Cat. No. 345),
who commissioned illustrations from Blake
for his translation of Virgil's *Eclogues.*

In 1823 Linnell commissioned Blake to produce engraved designs of the Book of Job, and
two years later bought his watercolours of
Paradise Regained. Varley too, with his passion for astrology, was fascinated by Blake
and worked with him on a series of 'Visionary
Heads', drawn at night. According to Linnell's *Autobiographical Notes* of 1864, quoted
by Butlin, 'Varley believed in the reality of
Blake's visions more than even Blake himself –
that is in a more literal and positive sense that

did not admit of the explanations by which
Blake reconciled his assertions with known
truth. I have a sketch of the two men as they
were seen one night in my parlour near mid-
night. Blake sitting in the most attentive attitude listening to Varley, who is holding forth
vehemently with his hand raised – the two attitudes are highly characteristic of the men, for
Blake, by the side of Varley, appeared
decidedly the most sane of the two.' **CF**

Peter De Wint
Stone 1784 –1849 London

240
Yorkshire Fells

Pencil and watercolour with gum arabic,
36.3 × 56.5 cm
Cambridge, Syndics of the Fitzwilliam
Museum
Inv. No. PD.130-1950
Provenance: T. W. Bacon, by whom given
to the Museum
Exhibitions: Reading, 1966, No. 61;
Cambridge, 1979–80, p. 5, Cat. No. 11,
Colour Plate 1; Queensland and Cambridge,
1982–83, p. 50, Cat. No. 61, Plate 32
Literature: Winter 1958, p. 388, No. 98,
Plate 98

De Wint first came to London from Staffordshire in 1802, as apprentice to the mezzotint
engraver, John Raphael Smith, for whom both
Turner and Girtin had worked in their youth.
Through his visits to Dr. Monro's house and

contact with John Varley, who gave him free
tuition, he entered, in 1809, the Royal
Academy Schools. He became an Associate of
the Society of Painters in Water-Colours in
1810 and a member a year later.

This watercolour is probably a relatively
early work, suggesting Girtin's influence in
the handling of the distance, but also displaying the artist's own breadth and spontaneity in
his treatment of alternating patches of shadow
and luminous glow of moorland colour across
the weighty sweep of landscape. **CF**

Joshua Cristall
Cambourne 1768–1847 London

241
Cottage of St. Lawrence, Isle of Wight

Watercolour with touches of white
bodycolour over pencil, 32.6 × 46.6 cm
Signed lower right: Joshua Cristall 1814
London, Trustees of the British Museum,
1980
Inv. No. 1980-10-11-1
Provenance: acquired by the Museum, 1980
Exhibitions: Society of Painters in Water-
Colours, 1814, No. 156; London, British
Museum, 1985, Cat. No. 69, Plate 48;
Cleveland and Raleigh, 1991, No. 36

Cristall was one of the original members of the
Society of Painters in Water-Colours; he was
president in 1816 and 1819 and again from 1821
until 1831. His early works in watercolour
were large historical and classical figure compositions, notable for their fine sense of design
and breadth of manner. In later years he
painted chiefly rustic and domestic subjects,
of which this is a typical example.

It was probably at the suggestion of one of
his patrons, James Vine, a merchant in the
Russia trade who had a house at Niton on the
Isle of Wight, that Cristall visited the island in
1812; between 1813 and 1820 he exhibited
eighteen Isle of Wight subjects at the Society,
including this, which he showed in 1814. A
link between the eighteenth-century rustic
genre of Thomas Gainsborough and Francis
Wheatley and their Victorian counterparts,
Cristall's work reflects a somewhat idealised
view of the charms of rural life. Writing about
a very similar work by Cristall, Ackermann's
Repository of Arts noted: 'Such as we wish to
meet in every village are here represented by
the elegant mind of this artist . . . the group of
figures, nay, the whole picture, raises in the
mind of the spectator none but images of pleasure.' **LS**

P. De Wint, *York-shire Fells*. Cat. No. 240

W. Turner 'of Oxford', *Oxford from Headington Hill*. Cat. No. 252

242

Joseph Mallord William Turner
London 1775–1851 London

242
Leeds, 1816

Watercolour and bodycolour over pencil,
29.1×43 cm
Signed and dated lower left: J M W
TURNER RA 1816
New Haven, Yale Center for British Art
Inv. No. B1981.25.2704
Provenance: John Allnutt; John Knowles,
Manchester; Thomas Agnew and Sons Ltd.,
from whom purchased by Paul Mellon
Exhibitions: Manchester, 1857, No. 312;
New York and London, 1972–73, Cat. No.
102; Royal Academy, 1974–75, Cat. No. 186;
New Haven, 1977, Cat. No. 136
Literature: Wilton 1979, p. 362, No. 544,
reproduced; Daniels 1986, pp. 10–17

Even after the recognition as a painter in oils
inherent in his election as a full member of the
Royal Academy in 1802, Turner maintained a

steady volume of topographical watercolours.
This watercolour of Leeds derives from draw-
ings made during visits of 1808 and after, to
Farnley Hall, close to the city.

The subject matter of a modern city of the
industrial revolution, with its huge mills and
factories – the type of functional architecture
so admired by Karl Friedrich Schinkel during
his visit to England in 1826 – is unusual in early
nineteenth century English watercolours.
Turner combines specific observation with
larger themes. On the crest of Beeston Hill, on
the left, tentermen are hanging the newly
woven and washed cloth to dry. Two figures
pick mushrooms in the distance, while on the
right, clothworkers trudge uphill alongside
milk carriers returning from the city, passing
labourers rebuilding the wall.

Leeds was the centre for not only the production of woollens used in uniforms, but also
flax spinning, used for naval ropes and sail-
cloth. Thus the view may be said to have
patriotic associations, as Daniels has pointed
out, the city's productivity helping the
country to conquer Napoleon. **SGW**

Joseph Mallord William Turner

243
The Field of Waterloo, *c.* 1817

Watercolour, 28.8×40.5 cm
Cambridge, Syndics of the Fitzwilliam
Museum
Inv. No. 2476
Provenance: Walter Fawkes; Major Richard
Fawkes; A.W. Fawkes, K.C., by whom
bequeathed to the Museum, 1942
Exhibitions: London, 45 Grosvenor Place,
1819, No. 34; Thomas Agnew and Sons Ltd.,
1967, p. 66, Cat. No. 53; Hamburg, 1980;
Cincinnati, 1986, p. 50, Cat. No. 32; Tokyo,
1990, p. 53, Cat. No. 37
Literature: Armstrong 1902, p. 284; Finberg
1961, p. 481, No. 243; Cormack 1975, pp. 11,
41, Cat. No. 14; Wilton 1979, p. 356, No.
494

From August to September 1817, Turner took
advantage of the travel opportunities opened
up by the peace of 1815 and made his first visit

to the Continent since 1802. On his way to the Rhine he stopped at Waterloo, sketching the site and recording the course of the battle in relation to the lie of the land. His terse notation of the thousands killed was transfigured into a painting of *The Field of Waterloo*, exhibited at the Royal Academy in 1818 (Tate Gallery), and this watercolour. Unlike George Jones's action-packed battle piece (Cat. No. 27) and Maclise's later heroic portrayal in fresco of the meeting of Wellington and Blücher for the new Palace of Westminster (1858–59), Turner focuses on the fate of the ordinary soldier. With its storm-ridden skies and alien wreckage of men and arms, it is a profoundly pessimistic work, out of sympathy with a celebratory view of war and victory and more in tune with the dislocations experienced at home in the immediate postwar years.

The watercolour was bought with the Rhine views by Turner's patron and close friend, Walter Fawkes of Farnley Hall, Yorkshire and exhibited together at Fawkes's London house in 1819. **CF**

243

Joseph Mallord William Turner

244
The Port of London, 1824

Watercolour and bodycolour over pencil, 29.2 × 44.5 cm
Signed and dated: J M W TURNER RA/24
London, Trustees of the Victoria and Albert Museum
Inv. No. 522-2882
Provenance: John Dillon; John Jones, by whom bequeathed, 1882
Literature: Wilton 1979, p. 358, No. 514, reproduced; Shanes 1981, pp. 36–37, Fig. 1

This watercolour is one of a group of four London subjects by Turner of 1824–25. It was engraved by Edward Goodall, along with two of the others, *Tower of London* and *The Custom House, London*, and it seems likely that all were intended as book illustrations. The 1820s witnessed a spate of publications celebrating the new public buildings of the capital, of which the best known was *Metropolitan Improvements: London in the Nineteenth Century* (1827–31).

Turner's view, with its exceptionally animated foreground, is taken from the Pool of London looking towards Old London Bridge. The famous medieval bridge, which until eighteenth century improvements by George Dance and Sir Robert Taylor carried houses and shops across its entire length, was soon to be rebuilt to the designs of John Rennie (Cat. Nos. 148–52). **SGW**

Richard Parkes Bonington
Arnold 1802–1828 London

245
The Château of the Duchesse de Berry

Watercolour and bodycolour, 20.3 × 27.2 cm
London, Trustees of the British Museum
Inv. No. 1910-2-12-223

244

Provenance: Lewis Brown; Christie's, 28 May 1835, Lot 18; Hixon; Christie's, 15 March 1848, Lot 182, bought by Shirley; George Salting, by whom bequeathed to the British Museum, 1910
Exhibitions: Nottingham, 1965, No. 208; London, British Museum, 1985, Cat. No. 165, Plate 116
Literature: Dubuisson and Highes 1924, p. 129; Cormack 1989, pp. 60, 63, Plate 43

Bonington died of consumption a month before his twenty-sixth birthday: his short creative life was concentrated into the years between 1817 and his death. When he was fifteen, his family left England and settled first in Calais, where his father (who had been a drawing master and painter) set up a lace manufacturing business, and then in Paris.

Apart from three visits to London, Bonington spent the rest of his life in France, and it may be argued that he belongs above all to that group of young French artists of the 1820s who rebelled against the neo-classical formulas of the previous generation.

They had in common an enthusiasm for painting landscape, an interest in the history and architecture of France, a fascination with the Near East and a passion for the poetry and novels of Sir Walter Scott: all of these tastes were reflected in Bonington's work.

Yet Bonington is also of considerable sig-

nificance as one of the chief links between English and French Romanticism. He absorbed the example of Girtin's mastery of watercolour through the latter's friend F. L. T. Francia, Bonington's first teacher, and transmitted his taste for the medium to a number of French contemporaries, most notably Delacroix. The brilliance and luminosity of his watercolours led Delacroix to write that 'I could never weary of admiring his marvellous understanding of effects, and the facility of his execution.' This watercolour, probably *c.* 1825, shows the château at Rosny belonging to Marie-Caroline, Duchesse de Berry (1798–1870), the anglophile collector and patron of the arts who was to commission one of Bonington's last historical paintings, *Quentin Durward at Liège, c.* 1827–28. **LS**

Thomas Stothard
London 1755–1834 London

246
Scene from the Conclusion of the Eighth Day of the Decameron, *c.* 1820–25

Watercolour over pencil, 27.3 × 20 cm
London, Trustees of the British Museum
Inv. No. 1886-6-7-3
Provenance: purchased from Mr. Allen, 1886
Exhibitions: London, Royal Academy, 1820, No. 71; Buxton, 1983, No. 3

Between 1811 and 1826 Thomas Stothard exhibited eleven subjects from the *Decameron* at the Royal Academy, each illustrating a general scene of festive pleasure rather than a specific incident, from the stories told by Boccaccio's young Florentine aristocrats who have fled the plague-ravaged city.

In 1825 Stothard provided ten illustrations for a new English translation by William Pickering; this watercolour was one of those used, and was engraved by Augustus Ford. Stothard had been a prolific book illustrator since *c.* 1780, working in a style influenced by the French rococo and later by elements of neoclassicism to form a distinctively sweet, yet elegant, manner. His characteristic elongated figures, with tiny tapering hands and feet, have parallels with the work of his friends Blake and Flaxman, although in Stothard's case they are a good deal more decorative in feeling. The *fêtes champêtres* of Watteau provided a model for these depictions of young people in a charmed rural idyll, a visit to Paris in 1815 sparking off a renewed interest in his paintings. **LS**

James Stephanoff
London 1787–1874 Bristol

247
Lalla Rookh, 1826

Watercolour and bodycolour, 35.6×42.3 cm
New Haven, Yale Center for British Art
Inv. No. B1977.14.4384
Provenance: J. S. Maas and Co.
Exhibitions: Society of Painters in Water-Colours, 1826, No. 277; New Haven, 1981, Cat. No. 60
Literature: Roget 1891, Vol. 1, pp. 533–34

The figure painters among the early nineteenth-century watercolourists (with the exception of Blake) have been remembered poorly in comparison with their contemporaries in landscape. After Thomas Stothard and Richard Westall (Cat. No. 440), came a generation of interesting draughtsmen including Henry James Richter (1772–1857), Thomas Uwins (1782–1857) and the brothers Stephanoff, James and Francis (1788–1860). All became regular exhibitors or members of the Old Water-Colour Society. The son of a Russian portrait painter, Stephanoff specialised in scenes from history and literature, and in 1830 was appointed Historical Painter in Water-Colour to the King, William IV.

Roget wrote that 'the kind of illustrative work introduced by the Stephanoffs was a novelty in the watercolour exhibitions. Before their time, drawings of such subjects had been executed with a more direct purpose of reproduction in plates for the embellishment of books, and not so much with a view to pleasing as pictures.' Indeed, when Thomas Moore's long narrative poem *Lalla Rookh* was

247

first published in 1817, it appeared with engraved illustrations by Westall, but within a decade it had become popular enough to serve as the inspiration for more ambitious exhibition pieces such as this. **SGW**

246

William Blake
London 1757–1827 London

248
The Simoniac Pope, 1824–27

Pen and ink and watercolour, 52.7×36.8 cm
Inscribed bottom left: W B HELL Canto 19
London, Tate Gallery
Inv. No. NO3357
Provenance: John Linnell; his heirs' sale Christie's, 15 March 1918, Lot 148, bought on behalf of the National Art-Collections Fund and presented to the Tate Gallery
Exhibitions: London, Royal Academy, 1893, No. 10; Paris, 1947, Cat. No. 29; New York, 1956, Cat. No. 10; London, Tate Gallery, 1978, Cat. No. 325; Pescara, 1983, Cat. No. 8
Literature: Butlin 1981, p. 567, No. 812.35; Butlin 1990, p. 212, No. 137

Blake evolved a complicated set of visual symbols and references to express his philosophy, which can often be both intensely personal and obscure. He illustrated his own writings, but also drew subjects from visions, the Bible, Milton and Shakespeare. His 102 illustrations to Dante's *Divine Comedy* were made in the final years of his life, encouraged by John Linnell. Blake learned Italian to read

the original text, but he also used Cary's translation to work on the series. His drawings both illustrate the text and act as a commentary upon it. He criticised Dante for his orthodox model of salvation, telling Crabb Robinson, 'Dante saw devils where I see none – I see only good', and inscribed the verso of one of the *Divine Comedy* drawings: 'it [Dante's Hell] must have been originally Formed by the Devil Him self . . . Whatever Book is for Vengeance for Sin & whatever Book is Against the Forgiveness of Sin is not of the Father but of Satan the Accuser & Father of Hell' (quoted Butlin 1990, p. 202).

The Simoniac Pope illustrates *Inferno* XIX, 31–126, and shows Pope Nicolas III. In punishment for his simony, he is condemned to hang upside down in a well of fire, until replaced by a pope guilty of the same sin. Virgil protects Dante from the wrath of Nicolas, who has mistaken him for his replacement. **RU**

William Blake

249
Beatrice Addressing Dante from the Car, 1824–27

Pen and watercolour on paper,
37.2×52.7 cm
Inscribed in ink: Pg Canto 29 and 30, Pg
Canto 29, 24
London, Tate Gallery
Inv. No. N.03369
Provenance: see under Cat. No.
Exhibitions: London, Tate Gallery, 1978,
Cat. No. 334, reproduced
Literature: Butlin 1981, p. 584, Nos. 812–88,
Plate 973; Bindman 1982–83, p. 44,
reproduced; Butlin 1990, No. 148

The absorbing complexity of Blake's personal imagery can be readily grasped from two opposing interpretations of this watercolour.

The scene depicted is the first meeting between Dante and Beatrice in the Terrestrial Paradise. Dante, at the right of the design, is now alone after bidding farewell to Virgil at the sight of Beatrice's approaching procession. Here he confronts the gryphon and Beatrice, representations of Christ and the church, accompanied by Faith, Hope and Charity, who are dressed in white, green and red. The four winged heads, the traditional symbols of the evangelists, and the vortex-like chariot wheel, spinning round filled with eyes and the spirits of the living, are images drawn by Blake from Ezekiel's vision (Ezekiel, I, 15–21).

One interpretation of the illustration, by Albert Roe, maintains that this work is central to Blake's commentary on Dante's text and is part of his criticism of Dante's materialistic conception of paradise. The inscription in the illustration suggests that Blake is addressing the descriptions in Cantos XXIX and XXX of the *Purgatorio*, but a number of details differ substantially from Dante's text. The thrust of this interpretation is that Dante, having crossed the River Lethe, seen in the preceding illustration in the series (now in the British Museum), is submitting to the mysteries of the church, a subjugation of Poetic Genius (the Natural Man) to the Female Will (the Goddess of Nature).

The opposing interpretation, put forward by David Fuller, also rests on the significance of Dante's passage across Lethe. This viewpoint claims that Blake avoids an easy identification of Beatrice with the church, instead representing her as Divine Wisdom. The vortex can then be understood as a means of conveying the light by which Dante is dazzled, contributing to the brilliant and apparently joyous effect of the watercolour, one of the most visually rich and technically inventive of the series. **IW**

David Cox
Birmingham 1783–1859 Birmingham

250
Buckingham House from Green Park, 1825

Watercolour, 22.4 × 44 cm
Signed and dated bottom left: D. COX 1825
Birmingham, Museums and Art Gallery
Inv. No. 6811
Provenance: John Palmer Phillips, by whom presented to Birmingham, 1911
Exhibitions: Swansea, 1953, Cat. No. 19;

250

Birmingham, 1959, Cat. No. 19; London, Guildhall Art Gallery, 1971, Cat. No. 45, reproduced; Birmingham and London 1983–84, Cat. No. 30, reproduced p. 8
Literature: Birmingham 1930, p. 54; Cox 1947, p. 50, Colour Plate 2

Apart from a number of scenes on the Thames, Cox seems to have painted few views of London. This delightful view of old Buckingham Palace is exceptional for its wealth of tiny animated figures, suggesting that it was made for engraving. It shows the red brick house built for the Duke of Buckingham in 1702–05 (designed either by William Winde or William Talman) and enlarged by Sir William

Chambers for George III in 1762–63. Effectively, the building survives, encased within the grandiose remodelling begun in 1825 by John Nash (Cat. No. 75) and continued by Edward Blore from 1832 to 1837. **SGW**

251
Near the Pont d' Arcole, Paris, 1829

Pencil and watercolour on paper,
24.5 × 37 cm
London, Tate Gallery
Inv. No. 4302

251

254

Provenance / Exhibitions (left column)

Provenance: bequeathed by J. Holliday, 1927
Exhibitions: Birmingham and London, Victoria and Albert Museum, 1983–84, Cat. No. 59
Literature: Solly 1873, pp. 63–65; Wilton 1977, No. 120; Egerton 1986, p. 14

By 1827 David Cox had returned to London, after a number of years spent in Hereford. He had travelled to Belgium and Holland in 1826 and was stimulated by a desire to see more of the Continent, which led to the trip he made to France in 1829. This watercolour reflects Bonington's example in its handling of paint and subject. Its spontaneity is heightened by the pencil notes on the colours to be used and the lettering on the buildings.

Cox and his son left London early in the summer of 1829. It had been intended that the tour would proceed from Paris to take in Orléans and the River Loire, but early in his stay Cox sprained his ankle rather badly. However, as his biographer Solly reported, this did not deter him from recording the monuments of the French capital: 'so, with his usual spirit, especially when the pursuit of art was in question, he used to drive out in a fiacre, or cab, every day, and making it stop when he came to an interesting subject that took his fancy, he painted away indefatigably for many weeks, seated in the cab, or occasionally, in a chair near the Seine or in some other not overcrowded spot. In this way he secured views of the Tuileries, Palais de Justice, Chambre des Députés, Rue St Honoré, Montmartre, the bridge over the Seine, and many others.' **IW**

William Turner 'of Oxford'
Black Bourton 1789–1862 Oxford

252
Oxford from Headington Hill

Watercolour over pencil with traces of gum arabic, 34.4×53 cm
Cambridge, Syndics of the Fitzwilliam Museum
Inv. No. 1484
Provenance: A. E. Anderson; gift to the Museum, 1928
Exhibitions: Queensland and Cambridge, 1982–83, p. 53, Cat. No. 67, Plate 35; Arts Council 1984–85, p. 66, Cat. No. 66

Having studied with John Varley, Turner became a member of the Society of Painters in Water-Colours in 1808. He returned to Oxford in 1811 where he took pupils, but he continued to exhibit in London as a country member of the society for fifty years.

Although he travelled extensively in England and, after 1838, in Scotland, he is best known for his views of Oxford and the surrounding countryside. In this typical example, the towers and spires of the university are seen from near the London road: left to right, Merton, Christ Church, Magdalen and All Souls colleges, the church of St. Mary's and the dome of the Radcliffe Camera. **CF**

Cornelius Varley
London 1781–1873 London

253
Regent's Canal looking towards Hampstead, 1827

Watercolour, 24.8×38.3 cm
Titled, signed and dated on verso: View on the Regent's Canal looking towards Hampstead. Cornelius Varley 1827. The spot is now/1841/Park Village east
London, The Museum of London
Inv. No. 58.69/6
Provenance: Frank T. Sabin
Exhibitions: London, The Museum of London, 1981, No. 70

The artist was the younger brother of John Varley and like him a founder member of the Old Water-Colour Society. However, having worked in his youth for his uncle Samuel Varley, a watch and scientific instrument maker, he resigned in 1820 and devoted the rest of his life principally to scientific pursuits.

The branch of the Regent's Canal shown here facilitated the daily supply of fresh vegetables from Middlesex to the markets behind Nash's great terraces on the east side of Regent's Park. The small villas which made up Park Village East and Park Village West were among Nash's last works and were planned in a picturesque Italianate or Gothic style. Varley's view shows, on the right, the space cleared for the construction of Park Village East, in front of the York and Albany Tavern, and a Park Village West villa on the left, with Primrose Hill in the middle distance. **CF**

George Fennel Robson
Durham 1788–1833 Stockton-on-Tees

254
Loch Coruisk, Isle of Skye, *c.* 1828–30

Watercolour and bodycolour with scratching-out, 45.1×65.4 cm
New Haven, Yale Center for British Art
Inv. No. B1977.14.6254
Provenance: Fine Art Society, London
Exhibitions: London, Society of Painters in Water-Colours, 1829, No. 127; New Haven, 1981, Cat. No. 62, reproduced

Robson enjoyed only limited tuition from a drawing master in Durham before coming to London in 1804. He was encouraged by John Varley, and exhibited in 1810 with the Asso-

255

ciated Artists in Water-Colours, alongside
David Cox. A speculative tour in Scotland that
year brought attention through the publication in 1814 of a book, *Scenes of the Grampian
Mountains*. Joining the Old Water-Colour
Society in 1813, he became its president in
1820. He capitalised on his previous success by
specialising in views of Scotland, especially the
Highlands, which were not so well known to
the art-buying public as those of Wales or the
Lake District. Dramatic light effects and the
use of deep shades of purple and brown made
his work instantly recognisable, but brought
criticism as a deliberate eccentricity. He died
of food poisoning, aged only forty-five,
during a journey by sea from London to Newcastle.

Robson exhibited six Loch Coruisk scenes
between 1826 and 1832, as well as several other
views of Skye. The size of the present watercolour suggests it is identifiable with the 1829
exhibit, *Lork Corisken and the Coolin
Mountains, in the Isle of Sky*, accompanied by
a quotation from Sir Walter Scott's poem *Lord
of the Isles*. **SGW**

Samuel Palmer
London 1805–1881 Redhill

255
A Cornfield by Moonlight with the Evening Star, *c*. 1830

Watercolour with bodycolour, pen and sepia
ink, varnished, 19.7 × 25.8 cm
London, Trustees of the British Museum
Inv. No. 1985-5-4-1
Provenance: A. H. Palmer; Christie's, 4
March 1929, Lot 23; Savile Gallery; Sir
Kenneth Clark; acquired by the Museum
after a public appeal, 1985
Exhibitions: London, Victoria and Albert
Museum, 1926, No. 64; Royal Academy,
1934, No. 769A; Tate Gallery, 1959, No.
797; Victoria and Albert Museum, 1978–79,
No. 10; New York, 1987–88, No.286, Fig.
176; Cleveland and North Carolina, 1991,
No. 81
Literature: Grigson 1947, pp. 93, 1967, No.
86; Lister 1988, pp. 74–75, No. 117

Palmer was born in London, the son of a
scholarly bookseller, and from his childhood
absorbed the poetry of Virgil and Milton as
well as the Old Testament. From around 1826
to 1832 he lived in seclusion as the leader of a
group of young artists, self-styled the
Ancients, in the village of Shoreham in the
Darent Valley, Kent, which he described as his
'Valley of Vision'. The works of the Shoreham
period, with their immediately distinctive anti--
naturalist style, mark the apogee of his near
mystical celebration of nature; his flocks of
sheep and sheaves of corn, harvest moons and
trees weighed down with blossom or fruit,
symbolising a passionate identification with a
life of pastoral simplicity. Nothing comparable
had previously been seen in British landscape
art. This watercolour, painted in about 1830, is
one of Palmer's undoubted masterpieces.

In later life, living again in London and then
in the suburbs, Palmer looked back nostalgically to his 'Valley of Vision'. It may perhaps
be argued that only a city dweller could have
had such an intense, self-aware and mystical
experience of nature. **LS**

David Roberts
Stockbridge, Edinburgh 1796–1864 London

256
The Debarkation of the Lord Mayor at Westminster, 1830

Watercolour, 33×47.2 cm
Signed and dated: D. Roberts 1830
London, Guildhall Art Gallery, Corporation
of London
Inv. No. 1246
Provenance: presented by Lord Wakefield,
1939
Exhibitions: London, The Museum of
London, 1981, No. 74; Barbican Art Gallery,
1982; The Museum of London, 1989
Literature: Norton 1972, p. 23; Knight 1986,
p. 244; Ellmers 1989, p. 8

Roberts' watercolour depicts an occasion
which never took place: the public celebrations for Lord Mayor's Day on 9 November
1830 were cancelled for fear of riots (Cat. Nos.
638–41). Nevertheless, the artist draws on his
training as a theatrical scene painter to conjure
up all the pageantry that had been associated

with the Thames since the fifteenth century.
Initially, both the mayor and the city livery
companies hired large barges, rowed by
watermen, for a variety of festive occasions. In
1453 the mayor, John Norman, had a barge
built to carry him from the city to Westminster to pledge his allegiance to the king, and
thus began the tradition of the river procession. Accompanied by a growing number of
specially built livery company barges, this
annual event transformed the Thames from a
working river into a grand spectacle.
Large ceremonial barges were expensive to
build, costing over £1,500 each by 1800. The
last City Corporation barge was built by
Searle and Godfrey of Lambeth, where most
barges were built and repaired, and launched
in 1807. This is the craft with the stern
head-on, alongside Westminster Bridge on the
right. The barge on the left belonged to the
Stationers' Company, whose Master, John
Key, was the new lord mayor. Roberts' depiction is suspiciously close to the etching of the
same barge by E. W. Cooke, dated 1829. The
towers of Westminster Abbey and roof of
Westminster Hall provided a suitably splendid backdrop. **CF**

John Constable
East Bergholt 1776–1837 London

257
London from Hampstead, with a double Rainbow, 1831

Watercolour, 19.7×32.4 cm
Inscribed verso: between 6 and 7 o'clock
Evening June 1831.
London, Trustees of the British Museum
Inv. No. 1888-2-15-55
Provenance: presented to the Museum by
Miss Isabel Constable, 1888
Exhibitions: London, Tate Gallery, 1976,
Cat. No. 283; British Museum, 1985, Cat.
No. 104, Plate 75; New York, 1987–88,
No. 218
Literature: Fleming-Williams 1976, p. 100;
Schweizer 1982, pp. 426–27; Reynolds 1984,
No. 31; Cormack 1986, p. 207

In 1827 Constable took a lease on a house in
Well Walk, Hampstead, a village on the northern heights of London, which became his
family's home for the next six years. From the
windows at the back of the house there were

258

magnificent views of London, and as he wrote to a friend in August 1827, 'It is to my wife's heart's content – our little drawing room commands a view unequalled in Europe – from Westminster Abbey to Gravesend. The dome of St. Paul's in the air – realises Michael Angelo's Idea on seeing that of the Pantheon – "I will build such a thing in the sky".'

Constable painted a sequence of watercolours from this vantage point, of which this is the most dramatic. Here he catches two phenomena that were of particular interest to him: the rainbow and the shaft of sunlight. Rainbows intrigued him both because of his serious scientific interest in meteorology and for their associative value; in other paintings and watercolours by Constable dating from this period they symbolised hope. The double rainbow appears through a shaft of light descending diagonally across the sky, a phenomenon then known as a 'sun pillar'. **LS**

John Frederick Lewis
London 1805–1876 London

258
The Alhambra, 1832

Watercolour and bodycolour, 25.8 × 36 cm
Inscribed bottom right: Alhambra, October 5, 1832
London, Trustees of the British Museum
Inv. No. 1885-5-9-1644
Provenance: acquired by the British Museum, 1885
Exhibitions: Cleveland and Raleigh, 1991, No. 80

Lewis was among the most successful of the members of the Society of Painters in Water-Colours; he was also a frequent contributor to the illustrated annuals and volumes of poetry which became so popular with British middle-class readers in the 1820s. Inspired by the example of his friend David Wilkie, Lewis travelled in Spain from 1832 to 1834, having, according to his patron Richard Ford, 'orders for young ladies' albums and from divers booksellers, who are illustrating Lord Byron'. Lewis used the sketches made on his Spanish tour as the basis for later watercolours, as well as for two volumes of lithographs; this view of the Alhambra was used as the background for *Distant View of the Sierra Nevada* published in Lewis's *Sketches of Spain and Spanish Character*, London, 1836.

The vibrant colouring of studies such as this astounded his fellow artists in England; John Sell Cotman commented when he saw Lewis's Spanish drawings in 1834 that 'words cannot convey to you their splendour, my poor Red, Blues and Yellows for which I have been so much abused and broken hearted about, are faded fades, to what I saw there.' **LS**

260

Samuel Prout

Plymouth 1783–1853 London

259
The Piazzetta and the Doge's Palace, Venice, *c.* 1831

Watercolour, 43×55 cm
London, Trustees of the Royal Watercolour
Society

Provenance: Parsons Bequest, 1979
Exhibitions: Birmingham, 1987, No. 27;
London, Bankside Gallery, 1991, No. 10

Samuel Prout was one of the most popular exponents of picturesque architectural topography. His views of foreign medieval cities became widely known, chiefly through engravings, and he also published a number of drawing manuals. Prout played a leading part in popularising illustrated travel books, the

'picturesque annuals' of the 1820s and 1830s, which appealed to a new middle-class public. As a boy, Ruskin had been a pupil of Prout, and his admiration of his work never ceased. A semi-invalid, most of Prout's travel took place in the 1820s and provided the material for subsequent compositions. **LS**

Thomas Shotter Boys

London 1803–1874 London

260
The Boulevard des Italiens, Paris, 1833

Watercolour heightened with bodycolour
and gum arabic, 32.7×59.7 cm
Signed and dated: Thos. Boys 1833
London, Trustees of the British Museum
Inv. No. 1870-10-8-2364
Provenance: P. and D. Colnaghi and Co.
Exhibitions: London, British Museum, 1985,
Cat. No. 167, Plate 115; Cleveland and
Raleigh, 1991, No. 78
Literature: Roundell 1974, pp. 96–97

Boys was one of a number of British artists who, following the example of Bonington, went to France where they were for a time able to exploit a vogue for watercolour, already perceived as a particularly British contribution to European art. In addition, he had been trained as an engraver in London, and he was able to take advantage of the dearth of French expertise in this area. He arrived in Paris *c.* 1823, and by 1826 was closely associated with Bonington, whose influence is apparent in his early watercolours, but from the outset his interests were different. Whereas Bonington's works reveal his romantic sensibility and subjective response to the atmospheric quality of his surroundings, Boys's studies of Paris are primarily topographical. *The Boulevard des Italiens* is a splendid example of his mastery of urban topography, showing his technical virtuosity and sense of design. **LS**

261

Joseph Mallord William Turner

London 1775–1851 London

261
Funeral of Sir Thomas Lawrence – a sketch from Memory, 1830

Watercolour and bodycolour, 61.6×82.5 cm
Inscribed lower left: Funeral of Sir Thos
Lawrence PRA/Jany 21 1830/ SKETCH
from MEMORY JMWT
London, Tate Gallery

Inv. No. CCLXIII 344; D25467
Provenance: bequeathed by the artist, 1856
Exhibitions: London, Royal Academy, 1830,
Cat. No. 493; Royal Academy, 1974–75,
Cat. No. 436
Literature: Williams 1831; Wilton 1979, No.
521; Gage 1980, p. 137, No. 161

This unusual subject was the last watercolour
Turner exhibited at the Royal Academy and
was evidently intended as a mark of personal
homage to Sir Thomas Lawrence. The
Academy's president had been ill for some
time and died on 7 January 1830. The two men
had been good friends for several years: apart
from personally intervening to obtain
Turner's only royal patronage, Lawrence
owned several works by Turner and was
among those who encouraged the artist to
make his important first visit to Italy in 1819.
The occasion of Lawrence's funeral at St.
Paul's Cathedral had a profound effect on
Turner, coming when it did, as the final blow
in a series of bereavements. He wrote of the
event in a state of dejection to George Jones,
then in Rome: 'My poor father's death proved
a heavy blow upon me, and has been followed
by others of the same dark kind. However, it is
something to feel that gifted talent can be acknowledged by the many who yesterday waded
up to their knees in snow and muck to see the
funeral pomp swelled up by the carriages of
the great, without the persons themselves.'

Burial in St. Paul's was an honour only merited by the nation's heroes: Lawrence was laid
to rest in the crypt amid a group of the first
Royal Academicians and other former presidents. **IW**

Edward Duncan
London 1803–1882 London

262
Windsor Castle, 1833

Watercolour and bodycolour with
scratching-out over pencil, 62.2×95 cm
Signed and dated: E. Duncan Del. 1833
Birmingham, Museums and Art Gallery
Inv. No. 116
Provenance: Arthur T. Keen, by whom
presented to Birmingham, 1916
Exhibitions: New Society of Painters in
Water-Colours, 1834, No. 120
Literature: Birmingham 1930, p. 76

Excelling as a painter of marine subjects, Duncan was one of the most skilful watercolourists
of his generation. After serving an apprenticeship with Robert Havell, Duncan set up his
own practice as an engraver, but turned to
watercolour in 1831. He was an exhibitor at the
New Society from its inception the following

262

year, although in 1848 he transferred his allegiance to the Old Society.

This watercolour was shown at the 1834 exhibition depicted in George Scharf's famous
view (Cat. No. 225). It has greater interest
than some previous views of Windsor Castle
in showing the full range of buildings as they
were newly revealed after the romantic medievalising improvements of the architect Sir Jeffry Wyatville (1766–1840). **SGW**

Anthony Vandyke Copley Fielding
Halifax 1787–1855 Worthing

263
Glen Lochy, Perthshire

Watercolour and dry oil paint, 64×85.9 cm
Signed and dated lower left: A.V. Copley
Fielding 1834

263

Cambridge, Syndics of the Fitzwilliam
Museum
Inv. No. PD.143-1961
Provenance: Dr. Louis C.G. Clarke;
bequeathed to the Museum, 1961
Exhibitions: Society of Painters in Water-
Colours, 1834, No. 218

The second son of the landscape painter
Nathan Theodore Fielding, and the best
known of five painter brothers, Copley Fielding settled in London in 1809, became a pupil
of John Varley and was one of the Monro
circle. In 1817, he became treasurer of the Old
Water-Colour Society and in 1818, secretary.
He was president from 1831 until his death.
Working from a studio in Newman Street, he
exhibited prolifically, producing a large number of marine subjects and landscapes based
on his extensive travels round the country.
Together with Constable and Bonington,
he was awarded a gold medal at the Paris
Salon of 1824.

In this impressive work, as in many large

scale exhibition watercolours of the 1830s, the
drama of the landscape is emphasised by the
rich colours and heightened by mixed-media
effects. **CF**

Samuel Jackson
Bristol 1794–1869 Bristol

264
Mail Coach Passengers at the New
Passage on the Severn, 1834

Watercolour, 13×18.75 cm
London, Baring Brothers and Co. Ltd.
Provenance: acquired at auction, 1983
Exhibitions: Bristol, 1834, No. 142; Bristol,
1986, No. 58
Literature: Greenacre and Stoddard, 1983

The son of a Bristol merchant, Jackson was
strongly influenced by Francis Danby (Cat.
No. 393), developing a complex watercolour
technique and building up a successful practice as a drawing master. This work shows the
passengers disembarking from the London
Mail coach on a stormy and turbulent night,
some to continue their journey to south Wales
by the ferry across the Severn. **MJO**

David Cox

Birmingham 1783–1859 Birmingham

265
Bolsover Castle, 1834–40

Watercolour and bodycolour, 74.7×99.6 cm
Signed bottom left: David Cox
London, University College
Inv. No. UCL 3664
Provenance: Henry Vaughan, by whom
bequeathed, 1930
Exhibitions: London, Society of Painters in
Water-Colours, 1840, No. 297
Literature: Solly 1873, p. 61

Cox spent the years 1815 to 1827 in Hereford,
earning a staple income as a drawing master in
a girls' school, while continuing to paint,
travel and exhibit at the Old Water-Colour
Society. He eventually returned to London,
playing a major part in the consolidation of the
society's reputation in the late 1820s and 1830s.
His watercolour style broadened, however,
and was increasingly at odds with a more
general move towards detail and finish. In 1841
he left London to return to his native Birmingham, partly in order to develop, undisturbed,
a personal style in oil painting which evolved
from his watercolour method.
   The famous old houses of the north
Midlands (chiefly in Derbyshire) afforded
plenty of picturesque subjects, especially
Haddon Hall and Bolsover, a huge half-ruined
pile of the seventeenth century. Cox peopled
several large watercolours of both houses with
figures in period costume, but this expansive
watercolour is more a celebration of a quintes-
sentially English landscape. Of the seven Bolsover Castle subjects exhibited by Cox between 1834 and 1843, it is most likely to be the
*Hardwick Park, Bolsover Castle in the dis-
tance,* shown in 1840. **SGW**

265

Exhibitions: Rome Academy, 1838; London,
Fine Art Society, 1881, No. 25; Sheffield,
1961, Cat. No. 45; Cambridge, 1984, Cat.
No. 36, reproduced
Literature: Malins 1968, pp. 52, 87, Plate 5;
Lister 1985, No. 42, reproduced in colour;
Powell 1987, pp. 182–84, Plate 176

English artists in Rome were fascinated by the
heady mixture of Mediterranean life conducted among substantial classical remains.
Both Turner and Palmer produced contrasting
pairs of paintings in the late 1830s: Turner's
Ancient Italy – Ovid banished from Rome and
Modern Italy – the Pifferari were shown at the

266

Samuel Palmer

London 1805–1881 Reigate

266
A View of Modern Rome during the
Carnival, 1838

Watercolour and bodycolour over pencil,
40.9×57.8 cm
Signed and dated lower right: Samuel Palme
Rome 1838
Birmingham, Museums and Art Gallery
Inv. No. P15'46
Provenance: A. H. Palmer; purchased
(Feeney Charitable Bequest Fund), 1946

267

wreckage in the foreground, 'including the gorgeous landscape of Rubens of the Wago-neer', and retitled the work to fit his fancy (there is no record that any of the consigned goods were lost at sea).

As a keen antiquarian and native of Nor-folk, Cotman would have known about the contents of the sale of the Walpole collection (made by the 3rd Earl of Orford in an effort to settle his father's debts), which took place in 1779. On his return to London in 1834 after twenty years in Norfolk and despite – or because of – health, money and family wor-ries, the generally impractical artist possibly tried to respond more to market forces, by in-troducing this sophisticated 'historical' ele-ment in an effort to meet the growing demand for works of narrative interest. **CF**

Royal Academy in 1838, followed in the next year by *Ancient Rome; Agrippina landing with the Ashes of Germancus* and *Modern Rome – Campo Vaccino*.

Cecilia Powell has pointed out how con-temporary guide books such as J.C. Eustace's *Tour through Italy* (1813) recommended that the visitor 'first contemplate the ancient, then visit modern Rome, and pass from the palaces of the profane, to the temples of the sacred city.'

Samuel Palmer married Hannah Linnell (daughter of John Linnell) on 30 September 1837, and the couple spent a two-year honey-moon in Italy, chiefly in Rome. This water-colour and its pair, *A View of Ancient Rome* (also in Birmingham), are the artistic high-lights of his stay. Interestingly, in a letter of 14 July 1838 to John Linnell, Palmer asked for details of Turner's oils: 'I should like very much to know which was the point of differ-ence between Turner's Ancient and Modern Italy – was it in the figures or buildings or both?' Palmer set his 'ancient' view in the Forum, contrasting its calm solitude with this festive scene of the Piazza del Popolo, looking towards St. Peter's. **SGW**

John Sell Cotman and Miles Edmund Cotman
Norwich 1782–1842 London,
Norwich 1810–1858 Norwich respectively

267
Lee Shore, with the Wreck of the Houghton Pictures, Books etc. sold to the Empress Catherine of Russia, 1838

Pencil and watercolour with bodycolour,
68×90.2 cm
Cambridge, Syndics of the Fitzwilliam Museum
Inv. No. 945
Provenance: the artist's sale, Christie's, 17–18 May 1843, Lot 160; bequeathed to the Museum by Joseph Prior, 1919
Exhibitions: London,Society of Painters in Water-Colours, 1838, No. 223; Arts Council, 1982, p. 140, Cat. No. 108; New Haven and London, National Maritime Museum, 1987, p. 60, Cat. No. 99, Fig. 26
Literature: Dickes 1905, pp. 392–94; Kitson 1937, pp. 343–44, Fig. 134; Boase 1959, pp. 332–46, Plate 33b; Mertens 1987, p. 179

This example of Cotman's late watercolour manner, though exhibited under his name, was in fact a fluent collaborative effort with his eldest son. From Cotman's letter to his third son of 7 April 1838, it appears that Miles had already painted the sea, sky and shipping when his father got to work on the figures and

William Henry Hunt
London 1790–1864 London

268
The Outhouse, 1838

Watercolour and bodycolour with scratching-out over pencil, 54×74.9 cm
Signed and dated lower right: W. Hunt 1838
Cambridge, Syndics of the Fitzwilliam Museum
Inv. No. 739
Provenance: Charles Fairfax Murray; gift to the Museum, 1912
Exhibitions: London, Society of Painters in Water-Colours, 1838, No. 262; P. and D. Colnaghi and Co. Ltd., 1973, No. 135; New Haven, 1981, p. 70, Cat. No. 66
Literature: Wilton 1977, p. 190, No. 139, reproduced; Witt 1982, p. 173, No. 321, Plate 15; Newall 1987, pp. 31–32, Plate 12

The son of a tin-plate worker of Covent Gar-den, Hunt was apprenticed to John Varley in 1806 where his fellow students included John Linnell and William Mulready (Cat. No. 410). He entered the Royal Academy Schools in 1808, and the following year worked as a scene painter at Drury Lane Theatre. Like many of the watercolour artists of his age, he knew Dr. Monro, attending his evening meetings in the Adelphi Terrace, and frequently sketched at Monro's house near Bushey. He first exhi-bited at the Royal Academy in 1807, and at the Society of Painters in Oil and Watercolours in

268

1814; ten years later, he was elected Associate of the Old Water-Colour Society, gaining full membership in 1826.

His early works were freely drawn with a reed pen and sepia ink (his skill in the technique acquired through copying Canaletto drawings at Dr. Monro's), but by the late 1820s he began to use a stipple method to add texture, and Chinese white to add light, appealing to the increasing middle-class demand for highly finished watercolours as substitutes for oil paintings. Specialising in still lifes to the extent that he became known as 'Bird's Nest' Hunt, he also exhibited scenes from rustic life. In this example, his meticulous observation of the differing textures of the timbers, shavings and straw is softened by the presence of the pretty young woman – probably the artist's wife, Sarah – again suggesting the artist was consciously appealing to middle-class tastes. **CF**

John Martin
Haydon Bridge 1789–1854 Douglas, Isle of Man

269 *(illus. p. 382)*
A Meadow, 1840

Watercolour with scratching-out,
25.4 × 34 cm
Signed bottom right: J. Martin 1840
London, Trustees of the British Museum
Inv. No. 1891-5-11-49
Provenance: purchased from Colnaghi, 1891
Exhibitions: Cleveland and Raleigh, 1991, No. 69
Literature: Balston 1947, pp. 254–55

John Martin made his name with a series of highly dramatic canvases and engravings depicting doom-laden scenes from the Bible or from mythology (Cat. No. 422). His first popular success was *Joshua Commanding the Sun to Stand Still* (Cat. No. 390), exhibited at the Royal Academy in 1816, which was followed in the 1820s with further 'catastrophic' subjects. His own mezzotints of these paintings and others illustrating *Paradise Lost* and the Bible were enormously successful with the public, although he had many harsh critics, including Charles Lamb and William Hazlitt.

A little known aspect of Martin's art is revealed in a group of landscape studies mostly dating from the 1840s. According to his son, Martin made frequent sketching expeditions in the environs of London. As a writer in the *Athenaeum* noted in 1854, 'These works, beautiful in execution . . . deep and bright in colour, presented us with a new view of the artist's character. He who revelled in vastness and sublimity, could go out and watch with a poet's love . . . the ripe corn rippling into furrows of exceeding lustre.' The gently lyrical quality of such works, with their distinctive stippled technique, contrasts greatly with his large scale paintings. **LS**

269

HOUSEHOLD FURNITURE AND INTERIOR DECORATION

As the meeting place of court and society, London provided the prime opportunity for conspicuous consumption, with changes in fashion catered for by the luxury trades. Virtually all the finest examples of furniture and works of art were designed in London, many manufactured and nearly all retailed in the capital. Leaders of taste – notably the Prince of Wales later George IV, Thomas Hope, John Soane, William Beckford – could draw on an eclectic range of historicist styles: Chinese, Greek, Egyptian or 'Louis XIV', besides commissioning unique commemorative pieces. In the increasingly scholarly revival of the Gothic, London led the rest of Europe.

Henry Holland
London 1745–1806 London

270
North Front of Carlton House and Screen Wall, 1794

Pen and ink and watercolour, 34.5×49.7 cm
Windsor Castle, H.M. Queen Elizabeth II
Inv. No. RL 18947
Literature: Stroud 1966, pp. 61–76; Crook and Port, 1973, pp. 307–22

For the London public the first manifestation of the Prince of Wales's architectural ambitions was the remodelling of the incoherent complex of buildings that comprised Carlton House, which he took over on attaining his

majority in 1783, and its transformation by Holland into elegant neo-classical mansion. The process took place slowly as the prince lurched from one financial crisis to another. But by 1794 work had been completed on the north front, which now presented a symmetrical rusticated stone façade and pedimented portico, supported on Corinthian columns, sufficiently deep to take carriages, an innovation which was widely copied.

The house was fronted on Pall Mall by a grand open screen wall inspired by those before the Palais Royal and Hôtel de Condé in Paris. It was composed of paired Ionic columns resting on a continuous podium, broken by two pedimented entrances. Thus the prince and his court were visibly part of London, yet separated from the life of the city by a real and symbolic barrier of status. **CF**

271
Ground Plan of the Principal Floor, Carlton House, October 1794

Pen and ink and watercolour, 34×49 cm
Windsor Castle, H.M. Queen Elizabeth II
Inv. No. RL18943
Literature: Stroud 1965, pp. 61–76; Crook and Port 1973, pp. 310–11

Carlton House was built on a slope so the principal floor appeared to be on the first floor viewed from the garden and on street level from the Pall Mall side. The rooms here comprised the grand reception rooms, but any impression of magnificence was marred by the prince's enormous debts (£630,000 in 1795), the misery of unpaid tradesmen and even the threat of bailiffs. An appropriate marriage was

272

272

held out as the only solution: Princess Caroline of Brunswick brought with her a generous settlement and the Prince's income was increased by the Establishment Act of 1795 to £138,000 per annum. During the course of the marriage negotiations in 1794, Holland was instructed to change the south-east rooms on the garden front, including the state bedchamber, into a suite for the princess, comprising drawing room, salon, bedchamber and boudoir, as indicated on this plan. The prince's own bedchamber was moved to the upper floor.

After the failure of the marriage, the princess's apartments reverted to being reception rooms for the prince, though he kept his bedchamber on the upper level, apart from a brief period *c.* 1805–07 on the basement floor. **CF**

Humphry Repton
Bury St. Edmunds 1752–1818 London

272
Designs for the Pavilion at Brighton

Published by J. C. Stadler, No. 15 Villiers Street, Strand, 1808
Folio, 53.3×36.5 cm
Cambridge, Graham Watson Collection, Master and Fellows of Emmanuel College
Literature: Abbey 1952, No. 55; Tooley 1973 ed., No. 396; Colvin 1978, pp. 679–81; Morley 1989, pp. 33–36

The Prince of Wales first rented a 'superior farmhouse' in Brighton in 1786 and immediately set about turning it into a marine pavilion to the design of Henry Holland. In 1802–04, the interiors were decorated in a fanciful Chinese style by the firm of Crace and further extensions were made. In 1803 an Indian style was used by William Porden for the design of the new stables, built behind the pavilion, one of the first manifestations of the influence of *Views of Oriental Scenery* by Thomas and William Daniell, published in 1795–1808. Repton evidently admired Porden's work and decided to make his own suggestions for rebuilding the whole pavilion, compiled in this volume. In it he gave his reasons for choosing the architecture of Hindustan as his inspiration in preference to other historicist styles.

The prince was initially enthusiastic, but did not take up the designs, possibly because he preferred fantasy to the purity, even pedantry, of Repton's approach. The architect he finally chose in 1815 for the remodelling was Repton's erstwhile partner, John Nash (Cat. No. 75), whose extravagantly idiosyncratic confection whipped up out of Indian and Gothick elements still adorns the town.

The work contains eight aquatinted plates and twelve vignettes, executed by Repton with the help of his architect sons, John Adey Repton (1775–1860) and George Stanley Repton (1786–1858), and engraved by Stadler. Though not trained as an architect, Repton believed architecture was 'an inseparable and indispensable auxiliary' to the art of landscape gardening, his first profession. He was also a talented watercolourist, a skill which enabled him to tempt his clients by illustrating his proposed improvements by means of a flap attached to his perspectives, which allowed them to make a direct 'before' and 'after' comparison. For his most important commissions, he prepared elaborate illustrated reports bound in red morocco, known as 'Red Books'. The present work, dedicated to the prince, may thus be regarded as a more public manifestation of the genre. **CF**

William Henry Pyne
London 1769–1843 London

273
The History of the Royal Residences of Windsor Castle, St. James's Palace, Kensington Palace, Hampton Court, Buckingham House and Frogmore

Published by Abraham Dry, 36 Upper Charlotte Street, Fitzroy Square, 1819
Printed book with coloured aquatint plates, Vol. 3, 34.2×27.5 cm
London, The Museum of London
Literature: Adams 1983, pp. 323–28, No. 132; Myers 1990, pp. 69–74

273

W. H. Pyne was employed in the production of several colour-plate books for Rudolph Ackermann. He resolved to publish a work in very much the same style which would describe and illustrate the royal palaces. The text would be written by himself. Charles Wild, James Stephanoff, Richard Cattermole, William Westall and George Samuel would draw the one hundred images.

Part 1 appeared in June 1816. Two years later it was clear that Pyne had over-reached himself financially. He sold out to Abraham Dry of 32 St. Martin's Lane. From Part 17 in December 1818, A. Dry's and W. H. Pyne's names alternate. Dry's name appears on the title page of the completed book. The view of the elaborate Gothic conservatory at Carlton House, designed for the Prince Regent in 1807 by Thomas Hopper, represents Plate 99 in the work – i.e. the penultimate plate. It was engraved by Thomas Sutherland after Charles Wild. **RH**

Charles Wild
London 1781–1835 London

274
The Crimson Drawing Room, Carlton House, *c.* 1816

Watercolour and gouache, 40.7 × 51 cm
Windsor Castle, H.M. Queen Elizabeth II
Inv. No. RL17603
Provenance: commissioned by the Prince Regent
Literature: Oppé 1950, p. 101, No. 654

The Crimson Drawing Room was situated in the north-west corner of the principal floor, created by Holland out of two rooms between 1788 and 1794 and first used as a dining room. In 1804 the decision was taken to convert it into a drawing room, symptomatic of the almost constant process of change which affected many of the apartments in Carlton House. The new room largely retained Holland's gilded plasterwork ceiling and coving. But the original scagliola walls and pilasters had been replaced first with stucco, to enable the prince to hang his pictures, and then *c.* 1805 with stretched panels of crimson silk damask, with matching curtains and draperies. The paintings included portraits by Lawrence and Reynolds, a Rubens of *St George* and Rembrandt's *The Jewish Bride*. The French-style neo-classical furnishings in the room were mainly supplied by Tatham, Bailey and Sanders between 1808 and 1814. The pair of female figure candelabra attributed to Thomire, placed in front of the windows, were delivered in 1812, but the maker(s) of the three chandeliers (that in the centre considered, according to Pyne, 'one of the finest in Europe') has yet to be firmly identified. **CF**

275
Chair, *c.* 1790

Possibly designed by Henry Holland; probably made by François Hervé
Beech, painted and parcel gilt, the upholstery modern, 93 × 63 × 62 cm
London, H.M. Queen Elizabeth II on loan to the Victoria and Albert Museum
Provenance: Carlton House

Most English furniture of the eighteenth century was based upon French prototypes though as with Cat. No. 276, the design was usually simplified and often muddled in the process. Here the original French design has been closely followed and this is no doubt a tribute to the client, for the Prince of Wales was a connoisseur of French art and design, and was at the time actively buying French furniture, new and old for Carlton House. The prince, therefore insisted that any English objects newly designed and made for him were sophisticated enough to stand beside the French originals. It is likely that this chair was designed by the distinguished architect Henry Holland who was involved at Carlton House from 1783 to 1802 and was particularly influenced by late eighteenth-century French neo-classicism. **CW**

276
Armchair, 1790

Made by François Hervé
Gilded beech, the upholstery modern, 103 × 60 × 63 cm
London, H.M. Queen Elizabeth II
Provenance: Carlton House
Exhibitions: London, Queen's Gallery, 1991–92, Cat. No. 54
Literature: de Bellaigue 1967, pp. 518–28, Fig. 31

This is one of a large set of chairs supplied by the London cabinet-maker François Hervé, to Carlton House in 1790 at a cost of £880.11s. Then in 1792 he supplied the Chinese figures which were applied to the top of the backs. They were made for the Chinese room which was the most sophisticated room in this style yet to have been created in England. The chairs were manufactured to complement two remarkable Chinese-style pier tables by the celebrated Parisian cabinet-maker Adam Weisweiler, which had been acquired for the room just before 1790. These tables are still in the royal collection. Whilst the chairs are London-made, in character they owe more to French prototypes than English. By 1820 these chairs and the pier table had been transferred to Brighton Pavilion where they joined other chinoiserie furniture. **CW**

276

277
Carlton House Table, *c.* 1790–95?

Rosewood with brass gallery, 79 × 140 × 84 cm
London, H.M. Queen Elizabeth II
Literature: Smith 1931, p. 237

A mystery still surrounds writing tables of this pattern which are popularly known as 'Carlton House Writing Tables'. As early as 1796, the records of the cabinet-makers Gillow illustrate a similar table and call it 'A Carlton House Table'. It has always been assumed that the original had therefore been made for the Prince of Wales at Carlton House earlier in the 1790s. No bills or other documentation have ever come to light to prove this to be true, although this table, or a very similar one, is recorded, *c.* 1826, in the king's bedroom situated on the attic floor at Carlton House. The form proved to be practical and popular and a considerable number of such tables survive from the late eighteenth and early nineteenth centuries, and they have frequently been reproduced since. **CW**

277

278
Upright Grand Pianoforte, 1808

Made by R. Jones & Co.
Ebony veneered case decorated with gilt
wood tracery, H 276 × W 114 × D 56 cm
Marks: inscribed on nameboard: R. JONES
UPRIGHT GRAND & SQUARE, Piano
Forte Maker, To His ROYAL HIGHNESS
the PRINCE of WALES, No.11, Golden
Square, London 1808; stamped on yoke,
R. Jones & Co. 855
London, H. M. Queen Elizabeth II, on loan
to the Museum of London
Inv. No. 38.208
Literature: Records of Fashion, 1808; James
1930, pp. 144-45

This instrument – essentially a grand piano
upended – was supplied to the Prince of Wales
at Carlton House and invoiced as follows on
15 August 1808 (RA 29011). 'A curious fine
toned Six Octave Upright Grand Piano
Forte/in black Ebony Case, designed from the
antique/Supported by four Strong Gothic
Columns; Moulding/and Cornice formed of
the best Workmanship/Carving & Gilding the
Columns, Moulding and/Cornice; in Burnish
and Mat Gold,/Ivory Balls Rosets & Orni-
ments for do/Japanning the Inside of the Case
a Royal Crimson/Fine Locks Water Gilt and
Hinges/Silk Curtains made full with gathered
Heads for do/An Elegant Bookcase Complete
in all respects to/Match the Piano Forte . . .
£680 0s'

The piano and matching bookcase formed part
of the decorative furnishings to the Gothic
library created in the basement storey of Carlton House in 1806.

The piano was illustrated 'exclusively' in a
colour engraving published in *Records of
Fashion* for 1808, and rediscovered by Simon
Jervis. The accompanying text recorded a visit
to Mr. Jones's premises in Golden Square,
'from a great number of our first amateurs,
whose curiosity led them to see and try the elegant upright grand piano . . . made for his
Royal Highness. The beauty of the workmanship, but above all, the rich quality of tone it
possesses, drew forth the most rapturous ex-
clamations, and must have proved the highest
gratification to Mr. Jones, who has spared
neither labor or expence, to produce an instrument which might not be excelled, either
for beauty or tone.'

The keyboard is of seventy-three notes,
CC-c and is trichord strung throughout. The
instrumental action has remained unaltered
since the day of its manufacture.

Both as prince and king, George enjoyed
music. He acquired a number of pianos from
Mott, Tomkinson and Broadwood among
others, and unusually, a Viennese grand of
1823 from Beethoven's piano-maker, Nan-
nette Streicher née Stein (H.M. Queen Elizabeth II, on loan to the National Trust, Hatch-
lands, Surrey). **TH**

279
Candelabrum, *c.* 1810

Possibly designed by Thomas Hopper; made
by Coade and Sealy
Coade stone, H 209 cm
London, Trustees of the Victoria and Albert
Museum
Inv. No. A.92-1980
Provenance: Carlton House
Literature: de Bellaigue 1972, p. 82

A set of ten of these were delivered to Carlton
House in February 1810. They were designed
for the Gothic Conservatory, and supported
oil lamps. They are of a most remarkable and
advanced Gothic Revival design for their date
and though it had often been assumed that
they were designed by Thomas Hopper who
designed the conservatory, they are rather
better than any of his known works.

They were made at the Coade and Sealy
works in London from their patent artificial
stone and Hopper may have provided the design. It is also possible that Coade commissioned a designer for them as they often did for
their various products, intending to produce a
number of them for sale. Coade stone was
used extensively at this period by architects in
many buildings and gardens. These candelabra
have such a sculptural quality that they could
have been designed by a sculptor rather than
an architect; if so, then a likely candidate
might have been Flaxman. **CW**

278

280
Coffer on Stand, 1813

Made by Thomas Parker
Inlay of tortoiseshell and pewter,
118.1×69.9×50.8 cm
Windsor Castle, H.M. Queen Elizabeth II
Provenance: Carlton House
Literature: Van Duin 1989, pp. 214–17

In January 1813, a pair of coffers, of which this is one, were delivered to Carlton House by the London cabinet-maker Thomas Parker. By 1817 they stood in the Rose Satin Drawing Room, and were later moved to Windsor. Parker specialised in Boulle marquetry, competing directly with George Bullock, and though neither of their workshops could match their Parisian counterparts, they produced Boulle of considerable quality. There are other pieces by Parker in the royal collection, including a Boulle drum table from Carlton House. **CW**

281
Pair of *lac burgauté* Vases

Chinese hard-paste porcelain, lacquered; gilt-bronze mounts, H 48.2 cm
London, H.M. Queen Elizabeth II
Inv. No. 2346
Literature: de Bellaigue 1967, pp. 45–53

These vases are first recorded by Benjamin Jutsham, the Prince Regent's inventory clerk, in an entry in his delivery book dated 27 March 1819 (Vol. 1, p. 312). It records their despatch from Carlton House to Brighton Pavilion and that they were 'said to have been presented by Her Late Majesty' (i.e. Queen Charlotte). The following year the mounts were altered and enriched by Benjamin Lewis Vulliamy, who charged £18.18s. for taking them to pieces 'adding a Bowl shell ornament to each & making 4 new masks gilding the new work strongly in ormolu and reglowing & refreshing the remainder of the gilt mountings' (PRO LCII/28. Qtr to 5 June 1820). *Lac burgauté* was a traditional method of decoration first applied to porcelain at the end of the Kangxi period and employed in the eighteenth century: unglazed porcelain was covered in black lacquer containing tiny pieces of mother-of-pearl, silver and gold.

No account has been traced for the original mounting but an attribution to the Vulliamys seems reasonable. They not only supplied clocks and watches, but also silver and ornamental work, particularly gilt-bronze mounts. Although skilled designers themselves, they

280

281

relied on a network of high quality craftsmen both in London and Paris to execute the work, giving them detailed drawings and specifications. The trade with J.-B. and P.-M. Delafontaine, who were among the finest bronze manufacturers in Paris, continued through the Napoleonic Wars conducted through the intermediary of the chinaman Robert Fogg, who undertook the delicate work of piercing the porcelain and cutting the bases for the attachment of the mounts. **CF**

Thomas Hope
Amsterdam 1769–1831 Deepdene

282
Household Furniture and Interior Decoration Executed from Designs by Thomas Hope, 1807

Published by Longman, Hurst, Rees, and Orme, Paternoster Row, 1 May 1807

Folio, 47×30 cm
Private Collection
Literature: Watkin 1968, pp. 51, 93–124, 214–18; Thornton and Watkin 1987, pp. 162–77

Thomas Hope belonged to a rich family of Amsterdam bankers (Cat. No. 66) who had fled to England in 1794 when Holland was occupied by the French. The house in Duchess Street, off Portland Place which he acquired in

View of the back front of H. Ph. Hope's house towards Hyde Park, in Seymour Place. 1813.

Artist unknown, *View of the back of Henry Philip Hope's house, Seymour Place*, 1813. Cat. No. 284

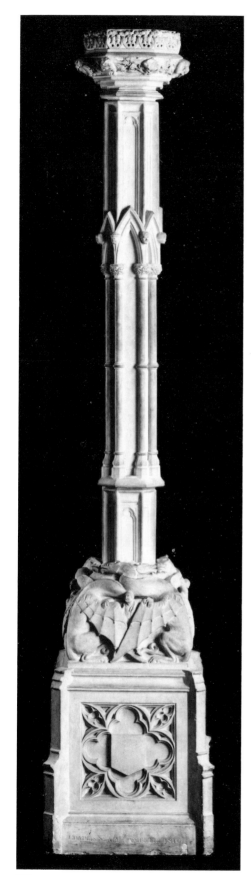

279

282

1799 had been built by Robert Adam *c.* 1768–71 and, unusually for London, had a forecourt as well as a back garden following the Parisian *hôtel particulier* model. He soon set about enlarging it and installing his important collection of antique and modern art, acquired on a lengthy Grand Tour of 1787–95, in appropriate classical and oriental settings; by 1804 the results could be viewed by the public on application or by invitation.

Hope's influential publication, in which the term 'interior decoration' was first used in English, followed three years later and contained views of the principal rooms on the first floor and measured drawings of individual pieces of furniture. The outline engravings were prepared by Edmund Aikin (1780–1820) and George Dawe (1781–1829) from Hope's own drawings.

Perhaps the most striking ensemble, the Egyptian Room, was by no means the largest apartment, but represents one of the earliest manifestations in London of the Egyptian influence in taste which received fresh momentum from Napoleon's brief period of conquest and the subsequent sequestration of antiquities by the British. The walls were decorated with a large frieze of figures drawn from Egyptian papyrus rolls, with the ceiling and double doors painted in a criss-cross pattern. The colour scheme was of suitably Egyptian shades of blue-green and pale yellow, relieved by black and gold. The sofas and armchairs (Cat. No. 286) designed by Hope had an archaic splendour and were taken from

Egyptian precedents. The materials used in the cups, canopic vases and figures displayed – including granite, porphyry and basalt – reflected Hope's determination to reflect the monumental character of Egyptian antiquities.

The first review of the work appeared in the *Edinburgh Review* in July 1807, written by Sydney Smith, and was damning: 'We confess we are not a little proud of this Roman spirit, which leaves the studies of those effeminate elegancies to slaves and foreigners, and holds it beneath the dignity of a free man to be eminently skilled in the decoration of couches and the mounting of chandeliers.' The *Monthly Review* of 1809 lumped him together with Soane: 'as little good taste is manifested in overloading our walls with symbolical images of antiquity, as in making our national Bank resemble a mausoleum.' **CF**

John Flaxman
York 1755–1826 London

283
Bust of Henry Philip Hope, 1803

Marble, H 54.2 cm
Provenance: Humbert and Flint, Deepende property sale, 1917, Lot 1130; Copenhagen, Thorvaldsen Museum

283

Artist unknown

284 (illus. p. 388)
View of the back of Henry Philip Hope's house, Seymour Place, 1818

Pen and ink and watercolour, 32.3 × 24 cm
Inscribed: View of the back front of H. Ph. Hope's house towards Hyde Park in Seymour Place 1818
New Haven, Yale Center for British Art
Inv. No. B1977.14.4765
Provenance: bought from Somerville and Simpson, 1970

Henry Philip Hope's first London home was situated in a cul-de-sac at the west end of Curzon Street and overlooked Hyde Park. This drawing shows the back of what was essentially a standard London town house, but embellished with a two-storey loggia supported on the first floor by four caryatids in the Greek Revival style associated with his brother Thomas. In 1833 he moved to Arklow House, Connaught Place, one-time home of Caroline, Princess of Wales (Cat. Nos. 617–30). Seymour Place was remodelled in 1835 by J. B. Papworth and two storeys were added with further ironwork. It was demolished early this century. **CF**

Exhibitions: London, Royal Academy, 1979, No. 125
Literature: Gentleman's Magazine, 1831, pp. 368–70; Watkin 1968, p. 118; Bindman 1979, p. 126; Fig. 125

Henry Philip Hope (1774–1839) was the brother of Thomas Hope, the gentlemen scholar and collector who befriended Flaxman in Rome and commissioned his illustrations for the works of Dante. The bust originally stood at the centre of a chimneypiece erected during Thomas Hope's remodelling of his London house in Duchess Street. Flaxman's account in the British Museum records that Thomas Hope paid £84 for the bust in October 1803. An engraving showing the bust in its original position appeared in Thomas Hope's *Household Furniture* of 1807 (illustration No. 48). Henry was much involved in the remodelling of the house at Duchess Street and erected a north gallery to exhibit his brother's Italian paintings and his own collection of Dutch and Flemish masters. A wealthy bachelor, he had the capital to devote extensive charitable works and the formation of a splendid collection of diamonds. He housed the majority of his collections at Chart Park in Surrey, a house built upon lands adjoining his brother's at Deepende. **MC**

285 (illus. p. 397)
Vase, c. 1802

Designed by Thomas Hope; manufacture attributed to Alexis Decaix
Copper, patinated to resemble bronze with applied ormolu mounts, 59 × 33.5 cm
London, Trustees of the Victoria and Albert Museum
Inv. No. 33-1983
Provenance: Duchess Street
Literature: Hope 1807, Plates 35, 36; Chapman 1985, pp. 217–28

This vase was designed by Thomas Hope for his celebrated London house at Duchess Street. The illustrations to *Household Furniture and Interior Decoration* show that massive forms with applied ornament, that parallel but are not strictly imitative of the contemporary French Empire style, were characteristic of his taste. One of the engravings, of a vase (Plates 35, 36), led to the identification of this vase with Thomas Hope's design. The attribution of a maker for the vase is less certain, although Chapman produced a strongly argued case for the French metalworker, Alexis Decaix. Hope made special reference to Decaix in his introduction to *Household Fur-*

niture, and stated that he had confidence in the skill of this 'bronzist' above all others.

Decaix was first mentioned in the London *Trade Directory* in 1799 where he was referred to as a 'bronze and ormolie (sic) manufacturer'. He worked for the prominent goldsmiths and retailers, Garrard, between 1799 and 1804, producing a range of objects in bronze and ormolu. The high quality of his work rapidly brought him to the attention of fashionable society in the period of his association with Garrard which coincided with Hope's decoration of Duchess Street. The evidence of the Frenchman's career, combined with the fine workmanship and the technical prowess manifested by the vase, would seem to confirm the maker as Decaix.

The original position of the vase in Hope's house has not been positively established, although the ornament, emblematic of Bacchus, would seem to indicate a position in the dining room, where such an iconographic scheme might appear to be appropriate. The form of the vase was based on that of an ancient Greek volute krater. Hope, however, seems to have copied elements of the form for his design from a vase that is now recognised to be a later Roman marble copy of the earlier ceramic type. The probable prototype is now in the Museo Archeologico Nationale in Naples. **AE**

286 (illus. p. 398)
Armchair, 1804

Designed by Thomas Hope; maker unknown
Painted and gilded wood with bronze mounts, 122 × 66 × 76 cm
Buscot Park, Berkshire, Trustees of the Faringdon Collection
Provenance: Thomas Hope, Duchess Street; by descent; Christie's, 18 July 1917, Lot 306; bought by Alexander Henderson, 1st Lord Faringdon
Exhibitions: London, Royal Academy, 1972, Cat. No. 1655; Washington, 1985, Cat. No. 525
Literature: Hope 1807, Plates 8, 46; Watkin 1968, pp. 115, 211, 256, Plate 40; Honour 1969, pp. 210–12; Musgrave 1970, pp. 5–11

This is one of four armchairs designed by Hope for the Egyptian Room of his house in Duchess Street and every part of the design is taken from an appropriately Egyptian source. Hope wrote that the 'crouching priests supporting the arms are copied from an Egyptian idol in the Vatican: the winged Isis placed in the rail is borrowed from an Egyptian mummy case in the Institute at Bologna: the Canopuses are imitated from the one in the

287

288

Capitol', and went on to describe the sources for the other motifs. In fact, Hope probably relied as much on engravings and replicas, which were widely available in Rome by the 1790s. These chairs are *en suite* with a pair of sofas which also stood in the same room. Though the maker is unknown they were certainly made in London. **CW**

287
Centre Table, 1804

Designed by Thomas Hope
Mahogany inlaid with silver and ebony,
74 × 106 cm
London, Trustees of the Victoria & Albert Museum
Inv. No. W. 13-1936
Provenance: Thomas Hope, Duchess Street
Literature: Hope 1807, Plate 39

Though we know that this piece were designed by Hope for his own house in Duchess Street it is not known in which room it stood. As with the Hope chair we do not know the cabinet-maker but it was certainly made in London. This table in both its design and ornament represents the most advanced aspect of the Greek Revival style in furniture. The combination of ivory and silver inlay and the inwardly curving pyramidal base is very unusual for England at this period, as indeed is the round centre table form itself. Following Hope's publication of the design as Plate 39 in *Household Furniture*, many commercial cabinet-makers produced versions of this table. **CW**

288
Klismos Chair, 1810–20

Painted beech, 84 × 66 × 45 cm
London, Trustees of the Victoria and Albert Museum
Inv. No. W.21-1958

It may never be possible to prove the country of origin and it is included here to illustrate the international character of neo-classicism in the opening decades of the nineteenth century. The form is directly derived from the ancient Greek Klismos chair widely illustrated in Greek vase painting. Indeed, the painted decoration upon this chair is taken directly from a Greek vase – now in the British Museum – from Sir William Hamilton's collection. Chairs of this type were designed and made throughout Europe from the 1780s to the 1840s; Thomas Hope had several which he published in 1807 and architects as diverse as Soane, Schinkel, Pelagi and Percier designed variations on this form. **CW**

Wedgwood

Literature: Kelly 1962; Farrer 1974; Reilly and Savage 1980, pp. 314–16, 364–66, 381

The Wedgwood company was founded by Josiah Wedgwood (1730–95) in 1759 at the Ivy House Pottery, Burslem, Stoke-on-Trent. From the eighteenth century, London was regarded as the 'window to the world' and it was therefore not surprising that in 1765 the newly established potter engaged his older brother John, of the firm of Wedgwood and Bliss, general warehouseman at No. 3 Cateaton Street in the City to provide an outlet for his new products. Free transport to the capital was provided by the company from what was at that time the rather rural Staffordshire Potteries, initially using the turnpike roads and later the canal system. The expansion of Wedgwood's manufacturing activities was mirrored by the increased size of its London premises: from Cateaton Street to the more fashionable West End, in Charles Street, Grosvenor Square, where Josiah received the patronage of Queen Charlotte, wife of George III. With the opening of Josiah's purpose-built manufactory called Etruria on the 13 June 1769 and his partnership with the merchant, Thomas Bentley (1730–80), who was ideally suited to organise the retailing of their products, the London premises moved to No. 1 Great Newport Street. In 1774 more impressive and prestigious rooms were leased at Portland House, Greek Street, Soho. The new showrooms were officially opened with the

289

display of the largest topographical cream coloured earthenware service commissioned by the Empress Catherine II of Russia. Again, the premises were used for a spectacular exhibition during the months of April and May 1790, when, by admission ticket only, London's fashionable society flocked to see Wedgwood's copy of the Portland Vase.

The end of the original lease on Portland House coincided with the death of Josiah Wedgwood I. Wedgwood's sons tried to renew the lease but difficulties arose because the Duke of Portland wished to dispose of his estate. With the Soho Square district becoming less fashionable, new premises were again sought. The choice eventually fell on a house in the aristocratic residential area at the corner of York Street (now Duke of York Street) in St. James's Square. The new rooms were opened in the summer of 1797. The location was not ideal for commercial activities as it was predominantly a residential area, but the York Street showrooms rapidly attracted many eminent visitors.

Josiah Wedgwood II (1769–1843) paid £8,500 for the initial purchase price and spent a further £7,400 on improving and refurbishing the York Street showrooms. The only picture of the interior is illustrated in Ackermann's *Repository of Arts* for February 1809 (p. 27). It shows a lofty colonnaded room with tall windows providing good natural light. 'Ornamental Wares' were displayed in imposing glass-fronted cabinets and on wall brackets, whilst the 'Useful Wares' were laid out on tables in the centre of the room. In a surviving manuscript (Mss. No. E141-28923) detailing an 'Examination of Plain Ware Stock

Account', various showrooms and storerooms are indicated including Ornamental Showrooms, Black Showroom (for Black Basalt), a Vase Garret and even a Chemical Ware Storeroom.

Queen Charlotte continued to patronise the firm but in a memorandum dated 20 April 1807 to the Etruria Works, the London showroom manager and Josiah I's nephew, Thomas Byerley, urged for 'all the aid you can give us with Novelties, for, though the town is very full, our rooms are very empty most days.' Despite Byerley's fears, sales were comparatively strong and the production of wares continued to be varied including Blue-printed wares, Rosso Antico, Black Basalt, Bone China, Queen's Ware, Drab and Dry-bodied Wares as well as Jasper. But by the 1820s, sales had declined and the fate of the showrooms was clear. Ultimately they closed in 1828, with a final sale of the stock and fixtures taking place in several parts, from September to December 1829. However, the company did not withdraw from the city completely, but sold through agents in Oxford Street. **GBR**

289
Portland Vase, *c.* 1790

Wedgwood; black Jasper with white bas-relief decoration, H 25.5 cm
Inscribed in pencil inside the neck: 25
Barlaston, Wedgwood Museum Trust
Inv. No. 4318
Exhibitions: London, Science Museum, 1978, Cat. No. 169
Literature: Reilly and Savage 1980, pp. 276–77, Plate XVII

This copy of the Portland Vase is Josiah Wedgwood's own, The Portland Vase was also called the Barberini Vase because the original cased glass vessel was sold to the Cardinal Francesco Barberini, nephew of Pope Urban VIII (1623–44). The glass original, dating from around 25 A.D., was subsequently sold in 1780 to James Byres the Scottish antiquary. He in turn sold the vase for £1,000 to Sir William Hamilton, British Ambassador to the Court of Naples, a renowned collector. On his return to London the vase was acquired by the Duchess of Portland for her private museum. On her death the glass vase was sold on 7 June 1786 as Lot 4155 in the sale of her Portland Museum. The vase was purchased on behalf of the 3rd Duke of Portland and within three days was lent to Josiah Wedgwood I to study and emulate its form in his Jasper body.

Josiah with his son Josiah II and two of his best workmen, Henry Webber and William Hackwood, commenced a series of experiments and trials to make a faithful copy. The first good copy was produced in October

1789. In April 1790 an exhibition to show the vase was arranged at Portland House, Greek Street, the Wedgwood London showrooms from 1774 to 1795.

A saturation campaign for publicising the Portland Vase was suggested by Josiah in a letter dated 2 July 1790 (Mss. No. E137-27399). A large quantity, 2,000 'Little pamphlets in French' were to be provided, 500 to be sewn into the existing French Ornamental Catalogues. Josiah II and Thomas Byerley were sent with a copy of the vase on a European tour to The Hague, Hanover, Berlin and Frankfurt.

Josiah Wedgwood's own copy is slightly imperfect and may have been one of the earliest successful copies. **GBR**

290
Copy of the Portland Vase, *c.* 1801–17

Wilson, Hanley, Staffordshire
Stoneware, brown-coloured with applied white relief-moulded decoration depicting Peleus and Thetis, and on the base, Paris, H 29.3 cm
Mark: Wilson, impressed
Stoke-on-Trent, City Museum and Art Gallery
Inv. No. 69–1988
Exhibitions: Barlaston and London, 1989–90

Other manufacturers in Staffordshire soon began to produce their own versions of Wedgwood's Portland Vase. In 1836, Edward Cowper, patentee of the Applegarth and Cowper steam-printing machine who also had an interest in the production of terracotta

290

vases based on classical forms, commented before the Select Committee on Arts and Manufactures (p. 50, qu. 590):

> Mr Wedgwood has improved the forms of pottery and diffused them more than any other person, but he retained a little of the prejudice of keeping art at a high price. His imitations of the Portland vase was justly celebrated, but after he had sold 30 of them at 25 guineas each, he destroyed the mould, in order to render them more rare, and that I consider a very erroneous feeling, because it was so far preventing the diffusion of taste throughout the country.

David Wilson, a master potter at the Church Works, Hanley, took over the business following his brother's death in 1801. Wilson himself died in 1816 and although the business was taken over by his son, also David, it was declared bankrupt in 1817. **DS**

292

291

291
Pastille or Incense Burner

Wedgwood; black Basalt, H 31.8 cm
Mark: WEDGWOOD impressed
Barlaston, Wedgwood Museum Trust
Inv. No. 1134
Exhibitions: London, Wedgwood House, 1984, Cat. No. N3

The pastille or incense burner is recorded in the 'Shape Number One' book as No. 496. In April 1807 Byerley wrote in a memorandum:

> I have just been attending the Bishop of Winchester, who has laid out some guineas

in ornaments, and wants a vase for perfuming large halls, of the form 290 Dolphin, Tripod, about 5 times as large as what we now make, that 3 or 4 pastiles may be burnt at once. I have promised him that one shall be made, and that he shall not be charged for the model, as it is a thing very likely to sell, and these things are coming more and more into use . . . It is to be in black, ornamented as the small ones are. **GBR**

292
Tea Set, comprising Teapot, Cream Jug and Sugar Box

Wedgwood; Rosso Antico body with white bas-relief 'Prunus' decoration, teapot H 10.2 cm
Mark: WEDGWOOD impressed
Barlaston, Wedgwood Museum Trust
Inv. Nos. 5042, 5043 and 5044 respectively
Exhibitions: London, Wedgwood House, 1984, Cat. No. N16
Literature: Reilly and Savage 1980, p. 302 illustrated

Rosso Antico (literally meaning antique red), an unglazed stoneware body which was first used by Josiah Wedgwood I from 1776 onwards especially for utilitarian objects such as teaware. It became more popular in the early years of the nineteenth century when effective use was made of white and black ornamentation on the red ground. The teapot is recorded in a price book watermarked 1805 (Mss. No. E54-30029) as 'New Low Oval Tea Pot . . . Brown with white Chinese Ornaments'. Wholesale prices ranged, according to size, for the teapots from 3s.6d. to 7.6d.; 3s. to 5s. for sugar basins and 1s.6d. to 3s.6d. for cream jugs. **GBR**

293
Tea Set, comprising Teapot, Cream Jug and Sugar Box, c. 1815–20

Wedgwood; Drabware body with white bas-reliefs in Egyptian style, teapot H 10.2 cm, cream jug H 7.6 cm, sugar box H 6.4 cm
Marks: teapot, WEDGWOOD in small capitals, impressed, and V incised; cream jug similar marks and 1 incised; sugar box similar marks and oo incised
London, Trustees of the British Museum
Inv. No. M&LA 1989, 11-2, 1 to 3
Literature: Conner 1983

The shape of the teapot is similar to the 'New Low Oval Tea Pot . . .' recorded in a Wedgwood price book for 1805. Fashionable taste at this period tended to the exotic but the styles were eclectic, borrowing and often combining elements from several ancient cultures. The individual could then choose between a chinoiserie, an Egyptian or perhaps a Roman style tea service happy in the knowledge that his choice would be in vogue.

Wedgwood had been producing wares using Egyptian styles and motifs as early as 1770. The main source for his designs was Bernard de Montfaucon's *L'Antiquité Expliquée* (1719–24) which reproduced antiquities from several ancient cultures including Egypt. The volumes were published in an English translation almost simultaneously with the French edition and they were widely read in England. Montfaucon had not personally visited Egypt but drew his information from the collections and publications available to him, inevitably including copies and pastiches. Wedgwood's designers in turn translated the images in a more neo-classical manner.

Popular interest in Egypt was rekindled by

293

Napoleon's expedition to Egypt in 1798 and Nelson's victory over the French fleet at the Battle of the Nile. Honoured with the title Baron Nelson of the Nile and Burnham Thorpe, Nelson is particularly remembered for his action in Egypt and it has been suggested that the popularity of the crocodile as a motif at this period may be patriotic in origin. Robert Southey in *Letters from England* (1807) directly related the fashion for the Egyptian style to the military campaigns, contrasting the returning wounded soldiers to the elegant modes inspired by Egypt, '... the ladies wear crocodile ornaments, and you sit upon a sphinx in a room hung round with mummies ...' **EE**

George Underwood
c. 1793–1829 Bath

294
The Courier newspaper office in the Strand, 1809

Pen and watercolour, 71×50 cm
London, Trustees of Sir John Soane's Museum
Inv. No. 27.6.11

Many London newspapers first appeared in the last decades of the eighteenth century: the *Morning Post* (1772), *The Times* (1785) and the *Observer* (1791). In 1792 John Parry launched the *Courier and Evening Gazette* as a liberal pro-French evening paper. In 1804 it became the *Courier*. In 1811 the circulation was 11,000 (more than that of *The Times*), but this success was not maintained and in 1842 the *Courier* ceased publication.

The paper had its offices at 348 the Strand and it was this street, rather than Fleet Street, which was the focus of newspaper publishing before about 1840. Neither the architect nor the date of the neo-Egyptian front of the *Courier* office is known. The drawing itself was prepared but not used for Sir John Soane's Academy lectures, which were first delivered in 1809, and was intended to illustrate his attack on '... the paltry attempt to imitate the character and form of [Egyptian] works in small and confined spaces ... particularly in many of the Shop Fronts of Metropolis'(Archives 1/35).

A British vogue for things Egyptian had been inspired by the drawings of Piranesi and by Denon's *Voyage dans la Basse et la Haute Egypte* (1802). Interest was catalysed by the publication of Thomas Hope's *Household Furniture* in 1807 (Cat. No. 282). The *Courier* office must have been one of the early fruits of the fashion. **NB**

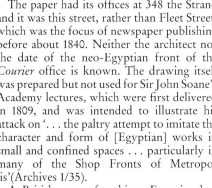

294

Artist unknown

295
Design perspective for the façade of No. 13 Lincoln's Inn Fields, 1812

Pen and watercolour, 78×45.5 cm
London, Trustees of Sir John Soane's Museum
Inv. No. 14.6.2
Literature: European Magazine 1812, p. 385; Stroud 1984, Fig. 40

This design perspective by one of Soane's pupils shows the house as it was built in 1812 when the openings of the projecting 'loggia', as Soane called it, were not glazed, the windows being set back in line with the houses on either side. Later in 1829 and 1834 the openings were glazed and the verandah became part of the internal space; Soane also added another storey in 1825.

This 'loggia', with its two tiers of round-headed openings and its Coade-stone caryatids, provoked a good deal of controversy in Soane's day. No sooner had the lower stage appeared in August and September 1812 than the district surveyor, William Kinnard, objected to it and took Soane to court alleging a contravention of the Building Act on the

295

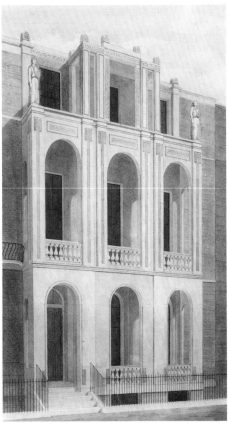

grounds that the loggia extended over 3 feet beyond the fronts of the adjoining houses. Soane argued that the projection was not a public nuisance as it was within the bounds of his own freehold property; the case was heard on 12 October 1912 at Bow Street and the magistrates declared in Soane's favour. **MAR**

Frank Copland

296
Section through the Museum and Breakfast Room at No. 13 Lincoln's Inn Fields, looking East, 1818

Pen, watercolour and black ink, 54.5×64 cm
Signed and dated: (recto), Drawn by F. Copland June 1817 (in George Bailey's hand) and (verso), F. Copland June 10th 181[-]
London, Trustees of Sir John Soane's Museum
Inv. No. PSA 1
Literature: Summerson, Watkin, Mellinghoff 1983, Fig. 23; Millenson 1987, pp. 55, 59, Fig. 37

John Soane began to build up his collections of antique fragments and vases, plaster casts and models in the 1790s when he was living at No. 12 Lincoln's Inn Fields, a smaller and more conventional townhouse than his later house and museum at No. 13. In 1808 Soane purchased the freehold of No. 13 and at first left the tenant, Mr. Tyndale, in residence in the front part of the existing house. He then rebuilt the stables at the back converting them into a museum and architectural office which were connected to the back of No. 12 by a narrow passage. Later, in 1812, Mr. Tyndale agreed to move into No. 12 which he rented from Soane, who was then free to demolish the front part of No. 13 which he rebuilt as his own home.

This section, drawn by his pupil Frank Copland, well shows the dual nature of Soane's house and museum. On the left is the double-height museum, top-lit by a conical skylight, providing an appropriate setting for the Apollo Belvedere and larger plaster casts, with the crypt below creating an emotive background for the more funereal *objets d'art*. The breakfast room, on the right, with its pendentive dome, is part of the house. It is lit by an octagonal lantern and two skylights, presenting, as Soane said in his Description, 'a succession of fanciful effects which constitute the *poetry* of architecture'. **MAR**

296

Joseph Michael Gandy
London 1771–1843 Devon

297
View of the Dome area at Sir John Soane's Museum, by lamplight, *c.* 1812

Pen and watercolour, 74×105.5 cm
London, Trustees of Sir John Soane's Museum
Inv. No. 14.6.5
Literature: Summerson, Watkin, Mellinghoff 1983, Fig. 17; Lutacher 1983, pp. 40–48, Fig. 6; Millenson 1987, pp. 98, 110, Fig. 60

The dome area of the museum, with its double-height tribune and shadowy galleries, best illustrates Soane's painterly vision. The walls are arranged in the manner of Piranesi with cinerary urns, models and the larger plaster casts, which include the huge cornice and architrave of the Temple of Castor and Pollux on the east wall and the large capital from the same order on the south.

In this perspective the scale of the interior is greatly exaggerated by the low viewpoint taken and the humble spectator dwarfed by the Piranesian arrangement of diverse objects. The dome area is seen by night, dramatically

lit by a shaft of light from a source of the crypt which is kept just out of sight. Of all Gandy's perspectives this is the one which best depicts the *lumière mystérieuse* which so strongly appealed to Soane. **MAR**

John Buckler
Calbourne, Isle of Wight 1770–1851 London

298
Fonthill Abbey, 1821

Grey wash with pen and grey and black ink, 35.2×45.6 cm
Inscribed below image: Drawn by J. Buckler July 1821, (beneath mount), South West View of Fonthill Abbey; the Seat of William Beckford Esqre
London, Trustees of the British Museum
Inv. No. 1944-10-14-24
Provenance: presented by Miss M. H. Turner, 1944
Literature: Lees-Milne 1976, pp. 1–76; Wainwright 1990, pp. 109–12

William Beckford (1760–1844), one of the most extraordinary personalities of his age, and a discerning if capricious collector and patron, was responsible for one of the most remarkable houses of the early nineteenth century, Fonthill Abbey in Wiltshire. He had inherited from his father in 1770 one of the largest Palladian mansions in the country, Fonthill Splendens, which he first adapted with the assistance of John Soane and James Wyatt, and eventually demolished when it no longer gave him sufficient scope for his progressively fantastic schemes. Between 1796 and 1818 Beckford supervised the construction of Fonthill Abbey, which was conceived from the outset in the Gothic style, with a tower.

Having appointed Wyatt as his architect, Beckford made constant changes to the original designs, and the process of construction was hindered by shoddy workmanship, so that by 1807 only the south wing was fit for habitation; the most striking feature of the whole ensemble, the great tower which was 278 feet high, was completed in 1809. Wyatt died in 1813, and Beckford himself subsequently directed the final phase of the building, under the shadow of impending financial ruin. The costs of building Fonthill were phenomenal, and at the same time Beckford's chief source of income, sugar from the West Indies estates he had inherited from his father, plummetted in price below the cost of production.

In 1822, only four years after the completion of the Abbey, Beckford sold it, complete with its contents, which were auctioned in 1823. Two books devoted to Fonthill were published in the same year, John Britton's *Graphical and Literary Illustrations of Fonthill* and John Rutter's *Delineations of Fonthill and its Abbey*. In 1825 the tower suddenly collapsed, only months after Wyatt's chief contractor confessed that he had never laid the foundation of the tower according to the specifications he had been given. **LS**

299
Cup and Cover, 1816

Designed by William Beckford and Gregorio Franchi; made by James Aldridge
Indian agate bowl and cover and chalcedony knops set with rubies in silver-gilt mounts, 24.2×14 cm
Marks: hallmark for 1815–16; maker's mark of James Aldridge
London, Trustees of the Victoria and Albert Museum
Inv. No. 428-1882
Provenance: Fonthill Abbey; Hamilton Palace
Exhibitions: London, British Museum, 1990, Cat. No. 19
Literature: Wainwright 1971, pp. 254–64; Snodin and Baker 1980, pp. 735–48, 820–34

Designed by the antiquary William Beckford and his Portuguese companion and agent, Gregorio Franchi, this piece in the Renaissance Revival style was made in London by the smallworker and jeweller, James Aldridge. At the centre of the luxury trade and catering for the most advanced taste, London's workshops supplied Beckford with some of the earliest examples of historicist English silver. Of the large number of pieces ordered by Beckford between 1812 and 1822 most were mounted hardstones and porcelain requiring the expertise to work with mixed materials and accomplish complex detailing, often on a small scale.

One of a number of independent London craftsmen employed for this purpose, James Aldridge, was recorded at 11 Northumberland Court, Strand, in 1817. He is notable for having provided more of the significant marked pieces for Beckford than any other maker. With only one exception, the eighteen items manufactured by Aldridge are mounted hardstone or porcelain. The cup and cover had been previously attributed to Joseph Angell, but as Snodin and Baker have shown, the evidence of Franchi's accounts and a signed design book in the Victoria and Albert Museum leave no doubt that Aldridge was, indeed, the maker.

Designed to complement Beckford's antiquarian collection, which included mounted pieces of genuine age, the cup and cover was displayed at Beckford's Gothic Revival house, Fonthill Abbey. It passed to his daughter, Susan Euphemia, wife of the 10th Duke of Hamilton and was purchased by the Victoria and Albert Museum from the Hamilton Palace sale of 1882 as an authentic Renaissance object. This was soon in dispute. It was taken from exhibition and remained in store until 1970 when its importance as an early example of the Renaissance Revival style was re-evaluated. **AE**

300 *(illus. p. 399)*
Cabinet, c. 1820

Probably made by Robert Hume
Ebony with *pietre dure* panels, Boulle side panels, gilt-metal mounts and mirror glass with a marble top, 105×99×49 cm
Windsor Castle, H.M. Queen Elizabeth II
Provenance: George Watson Taylor M.P., Cavendish Square, London; Christie's, 28 May 1825, Lot 68; Windsor Castle

298

Cup and Cover, 1816. Cat. No. 299

Vase, *c.* 1802. Cat. No. 285

Pietre dure panels from Rome and Florence were frequently purchased by collectors all over Europe from the late sixteenth century on and were incorporated into furniture by their local cabinet-makers. From the 1790s until 1820 William Beckford (Cat. No. 298), as part of the fabulous collection which he built up to furnish Fonthill Abbey, his vast Gothic Revival house in Wiltshire, gathered together a remarkable collection of *pietre dure*. Beckford had a number of pieces of furniture constructed around them – several still survive – and the work was probably carried out by the London cabinet-maker, Robert Hume.

This cabinet was, however, made for the London house of Beckford's Wiltshire neighbour and rival collector, George Watson Taylor, whose taste was very influenced by Beckford's. Taylor had several such cabinets both in his London house and in Erlestoke, his Wiltshire house. Not only do they represent the highest quality London cabinet making, but also the sophisticated furniture being made at this time specifically for collectors of ancient, fine and applied art to mix with their collections. In the 1820s, Taylor fell into financial difficulties and sold his London collection; this cabinet was bought on behalf of

George IV by Robert Fogg, one of the king's favourite antiquities brokers. **CW**

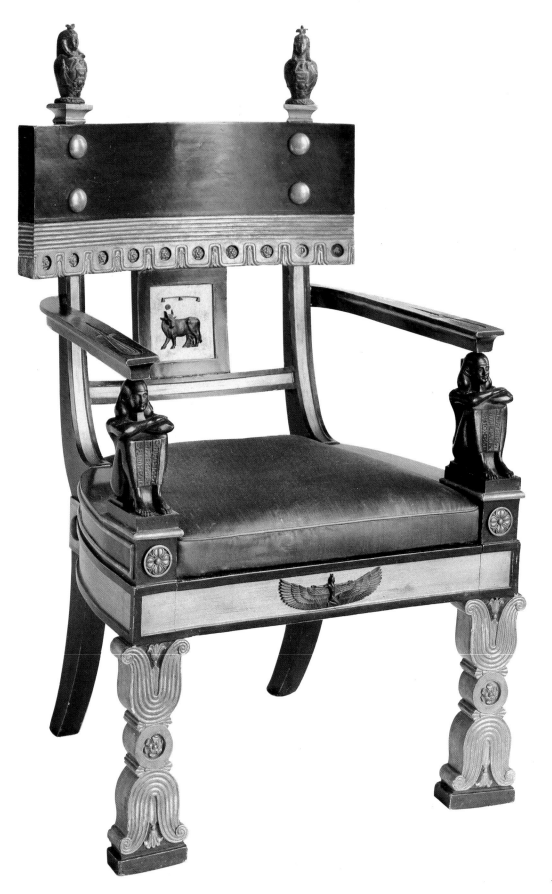

Armchair, 1804. Cat. No. 286

HOUSEHOLD FURNITURE

Cabinet, *c.* 1820. Cat. No. 300

J. M. Gandy, *View of the Dome area at Sir John Soane's Museum by lamplight, c.* 1812. Cat. No. 297

Inkstand, 1816. Cat. No. 303

Candlesticks, *c.* 1820. Cat. No. 305

HOUSEHOLD FURNITURE

Chair, 1823. Cat. No. 307

Fingerbowl, 1837. Cat. No. 306

Gilt beechwood frame, crimson velvet
upholstery, 99×65×68.5 cm
London, the Rt. Hon. the Lord Mayor and
Corporation of London
Inv. No. SF2/14
Provenance: Mansion House, London
Exhibitions: Brighton, 1948, Cat. No. 130
Literature: Beard and Gilbert 1986, p. 695;
documents in Corporation of London
Records Office: General Purposes
Committee (Common Council), minutes
and papers, 1803, 1835 and the Mansion
House Furniture Inventory 1804

This chair comes from a set of twenty-four
elbow chairs and three sofas supplied in 1803
for the Mansion House, the official residence
of the Lord Mayor of London, by John Phillips (1774–1812), an upholder who worked extensively for the City of London. The design
of anchors, ropes and sword has been connected with Nelson's naval victories, particularly the Battle of the Nile, and the presentation of the Freedom of the City of London to
Lord Nelson (Cat. No. 18). Such chairs were
fashionable, and Sheraton published designs
for 'Nelson's Chairs' in 1806.

In 1803 two inter-communicating drawing
rooms were created on the second floor of the
Mansion House, where the lord mayor and
lady mayoress had their private accommodation. The estimate for furnishings included '24
elegant arm Chairs, black Rose wood and rich
burnished gold, silk Cushions' as well as '3
elegant Sophas' similarly treated. The silk
damask for the chairs was to be yellow, as
chosen by the lady mayoress.

The city surveyor of the time was George
Dance the Younger (1741–1825), son of the designer of the Mansion House. He was asked to
present to the Committee 'a drawing and particular' of the furniture required 'with a Pattern Chair'. The records do not tell whether
Dance himself made the drawings, but they
say that he 'caused patterns to be produced'
for the chairs, and we know that John Phillips
was paid for supplying the pattern chair.
Advertisements were then placed in various
London morning newspapers inviting uphol-
ders and cabinet-makers to submit proposals.
The successful tenderer was John Phillips. The
new furniture was installed by 22 November
1803. The price originally estimated by Dance
for each chair was 10 guineas but Phillips was
finally only paid £246.14s. for all of the furniture he provided.

The Mansion House furniture inventory of
1804 lists the new chairs as rosewood and gold
with lions heads and claws, French stuffed and
covered with yellow silk damask, trimmed
with French gimp, with tablet backs and
stuffed elbows, with a set of covers in 'washing
leather' and a set of chintz cotton cases. **SJ**

302

302
Armchair, 1821

Designed by John Children and Thomas
Chippendale the Younger; made by
Chippendale the Younger

Elm, 116.8×69.2×68.5 cm
Windsor Castle, H.M. Queen Elizabeth II
Provenance: Windsor Castle
Literature: de Bellaigue 1978, pp. 14–18;
Haydon ed. Pope, Vol. 3, 1963, 10 June 1830,
pp. 452–53

In 1818 John Children, a librarian at the British Museum, whilst on a visit to Belgium purchased the historic elm tree under which the Duke of Wellington spent much of the day during the Battle of Waterloo. Several objects were made from the wood including two chairs in the London workshops of Thomas Chippendale the younger, one for the Duke of Wellington and still in the family collection, and this example which was delivered to King George IV at Carlton House on 24 February 1821. On the top rail is carved a representation of the village of Waterloo and the back is also decorated with a trophy of arms and two inscriptions. One inscription was composed by the Duke of Wellington's brother, the Marquess of Wellesley, and commences 'GREGORIO AUGUSTO EUROPAE LIBERATORI' (To George Augustus the Liberator of Europe).

The manufacture of such relics has always been a widespread practice but was not without its critics. In 1830 the artist Benjamin Haydon remarked of these chairs, 'This is exclusively an illustration of the English disease. They can't let a thing remain for all to enjoy. They have no poetry, no national feeling; they must have it to themselves, they must cut it up for their firesides ... You can't admit the English into your gardens but they will strip your trees, cut their names on your statues, eat your fruit, & stuff their pockets with bits for their museums ... In short the ignorance, vanity, want of feeling, grossness, rudeness, consequence, & impotent impertinence of any given number of English when they are uncontrolled, it a matter of great & just complaint from Petersburgh to Lisbon.' **CW**

303 (illus. p.401)
Inkstand, 1816

Made by T. Dudley
Brass and patinated bronze on black marble base supported on the backs of tortoises; drawer with handle in the form of the Prince of Wales's plume, fitted with trough for pens and compartments for ink- and sand-wells, 28 × 29.2 × 17 cm
Marks: engraved under each tortoise, T. Dudley (?Pub.^d) Aug 1816/London; along metal band of base, DUDLEY FECIT
Windsor Castle, H.M. Queen Elizabeth II Inv. No. 171
Exhibitions: London, Queen's Gallery, 1966–67, Cat. No. 51

The inkstand is a small scale model of the enormous mortar which still stands on Horse Guards' Parade and which was unveiled by the Prince Regent on his birthday, 12 August, in 1816. As the front plaque indicates, the original, which was capable of bombing Cadiz from a distance of 3½ miles, had been abandoned by the French outside the city after Wellington's victory at Salamanca in 1812. It was presented by the Spanish nation to the prince as a token of respect and gratitude. Unfortunately, it proved difficult to transport and was unmounted, so a special gun carriage was constructed by the Royal Arsenal to the design of the Earl of Mulgrave, the master general. This took the form of a monster, intended to represent Geryon (on account of his connection with Gades – Cadiz) symbolising Napoleon, overcome by Hercules, i.e. Wellington. Caricaturists had a field day, dubbing it 'THE REGENT'S BOMB' (pronounced 'bum') and the 'TREMENDOUS THING' erected in the park; it was also seen to symbolise the Prince's alliance with the restored absolutist monarchs of Spain and France.

According to Benjamin Jutsham's daybook, the manufacturer T. Dudley was based in King Street, Soho. **CF**

George Cruikshank
London 1792–1878 London

304
Making Decent – !! – A Hint to the Society for the Suppression of Vice ...

Coloured etching, 30 × 23 cm
Published by G. Humphrey, 27 St. James's Street, 8 August 1822
London, Guildhall Library, Corporation of London
Literature: Cohn 1924, No. 1713; George 1952, Vol. 10, pp. 302–03, No. 14383

304

The 20-foot-high bronze statue of Achilles in Park Lane was designed by Richard Westmacott and placed on its site in 1822. It was cast from guns captured from the French, and erected 'by the women of England to Arthur Duke of Wellington and his brave companions in arms'. It was the first public nude statue in England. A scandalised and embarrassed William Wilberforce, the philanthropist (Cat. No. 607), holds a top hat over Achilles' fig leaf and penis. A dedication below the image reads: 'This Print commemorative of Anglo French Brass & true British Chastity, is inscribed with veneration to that Worthy Man Mr. Willbyforce who with saintlike regard for the Morals of his Country, has undertaken to make the above fig. Decent, from 10 in the M[ornin]g till Dusk.'

The statue stands close by Apsley House, the London home of the Duke of Wellington. Leigh Hunt described it as 'manifesting the most furious intentions of self-defence against the hero whose abode he is looking at'. **RH**

305 (illus. p. 402)
Candlesticks, c. 1820

Pellatt and Green
Lead glass incorporating sulphide 'Crystallo-Ceramie' portraits, with polished deep-cut decoration, H 22 cm (Duke of Wellington), H 22.5 cm (Princess Charlotte)
London, Private Collection
Provenance: Jokelson Collection
Exhibitions: London, Mallett, 1991
Literature: Pellatt 1819; Pellatt 1821; Jokelson 1968; Einer, forthcoming

In 1819 Apsley Pellatt, twenty-nine-year-old member of a prominent London nonconformist family of iron merchants, glass sellers and owners of the Falcon Glassworks in Southwark (across Blackfriars Bridge from the City), took out a patent for 'Encrusting into Glass Vessels and Utensils White or other Coloured, Painted, or otherwise Ornamented Figures, Arms, Crests, Cyphers, and any other Ornaments made of Composition, Metal or other suitable Material'. The basic criterion of suitability was that the composition of the image to be 'encrusted' would not melt at the working temperature of the hot glass (Pellatt 1819). The idea appears to have been tried with little success in Bohemia about 1780. Further experiments were made by a number of Frenchmen in France and abroad. Pellatt (1821) notes that the French only made small objects and emphasises that his methods allow for a number of different kinds of objects, from door plates to decanters, jewellery to all kinds of lighting glassware, to be made in British glass which exceeded the productions of any other nation in 'its freedom from specks or rings' and its 'colourless transparency'. The sample objects illustrated include an imperial George IV, allegorical figures, 'Egyptian Cariatydes', muses, deities, Julius Caesar, Shakespeare, Wellington, and Napoleon.

These two different examples of 'a candlestick for the table or mantelpieces' contain profile portraits of Princess Charlotte, daughter of the Prince Regent, facing right, and the Duke of Wellington, facing left. No exact medallic reference has been found for Princess Charlotte but Joanna Marschner has pointed out that the princess was noted for the roses with which her hair was dressed at her wedding in May 1816 and these are suggested by the coiffure in this portrait. Objects commemorating the popular Princess Charlotte, who had problems with both of her parents, continued to be produced for some years after her agonising death in childbirth in 1817.

The particularly elegant likeness of the Duke of Wellington is probably adapted from one of two medals struck in France in about 1815 (Einer, forthcoming). **WE**

306 (illus. p.404)
Finger Bowl, 1837

Davenport, glass made by James Powell and Sons, Whitefriars glassworks
Lead glass coloured by uranium, wheel-engraved decoration, 13.1×9.5 cm
London, The Museum of London
Inv. No. 86. 411
Exhibitions: London, The Museum of London 1987–89
Literature: unpublished mss. in Whitefriars Archive, The Museum of London and elsewhere

This piece is one of twelve 'topaz coloured finger glasses' made for Her Majesty's table at the banquet given to Queen Victoria on Lord Mayor's Day, 9 November 1837.

The Corporation of London was accustomed to invite the new sovereign to dine, usually on the first Lord Mayor's Day of their reign. William IV had never been able to fulfil the engagement as there were fears for his safety at the hands of the London mob (Cat. Nos. 638–41). Consequently, in 1837, there was serious discussion as to whether the custom should be allowed to lapse. However, the young queen's visit was an outstanding success and the event contributed to the change in the popular attitude to royalty.

The preparations made by the entertainments committee for the banquet 'exceeded any thing ever attempted in the City of London'. Orders for food and drink, table equipment and decorations were placed less than one month before the event. All the special and general china and glass tableware (over 11,000 pieces) appears to have been provided by the firm of Davenport, whose showrooms were in Fleet Street. Although most of it had to be completed and sent hurriedly from their Midland factory it is probable that the glasses for the queen's table were in part supplied to Davenport by their neighbours James Powell and Sons at the nearby Whitefriars glassworks. Of the fifteen different glass items in the queen's service only the finger glasses and the hock glasses were in 'topaz coloured glass'. 'Topaz' was the name given to the yellow glass coloured by uranium which had been recently developed and perfected at the Whitefriars glassworks.

The Powells (who acquired the glassworks in 1834) possibly heard of central European experiments with uranium in glassmaking from their supplier P. N. Johnson of Hatton Garden. They began their experiments in February 1835 and in March 1836 record that the glass was good enough to be used for candlesticks presented to Queen Adelaide by Lord Howe. The term 'topaz' was in use by December 1836. The topaz glass finger bowls (of which at least two have survived) are thus the earliest known precisely datable pieces of uranium glass made in England. **WE**

307
Chair, 1823

Probably designed by Benjamin Dean Wyatt; made by Morel and Hughes
Aburra wood with carved and gilt decoration, modern upholstery,
88×65×77 cm
London, Trustees of the Victoria and Albert Museum
Inv. No. W.48-1979
Provenance: Northumberland House, London; Christie's, London, 1 June 1978, Lot 522

This chair represents the richest and most elaborate furniture being manufactured in London for aristocratic patrons. It was supplied at a cost of £112.18s. as part of the furnishings of the ante-room to the Crimson Drawing Room of Northumberland House in March 1823. Northumberland House in Trafalgar Square was one of the grandest houses in London with splendid eighteenth-century interiors by Robert Adam, including the celebrated glass Crimson Drawing Room – now in the Victoria and Albert Museum.

The alterations to Northumberland House at this period were designed to complement the Adam interiors and were in the fashionable Louis XIV style. These alterations were designed by Benjamin Dean Wyatt, the leading proponent of this style, which he was to deploy to great effect at two other grand London houses: Apsley House and Stafford House. Morel and Hughes were amongst the most famous London cabinet-makers for many aristocratic clients including the Prince Regent. **CW**

Charles Robert Leslie
London 1794–1859 London

308 (illus. p. 413)
The Grosvenor Family, 1831

Oil on canvas, 101.6×144.7 cm
Eaton Hall, Chester, His Grace the Duke of Westminster
Provenance: painted in 1831 for Robert Grosvenor, 1st Marquess of Westminster; by descent
Exhibitions: London, Royal Academy, 1832, No. 121; Tate Gallery, 1955; Royal Academy, 1957, No. 378; Washington, 1985, Cat. No. 517
Literature: Taylor 1860, Vol. 2, p. 224

This family portrait was commissioned to mark the elevation of Robert Grosvenor, 2nd Earl Grosvenor (1767–1845) to the marquessate of Westminster in 1831. Three generations of the family are represented. The marquess sits left centre, with his eldest son, Richard, Earl of Belgrave and later 2nd Marquess, standing behind him, and his grandson (Lord Belgrave's son), Hugh Lupus, later 1st Duke of Westminster, resting against his knee. The marchioness is seated at the piano and Lady Belgrave sits to the left, her three youngest daughters playing with a parrot at her feet, while the two elder girls dance in the foreground. The group behind them to the right comprise the marquess's second son Thomas, 2nd Earl of Wilton (a title inherited from his maternal grandfather) with his wife playing the harp and their daughter clasping his knee. The third son, Lord Robert Grosvenor, later 1st Lord Ebury, stands on the left in his uniform as comptroller of the household; the newly wedded Lady Robert Grosvenor, a niece of the Duke of Wellington, stands in the centre dressed in white.

Edward the Confessor, 54.5×38.7×7.5 cm
Windsor Castle, Royal Library, H.M.
Queen Elizabeth II
Inv. No. RCIN 1005092
Literature: Adams 1983, pp. 282–86, No. 123

Westminster Abbey provided the principal source of inspiration in London for antiquaries and designers seeking to re-establish the Gothic as a national style. Here the splendid binding reflects the contents within. This standard work on Westminster Abbey was issued in parts on an irregular basis from 1816 to 1823 to subscribers, headed by the Prince Regent, later George IV, to whom it was dedicated. It is generally known as 'Neale's Westminster Abbey' on account of the superb quality of the engravings after drawings by John Preston Neale (1779–1847). **CF**

309

The setting is the opulent picture gallery at Grosvenor House redecorated in 1805 at a cost of £17,000 and later extended to take four large tapestry designs by Rubens which were acquired in 1818. Two can be seen behind the columns: *Abraham and Melchizedek* and *The Fathers of the Church* (Ringling Museum, Sarasota); the painting immediately to the right of Lord Wilton is Velasquez' *Don Balthasar Carlos*. The collection also contained celebrated works by Claude, Rubens' *Adoration of the Magi* (King's College, Cambridge) and Gainsborough's *Blue Boy* (Huntington Collection, San Marino). The gallery was intended for great evening receptions but was also open to the public in May and June. **CF**

This print, originally designed by Gillray in 1802 and subsequently copied for later issues, satirised not *Tales of Wonder*, a harmless anthology of that title edited by M. G. Lewis, with contributions by Scott and Southey, but an earlier work that had made him a literary notoriety, *The Monk* (1795), which narrowly escaped prosecution for indecency; later editions were bowdlerised by the author. This, and its many imitations, achieved a good deal of popularity. The taste for such macabre gothic tales was criticised as 'horribly pathetic'; some critics saw a German influence. 'One needs only to look at the books that lie open in the lesser bookseller's shops,' complained an observer in 1810, 'They are nearly all ogres, ghosts, robbers, murder stories, with an accompanying engraving of the altogether most horrible contents.' **LS**

Richard Parkes Bonington
Arnold 1802–1828 London

311
Three Studies of Armour

Watercolour over pencil, each 21×10 cm, 23.2×11.4 cm, and 21.4×9.6 cm
London, Trustees of the British Museum
Inv. No. 1939-10-14-7,8,9
Provenance: Bonington sale, Sotheby's 29–30 June 1829, lot 14, 15 or 16; bought Colnaghi and Triphook; E. V. Utterson; by descent to Lt. Col. A. T. Utterson, by whom presented to the British Museum, 1939
Exhibitions: Nottingham, 1965, Nos. 155, 156, 157
Literature: Shirley 1940, pp. 26–28; Noon 1991, pp. 128, 130, 133, 135

In the summer of 1825, fired by the acclaim given to a group of paintings by British artists exhibited at the Paris Salon of 1824, Delacroix, Bonington and a number of other young painters in their circle visited England. Their shared antiquarian interests, reflected in their passion for the poetry of Byron and the romantic historical novels of Scott, was also manifested in the studies they made of tombs in Westminster Abbey and of armour in the Meyrick collection: these were subsequently to be employed as source material for history paintings. Bonington and Delacroix visited Dr Samuel Rush Meyrick's London house on 8–9 July 1825, probably through an introduction from watercolourist Samuel Prout. Dr. Meyrick (1783-1848), a distinguished antiquary and an advocate in the Admiralty Court who was later to be knighted by King William IV

James Gillray
London 1756–1815 London

309
Tales of Wonder!, 1802

Etching, coloured impression, 25.2×34.6 cm, a later copy of that published in 1802
Etched by W. Brocas and published by J. Sidebotham
London, Trustees of the British Museum
Inv. No. 1851-9-1-1066
Literature: George 1947, Vol. 8, pp. 118–19, No. 9932 A

Edward Wedlake Brayley
1773–1854

310
The History and Antiquities of the Abbey Church of St. Peter Westminster, 1818–23

Volume II of the presentation copy, bound in red morocco sumptuously tooled in gold with Gothic designs and the arms of King

for his work on the royal collection of armour, had just published his three volume *A Critical Inquiry into Antient Armour, as it existed in Europe, but particularly in England from the Norman Conquest to the Reign of Charles II* (London, 1824), and was the owner of one of the finest private collections of armour in Europe, much of which is now in the Wallace Collection, London; a full catalogue of Meyrick's armour was published in 1830. **LS**

312
Pier Table

Designed by Sir John Soane, 1806
Ebonised mahogany with ivory enrichments, 142×92×45 cm
London, Private Collection
Provenance: Stowe, Buckinghamshire; Christie's, Stowe sale, 1848, Lot 2508

Soane rarely worked in the Gothic Revival style but, displaying his genius for manipulating historic architectural forms, here he designed one of the most sophisticated pieces in the style known to exist from the very early nineteenth century. Though Stowe is a celebrated eighteenth-century neo-classical country house its owner, the Marquess of Buckingham, acquired an important collection of medieval manuscripts and commissioned Soane to design an appropriately Gothic library to house them.

Soane derived the Gothic motifs from Henry VII's Chapel at Westminster Abbey. The furniture consisted of a pair of pier tables, an octagonal table and arm chair all *en suite*. The room also contained ancient ebony and ivory chairs thought actually to be medieval. Therefore a combination of ebonising and ivory was used for the modern furniture. The cabinet-maker is not known but these pieces were certainly made in London. **CW**

313
Armchair, *c.* 1806

Oak, upholstery modern 91×56×47 cm
Marks: stamped 'Windsor Castle'
London, Trustees of the Victoria and Albert Museum
Inv. No. W.151-1978
Provenance: Christie's, 30 November 1978, Lot 12

Though this chair was once part of the furnishings of Windsor Castle and other examples still survive there, they are likely to have been designed for Carlton House and

311

312

313

314

This is one of a set of chairs made by George Bullock as part of the furnishings he supplied for the Gothic Revival interiors he created within the medieval abbey at Battle in Sussex. This was the seat of Sir Godfrey-Vassal Webster and his crest 'A dragon head couped, regardant' appears on the brass shield on the back of the chair. Though Bullock designed much of the furniture made in his London workshop, this piece was probably designed by his employee Richard Bridgens who seems to have specialised in the Gothic and Elizabethan style and who was also at this time helping Bullock at Abbotsford (Cat. No. 452). Though the interiors at Battle were Gothic in style, this chair is a sophisticated reworking of a seventeenth-century chair form, though it was probably considered Elizabethan by Bridgens. **CW**

315
Table, 1815–18

Designed and made by George Bullock
Inlay of ebony and brass with ormolu mounts, the top of various ancient Roman marbles, 74 × 86 cm
London, Trustees of the Victoria and Albert Museum
Inv. No. W.34-1978
Provenance: Thornbridge Hall, Derbyshire; Park Hall, Derbyshire; Phillips, Hepper House sale of the contents Park Hall, 5 April 1978, Lot 117
Literature: Bullock 1988, pp. 111–12

The top is made of ancient Roman marbles imported from Italy rather than the Welsh Mona marble which Bullock usually favoured. In line with Bullock's innovation of using British plant forms in his ornamental designs, though the elaborate brass inlay depicts the ancient Roman Thyrsus, it is entwined with British hops rather than grapes as is normally the case. **CW**

predate the publication of an illustration of a commercial adaptation of them by George Smith in his *A Collection of Designs for Household Furniture* of 1808. From about 1806, a series of Gothic Revival interiors were designed for Carlton House: some were executed and others not (Cat. No. 273). Oak chairs were certainly supplied, possibly for the library. Several of England's most talented architects, designers and cabinet-makers were working at Carlton House at this time and it is thus impossible to determine who designed and made the chairs. The design is, however, very assured and the most likely candidate is perhaps James Wyatt, who worked there in 1804 and 1805 and was then England's most talented Gothic Revival architect. **CW**

314
Chair, 1816

Designed by Richard Bridgens; made by George Bullock, 1816
Oak, painted and parcel gilt with gilt-brass mounts, 101 × 47 × 54 cm
London, Trustees of the Victoria and Albert Museum
Inv. No. W.53-1980
Provenance: Battle Abbey, Sussex; Christie's, 23 October 1980, Lot 91
Literature: Repository, September 1817; Bullock 1988, p. 75

316
Armchair, 1816

Designed and made by George Bullock
Mahogany, partly ebonised, 88 × 64 × 56 cm
Edinburgh, Dalmeny House, Earl of Rosebery
Provenance: Napoleon I, New Longwood House, St. Helena
Literature: Bullock 1988, pp. 82–83; Levy 1991, pp. 307–11, Fig. 4

Several armchairs were made to this design in Bullock's workshops as part of the furnishings which he supplied for New Longwood, the house built by the British government to house Napoleon on St. Helena. The surviving designs for these interiors show that this pattern of chair was used in the library, dining room, drawing room and breakfast room. Though a few pieces of the Bullock furniture remained on St. Helena and today furnish Old Longwood House, the contents of New Longwood were largely dispersed at auction after Napoleon's death in 1821. This chair was acquired in the later nineteenth century by the Earl of Rosebery, the celebrated British prime minister, who was an expert on Napoleon and in whose family it still remains. **CW**

317
Dressing Table, 1816

Designed by George Bullock
Oak inlaid with ebony, 50 × 81 × 54 cm
London, John Hardy
Provenance: Napoleon I, New Longwood House, St. Helena; Christie's, 6 July 1989, Lot 117
Literature: Levy 1991, pp. 307–11, Fig. 5

As with the chair, it is not known which of the rooms this piece furnished. It may of course have been Napoleon's own, but there were a number of similarly furnished bedrooms at

315

316

New Longwood. Here we see Bullock's preference for the use of native British wood, though Napoleon would no doubt have preferred his furniture to have been made from his favourite mahogany rather than plain British oak. **CW**

317

318
Cup and Saucer, c. 1815

Wedgwood; bone china moulded with vine leaves, gold edge line, D of saucer 15.5 cm, H of cup 6 cm
Mark: WEDGWOOD printed in red enamels
Barlaston, Wedgwood Museum Trust
Inv. No. 5792 a. and b.
Exhibitions: London, Wedgwood House, 1984, No. N44

The moulded design is traditionally to the hand of William Hackwood. A service of this moulded form was supplied for the use of Napoleon when in exile on St. Helena. A transcript of a note dated 24 October 1815 (Mss. No. E141-28830) refers to 'The Prince Regent at once ordered every requisite for his

319

A Bullock drawing for an almost identical lantern is known and an actual lantern of this form was recently discovered, which was supplied by Bullock in 1816 for New Longwood, Napoleon's house on St. Helena. These lanterns are the most splendid Gothic Revival light fittings of this period known to survive. Such metalwork was manufactured for Bullock by his near London neighbours W. and S. Summers of 105 New Bond Street. It is very likely that they went on selling the objects which they had in stock and indeed produced more to the original designs following Bullock's death in 1818.

The lantern certainly formed part of the furnishings of the elaborate Gothic Revival interiors created by Schinkel in the later 1820s during the restoration of Burg Rheinstein. The castle belonged to Friedrich Ludwig of Prussia, whose cipher appears on the glass, as does the eagle of Prussia. It hung in the bedroom of the Princess, Friedrich's wife. No documentation has been discovered to show how the lantern found its way to Rheinstein, but surely it is no coincidence that Schinkel was in London in 1826 looking at British architecture. He certainly visited a number of Gothic Revival buildings and was looking at the applied arts, for some of his later designs were influenced by English prototypes and Bullock would have still been a well-known name. Did Schinkel buy the lantern in New Bond Street? The glass is German and must have been especially made when it arrived in Germany. **CW**

320

320
Stool, c. 1827

Designed by A. W. N. Pugin; made by Morel and Seddon
Oak, original upholstery, 45 × 43 × 43 cm
Windsor Castle, H.M. Queen Elizabeth II
Provenance: Windsor Castle
Literature: de Bellaigue and Kirkham 1972, p. 27

321

(Napoleon's) establishment at St. Helena'. A memorandum from Mr. Mowbray (clerk of the Wedgwood Showroom, York Street) dated Friday, 1 December 1815 (Mss. No. E31-23623) reads:

> Mr. Bullock was here yesterday and made some trifling alterations in the assortment for St. Helena and has also made a few additions among which he has taken the two Tea & Coffee sets china embossed Vineleaf @ 5Gs . . .

Bullock was the government agent for all the stores to be despatched to St. Helena. **GBR**

319
Lantern, 1816–26

Designed by George Bullock; probably made by W. and S. Summers of New Bond Street
Gilt bronze with cut red overlay glass, 99 × 40 cm
London, Jonathan Harris Works of Art

C. R. Leslie, *The Grosvenor Family,* 1831. Cat. No. 308

Pugin at this time was fifteen years old, but his genius as a Gothic Revival designer was so apparent that he was employed by George IV to design furniture for the state rooms at Windsor. His office was in London where he was soon to set up his own furniture-making firm. All the furniture for Windsor was, however, made by the London firm of Morel and Seddon. Though much of this Windsor furniture was made from fashionable modern woods with gilt details (Cat. No. 321), these stools were plainly made in the English oak used in the middle ages. Their solid simple character which captures the essence of medieval furniture without in any way copying it, looks forward to Pugin's radical furniture designs of the 1840s. The extensive Gothic Revival additions and alterations which George IV made at Windsor had a widespread influence upon European domestic architecture of the 1830s. Schinkel for instance was well aware of the precedent which Windsor set. **CW**

321
Chair, *c.* 1827

Designed by A. W. N. Pugin; made by Morel and Seddon
Rosewood parcel gilt with gilt-bronze enrichments, the upholstery modern,
97 × 59 × 67 cm
Windsor Castle, H.M. Queen Elizabeth II
Provenance: Windsor Castle
Literature: de Bellaigue and Kirkham 1972, p. 26

Though the stool (Cat. No. 320) was thoroughly medieval in character, this chair designed at the same time shows how even Pugin was unable to break away completely from the elaborate version of the Gothic Revival established around 1800. This grand late Georgian style is represented by the table (Cat. No. 312), and the piano (Cat. No. 278). Even before Pugin established himself, there were a few designers who preferred to follow medieval precedent and use oak in the manu-

facture of furniture, as the oak armchair designed for Carlton House demonstrates (Cat. No. 313). **CW**

322 *(illus. p. 417)*
Standing Cup ('The Coronation Cup'), 1827

Designed by A. W. N. Pugin
Silver gilt and jewelled; bowl decorated with Gothic arcade, the spaces between the arches and the lip of the cup chased with quatrefoils, each set with a precious stone and contained within wavy lines; within the arches diamond rosettes alternating with other groups of precious stones; the lower part of the bowl decorated with kneeling figures of angels holding shields enamelled

E. W. Cooke, *The Antiquary's Cell,* 1836. Cat. No. 323

with the arms of George IV and emblems of the United Kingdom and Hanover; base of the bowl modelled like a fan vault with a central pendant, supported by pierced brackets which are held within a band of cresting at the top of the twisted stem; the stem engraved with a diaper pattern, Gothic collar at top set with small stones, rising from a gem-set Gothic crown; circular base decorated with foliage standing on eight arcaded feet, H 28 cm

Marks: London hallmark for 1826; maker's mark of John Bridge

Windsor Castle, H.M. Queen Elizabeth II Inv. No. GV598

Exhibitions: London, Victoria and Albert Museum, 1954, Cat. No. 128

Literature: Jones 1911, p. 172, Plate 87, No. 2; Bury, Wedgwood and Snodin 1979, pp. 343–53, Figs. 14, 16

By the mid 1820s, George IV was less concerned with amassing quantities of plate and more with acquiring suitable embellishments for Windsor Castle, where in 1824 Wyatville had begun to remodel the interiors and the refurnishing commenced two years later, supplied by Morel and Seddon. Possibly this Gothic cup was commissioned to stand on the new Gothic sideboard in the Gothic dining room. Rundells' bill for £400 (RA 26324), dated 11 September 1827, describes it as 'a very elegant silver gilt Gothic Cup with Angels bearing Armorial shields – enriched with Diamonds and colored stones'. Only in 1872 does it appear in the inventory as 'A Gothic Coronation Cup'.

Though its purpose was purely ornamental, it clearly drew its inspiration from medieval church architecture and woodwork, hence its quasi-religious character. Silver followed

belatedly the Gothic Revival in architecture and furniture, partly because most English examples of medieval silverwork had been destroyed during the Reformation, so there were few models available for study. Flaxman's design of 1819 for the 'National Cup' was a pioneer in the field and by 1821–22 Rundells were supplying copies of chalices in the revived Gothic style of the seventeenth century for the chapel at the Royal Pavilion, Brighton.

Bury, Wedgwood and Snodin make a convincing case for attributing the design to Augustus Welby Pugin (1812–1860). Though only fifteen at this date, he is known already to have been working for both the Rundells and for Morel and Seddon, his largest piece being the sideboard in the dining room with which the cup has stylistic affinities. The design of the cup bears a strong resemblance to a group

HOUSEHOLD FURNITURE

G. Cruickshank, *A Scene at London Museum, Piccadilly*, 1816. Cat. No. 327

T. Rowlandson, *Mr. Bullock's Exhibition of Laplanders*, 1822. Cat. No. 328

HOUSEHOLD FURNITURE

415

J. L. Agasse, *The Nubian Giraffe*, 1827. Cat. No. 341

322

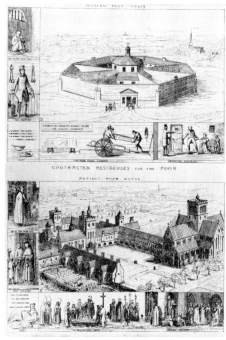

324

Edward William Cooke
London 1811–1880 Groombridge, Kent

323 *(illus. p. 414)*
The Antiquary's Cell, 1836

Oil on canvas, 58×76 cm
London, Trustees of the Victoria and Albert
Museum
Inv. No. FA 42
Provenance: Sheepshanks Collection
Literature: Wainwright 1989, pp. 39–40, Figs
29–31; Parkinson 1990, p. 42

This painting was commissioned from Cooke
by John Sheepshanks the collector of modern
paintings, who gave his collection to the South
Kensington Museum (now the Victoria and
Albert Museum). The subject is taken from
the well-known description of the 'Sanctum
Sanctorum' of Jonathan Oldbuck as described
in Walter Scott's novel *The Antiquary*. Cooke
had first-hand knowledge of collectors' interiors as he had trained as an artist in the
studios of A. C. Pugin along with the young
A. W. N. Pugin, and both the Pugins were
avid collectors. Cooke actually created the
'Romantic Interior' depicted in the painting in
his London studio and painted it by candle-
light. As he described in his diary, he bought
the ancient objects to furnish it from the shops
of antiquities brokers in London. **CW**

Augustus Welby Northmore Pugin
London 1812–1852 Ramsgate

324
Contrasts or a Parallel between the Noble Edifices of the Middle Ages and Corresponding Buildings shewing the Present Decay of Taste

Published by Charles Dolman, 61 New
Bond Street, 1841
28.5×23 cm
London, Private Collection
Provenance: William Burges

The first edition of *Contrasts* was published in
1836 at Pugin's own expense and bears the imprint 'London, Printed for the Author, and
Published by Him, at St. Marie's Grange,

Near Salisbury, Wilts'. St. Marie's was the remarkable Gothic Revival house that he had
designed and built for himself in 1834. *Contrasts* is one of the seminal books of the European Gothic Revival, both in the text and the
illustrations. Pugin attacked what he considered to be the feebleness and dishonesty of
late Georgian architecture when compared
with that of the middle ages. The illustrations
are arranged in pairs to contrast a modern
building with a medieval building of the same
type. His attack was not confined only to the
modern neo-classical buildings he hated so
much, but also to Gothic Revival buildings by
his contemporaries.

The book aroused a storm of protest not
only amongst architects, but also in the
Church of England because Pugin's Roman
Catholicism was – as in most of his later books
– prominently paraded in the text. This notoriety however meant that this second edition
was published. Interestingly the copy
belonged to the celebrated High Victorian
architect William Burges whose signature
appears on the title page. **CW**

of signed and dated but unexecuted designs
Pugin made for altar plate intended for St.
George's Chapel, Windsor. He was well
acquainted with medieval buildings and
woodwork, as is indicated by the high seriousness of the whole design. The virtuoso treatment of base of the cup as a fan vault with
pierced brackets to support it has no precedents and was possibly inspired by the vault of
Henry VII's Chapel at Westminster Abbey. It
is an astonishingly precocious piece of design.

As with the coronation cup the jewels (comprising in total, 106 diamonds, 32 rubies and 12
emeralds) might have been supplied from
Philip Rundell's extensive stock, but the price
for the cup which is less than half that for Flaxman's cup, could indicate that the pieces came
from the king's own surplus of old jewellery.
CF

Exploiting Britain's naval power, the 'Shows of London' brought a tangible taste of distant civilisations, both ancient and modern, before an enthusiastic public, eager to see the latest archaeological, anthropological, zoological and botanical attractions. But increasingly, the charismatic showmen who staged these displays gave way to a more professional, scientific approach, manifest in the foundation of learned societies and new museum buildings, intended for instruction rather than entertainment.

Lawrence Gahagen
Dublin *fl.* 1756–1820

325
Isis and Osiris, *c.* 1812

Portland stone, H 347 cm
Signed on rectangular base of Osiris:
L. Gahagen
London, Christopher Gibbs Ltd.
Provenance: removed from 170–71
Piccadilly, 1905; Sotheby's Sussex, 31 May
1989, Lot 802
Literature: Survey of London 1960, Vol. 29,
pp. 266–70; Altick 1978, pp. 235–37

325

William Bullock (*fl.* 1795–1836) first started in business as a jeweller-silversmith in Liverpool but, stimulated by the opportunities to acquire curiosities and natural history specimens off ships freshly arrived in that thriving port, he opened his own museum in 1795, adding material from other British collections when they closed (notably Dr. Richard Greene's in Lichfield in 1793 and Sir Ashton Lever's in London in 1806).

In 1809 he moved his collection to London, opening the Liverpool Museum at 22 Piccadilly, where it proved a popular success. A new home for the museum on the south side of Piccadilly, nearly opposite the end of Old Bond Street, opened in the spring of 1812. Though officially named the London Museum, its bizarre architecture ensured that it soon acquired the title of the Egyptian Hall by which it is remembered.

The Egyptian Hall was designed by Peter Frederick Robinson (1776–1858), a pupil of Henry Holland and master of many styles, who had worked under William Porden on Chinese interiors at the Brighton Pavilion in 1801–02. Here he turned his hand to the newly fashionable Egyptian style. Nominally inspired by the late Ptolemaic temple of Hat-hor at Dendera, the façade was designed like a great pylon; the entrance was framed by two stubby lotus columns and 'hieroglyphs' decorated the window frames. The central window above the entrance was flanked by these two stone statues of Isis and Osiris which supported the architrave head; this was broken and raised in the middle, where it was finished with a coved cornice surmounted by outward-facing sphinxes and a tablet bearing a large scarab. The sculptures bear a closer resemblance to conventional blackamoor figures than to Egyptian depictions of the deities (Cat. Nos. 371–74). Nor was there much regard for authenticity in J. B. Papworth's interiors where the Egyptian style entered the realms of

fantasy not matched until cinema architecture of the 1920s.

In 1819 Bullock converted his museum into a series of exhibition and sale rooms and auctioned off his collections; most of the ethnographical exhibits were acquired by the Berlin Museum and the arms and armour by Samuel Meyrick (Cat. No. 311). After continuing as an exhibitions and entertainments venue for the rest of the century, the Egyptian Hall was demolished in 1905. **CF**

325

326a

326b

George Scharf
Mainburg 1788–1860 London

326
Men and Boys with Advertising Boards, 1840

a) Watercolour over pencil, 13.6 × 22.1 cm
Signed bottom right: G. Scharf del.,
inscribed, 'N. 2', and also with various dates
London, Trustees of the British Museum

b) Watercolour over pencil, 13.4 × 21.9 cm
Signed bottom left: G. Scharf del., inscribed
'N. 9' and in pencil 'July 1840' and also with
various dates and notes

London, Trustees of the British Museum
Inv. Nos. 1862-6-14-1187, 1862-6-14-1188
respectively
Provenance: from a collection of the artist's
works purchased from his widow, 1862
Literature: Altick 1978, pp. 167–68, 275–79
and passim; Jackson 1987, p. 34

Based on hundreds of pencil sketches he had
made over a period of some twenty years since
first arriving in England, Scharf painted a
series of watercolours in 1840 showing the
eye-catching placard bearers who had become
a feature of the streets of London. The street
criers of the seventeenth and eighteenth centuries were succeeded by ever more ingenious
and exotic attempts to catch the attention of
the public, constituting in effect the birth of
modern advertising. One commentator writing in 1843 noted that these 'peripatetic pla-
cards' were a fairly recent innovation, and
compared them to Roman standard bearers.
These in their turn were to be ousted by what
Charles Dickens described as 'a piece of
human flesh between two slices of paste
board' – the sandwich man: the earliest
example of this form of advertising recorded

by Scharf was (according to his characteristically careful annotation) in 1828.

Most of the advertisements recorded here
were for popular entertainments (although a
boy sandwiched between turtle shells is promoting 'old port wine' and a Negro displays a
draper's placard). Among the best known
venues was the Egyptian Hall in Piccadilly.
(See Cat. Nos. 327–28, 331.) Another well-
known exhibition venue was the British Diorama at the Royal Bazaar, Oxford Street,
which opened in 1828 – Scharf records the inaugural attraction of four vast landscapes by
the leading scenic painters of the day (who
subsequently became famous landscape
artists), Clarkson Stanfield and David
Roberts, which were enhanced by dramatic
lighting and sound effects. **LS**

George Cruikshank
London 1792–1878 London

327 *(illus. p. 415)*
A Scene at the London Museum Piccadilly, – or – A Peep at the Spoils of Ambition, taken at the Battle of Waterloo

Coloured etching, 26 × 36 cm
Published by H. Humphrey, St. James's
Street, January 1816
London, Guildhall Library, Corporation of
London
Literature: Cohn 1924, No. 1951; George
1949, Vol. 9, p. 628, No. 12703; Altick 1978,
pp. 239–41

Crowds were drawn to the Egyptian Hall not
only to inspect Bullock's quadrupeds, fishes,
birds, fossils and other curiosities (a model of
the death of Voltaire, for instance, executed in
rice paste), but also to view its spectacular and
imaginative temporary shows. The first of
these was Napoleon's bullet-proof battlefield
carriage which, together with Napoleon's
actual coachman, Napoleon's folding bed and
the contents of the great man's travelling case,
went on show in January 1816.

A present from General Blücher to the
Prince Regent, Napoleon's carriage had been
acquired by Bullock from the prince for
£2,500. It attracted 10,000 people a day, far
more than any previous London exhibition.
By the time the exhibition closed on 24 August
the carriage had been inspected by 220,000 enthusiastic visitors. It then went on tour around
England, Scotland and Ireland, eventually
being viewed by 800,000 visitors. From his investment of £2,500 the proprietor achieved a
return of £35,000. **RH**

Thomas Rowlandson
London 1757–1827 London

328 *(illus. p. 415)*
Mr. Bullock's Exhibition of Laplanders, February 8th 1822

Coloured aquatint, 28 × 40 cm
London, Guildhall Library, Corporation of
London
Literature: George 1952, Vol. 10, p. 330, No.
14430; Altick 1978, pp, 273–274, reproduced

Like the exhibition of Napoleon's battlefield
carriage, William Bullock's exhibition of a
specimen family of Laplanders at the Egyptian
Hall appealed to the public imagination, was

329

topical (Ross and Parry's North Pole expeditions were then very much in the news) and was hugely successful. Bullock had encountered the diminutive herdsman, Jens, his wife Karlina, and their small boy whilst on a scientific excursion to Stavanger. With a vision of domesticating tens of thousands of reindeer in England on sub-standard agricultural land, he persuaded the family, accompanied by twelve reindeer, to return with him to London.

The plan for reindeer farms came to naught. Thomas Dibdin, it seems, was commissioned to write a two-act afterpiece for the Haymarket Theatre which would incorporate the family and their reindeer. According to Dibdin's account, eight of the beasts died before the first performance, and it was for this reason that the family became a living show at the Egyptian Hall.

To create the appropriate tone, a panoramic polar landscape was hung around the walls. Rowlandson's print shows seven reindeer (which casts doubt on Dibdin's story) and the male elk harnessed to a sledge which took small children on rides round the hall. Fashionable young ladies queue for the privilege of speaking with the Laplanders.

During the first six weeks of the show Bullock's takings amounted to £100 per day. 58,000 visitors viewed the family during the first season. **RH**

330

John Ross
Inch 1777–1856 London

329
A Voyage of Discovery

Published by John Murray, Albemarle Street, 1819
Quarto, 28×22 cm
London, Guildhall Library, Corporation of London
Inv. No. S919/8
Provenance: Worshipful Company of Clockmakers

John Ross entered the navy at the age of nine and served with distinction in the Napoleonic Wars. In 1818 he set off in command of H.M.S. *Isabella*, accompanied by H.M.S. *Alexander*, commanded by Lt. W. E. Parry, to explore Baffin's Bay and attempt a north-west passage. This work, published on his return and dedicated to Viscount Melville, 1st Lord of the Admiralty, was an illustrated account of the expedition. Some of the drawings – including scientific elevations of the coastline and depictions of the native inhabitants – and were made by A. M. Skene, H. P. Hoppner and J. Bushman, and engraved by Daniel Havell. The most exotic – almost surreal – landscape sketches were made by Ross himself.

331

One drawing was made by an Eskimo translator who accompanied the ships and is called variously, Sackheouse, Sacheuse or Sackheuse in the text. The illustration showed the *First Communication with the Natives of Prince Regents Bay* which Sackheouse presented to Ross. Ross describes (pp. 80–86) the encounter which took place on 9–10 August. At first the Eskimos feared the British, believing the ships had come from the sun or the moon. But once Sackheouse had managed to discover their dialect and could communicate, presents were given, including beads, clothing, knives and looking-glasses, which the Eskimos regarded with astonished delight. Equally the British learnt from the Eskimos how to survive the cold.

The ultimate purpose of the expedition – to discover the north-west passage – was thwarted, Ross maintained, by a range of mountains which he named the Croker Mountains (after John William Croker, 1st Secretary of the Admiralty), but by 1820 Parry's second expedition had confirmed that Ross was mistaken and his reputation suffered accordingly. In 1829–34, Ross undertook another Arctic expedition at the expense of Sir Felix Booth, the London gin distiller, enduring four winters in the ice, which resulted in extensive surveys and the discovery of the magnetic north pole by Ross's nephew, Lt. James Clark Ross. **CF**

William Bullock
fl. 1795–1840

330
Six Months' Residence and Travels in Mexico

Published by John Murray, Albemarle Street, 1824
Octavo, 22×14.5 cm
London, Guildhall Library, Corporation of London
Inv. No. Gresham 240
Provenance: Gresham College

Although somewhat diffident as an author, William Bullock published this work because there was no previous book of travels in Mexico by an Englishman and because of 'The rising interest attached to this portion of the world, and the growing importance of Mexico to the commercial enterprise of Britain.'

The book is mainly concerned with modern Mexico where Bullock had managed to travel widely (and be given a silver mine) despite the civil war taking place in the newly independent country, but there are two chapters on Ancient Mexico and Antiquities (pp. 296–

342). He describes how he persuaded the authorities to let him take casts from the great calendar and sacrificial stones in the Plaza Major, and the 10-foot basalt statue of the goddess of war, Teoyamiqui, buried under the gallery of the university. The local population was rather surprised by this activity and when the cast was being made of the sacrificial stone 'wished to be informed whether the English, whom they considered to be non-Christians, worshipped the same gods as the Mexicans did before their conversion'. (pp. 336–37)

Bullock made models of the two pyramids of San Juan de Teotihuacan and, most remarkably, brought back several of the manuscripts and hieroglyphic pictures sent to Montezuma to inform him of the transactions of the Spaniards, as well as the original map of the ancient city made by order of the Emperor for Cortez and intended to have been transmitted to the King of Spain. These were given on condition they would be returned when they had been copied in England. He also acquired a great number of ancient stones and antiquities (Cat. No. 332). **CF**

William Bullock
fl. 1795–1840

331
A Description of the Unique Exhibition called Ancient Mexico

Printed for the Proprietor, [1824]
21×14 cm
London, Guildhall Library, Corporation of London
Inv. No. Pam 1336
Provenance: transferred from the British Museum as duplicate, 1899
Literature: Altick 1978, pp. 246–48

This catalogue to the exhibition opened by William Bullock at his Egyptian Hall in April 1824 gives a history of Mexico and description of the exhibits. In the accompanying lithograph, drawn and printed by A. Aglio of 36 Newman Street, can be seen on the left the copy of a great serpent idol made from one in the cloisters of the Dominican Convent, opposite the Palace of the Inquisition, in the centre the cast of the calendar stone, 13 feet in diameter, and on the left the sacrificial stone, some 26 feet in circumference, in front of the goddess of war, Teoyamiqui. The lower gallery was devoted to modern Mexico, with samples of the flora and fauna, a young Mexican Indian in a hut, whom Bullock had brought back with him (see Cat. No. 333), and a panorama of Mexico City. **CF**

332

332
Kneeling figure of Chalchiuhtlicue

Basalt, H 28 cm
London, Department of Ethnography, Museum of Mankind, Trustees of the British Museum
Inv. No. 1825.12-10.6
Provenance: William Bullock; the Reverend Dr. Buckland, from whom purchased, 1825
Literature: Bullock 1824, illustrated opp. p. 27; Baquedano 1984, p. 32, No. 5

Among the antiquities that Bullock brought back from Mexico is this kneeling figure of Chalchiuhtlicue, illustrated but not specifically identified in his *Travels.* Chalchiuhtlicue was the Aztec goddess of fresh water, ruling over river and lakes, and hence the patron of fishermen. She is depicted in the pose typical of Indian women, squatting on her heels with her hands resting on her knees. She has a distinctive head-dress, consisting of three bands fringed with disks representing amaranth seeds (amaranth was an important part of the Mesoamerican diet) and with two large tassels on either side of her face; two plaits hang down below the knot at the back. Such elaborate hairstyles were worn by Aztec women on festive occasions and were indicative of status. She wears a shoulder-cape called the *quechquemitl* over a skirt. **CF**

Dorothy Wordsworth

Cockermouth, 1771–1855 Rydal

333
Letter to John Monkhouse, 16 April 1824

Manuscript, 19.5×11.4 cm
Grasmere, Wordsworth Trust
Inv. No. WLL/Wordsworth, William and
Dorothy/5/714
Literature: Hill 1978, pp. 258–63

Staying with John Monkhouse's brother
Thomas (cousins of Mary Wordsworth) at 57
Gloucester Place, Marylebone, Dorothy
Wordsworth sits down one cold, wet, windy
Good Friday to write of the sights she, her
brother William and his daughter Dora, then
aged nineteen, have seen – despite heavy colds
– in London. They have been to the Diorama
which had opened on 29 September 1823.
Dorothy went with Henry Crabb Robinson
(Cat. No. 431) to see the 'Swiss giantess', and
afterwards to breakfast with Samuel Rogers
(Cat. No. 433) and his sister at St. James's
Place.

Everyone went to Piccadilly to see the
Mexican Curiosities, 'the modern very amus-
ing and the live Mexican not the least interesting object – Mr R. talked Spanish with him.
The *Antient* Curiosities for which you pay
another shilling are but a collection of ugly
monstrous things.' Thence they went to the
Panorama of Pompeii where they were all
'much delighted – looked at Somerset House
and paid our Toll on Waterloo Bridge, for the
sake of the prospect – arrived at home not
tired.' The next day they walked through Regent's Park to Hampstead to see friends, and
then on to Hendon, to see more friends (a distance of some seven miles) 'none of us the
worse for the walk'. They were brought back
to London by carriage the following day and
proceeded to visit the British Museum with Sir
George and Lady Beaumont. **CF**

John Claude Nattes

c. 1765–1822 London

334
Two German dwarfs now exhibiting in the Publick room, Bond St – Janry 17th 1815

Pen and ink, 25.8×36.4 cm
London, The Museum of London
Inv. No. 62.186/5
Provenance: Frank T. Sabin

334

The exhibition of human freaks had long
attracted a credulous population to the fairs
and shows of London. But by the late
eighteenth century feelings of sympathy
towards the misfortunes of others and a sense

333

of decorum concerning the display of vulgar
appetites were becoming more prevalent. In
the 1770s and '80s, the midget Count Boruw-
laski enjoyed considerable social success in enlightened court and aristocratic circles across
Europe, gaining plaudits for his lively wit and
earning his keep, when necessary, through
private guitar concerts. Evidently, the two
German midgets depicted here – according to
Nattes's inscription 'John Hauptman 36
french inches high and the little Nannatte 33
french inches high' – sought to attract a similar
genteel audience, tempering the coarser appeal
of their size with musical accomplishments.

A founder member of Society of Painters in
Water-colours, Nattes was expelled in 1807
for exhibiting drawings executed by others
under his own name, so as to obtain larger
dividends from the year's profits. He reverted
to exhibiting at the Royal Academy and made
many informal sketches of the landscape, industrial and domestic life in the environs of
London. **CF**

335

Alfred Edward Chalon
Geneva 1780–1860 London

335
Carolina Crachami, the 'Sicilian Fairy'

Oil on canvas, 56×47 cm
London, The Royal College of Surgeons of
England, The Board of Trustees of the
Hunterian Collection
Inv. No. 252
Provenance: presented by Sir Everard
Home, 1827
Literature: Keith No.41; LeFanu 1960, p. 84,
No. 252; Altick 1978, pp. 257–60

When Carolina Crachami was first exhibited
as the 'Sicilian Fairy' in Bond Street in 1824,
she was nine years old, 19½ inches tall, her feet
three inches long and her waist 11¼ inches
around. The child was said to have been full-
term and was born to an Italian woman in or
near Palermo. Her Sicilian father, Fogell Crachami or Lewis Fogel, a musician had brought
his family to Ireland where he worked at the
Theatre Royal, Dublin. The child was entrusted by her parents to a Dr. Gilligan who,
having persuaded them that the English climate was better for her health, took her to
London, displaying her in Liverpool and Birmingham on the way. The parents only
learned of their child's death, due to a form of
respiratory infection in June 1824, from the
newspapers and Fogle immediately came to
London to take charge of her body. By this
time it had been offered for sale to Sir Everard
Home, then president of the Royal College of
Surgeons, who declined but subsequently
arranged for its purchase by the college. The
skeleton is still in the Hunterian Museum. **CF**

Carolina Crachami, *c.* 1824

336
Death mask, casts of arm and foot, with articles of clothing: shoes, stockings, thimble and ring

Box, 26×21.5 cm
London, Royal College of Surgeons of
England, The Board of Trustees of the
Hunterian Collection
Provenance: presented with the body, 1824

This preservation of these personal relics suggests the thin divide that then separated scientific curiosity and public interest. **CF**

James Spedding
Mirehouse near Keswick, 1808–1881 London

337
London Journal for December 1818–January 1819

Manuscript, 23.6×38.7 cm
Bassenthwaite, the Spedding family
Provenance: by descent

This diary describes the sights of London at
Christmas and the New Year through the eyes
of an eighteen-year-old visitor. James Spedding goes to various panoramas and theatres,
including the Drury Lane pantomime. He
visits the Exeter 'Change twice, once at night
to see the beasts fed. On 27 December he goes
to Hyde Park 'to see the Dandies and exquisites'. The following day he visits Bullock's
museum where he 'admired the Boa Constric-
tors squeezing the Tiger's and Deer's guts out.
And then we went to see the picture of Brutus
in which as Mama observed it was easy to
descern [sic] that he is half choking with a feeling of I know not what . . .' (The successful exhibition of the latter, *Brutus Condemning his
Son*, by Guillaume de Thière inspired Géricault to ask Bullock to exhibit *The Raft of the
Medusa* at the Egyptian Hall in 1820.)
Typically for his age, Spedding enjoyed the instruments of torture and the armour 'bulged
with bullets and stained with blood' at the
Tower, but had no comment to make on the
British Museum where he found 'a great many
rooms were shut up', and when taken to an
antiquarian society he could only comment 'I
do not know how I liked it'. Wisely, perhaps,
his aunt and uncle went without him to hear
Coleridge's lectures.
James Spedding is best known for his
edition of Francis Bacon's works, still a
standard text. **CF and RW**

337

Johannes Eckstein
fl. 1770–1802

338
The Camel at Exeter 'Change, 1798

Pen and watercolour, 35.6×44.5 cm
Signed, dated and inscribed: Eckstein.
Piddok. Exeter Change. Lond. 1798
Windsor, H.M. Queen Elizabeth II
Inv. No. 13312
Provenance: purchased by the Prince of
Wales from Colnaghi for 8 gns, 1800
Exhibitions: London, Royal Academy, 1799,
No. 610; The Museum of London, 1987
Literature: Oppé 1950, p. 45, No. 194, Plate
49; Marchand 1973, Vol. 3, pp. 206–07; Fox
1987, p. 29, Plate 8

Exeter 'Change was built in the 1670s on the
site of Exeter House, with a ground floor
arcade of shops and offices above. From the
1770s the upstairs rooms were let to a succession of showmen-dealers in wild animals: Gilbert Pidcock until his death in 1810, S. Polito
until around 1817 and finally Edward Cross.
With the help of street advertising, the 'troops
of wild Beasts' became a popular London
attraction. Moreover, artists – notably Stubbs,
Haydon, Agasse (Cat. No. 341) and Landseer
– came to draw the animals both from the life
and from dissected specimens.
Evidently during Gilbert Pidcock's ownership, some of the tamer animals kept at Exeter
'Change were allowed out in the streets. In the
Prelude, Book VII (Cat. No. 428), Wordsworth refers to a 'Dromedary, with an antic
pair/Of Monkies in his back'.
Both the drawing and its companion work,
Punch and Judy Show, were engraved by Eckstein with aquatint by C. F. Stadler. **CF**

339

Cross reluctantly decided to have him put down. But when both a civilian firing squad and soldiers from Somerset House also failed to have any impact, a cannon was sent for. At last, a keeper managed to pierce his vitals with a spear and, mortally wounded with 152 balls of ammunition inside him, he sank back on his haunches and expired.

Cross allowed the public to visit the enormous corpse for several days until the magistrates forced him to dispose of it. Eleven thousand pounds of meat were hauled off.

Chunee's demise was marked by poems and addresses, prints and even a successful play. Cross exhibited the bullet-ridden skeleton at the Exeter 'Change, round the country and back at the Egyptian Hall in 1829. It ended up in the Hunterian Museum of the Royal College of Surgeons (Cat. No. 343), but was destroyed by bombing in the Second World War. **CF**

Artist unknown

339
The Destruction of the Elephant at Exeter 'Change, 1 March 1826

Engraving, hand-coloured, 20×31 cm
Printed & Sold by W. Belch, 25, High
Street, Borough
London, The Museum of London
Inv. No. 60.43/16
Literature: Altick 1978, pp. 310–16

Chunee the elephant became the star attraction of the Exeter 'Change following an eventful stage debut (and farewell) in the Covent Garden pantomime, *Harlequin and Padmanaba*, of 1811. Always of uncertain temper during the mating season and having mortally wounded one keeper with a tusk – it was thought by accident – he finally departed this earth in sensational style. On 26 February 1826 he became violently enraged, threatened to bring down his specially strengthened cage and terrified the other animals with his trumpeting. All the usual palliatives having failed,

Thomas Hosmer Shepherd
France 1793–London 1864

340
Exeter 'Change, The Strand, 1829

Pencil and wash, 10×14.6 cm
Signed and dated lower right:
Tho. H. Shepherd
London, The Museum of London
Inv. No. 58.115/2
Provenance: Frank T. Sabin
Literature: Shepherd 1829, Plate 10, opp. p. 65; Altick 1978, pp. 38–39, 307–16, Fig. 105; Adams 1983, p. 392, No. 161/30

Shepherd made this view of the exterior knowing of its imminent demolition to widen the Strand (Cat. No. 80); it was engraved by T. Barber and published on 7 November 1829 as part of Shepherd's *London and its Environs in the Nineteenth Century*. By this time Cross had removed his animals to the King's Mews, nearby in Charing Cross. A permanent home was found for them in 1831 on a 13-acre site south of the river at Walworth, which became the Surrey Zoological Gardens. **CF**

Jacques-Laurent Agasse
Geneva 1767–1849 London

341 *(illus. p. 416)*
The Nubian Giraffe, 1827

Oil on canvas, 127×101 cm
Signed bottom right: J. L. A.

340

342a

342b

London, H.M. Queen Elizabeth II
Inv. No. Millar 651
Provenance: commissioned by King
George IV
Exhibitions: London, Tate Gallery, 1959,
Cat. No. 8; Queen's Gallery, 1966–67, Cat.
No. 26; Detroit 1968, Cat. No. 103; London,
Tate Gallery, 1989, Cat. No. 59
Literature: Millar 1969, pp. 3–4, No. 651,
Plate 284; Millar 1977, p. 137

Agasse was born in Geneva, where he started
his artistic training, but later moved to Paris to
study under Jacques Louis David. With the
onset of the French Revolution he returned to
Geneva in 1789, where he made the acquaintance of George Pitt, later Lord Rivers. Agasse
visited England with Rivers the following
year, but it was not until 1800 that he settled
permanently in London, where he led a successful career. Although he was an excellent
portrait and landscape painter, it was in the
field of animal painting that Agasse excelled
and for which he was principally known.

From 1803 he made frequent visits to work

at Polito's menagerie of wild and exotic
animals at Exeter 'Change in the Strand, one of
the most popular attractions of the city. Here
he was befriended by Polito's son-in-law
Edward Cross, who later supplied animals to
the king's menagerie at Windsor. It was probably Cross who obtained the royal commission for Agasse to paint the Nubian giraffe.

The giraffe was one of a pair raised from infancy on camels' milk, from Senaar in the
Nubian desert. In 1827 Mohammed Ali, Pasha
of Egypt, presented one each to George IV
and Charles X of France. The giraffes apparently made the 45-day journey to Cairo
strapped to the backs of camels. After travelling to Alexandria, the English giraffe was
shipped to Malta, and after a rest period, on to
London, arriving in August 1827. Agasse
shows the tame animal being fed cows' milk
by its Arab keepers at Windsor.

Unfortunately, weakened by the journey,
the giraffe became immobile, and despite the
construction of a special support, it died in
1829. It was eventually stuffed and presented
to the Zoological Society by William IV. **RU**

George Scharf
Mainburg 1788–1860 London

342
Zoological Gardens, Regent's Park, 1835

a) The Monkey House
Lithograph, hand-coloured, 20.3 × 30.8 cm

b) The Bear Pit
Lithograph, hand-coloured, 20.2 × 31.4 cm

c) The Aviary
Lithograph, hand-coloured, 20.3 × 30.8 cm

d) The Camel-House
Lithograph, hand-coloured, 20.2 × 31.3 cm

Printed by C. Hullmandel and published by
the Artist, 14 Francis St. Tottenham Court
Road, 1835
London, The Museum of London
Inv. No. Z3014-3017

342c

342d

343

Literature: Blunt 1976, pp. 23–41, colour plates facing pp. 48–49; Jackson 1987, pp. 106–07

The Zoological Society of London was founded on 29 April 1826, the East India Company administrator, scholar and zoologist, Sir Stamford Raffles, being principal promoter and first president. Based on the Jardin des Plantes in Paris, the society's aims were to introduce new varieties and breeds of animals which might be useful to the country's agriculture, and to promote the study of zoology with a museum of prepared specimens. Five acres of crown land at the north end of Regent's Park were offered by the Commissioners of Woods and Forests to form a zoological garden, which trebled in size in 1831 and gained a further 10 acres in 1834. Decimus Burton was appointed official architect in 1831.

The gardens were opened to non-members in 1828 and, as Scharf's views indicate, they became a fashionable place of resort, encouraged by the illustrious provenance of many of the animals. William IV presented the contents of the Tower menagerie to the society in 1831 and attendance that year reached a quarter of a million visitors. The Russian black bear visible in the pit was called Toby and was donated by the Marquess of Hertford. The camel house with its distinctive clocktower was built by Burton in 1831 to house two Peruvian llamas and only later adapted for camels.

But despite being an improvement on the Tower and on Exeter 'Change, conditions for the animals were still little understood. Their feeding by the public was permitted and indeed was one on the chief attractions. Behind the picturesque appearance of the monkey house, the sleeping quarters were ill ventilated and many animals died of tuberculosis.

The lithographs come from a set of six views made by Scharf with the society's permission and offered for sale in the gardens. **CF**

Richard Owen
Lancaster 1804–1892 Sheen

343
The Hunterian Museum, *c.* 1830

Pencil, 21.5 × 29 cm
Signed lower right: R O
London, The Royal College of Surgeons of England, The Board of Trustees of the Hunterian Collection
Inv. No. 316
Literature: Cope 1959, pp. 22–26, 42–56; Desmond 1989, pp. 240–54

John Hunter F.R.S. (1728–93), the founder of scientific surgery, was the most famous surgeon-anatomist in London in the second half of the eighteenth century. When Hunter died his museum of nearly 14,000 anatomical and morbid anatomy preparations and his folios of unpublished manuscripts were finally purchased by the government in 1799. The collection was entrusted to the Company of Surgeons on condition that it was catalogued, open to the public and an annual series of lectures instigated. The Company received its Royal Charter the following year, becoming the Royal College of Surgeons, and extended the house it had purchased in Lincoln's Inn Fields to store and display its new treasures. By the 1820s, some of the terms on which the collection had been transferred had not been properly fulfilled; moreover, Hunter's brother-in-law and co-executor, Sir Everard Home, had plagiarised, burnt and otherwise destroyed a large proportion of Hunter's manuscripts.

Nevertheless, the first museum was completed in 1813 but the collection expanded rapidly. The crowded display conditions of the collection may be gauged from this slight pencil drawing by Richard Owen who was appointed in 1827 to assist the conservator, William Clift, and to catalogue the collection. **CF**

Thomas Hosmer Shepherd
France 1793–1864 London

344
The Hunterian Museum

Watercolour, 18 × 16 cm
Signed and dated: T. H. Shephard
London, The Royal College of Surgeons of England, The Board of Trustees of the Hunterian Collection
Literature: Dobson 1959, pp. 274–305; Desmond 1989, pp. 240–54, Fig. 6.4

344

As a result of serious overcrowding, a new museum designed by Charles Barry was built in 1834–37. The new museum was opened in February 1837 in the presence of the Duke of Wellington, Sir Robert Peel and 500 guests. As portrayed by Shepherd, it was a handsome space, some 90 feet long with three-storey walls and a columned base, allowing the richest collection of comparative specimens and osteology in the capital to be seen properly for the first time. During the period of rebuilding Richard Owen completed his work on the production of a series of catalogues and, in 1836, was awarded the newly created Hunterian professorship in recognition of his work and growing reputation as one of the leading biologists in Britain. **CF**

Robert John Thornton
London *c.* 1768–1837 London

345
New Illustration of the Sexual System of Carolus Von Linnaeus . . . and The Temple of Flora, 1807

Imperial folio, 60 × 46.7 cm
Cambridge, Graham Watson Collection, Master and Fellows of Emmanuel College
Literature: Blunt 1950, pp. 203–08; Grigson and Buchanan 1956; Sitwell and Blunt 1956, pp. 26–28, 77

Having abandoned theology for medicine, Robert Thornton opened his own practice in London in 1797 and almost immediately embarked on one of the most ambitious pub-

346a

346b

lishing schemes of the day. He planned to produce the *New Illustration of the Sexual System of Linnaeus*. The work was advertised in 1797 and issued in parts at a guinea, then 25s. each, from 1799 to 1807. No trouble or expense was spared to produce a sumptuous work.

In order to stimulate subscriptions, the paintings from which the engravings were being made were exhibited at 49 New Bond Street in 1804, under the auspices of 'Dr. Thornton's Linnaean Gallery' in an indoor bower composed of foreign and native birds and butterflies. Unfortunately sales were slow, circumstances which Thornton attributed to the war. To save himself from ruin, he gained authorisation in 1811 to hold a 'Royal Botanic Lottery', under the patronage of the Prince Regent, the prizes being the paintings and prints. This was also a failure and the tickets were not drawn until 1813.

The Temple of Flora was the third section of the *New Illustration*, first published in 1807, republished separately in 1810 and in an octavo edition with re-engraved plates in 1812. It comprises some thirty magnificent colour engravings of flowers. Fourteen of the plates were based on paintings by Peter Henderson (*fl.* 1799–1829), eleven by Philip Reinagle, and

two by Abraham Pether (1756–1812); Thornton himself painted the Roses.

The plates were executed in a variety of media – stipple and line engraving, mezzotint and aquatint – in different combinations and were printed in basic colours with additional hand colouring. Most plates were altered or added to and for some there are as many as four different states. Therefore no two copies of *The Temple of Flora* are exactly alike.

Thornton claimed to set the specimens in their natural setting – tulips and hyacinths in Holland, mimosa in Jamaica – but he was frequently off course. The Sacred Egyptian Bean, *Nelumbo nucifera Gaertner* (also known as *Nelumbian speciosum*) was a native of southern Asia not Egypt. The subject was painted by Henderson and engraved in aquatint and stipple by Thomas Burke (1749–1815) and Frederick Christian Lewis (1779–1856).

The Temple of Flora was the product of romantic sensibility not botanical accuracy. Combining rustic, Gothic, exotic, primitive and even classical (passion flowers entwine fluted columns) elements in their settings, the plants themselves are portrayed with a vibrant intensity which suggests they possess a primeval force. **CF**

Philip Reinagle
Scotland 1749–1835 London

346
a) Cupid inspiring the Plants with Love

Oil on linen, 43.2 × 34.6 cm

b) Lilium superbum

Oil on canvas 45 × 34.7 cm

Cambridge, Syndics of the Fitzwilliam Museum
Inv. Nos. PD65.1974 and PD892.1973 respectively
Provenance: Robert John Thornton M.D.; sale of the Linnaean Gallery, Christie's, 2 July 1813, Lots 44 and 32; Levine and Mosley 1943; from whom bought by Henry Broughton, 2nd Lord Fairhaven; by whom bequeathed to the Museum, 1973–74
Exhibitions: a) London, Royal Academy, 1799, No. 111; b) Cambridge, 1974, p. 10, No. 3
Literature: Blunt 1950, Plate 35; Hulton and Smith 1979

Both paintings were executed for Thornton's *New Illustration of the Sexual System of Linnaeus* (1799–1807), the former being engraved by Thomas Burke with other matter preceding the twenty-eight plates of *The Temple of Flora* – as the third and most famous section was entitled on republication in 1810 – and for which the latter, engraved by Richard Earlom, was the first plate. *Strelitzia augusta*, depicted in *Cupid inspiring the Plants with Love*, was first introduced to Europe from South Africa by Francis Masson in 1791 and named after Charlotte of Mecklenburg-Strelitz, wife of George III. *Lilium superbum* was introduced from eastern North America in 1738.

Philip Reinagle, a pupil of the Royal Academy Schools and assistant to Allan Ramsay, exhibited at the Royal Academy from 1773, was elected a full Academician in 1812. He specialised first in portraits and then in landscape, botanical and sporting subjects. **CF**

347a

Robert Havell Junior
Reading 1793–1879 Tarrytown, Connecticut

after John James Audubon
San Domingo 1785–1851 New York

347
a) No. 83 Plate CCCCXI
Common American Swan. Cygnus Americanus, Sharpless. Nymphea flavae-Leitner
Coloured aquatint, 67.6×100 cm

b) No. 87 Plate CCCCXXXI
American Flamingo. Phoenicopterus ruber, Linn. Old Male.
Coloured aquatint, 101×68.6 cm

Cambridge, Syndics of the Fitzwilliam Museum
Literature: Chancellor 1978; Hyde 1984

Audubon's *Birds of America* presented the London print trade with its greatest challenge. When completed, it consisted of 435 double elephant-sized plates, every bird being represented in its natural habitat. The work would be issued in parts, each part consisting of five plates. A new part would appear every two months.

Audubon arrived in Britain in 1826 to seek a suitable engraver. The first part, published in February 1827, was printed by the Edinburgh firm of William Home Lizars. Lizars' colourists went on strike and so the artist resolved to have the work printed in London. The firm he selected was that of the aquatinters, Robert Havell and Son at 79 Newman Street, north of

347b

Oxford Street. From 23 June 1828, when the Havell partnership was dissolved, Audubon dealt exclusively with Robert Havell junior. The two men became friends, but this did not stop Audubon from being critical and exacting.

For a decade Robert Havell junior and his assistants (approximately fifty at one point) devoted themselves almost completely to Audubon's project. In 1831 Havell moved to 77 Oxford Street, opposite the Pantheon, and named his shop the Zoological Gallery. An interior view of the premises shows large bird paintings in heavy frames on the walls. (The sale of Audubon's oil paintings would, it was hoped, help to finance the undertaking.) A customer examines an Audubon plate. There are stuffed birds in glass-domed cases.

On 20 June 1838 Havell pulled an impression of the final plate of *Birds of America*. In all Audubon had spent £28,000 on the publication. 'I doubt if any other family with our pecuniary means will ever raise for themselves such a Monument. . .' he wrote proudly to his son.

The aquatint of the *Common American Swan* was based on a composition painted in London in 1838. *Nymphea flavae-Leitner* was named after the German botanist, Edward F. Leitner, who had just been killed in Florida by Seminole Indians. As a result the existence of this new plant could not be verified until 1867, when it was rediscovered and given its present name *Nymphea mexicana*.

Plate 431 represents one of the final plates in the *Birds of America* series. Though he had seen flocks of flamingos in the Florida Keys six years earlier, Audubon had difficulty in obtaining a specimen. He painted this one in London in 1838. **RH**

349

Peter Turnerelli
Dublin 1774–1839 London

348
Sir Joseph Banks, 1814

Marble, H 52 cm
London, Royal College of Surgeons of
England, Trustees of the Hunterian
Collection
Inv. No. 14
Provenance: commissioned by the College
Literature: Carter 1988

Born into the Lincolnshire gentry, Joseph
Banks (1743–1820) had a passion for natural
history from his Eton schooldays. His early
and lasting claim to fame rests on his role as
naturalist on Captain Cook's *Endeavour*
voyage to the South Pacific in 1768–71; largely
because of the botanical discoveries made, he
was elected President of the Royal Society in
1778 at the age of thirty-five, a post he held
until his death over forty years later.

In his role as the country's chief scientific
administrator, he was at the centre of scientific
progress in Britain, communicating with the
rest of Europe and the world. He was a munif-
icent patron of the Royal Botanic Gardens at
Kew and their living plant collections; he supported the founding of the Linnaean Society in
1788 and the Horticultural Society in 1804. He
was involved in matters celestial – the astronomy of William Herschel and lunar cartography of John Russell (Cat. No. 534) – and terrestrial with the expansion of the British
empire. His interest in the settlement of New
South Wales continued; he supported Mungo
Park and his exploration of Africa, helped to
establish the botany of India, and backed the

search for an Arctic north-west passage (Cat.
No. 329). Among his many academic and civic
honours and memberships of societies, he was
made a patron of the Royal College of Surgeons in 1805 and an honorary fellow in 1812,
the year before the bust was commissioned by
the College. But this time, Banks was chair-
bound from gout which crippled him, but still
keeping a lively interest in his learned empire.
CF

348

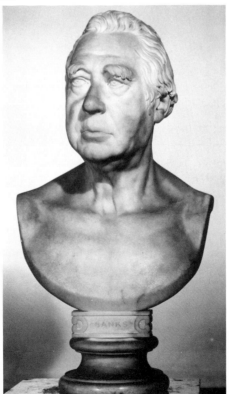

Francis Boott
Boston, USA 1792–1863 London

349
Sir Joseph Banks' Library and Study, c. 1828

Two watercolours, 19.8×25.4 cm and
19.8×26.1 cm
London, Natural History Museum
Literature: Boase 1886; Carter 1990

These two views of the interior of Sir Joseph
Banks' (1743–1820) home at 32 Soho Square,
London, were painted after Banks's death.
Banks lived in the house from 1777 for forty-
four years and it became the meeting point,
place of pilgrimage and focus of correspondence for men of science worldwide. Though
typical of many late Georgian London houses,
it was strategically placed near the Royal
Society and British Museum, and accessible
equally from Whitehall and the City. Moreover, there was a back building with a frontage
on Dean Street, designed by George Steuart
for the previous tenants and fitted out as a
library in the neo-classical style.

Here Banks installed his natural history
library on the first floor, as depicted by Boott
before the transfer of its contents to the British
Museum. His matchless herbarium was also
housed on the first floor and attic rooms immediately above. The small study was on the
ground floor of the main court, behind the
principal staircase, well placed to receive
visitors and connected to the library and herbarium by a passage to the back building. This
was the control room for the multifarious activities and enterprises in which Banks had a
hand. **AD and CF**

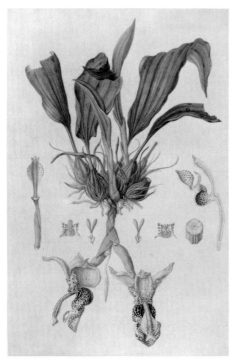

350

351

353

Franz Andreas Bauer
Feldsberg, Austria 1758–1840 Kew

350
Stanhopea insignis Frost

Watercolour on paper, 49×32.3 cm
London, Natural History Museum
Inv. No. 105
Provenance: The Royal Collection

The legacy left to botany by the Bauer brothers, much now held in London, is their illustrative excellence. Coming from a family linked with botanical painting since the mid eighteenth century, Franz and his brother had worked in Vienna with another famous artist and botanist, Nicolaus von Jacquin. Correspondence with Sir Joseph Banks and John Sibthorp, a professor of botany at Oxford University, eventually led to Franz Bauer's working for Banks and the king in England. During his work at Kew, he became a member of the Royal Society.

The orchid genus stanhopea was named in honour of Earl Stanhope (1781–1855), president of the London Medico-Botanical Society from 1829 to 1837. *Stanhopea insignis* was found in Brazil in 1826; it was introduced to the Royal Gardens at Kew prior to 1829, in which year it flowered for the first time. **MB**

351
Strelitzia augusta Thunb

Watercolour on paper, 52.6×35.8 cm

London, Natural History Museum
Inv. No. 140
Provenance: The Royal Collection

Franz Bauer, brother of Ferdinand Bauer, arrived in England in 1788 on a tour of Europe. He never finished his journey, for he was employed by Sir Joseph Banks as a botanical artist at the Royal Botanic Gardens, Kew, to illustrate plants growing there. Such was his expertise and scientific ability, he remained in that position of now immense historical significance, both to London and the rest of the world. Fifty years' work at the gardens followed, during which he painted hundreds of plants, but few were ever published. He became adept at microscopic illustration also, illustrating such plants as wheat and corn. Upon the death of Sir Joseph Banks, provision had been made in his will for Franz to continue his work at Kew until his own demise.

Strelitzia augusta, the Bird of Paradise flower, a native of South Africa, was named in honour of Charlotte of Mecklenburg-Strelitz, wife of King George III and is first recorded flowering in this country in 1791. **MB**

352 *(illus. p. 435)*
Protea

Watercolour on paper, 51×34.5 cm
London, Natural History Museum
Inv. No. 86
Provenance: The Royal Collection

The early nineteenth century saw many previously unknown plants being collected from around the world by adventurers and travellers. These were brought to Kew for cultivation within a scientific collection of plants. Experts in illustration, such as Bauer, recorded them to complement specimens in herbaria, against which determinations of plant families were made and scientific names formally allocated. Identification often depends upon fine detail and Bauer with his critical eye for colour and detail achieved near perfection in his paintings.

This is one of the most delicate examples of Franz Bauer's work. Protea is named after Proteus, the versatile sea god, an allusion of the diversity of the species. A genus of about ninety species of evergreen shrubs or (rarely) small trees, it was a native of South Africa and tropical Africa north to Abyssynia. **MB**

Ferdinand Lucas Bauer
Feldsberg 1760–1826 Vienna

353
Banksia speciosa, *c.* 1802

Watercolour on paper, 52.4×35.6 cm
Signed bottom right: Ferd. Bauer del.
London, Natural History Museum
Inv. No. 140
Provenance: Lords Commissioners of the Admiralty
Literature: Brown 1810, p. 396; Norst 1989, rear cover; Stearn 1976, Plate 18

This banksia is one of several hundred illustrations Bauer painted during the circumnavigation of Australia during the 1801–03 voyage of H.M.S. *Investigator*. Sir Joseph Banks had travelled to Australia on Captain Cook's first voyage. His personal wealth enabled him later to mount the expedition of the *Investigator* under the command of Captain Matthew Flinders, and to arrange for Ferdinand Bauer to be the official botanical artist. *Banksia speciosa* comes from a genus of forty-six species of Australian trees and shrubs, with often striking evergreen foliage; it was named in honour of Banks. **MB**

356

354 *(illus. p. 435)*
Koalas, Pharcolarctos cinereus, c. 1803

Watercolour on paper, 51×34.3 cm
London, Natural History Museum
Inv. No. 7
Provenance: Lords Commissioners of the Admiralty
Literature: Norst 1989

The koala was first discovered by the early colonists in New South Wales in 1798. However, it was not for five years that the first description was published (in 1803). Therefore when the *Investigator* returned to England in 1805 loaded with natural history drawings they caused great interest amongst the scientific fraternity. **AD**

355 *(illus. p. 345)*
Wombats. Vombatus ursinus, c. 1803

Watercolour on paper, 33.5×51 cm
London, Natural History Museum
Inv. No. 10
Provenance: Lords Commissioners of the Admiralty
Literature: Norst 1989, p. 33

The first report of wombats made by Europeans was surprisingly late – about 1797. Robert Brown (1773–1858) who was the naturalist on the *Investigator* and under whose guidance Bauer worked, collected a live male wombat which he brought back to England. **AD**

356
Platypus Ornithohynchus anatinus
c. 1803

Watercolour on paper, 33.2×50.8 cm
London, Natural History Museum
Inv. No. 14
Provenance: Lords Commissioners of the Admiralty
Literature: Norst 1989, p. 109

The platypus was first discovered in 1797 on the Hawkesbury River in New South Wales. It was an enigmatic animal with a rubber bill and webbed feet which proved difficult to classify as its fur coat placed it firmly in the mammalian class but it was also suspected of laying eggs, a characteristic of more ancient animals: final proof of its egg-laying was not obtained until 1884. It is one of only two kinds of egg-laying mammal and both are endemic of Australia. **AD**

357
Noisy Friarbird. Philemon
corniculatus c. 1803

Watercolour on paper, 50.7×33.7 cm
London, Natural History Museum
Inv. No. 27
Provenance: Lords Commissioners of the Admiralty
Literature: Norst 1989, p. 50

357

The discovery of colourful and unusual birds in Australia aroused considerable interest in London, even when they were brought back as skins and pickled specimens by the early colonists and explorers. **AD**

358 *(illus. p. 434)*
Volute Krater, c, 325 B.C.

Apulian, attributed to the Baltimore Painter, H 88.9 cm
London, Trustees of the British Museum
Inv. No. British Museum Catalogue of Vases F284
Literature: d'Hancarville 1766–76, Plates 52–6; Trendall and Cambitoglou 1978, No. 860.1

This was one of the star pieces of Sir William Hamilton's collection of vases bought by the British Museum in 1772. The main scene shows statues of a youth and a horse, set in a tomb monument (*naiskos*). Around the tomb are four figures, two women and two youths, holding offerings.

The vase was famous in Hamilton's day and retained its celebrity into the Regency period. It was reproduced by Josiah Wedgwood and was later featured in James Stephanoff's capriccio, *The Virtuoso* (Cat. No. 364).

The monumental shape and size of the volute krater made it, of all Greek vases, the most highly sought after among collectors. James Edwards, the bookseller (d. 1816), is said to have paid 100 guineas for the name-piece of the Capodimonte painter, a richly painted volute krater discovered near Tarentum in southern Italy in 1786, which is now in the Metropolitan Museum of Art, New York. **IJ**

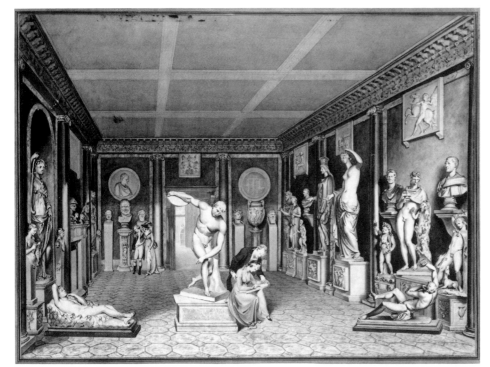

360a

360b

359
Vase, *c.* 1790–95

Etruria, Josiah Wedgwood's factory
Black basalt painted in encaustic colours
with offerings at a shrine to a hero, on one
side, and offerings at a stele (or
commemorative stone) on the other,
H 87.4 cm, W 54 cm
Marks: WEDGWOOD and Z, impressed
London, Trustees of the Victoria and Albert
Museum
Inv. No. 2419-1901
Provenance: Wedgwood's York Street
warehouse; purchased 1829 by Apsley
Pellatt, M.P.; presented by Pellatt to the
Museum of Practical Geology, Jermyn
Street, London, 1855; transferred from
Jermyn Street, 1901
Exhibitions: London, Victoria and Albert
Museum, 1972, Cat. No. 1844; Science
Museum, 1978, Cat. No. 132
Literature: Zeitlin 1968; Reilly 1989, pp.
101–02, Fig. C

This magnificent vase, which is the largest of
the encaustic-painted basalt vases made by
Wedgwood at Etruria, is a copy of a late
fourth-century B.C. Apulian (south Italian)
volute krater from the collection of Sir
William Hamilton, the British envoy at the
Court of Naples. The publication of d'Hancarville's *Antiquities Étrusques . . .*, a catalogue of Hamilton's collection, was begun in
Naples in 1766 and was a key event in the development of neo-classicism in Britain. The
first volume illustrated the Apulian krater as
Plate 52–6.
   Wedgwood thought sufficiently highly of
the publication to borrow proof plates from
Lord Cathcart; and he was subsequently presented with the published volumes by Sir Watkin Williams Wynn. Hamilton is known to
have lent Wedgwood vases for copying, and
his collection was readily accessible from 1772,
when it was purchased by parliament for the
British Museum. But that Wedgwood in this
instance based his copy on d'Hancarville's
illustration is suggested by the wave pattern
below the neck, the direction of which is reversed, as it is in engraving. It is reported that
in two years Josiah Wedgwood 'brought into
England, by sale of Wedgwood imitations of
the Hamilton vases, three times as much as the
£84,000 paid for the antiquities by parliament'.
   The vase was bought by glassmaker Apsley
Pellatt at the sale of Wedgwood's warehouse
in York Street, St. James's, in 1829, and was
presented to the Museum of Practical Geology. An almost identical vase is in the collection Mr. and Mrs. David Zeitlin, and a similar
but smaller version is in the Lenhart Collection, San Mateo, California. **HY**

432

359

tinued to amass Greek and Roman statuary, terracottas, gems and medals from agents and dealers operating abroad and through the London market. The public was allowed to visit and the collection became one of the sights of London.

Townley was a member of the Society of Dilettanti, vice-president of the Society of Antiquaries and a trustee of the British Museum to which he originally bequeathed his collection. He later bequeathed the marbles to his family on condition that a suitable gallery would be built to house them; when this condition could not be met the Townley marbles were purchased by act of parliament for £20,000 and deposited in the British Museum, where they were displayed in a new gallery, opened in 1808.

These watercolours may be compared with another, more famous record of the collection *in situ* at Park Street: in 1781–83 Zoffany painted the collector with his dog at his feet seated in the library, surrounded by his collection (including works that were never dis-

played in the library) and his friends – the self-styled Baron d'Hancarville (Pierre Franois Hugues), the palaeographer Thomas Astle and the Hon. Charles Greville, Emma Hart's protector before she became the mistress then wife of Sir William Hamilton (Towneley Hall Art Gallery and Museums, Burnley).

Unlike Zoffany, Chambers appears to have provided a generally faithful record of the entrance hall and dining room (the three statues in the foreground of the dining room were understandably moved from their place behind the artist's viewpoint). The presence of the Discobolus in the dining room dates the drawings to post 1793: it was found in the ruins of Hadrian's Villa in 1791, was purchased by Townley from the dealer Thomas Jenkins in 1792 and reached England the following year; Zoffany reworked his painting to include this celebrated addition to the collection. The costume of the figures in the Chambers drawings suggests a date closer to 1800.

Also in the dining room may be seen a num-

W. Chambers

360

a) The Dining-Room of Charles Townley's Residence, No. 7 Park Street, Westminster

b) The Entrance Hall of Charles Townley's Residence, No. 7 Park Street, Westminster

Watercolour, each 39.3×53.3 cm
Private Collection
Provenance: Lord O'Hagan; Sotheby's, 23 July 1985, Lot 559
Exhibitions: London, British Museum, 1985
Literature: Cook 1985, Figs. 1, 41, detail on cover; Walker 1986, pp. 320–21 (attributed to Maria Cosway)

Charles Townley (1737–1805) was one of the greatest English collectors of his day, spanning the eras of Horace Walpole and William Beckford. Born into a landed Lancashire family which adhered to the Catholic faith, he succeeded to the estate in 1742 and was educated at Douai, being received into Parisian society before settling down to improve his property. He went three times to Rome and travelled extensively in Italy between 1768 and 1777, collecting classical antiquities from the dispersal of old Roman collections and the new excavations taking place in and around Rome.

At his London house in Park Street (now Queen Anne's Gate), Westminster, he con-

'Clytie'; marble bust of a woman set in a calyx of leaves, A.D. 40–60. Cat. No. 361

Volute Krater, *c.* 325 B.C. Cat. No. 358

(left) F. L. Bauer, *Koalas, Pharcolarctos cinereus, c.* 1803, Cat. No. 354
(right) F. A. Bauer, *Protea.* Cat. No. 352

F. L. Bauer, *Wombats. Vombatus ursinus, c.*
1803. Cat. No. 355

D. Wilkie, *The Blind Fiddler*, 1806. Cat. No. 384

ber of other pieces from Hadrian's Villa, notably the second-century A.D. copy of an earlier Greek relief of a youth restraining a horse high on the right wall and the bust of Hadrian below it to the left. On the far right is the figure of Actaeon attacked by his own hounds acquired from Gavin Hamilton, who found it excavating the site of Monte Cagnolo near Lanuvium. The large marble vase decorated in relief with a Bacchic scene and known as the Townley Vase, displayed against the back wall, came from the same site. Two of the over-life-size female figures were excavated by Hamilton at Ostia: the statue of Thalia, half hidden in the niche on the left and the Townley Venus, with one (restored) arm raised on the right, which was much admired in England. Behind it stands the celebrated figure of a caryatid found near the Via Appia in the late sixteenth century, engraved by Piranesi, discussed by Winckelmann and acquired through Jenkins from the Villa Montalto. The

colossal head of Hercules to the left of the doorway was excavated by Hamilton at Hadrian's Villa but bought from Piranesi.

In the entrance hall, the large basalt *labrum* or bathtub was acquired from the Duke of Bracciano, heir to the Duke of Odescalchi, to whom it had been bequeathed by Queen Christina of Sweden. The cylindrical wellhead, carved in relief with Hercules and satyrs assaulting women and a youth, serving as a base for the sphinx, was acquired through Jenkins from the Palazzo Colombrano in Naples.
CF and IJ

361
'Clytie' *(illus. p. 433)*

Marble bust of a woman set in a calyx of leaves

Roman, A.D. 40–60, H 57 cm
London, Trustees of the British Museum
Inv. No. British Museum Catalogue of
Sculpture, 1874
Exhibitions: London, British Museum, 1990,
Cat. No. 3
Literature: Cook 1985, p. 15; Jucker 1961,
pp. 64–67; Ost 1984, passim; Walker,
forthcoming

Clytie, as she has long been known, was bought by Charles Townley as an *Agrippina* in 1772 from the Neapolitan Palazzo Laurenzano. She became one of the collector's most prized possessions among the marbles displayed in his house at Park Street.

In his biographical memoir of Charles Townley, James Dallaway recounts how, during the Gordon Riots of 1780, when Townley's house was threatened, along with those of other Catholics, he was forced to flee in haste. Having secured his cabinet of gems, he paused to take one last fleeting look at his marbles, but then seized the bust of Clytie and disappeared with her into a waiting carriage. The last part of the story is improbable, in view of the weight of the marble, but it serves to emphasise the special affection Townley felt for Clytie. She appears at the centre of Johan Zoffany's famous conversation piece portraying Townley with his circle of friends.

Townley came to call her by several names including Clytie, Libera or female Bacchus, and finally Isis set upon a lotus flower. Today the sculpture is still popularly known as Clytie, after the nymph who pined away in unrequited love for the sun god Helios, and was turned into a flower.

Some modern scholars have mistakenly doubted Clytie's authenticity as an ancient sculpture and would see her as a production of the early eighteenth century. A recent reappraisal of the problem, however, has argued persuasively in favour of her antiquity (Walker, forthcoming). **IJ**

362

Archibald Archer
c. 1790–1848 London

362
The Temporary Elgin Room at the British Museum, 1819

Oil on canvas, 76.2×102.7 cm
Signed bottom left: Archer 1819 ?
London, Trustees of the British Museum
Provenance: Edward Hawkins; Dr. J. E. Gray, by whom presented to the British Museum, 1872
Exhibitions: London, British Institution, 1819, No. 53; Royal Academy, 1972, No. 10; Iveagh Bequest, Kenwood, 1991, Cat. No. 41
Literature: St. Clair 1967, Fig. 9; Cook 1985, pp. 66–67

This painting shows the temporary, shed-like gallery constructed at the British Museum to house the Phigalian Sculptures that had arrived in 1815, which was extended a year later when the Elgin Marbles were purchased by the government (Cat. Nos. 363–64); they were exhibited here until 1831. The marbles had been offered to the nation by Lord Elgin in 1811 for £62,440 – the sum he calculated he had spent on their removal from the Parthenon and transport to London – but after a lengthy parliamentary investigation they were eventually acquired in 1816 for £35,000.

Several of the most celebrated pedimental sculpture and metopes from the collection are displayed here, including the *Dionysus of Thrasyllus* in the apse, and, on low pedestals with revolving tops, the *Illisus* (left) and *Theseus*, with the *Head of the Horse of Selene* on the floor. Archer shows himself in the foreground, assiduously sketching the marbles, in the company of a group of distinguished visitors and museum officials. These include the president of the Royal Academy, Benjamin West (Cat. No. 416), who is seated on the left, while to his right is Joseph Planta, principal librarian. At the extreme left, separated from these establishment figures (as in real life he felt himself to be) is the artist Benjamin Robert Haydon, the single most passionate admirer of the Parthenon Marbles. **LS**

363

Benjamin Robert Haydon
Plymouth 1786–1846 London

363
Horse of Selene, from the Elgin Marbles, 1809

Black and white chalks on grey paper, 55.5×75.8 cm
Dated bottom right: 1809
London, Trustees of the British Museum
Inv. No. 1881-7-9-346
Provenance: from an album of drawings by Haydon purchased from his son, Frederick Wordsworth Haydon, 1881
Literature: Taylor 1926, p. 67; Cummings 1964, pp. 323–28

The great fifth-century B.C. sculptured friezes from the Parthenon were brought to England between 1801 and 1811 under the auspices of Lord Elgin, ambassador at Constantinople from 1799 until 1803; Greece was under the rule of the Turks, and it was they who granted Elgin – who had a serious though amateur interest in classical archaeology and was concerned at the aimless destruction of many of the finest statues – permission to remove the reliefs. The arrival of the sculptures in England created considerable excitement in artistic circles from the time when they were first exhibited at Lord Elgin's London house

among their admirers, but their most passionate advocate was Benjamin Robert Haydon.

He began to study the Elgin Marbles in earnest in May 1808, attempting as far as possible to match their scale in his vast drawings, and became almost obsessive in his determination to analyse them, bribing Lord Elgin's porter to let him remain up to fifteen hours at a time in the cold, damp shed in which they were housed. 'I felt as if a divine truth had blazed inwardly upon my mind and I knew that [the marbles] would at last rouse the art of Europe from its slumber.' For Haydon, the Parthenon sculptures combined 'the most heroic style of art . . . with all the essential detail of actual life' and represented a central moment in the development of Greek art, sharing the same degree of inspiration as the writings of Homer.

The climax of this obsession came in 1816 when he published a pamphlet *On the Judgement of Connoisseurs being Preferred to that of Professional Men – The Elgin Marbles etc.*, an attack on the influential connoisseur (and trustee of the British Museum) Richard Payne Knight, whose taste had been formed on the ideals of Winckelmann, Mengs and Gavin Hamilton and who found difficulty in coming to terms with the dynamic aesthetic of the Parthenon sculptures.

In this drawing Haydon concentrates on one of the best preserved fragments in the collection, formerly at the extreme right of the east pediment of the Parthenon, the head of one of the horses that drew the chariot of Selene, the goddess of the moon. Haydon's notes and journals describe his fascination with the extraordinary life-like quality of the sculpture, the carefully observed differentiation between bony and fleshy areas, and he concluded that the Greeks had made anatomical dissections, yet elevated their scientific accuracy with a profound understanding of the animal's heroic nature. **LS**

in June 1807; in 1811 they were moved to Burlington House, Piccadilly, and in 1816 were purchased by the government and installed at the British Museum.

The Parthenon Marbles were the most important group of Greek sculptures to have been brought to Western Europe, and, at a period when neo-classical enthusiasm was at its height, aroused enormous interest and controversy, particularly among artists and connoisseurs. Canova, Sir Thomas Lawrence, Benjamin West, Fuseli and Flaxman were

James Stephanoff
London 1787?–1874 Clifton

364
a) An Apartment containing the Phigalian Marbles, and a Selection of the Elgin Marbles at the British Museum, 1818

Watercolour over pencil, 20.5×25 cm
Signed bottom left: J. Stephanoff 1818 ?
London, Trustees of the British Museum
Inv. No. 1935-3-9-3
Provenance: purchased from A. Zolotnitzky, 1935
Exhibitions: London, Society of Painters in Water-Colours, 1818, No. 354
Literature: Jenkins 1985, pp. 175–76, Fig. 3

b) The Virtuoso, 1833

Watercolour over pencil, 51×71.5 cm
Signed bottom left: I STEPHANOFF 1833
London, Trustees of the British Museum
Inv. No. 1934-1-13-1
Provenance: presented by G. A. Simonson
through the National Art-Collections Fund,
1934
Exhibitions: Society of Painters in Water-
Colours, 1833, No. 244
Literature: Jenkins 1985, pp. 1766–78, Fig. 6

Between 1817 and 1845 James Stephanoff exhibited a sequence of six watercolours at the
Society of Painters in Water-Colours which
were directly inspired by the British
Museum's collections of Greek and Roman
antiquities. None of them depicted actual galleries in the museum, but are ideal settings in
which the antiquities are displayed. Inspired
possibly by the example of Zoffany, Stephanoff made something of a speciality of depicting gallery interiors, and brought to this series
both his antiquarian and his painterly interest,
so that they are anything but dry records.

In the first of these two watercolours, exhibited in 1818, Stephanoff shows antiquities
from two collections very recently acquired
by the museum, the Phigalian Sculptures
which had arrived in October 1825, having
been recovered from the ruins of the Temple
of Apollo at Bassai by Charles Cockerell, and
the Parthenon Marbles, which had been purchased from Lord Elgin by the Government in
1816. Both collections were exhibited in a temporary gallery very different in reality from
the noble apartments shown by Stephanoff,
with their coved and gilded ceilings. As well as
idealising their setting, he also rearranged the
placing of the sculptures in this watercolour,
combining in the foreground gallery the Phigalian friezes, which are shown inset in two
bands around the walls, with a number of Par-
theon metopes which were in fact displayed in
the Elgin Room beyond the doorway.

The second watercolour shown here, *The
Virtuoso,* was exhibited fifteen years later, in
1833. In 1832 the Parthenon Marbles were re-
displayed in a new gallery, the Elgin Saloon,
an event which perhaps stimulated this watercolour. However, Stephanoff again fantasised
the setting, creating an elaborate architectural
ensemble with a floor inspired by mosaics in
the museum's collection and a grandiose ceiling decoration entirely different from the
simple neo-classical design of the new gallery,
while showing the marbles in an imaginary
grouping. A solitary figure, the 'Virtuoso' is
seated at a table on and beside which are placed
a carefully selected group of objects, intended
to suggest the arts of architecture, poetry and
paintings: a bust of Perikles, who masterminded the construction of the Parthenon, a
bronze head of a poet, then thought to represent Homer, and a number of vases, including

three of the finest from the Hamilton collection (Cat. No. 358), which may be supposed
to represent the art of painting in antiquity.

Stephanoff's museum series, sustained over
a period of twenty-seven years, is a remarkable testimony to the profound influence
exercised on the artist's imagination by the
great collections of classical sculpture assembled at the British Museum in the early years
of the nineteenth century. **LS**

William Gell
Hopton 1777–1836 Naples

365
Copies of Specimens of Papyri . . .

Manuscript volume, bound in red morocco,
gold tooled with lozenge shapes, spine
tooled *Herculaneum MSS,* light-blue
watered silk *doublures* tooled in gold; pen
and ink and watercolour illustrations,
45.3×29×2.5 cm.
Windsor Castle, Royal Library, H.M.
Queen Elizabeth II
Inv. No. RCIN 1005094
Literature: Davy 1821, pp. 191–208; Davy
1839–40, Vol. 6, pp. 160–76; Gigante 1979, p.
342; McIlwaine 1986, Vol. 1, pp. 321–29;
McIlwaine 1988, pp. 64–81, 753–99;
Auricchio 1989; McIlwaine 1989

The collection of Herculaneum papyri is
unique in being the only one to have been
found in Europe. It consists principally of
writings on Epicurean philosophy, the majority being in Greek. The papyri were discovered in a villa just outside the buried city in
1752–54. The rolls were carbonised, not
through heat but by chemical decomposition,
as Davy demonstrated in the chemical analysis
he carried out in England in 1818. They were
fragile and fell apart at the slightest touch and
the problems of unrolling them were colossal.

As a result of an appeal from the King of
Naples to the Vatican, Father Antonio Piaggio
was sent to Naples in 1753, where he remained
until his death in 1796. It took Piaggio about
ten years to perfect the machine that was to remain the principal means of unrolling the
papyri over the succeeding two centuries. This
consisted of attaching small pieces of gold-
beater's skin to the exterior of the roll using a
solution of isinglass. When the solution was
dried, the skin and the layer of papyrus that
was stuck to it were raised by means of thread
moved by wooden screws.

The considerable interest and speculation
about the contents of the papyri increased
after the publication of the first volume of
Herculanensium voluminum quae supersunt
in 1793. This was not sold but given to notable

European figures and institutions as a diplomatic gift. The challenge to find some means
of speeding up the process of unrolling and
publication captured the imagination of the
Prince of Wales and in 1800 he made a proposal to the Neapolitan government to pay for
the entire enterprise, sending the Rev. John
Hayter to Naples to oversee the work and
later hiring a Dr. Sickler to experiment on the
gift of rolls made to the prince.

Sickler's attempts were disastrous and were
the subject of a House of Commons enquiry.
Davy was a member of this committee of enquiry. He experimented on some fragments in
London and in 1819 he was sent to Naples by
the prince to conduct experiments on the rolls,
with a view to unrolling them by chemical
means. He was accompanied by the Reverend
Peter Elmsley, a notable Greek scholar and
later Camden Professor of Ancient History in
the University of Oxford. The artistic skill of
Sir William Gell, the classical archaeologist
and traveller, was employed to draw the
manuscripts as they were unravelled.

While at Naples in January and February
1820 Davy states that he succeeded (with
assistance) in partially unrolling twenty-three
manuscripts and in examining about 120
others, but he found the work unpleasant and
the local atmosphere suspicious and unhelp-
ful. On 29 February 1820 he paid and dismissed Elmsley, requested that Gell should be
paid for his drawings, and returned to
London. The whole enterprise cost between
£450 and £500.

This volume is referred to by Elmsley in his
papers, now in the Bodleian Library (Mss.
Clarendon Press d. 44), as the *King's Book,*
and was given to George IV (as the prince became in 1820) as a record of the work financed
by him in Naples. **IM**

Charles Roach Smith
Shanklin, Isle of Wight, 1806–1890 Strood

366
Illustrations of Roman London

Printed book with mss. notes and ills. in the
author's hand, 29.8×23 cm
Printed for the subscribers, 1859
London, The Museum of London
Inv. No. 77.109
Provenance: Charles Roach Smith's own
copy; Smith's Library sale 1890, Lot 270,
purchased by Bernard Quaritch; Images
Bookshop, from whom purchased, 1977
Literature: Rhodes, unpublished manuscript

367

By the late 1820s the City's extensive programme of road widening undertaken by the corporation's London Bridge Committee and a partly related programme of sewer construction by the Commissioners of Sewers, the rebuilding of London Bridge between 1824 and 1831 and construction of Smirke's General Post Office in 1826 had uncovered rich deposits of Roman antiquities which were brought to the attention of a new generation of London antiquarians.

Foremost among them was Charles Roach Smith, a native of the Isle of Wight who established his own business as a druggist at 48 Lothbury, behind the Bank of England, around 1832, moving in 1840 to larger premises at 5 Lothbury, where he was able to display his museum to much greater effect. Although it remained a private museum it was described as 'one of the sights of London'.

From these central locations Roach could visit sites and make purchases of coins and minor antiquities directly from the workmen. At the time, the British Museum only rarely bought London antiquities and the City had no local museum. Smith was unusual in that he attempted to understand the nature and layout of the whole Roman city. In recognition of his work he was elected to the Society of Anti-

quaries in 1836 and placed on its council four years later, an unusual honour when there was still a strong bias against men in trade.

This work was produced in retirement some twenty years after his most intense period of collecting activity and is an attempt to evoke the greatness of Roman London by reference to loose artefacts: stone sculpture, mosaics, wall paintings, bronzes, pottery, glass, coins &c. Relations between Smith and the corporation deteriorated after he received inadequate compensation for the compulsory purchase of his business for a road-widening scheme in 1840. He proceeded to lambaste the corporation on every possible occasion for what he saw as its complicity in archaeological destruction. The preface to this work is no exception. **MR**

367
Figure of Harpocrates

Silver with wrought gold chain and ring,
H 6.8 cm
London, Trustees of the British Museum
Inv. No. 1825.11-12.1
Provenance: gift of Messrs. Rundell, Bridge and Rundell
Literature: Smith 1859, p. 73, Plate 12; Brailsford 1964, p. 54, No. 6, Plate 15

This small figure of Harpocrates (the Graeco-Roman name for the Egyptian god Horus, son of Isis) found in 1825 while dredging for the foundations of new London Bridge was an unusual acquisition for the British Museum. The workmen who generally made such finds demanded cash on the spot, placing the museum, which required trustees' approval for every purchase, at a considerable disadvantage. However, on this occasion it appears that the find was taken to the royal goldsmiths, Rundell, Bridge and Rundell, situated conveniently nearby on Ludgate Hill. They in turn gave it to the museum via a solicitor, George Booth Tyndale of Lincoln's Inn Fields, writing on the same day (5 November 1825) directly to the trustees for permission to make a cast of the Cellini cup from the Payne Knight collection: permission was granted (British Museum Archives, Original Letters and Papers, 1825). **CF**

368
Bronze hand

32.5 cm
London, Trustees of the British Museum
Inv. No. 1856.7-1.18
Provenance: Charles Roach Smith
Literature: Smith 1859, pp. 65–66, illustrated; Brailsford 1964, p. 54

368

This bronze hand, found in Lower Thames Street, may be related to the bronze head of Hadrian, dredged up from the bed of the Thames, which passed immediately into the possession of John Newman of the Bridge House, and subsequently into the British Museum (1848.11-3.1). It evidently belonged to a colossal statue which once embellished Londinium, possibly erected in the forum or on the Roman bridge. **CF**

369
a) Fragment of a bronze figure of Apollo
H 11.3 cm

b) Bronze figure of Mercury
H 12 cm

c) Bronze figure of a hermaphrodite
H 13 cm

London, Trustees of the British Museum
Inv. Nos. 1856.7-1.14, 1856.7-1.15, 1848.8-3.44 respectively

369a

369b

369c

Provenance: a) and b), Charles Roach Smith from whom purchased, 1856; c), John Newman; Sotheby's, 19 July 1848
Literature: Smith 1840, pp. 36–46; Smith 1859, Plates 15, 16 and 17 respectively; Brailsford 1964, p. 54, No. 17, Plate 17; Rhodes 1991, pp. 183–84; Rhodes, unpublished manuscript

These bronze statuettes come from a group of five found in 1837 in the bed of the Thames, where dredging continued to make the river more navigable, and considered one of the finest groups of Roman bronzes from Britain.

The provenance of the figures is indicative of the problems attendant on the competition for Roman London antiquities in this period. William Edwards and his brother John made quick profits as middlemen, buying from the workmen and selling to collectors and dealers. Smith helped to identify some acquisitions, and in return they allowed him to record some of their finds and site observations. By 1836 the Edwardses had also agreed to act as agents for John Newman who, as comptroller of the Bridge House Estates, was in a position to build up a considerable collection.

Competition came to a head in 1837 when Smith bid against John Edwards for these

Roman bronzes. Edwards claimed to want them for Newman, but Smith bid well over the normal price. In the event, Newman obtained the figure of a hermaphrodite, and Smith obtained the rest. Despite their rivalry, Newman to his credit allowed Smith to publish them in the Society of Antiquaries' journal *Archaeologia* as a group. They were reunited when Smith's collection 'having been rejected by the corporation, . . . found a safe resting-place in the British Museum' in 1856, where works from Newman's collection had been deposited eight years previously, after purchase at Sotheby's. **MR**

Agostino Aglio

370
Memorial to Giovanni Belzoni, *c.* 1825

Lithograph, 43.2 × 33.5 cm
York, David Alexander
Exhibitions: Brighton, 1983, Cat. No. 131
Literature: Altick 1978, pp. 243–46; James 1981, pp. 9–14

Giovanni Battista Belzoni (1778–1823), a native of Padua, first came to England during the Napoleonic Wars as an itinerant show-

370

371
Plates Illustrative of the Researches and Operations of G. Belzoni in Egypt and Nubia

Published by John Murray, Albemarle
Street, 1821
Folio, 61×49 cm
London, Guildhall Library, Corporation of
London
Inv. No. 417.2

This handsome volume followed on the publication by John Murray in 1820 of Belzoni's *Narrative*, his account of the operations and discoveries in Egypt and Nubia. It contains forty-four hand-coloured plates – both lithographs and etchings after drawings by Belzoni and his wife Sarah, Alessandro Ricci and, rather curiously, one by George Scharf.

The subjects mainly comprise copies of wall paintings and topographical views, but there are also maps, plans and sections, and a single botanical drawing. They focus on the sites most associated with Belzoni – the second pyramid of Chephren at Giza, the tombs in the Valley of the Kings and the temples of Abu Simbel. Plate 19 shows a wall painting from one of the six tombs Belzoni discovered in the Valley of the Kings, depicting 'a great Tableau of Figures, large as life, in the Tomb of Psammuthis, supposed to represent when the Hero is presented to the God Osiris'. **CF**

372
Stela of Panes *c.* 650 B.C.

Wood, 40×27 cm
London, Trustees of the British Museum
Inv. No. 8504
Provenance: Henry Salt, from whom
purchased, 1823
Exhibitions: Brighton, 1983, Cat. No. 120
Literature: James 1981, pp. 9–14

Henry Salt (1780–1827) trained as a portrait painter and travelled to India in 1802 as draughtsman and secretary to Viscount Valentia (later 2nd Earl of Mountnorris). They visited Cairo on the journey home in 1806 and Salt's *Twenty-Four Views . . .'* (1809) illustrates the tour. Salt was appointed consul-general in Egypt in 1815 and between 1816 and 1827 he financed several excavations, including those of Belzoni, forming three separate collections of antiquities, many of which were eventually acquired by the British Museum.

The process of acquisition was fraught with

man, variously billed as the 'Patagonian Samson' or 'Roman Hercules' performing superhuman feats of strength (he was 6 feet 6 inches tall) including the lifting of a 'human pyramid' at Sadler's Wells.

On his travels in Europe he met an agent of Mohammed Ali who suggested Egypt would provide him with ample scope for his talents. He had some early training in hydraulics in Rome and he proposed to interest the Pasha in a new irrigation system. When this came to nothing, he turned to archaeology, where his spectacular discoveries and triumphs of engineering in bringing antiquities back to Europe earned him an international reputation. After a successful exhibition of his models and drawings at the Egyptian Hall in 1821, he set off to trace the source of the Niger, but died of dysentery on the road to Timbuktu.

This lithograph, published by Belzoni's

widow, Sarah, depicts the great man rising from the mist over Thebes, with some of the antiquities with which he is particularly associated arranged in the foreground. In the centre is the sarcophagus of Sethos I, which Belzoni considered his most important find and which is now in Sir John Soane's Museum. Behind it is the obelisk which Belzoni managed to get conveyed down the Nile from Philae for William Bankes and which still stands at Bankes's home, Kingston Lacy, Dorset. On the right is the colossal bust of Ramesses II known as 'Young Memnon'; Belzoni organised its removal on behalf of Salt and Burkhardt from the ruined mortuary temple of the king in western Thebes. On the left is the pyramid of Chephren at Giza which Belzoni opened in 1818, and in front of it the great red granite head of a king, probably Amenophis III, from the Temple of Mut in Karnak, now in the British Museum. **CF**

372

373

difficulties. The museum's collection of Egyptian antiquities had been greatly augmented by major works including the Rosetta stone sequestrated from the French in 1801. At first these were housed in temporary shelters in the garden of Montagu House and then in the new Townley range of galleries built at the north-west corner of the house. In 1817, Salt and the Swiss explorer Jean-Louis Burckhardt presented to the museum the great granite bust of Ramesses II, successfully removed by Belzoni from the Ramesseum at Thebes.

With the support of Sir Joseph Banks (Cat. No. 348), one of the trustees, Salt was encouraged to collect further antiquities on behalf of the museum. But in his eagerness to carry out the commission and need to recoup the costs he bore from his own modest fortune, he alienated the trustees. Basking in the glory conferred by the acquisition of the Townley, Phigalian and Elgin marbles, none could understand the importance of Egyptian sculpture, nor would even consider it as fine art.

After painful and protracted negotiations, Salt's collection was bought by the museum in 1823 for £2,000. This sepulchral tablet was among the acquisitions, having been purchased at Thebes by Salt. It depicts the four deities of Osiris, Isis, Nephthys and Duamutef being worshipped by the 'Master of the Secrets of Ma'at'. **CF**

Alessandro Ricci
d. 1832 Thebes

373
Copy of the Stela of Panes

Pen and ink and watercolour, 40.6 × 27.5 cm
Inscribed in ink: H. A tomb stone bought at Thebes – on wood. Copied by Dr. Ricci
Inscribed in pencil: Wooden sepulchral tablet
London, Trustees of the British Museum
Inv. No. 9

Provenance: probably acquired with the first Salt collection, 1823
Exhibitions: Brighton, 1983, Cat. No. 124

Dr. Ricci was an Italian-born physician who travelled widely in Egypt accompanying a number of patrons and making drawings for them of tomb paintings and antiquities. A group of these works commissioned by Henry Salt *c.* 1818 survives in the British Museum and may in some cases be compared with the originals. The difficulties of making a clear record without idealising the object are apparent. Yet the accuracy in the rendering of the hieroglyphics is remarkable for the date.

Such drawings might have been intended as the basis for a future publication or as part of Salt's presentation to the trustees of the museum, or simply to secure a copy against the risk of a sea voyage to Britain. Some certainly serve as the only record of objects lost or damaged since they were copied. Ricci died at Thebes in 1832 from a scorpion sting. **CF**

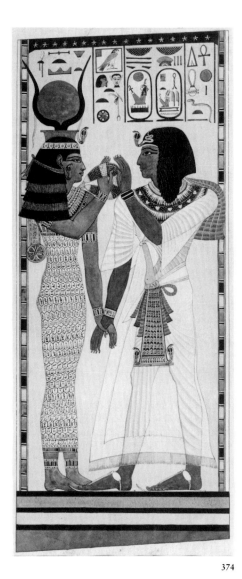

374

Henry Salt

Lichfield 1780–1827 Dessuke, Alexandria

374
Copy of a wall painting from the tomb of Sethos I

Pen, ink and watercolour, 86×66 cm
Signed and inscribed: E Drawn and finished on the spot by H. Salt on the right hand side of the . . . after descending the second or lower steps. This I consider to be the chef d'oeuvre of Egyptian painting. H. Salt
London, Trustees of the British Museum
Inv. No. E

Salt not only commissioned copies of antiquities from other artists, but was an able archaeological draughtsman himself, as demonstrated in a number of watercolours in the British Museum which he made of the tomb of Sethos I in 1817–18, soon after its dis-

covery by Belzoni. This scene depicts Sethos being embraced by the goddess Hathor. **CF**

375
Fragment of the lid of the sarcophagus of Sethos I, *c.* 1300 B.C. (19th Dynasty)

Alabaster, 30×30 cm
London, Trustees of the British Museum
Inv. No. 29948
Provenance: purchased, 1898
Exhibitions: Brighton, 1983, Cat. No. 29
Literature: James 1981, pp. 10–17

In October 1815, while exploring in the Valley of the Kings at Thebes, Belzoni discovered the many-chambered tomb of Sethos I, and 375 feet from the entrance, the king's alabaster sarcophagus. Henry Salt acquired the sarcophagus and tried to sell it to the British Museum. But so great was the classical bias of the then trustees that they rejected the purchase and it was bought by Sir John Soane for £2,000; it can still be seen at Sir John Soane's Museum in Lincoln's Inn Fields.

Salt was so disillusioned by his dealings with the British Museum that the second collection of antiquities he formed was only shipped to Leghorn, where it was bought through J. J. Champollion for the King of France. Salt died in Egypt in 1827 and his third collection was sold by Sotheby's in June–July 1835, with museum now a major purchaser. The trustees were belatedly aware of the opportunities they had missed and in 1834 Smirke's new gallery for Egyptian sculpture was completed with increasingly specialist curators to care for it. **CF**

George Scharf

Mainburg 1788–1860 London

376
The Entrance Hall of the Old British Museum, 1845

Watercolour over pencil, 31.5×43.8 cm
Signed bottom right: G. Scharf del. August 1845 and inscribed '28 feet wide from one door to the other'
London, Trustees of the British Museum
Inv. No. 1862-6-14-628
Provenance: from a collection of the artist's work purchased from his widow, 1862
Literature: Caygill 1982, p. 27, illustrated; Jackson 1987, p. 98, illustrated

George Scharf and his family lived within a few minutes of the British Museum from 1830 until 1856, and he carefully recorded the gradual demolition and rebuilding on the site that took place during this period.

Montagu House, the original house of the museum, had been one of the greatest London mansions of the late seventeenth century, but by 1800 the museum's collections had grown to such an extent that expansion was seen to be necessary, and a programme of rebuilding was gradually introduced. The original entrance hall and staircase were among the last part to be demolished, just a few weeks after this watercolour was painted in August 1845.

Scharf shows visitors entering and leaving the museum, and the visitors' book being signed under the watchful attention of the porters in their distinctive livery and one of the policemen assigned to the museum. The statues in the hall are of Sir Joseph Banks (Cat. No. 348), the naturalist, trustee and benefactor of the museum, by Chantrey, and the famous Roubiliac of Shakespeare, bequeathed by the actor David Garrick in 1779. In the background there is a glimpse of the lower part of the staircase cluttered with stuffed animals. **LS**

375

377

a) The Staircase of the Old British Museum, 1845
Watercolour over pencil, 24.1×28.7 cm

b) The Staircase of the Old British Museum, 1845
Watercolour over pencil, 36×27.9 cm
Signed bottom right: G. Scharf del. 1845
London, Trustees of the British Museum
Inv. Nos. 1862-6-14-631, 1862-6-14-629
respectively
Provenance: as for Cat. No. 376
Literature: Croft-Murray 1962, pp. 249–50, 255-57, Plate 117; Caygill 1981, p.28; Jackson 1987, pp. 98–99.

Montagu House, probably designed by the French architect Pierre Puget in the late 1680s, was the London house of the francophile 1st Duke of Montagu, and was subsequently bought by the trustees of the newly founded British Museum. The staircase and the principal state rooms were decorated by French artists, headed by a pupil of le Brun's, Charles de Lafosse (1636–1716); others included Jean-Baptiste Monnoyer (1634–99), Jacques Parmentier (1658–1730) and Jacques Rousseau (1630–93).

The building was particularly poorly suited for the display of the natural history collections, which were finally transferred to a purpose-built museum in South Kensington in

376

1883. Until 1845, however, some of the larger items were shown on the staircase. Although the first live giraffe to be seen in England was one given to George IV in 1827 (Cat. No. 341), stuffed examples were already to be seen in the British Museum: Prince Pückler Muskau noted that in October 1826 he had seen 'enormous giraffes, in the character of stuffed guards, or emblems of English taste' at the top of the stairs. **LS**

377a

377b

George Scharf

378
The Sculpture Gallery of the Old British Museum, 1827

Watercolour, 24×17.8 cm
Signed bottom right: G. Scharf del. 1827
London, Trustees of the British Museum
Inv. No. 1862-6-14-632
Provenance: as for Cat. No. 376
Literature: Jackson 1987, p. 99, illustrated

The collections of the British Museum developed so rapidly in the first fifty years of its existence that the construction of new gallery space became essential. In 1802 an important collection of antiquities from Egypt arrived in the museum, including the Rosetta stone (the key to the hieroglyphic script of dynastic Egypt), having been ceded to the British crown under the Treaty of Alexandria; this was the stimulus for building to begin in 1804. Three years later, the Townley collection of antique sculpture was acquired for the museum and the scheme for new galleries was expanded to allow space for its display. The new galleries were opened by Queen Charlotte in 1808.

Scharf's watercolour, made nineteen years later, shows the view into the Townley Gallery, with one of the most celebrated pieces just visible at the far end, the 'Discobolus' which had been excavated at Hadrian's Villa, Tivoli. In the left foreground are the 'Head of a Gaul' and 'Thalia' and on the right 'Bacchus and the Vine' and a bust of the Emperor Lucius Verus. **LS**

378

379
The Old and New Galleries of the British Museum, 1828

Pencil and watercolour, 18.9×28.2 cm
Signed right, below image: G. Scharf del.
and inscribed 'Fig A old gallery of Antiques in the British Museum B new gallery erecting July 1828'
London, Trustees of the British Museum
Inv. No. 1862-6-14-626
Provenance: as for Cat. No. 376
Literature: Caygill 1981, p. 23, illustrated;
Jackson 1987, p. 100, illustrated

Scharf recorded the changing appearance of the British Museum over a period of nearly thirty years. In this drawing, dated 1828, he shows a transitional phase in the redevelopment and enlargement of the buildings. In the early 1820s the architect Robert Smirke (1780–1867) was commissioned to undertake the project, and building began in earnest in 1823. King George IV had recently presented his father's extensive library to the museum, on condition that it was suitably housed. Public opinion, however, was not unanimous in welcoming such expansion: one writer in *The Times* complained 'in these times of general distress [of] so preposterous an intention of unnecessary expenditure of public money'.

In this drawing, three stages of the museum's development can be seen. On the far left is Montagu House, the original home of the museum. Joined to it at right angles is the Sculpture Gallery, leading to the Townley Gallery, and on the right is Smirke's new West Wing under construction; it was not completed until the Townley Gallery and Montagu House were demolished in 1846. The garden, here covered with building materials and men at work, was later the site of the great Reading Room. An informative note by Scharf states that 'There will be 44 Columns to the Facade and 10,000 tons of stone used as Mr. Baker the builder told me.' **LS**

380

Robert Smirke
London 1780–1867 Cheltenham

380
Proposed entrance façade of the British Museum

Pen and wash, 37.5×73 cm
Signed: Robt. Smirke
London, British Architectural Library
Drawings Collection, Royal Institute of British Architects
Inv. No. J11/41 [3]
Literature: Richardson ed. 1975, Vol. S, p. 65; Crook 1972, pp. 73–150, Fig. 49; Crook and Port 1973, pp. 403–21

Prophetically awarded the Royal Academy gold medal for his *Design for a National Museum* in 1799, Smirke's opportunity came some twenty years later when as one of the three attached architects to the Office of Works, he was directed to investigate the British Museum's future needs. Smirke proposed the building of two parallel wings running north of Montagu House but the gift by George IV of his father's library to the museum in January 1823 provoked a more radical solution. A new museum would be built round a quadrangle in stages, with the demolition of Montagu House only taking place as the new wings went up.

This drawing was part of the original plans approved in 1823 and as such predates Schinkel's Altes Museum in Berlin with which it is often compared. Smirke had an intense admiration for the 'primal simplicity' and unostentatious grandeur of Greek architecture and etymologically, museums were an attempt to recreate the concept of the antique temple. The façade was completed in 1848 with some alterations to the doorway, string course and parapet, and the insertion of Richard Westmacott's pedimental sculpture, *The Progress of Civilisation*. **CF**

PAINTING AND SCULPTURE

The annual exhibitions at the Royal Academy and from 1806, the British Institution, provided artists with the opportunity to present their works to an increasingly diverse public. Although the patronage of connoisseurs was important, some artists endeavoured to retain their independence by organising their own one-man exhibitions and to extend their income and reputation through the sale of prints after their work. While the primacy of history painting was still acknowledged in theory, in practice, there were few commissions and many artists earned their living from portraiture. It was the art of landscape that was advanced by Turner and Constable, and their achievement was matched in genre painting by Wilkie, gaining for the first time a European reputation for British art.

Thomas Rowlandson
London 1756–1827 London

381
The Exhibition 'Stare' Case, Somerset House, c. 1800

Ink and wash, 40×27 cm
London, University College London
Inv. No. 3677
Provenance: Henry Tonks, by whom bequeathed, 1936
Exhibitions: London, Goupil Gallery, 1922; Brussels, 1929, No. 154; London, Royal Academy, 1934, No. 1215, Cat. No. 693, Plate 161; Paris, 1938, No. 227; New York, Pittsburgh, Baltimore, 1990, Cat. No. 72
Literature: Grego 1880, Vol. 2, pp. 216–19; Oppé 1923, pp. 16–17, Plate 52; Falk 1949, pp. 144–47; Hayes 1972, p. 167, Plate 101; Paulson 1972, pp. 26, 81

This rapidly executed and curvilinear composition shows the staircase at Somerset House leading to the galleries of the Royal Academy, where the annual exhibitions had been staged since 1780. London society scrambles to get up or down the steps; the older men ogle ('stare' at) the women in their scanty apparel. **CF**

George Scharf
Mainburg 1788–1860 London

382
Austellung der Königlichen Academy London, 1828

Pen and ink and watercolour, 18.2×25.5 cm
Signed and dated bottom left: G. Scharf del London. 1828
London, The Museum of London

381

Inv. No. 63.86/35
Provenance: Sir Bruce Ingram
Exhibitions: London, The Museum of London, 1981, No. 76; Dulwich Picture Gallery, 1991–92, Cat. No. D7

Scharf's watercolour is one of a number of views depicting the Great Room, the largest of the top-floor galleries on the Strand frontage of Somerset House, where the annual exhibitions of the Royal Academy of Arts were held from 1780 to 1837. The earliest drawings of the room were made by Johann Heinrich Ramberg (1763–1840) from 1784 to 1787, engraved by Pietro Antonio Martini and published by A.C. de Poggi in 1787 and 1789; an aquatint after Rowlandson and Pugin was published as part of Ackermann's *Microcosm of London* (Cat. No. 176) in 1808. In this view Scharf's

proportions are faulty, the figures domesticating the scale of a room which was in fact over 52 feet long, 42 feet wide and 32 feet high. The artist nevertheless suggests the difficulties visitors experienced in attempting to see more than 1,100 works hung from floor to ceiling.

The Great Room was reserved for the largest and most important paintings, among them in this, the sixtieth exhibition, a number of full-length portraits by the president, Sir Thomas Lawrence: on the right, *The Marchioness of Londonderry and her son, Lord Seaham* (No. 140) and beyond that *The Countess Gower and her daughter* (No. 114). On the centre wall hangs Turner's *Dido directing the Equipment of the Fleet* (No. 70) and above it to the right, Lawrence's portrait of *Julia Beatrice Peel,* elder daughter of Sir Robert Peel (No. 77). Scharf himself exhibited *The Savoyards* (No. 813). **CF**

Alfred Joseph Woolmer
Hereford 1805–1892 London

383
The Interior of the British Institution, Old Master Exhibition, Summer 1832, 1833

Oil on canvas, 71.9×92 cm
Signed and dated lower right under bench: A. J . . . /1833
New Haven, Yale Center for British Art
Inv. No. B1981.25.694
Provenance: Mr. Campbell; Oscar and Peter Johnson, 1965; Paul Mellon
Exhibitions: London, British Instition, 1833, No. 509; New Haven, 1984, No. 12
Literature: Graves 1910, pp. 378–81

The British Institution was founded in 1805 with the aim to stimulate interest in British art and to encourage patronage. To these ends it

383

held an annual exhibition of contemporary artists' work and also awarded prizes each year for different categories of art, including landscape, portraiture and, importantly, history painting.

Despite its worthy intentions, and highly successful activities, the Institution attracted much criticism, for it was seen as a rival to the Royal Academy. Unlike the Academy its governing body excluded artists and consisted mainly of connoisseurs, anathema to the Royal Academy. Criticism was fuelled by the Institution's acquisition of a small collection of old master paintings in 1806, and from 1815 its inauguration of annual exhibitions of such works, the first in Britain. Students came to copy these pictures, leading the Academy to see its teaching facility threatened and other critics to accuse the Institution of promoting the collecting of the old masters rather than contemporary British work.

Woolmer shows the Institution's galleries at 52 Pall Mall on the occasion of their exhibition of old masters which opened in 1832. However, Woolmer's painting is an imaginative reconstruction of the rooms, for the order in which the pictures were actually displayed was different from that depicted here. Some paintings are identifiable, including works by Veronese, Ribera, Van Dyck, Poussin, Rembrandt, Reynolds and Gainsborough, then in British private collections. The Chantrey bust in the middle room was of the Marquess of Stafford who was president of the British Institution at the time; sculpted in 1829, the bust was installed in 1830. **RU**

Sir David Wilkie
Cults 1785–1841 Gibraltar

384 *(illus. p. 436)*
The Blind Fiddler, 1806

Oil on panel, 57.8×79.4 cm
Signed and dated: David Wilkie 1806
London, Tate Gallery
Inv. No. T.G.N00099
Provenance: commissioned by Sir George Beaumont, by whom presented to the National Gallery, 1826; transferred to the Tate Gallery, 1919
Exhibitions: London, Royal Academy, 1807, No. 147; Wilkie's Exhibition, 1812; British Institution 1825; . . . Edinburgh, 1985, Cat. No. 19; New Haven and Raleigh, 1987, Cat. No. 5
Literature: Cunningham 1843, Vol. 1, pp. 67, 95–96, 131, 143–46, 249, 332; Vol. 3, p. 512

With Turner and Constable, Wilkie was one of the three greatest British artists of the first three decades of the nineteenth century, his original achievement in figure painting matching theirs in landscape. *The Blind Fiddler* was among the most widely influential pictures exhibited in London in the early years of the century. It was the second work by Wilkie shown in the capital, and with his other youthful pictures, may be said to have established the fashion for popular and anecdotal genre that dominated painting in Europe and America for many years.

Born in Scotland, Wilkie first trained in Edinburgh and then in London at the Royal Academy, soon developing a type of narrative painting based on Dutch masters like Ostade and Teniers and on his own observation and experience. He was a marvellous story-teller in paint, and his pictures proved outstandingly successful, being regularly besieged by enthusiastic crowds in the London exhibitions.

This painting was commissioned by Sir George Beaumont (1753–1827), one of the most influential connoisseurs of Regency London and a collector of both old masters and modern artists. With his friend Lord Mulgrave (Cat. No. 303), Beaumont encouraged and supported Wilkie during his first difficult days in London. While the subject was of Wilkie's invention, the old masterly finish and subdued colouring of the picture were calculated to appeal to Beaumont's conservative tastes; it was the only modern picture of any significance to be included in Beaumont's gift to the National Gallery.

The painting portrays the mixed reactions of a rustic shoemaker's family to the music of a travelling fiddler, whose blindness renders him ignorant of the effect he has upon his listeners. Wilkie tempers the pathos of the scene with irony and humour, showing on the right a child mimicking the violinist by playing on a bellows with a poker. The writer and critic William Hazlitt (Cat. No. 458) dismissed this as a 'very bad' joke, but the musical imitation seems to have been an extension of the idea of learning by copying intrinsic in the artistic training Wilkie had recently undergone, exemplified in this picture by a child's copy of a print, pinned to the cupboard door above the boy's head. **DBB**

Joseph Mallord William Turner
London 1775–1851 London

385 *(illus. p. 457)*
London, 1809

Oil on canvas, 90×120 cm
Signed and dated, lower left centre: 1809
JMW Turner RAPP
London, Tate Gallery
Inv. No. N00483
Provenance: Walter Fawkes by 1811; returned to the artist by exchange at an unknown date; Turner Bequest, 1856
Exhibitions: London, Turner's gallery, 1809, No. 6; Royal Academy, 1974–75, Cat. No. 152, reproduced; Tate Gallery, 1990, No. 45
Literature: Ruskin 1857, Vol. 13, pp. 119–20; Butlin and Joll 1984, No. 97

Although Turner was born in Covent Garden and spent most of his life in London, he painted very few pictures of its famous views, the majority of his London subjects being closely observed topography executed during his adolescence. This canvas is the first to be inscribed with the letters 'PP' after Turner's own initials, referring to the post of Professor of Perspective at the Royal Academy, to which he had been appointed in 1807. The significance of his new role may explain the choice of a largely architectural subject in which the viewer looks down from the ridge in the park at Greenwich towards the Royal Naval Hospital designed by Wren and Hawksmoor and Inigo Jones's Queen's House.

The picture was among those exhibited at Turner's own gallery in 1809. He had created this gallery at his house in Harley Street as a means of providing a higher profile for his work, augmenting his success at the Royal Academy: the first exhibition took place in 1805. The display in 1809 included sixteen oil paintings and two watercolours. This view of London was bought by the Yorkshire landowner, Walter Fawkes (1769–1825), who acquired one of the biggest collections of works by Turner during the artist's lifetime and was an important friend until his death in 1825 (Cat. No. 243). Three of the pictures in the 1809 exhibition had verses by Turner appended to their titles. Those attached to this picture express Turner's regret at the ugly sprawling detritus of the great city. **IW**

William Collins
London 1788–1847 London

386
The Reluctant Departure, 1815

Oil on canvas, 88 × 112.4 cm
Signed and dated lower right: W. COLLINS 1815
Birmingham, Museums and Art Gallery
Inv. No. 2528'85
Provenance: J. Carpenter (brother-in-law of artist's wife, Harriet Gedes); Edwin Bullock, Birmingham; Bullock sale, Christie's, 21 May 1870, Lot 142; Timothy Kenrick, by whom presented to Birmingham, 1882
Exhibitions: London, Royal Academy, 1815, No. 29; British Institution, 1816, No. 109; Glasgow, 1888, No. 186; London, Tate Gallery, 1959, Cat. No. 58; Royal Academy, 1968–69, Cat. No. 209, reproduced p. 52
Literature: List of Pictures and Patrons 1808–27 (mss. notebook), Victoria and Albert Museum; Collins 1848, Vol. 1, p. 69; Birmingham 1960, p. 32

386

Through his father, a picture dealer and restorer, Collins was introduced at an early age to George Morland (1763–1804), and was encouraged to enter the Royal Academy Schools in 1807. He quickly started to exhibit, and achieved popular success with sentimental genre subjects such as *The Disposal of a Favourite Lamb* of 1813, which also gained admiration from the critic William Hazlitt (Cat. No. 458). Elected an Associate in 1814, he became a full Royal Academician in 1820.

The Reluctant Departure, his acknowledged masterpiece, is typical of his setting of rustic figures in a broad, bleak landscape (often coastal). There is a solemn dignity about the simple figure group, which has been rightly regarded as anticipating the poignant mood of Victorian painting. A certain stiffness of drawing may derive from the artist's habit, adopted from his friend Wilkie, of painting from clay models or dolls set in a lighted box. In a memoir of his father, the writer Wilkie Collins identified the subject as 'a mother taking leave of her child as it lies in the nurse's arms, ere she descends to a boat in the foreground, which a fisherman and his boy are preparing to push off from shore.' **SGW**

John Constable
East Bergholt 1776–1837 London

387 *(illus. p. 454)*
Ploughing Scene in Suffolk (A Summerland), 1814

Oil on canvas, 50.5 × 76.5 cm
Private Collection
Provenance: John Allnutt; probably the artist by *c.* 1825; George Simms; Miss Atkinson, 1891; her niece Mrs. L. Childs; Leggatt
Exhibitions: London, Royal Academy, 1814, No. 28; British Institution, 1815; Tate Gallery, 1976, Cat. No. 123; Tate Gallery, 1991, Cat. No. 71
Literature: Rosenthal 1983, pp. 18–21, 69–78, 83; Cormack 1986, pp. 80–84, 88, 91; Rosenthal 1987, pp. 76–81

This marvellously direct and simple painting was one of the masterpieces of Constable's early naturalism as finished for exhibition, and was painted at a turning point in his career. As early as 1802, the year of his first submission to the Royal Academy, he had declared his commitment to 'natural painture' – to a rendering of English landscape that owed most to direct observation rather to study of the old masters or the assimilation of compositional and colouristic conventions. In the intervening years he had pursued this mission, concentrat-

ing on the familiar landscape of his youth, the Stour valley near Dedham and his birthplace at East Bergholt, on the borders of the counties of Essex and Suffolk, about 50 miles from London. His summers were spent mainly at his family home, drawing and sketching, and his winters in London, where he worked up his materials in his studio. Besides filling sketchbooks, he made many superb oil sketches in the open air, which contributed to his finished pictures. No oil sketch for the *Ploughing Scene* is known, but there are related drawings in his sketchbook of 1813 (Victoria and Albert Museum).

The painting may be seen as marking the climax of this first phase of Constable's working practice. In the course of 1814 he began to give more urgency to a longstanding ambition – to paint not merely sketches and particular motifs out of doors, but to 'finish a small picture on the spot for every one I intend to make in future'. In fact, later in the year he went further than this, and began to paint directly from nature on his final canvases. It was at least partly his recognition of the difficulty of maintaining the freshness and truth of this scene from a Suffolk summer while working in a London studio in winter that spurred him to make this radical change. Even as it stands, the picture appeared before its London audience as a remarkable example of Constable's uncompromising honesty and verisimilitude, documenting agricultural activity in a straightforward and unromanticised way. The field is being ploughed in the summer to lie fallow until autumn, when it would be spread with manure and then sown in the winter. A 'summerland' was the name given by farmers to such a field, and Constable used it for the title for the print by David Lucas based on the

painting (Cat. No. 423). The view is of Dedham Vale from East Bergholt, literally rendered. Constable's one concession to compositional effect or sentiment is the motif of the dog asleep on a blanket – or perhaps the ploughman's coat – and the drinking bottle in the right foreground. **DBB**

Peter De Wint
Stone 1784–1849 London

388
A Cornfield, 1815

Oil on canvas, 104.8 × 163.8 cm
London, Trustees of the Victoria and Albert Museum
Inv. No. 258–1972
Provenance: presented to the Victoria and Albert Museum by the artist's daughter, Mrs. Helen Tatlock, 1872
Exhibitions: ? London, Royal Academy, 1815, No. 290; London, Thomas Agnew and Sons, 1966, Cat. No. 63; Norwich, 1969, Cat. No. 22; Tokyo, 1971
Literature: Smith 1982, pp. 62–9; Parkinson 1990, pp. 68–69

The first decades of the nineteenth century saw the consolidation of the development of British landscape painting away from the purely topographical tradition of the previous century. The pictorial subject matter and treatment of romantic landscape became more important than the mere recording of location in precise detail. Dramatic, poetic or evocative

landscapes became highly popular with collectors and critics alike, and they were to be found in some numbers in the annual exhibitions of the Royal Academy and British Institution and elsewhere. Turner and Constable were perhaps the leading and most distinctive exponents of this new approach to landscape, the latter producing harmonious portraits of the British countryside in a wholly original manner. Of all his fellow artists Peter De Wint reputedly admired only Constable, and he similarly produced landscapes which depicted the countryside as a place of beauty, harmony and productivity.

The Cornfield is perhaps his best oil painting, the simple yet highly effective composition, with its wide, almost panoramic sweep and complete lack of vertical axis, an unusual and innovative approach when it was first exhibited in 1815. Harvests were a favourite subject for De Wint, and as here (a scene near Horncastle, Lincolnshire), they invariably show agricultural life as one of pastoral perfection, where labourers, nature and rural society are in harmonious synthesis. The reality of rural existence was somewhat different; the year 1815 alone had seen food riots and action by the Luddites. The British countryside was also involved in a process of steady change, with new methods of farming being adopted, and the movement of many labourers away from the land and into the factory. Indeed, Britain itself was changing from an agricultural economy to an industrial one. De Wint therefore appears involved in a process of nostalgic idealisation. **RU**

Sir Augustus Wall Callcott
London 1779–1844 London

389 *(illus. p. 461)*
The Entrance to the Pool of London, 1816

Oil on canvas, 153 × 221 cm
Signed and dated: A.W.C. 1815
Bowood, Trustees of the Bowood Collection
Provenance: commissioned by the 3rd Marquess of Lansdowne; thence by descent
Exhibitions: London, Royal Academy, 1816, No. 185; Somerset House, 1977, Cat. No. 52; Tate Gallery, 1981, Cat. No. 15

The Pool of London situated down-river from the Tower and densely crowded with shipping, had long impressed Londoners and foreign visitors and attracted countless painters, but the activities of this great international trading port had been drastically reduced by the Napoleonic Wars. Callcott's picture, his masterpiece and a superlative example of tranquil marine painting, was exhibited in

1816, two years after the Congress of Vienna, and could hardly have been better calculated to celebrate the resurgence of the port after the war. In the foreground is moored a large Dutch boat, a representative of the United Netherlands, created by the Treaty of London in 1815 as part of the new Europe to build effective barriers against revived French ambitions. Callcott has cast his picture in a mood of timeless calm and bathed it in a warm glow that reflects the influence of the Dutch master Aelbert Cuyp, a painter then much admired by connoisseurs, whose great picture *The Passage Boat* had been bought by the Prince Regent in 1814.

Already a significant painter, recognised as the closest follower and friend of J. M. W. Turner, Callcott scored an enormous popular hit with *The Pool*. Turner himself admired it, declaring it to be worth 1,000 guineas – Callcott's price had been 200 – and it is generally acknowledged that Turner's own masterpiece of tranquil marine and tribute to Cuyp, *Dort, or Dordrecht*, of 1818 (Yale Center for British Art, New Haven) was a response to it. **DBB**

John Martin
Haydon Bridge 1789–1854 Douglas

390 *(illus. p. 459)*
Joshua commanding the Sun to stand still, 1816

Oil on canvas, 149.9×231.1 cm
Signed bottom right: J. Martin
London, United Grand Lodge of England
Provenance: William Collins; Thomas Wilson until 1848; John Naylor until 1889; John M. Naylor, his sale Leighton Hall, Welshpool, 23 January 1923, Lot 41; anonymous gift to the United Grand Lodge of England, 1924
Exhibitions: London, Royal Academy, 1816, No. 347; British Institution, 1817; Egyptian Hall, 1822; No. 152; Liverpool, 1854, No. 28; London, International Exhibition, 1862; Newcastle, 1970, Cat. No. 6; London, Tate Gallery, 1973, Cat. No. 276; Hazlitt, Gooden and Fox, 1975, Cat. No. 9
Literature: Feaver 1975, pp. 25–28, 54–56

With his large pictures of epic destruction, John Martin was one of the most popular exhibitors in the London art world. The public flocked to see his work, but the critics were less sure of his technical abilities and also accused him of vulgarity, no doubt because of his popularity. Martin's apocalyptic works usually employed the device of placing large numbers of tiny figures in an overpoweringly large and dramatic landscape, an approach

ideal for his many scenes from the Bible, although he used the same approach for his picture for Queen Victoria's coronation.

Joshua commanding the Sun to stand still was one of his first successes. It illustrates the book of Joshua, X, 10–14. The City of Gibeon had allied itself to Joshua and the Israelites, and was consequently besieged by the Amorites. When the Israelites came to Gibeon's aid, God destroyed the Amorites with hailstones; at the height of the carnage Joshua commanded the sun to be still. This is the moment Martin chose, Gibeon bathed in sunlight while the storm rages over the Amorites. *Joshua* owes much to J. M. W. Turner's similarly apocalyptic *Snow Storm: Hannibal and his Army crossing the Alps* which Martin undoubtedly saw at the Academy in 1812. Although *Joshua* proved highly popular with the public when Martin showed it at the Royal Academy in 1816, it did not secure a buyer, and he showed it again the following year at the British Institution where it was awarded the second premium of £100. **RU**

James Stark
Norwich 1794–1859

391 *(illus. p. 463)*
Lambeth looking towards Westminster Bridge, 1818

Oil on canvas, 88.3×137.2 cm
New Haven, Yale Center for British Art
Inv. No. B1976.7.76
Provenance: bought in 1818 by the Countess de Grey; by descent to the Baroness Lucas and Dingwall; her sale, Christie's, 16 November, 1917, Lot. 113, bought Leggatt; H.H. Illingworth; Major R. L. Farley; Thomas Agnew and Sons Ltd., from whom purchased, 1971
Exhibitions: London, British Institution, 1818, No. 10; Thomas Agnew and Sons Ltd., 1971, No. 8
Literature: Dickes 1905, p. 451; Cormack 1985, p. 212 reproduced

Having been indentured to John Crome as a pupil in 1811, and exhibiting at the Norwich Society of Artists from 1809 onwards, Stark moved to London in 1814, where he enrolled at the Royal Academy Schools in 1817. He was to achieve great success at the British Institution whose directors were among his earliest patrons, including Countess de Grey who purchased this painting, which won the Institution's £50 prize in 1818. **CF**

Joseph Mallord William Turner
London 1775–1851 London

392 *(illus. p. 456)*
England: Richmond Hill, on the Prince Regent's Birthday, 1819

Oil on canvas, 180×334.5 cm
London, Tate Gallery
Inv. No. N00502
Provenance: Turner Bequest, 1856
Exhibitions: London, Royal Academy, 1819, No. 206; Royal Academy, 1974–75, Cat. No. 167; Paris, 1983–84, Cat. No. 34; Birmingham, 1984; London, Tate Gallery, 1990, Cat. No. 67
Literature: Butlin and Joll 1984, pp. 106–07, No. 140; Golt 1987, pp. 9–20

Although he kept up a house and gallery in central London from 1804 onwards, it appears to have been important to Turner to maintain close links with the Thames by having a second residence on the banks of the river for much of his life. The Thames to the west of London seems to have held a particular attraction for him. In late 1804 or early 1805 he started living at the Ferry House at Syon, from 1806 to 1811 he kept up an address at Hammersmith and in 1812 he supervised the building of the Twickenham villa he had himself designed, Sandycombe Lodge. When he died in 1851 it was at his house in Cheyne Walk, Chelsea, not at his main residence in Queen Anne Street West near Cavendish Square.

Turner depicted the view from Richmond Hill several times, but never more eloquently than in the oil which shows the festivities on the Prince Regent's birthday. By 1817 the prince's birthday was celebrated publicly on 23 April – St. George's Day, which was also Turner's birthday – but other celebrations took place on his actual birthday, 12 August.

Golt has argued that *England: Richmond Hill* shows a widely reported fête held in August 1817 for the regent and his family by the Dowager Countess of Cardigan at her Richmond home. Turner's inclusion of the barge of the Lord Mayor of London, who waited to salute the arrival of the royal party, and the at-ease bandsmen of the First Regiment of Foot Guards, who played at the gathering, lend weight to this thesis.

In addition to showing a specific event, *England: Richmond Hill* embraces many themes, from patriotism, social harmony and thanksgiving for the ending of the Napoleonic Wars, to a celebration of the natural beauties of the Thames valley, and the poetic visions of Turner's heroes, Pope and Thomson. **RU**

Francis Danby
Wexford, Ireland 1793–1861 Exmouth

393 (illus. p. 470)
Disappointed Love, 1821

Oil on panel, 62.8 × 81.2 cm
Signed and dated bottom right: F Danby
1821
London, Trustees of the Victoria and Albert
Museum
Inv. No. FA65
Provenance: John Sheepshanks by 1850;
given by him to the Museum, 1857
Exhibitions: London, Royal Academy, 1821,
No. 210; Bristol, 1973, No. 7; Bristol and
London, Tate Gallery, 1988, pp. 91–93, Cat.
No. 19, illustrated
Literature: Adams 1973, pp. 17–27, p. 170,
No. 6; Parkinson 1990, pp. 58–59

Although Danby lived for many years in
Bristol, and is most often identified with the
circle of painters, both amateur and professional, known as the Bristol School, it was inevitable that he should seek to establish his
professional reputation in the annual exhibitions in London. In 1813 he visited London to
see the Royal Academy exhibition, and, after
exhausting nearly all his funds, was reduced to
walking the 120 miles back to Bristol. However, instead of directly obtaining a passage
back to his home in Ireland, he discovered a
market for topographical and genre subjects,
and remained in Bristol until 1824, when he
moved to London.

Between 1820 and 1860 he exhibited seventeen pictures at the British Institution, and
forty-eight at the Royal Academy. *Disappointed Love* was the first painting he contributed to a Royal Academy exhibition. The
use of varnish, now discoloured, is only partly
responsible for the gloomy and pessimistic
atmosphere of the scene, since nineteenth-
century writers on the pictures were unanimous in their opinion that the girl was about
to commit suicide. Lord Palmerston saw the
picture in 1856 while it was in John Sheepshanks' collection and, though impressed, said
it was a pity that the girl was so ugly, to which
his host replied, 'Yes . . . one feels that the
sooner she drowns herself the better.'

Danby apparently considered the picture
a kind of poem, and Thomson, Coleridge,
Blake and Cumberland have all been suggested as influences on the mood of innocence
corrupted and discarded. Certainly, the
prominent foliage in the foreground derives
from Erasmus Darwin's poem *The Loves of
the Plants.* Danby had been reading the poem
prior to commencing this painting, which
seems to echo Darwin's theory that plants
could experience pleasure and pain in a way
parallel to the emotions experienced by
humans. **IW**

Sir David Wilkie
Cults 1785–1841 Gibraltar

394 (illus. p. 460)
Chelsea Pensioners reading the Waterloo Despatch, 1822

Oil on wood, 97 × 158 cm
Signed and dated: 1822
London, Apsley House, Wellington
Museum, Trustees of the Victoria and Albert
Museum
Provenance: commissioned by the 1st Duke
of Wellington, 1816; by descent to the 7th
Duke; gift to the nation under the terms of
the Wellington Museum Act, 1947
Exhibitions: London, Royal Academy, 1822,
No. 126; British Institution, 1825, New
Haven and Raleigh, 1987, Cat. No. 23
Literature: Cunningham 1843, Vol. 2, pp.
170, 459; Vol. 2, pp. 13–14, 16–18, 25–26, 45,
48–51, 53–54, 58, 66, 68–69, 72–73, 109–10

This was, justifiably, one of the most celebrated pictures of its time. When exhibited at
the Academy, it attracted such a crush that
railings had to be erected to protect it, and it
reached a wide popular audience through
prints. It is undoubtedly Wilkie's masterpiece,
displaying all his gifts for the management of a
large cast of characters across a large composition, while portraying a wide variety of types
and emotions through their reactions to the
central incident. In retrospect it marks the culmination of the anecdotal manner which had
made his name, and point the way to his later
interest in grander and more elevated themes
through its treatment of a moment in recent
history.

The memory of Waterloo, which marked a
new epoch in European history and in British
fortunes in particular, was of universal concern to Wilkie's audience, but he depicted the
arrival of the news of the victory in a place and
among a crowd specially fitted to appreciate it.
The scheme is set outside the Royal Hospital
in Chelsea, opened in 1694 as a home for retired soldiers; its residents, the Chelsea Pensioners, feature prominently among the varied
London crowd assembled to hear the news,
and indeed it is a pensioner who reads it. The
exact spot chosen by Wilkie was apparently
Jew's Row – long since redeveloped but then
the 'Pall Mall of the pensioners' – outside the
Duke of York inn.

The picture was commissioned by the Duke
of Wellington in 1816 after he had visited Wilkie's studio with friends. It was his most important and costly act of patronage. Wilkie
eventually charged him the enormous sum of
1,200 guineas – which the duke paid in cash,
not wishing, as he told Wilkie's friend and fellow painter William Allan, his bank clerk to
know that he had 'been such a damned fool as
to pay a thousand guineas for a picture.' The

duke's idea was not at first very specific; he
proposed a scene of old soldiers reminiscing
outside an inn, perhaps in the King's Road,
Chelsea, and when Wilkie indicated the need
for some central incident to pull the subject together, suggested a game of skittles. Wilkie
proposed as an alternative that one of the
soldiers might be shown reading a newspaper
aloud to the rest, adding that other incidents
would occur as he worked.

Characteristically, he worked extremely
hard to make the picture as accurate as possible, whether by study of the topography of
Chelsea or correct observation of the habits of
the pensioners, who received their pay in summer and might indeed be found in what Wilkie
described as a 'glorious carouse' when inter-
rupted by the still more glorious news from
Waterloo. Wilkie had however forgotten one
detail. It was illegal to eat oysters in June – an
error committed at the very centre of the picture, and which was the subject of much
amusement at the time. **DBB**

Sir Charles Lock Eastlake
Plymouth 1793–1865 Pisa

395 (illus. p. 469)
The Colosseum from the Campo Vaccino, 1822

Oil on canvas, 52.7 × 64.8 cm
London, Tate Gallery
Inv. No. T00665
Provenance: painted for Greville Howard;
Colonel M. H. Grant, by 1932; Luther
Antiques, 1962; sold to the Friends of the
Tate Gallery and presented by them, 1964
Exhibitions: London, Royal Academy,
1951–52, No. 260; Plymouth, 1965, No. 6
Literature: Robertson 1978, p. 9, Fig. 3, pp.
254–55, No. 70

During the second half of his life, Eastlake was
one of the most important figures of the international art world. His own career as an artist
was eclipsed by his appointment to a number
of prominent public posts, spiralling upwards
from Secretary of the Fine Arts Commission
in 1841, to President of the Royal Academy in
1850, and culminated in his becoming first
Director of the National Gallery in 1855. The
foundation upon which all these appoint-
ments flourished was a scholarly connoisseur-
ship accumulated through years of diligent
study in picture collections across Europe. He
translated Goethe's *Theory of Colours* (1840)
and published his own writings on art.

While Director of the National Gallery,
Eastlake oversaw the arrival of the Turner
Bequest as well as being directly responsible
for the acquisition of 139 pictures, which remain at the heart of the national collection.

J. Constable, *Hampstead Heath with London in the Distance*, c. 1827–30. Cat. No. 407

Particularly significant was his interest in the early Italian painters, then still largely unfamiliar. He had studied both with Haydon and in the Royal Academy Schools, but his removal to Italy in 1816 provided a direct confrontation with the art of Italy from classical times to the present.

In Rome he mixed with a wide circle which included the archaeologist and architect C. R. Cockerell, the sculptors Canova and Thorvaldsen, and the German artists known as the Nazarenes. He worked hard painting many views of Rome and the surrounding countryside, also visiting Tivoli and Naples. His practice of relentlessly working out of doors throughout the fiery days of summer earned him the nickname the 'Salamander'.

This canvas was painted in the summer of 1822, and is one of several views he made of the Colosseum. Despite its title, the view is taken from a point to the south west of the Colosseum on the Palatine, from where the Arch of Constantine was visible. **IW**

Francis Danby
Wexford 1793 – 1861 Exmouth

396 *(illus. p. 488)*
Sunset at Sea after a Storm, 1824

Oil on canvas, 84.5×117 cm
Bristol, Museum and Art Gallery
Provenance: purchased from the artist by Sir Thomas Lawrence, 1824: his sale, 15 May 1830, No. 115; Edward W. Lake, Christie's, 11 July 1843, No. 64, bought Hogarth; Christie's, 13 June 1851, No. 95, bought J. Warrender; Gambart, Christie's, 3 May 1861, No. 278; Sotheby's, 17 March 1982, No. 68, from a foreign collection, bought Thomas Agnew and Sons Ltd. from whom purchased, 1982
Exhibitions: London, Royal Academy, 1824, No. 350; British Institution, 1825, No. 119; Bristol and London, Tate Gallery, 1988, pp.93–95, Cat. No. 20, Plate 8
Literature: Adams 1973, pp.44–45, p.193, No. 159

Although *Sunset at Sea after a Storm* was the fifth work Danby exhibited in the annual London exhibitions, it was the first to receive unqualified praise. The greatest recognition that the picture could perhaps achieve was its acquisition by the President of the Royal Academy, Sir Thomas Lawrence. Apart from generously allowing Danby to retain his picture for the purpose of its engraving by F. C. Lewis, Lawrence seems also to have ensured that in November of the following year Danby was elected an Associate of the Royal Academy. The impact the picture made was still vividly recalled almost forty years later by Richard Redgrave, who wrote, 'we could almost describe from memory the lurid red of the setting sun, the broken waves of the subsiding storm, the few survivors of the wreck, alone on a raft on the limitless ocean.'

The motif of a desolate raft may have been suggested by Géricault's famous painting, *The Raft of the Medusa*, which was exhibited in 1820 at the Egyptian Hall in Piccadilly (Cat. No. 325). Although Danby did not see Géricault's picture himself, it was described to him by Frank Gold, a Bristol acquaintance,

J. Constable, *Ploughing Scene in Suffolk (A Summerland)*, 1814. Cat. No. 387

and clearly left its mark on Danby: 'I stored what he said of this picture up in my memory.' Apart from the powerful impact that Danby's painting made at the Royal Academy, it can be seen to have had a direct influence on the work of his contemporaries, in particular on John Martin, whose picture of 1830, the *Destruction of Pharoah's Hosts* (Laing Art Gallery, Newcastle) bears more than a passing resemblance to Danby's picture. During the following years Danby set out to exploit what he called 'a rage for novelty in the public', and painted Biblical and Apocalyptic subject matter, a field with which Martin was also closely identified, inevitably resulting in a rivalry between the two artists and ultimately in accusations of plagiarism. **IW**

Charles Robert Leslie
London 1794–1859 London

397
Sancho Panza in the Apartment of the Duchess, 1824

Oil on canvas, 100.3 × 123.1 cm
Petworth House, Sussex, Lord Egremont
Provenance: commissioned by George O'Brien Wyndham, 3rd Earl of Egremont
Exhibitions: London, Royal Academy, 1824, No. 95
Literature: Waagen 1854, Vol. 3, p.37; Leslie ed. Hamlyn 1978, pp. 28–38

C. R. Leslie was one of a group of American artists drawn to London by its growing stature as a centre for the arts. Although actually born in London, he spent much of his childhood in his father's home city of Philadelphia. After showing artistic promise he returned to study in London on the proceeds of a subscription, arriving in 1811 with an introduction to Benjamin West. Once established in London his circle of American friends and fellow artists included Washington Allston and Washington Irving, through whom he met both Sir Walter Scott and Samuel Taylor Coleridge. His early works ranged from portraiture to history painting, but he came to be particularly associated with works such as the example displayed here.

Many of Leslie's most memorable paintings are taken from the central canon of Molière, Sterne, Shakespeare and Cervantes. The present picture was commissioned by George O'Brien Wyndham, 3rd Earl of Egremont, who gave Leslie complete freedom in the choice of subject. Egremont's regard for Leslie forged a close bond between the ageing peer and the artist: Leslie and his family often spent periods of a month or more as Egremont's guests at his home, Petworth House, in Sussex, along with other favoured artists, such as Jones, Haydon, Constable, Phillips, Beechey and, of course, Turner.

Petworth with its rich historic associations, paintings and decorative objects, and its unconventional artistic milieu proved the stimulus for many of Leslie's paintings. In this pic-

J. Constable, *The Leaping Horse*, 1825. Cat. No. 400

ture for example, Sir Francis Chantrey, a sculptor also of the Petworth circle, posed for the figure of Sancho Panza. Egremont, however, was not typical of Leslie's patrons, who by and large came from the class of newly rich industrialists, for whom Leslie's scenes drawn from everyday life and from the most familiar and accessible works of literature had an obvious appeal.

Leslie went on to paint many other scenes from Don Quixote, but it was this picture that was his most successful. When it was exhibited at the Royal Academy in 1824 one critic hailed it as 'the "Sancho" and will remain the stock squire for a thousand years'. Leslie painted at least three versions, including one for the poet Samuel Rogers (Cat. No. 433) and that for Robert Vernon which is now in the Tate Gallery. **IW**

Sir Charles Lock Eastlake
Plymouth 1793–1865 Pisa

398 *(illus. p. 467)*
The Champion, 1824

Oil on canvas, 122.5×174 cm
Inscribed and dated: ROME 1824
Birmingham, Museums and Art Gallery
Inv. No. P15'56
Provenance: Christie's, 28 May 1923, Lot 136; Henry Astley Ltd., Birmingham (Theatrical Costumiers); purchased from Messrs. Collins, Birmingham, 1956
Exhibitions: London, British Institution, 1825, No. 193; Plymouth, 1965–66, Cat. No. 8

Literature: Boase 1959, p. 171, Plate 65b; Birmingham 1960, p. 48; Robertson 1978, p. 25, Fig. 13

Eastlake lived in Italy until 1830, painting landscape and figure subjects which he began to submit to the Royal Academy and British Institution from 1823. *The Champion* was exhibited with this description: 'Near a castle occupied by the descendants of the Normans in Sicily a Knight is preparing to follow the enemy's herald to the scene of action, and receives a scarf from a lady.' Lady Eastlake, in a published memoir of her husband, remarked that it 'gave him the opportunity of painting armour, of which he always felt the picturesque capacities.' Haydon praised the painting for its bold colour and simplicity, calling it 'Titianesque', much to Eastlake's delight. **SGW**

J. M. W. Turner, *England: Richmond Hill on the Prince Regent's Birthday,* 1819. Cat. No. 392

James Ward
London 1769–1859 Cheshunt

399 *(illus. p. 458)*
Marengo, 1824

Oil on canvas, 81×109.2 cm
Signed and dated: J. Ward, R.A. 1824
Alnwick Castle, His Grace the Duke of
Northumberland
Provenance: Dukes of Northumberland
Exhibitions: London, Royal Academy, 1826,
No. 219; Royal Academy, 1951–52, No. 126;
Tate Gallery, 1959, Cat.No. 372; Richmond,
Virginia, 1960, No. 51; Detroit and
Philadelphia, 1968, Cat.No. 111
Literature: Phipps Jackson 1893, pp. 306–07;
Frankau 1904, pp. 106, 129; Grundy 1909,
pp. 46, 57, 58, 71; Walker 1954, pp. 72–74

Napoleon's famous horse Marengo was
named after the town in northern Italy where
his master first rode him, in battle against the
Austrians in 1800. Having survived Austerlitz,
Jena, Wagram and the retreat from Russia, he
was captured by the British at Waterloo and
brought to London by Lord Petre. By the time
Ward's picture was lithographed, in 1824, he
belonged to Captain Howard. Afterwards he
was bought by John Julius Angerstein, the
banker and collector, and kept at New Barnes,

near Ely, Cambridgeshire, where he died,
aged about thirty-eight, in 1831. In Ward's picture he is seen in a sombre and wasted landscape, which the painter's full title in the
Academy exhibition described as 'Emblematic
of his Master's Downfall'.

The son of a drunken warehouse keeper,
and largely self-taught as a painter, Ward had
shown his first bloodstock portrait in 1809.
Such training as he received was mainly in
mezzotint engraving – in 1794 he rose to
become mezzotint engraver to the Prince of
Wales – and he had been able to learn something of oil painting in the studio of his
brother-in-law, George Morland, as well as
through studying and copying the old
masters, especially Rubens whose influence
on his landscapes and historical compositions
was immense.

His large subject paintings were often over
ambitious, and his animal pictures are certainly his finest works. Like George Stubbs,
he studied animal anatomy, and could endow
his portraits with both perfection of physical
structure and nobility and character of expression. The portrait of Marengo was painted
during his period of most active involvement
in the 'grand department' of horse painting, in
1824, and was included in the series of fourteen
lithographs of *Celebrated Horses* published in
1823 and 1824 (Cat. No. 421). **DBB**

John Constable
East Bergholt 1776–1837 London

400 *(illus. p. 455)*
The Leaping Horse, 1825

Oil on canvas, 142×187.3 cm
London, Royal Academy of Arts
Provenance: William Taunton; his sale,
Christie's, 16 May 1846, Lot 42, bought in;
Christie's, 27 May 1849, Lot 111, bought in;
Charles Birch; his sale, Christie's, 7 July
1853, Lot 41, bought Ernst Gambart;
Charles Pemberton by 1863; Charles
Sartorious, whose wife presented it to the
Royal Academy, 1889
Exhibitions: London, Royal Academy, 1825,
No. 224; Tate Gallery, 1976, Cat. No. 238;
Munich, 1979, Cat. No. 353; London, Royal
Academy, 1982, Cat. No. 7; Washington,
1983, Cat. No. 32; Madrid, 1988–89, Cat.
No. 55; London, Tate Gallery, 1991, Cat.
No. 162
Literature: Smart and Brooks 1976, pp.
102–07, 139, Plate 60; Fleming-Williams
1976, p. 86, Fig. 60; Walker 1979, pp. 116–18,
Plates 32, 34; Rosenthal 1983, pp. 162–70,
245, Figs. 202–05; Reynolds 1984, No. 25. 1,
Plate 572; Cormack 1986, pp. 167–69, Plate
165; Rosenthal 1987, pp. 144–47; Plates
136–37; Fleming-Williams 1990, pp. 198, 295

J. M. W. Turner, *London*, 1809. Cat. No. 385

Constable decided early in his career that the landscape of Suffolk, where he had grown up and which was full of personal and associative meanings for him, would form the subject of his art. In 1821 he wrote of the area, 'the sound of water escaping from mill-dams, etc., willows, old rotten planks, slimy posts, and brickwork, I love such things . . . As long as I do paint, I shall never cease to paint such places . . . Those scenes made me a painter and I am grateful.'

The culmination of Constable's dedication to this landscape were the series of six-foot canvases, painted in London, which he sent to the Royal Academy for exhibition. These partly constituted a campaign for full membership of the Academy, but they also championed the legitimacy of landscape painting. In the academic hierarchies of art, landscape ranked lowest, even below portraiture and genre. History painting was placed highest,

and by making pictures such as *The Leaping Horse* the same large size as historical subjects were usually painted, Constable was challenging traditional perceptions.

The Leaping Horse is the last and perhaps most evocative of Constable's big Stour scenes. It shows Float Jump, upstream of Flatford, a barrier across the towpath to prevent cattle straying, and it also marked the border between Suffolk and Essex. Barge horses were forced to jump over it. Unusually for Constable, the picture was painted almost entirely from memory, instead of drawings, which was his normal practice. **RU**

Sir Edwin Henry Landseer
London 1803–1873 London

401 *(illus. p. 466)*
The Hunting of Chevy Chase, 1825–26

Oil on canvas, 143×170.8 cm
Birmingham, Museums and Art Gallery
Inv. No. P2'52
Provenance: commissioned by the 6th Duke of Bedford; Bedford sale, Christie's, 19 January 1951, Lot 186; National Art-Collections Fund, by whom presented 1952
Exhibitions: Royal Academy, 1826, No. 292; British Institution, 1827, No. 36; Royal Academy, 1951–52, Cat. No. 145; Tate Gallery, 1959, Cat. No. 240; Paris, 1972, Cat. No. 153; Philadelphia and London, 1981–82, Cat. No. 23
Literature: Boase 1959, pp. 167–68, Plate 25a; Birmingham 1960, p. 86, Plate 33a

J. Ward, *Marengo*, 1824. Cat. No. 399

E. Landseer, *The Old Shepherd's Chief Mourner*, 1837. Cat. No. 409

PAINTINGS AND SCULPTURE

J. Martin, *Joshua commanding the Sun to stand still*, 1816. Cat. No. 390

The third and youngest son of the engraver John Landseer (1769–1852), Edwin showed a precocious talent for drawing, especially animals, whose anatomy he studied in Haydon's informal 'school' before becoming a Royal Academy student (one of the youngest ever) in 1816. His first major paintings were also animal subjects, culminating in *The Cat's Paw*, shown at the British Institution in 1824; this unpleasantly realistic image of a monkey coercing a cat into fetching red-hot chestnuts off a stove attracted considerable attention and controversy.

A visit in Scotland in 1824 left an enduring impression on the artist. The wild scenery of the Highlands, to which he would return every autumn, soon became a regular, then a dominating, feature of his subsequent painting, in such famous works as *The Monarch of the Glen*, completed in 1851.

Chevy Chase is a well-known ballad of the Borders (the land between England and Scotland), and was published in Thomas Percy's celebrated *Reliques of Ancient English Poetry* in 1765. It describes the rivalry between Earl Percy of Northumberland and the Scottish Earl Douglas, centring on a hunt across disputed land: this led to a pitched battle in which both leaders and many of their men were killed. A surviving oil sketch suggests that Landseer may have intended a pendant battle scene, with *The Hunting of Chevy Chase* remaining essentially a sporting subject, as preferred by his patron, the Duke of Bedford. Its scale and drama owe a good deal to seventeenth-century Flemish painting, and there are direct references to works by Snyders and Rubens. **SGW**

Clarkson Frederick Stanfield
Sunderland 1793–1867 London

402 *(illus. p. 462)*
Market Boat on the Scheldt, 1826

Oil on mahogany panel, 82.9×126.4 cm
Signed and dated on barrel at left:
C STANFIELD 1826

London, Trustees of the Victoria and Albert Museum
Inv. No. FA189
Provenance: Sir Francis Freeling; his sale, Christie's, 15 April 1837, No. 91, bought Smith; John Sheepshanks, by whom presented in 1857
Exhibitions: London, British Institution 1826, No. 102; Sunderland 1979, pp. 93–94, Cat. No. 131, Plate 2
Literature: Parkinson 1990, pp. 270–71

Stanfield achieved a huge reputation during the nineteenth century as one of the greatest English landscape painters. He was born into a theatrical family in the north of England and spent his adolescent years at sea in the merchant service and then in the navy, into which he was press-ganged, before going on to make his name as a scene painter. After a number of engagements with the smaller London theatres, he took employment at the Theatre Royal, Drury Lane, early in 1823. For over twenty years his set designs were to be one of the principal attractions in any new production; his name appears on playbills in typeface

D. Wilkie, *Chelsea Pensioners reading the Waterloo Despatch*, 1822. Cat. No. 394

bigger than that used for the actors, and almost as large as that of the author.

It was during the 1820s that Stanfield began to exhibit oil paintings at the British Institution and the Royal Academy. This view of the Scheldt resulted from a tour of Belgium, Germany and Holland in 1823 and was one of several pictures of this scenery Stanfield painted in the following years. It was among the first of his works to be reviewed by the art critics, who were quick to note that Stanfield's skill in this field equalled his talent in the theatrical sphere. One aspect of Stanfield's easel paintings which is evident in this canvas, and which was remarked upon at the time, is the vivid clarity and brilliance of his realism. John Ruskin was particularly impressed by the verisimilitude of Stanfield's depictions of the sea and championed his pictures in the first volume of *Modern Painters* (1843).

Stanfield was keen that his pictures should retain their qualities of light and colour and preferred to paint with brighter tones, anticipating the darkening effects of time. He also chose not to use the standard heavy varnish for his pictures, a decision possibly based on an understanding of the reflective nature of paint when seen under artificial light.

Sir David Wilkie
Cults 1785–Gibraltar 1841

403
The Pifferari, 1827

Oil on canvas, 46×36.2 cm
Signed and dated: D Wilkie Roma 1827
London, H.M. Queen Elizabeth II
Provenance: King George IV
Exhibitions: London, Royal Academy, 1829, No. 298; British Institution, 1842; New Haven and Raleigh, 1987, Cat. No. 27
Literature: Cunningham 1843, Vol. 2, pp. 194, 414, 424; Vol. 3, pp. 4, 524; Millar 1969, pp. 138–39

Following a severe breakdown in his health in 1825, at the very peak of his career, Wilkie went on a long European tour to rest and recover. He travelled in Italy, Spain, northern and central Europe, at first doing no painting but observing continental life and traditions, and studying the old masters, with his unusually keen and sympathetic eye. When he began to paint again, in Italy, it was on a smaller scale and with greater immediacy. Instead of preparing numerous drawings and sketches, he worked directly on his final canvas with a looser and more painterly touch.

The Pifferari, which helped to announced his new style to the Academy audience, was one of four subjects of religious life in Rome – an aspect of Italian life that greatly interested him – painted while he was abroad. He worked on it probably between December 1826 and April 1827. On his first arrival in 1825 he had written excitedly of the arrival in Rome of 'Multitudes of pilgrims from all parts of Italy ... in costumes remarkably fine and poetical ... accompanied by one whose duty is to give music to the rest ... a piper, or pifferaro, provided with an immense bagpipe ... while another man plays on a smaller reed.'

Unpretentious though it is, Wilkie's picture nevertheless subtly blends direct recording – as in the pipers on the left – with a nobility of composition taken from the old masters – exemplified by the supplicants kneeling in prayer on the right, who might have stepped from a Titian or a Veronese. *The Pifferari* was bought by George IV, together with another of Wilkie's Roman subjects, *Roman Princess washing the Feet of Pilgrims* (likewise still in the Royal Collection), for £420. **DBB**

A. W. Callcott, *The Entrance to the Pool of London*, 1816. Cat. No. 389

Benjamin Robert Haydon
Plymouth 1786-London 1846

404 *(illus. p. 465)*
The Mock Election 1827

Oil on canvas, 144.8×185.4 cm
London, H.M. Queen Elizabeth II
Provenance: King George IV
Exhibitions: London, Egyptian Hall, 1828
Literature: Haydon 1828; Millar 1969, pp.
48–49, No. 829, Plate 297

Haydon was at once one of the most celebrated and least materially successful artists of his generation. Critic, pamphleteer, brilliant diarist and campaigner for improved art education and state support for the arts as well as painter, he was at the centre of London cultural life for thirty years. His fame spread to the Continent, Goethe being among the many great contemporaries who were persuaded by Haydon's genius for self-promotion. 'I am

adapted to great national work, to illustrate a National triumph or a moral principle,' Haydon once declared with characteristic lack of modesty, but his commitment to history painting in the grand manner won little patronage in an age increasingly devoted to the more modest and accessible subjects popularised by Wilkie, his old friend and fellow student at the Royal Academy. Under financial pressure Haydon was obliged to attempt more popular work directed at the taste Wilkie had created.

In June 1827 Haydon was for the second time imprisoned for debt in the King's Bench Prison. Before being released at the end of July he saw the prisoners, who had organised a college that arranged entertainments and masquerades, enact a mock election. The inmates formed a procession, headed by self-appointed officials, to open a poll for the election of two members to plead for their rights in the House of Commons. Deeply moved by the spectacle of the prisoners 'forgetting their sorrows at the humour, the wit, the absurdity

of what was before them the finest subject for humour and pathos on earth', Haydon worked quickly to record the scene as he recalled it, including portraits of fellow inmates. Conscious of the precedent of William Hogarth's London prison scenes, he displays an ironic, essentially urban wit in contrast to the sentiment and coy humour often evoked by contemporary genre painters. 'What a set of beings are assembled in that extraordinary place! – that Temple of Idleness and debauchery!' he wrote of the King's Bench. 'Good God! When you walk amongst them, you get amongst faces that are all marked by some decided expression, quite different from people you meet in the street.'

Besides being a remarkable revelation of the survival of the human spirit in a bleak corner of the metropolitan underworld, the picture must be seen in the context of the pressure for reform at this period. The issues of the franchise in general and of prisoners' rights in particular are clear enough, and Haydon intensifies the propaganda by alluding to his own

C. F. Stanfield, *Market Boat on the Scheldt*, 1826. Cat. No. 402

problem, imprisonment for debt. Among the crowd is a 'good family in affliction', the father holding an account in which unpaid legal costs vastly exceed paid debt; banners proclaim 'The Liberty of the Subject' and 'No Bailiffs'. In fact imprisonment for debt remained an evil for a number of years, and Charles Dickens was to spend much time attacking it. It was curtailed in 1842, and largely abolished in 1869.

Unsold after its exhibition at the Egyptian Hall, the picture was bought by King George IV for 500 guineas, a triumph for the painter in one of his darkest hours. **DBB**

William Etty
York 1787–1849 York

405 *(illus. p. 468)*
Sleeping Nymph and Satyrs, 1828

Oil on canvas 129.5 × 178.4 cm
London, Royal Academy of Arts
Provenance: presented by the artist to the Royal Academy as his diploma work, 1828
Exhibitions: London, Arts Council, 1962, Cat. No. 11
Literature: Gilchrist 1855, pp. 252–53; Farr 1958, pp. 54, 154, No. 85

Etty was the outstanding painter of the nude working in Britain in the first half of the century. Like Haydon, he had set himself first to paint history pictures in the grand style advocated by Reynolds, founded on the tradition of the old masters, but his commitment to moral themes and to the formal rules of classicism were tempered from the first by a love of the human body, above all the female form. As he wrote in his autobiography, he had found

'God's most glorious work to be WOMAN'.

Although he returned at the end of his life to his native York, he spent most of his career in London. His paintings were hugely popular, although they sometimes proved controversial for their frank portrayal of the naked body. A lifelong student and for many years a teacher in the Royal Academy life class, he brought to his art a full understanding of the structure and motions of the body, in addition to superb technical skill.

This picture, presented to the Academy as his diploma piece after he had been elected full Academician (having defeated Constable in the election), confirmed the essential characteristics of his art. It is a synthesis of favourite old masters, being based in part on Poussin's *Nymphs surprised by a Satyr* – of which a poor version is in the National Gallery – and on Titian's *Venus del Prado*. Etty has realised the design with his customary delight in the languid pose and soft texture of human flesh, and in rich and juicy paint whose warm colour and exuberant handling adds to the sensual and even erotic effect. **DBB**

PAINTINGS AND SCULPTURE

J. Stark, *Lambeth looking towards Westminster Bridge*, 1818. Cat. No. 391

Benjamin Robert Haydon
Plymouth 1786–1846 London

406 *(illus. p. 464)*
Punch, or May Day 1829

Oil on canvas, 150.5×185.1 cm
London, Tate Gallery
Inv. No. T.G.N00682
Provenance: Dr. George Darling, by whom
bequeathed to the National Gallery, 1862;
transferred to the Tate Gallery
Exhibitions: London, Western Bazaar, 1830
Literature: Haydon 1926, Vol. 2, pp.
465–66; Olney 1952, pp. 178–79; George
1967, pp. 158, 165–66, 187–89, 362, 364, 378

Haydon was a true lover of London, passionately devoted to his adopted city. He called it
'the city of the world our Babylon'; the sight
of it, shrouded by its inevitable canopy of
smoke, filled him 'with feelings of energy such
as no other spectacle could inspire'. He
planned this synoptic view of its citizens on a
festive day as a 'moral Satire', and thought it
'should rather be called "Life"'. He had

thought he might depict Ludgate Hill in the
City, but in the end chose a spot in the West
End near Marylebone church.

The occasion is a public holiday, and Haydon has assembled a rich variety of metropolitan types, treated with a certain comic
exaggeration. The focus is a Punch and Judy
show. A farmer, up from the country, watches
absorbed while a pickpocket rifles his pockets,
aided by an accomplice who tries to engage the
victim in conversation; a Bow Street police-
man moves in to intercept. A street sweeper, a
soldier and a sailor on leave, and a nursemaid
with a child also watch the show, but an apple
girl has fallen asleep over her stall. On the right
chimney sweeps are engaged in May Day re-
vels, led by a costumed Jack-in-the-Green and
his lady. Beyond, a funeral cortège and a wedding coach drive by; two dandies look down
from their horses; and an Italian image seller
fails to find buyers for his small casts after
antique statues.

Haydon intended this densely packed
assemblage as a hymn to metropolitan life, and
hoped it would be bought by George IV. But
although the king sent for it, he returned it,
thinking it overcrowded. **DBB**

John Constable
East Bergholt 1776–1837 London

407 *(illus. p. 453)*
Hampstead Heath with London in the Distance, *c.* 1827–30

Oil on canvas, 64.1×94.6 cm
Private Collection
Provenance: private collector, Pennsylvania;
sold American Art Association; Anderson
Galleries, New York, 8 April 1937, bought
Braus Galleries; John Phelan senior, Texas;
Margaret Phelan Reed; Peggy Reed;
Salander-O'Reilly Galleries, New York,
from whom bought by the present owners
Exhibitions: London, Thomas Agnew and
Sons Ltd., 1989, Cat. No. 9; London, Tate
Gallery, 1991, Cat. No. 128

While the landscape of his native Suffolk continued to be the mainstay and focus of his art,
after 1817 Constable returned there only for
brief visits and made London his home. From
1819 to 1826 Constable kept up a house in
central London, but spent his summers in

B. R. Haydon, *Punch, or May Day,* 1829. Cat. No. 406

rented properties at Hampstead, then a small village on the outskirts of the metropolis. In 1827 he made a more permanent move there, leasing 6 Well Walk and renting out part of his house in town. The move was precipitated by his wife's poor health, but Constable found Hampstead an ideal location, both for its proximity to London and, as he wrote to his friend Fisher, because 'I can get always away from idle callers – and above all see nature – & unite a town and country life.'

Constable found much to stimulate him artistically in Hampstead; he began making oil sketches of sky effects and clouds, and he resumed his practice for a time of painting some works to an almost finished standard on the spot. He also painted the views from Hampstead Hill. This view across Hampstead Heath to London is that from the garden of his house in Well Walk. It is a more refined version of a smaller oil sketch he had made in the open air probably in the first summer he was at the house; he exhibited a finished version of the composition at the Royal Academy in 1830. Two of London's landmarks can be identified on the horizon; to the left the dome of St. Paul's Cathedral, and further to the right, Westminster Abbey. **RU**

John Constable
East Bergholt 1776–1837 London

408 *(illus. p. 471)*
Salisbury Cathedral from the Meadows, *c.* 1829–31

Oil on canvas, 135.8 × 188 cm
London, Guildhall Art Gallery, Corporation of London
Provenance: ? the artist's administrators . . .
Charles Gassiot, by whom bequeathed to the Guildhall Art Gallery, 1902
Exhibitions: London, Tate Gallery, 1991, Cat. No. 209

B. R. Haydon, *The Mock Election*, 1827. Cat. No. 404

Literature: Cormack 1986, p. 205; Rosenthal 1987, p. 190; Fleming-Williams 1990, p. 237

Constable's most ambitious claims for his own vision of landscape were made in his series of large paintings known from their size as 'six-footers'. Exhibited in London from 1819, they maintained before the public a view of nature which, as a result of the artist's mission to assert the independent legitimacy and moral justification of pure landscape, had ironically lost touch with his original naturalistic impulses. Prepared from full-scale oil sketches after long meditation, involving considerable adaptation of material gathered on the spot for compositional effect, and increasingly impassioned and highly wrought in execution, they were heroic set-pieces in which the English landscape and its occupants func-

tioned almost as vehicles for a kind of natural history painting.

During the 1830s Constable's energies were increasingly taken up in the production, with David Lucas, of his series of characteristic images of *English Landscape Scenery* (Cat. No. 423), and he sent fewer large oils to exhibitions. *Salisbury Cathedral from the Meadows,* shown in 1831 (the Dowager Lady Ashton of Hyde, on loan to the National Gallery, London), was one of these, and perhaps the most magnificent of all Constable's 'six-footers'. Salisbury was the home and workplace of Constable's most loyal friend and patron, Archdeacon John Fisher, who was to die in 1832, and it was while on his last visits to him in 1829 that Constable made a start on the subject that Fisher himself – with questionable meaning – called the 'Church under a Cloud'.

Through oil sketches – of which this was the largest, on the scale of the picture, and was itself probably painted or at least begun in Salisbury – Constable prepared the final subject, which shows the great cathedral heroically transfigured, illuminated by lightning and a rainbow that marks the passing of a storm.

Some critics have seen the reference to the 'Church under a Cloud' as a political or social comment – Constable feared and opposed the reform movement and all it implied for traditions of church and state. Others, perhaps more convincingly, have interpreted the passing storm and bright rainbow as marking Constable's own sense of regeneration and hope, rooted in strong religious faith, following prolonged despair after the death of his wife in 1828. **DBB**

E. H. Landseer, *The Hunting of Chevy Chase*, 1825–26. Cat. No. 401

Sir Edwin Landseer
London 1803–1873 London

409 *(illus. p. 458)*
The Old Shepherd's Chief Mourner, 1837

Oil on canvas, 45.7×61 cm
London, Trustees of the Victoria and Albert Museum
Inv. No. FA93
Provenance: purchased from the artist by John Sheepshanks and presented to the Victoria and Albert Museum, London, 1857

Exhibitions: London, Royal Academy, 1837, No. 112; Dublin, 1865, No. 19; London, Royal Academy, 1968–69, Cat. No. 231; Paris, 1972, No. 155; London, Arts Council, 1978, Cat. No. 25; Munich, 1979, Cat. No. 364; London, Tate Gallery, 1982, Cat. No. 66
Literature: Manson 1902, pp. 89–91, reproduced; Reynolds 1966, pp. 15, 20, 27, Fig. 8; Lennie 1976, pp. 83, 91, 130, 131, 149

Landseer became one of the most successful British artists of the nineteenth century, his finely painted pictures of animals which display human emotions and sentiments per-

fectly matching contemporary taste and enjoying popularity with public, patrons and critics. His abilities were quickly recognised; he was elected an Associate of the Royal Academy at twenty four, the earliest possible age, and he became a full Academician in 1831. He secured important patrons, most notably Queen Victoria and the royal family; in 1850 he was knighted. Landseer always suffered from nervous anxiety, but in later life his mind gave way and he died in a lunatic asylum.

Animals had formed the chief subject for his art from the earliest years, particularly dogs. He took great care to ensure the animals he depicted were painted with anatomical exacti-

C. L. Eastlake, *The Champion*, 1824. Cat. No. 398

tude, in his youth, dissecting carcasses and regularly visiting the Exeter 'Change menagerie. Yet his subjects where made appealing by the character with which he invested them. *Blackwood's Magazine* wrote in 1840, 'His are not mere animals; they tell a story. You see them not only alive, but you see their biography, and know what they do, and if the expression be allowed, what they think.'

The Old Shepherd's Chief Mourner was one of Landseer's most famous pictures. It conveys in a simple yet moving and original way the devotion of the dog, the humble, solitary life of its departed master, and the harsh truth that it is the animal only who will truly mourn the shepherd's passing. **RU**

William Mulready
Ennis, Ireland 1786–1863 London

410
Open your Mouth and shut your Eyes, 1838

Oil on panel, 31.5 × 30.2 cm
London, Trustees of the Victoria and Albert Museum
Inv. No. FA143
Provenance: purchased from the artist by John Sheepshanks, 1838, and presented to the Victoria and Albert Museum, London, 1857
Exhibitions: London, Royal Academy, 1839, No. 143; Society of Arts, 1848, No. 48; South Kensington Museum, 1864, No. 79; Victoria and Albert Museum, 1986, Cat. No. 135
Literature: Heleniac 1980, pp. 130–32, 212–13, No. 145; Pointon 1986, pp. 106, 165; Parkinson 1990, pp. 202–04

Born in Ireland, Mulready and his family moved to London during his childhood, where he later studied at the Royal Academy and under John Varley. Although he experimented in his early career with historical subjects, landscape and portraiture, it was Mulready's genre scenes, influenced by Dutch art of the seventeenth century, which made him immensely popular with the public.

Open your Mouth and shut your Eyes is a subject which derives from a childhood game and saying, 'Open your eyes, shut your mouth and see what Providence will send you.' The complying recipient will then have something put into their mouth, usually something pleasant. Mulready's treatment of his subject has clear erotic overtones, as Pointon has noted. The contemporary public would have realised the game's *risqué* connotations, exacerbated by the girl's bare shoulders and forearms. This reading was without doubt intended by Mulready, who knew 'covertly exciting ... female beauty and innocence will be much talked about and sell well.' **RU**

W. Etty, *Sleeping Nymph and Satyrs*, 1828. Cat. No. 405

William Mulready

411 *(illus. p. 471)*
The Seven Ages of Man, 1836–38

Oil on canvas, 89.5 × 113.4 cm
London, Trustees of the Victoria and Albert
Museum
Inv. No. FA138
Provenance: purchased from the artist by
John Sheepshanks, 1839, and presented to
the Victoria and Albert Museum, 1857
Exhibitions: London, Royal Academy, 1838,
No. 122; Society of Arts, 1848, No. 26;
South Kensington Museum, 1864, Cat. No.
78; Tate Gallery, 1959, Cat. No. 264;
Bristol, 1977; London, Victoria and Albert
Museum, 1986, Cat. No. 118
Literature: Heleniac 1980, pp. 135–36,
213–14, No. 148; Pointon 1986, pp. 71, 99,
134–35; Parkinson 1990, pp. 198–99

The Seven Ages of Man was Mulready's only
attempt to paint a large-scale allegorical subject, as opposed to the purely genre pictures he
had attempted previously. It was also his first
and only attempt at a Shakespearean scene,
which were at that time highly popular both
with public and patrons alike, and which other
contemporary artists keenly contributed to
the market. Mulready illustrates the speech
made by Jacques in Act II, Scene 7 of *As You
Like It*, which begins 'All the world's a stage,
and all the men and women merely players:
They have their exits and their entrances; and
one man in his time plays many parts, His acts
being seven ages.' Each of the seven ages are
depicted: infancy, boyhood, youth, adult-
hood, middle age, old age and finally the 'Last
scene of all, That ends this strange eventful
history, Is second childishness and mere oblivion, Sans teeth, sans eyes, sans taste, sans
everything.'

Whilst Mulready's composition is not as
tautly constructed as his genre scenes, the picture attracted good reviews when it was first
exhibited at the Royal Academy. William
Thackeray writing as 'Michael Angelo Tit-
marsh' hailed Mulready as a king. It was purchased by the collector John Sheepshanks
(1784–1863), whose gift of his large collection
of pictures in 1857 formed the corpus of the
collection of British art in the South Kensington Museum, later the Victoria and Albert
Museum. **RU**

C. L. Eastlake, *The Colosseum from the Campo Vaccino*, 1822. Cat. No. 395

Daniel Maclise
Cork 1806–1870 London

412
Scene from Twelfth Night, *c.* 1840

Oil on canvas, 73.7×124.5 cm
London, Tate Gallery
Provenance: Robert Vernon, by whom
bequeathed to the National Gallery;
subsequently transferred to the Tate Gallery
Exhibitions: London, Royal Academy, 1840,
No. 381; . . . London, National Portrait
Gallery and Dublin, 1972, Cat. No. 76
Literature: Ormond 1968, p. 692

Maclise came to London from his native Ireland in 1827 to study at the Royal Academy
Schools. He made his mark during the 1830s as
a painter of literary portraits and of scenes of
literature, drama and frivolous genre. He later
turned also to history painting, and in his
breadth and variety of subject matter he would
emerge as the quintessential Victorian artist.
As a narrative painter he followed broadly in
the footsteps of Wilkie, usually conceiving
even the grandest and most serious of historical subjects in terms of domestic drama. His
style was slick and brilliant, and his fluent imagination sometimes overflowed into compositions that were over-crowded or exaggerated in gesture and expression. During the
1840s his style matured and became more con-

trolled under the influence of French and German painting, to which he turned in the
absence of suitable models in British art.

This painting was a much more successful
reworking of the theme Maclise had chosen
for his first Academy exhibit in 1829, *Malvolio
affecting the Count*. Malvolio, absurd and
foppish, plays up to Olivia and her companion, Maria. Here Maclise's grasp of composition and technique have improved almost
beyond recognition. Experience of the
London theatre has enabled him to construct
what is essentially a stage set, with subtle
characterisation and elegant and detailed execution. It was greatly admired by the actor
Macready, who was with Dickens among the
painter's earliest London friends. **DBB**

F. Danby, *Disappointed Love*, 1821. Cat. No. 393

William Dyce

Aberdeen 1806–1864 London

413

Joash shooting the Arrow of Deliverance, 1844

Oil on canvas, 77.6×110.4 cm
Hamburg, Kunsthalle
Inv. No. 1841
Provenance: purchased from the artist by G. C. Schwabe
Exhibitions: Royal Academy, 1844, No. 284; Royal Academy 1871, No. 99
Literature: Pointon 1797, pp. 72–79, 195; Vaughan 1979, pp. 199, 200, 236, 238, 239

The death of William Dyce in 1864 was noted in the minutes of the Royal Scottish Academy, who described him as 'one of the most remarkable men connected with the art of the present century; one whose learning, accomplishment, genius and artistic power would have secured for him a distinguished place in the art annals of any country.' Such fulsome praise would not have been felt contentious, for Dyce's clear artistic abilities were combined with lively and perceptive ideas about art education, industrial ornament and design, the National Gallery, architecture, religiosity and much else that placed him at the centre of many of the issues faced by the early Victorian art world. Following his publication of a leaflet which examined the role of art education and the function of design in art and industry, and called for a practical arrangement along Continental lines of design training, in 1838 Dyce was appointed first Superintendent of the School of Design. In its premises in Somer-

set House, the School was the only government sponsored institution for art education. Dyce proved a highly effective administrator, organising specialised training for differing crafts, but his time as Superintendent was beset by argument and controversy which centred upon the need for design students to study life drawing. Dyce considered the practice irrelevant except to those who would need to depict the human form, but this viewpoint was bitterly contested by some members of the artistic establishment, most notably Benjamin Robert Haydon. Amidst this criticism Dyce resigned his post in 1843, returning to painting full-time, having been able to complete little work during his busy years at the School of Design.

Dyce marked the resumption of his painting career with *Joash shooting the Arrow of Deliverance* which he exhibited at the Royal

J. Constable, *Salisbury Cathedral from the Meadows*, c. 1828–31. Cat. No. 408

W. Mulready, *The Seven Ages of Man*, 1836–38. Cat. No. 411

W. Dyce, *Joash shooting the Arrow of Deliverance*, 1844. Cat. No. 413

Academy in 1844, prompting *The Art Union* to praise him as 'one of the few British painters who may be described as learned – one of the few who consider it as much their duty to read and think as draw and paint.' *Joash* displays all the precision of detail and austerity of line for which Dyce was famous. On his visits to Italy in his youth Dyce had come to know the Nazarenes, becoming the friend of Franz Overbeck, and their commitment to religious subjects and purity of drawing echoed and perhaps developed his own. Such a rigorous linearity was first manifested in England with Flaxman, whose work was subsequently to influence the development of art in Germany. Under the influence of German painting in Britain felt during the 1830s and '40s, a new generation of British artists responded again to this style.

Joash shooting the Arrow of Deliverance illustrates 2 Kings XIII: 14–17. Joash, King of the Israelites, visits the prophet Elisha on his death bed, asking how to rid his country of the Syrians. Elisha tells him to fire an arrow eastwards through the window, and promises him that this will guarantee Israel's victory over Syria; Joash's actions with the bow bring about the promised victory, but not the complete annihilation of the Syrians Elisha had hoped for. Dyce rejects the narrative potential of his subject for a controlled and concentrated design, with taut lines and an enclosing space in which youth and vigour are contrasted with age and frailty.

A devout Christian, Dyce painted many religious subjects during his career, and he was an authority on church ritual and music. In 1850 he apparently persuaded John Ruskin to look at and study the Pre-Raphaelites for the first time, and also responded to them in his own work. Dyce executed a number of murals for the new Palace of Westminster, and also for Prince Albert at Osborne House. His interests were diverse, writing a prize winning essay on electro-magnetism in 1830 and in later life founding the Motett Society for early church music. **RU**

414

415

John Flaxman
York 1755–London 1836

414
Model for the monument to Barbara Lowther in Richmond Parish Church

Plaster, 116.2×66 cm
London, University College London
Inv. No. 107
Provenance: presented by Maria Denman, 1851
Exhibitions: London, Royal Academy, 1979, No. 130
Literature: Lyson 1811, Vol. 1. 1, p. 338; Croft-Murray 1939–40, p. 86; Whinney and Gunnis 1967, No. 107; Bindman 1979, p. 129, Fig. 130

John Flaxman, the son of a notable cast maker, was a figure whose fame and influence spanned Europe. He rose to fame during his years in Italy (1787–94) where part of his employment was as a designer for the Wedgwood firm. Here he produced his major graphic works illustrating Dante, Homer and Aeschylus which had an impact upon artists as diverse as Goya and Ingres. Brilliance as a designer and erudition as a classical scholar brought him the admiration, and even adulation, of many contemporary British artists of distinction.

On his return from Italy in 1794 he set up a

London workshop which was largely devoted to the production of monumental sculpture. The contents of his workshop, consisting of many of the casts and sketches which he produced for his studio, were given by his sister-in-law and heir to University College London in 1851.

This is not one of Flaxman's most original designs for funerary art. The standing mourner leaning against a pedestal was a frequently used convention of monumental sculpture in the period. Despite this, some care seems to have been taken to provide a design appropriate to the deceased and her relationship with the patron. Daniel Lyson observed in his *Environs of London* of 1811 that the monument had at its base a lily, '. . . one out of three blossoms being broken off'. This symbolised the fact that Barbara was the first of the three sisters to die. **MC**

John Flaxman

415
Monument to George Steevens, 1800

Marble, 173×108 cm
Signed on left edge of the inscription tablet: John Flaxman R.A. sculpt
London, Diocese of London, on loan to the Fitzwilliam Museum
Provenance: erected Poplar Chapel 1800
Exhibitions: London, Royal Academy, 1979, No. 124
Literature: Lyson 1811, Vol. 2. Part 2, p. 700; Reed Diaries 1946, p. 224; Croft-Murray 1939–40, p. 69; Bindman 1979, pp. 124–25

The celebrity of George Steevens, a noted Shakespearean scholar of the late eighteenth century, ensured that this was amongst the best known of Flaxman's smaller monumental compositions. Flaxman's account books record a payment of £100 made to the sculptor in August 1800 by Isaac Reed of Staples Inn. Reed was one of Steevens' closest friends who had assisted him in the publication of several of his editions of Shakespeare. This sum corresponds with Steevens' bequest to Reed, made as a token of friendship.

Isaac Reed's diary entry for 12 June 1800 records that he 'Went to Poplar Chapel with Mr. Flaxman the statuary, Mr. Long and Mr. Braithwaite to fix a place for Mr. Steevens monument.' It would seem, therefore, that the monument was set up by a group of Steevens' London friends including the surgeon, William Long and the amateur poet and post office official, Daniel Braithwaite.

Steevens was a colourful character who be-

came exceedingly eccentric in his old age. Always a gourmand, it is recorded that he purposefully finished his life by indulging in a bout of gluttony. It has been suggested that the particular pose of Flaxman's figure – with the nearest leg stretched out – reflects Steevens' admiration of his own 'remarkably handsome' legs. If this reference was intended, it would seem that the design of the monument retains a touch of the humour which was a characteristic of the London literary circles to which Steevens and Reed belonged. **MC**

Sir Francis Chantrey
Norton 1781–London 1841

416
Bust of Sir Benjamin West, P.R.A., *c.* 1818

Marble, 65×42×26 cm
Signed and dated on back; Chantrey. SC./ 1818. B. West P.R.A.
London, Royal Academy of Arts
Provenance: presented by the artist to the Royal Academy as his diploma work, 1818
Exhibitions: London, Royal Academy, 1818, No. 1104, plaster; Manchester, 1857, No. 149; Philadelphia, 1876; London, Royal Academy 1963, No. 232, 1968, No. 205
Literature: Whinney 1988, p. 422; Radcliffe 1969, p. 48; Fig. 15; Potts 1980, Fig. 11, p. 19

416

Francis Chantrey was the greatest entrepreneur of the London sculpture profession in the early nineteenth century. He was said to have left £150,000 at his death. A man of formidable intellect and great personal charm, he rose to dominate the London sculpture market from the humble origins of an apprentice carver in the environs of Sheffield. His London business was not dissimilar from that run by Joseph Nollekens (1737–1823), the greatest entrepreneur of the metropolitan sculpture profession of the late eighteenth century. The two sculptors knew and admired each other. Like Nollekens, Chantrey excelled at the production of animated portrait busts.

The court minutes of the Royal Academy record that Chantrey presented this bust to the Academy in December 1818, when West was entering his last year as president of the Academy. It is a version of a bust first exhibited in the Academy in 1811. Its exhibition together with those of Horne Took and J. R. Smith brought a flood of commissions and effectively launched his career. West recognised the talents of Chantrey while still in comparative obscurity and commissioned him to design a medal for presentation to the patrons of the British Institution upon their purchasing his massive painting of *Christ healing* in 1810. Chantrey's success at the Academy and the president's favour were vital in establishing the kudos upon which his commercial success was founded. He repaid this by leaving the Academy his fortune. **MC**

John Rossi
Nottingham 1762–London 1839

417
British Athlete, 1828

Marble, H 198 cm
Petworth, National Trust
Provenance: purchased by the 3rd Earl of Egremont, 1828
Exhibitions: Royal Academy, 1828
Literature: Kenworthy-Brown 1977, pp. 367–73; Pointon 1978, pp. 131–40

John Rossi, the son of an Italian merchant living in Nottingham, had a career of sharply varying fortunes. He received enough public acclaim to be awarded a number of commissions for great public monuments at St. Paul's and yet was on a number of occasions without employment or close to ruin.

The statue of a British athlete or boxer, completed in 1828, was one of two major commissions given to Rossi by the 3rd Earl of Egremont. It was placed in the Earl's famous north gallery at Petworth House. The 3rd Earl of Egremont was amongst the most important patrons of British statuary of the early nineteenth century. Despite the Earl's geniality towards artists, Rossi managed to irritate him by demanding further payments for his statue of the boxer. It was, not surprisingly, the last work he made for the Petworth collection.

Rossi's figure of the pugilist was first seen at the Academy in 1828. J. T. Smith, who saw it there, described it as 'truly vigorous and masterful'. The work publicly demonstrated Rossi's claim to technical virtuosity and anatomical knowledge. George Jones records that Chantrey described the carving of a freestanding athlete or boxer as 'the most difficult task in the art of sculpture'. As Pointon has shown, the physical prowess of professional boxers was fascinating to the artists of the Royal Academy in the period. Rossi was present at the meeting of a group of Academicians who posed the prize-fighter Gregson amongst the Elgin Marbles in 1808. As the title of his statue *athleta Britannicus* suggests, this fascination with contemporary British boxers was founded upon the patriotic notion that Britain could produce men of equal stature to the heroes of antiquity. The placement of the statue in a gallery which also contained Roman marbles, collected by the 3rd Earl's father, suggested the complementary idea that modern British sculptors were capable of attaining the artistry of ancients. **MC**

418

John Gibson
Conway 1790–Rome 1866

418
Narcissus, 1833?

Marble, 108 × 71 × 48 cm
Signed on right hand side of base:
IOANNIS GIBSON
London, Royal Academy of Arts
Provenance: mentioned in inventories of Gibson's studio received into the Royal Academy collection, 1868
Exhibitions: identical to diploma work exhibited Royal Academy, 1838, No. 1255
Literature: Eastlake 1870, p. 250; Matthews, 1911, pp. 83, 243; Hartmann, 1955, pp. 223–24; Fig. 17; Radcliffe, 1969, p. 48

Gibson spent the major part of his working life in Rome where he concentrated upon the production of statues or statue groups inspired by his reading of classical literature. Most of his work was sold to wealthy Englishmen visiting Rome for cultural edification. In Rome Gibson moved in the social milieu of Thorvaldsen and Canova, artistic contacts which are reflected in the style of his work.

Gibson rose from humble origins in Liverpool and was, like Chantrey, proud of having risen upon his own talents. Unlike Chantrey, however, he went to great lengths to disassociate himself from entrepreneurial values.

The statue of Narcissus is one of five made by the sculptor's workshop. Gibson's biographer, Matthews, records that the sculptor made the model for the statue after seeing a boy sitting on the edge of a fountain whilst walking in the Pincio. The first image was

419

made for Lord Barrington who paid £300 for the statue in February 1833. Gibson's account books record that a statue of Narcissus was made for presentation to the Academy at a cost of £160. This would appear to be the diploma work in the Academy collection signed by Gibson and dated 1838. The version of the statue exhibited here came into the Academy collection as part of the stock of Gibson's Italian workshop bequeathed to the Academy. It may be the statue made in 1833, which according to the sculptor's accounts were made 'on spec' without a client in mind. The sculptor either kept this version as his own or was unable to find a buyer for it. **MC**

William Blake
London 1757–1827 London

419
The Canterbury Pilgrims, *c.* 1810–20

Engraving, 35.5×97 cm, third state
Published by W. Blake, *c.* 1810–20
London, Trustees of the British Museum
Inv. No. 1846–2–9–326
Literature: Essick 1980, p. 188 passim;
Essick 1983, No. XVI, pp. 60–89, illustrated

One of the 'fresco' paintings shown at Blake's 1809–10 exhibition in Soho was *The Canterbury Pilgrims* (Pollok House, Glasgow), which was considered at length in the *Descriptive Catalogue* (Cat. No. 227), with thirty-six pages devoted to an analysis of Chaucer's characters, which Blake regarded as 'the physiognomies or lineaments of universal life', eternal archetypes of human character. The painting was the occasion of a serious quarrel between Blake and two former friends, Robert Cromek and Thomas Stothard. According to Blake (although others gave differing accounts), Cromek had commissioned the painting but secretly planned to have it engraved by someone else; Blake therefore refused to release the painting to him and Cromek then commissioned Stothard to paint his version of the subject exactly the same size (now in the Tate Gallery), and had it engraved. Stothard's version was a considerable popular success, but he was never forgiven by Blake.

The importance Blake attached to this subject is further shown in other writings of the time. The print, published in October 1810, was by far the largest of his engravings. Most contemporary connoisseurs found it mannered and heavy in execution, 'Gothic' in a pejorative sense. In fact, Blake here combined a number of widely different influences in a design now recognised as among his greatest, including that of Flemish and German Primitive painting, and the recently arrived Elgin Marbles (Cat. Nos. 362–63). **LS**

420a

420b

Joseph Mallord William Turner and Charles Turner

London 1775–1851 London,
London 1774–1857 London respectively

420a
Little Devil's Bridge, 1809

Etched outline by J. M. W. Turner,
mezzotint by Charles Turner,
20.8×28.9 cm, 2nd state
Published by C. Turner, 29 March 1809

Joseph Mallord William Turner and Henry Dawe

London 1790–1848 Windsor

420b
Isleworth, 1819

Etched outline by J. M. W. Turner,
mezzotint by Henry Dawe, 20.8×29 cm,
trial proof
Published by J. M. W. Turner, 1 January
1819
London, Trustees of the British Museum
Inv. Nos. 1869–11–940, 1972. u.929
Literature: Finberg 1924, Nos. 19 and 63;
Herrmann 1990, pp. 47, 65–66

Turner's *Liber Studiorum* (1807–19) was conceived from the outset as a visual treatise on
landscape art; it was also the most important
of all his ventures into printmaking. It imitated, both in title and medium, the famous
series of prints by Richard Earlom after
Claude's *Liber Veritatis* drawings published
in the 1770s.

The *Liber Studiorum* had a didactic purpose: to illustrate, with suitably designed
examples, the various categories into which
landscape painting could be divided. Seventy-
one plates were published in fourteen parts.
Originally it was intended to be a series of one
hundred plates, but the scheme petered out,
perhaps because by 1819 his ideas and taste had
changed. It was also a financial failure, inadequately advertised, published at erratic
intervals, and Turner antagonised the chief
distributors of the prints by cutting their trade
discount from 20 per cent to nothing.

Turner was determined to oversee the engraving process in minute detail; heavily
annotated proofs confirm his vigilance. He
himself etched the outlines for almost all the
series. The two subjects shown here span ten
years of the project and demonstrate the considerable contrasts of mood that Turner expressed in the different categories of landscape
types. *Little Devil's Bridge over the Reuss
above Altdorf* was derived from a drawing
made by Turner during his first visit to

421

Switzerland in 1802. *Isleworth* was among the
last of the series to be published, and was
among the most Claude-like in mood and
composition, it shows a stretch of the River
Thames which Turner knew well. **LS**

James Ward
London 1769–1859 London

421
Marengo, 1824

Lithograph, 33.7×45.5 cm
Published by R. Ackermann, 1 August 1824
London, Trustees of the British Museum
Inv. No. 1917–12–8–2886
Literature: Phipps-Jackson 1893, pp. 306–07;
Trankan 1904, pp. 106, 129; Grundy 1909,
p. 46

This print is one of a series of twenty-four
portraits of famous horses painted and engraved by James Ward between 1823 and 1826;
the two most celebrated were Wellington's
horse Copenhagen and Napoleon's Marengo,
both ridden at the Battle of Waterloo in 1815,
and painted by Ward in 1824 (Cat. No. 399).
Their publication was influenced mainly by
Stubb's *Review of the Turf* (1794) but also perhaps by Carle Vernet's prints of thorough-
breds which had appeared anonymously in
London. In turn, Ward's lithographs were
much admired by Géricault. **LS**

John Martin
Haydon Bridge 1789–1854 Douglas

422
Belshazzar's Feast, 1826

Mezzotint, 59.8×81.6 cm, proof impression,
before lettering, 1826
London, Trustees of the British Museum
Inv. No. Mm 10–1
Literature: Balston 1947, p. 281, No. 5; Wees
and Campbell 1986, No. 74

Belshazzar's Feast was John Martin's most
successful composition. The painting on
which the mezzotint is based was exhibited at
the British Institution in 1821, where it had to
be roped off to protect it from the crowds.

Belshazzar's Feast displays all the elements
that characterise Martin's most dramatic
works, including architectural settings conceived on a vast scale, dwarfing human figures
who are caught up in cataclysmic events. Martin was certainly influenced by popular millenarianism, the belief that the end of the world
was imminent, and it may be that his paintings
were to some extent allegories of contemporary life. He also had a passionate interest in
urban improvements, and devoted a considerable amount of time and money to planning
engineering schemes for improving the quality
of London's water supply, publishing a series
of pamphlets in which he discussed sewage
schemes and provision of pure water. Perhaps,
as in his paintings, this reflects a desire to

422

transform London from a Babylon into a New Jerusalem as biblical prophesy foretold.

The popularity of the painting led Martin to make it the subject of the first of his large-scale mezzotints, which he probably began to work on in 1822, although it was not published until 1826. Martin himself engraved, published and distributed his large single sheet prints; his success can be gauged from the fact that within eighteen months the proceeds from the sale of impressions of *Belshazzar's Feast* and *Joshua Commanding the Sun to Stand still* were over £2,900. **LS**

John Constable and David Lucas
East Bergholt 1776–1837 London,
London 1802–1881 London respectively

423
A Summerland, 1831

Mezzotint, 17.6×25.2 cm, published state
Engraved by David Lucas, published by
J. Constable, October 1831
London, Trustees of the British Museum

423

Inv. No. 1842–12–10–107
Literature: Wedmore 1914, No. 15; Shirley 1930, No. 10; Wilton 1979, Plate 15

It was only in his last decade that Constable seriously devoted himself to seeking a wider public for his art through the publication of engravings after his works. In 1829 he conceived the idea of a series of mezzotints based on a wide range of finished paintings, oil sketches and drawings made during the preceding thirty years, and chose David Lucas to engrave them under his close supervision. In all, twenty-two plates were published in five parts between June 1830 and July 1832, and twenty further subjects were issued posthumously.

The first edition was entitled *Various Subjects* of *Landscape Characteristic of English Scenery, from Pictures Painted by John Constable R.A.*, now generally known as *English Landscape Scenery*. It was financed by Constable himself, and although it does not seem to have been particularly successful he issued a second edition in 1833 in which he arranged the order of the plates, accompanying them with an explanatory text.

English Landscape Scenery had an obvious precedent in Turner's famous *Liber Studiorum* (Cat. No. 420); although Constable once referred to it as Turner's *Liber Stupidorum*, his own publication was evidently modelled in many respects on the *Liber*, not least in his plan to present a balance of landscape types in each issue, as well as to use mezzotint.

Such qualities are particularly well shown in *A Summerland*, based on the painting exhibited by Constable in 1814, *Ploughing Scene in Suffolk (A Summerland)* (Cat. No. 387). Lucas had a considerable challenge in translating the painting into a much smaller mezzotint, but his achievement in capturing the shifting light and sparkling feel of the original was remarkable. **LS**

Benjamin Gibbon after Sir Edwin Landseer
Penally 1802–1851 London,
London 1802–1873 London respectively

424
The Old Shepherd's Chief Mourner, 1838

Engraving, 34.6×37.4 cm
Published by F. G. Moon, 2 June 1838
London, Trustees of the British Museum
Inv. No. 1850–5–25–30
Literature: Beck 1973, pp.34, 57–58

PAINTINGS AND SCULPTURE

Landseer was arguably the most popular painter of his day, known particularly through the medium of engravings. His remarkable gift for animal observation was both the source of his extraordinary public success and of his ultimate failure to achieve real greatness as an artist; by endowing his animals with human sentiments and expressions he too often pandered to popular taste. Yet at his best, subjects such as *The Old Shepherd's Chief Mourner* convey a genuine sense of heroic pathos. Exhibited at the Royal Academy in 1837 this was one of Landseer's most famous paintings (Cat. No. 409), and was engraved in the following year.

With Ruskin's eulogy in *Modern Painters* both painting and artist were elevated to near legendary status '... the close pressure of the dog's breast against the hood, the convulsive clinging of the paws, which has dragged the blanket off the tressle, the total powerlessness of the head laid, close and motionless, upon its folds ... the rigidity of the repose which marks that there has been no motion nor change in the trance of agony since the last blow was struck on the coffin lid, the quietness and gloom of the chamber, the spectacles marking the place where the Bible was last closed, indicating how lonely has been the life, how unwatched the departure of him, who is now laid solitary in his sleep; – these are all thoughts – thoughts by which the picture is separated at once from hundreds of equal merit, as far as mere painting goes, by which it ranks as a work of high art, and stamps its author, not as the neat imitator of the texture of a skin, or the fold of a drapery, but as the Man of Mind.' **LS**

424

LITERARY LONDON

London was at the heart of the country's literary life. Men of letters could derive support from the company of fellow writers, the initiative of enterprising publishers and the notice of a cultivated and extensive reading public. But the attitude of the Romantic poets towards London was at best equivocal, at worst hostile. Only in the 1820s was London as an environment treated by essayists with emotional rapport, understanding and even sometimes with affection.

William Blake
London 1757–1827 London

425 *(illus. p. 478)*
Songs of Experience, c. 1794–1825

Relief etchings, finished in watercolour, each approximately 11×7 cm; copy T
London, Trustees of the British Museum
Inv. No. 1856-2-9
Literature: Bentley 1977, No. 139 T

Songs of Innocence published in 1789, Blake's most famous collection of poems as well as his best know illuminated book, are pastoral lyrics which may be read as children's verses, but at another level they are meditations on the state of childhood and the presence of Christ. In 1794 Blake added *Songs of Experience*, a sequence of poems illustrating man's spiritual development in the period which succeeds the joyful state of Innocence, when beauty and love were supreme. In Experience, mankind becomes conscious of sorrow, social evils, conventional morality and disappointment. Blake contrasts the carefree child with the hardened adult, the innocent virgin with a harlot, and in nature contrasts the innocent lamb with the awful 'tyger'. In the plate shown here,

The Chimney Sweeper, Blake reveals his scorn of established religion. The young sweep's parents have left him to go to church, 'And are gone to praise God and Priest and King/ who made up a heaven of our misery'; Blake stresses the child's woe.

The book is dated 1794 on the title page and was probably intended to be sold on its own although most surviving copies were bound with *Songs of Innocence*. The order of the plates and their colouring underwent great variation during Blake's lifetime; in its combined form it was the one illuminated book that sold at all steadily over the years, and he seems to have printed copies on request. **LS**

527

William Blake

426
Jerusalem, 1804–27?

Relief etching, each *c.* 22×16 cm
London, Trustees of the British Museum
Inv. No. 31* a.11
Literature: Bindman 1978, Nos. 480–579

Jerusalem, the Emanation of the Giant Albion
was Blake's last illuminated book, the culmination of his prophetic works. He began it in
1804 and was still working on it well into the
1820s. Only one complete coloured copy is
known (Mr. Paul Mellon); there is another incomplete coloured version, and four other uncoloured copies. The boldness of the designs is
even more apparent in the monochrome versions than in the one exquisitely coloured
copy. The theme of Blake's poem is the redemption of Albion's lost soul, Albion being
identified both with mankind and with
England. Jerusalem is his female counterpart,
separated from him at the Fall. They are reunited through Christ. The struggle between
Jerusalem and Albion is paralleled by the
struggle of Los, the poetic principle, with his
emanation Enitharmon as he tries to give form
to the actual poem *Jerusalem.*

Plate 84 of the hundred plates, 'An old man
led by a child', is a revival, in reverse, of one of
the illustrations to *Songs of Experience,* 1794,
the headpiece to *London.* This touching image

illustrates the lines, 'I see London blind and
age-bent begging through the streets of Babylon, led by a child; his tears run down his
beard'. The child leads him towards the
Gothic church, on the top of which the cross is
silhouetted against the sky. It can be related to
other images of redemption in Blake's work,
where an old man rises as a regenerate youth
from the grave.

Throughout the poem Blake recalls the unspoilt semi-rural outskirts of his London
childhood, transfigured into a vision of the
millenium to come. **LS**

William Wordsworth
Cockermouth 1770–1850 Rydal

427

Poems in two volumes, Volume 1
Published by Longman, Rees and Orme,
1807
Printed book, 17×10.9 cm
Inscribed: William Wordsworth / Stow June
1849
Grasmere, The Wordsworth Trust
Inv. No. WW(a)1807
Provenance: author's presentation copy to
Isabella Monkhouse, May 1807; gift of
William Knight

Certainly the best known poem written about
London in the nineteenth century, *Westminster Bridge,* first published in this work, was
composed by Wordsworth in September 1802,
during a stay in London on the way back from
visiting Annette Vallon, the mother of his
child, Caroline, in France. In an unusual
moment of enthusiasm for the city inspired by
its taking on the appearance of one of nature's
sublime scenes, Wordsworth looks downriver
and takes in a panoramic sweep of skyline
from St. Paul's to Holland's Theatre Royal,
Drury Lane, sparkling and for once tranquil in
the early morning sun. Dorothy Wordsworth,
who accompanied her brother, recorded in her
'Journal', 'the sun shone so brightly, with such
a pure light, that there was even something like
the purity of one of Nature's own grand spectacles.'

In contrast, the poems of 1807 also include
some bitter accounts of the over-commercial
city. One sonnet entitled 'London 1802' has
this serious, satirical tone:

> The world is too much with us; late and
>   soon,
> Getting and spending, we lay waste our
>   powers:
> Little we see in nature that is ours;
> We have given our hearts away, a sordid
>   boon!

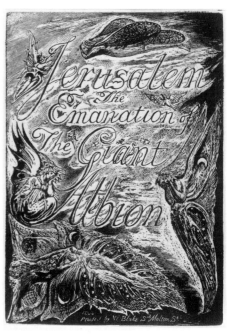

426

Two of Wordsworth's greatest poems were
also first published in the volumes: *Resolution
and Independence* and *Ode: Intimations of
Immortality.* Both reveal Wordsworth's capacity for what John Stuart Mill called 'a medicine for my mind'. For in both poems, his
meditation leads him through depression and
despondency to a renewed, if hard-won, recovery. **RW**

William Wordsworth

428
The Prelude, Book VII, Mss. D, *c.*
1839, composed 1804

19.5×15 cm
Grasmere, The Wordsworth Trust
Inv. No. DCMS: 124
Provenance: Gordon Graham Wordsworth
Bequest
Exhibitions: London, British Museum,
1988–89, Cat. No. 78b
Literature: Wordsworth, Jaye and Woof
1987, pp. 138–42; NHMF 1988, pp. 108–12

In September 1802 Charles Lamb and his sister
Mary acted as guides for Wordsworth and his
sister Dorothy when they paused in London
after meeting Annette Vallon and Caroline in
France. Among the sights they saw was Bartholomew Fair which acted as one of the cata-
lysts for Wordsworth's imagination when he

came to write *The Prelude*, his great verse autobiography completed in 1805 but not finally published in revised form until after his death in 1850. In Book VII, entitled *London*, Wordsworth describes the city as a great vortex which has latent energy, but is something that is, in the last analysis, spurious and grotesque compared with the more appropriate order of the natural green world. Bartholomew Fair, with its nightmare images, sums up the worst aspects of the city:

> All out-o'-the-way, far-fetched, perverted
>   things,
> All freaks of Nature, all Promethean
>   thoughts
> Of man – his dulness, madness and their
>   feats,
> All jumbled up together to make up
> This parliament of monsters. Tents and
>   booths
> Meanwhile – as if the whole were one vast
>   mill -
> Are vomiting, receiving on all sides,
> Men, women, three-years' children, babes
>   in arms.

This manuscript is a fair copy of *The Prelude* in fourteen books, made by Mary Wordsworth early in 1832. It was very extensively revised both in 1832 and 1838–39, in preparation for mss. E. **RW**

429

John Bluck
after
Thomas Rowlandson and
Augustus Charles Pugin
London 1756–1827 London,
France 1762–1832 London respectively

429
Bartholomew Fair, 1808

Coloured aquatint, 21.5 × 26.8 cm
Published by R. Ackermann, 1 February 1808
London, The Museum of London
Inv. No. A9876

Bartholomew Fair was held annually in August, later September, at Smithfield, taking its name from the Austin Friars' foundation of St. Bartholomew's in 1133. As its trade function declined, the fair's importance as a centre for all kinds of entertainment increased, despite almost constant complaints about the disorder it encouraged. From the small-scale performances of political squibs and puppet shows, there developed in the eighteenth century more elaborate shows performed by actors taking a summer break from the licensed theatre companies. There were added attractions of rope dancers, waxworks, freaks and quacks, bawds and prostitutes, and a wide variety of refreshments.In this plate from the *Microcosm*, Rowlandson and Pugin depict the fair in its last period of brilliance. It was finally closed in 1855. **CF**

George Dance
London 1741–1825 London

430
Samuel Taylor Coleridge, 1804

Pencil, 19.7 × 16 cm
Signed and dated: Geo. Dance/March 21st 1804
Grasmere, The Wordsworth Trust
Inv. No. GRMDC: B129
Provenance: Beaumont family until 1984
Exhibitions: New York, Bloomington and Chicago, 1988, Cat. No. 281, Fig. 160; London, British Museum, 1988–89, Cat. No. 78d; Osaka, 1991

By 1804 Coleridge's career as a poet was largely over: the first letter to Sara Hutchinson (with whom he had fallen in love), dated 4 April 1802, and later published as *Dejection: An Ode* describes self-contempt and baffled creativity. But even his less confessional and perhaps greatest poetry – *Kubla Khan, Christabel* and *The Ancient Mariner* – celebrate a psychological plight – that of wanting to act, but being rendered impotent by some constitutional defect and arbitrary game of dice in which the figure of life in death had played his own gambling hand. Without a sense of joy, he suggests, one cannot have a rich relationship with the world that Wordsworth had discovered. Before leaving Keswick for his journey to the Mediterranean in search of a better climate for his health, wrecked by

428

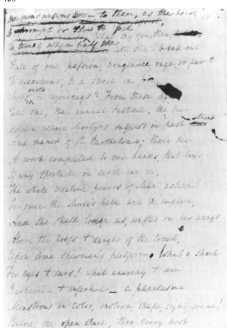

opium addiction, he urged Wordsworth to complete *The Prelude*. Wordsworth in turn urged him to map out the structure of his own philosophic poem to be written abroad, and arranged a loan of £105 for the journey.

The drawing was probably commissioned by Sir George Beaumont when Coleridge was in London waiting for his passage, because of delays attendant on the wartime convoy system. During his last weeks, he stayed with the Beaumonts at their insistence, in the comfort of their town house in Grosvenor Square. As it was feared he might die abroad, Sir George wished to preserve his likeness and certainly commissioned an oil from James Northcote, made on 25–26 March (The Wordsworth Trust). He also gave him £100 for the journey and Lady Beaumont sent him a specially made travelling desk with hidden drawers full of comforts. **RW**

430

Henry Crabb Robinson
Bury St. Edmunds 1775–1867 London

431
Diary for 11 December 1811 to 22 January 1813

11 × 19 cm
London, Dr. Williams's Library Trust
Literature: Morley 1938, Vol. 1, pp. 74–75; Hudson 1967, pp. 7–19

The journalist and barrister Henry Crabb Robinson was the friend of many of the most notable men of his generation in Europe. Relentlessly sociable, over a hundred volumes of his diaries, journals, correspondence and re-

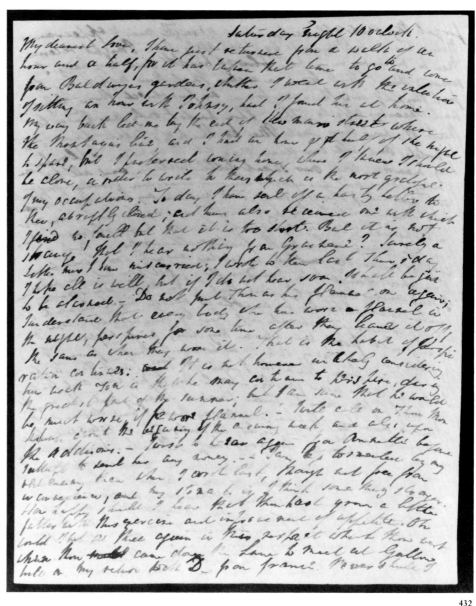

432

miniscences, extracts from which were only published posthumously, provide invaluable background for literary and intellectual life in London. He first met Wordsworth at Charles Lamb's house in 1808 and four years later attempted to mediate in the quarrel which had arisen between Wordsworth and Coleridge, over some thoughtless remarks the former had made regarding Coleridge's disruptive presence in the Wordsworth household, which were reported back to Coleridge by Basil Montagu. The following extract (p. 70) dates from 8 May 1812: 'I delivered C's message to W. and this led . . . to a commission which W. gave me, viz. in answer to C's message to say to him the following:

1. That he, W. denied most positively having ever given to M. any commission whatever

to say anything as from him W. to C. . . .
2. He denies ever having used such a phrase as <u>rotten drunkard</u>; such as expression he could not, as a man of taste, merely, have made use of.
3. Neither did he ever say that C. <u>had been a Nuisance in his family</u>. He might have in the course of conversation, and in reference to certain particular habits have used the word nuisance which is a word he frequently makes use of, but he never employed it as the result or summary of his feelings towards C. He never said he was a nuisance . . .

Though the quarrel was patched up, relations between the two poets were never quite the same again. **CF**

433

through my mind of thee & Dorothy and home soon after I heard, first or almost in the moment in which I heard, of Mr Perceval's death. I saw him only ten short days before his death upon the floor of the house of Commons, and admired the spirit and animation with which he suppressed & chastized that most dangerous & foolish Demogogue Sir Francis Burdett ... the lower orders of the People in London cry out Burdett for ever in the Pot houses, deeming him their champion and the Man who is rid them of all their sufferings real and imaginary.

To economise, Wordsworth usually sent his letters to the Lake District franked by M.P.s, who were exempt from postal payment. On this occasion, he says, the 'Letter will be franked by Lord Byron, a Man who is now the rage in London, in consequence of his Late Poem Childe Haroldes pilgrimage ... it was from his mouth that [Samuel] Rogers first heard, and in his presence told us, the murder of Perceval.' **CF**

Jean Pierre Dantan
Paris 1800–1869 Baden-Baden

433
Samuel Rogers, 1833

Plaster caricature bust (*portrait chargé*), painted to imitate bronze, H 31.1 cm
Marks: incised on the back of the sockle, Published by Dantan . . . . . . London
London, National Portrait Gallery
Inv. No. 3888
Provenance: probably Sir Edmund Gosse; given by his son Dr. Philip Gosse, 1953
Exhibitions: London, ?Dantan's lodgings, 18 Leicester Square, 1833; National Portrait Gallery, 1976, Cat. No. 1
Literature: Walker 1985, Vol. 1, p. 420; Vol. 2, Plate 1012

The poet, banker and connoisseur Samuel Rogers (1763–1855) was at the centre of literary and cultural life in London, entertaining friends at his house in St. James's Place. It was at Rogers' house that Wordsworth met Byron and learnt from him of the assassination of Spencer Perceval. Rogers' best known work, *The Pleasures of Memory*, was published anonymously in 1792 but by 1794 it had reached its seventh edition and the author was recognised as a rising poet. This youthful promise was largely unfulfilled, though he was canny enough to hire Turner and Stothard to supply engravings for his books *Italy* (1830) and *Poems* (1834), thus ensuring they sold.

Dantan's vivid *portrait chargé* presents the

434

image of a cantankerous elderly man; not surprisingly, Rogers held it in especial horror. Despite acts of kindness to his friends, he had a reputation for caustic wit and for being a gossip: Byron wrote a devastating verse attack on him in 1818 for his behaviour at the time of Byron's separation from his wife (Cat. No. 441):

Nose and chin would shame a knocker,
Wrinkles that would puzzle Cocker;
Mouth which marks the envious scorner,
With a scorpion at each corner,
Turning its quick tail to sting you,
In the place that most may wring you;
Eyes of lead-like hue, and gummy;
Carcase picket out from some mummy ...

CF

434
Life Mask of William Wordsworth, 1815

Plaster cast, 25.5 × 15 × 13 cm
Grasmere, The Wordsworth Trust
Inv. No. GRMDC: L9
Provenance: gift of Ernest H. Coleridge
Literature: de Selincourt 1911; Blanchard 1959, p. 144; Walker 1985, Vol. 1, pp. 572–73, No. 2020; Haydon ed. Pope 1960, Vol. 1, p. 450

William Wordsworth
Cockermouth 1770–1850 Rydal

432
Letter to Mary Wordsworth, 9–13 May 1812

Manuscript, 22.6 × 36.8 cm
Grasmere, The Wordsworth Trust
Inv. No. WLMS G1/4/4
Provenance: Sotheby's 1977; purchased 1978
Exhibitions: New York, Bloomington and Chicago, Cat. No. 118, Fig. 74
Literature: Darlington ed. 1981, pp. 138–49

Wordsworth's letter to his wife from London reveals how much he missed his family and disliked the capital. 'The life which is led by the fashionable world in this great city is miserable; there is neither dignity nor content nor love nor quiet to be found in it.' Nevertheless, the letter is full of news. He misses seeing Coleridge (their quarrel now patched up) because the latter is busy at the *Courier* office (Cat. No. 294) assisting the editor, Daniel Stuart, 'in writing upon the late most dreadful event the Assassination of Mr Perceval' (Cat. No. 615), but Wordsworth himself, typically, reacts to the public crisis on a personal level:

oh my Joy & my comfort, my hope & my repose, what awful thoughts passed

remember you & [illegible] & Monkhouse
getting Lamb out of the parlour
into the painting Room by force, putting
on his great Coat, he, reiterating, being
down to look at the Commissioner & [illegible]
[illegible] man! – Do you remember Keats' proposing
confusion to the memory of Newton, and on
your insisting on an explanation before you
drank it, & his "saying
Because he destroyed the Poetry of the Rainbow
By reducing it to a Prism!
Ah My dear old Friend, we shall never see such
days again. "The Peaches are not so big as they
were in our days" – many [illegible] the immortal
dinner which took place in my painting
room – where the food was simple but the
Wine good, & the Poetry first rate – Wordsworth
Walter Scott – David Wilkie – Lamb – Hazlitt, Keats,
Leigh Hunt, Talfourd – &c. attended my call – [illegible]
my Talk –
I have got through a Cartoon, to the utmost
of my power – from Milton – Christ
as Judge cursing Adam, after having
cursed Eve & the Serpent – I have introduced
the Evil Principle – Satan, opposed to Christ,
but tormented yet fierce – [illegible], – Sketch
grand; & [illegible] –
I have no hesitation whatever
now, in deciding, to the habit, of making
Cartoons an end, instead of a Means

to the babyish habit of devoting years to
polishing up Cartoon Pictures in chalk
Europe has produced no great handler
of the brush since Rubens, Rembrandt, Velasquez,
& Murillo –
That Raphael made merely correct Sketches
that something might be left for the hand
& mind to do on the Wall, the German
French & Italians have devoted to make
complete works – which Raphael never
dreamt of – he was but 12 years in
the Vatican if I had been Spent on one
Cartoon – How many Frescoes would
he have painted!
After years of labor, the present race of
Cartoon Men (not excepting Cornelius)
are helpless with the brush –
After Laurence's visit to Camuccini's –
Cartoon of several years' labor, as he came
out – he said to Evans the Portrait painter
"and after all this, comes a d— n bad
Picture"
The use of Cartoon is to save the design
on the Wall from gross alterations, but
if the utility be overrated, it will ruin any
School on Earth – and it will ruin ours
if repeated per se, without reference
to Wall application – Fresco implies
Cartoons – but Cartoons do not imply
Fresco – and here's the danger ——
I wish Rumohr, those conclusions

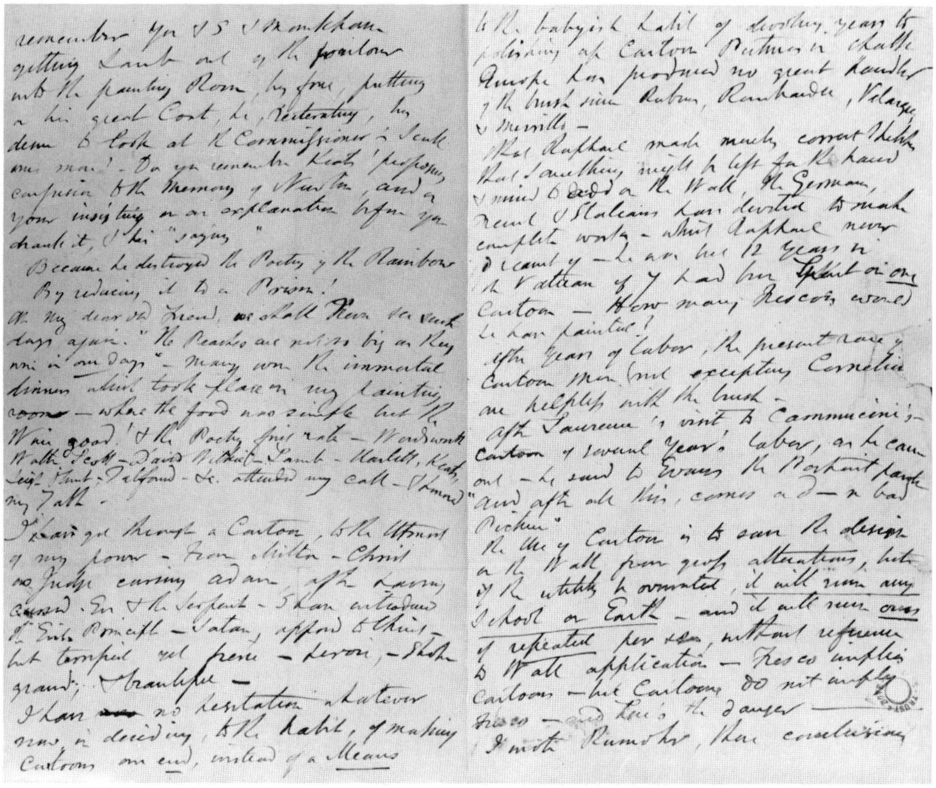

436

This mask was made for Benjamin Robert Haydon at the time he was working on *Christ's Entry into Jerusalem* in which Wordsworth appeared with Keats (whose mask was also made) among the crowd of onlookers. Life masks were obviously an aid to artists and sculptors but they also reflected the contemporary obsession with phrenology. According to Haydon, Wordsworth bore the ordeal 'like a philosopher', although the artist could not resist allowing John Scott (editor of *The Champion* and later editor of the *London Magazine*) to see him in this state, 'that he might say the first sight he ever had of so great a poet was such a singular one as this. I opened the door slowly, & there he sat innocent and unconscious of our plot against his dignity, unable to see or to speak, with all the mysterious silence of a spirit.' **CF**

Benjamin Robert Haydon
Plymouth 1786–1846 London

435
John Keats, 1816

Pen and ink, 31.7×20.3 cm
Signed and dated: Nov 1816/BRH
London, National Portrait Gallery
Inv. No. 3251
Provenance: B. R. Haydon; Frederick Wordsworth Haydon; Henry Buxton Forman and bought from his son, 1945
Exhibitions: Paris, 1972, No. 136; New York, Bloomington and Chicago 1988, Cat. No. 73, Fig. 47
Literature: Walker 1985, Vol. 1, p. 287, Vol. 2, Plate 671

This drawing was executed on a sheet torn from November 1816 of Haydon's 'Diary' and the entry on the verso contains, typically, vituperative criticism of the Royal Academicians, reflecting his own struggles to achieve reputation. He inscribed the drawing later, 'Keats was a spirit that in passing over the Earth came within its attraction, and expired in fruitless struggles to make its dull inhabitants comprehend the beauty of his soarings' – a fate which the artist felt no doubt seemed to mirror his own. In attempting to return the compliment with a pen portrait profile of Haydon made on a second sheet from the 'Diary', Keats produced what Haydon considered to be a 'vile caricature' of him, also in the National Portrait Gallery (Inv. No. 3250). More flatteringly, the poet compared Haydon with Raphael in his sonnet *Great Spirits Now on Earth are Sojourning*. **CF**

Benjamin Robert Haydon

436
Letter to William Wordsworth, 16 October 1842

Manuscript, 31.7×39.5 cm
Grasmere, The Wordsworth Trust
Inv. No. WLL/Haydon, Benjamin Robert/26
Provenance: Gordon Graham Wordsworth Bequest
Exhibitions: New York, Bloomington and Chicago, 1988, Cat. No. 133
Literature: Haydon ed. Pope 1960, Vol. 2 , pp. 173–76

Haydon's letter recalled that 'Immortal Dinner' held on 28 December 1817 in Haydon's London house, when Leigh Hunt, Charles Lamb, John Keats, Wordsworth and Mary Wordsworth's cousin, Thomas Monkhouse, were present. Keats proposed a toast of 'confusion to the memory of Newton' because 'he destroyed the poetry of the rainbow by reducing it to a prism!'

His diary entry written twenty-five years earlier gives more details of the table talk and sets the scene. Behind them towered Haydon's enormous canvas of *Christ's Entry into Jerusalem* (in which Keats, Wordsworth and Newton were all portrayed)

> occasionally brightened by the gleams of flame that sparkled from the fire ... the voice of Wordsworth repeating Milton with an intonation like the funeral bell of St. Paul's, & the music of Handel mingled – & then Lamb's wit came sparkling in between, & Keats's rich fancy of Satyrs & Fauns & doves and white clouds ... It was an evening worthy of the Elizabethan age, and will long flash upon 'that inward eye which is the bliss of Solitude'.

The letter continues on an elegiac note: 'Ah My dear old friend. we shall never see such days again. "The Peaches are not so big as they were in our days".' **CF**

Joseph Severn
London 1793–1879

437
John Keats, 1819

Watercolour on ivory over a pencil outline, 10.8×8.3 cm, framed with a lock of Keats's hair
Cambridge, Syndics of the Fitzwilliam Museum
Inv. No. 713

Provenance: Miss Fanny Brawne; Charles W. Dilke; by descent to the Rt. Hon. Sir Charles W. Dilke, by whom bequeathed to the museum, 1911
Exhibitions: London, Royal Academy, 1819, No. 940
Literature: Bayne-Powell 1985, pp. 194–96, illustrated; Walker 1985, Vol. 1, p. 288, No. 1605

This portrait miniature was probably commissioned by Keats for Fanny Brawne. Ironically, it hung in the Royal Academy exhibition at Somerset House near her portrait miniature by A. E. Chalon, but as Keats had gloomily predicted when Severn had suggested exhibiting it, his miniature remained unnoticed, 'a drop of water in the ocean'. Mortally threatened with consumption, Keats left England for Italy in September 1820, accompanied by his friend Severn, who nursed him devotedly until his death in Rome the following February. **CF**

437

the first two cantos of *Childe Harold's Pilgrimage*. The verses are openly autobiographical. Byron originally called his hero 'Childe Burun', but changed the name when he was persuaded to publish the verses by his kinsman Robert Dallas. Dallas also unsuccessfully tried to persuade him to omit some of the verses on religious and political grounds. Byron did agree to omit a satirical passage on Sunday in London. Dallas offered the manuscript to John Murray who accepted the work after consulting William Gifford, the editor of the *Quarterly Review* and his chief literary adviser. He too failed to persuade Byron to remove the controversial passages.

The publication went ahead and as the work was on the press Byron made constant alterations and additions. Murray exercised great patience and the work was finally published on 10 March 1812. It was an immediate success and the 500 copies which had been produced sold within three days. Five editions were printed in 1812 alone. **EE**

Richard Westall
Hertford 1765–1836 London

438 *(illus. p. 487)*
Lord Byron, 1813

Oil on canvas, 91.8×71.1 cm
Inscribed on the rock top right: Gordon Lord Byron/Painted by/ Richd Westall, R.A./1813
London, National Portrait Gallery
Inv. No. 4243
Provenance: probably Sir Francis Burdett; first recorded in the collection of his daughter Baroness Burdett-Coutts, 1891; Burdett-Coutts sale, Christie's, 4 May 1922, Lot 80, bought Vicars; Lady Wentworth, Crabbet Park; Gladstone E. Moore, by whom sold to the gallery, 1961
Exhibitions: London, ?Royal Academy, 1825, No. 41; New Gallery, 1891, No. 213
Literature: Walker 1985, Vol. 1, pp. 81–82, Vol. 2, Plate 176

Westall's portrait of Byron, undertaken at the request of an unidentified friend of the poet, was painted the year after Byron's burst into literary celebrity with the publication of *Childe Harold's Pilgrimage* and into social notoriety through his brief, melodramatic affair with Lady Caroline Lamb, who still hounded him. Burdened by debt, he was contemplating marriage with the heiress Annabella Milbanke, but was closer to his half-sister Augusta and to his confidante, Lady Melbourne, to whom he wrote on 1 October:

Ldy H[olland] says I am <u>fattening</u>, and you

say I talk '<u>nonsense</u>'. Well – I must fast and unfool again, if possible. But, as Curran told me last night that he had been assured upon oath by half the Court, that 'the Prince was not at all <u>corpulent</u>, that he was stout certainly, but by no means protuberant, or obese,' 'there's comfort yet.' As to folly, that's incurable . . .

The Giaour was published in June and *The Bride of Abydos* in December the same year.

The portrait was much copied and adapted by Westall and other artists. **CF**

Lord Byron
London 1788–1824 Missolonghi

439
Childe Harold's Pilgrimage, 1st edition, 5th printing with MS proof corrections, 1812

Bound volume, 23×15 cm
London, John Murray
Provenance: bookplate of John Murray, Newstead, Wimbledon Park
Exhibitions: London, Victoria and Albert Museum, 1974, D9

In July 1811 Byron returned to England from his travels in Europe and the Middle East with

Richard Westall
Hertford 1765–1836 London

440
Bride of Abydos Canto I Stanza 12, 1813

Watercolour, 12.7×10.2
London, John Murray
Exhibitions: London, Victoria and Albert Museum 1974, S 51

440

He lived – he breathed – he moved – he felt:
He raised the maid from where she knelt

Richard Westall was principally a watercolourist best known for his book illustrations, although his range also included topographical and historical works and portraits. As an illustrator he worked for many of the London publishing houses including Longman's and John Murray. In 1813 he was approached by Murray's to illustrate *Childe Harold* and *The Giaour* and other works, which may well have included a commission for illustrations for *The Bride of Abydos*. **EE**

Lord Byron
London 1788–1824 Missolonghi

441
Lord Byron to John Murray, 2 April 1816

Pen and ink on paper, 18 × 22.5 cm
London, John Murray
Literature: Marchand 1976, Vol. 5, p. 60

Foe to all Vice – yet hardly Virtue's friend –
For Virtue pardons those she would amend

These amended verses from *A Sketch from*

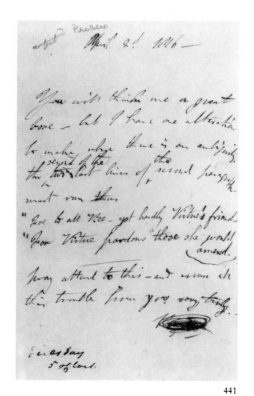

441

Private Life (1816, lines 35–36) refer to Lady Byron's refusal to acknowledge Byron's approaches to her after their separation.

The success of Byron's marriage to Annabella Milbanke was in doubt even before the

wedding took place in 1815. It lasted just over a year and became increasingly painful for both partners. Aware that he had made a mistake, plagued by debts and harassed by rumours about his private life, Byron behaved with mounting irrationality and doubts were cast on his sanity. His wife left him to live with her parents and eventually agreed to the arrangement of a separation.

Immediately after reluctantly signing the preliminary agreement for the separation, Byron wrote to Lady Byron expressing his continuing devotion. Entitled *Fare thee Well*, these sentimental verses reveal more of Byron's wounded pride and frustration than love for his wife. Annabella did not respond and the verses were privately circulated to Byron's friends by John Murray. Byron then made a vitriolic attack on Mrs. Clermont, Lady Byron's old governess, whom Byron felt had influenced his wife against him.

After taking legal advice over the libellous nature of the work, John Murray agreed to print fifty copies for private distribution. Both *Fare thee Well* and *A Sketch* found their way into the newspapers and the consequent publicity (Cat. Nos. 668–69) increased public feeling against Byron, who, embittered and ostracised, left England for ever in April 1816. **EE**

Lord Byron

442
Don Juan, Cantos I and II, 1819

Bound volume of proofs, annotated with John Cam Hobhouse's mss. comments and criticism and Byron's answers, 24 × 15.5 cm
London, John Murray

In 1818 Byron sent the first canto of *Don Juan* to his friend John Cam Hobhouse, among others, eager to hear his opinion of a work which he recognised was 'too free for these very modest days' but which he felt had great literary merit, being the product of a period of intense creativity. Byron's fears about his friends' reaction to its content were justified when they urged total suppression of the verses.

Byron at first acceded to their wishes but later, assessing his debts and confident of the quality of the poetry, determined to ask Murray, or the highest bidder, to publish. Murray eagerly took the work which he described as 'seductive' but encouraged Byron to reconsider the 'indelicacies'. Byron's reply was direct, 'The poem will please, if it is lively, if it is stupid, it will fail; but I will have none of your damned cutting and slashing. If you please, you may publish anonymously; it will

442

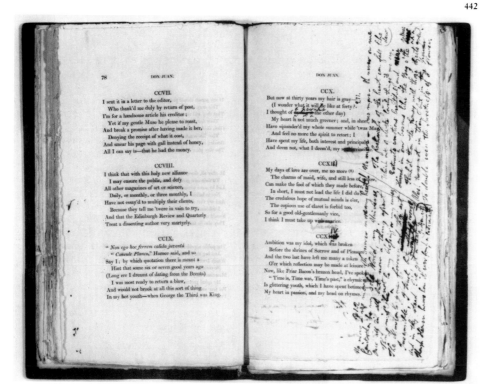

perhaps be better; but I will battle my way against them, like a Porcupine.'

Murray offered 1,500 guineas for the first two cantos of *Don Juan* and *The Ode to Venice* and the work was published on 15 July with only the printer's name on the title page.

The public reaction was as Hobhouse had feared. The Edinburgh publishers Blackwood's refused to distribute the book and it was attacked on all sides for immorality. EE

Lord Byron

443
Werner, 1823

Bound volume, 22.5×15 cm
London, John Murray
Provenance: bookplate of John Murray, Newstead, Wimbledon Park

Werner was dedicated by Lord Byron: To/The Illustrious Goethe/By One of His Humblest Admirers/This Tragedy Is Dedicated

Werner, published in 1822, was based on *The German Tale* in Sophia and Harriet Lee's *Canterbury Tales*. It was among the manuscripts that Byron had instructed John Murray to hand over to John Hunt. Murray however retained and published *Werner* whilst giving the potentially damaging *Heaven and Earth* to Hunt. Six thousand copies were sold within four days. Byron did not blame Murray for his deception but looked forward to payment for the work.

Byron and Goethe rapidly came to be seen as spiritual representatives of their age in the broader European context of romanticism. Goethe's concepts of *Weltschmerz* and *Ischschmerz* were in essence part of Byron's own character and his and Byron's autobiographical verses had a profound influence on subsequent European literature. EE

Lord Byron

444
Facsimile of the Dedication of Sardanapalus to Goethe, 1821

25.3×20.1 cm
London, John Murray
Provenance: John Murray from Leonard L. Mackall, 1923

444

To the illustrious Goethe
a stranger presumes to offer the homage of a literary vassal to his liege Lord, the first of existing writers, who has created, the literature of his own country, and illustrated that of Europe. The unworthy production which the author ventures to inscribe to him is entitled "Sardanapalus".

Byron first acknowledged a debt to Goethe in the construction of his experimental play *Manfred* (1817), which Goethe subsequently praised for its completely original interpretation of his drama *Faust*, from which Byron admitted he had derived his inspiration. After reading *Manfred*, Goethe wrote, 'This strange and gifted poet has completely assimilated my *Faust* and derived the strangest nourishment from it for his hypochondria. He has used all the motifs in his own way, so that none remains quite the same . . .' (Briefe XXVIII, p. 277ff, 13 October 1817).

Byron sought to dedicate Sardanapalus to Goethe, but failed to receive permission in time before the first edition was printed. A manuscript dedication was sent to Goethe who immediately had a small number of facsimiles made, examples of which are also in the Goethe-Schiller Archive in Weimar.

Though Byron denied that his verse drama was intended to be read politically, many readers must have drawn the parallel between the Assyrian king's dissolute court and that of George IV. EE

445
The Liberal

Verse and Prose from The South, Volume 1, 1st edition, London, 1822

Bound volume, 22×14 cm
London, John Murray
Provenance: inscribed on flyleaf, John Murray, 32 Onslow Sq.

The publication of *The Liberal* in October 1822 led to a break in the commercial relations between Byron and John Murray. The idea for a new literary journal had been raised by Shelley and Leigh Hunt who arrived in Italy in 1821 to discuss the proposal. Byron had misgivings about the enterprise from the outset but he admired Hunt's radical politics and style of journalism and after Shelley's death in May 1822, felt an increased obligation towards him. Relations with Murray had soured over the potential prosecution of *Cain* and Byron asked him to hand over all his prose works including *The Vision of Judgement*, his satirical masterpiece attacking Southey, to Hunt's brother, John, who was to print *The Liberal*.

However when *The Vision* was printed in the first volume of *The Liberal*, it appeared without its explanatory preface and Byron accused Murray of deliberately holding it back. The quarrel escalated and Byron withdrew all his manuscripts from Murray. EE

Henry Crabb Robinson
Bury St. Edmunds 1775–1867 London

446
Travel Journal for August 1829

10×17 cm
London, Dr. Williams's Library Trust
Literature: Morley 1938, Vol. 1, pp. 367–68;
Hudson 1967, pp.vii-xix

From 1800 to 1805 Crabb Robinson was in Germany, where he met the leading writers and made a close study of German life and literature. Thereafter, more than anyone before Carlyle, he brought German philosophy and literature to England, serving as an intellectual mediator between the two countries. He was a keen advocate of the works of Goethe and Kant and a upholder of German transcendental thought in the largely hostile utilitarian climate of London University. He first met Goethe in 1805, an experience which he compared with seeing Sarah Siddons (Crabb Robinson was a keen theatre goer). On this occasion in 1829, he is only marginally less awestruck:

Sunday 2. Aug. 1829
A Golden day! But I feel ashamed at my inability to leave a memorial at all worthy of it . . . It was between ten and eleven when I left my card at Goethe's house for his daughter-in-law, and we proceeded then to the small house in the park, where we were at once admitted to the Great Man. I was oppressed by the cordial reception. And as the cordiality increased during two most interesting conversations, the sense of unworthiness but increased . . . We spoke of Lord Byron and I mentioned *The Vision of Judgement.* He called it sublime and laughed while he referred to the summoning of Junius and Wilkes as witnesses and to the letting the king slip into heaven, &c., as admirable hits. He said: 'Er sind keine Flickwörter im Gedichte,' and he compared the brilliancy and clearness of his style to a metal wire drawn through a steel plate! I informed him of my having brought Flaxman's lectures, which he politely accepted, and spoke of Flaxman's *Homer* with great respect.' **CF**

447
Lord Byron's Hair and Visiting Card, 1815–1824

Framed, 23×17 cm
London, John Murray
Provenance: noted in a supplement to an official list of Byron relics after the death of John Murray IV in 1928

Locks of hair were frequently exchanged as tokens of love or regard. Found among Lord Byron's memorabilia are both locks and tresses of hair which he had accepted from lovers and friends. **EE**

448

Count Alfred d'Orsay
Paris 1801–1852 Dieppe

448
Lord Byron

Pencil, 29.4×22 cm
London, John Murray
Provenance: Sir Thomas Phillips, sold by Sotheby's 13 February 1950

Count d'Orsay was a celebrated wit and dandy who impressed Byron with his handsome and youthful good looks, suavity and what Byron saw as his acute perception of the English character. D'Orsay had been travelling on the Continent since August 1822 with the Earl and Countess of Blessington, the latter a noted beauty and society hostess, and the party travelled to Genoa specifically to meet Byron in the spring of the following year. D'Orsay was also a talented artist and sculptor and he is known to have drawn a full-length profile sketch of Byron at this time. During their visit Byron was preoccupied with raising money to aid the Greek cause and with his desire to go in person to Greece. Lady Blessington later recalled his frequent changes of mood, his remorse at leaving Teresa Guiccioli and his presentiments of death. **EE**

M. A. Kornicker

449
Letter to John Murray, 15 March 1829

Pen and ink on paper, 24.4×20 cm
London, John Murray

This letter describes the publication by Kornicker of Stuttgart of a German translation of Murray's edition of Byron's works. The bookseller wishes to preface the first volume of the translation with the engraving of Thomas Phillips' *Portrait of Lord Byron* by Edward Finden (1791–1857) which was included in the Murray edition. He asks for a price for 1,000 copies of the engraving.

The painting of Lord Byron by Thomas Phillips (1770–1845) to which Kornicker refers was commissioned by John Murray in 1814 and a rough impression of it can be seen hanging over the fireplace in Cat. No. 00. It hangs in the same position today.

Byron's work was extremely popular abroad and he noted in his journal in 1822 that his sales were better in Germany, France and America than in England. **EE**

Grieve Family

450 *(illus. p. 489)*
Three-dimensional model set design for Manfred, Act II, scene iv, The Hall of Arimanes, 1834

Pen and ink and watercolour over pencil, 19.8×29 cm
Signed: C? G.
London, University of London, Sterling Library
Inv. No. Grieve Collection 604
Literature: Robinson 1966 ed., pp. 144–45; Rosenfeld 1973, p. 104; Howell 1982, pp. 97–106

The Grieve family dominated scene design on the London stage from the 1820s to the 1840s. John Henderson Grieve (1770–1845) started his fifty-year career with the Theatre Royal, Covent Garden in 1795. His sons Thomas (1799–1882) and William (1800–44) worked with him on a collaborative basis. The Grieves excelled in special effects, exploiting the gas lighting installed in Covent Garden in 1817, and drawing on an eclectic range of antiquarian sources, travel illustrations and sheer fantasy, which they put to good use in a range of operas, ballets, dramas and pantomimes.

Eight months after a successful staging of Byron's *Sardanapalus,* the Theatre Royal,

R. Westall, *Lord Byron*, 1813. Cat. No. 438

F. Danby, *Sunset at Sea after a Storm*, 1824. Cat. No. 396

Covent Garden, embarked on a production of *Manfred*, Byron's lyrics being set to music by Henry Bishop. In an attempt to repeat the success of Weber's *Der Freischutz* ten years earlier, the supernatural effects were played up, while Byron's political and religious opinions, not to mention his hints of incest, were cut.

The play opened to much publicity on 29 October 1834. In this scene Arimanes sits on his throne of fire surrounded by spirits, a setting based on John Martin's painting, *Satan in Council*. A new stage allowed for tiers of demonic spectators to look down from the back. Dancers placed sepulchral urns at Arimanes' feet before departing with Nemesis and other spirits in mechanical clouds.

The play's reception was mixed. The *Literary Gazette* found the 'little ginger-bread things behind the Principle of Evil', whose attendant spirits were dressed like lifeguardsmen, very laughable. Henry Crabb Robinson, who went on the first night, got little pleasure from it apart from the scenery, 'There must be some merit in this poem since Goethe admired it – but as a drama nothing could be worse … Action there is not. It is a sort of Don Juan without wit or fun or character.' **CF**

L. Werner
1824–1901

451 *(illus. p. 489)*
The Meeting of Byron and Scott at Albemarle St. Spring 1815, an imaginary reconstruction, *c.* 1850

Watercolour, 31.8×40 cm
Signed bottom left: L Werner
London, John Murray
Exhibitions: London, Victoria and Albert Museum, 1974, E15
Literature: Smiles 1891, p. 267

At the table, left to right: Isaac D'Israeli, John Murray, Sir John Barrow; standing in front of the fireplace: George Canning; in the armchair: William Gifford; on the right: Sir Walter Scott and Lord Byron.

John Murray was instrumental in bringing Scott and Byron together at Albemarle Street, which, due to Murray's personality, had become a favoured meeting place for the literary figures of the day. Both Walter Scott and

Lord Byron had a talent for forming deep friendships. Soon after the meeting at Albemarle Street, Scott wrote to Thomas Moore 'Like the old heroes in Homer we exchanged gifts' (Cat. No. 452). This friendship, once struck, together with their mutual admiration for each other's work, overcame their very deep differences of opinion in the spheres of politics, religion and morality.

Byron had all the Waverley novels sent out to Italy as they appeared and he wrote in his journal, 5 January 1821, 'Read the conclusion for the fiftieth time (I have read all W Scott's novels at least fifty times), of the third series of *Tales of my Landlord* – grand work – Scotch Fielding, as well as great English poet – wonderful man! I long to get drunk with him …'

Scott felt a similar warmth for Byron and showed a sensitive insight into his melancholy. His review of *Childe Harold*, Canto III and *The Prisoners of Chillon* (*Quarterly Review*, Vol. 31, October 1816) discusses the Byronic hero, suggesting the unstated possibility of an autobiographical source. He also offered support to Byron through the period of Byron's separation and Byron dedicated *Cain* to Scott in 1821. **EE**

452

450

original stand left the house many years ago and that shown, though identical to it, was discovered by Martin Levy in 1980 and purchased for the house. Abbotsford was designed in what Scott called the 'Old Scotch Style' and contained remarkable 'Romantic Interiors' in the same style. Both the urn and the stand, however, represent British Greek Revival design and craftsmanship at their best – an entirely appropriate style to associate with ancient Athenian bones, and indeed with Byron. **CW**

452
Urn on Stand, 1816

Stand designed and made by George Bullock; urn probably designed by George Bullock
Urn, silver; stand, yew inlaid with ebony with gilt-brass mounts, Mona marble top
Urn H 58 cm; stand H 92 cm
Abbotsford, The Abbotsford Collection
Provenance: Abbotsford
Exhibitions: Washington, 1985, Cat. No. 527
Literature: Bullock 1988, p. 78; Wainwright 1989, p. 63, Fig. 141

This silver urn was presented by Lord Byron to Walter Scott soon after their last meeting in 1815 and bears several inscriptions, one of which describes its purpose: 'The bones contained in this urn were found in certain ancient sepulchres within the long walls of Athens in the month of February 1811'. Although the designer is not documented, silver designs of very much this character by Bullock exist and make an attribution to him likely. He certainly designed and supplied a stand for it which arrived at Abbotsford in November 1816. The

451

453

mously in 1814, that most profoundly changed the image of that country, its history and landscape for an international audience. *Ivanhoe* (1819) was a new departure, a vivid representation of medieval life which achieved even greater success in England than the 'Waverley Novels'; *Quentin Durward* (1823) was a comparable success in France.

Scott was created a baronet in 1820; George IV commissioned Lawrence to paint his portrait for the Waterloo Chamber at Windsor Castle, and Scott took a leading role in organising the 1822 reception of the king in Edinburgh. Scott's literary and material prosperity found expression in his conversion of Abbotsford, the modest farmhouse he had acquired in 1812 on the river Tweed near Melrose Abbey, into a Scottish baronial castle (with gas lighting) at an estimated total cost of £76,000. The bankruptcy of his publishers, Constable, left him deeply in debt but he heroically resolved to repay his creditors, which further confirmed his popularity. Nevertheless, his health declined and after a number of paralytic seizures he died at Abbotsford. **CF**

454
Sir Walter Scott's Travelling Desk

Mahogany, bound and fitted with brass, 24.3×30×11.3 cm
London, John Murray
Provenance: after Sir Walter Scott's death given by his daughter Anne to the wife of Daniel Terry and thence to her brother James Nasmyth, by whom it was bequeathed to John Murray IV, May 1890
Literature: Smiles 1891, pp. 243–44

454

Sir William Allan
Edinburgh 1782–1850 Edinburgh

453
Sir Walter Scott, 1831

Oil on board, 81.6×64.5 cm
Signed and dated indistinctly on the belt in foreground: William Allan Pinxt 1831
London, National Portrait Gallery
Inv. No. 321
Provenance: bought from the artist by Robert Nasmyth, 1833; his sale, Christie's, 11 March 1871, Lot 47
Literature: Lockhart 1837; Walker 1985, Vol. 1, p. 441; Vol. 2, Plate 1064

This portrait shows Sir Walter Scott (1771–1832) in his study at Abbotsford, reading the Proclamation of Mary Queen of Scots prior to her marriage with Henry Darnley. He is surrounded with relics and mementos which relate to his works, with a bust of Shakespeare on the mantelpiece and Maida, his favourite stag hound, at his feet. Lord Byron's urn is placed on the table by the window.

The son of an Edinburgh lawyer, Scott also trained for and practised at the Scottish bar, even when the *Border Minstrelsy* (1802–03), the *Lay of the Last Minstrel* (1805), *Marmion* (1808) and *The Lady of the Lake* (1810) established him as the most famous poet of his day before Byron. But it was his Scottish novels, starting with *Waverley*, published anony-

The manuscript of *Waverley* was reputed to have been left forgotten in one of the inner compartments of this desk until it was accidentally discovered by Sir Walter Scott who then proceeded to complete and publish the novel. John Murray himself discounted this story. Another version describes how Scott came across the manuscript whilst searching for fishing tackle in a drawer at his home, Abbotsford. Whatever the truth it is a fact that Scott started writing *Waverley* some years earlier but laid the manuscript aside. It was finally published anonymously in 1814 but immediately recognised by both Byron and Murray as Scott's work.

Murray's association with Walter Scott dates back to the start of his career as a bookseller when he was appointed London agent for the Edinburgh firm of Constable by whom he was introduced to Scott. Their friendship thrived and together with George Canning, George Ellis and William Gifford they were instrumental in founding the *Quarterly Review* in 1809, as a Tory counter-measure to the Whig *Edinburgh Review*. Scott was a regular contributor to the *Quarterly*, reviewing many of Byron's works and Jane Austen's *Emma*.
EE

455

Grieve Family

455
Three-dimensional model set design for A Vision of the Bard, 1832

Pen and ink and wash, 21.5 × 27.2 cm
London, University of London, Sterling Library
Inv. No. Grieve Collection 473
Exhibitions: Sunderland, 1979, p. 76, Cat. No. 93
Literature: Rosenfeld 1965, p. 42, p. 86, Fig. 6; Rosenfeld 1973, p. 104

This model shows the Grieves working in the fashionable Gothic mode. The subject, *A Vision of the Bard*, was a masque by Sheridan Knowles, first performed at Covent Garden on 22 October 1832, in honour of Sir Walter Scott, who had died a month earlier. The setting is Dryburgh Abbey, where the Bard was buried. In the first scene, the spirit of Scott's 'Immortality' rose from his tomb, which then sank through a trap, and the background gave way to a series of tableaux from Scott's novels, managed by invisible strong lights. **CF**

Attributed to Mrs. Collins

456
Jane Austen, *c.* 1801

Silhouette, hollow-cut paper, 10 × 8 cm
Inscribed: L'aimable Jane
London, National Portrait Gallery

456

Inv. No. 3181
Provenance: pasted into a copy of *Mansfield Park,* Vol. 2, 2nd edn., bearing the owner's name A. E. Oakley in Vol. 1; Archie Miles; Arthur Rogers; purchased, 1944
Literature: Chapman 1948, pp. 30–31, 212–14; Hickman 1968, pp. 9–11; Piper 1970, p. 59; Walker 1985, Vol. 1, p.16; Vol. 2, Plate 30; Butler 1987, pp. 219–49

Jane Austen (1775–1817) was born into the impecunious lesser gentry and lived most of her life in the Hampshire countryside, with an eight-year interlude from her late twenties in Bath and Southampton. The world she wrote about in her novels was largely confined to the great houses, mansions and rectories of southern England, in which the moral progress of her heroines was acutely observed from a conservative standpoint. Yet larger forces intruded to threaten this traditional world, never more so than in *Mansfield Park* (1814), where they are represented by Mary Crawford and her brother Henry who, though superficially lively and attractive, are cynical, selfish, worldly, and metropolitan. London is the place which coarsens and corrupts, where, as Mary Crawford says, 'everything is to be got with money' and people are judged by outward appearances.

The identity of this profile silhouette is not absolutely proven, but it is difficult to think of any other reason for inserting a portrait inscribed 'L'aimable Jane' in this work. **CF**

458

Jane Austen
Steventon 1775–1817 Winchester

457
Letter to John Murray, 11 December 1815

Pen and ink on paper, 22.6×18.5 cm
London, John Murray
Literature: Modert 1990, F–286–387, p. 55;
Smiles 1891, pp. 282–83; Paston 1932, pp.
10–11

The Title page must be, Emma, Dedicated
by Permission to H.R.H. the Prince Regent
– And it is my particular wish that one set
should be completed and sent to H.R.H.
two or three days before the work is
generally public –

Published by John Murray in 1817 *Emma* was
dedicated, according to Jane Austen's instruction, to the Prince Regent. A professed
admirer of her work, the prince kept a set of
her novels in each of his residences. Although
three of Jane Austen's novels *Sense and Sensibility'* (1811), *Pride and Prejudice* (1813) and
Mansfield Park (1814) had been previously
published, *Emma* was her first novel to make
an impact on the critics. Walter Scott praised it
in the *Quarterly Review*, noting the originality with which she treated the mundane; years
later he echoed this observation when he recalled in his journal, 'That young lady had a
talent for describing the involvements, and
feelings and characters of ordinary life, which
is to me the most wonderful thing I ever
met with.' **EE**

William Hazlitt
Maidstone 1788–1830 London

458
Self Portrait, *c.* 1802

Oil on canvas, 69.3×58.8 cm
Maidstone, Museum and Art Gallery
Inv. No. 67–1909.26
Provenance: bequest of William Carew
Hazlitt, 1909
Literature: Hazlitt 1970 edn.; Barrell 1986,
pp. 314–38

The son of a Unitarian minister, William
Hazlitt rejected his father's wish that he too
should study for the ministry, and on hearing
Coleridge deliver his last inspiring sermon in
Shrewsbury in 1798, turned to philosophy and
art. Hazlitt studied painting in London.
Although he soon gave up his ambition to
become a professional portrait painter, he
never lost his passion for art, and it was a subject on which he wrote frequently. Raphael
and Titian were for Hazlitt the supreme
masters, and it is they whom he sought to follow in his own work, including this introspec-
tive self-portrait. He also completed portraits
of Wordsworth, Coleridge and Lamb in the
manner of Titian (the last is in the National
Portrait Gallery).

Coleridge described Hazlitt in 1803 as 'a
thinking, observant, original man, of great
power as a Painter of Portraits', but that 'His
manners are to 99 in 100 singularly repulsive–:
brow-hanging, shoe-contemplative, <u>strange'</u>.
But he added prophetically, 'He sends well-
headed & well-feathered Thoughts straight
forwards to the mark with a Twang of the
Bow-string.'

Hazlitt was among the first critics to assert
that art offered private satisfactions to a
private audience and was not intended to serve
a public function. His essay, *On the Pleasure
of Painting,* first published in the *London
Magazine* in December 1820 and reprinted in
Table-Talk the following year, celebrates the
personal happiness art brings. **CF**

William Bewick
Hurworth 1795–1866 Darlington

459
William Hazlitt, 1822

Black chalk heightened with white chalk,
29×22.1 cm
Maidstone, Museum and Art Gallery
Inv. No. 67–1909.13
Provenance: bequest of William Carew
Hazlitt, 1909

459

Unlike many of his fellow writers, notably
Coleridge and Wordsworth, Hazlitt remained
a radical throughout his life, and was a passionate advocate of man's rights and liberties.
He was a deadly controversialist starting with
A Reply to the Essay on Population (1807) – a
fierce attack on Thomas Malthus's pessimistic
views on overpopulation and the poor – and
continuing in his essays for Leigh Hunt's
Examiner, republished under the title of *The
Round Table* (1817).

His subject matter was wide ranging: from
parliamentary reports for the *Morning Chronicle*, incisive dramatic criticism for *The Times*,
brilliantly racy essays on the amusements of
the day, such as *The Indian Jugglers* (who performed at the Olympic New Theatre, Newcastle Street, Strand, during the winter of 1815)
and *The Fight* (on an outing to a famous box-
ing contest which took place at Hungerford in
1821), and portraits of leading contemporaries
collected together in *The Spirit of the Age*
(1825).

He had a talent for invective and for the cutting epigram arising from a keenly observed, if
cynical, view of human nature, but he himself
revealed his vulnerability when he fell in love
in 1820 with the nineteen-year-old daughter of
his landlord in Southampton Buildings, Chancery Lane. His frantic and, for his friends,
embarrassingly frank account of his obsession, written around the time this portrait
was drawn, was published as *Liber Amoris*
in 1823. Both his marriages were unsuccessful.
He died of cancer at 6 Frith Street, Soho,
aged fifty-two. **CF**

Attributed to Henry Hoppner Meyer
c. 1783–1847

460
Charles Lamb, 1826

Oil on canvas, 34.2×27.5 cm
London, National Portrait Gallery
Inv. No. 1312
Provenance: purchased from Miss Emily Collyer, 1902
Literature: Lamb ed. 1985, pp. 260, 316–18; Walker 1985, Vol. 1, pp. 1312, Vol. 2, Plate 718; Archer 1986, p. 38, No. 48

Charles Lamb (1775–1834) was born in the Inner Temple and educated at Christ's Hospital; he served as a clerk in the accountants office of the East India Company for thirty-three years, from 1792 to 1825. But it is as a quirkily original and good-humoured essay writer that he is remembered. He revived interest in the neglected English dramatists contemporary with Shakespeare and was the first critic to draw attention to the 'genius and character' of Hogarth, in an age which still played lip service to the primacy of history painting. Through the recommendation of Benjamin Robert Haydon, in August 1820 he began to contribute pieces under the pen-name of 'Elia' to John Scott's *London Magazine*, founded in January that year; the collected edition of these *Essays of Elia* (1823) made Lamb's name.

Despite a tragic personal life (his sister Mary stabbed their mother in a mad seizure and thereafter he agreed to take responsibility for her, although her condition steadily deteriorated), he celebrated the ordinary sights and sounds of London life, from its theatres to its beggars, avowing a passion for crowds and aversion to solitude: 'I love the very Smoke of London, because it has been the medium most familiar to my vision.'

This painting shows him seated surrounded by official papers with East India House in the background. In an autobiographical note he said his true works were not the 'Recreations' pompously christened his 'Works', but were to be found on the shelves of Leadenhall Street, filling some hundred volumes. Henry Crabb Robinson recorded calling on the artist Meyer in Red Lion Square on 26 May 1826,

460

when Lamb was sitting for the large-scale original version of this work, and commented, 'A strong likeness but it gives him the air of a thinking man and is more like the framer of a system of Philosophy than the genial and gay author of "The Essays of Elia".' That version belonged to Lamb's friend and biographer Sir Thomas Talfourd, and was bought at the sale of his effects by the India Office in 1902; it now hangs in the Foreign and Commonwealth Office. **CF**

Thomas De Quincey
Manchester 1785–1859 Lasswade

461
Confessions of an English Opium Eater, 1822

Published by Taylor and Hessey, 1822
16.8×10.2×1.8 cm
Grasmere, The Wordsworth Trust
Inv. No. DEQ (b) 1822
Exhibitions: New York, Bloomington and Chicago, 1987–88, Cat. No. 67

De Quincey's *Confessions* was an account of his early life and opium experiences, the latter used as a metaphor for the imagination and a means of exploring the mind. Born in Manchester the son of a textile merchant, De Quincey ran away from school to wander in north Wales and London. Sick and penniless in the capital, he was befriended by a prostitute, Ann, who was his own age of sixteen, and who looked after him when he fell ill in Soho Square off Oxford Street. It was in Oxford Street too that as an Oxford undergraduate suffering from toothache, De Quincey first bought opium from a druggist, a source of relief which developed into a lifelong addiction.

De Quincey's writing is often a celebration of loss and nothing is more poignant than his handling of irrecoverable beauty in the form of Ann, who returns to haunt his opium dream. In one passage he records their re-encounter on Easter morning, outside Dove Cottage, the house he took over from the Wordsworths at Grasmere in the Lake District:

And at a vast distance were visible, as a stain upon the horizon, the domes and cupolas of a great city – an image or faint abstraction, caught perhaps in childhood from some picture of Jerusalem. And not a bow-shot from me, upon a stone, and shaded by Judean palms, there sat a woman; and I looked; and it was – Ann! She fixed her eyes upon me earnestly; and I said to her at length: 'So then I have found you at last.' I waited: but she answered me not a word. Her face was the same as when I saw it last, and yet again how different! Seventeen years ago, when the lamp-light fell upon her face, as for the last time I kissed her lips . . . but suddenly her countenance grew dim; and, turning to the mountains, I perceived vapours rolling between us; in a moment, all had vanished; thick darkness came on; and, in the twinkling of an eye, I was far away from the mountains, and by lamp-light in Oxford-street, walking again with Ann – just as we walked seventeen years before, when we were both children.

CF and RW

Visitors to London always marvelled at the range and quality of the goods on sale in the shops. Many luxury items – silver and jewellery, clocks, watches and scientific instruments – were made by highly skilled craftsmen in the capital. And though the manufacture of porcelain had ceased in the late eighteenth century, there were still painting studios for decorating wares. All manufacturers of high quality products had to have London outlets to display their finest work, where prestigious potential clients could visit and where orders could be taken. Their managers kept the manufacturers aware of the latest fashion trends. London also served as the main port supplying valuable export markets.

462
The Islington Cup

Silver, parcel gilt, 49×31×21.5 cm
Marks: London hallmark for 1802–03; mark of Joseph Preedy.
The cup bears a shield cast with the arms of Alexander Aubert, and on the back, a shield engraved with an inscription recording its presentation by the former Corps of the Loyal Islington Volunteers, to Alexander Aubert, their Lt-Col. Commandant. The foot is engraved 'Designed by I. THURSTON, Modeled by E. COFFEN, EXECUTED BY J. Preedy GREAT NEWPORT STREET LONDON', and

'The whole Completed under the direction of MR. POWNALL & MR. WARREN December 20, 1802'
London, Trustees of the Victoria and Albert Museum
Inv. No. M12 to B–1987
Provenance: Alexander Aubert; Major William DuCane Luard; by descent; Gleneagles sale, Sotheby's, 26 August 1971, Lot. 144; Phillips, Edinburgh, 20 December 1985, Lot. 250, acquired with the aid of the National Art Collections Fund, the Associates of the V & A, the Worshipful Company of Goldsmiths, and the citizens of Islington, 1986
Literature: Nelson 1811, pp. 145–47, and 1829, p. 143; Culme 1977, pp. 100, 130–31

'A magnificent Silver Cup, of the value of 250 guineas' (*The Times,* 22 January 1803) was presented at the Canonbury Tavern, Islington, on 20 January 1803 to Alexander Aubert, the commanding officer of the Loyal Islington Volunteers, a regiment of local part-time volunteers formed in 1797 in response to the threat from post-Revolutionary France. The regiment never saw active service, but was jealous of its honour and disbanded in 1801.

The date of the presentation to Aubert was the second anniversary of the general resignation. Alexander Aubert (1730–1805) was a director of the London Assurance Company, a friend and champion of the engineer John Smeaton, and at Highbury House, Islington, the owner of one of the finest observatories in Britain. Although the cup celebrates the arts of war, it also alludes to Aubert's interest in astronomy by means of the head of Mercury with a star above it and the groups of astronomical instruments on the base. A chart engraved 'Transit of Venus', refers to the transit which Aubert observed on 3 June 1769.

The designer, John Thurston (1774–1822), was a book illustrator and exhibited at the Royal Academy from 1794 to 1812. The modeller, Edmund Coffin (or Coffen; born 1761), was a sculptor known from wax models and church monuments, who also exhibited models for candelabra at the Royal Academy. Joseph Preedy, the silversmith, first registered his mark in 1773 and was a partner of William Pitts in the 1790s. The presentation inscription on the shield is signed by John Roper, who is recorded as an engraver of city plans in 1805–07. **RE**

Rundell, Bridge and Rundell

Rundell, Bridge and Rundell, the royal goldsmiths, dominated the London trade in the first decades of the nineteenth century. The firm had its origins in the early eighteenth century in St. Paul's Churchyard in the City, moving to 32 Ludgate Hill in 1745. It was here that the Bath-trained jeweller Philip Rundell (1746–1827) was first employed by the then owner William Pickett, being taken into

462

463

464

partnership and eventually assuming outright control around 1785. In 1788 he took into partnership another Bath jeweller, John Bridge (1755–1834) and thereafter the firm's prosperity was assured. Acting both as manufacturers and retailers, Rundell and Bridge were concerned with most aspects of the trade in precious and semi-precious materials, with agents in the Middle and Far East and in South America. Their shop in Ludgate Hill sold all types of jewellery, gold boxes, watches and objects of vertu. John Bridge dealt with clients, including the royal family; Philip Rundell was an astute businessman (known by his employees as 'Vinegar' to Bridge's 'Oil'), concentrating on the jewel trade which supplied the firm's capital. Around 1805, they were joined by Philip Rundell's nephew, Edmond Waller Rundell.

Rundells were involved in a number of subsidiary businesses which supplied them with their stock and commissioned work, including a diamond-cutting business in Brick Lane, Spitalfields. To produce their modern plate, they established a workshop in Lime Kiln Lane, Greenwich in 1801 or 1802, managed by Benjamin Smith senior and Digby Scott, and when Smith set up on his own account around 1807, another in Dean Street, Soho, managed by Paul Storr until 1819. During this period the firm's products were registered under the

marks of Smith and Storr respectively, meaning that they as managers took responsibility for the fineness of the metal. Philip Rundell adopted this role in 1819, registering his mark on behalf of the firm in 1819–22, and John Bridge in 1823. The design of the pieces was undertaken by a variety of artists. William Theed senior R.A. (1764–1817) was in charge of the art department until his death, when John Flaxman (1755–1826) took over in an advisory capacity: he was more responsible than anyone for the firm's artistic reputation. His pupil, Edward Hodges Baily (1788–1867), acted as his assistant on the staff.

Three distinct styles can be associated with Rundells, who were, for much of the period, cut off from the influence of French design. Firstly, through Flaxman, they produced extremely chaste, simple neo-classical pieces inspired by Greek models. Secondly, through their role as royal goldsmiths and access to the royal collection, they (and Garrard) revived rococo styles from 1809. Thirdly, they were involved in the burgeoning antiquarian movement not only through discreet sales of late Stuart royal plate from the jewel-house in 1808 and onwards, purchases of antique plate for the Prince of Wales, among other clients, but also the production of Gothic Revival pieces designed both by Flaxman and the youthful Augustus Welby Pugin. **JC**

463

Two-handled Vase (The Theocritus Cup), 1812

Designed by John Flaxman
Silver-gilt *krater* form with handles of twisted vine stems and plain circular foot; chased on a matted ground with scenes on one side of two youths competing for the favours of a girl and on the other with a fisherman hauling a net and a boy in a vineyard with foxes approaching; lip and sides chased with fruiting vines; lower border chased with acanthus whorls,
H 24 cm, D 25 cm
Marks: London hallmark for 1812–13; maker's mark for Paul Storr
Engraved: RUNDELL BRIDGE ET RUNDELL AURIFICES REGIS ET PRINCIPIS WALLIAE LONDIN FECERUNT; Prince of Wales's feathers and motto within crowned Garter motto; CR (cipher of Queen Charlotte) within crowned chain collar
Windsor Castle, H.M. Queen Elizabeth II Inv. No. GV 526
Exhibitions: London, Queen's Gallery, 1991–92, Cat. No. 86
Literature: Jones 1911, p. 120, Plate LXI; Culme 1977, p. 19

465

465
The Shield of Achilles, 1822

Designed and modelled by John Flaxman
Silver-gilt circular shield; the centre cast in high relief with Apollo driving his chariot over a full moon flanked by the Pleiades; the border cast and chased in medium and low relief with seven scenes: marriage procession and banquet; quarrel and judicial appeal; siege, ambush and battle; harvest; vintage; oxherds defending their beasts against lions; Cretan dance; within a border of ocean waves; D 99 cm
Marks: London hallmarks of 1822–23; maker's mark of Philip Rundell; inscribed on reverse 'Designed and Modelled by John Flaxman R.A. Executed and Published by Rundell, Bridge and Rundell, Goldsmiths and Jewellers to His Majesty, London MDCCCXXII'
Anglesea Abbey, National Trust
Provenance: William Lowther, 2nd Earl of Lonsdale; by descent to the 6th Earl; his sale, Christie's, 20 February 1947, Lot 136; bought Huttleston Broughton, 1st Lord Fairhaven; bequeathed with Anglesea Abbey and its contents to the National Trust, 1966
Exhibitions: Washington, 1985, Cat. No. 529
Literature: Jones 1911, pp. 17–18, Plate 54; Wark 1970, No. 58; Bury and Snodin 1984, pp. 274–83

The Shield of Achilles was John Flaxman's masterwork in silver. It represents the episode in the eighteenth book of the *Iliad* in which Hephaestus, lame god of metalworking, made a large and powerful shield for Achilles, conceived as a mirror of the world of gods and men, with 'the mighty stream of ocean' round the rim. Flaxman evidently was familiar with the passage in the original Greek and persuaded Rundells to commission him to re-create it around 1810, when he received 100 guineas for four models and six drawings.

Unlike his other undertakings for the royal goldsmiths, Flaxman not only provided detailed drawings but also made the model for the shield, first as a general design and then moulded in compartments and cast in plaster. Finally, he made the necessary additions or subtractions to form a harmonious and technically feasible whole. The finished model was handed over in 1818 after payment of £200 in January 1817 on account, and £525 on delivery. Four copies were made in silver gilt: two hallmarked 1821–22 went to the king and to the Duke of York (Huntington Collection,

The scenes on the vase are based on the description in the First Idyll of Theocritus of the cup that was given by a goatherd to the shepherd Thyrsis in return for singing his song about Daphnis. Though of Greek *krater* form, the handles are inspired by Roman models.

The cup was given to the Prince Regent by Queen Charlotte. There are at least two other versions, both hallmarked for 1811–12: one with a stand was presented by the Mayor and Corporation of Liverpool to Alderman Thomas Earle for the improvements he made to the town and port (Merseyside County Museums); the other is in an American collection. The same shape and decoration were also used for wine coolers. CF

John Flaxman
York 1755–1826 London

464 *(illus. p. 495)*
Study for the Theocritus Cup, c. 1811

Pen and ink and wash, 27.7 × 23.8 cm
London, Trustees of the Victoria and Albert Museum
Inv. No. 2410
Exhibitions: London, Royal Academy, 1979, Cat. No. 193
Literature: Wark 1970, No. 59, pp. 77–79

The suitors' group is based on the 'Orpheus' relief in the Villa Albani, for which a study exists in Flaxman's Italian sketchbook (Victoria and Albert Museum, E. 90–1964, fo. 41). There is a study for the figures on the reverse of the cup in the British Museum, which also holds an etching of the completed work, perhaps made for Rundells. This preliminary

Tea/Coffee/Breakfast Service. Cat. No. 468

Tureen, Cover and Stand, *c.* 1795. Cat. No. 476

Dessert Dish, *c.* 1815. Cat. No. 479b

Pair of Ice Pails, *c.* 1800. Cat. No. 477

SILVER AND JEWELLERY

499

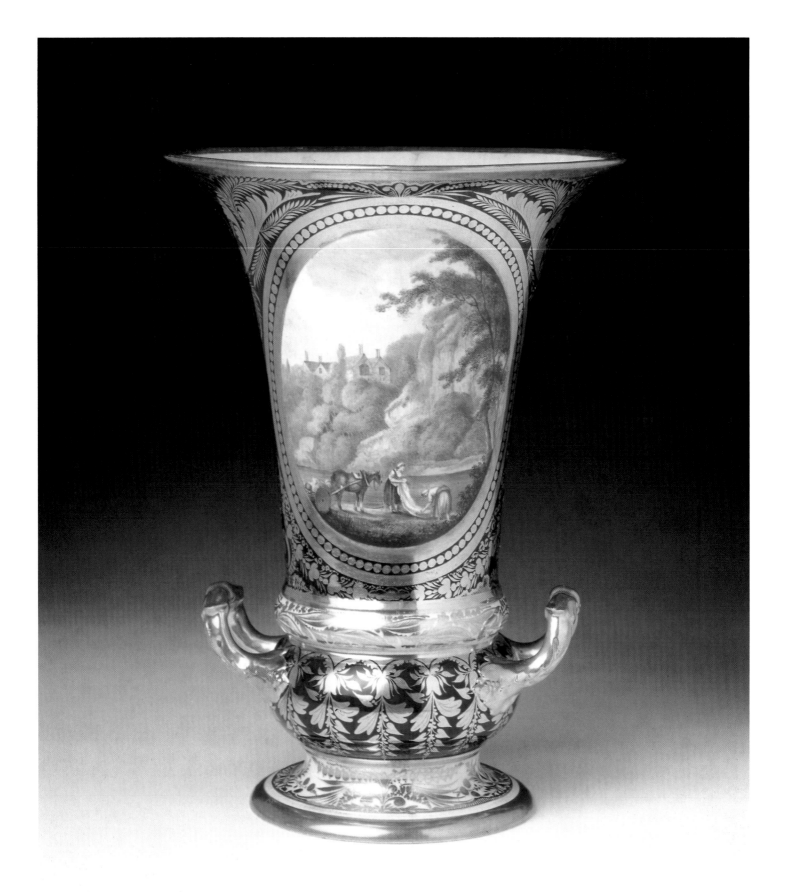

Elongated, Campana-Shaped Vase, *c.* 1812. Cat. No. 484

San Marino). The third and fourth, hall-marked 1822–23, went to the Duke of Northumberland (Al-Tajir Collection) and to the Earl of Lonsdale, the present example.

When first placed on display in Rundells' Ludgate Hill premises in 1823, the street outside was blocked with carriages and pedestrians anxious to see this 'masterpiece of modern art', as the Rundells' inventory for William IV in 1832 described it. It was rotated on a stand so that the different scenes could be better appreciated. **CF**

466
Two-Handled Vase (The Age of Gold and Age of Silver), 1826

Designed by John Flaxman
Skyphos form gilt on one side, silver on the other; two rectangular plaques cast and chased in low relief on one side with a family group representing the Golden Age and on the other with two figures, male and female with libation vessels, representing the Silver Age; H 15.6 cm, W 24.3 cm
Marks: London hallmark for 1826–27; maker's mark for John Bridge
Engraved: RUNDELL BRIDGE ET RUNDELL AURIFICES REGIS LONDINI; lion on a crown within crowned Garter motto
Windsor Castle, H.M. Queen Elizabeth II Inv. No. GV521
Exhibitions: London, Queen's Gallery, 1991–92, Cat. No. 134
Literature: Jones 1911, p. 108, Plate 55

In this piece Flaxman sought to revive the simple form of the Athenian *skyphos* or deep cup, as well as the linear purity of Grecian painted decoration and low-relief ornament. The design of the plaques is taken from plates nine and eleven of Flaxman's *Compositions from the Works, Days and Theogony of Hesiod*, published by Longman in 1817. The vase was invoiced by Rundells on 13 March 1827 at £51.19s. (RA 26116). **CF**

467
Tureen and Cover, 1826–27

Design attributed to John Flaxman
Silver gilt, in the form of a clam shell borne on three seahorses rising from a triangular base worked in imitation of waves; the cover surmounted by lobsters, serpents, lizards, etc., with a triton seated on the whorl blowing a conch shell; the feet comprising tortoises, shells and seaweed; H 44.5 cm
Marks: London hallmark for 1826–27;

467

maker's mark of John Bridge; the Garter and motto engraved inside
Windsor Castle, H.M. Queen Elizabeth II Inv. No. GV 234
Exhibitions: London, Royal Academy, 1979, Cat. No. 189
Literature: Jones 1911, p. 160, Plate 81; London 1954, No. 109; Bury 1966, pp. 152–58

The tureen is one of four which were part of the Grand Service, a collection of plate started by the Prince of Wales *c.* 1804 and added to for

466

the rest of his life. Rundells were from the early years of the century in the forefront of the rococo revival. Their source of inspiration was a fine mid eighteenth-century service in the royal collection, which had been made for Frederick, Prince of Wales, by Nicholas Sprimont. By the 1820s they were supplying silver in increasingly naturalistic forms, rather than works which merely displayed a superficial embellishment of rocaille motifs. Moreover, antiquarian tastes were developing, including that of the king: a late sixteenth century Nautilus cup by Nicolaus Schmidt of Nuremburg was bought in 1823 by George IV from Rundells, who had themselves bought it at the Wanstead sale of 1822. It too was adorned with marine motifs, and was considered by Flaxman to be by Cellini.

The attribution of this design to Flaxman is based on that given to the uncovered version of the tureens in the 1840s and to the massive wine cooler of 1829, similarly ornamented, in the royal collection. Moreover, there are two sheets of designs by Flaxman, one in the Victoria and Albert Museum, the other in the British Museum, which include related motifs.

The tureens were delivered on 5 November 1829 (RA 26245) and charged, with a wainscot box, at £2,452.16s.9d. The same account lists six soup ladles *en suite*. (H.M. Queen Elizabeth II). **CF**

470

468 *(illus. p. 497)*
Tea/Coffee/Breakfast Service

Philip Rundell, John Bridge, Charles Eley, Robert Jones; Flight, Barr and Barr, Worcester
Sterling silver with repoussé and chased decoration and cast finials, gold plated, carved ivory handles; rattle, 22 carat gold and coral; soft-paste porcelain cups and saucers
Marks: Grimwade, 2228, 1172, 298; Godden No. 4344
Dimensions of case: 20.3 cm. × 80.4 cm. × 41.1 cm
Toronto, Canada, Royal Ontario Museum Inv. No. 969.367.1.1-76
Provenance: Elizabeth, Marchioness of Conyngham; ... H. R. Jessop Ltd; Mr. William Bell, art dealer, Aberdeen, *c.* 1949–50; Mr. and Mrs. D. Lorne Pratt, by whom bequeathed to the Museum
Literature: Penzer 1954, p. 188; Hunt 1984, pp. 347–348; Kaellgren 1992

This set, which is part of Rundells' invoice of 14 March, 1827 (RA 26116), was a gift to Elizabeth, Marchioness of Conyngham (1768–1861), George IV's mistress from 1820 until his death.
The service is exemplary of the evolving taste of the 1820s, as well as the shop practices of important goldsmiths. Like French Empire silver, the service is decorated with contrasting polished and chased textures and with Regency/Empire motifs. However, the robust proportions, the lobed bodies and the richness of decoration are indicative of the emerging Rococo Revival style, which was to dominate British manufactures by the 1850s.
Large workshops like Rundells could assemble a de luxe set like this from existing stock (the galvanic goblet of 1818, the three-piece tea set and large salver of 1821), from pieces made for the order and from items supplied by specialists. The latter include: silver forks and spoons, 1825, from Charles Eley; a 'very elegant Gold coral' from Robert Jones, who registered his mark in 1822; and two pairs of tea and coffee cups with saucers from the Flight, Barr and Barr factory at Worcester. The handsome mahogany case, which at £48 was the third most expensive piece in the set, was produced by a specialist case maker. It retains its original lining and fittings and is inlaid with silver plates for Lady Conyngham's engraved cipher and the lock. The intended use of the set by George IV and Lady Conyngham is signalled by their ciphers engraved on each and every piece and by the pairs of plates, cups and saucers. The pap boat with spoon, small mug, and porringer, along with the unengraved gold rattle, were possibly intended to serve visiting grandchildren, nieces and nephews.
As a rare, nearly intact survival, this service constitutes an unusual study in the luxury and formal display of the court of George IV. **PK**

469
Medallion, 1814–15

Profile head under glass of the Prince Regent flanked by sprays, in gold, of palm and laurel mounted on dark blue enamel on an engine-turned radiating ground, with gold back, 8.8 × 6.5 × 1.5 cm
Medallion supplied by Rundell, Bridge and Rundell; head modelled by Peter Rouw (1770–1852), and made by John Barber
Inscription at the truncation: 'RUNDELL BRIDGE ET RUNDELL./J. BARBER. F'
London, Trustees of the Victoria and Albert Museum
Inv. No. M.104–1966
Provenance: presented by the Prince Regent to Sir William Knighton, Bart.; thence by descent to J. L. Jervoise Esq.
Literature: Bury 1982, p. 107 (Case 17, Board E, No. 10); Tait ed. 1984, Vol. 1, No. 390; Bury 1991, Vol. 1, p. 82

George IV, both as regent and as king, distributed splendid relief portraits, mounted in boxes and set in medallions. Sir William Knighton, believed to have been given this example, attended the Marquess of Wellesley as a doctor on his mission to Spain in 1809, was recommended by him to the Prince of Wales in 1810, became one of the prince's physicians, and was created a baronet on 1 January 1813. He won the complete confidence of George IV, and from 1822 served him as private secretary and keeper of the privy purse. A date of 1814 or 1815 for the medallion is suggested by the inclusion of the attributes of peace and victory in the design. **RE**

470
Box, 1815

Probably Rundell, Bridge and Rundell
Gold, enamel and tortoiseshell, L 8 × D 3 cm
Marked in relief on the truncation: ROUW CER. EF^T/BARBER FEC^T (i.e. Rouw cera effinxit, Barber fecit; Rouw modelled it in wax, Barber made it)
London, British Museum, Hull Grundy Gift Inv. No. 1978, 10–2, 228
Literature: Tait ed. 1984, p. 68, No. 390, Vol. 1, pp. 98–99, Fig. 390, Vol. 2, Plate 20

The inscription inside the lid of this exquisitely crafted box records that it was a gift from the Prince Regent to John Watier, his former chef, who had founded Watier's club under the prince's patronage in 1807. Watier's was the dandy club *par excellence* and remained extremely fashionable until 1819. It was noted both for its outstanding food and for the reckless and extravagant gambling its members indulged in. The most popular game was macao in which only one card was dealt to each player and the winning number was nine. The stakes were high and huge sums were made and lost. Scrope Davies won £6,065 in one evening playing macao at Watier's, but two years later he was in debt to the tune of £1,110.13s. to the club.

Peter Rouw was appointed sculptor and modeller of gems to the Prince of Wales in 1807. The association of Rouw and Barber as modeller and engraver suggests that the box was probably made by Rundell, Bridge and Rundell. Barber was employed by Rundells at the time and his name appears, together with theirs, on Cat. No. 469. **EE**

471

471
Box, 1829

Gold, 10×6.8×2.7 cm
Marks: stamped inside the lid with a full set of London hallmarks for 1828–29, with maker's mark in a rectangular shield; partial hallmarks stamped inside the base and on rim of base, which is engraved S JONES, FECIT, CHEAPSIDE
London, Trustees of the British Museum
Inv. No. 1921, 6–18, 1
Provenance: given by Lady Emily Peel
Literature: London's Roll of Fame 1884, pp. 140–41

On 26 February 1829 the Court of Common Council in the presence of the lord mayor and chamberlain of the City of London, resolved to present the Freedom of the City in a gold box valued at 100 guineas to the Rt. Hon. Robert Peel M.P. This gold box, ornately embellished on the lid with the arms of the City of London in high relief, still contains the original parchment granting the Freedom. The base of the box bears the arms of Peel with crest and motto, 'INDUSTRIA', also in high relief. Peel was honoured for the support he gave the prime minister, the Duke of Wellington, in pressing for Catholic emancipation.

Peel had in fact staunchly opposed emancipation throughout his political career but after he accepted office under Wellington in 1828 as home secretary and leader of the House of Commons, he came to the conclusion that the troubles in Ireland had reached such a crisis point, that to persist in opposition might lead to civil strife. He thereafter, together with Wellington, urged the king to accept the reform. The box was presented to Peel on 8 April 1829, two days before the king finally and reluctantly gave his consent to the Roman Catholic Relief Bill. **EE**

472
Pair of Telescopic Argand Lamps

Sheffield plate, 79×35.5 cm
Birmingham, *c.* 1814–23
Marks: maker's marks for Matthew Boulton and Co.

London, Trustees of the Victoria and Albert Museum
Inv. No. M.14a and b–1987
Provenance: each lamp is engraved on the stem with the Arms of Charles William Stewart, 1st Baron Stewart, later 3rd Marquess of Londonderry (d. 1854),

472

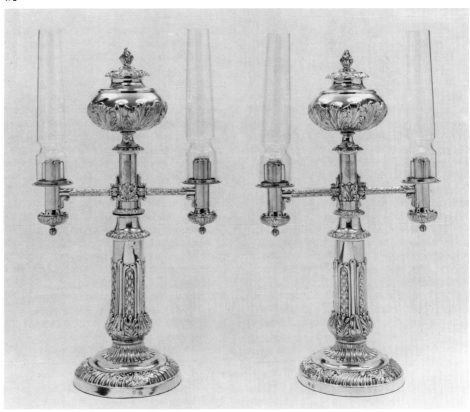

473

Thomas Baxter Junior
Worcester 1782–1821 Worcester

473
China Painters: The Painting Room of Mr. Baxter, No. 1 Goldsmith Street, Gough Square, 1810

Watercolour over pencil, 47×43.5 cm
Signed and dated: T. Baxter 1810
London, Trustees of the Victoria and Albert
Museum
Inv. No. 782–1894
Provenance: G. Underwood
Exhibitions: London, Royal Academy, 1811,
No. 722; The Museum of London, 1987;
Victoria and Albert Museum, 1992
Literature: Fox 1987, pp. 106, 259; Sandon
1987, pp. 6–8; Godden 1988, pp. 129–31

Thomas Baxter senior was a painter and gilder
who ran a porcelain decorating studio in
London, buying in his supplies of porcelain
blanks direct from manufacturers, notably
John Rose of Coalport. Thomas junior was
one of the most skilful of porcelain painters
active in the early nineteenth century. He
studied under Henry Fuseli at the Royal
Academy and was a regular exhibitor there
from 1802 until his death. He remained at his
father's studio until 1814 when ill health forced
him to return to his native Worcester. He then
worked for Flight, Barr and Barr, and subsequently for Chamberlain's factory and at
Swansea.
   His name is generally associated with cabinet porcelain bearing fine enamelled decoration, but virtually all the pieces shown in this
watercolour are relatively plain. The one exception is the plate in the foreground, which
commemorates the death of Nelson (Cat. No.
474). The upright figure holding a dividing
plate for transferring and centring patterns is
thought to represent the artist; his father is
thought to be the seated figure decorating a
saucer. **HY**

474
Plate, 1806

Coalport, decorated in London by Thomas
Baxter junior
Hard-paste porcelain with low-fired glaze,
gilded, and enamelled in colours with scenes
commemorating the life of Viscount Nelson,
D 24 cm
Signed and dated: T. Baxter 1806
London, Trustees of the Victoria and Albert
Museum
Inv. No. C.67–1984

encircled with the collar of the Order of the
Bath; purchased by the Museum, 1987
Literature: Turner 1989, p. 390

The Sheffield plate industry, pioneered by
Thomas Boulsover (1705–1788) and exploited
by Matthew Boulton (1728–1809) in Birmingham, introduced new industrialised processes
which simultaneously lowered manufacturing
costs while at the same time boosting the rate
of production to give the Sheffield plates a
highly competitive edge. However, until the
late eighteenth century, the majority of goods
using fused plate from Sheffield or Birmingham, only competed directly with the
standard ware produced by the London silversmiths. For the prestigious single commissions, the London silversmiths dominated.
   During the first half of the nineteenth
century, when the fused plate industry continued to flourish and expand until the introduction of electroplating in 1840, there was
increasing competition by the Sheffield platers
to compete for these highly lucrative commis-

sions on equal terms, seeking to boost their
market through the establishment of lavish
London salerooms. These lamps illustrate that
they could compete very successfully.
   Since no marking system was ever introduced for the industry, which dated the production (unlike the date letter on sterling
silver), it is most unusual to be able to date a
piece of Sheffield plate with any degree of
accuracy, but in the case of these lamps the
heraldic inscriptions enable us to do this. Since
Stewart became Baron Stewart in 1814 and was
created Viscount Seeham only six years later in
1823, these lamps must have been made between these dates. **ET**

474

Provenance: Blenstock House sale, Phillips, 7 December 1983, Lot 232
Exhibitions: London, Victoria and Albert Museum, 1991
Literature: Mallet 1987; Sandon 1991, pp. 34–36

The central panel contains a figure of Britannia mournfully unveiling a bust of Nelson. The boarded panels represent his victories (the battles of the Nile and Copenhagen, the surrender of San Josef, the last after a painting by Daniel Orme), and his death at Trafalgar, possibly based on the painting by Benjamin West.

During the period immediately after Nelson's death in 1805 a great many commemorative objects were produced, inspired by national sentiment as much as by desire for profit. Baxter's plate is an exception, not only because of the quality of design and finish, but because the artist had personal ties with Nelson's household – and the plate itself seems to have been his personal memorial of Nelson, one that he kept for at least four years after its completion.

A preliminary design for the central figure of Britannia survives in an album of Thomas Baxter's drawings (National Maritime Museum) in which she is clearly identifiable as Emma Hamilton, with whom Nelson shared a house at Merton and where Baxter is known to have spent some time as Emma's guest in 1802–03. He is also recorded as having exhibited an enamel portrait of Emma's husband, Sir William Hamilton, at the Royal Academy in 1805; and in 1814, when working at the Worcester factory of Flight, Barr and Barr, he modelled a portrait medallion of Nelson, Sir William's successor in Emma Hamilton's affections.

This plate is an impressive documentary piece, one that was clearly highly valued by Baxter himself as it features prominently in the foreground of this father's china-decorating workshop (Cat. No. 473). **HY**

Derby China Works

The foundation of the china works in Derby around 1748 can probably be attributed to Andrew Planché, son of Paul Planché, a London coffee-house man of Huguenot descent. By 1756, an agreement had been drawn up between John Heath, a banker, Planché, the chinamaker and William Duesbury, an enameller and repairer from Staffordshire, forming the first William Duesbury and Company. The second Duesbury had created an international name for Derby, alongside Meissen and Sèvres, his father having taken over the Chelsea Porcelain Manufactory in 1770. By 1775, the Derby factory had received the royal warrant and therefore the right to use the crown. In 1795, Michael Kean, an Irish miniaturist, was taken into partnership. Two years later, he married Duesbury's widow and ran the factory until 1811. That year, Robert Bloor, clerk to the partnership, leased the factory, inaugurating the Bloor period, which continued until 1848.

A London showroom was opened in 1773 in Bedford Street, Covent Garden, run from 1777 by the celebrated Joseph Lygo, whose letters to Derby form a basis for modern research on the factory. During the 'Bloor period', the business was based at 34 Old Bond Street and managed by Mr. Courtney. **JT**

William 'Quaker' Pegg
Whitmore 1775–1851 Derby

475 *(illus. p. 509)*
Sketchbook, 1813

Pencil and watercolour on paper, 33 × 21 × 2.3 cm
Signed and dated top of page two: Wm Pegg/Seventh Mo. 1st 1813
Derby, Royal Crown Derby Museum
Provenance: William Pegg; Thomas Martin Randall; by descent
Exhibitions: London, Victoria and Albert Museum, 1987, No. 30; Toronto, 1988; Derby, 1990, No. 65
Literature: Twitchett 1980, pp. 174–78, Colour Plates 55–62

William Pegg is generally considered to be one of the finest natural flower painters ever to paint on china. Apprenticed to a china painter in 1790, he extended his range through the study of botanical prints and joined the Derby factory in 1796. But because of his religious beliefs as a Quaker he gave up painting in 1801 and burnt most of his sketches. When he returned to work for Robert Bloor in 1813, he wrote he had 'Lost the feeling which induced

me to give up china painting . . .' Some of the sketches here demonstrate his great knowledge of plants; many reveal the new freedom with which he now brought to his art (Cat. Nos. 478–79). **JT**

476 *(illus. p. 498)*
Tureen, Cover and Stand, *c.* 1795

Derby, Duesbury and Kean
Soft-paste porcelain, gilded and enamelled in colours, H 31.7 × D 45.2 cm
Marks: blue crown, crossed batons with six dots and D; pattern number 197; the tureen also marked W. 676, and the stand with a cross incised; inscribed in blue with the names in English of the plants depicted
London, Trustees of the Victoria and Albert Museum
Inv. No. 3068 to 3068b–1901
Provenance: transferred from the Museum of Practical Geology
Exhibitions: London, Victoria and Albert Museum, 1987, Cat. No. 14b (also Toronto 1988)
Literature: Haslem 1876, p. 95; Mortimer 1979, p. 24

The painting on this piece is of the highest quality and has been attributed by Haslem to William 'Quaker' Pegg. However, among a group of recently rediscovered drawings by Derby painters is a closely related design for a comport bearing the same arrangement of tulips and lilac as here. The back of this drawing bears the inscription 'by Billingsley', which was perhaps added by Bemrose. The attributions on Bemrose's drawings are not always infallible but this drawing, which corresponds to a comport at Castle Howard, is by the same hand as other designs that can be firmly linked to pieces by William Billingsley. It therefore seems more likely that the painting here is by Billingsley than by Pegg, though since the named flowers are all copied from the plates of John Edwards' *A Collection of Flowers drawn after Nature . . .* (London, 1783–95), a publication that may have been available to other Derby painters, there remains some room for doubt.

If the painting here is indeed attributable to Billingsley then the tureen can be dated before October 1796, when the artist left Derby for Pinxton. Billingsley was a figure of considerable importance for British ceramics: he was apprenticed at Derby and he is generally regarded as the finest of the flower painters working there until his departure in 1796. In that year he embarked on a remarkable odyssey that took him from one porcelain factory after another – Pinxton, Mansfield, Torksey, Worcester, Coalport, Nantgarw, and Swansea – where he worked not only as a painter, but also as a body-mixer developing soft-paste porcelain recipes. **HY**

477 *(illus. p. 499)*
Pair of Ice Pails, *c. 1800*

Derby, Duesbury and Kean
Soft-paste porcelain, painted with flowers,
H 36 cm
Marks: blue crown, crossed batons and D;
one inscribed on base 'Eastern Poppy, &
Piquette Carnation/China Aster, Dwarf
Double Poppy, & Hyacinth'; the other,
'Tulips, French Marigold, & Larkspur/
White & Strip'd Roses'
Derby, Derby Museums and Art Gallery
Inv. No. 636-1964
Provenance: Boswell and Ward
Literature: Barrett and Thorpe 1971, p. 65,
Fig. 152

As with Cat. No. 476, the flowers are based on
the plates for John Edwards' *A Collection of
Flowers drawn after Nature.* **AB**

478
Pair of Plates, *c. 1813–15*

Derby, Robert Bloor and Co.
Soft-paste porcelain, gilded and enamelled in
colours with flowers, D 22.4 cm and 22.7 cm
Marks: red crown with crossed batons, six
dots and D; inscribed in red on base 'Lilies
of the Valley, Large Pinks & Carnation' and
'Convolvulus Major, & Bloody-wall-flower'
London, Trustees of the Victoria and Albert
Museum
Inv. Nos. Circ.125–1931, Circ.126–1931
Provenance: Mrs. A. W. Hearn Collection;
bequeathed, 1935
Literature: Mortimer 1979

The painting on these plates has been attributed to William 'Quaker' Pegg since at least
the 1930s. The plates are clearly related to both
the service cited by Mortimer as the touchstone of Pegg's style, and to the plate and dessert dish, Cat. No. 479. **HY**

479
a) Dessert Plate, *c. 1815*

Derby, Robert Bloor and Co.
Soft-paste porcelain, painted with flowers,
D 22.4 cm
Marks: red crown, crossed batons and D;
inscribed in red on base 'Great Bluebottle,
Mountain Primula, & Rose Cistus'

b) Dessert Dish, *c. 1815*

Derby, Robert Bloor and Co.
Soft-paste porcelain, painted with flowers,
29.2×21.5 cm

479a

Marks: red crown, crossed batons and D;
number 2; inscribed in red on base 'Peony,
Great Honey-flower, & Viper Buglass'

Derby, Derby Museums and Art Gallery
Inv. Nos. 376–49–1904 and 376–88–1904
Provenance: Henry Evans Bequest
Exhibitions: Derby, 1877
Literature: Derby Corporation Art Gallery
1905, pp. 9–10, Nos. 49, 82 respectively

480
Ice Pail and Cover (Fruit Cooler) *c.
1811*

Derby, Duesbury and Kean
Soft-paste porcelain, gilded and painted with
full-blown pink roses on a blue ground,
bearing the quartered arms of Pendock
Barry of Roclaveston Manor Estate,
Tollerton, Nottingham within a circle of oak
leaves and acorns, H 26.5×D 26 cm
Marks: gold crown, crossed batons, six dots
and D
Derby, Royal Crown Derby Museum
Provenance: Pendock Barry; Pendock Barry
Barry; Miss Elizabeth Jones; Herbert L.
Satterlee; Parke Bernet, New York, 18
October 1947
Exhibitions: London, Royal Academy, 1985,
Cat. No. 64
Literature: Swain 1984, pp. 68–72; Twitchett
1980, p. 194

The ice pail, one of a pair in the Royal Crown
Derby Museum, comes from one of the most
celebrated services produced by the Derby
factory. The distinctive rose decoration is in
the tradition of William Billingsley (1758–
1828), son of a Chelsea flower painter, who
brought a meticulous delicacy to the painting
of flowers on porcelain. He had however
moved from Derby to Pinxton in 1796 and
the artist most likely to have undertaken such

high quality work is Thomas Martin Randall
(1786–1859), who left Derby for London in
1813 and established an enamelling business in
Islington.
   The ninety pieces offered for sale separately
in 1894 realised £496.11s., then the highest
price ever obtained for a dessert service of old
Derby. Evidently they did not include the ice
pails, it being sometimes the custom to remove
the most valuable items, such as the pails, and
to sell them separately. The pails appeared in a
1947 New York sale of forty pieces from the
service. **JT**

481
**Ice Pail, Cover and Liner (Fruit
Cooler),** *c. 1810*

Derby, Duesbury and Kean
Soft-paste porcelain, gilded and decorated
with named views 'Near Broseley,
Shropshire' and 'In Llangollen Vale,
Denbighshire', attributed to George
Robertson, H 28×D 25.5 cm
Marks: red crown, crossed batons, six dots
and D, with the descriptions of the scenes
Derby, Royal Crown Derby Museum
Literature: Twitchett 1980, pp. 226–27, Fig.
291, pp. 263–64; Fy-Hall and Mundt 1983,
p. 84, Fig. 120

George Robertson (1777–1833) was one of the
most distinguished landscape and marine
painters to work in ceramics, displaying a fine
sense of colour and meticulous attention to
detail. He came to the Derby factory from
Scotland in 1797, later setting himself up as a
drawing master. The highly worked-up and
burnished gilding is typical of the factory in
this period. **JT**

482
Covered Urn, *c. 1810*

Derby, Duesbury and Kean
Soft-paste porcelain, ground gilded by
Samuel Keys and painted with two panels of
flowers by John Brewer, H 34.5×D 21 cm
Marks: red crown, crossed batons, six dots
and D; gilder's number 1; number 38
Derby, Royal Crown Derby Museum
Provenance: David Holborough Collection
Literature: Twitchett 1980, p. 231, Colour
Plate 50

The gilder's mark, number 1, indicates Samuel
Keys' position as head gilder at this date. The
piece also shows the use of simulated bronze
decoration in the band above the snake
handles and on the base. **JT**

480

481

482

483

483
Coffee Pot and Cover, *c.* 1810

Derby, Duesbury and Kean
Soft-paste porcelain, painted by Robert
Brewer with named views 'Castle at
Spolleto' and 'The Approach to the Cascade
at Terni', H 24.5 × D 23.5 cm
Marks: red crown, crossed batons, six dots
and D
Derby, Royal Crown Derby Museum
Provenance: George Woods Esq.

Robert Brewer (1775–1857), the younger
brother of John Brewer (see Cat. No. 484) was
almost certainly a pupil of the watercolour
artist Paul Sandby (1725–1809) and lived in
Bloomsbury before joining his brother in
Derby in 1797. **JT**

484 *(illus. p. 500)*
Elongated Campana-Shaped Vase, *c.* 1812

Derby, Robert Bloor and Co.
Soft-paste porcelain, gilded on blue ground
and painted by John Brewer with a view
'Near Lismore, Ireland', H 26.5 × D 19 cm
Marks: red crown, crossed batons, six dots
and D, with description of the scene;
workman's numeral No. 44
Derby, Royal Crown Derby Museum
Exhibitions: Derby, 1990, No. 10
Literature: Twitchett 1980, p. 232, Plate 52

John Brewer (1764–1816), the elder son of two
London-based artists, John and Ann Brewer,
came to work in Derby as a china painter and
drawing master in the 1793. With the help of
such skilled watercolourists, Derby pioneered
the painting of topographical scenes on British
ceramics. **JT**

486

485
Pair of Flower Pots and Stands, *c.* 1820

Derby, Robert Bloor and Co.
Soft-paste porcelain, gilded and enamelled in
colours with a board band of naturalistic
flowers, H 19 cm × D 16.8 cm
Marks: red crown and crossed batons with
six dots and D; pattern number 2
London, Trustees of the Victoria and Albert
Museum
Inv. No. C.229 to C.299C–1935
Provenance: Herbert Allen Collection;
bequeathed, 1935
Exhibitions: London, Victoria and Albert
Museum, 1987, Cat. No. 80A

This style of decoration, in which flowers are
set against a solid background of gilding, was
carried out at Derby from the 1770s onwards.
The intensity of the enamelled colours is in
part due to the fact that they must compete
with the strength of the gilt background; it
also accords with what little is known of the
work of George Hancock, with whose name
these pieces have recently been associated.
Hancock was one of the numerous family of
highly mobile painters and gilders active in the
Derby and Staffordshire ceramic industries in
the late eighteenth and nineteenth centuries.
Among them George is of particular interest
as he was the link between the generation of
Billingsley, by whom he was taught flower
painting, and John Haslem, who he in turn
taught to enamel flowers on porcelain and
who acknowledged him as the source of much
of the information given in his pioneering
study, *The Old Derby China Factory* (1876).
HY

486
Porter Mug, *c.* 1820

Derby, Robert Bloor and Co.
Bone china, painted with fruit, H 12.9 × D
12.7 cm
Marks: red crown, crossed batons and D on
base; gilder's number 2; number 61 in blue
inside foot rim
Derby, Derby Museums and Art Gallery
Inv. No. 255–1892
Provenance: Felix Joseph Collection,
No. 556
Literature: Derby Corporation Art Gallery
1892, p. 20, No. 556; Haslem 1876, p. 230

Thomas Steel (1772–1850), a native of the Staffordshire potteries, worked at Derby from *c.*
1815, excelling in the painting of fruit. Haslem
states that *c.* 1820, the gilder James Clarke was
using the number 2. **AB**

487

485

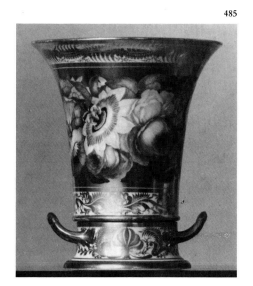

W. 'Quaker' Pegg, *Sketchbook*, 1813. Cat. No. 475

487
Figure of King George IV, *c.* 1820–25

Derby, Robert Bloor and Co.
Biscuit porcelain, H 32 cm
Derby, Derby Museums and Art Gallery
Inv. No. 241–142–1990
Provenance: Felix Joseph Collection,
No. 142
Literature: Derby Corporation Art Gallery
1892, p. 9, No. 142; Bradshaw 1990, pp.
422–23, G28, Fig. 353

The scale and quality of Derby's figure
making in biscuit were unrivalled by any
European factory, with the possible exception
of Sèvres. It has been suggested that the figure
of George IV was modelled by the sculptor
François Hardenburg, who worked briefly in
Derby in the 1790s before establishing his own
atelier in London, but possibly still continued
to supply the factory with master models. The
head may be based on Sir Francis Chantrey's
portrait bust of the king of *c.* 1821. **AB**

488
**Soup Plate from the 'Trotter Service',
c. 1825**

Derby, Robert Bloor and Co.
Bone china, painted with flowers by Moses
Webster, D 24.5 cm
Marks: gold crown, crossed batons, six dots
and D, with the name 'John Trotter Esq.
Durham Park'
Derby, Royal Crown Derby Museum
Exhibitions: London, Victoria and Albert
Museum, 1987, Cat. No. 36a; Toronto, 1988;
Derby, 1990, No. 59
Literature: Twitchett 1980, pp. 272–73, Fig.
375, p. 281

Patrons could visit the London showrooms
and commission pieces, such as the celebrated
service commissioned by John Trotter Esq. of
Durham Park, near Barnet in Hertfordshire
on the outskirts of London. Moses Webster
(1792–1870), who was responsible for most of
the fine decoration on the service, specialised
in flower painting and was much influenced

by Pegg the Quaker. He worked in London
around 1815–20 as an independent decorator
for various china studios before returning to
Derby. **JT**

488

489
Vase, c. 1835

Derby, Robert Bloor and Co.
Soft-paste porcelain, gilded and enamelled in colours, H 42.3 cm
London, Trustees of the Victoria and Albert Museum
Inv. Nos. 3071 and A–1901
Provenance: transferred from the Museum of Practical Geology, London
Literature: Haslem 1876, pp. 36–37, 119–21; Honey 1948, p. 129

According to John Haslem this vase was made from the same moulds as a pair designed for presentation to King William IV after the passing of the Reform Bill in 1832, which redistributed parliamentary seats in favour of the growing industrial areas, Derby among them. These royal presentation pieces – which had landscape panels painted by Daniel Lucas, and covers surmounted by figures – were paid for by subscriptions raised from the workforce at the Derby factory; but they were rejected by the king's ministers on the grounds that he could not receive presents expressive of political sentiments.

The list of subscribers is reprinted by Haslem, and as virtually the whole adult workforce subscribed this gives a remarkably precise picture of the organisation of the factory in the early 1830s. There were then thirteen potters, one body-mixer, six figure makers, eighteen painters, forty-one gilders, thirty-two burnishers, seven kilnmen, seven slipmen, packers and washers, three clerks, one salesman and the manager, James Thomason; in addition there would have been in the region of forty to fifty boys, which gives a total workforce of between 170 and 180.

The flower painting here has been attributed to both Thomas Steel and his son Horatio Steele (who added an additional, terminal 'e' to his surname), more probably the latter. **HY**

The Royal Porcelain Works at Worcester

When King George III visited the porcelain works of Messrs. Flight in Worcester on 9 August 1788, not only did the firm receive its first royal warrant but also advice that they should open a London retail establishment. A warehouse known as 'London House' was swiftly opened at No. 1 Coventry Street in the West End, which was liberally patronised by the royal family and London society. It also provided the opportunity for securing many foreign orders of importance.

During the period 1801–40, there were three separate porcelain factories in the city of Worcester, working in direct competition. The families of Flight and Barr managed what had formerly been the original Warmstry House Factory of Dr. Wall. Messrs. Chamberlain managed their own establishment in the Diglis area of Worcester, where the present works continue to this day. Messrs. Grainger had formed their own establishment in St. Martinsgate in 1801.

This period of competition coincided with the creation of some of the finest and most lavish decorations to issue forth from Worcester. Pre-eminent among the Worcester factories was that of Flight and Barr (1792–1804), Barr, Flight and Barr (1804–13) and Flight, Barr and Barr (1813–40). The quality of the body, the finesse of the shapes, the glaze and potting skills were brought to perfection.

Some of the most accomplished ceramic decorators of the day made their home at Worcester. Thomas Baxter junior (Cat. No. 473), worked for Flight, Barr and Barr from 1814 to 1816 and formed a school for painting in Edgar Street, which became the nursery for some of the factory's foremost painters. Baxter left for Wales, but on his return he assisted Messrs. Chamberlain from 1819 until his death in 1821. **HF**

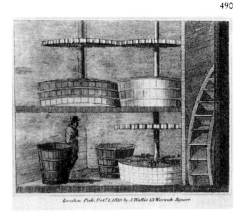
490

490
Booklet, The Process of Making China

Published by Barr, Flight and Barr, 1813
12.5 × 10.5 cm
Worcester, Dyson Perrins Museum Trust
Literature: Sandon 1978, p. 99, Plate 91

This educational booklet for the young accompanied a jigsaw and was published in 1813. The illustrations are the only record of the interior of the original Warmstry porcelain factory. They depict twelve different departments from the grinding mill to 'the enamelling kiln and burnishing'. **HF**

491
Cabinet Cup and Saucer, c. 1800

Worcester, Flight and Barr
Soft-paste porcelain, H 8 cm (cup), D 13 cm (saucer)
Mark: scratch B
Worcester, Dyson Perrins Museum Trust
Inv. No. L.4139
Provenance: private donation

It is likely that the panels of dogs were painted by John Pennington, a clever artist who was apprenticed to Wedgwood and had come from London. Recruited in 1789, he became Flight and Barr's chief artist, retiring as foreman painter in 1840. He specialised in figures and landscapes and is most famous for the scenes he painted on the Hope Service for the Duke of Clarence in 1792. **HF**

492
Cup and Saucer, c. 1810

Worcester, Barr, Flight and Barr
Soft-paste porcelain, H 6.5 cm (cup),
D 14 cm (saucer)
Marks: cup, scratch B on base; saucer, full painted mark on back
Worcester, Dyson Perrins Museum Trust
Inv. No. L.1667
Provenance: Royal Worcester Works Museum

The first two decades of the nineteenth century saw British porcelain painters experimenting with a number of short-lived styles of decoration which broke away from the floral patterns, landscape painting and Imari patterns that had dominated output at the close of the eighteenth century. This development gave rise to the vogue for shells and seaweed, feathers, vermicular designs, Egyptian motifs, 'Etruscan' figures, Pompeian grotesques, bold classical strip ornament, and for marbled and *trompe l'oeil* designs. **HY**

493
Pair of Slop Bowls, c. 1810

Worcester, Barr, Flight and Barr
Soft-paste porcelain, H 7.7 × D 17 cm
Mark: scratch B to base on one
Private Collection

The fashion for shell painting sprang from the collections of real shells formed by the nobility and connoisseurs of the day. Foremost among the shell painters was Samuel Smith, who probably painted these examples. **HF**

491

492

494

494
Oval Sugar Bowl, *c.* 1810

Worcester, Barr, Flight and Barr
Soft-paste porcelain, H 11×D 17 cm
Marks: B.F.B. and crown impressed on base
Worcester, Dyson Perrins Museum Trust
Inv. No. L.1696
Provenance: Royal Worcester Works
Museum

This type of decoration, known as bat printing, was used over a period of ten or so years at Worcester, from 1804 to 1815. Elegant in conception and exceptionally fine in detail, it required all an engraver's skills to create the original copper plates. **HF**

495
Warwick Vase on Pedestal, 1815

Worcester, Flight, Barr and Barr
Soft-paste porcelain, H 24×D 20 cm
Mark: painted Flight Barr and Barr mark on base
Worcester, Dyson Perrins Museum Trust
Inv. No. L.1736
Provenance: Royal Worcester Works
Museum
Literature: Sandon 1978, Plate 110

An old inventory states that this piece was 'either painted by Solomon Cole or [Thomas] Lowe'. Both men were pupils of Thomas Baxter junior. The scene depicted comes from Shakespeare, *King John*, Act IV, scene i, 'For heaven sake Herbert, let me not be bound!' **HF**

496
Ice Pail, *c.* 1815

Worcester, Flight, Barr and Barr
Soft-paste porcelain, H 26×D 30 cm
Mark: impressed F.B.B. under crown on base

Worcester, Dyson Perrins Museum Trust
Inv. No. L.1735
Provenance: C. W. Perrins
Literature: Sandon 1978, Plate 96

This is typical of the sophisticated palette and scale where Baxter felt most comfortable. In a letter to his friend, Benjamin Robert Haydon (Cat. Nos. 363, 404, 406), dated 21 July 1819, he is rather scathing of his lot at Chamberlain's, 'I am employed here on little things and the "littler the prettier" the dear little things and the dearer they are made the better!' **HF**

497 *(illus. p. 514)*
Cabinet Plate, *c.* 1815

Worcester, Flight, Barr and Barr
Soft-paste porcelain, D 21 cm
Marks: impressed BF.B with printed Flight, Barr and Barr mark on back
Worcester, Dyson Perrins Museum Trust
Inv. No. L.1712
Provenance: Royal Worcester Works
Museum

An exercise in the antique, the underglaze-blue ground is broken with gilt veining and a stylised anthemion border. The architecturally inspired decoration was in sympathy with the taste for pure and austere neoclassical interiors. Such sophisticated styles were intended for the London trade, where they found a ready market. **HF**

495

498
Cabinet Cup, *c.* 1815

Worcester, Flight, Barr and Barr
Soft-paste porcelain, H 8.5×D 9 cm
Marks: painted Flight Barr and Barr mark
B.F.B. impressed on base
Worcester, Dyson Perrins Museum Trust
Inv. No. L.1739
Provenance: Royal Worcester Works
Museum

With its classical form and decoration, this is a good example of the close working relationship between the modellers and artists. Individually hand-rolled clay beads, known as pearls, were a popular decorative device. **HF**

499
Vase, *c.* 1816

Worcester, Flight, Barr and Barr
Soft-paste porcelain, gilded and enamelled in colours, each side painted with the arms and motto (Auspicio Regis et Senatus) of the Honourable East India Company,
H 38.2 cm
Mark: FBB under a crown, impressed
London, Trustees of the Victoria and Albert Museum
Inv. No. C.439–1935
Provenance: Herbert Allen Collection; bequeathed, 1935
Literature: Godden 1982, p. 130

The shape of this piece is based on the Medici Krater, a Hellenistic marble vase that was much illustrated in books of vases and classical antiquities published in the late eighteenth and early nineteenth centuries. It was initially taken up in England by London goldsmiths towards the end of the first decade of the century, and shortly thereafter by porcelain manufacturers. However, the surface decoration – with its salmon-pink border pattern, gilt scrollwork and elaborate mantling – is in an advanced Rococo Revival style, one that the firm of Flight, Barr and Barr and their successors at Worcester pioneered in English porcelain during the second decade of the century.

In reviving the rococo, Worcester was very much at the cutting edge of fashion, for the style was only then being taken up by the foremost London goldsmiths, Rundell, Bridge and Rundell, most notably in the work carried out for the Prince of Wales (Cat. No. 467).

The vase here is from one of two large Worcester services commissioned by the East India Company during the second decade of the century, the other being made by the breakaway and rival Chamberlain factory in 1817–20 (Cat. No. 504).

The East India Company had been respon-

496

sible for bringing vast amounts of Chinese export porcelain to Britain during the eighteenth century, and it is a measure of the aesthetic and technical success of the Worcester firms, and of the declining quality of Chinese export wares, that these two large services should have been commissioned from them. Specimens from a contemporary Chinese export service made for the East India Company survive; poorly potted and decorated, these serve to emphasise the excellence of the English work. **HY**

500
Hot Water Dish and Cover and two Eggcups, *c.* 1802

Worcester, Chamberlain
Soft-paste porcelain, painted in colours and gilt with Japan design; the base of dish made in one piece with double skin and hollow gilt loop handles for filling with hot water; eggcups decorated en suite; H 13 × D 21 cm (dish), H 6.5 × D 4.3 cm (eggcups)
Marks: indecipherable cursive inscription

498

499

inside cover, 240 painted on eggcup base
London, National Maritime Museum
Inv. No. 46.437
Provenance: Horatia Nelson; by descent;
Reverend Hugh Nelson Ward, by whom
presented to the Museum, 1939
Literature: Binns 1865, pp. 144–47; Fisher
1955, p. 886; Godden 1982, Plates 117, 118;
Sandon 1989, pp. 45–47

In 1802 Lord Nelson undertook a triumphant
tour of the country as national hero, accompanied by Sir William and Lady Hamilton.
When they arrived in Worcester on 26 August,
they visited the Chamberlain factory. Having
declared that 'although possessed of the finest
porcelain the Courts of Dresden and Naples
could afford, he had seen none equal to the
productions of their manufactory', Nelson
left a large order for china to be decorated in
one of the most popular Japan-based patterns
with the addition of his arms and insignia, and
the crest of Nelson's flagship from 1801–03,
the San Josef, taken by boarding off Cape St.
Vincent in 1797.

The full order was for a breakfast, dinner
and dessert service but only the breakfast service, comprising 151 pieces, was completed at a
cost of £69.3s.(with an additional £44 for
painting the crests and armorials) before the
admiral's death. The account was not settled
until 1808. The hot water dish was used for
keeping muffins warm. **CF**

The Chamberlain Harlequin Service for the Prince Regent

Windsor Castle, H.M. Queen Elizabeth II
Inv. No. 832
Literature: Binns 1865, pp. 239–43; Godden
1982, p. 101

Robert Chamberlain is reputed to be the first
apprentice at the original Worcester Warmstry factory, founded by Dr. Wall and his
partners in 1751. After an accomplished career
as an extremely talented porcelain decorator,
he left these works in 1783 to undertake his
own business, formed with his sons in King

500

Street, Worcester. The business grew rapidly from its origins as a decorating workshop to become one of the most prestigious porcelain manufactories in Britain. On 25 September 1807, the Prince of Wales visited the factory. The press reports were glowing. The Prince inspected highly finished services being produced for the aristocracy and impressed with the abundant variety of patterns presented for his inspection, ordered a full table service, each piece of a different pattern (hence the description Harlequin), and in the Japan taste.

Mr. Chamberlain, sufficiently honoured, produced a new porcelain body known as 'Regent', of good colour, closeness of texture and generally rich in appearance. A special book of designs was also created, still in existence, with several hundred patterns from which the prince could choose. It dates from 1811, the year when the dessert service was ready for despatch to Carlton House, on 31 July, at a cost of £837.6s.

It was not until 1816 that the Harlequin dinner and breakfast services were complete. Such was the appeal of the Harlequin style to fashionable society that the service for the regent was delayed in manufacture. Flushed with their success, Messrs. Chamberlain decided to open their own London showrooms in 1814 at 63 Piccadilly, moving to 155 New Bond Street in July 1816. **HF**

501a
Soup Tureen and Cover, Harlequin Dinner Service, 1807–16

Worcester, Chamberlain
Regent porcelain, painted with dragons cavorting in an exotic garden on a chocolate ground with green foliage borders; the base supported by two handles issuing out of lion's head terminals; the lid surmounted by a pineapple finial surrounded by five leaves, H 24.5 × D 32.2 cm

501c

Mark: Chamberlains Worcester in red inside lid

This is one of the six 'soup tureens richly gilt' supplied at a princely £24 each. **HF**

501b
Dinner Plate, Harlequin Dinner Service, 1816

Worcester, Chamberlain
Regent porcelain, decorated in the Isnik style and gilt, D 28.2 cm
Marks: '155 New Bond Street' in part cartouche, 'Royal Porcelain manufactures' with crown, printed

This vigorous design is typical of the dramatic effects the Worcester artists could achieve. The rust-red colour known as Lac Red (short for the Chinese lacquer red) used so much in the Harlequin services is still in use today, known by the same name. **HF**

501b

501c
Dinner Plate, Harlequin Dinner Service, 1807–16

Worcester, Chamberlain
Regent porcelain, decorated to the centre with an exotic bird perched in a landscape, the stylised floral Japan borders in underglaze blue and lacquer red with rich gilding, D 28.2 cm
Mark: Chamberlains in red script

The Regent body was not easy to control in the kiln and for stability the plates were potted slightly heavier than usual. One hundred and forty four table plates were ordered in the original service at a cost of 3 guineas each. **HF**

501d
Round-Shaped Dish, Harlequin Dinner Service, 1806–16

Worcester, Chamberlain
Regent porcelain, decorated with three Asiatic pheasants against a flowering prunus in sky blue and lacquer red on a chocolate ground, a jewelled green border against a red diaper to edge, D 30.8 cm

This is one of the nine 'Round shaped dishes 12 inches' supplied at 185 shillings each. It is an extremely early date for jewelling enamel to be used. **HF**

501e
Oval Dish, Harlequin Dinner Service, 1816

Worcester, Chamberlain
Regent porcelain, decorated with a dramatic design on a purple ground, the central oval radiating sections containing dianthus, tiger lily, passion flower, roses, exotic birds, flies and strawberries with gilt and green stems entwined, 44 cm × 56 cm
Marks: '155 New Bond Street' in oval wreath and crown, printed

Chamberlain's order books survive at the Dyson Perrins Museum, Worcester. The order for this dinner service is recorded on 31 July 1816 at a cost of £2,539.1s.0d., a very high sum indeed. Adding the cost of the breakfast and dessert services, the whole amounted to over £4,000. This is one of the three 'Oval dishes 22 inches' at 414 shillings each. **HF**

501e

501a and 501d

502

502
Grace Mug, 1813

Worcester, Chamberlain
Soft-paste porcelain, H 17.5×D 20.5 cm
Marks: signed by Humphrey Chamberlain
with painted factory mark on base
Worcester, Dyson Perrins Museum Trust
Inv. No. M.4180
Provenance: purchased with the assistance of
the V & A Purchase Grant Fund, 1973
Literature: Godden 1982, p. 102, Plate 106,
p. 188, Plate 227

One of a pair of 'Grace' mugs painted by
Humphrey Chamberlain, the armorial bearings are those of the Marquess of Abergav-
venny. They were invoiced at 40 guineas for
the pair in 1813. **HF**

503 *(illus. p. 514)*
Cabinet Cup, Cover and Stand, 1815

Worcester, Chamberlain
Soft-paste porcelain, H 14×D 14 cm
Marks: painted 'Chamberlains Worcester',
inscribed 'King Henry VI pt. 3rd. War.' and
'of all my lands is nothing left me but my
bodies length'
Worcester, Dyson Perrins Museum Trust
Inv. No. M.1958
Provenance: C. W. Dyson Perrins

This Shakespearean scene, by either Humphrey or Walter Chamberlain, was possibly
taken from prints after the paintings made for
John Boydell's Shakespeare Gallery. A similar
example is noted as having been returned from
the London warehouse, its cost being
7 guineas. **HF**

504
Kidney Shaped Dish, 1818

Worcester, Chamberlain
Soft-paste porcelain, 18×26 cm
Mark: printed on reverse 'Chamberlains 155
New Bond St'
Worcester, Dyson Perrins Museum Trust
Inv. No. M.3949A
Provenance: purchased in 1965
Literature: Godden 1982, p. 130

The order by the Honourable East India
Company in 1817–18 for their headquarters at
Fort St. George, Madras, was one of the most
important commissions received from Messrs.
Chamberlain. It took a considerable time to
complete and was not invoiced until 1820, at a
total cost of £4,190.4s. **HF**

504

Spode

Josiah Spode II led the way in establishing the
market for bone china (a type of porcelain
made with the addition of bone ash, which is
pure white in colour) as an alternative to soft-
paste porcelain. It received its first accolade
when the Prince of Wales visited the Spode
factory in 1806. It was more durable and less
expensive to produce than soft-paste and
swiftly became the standard English body for
fine ceramics. **CF**

505

505
Jug, c. 1810–15

Spode; bone china, bat printed in black with
children's scenes, H 15.8 cm
Stoke-on-Trent, The Spode Museum Trust
Collection
Inv. No. AGC 1406
Literature: Drakard and Holdway 1983, pp.
10–13, 40–49; Copeland 1980, pp. 26–30;
Wyman 1980, pp. 187–99

The shape is known as Low Dutch. **RC**

506 *(illus. p. 521)*
Suite of Tea Ware, c. 1812

Spode; bone china, H 16.8 cm (teapot)
Marks: on the teapot, covered sugar box and
cream jug '1709' in red
Stoke-on-Trent, The Spode Museum Trust
Collection
Inv. No. WTC 3
Exhibitions: Oslo, 1966, No. 42; London,
Royal Academy, 1970, No. 161
Literature: Whiter 1970, Plate 274 (centre)

The shape is known as New Oval with Bute
tea cup and saucer. **RC**

507

507
Cream Bowl, Cover and Stand, *c.* 1812

Spode; bone china, bat printed in gold with sprays of fruit, H 14.8×D 21.5 cm (bowl and cover, length over handles), D 19.6 cm (stand)
Unmarked, but the pattern is 1696
Stoke-on-Trent, The Spode Museum Trust Collection
Inv. No. WTC 32
Exhibitions: London, Royal Academy, 1970, No. 194
Literature: Drakard and Holdway 1983, p. 42, Plate 7; Whiter 1970, p. 184, Plate 277.

The shape is known as Dolphin embossed, with swan handles and knob. The decorations on the sides are catalogued by Drakard and Holdway as P192 and P185: on the cover and stand, P175. **RC**

508

509

508
Suite of Dinner Ware, *c.* 1820

Spode; bone china, 29.8×23.1 cm (rectangular dish) H 14.2×D 18.5 cm (cream tureen) D 20.4 cm (stand), D 24.9 cm (plates)
Unmarked, but the pattern is 2970
Stoke-on-Trent, The Spode Museum Trust Collection
Inv. No. WTC 235

The rich royal blue rim is gilded with seaweed and bladderwrack. In the centre of each piece is a shell, painted in royal blue and traced with gold, with gilded seaweed on one side of the shell. **RC**

509
Dessert Dish, *c.* 1823

Spode; bone china, 28.7 ×17.8 cm
Mark: SPODE 3663 (RC22)
Stoke-on-Trent, The Spode Museum Trust Collection
Inv. No. WTC 17
Exhibitions: Oslo, 1966, No. 45
Literature: Whiter 1970, Plates 71, 213

Known as a twig-handled comport, the leaves flow over the edge on to the underside. The intricate gilded pattern of scrolls on the deep royal blue band is known as Dresden border. The centre displays a botanical study of a yellow narcissus with a red eye (like a daffodil) and a yellow poppy edged in red. A gold line finishes the edge. **RC**

Suite of Tea Ware, *c*. 1812. Cat. No. 506

The Rockingham Dessert Service for King William IV

Windsor Castle, H.M. Queen Elizabeth II
Literature: Rice 1971, pp. 37–43; Eaglestone and Lockett 1973, pp. 107–10; Cox 1975, pp. 90–97; Cox 1983, pp. 134–38

This service, the *chef-d'oeuvre* of the Rockingham works, was ordered in 1830 for the new king, William IV. Both technically and aesthetically, it was ambitious, proud and powerful, reflecting the period in which it was created. The service was not only of outstanding splendour but for the porcelain factory established only five years previously at Swinton, Yorkshire, by the Brameld brothers, under the patronage of the 2nd Earl Fitzwilliam, it was intended as a brave new ceramic statement, surpassing anything that had gone before. The design was entrusted to John Wager Brameld who, although an excellent artist, spent much of his time as the firm's travelling agent, eventually becoming the manager of the London shop and warehouse. From 1828 the firm had a wholesale warehouse at 13 Vauxhall Bridge Road, but from 1832–34 they also leased part of 174 Piccadilly, 'The Griffin', as a showroom and by 1837, they had taken premises at 3 Tichbourne Street.

By May 1837, the service was finally complete and packed for its journey in mahogany boxes, being conveyed to the capital, it is said, under mounted escort. With the king's agreement, the service was placed on public exhibition at the Piccadilly showroom, where it was greatly admired by London society; it was still on display when the king died on 20 June 1837. It is believed that the service was first used at Queen Victoria's coronation. **HF**

510a

510c (illus. p. 525)
Pineapple Comport, William IV
Dessert Service, 1830–37

Rockingham, Brameld
Bone china, the basket supported by a
realistically modelled and coloured pineapple
surmounting views of 'Wynyard Durham
seat of the Marquess of Londonderry' and
'Brothers Water from Kirkstone Foot
Westmorland' entitled in red script below,
H 27.5 cm × D 24 cm
Marks: cartouched griffin in puce;
'Rockingham Works Brameld Manufacturer
to the King Queen and Royal Family'
printed twice
Inv. No. 1234

Four pineapple comports were made. All the
views painted on the service were of British or
colonial origin. **HF**

510d

510a
Tropical Comport, William IV Dessert
Service, 1830–37

Rockingham, Brameld
Bone china, supported on stems of twisted
sugar cane; the tropical fruits and entitled in
red script below; the whole rising from
painted views of 'Spring Garden Estate, St.
Georges, Jamaica' and 'Mausoleum of Sufter
Jung Delhi'; H 24.5 × D 27.5 cm
Marks: cartouched griffin in puce;
'Rockingham Works Brameld Manufacturer
to the King Queen and Royal Family'
printed twice
Inv. No. 1240

The depth of research required for such a de-
sign would have been immense. The East and
West Indian fruits, probably based on F. R. de
Tussac, *Flores des Antilles* (Paris, 1808–27), or
M. E. Descourtilz, *Flore pittoresque et medi-
cale des Antilles. . .* (Paris, 1821–29) (informa-
tion kindly supplied by Jennifer Vine, Royal
Horticultural Society library), are echoed in
the painted scenes of the East and West Indies.
HF

510b
Shell Comport, William IV Dessert
Service, 1830–37

Rockingham, Brameld
Bone china, a limpet shell with mussel and
samphire at its edge supported on red coral
above views of 'The Clyde from Erskine
Ferry' and 'A Breeze' – a seascape, both
entitled in red script below, H 18.8 ×
D 25.5 cm
Marks: cartouched griffin in puce;
'Rockingham Works Brameld Manufacturer
to the King Queen and Royal Family'
printed twice
Inv. No. 1228

These curiously original comports, of which
four were made, are possibly based on rococo
precedents. Thomas Brameld is believed to
have designed these shapes which are thought
to have been executed by Thomas Griffin, a
fine modeller originally employed at the
Derby China Works. The marine imagery is
carried through from the modelling to the
choice of painted views. **HF**

510d *(illus. p. 523)*
Double Dress Stand, William IV
Dessert Service, 1830–37

Rockingham, Brameld
Bone china, two plateaus encrusted with all manner of British garden flowers sensitively coloured and supported on a continuous pineapple stem springing from a base with exquisitely painted views of 'Kutnnallee Gate Gour' and a 'View of a house built by Colonel Claude Martin at Lucknow Bengal', entitled in red script below; the whole surmounted by a small vase painted with scenes of Italian peasants possibly by John Wager Brameld himself; H 48.2×D 24.5 cm
Marks: cartouched griffin in puce; 'Rockingham Works Brameld Manufacturer to the King Queen and Royal Family' printed twice
Inv. No. 1252

These elegant stands in use would carry delicate almond confections such as *petits fours*, the vase being dressed with real flowers. **HF**

511

510e *(illus. p. 526)*
Dessert Plate, William IV Service, 1832

Rockingham, Brameld
Bone china, the centre painted with the arms of King William IV, the border of Brunswick blue ground overlaid with gold trellis of embossed, burnished and chased gold over which creeps a wreath of English oak; minute border on the shoulder of white and red roses, thistles, shamrocks and leeks symbolising the Union of Great Britain; D 23.5 cm
Marks: cartouched griffin mark in puce; 'Rockingham Works Brameld Manufacturers to the King Queen and Royal Family' printed twice; dated 1832 in gilt
Inv. No. 5223

One hundred and forty-four dessert plates were completed for the service. The symbolic wreath of English oak was added, apparently, at the suggestion of the king. **HF**

Watch and Clockmaking

By 1790 the London watch and clockmaking industry had established both a technical and economic supremacy in national and international trade. Market factors, especially the ever growing concentration of purchasing power in London and access to very diverse and valuable home and foreign markets, pro-vided the financial stimulus. London had greatly benefited from the scientific lead developed by John Harrison, Thomas Mudge, John Arnold and Thomas Earnshaw, whose inventive talents led to the perfection of the marine chronometer by the early 1780s. From that date on, a number of London makers were developing the lever escapement, invented earlier by Mudge and pioneered the duplex escapement, patented by the Clerkenwell watch-maker, Thomas Tyrer, in 1782.

Business entrepreneurship paralleled these technological developments and clock and watchmaking emerged as one of London's leading trades by the opening years of the nineteenth century, when some 120,000 watches were being produced each year. Contemporary estimates valued the annual output of London made clocks, watches and chronometers at £½–1 million.

To achieve such a high volume of production the watchmaking trade had become highly specialised. The secret of success lay in a progressive move towards increased sub-division of labour. The system was dominated by the West End and City makers, and a small group of wholesale traders working in the watchmaking parishes. These were the men whose names appeared on the actual clocks and watches. Working for both groups were the smaller tradesmen and artisans who found employment in the sixty or so major branches of the horological trades. Such a structure was encouraged by the market and facilitated by the wide range of available tools, machines and materials, which enabled workers to become more specialised and productive. One effect of all this was that the retail price of good quality London pair-case silver watches fell from £8.10. to £2.10. in the period 1710–1810.

Ever increasing subdivision of labour was accompanied by a greater localisation of the workforce. By 1800, most of London's working watch and clockmakers lived in a belt which ran from the eastern fringe of Holborn, through Clerkenwell and St. Luke's, Old Street, to the western part of Shoreditch, and extended southwards to Smithfield, Cripplegate and Moorfields, and northwards to Islington.

Despite its many achievements, however, London's watch and clockmaking trade was at a watershed by 1820. The war with France and the trade depression which followed the cessation of hostilities in 1815, government taxation and, more importantly, competition from cheaper watches made in Coventry and Switzerland, all conspired to diminish the lead which London had built up. Furthermore, the technical ascendancy was passing to the Continent. Swiss makers were already producing slimmer, and more popular, watches with going barrels and bar plates to the movement, along the lines of those first introduced by Jean-Antoine Lépine in 1770. None of London's eminent makers had quite the innovative edge and reputation of the Swiss horological genius, Abraham-Louis Breguet, who worked in Paris. Time – quite literally – was running out for the London trade. **CE**

Pineapple Comport, William IV Dessert Service, 1830–37. Cat. No. 510c

Dessert Plate, William IV Service, 1832. Cat. No. 510e

WATCH AND CLOCK MAKING

T. Lawrence, *Kemble as Coriolanus*, 1798. Cat. No. 546

Marine Chronometer, 1795. Cat. No. 525

WATCH AND CLOCK MAKING

M. A. Shee, *Thomas Earnshaw*, 1798. Cat. No. 522.

Silver-Cased Stop-Watch, 1802. Cat. No. 514

Gold Pair-Cased Pocket Chronometer, 1800. Cat. No. 523

Lunar globe, 'Selenographia', 1977. Cat. No. 534

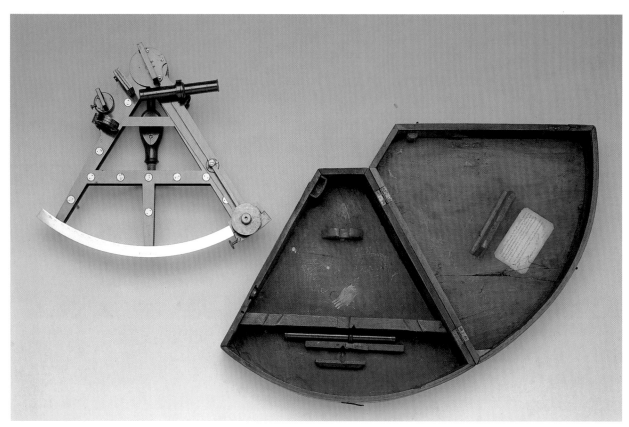

Sextant, 1797. Cat. No. 530

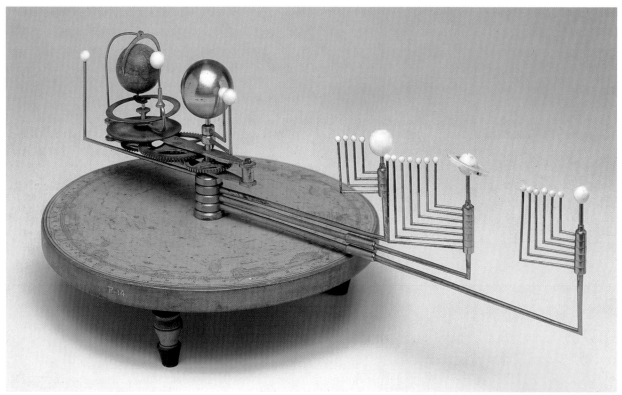

Orrery, 1823–27. Cat. No. 537

512

513

piece protected by a glass dome, appear on the shelves behind. It has been suggested that this portrait might be by the artist Benjamin West.

Benjamin Vulliamy's father, Justin, had come to London from the Pays de Vaud, Switzerland. He married Mary, the daughter of his famous partner Benjamin Gray, in 1746. Benjamin Vulliamy became clockmaker to the king in 1773, a position which he held until his death in 1811, when the warrant passed to his son Benjamin Lewis Vulliamy. **CE**

512
Clockmaker's Uprighting Tool

Bronze and iron, 52×28 cm
Inscribed: VULLIAMY
Brighton, Laurence Harvey
Provenance: workshop of Benjamin Lewis Vulliamy, 68 Pall Mall, 1810–54
Literature: Crom 1980, p. 614

This large clockmaker's uprighting tool, which can accommodate movements up to around 6 inches wide, was mainly used for repair work. The bottom and upper centres are moveable to enable pairs of pivot holes, on clock movement plates, to be lined up, making it an easy task to undertake jobs such as the re-bushing and drilling of new pivot holes. The tool shown here would have been very useful in Benjamin Lewis Vulliamy's workshop, which undertook extensive repair, restoration and renewal work for royal and other customers. **CE**

Artist unknown

511 *(illus. p. 524)*
Benjamin Vulliamy, c. 1790

Oil on canvas, 68.9×83.3 cm
London, Worshipful Company of Clockmakers
Inv. No. 1086
Literature: Jagger 1983, pp. 86–88, 112–19; Clifford 1990, pp. 226–37

Benjamin Vulliamy (1747–1811), one of London's leading clock and watchmakers, is pictured here in his shop in Pall Mall. To Vulliamy's right is a splendid sculptural clock of the type which he produced from the 1780s. Standing on a marble base, the ormolu clock case is surmounted by a globe and flanked by a putti and a female figure. Vulliamy employed London sculptors to model figures which were then produced, in biscuit, by William Duesbury's Derby porcelain works. An identical clock to that seen here is now at Syon House, Middlesex. Other items produced by Vulliamy, including the movement of a time-

513
Saddle Watch and Pedometer, c. 1800

Ralph Gout; verge escapement; fusee and chain; spiral steel balance spring with plain steel balance; gilt-brass dust cap, signed and numbered, L 23.5 cm
Inscribed on back of movement: By the King's Letters PATENT Ralph Gout London 365
White enamel dial with upper subsidiary dial for hours and minutes and two lower subsidiary dials for the pedometer register 0–10 and 10–100 paces. Perimeter of dial calibrated with 0–10,000 paces. Signed 'Weston' on the counter enamel. Gilt-brass hands
Gilt-brass watch case, punched with maker's mark IN, and 0 and 365; gilt-brass and glass saddle mount engraved
London, Trustees of the British Museum

Inv. No. MLA CA1–355
Provenance: C. A. Ilbert Collection, bought 1938; bought by the British Museum, 1958

Ralph Gout (*fl.* 1770–1829) was a wholesale watchmaker active in St. Luke's parish, Old Street, from around 1770 to 1829. In 1799, he obtained a patent (No. 2351) covering improvements to watch mechanisms designed to record the steps of a pedestrian, the paces of a horse, and the revolution of a carriage wheel. In the one shown here, the movement of the horse causes the watch and outer case to jerk up and down and the chain to index the pedometer mechanism and record the number of paces. The decoration suggests that it was probably destined for the Turkish market, where such objects were highly prized. **DRT and CE**

515

Bailey – their horological business was also significant: as well as more ordinary pieces, pedometer wind watches signed 'Recordon, Spencer & Perkins' survive (Louis Recordon was the patentee); and they are known to have ordered at least 106 clocks from John Thwaites, manufacturing clockmaker, Rosoman Street, Clerkenwell. **CE and DT**

516
Gold Pair-Cased Watch, 1808

William Ilbery; spring detent escapement of Peto type; three-arm bi-metallic compensation balance; helical steel balance spring; fusee and chain; white enamel dial with subsidiary seconds dial; gold hands
Inscribed on back of movement: Ilbery, London, 5762
Gold inner case engine turned and engraved, D 5.2 cm
Outer case engine turned and decorated in enamelling, D 6 cm
Marks: London hallmark for 1808–09; maker's mark WM for William Mansell, 32 Rosoman Street, Clerkenwell
London, The Museum of London
Inv. No. C1512
Provenance: J. G. Joicey, given to the London Museum, 1912

William Ilbery (*fl.* 1780–1840) is recorded as working at Goswell Road in 1780, and in 1814 at 24 York Place, City Road. He specialised in organising the manufacture of costly and complicated pieces for the Chinese and oriental markets. The watch shown here is a pocket chronometer with a spring detent escapement credited to one Peto, who worked for John and Myles Brockbank, 6 Cowper Court, Cornhill, in the City, who were amongst the

514 (illus. p. 530)
Silver-Cased Stop-Watch, 1802

Vulliamy; duplex escapement; temperature compensation balance and spiral balance spring; fusee and chain, and Harrison's maintaining power; stop lever to intercept the balance; gilt-brass dust cap; white enamel dial; blued steel hands
Inscribed on back of movement: Vulliamy LONDON zmx
Silver case, D 6.3 cm
Marks: London hallmark for 1802–03; casemaker's mark RW
London, Trustees of the British Museum
Inv. No. MLA CA1–1310
Provenance: C. A. Ilbert Collection, bought 1939; bought by the British Museum, 1958

Benjamin Vulliamy was in business at 74 Pall Mall from 1775 to 1811 (Cat. No. 511). In 1781, together with a large number of other prominent London makers, he was made an honorary freeman of the Clockmakers' Company. Despite his father being Swiss, and having married a Swiss girl, Benjamin Vulliamy was one of the foremost opponents of the importation (mostly smuggled) of watches from Switzerland and France.

The duplex escapement was patented in 1782 by Thomas Tyrer, Red Lion Street, Clerkenwell, and described as a 'horizontal escapement to act with two wheels'. By around 1790, however, leading London makers had developed this into a single escape wheel with two rows of teeth. It became especially popular with English makers of high quality pocket watches in the period 1810–50. **CE and DRT**

515
Pair-Cased Gold Watch, 1806

Spencer and Perkins; verge escapement; fusee and chain; diamond endstone to balance cock; white enamel dial; gold hands
Inscribed on dial: SPENCER & PERKINS LONDRES
Inscribed on back of movement: Spencer & Perkins 17009
Gold inner case, D 5 cm
Marks: London hallmark for 1806–07; makers' marks TC/RC for Thomas and Richard Carpenter, 5 Islington Road, Clerkenwell
Brass outer case, not marked, overlaid with horn and under painted with a harbour scene and two warships, D 6 cm
London, The Museum of London
Inv. No. A9883
Provenance: J. G. Joicey, given to the London Museum, 1912
Exhibitions: London, The Museum of London, 1991–92
Literature: Murdoch ed. 1991, p. 144

Emmanuel Spencer and John Perkins carried on an extensive business from 44 Snow Hill (1772–1802) and 115 Newgate Street (1802–08).

The regulator of the watch shown here is inscribed with the Spanish words for fast and slow, indicating that it was probably intended for export to Spain or South America. The combination of gold inner case and painted horn outer case is unusual.

Although Spencer and Perkins were noted as tools and material dealers – with their own metal flatting mill in Bishops Court, Old

516

leading London pioneers of chronometer manufacture. The Peto escapement, however, was somewhat anachronistic by the time this watch was made. Ilbery also imported complex Swiss movements and had them signed 'Ilbery London', and then exported to China. Together with his son he also had an address in Fleurier, Switzerland – a centre for the manufacture of complicated watches for the Chinese market – and they later set up in Canton, China. **CE**

517
Gold-Cased Watch, 1810

Vulliamy; Savage two-pin lever escapement; temperature compensation balance and spiral balance spring; fusee and chain, and Harrison's maintaining power; gilt-brass dust cap punch marked IB on the inside; white enamel dial; blued steel hands
Inscribed on back of movement:
VULLIAMY LONDON msza
Gold case, D 4.5 cm
Marks: London hallmark for 1810–11; casemaker's mark AC and numbered 5079
London, Trustees of the British Museum
Inv. No. MLA CA1–1107
Provenance: C. A. Ilbert Collection, bought 1930; bought by the British Museum in 1958

Benjamin Lewis Vulliamy (1780–1854) began working with his father Benjamin Vulliamy (Cat. No. 511) in 1793. He became free of the Clockmakers' Company, by redemption, in 1809. He succeeded as head of the family business, at 74 Pall Mall, on his father's death in 1811 and held the warrant of royal clockmaker from then up to his own death in 1854. He served as a warden of the Clockmakers' Company from 1815 to 1820, and held the office of master in 1821, 1823, 1825, 1827 and 1847. Over this time, he presented some forty-seven watches, by various makers, to the Clockmakers' Company, forming the nucleus of their present museum.
  The particular form of lever escapement found in this watch was developed by George Savage, originally from Huddersfield, but later working at 5 St. James's Street, Clerkenwell. The Royal Society of Arts awarded their silver medal to Savage for his detached watch escapement in 1822. **DRT and CE**

518
Gold-Cased Watch, 1811

Charles Smith; cylinder escapement; fusee and chain; diamond endstone to balance cock; matt gold dial, with polished raised numerals and engine-turned centre;

518

blued steel hands
Inscribed on the back of the movement:
Chas Smith London 100523
Back of the case three-colour gold, decorated with engine turning, D 4.6 cm
Marks: London hallmark for 1811–12; the maker's mark TH; for Thomas Hardy, Rosoman Row, Clerkenwell
London, The Museum of London
Inv. No. C34
Provenance: J. G. Joicey, given to the London Museum, 1912

Charles Smith (*fl.* 1784–1823) was the son of James Smith, watchmaker, of Bunhill Row, in the parish of St. Luke's, Old Street. He set up on his own account, from around 1784, at 122 Bunhill Row. Between 1790 and 1823 he traded at 118 Bunhill Row, his father's old address. Charles Smith described himself in the Post Office London Directories as a 'wholesale watchmaker'. He had substantial business acumen and became one of the most productive of London makers. **CE**

519
Pair-Cased Silver Watch, 1813

Robert Chassereau; verge escapement; fusee and chain; white enamel dial; copper hands
Inscribed on back of the movement: Robt Chassereau London No. 2026
Silver inner case, D 5.1 cm
Marks: London hallmark for 1813–14; unidentified maker's mark WH; pendant

marked MA for Michael Atkins, pendant maker, 4 Red Lion Street, Clerkenwell
Brass outer case, also marked WH, overlaid with tortoiseshell and horn, and under painted with a rustic scene, D 5.8 cm
London, The Museum of London
Inv. No. A1533
Provenance: J. G. Joicey, given to the London Museum, 1912
Exhibitions: London, The Museum of London, 1985
Literature: Murdoch 1985, p. 254

519

520

Robert Chassereau (*fl.* 1799–1814) was of Huguenot descent, his great-grandfather, Jacob, having been naturalised in 1709. Robert was not apprenticed through the Clock-makers' Company, but obtained the Freedom of the Company in 1803. Chassereau is recorded as working at 10 Rosoman Street, Clerkenwell, in 1799, and 4 Beech Street, Barbican, 1804–08. From 1811 to 1813 he was working at 34 Coppice Row, Clerkenwell.

Chassereau's output of watches, under his own signature at least, was modest. But according to his insurance policy with the Sun Insurance Company, dated 1 December 1807, he was also a 'dealer in skins'. **CE**

520
Gilt-Brass Alarm Watch, c. 1820

Joseph Anthony Berrollas; movement with going barrel; duplex escapement; spiral balance spring and steel balance; Berrollas's patent alarm mechanism; white enamel dial with hours and quarter hours for alarm setting
Movement inscribed: BERROLLAS 194 Strand PATENT 582
Gilt-brass, engine-turned hunter case with armorial crest, D 5.55 cm
London, Trustees of the British Museum
Inv. No. MLA CA1–1392
Provenance: Ilbert Collection, bought 1925; bought by the British Museum, 1958

Joseph Anthony Berrollas was an inventive watchmaker who took out a number of patents for innovative designs relating to watchwork: in October 1808 (No. 3174) for a

repeating mechanism; in March 1810 (No. 3342) and April 1827 (No. 5489) new systems for alarm watches; and in December 1827 (No. 5586) to cover a new pendant-operated pull-winding mechanism and hand-setting device. **DRT and CE**

521
Silver-Gilt-Cased Watch, 1829

Henry Borrell; ratchet tooth lever escapement; fusee and chain, and Harrison's maintaining power; spiral balance spring with steel balance; gilt-brass dust cap signed and numbered on the outside and the maker's mark TF in cameo on the inside; white enamel dial; gold hour and minute hands, blued steel seconds hand
Inscribed on back of movement: Heny. Borrell London 30688
Silver-gilt case, D 5.35 cm
Marks: London hallmark for 1829–30; casemaker's mark GR for George Richards, 17 Bridgewater Square; pendant marked JP
London, Trustees of the British Museum
Inv. No. MLA CA1–1184
Provenance: C. A. Ilbert Collection, bought 1925; bought by the British Museum, 1958

Henry Borrell traded at 15 Wilderness Row, Clerkenwell, between 1795–1840. During the early part of his career he was supplying both regulators and musical bracket clocks for the Turkish and Chinese markets. From the serial number on the movement it is clear that Borrell was retailing a significant number of watches, made and finished by local outworkers. George Richards, the casemaker, lived nearby in Bridgewater Square and the pendant maker's mark, is almost certainly that of James Pascall, living even closer at 18 Wilderness Row. The maker of the dust cap can be identified as Thomas Furneaux, 5 St. James Street, Clerkenwell. **DRT and CE**

Martin Archer Shee
Dublin 1769–1850 Brighton

522 (*illus. p. 529*)
Thomas Earnshaw, 1798

Oil on canvas, 92 × 71 cm
London, Trustees of the Science Museum
Inv. No. 1962–372
Provenance: Earnshaw family, by descent, probably from sitter; Mrs. W. Earnshaw, 1861; Richard Russell Earnshaw, 1962, lent to the Science Museum; bequeathed, 1968
Exhibitions: London, Royal Academy, 1798, No. 110

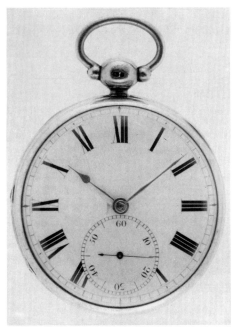

521

Thomas Earnshaw (1749–1829) was a pioneer of chronometer manufacture. A watchmaker from Lancashire, by 1800 he had a well established shop for clock and watchmaking at 119 High Holborn. Earnshaw recognised the needs of a mass market. His instruments were made simple and cheap, for private use and for the Admiralty for issue to naval officers. By 1829 the marine chronometer was commonplace, while Earnshaw's spring detent escapement of 1782 has remained the standard chronometer escapement almost without alteration up to modern times.

Before accurate marine timekeepers were available, navigators on ocean voyages could only roughly estimate their longitude. Mistakes cost many shipwrecks. John Harrison from 1728 to 1759 was pre-eminent for producing chronometers whose accuracy of performance was above that required by the Longitude Acts, with much saving of life. However, Harrison's chronometers were individually crafted and expensive to produce.

Earnshaw, and his contemporary John Arnold in Cornhill, each set up an organisation for large scale production in which each process was carried out by specialist craftsmen. Earnshaw and Arnold worked only on the final springing and adjustment. Over forty years they produced about 1,000 chronometers at the relatively cheap price of £40 each. Until 1790, Earnshaw worked almost entirely for trade, and his name seldom appeared on his instruments. In 1793 he applied unsuccessfully for recognition as discoverer of longitude, but he and Arnold were each awarded £3,000 for their improvements to chronometers. His pamphlets, *Explanations of Timekeepers* (1806) and *Longitude* (1808) acknowledge the contribution of Arnold. **WS**

523
Gold Pair-Cased Pocket Chronometer, 1800

Thomas Earnshaw; Earnshaw's spring detent escapement; steel balance and spiral steel balance spring with Earnshaw's 'sugar tongs' temperature compensation; fusee and chain, and Harrison's maintaining power; white enamel dial; gold hands; Gold pair-cases, D of outer case 5.8 cm
Marks: London hallmark for 1800–01; casemaker's mark TC surmounted by an axe; inside the outer case a watchpaper printed with a coat of arms
London, Trustees of the British Museum
Inv. No. MLA CA1–1731
Provenance: C. A. Ilbert Collection, bought 1933; bought by the Museum, 1958
Literature: Randall and Good, 1990, p. 82 and Plate 43a–c

The casemaker, Thomas Carpenter junior registered his punch mark – TC surmounted by an axe – at Goldsmiths' Hall on 20 July 1797, his address being given as 9 Islington Road, Clerkenwell.

The watchpaper in the outer case is printed with the arms of the barony of Arden. Charles George Perceval (1756–1840) who owned this watch, was the 2nd Baron Arden. In addition to being an M.P., he was Lord of the Admiralty and registrar of the Admiralty Court and thus would have been well acquainted with Earnshaw's reputation. **DRT and CE**

524
Marine Chronometer, c. 1802

Thomas Earnshaw; brass and steel movement in mahogany box with gimbals and sliding lid, 17.5 × 22 × 20 cm
Two-day chronometer with Earnshaw spring detent escapement and Earnshaw compensation balance
Signed: Thomas Earnshaw Invt. et Fecit No. 524/2869 London
Greenwich, National Maritime Museum
Inv. No. CH.629
Provenance: Robert Foulkes Collection
Exhibitions: Armagh, 1989
Literature: Earnshaw 1806; Earnshaw 1808; Gould 1923, pp. 113–27

Marine chronometers are mechanical timekeepers specially designed to keep accurate time on board ship. The series of rewards offered by the government from 1714, to encourage an accurate method of determining longitude at sea stimulated work in both the astronomical and horological fields.

524

Earnshaw settled in London around 1763, and worked as a finisher and escapement maker. Of humble origins, he turned to chronometer making out of necessity, wanting to receive a prize payment. By c. 1780–81, he had already developed a chronometer with a spring detent escapement, but did not have the necessary capital (around £100) to have it patented. This chronometer was left with Thomas Wright, a watchmaker operating at 6 Poultry in the City, who had agreed to meet the costs of patent registration in return for a royalty on subsequent chronometers manufactured. Wright was slow in submitting it for patent registration (1783), and Earnshaw contended that Arnold, alerted by John Brockbank (Cat. No. 529), saw it at Wright's shop and copied it. Arnold registered his own patent in 1782. Earnshaw's spring detent, together with his fused brass and steel compensation balance, however, proved more easy to make than Arnold's and they quickly became the standard for chronometer manufacture, remaining barely changed until the introduction of quartz technology to chronometers in the 1970s. **CE and JB**

525 *(illus. p. 528)*
Marine Chronometer, 1795

Howells and Pennington; brass and steel movement in later mahogany gimballed box, 19 × 20 × 18 cm
Two-day chronometer with later Arnold sprint detent escapement, compensation balance and blued steel helical spring; dial with applied silver filigree work, incorporating three enamel dials – for hours, minutes and seconds – and a crescent-shaped 'up and down' indicator, which shows the

need for rewinding
Signed: Howells and Pennington FOR Thos Mudge No. 4, 1795
Greenwich, National Maritime Museum
Inv. No. CH.155
Provenance: Hydrographic Department, Ministry of Defence
Literature: Mudge 1799; Gould 1923, pp. 81, 121ff

This chronometer was one of a series constructed to the order of Thomas Mudge junior between c. 1794–99. Thomas Mudge senior (1715–1794) had been experimenting with marine timekeepers in the 1760s. In 1771 he left London for Plymouth to develop a marine timekeeper that could become commercially viable. During tests at Greenwich between 1778 and 1790, however, Mudge's timepieces failed to meet the very exacting standards of the astronomer royal. Mudge's son, Thomas junior, a lawyer, realising that his aged father's chance of receiving any reward from the Board of Longitude was slipping away in the light of John Arnold's work (Cat. No. 526), petitioned parliament and in 1793 Thomas senior was awarded £2,500.

In 1794 Thomas Mudge junior contracted two watchmakers – William Howells of Kennington and Robert Pennington of Camberwell – to make replicas of his father's timepieces. Howells and Mudge, however, fell out in 1795 and the former was replaced as head workman by Pennington. **CE and JB**

526
Silver Pocket Chronometer, 1806

John Roger Arnold; Arnold's spring detent escapement; Arnold's Z-type compensation balance with gold helical spring; fusee and chain with Harrison's maintaining power; white enamel dial; blued steel hands
Movement inscribed: Jno. R. Arnold London Invt. et Fecit No. 1984
Silver consular case, D 5.82 cm
Marks: London hallmark for 1806–07; casemaker's mark TH; coat of arms on back with the motto REGARD BIEN
London, Trustees of the British Museum
Inv. No. MLA CA1–1842
Provenance: C. A. Ilbert Collection, bought 1935; bought by the Museum, 1958
Literature: Mercer 1972, Plate 179; Randall and Good 1990, pp. 70–71, Plate 34c–f

John Roger Arnold (1769–1843) was the son of John Arnold (1736–99), one of the great pioneers of the chronometer. He patented his spring detent escapement in 1782, drawing vitriolic complaints of plagiarism from Thomas Earnshaw. Arnold's design of a hel-

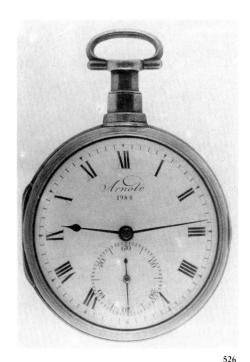

526

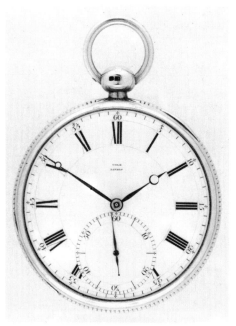

528

Greenwich, National Maritime Museum
Inv. No. CH 192
Provenance: Hydrography Department,
Ministry of Defence
Literature: Gould 1923, pp. 115, 118, 124–25

Following the death of his father, John Arnold in 1799, John Roger Arnold carried on the family business making marine and pocket chronometers as well as fine pocket watches and regulators. Many of the chronometers incorporated his latest innovations. Small un-gimballed chronometers like this example, which became known as deck watches, could be purchased at around half the cost of large boxed chronometers and proved especially popular with ships' captains. This chronometer, typical of John Roger's work, spent its working life on H.M. Navy ships, including the Arctic expedition of 1852, remaining in use until 1910. **CE and JB**

ical balance spring with terminal curbs (patented in 1775) proved of lasting use in chronometer design, but it was to be Earnshaw's escapement and balance which were to prove more popular with later makers.

John Arnold operated an embryonic factory producing chronometers at Chigwell, Essex, and took John Roger into partnership, at his shop at 112 Cornhill, where they traded as 'Arnold & Son' until John's death in 1799. John Roger – who became master of the Clockmakers' Company in 1812 – moved from Cornhill to 27 Cecil Street, Strand in 1820. In 1830, he moved to 84 Strand, where he was in partnership with Edward John Dent until 1840 and then traded independently up to his death.

From the engraved coat of arms, it is likely that this watch belonged to Robert John Milliken Napier (1764–1808) who became a colonel in the British army, commanding at the Siege of Mangalore. **DRT and CE**

527
Pocket Chronometer, *c.* 1818

John Roger Arnold; gilt-brass movement in a silver case and mahogany deck box, 5.5 × 8.5 × 12 cm
One-day chronometer with Arnold spring escapement; Arnold Z-type compensation balance oversprung with helical blued steel spring
Marks: silver inner case with the London hallmarks for 1818–19
Signed: Jn. R. Arnold London Invt. et Fecit
No. 2168

528
Gold-Cased Pocket Chronometer, 1820

James Fergusson Cole; pivoted detent escapement; fusee and chain, and Harrison's maintaining power; spiral steel balance spring with micrometer screw adjustment; white enamel dial signed COLE LONDON; blued steel hands
Inscribed on back of movement: JAMES FERGUSSON COLE N0. sx LONDON Invt. et Fecit

527

Inscribed on silver-plate on balance cock: PATENT
Gold open-faced case, D 6.03 cm
Marks: London hallmark for 1820–21, 18 carat; indistinct casemaker's mark, possibly HJ; pendant maker's mark IHG
London, Trustees of the British Museum
Inv. No. MLA CA1–1726
Provenance: C. A. Ilbert Collection, 1934; bought by the Museum, 1958
Literature: Clutton and Daniels, 1979, p. 270; Randall and Good, 1990, Plates 12e–f and 13a–b

James Fergusson Cole (1798–1880), named after the famous eighteenth century astronomer James Fergusson, became known as the 'English Breguet' because of his innovative and finely made clocks and watches.

This particular example of his work was made very soon after he finished his apprenticeship. Its characteristics suggest that it may well have been an experimental work, a fact born out by a patent which Cole took out on 27 January 1821 (No. 4530) which describes 'various improvements in the design of a pivoted detent escapement and a compensation curb added to the watch index, including a fine adjustment for mean time'.

Cole experimented with various escapements and often used the Lépine type of calibre for his movements. He was a close friend of the Swiss watchmaker Sylvain Mairet (1804–90), who worked in London during the 1830s and supplied watches to Hunt and Roskell, and Benjamin Lewis Vulliamy. Like other London makers, however, Cole was dependent upon the Clerkenwell trade. **DRT and CE**

529
Marine Chronometer, *c.* 1825

Brockbank and Atkins; brass and steel
movement in mahogany gimballed box,
18.5 cm × 21 × 18.5 cm
Two-day chronometer with Earnshaw type
spring detent escapement; Brockbank's
three-arm compensation balance, oversprung
with helical blued steel spring
Signed: Brockbank and Atkins, London
No. 841
Greenwich, National Maritime Museum
Inv. No. CH. 45
Provenance: Doyle Bequest, 1959
Literature: Gould 1923, pp. 117–24

By the time Brockbank and Atkins' No. 841
was manufactured, chronometers had ceased
to be rarities as a result of the increasing output of the ten or so London firms engaged in
this trade. They had also been perfected to
such a degree that subsequent makers were
only able to make minor improvements by
way of new types of compensation balances.
The firm of Brockbank and Atkins had originated with John Brockbank, who operated at
17 Old Jewry from around 1769. He entered
into a partnership with his brother, Myles, and
they had a shop at 6 Cowpers Court, Cornhill
from 1776 to 1808, where some fine chronometers were made. They were succeeded by
their nephews, also called John and Myles,
from 1808 to 1814. Between 1814 and 1840, the
firm traded at 6 Cowpers Court as 'Brockbank
and Atkins', with George Atkins as partner.
CE and JB

529

531

530 *(illus. p. 532)*
Sextant, *c.* 1797

John and Edward Troughton; brass,
11 × 38 × 37 cm, R 29.9 cm; box,
13 × 42.5 × 38 cm
Signed on limb: Troughton London 294
Greenwich, National Maritime Museum
Inv. No. S. 104/37–1400
Provenance: Gift of Captain James Brisbane
to T. H. Hoskins, Master of H.M.S. Saturn
in 1802; presented to the Museum, 1937
Literature: Taylor 1966, pp. 298–99; Brown
1979, pp.41, 52, 76–78

The sextant was developed as a result of the
lunar-distance method of determining longitude at sea in the 1760s. Its design, incorporating an arc the sixth of a circle, enabled it to
measure large angles by reflection in a more
accurate way than the earlier octant.

After the death of Jesse Ramsden in 1800,
Edward Troughton (1753–1835) became
Britain's leading instrument maker. He was
apprenticed to his brother, John and together
they developed their own dividing engine by
around 1778, which enabled them more accurately and speedily to calibrate their instruments. They traded as partners between 1788
and 1804 at 136 Fleet Street. Following John's
death, Edward operated there under his own
name until 1826, when he took William Simms
(1793–1860) into partnership. In 1788 Edward
Troughton patented the pillar or double-
framed sextant, and around 1800 designed the
surveyor's 'snuff-box' pocket sextant. He
began supplying large observatory-type instruments around 1805, and many were seen in
use around the world, as were his surveying
instruments. His standing was recognised by
his election as fellow of the Royal Societies of

London and Edinburgh in 1812 and 1822 re-
spectively. He was a founder member of the
Royal Astronomical Society in 1820. **CE and
KL**

531
Sextant, *c.* 1825

Ripley and Son; brass, 12 × 32 × 29 cm, R
22.2 cm; box, 13 × 36.5 × 32 cm
Signed on limb: Ripley & Son, Hermitage,
London
Greenwich, National Maritime Museum
Inv. No. S. 126/46–295
Provenance: F. N. Adams Collection; on
loan to the Museum, 1946–74; bequeathed to
the Museum, 1974
Literature: Taylor 1966, pp.295, 373; Brown
1979, pp.43, 76, 85–86

The Ripleys were one of a significant number
of instrument makers who operated in the
riverside parishes east of the Tower, where
they developed a flourishing trade with
mariners, ships' husbands, ship chandlers and
merchants. Thomas Ripley, the founder of the
business, operated from around 1765 at an
address given variously as 364 Hermitage and
364 Wapping (High Street). His son, James,
was apprenticed to him, and they are recorded
as working together at 364 Wapping (*c.* 1791–
1800) and 335 Wapping (*c.* 1800–07). In 1807,
James took over the premises at 335 Wapping,
and by 1813 he was also operating a shop in the
newly built Commercial Road (which linked
the City to the recently opened West and East
India Docks), with an adjoining store-room
above the Excise Office. **CE and KL**

members of the Tulley family were involved in telescope making in North London over the years 1782 to 1846, and this telescope cannot be assigned to any particular maker.

Francis Baily was active in the financial world in the City of London and was able to retire after amassing a considerable fortune and devote himself to intellectual activity, especially but not exclusively astronomy; he also wrote on British history and on actuarial theory (as had a number of earlier astronomers). Principally remembered today for his first description of 'Baily's Beads', the necklace-like effect seen just before totality during a solar eclipse, he was also notable as the first secretary when the Royal Astronomical Society was founded in 1820, and was later its president. Perhaps his most important contribution, however, was the collection, editing, and reinterpretation of the many early star catalogues dating in some cases back to the Greeks which built a firm foundation for the flowering of positional astronomy which followed.

The telescope also well represents the attractive appearance of the numerous small instruments purchased for interest and occasional use in the wealthier households at a period when science could be a 'polite accomplishment'; perhaps in conjunction with an aid to star finding such as *Urania's Mirror* (Cat. No. 540). **PH**

533

532
Azimuth Compass, *c.* 1830

William and Thomas Gilbert; brass,
36×25×23 cm
Signed on compass card: W. & T. Gilbert, London
Greenwich, National Maritime Museum
Inv. No. ACO.8/69.19N
Provenance: transferred to the National Maritime Museum from the Admiralty Compass Observatory, 1969
Literature: Fanning 1986; Taylor 1954, p. 134; Taylor 1966, p. 393; Brown 1979, pp. 47, 83

Azimuth compasses were used to determine magnetic variation – the difference between true north and magnetic north – on board ship. In common with other compasses of the period, the one shown here has azimuth sights fixed to the bowl, which had to be rotated about its centre when taking bearings. The bowl is fitted with a spring stop, operated through one of the gimbal pins, for checking the movement of the card. It also has a card lifter, operated by folding down the sight vane to prevent unnecessary wear on the pivot. The compass is certified on the underside of the card as being correct on 19 April 1838. This is probably the date upon which it was examined by the Admiralty Compass Committee.

William and Thomas Gilbert were appren-

ticed to their father, also William, through the Grocers' Company in 1795 and 1801 respectively. The business operated as Gilbert and Sons from 1806–18, as W. and T. Gilbert from about 1819–31, and as William Gilbert from 1832. The Gilberts were one of the largest producers of mathematical and optical instruments in the early nineteenth century. Thomas Gilbert became mathematical instrument maker to the East India Company in 1820. **CE and KL**

533
Three-Draw Hand-Held Achromatic Telescope

Tulley and Sons; object glass, D 4.8 cm; tube overall, D 5.8 cm, L (folded) 29 cm, L (extended) 83 cm; stand, H 37 cm
Signed: Tulley and Sons, Islington,/ /FB
London, Royal Astronomical Society
Inv. No. R.A.S. Instrument Collection No. 150
Provenance: presented by Lt. Col. John Day, R.E., 1929
Literature: Howse 1986, p. 229

This small early nineteenth-century refracting telescope is preserved as a relic of Francis Baily (1774–1844), whose monogram can be seen on the brass ring of the upper course. Several

532

535

Provenance: bought with two others at Christie's, 9 March 1895; presented to the Society by Dr. McClean
Literature: Ryan 1966, pp. 27–48

Russell was determined to produce the largest and most accurate picture of the moon ever made, finding all previous efforts at lunar map making deficient. His serious studies began in 1785 with the help of professional astronomers and two telescopes, by Herschel and Dollond. From around 1795 he made finished pastel drawings such as this of the moon at various phases. **PH**

538

534 *(illus. p. 531)*
Lunar Globe, 'Selenographia', 1797

John Russell; printed paper gores on plaster, brass stand, 51×42 cm
Signed: Invented by J Russell . . . Published by the Author
Stamford, Burghley House Collection
Provenance: acquired by Henry Cecil, 10th Earl and 1st Marquess of Exeter
Exhibitions: Burghley, 1986, Cat. No. 26

John Russell R.A. (1745–1806) was best known as an artist in pastels, but he was also an active amateur astronomer, with a particular interest in the moon. His 'Selenographia', as he named this invention, is more than a simple lunar globe; it is rather an instrument for demonstrating the effect of what is called lunar libration. The moon always presents the same face to earth, so that before the space age, only this side was known. However, because there is a complex combination of real and apparent oscillations (the libration) about this mean presentation, a little more than half the lunar surface can be seen from Earth. Russell's instrument has the very specialised function of demonstrating this phenomenon.

This example was acquired by the 10th Earl of Exeter – who had a keen interest in science and technology – probably when Russell visited Burghley House to paint portraits of the Earl and his children. **JB**

John Russell
Guildford 1745–1806 Hull

535
Drawing of the Full Moon

Pastel, 46×38 cm
London, Royal Astronomical Society

536
Lunar Planisphere under oblique observation, 1805–06

Etching, 40.7×40.2 cm
London, Christopher Mendez
Literature: Ryan 1966, pp. 27–48

Russell's two etchings of the moon, which he entitled 'lunar planispheres', were published after his death by his son. One showed the full moon under direct illumination; the other – the present example – showed the moon under oblique illumination of each part, when the forms became more clearly defined. The first print was dedicated to the Astronomer Royal, Nevil Maskelyne; this the second to William Herschel. **CF**

537 *(illus. p. 532)*
Orrery, 1823–27

John Addison; wooden baseboard with varnished paper scale; brass gearing, with brass and ivory planets, hand-painted earth;

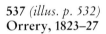

536

engraved silver scale beneath Sun/Moon group, 17×53×28 cm
Signed on paper scale above the Gemini: Published for & Sold by J. ADDISON, / 116, Regent Street St. James's / GLOBE MAKER to His Most Gracious Majesty, Geo. III
Greenwich, National Maritime Museum Inv. No. P. 14/37–201
Provenance: George H. Gabb Collection (No. R.3); presented to the Museum by Sir James Caird, Bart., 1937
Literature: King 1978, pp. 150–58, 210; Taylor 1966, p. 412

John Addison (*fl.* 1820–38) moved from his premises at 9 Skinner Street to Regent Street in 1823. By 1826 he was at 50 London Street, Fitzroy Square, moving on to Hampstead Road in 1827. Addison and Co. were described by Thomas Keith in his influential *Treatise on the use of Globes with a Philosophical View of the Earth and Heavens* (1806) as among the most important and prosperous globemakers in London.

The orrery is a mechanical model which demonstrates the relative motions of the planets and their satellites. The name 'orrery' comes from the now defunct title of Charles Boyle, 4th Earl of Cork and Orrery, who bestowed his name on the mechanical planetary model given to him by the instrument maker John Rowley (*fl.* 1698–1728). **KL**

538 (*illus. p. 541*)
Theodolite, *c.* 1840

Troughton and Simms; brass with silvered scales, D of horizontal circle, 16.5 cm
Signed: Troughton and Simms, LONDON
Cambridge, Whipple Museum of the History of Science
Inv. No. 2116
Provenance: Reverend Richard Sheepshanks; presented by his family to the Royal Astronomical Society in 1857

Troughton and Simms were the leading British makers of precision instruments in the first half of the nineteenth century. The high regard in which their instruments were held is borne out by the fact that in 1826–27 they supplied the two 10-foot Ordnance Standards for the Ordnance Survey Department, and that they were used, with other instruments made by them, in the Principal Triangulation of Great Britain and Ireland. They also provided most of the theodolites used in the Survey of India. **JB and CE**

539
Compound Microscope, *c.* 1840

Andrew Ross; brass, length of limb, 40.5 cm
Signed on foot: ANDW ROSS & Co Opticians 33 Regent St. Piccadilly
Cambridge, Whipple Museum of the History of Science
Inv. No. 2385

This is a relatively early example of the work of Andrew Ross (1798–1859), who was to become one of the world's leading makers of fine microscopes. At a time when the established supremacy of London makers in the field of precision instruments for astronomy and navigation was coming under increasing threat from Germany and France, the microscope makers benefited from their familiarity with achromatic objective lenses and for much of the century the best microscopes were to be had in London. **JB**

Jehoshaphat Aspin
fl. 1814–1835

540
a) A Familiar Treatise on Astronomy
Published by M. A. Leigh, 421 Stand, 1834
Book, 22 × 14 cm

b) Urania's Mirror
32 cards, 20 × 13.5 cm, engraved by Sydney Hall and perforated with hand-applied watercolour, in box with printed labels

540a and b

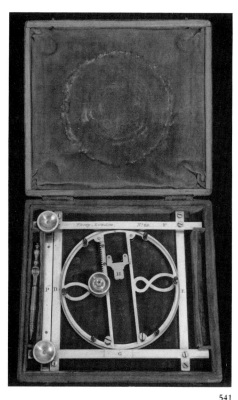

541

London, Royal Astronomical Society
Inv. Nos. 19308, 24267 respectively
Provenance: book bought 1975; cards donated by R. Mumford, 1958
Literature: Sperling 1981, pp. 398–99

Astronomy participated in the rise of popular education in two ways. Firstly, the need of the mariner for astronomical knowledge for practical navigation (enabling seafarer to progress to mate and master in the deep water trades) resulted in astronomical instruction being given in the many local nautical schools in seaport towns. Secondly, a much wider desire for general scientific knowledge led to many popular astronomical books and articles in general magazines.

Among the great number of works intended to facilitate identification of the constellations possibly the most ingenious and beautiful is the set of thirty-two cards entitled *Urania's Mirror*. The unique feature is that the cards are perforated with holes in the positions of the brighter stars with the diameters of the holes corresponding to their magnitudes. Thus if the cards are held up to the light the constellation patterns are represented in a most realistic way.

The books which went with the cards, Jehoshaphat Aspin's *Family Treatise on Astronomy*, went through numerous editions and there appear to be two states of the cards. A pleasant mystery is attached to the cards as they are described as 'On a plan entirely

539

original, designed by a Lady'. There were several female astronomers active at this period but none of them are associated with elementary treatises and it seems likely that the conundrum will never be solved. **PH**

541
Farey's Ellipsograph c. 1814

John Farey; steel and brass in shagreen-covered wooden box, 15.8×16.6×3.1 cm; instrument, 13.5×15×2.1 cm
Signed: FAREY, LONDON, NO.20
London, Trustees of the Science Museum
Inv. No. 1922–108
Literature: Farey 1812; Farey 1813, pp. 117–30; Taylor 1966, p. 391; Hambly 1988, pp. 89–90

This instrument is one of several surviving examples of the ellipsograph invented by John Farey in about 1810. It was the first such instrument to be designed in Britain. It satisfied the demand for a device which would enable architects and engineers to draw smaller ellipses than had previously been possible. Ellipses were required whenever a circle was depicted in perspective, but the earlier trammels had only allowed large figures to be constructed. The ellipsograph can be used to draw on to paper or engrave on to copper plate.

The instrument consists of two circles which slide between two parallel rulers fixed at right angles to each other. The distance between the centres of the circles can be varied for each ellipse, but the circles move as one while the ellipse is drawn. Attached to the upper circle is a swivel socket in which a pair of compasses may be fixed; this enables the position of the describing point to be adjusted.

John Farey's father, also John Farey, was a mineral and land surveyor who worked from Howland Street, London, and Upper Crown Court, Westminster. John junior used the latter address. From an early age, John junior became renowned for his technical engravings, producing plates for Rees's *Cyclopaedia* from 1805 to 1830 (Cat. No. 198). He demonstrated the ellipsograph at the Society of Arts in 1813 where it won a gold medal. **JW**

542
Pocket Set of Drawing Instruments

William Cary; brass, steel, ivory and ebony in a fishskin-covered wooden case, 13.5×7.5×2.1 cm
Signed: CARY LONDON
London, Trustees of the Science Museum
Inv. No. 1938–167

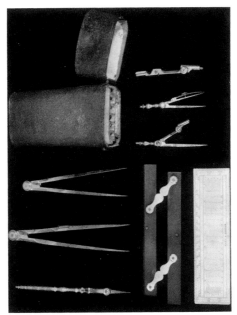

542

Provenance: gift of H.M. Queen Mary to the Museum, 1938
Literature: Taylor 1966, pp. 692–93; King 1979, pp. 170–72

This standard set of the period comprises a pair of compasses, a pair of dividers, ink point, pencil point, two small bows, ruling pen, scale rule, sector and parallel rule. The scale rule incorporates a protractor and bears the signature.

The Cary family was active in the scientific instrument making society of London from the late eighteenth century until the mid nineteenth century. William's elder brother John (1754–1835) was a cartographer who worked in the Strand from 1783 and also at St. James's Street. In 1820 a fire burnt the Strand workshop but it was subsequently rebuilt and occuped by William (1759–1825). Another property in the Strand was used by John's sons who kept the family business going until 1853.

William Cary was apprenticed to Jesse Ramsden, the leading maker of scientific instruments at the end of the eighteenth century. Before Ramsden died, Cary was able to pick up assignments which Ramsden was not able to fulfil. The most important of these was for Francis Wollaston for whom he attached a graduated circle to a transit telescope to enable him to measure altitudes. In 1805 Brewster communicated the idea of his variable eye piece to Cary, demonstrating the esteem in which he was held. In the same year, Cary built a transit instrument for the Moscow Observatory. **JW**

543
Terrestrial Globe, 1842 impression of 1816 edition

J. and W. Cary; hand-coloured, printed paper gores, brass and walnut stand, D 46 cm
Signed: CARY'S NEW TERRESTRIAL GLOBE . . . LONDON Made and Sold by J. & W. Cary, Strand, March 1st 1818. WITH ADDITIONS AND CORRECTIONS TO 1842
Cambridge, Whipple Museum of the History of Science
Inv. No. 2693
Provenance: Park Street School, Cambridge

The Cary family were the principal London globe and map makers of the period with a large trade in relatively inexpensive products, always marked with the latest celebrated voyages, discoveries and cartographic refinements. By the time this example was printed, both the original partners, John and William, were dead and the business had moved from the Strand, and was in the hands of two sons of John Cary, George and John. **JB**

543

544
Set of Amputation Instruments

Savigny and Co., 67 St. James's Street
Wood and steel, 7×17.2×41.6 cm
Signed: Savigny & Co.
London: Trustees of the Science Museum
Inv. No. A600571
Literature: Savigny 1798; Weston-Davies
1989, pp. 40–43

There was considerable demand for London-made surgical instruments not only for the home market but also for export to the British colonies, and for supplies to the army and navy medical services. This amputation set is typical of the period, comprising bone saw and forceps, and knives to sever the limb muscles, together with needles, ligatures and other small instruments. A tourniquet, of the type devised by the Frenchman, Jean-Louis Petit, is included.

Savigny was one of the foremost London instrument makers, the family business having been in existence since at least 1720. He probably subcontracted the initial forging required to blacksmiths, then carried out the necessary grinding, polishing, assembly and handle making. Case makers belonged to a separate trade, a branch of cabinet making. **GL**

THEATRE AND MUSIC

Theatre was the most popular form of public entertainment, uniting all classes and fanned by a buoyant market in souvenirs. The London stage was dominated by three great tragedians: John Philip Kemble, Sarah Siddons and Edmund Kean. Their stature was matched by the ever increasing ambitions of scale and spectacle at the two Theatres Royal, Covent Garden and Drury Lane. At the same time the growing number of minor theatres in the suburbs of London encouraged the new forms of melodrama, pantomime, equestrian and aquatic shows. Though foreign singers and musicians visited London in exchange for lucrative contracts, they found the audiences largely ignorant and musical standards disappointing.

John Orlando Parry
1810–1879

545 *(illus. p. 559)*
A London Street Scene

Watercolour, 70.2×100.3 cm
Signed and dated lower right: John Parry
1835
London, Alfred Dunhill Ltd.
Literature: Motif, Vol. 1, 1958, pp. 72–73

Parry's painting gives a vivid impression of the rapid change taking place in London in the 1830s. Buildings about to be demolished and the temporary wooden hoardings around the sites of those that had been torn down were immediately exploited as a site for the printed posters which competed for the attention of the passer-by. The most prominent of the posters shown are for entertainments, theatrical and musical; steam ships are also advertised, and the *Comet*, a horse-drawn coach running from London to Liverpool in twenty-four hours.

Parry conveys the visual chaos of the scene, the fierce competition for space and the ephemeral nature of the poster, which rapidly became prey to the destructive force of the weather, small boys and rival advertisers. Variety was created by the exploitation of colour, different letter forms, from 'fat face' to 'sans serif', and the treatment of the letter, using reversed-out (or negative) letters, and shaded forms emulating inscriptions in relief. **JM**

547a

Sir Thomas Lawrence
Bristol 1769–1830 London

546 (illus. p. 527)
John Philip Kemble as Coriolanus, 1798

Oil on canvas, 113×70 cm
London, Guildhall Art Gallery
Inv. No. 844
Provenance: purchased from the artist by Sir Richard Worsley; thence by marriage to the Earls of Yarborough; by descent, presented to the Gallery by the 4th Earl, 1906
Exhibitions: London, Royal Academy, 1798, No. 225; British Institution, 1845, No. 80 and 1848, No. 30; Manchester, 1857, No. 173; Port Sunlight, 1948; London, Royal Academy, 1951, Cat. No. 415; Hayward Gallery, 1975, Cat. No. 136; National Portrait Gallery, 1979, Cat. No. 12; Royal Academy, 1982–83, Cat. No. 136
Literature: Garlick 1989, p. 216; West 1991, pp. 226–48

John Philip Kemble (1757–1823) was one of the most capable and famous actors of his generation, and an important figure in the development of the theatre in London. The son of the actor-manager Roger Kemble, his first appearance in London in 1783, at Drury Lane as Hamlet, was greeted with excitement by the critics, and he subsequently appeared at the

theatre in many of Shakespeare's plays. It was generally agreed, however, that it was in tragic roles that Kemble showed his true brilliance. Kemble served as actor and manager at Drury Lane until 1802, drawing a salary of £55.14s. per week, which shows clearly his measure of success. He later became actor-manager at Covent Garden, where he spent the remainder of his career.

One of Kemble's greatest roles was as Coriolanus, which he first performed in 1789, and it was in this part that the actor gave his farewell performance in June 1817. The play was attended by an immense crowd who chanted 'No farewell!' at the prospect of his retirement. Lawrence knew him well, painting his portrait several times, most notably as Coriolanus. Kemble is shown at the hearth of Tullus Aufidius, waiting in disguise for his enemy with whom he intends to join against Rome, following his exile from the city. Lawrence appears to have thought it more than a portrait, describing it in a letter as 'a sort of half-history picture'. **RU**

George Henry Harlow
London 1787–1819 London

547
**a) Sarah Siddons as Lady Macbeth
Act I, scene v: Come all ye spirits/
That tend on mortal thoughts, unsex me here**
Oil on canvas 61×38 cm

**b) Sarah Siddons as Lady Macbeth
Act V, scene i: Out, damned spot!
Out, I say!**
Oil on canvas, 61.6×37.5 cm

London, The Garrick Club
Inv. Nos. Mathews 147, 137; RW/CKA 31, 43 respectively
Provenance: Charles Mathews
Exhibitions: London, Royal Academy 1833, Nos. 147 and 137; Hayward Gallery, 1975, Cat. Nos. 100, 101
Literature: Ashton mss., Nos. 742, 743

Sarah Siddons (1755–1831) was the eldest of Roger Kemble's twelve children, making her London stage debut in Garrick's last season at Drury Lane in 1775–76. But it was only in 1782 that she achieved success in Southerne's *Isabella; or the Fatal Marriage* and thereafter came to be regarded as the apotheosis of tragedy, a legend sustained by Reynolds' famous painting of her as *The Tragic Muse* (Royal Academy, 1784, No. 190. Huntington Library, San Marino, California). Lady Macbeth was the role most closely associated with Mrs. Siddons, from her first appearance in

548

London in the part on 2 February 1785 until her last official performance on stage, at Covent Garden on 22 June 1812, when the audience would not allow the play to continue after the sleep-walking scene (b).

Harlow charged 20 guineas for such small full lengths and is it probable that they were commissioned directly from the artist by Charles Mathews, a close friend and patron. A large-scale version of (a), exhibited at the British Institution in 1814 (No. 93) is in the collection of Bob Jones University, Southern California. **CF**

Samuel Drummond
London 1763–1844 London

548
Edmund Kean as Richard III, 1813

Oil on canvas, 203×122 cm
London, Sadler's Wells Trust Ltd.
Provenance: believed to have been given to Lilian Baylis
Exhibitions: London, Royal Academy, 1814, No. 315; Sydney, 1973; London, Hayward Gallery, 1975, Cat. No. 203, reproduced
Literature: Moore 1888, p. 228; Hackett 1959

550

Edmund Kean (1787?-1833) was a tragedian whose intensely expressive style of acting typified the romantic and radical preoccupations of his age. He made his debut at Drury Lane on 26 January 1814 as Shylock, followed on 12 February by Richard III, which became his most famous role. His appearance was startling to theatre goers accustomed to Kemble's dignity and physical grandeur; small, notably lacking in grace but with a dark piercing eye, Kean acted with all the muscles in his body, using every physical recourse to create drama of passionate intensity. His range was narrow, a dull Romeo and disappointing Lear, but he excelled in the portrayal of malign and frenzied evil. Racked with emotion, his voice was harsh and broken and sometimes even choked; he moved from measured speech to 'rapid and familiar utterance' producing tremendous excitement and involvement in his audience. EE

549
Edmund Kean's stage costume for Richard III, London, c. 1830

Crimson cotton velvet and silk satin surcoat, lined with canvas and silk, decorated with leather, overlaid with appliqué spangles and trimmed with imitation ermine; similarly decorated black doublet fastened with brass buttons, the upper sleeves paned to reveal the silk beneath, with integral sword belt of crimson velvet ornamented with paste

diamonds and amethysts; matching trunk-hose wig and crown of gilded pasteboard edged in imitation ermine decorated with imitation pearl and paste gems; sword associated with Kean

London, The Museum of London
Inv. No. 53.96 (costume); 49.76/1 (sword)
Provenance: costume, Russell Thorndike, loaned to the London Museum in 1953 and given 1975; sword, Sir John Martin-Harvey; presented by Mrs. Huntley Gordon to the Museum, 1949
Literature: Holmes 1965, pp. 8, 27; de Marly 1982, p. 45

The traditional style of stage costume for Richard III was a pastiche of sixteenth-and early seventeenth-century fashions. The doublet, trunk-hose and surcoat were variants of the costume depicted in J. van der Gucht, *The Works of William Shakespear*, (1709), seen in paintings and engravings of David Garrick (who first played the role in 1741) and in the anonymous portrait of George Frederick Cooke in the role, of 1801. Attempts to dress Richard III in the fashions of the late fifteenth century (he reigned from 1483 to 1485) came later in the nineteenth century. Kean played Richard III throughout his career on the London stage, his last performance in the role taking place on 12 March 1833, a few weeks before his death on 15 May. All leading actors of this period owned their stage costumes and were rarely persuaded to wear costumes from the theatre wardrobe. VC

550
Figure of Edmund Kean in the role of Richard III

Robert Bloor and Co., c. 1815

Soft-paste porcelain, H 29 cm
Marks: crown over D in red; incised number 21 and 1 size; workman's mark 45 in blue
Derby, Royal Crown Derby Museum
Literature: Twitchett 1980, pp. 228–29, Fig. 296; Bradshaw 1990, p. 418, G4, p. 187, Fig. 144

Derby produced three versions of models of Richard III, as portrayed by David Garrick, John Philip Kemble and Kean, the present example. Only the head decoration was changed for each actor, illustrating the thrift of the Midlands china works. The original model was based on the portrait of Garrick by Nathaniel Dance, commissioned by Garrick, exhibited at the Royal Academy in 1771 and acquired by Sir Watkin Williams-Wynn; it was widely known through engravings, one by J. Dixon, who also exhibited a *grisaille* version at the Society of Artists in 1772. JT

551
Tuppence Coloured Print

Edmund Kean as Richard III

Lithograph, 24.2 × 19.7 cm
Published by W. S. Johnson
London, The Raymond Mander and Joe Mitchenson Theatre Collection
Exhibitions: London, Hayward Gallery, 1975, Cat. No. 216

In the first half of the nineteenth century all the major actors were commemorated in their most famous roles in prints which sold at a 'Penny Plain' and 'Tuppence Coloured'. The latter were sometimes 'tinselled', or embellished with coloured foil. CF

552
Playbill, Theatre Royal, Drury Lane. 10 June, 1822

King Richard the Third, Duke of Glo'ster, Mr. KEAN, Being his last appearance in that Character this Season . . .
Wove paper, letter press, 33.4 × 25 cm
London, The Museum of London
Inv. No. Drury Lane Playbills 459

552

555

Garrick was the first actor to have his name printed more prominently that any other on a playbill, but with the advent of new typefaces at the beginning of the nineteenth century, the practice received fresh impetus. Kean is said never to have agreed to play second lead, and to demand and get star billing for every performance. EE

Samuel de Wilde
Holland 1748–1832 London

553 *(illus. p. 558)*
Thomas Collins as Slender in *The Merry Wives of Windsor*

Oil on canvas, 73.7×57.2 cm
Signed on step, lower left: S. De Wilde
London, Royal National Theatre, Maugham Collection
Provenance: W. Somerset Maugham, by whom bequeathed to the Shakespeare Memorial National Theatre Trust (Royal National Theatre) in 1951
Exhibitions: London, Royal Academy, 1803, No. 652; Victoria and Albert Museum, 1951; Hayward Gallery, 1975, Cat. No. 128
Royal Academy, 1982–83, pp. 83–84, Cat. No. 140
Literature: Mander and Mitchenson 1955, p. 113; Mander and Mitchenson 1980, Cat. No. 28

The revival of *The Merry Wives of Windsor* took place at Drury Lane Theatre, on 26 October 1802 with a fine cast of comedians; Falstaff was played by Stephen Kemble who, in contrast to his outstandingly handsome elder brother, was remarkable for his enormous bulk which enabled him to play the part without padding. Thomas Collins (1775–1806) had made his first appearance in London at

Drury Lane earlier in 1802 and remained at the theatre until his death at the age of thirty-one.

Samuel de Wilde was one of the first students at the Royal Academy Schools in 1769 and exhibited there from 1778 to 1821. His studio was in Tavistock Row, conveniently placed between Covent Garden and Drury Lane, and he painted hundreds of theatrical portraits in oil and watercolour. IM

Samuel de Wilde

554 *(illus. p. 558)*
Charles Farley as Francisco in *A Tale of Mystery* by Thomas Holcroft, 1803

Oil on canvas, 89.5×69.2 cm
London, Royal National Theatre
Provenance: as for Cat. No. 553
Exhibitions: London, Royal Academy, 1803, No. 191; Victoria and Albert Museum, 1951; Hayward Gallery, 1975, Cat. No. 129
Literature: Mander and Mitchenson 1955, p. 117; Mander and Mitchenson, 1980, Cat. No. 29

A Tale of Mystery, based on the French drama by Pixercourt called *Coelina, ou l'Enfant du Mystère,* was the first play in London to be entitled a 'melo-drama', in other words, a play in which a musical accompaniment was used to heighten the reactions of the characters at dramatic climaxes. The plot turns on the parentage of Francisco, who has been attacked and rendered dumb, but is still able to write. In answer to the question posed by Selina, his rich protectress, as to the identity of his attackers, he writes on the paper he holds 'the same who stabbed me among the rocks'. The first act takes place in a Gothic hall in the house of Selina's guardian and Farley wears a version of mid-European mountain costume – the drama growing out of the popular Gothic novels of the late eighteenth century.

Charles Farley (1771–1859) first appeared at Covent Garden in 1782 and was the original Francisco in the play's first performance on 13 November 1802 at the same theatre. From 1806 until 1834, he was responsible for all the pantomimes at Covent Garden. IM

555
Patchbox, 1804

Soft-paste porcelain, silvered barrel and gold-rimmed lid, decorated in enamel with the head of Master Betty in profile, 2.8×5.5×5.5 cm
Inscribed on lid: 'William Henry West Betty/Born 13th Sept. 1791', and on base, 'British tragedian with feeling and propriety

he astonishes the judicious observers of human nature 1804'
Brighton, Royal Pavilion, Art Gallery and Museums
Inv. No. C.HW.926
Exhibitions: London, Bethnal Green, 1899, No. 926

William Henry West Betty (1791–1874) enjoyed adulatory praise and attention for his dramatic performances on the London stage during the early years of the nineteenth century. The son of a linen manufacturer, he visited the theatre for the first time at the age of ten when he saw Mrs. Siddons as Elvira. This experience inspired him to become an actor himself, and less than two years later he made his first appearance, at Belfast.

He appeared for the first time in London in 1804 at Covent Garden to instant acclaim. Admiration of the prodigy verged on the hysterical; his appearance in *Barbarossa* in December 1804 provoked a near riot, the military having to be deployed to preserve order. Many people were injured in the crush to get into the theatre to see him. He was universally known as 'The Young Roscius' and Hazlitt described him as 'almost like some gay creature of the elements moving about gracefully with all the flexibility of youth and murmuring Aeolian sounds with plaintive tenderness.' Betty was particularly famous for his performances as Hamlet, on one occasion Pitt adjourning the Commons so that members would be able to see him in the play. RU

556
Medal

Master Betty, 1804

White metal, D 4.2 cm
Engraved by T. Webb

556

559

daughter of the famous engraver Francesco Bartolozzi. At sixteen she married the dancer Armand Vestris from a leading Franco-Italian stage family, but by 1815, she had separated from him and went on the stage in Paris, returning to make her London debut at Drury Lane five years later. Most successful in light comedy and burlesque, she subsequently managed the Olympic, Covent Garden and Lyceum theatres, marrying the comedian Charles Mathews.

Madame Vestris first sang the German 'Broom Girl' song, arranged by Alexander Lee, at the Theatre Royal Haymarket on 18 September 1826. The 'Broom Girl' song was introduced into the farce *The £100 Note* by Richard Brinsley Peke at Covent Garden the following year and long remained a popular favourite. At her benefit at the Haymarket on 6 November 1826, she sang her song as a duet with John Liston, the occasion giving rise to numerous prints and figurines. **IM**

George Cruikshank
1792 London–1878 London

559
J. Grimaldi. Song in Character – All the world's in Paris, *c.* 1814

Etching, hand-coloured, 17 × 20.3 cm
London, The Museum of London
Inv. No. A6897
Literature: Reid 1871, No. 457; Cohn 1924, p. 249, No. 880; George 1949, Vol. 9, p. 623, No. 12698

The print was originally published by Whittle and Laurie as the heading to a song 'Sung with great Applause by Mr Grimaldi, in the popular Pantomime of "Harlequin Whittington",' first performed at Covent Garden on 26 December 1814. Joseph Grimaldi (1779–1837) was the greatest clown in British stage history. Born the son of a ballet master and clown at Drury Lane, Grimaldi was an infant prodigy, making his stage debut at the age of three. His first performance as a clown took place at Sadler's Wells (Cat. No. 572) in 1800 and it is with this theatre that he is particularly associated. Here he is disguised as an English tourist *en route* to Paris. Napoleon's exile in Elba led the country to assume, somewhat prematurely, it was safe to visit the Continent again. **CF**

Obverse: draped bust of William Betty. THE YOUNG ROSCIUS
Reverse: sword, goblet, trumpet and manuscript enclosed by a wreath NOT YET MATURE YET MATCHLESS BORN SEPTr 13th 1791. MDCCCIV
London, Trustees of the British Museum
Inv. No. Banks NTC. 185
Literature: Brown 1980, p. 137, No. 558

At least seven medals were struck celebrating William Henry West Betty. **EE**

557
Figure of John Liston as Paul Pry, *c.* 1826–30

Staffordshire; earthenware, press-moulded, hand-painted overglaze enamel colours, H. 15 cm
Stoke-on-Trent, City Museum and Art Gallery
Inv. No. 371–1949
Provenance: formerly in the collection of Miss M. D. Wood, descendant of the Wood family of potters, Burslem, Staffordshire
Exhibitions: Stoke-on-Trent, 1991, No. 10
Literature: Pückler Muskau 1832, Vol. 3, pp. 119–20; Halfpenny 1991

John Liston (1776–1846) was one of the most successful comic actors of the day, appearing on the London stage between 1805 and 1837.

In 1826 a set of coloured lithographs was issued depicting Liston in eight of his celebrated roles. These were a source of inspiration for the Staffordshire potters as well as the upmarket Derby and Rockingham Factories.

The comedy *Paul Pry* by John Poole was first produced at the Haymarket Theatre on 13 September 1825 with Liston in the title role. It was immediately successful and sustained its appeal throughout the nineteenth century. Prince Pückler Muskau described the character on 21 November 1826 as 'a sort of foolish lout. The actor, who is said to have made a fortune of six thousand a-year, is one of those whom I should call natural comic actors.' Paul Pry became an affectionate term for an inquisitive person; Pry's catch-phrases 'I hope I don't intrude', 'It's nothing to me' and 'Just drop't in' became part of the patter of the day. **DS**

L. H. Lynch

558
John Liston and Madame Vestris as Broom Girls, 1826

Lithograph, 130 × 24 cm
London, The Raymond Mander and Joe Mitchenson Theatre Collection
Exhibitions: London, Hayward Gallery, 1975, Cat. No. 166, illustrated

Madame Vestris, née Lucia Elizabeth Bartolozzi (1797–1856) was born in London, grand-

T.M. Grimshaw

560
a) Mr Grimaldi in his Fav'rite Dance of "Fun and Physic" . . . 1814

560a

Watercolour over pencil, 38×28 cm
Signed: Drawn by T. M. Grimshaw, who
performed with Grimaldi at Covent Garden
and Sadlers Wells Theatres in 1814, 15, 19, 20,
21, 22, 23

b) Grimaldi and his "pugilistic vegetable Figure" ... 1816

Watercolour over pencil, 38×27.7 cm
Signed: Drawn by T. M. Grimshaw who
performed with Grimaldi at 1814 to 23 at
Covent Garden, Sadlers Wells and Coburg
Theatres

London, The Museum of London
Inv. No. 39.85/4-5
Provenance: A. W. Fuller
Exhibitions: Sunderland, 1988, pp. 7, 9, 55
Literature: Dickens 1833, pp. 185–86, 209–10

According to Charles Dickens (who edited the
clown's *Memoirs*), Grimaldi's comic dance of
'Fun and Physic' was one of two new songs
he sang in *Rival Genii; or Harlequin Wild
Man*, which opened at Sadler's Wells on Easter
Monday, 11 April 1814: the other was the topical *Frost Fair; or the Disasters of Mr. Higgins
and Mrs Wiggins*. At the same time, Grimaldi
was performing in the Great Asiatic Spectacle
of *Sadak and Kalasrade* at Covent Garden,
frequently on the same evening. Before the
1816 winter season commenced, Grimaldi fell
out with Dibdin over an increase in salary and
he did not return to Sadler's Wells until 1818
on terms which included a share in the profits.
CF

561
Figure of Joseph Grimaldi, *c.* 1828

Staffordshire, Enoch Wood factory
Earthenware, enamelled, 14.5×10×5 cm
Brighton, Royal Pavilion, Art Gallery and
Museums
Inv. No. 320000
Provenance: Hoare Collection
Exhibitions: Louisville, 1990, No. 15
Literature: Horne 1987, Fig. 191

This figure depicts Grimaldi in his famous role
in *Harlequin and Mother Goose*. It seems
likely that these figures were made to celebrate
the benefit performance given for Grimaldi at
Drury Lane on 27 June 1828. Undecorated
fragments of a Grimaldi figure were found in a
deposit together with other wasters beneath
the cornerstone of St. Paul's Church, Burslem,
when it was demolished in 1974. The cornerstone was laid in June 1828. All the marked
pieces related to Enoch Wood. A similar
figure modelled in porcelain by Thomas Griffin at the Derby factory would have been
aimed at wealthier enthusiasts.

Enoch Wood made a large collection of pottery in order to illustrate the history of the industry, presenting in 1835 the King of Saxony
with 182 pieces (now in the Museum für Kunsthandwerk, in Dresden). **EE**

562
Playbill, Theatre Royal, Drury Lane. 17 November, 1838

MR. DUCROS, With the introduction of
his Double Stud of highly trained Palfreys
and ... MR. VAN AMBURGH and his
celebrated Lions ... a grand Fairy Ballet ...
The SPIRIT OF AIR!
Wove paper and letter press, 34.4×20 cm
London, The Museum of London
Inv. No. Drury Lane Playbills 157

Isaac van Amburgh (1811–1865) and Andrew
Ducrow (1793–1843) were showmen celebrated in their time and influential in the development of the circus.

Descended from an American Indian, Van
Amburgh first appeared as a lion tamer at
Richmond Hill Theatre, New York in 1833
and his control, and relaxed and playful handling of his animals created a sensation. He
came to England in 1838 and presented his
lions, tigers and leopards at Astley's Amphith-
eatre which had been under the management
of Ducrow and James West since 1825.
Ducrow played many roles, as tightrope
dancer, contortionist and animal trainer, as
choreographer and costume designer but he
was famed for his horsemanship which he
combined with a startling talent as a mimic.

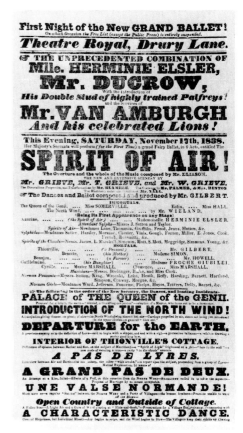

562

Ducrow and Van Amburgh performed together at Drury Lane in the autumn of 1838
opening on Monday 22 October with a new
drama entitled *Charlemagne*. Van Amburgh
was subsequently portrayed by Edwin Landseer reclining surrounded by his animals in
their cage (H.M. Queen Elizabeth II). **EE**

Grieve Family

563
Three-dimensional stage model set for *Harlequin and Number Nip,* The Dolphin's Abode, 1827

Pen and ink and watercolour, 14.4×23.5 cm
London, University of London, Sterling
Library
Inv. No. Grieve Collection No. 59
Literature: Pückler Muskau 1832, Vol. 3, p.
284; Rosenfeld 1973, pp. 91, 96, 158, Plate
56; Mayer 1969, p. 32, Fig. 7

The pantomime *Harlequin and Number Nip;
or, The Giant Mountain* was first performed at
Covent Garden on 26 December 1827. It was

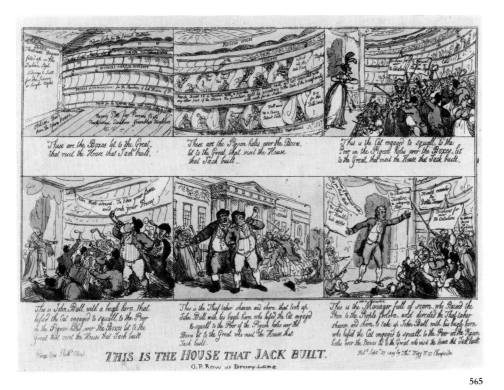

These are the Boxes let to the Great, that visit the House that Jack built. *These are the Pigeon holes over the Boxes, let to the Great, that visit the House that Jack built.* *This is the Cat engaged to squall, to the Poor in the Pigeon holes over the Boxes, let to the Great, that visit the House that Jack built.*

This is John Bull, with a bugle horn, that hlisd the Cat engaged to squall, to the Poor in the Pigeon holes over the Boxes let to the Great that visit the House that Jack built. *This is the Thief taker shaven, and shorn, that took up John Bull with his bugle horn, who hlisd the Cat engaged to squall to the Poor of the Pigeon holes over the Boxes let to the Great, who visit the House that Jack built.* *This is the Manager full of scorn, who Raised the Price, to the People forlorn, and directed the Thief taker shaven and shorn, to take up John-Bull, with his bugle horn, who hlisd the Cat engaged to squall, to the Poor in the Pigeon holes over the Boxes let to the Great, who visit the House that Jack built.*

THIS IS THE HOUSE THAT JACK BUILT.

O.P. Row at Drury Lane

565

principally noted for a seascape panorama painted by David Roberts (Cat. No. 256), which extended from the Chain Pier, Brighton, to Gibraltar, the Archipelago, and the Battle of Navarino, ending with an allegorical group representing the Triumph of Britannia. The Grotto of the Dolphins, represented here, was the final scene. **CF**

Thomas Hosmer Shepherd
France 1793–1864 London

564
Theatre Royal, Covent Garden, *c.* 1825

Pencil, pen and ink and wash, 20.7×30 cm
Private Collection
Exhibitions: London, Royal Academy, 1982–83, p. 112, Cat. No. 175, illustrated

Following the Commonwealth ban on stage plays, in 1662–63 King Charles II granted two patents, one to Sir William Davenport and the other to Thomas Killigrew, to present theatrical entertainment again in London. The Davenport patent was transferred from Lincoln's Inn Fields to Covent Garden in 1732, where the first of six successive theatres on the site was built. John Inigo Richards' second theatre of 1782 was remodelled by Henry Holland ten years later on a somewhat larger scale, in the neo-classical style – the first of its type in

London. But when it was totally destroyed by fire on 20 September 1808, the opportunity was seized to build a much larger theatre to the design of the young Robert Smirke (1780–1867). Under the direction of John Philip Kemble and his senior partner Thomas Harris, the rebuilding only took ten months. Smirke produced an austere Hellenic exterior, enlivened with bas-relief panels by Flaxman and statues by Rossi, with an auditorium holding over 2,800 people. But the attempt by the management to recoup their outlay by squeezing in more boxes at the expense of the galleries, led to the O.P. Riots (Cat. No. 565). **IM**

Thomas Rowlandson
London 1756–1827 London

565
a) This is the House that Jack Built, 1809

Etched, coloured impression, six designs on one sheet, each *c.* 8×10.5 cm
Published by Thos. Tegg, 111 Cheapside, 27 September 1809
London, Trustees of the British Museum
Inv. No. 1868-8-8-7878
Literature: George 1947, Vol. 8, pp. 863–65, No. 11414

b) These are the Boxes let to the Great, that visit the House that Jack built
Pen and ink, 10.3×11 cm

c) These are the Pigeon holes over the Boxes, let to the Great . . .
Pen and ink, 9×11.2 cm

d) This is the Cat, engaged to squall, to the Poor in the Pigeon Holes . . .
Pen and ink, 9×10.2 cm

London, The Museum of London
Inv. No. 64.139/1-3
Exhibitions: London, Royal Academy, 1982–83, Cat. No. 172

In order to offset the building costs of the new Covent Garden Theatre, seat prices were raised, provoking the Old Price Riots, violent protests against the theatre's management which continued until John Philip Kemble, who had become a part owner of the theatre, promised scrutiny of the accounts; he is shown addressing the Covent Garden audience in the last design in the sequence, and is the 'Jack' of the title, against whom the satire was directed. Many of the mob believed that the increase of prices was chiefly due to the rapacity of the leading singer, the Italian Mrs. Catalani (Cat. No. 577), caricatured elsewhere by Rowlandson as 'Mrs. Catsqualani', who can be seen in the third design.

Another source of grievance was the existence of private boxes (see the first two designs), reserved for the rich and the aristocracy, each having its own ante-room, where amorous intrigues were said to flourish. The O.P. riots were partly political, fostered by the rivalry with Drury Lane Theatre, the management of which was Whig in sympathy, and which Kemble had deserted for Covent Garden. **LS**

Robert William Billings
1815–1874

566
Theatre Royal, Covent Garden, 1833

Engraving, 48.3×63.5 cm
Private Collection
Exhibitions: London, Hayward Gallery, 1975, Cat. No. 258; Royal Academy, 1982–83, p. 112, Cat. No. 177

This print shows the interior of the Covent Garden after alterations were made in 1813 and 1819. A semi-dome was introduced over the proscenium, probably for accoustical reasons, and an elliptical arch replaced the square-topped proscenium in 1819, when the proscenium arch doors were also removed. By this date all the causes of the O.P. Riots had disappeared: the notorious 'pigeon-holes' in the attic storey went in 1812 to be replaced by the one-shilling gallery benches in the foreground, while the private boxes were taken from the often absentee subscribers and reopened to public booking. **IM**

Henry Andrews
d. 1868

567
The Trial of Queen Katherine, from Henry VIII by William Shakespeare, Act II, scene iv, Theatre Royal, Covent Garden, 1831

Oil on canvas 92.7 × 85.7 cm
Stratford, Governors of the Royal
Shakespeare Theatre
Exhibitions: London, Hayward Gallery, 1975, Cat. No. 258; Royal Academy, 1982–83, p. 99, Cat. No. 154

The cast includes even more Kembles: Charles Kemble (1775–1854) plays Henry VIII and his daughter Frances Anne ('Fanny') (1809–93), Queen Katherine. The part of Wolsey was played by Charles Young. The painting gives some idea of the scale of Covent Garden and the necessity of playing down-stage, because although gas lighting had been introduced to the auditorium, it was not yet dimmed during performances. Nevertheless, as stated in Britton and Pugin's *Illustrations of Public Buildings of London* (1824), 'The appearance of the house is very imposing: the colour is a subdued yellow, relieved by white, and superbly enriched with gilding.' **IM**

Benjamin Dean Wyatt
London 1775–1850

568
Perspective Elevation of the new Theatre Royal, Drury Lane, 1810

Pen and ink and watercolour, 44.2 × 70.7 cm
Inscribed: B. Wyatt Feby.1810/Perspective Elevation, shewing the principal Front and one side of the Theatre
London, Theatre Royal, Drury Lane Archives

567

Exhibitions: London, The Museum of London, 1984, pp. 97–99, Cat. No. 98c
Literature: Binney 1970, pp. 1116–19

The Theatre Royal, Drury Lane was the outcome of the patent granted to Thomas Killigrew by King Charles II in 1662. The third theatre on the site, built by Henry Holland in 1793, cost £150,000 to construct and had a seating capacity of 3,900, one of the largest in Europe.

When it was gutted by fire on the night of 24 February 1809, a joint-stock company (the first in the theatre business) was formed under the chairmanship of the Whig politician, brewer, and patron of the arts, Samuel Whitbread II (1758–1816) to undertake its rebuilding. Architects were invited to compete for the commission, which went to Benjamin Wyatt, largely through the support of Whitbread, and to the annoyance of his brother Philip, who had also submitted designs. Benjamin Wyatt prepared himself well for the commission, making designs such as this, well before the competition was announced. **CF**

Benjamin Dean Wyatt

569
Section through the Rotunda and principal Staircases of the Theatre Royal, Drury Lane

Pen and wash, 19.1 × 29.5 cm
Private Collection
Exhibitions: London, Hayward Gallery, 1975, Cat. No. 237, reproduced
Literature: Binney 1970, pp. 1116–19

In his design for Drury Lane, Wyatt attempted to solve two problems that had plagued theatres in London. Firstly, he cut down the fire risk (since 1789 alone there had been seven major theatre conflagrations – at a time when there were only nine London theatres in regular use). He encased the auditorium in a brick wall over three feet thick, as opposed to the usual timber frame, and William Congreve installed a primitive

571a

571b

'sprinkler' system. The staircases were constructed entirely of stone.

The second problem Wyatt sought to overcome was social: through placing the entrances to the most important seats, the dress boxes, on a mezzanine level between the ground and first floors the 'respectable class of spectators' were subtly segregated from the disreputable (Cat. No. 570) who instead made use of a spacious suite of rooms away from the auditorium on the far side of the stairs and rotunda. **CF**

(Isaac) Robert Cruikshank
London 1789–1856 London

570
Lobby Loungers (taken from the Saloon of Drury Lane Theatre), 1816

Etching coloured impression, 23.9×40 cm
Published by J. Sidebotham, 1816
London, Trustees of the British Museum
Inv. No. 1866-10-13-961
Literature: George 1949, Vol. 9, p. 713, No. 12826

Numerous satires were published at the time of Byron's separation from his wife Annabella in the spring of 1816 (Cat. Nos. 668–69). It was popularly rumoured that Lady Byron had found her husband's reported dalliances with actresses intolerable. In 1814 Bryon had joined the committee of management of the newly re-built Drury Lane Theatre, and devoted a good deal of his time to the oversight of theatrical business. He is shown here on the left, in his pocket a piece of paper inscribed with the title of two of his poems, *The Corsair* (1814), and

Farewell etc, a reference to *Fare Thee Well*.

Byron is staring fixedly at Mrs. Mardyn, an actress in the Drury Lane Theatre company, commonly thought to be Byron's mistress, although she denied this and subsequently protested in the *Morning Chronicle* that she had been falsely associated 'with the recent domestic disagreements of a Noble Family'. The satire exploits not only Byron's reputation as a philanderer but also the popular notion of the moral laxity of the theatre, as well as ridiculing contemporary fashions worn by men and women. **LS**

Robert Blemmell Schnebbelie
London 1790–1849 London

571
a) Interior View of the Royal Coburg Theatre, 1818

Pencil, pen and ink and watercolour, 17.1×22.2 cm
Signed and inscribed: Orig. Sketch of the Coburg Th.Monday 25th May Robert Blemmime (sic) Schnebbelie 1818

b) Exterior View of the Royal Coburg Theatre, 1818

Pencil, pen and ink and watercolour, 19.1×26.7 cm
Signed and inscribed: Sketched 11th May Monday 1818 (Fourteen days) after which the theatre was opened, by Robert Blemime Schnebbelie

Private Collection
Exhibitions: London, Hayward Gallery, 1975, Cat. Nos. 336–37

The artist, son of J. C. Schnebbelie who was also a topographical draughtsman, produced many watercolours of the theatres of London, providing an unrivalled record of the minor playhouses which mushroomed in the twenty years before the Licensing Act of 1843, which revoked the monopoly on drama held by the two Patent Theatres.

The interior view was taken on the opening night of the theatre, built in 1816–18 to the design of Rudolph Cabanel of Aachen near the south bank, newly made accessible by the opening of Waterloo Bridge. Named in honour of its patrons Prince Leopold and Princess Charlotte (renamed in 1833 the Royal Victoria Theatre in honour of the young princess and now known universally as the Old Vic), it specialised in melodrama. The play depicted is *Trial by Battle*. Henry Crabb Robinson recorded in his diary on 28 May 1819, 'This is a very pretty suburban playhouse not so large, but a fit match for the Paris minor Theatres.' **CF**

Augustus Charles Pugin
France 1762–1832 London

572a
Sadler's Wells Theatre, *c.* 1809
Watercolour, 19.4×25.6 cm

John Bluck after
Augustus Charles Pugin and Thomas Rowlandson

572b
Sadler's Wells Theatre, 1809
Coloured aquatint, 19.2 × 25.5 cm
Published at R. Ackermann's Repository of
Arts 101, Strand, 1 June 1809

London, The Museum of London
Inv. Nos. 52.71/7-8
Exhibitions: London, Hayward Gallery,
1975, Cat. No. 333; The Museum of
London, 1981, Nos. 64, 65
Literature: Arundell 1978, pp. 1–121

Sadler's Wells, on the foothills of Islington
north of the City, was a popular spa and place
of entertainment by the late seventeenth
century, becoming an established theatre in
the mid eighteenth century under the ownership of a local builder, Thomas Rosoman. The
auditorium sketched by Pugin dates from between 1795 and 1809 and is probably contemporary with the water tank (fed from the
New River which ran alongside the theatre)
installed by the playwright Charles Dibdin,
and used to stage aquatic spectacles.

Pugin's watercolour sketch is part of a series
of drawings made prior to the aquatint image,
published as Plate 69 in Ackermann's *Microcosm of London* (see p. 207). **IM**

572a

George Cruikshank
London 1792–1878 London

573
Pit, Boxes & Gallery

Etching, hand-coloured 17 × 23 cm
Designed, Etched & Published by George
Cruikshank, 23 Myddelton Terrace
Pentonville, 25 June 1836
London, Iain Mackintosh
Exhibitions: London, Hayward Gallery,
1975, Cat. No. 326

For George Cruikshank, the theatre was a lifelong obsession. In 1836 he was engaged in providing etchings for Charles Dickens' portraits
of Londoners entitled *Sketches by 'Boz'*, and
Pit, Boxes & Gallery evokes faithfully the
theatre of Dickens. This was the world of the
'minor theatres' in London, so called to contrast with the 'major' theatres of Drury Lane
at Covent Garden, or any of England's hundreds of provincial theatres. Common to all
was a carefully graduated price scale. At such
theatres this would have been Boxes 2s., Pit 1s.
and Gallery 6d. unless the presence of a great
star justified the doubling of prices. The four-
to-one price ratio would have been wide
enough to bring together into a single space all
strata of society as was the tradition in the
Georgian playhouse and as Cruikshank suggests in this etching. **IM**

Edward Francis Burney
Worcester 1760–1848 London

574 *(illus. p. 557)*
The Waltz

Pen and ink and watercolour, 47.5 × 68.6 cm
Signed: Ed Burney Fecit/London
London, Trustees of the Victoria and Albert
Museum
Inv. No. P129–1931
Provenance: Bernard Squire, from whom
bought, 1931
Exhibitions: London, Victoria and Albert
Museum, 1974, Cat. No. G13; Tokyo, 1987
Literature: Pückler Muskau 1832, Vol. 3, pp.
330-31; Crown 1980, pp. 435–42

This watercolour, together with Cat. No. 575,
comes from a group of four by the artist on
different aspects of music and society in early
nineteenth-century London. A nephew of the
eminent musicologist Dr. Charles Burney
(1726–1814), Edward Burney was himself a
talented amateur musician and played the violin. He studied at the Royal Academy Schools
from 1776 to the early 1780s and specialised
principally in book illustration.

The waltz, imported from southern Germany via France, was introduced to London at
Almack's assembly rooms in 1812. The first
dance in which partners were in close physical
contact, it was greeted with ridicule by some,
notably Gillray, Cruikshank and Lord Byron,
and outrage by others on account of its supposed immorality. In this dense, swirling
composition, Burney echoes the giddy-
making movements of the waltz itself. The
text is alive with puns, double meanings and
esoteric references. But in general all point to
the waltz's immoral social connotations. Lud-
icrously stiff rules regulating the behaviour of
the participants at the assembly are given in
the top panels; they are designed to ensure that
classes of society retain their proper station
and distance from one another. **CF**

Edward Francis Burney

575 *(illus. p. 557)*
The Glee Club or, The Triumph of
Music, c. 1815

Pen and ink and watercolour, 30.8 × 45.8 cm
New Haven, Yale Center for British Art
Inv. No. B1975.4.1407
Provenance: Christie's, 22 June 1962, Lot 31;
Paul Mellon
Exhibitions: Richmond USA, 1963, No. 434;
London, Colnaghi and New Haven,
1964–65, No.30; New York and London,
Royal Academy, 1972, Cat. No. 81; New
Haven, 1985–86, Cat. No. 41
Literature: Crown 1980, pp. 461–72

577b

By the late eighteenth century there were numerous Glee Clubs in London, where gentlemen met to eat, drink and sing English 'glees' or part songs. The degree of bawdiness in the punning lyrics depended on whether ladies were admitted, though their presence in this watercolour does not entirely exclude risqué material.

Above the doorway the bust of 'Glorious Apollo' (title of a famous glee), ominously flanked by anti-musical birds, looks down on a chandelier which drips oil on the music for 'Life's a Bum per' (a pun on the shape revealed by the pianist's parted tailcoat). On either side of the songsters sit groups of women of different ages, suggesting the round of the glee, the three younger women on the left making an ironic refrain to the three old women to the right. **CF**

576
Viol da Gamba Vase, c. 1801–03

Wedgwood; Jasper, solid blue body with bas-relief decoration, H 16.2 cm
Barlaston, Wedgwood Museum Trust
Inv. No. 1270
Exhibitions: London, Wedgwood House, 1984, No. N6
Literature: Reilly and Savage 1980, p. 354

Thomas Byerley, Wedgwood's London manager wrote in a memorandum dated 21 February 1801, 'You will receive this week four new ornaments in form of Viol del Gamba or Violoncello for Musical Amateurs – to be used either as flowerpot, bulbous roots, or candlestick. They belong to a set intended to captivate musical people.' **GBR**

Alfred Edward Chalon
Geneva 1780–1860

577
a) Angela Catalani as Elfrida, 1814
Pencil, pen and wash, 12.7 × 8.7 cm
Inscribed: Elfrida/Catalani 1814

b) Maria Dickons as the Contessa from *Nozze di Figaro*, 1815
Pen and ink, 14.9 × 12.6 cm
Inscribed: Dickons 1815 Contessa Figaro/sospir
London, National Portrait Gallery
Inv. Nos. 1962 (a), (c) respectively
Literature: Ebers 1828, pp.215–16, 283–85; Nalbach 1972, pp. 96, 99, 118–19; Walker 1985, Vol. 1, pp. 102–03, 157–58, 632, Vol. 2, Plates 224, 369

Angelica Catalani was the unrivalled dramatic soprano of her age; she figured heavily in caricatures partly on account of the punning version of her name (Cat), and partly on account of her supposed greed. Paisello's *Elfrida* was first performed in London in 1792. Among her other roles was that of Susanna in *Nozze di Figaro*, which she introduced to London. According to Leigh Hunt, 'She was a Roman with the regular Italian antelope face (if I may so call it); large eyes, with a sensitive elegant nose and lively expression.'

Maria Dickons (*c.* 1770–1830) was, from Chalon's drawing, not endowed with the same looks as Catalani but she had a powerful mellifluous voice and sang the sang the Contessa in *Nozze di Figaro*, first performed by her to Catalani's Susanna at the King's Theatre, Haymarket on 18 June 1812. When Catalani left England she took Dickons with her to Paris, where the latter was not a success, but she was highly regarded in Italy. Both singers returned to London in the 1820s, Catalani with her manager-husband Valabreque to shock the theatres further with the scale of her demands. **CF**

Alfred Edward Chalon

578
Maria Taglioni, in *William Tell*, c. 1831

Watercolour, 29.8 × 23.2 cm
Inscribed: Taglioni
London, National Portrait Gallery
Inv. Nos. 1962 (l)
Literature: Ormond 1973, Vol. 1, p. 443; Vol. 2, Plate 883; Binney 1984

Maria Taglioni (1800?–84) was the leading ballerina of her age, breaking with outworn neo-classical themes to perform in poignantly romantic ballets – notably *La Bayadère* and *La Sylphide* – with supple grace, poetic execution and flawless pointe work The daughter of an Italian ballet-master father and a Swedish mother, her first season at the King's Theatre in London in 1830 was cut short by the death of George IV, but the second in 1831 was a triumph.

A series of six lithograph sketches after Chalon's drawings of the dancer in the characters in which she appeared in the 1831 season was published by J. Dickinson the same year, of which the second was 'La Tirolienne', the role played here, from *William Tell*. **CF**

Alfred Edward Chalon

579
La Camporese, 1829

Watercolour, 35 × 22.7 cm
Inscribed: La Camporese. 1829.
London, Trustees of the Victoria and Albert Museum
Inv. No. E963-1924
Exhibitions: Leicester, 1968, Cat. No. 126; New Haven, Washington D.C., Ottawa and London, Victoria and Albert Museum, 1984–85, Cat. No. 155

579

The Italian soprano Violante Camporese (1785–1839) sang at Napoleon's private concerts in Paris. She made her début in London on 11 January 1817 in Cimarosa's *Penelope*. By the time she made her last appearance in 1829 her voice was worn, but judging from this spirited sketch possibly made at her benefit concert on 12 June, she still enjoyed singing. Her headdress is a magnificent ensemble of bows and feathers. **CF**

580
Playbill, Theatre Royal, Drury Lane. 16 October, 1826

Performance of *Faustus* and *Der Freischutz*
Wove paper, letter press, 33×21.5 cm
London, The Museum of London
Inv. No. Drury Lane Playbills 393
Literature: Murray 1971, pp. 102–13

Carl Maria von Weber (1786–1826), composer, conductor, pianist and critic, was a leading figure in the German romantic movement and one of its foremost composers. He discovered the story of *Der Freischutz* in 1809 but was not able to begin work on it until 1817 after his appointment as music director of the German opera in Dresden. It had its première in Berlin on 18 June 1821 and was rapturously received. On 18 August 1824 Weber received a letter from Charles Kemble, the manager of Covent Garden, asking him to write an opera for the 1825 season and to come and conduct that and *Der Freischutz*. Kemble proposed either 'Faust' or 'Oberon' for the new opera and Weber chose the latter giving 'Faust' to his colleague Spohr. The premier of *Oberon* on 12 April 1826 was well received and Weber was called to the stage at the end. His health was however rapidly declining and he died whilst still in London on 5 June. He was buried in Moorfields amid great public mourning. In 1844 Richard Wagner arranged for his coffin to be returned to Dresden to be interred.

Faustus was produced by Robert William Elliston who leased the Drury Lane Theatre from 1819 to 1827. It opened on 16 May 1825 and was noted for its spectacular effects, inspired by *Der Freischutz*. **EE**

Grieve Family

581
Three-dimensional model stage set for *Oberon*, Act I, scene iii, Vestibule and Terrace in the Harem of the Caliph overlooking the Tigris

580

Pen and ink and watercolour, 13.7×18 cm
London, University of London, Sterling Library
Inv. No. Grieve Collection 597
Literature: Pückler Muskau 1832, Vol. 3, pp. 162–63; Crabb Robinson ed. 1966, p. 114; Rosenfeld 1973, pp. 105–06

The scenery made for the world première of Weber's *Oberon* at the Theatre Royal Covent Garden on 12 April 1826 was said to have cost £6,000. Several sets such as the present example were of oriental splendour, but the Grieves also surpassed themselves with special effects and transformations. For Crabb Robinson, 'the paintings are magnificent and for the greater part in very fine taste – The machinery, flying cupids, sea nymphs, aerial cars approach to the perfection of the French Opera and Milan Theatre de la Scala.' Prince Pückler Muskau was more lukewarm in his report to his wife on 5 December 1826, 'the execution of both the instrumental and vocal parts left much to desire; but on the whole the Opera was well performed, for London.' However, he reserved special praise for the sets, 'especially at the conjuration of the spirits.' **CF**

582
Three-dimensional model stage set for *Norma*

Pen and ink and watercolour, 21×30.1 cm
London, University of London, Sterling Library
Inv. No. Grieve Collection 518

Bellini's *Norma*, premièred at la Scala Milan in 1831, was first performed in London at the King's Theatre, Haymarket on 20 June 1833, with Giuditta Pasta (1797–1865) taking the lead role on each occasion. Act I takes place in the sacred grove of the Druids during the Roman occupation of Gaul *c.* 50 B.C. The Grieves' reconstruction of a Stonehenge-style shrine is symptomatic of the renewed antiquarian interest in pre-Roman Britain. The association of Stonehenge with the Druidic priesthood was first made in the late seventeenth-century by John Aubrey and his circle, and championed by William Stukeley in *Stonehenge, a Temple restor'd to the British Druids* (1740). By the nineteenth century, Druids had become stock characters in romantic landscape and literature. **CF**

Daniel Maclise
Cork 1806–1870 London

583
Nicolo Paganini, *c.* 1831

Pencil and wash, and chalk, 35.9×27.3 cm
Inscribed in pencil: The Debut of Paganini/ Harmonics & Seul Corde/Sketched at Opera House

583

London, Trustees of the Victoria and Albert Museum
Inv. No. F.81
Provenance: artist's sale, Christie's, 24 June 1870, Lot 33; Forster Bequest to the Museum, 1876
Exhibitions: Philadelphia and Detroit, 1968, Cat. No. 192; Cork, 1971, Cat. No. 78; London, National Portrait Gallery, 1972, Cat. No. 35, illustrated
Literature: Forster 1893, p. 8; V & A 1927, p. 345; V & A 1953, Plate 21

Nicolo Paganini (1784–1840) made his London debut at the King's Theatre on 3 June 1831 and immediately became the subject of innumerable portraits and caricatures. Like other foreign performers, he was also attacked in the Press for the high prices charged for his concerts. This drawing was adapted for a lithograph entitled *The Modern Orpheus*, published by Thomas McLean in 1831. **CF**

Robert Seymour
Somerset 1798–1836 London

584
Fiddlestick versus Broomstick

Coloured lithograph, 25 × 37 cm
Published by Thos. McLean, 26 Haymarket, 19 July 1831
London, Guildhall Library, Corporation of London
Literature: George 1954, Vol. 11, p. 506, No. 16734

At a dinner in the Mansion House, the Lord Mayor's official residence, Paganini (Fiddlestick), who was then visiting London, stands upon a chair with his violin and bow. He is applauded wildly by guests: one uncultured but appreciative 'cit' imagines the musician's name to be 'Baganinni'. The reformist lord mayor, Alderman John Key (Cat. Nos. 638–41), tipsily cries: 'Your very good health, Mr. Paganini!' Henry Brougham, lord chancellor (Broomstick), standing next to him, looks thoroughly displeased. The purpose of the occasion was to celebrate the presentation of the Freedom of the City to Lord John Russell, paymaster general, not Paganini's visit. Russell, who had recently introduced the Reform Bill, was the hero of the hour. Before the toast to Lord Russell, Paganini stood on his chair and played a concerto. Brougham was apparently annoyed at being upstaged not only by Paganini and Russell but by Lord Grey, prime minister, who sits next to him and was asked to return the toast on behalf of the ministers. **RH**

THE CULTURE OF REFORM

If London was the base for court and government, it also set the pace for opposition to these traditional sources of wealth and power. Here too the economic distress which followed the ending of the Napoleonic wars was visible in its most concentrated form. Freedom of expression was a cherished right upheld by cheap periodicals and caricatures, despite attempts at censorship. Mass meetings kept political, economic and social grievances before the public eye. The repertoire of popular agitation reached a sensational climax with the return of Queen Caroline in 1820 to claim her rightful position. The ideological arguments for reform were rehearsed in the intellectual circles of the capital. Many saw political reform as the key to change, and though the first Reform Act benefited only a limited sector of the population, it was passed under the threat of popular revolt, a threat which would inevitably lead to further reform.

585
Stanhope Press

Cast iron and forged steel, on a timber base, 160 × 144 × 115 cm
Inscribed: STANHOPE INVENIT/ WALKER FECIT/No. 5/1804
London, Gunnersbury Park Museum
Provenance: Chiswick Press
Literature: Mosley 1966, pp. 19–33

The Stanhope Press was the first printing press for commercial use to be made wholly of iron and steel, and it was the first press to derive additional power from 'compound levers'. It was the invention of Charles, 3rd Earl Stanhope (1753–1816), whose radical politics and keen interest in practical technology led him to promote several improvements to processes relating to printing.

The press used for printing books and newspapers in Europe and America until the first decades of the nineteenth century was made largely of wood, and its design did not change significantly during 300 years. In substituting a rigid iron-cast frame for the timber framework of the traditional press, Stanhope was probably aware of the experimental iron press made in 1772 by the printer and typefounder Wilhelm Haas of Basel. However, the 'compound' or 'Stanhope' levers, which progressively increased the power of the screw during the pull, were wholly original. All subsequent iron presses, of which many different kinds were designed and made during the decades that followed, incorporated the principle of compound leverage.

The Stanhope Press was expensive, and its increased power and rigid frame were advantages that were at first exploited by printers of fine editions. One of the earliest users is known to have been William Bulmer, of the Shakspeare Printing-Office, and the press exhibited here belonged to Charles Whittingham (1767–1840), whose Chiswick Press was distinguished for fine presswork from type and wood engravings. However, the power of the iron presses is also clearly seen in posters and handbills using the new display types, 'fat faces' and 'antiques' whose size and blackness would have been beyond the capability of the wooden press (Cat. No. 679). **JM**

E. F. Burney, *The Glee Club or, The Triumph of Music, c.* 1815. Cat. No. 575

E. F. Burney, *The Waltz.* Cat. No. 574.

S. de Wilde, *Charles Farley at Francisco in a 'Tale of Mystery' by T. Holcroft*, 1803. Cat. No. 554

S. de Wilde, *Thomas Collins as Slender in 'The Merry Wives of Windsor' by W. Shakespeare*. Cat. No. 553

George Cruikshank
London 1792–1878 London

586
Liberty Suspended! with the Bulwark of the Constitution, 1817

Etching, coloured impression, 24.1×34.4 cm
Published by J. Sidebotham, March (date erased) 1817
London, Trustees of the British Museum
Inv. No. 1868-8-8-8364
Literature: George 1949, Vol. 9, pp. 741–42, No. 12871

The threat of popular uprising was never very distant in this period, and in January 1817 when the Prince Regent escaped an assassination attempt, the Archbishop of Canterbury described it as an expression of 'The Madness of the People', a phrase which the radical press felt was an insult to the nation. In March, the temporary Seditious Meetings Bill, popularly known as the Gagging Act, was passed, and

Habeas Corpus (the right of a citizen not to be imprisoned without being brought before a court) was suspended for persons committed to custody for treason or on suspicion of treason under a warrant of the secretary of state or of six privy councillors.

The Gagging Act was particularly directed against the Press, as this radical print by George Cruikshank makes clear. Liberty is gagged and bound, and hangs from a gibbet which projects from a dismantled printing press. To the right, the lord chancellor, Lord Eldon, holds a large bag inscribed with a reference to the Spa Fields Plot, a minor riot, '3 or 4 rusty fire arms and a few bullets too large to fit the barrels!!', which the government interpreted as a grave threat to the order of the nation, while Lord Castlereagh attempts to justify the emergency legislation, 'It is better to do this, than "Stand Prostrate" at the feet of Anarchy'. To the left, the Archbishop of Canterbury is ridiculed for the 'Cant' he had talked. Approving the government's actions are the 'Gentlemen Sinecurist' and 'Gentlemen Pensioners', targets of much radical criticism. In

the distance, on the right, is a plumed hearse driving towards the gibbet, labelled 'For the funeral of British Liberty who died near St. Stepens (sic; i.e. The Houses of Parliament) – March 1812'. Sitting on the ground nearby and weeping is John Bull, the popular symbol of the ordinary Briton and the epitome of freedom-loving patriotism. LS

J. O. Parry, *A London Street Scene*, 1835. Cat. No. 545

William Hone
Bath 1780–1842 London,
and
George Cruikshank
London 1792–1878 London

587b

587
a) The Political House that Jack Built
Printed by and for William Hone, Ludgate
Hill 1819, 30th edition
Octavo, 22×28 cm (open)

b) The Man in the Moon
Printed by and for William Hone, 45,
Ludgate Hill, 1820, 2nd edition
Octavo, 22×28 cm (open)

London, Guildhall Library, Corporation of
London
Inv. Nos. Pamph. 7345 and 7350
Literature: Hackwood 1912, pp. 131–34;
Wickwar 1928, pp. 131–34, 163–65, 192–93;

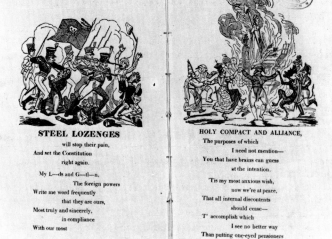

STEEL LOZENGES
will stop their pain,
And set the Constitution
right again.

My L——ds and G——tl——n,
The foreign powers
Write me word frequently
that they are ours,
Most truly and sincerely,
in compliance
With our most

HOLY COMPACT AND ALLIANCE,
The purposes of which
I need not mention—
You that have brains can guess
at the intention.
'Tis my most anxious wish,
now we're at peace,
That all internal discontents
should cease—
T' accomplish which
I see no better way
Than putting one-eyed pensioners
on full pay.

Jeremy Bentham, Auto Icon. Cat. No. 595

George 1949, Vol. 9, pp. 945–48, Nos. 13292–304; George 1952, Vol. 10, pp. 508, Nos. 13508–21; Rickword 1971; Fox 1978, pp. 226–35

William Hone was a radical publisher and satirist of exceptional skill. He first rose to notoriety in 1817 through his parodies of the Liturgy from the Book of Common Prayer, in which he denounced the corruption of parliament. Arrested and tried on the charge of blasphemous libel, he defended himself and was acquitted by three London juries, becoming a popular hero.

Two years later in the tense political climate following Peterloo, he launched the first of a series of brilliant parodies of children's nursery-rhyme chapbooks, illustrated with bold wood engravings by George Cruikshank. *The Political House that Jack Built* is said to have sold over 100,000 copies, going through fifty-two editions between December 1819 and March 1820. Though ostensibly attacking all manifestations of 'old corruption', notably 'THE DANDY OF SIXTY' (the Prince Regent), its main thrust was to advocate parliamentary reform and the freedom of the Press.

The Man in the Moon, published early in January 1820, parodied the threatening speech made by the Prince Regent at the opening of parliament on 23 November 1819 and the six repressive acts introduced, two of which – the Blasphemous and Seditious Libels Act and the Publications Act – affected Press freedom. The army bayonet the people with 'STEEL LOZENGES', while the 'HOLY COMPACT AND ALLIANCE', comprising the Prince Regent with Ferdinand II of Spain (in a biretta and the embroidered petticoat he is said to have made for a statue of the Blessed Virgin) on one side and the Devil on the other, linking hands with (left to right) the pope, Louis XVIII, Frederick William III, Francis I and Czar Alexander, dance round the figure of Liberty, her hands tied behind her, on a funeral pyre made of a printing press. **CF**

M. Adams

588
A Parody on the Political House that Jack Built: or the Real House that Jack Built

Published by C. Chapple, Pall Mall, 1820
Octavo, 23 × 29.5 cm (open)
London, Guildhall Library, Corporation of London
Inv. No. Pamph. 5068
Literature: George 1952, Vol. 10, pp. 35–36, Nos. 13678–90

Hone's verse pamphlets provoked many loyalist responses disguised in the same format. In this example, 'THE VERMIN' are the reformers, notably Henry Hunt (Cat. No. 637), William Cobbett and Richard Carlile, while the army are 'THE MEN WHO OPPOSE LAWLESS POWER'. The text also refers to the 'CATO STREET MEN'. The pamphlet contains a flattering portrait of George IV, 'THE MONARCH OF SIXTY' signed by Isaac Robert Cruikshank, George's older brother. **CF**

589

'Paul Pry' William Heath
London 1795–1840 London

589
The Man Wots Got the Whip Hand of 'Em All, 1829

Etching, coloured impression, 34.1 × 24.9 cm
Published by T. McLean, 30 May 1829
London, Trustees of the British Museum
Inv. No. 1868-8-8-8994
Literature: George 1954, Vol. 11, pp. 148–49, No. 15776

A monstrous creation, a Stanhope hand printing press is shown supported on the robust legs of a man, perhaps John Bull, who kicks aside tiny humans. A little printer's devil, brandishing an ink ball, rushes in towards the

press. The creature's arms are formed by two levers, and one hand grasps a giant quill pen, around which three serpents are entwined, spitting fire at the departing legs and distinctive cocked hat of the Duke of Wellington. On the left, another pair of legs with the black stockings and buckled shoes of Lord Chancellor Eldon, as well as a single leg and a broom signifying Lord Brougham, disappear from the scene. A second lever holds a print, 'The Man Wot Drives the Sovereign' – the Duke of Wellington. Topping the press is a Cap of Liberty, inscribed Free Press and crowned with a wreath. The implication of the print seems to be that though Wellington controls the king, the Press has the ultimate whip-hand. **LS**

John Thomas Smith
London 1766–1833 London

590
Vagabondiana; or, Anecdotes of Mendicant Wanderers through the Streets of London; with Portraits of the most Remarkable drawn from the Life, 1817

Bound volume, 35.5 × 30.5 cm
London, Guildhall Library
Inv. No. AN.9.1
Literature: Fox 1988, pp. 64–65, Fig. 46

Smith's pioneering work first took the form of a series of twenty-three etchings, with a title page headed 'Etchings of Remarkable Beggars, Itinerant Traders and other Persons of Notoriety in London and its Environs', published in 1815–16. This series had no accompanying text and being principally devoted to street sellers, was simply a continuation of the *Street Cries* tradition. But the present work, first published in 1817, concentrated on the blind and crippled, and was accompanied by fifty-two pages of text which explain the artist's intention.

The change of emphasis was made to meet a change in circumstances. The rapid demobilisation and cessation of government orders which followed the Napoleonic Wars brought about a fall in urban employment and the consequent swelling of the poor rate. The most outward, visible result was the hoards of beggars who roamed the city streets in search of casual labour or charitable relief. The 1815–16 Select Committee of Vagrancy and the subsequent tightening up of the legislation against vagrants had already, according to Smith, resulted in a reduction in the number of beggars in the metropolis, and these circumstances account for his shift of focus: to record them before they entirely disappeared. **CF**

591b 591c

Theodore Géricault
Rouen 1791–1824 Paris

591
a) The Piper, 1821

Lithograph, 2nd state, 31.4×23.3 cm
Published by Rodwell & Martin, New Bond
St., 1 February, 1821
London, Trustees of the British Museum
Inv. No. 1876-11-11-320
Provenance: Burty Collection
Literature: Clément 1879, No. 26; Delteil
1924, No. 30; Eitner 1983, pp. 228–29, Fig.
180; Fox 1988, pp. 62–66, Fig. 43

b) Pity the Sorrows of a Poor Old Man whose Trembling Limbs have Born him to Your Door, 1821

Lithograph, 2nd state, 31.5×37.4 cm
Published by Rodwell & Martin, New Bond
St., 1 February 1821
London, Trustees of the British Museum
Inv. No. 1876-10-12-3778
Literature: Clément 1879, No. 27; Delteil
1924, No. 31; Eitner, pp. 213, 228–29, Fig.
182; Fox 1988, pp. 61–66

c) A Paraleytic Woman, 1821

Lithograph, only state, 22.5×31.7 cm
Published by Rodwell & Martin, New Bond
St., 1 April, 1821.
London, The Museum of London
Inv. No. 86.357
Provenance: A. Beurdeley; sale, Paris, 15–16
December 1920, Lot 421; Hans E. Bühler;
Christie's 15 November 1985, Lot 100

Literature: Clément 1879, No. 30; Delteil
1924, No. 38; Eitner 1983, p. 213; Fig 183,
229, 230, 351, Note 78; Fox 1988, pp. 61–66,
Fig. 44

Shortly after his arrival in England in 1820 to
exhibit *The Raft of the Medusa* at the Egyptian
Hall, Géricault arranged with the firm of Rodwell and Martin and the printer, Charles Hullmandel, to produce a set of twelve lithographs.
Published on Géricault's return visit the following year, the work was described on the
title page as *Various Subjects drawn from life
and on stone by J. Gericault.* The majority
were devoted to equestrian subjects, depicting
both working and high-bred horses, and the
labour of farriers. But the three most powerful
images show scenes of urban poverty.

Poverty on the streets of London was a
peculiarly live issue in 1821. The government
appointed no less than four parliamentary
select committees between 1815 and 1820 to investigate the workings of the Poor Law,
besides others on the related subjects of
vagrancy and immigration. Géricault might
not have been aware of Smith's *Vagabon-
diana*, but in this climate, Géricault's choice of
subject matter appears to have been less arbitrary and idiosyncratic than might appear. He
was demonstrably not alone in thinking that
sufficient interest had been aroused for the
subject to be reflected in visual form.

In these works Géricault interweaves
observed reality with visual precedent, tran-
scending the merely documentary through his
power of expression and achieving an
ominous intensity of atmosphere through exploiting the lithographic medium to the full.
The architect C. R. Cockerell (Cat. No. 100),
who admired Géricault's talent, modesty and
'deep feeling of pity', was much struck by

these three lithographs when he first saw them
in November 1821, believing they showed
'when works of art attain their utmost perfection they are eminently calculated to awaken
thoughts of energy and virtue.'

The title of *Pity the Sorrows* is taken from an
English nursery rhyme. The scene is set in
Southwark, south of the river near Blackfriars
Bridge. In a *Paraleytic Woman*, the girl with
her young charge pauses to look back furtively
at the invalid passenger. The sense of aliena-
tion is accentuated by the bars on the window
behind her and the carriage being driven
through the fog in the background, oblivious
to this small tableau of urban misery. **CF**

Thomas Rowlandson
London 1757–1827 London

592
A Watchman making his Rounds, *c.* 1800

Pen and watercolour over pencil,
35.9×25.3 cm
London, The Museum of London
Inv. No. 60.89/1
Provenance: Bovill family; Abbott & Holder
Literature: Hayes 1960, p. 13

Watchmen were appointed by the tangle of
overlapping authorities responsible for the
administration of London – parish vestries,
highway commissions, turnpike and square
trusts – to call the hours at night and keep the
peace. But being notoriously underpaid and
inadequately supervised, they seldom discharged their duties properly. **CF**

593

William Heath after
London 1795–1840 London
Charles Jameson Grant
fl. 1828–1846

593
Drunkards on Duty, 1830

Etching, hand-coloured, 25.5×18 cm
Published by T. McLean, 26 Haymarket,
May 1830
Inscribed in pen by Grant: drawn by C. J.
Grant, William Heath etc.
London, Richard Godfrey
Literature: George 1954, Vol. 11, pp. 408–09,
No. 16430

This is the right half of a design by Grant, the
left half showing a drunken army officer. This
impression is from Grant's own album of his
prints and designs which was discovered and
unfortunately dispersed in recent years. A
number of prints were inscribed in pen by
Grant with the identical legend, showing that
he was in the habit at this period of providing
designs for Heath which were unacknowledged in the published prints. No doubt this
was to supplement an irregular income. Grant
was one of the most ferocious caricaturists of
the 1830s, executing coloured etchings, lithographs and, finally, brutally simple woodcuts
aimed at a popular market.

    Founded by Sir Robert Peel in 1829, the
Metropolitan Police attracted much unfavourable comment for the character and appearance of its earliest recruits. **RG**

Samuel Drummond
London 1765–1854 London

594
Elizabeth Fry, *c.* 1815

Watercolour miniature on ivory,
11.4×8.3 cm
London, National Portrait Gallery
Inv. No. 118
Provenance: the artist; purchased from his
son by James Roffway, who sold it to the
Gallery, 1861
Literature: Walker 1985, Vol. 1, p. 193; Vol.
2, Plate 449

Elizabeth Fry (1780–1845), was born into a
Quaker banking family in Norfolk, the Gur-
neys, and married a London merchant in 1800.
In February 1813, she visited Newgate prison
and found 300 women, tried and untried, and
their children, living in cramped and filthy
conditions without employment. By her
efforts, a school and manufactory were organised, dress and cleanliness improved, religious
instruction given and the women submitted to
rules for their well-being. She devoted the rest
of her life to prison reform at home and
abroad, founded shelters for the homeless and
libraries in naval hospitals and coastguard
stations. **CF**

Jeremy Bentham
London 1748–1832 London

595 *(illus. p. 560)*
Auto-Icon

Case, 196×98×120 cm
London, University College London
Provenance: Dr. Thomas Southwood Smith
Literature: Bentham 1842; Marmoy 1958;
Richardson and Hurwitz 1987, pp. 195–98

Jeremy Bentham was the leading figure in
London's intellectual life in the 1820s and up
to his death. He corresponded with an international network of liberally minded politicians, jurists, reformers, and thinkers. His
life's work was the reformation of society, law
and thought on the basis of a philosophy that
he was the first to develop systematically, the
philosophy of utilitarianism. The central principle on which the great reforming work was
to be based was that it should be carried out
with the aim of maximising the happiness of
the greatest number. It was an approach that
subsequently motivated many important
social and legal improvements.

    Bentham's greatest memorial is University

594

College London, founded in 1826 by a group
largely composed of his friends and followers.
It was the first university-level institution in
the metropolis, and the first university in
England to offer open access to all regardless
of creed or opinion (Oxford and Cambridge
were open only to Anglicans).

    It was typical of Bentham's systematic all-
embracing vision that even a dead body was to
be regarded from the point of view of how it
might yield pleasure and profit. He directed
that his body be dissected in the interests of
anatomical science. Three days after his death
on 6 June 1832, his friend Southwood Smith
delivered a public lecture over his corpse at the
Webb Street School of Anatomy and Medicine. After the usual anatomical demonstrations, Southwood Smith had a skeleton made
of the bones. He tried unsuccessfully to preserve the head untouched, so he had a wax
head sculpted by a French doctor, Jacques
Talrich, a noted anatomical modeller. (The
original head is preserved in the vaults of University College London.) The auto-icon remained in Southwood Smith's possession
until 1850, when it was given to University
College in a mahogany and plate-glass case.
Bentham imagined a whole range of possible
uses for dead bodies treated as his was. They
could be placed in churches in place of marble
monuments. Those of heroes would elevate
viewers and those of villains horrify them
appropriately. Auto-icons could be used for
stage dialogues between great men.

    Bentham's proposals on this subject
demonstrate in typically trenchant manner his
determination to rid thinking of taboo and
prejudice and to subject every question
systematically to rational consideration. In
this he was a precursor of the 'scientific' outlook so typical of modernity. **CPB**

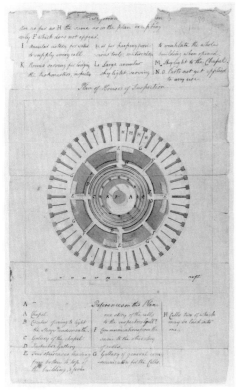

596

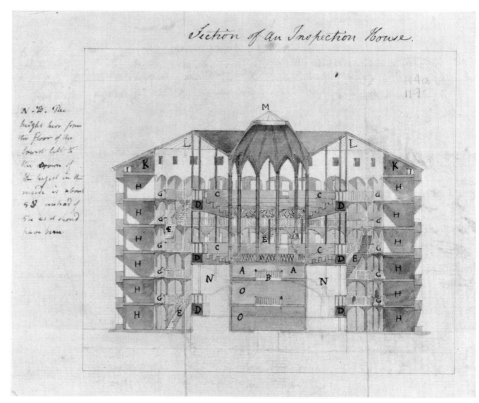

597

Willey Reveley
Newby Wiske 1760–1799 London

596
Plan of a House of Inspection, 1791

Watercolour and ink writing, 32.5×20 cm
London, University College London
Library
Inv. No. Bentham Papers, CXIX, 121
Literature: Evans 1982, pp. 195–230, Fig. 105

The Panopticon, or Inspection House, was designed by Samuel Bentham (1757-1831) while in the service of Prince Potemkin. Its original purpose was for a factory in which ignorant Russian workmen could be efficiently supervised. His elder brother, Jeremy Bentham, seized on the idea and created an ideal instrument of management that would combine maximum efficiency and minimum expense. His project was for a contract prison; the essence of the design was that prison officials in the central tower could see into every cell on the perimeter and could monitor every movement of their charges. But they themselves would be invisible, shrouded from the sight of the inmates. This would have the psychological impact of total unremitting inspection. He first described this project in a series of letters to his father written from Krichev in 1786. This drawing and Cat. No. 597

were commissioned from the architect Willey Reveley after his return to London. For twenty years after this, Bentham attempted to persuade the British government to build a panopticon penitentiary of which he and his brother would have been the contractor governors. He believed that he had devised the perfect instrument for rational humane punishment. **JES**

597
Section of an Inspection House

Watercolour and ink writing, 16×20 cm
Unsigned, but Jeremy Bentham's handwritten annotations left hand margin
London, University College London
Library
Inv.No. Bentham Papers, cxix, 119
Literature: Evans 1982, pp. 195–230, Fig. 106

The Panopticon was an architectural extravaganza. Built of iron and glass it would have been in the forefront of the technology of the time. This drawing conjures up its Utopian element. Bentham envisaged a beautiful structure, comparable to the Rotunda at Ranelagh, full of flowers and music and surrounded by gardens. The convicts would sing as they worked the wood and stone finishing machines of Samuel Bentham's invention.

They would be happy, healthy and industrious. They would earn wages and could look forward to a pension. But they would have to work 14 hours a day and the Bentham brothers, as contractors, could hope to make an immense fortune from their labours. Nevertheless, the accounts and records would be freely available and anyone – journalists, philanthropists or the merely curious – would have access to the central inspection tower where they could watch the inmates and the officers at work and so supervise every aspect of the administration of the prison. **JES**

John Varley
London 1778–1842 London

598
Millbank Penitentiary from Vauxhall Bridge Road, *c.* 1820

Watercolour, 27.4×40.8 cm
London, The Museum of London
Inv. No. 66.25
Provenance: Sotheby's, 22 March 1966, Lot 83
Exhibitions: London, The Museum of London, 1981, No. 69
Literature: Evans 1982, pp. 227–28, 243–50

Bentham's schemes for a panopticon penitentiary foundered on the government's unwillingness to support the principle of private contract management of prisons. Instead, the largest prison in Europe was constructed at a cost of £458,000 to the design of William Williams and Thomas Hardwick on a marshy riverside side at Millbank, south of Westminster to house 1,200 convicts from London and Middlesex awaiting transportation or referral.

Superficially resembling Bentham's design based on centralised inspection, the Millbank prison in fact consisted of six pentagons within a hexagon (like a large snowflake in plan), each component being independently managed; there were three miles of labyrinthine passages. As a building it was a disaster. The engineer John Rennie (Cat. No. 145) and architect Robert Smirke (Cat. No. 380) were called in soon after its completion in 1816 to underpin the sinking structure. Within a few years, Sir Humphry Davy (Cat. No. 200) had to supervise its ventilation and Michael Faraday (Cat. No. 202) its fumigation. The prison was closed in 1890 and part of the site used for the Tate Gallery. **CF**

William Wilkins
Norwich 1778–1839 Cambridge

599
Façade of University College London, between August 1825 and March 1826, with alterations probably made before December 1827

Pencil and wash, 39.4 × 86.9 cm
London, University College London, Strang Print Room
Inv. No. G4393
Exhibitions: London, Royal Academy, 1827, Cat. No. 969; University College London, 1985, Cat. No. 1, passim
Literature: University College 1927, p. 976, Fig. 1; Harte and North 1991, pp. 9–33; Liscombe 1980, pp. 156–69, Fig. 86

University College London, the capital's first university, was the brainchild of Henry Brougham and a group of social reformers who shared a sense of frustration at the lack of scientific teaching at the older universities and resented the exclusive power of the Anglican church in the field of higher education. In an open letter to Brougham, published in The Times on 9 February 1825, Thomas Campbell called for

'a great London University . . . for effec-

599

tively and multifariously teaching, examining, exercising and rewarding with honours in the liberal arts and sciences, the youth of our middling rich people between the age of fifteen or sixteen and twenty . . .'

A competition for designs was announced six months later, and the foundation stone of Wilkins' winning entry was laid on 30 April 1827. The Greek Revival was then at its most fashionable, and Wilkins' design takes its place alongside a series of imposing buildings in the style erected in London in the 1820s and 1830s.

In Wilkins' scheme as initially planned, three continuous ranges of buildings were to be laid out around a quadrangle, whose fourth side was to be enclosed by a colonnaded screen with a centrally placed Doric propylaeum. The central section of the drawing exhibited here, which almost certainly formed part of Wilkins' original submission, shows in elevation the central range as first envisaged. The project ran into financial difficulties, however, and when it became clear that the lateral wings as planned were beyond the resources of the college, these parts of the drawings were cut away. New wings were then added in perspective according to a truncated design.

The centre-piece of the composition is a decastyle Corinthian portico, modelled on that of the temple of Olympian Zeus at Athens. Raised on a high podium, the portico was given greater prominence by its position at the front of the great hall, an imposing building intended to project forward into the centre of a quadrangle. The effect of restrained grandeur was to be further enhanced by a programme of figure sculpture in the pediment and an erudite display of classical ornament around the main door, the latter directly inspired by the Erechtheum. The point where the hall joined the main block was to be accentuated by a dome.
The founders went to great lengths to ensure that the new building would be well suited to its educational function, turning to Germany and Scotland, where many of the techniques of scientific education had been pioneered. **ND**

600
Share Certificate

No. 440, made out to Joseph Freeman, 24 November 1826
16.7 × 26 cm
London, University of London
Inv. No. U.L.C./P.C.3/10(i)
Literature: Bellot 1929, pp. 32–34; Turner ed. 1978, p. 9, No. 10; Harte and North 1991, pp. 14, 22; Dawton, 1985, pp. 6–9

The Deed of Settlement formally establishing University College London, then called simply the London University, was signed on 11 February 1826. Shares of £100 were to be sold, with the aim of raising between £150,000 and £300,000, and the commencement of building operations was made conditional on receiving deposits of £25 on at least 1,500 shares. After some initial success, a general downturn in confidence in joint-stock companies caused the sale of shares to flag. By October, only £130,000 had been raised, and although the minimum number of shares had been sold by February 1827, the generally poor sale imposed a financial stringency on the Council, which directly affected the progress of the building. The problem was compounded by Wilkins' estimate of £87,000 for the cost of construction, which proved to be over optimistic by £20,000. Wilkins had consistently refused to guarantee this figure, arguing that 'an architect ought never to be concerned with the executive part of building.' After independent valuations, it was decided to erect the college in stages. **ND**

Thomas Higham
1796–1844
after Frederick Mackenzie
1787–1854

601
University of London, 1828–29

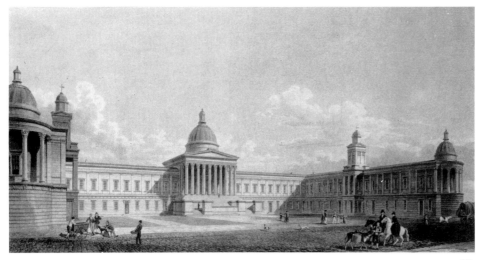

601

Engraving, hand-coloured, 26.5×44.5 cm
London, University College London, Strang
Print Room
Inv. No. G3651
Exhibitions: London, University College
London, 1985, Cat. No. 19, passim
Literature: Alternative Design 1904, p. 16;
Bellot 1929, p. 437; Summerson 1983, pp.
514–15, Fig. 417; Harte and North 1991, pp.
28–29, Fig. 36; Liscombe 1980, p. 164

Higham's print, engraved for the *Stationers'
Almanack* of 1829 after a drawing by Frederick Mackenzie, shows the altered scheme for
the central range that was finally built.

The plan to build the college in stages provided Wilkins with an opportunity to revise
his design for the lateral ranges. But when the
college opened in October 1828, only the
central range was standing. Wilkins' building
was left incomplete until the later years of the
century, when the existing wings were added
according to a revised design by Professor
Hayter Lewis. This in no way diminished the
public acclaim with which Wilkins' building
was greeted. **ND**

(Isaac) Robert Cruikshank
London 1786–1856 London

602
The Political, Toy-Man, 1825

Engraving, hand-coloured, 28.2×20 cm
Published by G. Humphrey, St James's
Street, July 1825
London, University College London
Library

Literature: George 1952, Vol. 10, pp. 481–82,
No. 14788; Harte and North 1978, pp. 14–15,
reproduced

Henry Brougham, with legal wig and gown, is
portrayed in the guise of a toy-man, as those
(usually Italians) who traded in plaster-of-
Paris models on the streets of London were
called. His model is that of the newly projected London University, here conceived in
the Gothic style of Oxford and Cambridge
colleges. But as opposed to the classical education given in the old universities, Cruikshank
suggests that the new foundation will confine
itself to the pedantic study of English grammar. Brougham himself had long advocated a
scientific education for the upper classes and
attacked the abuse of charitable foundations,
including Oxford, Cambridge and the public
schools of Eton and Winchester. The list of
shareholders and brief-bag of subscriptions he
carries refer to the flotation of the joint-stock
company to pay for the university. John Bull
on a hobby horse looks sceptical.

The same year, Brougham published
Observations on the Education of the People,
which advocated the publication of cheap useful works for the lower classes, went through
twenty editions and led to the foundation of
the Society for the Diffusion of Useful Knowledge. **CF**

M. R. Giberne

603
St. Mary's Infant School,
Walthamstow, *c.* 1824

Etching, 37.5×45.7 cm
Printed by N. Chater and Co., 33 Fleet
Street

London, Vestry House Museum,
Walthamstow
Inv. No. N5946
Literature: Law 1978; McCann and Young
1982, pp. 58, 71, Plate 4

St. Mary's Infant School at Walthamstow,
north east of the City, was the first Church of
England infants school in the country. The
parochial schools – the Anglican 'National'
and the nonconformist 'British' schools – only
took children from the age of six or seven. But
the pioneer educationalist Samuel Wilderspin
(*c.* 1799–1866) believed that much younger
children could usefully be introduced to the
rudiments of knowledge, as was clearly
demonstrated by the standards achieved by
the privately educated children of the affluent.
He first opened an infant school in Spitalfields
in 1822 and under the patronage of George IV,
others swiftly followed at Brighton, Lewes
and Worthing.

The Vicar of Walthamstow, the Reverend
William Wilson, was encouraged by his
brother to follow suit and with Wilderspin's
help, a small school was opened in March 1824
in a barn appropriated for the purpose. The
experiment proved a success and a permanent
school building was erected on glebe land in
1828. **CF**

'Paul Pry' William Heath
London 1795–1840 London

604
March of Intellect, 1829

Etching, coloured impression, 30.5×42.1 cm
Published by T. McLean, May (?) 1829
London, Trustees of the British Museum

603

Inv. No. 1948-2-17-34
Literature: George 1954, Vol. 11, pp. 152–53, No. 15779

One of the most extraordinary and inventive satires published in this period, the *March of Intellect* reflects contemporary awareness of profound social change. Although welcomed by those of radical sympathies, such changes were feared by the more conservative, illustrated by the extreme ridicule directed at the more spectacular manifestations of technological innovation, notably the development of steam power, which is the chief theme of this print. In the foreground is the suggestion that social distinctions have disappeared: the working classes have discovered luxury in the form of exotic foods formerly available only to the rich – a dustman gnaws at a pineapple, his companion eats an ice-cream. On the left, modern architecture is ridiculed: a gibbet, labelled 'Designed to Elevate the Architects', is shown above the Marble Arch (a new London landmark) and beyond is a fantastic hybrid neo-Gothic church. There are flying machines, including a monstrous webbed-wing creature labelled 'For New South Wales' and 'with convicts'. In the sky, cloud-borne castles are labelled 'Scheme for the Payment of the National Debt'. **LS**

604

605

Slave Medallion, from 1787

Wedgwood; Jasper, solid yellow body, black relief, D 3.3 cm
Mark: WEDGWOOD impressed
Barlaston, Wedgwood Museum Trust
Inv. No. 4275
Exhibitions: London, Science Museum, 1978, No. 194
Literature: Reilly and Savage 1980, p. 319, Plate 7

605

The medallion depicts the figure of a kneeling supplicant Negro slave in chains and bears the inscription, 'Am I not a Man and a Brother?', taken from the seal of the committee of the Slave Emancipation Society. It was modelled by William Hackwood (c. 1757–1839) in 1787. Josiah Wedgwood I (1730–95) played an active part in the affairs of the society and became a member of the committee. The medallion was contributed by Wedgwood to the movement and they were freely distributed. A parcel with slave medallions was sent to Benjamin Franklin in America, who was, 'persuaded [they] may have an Effect equal to that of the best written Pamphlet in procuring Favour to these oppressed People.' **GBR**

606

Medal

Abolition of Slave Trade, 1807

Silver, D 5.3 cm
Engraved by T. Webb
Obverse: head of William Wilberforce
Reverse: Britannia seated on a dais, attended by 3 allegorical figures, with Victory above.
I HAVE HEARD THEIR CRY. In exergue: SLAVE TRADE ABOLISHED MDCCCVII
London, Trustees of the British Museum
Inv. No. M.5319
Literature: Brown 1980, p. 154, No. 627; Eimer 1987, p. 125, No. 983, Plate 27

The movement against slavery had been gathering force since the 1770s with the Quak-

ers forming the backbone of the campaign. However Quaker and non-Quaker movements were brought together in 1787 with the formation of the Society for the Abolition of the Slave Trade under the chairmanship of Granville Sharp. Whilst Thomas Clarkson toured the provinces promoting the cause, William Wilberforce (Cat. No. 607), an Evangelical Christian and political and social reformer, used his position as M.P. for Hull to work through parliamentary and government channels. Known as 'the nightingale of the house' his eloquence and fluency won widespread support. The slave trade in England was finally abolished in 1807 but the campaign against slavery in general was to continue well into the nineteenth century. **EE**

606

George Richmond
London 1809–1896 London

607
William Wilberforce, 1832–33

Watercolour, 45.2×33.8 cm
Signed and dated lower right: George
Richmond delnt. 1833
London, National Portrait Gallery
Inv. No. 4997
Provenance: commissioned by Sir Robert
Inglis; bequeathed by his widow to
Marianne Thornton, who gave it to
Wilberforce's son Samuel; by descent to his
granddaughter Dr. Octavia Hill; her sale,
King and Chasemore, Pulborough, 12 June
1974, Lot 1273
Exhibitions: London, Royal Academy, 1833,
No. 538
Literature: Wilberforce 1838; Walker 1985,
Vol. 1, pp. 555–56, Vol. 2, Plate 1387

This portrait of the famous slavery abolitionist
and reformer William Wilberforce (1759–
1833) depicts the frail seventy-four-year-old
seated in the dining-room of his house in Battersea Rise. The pose was clearly influenced by
Sir Thomas Lawrence's unfinished portrait of
Wilberforce, which was also owned by Richmond's friend and patron, Sir Robert Inglis.
CF

608
Sugar Bowl, *c.* 1820-30

Earthenware, on-glaze polychrome enamels,
on one side the image of a suppliant slave
beneath palm tree, on the other in gold:
'East India Sugar not made / By Slaves / By
six Families using / East India,/ instead of /
West India Sugar, one / Slave less is
required,' H 11.8×D 10.9 cm
London, The Museum of London
Inv. No. 87.213/4
Provenance: John May
Literature: London Encyclopedia, Vol. 21
(1829), p. 365; Deer 1949, pp. 296–301, Plate
22

The urn-shaped basin is similar to some adver-
tised by a china warehouse in an area of South
London with strong nonconformist connec-
tions; the owner 'Respectfully informs the
Friends of Africa, that she has on Sale an
Assortment of Sugar Basins, handsomely
labelled in Gold Letters: "East India Sugar not
made by Slaves".'
Attempts had been made to promote East
Indian sugar in Britain since the 1780s but it

609

carried much more duty that sugar from the
West Indies. The working conditions of its
labour force were questionable but supporters
of the anti-slavery movement seemed to be
ignorant of the real state of affairs; and those
with East India interests were very pleased to
be so popular. The *London Encyclopedia*
(1829) follows its description of sugar production in the West Indies '. . . where slaves alone
are employed: but we feel a peculiar pleasure
in having it in our power to add a short
description of the method used in the East In-

dies, because there sugar is manufactured by
free men, on a plan much more economical
than what is followed in the West Indies.'
Whether the sugar basins were produced for,
distributed or subsidised by the East India
merchants, or by groups of reformers anxious
to support the cause is not known. **WE**

609
Figure of a Negro Slave, 1820s

Unknown factory, probably Staffordshire
Earthenware, decorated with enamels,
H 18 cm
Brighton, Royal Pavilion, Art Gallery and
Museums
Inv. No. HW 589
Provenance: Henry Willett Collection
Exhibitions: London, Bethnal Green
Museum, 1899, p. 48, No. 589
Literature: Horne 1986, Fig. 161

The slave released from his shackles kneels
praising God for his freedom. The open book
on his knee is inscribed 'Bless God Thank
Britton Me No Slave'. In the 1820s the anti-
slavery movement gained new impetus both
from Henry Brougham (Cat. No. 00) and the
Whig reformers in London and from the foundation of the Society for the Total Abolition of
Slavery by John Cropper, a Quaker, in Liverpool, the city whose wealth had been founded
on slavery. An Act for the Abolition of
Slavery was passed in 1833 under which all
slaves in British colonies were granted emancipation from 1 August 1834. Slavery continued
in the United States for almost another thirty
years. **EE**

610

610
Medal: Abolition of Slavery, 1834

Engraved by J. Davis
Bronze, D 4.3 cm
Obverse: Negro kneeling in chains AM I
NOT A MAN AND A BROTHER. In
exergue: A VOICE FROM GREAT
BRITAIN TO AMERICA 1834
Reverse: Negro standing amid palm trees,
arms raised showing broken chains, THIS IS
THE LORD'S DOING: IT IS
MARVELLOUS IN OUR EYES. PSALM
118 V. 23. In exergue: JUBILEE AUGt 1
1834
London, Trustees of the British Museum
Inv. No. M. 6227
Literature: Brown 1980, p. 398, No. 1666

G. Richmond, *William Wilberforce*, 1932-33. Cat. No. 607

G. Hayter, *Queen Caroline*, 1820. Cat. No. 619

611

The obverse of this medal recalls the Society for the Abolition of the Slave Trade's plaque designed for Wedgwood (Cat. No. 605). Many anti-slavery campaigners saw the issue as a purely religious one and zealously roused public opinion with quotations from the Testaments and threats of just retribution against those profiting from slavery, which some took to involve the whole nation.

The call to America should be noted. American Quakers had been speaking out against slavery since the seventeenth century and leading anti-slavery movements in New York and Philadelphia were in contact with the campaigners in England. **EE**

611
Medal: Abolition of Slavery

Bronze, D 4.2 cm
Engraved by T. Halliday
Obverse: Enchained slave kneeling before Justice. AM I NOT A WOMAN AND A SISTER. In exergue: LET US BREAK THEIR BANDS ASUNDER AND CAST AWAY THEIR CORDS PSALM. 11.3
Reverse: TO THE FRIENDS OF JUSTICE, MERCY, AND FREEDOM, and: PENN / GRANVILLE SHARP / WILBERFORCE / BENEZET / CLARKSON / TOUSAINT LOUVERTURE / STEPHEN / D BARCLAY
London, Trustees of the British Museum
Inv. No. M. 6225
Literature: Brown 1980, p. 399, No. 1669

Here the motto of the anti-slavery movement is adapted to refer to the many women held in slavery. Ladies' anti-slavery societies were extremely active and well subscribed. The men listed on the reverse of the medal include many

of the leading figures of the movement in England and abroad. William Penn and Anthony Benezet were both American Quakers. The exception is Tousaint Louverture who led the successful and bloody slave uprising in San Domingo in 1791. San Domingo became the first black independent state of Haiti after the defeat by the ex-slaves of Napoleon's expedition to the island in 1803. **EE**

William Sharp
1749–1824

612
Joanna Southcott, c. 1812

Pencil, 35.5 × 27 cm
Dated and inscribed: Jany. 1812 Isaiah Ch.65 & 66 Joanna Southcott
London, National Portrait Gallery
Inv. No. 1402
Provenance: purchased from S. G. Fenton, 1905
Literature: Harrison 1979, pp. 86–134; Walker 1985, Vol. 2, p. 468, Plate 1144

William Sharp was an engraver who was so peculiarly impressed with the prophecies of Joanna Southcott (1750–1814), a farmer's daughter from Devon, that he persuaded her in 1802 to come to London. She settled in Paddington and began the practice of 'sealing' the faithful as a form of initiation, these 'seals' were soon seen to possess talismanic qualities. Her following grew from fifty-eight in 1803 to 14,000 by 1807 and 20,000 by 1815, nearly a third coming from London.

The engraver never lost his belief in her even when she announced in 1814 that she was destined to give birth to Shiloh or the second Christ on 19 October. Seventeen out of twenty-one doctors attested to her pregnant condition. Such was her credibility that among the many gifts she received was a satin-wood cradle costing £200, from Seddon, the furniture manufacturers (Cat. Nos. 652–53). Instead, she fell into a trance, became a figure of fun for caricaturists and died of dropsy on 27 December. **CF**

Artist unknown

613
The Rev. Edward Irving, c. 1823

Watercolour, 61.9 × 45 cm
London, National Portrait Gallery
Inv. No. 2757
Provenance: gift of his granddaughter, Miss Margaret Gardiner, 1935

613

Literature: Walker 1985, Vol. 1, pp. 275–76; Vol. 2, Plate 642; Tierney 1990, pp. 289–314

The fashionable Scottish preacher Edward Irving (1792-1834) and founder of the Irvingite Church is depicted in characteristically flamboyant pose. Having been educated and licensed to preach in Scotland, he first came to London in 1822 where his success as a preacher at the Caledonian Church in Hatton Garden was unrivalled. A new church was built in Regent Square, where every Sunday Irving would expound for three hours at a stretch to a thousand followers. He began to prophesy that a second coming of the Messiah was imminent and further prophecies followed. Deeply socially conservative, his brand of millenarianism appealed to the rich and privileged who were the elect. But when his followers began to 'speak in tongues', he was convicted of heresy and ejected from his new church in 1833. **CF**

Lawrence Gahagan
Ireland *fl.* 1756–1820

614
Mary Anne Clarke, 1811

Marble bust, H 64 cm
Incised at back: 'L. Gahagan fecit & pub. Nov.1 1811' and under the base 'M. A. Clarke executed from life per her order November 1811 by L. Gahagan'
London, National Portrait Gallery
Inv. No. 4456

Provenance: commissioned by the sitter and in her collection; . . . H. M. Calmann, from whom purchased, 1965
Literature: Walker 1985, Vol. 1, pp. 112–13, Vol. 2, Plate 254; McCalman 1988, pp. 164–65, 236

Mary Anne Clarke (1776–1852), was from 1803 to 1809 the mistress of George III's second son, Frederick, Duke of York and Albany, Commander in Chief of the army, and was at the centre of a scandal which involved trafficking in army commissions. The duke was indicted for having allowed the sale of promotions to those officers who had paid a suitable bribe to Mrs. Clarke. After questions and motions in parliament, the duke was forced to resign in March 1809 and radicals demanded the reform of 'old corruption'. Renounced by her protector, Mrs. Clarke took to blackmail on the basis of her knowledge of the royal family's private life and in particular, the government plot to incriminate the Prince of Wales's estranged wife, Princess Caroline. In exchange for suppressing her printed memoirs, *Recollections,* she extracted the colossal sum of £10,000 and life annuities for herself and her daughter. Nevertheless, she saw in her circumstances a parallel to those of Clytie, the deserted lover of Helias, who changed into a flower. The pose echoes that of the famous bust in the Townley Collection (Cat. No. 361) and was no doubt deliberately chosen to extend the allegory. Mrs. Clarke's end was more prosaic. She was imprisoned for libel in 1813 and moved to Paris in 1815; she died at an advanced age in Boulogne. **CF**

614

616

Artist unknown

615
The Assassination of the Right Hon: Spencer Perceval, 1812

Aquatint, 27.5 × 37 cm
London, The Museum of London
Inv. No. Z1288

The prime minister, Spencer Perceval (1762–1812) was shot as he entered the lobby of the House of Commons at 5.15pm on 11 May. His assassin was John Bellingham, a bankrupt Liverpool broker who had a grievance against the government for failing to intercede when he had been arrested in Russia. Perceval, second son of the 2nd Earl of Egmont, came to the attention of Pitt through his skill as a barrister: he was given the crown brief in the prosecutions of Tom Paine, Horne Tooke and later, William Cobbett. He entered parliament in 1796 and in the Portland administration was chancellor of the exchequer, a position he still held when he became prime minister in 1809 following Portland's death. He presided over a weak government, plagued by scandals and by increasing radical activity. **CF**

George Cruikshank
London 1792–1878 London

616
The Cato Street Conspirators, on the Memorable Night of 23 February 1820, at the Moment when Smithers the Police Officer was Stabbed

Coloured aquatint, 25 × 38 cm
Published by G. Humphrey, 27 St. James's Street, 9 March 1820
London: Guildhall Library, Corporation of London
Literature: Cohn 1924, No. 177; George 1952, Vol. 10, pp. 42–43, No. 13707; Anand and Ridley 1977

Cato Street, built in 1803, lies in the parish of St. Marylebone, close to and parallel with the Edgware Road. It was here that a group of conspirators, led by Arthur Thistlewood, met in a stable loft and planned the murder of the entire British cabinet. This was to take place on 23 February 1820 when the ministers were due to dine at 44 Grosvenor Square with Lord Harrowby. The heads of Lord Sidmouth and Lord Castlereagh were to be carried off in a bag; cannons were to be grabbed from the Artillery Ground; and Coutts Bank, the Bank of England, the Mansion House and the Tower of London were to be taken over. A provisional government would be proclaimed.

One of the conspirators, in fact a government spy, passed details of the plan to the Home Office. On 20 February Bow Street police officers and Coldstream Guards attacked the Cato Street premises. In the commotion Thistlewood ran through a police officer, Richard Smithers, with a sword. Smithers was caught by a second police officer, Mr. Ruthven, as he fell. Some of the conspirators were arrested whilst others succeeded in making their escape through a skylight. Thistlewood was captured the following day. The five ringleaders were hanged at Newgate on 1 May 1820. **RH**

[?T. Lane]

617
Carrying Coals to Newcastle!!

Coloured etching, 26×40 cm
Published by G. Humphrey, 27 St. James's
St., 16 February 1821
London, Guildhall Library, Corporation of
London
Literature: George 1952, Vol. 10, pp. 189–90,
No. 14119; Richardson 1960

George, Prince of Wales, married Princess
Caroline of Brunswick, at a ceremony at Carlton House on 8 April 1795. One year later,
'because nature had not made us suitable to
each other', the couple informally separated.
In the following years the princess was the
centre of scandalous gossip. She had committed adultery, it was said, and had given
birth to a son, William Austin. Leaving her
home, Ranger's House in Blackheath, she
settled in Italy, taking a lover, Bartolomeo
Bergami ('six feet high, a magnificent head of
black hair, pale complexion, mustachios
which reach *from here to London,*' as one of
Caroline's friends described him). Her frolics
with Bergami became the subject of investigation by the House of Lords intended to
deprive her of her title, rights and privileges.

Learning of the death of George III in 1820
she set off for England. At Montbarde in Burgundy she was met by Alderman Matthew
Wood. After a triumphal procession from
Dover she arrived in London on 6 June, and
took up temporary residence in Wood's house
in South Audley Street. In the summer she
moved to Brandenburgh House on the banks
of the Thames at Hammersmith. A pilgrimage
to Brandenburgh House immediately became
a social necessity for radicals.

The Press, *The Times* in particular, took the
side of the 'wronged woman', against her husband, George IV, who was never less popular
than at this moment. The caricaturists were
divided. G. Humphrey, nephew of Gillray's
publisher, Hannah Humphrey, was the most
outspoken in his opposition to her.

In this caricature braziers (brassfounders)
march to Brandenburgh House to express
their support for Caroline and deliver an
address (compare with Cat. No. 121). Their
emblems include a figure of Bergami carrying
Caroline piggy-back, and a bust of Alderman
Wood.

On 22 January Caroline received sixty-five
addresses. Some trades formed their own distinctive processions. *The Examiner,* 28
January 1821, described that of the braziers as
being conspicuously brilliant: 'There were a
number of men in complete suits of brass and
steel armour, and a variety of splendid insignia
of the trade.' **RH**

618

618
Handkerchief

**A Faithful Representation of the Trial
of Her Most Gracious Majesty . . .**

Cotton, plate printed after a drawing by I.
Slack, 47×58 cm
London, The Museum of London
Inv. No. 53.123
Provenance: Lady Florence Pery
Exhibitions: London, The Museum of
London, 1988
Literature: Schoeser 1988, Fig. 25

The handkerchief represents the 'trial' of
Queen Caroline who was accused of 'licentious and adulterous Intercourse' with Bartolomeo Bergami, her Italian chamberlain,
whom she initially engaged as a courier but
later made baron and in 1817 Grand Master of
the Order of St. Caroline of Jerusalem. The
hearing took place in the House of Lords and a
Bill of Pains and Penalties was proposed, designed to remove the queen's name from the
liturgy and her presence from the country.

The evidence submitted against the queen
had been collected by the 'Milan Commission'
despatched to Italy some years previously to
gather evidence of the Princess of Wales's immorality and thus to provide information that
might be used against her in the divorce proceedings the Prince of Wales hoped for. The

'trial' opened on 17 August with Henry
Brougham acting as the queen's attorney-general. When the vote was taken after the
third reading on 10 November the majority in
favour of the bill had shrunk from twenty-eight to nine and the prime minister, Lord
Liverpool, decided that the bill should be
withdrawn. **EE**

Sir George Hayter
London 1792–1871 London

619 *(illus. p.570)*
Queen Caroline, 1820

Oil on panel, 34.9×29.2 cm
London, National Portrait Gallery
Inv. No. 4940
Provenance: sketch for a commission by
George Agar Ellis M.P. (later 1st Baron
Dover); Hayter family; Hayter sale,
Christie's, 21 April 1871, Lot 587; Bonham's,
14 November 1972, Lot 208; Mrs Amanda
Bruce-Mitford, from whom purchased, 1972
Exhibitions: London, Victoria and Albert
Museum, 1974, F8
Literature: Creevey ed. 1904, Vol. 1, p. 307;
Walker 1985, Vol. 1, p. 99, Vol. 2, Plate 215

621b

The artist was commissioned by George Agar Ellis (1797–1833), a rising young Whig politician and art patron, supporter of the queen and director of the British Institution, to produce a large-scale painting of the queen's 'trial' in the House of Lords, anticipating that it would be an event of extraordinary national significance. Hayter attended the trial, making extensive annotated notes in pencil, pen and watercolour wash in preparation for the main composition. These were followed with 161 sittings given by the main protagonists (whereabouts not known). The present work is based on several candid sketches of the queen, and bears out the description of 17 August 1820 given by the convivial Whig M.P. Thomas Creevey who, though he could not see her face through her veil, noted 'a few straggling ringlets on her neck, which I flatter myself from their appearance were not her Majesty's own property.'

Hayter received 2,000 guineas for the completed work, which was exhibited in Pall Mall in 1823 to great acclaim (it now hangs in the National Portrait Gallery). Creevey was an exception, pronouncing it 'a regular daub' but conceding 'I find myself singular in this opinion so far.' **CF**

Sir George Hayter

620
Theodore Majocchi, 1820

a) chalk, 17.6 × 10.9 cm
Inscribed : non mi ricordo

b) chalk, 9.5 × 13.4 cm

London, National Portrait Gallery
Inv. Nos. 1695 (c) and (d)
Provenance: Sir George Hayter and probably his sale, Christie's, 19 April 1871, Lot 349, bought Noseda; Edward Basil Jupp; Matthew B. Walker, from whom purchased, 1913
Literature: New 1961, pp. 249–51; Walker 1985, Vol. 1, pp. 620–23, Vol. 2, Plates 1535, 1537

Theodore Majocchi, a former servant of the queen, was the first witness for the prosecution. His evidence was extensive and damning, but under cross-examination from Brougham, he got confused, contradicted himself and was thoroughly discredited. This was the high point of the 'trial', which Hayter used for his finished painting. In sixteen pages of solid print recording the cross-examination, 'I do not remember' – 'Non mi ricordo' before translation – occurs eighty-seven times. The expression instantly became a catch-phrase and was endlessly employed in satires attacking the 'trial'. **CF**

Sir George Hayter

621
a) Sir Christopher Robinson, James Parke and Dr. Adams, 1820
Ink and sepia wash, 20.4 × 28.1 cm
Signed and inscribed upper left: G. Hayter/ for the Trial/of the Queen/1820

b) Sir Robert Gifford, Sir John Singleton Copley, Thomas Wilde, Dr. Stephen Lushington, Marchese di Spineto, and others
Ink and sepia wash, 14.5 × 21.5 cm
Signed and inscribed lower right: House of Lords Trial of the Queen/ GH Sept 1820

London, National Portrait Gallery
Inv. Nos. 1695 (h) and (i)
Provenance: as for Cat. No. 620
Literature: New 1961, pp. 248–49; Walker 1985, Vol. 1, p. 621, Vol. 2, Plates 1540–41

Hayter's *ad vivum* sketches include some of the legal protagonists in the queen's 'trial' but omit the undoubted star, Henry Brougham (Cat. No. 602), the leading Queen's Counsel. Also defending the queen were Lushington, an accomplished and humanitarian lawyer, who was later to become a judge of the High Court of the Admiralty, and Wilde (later Lord Truro) who like Brougham was to become a Whig lord chancellor. Counsel for the crown was led by the attorney-general, Gifford, but Brougham's real opponent was the solicitor-general, Sir John Copley (later Lord Lyndhurst). He was to precede and succeed Brougham as lord chancellor in Tory administrations, but both became allies in the cause of law reform and a close friendship developed between them. **CF**

622

George Cruikshank
London 1792–1878 London

622
The Radical Ladder, 1820

Etching, 20×14 cm
London, The Museum of London
Inv. No. Z6785
Literature: George 1952, Vol. 10, pp. 11–13,
109–10, No. 13895

Originally published as a plate to the *Loyalist's
Magazine*, the image reflects a change of political heart by Cruikshank presumably not
unconnected with his receipt of £100 from
Carlton House. The queen reaches to top of a
flimsy ladder with steps labelled 'RUIN',
'ANARCHY', 'REVOLUTION', 'MOB
GOVERNMENT' &c., pushed by Jacobins
behind her, and . threatens the pillar of the
constitution **CF**

William Hone
Bath 1780–1842 London
and
George Cruikshank

623
a) The Queen's Matrimonial Ladder
Printed by and for William Hone, Ludgate-
Hill, 1820
Octavo, 22×28 cm (open)

b) "Non Mi Ricordo!"
Printed by and for William Hone, Ludgate
Hill, 1820
Octavo, 22×28 cm (open)

London, Guildhall Library, Corporation of
London
Inv. Nos. A.6.2.1 in 10 and A.6. 4 in 9
Literature: Hackwood 1912, pp. 223,
236–37; George 1952, Vol. 10, pp. 78–82,
92–93, Nos. 13790–805, 137808 and
13844–46; Rickword 1971

The Queen's Matrimonial Ladder was the result, evidently based on a toy entitled 'the
matrimonial ladder' which Hone saw in a shop
in Pentonville. The sad story of the royal marriage is related in a series of steps explained
from the queen's viewpoint. *Non Mi Ricordo!*
parodies the cross-examination of Majocchi,
placing George IV in the dock. In Hone's accompanying text, the king is questioned on his
past and present life, with allusions to the
queen and his mistresses. Both pamphlets
were prosecuted unsuccessfully for libel. **CF**

"NON MI RICORDO!"
&c. &c. &c.

"This will witness outwardly, as strongly as the conscience does within"
Cymbeline.

"Who are you?"
Thirty-First Edition.
LONDON:
PRINTED BY AND FOR WILLIAM HONE, LUDGATE HILL.
1820.
SIXPENCE.

623b

[?T. Lane]

624 *(illus. p.579)*
Honi Soit qui Mal y Pense

Coloured etching, 30×42 cm
Published by G. Humphrey, 27 St. James's
St, 12 August 1821
London, Guildhall Library, Corporation of
London
Literature: George 1952, Vol. 10, pp. 233–34,
No. 14206; Richardson 1960

The print consists of an exterior view of G.
Humphrey's print shop. A crowd of citizens,
some amused, some puzzled, gathers on the
pavement to view no less than forty-two anti-
Caroline caricatures displayed in the shop
window. All of them can be identified with
actual caricatures (see below) Humphrey had
published when the Caroline affair was in full
swing. Through the glass-fronted door we see
a man (who must be G. Humphrey) holding a
print entitled *Folly as it flies*, a quote from
Pope's *Essay on Man*. A second man (John
Bull, one assumes) congratulates the print-
maker and laughs. **RH**

(Isaac) Robert Cruikshank
London 1789–1856 London
and
George Cruikshank

625 *(illus. p.579)*
The Royal Extinguisher, or the King of Brobdinag & the Lilliputians

Coloured etching, 24×33 cm
Published by G. Humphrey, 27 St. James's
Street, 7 April 1821
London, Guildhall Library, Corporation of
London
Literature: George 1952, Vol. 10, pp. 204–05,
No. 14145; Richardson 1960

George IV in military uniform is surrounded
by delighted and well-satisfied ministers. He
holds a large paper extinguisher consisting of
his speech from the throne. Beneath it on the
table and about to be extinguished, is a mob of
terrified Lilliputian Jacobeans, Queen Caroline and Alderman Wood.
   The king's speech, delivered from the
throne on 23 January, helped turn the tide of
popular opinion in his favour. The queen's
reputation declined thereafter. The bag of cash
which she holds refers to a grant from parliament of £50,000 a year which she accepted,
though earlier she had solemnly vowed that
she would refuse all offers of money. **RH**

[? T. Lane]

626 *(illus. p.580)*
Delicious Dreams!

Coloured etching, 39×29 cm
Published by G. Humphrey, 27 St. James's
St., 30 April 1821
London, Guildhall Library, Corporation of
London
Literature: George 1952, Vol. 10, pp. 213–14,
No. 14175; Richardson 1960

Following dinner at Brandenburgh House,
Queen Caroline and her supporters sleep
around the table. Their dreams are to be seen
in the cloud above them. The dream at the top
is of the coronation, George and Caroline
kneeling together before the Archbishop of
Canterbury, the queen about to be crowned.
Below on the left is a dream of Buckingham
House where the queen would live. The dream
on the right shows the queen receiving lady
courtiers. Pictures of the queen and Bergami
hang on the wall. Caroline wears a miniature
of her lover. **RH**

628a

628b

[?T. Lane]

627 (illus. p.581)
The Effusions of a Troubled Brain . . .

Coloured etching, 39×29 cm
Published by G. Humphrey, 27 St. James's
St., 10 July, 1821
London, Guildhall Library, Corporation of
London
Literature: George 1952, Vol. 10, pp. 228–29,
No. 14196; Richardson 1960

Queen Caroline writes, 'To the King's most
Excellent Majesty in Council . . .' praying that
she be crowned at the forthcoming coronation. On the left stands Matthew Wood,
with devil's body though dressed in alderman's gown. On the extreme right is a broom
(Henry Brougham, the queen's legal adviser)
clad in a wig and gown. Behind are dark forces
of revolution. A figure of Bergami stands on
the table. Above the Queen hovers an owl
wearing a fool's cap, and above the owl a
variety of objects which include caps of liberty
marked Bat, Mat, and Cat (Bartolomeo Bergami, Matthew Wood, and Caroline), open
sketchbooks of the queen's travels and
'Letters to Watch Makers [of] Coventry' with
a watch and chain. (A watch was presented to
Caroline on 14 June by a deputation from
Coventry.) Between 5 and 6 June it had been
exhibited in Coventry to raise the needed subscriptions. *John Bull* on 10 June cattily noted
that 20,000 inhabitants had not yet raised £60.
RH

628
Medals

a) Caroline of Brunswick and Count Bergami, 1820

Engraved by P. Kempson
Bronze, D 4.1 cm

Obverse: Laureate, draped bust of Queen
Caroline, head left CAROLINE D: G.
BRITT: REGINA
Reverse: Bust of Count Bergami facing, head
right. COUNT B. BERGAMI
London, Trustees of the British Museum
Inv. No. M.5652
Literature: Brown 1980, p. 250, No. 1030;
Eimer 1987, p. 140, No. 1132

b) The Trial of Queen Caroline, 1820

Engraved by A. Desboeufs or Durand
Bronze, D 8.2 cm
Obverse: Draped bust of Queen Caroline
(to left) CAROLINE QUEEN OF
ENGLAND
Reverse: Minerva holding a tablet inscribed
QUEEN'S TRIAL and dismissing Discord.
In exergue: MDCCCXX
London, Trustees of the British Museum
Inv. No. M.5658
Literature: Brown 1980, pp. 248, 249, No.
1026; Eimer 1987, p. 140, No. 1131

Both these souvenir medals allude to the 'trial'
of Queen Caroline. The first is undated and of
simple design; the more sophisticated second
design, despite the English inscription,
appears to have been produced by a French
engraver and was possibly struck in France for
the English market. **EE**

629
Commemorative Wares, Queen Caroline

a) Beaker, c. 1820

Staffordshire; earthenware with maroon on-
glaze transfer print of a young Queen
Caroline described as 'The Royal Wanderer';
pink lustre banding, H 7.4×D 6.8 cm
Mark: 4 impressed on base
London, The Museum of London
Inv. No. A12972
Provenance: E. J. Sidebotham, H.M. Queen
Mary
Literature: May 1972, p. 42, Fig. 62

b) Jug, c. 1820

Staffordshire; Earthenware, printed in black
and enamelled with portrait of a young
Queen Caroline and a naval scene, with the
verse, 'May Peace and Plenty / On our
Nation smile / And Trade & Commerce /
Bless the British Isle / Success to Ship
Trade.' H 14.5 cm
Brighton, Royal Pavilion, Art Gallery and
Museums
Inv. No. EH/A/10

Provenance: Sir Eardley Holland

c) Jug, c. 1820

Probably Staffordshire; earthenware, printed
in black, with the verse 'When man
presumes to chuse a wife / He takes his
lovely spouse for life / Who can judge and
not repine /The Wofull case of
CAROLINE; applied copper lustre, H 16cm
Brighton, Royal Pavilion, Art Gallery and
Museums
Inv. No. HW 63
Provenance: Henry Willett Collection
Exhibitions: London, Bethnal Green, 1899,
p. 6, No. 63

d) Jug, c. 1820

Staffordshire; pearlware, transfer-printed
overglaze in black with a caricature 'Public
Opinion' after I. R. Cruikshank and a rhyme
entitled 'Caroline Our Much Injured
Queen'; painted with overglaze enamel
colours and pink lustre bands, H 10.4 cm
Stoke-on-Trent, City Museum and Art
Gallery
Inv. No. 1495

e) Plate, c. 1820

Probably Staffordshire; earthenware with
moulded floral border, transfer printed and
painted in green, yellow and orange with a
profile bust of Queen Caroline with 'Long
live Queen Caroline' beneath, under blue-
tinted glaze, D 15.5 cm
Cambridge, Syndics of the Fitzwilliam
Museum
Provenance: bequeathed by J. W. L.
Glaisher
Inv. No. C.27-1928

f) Plate, c. 1820

Staffordshire; earthenware, printed in black
and enamelled, with the adapted nursery

629d

629h

queen's 'trial' and of the popular sympathy for Caroline is supported by the large number of pieces of commemorative pottery which survive referring to the events of 1820. They were decorated with portraits (some, suspiciously youthful looking and probably adapted from prints of the queen's daughter, Princess Charlotte),verses – some satirical, others patriotic – and crude versions of caricatures. **EE**

rhyme 'I'll sing a song of sixpence, /A green Bag full of lies, / Four and Twenty witnesses, / All proved to be spies; /When the Bag was open'd,/ The Lords began to stare, /To see their precious evidence, / All vanish'd into air', surrounded by a ribbon inscribed 'LONG LIVE CAROLINE / QUEEN OF ENGLAND' and with the names of her lawyers, D 6.7 cm
London, Trustees of the British Museum
Inv. No. R27
Literature: Hobson 1903, p. 289, R27

g) Dish, *c.* 1820

Staffordshire; bone china with magenta on-glaze transfer print of Queen Caroline; pink lustre banding, D 21.5 cm
London, The Museum of London
Inv. No. C1676
Provenance: Dr. F. Corner

h) Plaque, *c.* 1820

Staffordshire; earthenware, enamelled, 14×12×1 cm
Brighton, Royal Pavilion, Art Gallery and Museums
Inv. No. EH/A/7
Provenance: Sir Eardley Holland

Commemorative pottery was mass produced at prices that large numbers of the population could afford. Due to improved transport and a more efficient postal system and the growing numbers of provincial newspapers, information was disseminated more quickly than ever before and with the increasing literacy of the artisan classes, that information was available to a far wider range of people than previously. The transfer-printed pottery that these people were able to buy was highly decorative, but its celebratory and propagandist nature also revealed their interest in and awareness of national issues.
    Evidence of the interest aroused by the

629e

630 *(illus. p.582)*
Figure of Queen Caroline

Probably Staffordshire, *c.* 1820

Bone china, decorated with enamels,
H 15.3 cm
Brighton, Royal Pavilion, Art Gallery and Museums
Inv. No. HW 58
Provenance: Henry Willett Collection

This finely made figure of Queen Caroline was probably intended for display on a mantelpiece as it is worked in relief rather than modelled in the round. As such figures were often made in pairs it may once have been accompanied by a figure of the king. **EE**

631
Figure of George IV

Derby, Robert Bloor and Co., *c.* 1820–8

Bone china, enamelled and gilt, H 31.8 cm
Mark: crown, crossed batons and dots over BLOOR DERBY in red
Cambridge, Syndics of the Fitzwilliam Museum
Provenance: given by Mrs. W. D. Dickson
Inv. No. C.113-1932

The production of this handsome figure suggests that the king enjoyed some support, although compared with the biscuit porcelain version (Cat. No. 487) it lacks finesse, the enamelling having coarsened the modelling. **CF**

633

zotints were produced after the watercolours, and the artists were there identified as Stephanoff for the composition and figures, Bowyer for the portraits and Pugin for the architectural parts.

The chamber as shown is the final state of the medieval upper chapel of St. Stephen before it was destroyed by fire in 1834. The two-storey royal chapel of St. Stephen, built between 1290 and 1344, was one of the glories of medieval England. Following the suppression in 1547 of the collegiate foundation that served the chapel, the House of Commons took it over for their chamber. In 1692 and 1707 Sir Christopher Wren reconstructed the interior, including the north and south galleries seen in the picture. Between 1800 and 1812 James Wyatt further modified the chamber to accommodate the Irish members who sat at Westminster following the Act of Union of 1800. **AW**

Robert Havell Junior
1798–1878
after
George Scharf
Mainburg 1788–1860 London

632
Representation of the Election of Members of Parliament for Westminster, 1818

Coloured aquatint, 40.4×51.5 cm
Published by G. Scharf, 3 St. Martins Lane, Charing Cross and Colnaghi & Co., Printsellers, Cockspur Street, November 1818
London, The Museum of London
Inv. No. 59.81
Literature: George 1949, Vol. 9, No. 13006, pp. 812–13; George 1952, Vol. 10, No. 13006A, p. 39; Jackson 1987, pp. 78–79

Depictions of the electoral hustings – a temporary wooden shed from which the candidates addressed the crowd – in front of St. Paul's Church, Covent Garden, came to symbolise the political process at work in London. Westminster enjoyed one of the most democratic franchises in the country, being a 'scot-and-lot' borough where any man who paid the poor rates could vote. As a result, its M.Ps. tended to be radical and the process by which they were returned to parliament was inclined to be riotous. Here Scharf depicts the election brought about by the dis-

solution of parliament on 10 June 1818. The six candidates ranged from the Tory candidate Sir Murray Maxwell to the extreme radical Henry Hunt, (Cat. No. 637). But the election was won by the moderate Whig legal reformer Sir Samuel Romilly and an increasingly conservative Sir Francis Burdett (Cat. No. 634), despite the fact that neither deigned to appear on the hustings. **CF**

James Stephanoff
London *c.* 1786–1874 Bristol

Robert Bowyer
1758–1834 Byfleet

Augustus Charles Pugin
Normandy *c.* 1769–1832 London

633
The House of Commons, 1821–23

Watercolour, 34.3×49.6 cm
London, Palace of Westminster Collection
Literature: Walker 1988, p. 58, No. 131

The picture shows a view of the crowded chamber of the House of Commons looking towards the speaker. The exact occasion represented has not been identified but, because there is a companion watercolour of the House of Lords made during the trial of Queen Caroline in 1820, probably this picture is connected with the same proceedings. Mez-

Adam Buck
Cork 1759–1833 London

634
Sir Francis Burdett, 1810

Watercolour, 19.5×16.2 cm
London, National Portrait Gallery
Inv. No. 1229
Provenance: Arthur L. Collie, from whom purchased, 1899
Exhibitions: London, Royal Academy, 1817, No. 30
Literature: Hone 1982; Walker 1985, Vol. 1, p. 75; Vol. 2, Plate 163

634

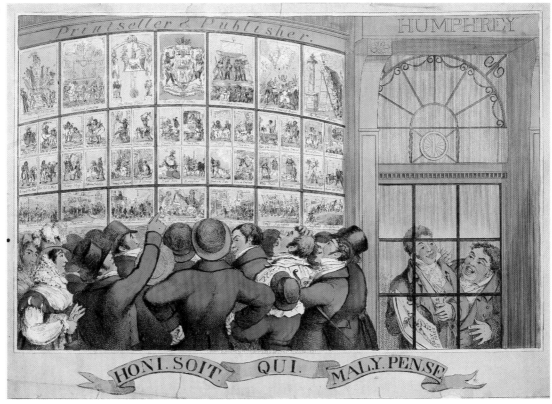

T. Lane (?), *Honi Soit qui Mal y Pense*, 1821. Cat. No. 624

I. R. and G. Cruikshank, *The Royal Extinguisher . . .* 1821. Cat. No. 625

T. Lane (?), *Delicious Dreams!* 1821. Cat. No. 626

The Effusions of a Troubled Brain.
"Evil communications" corrupt good Manners.

ALARMING!!! REVOLUTION in the CITY

Wots to become of all the Wittles let me ax you that — wot are we to do with the Wittles eh?

DON MAYO

LORD MAYORS DAY and no DINNER

(left) T. Lake (?), *The Effusions of a Troubled Brain . . .* 1821. Cat. No. 627

(right) W. Heath, *Alarming!!! Revolution in the City,* 1830. Cat. No. 640

My lords & gentlemen. I am well satisfied with your Loyalty & attachment. receive my thanks. & Kiss my hand

Loyal Address's & Radical Peteions, or the R—— is most gracious answer to both sides of the question at once.

G. Cruikshank, *Loyal Address's & Radical Petitions,* 1819. Cat. No. 636

Figure of Queen Caroline, *c.* 1820. Cat. No. 630

Sir Francis Burdett (1770–1844) was as unlikely a figure to lead the radical cause as his patrician appearance would suggest. He was educated at Westminster and Oxford and having spent the years 1790–93 on the Continent, where he witnessed the French Revolution, he married the youngest daughter of Francis Coutts, the banker; in 1797 he succeeded to a baronetcy. Having been returned as M.P. for Boroughbridge in 1796, he made himself conspicuous through his opposition to the war, and his advocacy of reform. In 1802 he was returned for the county of Middlesex, but two years later his election was declared void and he eventually lost the seat after lengthy and costly litigation. In 1807, thanks to the support of the Westminster committee of radicals, he was returned for Westminster, a seat which he held for thirty years.

When he published a letter to his constituents in Cobbett's *Political Register* in 1810, in support of the reporting of parliamentary debates and declaring the conduct of the House of Commons illegal in imprisoning a radical orator who had advocated this elementary freedom, he was arrested and was imprisoned in the Tower. This watercolour was executed at the time, possibly in prison. The etching published after it by the artist, inscribed 'Plate 2 of Friends to a Constitutional Reform of Parliament', was certainly designed to cash in on his popularity. Burdett was released after a few weeks and continued to support reform. Ten years later a letter on the 'Peterloo Massacre' involved him in a further period of imprisonment, for three months, and a £1,000 fine. **CF**

Artist unknown

635
Smithfield Meeting London, 1819

Coloured etching, 38×48 cm
Published by C. Thompson, 40 Long Lane, Smithfield, August 9 1819
London, Guildhall Library, Corporation of London

On 21 July 1819 Henry 'Orator' Hunt (Cat. No. 637) presided at a reform meeting held in the open space of the City's live meat market at Smithfield (Cat. No. 178). Hunt, a fiery, egotistical politician, was an energetic campaigner for universal suffrage and vote by ballot, and a pioneer fighter for women's rights. The authorities anticipated the meeting with trepidation. Alderman John Atkins, lord mayor, called a meeting of the Court of Aldermen in the hope of finding a way of stopping it. Whether he had the power to do so was in doubt. However, he was advised that once the meeting was under way it could be halted if the speakers propagated sedition or excited riot.

The print, published by a Smithfield print-maker, shows the great meeting in progress, with 'Orator' Hunt haranguing the thousands of citizens who turned up. In the event, the crowd remained 'peaceable and went away in good Order, and no the least disturbance'. **RH**

George Cruikshank
London 1792–1878 London

636 *(illus. p. 581)*
Loyal Address's & Radical Petitions

Coloured etching, 24×33 cm
Published by T. Tegg, 111 Cheapside, 4
December 1819
London, Guildhall Library, Corporation of
London
Literature: George 1949, Vol. 9, pp. 935–36,
No. 13280; Cohn 1924, No. 1705

The Prince Regent proffers his hand to be kissed by obsequious loyal subjects who grovel in front of him, simultaneously turning his back on a group of unruly radical petitioners in *bonnets rouge*, and farting into their faces. On the wall is a picture of the Regent's Bomb (pronounced 'Bum'), fire blasting from its muzzle (Cat. No. 303). The radicals are Alderman Waithman, who holds aloft a 'City Petition for Reform Three <u>Yards</u> long'; Francis Burdett and Henry 'Orator' Hunt with their petitions; and Dr. Watson who is lying on the floor, his clyster-pipe squirting its contents at the regent.

Following the 'Peterloo Massacre' at Manchester on 16 August 1819, many protest meetings were held and petitions to the regent voted. The City of London presented a critical City address to the regent on 17 September. In his reply the regent, much displeased, expressed his 'deep regret' at their action. At the same time, loyal addresses to the regent were being voted by conservative forces fearful of unrest and revolution. **RH**

J. Wiche
fl. 1811–1827

637
Henry Hunt, 1822

Watercolour, 31.3×23.4 cm
London, National Portrait Gallery
Inv. No. 957
Provenance: Henry Hunt; donated by
Henry Willett, 1894
Literature: Huish 1836; Walker 1985, Vol. 1,
p. 267, Vol. 2, Plate 621

635

Henry 'Orator' Hunt (1773–1835) came from a wealthy Wiltshire farming background but championed many reforming causes, especially annual parliaments, universal suffrage, votes by ballot, women's rights and the abolition of the Corn Laws. His oratorical skills drew large crowds to mass meetings organised to press for parliamentary reform, notably at Spa Fields, Islington, in November and December 1816; the violent actions of extre-

637

mists on the latter occasion even before Hunt had arrived led to repressive government legislation.

In 1819, he was the principal speaker at the rally at St. Peter's Fields, Manchester, which ended in the 'Peterloo Massacre'. This watercolour was painted after his release from Ilchester Gaol, where he was imprisoned for two years following Peterloo. The 'REPORT' on the table refers to the discussion in the House of Commons of his ill treatment in the gaol, the paper inscribed, 'Roasted Corn' to his prosecution by the Excise for manufacturing it as a substitute for coffee: it was dubbed 'Radical Coffee'. **CF**

'A Sharpshooter'

638
Conjunction of Talent. The Great Dictator and his Mighty Councillor, the Donkey Mare

Coloured etching, 35×25 cm
Published by S. Gans, 15 Southampton
Street, Strand, November 13 1830
London, Guildhall Library, Corporation of
London
Literature: George 1954, Vol. 11, p. 365;
Hyde 1976, pp. 54–63

By tradition Lord Mayor's Day in the City of London took place on 9 November. It was the tradition too that the monarch be invited to the City in the first year of his or her reign. When William IV came to the throne in 1830 the City fathers resolved that the royal visit should coincide with the 9 November celebrations, and that the banquet should be the most splendid and lavish of entertainments.

The preparations were presided over by the lord mayor elect, Alderman John Key, a reformer and master of the Stationers' Company. Caricatures were published showing John Key welcoming William and Adelaide to Guildhall. Key becomes 'Donkey'. When not a 'mare' he is the 'new Vicar of Bray', and shown as a donkey in mayoral attire. The king rewards him with a Spanish title, 'Don Key'. As a stationer he is 'John Fool's Cap'.

Three days before the feast Key wrote to the prime minister, the anti-reform Duke of Wellington, informing him that a 'set of desperate and abandoned characters' were intending to use the occasion to create 'tumult and confusion'. He advised the duke to come 'strongly and sufficiently guarded'. **RH**

Henry Heath
fl. 1824–1850

639
The Great General Frightened by Don-Key!

Coloured etching, 24 × 35 cm
Published by S. W. Fores, 41 Piccadilly, 1830
London, Guildhall Library, Corporation of London
Literature: George 1954, Vol. 11, p. 538, No. 16305; Hyde 1976

On 6 November Sir Claudius Hunter, the *locum tenens* of the retiring lord mayor, together with John Key, visited the home secretary, Sir Robert Peel ('Bob'), and warned him of the danger of disorder. Peel discussed the matter with Wellington. An audience was sought with the king. Wellington and Peel urged the king to postpone his visit. The king decided that they were right. The visit was off. **RH**

William Heath
1795–1840 London

640 *(illus. p. 581)*
Alarming!!! Revolution in the city. Lord Mayors Day and no Dinner

Coloured etching, 35 × 24 cm
Published by T. McLean, 26 Haymarket London, 10 November 1830
London, Guildhall Library, Corporation of London
Literature: George 1954, Vol. 11, pp. 356–57, No. 16303; Hyde 1976

An obese, brandy-faced, goggle-eyed 'cit', dressed in an old-fashioned court dress, on hearing that the royal visit and Lord Mayor's Banquet have been cancelled, wails: 'Wots to become of all the Wittles . . . ?' The news of the cancelled visit was greeted with dismay by the City fathers. Key was angrily ordered to explain his part in the fiasco. As the news became general knowledge alarm spread through the metropolis, business was suspended, the funds fell 3 per cent, the Tower of London's moat was flooded by way of precaution, and the guards at the Bank of England were doubled. A mob marched through the City to Westminster where a conflict took place with Peel's new police. A dinner was held at Stationers' Hall. When a toast was proposed to the new lord mayor the assembly booed, hissed, and shouted, 'No! No! No!' **RH**

Henry Heath

641
Ahithophel in the Dumps

Coloured etching, 23 × 33 cm
Published by S. W. Fores, 41 Piccadilly, 1830
London, Guildhall Library, Corporation of London
Literature: George 1954, Vol. 11, p. 373, No. 16343; Hyde 1976

Key's clumsy action saved Wellington from having to make physical contact with a hostile mob on Lord Mayor's Day. However, the duke's role in the fiasco caused bitter attacks to be made on him inside and outside parliament. That the King of England dared not dine with his loyal citizens because his ministers were too unpopular to be seen in public was considered a scandal. Ironically, it was in part the 9 November calamity, together with Wellington's declaration on reform, that precipitated Wellington's downfall one week later.

Heath's caricature is an adaptation of a print by James Gillray, Wellington being substituted for Fox. The donkey, which carried the arms of the Corporation of London on its saddle, represents the new lord mayor, Alderman John Key. **RH**

642
Handkerchief

The Reformers' Attack on The Old Rotten Tree

After an engraving published by E. King, Chancery Lane, 1831
Cotton, block- and plate-printed, 73 × 85 cm
London, The Museum of London
Inv. No. 35.89/1
Provenance: Miss Moseley
Exhibitions: London, The Museum of London, 1988, No. 23
Literature: Schoeser 1988, Fig. 23; George 1954, No. 16650

The foremost reformers can be identified as Henry Brougham, in an exaggerated wig with an axe shaft fashioned from a mace, Earl Grey and the Marquess of Lansdowne whose axes bear their names and Viscount Althorp whose axe is inscribed 'Bum Chopper'. Opposing them are Sir Robert Peel with his back to the trunk whilst Wellington strains above him. Ellenborough, with an elephant's trunk attached to his profile, recalling a recent scandal over his description, whilst president of the India Board, of a judge of the Supreme Court of Bombay as 'a wild elephant', pushes with outstretched arms. In the background on Constitution Hill stand the king and queen and an Englishman, Irishman and Scotsman. **EE**

643
Handkerchief, 1831

The Glorious Reform in Parliament

After a design by Robert Cruikshank, 1831
Silk, plate-printed, additional colours added by hand, 84 × 87 cm
London, The Museum of London
Inv. No. 29.25
Provenance: Miss M. Coles
Exhibitions: London, The Museum of London, 1988
Literature: Schoeser 1988, Fig. 22; George 1954, No. 16676

According to *The Times*, 9 May 1831, the image printed on this handkerchief was designed by Robert Cruikshank specifically for a handkerchief it was afterwards published as a lithograph by Alfred Miller, 137 Oxford Street (BM No. 16676).

After the middle of the eighteenth century fewer existing engravings seem to have been used as a source for pictorial handkerchiefs. New designs were specifically commissioned. Cruikshank describes himself in the lower left hand corner as a 'Friend of Reform'. This suggests that the handkerchief might be bought as a gesture of political allegiance. **EE**

642

643

644
Medals

a) The Reform Bill Presented, 1831

Bronze, D 4.6 cm
Engraved by T. Halliday
Obverse: Heads of William IV, Earl Grey,
Lord Brougham and Lord Russell with
inscription: THE CONFIDENCE OF
THE PEOPLE
Reverse inscribed: THE REFORM BILL /
THE DESIRE OF THE PEOPLE / NO
UNMERITED PENSIONS / NO TITHES
/ NO CORN LAWS / NO GAME LAWS /
NO STAMP TAXES / NO EAST INDIA /
MONOPOLY / NO COLONIAL
SLAVERY
London, Trustees of the British Museum
Inv. No. M.6073
Literature: Brown 1980, p. 369, No. 1535;
Eimer 1987, p. 151, No. 1244

b) The Reform Bill, 1832

Bronze, D 5.1 cm
Engraved by J. Davis
Obverse: The king enthroned, attended by
four people to left, Britannia holding a
banner inscribed UNION attended by the
British lion whose paws rest on a slain
dragon. OUR CAUSE HATH
TRIUMPHED GLORIOUSLY THE
HORSE & HIS RIDER HATH HE
THROWN INTO THE SEA. In exergue:
EXODUS CHAP. 15.V.21
Reverse: A table in the centre showing the
Bill's stages: times, dates, readings, votes

London, Trustees of the British Museum
Inv. No. M 6163
Literature: Brown 1980, p. 379, No. 1578;
Eimer 1987, p. 153, No. 1255

644a

644b

645
Commemorative Wares, Reform Bill

a) Reform Mug, *c.* 1832

Staffordshire; perhaps Chetham and
Robinson or Chesworth and Robinson,
Lane End, Longton
Earthenware, transfer printed in black with a
bust of Earl Grey signed 'Kennedy', and a
wreath of roses, thistles and shamrock
enclosing the word 'REFORM', and lustred
pink overall, H 8.2 cm
Mark: C & R in rosette, transfer printed in
black
Cambridge, Syndics of the Fitzwilliam
Museum
Inv. No. C.1145-1928
Provenance: J. W. L. Glaisher Bequest
Literature: Rackham 1935; Vol. 1, p. 148,
No. 1145

b) Reform Mug, *c.* 1832

Staffordshire; perhaps Chetham and
Robinson or Chesworth and Robinson,
Lane End, Longton
Earthenware, transfer printed in black with a
bust, titled below 'LORD BROUGHAM
AND VAUX./Lord High Chancellor' and a
wreath of roses, thistles and shamrock
enclosing the word 'REFORM'; pink lustre
bands round rim and foot, H 11.7 cm
Cambridge, Syndics of the Fitzwilliam
Museum
Inv. No. C. 1137-1928
Provenance: J. W. L. Glaisher Bequest
Literature: Rackham 1935; Vol 1, p. 147, no.
1137

645c

645d

c) Jug, 'The Old Rotten Tree', 1832

Staffordshire; earthenware, with underglaze
transfer print, H 15 cm
London, The Museum of London
Inv. No. 33.3/1
Provenance: H.M. Queen Mary
Literature: May 1972, p. 144, Fig. 212;
George 1954, Vol. 11, p. 471, No. 16650

d) Punch Bowl, *c.* 1832

Probably Goodwin, Bridgwood and Harris
Earthenware, printed in mauve, H 18 × D
28 cm
Brighton, Royal Pavilion, Art Gallery and
Museums
Inv. No. HW 509
Provenance: Henry Willett Collection
Exhibitions: London, Bethnal Green
Museum, 1899, p. 42, No. 509

The parliamentary Reform Bill of 1832 provoked another flood of popular commemorative ceramics, often decorated with portraits
of the leading reformers. Earl Grey was prime
minister in the administration which proposed
the First Reform Bill. Lord Brougham (Cat.
No. 602) who had already achieved a high
public profile through his role in the Queen
Caroline affair and his advocacy of popular
education, was lord chancellor in Grey's pro-
reform administration.
The imagery on the jug, like the handkerchief Cat. No. 642, is derived from an engraving published by E. King of Chancery

Lane (BM No. 16650) although in a much simplified form. On the reverse of the jug are
depicted King William IV and Queen Adelaide on Constitution Hill together with the
Englishman John Bull, Paddy the Irishman
and Sandy the Scotsman. The punch bowl is
decorated with three well-known transfer
prints associated with the Reform Bill. **EE**

646
Spirit Flasks

a) Lord Brougham, 1832

Doulton and Watts; grey stoneware with tan
dip, H 18 cm
Mark: Lambeth Pottery, DOULTON &
WATTS 15 HIGH STREET *LAMBETH*,
impressed
London, The Museum of London
Inv. No. C559
Provenance: Frank Crace; Dr. F. Corner
Literature: Hildyard 1985, p. 60

b) Spirit Flask, Lord John Russell, 1832

Doulton and Watts; grey stoneware with
dark tan dip, H 17.9 × 8.5 cm
Mark: Lambeth Pottery, DOULTON &
WATTS, 15 HIGH STREET, *LAMBETH*,
impressed
London, The Museum of London
Inv. No. A23688
Provenance: Sir Frank Crisp

c) Spirit Flask, Earl Grey, *c.* 1832

Belper and Denby, Derbyshire; stoneware
with tan dip, H 19 cm
Mark: BELPER & DENBY BOURNES
POTTERIES DERBYSHIRE
Brighton, Royal Pavilion, Art Gallery and
Museums
Inv. No. R 2878/40
Provenance: Stuart Robertson Collection

Under the Reform Act which brought about
redistribution of parliamentary seats and a
modest extension of the franchise, some
boroughs with a very small electorate were
abolished whilst others in industrial areas
were represented for the first time. The
London borough of Lambeth where the
Doulton and Watts pottery was situated came
into the latter category. When the news came
that the bill had been passed, the factory was
decorated and illuminated and John Doulton
took his children to see the fireworks display
in Vauxhall Gardens. Doulton and Watts produced Reform flasks modelled as busts of the
leading proponents of the bill, which often
bore legends such as the one seen on this
model of Lord John Russell: he carries a scroll
inscribed 'THE True Spirit of REFORM'.
The flask, moulded to resemble Lord
Brougham, was made for a London wine and
spirit merchant, W. Firth of 13 Middle Row,
Holborn, and would have contained gin. The
Russell flask was produced for W. Sharp's
Wine & Spirit Establishment of 7 High Street,
Gravesend, whose name and address are impressed on the reverse of the bottle. **EE**

Benjamin Robert Haydon
Plymouth 1786–1846 London

647
The Reform Banquet, 1832–34

Oil on canvas, 255 × 310 cm
Private Collection
Provenance: commissioned by Lord Grey
Exhibitions: The Great Room, 26 St. James's
Street, London, 1834
Literature: George 1967, pp. 206–11

The Reform Banquet was held in Guildhall, in the City of London, on 11 August 1832, to commemorate the passing of the Reform Bill. It was a magnificent occasion, not least, according to Haydon, because of the splendour of the decorations and the gas lighting. At one end of the hall the word REFORM was spelt out in coloured gas jets, while at the other blazed a gas star; down the side of the hall were flags, and more gas stars.

Haydon's commission to paint the banquet sprang indirectly from another related enterprise. A committed supporter of the reform movement in all its aspects, he had read in May 1832 of a gathering of the Political Union at Hewhall Hill, Birmingham, held to campaign for the passing of the bill in full. Thinking this 'the finest thing in history' he set about painting it, and approached Lord Grey for his patronage. This was refused, but Grey did offer to subscribe to 'any other subject connected with Reform' and proposed that Haydon should attend and paint the banquet to be held in Guildhall when the bill was finally carried. Haydon seized on the opportunity to associate himself with what he justifiably con-

647

sidered an epoch-making event, and to promote his claims for history painting of national significance that could attract public patronage.

Haydon sketched the background of the picture in Guildhall during the day before the dinner, worked on it in the course of the evening itself, and a week later received Grey's confirmation of his commission, at 500 guineas. Subsequently he developed the heads of the individual diners – numbering nearly a hundred – through individual sittings, and the picture took a year and a half to complete. Despite its mixed reception at the time, *The Reform Banquet* retains considerable documentary value, and stands as a testament of Haydon's own intense commitment to political causes. **DBB**

Attributed to John Francis
Lincolnshire 1780–1861 London

648
Earl Grey, Lord Brougham and Lord John Russell

Marble, carved in low relief within an oval, held by a bracket inscribed EARL GREY LORD BROUGHAM LORD J. RUSSELL, surmounted with spray of oak and laurel leaves, H 64 × W 50 cm

Private Collection
Literature: Brock 1973, passim

This memorial, attributed to the unofficial sculptor of the Whig party, depicts the protagonists in the passage of the First Reform Bill. Grey was leader of the reforming Whigs who came to power pledged to parliamentary reform in November 1830. 'The principle of my Reform,' he said, 'is to prevent the necessity for revolution.' Lord Brougham was lord chancellor in his cabinet and played a leading role in rousing the country. Russell helped to draft the successive bills and to steer their passage through the Commons.

The bill that was finally passed on 4 June 1832 was the third to be introduced since March 1831 after many amendments and against a background of tension and violence in the country at large. Though many of the worst electoral anomalies were eliminated and some redistribution of seats took place to reflect new centres of population, the right to vote did not extend beyond the middle classes and there was little change in the class of member returned to parliament. Nevertheless, if the conservatives' worst fears were unrealised, they were right in anticipating that a reform bill, if passed, would serve as a precedent for future reform to a system of government which had not changed for centuries. It was a symbolic first step on the path towards universal suffrage. The Corn Law reformer, John Bright, concluded, 'It was not a good Bill, but it was a great Bill when it passed.' **CF**

648

CLUBLAND

The main prerequisites for the fashionable man about town were a healthy income and good social connections. His life centred on the London club which provided ample opportunity for gambling and drinking in the company of like-minded spirits. The rest of London catered for his sartorial, sexual and sporting proclivities, on both high and low social levels. But by the 1820s, extravagances of behaviour and dress were going out of style, to be replaced by a new sobriety, exemplified in the dignified clubs constructed along Pall Mall.

The London Dandy

Literature: Adburgham 1979, p. 77; Adburgham 1983, pp. 6, 127, 130–31, 203; Ribeiro 1986, pp. 111, 114; Walker 1988, pp. 19, 20, 35

One of the fashionable archetypes of this period is the London dandy. He is usually portrayed satirically in caricatures, novels, correspondence and diaries. A brief glance at Richard Dighton's *West End Characters* (1825) introduced the uninitiated to the absurdities of 'The Dandy Club', a group of fashionable exquisites apparently united by carefully coiffured hair, starched cravats of such height that their heads and bodies seem divorced, tightly laced waist-lines and expressions which combine *ennui* and self-regard in equal proportions. Dighton's two volumes: *City Characters* and *West End Characters* illustrate the sharp contrast between men of business whose appearance and clothes were purely functional, even old-fashioned, and those men to whom appearance was all-important.

Dandies are an early nineteenth-century species of a type of young man who, in the eighteenth century might have been a 'macaroni' of the 1760s or a 'jessamy' *c.* 1790. Both groups enjoyed bright colours and a type of precious elegance which were easy to mock and caricature. The dandy, however, eschewed bright colours in favour of a restrained elegance which, in the hands of a master such as George 'Beau' Brummell (1778–1840), was impressive in its simplicity. Less discriminating dandies were exemplars of the dictionary definition of dandy, 'One who studies ostentatiously to dress elegantly and fashionably; a fop, an exquisite'.

At the end of the eighteenth century Bond Street provided hotels and apartments for gentlemen in central London, but soon after 1800 it became established as a centre for shop-keepers and crafts required by the dandies: tailors, barbers, wigmakers, perfumers, hatters etc., all clustered in or around this one street. Some of the traders became arbiters of taste; Robert Southey parodied 'a professor in the famous Bond-street who, in lessons at half-a-guinea instructs gentlemen in the art of tying their neck-hankerchiefs in the newest and most approved style'. This anxiety about the correct arrangement of a linen or cotton cravat, an art in which Brummell and his valet were acknowledged masters, led to the satirical pamphlet *Neckclothiana* (1818) which suggested that only correctly starched and arranged neckcloths distinguished the refined man of fashion from lesser mortals. It was the relatively uniform quality of men's clothing which, in part, led to such excesses. Beau Brummell's biographer insisted that

> His chief aim was to avoid anything marked; one of his aphorisms being that the severest mortification that a gentlemen could incur was to attract observation in the street by his outward appearance . . . There was, in fact, nothing extreme about Brummell's personal appearance but his extreme cleanliness and neatness, and whatever time and attention he devoted to his dress the result was perfection; no perfumes, he used to say, but very fine linen, plenty of it, and country washing.

In his blue coat of the finest Bath wool coating, perfectly cut to fit by John Weston (or John Meyer), a pristine starched cravat, skin-tight buckskin pantaloons and shiny black boots, his only ornaments the simplest brass buttons and gold watch-chain, Brummell was the perfect dandy. Nature had been improved by art, but not excessively so.

There were many, however, like Brummell's friend the Prince of Wales, who were not as young, naturally slender, graceful, clear-complexioned and possessed of a fine head of hair and side-whiskers. It was their desire to improve on nature by corsetting tightly, using false hair, make-up and perfume and generally forgetting the need for simplicity in pursuit of elegance which led to the caricatures and satires. The apogee of the dandy was just before and just after the battle of Waterloo, a period particularly rich in caricatures (Cat. Nos. 663–65).

In the 1820s and 1830s dandies were recorded in various fashionable novels, often thinly disguised fictions based on real characters. Thomas Lister's *Granby* (1826) had a dandy hero called Trebeck, and Disraeli's *Vivien Gray* (1826/27) and Bulwer Lytton's *Pelham* (1828) created eponymous heroes who had much in common with their authors: dandies with political ambitions.

In 1828 *The Gentlemen's Magazine of Fashion, Fancy Costumes and the Regimentals of the Army* first appeared. Although not wholly concerned with matters of dress it was the first English magazine for men which emphasised this, to its compilers, crucial matter. It reinforced the major role of fine tailoring in the presentation of a London man of fashion, and his more conservative contemporaries. The best men's tailors in the early nineteenth century were London tailors, a position they retained throughout the century despite the initial cynicism of the older, more conservative men in society.

Although the dandy disappeared around 1840 his influence and his absurdities live on in caricature and literature. Those distinguished 'Victorians', like Disraeli, who had been dandies in their youth, were never allowed to forget this fact. Later in the century 'dandy' became a synonym for foolish, idle, spendthrift and dissolute behaviour, as it had been during its hey-day for certain contemporaries. **VC**

649
A Dandy
London *c.* 1795–1840

Dressing gown *c.* 1825–30; double-breasted; of Spitalfields dress fabric, made *c.* 1765
Shirt *c.* 1800; linen
Cravat; cotton cambric
Waistcoat *c.* 1795; front and collar of Spitalfields silk satin
Stockings *c.* 1820–30; black silk; woven monogram GR at top of each leg
Slippers *c.* 1820–30; cloth of silver edged, lined with salmon pink taffeta
'Wellington' boots *c.* 1840; black patent leather with black Morocco leather leg and shallow band of crimson Morocco leather lining

Gloves c. 1825–40; ivory suede
Umbrella, with cover case c. 1830–40, metal frame and bamboo handle; silk
Reproduction cravat, pantaloons and body belt, the last taken from a surviving paper pattern of George IV's 1824 body belt
London, The Museum of London
Inv. Nos. 37.100 (dressing gown); 87.194 (shirt); 59.28/9 (cravat support); 34.167/3 (waistcoat); 39.54 (stockings); A3833 (slippers); 60.131/3 (boots); 60.106/49 (gloves); 53.173 (umbrella)
Provenance: dressing gown given by Miss C. Gadsall, 1937; shirt purchased, 1987; cravat support associated with William IV given to by Mrs. M. Turner, 1959; waistcoat given by Mrs. Chamberlayne, 1934; stockings given anonymously 1939; slippers made for George IV, bought at auction in 1830 by his shoemaker Mr. White of King Street, S.W.1, sold to the London Museum; boots from a uniform of the 1st Duke of Wellington, later used by the Marquess of Crewe, by whom given to the 7th Duke of Wellington, 1944, who presented it to the Museum; gloves, given by Mrs. I. Hockstetter, 1960; umbrella formerly owned by the 1st Duke of Wellington and given by Lady Harnon, 1953
Literature: Pückler Muskau 1832, Vol. 4, pp. 47–48; Cruso, 2nd ed. 1946, p. 186

This group draws together items which might have been worn by a London dandy at any date between the late 1790s and the late 1830s. Some belonged to George IV who was a dandy in his youth and retained a lifelong delight in clothing; others to men like his brother William IV and the Duke of Wellington, who were never dandies but whose tastes were influenced by the fashions which dandies introduced.

Prince Pückler Muskau, described in a letter of June 1827 the requirements of the dandy:

As a sample of the necessities of a London dandy, I send you the following statement by my 'fashionable' washerwoman, who is employed by some of the most distinguished 'élégan[t]s', and is the only person who can make cravats of the right stiffness, or fold the breasts of shirts with plaits of the right size. An 'élégant', then, requires per week, – twenty shirts; twenty-four pocket handkerchiefs; nine or ten pairs of 'summer trousers'; thirty neck handkerchiefs (unless he wears black ones); a dozen waistcoats; and stockings, 'a discrétion'.

I see your housewifely soul aghast. But as a dandy cannot get on without dressing three or four times a day, the affair is 'tout simple', for he must appear: 1st. Breakfast toilette, – a chintz dressing gown and Turkish slippers; 2nd. Morning riding dress – a frock coat, boots and spurs; 3rd. Dinner dress – dress coat and shoes; 4th. Ball dress, with 'pumps', a word signifying shoes as thin as paper.

VC

649

650
Gentleman's Greatcoat, 1803

Made by John Weston, tailor of Old Bond Street.
Dark blue cloth coat, double-breasted with gilt metal buttons; velvet collar
London, The Museum of London
Inv. No. 56.69
Provenance: deposited with Coutts Bank in 1803 by Mr. John Gordon on behalf of an unnamed friend, it was never claimed and was presented by Messrs. Coutts to the London Museum on permanent loan, 1956

John Weston was one of the most prominent London tailors; amongst his many clients he numbered the Prince of Wales, later George IV. A letter from him to John Gordon in regard to the order mentions despatch of 'an exceed[ingly] good blue cloth great coat for your friend, made in evry (sic) respect in the best manner'. This style of greatcoat was favoured for winter and outer wear; a caricature of Nathan Meyer Rothschild in Dighton's *City Characters* (Cat. No. 673) indicates that a variant of this style was still worn in the late 1810s and early 1820s. Fine English cloth, cut with an almost military precision to fit the upper body like the proverbial glove, was a distinctive feature of the best quality London tailoring. **VC**

651
Gentleman's Tailcoat, *c.* 1825–28

Dark blue cloth coat; double-breasted with
gilt metal buttons; velvet collar with full
notched revers; no known maker but
buttons marked Jennens and Co., London
London, The Museum of London
Inv. No. 53.101/12
Provenance: studio of the artist J. L.
Meissonier; acquired by the painter F. M.
Bennett and after his death bought by the
London Museum, 1953

This type of dark blue tailcoat is a later and
more formal version of the simple coat of light
blue cloth which George 'Beau' Brummell had
designated as appropriate wear for dandies in
the early years of the century. The highly decorative buttons came from the family firm of
Joseph Jennens, located at 316 Oxford Street.
VC

652
Bonheur du Jour, 1794

Seddon and Co.
Mahogany with Wedgwood plaques,
142×92×52 cm
Marks: signed in ink under the drawer, July
17 1794 No. 4402 Seddon & Co
London, Trustees of the Victoria and Albert
Museum

Inv. No. W.40-1987
Provenance: Christie's, London, 19
November 1987, Lot 74

Seddon and Co. were in the 1790s the largest
cabinet-making firm that had ever existed in
London. They were founded in 1753 in
Aldersgate Street where they remained until
1826, but continued in business until 1868.
Comparatively little Seddon furniture has
been identified because they rarely their
pieces. The grand pieces such as those for
Windsor Castle are identified by surviving
bills, but such commissions were a small part
of their output. Most of their production consisted of plain furniture for the professional
and mercantile classes like this bonheur du
jour. The design is a simplification of a French
original, from the 1770s. **CW**

653
Pair of Chairs, 1790–1795

Seddon Shackleton and Co.
Painted satinwood, 93×54×54 cm
London, Trustees of the Victoria and Albert
Museum
Inv. Nos. W.59-1936 and W.1-1968
Provenance: Hauteville House, Guernsey
Literature: Tomlin 1972, p. 129

A surviving bill shows that these chairs are
part of a suite of eighteen supplied by Seddon
to Hauteville House, St. Peter Port, Guern-

sey. From 1790 to 1795 the firm traded under
the name of Seddon Shackleton and Co;
Thomas Shackleton was the son-in-law of
George Seddon. They cost a relatively modest
£3.13s.6d. each. Ironically these plain English
versions of French pieces, through the
medium of London publications such as the
pattern books of Hepplewhite and Sheraton,
were much admired and copied in places as
diverse as Scandinavia, Austria, Hungary,
Spain, Berlin and Munich. **CW**

654
Wine Glasses

Lead glass with polished deep cutting and
engraving, goblet H 14.2×D 10 cm; port
glass H 13.8×D 6 cm
London, The Museum of London
Inv. No. A19854 goblet; D13 port glass
Provenance: H.M. Queen Mary (D13)
Exhibitions: London, London Museum, 1970
Literature: Repository of the Arts 1823, pp.
210–13; Gray, Cherry and Richard 1987, pp.
11–18; Truman 1984, p. 27

This distinctive and unusual service of wine
glasses is engraved with the crest of the Prince
of Wales. There are a number of these glasses
in the Royal Collection. The glasses have, in
the past, been attributed to leading London

glass suppliers, particularly John Blades of 5 Ludgate Hill. His imposing showroom (p. 109), designed by Papworth, had a large glass-cutting manufactory in an adjacent building where glass blanks from a number of English manufacturers would be cut in the latest fashion.

The most recent attribution by Gray is that the glasses derive from a service supplied by Messrs. Perrin Geddes of Warrington, Cheshire, to the Corporation of Liverpool for a dinner given to the Prince of Wales and his brother, the Duke of Clarence, in 1806. The original glassware which bore the arms of Liverpool was greatly admired by the prince and he 'requested the mayor to order him a few dozen glasses of the same sort'.

The council thereupon ordered a large service to be made for the prince which was finally paid for in 1811. The attribution is based on similarities between the decanters with the Liverpool crest and more elaborate ones with the crest of the Prince of Wales. **WE**

Thomas Rowlandson
London 1757–1827 London

655
Gaming at Brooks's Club, *c.* 1810

Pen and ink and watercolour over pencil, 14.9×23.7 cm
London, The Museum of London
Inv. No. 13984
Provenance: Christie's, 20 July 1914, Lot 4
Literature: Hayes 1960, p. 21, No. 26, Fig. 16; Eeles and Spencer 1964, pp. 13–102; Ziegler and Seward 1991, pp. 25–58, 153–54, 173–75

Brooks's Club derives its name from William Brooks who ran the original club on behalf of William Almack until establishing it under his own name in 1778, in a grand neo-classical building designed by Henry Holland on the west side of St. James's Street. Originally intended purely as a social club for aristocratic young men, it soon gained a reputation for heavy gambling. The large round table depicted by Rowlandson still survives, as does the club's betting book. The scene is set in Holland's Great Subscription Room. Through the club's long connection with Charles James Fox, Brooks's became associated with the Whig cause, attracting politicians of reformist inclinations, alongside those more socially inclined, notably Beau Brummell and Scrope Davies (Cat. No. 270). When the Whigs eventually came to power in 1830, all but four members of the Grey administration were members of Brooks's. **CF**

654

656

656
Counter Box and Cover, *c.* 1805–10

Derby, Duesbury and Kean
Soft-paste porcelain, gilded and enamelled in colours, H. 13.4 cm
Marks: red crown crossed batons three dots and C; pattern number 37
London, Trustees of the Victoria and Albert Museum
Inv. No. C. 306-1935
Provenance: Herbert Allen Collection; bequeathed, 1935
Literature: Twitchett 1980, p. 239

The *trompe l'oeil* pattern is of scattered playing cards, which suggests that the piece was intended for gaming counters. The same design is also known on a spill vase and a circular dish. **HY**

657
Gambling Tokens

Ivory and stained ivory, two 3.6×3.5 cm, one D 3.8 cm
Marks:

Gs	Gs
100 on face	100 on reverse
GR	54

Gs	Gs
100 on face	100 on reverse
GR	35

239 Brook's on reverse; 25 Guineas on face

London, The Museum of London
Inv. No. A7697, A7698, A7685
Provenance: the Hon. Algernon Bourke

The square tokens were used at White's Club. Large sums of money were lost and won at London clubs, where wealthy members gathered to talk, dine and gamble. **EE**

658
Duelling Pistols, *c.* 1815

W. A. Jones, London
A pair of saw-handled flintlock duelling pistols with finely figured half stocks and chequered grips, engraved silver and blued steel furniture, bearing later oval plaques engraved: 'Presented to H. G. The Duke of Wellington K.G.' and 'By the Honorable East India Company'; 14×40 cm
Signed on lockplates and barrels: W. A. Jones London
London, The Museum of London
Inv. No. 61.192/1–2

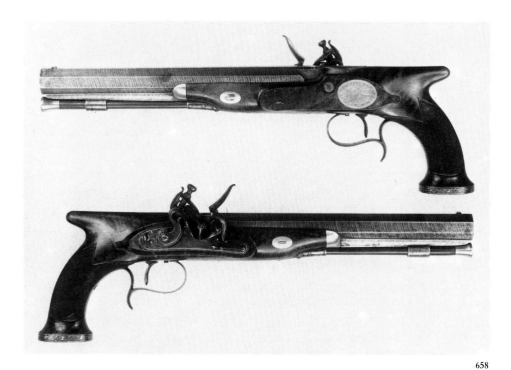

658

Royal Academy in 1814 (No. 757) as *Boxers: taken from a point of time in the late celebrated combat between the Champion and the Black*. The latter was Tom Molineux, a Negro challenger twice defeated by the champion, Tom Cribb. This work supposedly represents their second meeting on 28 September 1811 at Thistleton Gap, Leicestershire. Garrard enjoyed the patronage of the reforming Whig brewer, Samuel Whitbread II (1764–1815), who bought the plaster model of this work. **CF**

William Mulready
Ireland 1786–1863 London

661
John Thurtell, 1824

Pen and ink, 15 × 5.2 cm
London, Trustees of the Victoria and Albert
Museum
Inv. No. 6185
Exhibitions: London, Victoria and Albert
Museum, 1986, Cat. No. 84
Literature: Pointon 1978, pp. 138–39

John Thurtell was a leading member of the London Fancy, training and promoting boxers. He was first commemorated in a celebrated essay on *The Fight* by William Hazlitt (Cat. No. 459), published in the *New Monthly Magazine* in February 1822. Less than two years later, Thurtell was arrested, tried at Hertford assizes and hanged for the murder of a moneylender, confirming to many the intimate connection between crime and the prize ring. Pierce Egan wrote a gallows biography of his old acquaintance. Mulready, a keen boxer, attended the trial and made a series of sketches which indicate that Thurtell, though understandably apprehensive, at least kept up a dandified appearance.

Thurtell's body went St. Bartholomew's hospital for dissection; his skeleton, presented by the widow of the anatomy demonstrator in 1874, is in the Hunterian Museum. **JF and CF**

Literature: Atkinson 1978, p. 84, Plate 63 on p. 84

The distinctive saw-handled butt was introduced about 1805 and may have been designed to make it easier to steady the heavy pistol when aiming with an extended arm. The pistols are fitted with hair triggers and regulating set screws, and the breeches are designed to bring the touch holes nearer the powder in the chamber.

The Duke of Wellington fought a duel in 1829 with the Earl of Winchelsea at Battersea Fields In the event random shots were fired and neither man was injured. **EE**

Pierce Egan
London 1774–1849 London

659
Boxiana: Sketches of Ancient and Modern Pugilism

Published by G. Smeeton, 139 St. Martin's
Lane, Charing Cross
5 volumes, 22 × 14 cm, 1812-29
Brighton, John Ford
Literature: Reid 1971; Ford 1971

Prize-fighting, which flourished from 1780 to 1824, had its unofficial headquarters in London. Although magistrates often endeavoured to prosecute the participants (prize-fighting had been declared illegal in 1750), hundreds of bare knuckle fights took place. The sport brought together wealthy, often aristocratic patrons and the lower orders of society and crowds of up to 20,000 attended the fights, the principal venue becoming Moulsey Hurst, near Hampton Court.

Pierce Egan was a journalist who reported the fights in the *Weekly Dispatch* and reprinted and expanded these reports into *Boxiana*. Egan's work both recorded and influenced the style and fashion of the sport. It provides colourful and individual portraits of the prize-fighters themselves, probably the first sportsmen to be so intimately revealed in print. **JF**

George Garrard
1760–1826 London

660
Boxers, either 1816 or 1819

Bronze, H 69.2 cm
Inscribed: G GARRARD ARA/Oct 1
181-(?6 or 9)
London, Humphrey Whitbread
Provenance: purchased *c.* 1950
Exhibitions: London, ?British Institution,
1815, No. 239; Bedford 1961, p. 5, Cat. No.
13; London, The Museum of London, 1984,
Cat. No. 70

The original plaster model was exhibited at the

660

John Augustus Atkinson
London *c.* 1775–*c.* 1833

662
The Berners Street Hoax, 1809

Watercolour, 19 × 15.9 cm
London, The Museum of London
Inv. No. 87.57
Provenance: Ray Livingstone Murphy; P.
and D. Colnaghi and Co. Ltd.; Christie's, 19
November 1985, Lot 1; Leger Galleries Ltd.
Literature: Quarterly Review 1843, 72, p.
62–63; George 1947, p. 959, Cat. No. 11603;
Barker and Jackson 1974, p. 248

One of the most famous practical jokes ever
perpetrated in London may be seen to parody
the aggressive service trades and insatiable
consumption patterns developed in the capital
during the late Georgian period. In 1809, while
walking with a friend in an eminently respectable West End neighbourhood, the writer
and wit Theodore Hook (1788–1841) wagered
a guinea that within a week the 'nice modest
dwelling' they were passing would be the most
famous in all London. Over the next few days
Hook wrote hundreds of letters (by some
accounts as many as 1,000) to tradesmen of
every sort asking them to deliver goods to No.
54 Berners Street – the house of the luckless
Mrs. Tottenham, a wealthy widow – at a certain time on a certain day. At the appointed
hour, the street was blocked with draymen,
delivery boys and dealers clamouring to get to
the door with their goods. The lord mayor
arrived on the promise of a deathbed con-
fession of a financial fraud; the Duke of York,
Archbishop of Canterbury, governor of the
Bank of England and chairman of the East
India Company were similarly appealed to on
pious or patriotic grounds. All the while,
Hook watched the affray from the window of
a house opposite. **CF**

(Isaac) Robert Cruikshank and
George Cruikshank
London 1789–1856 London,
London 1792–1878 London respectively

663
Dandies Dressing, 1818

Etching, coloured impression, 22 × 32 cm
Published by T. Tegg, 2 November 1818
London, Trustees of the British Museum
Inv. No. 1865-11-11-2096
Literature: George 1949, Vol. 9, p. 844, No.
13062

In this satire, a fully dressed dandy remarks,

663

'Pon honor Tom, you are a charming figure!
You'll captivate the girls to a nicety!', to which
he replies, 'Do you think so Charles? – I shall
look more the thing when I get my other calf
on.'

In its more extreme forms, dandyism was an
eminently suitable subject to satire, but the
essential elements of this style of male dress,
with its emphasis on fastidiousness, on a
simple but elegant line and on meticulous
tailoring enlivened with some personal touch,
formed the basis for the development later in
the century of the Savile Row gentleman's
suit, arguably Britain's most significant contribution to the history of dress. **LS**

662

(Isaac) Robert Cruikshank
London 1786–1856 London

664
Dandy Pickpockets, diving . . . 1818

Engraving, hand-coloured, 24.5 × 35 cm
Published by T. Tegg, 111 Cheapside, 2
December 1818
London, The Museum of London
Inv. No. 91.165/2

The focus of this caricature is the countryman
studying dandy caricatures in a printshop
window, presumably intended to represent
one of Tegg's major rivals, G. Humphrey at 27
St. James's Street. The old man is being dis-
tracted by the woman dressed in the height of
fashion, while her male accomplices, both in
extreme dandy dress, 'dive' or steal from his
pockets. **CF**

George Cruikshank
London 1792–1878 London

665
Monstrosities of 1822

Engraving, 1st state, hand-coloured,
26 × 37.8 cm
Published by G. Humphrey, 27 St. James's
Street, 19 October 1822

London, The Museum of London
Inv. No. P888
Literature: Reid 1871, No. 1094; Cohn 1924, No. 1752; George 1952, Vol. 10, p. 333, No. 14438

The scene is set on the eastern side of Hyde Park, with Westmacott's statue of Achilles (Cat. No. 304) in the background. The principal characters are dressed in absurd parodies of contemporary fashion. Cruikshank also records a change in deportment. The women, who stoop in prints of around 1817, now lean backwards, daintily revealing an ankle in front. **CF**

C. Williams

666
City Scavengers Cleansing the London Streets of Impurities!!

Coloured etching, 26 × 39 cm
Published by T. Sidebottom, 96 Strand, *c.* November, 1816
London, Guildhall Library, Corporation of London
Literature: George 1949, Vol. 9, pp. 706–07, No. 12814

The scene is in front of the Mansion House, the official residence of the Lord Mayor of London. Alderman Matthew Wood, assisted by others who include Alderman Waithman (on the left) and Alderman William Curtis (in striped sailor's trousers), clear the streets of

prostitutes, pitching them unceremoniously on to a cart which is marked, 'Magdalen and Female Penitentiary Asylum'. Standing on the balustrade of the Mansion House is Sir John Silvester, the recorder. The Society for the Suppression of Vice had been founded in 1802; Silvester held harsh reactionary opinions on crime and punishment. **RH**

667 (illus. p. 599)
Lady Byron's Pelisse, 1815

Grey silk satin
Bath, Museum of Costume
Provenance: Lady Byron, by descent to the 4th Earl of Lytton (her great-great-grandson), by whom loaned to the Museum of Costume, 1969; continuing on loan by permission of the 5th Earl of Lytton
Literature: Burton and Murdoch 1974, p. 65; Langley Moore 1971, pp. 1–13; Marchand 1975, Vol. 4

Lady Byron (1792–1860) was the only daughter of Sir Ralph and Lady Milbanke of Seaham in the county of Durham; she was christened Anne Isabella. Her marriage to George Gordon, 6th Lord Byron took place at Seaham on 2 January 1815. In a letter written the following day to Lady Melbourne, Byron's friend and his wife's aunt, Lord Byron said: 'Lady Mil was a little hysterical and fine feeling and the kneeling was rather tedious and the cushions hard but upon the whole it did vastly well – and thus we set off

according to approved custom to be shut up by ourselves.' Lady Byron wore the pelisse for the journey from her parents' home to Halnaby Hall about forty miles away. The union was ill fated and Lady Byron was legally separated from her husband early in 1816, shortly after their only child Augusta Ada was born, on 10 December 1815. **RJH**

George Cruikshank
London 1792–1878 London

668
Fare Thee Well, 1816

Etching, coloured impression, forming the heading to a broadsheet, 38.1 × 25.9 cm
Published by J. Johnston, *c.* April 1816
London, Trustees of the British Museum
Inv. No. 1862-17-12-290
Literature: George 1949, Vol. 9, pp. 713–14, No. 12827

Following the separation from his wife which was legally ratified on 21 April 1816, Bryon left England for good four days later. In the previous month he had written a poem addressed to his wife in which he expressed his sadness at the failure of their marriage – *Fare Thee Well.* Originally privately printed, the verses soon appeared in the Press, together with much scurrilous comment on Byron's conduct.

In this satirical broadsheet the poem is printed in full, headed by a print in which Byron is shown standing in a rowing boat embracing Charlotte Mardyn (Cat. No. 570), the actress from Drury Lane Theatre, while two other women caress him (in fact, Byron left England in the company of Dr. John Polidori and three servants). In the distance on the right is a glimpse of Lady Byron holding their infant daughter. **LS**

FARE THEE WELL.

Isaac Robert Cruikshank
London 1789–1856 London

669
The Separation, a Sketch from the private life of Lord Iron ... 1816

Etching, uncoloured impression,
24.9×34.9 cm
Published by J. Sidebotham, April 1816
London, Trustees of the British Museum
Inv. No. 1868-8-8-8316
Literature: George 1949, Vol. 9, pp. 714–15,
No. 12828

The public hostility felt towards Byron at the
time of his separation from his wife was expressed in satires such as this. When Annabella
failed to respond to his poem *Fare Thee Well*,
fury succeeded his initial feelings of sadness
and injured pride. He felt particular rage
against his wife's old nurse, Mrs. Clermont,
whom he suspected of being the instigator of
the separation and wrote some vicious verses
aimed at her, *A Sketch from Private Life*, from
which the title of this satire was taken. The
print conflates several episodes in the separation crisis that took place between January and
April 1816. The room is strewn with references
to the scandal, including extracts from
Byron's poems and reflects the generally held
opinion that it was his philandering which
caused the crisis. **LS**

669

670
Trunk, Kid Gloves and Leather Wallet

Leather; brass studs and plate on the lid
inscribed 'Mr Scrope Davies'; remains of
wax seal on lid bearing the arms of Douglas
Kinnaird in whose bank Scrope Davies
deposited the trunk; inside trunk lid, label of
'J. and W. Lowndes, Military and Camp
Equipage Warehouse, No. 18 Haymarket';
55×32×24 cm
London, Barclays Bank on deposit
Provenance: Scrope Berdmore Davies, by
whom deposited with Ransom, Morland and
Co., 1820
Literature: Burnett 1981

In 1976, during alterations, the No. 1 Pall Mall
East branch of Barclays Bank discovered this
trunk in their vaults. It had been deposited in
1820 with Ransom, Morland and Co., a private
bank which subsequently amalgamated with
others to form Barclays. The trunk had
belonged to Scrope Berdmore Davies (1782–
1852) – one of Byron's closest friends, scholar,
gambler, drinker, womaniser and ace tennis

player – who left the country in 1820 to escape
his debts. Within the trunk were found a mass
of bills etc; correspondence from the Byron
circle; Byron manuscripts and poems by Shelley; besides drawings of Napoleon and of
Longwood, Napoleon's home on St. Helena,
made by Scrope Davies's brother, Samuel
Decimus Davies (1797–1824).

In 1816 he stood by Byron during his
separation from Annabella and visited him at
the Villa Diodati on Lake Geneva in the early
autumn. Here Byron gave him the original
manuscript of *Childe Harold's Pilgrimage*,
Canto III. In another manuscript volume is a
transcript of Byron's *The Prisoner of Chillon*
in Mary Godwin's hand (Shelley's mistress,
later wife) extensively amended by Byron, a
fair copy – also in Mary Godwin's hand – of
Shelley's *Hymn to Intellectual Beauty* and
Mont Blanc, as well as two hitherto unknown
sonnets in Shelley's hand. Further manuscript

670

correspondence reveals how Davies supported the reform section of the Whig party in
1818–20. **CF**

Pierce Egan
London 1771–1849 London

671 (illus. pp. 188–89)
Life in London

Published by Sherwood, Neely and Jones,
Peternoster Row, 1821
Octavo, bound in gold-tooled brown
morocco, 22.9×14.3 cm
Cambridge: The Graham Watson
Collection, The Master and Fellows of
Emmanuel College

Life in London provides a visitor's *vade
mecum* to the fashionable sights of London. It
delineates the haunts of the fashionable world,
of the demi-monde and the working classes.
The book, describes the London scene visited
by a man of fashion, Corinthian Tom, with his
good-natured country cousin, Jerry Hawthorn, and a whimsical Oxonian, Bob Logic.

Egan's London was a city of contrasts, of
high life and low life, west end and east end,
aristocrats and bargehands, wealth and
poverty. But is was a unified world with

673b

society inextricably connected. Egan's analogy was a Corinthian column with its decorative capital supported by its lowly, but essential base. *Life in London* reflected the vigorous democracy of the London streets, a phenomenon so often remarked by foreign visitors. The illustrations by the Cruikshank brothers, George and Robert, complement Egan's racy text, and the book became a runaway bestseller. Egan wrote a sequel, *Finish to a Life in London* and he turned the original into a theatrical extravaganza. **JF**

'Peter Quiz' D. T. Egerton

672
Fashionable Bores or Coolers in High Life

Published by Thos. McLean, 26, Haymarket, 1824
27×37 cm
London, Guildhall Library, Corporation of London
Inv. No. GR 1.1.3

This work, probably the vanity publication of an amateur, illustrates in twelve plates, designed and etched by the author, a series of embarrassing or 'boring' incidents in which a dandy could find himself. Some revolve round his financial problems: tradesmen pressing for payment of bills when he is trying to impress a lady; others deal with his sexual conduct: being subject to a paternity suit and being spotted by his fiancée emerging from a Soho brothel. **CF**

Richard Dighton
London 1795–1880 London

673
a) Characters at the West End of the Town
Published by Thomas M'Lean (sic), Repository of Wit and Humour, No. 26, Haymarket, 1825
37×27.5 cm

b) City Characters
Published by Thomas McLean, 1825
35×27 cm
(open)

London, The Museum of London
Inv. Nos. A1839/62.70
Literature: Oppé 1950, pp. 42–43, 118–21

Richard Dighton was the son of the accomplished artist and printseller Robert Dighton (1752–1815) and brother of Denis Dighton (Cat. No. 38). He specialised in profiles which, though not caricatures with the wit and ferocity of Cruikshank or Gillray, afforded purchasers the fun of identifying the characters. The Prince Regent bought many of the original drawings which are now bound in two volumes in the Royal Library.

Although Dighton made the drawings over a number of years, the publisher Thomas McLean produced two companion volumes of the etched versions in 1825, selected so as to illustrate the difference between City and West End types. The dress of the City is decidedly sombre and old fashioned. In contrast, nearly all the West End characters wear trousers with varying degrees of elegance and carry a variety of fashionable accessories. **CF**

'H. B.' John Doyle
Dublin 1797–1868

674
HB Sketches:
No. 83. John Bull or the Man Wot is Easily Led by the Nose
Lithograph, 34×25.7 cm
Published by Thos. McLean, 26 Haymarket, 10. Sep. 1830

London, The Museum of London
Inv.No.37.86/2
Literature: Fox 1988, pp. 78, 86–88

'H. B.' came from a highly respectable Dublin family, received academic art training and from the start of his career, was patronised by the gentry to delineate their families and horses, both in oils and later, using the lithographic stone. Unlike the caricaturists of earlier generations, although conservative by inclination, he never sought bribes or pensions from any political party.

The publication of another batch of his Sketches was eagerly awaited, commented upon in *The Times*, noted in political diaries of the period and collected in the great houses of the land. They mark, like Dighton's profile portraits, a change in the tenor of political prints. As Thackeray noted, they did not appeal to 'grinning good-natured mechanics', who used to crowd round the windows of print sellers (Cat. No. 624), but caused one to smile 'in a quiet, gentleman-like kind of way'. For *The Times*, there was 'humour without coarseness, and satirical representation without any extravagant or offensive deviation from resemblance'. The artist's admirers included Metternich and Wellington; Grey had his own collection and people were flattered to be depicted by him. Benjamin Robert Haydon recorded in his Diary, 'he is a man of genius. He has an instinct for expression and power of drawing, without academical cant, I never saw before; but evidently an amateur from the delicacy of his touch, or timidity rather.'

John Bull, or the Man Wot is Easily Led by the Nose (British Museum Satires, No. 16265) reflects the claim made by the editor Thomas Barnes of *The Times* that he could direct the opinion of his readers. John Bull exclaims 'What a glorious thing it is to enjoy the liberty and independence of an Englishman!' **CF**

674

Benjamin Robert Haydon
Plymouth 1786–1846 London

675 (illus. p. 602)
Waiting for The Times, the Morning after the Debate on Reform, 8 October 1831

Oil on canvas, 64×75 cm
London, Simon Jenkins, Editor of The Times
Provenance: painted either for Thomas Kearsey or for Lord Stafford
Exhibitions: London, Egyptian Hall, 1832
Literature: Olney 1952, pp. 190, 193–94; George 1967, pp. 193, 344

On 7 October the Reform Bill was defeated by the House of Lords: it was finally carried in June 1832. The setting was probably the White Horse Cellar in Piccadilly, but is reminiscent of the gentlemen's political clubs that were flourishing in London. The impatience to share a newspaper, the humorous point of the picture, arose from a shortage of newsprint that was then restricting the Press, as well as the urgent concern to read of the progress of reform.

Founded in 1785, *The Times* was London's greatest national newspaper. Printed by steam-driven machinery since 1814, it was both technologically advanced and magisterial in its views. Under the editorship of Haydon's friend Thomas Barnes, the paper was a qualified supporter of the reform movement, as was the painter himself, who contributed three letters to the paper on the subject, under the pseudonym 'Radical Junior'. **DBB**

676
Table and Chair, c. 1928–30

Designed by Decimus Burton; made by Taprell and Holland
Rosewood, table H 73.5 cm, D 61 cm, chair 94×59×61 cm
Carved: 'Athenaeum' on edge of table base and lower fore edge of seat of chair
London, The Athenaeum
Literature: Ward 1926, pp. 3–57; Nares 1951, pp. 1018–22; Jervis 1970, pp. 43–61; Cowell 1975, pp. 1–20

The Athenaeum was founded in 1824 by John Wilson Croker, M.P. and secretary to the Admiralty, as a club for 'Literary and Scientific men and followers of the Fine Arts'; trustees (not officials) of the British Museum, Royal Academicians and Life Governors of the British Institution were also allowed to join, as well bishops and judges. Though it had titled members, it was not the preserve of the

676

merely aristocratic or wealthy. Sir Humphry Davy, Sir Thomas Lawrence, Sir Francis Chantrey, Robert Smirke and Samuel Rogers were among its founder members and Michael Faraday was its first secretary.

When Carlton House was demolished in 1827, a site was procured on which to build a new clubhouse, to the design of Decimus Burton. This was completed in April 1830 in the Greek Revival style. Out of a total cost of £43,000, £6,700 was spent on the furniture, with Burton providing the designs for pieces in the principal reception rooms. Simple in outline and chaste in detail, his furniture complemented the architecture and possibly the intellectual pretensions of the members.

Other London clubs were furnished in a similar manner. As Holland and Sons, the manufacturers went on to become the largest furniture makers in nineteenth-century Britain. **CF**

Charles Barry
London 1795–1860 London

677
Travellers' Club, North Elevation, 1829

Pen and ink, 47.5×59 cm
Signed and dated: Charles Barry, 17 July, 1829

London, Public Record Office
Inv. No. MPE 787, LRRO 1/913(1)

Gentlemen's clubs were a phenomenon of the early nineteenth century. They replaced the earlier dining clubs and coffee house groups, providing a place of common resort for those of the same social class, interests or political affiliation. The Travellers' Club was founded in 1819 specifically 'to form a point of re-union for gentlemen who had travelled abroad'. Foreign travel – at least to France and Italy – had long been an element in the education of most gentlemen, but it is plain that the club was intended to cater for those with a more particular interest in foreign countries. Among the founder members were Lord Castlereagh and Lord Palmerston, both influential shapers of British foreign policy, the architect C. R. Cockerell who had made a detailed study of a wide range of Greek architecture, and W. R. Hamilton, who as secretary to Lord Elgin had supervised the shipping of the Parthenon frieze.

At first the club existed in rented accommodation, but after the demolition of Carlton House in the late 1820s a site was obtained in Pall Mall, immediately next to Decimus Burton's Athenaeum, for the building of a new clubhouse. Seven leading architects submitted competing designs and the job was awarded to Charles Barry. The building was completed in 1832. Barry broke new ground with his introduction of the Italian Renaissance style into London. **NB**

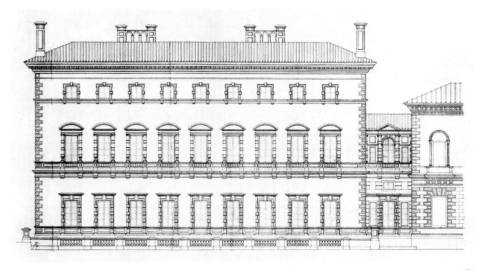

was a striking but fragile letter. Another novel style was the 'egyptian', 'sans serif' or 'grotesque', a geometrical letter with no endstrokes or serifs and no variety at all in the weight of its strokes. The 'antique', occasionally also known as 'egyptian', was a letter with all its strokes more or less the same thickness, like the 'sans serif', but with heavy block-like serifs.

There is some evidence that the adoption of these new letter forms was due to the entrepreneurial advertisers of the first decades of the nineteenth century. Among the most prominent of these were the agents for the tickets of the state lotteries, the last of which was drawn in 1826. One of the most inventive of these agents, visually and verbally, was Thomas Bish, with his printers Gye and Balne, whose handbills and posters may well have helped to transform the appearance of printed matter. **JM**

Artist unknown

678
Elevation of Front Façade of the Reform Club, *c.* 1837

Pen and ink, 52×72.5 cm
London, British Architectural Library, Drawings Collection, Royal Institute of British Architects
Inv. No. C1/4(2)
Provenance: by descent; Caryl Arthur Ransome Barry
Literature: Richardson ed. 1972, Vol. B, p. 27, No. 32, Fig. 15

The electoral defeat of the Tory party and the passing of the Reform Bill created a climate friendly to radical political groups. One of these was the Westminster Reform Club. In 1837 the club acquired an interest in a large site next to the Travellers' Club, with the intention of building clubhouse. Charles Barry was chosen as architect; his design was in the High Roman Renaissance style and a full extra storey made it the dominant building in Pall Mall. This top storey was given over to bedrooms for club members, a new development in club accommodation. The new building was opened in 1841. The club interior was fitted up with unparalleled richness and every modern convenience including central heating. The original cost estimate was £38,000, the final cost £82,000. **NB**

Lottery Bills

679

Woodcut and letterpress, 54.2×42.6 cm
Printed by W. J. Ruffy at the Farmers' Journal Office, Bridge Row, 15 July 1825
London, The Museum of London
Inv. No. Upcott Collection, Vol. 2, pp. 379 and 417

During the first two decades of the nineteenth century the appearance of commercial printing was transformed by the creation of new kinds of printing type of which the chief purpose was to attract attention and to convey information aggressively. The first of these types was the 'fat face'. Created by retaining the thin strokes but increasing the weight of the thick ones beyond all precedent. The result

Artist unknown

680
The Shoemaker's Shop, *c.* 1828

Oil on canvas, 63.5×51 cm
Cambridge, Wimpole Hall, National Trust
Inv. No. CI B85/357
Provenance: London, Leicester Galleries, from whom purchased by Captain Bambridge, 1941
Exhibitions: London, Leicester Galleries, 1941, No. 14
Literature: Souden 1991, p. 48 reproduced, p. 71

From the trade directories of the period, Edward Pattison's shoe shop opened at 129 Oxford Street in 1820, moving in 1835 to 74 Oxford Street, where it remained until the 1860s. In this unusual view for the date of a shop interior in oils, possibly the owner's wife supervises two assistants helping a boy and a female customer try on shoes. Around 1825, the fashion for plain black shoes – like the pair the lady is trying on – was imported from France and caught on, much to the dismay of English makers.

Once it lost its insalubrious association with the Tyburn gallows in 1783, Oxford Street developed as a middle-class shopping street. The ladies depicted here are fashionably dressed, the one in a light muslin dress, flower-decorated bonnet and an extravagant mantle, the other more soberly, but wearing a vivid saffron-ground shawl with a popular oriental motif. **VC and CF**

George Cruikshank
London 1798–1878 London

681
Anticipated Effects of the Tailors 'Strike' – or Gentlemen's Fashions for – 1834

Etching, hand-coloured, 27.4 × 37.4 cm
Published by George Cruikshank No 23
Myddelton Terrace Pentonville and sold by
Charles Tilt, Fleet St, 22 May 1834
London, The Museum of London
Inv. No. 66.11

Published twelve years after Cat. No. 665, the setting is the same but the fashions have changed and those on parade are reduced to rags and patches. An erstwhile dandy proudly clutches a card addressed 'LEVY Monmouth Street' – a reference to the street in Seven Dials famed 'as the only true and real emporium for second hand wearing apparel ... the burial place of the fashions,' as Dickens memorably described it in *Sketches by Boz* (1833–35).

In the 1790s the tailors possessed the strongest of all the trades unions. But by the 1820s much of the trade was in the hands of show shops selling cheap, inferior articles to order and slop shops selling ready-made goods, both exploiting cheap labour. The 1826 depression drained unemployment funds; in 1827 the union lost a strike against female labour. On the death of George IV in 1830, employers refused to adhere to the old custom of double pay during court mourning and defeated the tailors' response of a general strike. A Grand Lodge of Operative Tailors of London was formed in September 1833 to operate a closed shop, abolish outwork and piece work, limit hours and set a fixed day rate. To press their demands, the tailors went on strike at the beginning of the next brisk season in April 1834, but the Lodge's resources ran out and the strike was crushed. **CF**

Artist unknown

682
a) View in the Queen's Bazaar, London. Winter Fashions from Novr. 1833 to April 1834

Coloured aquatint, 41 × 54 cm
Published by B. Read, Pall Mall, St. James's
and 12 Hart St., Bloomsbury Square
London: Guildhall Library, Corporation of
London
Literature: Altick 1978, pp. 167–68; Wilcox 1976, pp. 107–08; Hyde 1988, pp. 112–13, 121–23; Hyde and Van der Merwe 1987, pp. 10–15

Lady Byron's Pelisse, 1815. Cat. No. 677

VIEW CARLTON TERRACE NEAR THE YORK PILLAR LONDON.

WINTER FASHIONS for 1837 & 38 by B. READ & H. BODMAN 12 Hart St. Bloomsbury Sq.t & 95 Strand LONDON also Broad Way New York AMERICA.

682b

b) View (of) Carlton Terrace near the York Pillar, London. Winter Fashions for 1837 and 38

Coloured aquatint, 42 × 56 cm
Published by B. Read and H. Bodman, 12 Hart St., Bloomsbury Square and 95 Strand, also Broadway, New York, America
London, Guildhall Library, Corporation of London
Literature: Splendid Views 1984, Plate 3

These prints are examples of topographical fashion plates issued by an enterprising Bloomsbury tailor-printmaker, Benjamin Read. The prints were directed at the *nouveaux riches* who aspired to high society. Provincial tailors paid one pound a year and received a fine aquatint showing the summer fashions, another showing the winter fashions, collections of patterns related to the fashions displayed in the plates and cutting instructions.

The prints began to be published in the mid 1820s. Isaac Robert Cruikshank was commissioned to draw some of the earliest ones. They continued to appear until the late 1840s. There were approximately forty-six in all. Right until the end they maintained their original Regency style. The figures serve as tailors' dummies, announcing the fashions of the coming season, and even showing the position of seams.

The backgrounds against which Read's figures preen themselves were selected with great care, since the clothes were intended to benefit from the association. They include the Diorama, the Pantheon, the Queen's Bazaar, Gloucester Gate, Cumberland Terrace, Regent's Park (frequently) and the various royal palaces. The popularity of zoology in the 1820s and 1830s was acknowledged: Regent's Park Zoo and the Surrey Zoological Gardens feature in at least four prints. The Colosseum is to be seen in at least five. Madame Tussaud's waxworks, wildly popular in the 1840s, provide the setting for 1842–43.

On two occasions Benjamin Read chose Oxford Street bazaars (the forerunners of the street's modern department stores) as backgrounds to his fashion plates, the Pantheon featuring in 1834–35, and the Queen's Bazaar in 1833–34. Such shopping places had existed in London since the seventeenth century when Exeter 'Change was established in the Strand. The Queen's Bazaar was established in 1828 by the goldsmith, Thomas Hamlet, on the north side of Oxford Street. In addition to the usual counters in the Great Room with their bijouterie, song sheets, inkstands, toys, framed pictures, fleecy hosiery and pastries, there was a British Diorama which rivalled the French Diorama a mile away in Regent's Park. The entrance to it can be seen on the left of the image. In June 1833 a large diorama of *Belshazzar's Feast* (Cat. No. 422) went on show. British Diorama publicity claimed it was by John Martin though, in fact, it was an unauthorised copy by Hippolyte Sebron. An infuriated Martin applied for a court order to have the exhibition halted. He failed. You can see Martin's diorama advertised on a poster down the stairs to the right in Benjamin Read's image.

The topographical background selected by Read for his winter 1837–38 fashion plate is the site of the Regent's palace, Carlton House, demolished in 1827. Pall Mall can be seen extending across the print from left to right. In 1807 it was the first street in London to be provided with gas street lighting, and gas lampposts are much in evidence. In Pall Mall, to the left of the Duke of York's Column, can be seen the United Services Club. This, and the Athenaeum clubhouse (Cat. No. 676) – the building on the right – were both designed by Decimus Burton. **RH**

Samuel Laurence
Guildford 1812–1884 London

683
Charles Dickens, 1838

Chalk, 52.7×36.4 cm
Signed and dated lower right: Samuel
Laurence 1838; and autographed 'Boz'
London, National Portrait Gallery
Inv. No. 5207
Provenance: Charles Dickens; given by
Dickens to his sister Frances Burnett; . . .
Lord Glenconner
Exhibitions: London, Royal Academy, 1838,
No. 858; Earl's Court, 1897, No. 239
Literature: Ormond 1973, Vol. 1, p. 143

By 1838 and while still in his twenties Charles Dickens (1812–69) had established himself as the country's leading novelist. His first attempts at fiction, a series of sketches of London, written for various London magazines and newspapers, was republished by John Macrone in 1836 under the title *Sketches by Boz*, with illustrations by George Cruikshank. Chapman and Hall then commissioned the young author to write a serial story to accompany etched illustrations by Robert Seymour (1798–1836); this work developed into Dickens's first novel, *The Pickwick Papers*. While *Pickwick* was still appearing in monthly parts, Dickens was already writing his second

683

novel, *Oliver Twist*, which appeared in 1837–38 with illustrations again by Cruikshank in the magazine Dickens had agreed to edit for Richard Bentley, *Bentley's Miscellany*. In April 1838 Chapman and Hall started to publish his third work *Nicholas Nickleby*, also in monthly parts. Although his publishing career largely falls outside the period covered by this exhibition, the London of nearly all his novels is the London of his youth, where his imagination continued to live.

This portrait was was considered by Dickens's brother-in-law a 'facsimile' of the man. **CF**

Charles Dickens
Portsmouth 1812–1869 Rochester

684
Autograph Manuscript Page from The Pickwick Papers, Chapter thirty-seven

23×18.5 cm
London, Trustees of the Dickens House
Museum

The success of *The Pickwick Papers* began to happen at the time of the fourth number, when the character of Sam Weller was introduced and Hablot K. Browne's illustrations appeared for the first time. Sam Weller is the archetypal cockney manservant who cheer-

fully steers his innocent master, Mr. Pickwick, through the dangerous ways of the world. He has been well trained in metropolitan life by his father, Mr. Weller, a stage coachman who, when reassured by Mr. Pickwick that his son is a model employee, replies that he is very glad to hear it for, 'I took a good deal o' pains with his eddication, sir; let him run in the streets when he was wery young, and shift for his-self. It's the only way to make a boy sharp, sir.' Here Sam tests his wits against the snobbish footmen of Bath. **CF**

'Boz' (Charles Dickens)
Portsmouth 1812–1869 Rochester

685
The Posthumous Papers of the Pickwick Club

Published by Chapman and Hall, 186,
Strand, 1836–37
Octavo, 32 pp, 4/2 etchings
London, Trustees of the Dickens House
Museum
Literature: Patten 1978, pp. 45–74

Seymour's idea to illustrate the exploits of a club of cockney sportsmen was not original: the figure of the London 'Cit' who was out of touch with the realities of country living was a stock character in literature and had recently been revived in R. S. Surtees, *Jorrocks's Jaunts and Jollities* (1831–34). The job of providing the accompanying words was offered to Dickens, who accepted, and when Seymour committed suicide after the second number, his subsidiary role quickly became the dominant, with the illustrations provided first by R. W. Buss and then by Hablot K. Browne ('Phiz') being reduced to two each number.

The form and manner of publishing *The Pickwick Papers* in twenty monthly parts from April 1836 to November 1837, at a shilling each in distinctive green wrappers, heralded a revolution in the circulation and appeal of narrative fiction. Serialisation of light humour and classic fiction in magazines was common, but the usual method of publishing newly written novels was in three volumes. Chapman and Hall had printed c. 400 copies of the first monthly number. But as circulation began to rise, they placed advance notices in the newspapers announcing when the next part would be available. This also meant that the reviews were staggered. The revealing of Boz's identity in July 1836 brought more publicity. By the end, 40,000 copies were being printed. The relative cheapness of each part democratised and enormously expanded the book-buying and book-reading public. **CF**

B. R. Haydon, *Waiting for The Times, the Morning after the Debate on Reform, 8 October 1831.* Cat. No. 675

Charles Dickens
Portsmouth 1812–1869 Rochester

686
Autograph Letter to Chapman and Hall, 1836

19×11.3 cm
London, Trustees of the Dickens House Museum
Literature: House and Storey eds. 1965, Vol. 1, pp. 129, 161, 647–62; Patten 1978, pp. 9–74

Furnivals Inn/ Saturday
D[r] Sirs,

When you have quite done counting the sovereigns, received for Pickwick, I should be much obliged to you, to send me up a few . . .

As this letter to Chapman and Hall of August 1836 suggests, Dickens's relations with his publishers were often testy, the example of his father's profligacy making him acutely conscious of money and his own rising value. Chapman and Hall had offered Dickens the job of providing the text to Robert Seymour's illustrations at 9 guineas a sheet, at a rate of one and a half sheets (sixteen pages of printed text) a month, a proposal which he gladly accepted when his marriage to Catherine Hogarth was imminent.

Once *Pickwick* was a success, however, the rate was increased and by August 1837, Chapman and Hall had agreed to pay Dickens £2,000 for all the monthly parts. They in turn cleared £14,000 on the numbers alone; more was made from the advertisements which were placed in front of the main text. Meanwhile, Dickens signed agreements in August and November 1836 with Richard Bentley to write two novels and edit a new magazine, *Bentley's Miscellany*, in which *Oliver Twist* first appeared in 1837. **CF**

687

Charles Robert Leslie
London 1794–1859 London

687
Lord and Lady Holland, Dr. Allen and William Doggett in the Library at Holland House, 1839

Oil on canvas, 57.8×73.7 cm
Private Collection
Provenance: commissioned by Henry Richard Vassall Fox, 3rd Baron Holland for his wife; given by Lady Holland to Lord Grey; by descent
Exhibitions: London, Royal Academy, 1841, No. 340; Victoria and Albert Museum, 1974, Cat. No. F3
Literature: Ilchester 1937, pp. 106–07, 245–46, 290

Leslie's conversation piece gives a unique glimpse of Whig intellectual society at home in London. Since his father died when he was one, the 3rd Lord Holland (1773–1840) was brought up and profoundly influenced by his uncle, the rakish leader of the Whig parliamentary opposition, Charles James Fox (1749–1806). Renowned for his kindness, tolerance and urbanity, Holland supported many liberal causes, including the emancipation of slaves, despite his wife's extensive plantations in the West Indies.

The first marriage of Elizabeth Vassall Fox (1770–1845) to Sir Godfrey Webster was dissolved in 1797 on the grounds of her adultery with Lord Holland, whom she married the same year. Ostracised from court, Lady Holland established herself as one of the leading hostesses of her day, drawing to her salon at Holland House the most brilliant politicians

and writers. Dr. John Allen (1771–1843) lived at Holland House as one of the family. He acted as librarian, assisted Holland and devoted any spare time to his own writings and Dulwich College, where he was warden and then master. Byron considered Allen 'the best informed and one of the ablest men he knew'. Excluded from public office until the Whigs came to power in 1830, Holland held the cabinet post of Chancellor of the Duchy of Lancaster in the Grey and Melbourne administrations. Here Lord Holland is depicted at a French writing table, while Lady Holland sits in her favourite armchair. Dr. Allen stands between them while Lady Holland's erstwhile page, William Doggett, preferred to the post of Groom of the Library, appears by the bookcases. The library was a long gallery occupying the length of the west wing on the first floor. **CF**

688a

688b

Thomas Shotter Boys
London 1803–1874 London

688
Original Views of London as it is, 1842

a) The Club Houses etc., Pall Mall
Plate 13, coloured tinted lithograph,
31.4×44.7 cm

b) Hyde Park, near Grosvenor Gate
Plate 16, coloured tinted lithograph,
24.5×46.3 cm

c) Piccadilly Looking towards the City
Plate 17, coloured tinted lithograph,
31×42 cm,

**d) Regent Street, Looking towards the
Duke of York's Column**
Plate 19, coloured tinted lithograph,
31×43 cm

e) St. Dunstans etc. Fleet Street
Plate 23, coloured tinted lithograph,
42.9×31.4 cm

London, Guildhall Library, Corporation of
London
Literature: Roundell 1974, pp. 49–52,
illustrated; Adams 1983, pp. 468–71,
No. 196

Thomas Shotter Boys was primarily an architectural perspectivist, and his understanding and love of perspective is most apparent in the series of twenty-six views entitled *London as it is*. Unlike Boys's earlier *Picturesque Architecture in Paris* series, innovatively printed in chromolithography, *London as it is* was printed in tinted lithography, and when coloured, the prints were hand coloured. The colouring of the Guildhall Library set is particularly fine; tradition has it that it was coloured by Thomas Shotter Boys himself.

The Pall Mall view shows clubhouses, stretching down the right hand side of the street like a row of Italian palazzi. In the distance is the National Gallery and St. Martin-in-the-Fields. The charm of Boys's images is that they show not only the buildings, but also the everyday life of London. On the left, workmen are seen erecting scaffolding against one of the houses.

The eastern edge of Hyde Park, towards the north end of Park Lane, is seen on a Sunday afternoon. High society is on parade. Unusually for Boys, topography takes second place. In the distance is a Grecian lodge, designed by Decimus Burton. On the right is Grosvenor House, formerly Gloucester House, the London residence of the Marquess of Westminster.

In Plate 17, we look westwards down Piccadilly towards present-day Piccadilly Circus.

688c

On the left is the entrance to Burlington Arcade and just beyond that the wall of Burlington House. The building on the extreme right is the Egyptian Hall.

Lower Regent Street is seen from Regent's Circus, today's Piccadilly Circus. In the distance is the Duke of York's Column, and on the right St. Philip's Chapel. Next door to the chapel, immediately beyond it, were the premises of Christopher Greenwood, who was responsible for the large survey of London made in 1827 (Cat. No. 2).

Boys frequently alludes to himself in his images. In the Strand his name appears on a phaeton, whilst in Regent Street the board of a sandwich-board man announces, 'Vote for Boys!' In the foreground of the Tower of London print Boys depicts himself at work sketching the scene, closely watched by two curious boys. **RH**

688d

The death of George IV marked the end of an extravagant and dissipated era at court. The new Whig administration succeeded in passing the Reform Bill in 1832, which initiated the process of dismantling aristocratic power. The burning of the Houses of Parliament and the plans for the new Palace of Westminster symbolised the process of change. The coming of the railways caused the greatest upheaval that had taken place in London since the great fire of 1666. But the speed of communications facilitated by the steam transport on land and sea contributed greatly to the country's economic might and confirmed London's status as world city.

Sir Francis Chantrey
Norton 1781–London 1841

689
King William IV, 1841

Marble bust, 84×75×29 cm
Signed and dated on back: Sir Francis
Chantrey / sculptor / 1841 London, Royal
Academy of Arts
Provenance: presented by the artist's widow
Exhibitions: Royal Academy, 1873; Royal
Academy, 1956, No. 522
Literature: Potts 1980, p. 14; Fig. 3

This bust of William IV is one of many to
derive from a portrait made by Chantrey in
1829 and exhibited at the Academy in 1831, the
year of William's coronation. The painter C.
R. Leslie described the work as a '. . . triumph
of the art. He managed to preserve a very
strong likeness, and without gross flattery
contrived to give a kingly air to it, of which
certainly honest King William had very little.'
MC

689

George Cattermole
Dickleburgh 1800–1868 London

690 *(illus. p. 608)*
**Coronation Procession of King
William IV and Queen Adelaide, 1831**

Watercolour and bodycolour, 38.7×51.8 cm
London, The Museum of London
Inv. No. A16163
Literature: Greville 1874, Vol. 2, p. 193;
Ziegler 1971, pp. 192–94

In contrast to the ostentatious coronation of
his brother ten years earlier (Cat. Nos. 00–00),
that of William IV was a modest affair costing
little over £30,000. Taking after his father, the
new king deplored needless expense, had little
sympathy with ceremony for its own sake and
was fearful of exciting further agitation in the
middle of the reform crisis. He proposed
merely to take the oath before the assembled
Lords and Commons. But the more traditionalist Tory peers persuaded him to go
through with what became known as the 'Half
Crownation' on 8 September 1831. The banquet in Westminster Hall (Cat. No. 00) was
dispensed with and no crown was hired for the
queen. Charles Greville commented in his
journal, 'The coronation went off well, and
whereas nobody was satisfied before it everybody was after it.'
  Nevertheless, in this watercolour Cattermole manages to invest the event with
glamour by virtue of his superb rendering of
the architecture of Westminster Abbey. An
engraving after the work was made by William
Woolnoth and published by H. Teesdale and
Co. Cattermole went on to contribute to John
Britton's *English Cathedrals* (1832–36) and to
illustrate Dickens' *The Old Curiosity Shop*
and *Barnaby Rudge* from *Master Humphrey's
Clock* (1841). The artist was best known for his
lively watercolours of characters and scenes
from historical romances. **CF**

Joseph Mallord William Turner
London 1775–1851 London

691
**The Burning of the Houses of
Parliament, 1834**

Watercolour, 30.2×44.4 cm
London, Tate Gallery
Inv. No. D36235, TB CCCLXIV-373
Provenance: bequeathed by the artist, 1856
Exhibitions: Washington, 1963, Cat. No. 54;
New York, 1966, Cat. No. 71; Hamburg,
1976, Cat. No. 125; The Hague, 1978–79,
Cat. No. 88; Mexico City, 1979, Cat. No.
86; Paris, 1983–84, Cat. No. 225; Cleveland,
1984, Cat. No. 10
Literature: Wilton 1979, p. 359, No. 522;
Butlin and Joll 1984, pp. 207–09, No. 359;
Wilton 1988, p. 129; Shanes 1990, p. 244

On the night of 16 October 1834 the complex
of buildings that made up the Palace of Westminster, the seat of the British parliament,
burnt to the ground. The fire was caused by
overloading the furnaces with large numbers
of wooden tally sticks, the ancient method of
recording tax payments, used from the twelfth
century until 1826. Fire spread quickly
through the buildings, many of timber-framed
construction dating back to medieval times.
Attempts to quell the blaze were useless.
When the fire was finally subdued next morning, most of the palace had been destroyed,
although Westminster Hall had been saved.
  The event was a significant one in the popular consciousness. Some commentators saw in
the fire God's displeasure with the Reform Bill
which brought greater democracy to the parliamentary system, but was bitterly opposed
by the ruling classes. Conversely, others saw a
divine reaction to parliament's recent revision
of the Poor Law. What is more clearly discernible is the sentiment of the large crowd
that watched the fire, who at times clapped
and cheered. Turner too was present, watching the fire's progress from a boat on the
Thames. He made a series of free and vibrant
watercolour sketches in a sketchbook; this
more detailed design indicates the possibility
of its use as a subject for an engraving. **RU**

691

Joseph Mallord William Turner
London 1775–1851 London

692 *(illus. p. 609)*
**The Burning of the House of Lords
and Commons, 16 October 1834, 1835**

Oil on canvas, 92×123 cm
Philadelphia, Museum of Art, McFadden
Collection
Inv. No. M'1928-001-041
Provenance: bought at the British Institution
1835 by Chambers Hall; . . . Christie's, 24
June 1909, Lot 97, bought Agnew, from
whom bought by J. H. McFadden, by whom
bequeathed to the Philadelphia Museum of
Art, 1921
Exhibitions: London, British Institution,
1835, No. 58; . . . New York, 1966, Cat. No.
9; Detroit and Philadelphia 1968, Cat. No.
120; Berlin, 1972, Cat. No. 18; London,
Royal Academy, 1974–75, Cat. No. 512;
Paris, 1983–84, Cat. No. 60

Literature: Butlin and Joll 1984, pp. 207–10,
No. 359

The spectacle and drama of the great fire
which destroyed the Houses of Parliament
was a naturally attractive subject for Turner's
art, and he exhibited two oils of the scene the
following year. The present picture was the
first of these, and shows the fire from the
south bank of the Thames at a point beside
Westminster Bridge. Turner exhibited the picture at the British Institution annual exhibition. As at the Royal Academy, the Institution
allowed exhibitors a number of 'varnishing
days' prior to the opening so that they might
make slight adjustments to their work. Whilst
usually secretive about his working methods,
Turner used these occasions to show off his
abilities of bringing in barely laid-in canvases
and working them up wholly *in situ.*

E. V. Ripingille published a detailed
account of Turner's completion of *The Burning of the Houses of Parliament:*

The picture sent in was a mere dab of several

colours, without form . . . All lookers-on
were amused by the figure Turner exhibited
in himself, and the process he was pursuing
with his picture. A small box of colours, a
very few small brushes, and vial or two,
were at his feet, very inconvenient placed;
but his short figure, stooping, enabled him
to reach what he wanted . . . Presently the
work was finished: Turner gathered his
tools . . . and then, with his face still turned
to the wall, went sidling off, without speaking a word to anybody . . . Maclise, who
stood near, remarked, 'There, that's
masterly, he does not stop to look at his
work; he knows it is done, and he is off.'

RU

G. Cattermole, *Coronation Procession of King Willian IV and Queen Adelaide,* 1831. Cat. No. 690

Charles Barry
London 1795–1860 London

693
New Houses of Parliament (or New Palace of Westminster) West elevation, 1836

Blue and brown pen and wash,
21.5×58.5 cm
London, British Architectural Library
Inv. No. S8/6 (2)
Provenance: Barry family by descent
Literature: Stanton 1971; Crook and Port 1973, pp. 573–626; Port ed. 1976

Westminster Hall and the Law Courts survived the burning of the Houses of Parliament, as did Soane's new buildings for the House of Lords to the south (Cat. No. 56). It was decided to plan an entirely new building and to choose the architect by means of a competition. There were ninety-seven entries and in February 1836 Charles Barry was declared the winner. He won in part because of the efficiency of his plan and in part because of the glamorous and convincing Gothic detail shown in his entry, which was prepared by the young A. W. N. Pugin.

By embanking the Thames a large area was gained for a modern legislature. The central range of the building contained both chambers with their lobbies in a straight line to either side of a central lobby. The libraries, committee rooms, refreshment rooms, and some residencies, including a house for the speaker, were placed on the river, or east front.

This drawing shows the façade facing Parliament Square and Westminster Abbey and demonstrates how the perpendicular architecture of the Henry VII chapel was a powerful influence on Barry's design. It also shows how Barry was seeking to impose uniformity on a very disjointed façade, by carrying the same elevation across it all, including lapping around Soane's Law Courts and the adjoining eighteenth-century buildings. Although the outlines of Barry's plan remained unchanged, innumerable revisions were made to his designs before building began and most of the details shown here were altered in the finished building: Barry never built an arcade, the Law Courts were not refronted and a central tower was added. Construction began from the river, and this west front and the towers were not completed until the 1850s. **AW**

J. M. W. Turner, *The Burning of the House of Lords and Commons, 16 October 1834*, 1835. Cat. No. 692

Augustus Welby Northmore Pugin

London 1812–1852 Ramsgate

694
New Houses of Parliament, plans, elevations and section of the King's Tower, 1836–37

Pen and wash on tracing paper,
44.8×59.8 cm
London, Society of Antiquaries
Provenance: G. Somers Clarke
Literature: Stanton 1971; Crook and Port 1973, pp. 537–626; Port ed. 1976

A. W. Pugin (Cat. Nos. 320–22, 324) had an adventurous youth, working for the theatre, passionately studying medieval art and attempting to run his own decorative arts business. By 1834, with growing family responsibilities, he was settling down and looking for openings, particularly with architects who needed help with the new Gothic Revival style. He found one in Charles Barry, for whom he designed the Gothic decorative details for King Edward VI Grammar School, Birmingham. Then between August and the end of November 1835 Pugin helped Barry with his entry for the competition for the Houses of Parliament. Barry was declared the winner in February 1836, and Pugin's next work for the project, between August 1836 and March 1837, was to prepare the drawings needed to make a detailed estimate of the building.

The *King's Tower* shows his brilliant draughtsmanship and ability to design convincing Gothic detail. The King's Tower (now called the Victoria Tower) was intended to form the entrance for the monarch, and it is still so today. The plans in Pugin's drawing show that the Tower was to be used for the storage of documents and today it holds the House of Lords Records Office. The 'Estimate Drawings' were only intended to give an impression of the final result, and all the designs were substantially altered in the finished building.

After this episode Pugin and Barry ended their collaboration until September 1844, when Barry asked Pugin to help him with the fittings for the House of Lords. From then until his early death in 1852 Pugin produced innumerable designs for internal fittings and furnishings for the Houses of Parliament. **AW**

695

Sir David Wilkie

Cults 1785–Gibraltar 1841

695
The First Council of Queen Victoria, 1838

Oil on canvas, 151.8×238.8 cm
Signed and dated: David Wilkie f 1838
Windsor Castle, H.M. Queen Elizabeth II
Provenance: painted for Queen Victoria, 1837–38; has since remained at Windsor
Exhibitions: London, Royal Academy, 1838, Cat. No. 60
Literature: Cunningham 1843, Vol. 3, pp. 226–27, 229, 233, 235, 237–39, 241–42, 252–54, 531; Millar 1969, Vol. 1, p. 144, No. 1188, Vol. 2, Plate 279

Queen Victoria appears at her Accession Council, held in the Red Saloon at Kensington Palace on 20 June 1837. In her hand is a declaration addressed 'to the Lords and others of the Council then assembled'. Before the queen near the centre stands her prime minister,

Lord Melbourne, with the first state paper signed by Her Majesty. Lower down the table are the royal dukes, the Archbishop of Canterbury, and, in front of the column at right, the Duke of Wellington. The Declaration of the Queen's Accession lies on the table, for signature by the Privy Council.

Queen Victoria began to sit for Wilkie for a state portrait at Brighton in October 1837. However, hearing of a sketch he had made at her Accession Council she ordered a picture of the occasion, giving him special sittings and advising which of her ministers and courtiers should appear with her. For the sittings, she wore a white satin dress, 'covered with gauze embroidered', instead of the black mourning dress she had actually worn at the Council.

Wilkie was obliged to work rapidly as she expected the picture to be ready for the Royal Academy exhibition the next spring. He had difficulties arranging so large a group of people, and in obtaining sittings; nor was he helped by the sitters' rather undignified scramble for position and precedence in the composition, and their insistence on appearing at their best. Court intrigue and pique per-

haps contributed to the queen's growing disillusionment with the picture once completed, and ultimately to Wilkie's fall from court favour. **DBB**

Robert Blemmel Schnebbelie

London 1790–1849 London

696
Spa Road temporary terminus, London and Greenwich Railway, 1836

Watercolour, 16.1×23.5 cm
London, The Museum of London
Inv. No. 63.66/1
Literature: Thomas 1972, pp. 11–62, Fig. 21

The opening on 8 February 1836 of the section from Deptford to Spa Road, Bermondsey of the London and Greenwich Railway, brought the first railway to London. The successful

697a

697b

scheme was launched in 1831 by a retired lieutenant-colonel of the Royal Engineers, George Thomas Landmann with the help of City men and £400,000 share capital, despite the opposition from steam-boat companies and George Shillibeer (Cat. No. 165), who had unfortunately just abandoned his central London omnibus routes in favour of a service to Greenwich and Woolwich. The railway was carried over sparsely populated marshy country by means of a brick viaduct, only necessitating evictions from dwellings in the slums near London Bridge. **CF**

John Cooke Bourne
London 1814–1896

697

a) **London & Birmingham Railway Hampstead Road Bridge, 1836**
Pencil, ink and wash with white heightening on paper, 25×42.5 cm
Signed on mount: JCB September 6 1836

b) **Park Street, Camden Town, 1836**
Pencil, ink and wash with white heightening on paper, 25×42.5 cm
Signed and dated bottom left: JCB September 17 1836

c) **Park Street, Camden Town, 1836**
Pencil, ink and wash with white heightening on paper, 25×42.5 cm
Signed and dated bottom centre: JCB September 1836

d) **Stationary engine house, Camden Town, 1837**
Pencil, ink and wash with white heightening on paper, 25.5×43 cm
Signed and dated on mount: JCB April 6 1837

York, National Railway Museum

Inv. Nos. 1990-7195, 7201, 7202, 7205
Provenance: York, National Railway Museum; acquired from British Rail (London Midland Region), 1987
Exhibitions: York, 1988

These four drawings form part of a series of seventy-five by John Cooke Bourne showing the construction of the London and Birmingham Railway. The London and Birmingham was the first main line to be built from London and was completed in 1838. The engineer was Robert Stephenson and the route was constructed to a high standard over its 112-mile length. Much was in cuttings or on embankments and no fewer than eight tunnels were built to keep it as level as possible. The views included here are all of the section from the London terminus at Euston to Camden Town, a distance of just over a mile, where the line passed through crowded suburbs before entering open countryside.

The steep descent from Camden Town to Euston meant that this was a very difficult section to build and it was constructed almost entirely in a deep cutting. High retaining walls, shown in the two views of Park Street, were needed to hold back the soft clay subsoils of north London and several bridges had to be built. The gradient was too steep for early locomotives to tackle and carriages were hauled from (and lowered to) Euston by means of cables worked from stationary engines at Camden Town. Locomotives were attached and detached at Camden and it was not until 1844, with the development of more powerful locomotives, that cable haulage was abandoned and locomotives were able to reach the terminus itself.

Bourne lived at Hatton Garden in London, less than a mile from Euston, and at first seems to have made drawings for his own interest although thirty-six were later published. The novelist Charles Dickens, who knew Camden Town well, provides a vivid account in *Dombey and Son* (1848) of the chaos that the construction of the railway brought to the suburb of 'Camberling Town'. **RD**

Thomas Talbot Bury
1811–1877

698
Six Coloured Views on the London and Birmingham Railway, from Drawings Made on the Line

Published by Ackermann and Co., 1837
Folio, 35×30 cm
London, Guildhall Library, Corporation of London
Literature: Adams 1983, p. 515, No. 230

The London and Birmingham Railway was probably the largest public work ever undertaken at that date, with the exception of the Great Wall of China. Five and a half million pounds of capital had to be raised to finance it. For some while the mile-long railway tunnel at Watford was the longest railway tunnel in the world. Yet the London terminus, Euston Station shown in Plate 1, the first of six aquatints after Bury, was initially a very modest temporary building. Soon it was to be replaced by Philip Hardwick's infinitely grander and more ambitious station building and the Euston Arch. **RH**

698

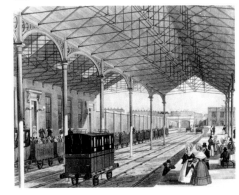

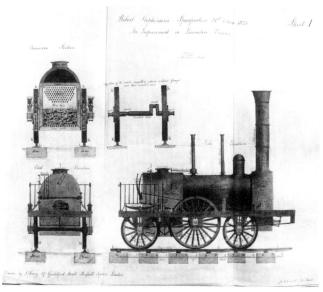

669

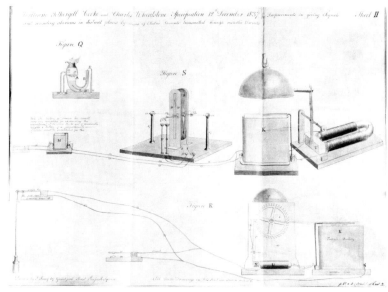

701

John Farey for Robert Stephenson

Newcastle 1803–1859 London

699
Specification for 'An Improvement in Locomotive Engines', 31 October 1833

Pen, ink and watercolour, 49.3×59.5 cm
Signed: Stephenson, Drawn by J. Farey, 67,
Guildford Street, Russell Square, London
London, Public Record Office
Inv. No. C73/44/10 Sheet I
Literature: Warner 1923, p. 79

Robert Stephenson is known primarily as a civil engineer. He worked initially with his father George managing the Stephenson locomotive factory in Newcastle and assisting his father with the Liverpool and Manchester Railway and other lines. In 1833 he was appointed engineer for the London and Birmingham Railway (Cat. No. 697) whose construction posed severe technical problems. He continued to be involved with the construction of railways both in England and abroad until his death. He is particularly famous for his bridges which include the Menai Straits Bridge, built in tubular girder form, and the Victoria Bridge over the St. Lawrence River in Montreal, Canada, at the time the longest bridge in the world.

He was also an outstanding engineer. *The Rocket* was completed under his supervision and he continued to refine and develop the steam locomotive. The 'improved' locomotive registered in this specification is similar to Stephenson's 'Planet' type locomotive but is enlarged with the addition of a pair of wheels behind the firebox. The first locomotive built

at Stephenson's Newcastle factory which incorporated these improvements was bought by the Liverpool and Manchester Railway for £1,000 and was referred to as the 'Patentee'. The design was much admired and many were made both for the domestic and overseas markets by Robert Stephenson and Co. and other manufacturers to whom they supplied drawings. **EE**

Edward Bury

Salford 1794–1858 Scarborough

700
Steam Locomotive, 1840

Model, scale 1:12, steel and brass,
50×30×85 cm
London, Trustees of the Science Museum
Inv. No. 1905–8
Literature: Ellis 1950; White 1971;
Westwood 1977; Marshall 1978

Bury and Co. built locomotives from 1829. They were the most serious competitor of Robert Stephenson and Co. and over the next twenty years built 324 locomotives. In 1837 Bury was appointed locomotive superintendent of the London and Birmingham Railway which started operating that year. Consequently, almost all their locomotives were built or designed by him until his resignation in 1846.

Bury was a champion of four-wheeled barframed locomotives and many were exported to America. He introduced engines of this

type in 1832 but they were found to oscillate at high speeds. This was remedied by introducing a pair of trailing wheels, as shown on the model, which is probably of an engine built about 1840. This engine model was purchased in 1905 for £25 from James Pattison who operated a travelling exhibition of high quality models. It was accompanied by a coloured drawing entitled *A model of a locomotive engine made by William Eaves, Derby, 1846. Drawn full size.* The tender was added in 1906, commissioned from J. Leber for £25. **PM**

John Farey

701
Specification drawing for improvements in giving signals and sounding alarms in distant places by means of Electric Currents transmitted through metallic Circuits by William Fothergill Cooke and Charles Wheatstone, 12 December 1837

Pen and ink and watercolour, 51.6×71.1 cm
Public Record Office
Inv. No. C73/81

Charles Wheatstone was born in Gloucester in 1802 but lived in London from 1806, becoming professor of experimental philosophy at King's College London in 1834. In partnership with William Cooke, an ex-army officer born

700

in 1806 in what is now part of Greater London, he developed the first practical electromagnetic telegraph.

Cooke and Wheatstone were granted a patent for their invention in June 1837. The full specification, of which this drawing forms a part, was enrolled in December. It is signed by John Farey, a consulting engineer engaged by Cooke and Wheatstone in October 1837.

The drawing illustrates two of the patent's six claims. Both are methods of 'sounding alarms in distant places'. One magnetically releases a clockwork mechanism; the other employs a local battery instead of clockwork. For the latter, relays were needed. Two types are shown, one electromagnetic and another relying on displacement of mercury by the electrolysis of water.

The patent's major claim was the use of the five magnetic needles, deflected in pairs by electromagnets, to indicate twenty letters of

the alphabet. Although it needed a five-wire connection, this system was adopted for the first commercial electric telegraph, installed in 1838 extending about 15 miles westward from London along the Great Western Railway.

Cooke and Wheatstone soon realised that it was cheaper to use a single wire controlling a single needle. This could still, using a suitable code interpreted by a skilled operator, convey any desired message. Their 'ABC' telegraph, patented in 1840, similarly needed only a single line but could be used by an untrained clerk.

The telegraphs of Cooke and Wheatstone, and the later development of telegraphs based on the work of Morse and Vail in the U.S.A., were to contribute greatly, in the period after 1840, to Britain's economic power and the confirmation of London's status as capital city and world centre. **RB**

Isambard Kingdom Brunel
Portsmouth 1806–1859 London

702
Facts 1830–1837

Manuscript, 33.1×41.5 cm (open)
London, Public Record Office
Inv. No. RAIL 1149/8
Literature: Brunel 1870, passim

The diversity and scope of the information recorded in this notebook bears witness to Brunel's driving curiosity and tenacious and highly creative intelligence. Cuttings, records of prices, measurements and calculations are interspersed with sketches and drawings, details ready to be absorbed and applied into larger schemes.

Isambard Kingdom Brunel, the only son of

THE NEW AGE

703

704

Marc Isambard Brunel, gained his early experience as a civil engineer assisting his father in the construction of the Thames Tunnel (Cat. No. 214). He became an inventor of marked originality combining his knowledge of engineering science and mathematical skills with a practical understanding of materials and mechanics, and a strong sense of design. Probably his best known and first independent design was for the Clifton Suspension Bridge which spans the Avon Gorge.

In 1833 he was appointed engineer to the Great Western Railway for whom he constructed over 1,000 miles of broad gauge track (7 feet wide as opposed to the standard narrow gauge of 4 feet 8½ inches) and the *Great Western* steamboat, the first regularly to cross the Atlantic. Contrary to current thought, Brunel insisted that resistance did not increase in proportion to the tonnage of a vessel and that high speeds could be achieved by larger ships. Amongst the data recorded in his notebook are some detailed notes on the speeds and velocity of steamboats. EE

703
Oscillating-Cylinder Marine Steam Engine, patented 1827

Working model, iron, steel, brass and copper, 89×127×61 cm
London, Trustees of the Science Museum
Inv. No. 1857-76
Provenance: Maudslay, Sons and Field, Lambeth; Patent Office Museum; Loan Collections of Scientific Apparatus, South Kensington
Exhibitions: London, Great Exhibition, 1851
Literature: Gilbert 1971; Matschoss 1901, 1978; Wagenbreth and Wächtler 1986

During the early decades of the nineteenth century, the principal English builders of marine steam engines were Maudslay, Sons and Field, who established an extensive ironworks at Lambeth Marsh and a riverside depot at Belvedere Road, Lambeth. Subsequently they occupied a second riverside yard at East Greenwich, which later became a boilerworks when shipbuilding on the Thames ceased.

Because of the low boiler pressures then prevalent, early marine steam engines had a poor power output relative to their weight. The oscillating engine represented an attempt to improve on the cumbersome and top-heavy beam engine for driving paddle wheels. Each piston rod was directly coupled to the crank, and the steam cylinders were suspended in trunnions so that they could swing to follow the throw of the cranks. The trunnions, being hollow, also served as passages for the admission of steam to the cylinders, and for its exhaust to the condenser mounted between them. Reactive forces were contained within the iron framing and not transmitted to the hull of the ship, which could thus be built lighter.

The use of these ingenious engines depended on the development of a satisfactory valve gear to control the admission and exhaust of steam. Joseph Maudslay's solution to this problem and the firm's superior workmanship made the type a success. His valve gear and other features described in his patent of 1827 are represented in this model which originated in the firm's workshop. The arrangement for working the air pump between the cylinders has been modified. **JR**

705

704
Side-Lever Marine Steam Engine, 1832

Model, scale 1:32, wood and metal, 28×38×36 cm
London, Trustees of the Science Museum
Inv. No. 1900–41
Provenance: Maudslay, Sons and Field, Lambeth; South Kensington Museum
Exhibitions: London, Great Exhibition, 1851
Literature: Verhandlungen des Vereins zur Beförderung des Gewerbfleisses in Preussen, Vol. 12, 1833

Henry Maudslay was only twelve years old when he began work at Woolwich Arsenal near London in 1783. Initially employed on the lowly task of filling cartridges, the boy rapidly showed his interest in metalworking. He was moved to the carpenters' shop two years later and then to the smithy where he acquired a reputation both for practical ability and for resource in solving problems. Those skills recommended him to Joseph Bramah, whose 'unpickable' lock depended on close engineering tolerances for its success.

By 1797 he was married with several children, and sufficiently confident of his abilities to establish his own workshop at 64 Wells Street, off Oxford Street in London, where his first order was for the ironwork of an artist's easel. Maudslay consistently advocated the importance of accuracy in making mechanical parts, and this helped to assure his success

when he began making steam engines in 1808. Two years later the increase in business obliged him to move his works to the site of a former riding school at Lambeth Marsh, south of the Thames.

The superior workmanship of Maudslay's engines caused them to be chosen for many pioneering applications in steam ships. Ships fitted with Maudslay's engines traded to ports throughout Europe and his name became widely known. In 1829 he was elected an honorary member of the Verein zur Beförderung des Gewerbfleisses in Preussen, whose technical report on his Lambeth works was published in Berlin in 1833. An engraving in that report illustrates the Main Erecting Shop; one of the two marine engines under construction at that time was this side-lever engine of 200 n.h.p. supplied by Maudslay to propel the Post Office mail packet P.S. *Dee*. The side-lever layout was first evolved in Birmingham by Boulton Watt and Co., and was particularly suited to marine use because its centre of gravity was low. Such engines continued to be built on the Rivers Clyde and Tyne until the final decades of the nineteenth century.

This model is believed to have been made by Henry Maudslay himself and his personal assistant James Nasmyth who later invented the steam hammer. It was among his firm's exhibits at the Great Exhibition in Hyde Park in 1851. It was purchased when the works closed in 1900. **JR**

705
PS Lord William Bentinck, 1832

Model, scale 1:48, wood and metal, 33.5×86.5×25.5 cm
London, Trustees of the Science Museum
Inv. No. 1866-6
Provenance: Maudslay, Sons and Field, Lambeth; Patent Office Museum; South Kensington Museum
Literature: Henry Maudslay 1949

Henry Maudslay's foundry produced in 1815 the 17 hp engine for P.S. *Richmond,* the first steam passenger vessel on the River Thames. In 1823 they engined H.M.S. *Lightning*, the first steam vessel in the Royal Navy. Always progressive and innovative, Maudslay put his skills in metal fabrication at the disposal of the East India Company when in 1831 four shallow-draught steamers were required for service on the River Ganges. *Lord William Bentinck* was the first of these, and was the first iron steamer built on the River Thames. After trials in London the steamer was dismantled and shipped to India where she was reassembled on the Ganges. With a draught of only two feet, she was able to reach almost every landing on that shallow and meandering river. Maudslay's subsequently built nine similar steamers for service in India. **JR**

BIBLIOGRAPHY

Abbey, J. R., *Scenery of Great Britain and Ireland in Aquatint and Lithography 1770-1860 from the Library of J.R. Abbey*. London, 1952.
Abbey, J. R., *Life in England in Aquatint and Lithography, 1770-1860, from the Library of J.R. Abbey*. London, 1953.
Abell, Sydney G., *A Contribution towards a Bibliography of . . . the Literature of the Art of Turning*. Society of Ornamental Turners, 1950.
Abrams, M. H., *Natural Supernaturalism: Tradition and Revolution in Romantic Literature. New York*, 1971.
Acres, W. Marston, *The Bank of England from Within 1694–1900*, 2 vols. London, 1931.
Adams, Bernard, *London Illustrated 1604–1851*. London, 1983.
Adams, Eric, *Francis Danby: Varieties of Poetic Landscape*. New Haven and London, 1973.
Adburgham, Alison, *Shopping in Style*. London, 1979.
Adburgham, Alison, *Silver Fork Society*. London, 1983.
Albion, R. G., *Forests and Sea Power*. Cambridge, Massachusetts 1926.
Alex, Reinhard, *Friedrich Erdmannsdorff 1736–1800 zum 250 Geburtstag*. Wörlitz, 1986.
Alex, Reinhard, *Schlösser und Gärten um Wörlitz*. Leipzig, 1988.
Alexander, Boyd, *Life at Fonthill 1807–1822*. London, 1957.
Alexander, David and Godfrey, Richard T., *Painters and Engraving. The Reproductive Print from Hogarth to Wilkie*. New Haven and London, 1980.
Alexander, Levy, *Memoirs of the Life and Commercial Connections, Public and Private, of the Late Benjamin Goldsmid of Roehampton*. London, 1808.
Allen, C. Robert, 'The Efficiency and Distributional Consequences of Eighteenth-century Enclosures', *Economic Journal*, vol. 92, 1982.
'Alternative Design by Wilkins for University College', *The Builder*, vol. 87, no. 3204, 2 July 1904.
Altick, Richard D., *The Shows of London*. Cambridge, Massachusetts and London, 1978.
Ambulator: or, a Pocket Companion in a tour round London. London,1796.
Anand, Vidlya Sagar and Ridley, Francis A., *The Cato Street Conspiracy*. London, 1977.
Andersen, J. A. (A. A. Feldborg), *A Dane's Excursions in Britain*. London, 1809.
Annals of the Fine Arts, 5 vols., 1817–20.
Annual Register 1817, 1821, 1831.
Armstrong, Walter, *Turner*. London, 1902.
Arundell, Dennis, *The Story of Sadler's Wells*. Newton Abbot, 2nd edn. 1978.
Ashmole, Bernard, *The Classical Ideal in Greek Sculpture, Lectures in Memory of L. Taft Semple*. Cincinnati, 1964.
Ashton, Geoffrey and Mackintosh, Iain, *Royal Opera House Retrospective 1732–1982*. London, 1982–83.
Ashton, Geoffrey, *MSS Catalogue of Paintings in the Garrick Club*.
Ashton, Thomas, S., 'The Bill of Exchange and Private Banks in Lancashire, 1790–1830', *Economic History Review*, vol. 15, 1945.
Aspinall, A., ed., *Letters of King George IV, 1812–1830*, 3 vols. London, 1938.
Aspinall, A., ed., *The Letters of Princess Charlotte 1811–1817*. London, 1949.
Aspinall, A., ed., *Correspondence of George, Prince of Wales*, 1770–1812, 8 vols. London, 1963–71.
Atkinson, A. John, *The British Duelling Pistol*. London, 1978.
Austen, Brian, 'William & Richard Gomm', in Geoffrey Beard and Christopher Gilbert, *Dictionary of English Furniture Makers 1660–1840*. Leeds, 1986.
Babbage, Charles, *Passages from the Life of a Philosopher*. London, 1864.
Baer, Winifred, Baer, Ilse and Grosskopf-Knaack, Suzanne, *Von Gotzkowsky zur KPM*. Berlin, 1986.
Balston, Thomas, *John Martin 1789–1854: His Life and Works*. London, 1947.
Banbury, Philip, *Shipbuilders of the Thames and Medway*. London, 1971.
Bank of England. An Historical Catalogue of Engravings, Drawings and Paintings in the Bank of England. London, 1928.
Bankers' Magazine, 'Obituary of Abel Smith', vol. 19, 1859; 'Obituary of Isaac Lyon Goldsmid', vol. 20, 1860.
Baquedano, Elizabeth, *Aztec Sculpture*. London, 1984.
Barker, Felix and Hyde, Ralph, *London As It Might Have Been*. London, 1982.
Barker, Felix and Jackson, Peter, *London 2000 Years of a City and its People*. London, 1974.
Barker, T. C. and Robbins, Michael, *A History of London Transport*. London, 1975.
Barrell, John, *The Dark Side of the Landscape: The Rural Poor in English Painting, 1730–1840*. New Haven and London, 1980.
Barrell, John, *The Political Theory of Painting from Reynolds to Hazlitt, 'The Body of the Public'*. New Haven and London, 1986.
Barrett, A. Franklin, and Thorpe, L. Arthur, *Derby Porcelain*. London, 1971.
Barty-King, Hugh, *The Baltic Exchange: The History of a Unique Market*. London, 1922.
Bayard, Jane, *Works of Splendor and Imagination: The Exhibition Watercolour 1770–1870*. New Haven, 1981.
Bayne-Powell, Robert, *Catalogue of Portrait Miniatures in the Fitzwilliam Museum, Cambridge*. Cambridge, 1985.
Beales, H. L., *The Early English Socialists*. London, 1933.
Beard, Geoffrey, and Gilbert, Christopher, *Dictionary of English Furniture Makers 1660–1840*. Leeds, 1986.
Beck, Hilary, *Victorian Engravings*. London, 1973.
Beckett, John, 'The Pattern of Landownership in England and Wales, 1660–1880', *Economic History Review*, 2nd ser. vol. 37, 1984.
Beckett, John and Turner, Michael, 'Taxation and Economic Growth in Eighteenth-century England', *Economic History Review*, 2nd ser. vol. 43, 1990.
Bedarida, Franois, 'Urban Growth and Social Structure in Nineteenth-century Poplar', *London Journal*, vol. 1, 1975.
Behagg, Clive, *Politics and Production in the Early Nineteenth Century*. London, 1990.
Belchem, C. John, 'Henry Hunt and the Evolution of the Mass Platform', *English Historical Review*, vol. 93, 1978.
Belchem, C. John, *'Orator Hunt': Henry Hunt and English Working-Class Radicalism*. Oxford, 1985.
Bellaigue, Geoffrey de, 'The Furnishings of the Chinese Drawing Room, Carlton House', *Burlington Magazine*, vol. 109, no.774, 1967.
Bellaigue, Geoffrey de, 'The Vulliamys and France', *Furniture History*, vol. 3, 1967.
Bellaigue, Geoffrey de, and Kirkham, Pat, 'George IV and the Furnishing of Windsor Castle', *Furniture History*, vol. 8, 1972.
Bellaigue, Geoffrey de, 'The Waterloo Elm', *Furniture History*, vol. 14, 1978.
Bellot, Hugh Hale, *University College London, 1826–1926*. London, 1929.
Benjamin, Marina, 'Elbow Room: Women Writers on Science, 1790–1840', in Marina Benjamin ed., *Science and Sensibility: Gender and Scientific Enquiry 1780–1945*. Oxford, 1991.
Bennett, Jim, 'Instrument Makers and the "Decline of Science in England": the Effects of Institutional Change on the Elite Makers of the Early Nineteenth Century', in P.R. de Clercq ed., *Nineteenth Century Scientific Instruments and their Makers*. Amsterdam, 1985.
Bentham, Jeremy, *Auto-Icon; or, farther uses of the dead to the living. A Fragment*. From the mss. of Jeremy Bentham. London, printed but unpublished, 1842.
Bentham, Jeremy, *The Handbook of Political Fallacies*. New York, 1962.
Bentley, G. E., *Blake Records*, Oxford, 1969.
Bentley, G. E., *Blake Books* , Oxford, 1977.
Berg, Maxine, *The Machinery Question and the Making of Political Economy 1815–1848*. Cambridge, 1980.
Bergot, François, *Géricault: Tout l'Oeuvre Gravé*. Rouen, 1981–82.
Berkowitz, Roger M., 'Patriotic Fund Vases: Regency Awards to the Navy', *Apollo*, vol. 113, no. 228, 1981.
Berlin, Kunstbibliothek, Katalog der Ornamentstich-Sammlung. Utrecht, 1986.
Berman, Morris, *Social Change and Scientific Organization: The Royal Institution 1799–1844*. London, 1978.
Berry, John, '"The Fracas": Echoes and Pre Echoes', *Playing Card World*, November, 1991.
Berry, John, *Catalogue of the Playing Cards of the Worshipful Company of Makers of Playing Cards*, 1991.
Bessborough, 9th Earl of, ed., *Extracts from the Correspondence of Georgiana, Duchess of Devonshire*. London, 1955.
Betthausen, Peter, *Philipp Otto Runge, Briefe und Schriffen*. Berlin, 1983.
Bickley, F., ed., *Diaries of Sylvester Douglas, Lord Glenbervie*. London, 1928.
Bicknell, Peter and Munro, Jane, *Gilpin to Ruskin, Drawing Masters and their Manuals, 1800–1860*. Cambridge, 1988.
Bindman, David, ed., *William Blake Catalogue of the Collection in the Fitzwilliam Museum, Cambridge*. Cambridge, 1970.
Bindman, David, *Blake as an Artist*. Oxford, 1977.
Bindman, David, *The Complete Graphic Works of William Blake*. London, 1978.
Bindman, David, ed., *John Flaxman, Mythology and Industry*. Munich and London, 1979.
Bindman, David, *William Blake: His Art and Times*, New Haven and Toronto, 1982–83.
Bingham, Neil, *C. A. Busby, The Regency Architect of Brighton and Hove*. London, 1991.
Binney 3rd, Edwin, *Longing for the Ideal: Images of Marie Taglioni in the Romantic Ballet*. Cambridge, Massachusetts, 1984.
Binney, J. E. D., *British Public Finance and Administration, 177492*. London, 1959.
Binney, Marcus, 'The Theatre Royal, Drury Lane', *Country Life*, vol. 148, no.3836, 1970.
Binney, Marcus, *Sir Robert Taylor: From Rococo to Neoclassicism*. London, 1984.
Binns, Richard William, *A Century of Potting in the City of Worcester*. London and Worcester, 1865.
Bird, James, *The Geography of the Port of London*. London, 1957.
Birmingham, City Museum and Art Gallery, Catalogue of Paintings. Birmingham, 1960.
Birmingham, City Museum and Art Gallery, Catalogue of the Permanent Collection of Paintings. Birmingham, 1930.
Black, Iain, 'Geography, Political Economy and the Circulation of Capital in Early Industrial England', *Journal of Historical Geography*, vol. 15, 1989.
Black, Robert A. and Gilmore, Claire G., 'Crowding Out during Britain's Industrial Revolution', *Journal of Economic History*, vol. 50, 1990.
Blair, Claude, *Three Presentation Swords in the Victoria and Albert Museum*... London, 1972.
Blanshard, Frances, *Portraits of Wordsworth*. London, 1959.
Bloom, H., *The Visionary Company*. Ithaca, New York, 1961.
Bloom, H., *Romanticism and Consciousness*. New York, 1970.
Blunt, Anthony, *The Art of William Blake*. London, 1959.
Blunt, Wilfrid, *The Art of Botanical Illustration*. London, 1950.
Blunt, Wilfrid, *The Ark in the Park. The Zoo in the Nineteenth Century*. London, 1976.
Boase, G. C. Boott, 'Francis Boott', *Dictionary of National Biography*, vol. 5. Oxford, 1886.
Boase, G. C. Boott, 'Frederic Schobel', *Dictionary of National Biography*, vol. 18. Oxford, 1897.
Boase, T. S. R., *English Art 1800–1870*. Oxford, 1959.
Boase, T. S. R., in M. H. Port ed., *The Houses of Parliament*. New Haven and London, 1976.
Boettiger, Carl August, *Reise nach Wörlitz 1797*. Wörlitz, 1982.
Bolton, Arthur T., *The Works of Sir John Soane*. London, 1924.
Bolton, Arthur T., *Portrait of Sir John Soane*. London, 1927.
Bolton, Arthur T., ed., *Lectures on Architecture by Sir John Soane*. London, 1929.
Bolton, Arthur T., *A Short Account of the Evolution of the Design of the Tivoli Corner of the Bank of England Designed by Sir John Soane, R.A. in 1804–05*. London, 1933.
Bonwitt, W., *Michael Searles: A Georgian Architect and Surveyor*. London, 1987.
Booker, John, *Temples of Mammon: The Architecture of Banking*. Edinburgh, 1990.
Booth, Charles, *Life and Labour of the People in London*, vol. 5. London, 1903.
Borsay, Peter, 'The English Urban Renaissance: the Development of Provincial Urban Culture, c.1680–c.1760', *Social History*, vol. 5, 1977.
Börsch-Supan, Helmut, *The Pfaueninsel*. Berlin, 1977.
Boswell, James, *Life of Johnson*. London, 1791.
Bourhis, Katell le, ed., *The Age of Napoleon, Costume from Revolution to Empire 1789–1815*. New York, 1989.
Bowers, Brian, *Michael Faraday and the Modern World*. Saffron Walden, 1991.
Bradley, M., and Perrin, F., 'Charles Dupin's Study Visits to the British Isles 1816–1824', *Technology and Culture*, vol. 32, no. 1, 1991.
Bradshaw, Peter, *Derby Porcelain Figures 1750–1848*. London, 1990.
Brailsford, John William, *Guide to the Antiquities of Roman Britain*. London, 1964.
Bray, Mrs. Anna Eliza, *Life of Thomas Stothard R. A.* London, 1851.
Brewer, John, *The Sinews of Power: War, Money and the English State 1688–1783*. London, 1989.
British Almanac and Companion, 1830.
Britton, John and Brayley, Edward Wedlake, *Illustrations of Public Buildings of London*, 2 vols. London, 1823–28.
Britton, John and Pugin, Augustus Charles, *Illustrations of the Public Buildings of London*, 2 vols. London, 1825–28.
Brock, Michael, *The Great Reform Act*. London, 1973.
Brooke, John, *George III*. London, 1972.
Brooks, Chris, *Mortal Remains*. London, 1989.
Brown, David Blayney, *Augustus Wall Callcott*. London, 1981.
Brown, David Blayney, *Oil Sketches from Nature*. London, 1991.
Brown, Ford K., *Fathers of the Victorians: The Age of Wilberforce*. Cambridge, 1961.
Brown, Joyce, *Mathematical Instrument-Makers in the Grocers' Company 1688–1800*. London, 1979.
Brown, Laurence, *British Historical Medals 1760–1960, Vol. I, The Accession of George III to the Death of William IV*. London, 1980.
Brown, Robert, *Prodromus Florae Novea Hollandiae et Insulae Van Diemen, Exhibens Characteres Plantarum Quas Annis 1802–1805*. London, 1810.
Brown, Sanborn C., *Benjamin Thompson, Count Rumford*. Cambridge, Massachusetts, 1979.
Brunel, Isambard, *The Life of Isambard Kingdom Brunel Civil Engineer*, London, 1870 and Newton Abbot, 1971.
Bryne, Andrew, *Bedford Square, An Architectural Study*. London, 1990.
Bullock, George, Cabinet Maker, introd. Clive Wainwright. London, 1988.
Bullock, William, *Six Months' Residence and Travels in Mexico*. London, 1824.
Burnett, T. A. J., *The Rise and Fall of a Regency Dandy. The Life and Times of Scrope Berdmore Davies*. London, 1981.
Burton, Anthony and Murdoch, John, *Byron*. London, 1974.
Bury, Shirley, 'The Lengthening Shadow of Rundells', parts 1 and 2, *Connoisseur*, vol. 161, 1966.
Bury, Shirley, Wedgwood, Alexandra and Snodin, Michael, 'The Antiquarian Plate of George IV: a Gloss on E. A. Jones', *Burlington Magazine*, vol. 121, no. 915, 1979.
Bury, Shirley, *Jewellery Gallery Summary Catalogue, Victoria and Albert Museum*. London, 1982.
Bury, Shirley and Snodin, Michael, 'The Shield of Achilles by John Flaxman, R.A.', *Art at Auction 1983–84*. London, 1984.

Bury, Shirley, *Jewellery 1789–1910,* 2 vols. Woodbridge, 1991.
Butler, Marilyn, *Jane Austen and the War of Ideas.* Oxford, 1987 edn.
Butlin, Martin, *The Paintings and Drawings of William Blake,* 2 vols. New Haven and London, 1981.
Butlin, Martin and Joll, Evelyn, *The Paintings of J.M.W. Turner,* 2 vols. New Haven and London, revised edn. 1984.
Butlin, Martin, Luther, Mollie and Warrell, Ian, *Turner at Petworth: Painter and Patron.* London, 1989.
Butlin, Martin, *William Blake 1757–1827. Tate Gallery Collection Catalogue: Volume Five.* London, 1990.
Campbell, Una, *Robes of the Realm, 300 Years of Ceremonial Dress.* London, 1989.
Cannon, John, *Parliamentary Reform 1640–1832.* Cambridge, 1973.
Cantor, Geoffrey, Gooding, David and James, Frank, *Faraday.* London, 1991.
Capper, Charles, *The Port and Trade of London.* London, 1862.
[Carey, William Paulet], *Observations on the Probable Decline or Extinction of British Historical Painting from the effects of the Church Exclusion of Paintings.* London, 1825.
Carlile, Richard, 'Address to Men of Science', 2nd edn. 1822, in Brian Simon ed., *The Radical Tradition in Education in Britain.* London, 1972.
Carlsund, R., *Anteckningar under Resor . . . 1825 till 1828.* Stockholm, 1834.
Carlton House the Past Glories of George IV's Palace. London, 1991.
Carr, Gerald L., *The Commissioners' Churches of London 1818–1837,* University of Michigan, Ph.D., 1976. University Microfilms International, 1979.
Carter, Harold B., *Sir Joseph Banks.* London, 1988.
Carter, Harold B., *Sir Joseph Banks and his House in Soho Square.* Unpublished paper read to the Soho Society, 1990.
Cassis, Youssef, *Les Banquiers de la City à l'Epoque Edouardienne.* Geneva, 1984.
Catalogue Raisonee of the Pictures now Exhibiting at the British Institution. London, 1815.
Caygill, Marjorie, *The Story of The British Museum.* London, 1981.
Chadwick, George F., *The Park and the Town: Public Landscape in the 19th and 20th Centuries.* London, 1966.
Chaffers, William, *Marks & Monograms on European and Oriental Pottery and Porcelain,* Geoffrey A. Godden ed. British Section, 15th revised edn., 2 vols. London, 1965.
Chancellor, Beresford, E., *Annals of Fleet Street.* London, 1913.
Chancellor, John, *Audubon: A Biography.* New York, 1978.
Chapman, Martin, *Thomas Hope's Vase and Alexis Decaix.* London, 1985.
Chapman, Stanley D., 'Enterprise and Innovation in the British Hosiery Industry, 1750–1850'. *Textile History,* vol. 5, 1974.
Chapman, Stanley D., 'The Foundation of the English Rothschilds: N. M. Rothschild as a Textile Merchant, 1794–1811', *Textile History,* vol. 8, 1977.
Chapman, Stanley D., 'The International Houses: the Continental Contribution to British Commerce, 1800–60', *Journal of European Economic History,* vol. 6, 1977.
Chapman, Stanley D., 'British Marketing Enterprise: the Changing Roles of Merchants, Manufacturers and Financiers, 1700–1860,' *Business History Review,* vol. 53, 1979.
Checkland, Sidney, G., 'The Birmingham Economists, 1815–50', *Economic History Review,* 2nd ser. vol. 1, 1948.
Checkland, Sidney, G., 'The Lancashire Bill System and its Liverpool Protagonists, 1810–37', *Economica,* new ser. vol. 21, 1954.
Civil Engineer and Architect's Journal, vol. 1, 1838 and vol. 6, 1842.
Clapham, John H., *The Bank of England: A History,* 2 vols. Cambridge, 1944.
Clarke, Martin Lowther, *George Grote: A Biography.* London, 1962.
Clay, Christopher, 'Lifeleasehold in the Western Countries of England, 1650–1750', *Agricultural History Review,* vol. 29, 1981.
Clayden, Peter, *The Early Life of Samuel Rogers.* London, 1887.
Clment, C., *Géricault, Etude Bibliographique et Critique.* Paris, 1879.
Clements, Paul, *Marc Isambard Brunel.* London, 1970.
Clifford, Timothy, 'Vulliamy Clocks and British Sculpture', *Apollo,* vol. 132, No. 344 new ser., 1990.
Clunn, Harold, *London Rebuilt.* London, 1924.
Clutton, Cecil and Daniels, George, *Watches.* London, 1979.
Cobbett, William, *Rural Rides.* 2 vols. London, 1912 edn.
Cohen, Bernard, I., 'Babbage and Aiken, with Notes on Henry Babbage's Gift to Harvard, and to Other Institutions, of a Portion of His Father's Difference Engine', *Annals of the History of Computing,* vol. 10, no. 3, 1988.
Cohn, Albert M., *George Cruikshank, a Catalogue Raisonn of the Work Executed 1806–1877.* London, 1924.
Colley, Linda, 'Whose Nation? Class and National Consciousness in Britain 1750–1830', *Past and Present,* no. 113, 1986.
Collins, Wilkie, *The Life of William Collins Esq., R.A.,* 2 vols. London, 1848.
Colvin, Howard, *A Biographical Dictionary of British Architects 1600–1840.* London, 1978.
Commons Journals, vols. 42–48. London, 1959.
Concise Catalogue of Oil Paintings in the National Maritime Museum. London, 1988.
Conner, Patrick, ed., *The Inspiration of Egypt.* Brighton, 1983.
Cook, Brian, 'The Townley Marbles in Westminster and Bloomsbury', in *Collectors and Collections, British Museum Yearbook,* vol. 2. London, 1977.
Cook, Brian, *The Townley Marbles.* London, 1985.
Cooney, E. W., 'The Origins of The Victorian Master Builders', *Economic History Review,* vol. 8, 1955–56.
Cope, S.R., *Walter Boyd: A Merchant Banker in the Age of Napoleon.* Gloucester, 1983.
Cope, Zachary, *The Royal College of Surgeons of England – A History.* London, 1959.
Copeland, Robert, *Spode's Willow Pattern and Other Designs after the Chinese.* London, 1980.
Copeland, Robert, *Spode and Copeland Marks and other Relative Intelligence.* London, 1992.
Cormack, Malcolm. *J.M.W. Turner, R.A. 1775–1851. A Catalogue of Drawings and Watercolours in the Fitzwilliam Museum, Cambridge.* Cambridge, 1975.
Cormack, Malcolm, *A Concise Catalogue of Paintings in the Yale Center for British Art.* New Haven, 1985.
Cormack, Malcolm, *Constable.* Oxford, 1986.
Cormack, Malcolm, *Bonington.* Oxford, 1989.
Cowell, F. R., *The Athenaeum Club and Society Life in London 1824–1974.* London, 1975.
Cox, Alwyn and Angela, 'The Rockingham Dessert Service for William IV', *Connoisseur,* vol. 188, no.156, 1975.
Cox, Alwyn and Angela, *Rockingham Pottery and Porcelain 1745–1842.* London 1983.
Cox, Trenchard, *David Cox.* London, 1947.
Coysh, A. W. and Henrywood, R. K., *The Dictionary of Blue and White Printed Pottery 1780–1880.* Woodbridge, 1982.
Cranfield, G. A., *The Press and Society.* London, 1978.
Creevey, Thomas, *The Creevey Papers,* ed. Sir Herbert Maxwell, 2 vols. London, 1904.
Cresy, E., *Encyclopaedia of Civil Engineering,* vol. 1. London, 1847.
Croft-Murray, Edward, 'An Account Book of John Flaxman R.A.', *The Walpole Society,* vol. 28, 1939–40.
Crom, Theodore R., Horological Shop Tools 1700 to 1900. Melrose, Florida, 1980.
Crook, J. Mordaunt, 'Sir Robert Smirke, A Pioneer of Concrete Construction', *Transactions of the Newcomen Society,* vol. 38, 1965–66.
Crook, J. Mordaunt, 'The Villas of Regent's Park,' *Country Life,* vol. 150, no. 144, 1968.
Crook, J. Mordaunt. 'The Pre-Victorian Architect: Professionalism and Patronage,' *Architectural History,* vol. 12, 1969.
Crook, J. Mordaunt, *The Greek Revival: Neo-Classical Attitudes in British Architecture, 1760–1870.* London, 1972.
Crook, J. Mordaunt and Port, Michael, *The History of the King's Works, Vol.6, 1782–1815,* ed. H. M. Colvin. London, 1973.
Crouzet, François, 'Les Importations d'Eaux-de-Vie et de Vins Franais en Grande-Bretagne pendant le Blocus Continental', *Annales du Midi,* 1953.
Crouzet, François, *The First Industrialists: The Problem of Origins.* Cambridge, 1985.
Crown, Patricia, 'Visual Music: E. F. Burney and a Hogarth Revival', *Bulletin of Research in the Humanities,* vol. 83, 1980.
Cruickshank, Dan, 'Gwilt Complex', *Architectural Review,* vol. 185, no.1106, 1989.
Cruickshank, Dan, and Burton, Neil, *Life in the Georgian City.* London, 1990.
Cruso, Thalassa, *Costume: London Museum Catalogue No. 5.* London, 2nd edn., 1946.
Culme, John, *Nineteenth-Century Silver.* London, 1977.
Cumberland, George, *Thoughts on Outline Sculpture, and the System that Guided the Ancient Artists in Composing their Figures and Groupes.* London, 1794.
Cummings, Frederick, 'B.R. Haydon and his School', *Journal of the Warburg and Courtauld Institutes,* vol. 26, 1963.
Cummings, Frederick, 'Phidias in Bloomsbury: B.R. Haydon's Drawings of the Elgin Marbles', *Burlington Magazine,* vol. 106, no. 736, 1964.
Cunningham, A., *The Life of Sir David Wilkie with his Journals, Tours, and Critical Remarks on Works of Art; and a Selection from his Correspondence,* 3 vols. London, 1843.
Curl, James Stevens, *The Art and Architecture of Freemasonry.* London, 1991.
D'Hancarville (P. F. Hughes), *Collection of Etruscan, Greek and Roman Antiquities from the Cabinet of the Hon ble W m Hamilton,* 4 vols. London, 1766–67.
D'Israeli, Isaac, *Curiosities of Literature.* London, 1791.
D'Israeli, Isaac, *Calamities of Authors.* London, 1812–13.
D'Sena, Peter, 'Perquisites and Casual Labour on the London Wharfside in the Eighteenth Century', *London Journal,* vol. 14, 1989.
Daniels, Stephen, 'The Implications of Industry: Turner and Leeds', *Turner Studies,* vol. 6. no.1, 1986.
Darlington, Beth, ed., *The Love Letters of William and Mary Wordsworth.* Ithaca, New York, 1981.
Darwin, Charles, *Correspondence, Volume 2: 1837–1843,* eds. Frederick Burkhardt and Sydney Smith. Cambridge, 1986.
Davidoff, Leonore, *The Best Circles: Society, Etiquette and the Season.* London, 1973.
Davis, Terence, *The Architecture of John Nash.* London, 1960.
Davis, Terence, *John Nash, the Prince Regent's Architect.* London, 1966.
Davy, John, ed., *The Collected Works of Sir Humphry Davy,* 9 vols. London 1839–40.
Davy, Sir Humphry, *A Discourse, Introductory to a Course of Lecture on Chemisty, Delivered in the Theatre of the Royal Institution on the 21st of January, 1802, Royal Institution.* London, pt. 1, 1802.
Davy, Sir Humphry, 'Some Observations and Experiments on the Papyri found in the Ruins of Herculaneum', *Philosophical Transactions of the Royal Society of London,* pt. 1, 1821.
Dawson, Frank Griffith, *The First Latin American Debt Crisis: The City of London and the 1822–25 Loan Bubble.* New Haven and London, 1990.
Dawson, Warren R., *The Nelson Collection at Lloyd's.* London, 1932.
Dawton, Nicholas, *William Wilkins, R. A., Architect and Antiquary.* London, 1985.
Day, John R, *The Story of the London Bus.* London, 1973.
Dayes, Edward, *The Works of the Late Edward Dayes.* London, 1805.
De Marly, Diana, *Costume on the Stage 16001940.* London, 1982.
De Morgan, Sophia Elizabeth, *Memoir of Augustus De Morgan.* London, 1882.
De Quincey, Thomas, *Reminiscences of the Lake Poets.* London, 1837.
De Selincourt, Ernest, ed., *Letters of William and Dorothy Wordsworth,* 6 vols. Oxford, 1935–39.
Deerr, Noel, *The History of Sugar,* 2 vols. London, 1949.
Delpierre, Madeleine, 'Les Costumes du Cour et les Uniformes Civils du Premier Empire', *Bulletin du Musée Carnavalet,* No. 2, 1958.
Delpierre, Madeleine, 'A propos d'un Manteau de Représentant du Peuple de 1798 rcemment offert au Muse du Costume', *Bulletin du Muse Carnavalet,* No.1, 1972.
Delteil, Loys, *Théodore Géricault: Le Peintre-Graveur Illustr,* vol. 18. Paris, 1924.
Derby Corporation Art Gallery, Catalogue of the Felix Joseph Collection of Derby China. Derby, 1892.
Derby Corporation Art Gallery, Catalogue of the Porcelain, Pictures, etc. forming the 'Henry Evans' Bequest. Derby, 1905.
Desmond, Adrian, 'The Making of Institutional Zoology in London, 1822–1836', *History of Science,* vol. 23, 1985.
Desmond, Adrian, 'Artisan Resistance and Evolution in Britain, 1819–1849', *Osiris,* ser. 2, 3, 1987.
Desmond, Adrian, *The Politics of Evolution: Morphology, Medicine and Reform in Radical London.* Chicago, 1989.
Dickens, Charles, *Memoirs of Joseph Grimaldi.* London, 1833.
Dickens, Charles, *The Pickwick Papers.* London, 1836–37.
Dickens, Charles, *Nicholas Nickleby.* London, 1838.
Dickens, Charles, *The Life of C. J. Mathews.* London, 1879.
Dickes, W. F., *The Norwich School of Painting.* London, 1905.
Dickinson, H. T., *Liberty and Property.* London, 1977.
Dickinson, H. T., ed., *The Political Works of Thomas Spence.* Newcastle upon Tyne, 1982.
Dickinson, H. T., *British Radicalism and the French Revolution 1789–1815.* Oxford, 1985.
Dickinson, H. T., 'The Rights of Man in Britain: From the Levellers to the Utopian Socialists' in Gnter Birtsch ed., *Grund und Freiheitsrechte von der stndischen zur sptburgerlichen Gesellschaft.* Göttingen, 1987.
Dickinson, H. W., 'Jolliffe and Banks, Contractors', *Transactions of the Newcomen Society,* vol. 12, 1933.
Dickinson, H. W. and Titley, A., *Richard Trevithick.* Cambridge, 1934.
Dickinson, H. W., *Water Supply of Greater London.* London, 1954.
Dictionary of National Biography. 63 vols. Oxford, 1885–1900.
Dinwiddy, John R., '"The Patriotic Linen-draper": Robert Waithman and the Revival of Radicalism in the City of London, 1795–1818', *Bulletin of the Institute of Historical Research,* vol. 46, 1973.
Dinwiddy, John, 'Charles Hall, Early English Socialist', *International Review of Social History,* vol. 21, 1976.
Dinwiddy, John 'Sir Francis Burdett and Burdettite Radicalism', *History,* vol. 65, 1980.
Dinwiddy, John, *From Luddism to the First Reform Bill.* Oxford, 1986.
Dobson, J., 'The Story of Caroline Crachami – the "Sicilian Dwarf"', *Annals of the Royal College of Surgeons of England,* vol. 16, 1955.
Dobson, Jessie, 'The Hunterian Museum', in Zachary Cope, *The Royal College of Surgeons of England – A History.* London, 1959.
Docklands: An Illustrated Historical Survey. London, 1986.
Dodd, George, *Days at the Factories.* London, 1843.
Drakard, D. and Holdway, P, *Spode Printed Ware.* London, 1983.
Dreyer, John Louis Emil and Turner, Herbert Hall, *History of the Royal Astonomical Society 1820–1920.* London, 1923.
Du Prey, Pierre de la Ruffinière, *Sir John Soane, The Making of an Architect.* Chicago, 1982.
Du Prey, Pierre de la Ruffinière, *Sir John Soane, Catalogue of Drawings. London,* 1985.
Dubuisson, A., *Richard Parkes Bonington,* translated with annotations by C.E. Hughes. London, 1924.
Dupin, Charles, *Notice Nécrologique sur John Rennie, Esq.* London, 1821.
Dupin, Charles, *View of the Actual State of the Military Force of Great Britain.* London, 1822.
Dupin, Charles, *Voyages dans la Grande-Bretagne, Entrepris relatives aux Services Publics 1816–19,* vol. 6. Paris, 1824.
Eaglestone. A. A., and Lockett, T. A., *The Rockingham Pottery.* Newton Abbot, revised edn., 1973.
Earnshaw, Thomas, *Explanation of Timekeepers Constructed by Mr. Thomas Earnshaw.* London, 1806.
Earnshaw, Thomas, *Longitude: An Appeal to the Public...* London, 1808.
Eastlake, C.L., *Contributions to the Literature of the Fine Arts,* 2nd ser. London, 1870
Eastlake, Lady, *John Gibson.* London, 1870.
Easton, Harry Tucker, *The History of a Banking House, Smith, Payne and Smiths.* London, 1903.
Eatwell, Ann and Werner, Alex, 'A London Staffordshire Warehouse, 1794–1825', *Journal of the Northern Ceramic Society,* vol. 8, 1991.
Ebers, John, *Seven Years of the King's Theatre.* London, 1828.
Edwards, Edward, *The Administrative Economy of the Fine Arts in England.* London, 1840.
Edwards, Michael M., *The Growth of the British Cotton Trade, 1780–1815.* Manchester, 1967.
Eeles, Henry S. and Spencer, Earl, *Brooks's 1764–1964.* London, 1964.
Egerton, Judy, *British Watercolours.* London, 1986.
Eimer, Christopher, *British Commemorative Medals.* London, 1987.
Eimer, Christopher, *The Medallic Portraits of*

the Duke of Wellington, forthcoming.
Eitner, Lorenz E. A., *Géricault: His Life and Work*. London, 1982.
Ellis, Hamilton, *Four Main Lines*. London, 1950.
Ellmers, Chris, *City and River*. London, 1989.
Elmes, James, and Shepherd, Thomas Hosmer, *Metropolitan Improvements; or London in the Nineteenth Century*, 2 vols. London, 1827–29; reprinted New York, 1978.
Elmes, James, *Survey of the Harbour and Port of London*. London, 1838.
Elster, J., *Fahrten eines Musikanten*. Frankfurt, 1854.
Erffa Helmet von, and Staley, Allen, *The Paintings of Benjamin West*, 2 vols. New Haven and London, 1986.
Errington, Lindsay, *Tribute to Wilkie*. Edinburgh, 1985.
Essick, Robert N., *William Blake Printmaker*. Princeton, 1980.
Essick, Robert N., *The Separate Plates of William Blake; a Catalogue*. Princeton, 1983.
European Magazine. London, 1824.
Evans, David Morier, *City Man and City Manners. The City; or, The Physiology of London Business; with Sketches on 'Change and the Coffee Houses*. London, 1852.
Evans, Hilary and Mary, *The Man Who Drew the Drunkard's Daughter*. London, 1978.
Evans, Robin M., *The Fabrication of Virtue. English Prison Architecture,1750–1840*. Cambridge, 1982.
Exhibition of the Society of British Artists, Suffolk Street, Pall Mall East. London, 1824.
Falk, Bernard, *Thomas Rowlandson, His Life and Art*. London, 1949.
Fanning, A. E., *Steady as She Goes: The History of the Compass Department of the Admiralty*. London, 1986.
Faraday, Michael, *Selected Correspondence*, ed. L. Pearce Williams. Cambridge, 1971.
Faraday, Michael, *Correspondence*, ed. F. A. J. L. James, vol. 1. London, 1991.
Farey, John, *Description of an Instrument for Describing Ellipses*. London, 1812.
Farey, John, *Transactions of the Society of Arts*, vol. 31, 1813.
Farington, Joseph, *The Diary of Joseph Farington*, eds. Kenneth Garlick and Alistair Macintyre vols. 1–4; ed. Kathryn Cave vols. 7–14. New Haven and London, 1978–84.
Farr, Dennis, *William Etty*. London, 1958.
Fy-Hall, Antoinette and Mundt, Barbara, *Nineteenth-Century European Porcelain*. London, 1983.
Feaver, William, *The Art of John Martin*. Oxford, 1975.
Ferriday, P., ed., *Victorian Architecture*. London, 1963.
Fetter, Frank, W., *Development of British Monetary Orthodoxy, 1797–1875*. Cambridge, Massachusetts, 1965.
Finberg, Alexander J., *The History of Turner's 'Liber Studiorum' with a New Catalogue Raisonn*. London, 1924.
Finberg, Alexander J., *Life of J. M. W. Turner, R. A.*. Oxford, 1939, revised edn., 1961.
Findlay, J. A., *The Baltic Exchange. Being a Short History of the Baltic Mercantile and Shipping Exchange from the Days of the Old Coffee House*. London, 1927.
Finer, Samuel, 'The Transmission of Benthamite Ideas', in Gillian Sutherland ed., *Studies in the Growth of Nineteenth Century Government*. London, 1972.
Finlay, George, *History of the Greek Revolution*. Oxford, 1877, reprinted London, 1971.
Fitton, Robert, S., 'Samuel and William Salte: an Eighteenth-century Linen House', *Exploration in Entrepreneurial History*, 2nd ser. vol. 6, 1969.
Fleming-Williams, Ian, *Constable: Landscape Watercolours and Drawings*. London, 1976.
Fleming-Williams, Ian, *Constable and his Drawings*. London, 1990.
Fletcher, William, *Steam Locomotion on Common Roads*. London, 1891.
Flower, Raymond and Wynn Jones, Michael, *Lloyd's of London. An Illustrated History*. London, 1974.
Forbes, Eric, *Greenwich Observatory: Origins and Early History 1675–1835*. London, 1975.
Ford, Jill, 'Ackermann's *History of Westminster Abbey*: its Publishing History and the Unique Copy in Westminster Abbey', *Book Collector*, Winter 1981.
Ford, Jill, 'Ackermann's *History of the Colleges*: an Identification of its Authors and Notes on its Publishing History', *Library*, 6th ser. vol. 6, no. 1, 1984.
Ford, John A., *Prizefighting: the Age of Regency Boximania*. Newton Abbot, 1971.
Ford, John, *Ackermann 1783–1983, the Business of Art*. London, 1983.
Forster Collection Catalogue. London, 1893.
Forster, E.M., *Marianne Thornton 1797–1887*. London, 1956.
Fox Bourne, Henry Richard, *English Merchants*. London, 1886.
Fox, Celina, 'Political Caricature and the Freedom of the Press in Early Nineteenth-century England', in George Boyce, James Curran and Pauline Wingate eds., *Newspaper History*. London, 1978.
Fox, Celina, *Londoners*. London, 1987.
Fox, Celina, 'Géricault's Lithographs of the London Poor', *Print Quarterly*, vol.5, no.1, 1988.
Fox, Celina, *Graphic Journalism in England during the 1830s and 1840s*. New York and London, 1988.
Foxley Papers, Pottery Correspondence 1812–35, unpublished. Hereford County Records Office.
Francis, A.J., *The Cement Industry 1796–1914; A History*. Newton Abbot, 1977.
Frankau, Julia, *William Ward A.R.A. and James Ward R.A.* London, 1904.
Franzero, Carlo Maria, *A Life in Exile: Ugo Foscolo in London, 1816–1827*. London, 1977.
Fraser, Edward, *The Londons of the British Fleet*. London 1908.
Frostiana. London, 1814.
Frye, Northrop, *A Study of English Romanticism*. New York, 1968.
Fulford, Roger, *The Trial of Queen Caroline*. London, 1967.
Fullerton, Peter, 'Patronage and Pedagogy: The British Institution in the Early Nineteenth Century', *Art History*, vol. 5, no. 1, 1982.
Fussell, G. E., *James Ward, R. A.* London, 1974.
Gage, John, *A Decade of English Naturalism 1810–1820*. Norwich and London, 1969.
Gage, John, ed., *The Collected Correspondence of J.M.W. Turner*. Oxford, 1980.
Gage, John, *Turner, A. Wonderful Range of Mind*. New Haven and London, 1987.
Gardeners' Magazine, vol. 16, 1840.
Garlick, Kenneth, *Sir Thomas Lawrence. A Complete Catalogue of the Oil Paintings*. Oxford, 1989.
Gash, Norman, 'After Waterloo: British Society and the Legacy of the Napoleonic Wars', *Transactions of the Royal Historical Society*, 5th ser. vol. 28, 1978.
Gatty, Richard, *Portrait of a Merchant Prince: James Morrison, 1789–1857*. Northallerton, 1976.
Gee, Brian, 'Joseph Henry's Trade with Instrument Makers in London and Paris', *Bulletin of the Scientific Intrument Company*, vol. 25, 1990.
Gentleman's Magazine, 1791, 1809, 1817, 1820, 1831, 1848.
George, Eric, *The Life and Death of Benjamin Robert Haydon 1786–1846*. Oxford, 1948 and 2nd edn., 1967.
George, M. D., *London Life in the Eighteenth Century*. London, 1930.
George, Mary Dorothy, *Catalogue of Personal and Political Satires Preserved in the British Museum*, vols. 7, 8, 9, 10, 11. London, 1942, 1947, 1949, 1952 and 1954.
George, Mary Dorothy, *Hogarth to Cruikshank: Social Change in Graphic Satire*. London, 1967.
Gibbon, Edward, *The History of the Decline and Fall of the Roman Empire*, ed. J. B. Bury, vol. 6. London, 1898.
Gibson-Jarvie, Robert, *The City of London: A Financial and Commercial History*. Cambridge, 1979.
Gigante, Marcello, ed., *Catalogo dei Papyri Erconanesi Bibliopolis*. Naples, 1979.
Gilbart, James William, *The History and Principles of Banking*. London, 1834.
Gilbert, Christopher, *The Life and Work of Thomas Chippendale*. London, 1978.
Gilbert, K. R., *Henry Maudslay, Machine Builder*. London, 1971.
Gilbert, L. F. 'The Election to the Presidency of the Royal Society in 1820', *Notes and Records of the Royal Society of London*, vol. 11, 1955.
Gilchrist, Alexander, *Life of William Etty, R. A.*, 2 vols. London, 1855.
Gilchrist, Alexander, *Life of William Blake*. London, 1863.
Gilpin, Rev. William, *Three Essays on Picturesque Beauty; on Picturesque Travel; and on Sketching Landscape*. London, 1792.
Girtin, Thomas and Loshak, David, *The Art of Thomas Girtin*. London, 1954.
Godden, Geoffrey A., *Encyclopaedia of British Pottery and Porcelain Marks*. London, 1964 and later editions.
Godden, Geoffrey A., *Chamberlain-Worcester Porcelain*. Woodbridge and London, 1982.
Golden, Jacqueline, *A List of the Papers and Correspondence of George Bellas Greenough*. London, 1981.
Goldman, Paul, *Sporting Life: An Anthology of British Sporting Prints*. London, 1983.
Golinski, Jan, 'Humphry Davy and the "Lever of Experiment"', in Homer Le Grand ed., *Experimental Inquiries*. Dordrecht, 1990.
Golt, Jean, 'Beauty and Meaning on Richmond Hill: New Light on Turner's Masterpiece of 1819', *Turner Studies*, vol. 7, no.2, 1987.
Goodfield, June, 'Some Aspects of English Physiology 1780–1840', *Journal of the History of Biology*, vol. 2, 1969.
Gooding, David and James, Frank, eds., *Faraday Rediscovered*. London, 1965 and 1985.
Goodway, David, *London Chartism, 1838–48*. Cambridge, 1982.
Gordon, Alden and Dchery, Maurice, 'The Marquis de Marigny's Purchases of English Furniture and Objects', *Furniture History*, vol. 25, 1989.
Gough, B. G., 'Dr. Syntax, Rowlandson's Popular Schoolmaster, in Print and Porcelain', *Antique Collector*, vol. 38, 1967.
Gould, Nathaniel, *Historical Notice of the Commercial Docks*. London, 1844.
Gould, Rupert T., *The Marine Chronometer: Its History and Development*. London, 1923.
Graves, Algernon, 'The British Institution', *Art-Journal*, vol. 72, 1910.
Gray, Cherry and Richard, 'The Prince's Glasses: Some Warrington Cut Glass, 1806–11', *Journal of the Glass Association*, vol 2, 1987.
Green, Henry and Wigram, Robert, *Chronicles of Blackwall Yard Part 1*. London, 1881.
Greenacre, Francis and Stoddard, Sheena, *Bristol: The Landscape. The Watercolours of Samuel Jackson*. Bristol, 1983.
Greenacre, Francis, *Francis Danby, 1793–1861*. Bristol and London, 1988.
Greeves, Ivan S., *London Docks 1800–1980, a Civil Engineering History*. London, 1980.
Grego, Joseph, *Rowlandson the Caricaturist*, 2 vols. London, 1880.
Greville, Charles C. F., *A Journal of the Reigns of King George IV and King William IV*, ed. Henry Reeve, 3 vols. London, 1874.
Griffin, Josiah, *History of the Surrey Commercial Docks*. London, 1877.
Griffith Dawson, Frank, *The First Latin American Debt Crisis*. New Haven and London, 1990.
Grigson, Geoffrey and Buchanan, Handasyde, *Thornton's Temple of Flora*. London, 1956.
Grigson, Geoffrey, *Samuel Palmer: The Visionary Years*. London, 1947.
Grimwade, Arthur G., *London Goldsmiths 1697–1837; Their Marks and Lives from the Original Registers at Goldsmiths' Hall and other Sources*. London, 1990.
Grote, Harriet, *The Personal Life of George Grote*. London, 1873.
Grundy, Reginald C., *James Ward R.A.: His Life and Works with a Catalogue of his Engravings and Pictures*. London, 1909.
Gunnis, Rupert, *Dictionary of British Sculptors 1660–1851*. London, 1953.
Guthrie, Tyrone, *A Life in the Theatre*. London, 1960.
Hackett, James H., *King Richard III, Edmund Kean's Performance, as recorded by James H. Hackett*, ed. Alan S. Downer. London, 1959.
Hackwood, F.W., *The Life and Times of William Hone*. London, 1912.
Hadfield, Charles and Skempton, A. W.,*William Jessop, Engineer*. Newton Abbot, 1979.
Halevy, Elie, *The Growth of Philosophic Radicalism*. London, 1972.
Halfpenny, Pat, *English Earthenware Figures 1740–1840*. Woodbridge, 1991.
Hall, Peter, G., 'The East London Footwear Industry: an Industrial Quarter in Decline', *East London Papers*, vol. 5, 1962.
Hall, Peter, G., *The Industries of London since 1861*. London, 1962.
Halls, Zillah, *Coronation Costume and Accessories 1685–1953*. London, 1973.
Hambly, M., *Drawing Instruments 1580–1980*. London, 1988.
Hamlyn, Robin, *The Vernon Collection*. London, forthcoming 1993.
Hardie, Martin, *Water-Colour Painting in England*, 3 vols. London, 1966–68.
Harley, J. B., *Christopher Greenwood, Country Mapmaker and His Worcestershire Map of 1822*. Worcester, 1962.
Harris, John, de Bellaigue, Geoffrey and Millar, Oliver, *Buckingham Palace*. London, 1968.
Harrison, J. F. C., *The Second Coming. Popular Millenarianism 1780–1850*. London, 1979.
Harrison, Michael, *London beneath the Pavement*. London, new edn., 1971.
Harte, Negley Boyd, 'The Growth and Decay of a Hosiery Firm in the Nineteenth Century', *Textile History*, vol. 8, 1977.
Harte, Negley and North, John, *The World of University College London, 1828–1978*. Portsmouth, 1978; *18281990* revised edn., 1991.
Hartman, G. H., *Wordsworth's Poetry, 1787–1814*. New Haven and London, 1964.
Hartmann, J.B., Canova, *Thorvaldsen and Gibson, English Miscellany*. London, 1955.
Harwood, Elain, and Saint, Andrew, *Exploring England's Heritage: London*. London, 1991.
Haskell, Francis and Penny, Nicholas, *Taste and the Antique*. New Haven and London, 1981.
Haslem, John, *The Old Derby China Factory: The Workmen and Their Productions*. London, 1876.
Hatfield, C. and Skempton, A. W., *William Jessop, Engineer*. London,1979.
Haydon, Benjamin Robert, *Explanation of the Picture of the Mock Election, which Took Place at the King's Bench Prison, July 1827*. London, 1828.
Haydon, Benjamin Robert, *Autobiography and Memoirs*, ed. Tom Taylor, 3 vols. London, 1853, new edn. with introduction by Aldous Huxley, 1926.
Haydon, Benjamin Robert, *Autobiography*, ed. Edmund Blunden. Oxford, 1927.
Haydon, Benjamin Robert, *The Diary of Benjamin Robert Haydon*, ed. William Bissell Pope, 5 vols. Cambridge, Massachusetts, 1960–63.
Haydon, Benjamin Robert, *Neglected Genius, The Diaries of Benjamin Haydon 1808–1846*, ed. John Joliffe. London, 1990.
Hayes, John, *A Catalogue of Watercolour Drawings by Thomas Rowlandson in the London Museum*. London, 1960.
Hayes, John, *Catalogue of Oil Paintings in the London Museum*. London. 1970.
Hayes, John, *Rowlandson: Watercolours and Drawings*. London, 1972.
Hays, J. N., 'Science and Brougham's Society', *Annals of Science*, vol. 20, 1964.
Hays. J. N., 'The London Lecturing Empire, 1800–50', in Ian Inkster and Jack Morrell eds., *Metropolis and Province: Science in British Culture 1750–1850*. London, 1983.
Hayward, Helena and Kirkham Pat, *William and John Linnell, Eighteenth Century London Furniture Makers*. London, 1980.
Hazlitt, William 'On My First Acquaintance with the Poets', *The Liberal*, 1823.
Hazlitt, William, *The Spirit of the Age*. London 1825.
Hazlitt, William, *Selected Writings*, ed. and introd. Ronald Blythe. London, 1970.
Heim, Carol, E., and Mirowski, Philip, 'Interest Rates and Crowding Out during Britain's Industrial Revolution', *Journal of Economic History*, vol. 47, 1987.
Heleniac, Kathryn Moore, *William Mulready*. New Haven and London, 1980.
Henry Maudslay 1771–1831 and Maudslay, Sons & Field, a commemorative brochure. London, 1949.
Herrmann, Luke, *Turner Prints: the Engraved Work of J. M. W. Turner*. Oxford, 1990.
Hibbert, Christopher., *George IV 1762–1811*. London, 1972.
Hibbert, Christopher, *George IV 1811–1830*. London, 1973.
Hichberger, Joany, 'Captain Jones of the Royal Academy', *Turner Studies*, vol. 3, no.1, 1983.
Hichberger, Joany, *Images of the Army: the Military in British Art 1815–1914*. London, 1988.
Hidy, Ralph, W., *The House of Baring in American Trade and Finance: English Merchant Bankers at Work, 1763–1861*. Cambridge, Massachusetts, 1949.
Hildyard, R. J. C., *Browne Muggs: English Brown Stoneware*. London, 1985.
Hill, Alan G., *The Letters of William and Dorothy Wordsworth, vol. 3: The Later Years, Part 1, 1821–1828*. Oxford, 1978.
Hill, Draper, *Fashionable Contrasts: Caricatures of James Gillray*. Oxford, 1966.
Hilton, Boyd, *Corn, Cash and Commerce: The Economic Policies of the Tory Governments, 1815–30*. Oxford, 1977.
Hilts, Victor, 'Alliis exterendum, or, the Origins of the Statistical Society of London', *Isis*, vol. 69, 1978.
Himmelheber, Georg, *Biedermeier Furniture*. London, 1974.
Hirsch, Erhard, 'Erdmannsdorffs Kultur- und Kunstpädagogisches Wirken', in *Friedrich Erdmannsdorff 17361800 zum 250 Gerburstag*.

Wörlitz, 1986.
Hoare, Prince, *Extracts from a Correspondence with the Academies at Vienna and St. Petersburg*. London, 1802.
Hoare, Prince, *Academic Correspondence, 1803, Containing Extracts, No. 2, from a Correspondence with the Academies of Vienna and St. Petersburg*. London, 1804.
Hoare, Prince, *An Inquiry into the Requisite Cultivation and Present State of the Arts of Design in England*. London, 1806.
Hoare, Prince, *Academic Annals of Painting, Sculpture and Architecture*. London, 1809.
Hoare, Prince, *Epochs of the Arts, Including Hints on the Use and Progress of Painting and Sculpture in Great Britain*. London, 1813.
Hobhouse, Hermione, *Thomas Cubitt*. London, 1971.
Hobhouse, Hermione, *A History of Regent Street*. London, 1975.
Hobson, Robert Lockhart, *British Museum Department of British and Mediaeval Antiquities. Catalogue of the Collection of English Pottery*. London, 1903.
Hoffmann, Friedrich Gottlob, *Neues Verzeichnis und Muster-Charte des Meubles-Magazin*. Leipzig, 1981.
Holcomb, Adele, ' "Indistinctness is my fault". A Letter about Turner from C. R. Leslie to James Lenox', *Burlington Magazine*, vol.114, no. 833, 1972.
Holcomb, Adele M., *John Sell Cotman*. London, 1978.
Hole, Robert, *Pulpits, Politics and Public Order in England 17601832*. Cambridge, 1989.
Holland, Henry, *Lectures on Paintings*. London, 1848.
Hollis, Patricia, *The Pauper Press: A Study in Working-class Relations of the 1830s*. Oxford, 1970.
Holmes, Martin, *Stage Costume*. London, 1965.
Holtzapffel, C., *Turning and Mechanical Manipulation*, vol. 2. London, 1846.
Hone, J. Ann, *For the Cause of Truth: Radicalism in London 1796–1821*. Oxford, 1982.
Honey, W. B., *Old English Porcelain*. London, 1948.
Honour, Hugh, *Cabinet Makers and Furniture Designers*. London, 1969.
Hope, Thomas, *Household Furniture and Interior Decoration Executed from Designs by Thomas Hope*. London, 1807.
Hope, Thomas, *An Historical Essay on Architecture*. London, 1835.
Hoppit, Julian, 'Attitudes to Credit in Britain, 1680–1790', *Historical Journal*, vol. 33, 1990.
Horne, Jonathan, *A Collection of Early English Pottery, Part 6*. London, 1986.
Horne, Jonathan, *A Collection of Early English Pottery, Part 7*. London, 1987.
Horsefield, J. Keith, 'The Bankers and the Bullionists in 1819', *Journal of Political Economy*, vol. 57, 1949.
Hoskin, Michael, 'Astronomers at War: South v. Sheepshanks', *Journal for the History of Astronomy*, vol. 20, 1989.
Houfe, Simon, 'To Market, To Market', *Country Life*, vol. 184, no. 47, 1990.
House, Madeline, and Storey, Graham, *The Letters of Charles Dickens*, vol. 1. Oxford, 1965.
Howard, Seymour, 'Winckelmann's Daemon: the Scholar as Critic, Chronicler and Historian', *Antiquity Restored, Essays on the Afterlife of the Antique*. Vienna, 1990.
Howarth, David, *Lord Arundel and his Circle*. London, 1986.
Howell, Margaret J., *Byron Tonight*. Windlesham, 1982.
Howgego, James Laurence, *Printed Maps of London, c. 1553–1850*. Folkestone, 1978.
Howse, Humphrey D., 'The Royal Astronomical Society Instrument Collection, 18271985', *Quarterly Journal of the Royal Astronomical Society*, vol. 27, 1986.
Hubbard, Geoffrey, *Cooke and Wheatstone and the Invention of the Electric Telegraph*. London, 1965.
Hubbard, Hesketh, *An Outline History of the Royal Society of British Artists: Part I, 18231840, The Foundation and Early Years*. London, 1937.
Hudson, Pat, *The Genesis of Industrial Capital: A Study of the West Riding Textile Industry, c. 17501850*. Cambridge, 1986.
Huish, R., *Life of Henry Hunt Esq*. London, 1835–36.
Hulton, Paul and Smith, Lawrence, *Flowers in Art from East and West*. London, 1979.
Hunt, Leslie B., 'The Mystery of the Galvanic Goblet', *Burlington Magazine*, vol. 126, no. 975, 1984.
Hunting, Penelope, *Cutlers Gardens*. London, 1984.
Hussey, Christopher, *The Picturesque. Studies in a Point of View*. London, 1927.
Hutchison, Sidney, *The History of the Royal Academy*. London, 1968.
Hyde, Ralph, 'Wellington's Downfall and the Reformist Donkey', *British History Illustrated*, 1976.
Hyde, Ralph, *The Rhinebeck Panorama of London*. London, 1981.
Hyde, Ralph, *The Regent's Park Colosseum*. London, 1982.
Hyde, Ralph, 'Robert Havell Junior, Artist and Aquatinter', in Robin Myers and Michael Harris eds., *Maps and Prints: Aspects of the Print Trade*, Oxford, 1984.
Hyde, Ralph, and van der Merwe, Pieter, 'The Queen's Bazaar', *Theatrephile*, vol. 2, no. 8, 1987.
Hyde, Ralph, *Panoramania! The Art and Entertainment of the 'All-Embracing View'*. London, 1988.
Hyman, Anthony, *Charles Babbage: Pioneer of the Computer*. Oxford, 1982.
Ilchester, Earl of, *Chronicles of Holland House 1820–1900*. London, 1937.
Inkster, Ian, 'Science and Society in the Metropolis', *Annals of Science*, vol. 34, 1977.
Irwin, David, *English Neo-Classical Art*. London 1966.
Jackson, Gordon, *The History and Archaeology of Ports*. Tadworth, 1983.
Jackson, Peter, *George Scharf's London. Sketches and Watercolours of a Changing City, 1820–50*. London, 1987.
Jackson, Robert V., 'Growth and Deceleration in English Agriculture, 1660–1790', *Economic History Review*, 2nd ser. vol. 38, 1985.
Jagger, Cedric, *Royal Clocks: The British Monarchy and its Timekeepers 1300–1900*. London, 1983.
James Ward, exhibition catalogue. Arts Council of Great Britain, 1960.
James, Philip, *Early Keyboard Instruments from their Beginnings to the year 1820*. London, 1930.
James, T. G. H., *The British Museum and Ancient Egypt*. London, 1981.
James. J. G., 'Ralph Dodd, the Very Ingenious Schemer', *Transactions of the Newcomen Society*, vol. 47, 1974–76.
Jenkins, Ian, 'James Stephanoff and the British Museum', *Apollo*, vol. 121, no. 277, March, 1985.
Jenkins, Ian, 'Adam Buck and the Vogue for Greek Vases', *Burlington Magazine*, vol. 130, no. 1023, 1988.
Jenkins, Ian, 'Acquisition and Supply of Casts of the Parthenon Sculptures by the British Museum, 18351939', *Annual of the British School of Archaeology at Athens*, vol. 85, 1990.
Jenkins, Ian, *Archaeologists and Aesthetes: The Sculpture Collections of the British Museum in the Nineteenth Century*. London, 1992.
Jervis, Simon, 'Holland and Sons and the Furnishing of the Athenaeum', *Furniture History*, vol. 6, 1970.
Jervis, Simon, 'The Pryor's Bank Fulham. Residence of Thomas Baylis Esquire F.S.A. An Illustration of the Preservation of Ancient Works by their Application to Modern Purposes', *Furniture History*, vol. 10, 1974.
Jervis, Simon, *The Penguin Dictionary of Design and Designers*. London, 1984.
Jervis, Simon, 'Introduction: Europe, America and England', *Art and Design in Europe and America 1800–1900*. London, 1987.
Johnson, Richard, 'Educating the Educators: Experts and the State 1833–9', in A. P. Donajgrodzki ed., *Social Control in Nineteenth Century Britain*. London, 1977.
Johnson, Samuel, *Lives of the Poets*. London, 1779–81.
Jokelson, Paul, Sulphides. *The Art of Cameo Incrustation*. New York, 1968.
Jones, Alfred E., *The Gold and Silver of Windsor Castle*. London, 1911.
Journal der Moden, 1786; Journal des Luxus und der Moden, 1787–1812; Journal fr Literatur, Luxus und Mode, 1814–1827. Weimar, 188690; Leipzig, 1791–1827.
Jucker, H. *Das Bildnis im Blätterkelch*. Basel, 1961.
Kaellgren, Peter, 'Lady Conyngham's silver gilt in the Royal Ontario Museum', *Burlington Magazine*, vol. 134, no. 1071, 1992.
Kaiser, Paul, *Das Haus am Baumgarten*, vol. 1. Weimar, 1980.
Kauffmann, C.M., *John Varley 1778–1842*. London, 1984.
[Keith, Arthur], *Hunterian and other Pictures in the Museum Collection of the Royal College of Surgeons*. London, *c.* 1930.
Kellet, John R., 'The Breakdown of Guild and Corporation Control over the Handicraft and Retail Trade in London', *Economic History Review*, 2nd ser. vol. 10, 1957–58.
Kelly, Alison, *The Story of Wedgwood*. London, 1962 edn.
Kenworthy-Brown, John, 'The Third Earl of Egremont and Neo-Classical Sculpture', *Apollo*, vol. 105, no. 183, 1977.
Keynes, Geoffrey, *A Bibliography of William Blake*. London, 1921.
Keynes, Geoffrey ed., *The Complete Writings of William Blake*. Oxford, 1957, 1966, and new edn., 1977.
King, Charles R., 'Site of the First Passenger Steam Railway in the World', *The Locomotive*, 14 June 1930.
King, Henry C. and Millburn, John, *Geared to the Stars: the Evolution of Planetariums, Orreries and Astronomical Clocks*. Bristol, 1978.
King, Henry C., *The History of the Telescope*. New York, 1979.
Kirk, *Outlines from the Figures and Compositions upon the Greek, Roman and Etruscan vases of the late Sir William Hamilton; drawn and engraved by the late Mr. Kirk*. London, 2nd edn., 1814.
Kitson, Sydney D., *The Life of John Sell Cotman*. London, 1937.
Knight's Cyclopaedia of London, 1851. London, 1851.
Knight, Richard Payne, *An Analytic Inquiry into the Principles of Taste*. London, 1805.
[Knight, Richard Payne], 'The Works of James Barry Esq., Historical Painter', *Edinburgh Review*, vol. 16, 1810.
Kratz, Annette-Isabell, *Altonaer Möbel des Rokoko und Klassizismus*. Hamburg, 1988.
Lacqueur, Thomas W., 'The Queen Caroline Affair: Politics as Art in the Reign of George IV', *Journal of Modern History*, vol. 54, 1982.
Lamb, Charles, *Selected Prose*, ed. Adam Phillips. London, 1985.
Lambourne, Lionel and Hamilton, Jean, *British Watercolours*. London, 1980.
Lampe, David, *The Tunnel: The Story of the World's First Tunnel under a Navigable River*. London, 1963.
Landers, John, 'Mortality and Metropolis: the Case of London 1675–1825', *Population Studies*, vol. 41, 1987.
Landseer, John, ed., *Review of Publications of Art*. London, 1808.
Langley Moore, Doris, *Guidebook to the Museum of Costume*. Bath, 1965.
Langley Moore, Doris, 'Byronic Dress'. *Costume*, no. 5, 1971.
Larrabee, Stephen, *English Bards and Grecian Marbles*. New York, 1943.
Lavessière, Sylvain and Michel, Régis, *Géricault*. Paris, 1991.
Law, A.D., *St. Mary's Infant School*. London, 1978.
Lawrence, Christopher, 'The Power and the Glory: Humphry Davy and Romanticism', in Andrew Cunningham and Nicholas Jardine eds., *Romanticism and the Sciences*. Cambridge, 1990.
Lawrence, Jon, *From Counting-House to Office: The Transformation of London's Central Financial District, 16931871*. Unpublished study for the Centre for Metropolitan History, University of London, 1991.
Lee, Charles E., 'Early Railways in Surrey', *Transactions of the Newcomen Society*, vol. 21, 1940–41.
Lee, Charles E., 'Early Railways in Surrey', *The Railway Gazette*, 1944.
Lee, Charles E., *St. Pancras Church and Parish*. London, 1955.
Lee, Charles E, *The Horse Bus as a Vehicle*. London, 1962.
Lee, Charles E., 'A Family of Architects: The Inwoods of St. Pancras', *Camden History Review*, vol. 4, 1976.
Lees-Milne, James, *William Beckford*. Tisbury, 1986.
LeFanu, William, *A Catalogue of the Portraits and other Paintings, Drawings and Sculpture in the Royal College of Surgeons of England*. London, 1960.
Leighton-Boyce, J. A. S. L., *Smiths and Bankers, 1658–1958*. London, 1958.
Lemmerich, Jost, *Michael Faraday 1791–1867; Erforcher der Elektrizitt*. Munich, 1991.
Lennie, C., *Landseer, Victorian Paragon*. London, 1976.
Leslie, C. R., *Autobiographical Recollections*, edited with a prefatory essay on Leslie as an artist, and selections from his correspondence by Tom Taylor, 1860, 2 vols; reissued with a new introduction by Robin Hamlyn. Wakefield, 1978.
Leslie, C. R., *Memoirs of the Life of John Constable*, ed. Jonathan Mayne London, 1951.
Letters from Albion to a Friend on the Continent, written in the years 1810, 1811, 1812, and 1813. London, 1814.
Levy, Martin, 'George Bullock's Partnership with Charles Fraser, 1813–1818, and the Stock-in-Trade Sale, 1819', *Furniture History*, vol. 25, 1989.
Levy, Martin, 'Napoleon's Fauteuil de Malade. A New Identification', *Apollo*, vol. 133, no. 351, 1991.
Levy, Michael, *Sir Thomas Lawrence*. London, 1979.
Lievre, Audrey le, 'Herbstrewer to the King'. *Country Life*, vol. 181, no. 7, 1987.
Lillywhite, Bryant, *London Coffee Houses*. London, 1963.
Liscombe, R. W., 'The Commencement of Real Art', *Apollo*, vol. 103, no. 167, 1976.
Liscombe, R. W., *William Wilkins, 17781839*. Cambridge, 1980.
'List of Pictures and Patrons 1808–27'. William Collins mss. notebook, Victoria and Albert Museum. London, 1848.
Lister Raymond, ed., *The Letters of Samuel Palmer*, 2 vols. Oxford, 1974.
Lister, Raymond, *The Paintings of Samuel Palmer*. Cambridge, 1985.
Lister, Raymond, *Catalogue Raisonné of the Works of Samuel Palmer*. Cambridge, 1988.
Lister, Raymond, *British Romantic Painting*. Cambridge, 1989.
Lockhart, J. G., *Memoirs of the Life of Sir Walter Scott, Bart.*, 7 vols. Edinburgh and London, 1837–38.
London's Roll of Fame, 1757–1884. London, 1884.
Longo Auricchio, Francesca, 'Lesperienza Napoletanas de Davy'. *Proceedings of the XIX International Congress of Papyrology*. Cairo, 1989, forthcoming.
Loudon, J. C., *The Suburban Gardener and Villa Companion*. London, 1838.
Lubbock, Basil, *Old East Indiamen. The Blackwall Frigates*. London, 1922.
Lukacher, Brian, 'Phantasmogoria and Emanations: Lighting Effects in the Architectural Fantasies of Joseph Michael Gandy', *A. A. Files*, vol. 4, 1983.
Lukacher, Brian, 'John Soane and his Draughtsman Joseph Michael Gandy', *Daedalus*, September 1987.
Lyles, Anne and Perkins, Diane, *Colour into Line: Turner and the Art of Engraving*. London, 1989.
Lyson, Daniel, *The Environs of London*, 2nd edn., vol. 1. London, 1811.
Lytton, Edward Bulwer, *England and the English*. London, 1833.
MacDougall, Philip, *Royal Dockyards*. London, 1982.
Mace, Rodney, *Trafalgar Square*. London, 1976.
Mackay, David, *In the Wake of Cook: Exploration, Science and Empire, 1780–1801*. London, 1985.
Mackintosh, R. J. *Memoirs of the Life of Sir James Mackintosh*, 2 vols. London, 1835.
Macleod, Roy, 'Whigs and Savants: Reflections on the Reform Movement in the Royal Society, 1830–48', in Ian Inkster and Jack Morrell eds., *Metropolis and Province: Science in British Culture 17801850*. London, 1983.
Macmillan, Duncan, 'Blake's Exhibition and "Catalogue" Reconsidered', *Blake Newsletter*, vol. 5, 1971–72.
Maddison, John, 'Architectural Drawings at Blickling Hall', *Architectural History*, vol. 34, 1991.
Madsen, Stephen Tsudi, *The Works of Alexis de Chateauneuf in London and Oslo*. Oslo, 1965.
Main, J. M., 'Radical Westminster, 1805–1820', *Historical Studies (Australia and New Zealand)*, vol. 12, 1966.
Malcolmson, Robert, W., *Popular Recreations in English Society, 1700–1850*. Cambridge, 1973.
Malden, John, *John Henning, 1771–1851 '...a very ingenious Modeller'*. Paisley, 1977.
Malins, Edward, *Samuel Palmer's Italian Honeymoon*. London, 1968.
Mallet, J. V. G., 'Recent Accessions in the Victoria and Albert Museum's Department of Ceramics and Glass', *Burlington Magazine*, vol. 129, no. 1010, 1987.
Mander, Raymond and Mitchenson, Joe, *Theatrical Companion to Maugham*. London, 1955.
Mander, Raymond and Mitchenson, Joe, *Catalogue of the Paintings in the Maugham Collection*, 1980.
Mansbridge, Michael, *John Nash. A Complete*

Catalogue. Oxford, 1991.
Mansfield, Alan. *Ceremonial Costume*. London, 1980.
Manson, J., *Sir Edwin Landseer*. London, 1902.
Marchand, Leslie A., ed., *Byron's Letters and Journals,* vols. 3, 4, 5. London, 1973, 1975, 1978.
Märker, Peter, *Daniel Chodowiecki Bürgerliches Leben im 18. Jahrhundert*. Frankfurt on Main, 1978.
Marks, Richard and Payne, Ann, *British Heraldry*. London, 1978.
Marmoy, C. F. A., 'The "Auto-Icon" of Jeremy Bentham at University College London', *Medical History,* vol. 2, no. 2, 1958.
Marshall, John, *A Biographical Dictionary of Railway Engineers*. Newton Abbot, 1978.
Martin, Frederick, *The History of Lloyd's and of Marine Insurance in Great Britain*. London, 1876.
Mathias, Peter and O'Brien, Patrick K., 'Taxation in Britain and France, 1715–1810: A Comparison of the Social and Economic Incidence of Taxes Collected for the Central Governments', *Journal of European Economic History,* vol. 5, 1976.
Matschoss, C., *Geschischte der Dampfmaschine*. Berlin, 1901 and Hildesheim, 1978.
Matthew, William, M., *The House of Gibbs and the Peruvian Guano Monopoly*. Woodbridge, 1981.
Matthews, Thomas, *John Gibson*. London, 1911.
May, John and Jennifer, *Commemorative Pottery 17801900*. London, 1972.
Mayer, Luigi, *Views in the Ottoman Empire chiefly in Caramania, a Part of Asia Minor Hitherto Unexplored*. London, 1801–04.
McCalman, Iain, 'Ultra-Radicalism and Convivial Debating-Clubs in London, 1795–1838', *English Historical Review,* vol. 102, 1987.
McCalman, Iain, *Radical Underworld*. Cambridge, 1988.
McCann, Philip and Young, Francis A., *Samuel Wilderspin and the Infant School Movement*. London, 1982.
McHardy, George, *Catalogue of the Drawings Collection of the Royal Institute of British Architects Office of J. B. Papworth*. London, 1977.
McIlwaine, Ia Cecilia, 'British Interest in the Herculaneum Papyri, 1800–1820', *Proceedings of the XVIII International Congress of Papyrology,* vol. 1. Athens, 1986.
McIlwaine, Ia Cecilia, *Herculaneum: a Guide to Printed Sources*. Naples, 1988.
McIlwaine, Ia Cecilia, 'Davy in Naples: the British Viewpoint', *Proceedings of the XIX International Congress of Papyrology*. Cairo, 1989, forthcoming.
McKendrick, Neil, Brewer, John and Plumb, John, *The Birth of a Consumer Society: The Commercialization of Eighteenth-century England*. London, 1982.
McNeil, Ian, *Joseph Bramah. A Century of Invention 1749–1851*. Newton Abbot, 1968.
Mellor, Anne, '*Frankenstein*: a Feminist Critique of Science', in George Levine ed., *One Culture: Essays in Science and Literature*. Wisconsin, 1987.
Mercer, Vaudrey, *Arnold and Son*. London, 1972.
Metken, Gnter. 'Les Ruines Anticipes', in Anne and Patrick Poirier eds., *Domus Aurea. Fascination des Ruines*. Paris, 1978.
Michaelis, Adolph, *Ancient Marbles in Great Britain*. Cambridge, 1882.
Miles, Dudley, *Francis Place 1771–1854*. Brighton, 1988.
Millar, Oliver, *The Later Georgian Pictures in the Collection of Her Majesty the Queen,* 2 vols. London, 1969.
Millar, Oliver, *The Queen's Pictures*. London, 1977.
Millensen, Susan Feinberg, *Sir John Soane's Museum*. Ann Arbor, Michigan, 1987.
Miller, David Philip, 'Between Hostile Camps: Sir Humphry Davy's Presidency of the Royal Society of London, 1820–1827', *British Journal for the History of Science,* vol. 16, 1983.
Miller, David Philip, 'Sir Joseph Banks: an Historiographical Perspective', *History of Science,* vol. 19, 1981.
Miller, Naomi C. 'Major John Cartwright and the Founding of the Hampden Club', *Historical Journal,* vol. 17, 1974.
Miller, Naomi C., 'John Cartwright and Radical Parliamentary Reform, 18061819', *English Historical Review,* vol. 83, 1968.
Minihan, Janet, *The Nationalization of Culture: The Development of State Subsidies to the Arts in Great Britain*. London, 1977.
Miracco, Franco, ed., *Venezia nell' Et di Canova 1780–1830*. Venice, 1978.
Modert, Jo, *Jane Austen's Manuscript Letters in Facsimile*. Carbondale and Edwardsville, 1990.
Momigliano, Arnaldo, *George Grote and the Study of Greek History, An Inaugural Lecture Delivered at University College*. London, 1952.
Montefiore, Joshua, *A Commercial Dictionary: Containing the Present State of Mercantile Law, Practice and Custom*. London, 1803.
Moore, Thomas, *Letters and Journals of Lord Byron, with Notices of his Life,* 2 vols. London, 1830 and 1888 edn.
Morley, John, 'King George IV and the Building of the Royal Pavilion', *The Royal Pavilion Brighton*. Brigton, 1989 edn.
Morrell, Jack and Thackray, Arnold, *Gentlemen of Science: the Early Years of the British Association for the Advancement of Science*. Oxford, 1981.
Morrell, Jack, 'Individualism and the Structure of British Science in 1830', *Historical Studies in the Physical Sciences,* vol. 3, 1971.
Morrell, Jack, 'London Institutions and Lyell's Career, 1820–1841', *British Journal for the History of Science,* vol. 9, 1976.
Morris, Susan, *Thomas Girtin 1775–1802*. New Haven, 1986.
Morriss, Roger, *The Royal Dockyards during the Revolutionary and Napoleonic Wars*. London, 1983.
Mortimer, F.C. Martin, ' "Quaker" Pegg's First Period?', *Connoisseur,* vol. 200, no. 803, 1979.
Morus, Iwan Rhys, "Telegraphy and the Technology of Display', *History of Technology,* vol. 13, 1991.
Morus, Iwan Rhys, 'Different Experimental Lives: Michael Faraday and William Sturgeon', *History of Science,* 1992, forthcoming.
Mosley, James, ed., *Horace Hart, Charles Earl Stanhope and the Oxford University Press; reprinted from Collectanea, vol. 3, 1896 of the Oxford Historical Society*. London, 1966.
Motif, no. 1. London, 1958.
Mudge Jnr., Thomas, *A Description with Plates, of the Time-keeper Invented by the late Mr Thomas Mudge, to which is Prefixed a Narrative, by Thomas Mudge, His Son*. London, 1799.
Murdoch, John, and Twitchett, John, *Painters and the Derby China Works*. London, 1987.
Murdoch, Tessa ed., *The Quiet Conquest: The Huguenots 1685–1985*. London, 1985.
Murdoch, Tessa ed., *Treasures & Trinkets: Jewellery in London from pre-Roman times to the 1930s*. London, 1991.
Murray, Christopher, 'Robert William Elliston's Production of Faust', *Theatre Research,* vol.11, 1971.
Musgrave, Clifford, *Regency Furniture 1800–1830*. London, 1961, new edn., 1970.
Myers, Harry, *William Henry Pyne and his Microcosm*. unpublished mss., 1990.
Nalbach, Daniel, *The King's Theatre 1704–1867*. London, 1972.
Nares, Gordon, 'The Athenaeum', *Country Life,* vol. 109, no.2829, 1951.
Nash, J. K. T. N., 'The Foundations of London Bridge', *Canadian Geotechnical Journal,* vol. 18, 1981.
National Art-Collections Review. London, 1990.
Nayler, Sir George, *The Coronation of His Most Sacred Majesty King George IV*. London, 1837.
Neal, Larry, *The Rise of Financial Capitalism: International Capital Markets in the Age of Reason*. Cambridge, 1990.
Nelson, *John, History, Topography, and Antiquities of the Parish of St. Mary Islington*. London, 1811, 3rd. edn., 1829.
New, Chester W., *The Life of Henry Brougham to 1830*. Oxford, 1961.
Newcastle upon Tyne, British Water-Colours in the Laing Art Gallery. Newcastle upon Tyne, 1976.
Newcastle upon Tyne, Laing Art Gallery, Illustrated Catalogue of the Permanent Collection of Water Colour Drawings. Newcastle upon Tyne, 1939.
Newell, Christopher, *Victorian Watercolours*. Oxford, 1987.
Nichols, J., *Literary Anecdotes of the Eighteenth Century*. London, 1812–15.
Noble, Thomas, *The Professional Practice of Architects*. London, 1836.
Noon, Patrick, *Richard Parkes Bonington: 'On the Pleasure of Painting'*. New Haven and London, 1991.
Norst, Marlene F., *Ferdinand Bauer: the Australian Natural History Drawings*. London, 1989.
North, A. R. E., *European Swords*. London, 1982.
Norton, Peter, *State Barges*. London, 1972.
Nygren, Edward J., *James Ward's Gorsdale Scar, An Essay in the Sublime*. London, 1982.
O'Brien, Patrick K., 'Agriculture and the Industrial Revolution', *Economic History Review,* 2nd ser. vol. 30, 1977.
O'Brien, Patrick K., 'The Political Economy of British Taxation, 16601815', Economic History Review, 2nd ser. vol. 41, 1985.
O'Brien, Patrick K., 'Agriculture and the Home Market for English Industry, 16601820', *English Historical Review,* vol. 100, 1985.
Oechslin, Werner. 'Die Bank of England – und ihre Darstellung als Ruine,' *Archithese* , vol. 2, no. 81, 1981.
Ogden Jnr., Warren Greene, *Notes on the History and Provenance of Holtzappfel Lathes; With Numerous Corrections and Additions to the Transcript of the Holtzapffel Register of Lathes*. North Andover, Massachusetts, 1987.
Ollier, Charles, *Literary Pocket Book*. London, 1823.
Olney, C., *Benjamin Robert Haydon, Historical Painter*. Athens, Georgia, 1952.
Olsen, Donald J., *Town Planning in London: The Eighteenth and Nineteenth Centuries*. New Haven and London, 1964.
Olsen, Donald J., *The City as a Work of Art: London, Paris, Vienna*. New Haven and London, 1986.
Oman, Charles, 'The Plate at the Wellington Museum', *Apollo,* vol. 98, no. 139 new ser., 1973.
Opp, A. P. *English Drawings, Stuart and Georgian Periods, in the Collection of His Majesty the King at Windsor Castle*. London, 1950.
Opp, A. P., *Thomas Rowlandson: His Drawings and Water-Colours*. London, 1923.
Ormond, Richard, 'Daniel Maclise', *Burlington Magazine,* vol. 110, no. 789, 1968.
Ormond, Richard, *Early Victorian Portraits,* 2 vols. London, 1973.
Ost, Hans, *Falsche Frauen*. Cologne, 1984.
Owen Pughe, W. and Williams, E., *Myvyrian Archaeology,* 3 vols. London, 1801–07.
Owen, David, *The Government of Victorian London 1888–1889. The Metropolitan Board of Works, the Vestries and the City Corporation*. London, 1982.
Owen, Felicity and David Blayney Brown, *Collector of Genius: A Life of Sir George Beaumont*. New Haven and London, 1988.
Paley, Morton D., *William Blake*. Oxford, 1978.
Palmer, Sarah, *Politics, Shipping and the Repeal of the Navigation Laws*. Manchester, 1990.
Papworth, Wyatt, *J. B. Papworth*. London, 1879.
Parkinson, Ronald, *Victoria and Albert Museum: Catalogue of British Oil Paintings 18201860*. London, 1990.
Parliamentary Debates: Cobbett and Hansard, 1803 onwards; 3rd ser., 1835.
Parliamentary Papers, (House of Commons) 1812–31.
Parliamentary Papers: Reports of the Commissioners of H.M. Woods, Forests and Land Revenues, nos.117, 178793.
Parliamentary Papers: Triennial Reports of the Surveyor-General of Land Revenues. Nos. 1–4, 1797, 1802, 1806, 1809.
Parliamentary Papers: Report of the Commissioners of H.M. Woods, Forests and Land Revenues, nos. 1–120, 18121942.
Parliamentary Papers: Report of the Commissioners of Inquiry into the Office of Works, vol. 5, 181213.
Parliamentary Papers: Report from the Select Committee of the House of Commons on the Earl of Elgin's Collection of Sculptured Marbles etc., 1816.
Parliamentary Papers: Report from the Select Committee of the House of Commons on the Office of Works, vol. 4. 1828.
Parliamentary Papers: Report from the Select Committee of the House of Commons on Crown Leases, vol. 3. 1829.
Parliamentary Papers: Second Report of the Select Committee of the House of Commons on Windsor Castle and Buckingham Palace, vol. 4. 1831.
Parliamentary Papers: Report from the Select Committee of the House of Commons on Arts and Manufactures. 1836.
Parris, Leslie and Fleming-Williams, Ian, *Constable*. London, 1991.
Parssinen, T. M., 'The Revolutionary Party in London, 1816–20', *Bulletin of the Institute of Historical Research,* vol. 45, 1972.
Passavant, M. J. D., *Tour of a German Artist in England,* vol. 1. London, 1836.
Paston, George, *At John Murray's, 1843–1892, Records of a Literary Circle*. London, 1932.
Patten, L. Robert, *Charles Dickens and his Publishers*. Oxford, 1978.
Paulson, Ronald, *Rowlandson: a New Interpretation*. London, 1972.
Pecchio, Count, *Semi-Serious Observations of an Italian Exile during his Residence in England*. London, 1833.
Pellatt, Apsley, *Ornamenting Glass, Patent Specification No. 4424*. London, 1819.
Pellatt, Apsley, *Memoir on the Origin, Progress and Improvement of Glass Manufactures*. London, 1821.
Pelzet, Michael and Wackernagel, Rudolf, *Bayerische Krönungswagen*. Munich, 1967.
Pendred, Loughnan St. L., 'The Mystery of Trevithick's London Locomotives', *Transactions of the Newcomen Society,* vol. 1, 1920–21.
Penzer, N. M., 'Galvanic Goblet: Paul Storr', *Connoisseur,* vol. 133, no. 537, 1954.
Pevsner, Nikolaus, *Academies of Art Past and Present*. Cambridge, 1940.
Pevsner, Nikolaus, *A History of Building Types*. Princeton, 1976.
Phipps-Jackson, M., 'Two famous Chargers "Marengo" and "Copenhagen", *Magazine of Art,* vol. 16, 1893.
Picciotto, James, *Sketches of Anglo-Jewish History*. London, 1875.
Pirzio Biroli Stefanelli, Lucia, 'I Modelli in Cera di Benedetto Pistrucci', *Bollettino di Numismatica, Monographia,* 2 vols. Rome, 1989.
Pocock, John G.A., *Virtue, Commerce and History: Essays on Political Thought and History, Chiefly in the Eighteenth Century*. Cambridge, 1985.
Pocock, Tom, *Horatio Nelson*. London, 1987.
Podro, Michael, *The Critical Historians of Art*. New Haven and London, 1982.
Pointon, Marcia, 'Painters and Pugilism in Early Nineteenth-Century England', *Gazette des Beaux Arts,* 5ième période, vol. 92, 1978.
Pointon, Marcia, *William Dyce 1806–1864; a Critical Biography*. Oxford, 1979.
Pointon, Marcia, *Mulready*. London, 1986.
Pollard, Sidney, 'The Decline of Shipbuilding on the Thames', *Economic History Review,* 2nd ser. vol. 3, 1950–51.
Port, Michael, *Six Hundred New Churches*. London, 1961.
Port, Michael, 'The Office of Works and Building Contracts in Early Nineteenth-Century England', *Economic History Review,* vol. 20, 1967.
Port, Michael, ed., *The Houses of Parliament*. New Haven and London, 1976.
Postle, Martin, 'The Artist's Model: from Reynolds to Etty', in I. Bignamini and M. Postle eds., *The Artist's Model: its Role in British Art from Lely to Etty*. Nottingham and London, 1991.
Potts, Alex, 'Die Skulturenaufstellung in der Glyptothek', in K. Vierneisel and G. Leinz eds., *Glyptothek Munchen, 1830–1980*. Munich, 1980.
Potts, Alex, *Sir Francis Chantrey, 1781–1841*. London, 1980.
Powell, Cecilia, *Turner in the South: Rome, Naples, Florence*. New Haven and London, 1987.
Pressly, William L., *The Life and Art of James Barry*. New Haven and London, 1981.
Pressnell, Leslie S., *Country Banking in the Industrial Revolution*. Oxford, 1956.
Preston, J. M., *Industrial Medway: An Historical Survey*. Rochester, 1977.
Price, George, *Treatise on Fire and Thief-Proof Depositories, and Locks and Keys*. London, 1856.
Price, Sir Uvedale, *Three Essays on the Picturesque,* 2 vols. London, 1810.
Prochaska, Alice, 'The Practice of Radicalism: Educational Reform in Westminster', in John Stevenson ed., *London in the Age of Reform*. Oxford, 1977.
Prothero, Iorwerth J., *Artisans and Politics in Early Nineteenth-Century. London: John Gast and His Times*. Folkestone, 1979.
Prothero, Iorwerth, *Artisans and Politics and the Destitute*. London, 1987.
[Pckler Muskau, H. L. H. V.], *Tour in Germany, Holland and England, in the years 1826, 1827, & 1828,* translated by Sarah Austin, vols. 3, and 4. London, 1832.
Pckler Muskau, H. L. H. V., *Tour of England, Ireland and France*. Zurich, 1940.
Pckler Muskau, H. L. H. V., *A Regency Visitor: the English Tour of Prince. Describe in his Letters, 1826–1828,* ed. E. M. Butler. London, 1957.

Pudney, John, *London's Docks*. London, 1975.
Pugh, Ralph B. *The Crown Estate*. London, 1960.
Pugin, Augustus Welby Northmore, *Contrasts*. London, 1836.
Purcell, Edmund Sheridan, *Life of Cardinal Manning, Archbishop of Westminster, vol. 1, Manning as an Anglican*. London, 1986.
Quarterly Review, vol. 72, 1843, 'Theodore Hook'.
Quennell, Peter, *The Private Letters of Princess Lieven to Prince Metternich, 18201826*. London, 1937.
Rackham, Bernard, *Catalogue of the Glaisher Collection of Pottery and Porcelain in the Fitzwilliam Museum, Cambridge*. Cambridge, 1935.
Radcliffe, Anthony, 'Acquisitions of Sculpture by the Royal Academy', *Apollo*, vol. 89, no. 83 new ser., 1969.
Rajnai, Miklos, ed., *John Sell Cotman*. London, 1982.
Randall, Anthony and Good, Richard, *Catalogue of Watches in the British Museum*, vol. 6. London, 1990.
Raumer, Frederick von, *England in 1835*, translated by Sarah Austin, vols. 1 and 2. London, 1836.
Reader, W.J., *Macadam*. London, 1980.
Records of Fashion. London, 1808.
Reed, Isaac, *Diaries 1762–1804*. University of California publications, vol. 10, 1946.
Reese, M. M., *Master of Horse*. London, 1976.
Reid, George William, *A Descriptive Catalogue of the Works of George Cruikshank*. London, 1871.
Reid, John C., *Bucks and Bruisers: Pierce Egan and Regency England*. London, 1971.
Reilly, Robin and Savage, George, *The Dictionary of Wedgwood*. Woodbridge, 1980.
Reilly, Robin, *Wedgwood*. London, 1989.
Rennie, Sir John, *Autobiography*. London, 1875.
Repertory of Arts, *Some Account of the Archway or Tunnel Intended to be Made under the River Thames*. London 1805.
Repertory of Arts, *An Account of the Progress and Present State of the Works Undertaken with a View of Forming a Tunnel under the Thames*. London, 1809.
Repository of Arts, Literature, Commerce, Manufactures, Fashions and Politics, 40 vols. London, 1809–28.
Repton, Humphry, *Fragments on the Theory and Practice of Landscape Gardening*. London, 1816.
Review of Publications of Art, ed. John Landseer, one vol. only. London, 1808.
Reynolds, Graham, *The Later Paintings and Drawings of John Constable*, 2 vols. New Haven and London, 1984.
Reynolds, Graham, *Victorian Paintings*. London, 1966.
Reynolds, Joshua, *Discourses on Art*, ed. R. R. Wark. San Marino, California, 1959.
Reynolds, Sir Joshua, *Works*, ed. Edmond Malone. London 1801.
Rhodes, Michael, 'The Roman Coinage from London Bridge and the Development of the City and Southwark', *Brittania*, vol. 22, 1991.
Rhodes, Michael, *Some Aspects of the Contribution to British Archaeology of Charles Roach Smith (1806–90)*, unpublished PhD thesis mss., University of London, 1992–93.
Rhyne, Charles, 'Changes in the Appearance of Paintings by John Constable', *Appearance, Opinion, Change: Evaluating the Look of Paintings*. United Kingdom Institute for Conservation, 1990.
Ribeiro, Aileen, *Dress and Morality*. London, 1986.
Ribeiro, Aileen, *Fashion in the French Revolution*. London, 1988.
Rice, Dennis G., *The Illustrated Guide to Rockingham Pottery and Porcelain*. London, 1971.
Richardson, Joanna, *The Disastrous Marriage*. London, 1960.
Richardson, Margaret, ed., *Catalogue of the Drawings Collection of the Royal Institute of British Architects*, vols.C-F, S. London, 1972, 1976.
Richardson, Margaret, 'Soane's Use of Drawings', *Apollo*, vol. 131, no. 338, 1990.
Richardson, Ruth and Hurwitz, Brian, 'Jeremy Bentham's Self Image: an Exemplary Bequest for Dissection', *British Medical Journal*, 18 July 1987.
Richardson, Ruth, *Death, Dissection and the Destitute*. London, 1987.
Rickwood, Edgell, *Radical Squibs and Loyal Ripostes*. Bath, 1971.
Riemann, Gottfried, *Karl Friedrich Schinkel, Reisen nach England, Schottland und Paris im Jahre 1826*. Berlin, 1986.
Roberts, William, *Memoirs of Mrs. Hannah More*, vol. 1. London, 2nd edn., 1834.
Robertson, David, *Sir Charles Eastlake and the Victorian Art World*. Princeton, 1978.
Robinson, Henry Crabb, *MS Diary*. London, Dr. Williams's Library.
Robinson, Henry Crabb, *Blake, Coleridge, Wordsworth, Lamb &c.*, ed. Edith J. Morley. Manchester, 1932.
Robinson, Henry Crabb, *The London Theatre 1811–1866*, ed. Eluned Brown. London, 1966.
Robinson, Henry Crabb, *Diary, An Abridgement*, ed. Derek Hudson. Oxford, 1967.
Robinson, J. M., 'Sir Frederick Trench and London Improvements', *History Today*, May 1977.
Robinson, Ralph M., *Coutts': the History of a Banking House*. London,1929.
Roe, F., 'Nelson's Sword of Honour at the Guildhall', *Connoisseur*, vol. 83, no. 329, 1929.
Roget, J. L., *A History of the 'Old Water-Colour' Society*, 2 vols. London, 1891.
Rolt, L. T. C., *Thomas Telford*. London, 1958.
Rose, Dennis, *Life, Times and Recorded Works of Robert Dighton and Three of his Artist Sons*. Privately published, 1981.
Rosenfeld, Sybil, 'The Grieve Family' in *Anatomy of an Illusion, Lectures of the 4th International Congress on Theatre Research*. Amsterdam, 1965.
Rosenfeld, Sybil, *A Short History of Scene Design in Great Britain*. Oxford, 1973.
Rosenfeld, Sybil, *Georgian Scene Painters and Scene Painting*. Cambridge, 1981.
Rosenthal, Michael, *Constable: The Painter and his Landscape*. New Haven and London, 1983.
Rosenthal. Michael, *Constable*. London, 1987.
Rossetti, William Michael, 'Annotated Catalogue' of Blake's works in Alexander Gilchrist, *Life of William Blake*, 2 vols. London, 1880.
Rothenburg, Jacob, *'Descensus ad Terram': The Acquisition and Reception of the Elgin Marbles*. New York and London, 1977.
Rougemont, Herbert de, *A History of Lloyd's Patriotic Fund from its Foundation in 1803*. London, 1914.
Roundell, James, *Thomas Shotter Boys, 1803–1874*. London, 1974.
Rowe, D. J., 'The Failure of London Chartism', *Historical Journal*, vol. 11, 1968.
Rowe, D. J., ed., *London Radicalism 1800–1843*. London, 1970.
Rowe, D. J., 'London Radicalism in the Era of the Great Reform Bill', in John Stevenson ed., *London Radicalism 1800–1843*. London, 1970.
Royal Academy, Vol. of Press Cuttings and Letters, mostly relating to 1803 disputes. London, Royal Academy of Arts, RAA F3.
Royal Academy, Lawrence Papers, MS letters, Addresses to the the Royal Academy and miscellaneous papers of Sir Thomas Lawrence, 9 vols. London, Royal Academy of Arts, LAW/1–9.
Royal Plate from Buckingham Palace and Windsor Castle. London, 1954.
Rubinstein, William D., *Men of Property: The Very Wealthy in Britain since the Industrial Revolution*. London, 1981.
Ruch, John E., 'Regency Coade: A Study of the Coade Record Books 1813–21', *Architectural History*, vol. 11, 1968.
Ruddock, Ted, *Arched Bridges and their Builders 1735–1835*. Cambridge, 1979.
Rud, George, *Hanoverian London 17141808*. London, 1971.
Rudwick, Martin, *The Great Devonian Controversy: The Shaping of Scientific Knowledge among Gentlemanly Specialists*. Chicago, 1985.
Rush, Richard, *A Residence at the Court of London*. London, 1833.
Ruskin, John, *Praeterita,* 3 vols. Orpington, 1885.
Ruskin, John, *Modern Painters,* vol. I. London, 1888.
Ruskin, John, *The Works of John Ruskin*, eds. E.T. Cooke and Alexander Wedderburn, 39 vols. London, 1902–1914.
Russell, Lord John, ed., *Memoirs of Thomas Moore*, 8 vols. London, 1853–56.
Rutherford, A. ed., 'The Impact of Byron's Writings: an Evidential Approach', *Byron: Augustan and Romantic*. London, 1990.
Ryan, W. F., 'John Russell, R. A., and Early Lunar Mapping', *Smithsonian Journal of History*, vol. 1, 1966.
Saint, Andrew, *The Image of the Architect*. New Haven and London, 1983.
Sandner, Oscar ed., *Angelika Kauffman und ihre Zeitgenossen*. Bregenz, 1968.
Sandon, Henry, *Flight & Barr Worcester Porcelain*. Woodbridge, 1978.
Sandon, John, 'Thomas Baxter', *Northern Ceramic Society Newsletter*, no. 66, June 1987.
Sandon, John, 'Nelson's China', *Antique Dealer and Collector's Guide*, vol. 42, no. 8, 1989.
Sandon, John, 'The Regency Decorators of Worcester'. *International Ceramics Fair and Seminar*. London, 1991.
Santanello, A.E. introd., *The Boydell Shakespeare Prints*. New York, 1968.
Sargent, Edward, 'The Planning and Early Buildings of the West India Docks', *Mariner's Mirror*, vol. 77, no. 2, 1991.
Saunders, Ann, *Regent's Park*. Newton Abbot, 1969.
Savigny, H. John, *A Collection of Engravings Representing the Most Modern and Approved Instruments Used in the Practice of Surgery*. London, 1798.
Scharf, George, *A Descriptive and Historical Catalogue of the Collection of Pictures at Woburn Abbey*, 2 parts. London, 1877.
Schoeser, Mary, *Printed Handkerchiefs*. London, 1988.
Schumann-Bacia, Eva-Maria, *Die Bank von England und ihr Architekt John Soane*. Zurich, 1989.
Schumann-Bacia, Eva-Maria, *John Soane und die Bank of England. 1788 bis 1833*. Hildesheim, 1990.
Schwarz, Leonard D., 'Income Distribution and Social Structure in London in the Late Eighteenth Century', *Economic History Review*, vol. 32, 2nd ser., 1979.
Schwarz, Leonard D., 'Social Class and Social Geography: the Middle Classes in London at the End of the Eighteenth Century', *Social History*, vol. 7, 1982.
Schwarz, Leonard D., 'The Standard of Living in the Long-run: London, 1700–1860', *Economic History Review*, 2nd ser. vol. 38, 1985.
Schweber, Silvan, 'Scientists as Intellectuals: the Early Victorians', in James Paradis and Thomas Postlewait eds., *Victorian Science and Victorian Values: Literary Perspectives*. New Brunswick, 1985.
Schweizer, Paul, 'John Constable, Rainbow Science, and English Color Theory', *Art Bulletin*, vol. 64, no. 3, 1982.
Scrase, David, *Drawings and Watercolours by Peter de Wint*. Cambridge, 1979.
Seaborne, Malcolm, *The English School, 1370–1870*. London, 1971.
Seaby, H. A and P. J. *Coins of England and the United Kingdom, Standard Catalogue of British Coins*, vol. I. London, 1991 edn.
Searle, Mark, *Turnpikes and Toll-Bars*. London, 1930.
Second, James Andrew, 'King of Siluria: Roderick Murchison and the Imperial Theme in Nineteenth-century British Geology', *Victorian Studies*, vol. 25, 1982.
Second, James Andrew, The Geological Survey of Great Britain as a Research School, 1839–1855', *History of Science*, vol 24, 1986.
Sekora, John, *Luxury: The Concept in Western Thought, Eden to Smollett*. Baltimore, 1977.
Shanes, Eric, 'Turner's "Unknown" London Series'. *Turner Studies*, vol.1, no.2, 1981.
Shanes, Eric, 'Picture Notes', *Turner Studies*, vol. 3, no. 2, 1984.
Shanes, Eric, *Turner's England*. London, 1990.
Shapin, Steven and Barnes, Barry, 'Science, Nature and Control: Interpreting Mechanics' Institutes', *Social Studies of Science*, vol. 7, 1977.
Shaw, Henry, *Specimens of Ancient Furniture. . . with descriptions by Sir Samuel Rush Meyrick*. London, 1836.
Shee, Martin Archer, *A Letter to the President and Directors of the British Institution*. London, 1809.
Shee, Martin Archer, *Rhymes on Art*. London, 1805.
Shelley, Percy Bysshe, 'On the Devil and Devils' 1819–20, in D. L. Clark ed., *Shelley's Prose*. Durham, North Carolina, 1972.
Sheppard, F. H. W., *Local Government in St. Marylebone 1688–1835*. London, 1958.
Sheppard, Francis, *London, 1808–1870: The Infernal Wen*. London, 1971.
Sheppard, Francis, Belcher, Victor, and Cotterell, Philip, 'The Middlesex and Yorkshire Deeds Registries and the Study of Building Fluctuations', *London Journal*, vol. 5, no. 2, 1979.
Sheraton, Thomas, *The Cabinet Dictionary*, 2 vols. London, 1803.
Shirley, Andrew, *Bonington*. London, 1940.
Shirley, Andrew, *The Published Mezzotints of David Lucas after John Constable R.A.: A Catalogue and Historical Account*. Oxford, 1930.
Sichel, W., ed., *Glenbervie Journals*. London, 1910.
Siegfried, Robert, 'Davy's "Intellectual Delight" and his Lectures at the Royal Institution', in Sophie Forgan ed., *Science and the Sons of Genius: Studies on Humphry Davy*. London, 1980.
Simond, Louis, *Journal of a Tour and Residence in Great Britain during the years 1810 and 1811*. London, 1817.
Sitwell, Sacheverell and Blunt, Wilfrid, *Great Flower Books 1700–1900*. London, 1956.
Skempton, A. W., 'Samuel Wyatt and the Albion Mill', *Architectural History*, vol. 14, 1971.
Skempton, A. W., 'Engineering in the Port of London, 1798–1808', *Transactions of the Newcomen Society*, vol. 50, 1978–79.
Skempton, A. W.,'Engineering in the Port of London, 1808–1834', *Transactions of the Newcomen Society*, vol. 53, 1981–82.
Sloan, Kim, *Alexander and John Robert Cozens, The Poetry of Landscape*. New Haven and London, 1986.
Smart, Alastair, and Brooks, Artfield, *Constable and his Country*. London, 1976.
Smiles, Samuel, *Lives of the Engineers*, 3 vols. London, 1861–62.
Smiles, Samuel, *A Publisher and His Friends, Memoir and Correspondence of the Late John Murray*. London, 1891.
Smith, Arthur, 'Lord Elgin and his Collection', *Journal of Hellenic Studies*, vol. 36, 1916.
Smith, Arthur, 'The Gurney Steam Carriage', *Journal of the Society of Model and Experimental Engineers,* vol. 3 , no. 3, 1959.
Smith, Charles Roach, 'On some Roman Bronzes discovered in the Bed of the Thames,' *Archaeologia*, vol. 28, 1840.
Smith, Charles Roach, *Illustrations of Roman London*. Privately printed, 1859.
Smith, Clifford, *Buckingham Palace*. London, 1931.
Smith, George, *A Collection of Designs for Household Furniture and Interior Decoration*. London, 1808.
Smith, Hammond, *Peter De Wint*. London, 1982.
Smout, T. Christopher, *A History of the Scottish People, 1560–1830*. London, 1969.
Snodin, Michael, and Baker, M., 'William Beckford's Silver', *Burlington Magazine*, vol. 122, nos. 932 and 933, 1980.
Snodin, Michael, 'Charles and Edward Crace and Rococo Coach Painting', *The Craces, Royal Decorators 1768–1899*. Brighton, 1990.
Soane, Sir John, *Designs for Public and Private Buildings*. London, 1828.
Soane, John, *Description of the House and Museum*. London, 1835.
Solly, N. Neil, *Memoir of the Life of David Cox, Member of the Society Painters in Watercolours, with Selections from his Correspondence, and Some Accounts of his Works*, 1873, reprinted London 1973.
Souden, David, *Wimpole Hall*. London, 1991.
Southall, Humphrey, 'The Origins of the Depressed Areas: Unemployment, Growth and Regional Economic Structure in Britain before 1914', *Economic History Review*, 2nd ser. vol. 41, 1988.
Southey, Robert, *Letters from England*. London, 1807, ed. Jack Simmons. London, 1951.
Southwick, Leslie, 'Swords of Honour. City of London Presentation Awards', *Antique Dealer & Collector's Guide*, vol. 38, no. 6, 1983.
Southwick, Leslie, 'Patriotic Fund Swords', *Journal of the Arms and Armour Society*, vol. 12, 1987–88.
Southwick, Leslie, 'The Silver Vases Awarded by the Patriotic Fund', *Silver Society Journal*, vol. 1, 1990.
Spater, George, *William Cobbett: The Poor Man's Friend,* 2 vols. Cambridge, 1982.
Speler, Ralf Torsten, 'Erdmannsdorff, Palladio und England', *Friedrich Erdmannsdorff 1736–1800 zum 250 Geburtstag*. Wörlitz, 1986.
Spencer, Herbert, *London's Canal*. London, 1961.
Spencer, Terence, *Fair Greece Sad Relic: Literary Philhellenism from Shakespeare to Byron*. Bath, 1974.
Sperling, Norman, 'The Mystery of Urania's Mirror', *Sky and Telescope*, vol. 61, 1981.
Splendid Views, Portfolio of Reproductions of Benjamin Read Topographical Fashion Plates, with notes by Anne Buck, Ralph Hyde and

Ann Saunders. London, 1984.
St. Clair, William, *Lord Elgin and the Marbles*. London, 1967 and 2nd edn. Oxford, 1983.
St. Clair, William, *That Greece Might Still Be Free: The Philhellenes in the War of Independence*. London, 1972.
St. Clair, William, 'The Impact of Byron's Writings: an Evidential Approach' in A. Rutherford ed., *Byron: Augustan and Romantic*. London, 1990.
St. Quintin, A. N., *Patriotic Fund at Lloyd's*. London, 1923.
Stafford, Robert, *Scientist of Empire: Sir Roderick Murchison, Scientific Exploration and Victorian Imperialism*. Cambridge, 1989.
Stamp, Gavin, *The Great Perpectivists*. London, 1982.
Stamp, Gavin, 'Hungerford Market', *A. A. Files*, vol. 11, 1986.
Stanton, Phoebe, *Pugin*. London, 1971.
Stearn, T. William, *The Australian Flower Paintings of Ferdinand Bauer*. London, 1976.
Stedman Jones, Gareth, *Outcast London: A Study in the Relationship between Classes in Victorian Society*. Oxford, 1971.
Steele, H. Rooksby and F. R. Yerbury, *The Old Bank of England, London*. London, 1930.
Stern, Walter M., 'The First London Dock Boom and the Growth of the West India Docks', *Economica*, vol. 19, 1952.
Stern, Walter M., 'The Isle of Dogs Canal. A Study in Early Public Investment', *Economic History Review*, 2nd ser. vol. 4, no. 3, 1952.
Stevenson, John, 'The Queen Caroline Affair', in John Stevenson ed., *London in the Age of Reform*. Oxford, 1977.
Stevenson, Sara and Bennett, Helen, *Van Dyck in Check Trousers*. Edinburgh, 1978.
Stewart, Bertram, *The Library and the Picture Collection of the Port of London Authority*. London, 1955.
Stigand, William, *The Life, Work and Opinions of Heinrich Heine*, 2 vols. London, 1875.
Stokes, M. V., 'The Lowther Arcade in the Strand', *London Topographical Record*, vol. 23, 1974.
Stoneman, Richard, *A Literary Companion to Travel in Greece*. London, 1984.
Stoneman, Richard, *Land of Lost Gods: The Search for Classical Greece*. London, 1987.
Story, T. Alfred, *The Life of John Linnell*. 2 vols. London, 1892.
Stroud, Dorothy, *The Thurloe Estate, South Kensington*. London, 1959.
Stroud, Dorothy, *Capability Brown*. London, revised edn. 1975.
Stroud, Dorothy, *John Soane, Architect*. London, 1984.
Sturmer, Michael, 'An Economy of Delight: Court Artisans of the Eighteenth Century', *Business History Review*, vol.53, 1979.
Summerson, John, *John Nash. Architect to George IV*. London, 1935.
Summerson, John, *Georgian London*. London, 1945 and edns. 1947, 1978, 1962, 1988.
Summerson, John, *Heavenly Mansions*. London, 1949.
Summerson, John, introduction to Terence Davies, *John Nash*. London, 1960.
Summerson, John, 'The Beginning of Regent's Park', *Architectural History*, vol. 20, 1977.
Summerson, John, *The Life and Work of John Nash, Architect*. London, 1980.
Summerson, John, Watkin, David and Mellinghoff, G.-Tilman, *John Soane*. London, 1983.
Summerson, John, *Architecture in Britain, 1530–1830*. London, 1970, 3rd edn. 1983
Summerson, John, *Architecture in the Eighteenth Century*. London, 1986.
Summerson, John, 'The Evolution of Soane's Bank Stock Office in the Bank of England', *The Unromantic Castle*. London, 1990.
Summerson, John, 'John Nash, "Statement", 1829,' *Architectural History*, vol. 34, 1991.
Supple, Barry, *The Royal Exchange Assurance: A History of British Insurance, 1720–1970*. Cambridge, 1970.
Survey of London, vols. 21, 29, 36, 39, 40, 42. London,1949, 1960, 1970, 1977, 1980, 1986.
Sutton, Thomas, *The Daniells: Artists and Travellers*. London, 1954.
Swade, Doron, *Charles Babbage and his Calculating Engines*. London, 1991.
Swain, Marilyn, 'Pendock Barry and his Derby Dessert Service', *Antique Collector*, vol. 55, no.9, 1984.
Sykes, Christopher Simon, *Private Palaces: Life in the Great London Houses*. London, 1985.
Tait, Hugh and Gere, Charlotte, *The Jeweller's Art, An Introduction to the Hull Grundy Gift to the British Museum*. London, 1978.
Tait, Hugh, ed., *The Art of the Jeweller, A Catalogue of the Hull Grundy Gift to the British Museum*. London, 1984.
Tallis, John, *Street Views of London*. London, 1838–40, reprinted 1969.
Tanner, L. E., *The History of the Coronation*. London, 1952.
Taylor, Basil, ed., *Painting in England 17001850*. London, 1966.
Taylor, Basil, *The Old Watercolour Society and its Founder-members*. London, 1973.
Taylor, Basil, *Joshua Cristall 1768–1847*. London, 1975.
Taylor, Eva Germaine Rimington, *The Mathematical Practitioners of Tudor and Stuart England*. Cambridge, 1954.
Taylor, Eva Germaine Rimington, *The Mathematical Practitioners of Hanoverian England, 1714–1840*. Cambridge, 1966.
Taylor, George Ledwell, *The Autobiography of an Octogenarian Architect*, 2 vols. London, 1870–72.
Taylor, N. *Monuments of Commerce*. London, 1968.
Tedder, Henry Richard, 'Rudolph Ackermann', *Dictionary of National Biography*, vol 1. Oxford, 1885.
Telford, Thomas, *Life of Thomas Telford, Civil Engineer, Written by Himself*. London, 1838.
Teyssot, Georges. *Città e Utopia nell'Illuminismo Inglese: George Dance il giovane*. Rome, 1974.
Thackeray, W. M., *Sketches and Travels in London*. London, 1844–50; Gloucester edn., 1989.
The Cabinet or Monthly Report of Polite Literature, 1807.
The Gurney Steam Carriage', *Engineering*, 3 April 1959.
The Sun, coronation supplement, 28 June 1838.
Thomas, John Meurig, *Michael Faraday and the Royal Institution (The Genius of Man and Place)*. Bristol, 1991.
Thomas, Matthews, *John Gibson*. London, 1911.
Thomas, R. H. G., *London's First Railway – The London and Greenwich*. London, 1972.
Thomas, William, *The Philosophic Radicals*. Oxford, 1979.
Thompson, E. P., *The Making of the English Working Class*. London, 1968.
Thompson, F. M. L., *Hampstead: Building a Borough 1650–1964*. London, 1974.
Thoms, W. J., *The Book of the Court*. London, 1838.
[Thomson, Richard], *Chronicles of London Bridge*. London, 1827.
Thorne, Robert, 'Origins of the Skin Floor', *Architect's Journal*, vol 184, no. 30, 1986.
Thorne, Robert, ed., *The Iron Revolution – Architects, Engineers and Structural Innovation 1780–1880*. London, 1990.
Thorne, Roland, *The History of Parliament, The House of Commons, 1790–1820*, vol.3 Members A-F, vol. 4 Members G-P, vol. 5 Members Q-Y. London, 1986.
Thornton, Peter and Fitz-Gerald, Desmond, 'Abraham Roentgen – 'Englische Kabinettmacher', *Victoria and Albert Museum Bulletin*, vol. 2, 1966.
Thornton, Peter, *Authentic Decor The Domestic Interior 1620–1920*. London, 1984.
Thornton, Peter and Watkin, David, 'New Light on The Hope Mansion in Duchess Street', *Apollo*, vol. 126, no. 307, 1987.
Tierney, David, 'The Catholic Apostolic Church: a Study in Tory Millenarianism', *Historical Research*, vol. 63, 1990.
Tindall, Gillian, *The Fields Beneath*. London, 1977.
Tischbein, J. H. W., *Recueil de Gravures d'aprs des Vases Antiques. Cabinet Hamilton*, 4 vols. Naples, 1791–95 and 1803 edn..
Tomlin, Maurice, *Catalogue of Adam Period Furniture, Victoria and Albert Museum*. London, 1972.
Tooley, R. V., *English Books with Colour Plates 1790 to 1860*. London, 1954 and Folkestone, 1973.
Townsend, Charles E. G, 'Further Notes on Early Railways in Surrey'. *Transactions of the Newcomen Society*, vol. 27, 1949–51.
Trench, Frederick William, *A Collection of Papers Relating to the Thames Quay*. London, 1827.
Trench, Frederick William, *Royal Palaces*. London, 1846.
Trench, Richard and Hillman, Ellis, *London under London*. London, 1985.
Trendall, A. D. and Cambitoglou, Alexander, *The Red-Figured Vases of Apulia*. Oxford, 1978.
Truman, Charles, *English Glassware to 1900*. London, 1984.
Turner, A. J., ed., *University College London, Past and Present 1828–1978*. London, 1978.
Turner, Eric, 'Metalwork Acquisitions at the V&A 1978–88, No. XVI', *Burlington Magazine*, vol. 131, no. 1034, 1989.
Turner, Frank, *The Greek Heritage in Victorian Britain*. New Haven and London, 1981.
Twitchett, John, *Derby Porcelain*. London, 1980.
Twyman, Michael, *Lithography 1800–1850*. London, 1970.
'University College London', *Country Life*, vol. 61, no.1587, 1927.
Unwin, George, *Samuel Oldknow and the Arkwrights: The Industrial Revolution in Marple and Stockport*. Manchester, 1924.
Van der Merwe, Pieter, *Clarkson Stanfield*. Sunderland, 1979.
Van Duin, Paul, 'Two Pairs of Cabinets on Stands by Thomas Parker', *Furniture History*, vol. 25, 1989.
Vaughan, William, *German Romanticism and English Art*. New Haven and London, 1979.
Vaughan, William, *Tracts on Docks and Commerce, Printed between the years 1793 & 1800, . . . with an Introduction, Memoir, and Miscellaneaous Pieces*. London, 1839.
Venning, Barry, 'Turner's Annotated Books: Opie's "Lectures on Painting"and Shee's "Elements of Art"', *Turner Studies*, vol. 2, nos. 1 and 2, 1982.
Verhandlungen des Vereins zur Beförderung des Gewerbfleisses in Preussen, vol. 12, 1833.
Vermeule, Cornelius, *European Art and the Classical Past*. Cambridge, Massachusetts, 1964.
Vickers, Michael, 'Value and Simplicity: Eighteenth-century Taste and the Study of Greek Vases', *Past and Present*, no. 116, 1987.
Victoria and Albert Museum Catalogue of Water Colour Paintings. London, 1927.
Victoria and Albert Museum Portrait Drawings. London, 1953.
Waagen, Dr. Gustav, *Works of Art and Artists in England*, vol. 2. London, 1838.
Waagen, Dr. Gustav, *Treasures of Art in Great Britain: being an account of the Chief Collections of Paintings, Drawings, Sculptures, Illuminated MSS &c. &c.*, 3 vols. London, 1854.
Wagenbreth, D., and Wchtler, E., *Dampfmaschinen*. Leipzig, 1986.
Wainwright, Clive, 'Some Objects from William Beckford's Collection now in the Victoria and Albert Museum', *Burlington Magazine*, vol. 113, 1971.
Wainwright, Clive, 'Pugin's Early Furniture', *Connoisseur*, vol. 191, 1976.
Wainwright, Clive, *The Romantic Interior: The British Collector at Home 1750–1830*. New Haven and London, 1989.
Waldron, Peter and Culme, John, 'The Newborough Plate', Sotheby's London sale catalogue, 27 February 1992.
Walker Richard, *Regency Portraits*, 2 vols. London, 1985.
Walker, John, *John Constable*. London, 1979.
Walker, John, 'Maria Cosway: An Undervalued Artist'. *Apollo*, vol. 123, no.291, 1986.
Walker, R. J., *A Catalogue of Paintings, Drawings, Engravings and Sculpture in the Palace of Westminster, compiled during 1959–72*, 4 vols. in typescript, 1988.
Walker, Richard, *The Savile Row Story*. London, 1988.
Walker, Stella A., *Horses of Renown*. London, 1954.
Walker, Susan, 'Clytie – a False Woman', in *Proceedings of the Colloquium held at the British Museum in conjunction with the exhibition Fake? The Art of Deception*. London, 1990.
Ward, Humphry, *History of the Athenaeum 1824–1925*. London, 1926.
Wark, Robert R., *Drawings by Flaxman from the Huntington Collection*. San Marino, California, 1970.
Warner, J. G. M., *A Century of Locomotive Building by Robert Stephenson & Co. 18231923*. London, 1923.
Warner, Oliver, *A Portrait of Lord Nelson*. London, 1968.
Watkin, David, *The English Vision. The Picturesque in Architecture, Landscape and Garden Design*. London, 1982.
Watkin, David, *The Life and Work of C.R. Cockerell*. London, 1974.
Watkin, David, *Thomas Hope 1769–1831 and the Neo-Classical Idea*. London, 1968.
Webb, Mrs. *The Annotated Index of the Royal Academy Lectures in the V&A Sculpture Collection*.
Weber, C. von, ed., *Reise-Briefe von Carl Maria von Weber an seine Gattin Carolina*. Leipzig, 1886
Webster, A. B., *Joshua Watson, The Story of a Layman 1771–1835*. London, 1954.
Wedmore, Frederick, *Constable: Lucas: With a Descriptive Catalogue of the Prints They did between Them*. London, 1914.
Weedon, Cyril, 'Dr. Syntax in the Glasshouse', *Glass Circle News*, no. 36, July 1987.
Wees, J. Duston and Campbell, Michael, *'Darkness Visible': The Prints of John Martin*. Williamstown, Massachusetts, 1986.
Werner, Alex and Lane, Nick, *Gateway to the East*. London, 1991.
Werner, J. G. M., *A Century of Locomotive Building by Robert Stephenson and Co 1823–1923*. London, 1923.
West, Shearer 'Thomas Lawrence's "Half History" Portraits and the Politics of Theatre', *Art History*, vol. 14, no. 2, 1991.
Westmacott, C. M., *Minutes of Council, A. Pindaric, The British Press, reprinted in The Spirt of the Public Journals for the year 1825*. London,1826.
Weston-Davies, W. H., 'The Surgical Instrument Maker: An Historical Perspective', *Journal of the Royal Society of Medicine*, vol. 82, 1989.
Westwood, J. N., *Locomotive Designers in the Age of Steam*. London, 1977.
Whinney, Margaret and Gunnis Rupert, *The Collection of Models of Joseph Flaxman R.A. at University College London*. London, 1967.
Whinney, Margaret, *Sculpture in Britain 1530–1830*. London 1988.
White, Elizabeth, *Pictorial Dictionary of English Eighteenth Century Furniture Design*. Woodbridge, 1990.
White, H. P., *A Regional History of the Railways of Great Britain, Vol. 3 Greater London*. Newton Abbot, 2nd edn. 1971.
White, John, Jr., *Some Account of the Proposed Improvements of the Western Part of London, by the Formation of Regent's Park*. London, 1813.
Whiter, Leonard, *Spode, A History of the Family, Factory and Wares from 1733–1833*. London, 1970.
Whitley, William T., 'Girtin's Panorama', *Connoisseur*, vol. 69, 1924.
Whitley, William T., *Art in England 1800–1820*, 2 vols. Cambridge, 1928.
Whitley, William T., *Art in England, 1821–1837*. Cambridge, 1930.
Whitley, William T., *Thomas Heaphy (1775–1835) First President of the Society of British Artists*. London, 1933.
Whittingham, Selby, 'A Most Liberal Patron: Sir John Fleming Leicester Bart., 1st Baron de Tabley, 1762–1827', *Turner Studies*, vol. 6, no. 2, 1986.
Wickwar, W. H., *The Struggle for the Freedom of the Press 1819–32*. London, 1928.
Wiener, J. H., *Radicalism and Freethought in Nineteenth-century Britain: The Life of Richard Carlile*. Westport, Connecticut, 1983.
Wightwick, George, 'The Life of an Architect', *Bentley's Miscellany*, vol. 34, 1853.
Wilcox, Scott Barnes, *Panoramas and Related Exhibitions in London*. M. Litt thesis, University of Edinburgh, 1976.
Wilcox, Scott, *David Cox: His Development as a Painter in Watercolours*. Yale University, New Haven, dissertation, 1984.
Wildman, Stephen, *David Cox, 1783–1859*. Birmingham, 1983.
Wilkins, William, *Letter to Lord Viscount Goderich on the Patronage of the Arts by the English Government*. Privately printed, 1831.
William Turner of Oxford (1789–1862). Arts Council, 1984–85.
Williams, D. E., *Life and Correspondence of Sir Thomas Lawrence*, 2 vols. London, 1831.
Williams, L. Pearce, *Michael Faraday*. London, 1965.
Williams, S. B., *Antique Blue and White Spode*. London, 1949.
Williamson, G. Jeffrey, 'Why was British Growth so Slow during the Industrial Revolution?', *Journal of Economic History*, vol. 44, 1984.
Wilton, Andrew, *British Watercolours 1750 to 1850*. Oxford, 1977.
Wilton, Andrew, *Constable's 'English Landscape Scenery*. London, 1979.
Wilton, Andrew, *The Life and Work of J. M. W. Turner*. Fribourg and London, 1979.
Wilton, Andrew, *Turner Watercolours in the Clore Gallery*. London, 1988.
Wilton, Andrew, 'The Keepsake Convention: Jessica and some related Pictures', *Turner Studies*, vol. 9, no. 2, 1989.
Wilton, Andrew, *Painting and Poetry: Turner's Verse Book and his Work of 1804–1812*. London, 1990.

Wilton-Ely, John, 'The Architectural Models of Sir John Soane: A Catalogue', *Architectural History*, vol. 12, 1969.

Wirth, Irmgard, *Johann Wilhelm Meil*. Berlin, 1970.

Witt, John, *William Henry Hunt*. London, 1982.

Woodforde, John, *The Story of the Bicycle*. London, 1970.

Woodhouse, Christopher, *The Philhellenes*. Princeton, 1971.

Woods, R. A., *The Bank of England: An Illustrated Visit Bank of England*. London, 1975.

Wormsbcher, Elisabeth, *Daniel Nikolaus*

Chodowiecki, Erklrungen und Erluterungen zu seinen Radierungen. Hanover, 1988.

Worsley, Giles, *Architectural Drawings of the Regency Period, 1790–1837*. London, 1991.

Worthington, J.H., 'Drawings by Charles Robert Cockerell R.A.', *Royal Institute of British Architects Journal*, vol. 29, 1932.

Wright, Charles and Fayle C Ernest, *A History of Lloyd's from the Founding of Lloyd's Coffee House to the Present Day*. London, 1928.

Wrigley, E. Anthony, 'Metropolitan Cities and their Hinterlands', in Erik Aerts and Peter Clark eds., *Metropolitan Cities and their*

Hinterlands in Early Modern Europe, Proceedings of Tenth International Economic History Congress. Leuven, 1990.

Wrigley, E. Anthony, *Continuity, Chance and Change: The Character of the Industrial Revolution in England*. Cambridge, 1988.

Wrigley, E. Anthony, *People, Cities and Wealth: The Tranformation of Traditional Society*. Oxford, 1987.

Wyman, C., 'The Early Techniques of Transfer Printing', *Transactions of the English Ceramic Circle*, vol. 10 part 4.

Yorke, James, 'Table of Triumph', *Country Life*, vol. 182, no. 44, 1988.

Young, Arthur, *Annals of Agriculture*, vol. 2. London, 1784.

Young, G. M., ed., *Early Victorian England*. London, 1934 and 1951 edn.

Zeitlin, Charlotte, 'Wedgwood Copies of a Vase in the Hamilton Collection', *Proceedings of the Wedgwood Society*, no. 7, 1968.

Ziegler, Philip, *King William IV*. London, 1971.

Ziegler, Philip, *The Sixth Great Power. Barings 1762–1929*. London, 1988.

Ziegler, Philip and Seward, Desmond, *Brooks's A Social History*. London, 1991.

EXHIBITIONS

Arts Council of Great Britain, 1961–62. Birmingham, City Art Gallery; Sheffield, Graves Art Gallery; Bolton, Bolton Museum and Art Gallery; Swansea, Glynn Vivbian Art Gallerty; Plymouth, City Art Gallery. *Diploma and other Pictures from the Collection of the Royal Academy*.

Arts Council of Great Britain, 1978. Leeds, Leeds City Art Gallery; Leicester, Leicester Museum and Art Gallery, Bristol, City of Bristol Museum and Art Gallery and London, Royal Academy of Arts, *Great Victorian Pictures*, catalogue by Rosemary Treble.

Arts Council of Great Britain, 1980–81. *British Watercolours 1760–1930 from the Birmingham Museum and Art Gallery*, catalogue by Richard Lockett.

Arts Council of Great Britain, 1982–83. London, Victoria and Albert Museum; Manchester, Whitworth Art Gallery; Bristol, City of Bristol Museum and Art Gallery, *John Sell Cotman 1782–1842*, catalogue by Miklos Rajnai

Arts Council of Great Britain, 1984–85. Woodstock, Oxfordshire County Museum; London, Bankside Gallery; Bolton, Bolton Museum and Art Gallery. *William Turner of Oxford*, catalogue by Timothy Wilcox and Christopher Titterington.

Barlaston, Staffordshire, Josiah Wedgwood and Sons and London, Wigmore Street, 1989–1990. *The Portland Vase*.

Bedford, Cecil Higgins Museum, 1961. *George Garrard*.

Berlin, Nationalgalerie, 1972. *William Turner 1775–1851*.

Birmingham, Birmingham Museums and Art Gallery, 1959. *David Cox 1783–1859*, catalogue by John Rowlands.

Birmingham, Birmingham Museums and Art Gallery, and London, Victoria and Albert

Museum, 1983–84. *David Cox 1783–1859*, catalogue by Stephen Wildman, John Murdoch and Richard Lockett.

Birmingham, Birmingham Museums and Art Gallery, 1984. *J. M. W. Turner*.

Birmingham, Birmingham Museums and Art Gallery, 1987. *The Glory of Watercolour*.

Birmingham, *Birmingham Society of Artists*, 1852.

Brighton, Royal Pavilion, Art Gallery and Museums, 1951. *John Nash Exhibition*.

Brighton, Brighton Museum and Manchester, Manchester City Art Gallery, 1983. *The Inspiration of Egypt*, catalogue edited by Patrick Conner.

Bristol, Bristol Art Gallery, 1973. *The Bristol School of Artists: Francis Danby and Painting in Bristol 1810–1840*, catalogue by Francis Greenacre.

Bristol, Bristol Art Gallery and London, Tate Gallery, 1988. *Francis Danby, 1793–1861*, catalogue by Francis Greenacre.

Bristol, Bristol Cathedral, 1977. *Victorian Narrative Painting*.

Brussels, Muse Moderne, 1929. *Exposition Rtrospective de Peinture Anglaise (XVIIIᵉ et XIXᵉ siècles)*.

Buxton, Buxton Museum and Art Gallery, 1983. *Tales Retold: Boccaccio's Decameron from the 17th Century to the 19th Century*.

Cambridge, Fitzwilliam Museum, 1970. *William Blake*, catalogue edited by David Bindman.

Cambridge, Fitzwilliam Museum, 1974. *Botanical Drawings from the Broughton Collection*, catalogue by John Raven.

Cambridge, Fitzwilliam Museum, 1979. *Drawings and Watercolours by Peter de Wint*, catalogue by David Scrase.

Cambridge, Fitzwilliam Museum and New Haven, Yale Center for British Art, 1982–83. *John Linnell, A Centennial Exhibition*,

catalogue by Katharine Crouan.

Cambridge, Fitzwilliam Museum, 1984. *Samuel Palmer and 'The Ancients'*, catalogue by Raymond Lister.

Cincinnati, Ohio, Taft Museum, 1986. *J. M. W. Turner: The Foundations of Genius*.

Cleveland, Ohio, Cleveland Museum of Art, 1984. *Dreadful Fire! Burning of the Houses of Parliament*, catalogue by Katherine Solender.

Cleveland, Ohio, Cleveland Museum of Art and Raleigh, North Carolina Museum of Art, 1991. *Nature into Art: English Landscape Watercolours from the British Museum*.

Derby, Royal Crown Derby Museum, 1990. *Painters and the Derby China Works*.

Detroit, Detroit Institute of Arts and Philadelphia, Philadelphia Museum of Art, 1968. *Romantic Art in Britain: Paintings and Drawings 1760–1860*, catalogue by Frederick Cummings and Allen Staley.

Dublin, *International Exhibition*, 1865.

Edinburgh, National Gallery of Scotland, 1985. *A Tribute to Wilkie*, catalogue by Lindsay Errington.

Edinburgh, Royal Scottish Museum, 1969. *Pomp: a Tribute from the City of London to the City of Edinburgh*.

Frankfurt on Main, Kunsthandwerk Museum, 1965. *Spode Copeland 1765–1965. Steingut und Porzellan*.

Glasgow, *International Exhibition*, 1888.

Hamburg, Kunsthalle, 1976. *William Turner und die Landschaft seiner Zeit*.

Hamburg, Kunsthalle, 1980. *Goya: The Age of Revolution*.

Leicester, Leicester Museums and Art Gallery, 1968. *The Victorian Vision of Italy*.

Liverpool, *Liverpool Academy*, 1854.

London, Thomas Agnew and Sons Ltd., 1966. *Peter de Wint*.

London, Thomas Agnew and Sons Ltd., 1967.

Loan Exhibition of Paintings and Watercolours by J. M. W. Turner, R. A.

London, Thomas Agnew and Sons Ltd., 1971. *English Pictures 1730–1870*.

London, Thomas Agnew and Sons Ltd., 1983. *110th Annual Exhibition of Watercolours and Drawings*.

London, Thomas Agnew and Sons Ltd., 1989. *Master Paintings*.

London, Arthur Ackermann and Son Ltd., 1983. *Ackermann 1783–1983: Bicentennial Exhibition*.

London, Bankside Gallery, 1991. *Visions of Venice: Watercolours and Drawings from Turner to Procktor*.

London, Barbican Art Gallery, 1984. *Capital Paintings*.

London, Barbican Art Gallery, 1984. *Getting London in Perspective*, catalogue by Gavin Stamp and Ralph Hyde.

London, Barbican Art Gallery, 1988–89. *Panoramania!*, catalogue by Ralph Hyde.

London, Bethnal Green Museum, 1899. *A Collection of Pottery and Porcelain illustrating Popular British History. Lent by Henry Willett Esq., of Brighton.*

London, British Institution, annual exhibitions of British paintings, 1805–67.

London, British Museum, 1957–58. *William Blake and his Circle*.

London, British Museum, 1985. *British Landscape Watercolours 1660–1860*, catalogue by Lindsay Stainton.

London, British Museum, 1985. *Charles Townley 1737–1805*.

London, British Museum, 1988–89. *Treasures for the Nation*.

London, British Museum, 1990. *Fake? The Art of Deception*, catalogue edited by Mark Jones.

London, 28 Broad Street, 1809–10. *William Blake Exhibition*.

London, Burlington Fine Arts Club, 1888. *Exhibition of Drawings in Water Colour and in Black and White by John Sell Cotman.*

London, P. and D. Colnaghi and Co. Ltd. and New Haven, Yale University Art Gallery, 1964–65. *English Drawings and Watercolours from the Collection of Mr. and Mrs. Paul Mellon.*

London, P. and D. Colnaghi and Co. Ltd., 1973. *A Loan Exhibition of Drawings, Watercolours, and Paintings by John Linnell and his Circle.*

London, Dulwich Picture Gallery, 1992. *Palaces of Art. Art Galleries in Britain 1790–1990*, catalogue edited by Giles Waterfield.

London, Earl's Court, 1897. *Victorian Era Exhibition.*

London, Egyptian Hall, 1822. *John Martin Exhibition.*

London, Egyptian Hall, 1828. *Benjamin Robert Haydon Exhibition.*

London, Goupil Gallery, 1922. *Loan Exhibition.*

London, *Great Exhibition*, 1851.

London, Guildhall Art Gallery, 1971. *London and the Greater Painters,* catalogue by J. L. Howgego.

London, Hayward Gallery, 1975. *The Georgian Playhouse. Actors, Artists, Audiences and Architecture 1730–1830*, catalogue by Iain Mackintosh and Geoffrey Ashton.

London, Hazlitt, Gooden and Fox, 1975. *John Martin.*

London, Heinz Gallery, Royal Institute of British Architects, 1984. *The Art of the Architect*, with catalogue by Margaret Richardson and Jill Lever.

London, Heinz Gallery, Royal Institute of British Architects, 1991. *Architectural Drawings of the Regency Period, 1790–1837*, catalogue by Giles Worsley.

London, *International Exhibition*, 1862.

London, Kenwood, Iveagh Bequest and Nottingham, University Art Gallery. 1991. *The Artist's Model*, catalogue by Ilaria Bignamini and Martin Postle.

London, M. C. C., 1987. *M. C. C. Bicentenary Exhibition.*

London, Mallett and Son Ltd. *The Jokelson Collection*, 1991–92.

London, The Museum of London, 1980. *Covent Garden.*

London, The Museum of London, 1981. *London Delineated.*

London, The Museum of London, 1984. *Paintings Politics & Porter. Samuel Whitbread II 1764–1815 and British Art,* catalogue by Stephen Deuchar.

London, The Museum of London, 1987. *Londoners,* catalogue by Celina Fox.

London, The Museum of London, 1987–89. *Whitefriars, The Unique Glasshouse.*

London, The Museum of London, 1989. *The Lord Mayor, The City and the River.*

London, The Museum of London, 1989. *This Gorgeous Mouchoir.*

London, The Museum of London, 1991. *Treasures and Trinkets*, catalogue by Tessa Murdoch.

London, National Army Museum, 1973. *London's Citizen Soldiers.*

London, National Portrait Gallery and Dublin, National Gallery of Ireland, 1972. *Daniel Maclise 1806–1870*, catalogue by Richard Ormond and John Turpin.

London, National Portrait Gallery, 1976. *Vanity Fair,* catalogue by Eileen Harris and Richard Ormond.

London, National Portrait Gallery, 1979. *Sir Thomas Lawrence 1769–1830,* catalogue by Michael Levey.

London, National Portrait Gallery, 1981. *Sir Francis Chantrey 1781–1841, Sculptor of the Great,* catalogue by Alex Potts..

London, National Portrait Gallery, 1991–92. *Michael Faraday 1791–1867.*

London, New Gallery, 1891. *Exhibition of the Royal House of Guelph.*

London, 145 Piccadilly, 1939. *Royal and Historical Treasures.*

London, Queen's Gallery, 1966–67. *Animal Painting: Van Dyke to Nolan.*

London, Queen's Gallery, 1991–92. *Carlton House. The Past Glories of George IV's Palace.*

London, Royal Academy of Arts Summer Exhibitions, 1798–

London, Royal Academy of Arts Winter Exhibitions, 1885, 1889, 1907. *The Old Masters.*

London, Royal Academy of Arts and Victoria and Albert Museum, 1972. *The Age of Neo-Classicism.*

London, Royal Academy of Arts, 1893. *Works by Old Masters including a Collection of Water Colour Drawings &c. by William Blake.*

London, Royal Academy of Arts, 1934. *Exhibition of British Art c.1000–1860.*

London, Royal Academy of Arts, 1951–52. *The First Hundred Years of the Royal Academy.*

London, Royal Academy of Arts, 1957. *British Portraits.*

London, Royal Academy of Arts, 1961. *Sir Thomas Lawrence P. R. A.*

London, Royal Academy of Arts, 1964–65. *Painting in England 1700–1850*, catalogue by Basil Taylor.

London, Royal Academy of Arts, 1968–69. *Royal Academy of Arts Bicentenary Exhibition 1768–1968.*

London, Royal Academy of Arts, 1970. *Two Hundred Years of Spode.*

London, Royal Academy of Arts, 1974–75. *Turner 1775–1851*, catalogue by Martin Butlin, Evelyn Joll, Andrew Wilton and John Gage.

London, Royal Academy of Arts, 1979. *John Flaxman, R.A.*, catalogue edited by David Bindman.

London, Royal Academy of Arts, 1982–83. *Royal Opera House Retrospective 1732–1982*, catalogue by Geoffrey Ashton and Iain Mackintosh.

London, Science Museum, 1969. *Brunel Bicentenary Exhibition.*

London, Science Museum, 1978. *Josiah Wedgwood: The Arts and Sciences United.*

London, Science Museum, 1991. *Charles Babbage and his Calculating Engines*, catalogue by Doron Swade.

London, Science Museum, 1991–92. *Michael Faraday and the Modern World.*

London, Society of Painters in Water-Colours, annual exhibitions, 1804–

London, Somerset House, 1977. *London and the Thames: Paintings of Three Centuries,* catalogue by Harley Preston.

London, South Kensington Museum, 1864. *William Mulready.*

London, South Kensington Museum, 1866–68. *First, Second and Third Exhibitions . . . of National Portraits.*

London, Spink and Son, 1973. *The Old Watercolour Society and its Founder Members 1804–1812.*

London, Tate Gallery, 1959. *The Romantic Movement*, catalogue by Geoffrey Grigson, Michael Kitson and others.

London, Tate Gallery, 1960. *William Hogarth.*

London, Tate Gallery, 1973. *Landscape in Britain c.1750–1850*, catalogue by Leslie Parris.

London, Tate Gallery and Royal Academy of Arts, 1974–75. *Turner 1775–1851*, catalogue by Martin Butlin, Andrew Wilton and John Gage.

London, Tate Gallery, 1976. *Constable: Paintings, Watercolours and Drawings*, catalogue by Leslie Parris, Ian Fleming-Williams and Conal Shields.

London, Tate Gallery, 1978. *William Blake*, catalogue by Martin Butlin.

London, Tate Gallery, 1981. *Augustus Wall Callcott*, catalogue by David Blayney Brown.

London, Tate Gallery, 1982. *James Ward. Gordale Scar. An Essay in the Sublime,* catalogue by Edward J. Nygren.

London, Tate Gallery, 1982. *Sir Edwin Landseer*, catalogue by Richard Ormond.

London, Tate Gallery, 1989. *Jacques-Laurent Agasse,* catalogue by Rene Loche, Colston Sanger and others.

London, Tate Gallery, 1990. *Painting and Poetry: Turner's Verse Book and His Work of 1804–12*, catalogue by Andrew Wilton.

London, Tate Gallery, 1991. *Constable*, catalogue by Leslie Parris and Ian Fleming-Williams.

London, Tate Gallery, 1991. *Turner's Rivers of Europe: The Rhine, Meuse and Mosel*, catalogue by Cecilia Powell.

London, University College London, Strang Print Room, 1985. *William Wilkins, R.A., Architect and Antiquary*, catalogue by Nicholas Dawton.

London, Victoria and Albert Museum, 1926. *Exhibition of Drawings, Etchings and Woodcuts by Samuel Palmer and other Disciples of William Blake.*

London, Victoria and Albert Museum, 1951. *The Artist and the Theatre.*

London, Victoria and Albert Museum, 1954. *Royal Plate from Buckingham Palace and Windsor Castle.*

London, Victoria and Albert Museum, 1967. *Great Britain – USSR: an historical Exhibition.*

London, Victoria and Albert Museum and Royal Academy of Arts, 1972. *The Age of Neo-Classicism.*

London, Victoria and Albert Museum, 1974. *Byron*, catalogue by Anthony Burton and John Murdoch.

London, Victoria and Albert Museum, 1978–79. *Samuel Palmer: A Vision Recaptured.*

London, Victoria and Albert Museum, Manchester, Whitworth Art Gallery, Bristol, City of Bristol Art Gallery, 1982–83. *John Sell Cotman 1782–1842*, catalogue edited by Miklos Rajnai.

London, Victoria and Albert Museum, 1986. *William Mulready,* catalogue by Marcia Pointon.

London, Victoria and Albert Museum, 1987. *Painters and the Derby China Works,* catalogue by John Murdoch and John Twitchett.

London, Victoria and Albert Museum, 1992. *The Art of Death: Objects from the English Death Ritual.*

London, Wedgwood House, 1984. *Wedgwood in London. 225th Anniversary Exhibition 1759–1984.*

London, Western Bazaar, Bond Street, 1830. *Benjamin Robert Haydon Exhibition.*

London, Wildenstein, 1986. *William Blake and his Contemporaries.*

Louisville, Kentucky, J. B. Speed Museum, 1990. *Circus and Sport: English Earthenware Figures 1780–1840*, catalogue by Pat Halfpenny and Stella Beddoe.

Madrid, Prádo, 1988–89, *Pinctura Britanica de Hogarth a Turner.*

Manchester, *Art Treasures exhibition,* 1857.

Manchester, City Art Gallery, 1968. *Art and the Industrial Revolution*, catalogue by Arthur Elton.

Manchester, Whitworth Art Gallery, 1961. *The Norwich School: Loan Exhibition of Works by Crome and Cotman and their Followers*

Mexico City, Museo de Arte Modero,1979. *Exposicion del gran pintor ingles William Turner: oleos y acuarelas.*

Munich, Haus der Kunst, 1979–80, *Zwei Jahrhunderte Englische Malerei.*

New Haven, Yale Center for British Art, 1977. *English Landscape 1630–1850: Drawings, Prints and Books from the Paul Mellon Collection*, catalogue by Christopher White.

New Haven, Yale Center for British Art, 1977. *The Cottage of Content; or, Toys, Games, and Amusements of Nineteenth Century England*, catalogue by John Brewer, John B. Thomas, Paula D. Matthews and Deborah S. Berman.

New Haven, Yale Center for British Art, 1980. *Painters and Engraving, The Reproductive Print from Hogarth to Wilkie*, catalogue by David Alexander and Richard T. Godfrey.

New Haven, Yale Center for British Art, 1981. *Works of Splendour and Imagination: The Exhibition Watercolour, 1770–1870*, catalogue by Jane Bayard.

New Haven, Yale Center for British Art, 1984. *Painting in Focus: John Scarlett Davies 'The Interior of the British Institution Gallery'.*

New Haven, Yale Center for British Art; Washington D. C., Library of Congress; Ottawa, National Gallery of Canada and London, Victoria and Albert Museum, 1984–85. *English Caricature 1620 to the Present,* catalogue by Richard Godrey, John Riely and Linel Lambourne.

New Haven, Yale Center for British Art and Raleigh, North Carolina Museum of Art, 1987. *Sir David Wilkie of Scotland*, catalogue by H. A. D. Miles and D. B. Brown.

New York, Frick Collection; Pittsburgh, Frick Art Museum and Baltimore, Baltimore Museum of Art, 1990. *The Art of Thomas Rowlandson,* catalogue by John Hayes.

New York, Museum of Modern Art, 1956. *Masters of British Painting 1800–1950.*

New York, Museum of Modern Art, 1966. *Turner: Imagination and Reality.*

New York, New York Public Library; Bloomington, Indiana University Art Museum and Chicago, Chicago Historical Society, 1987–88. *William Wordsworth and the Age of English Romanticism*, catalogue by Jonathan Wordsworth, Michael C. Jaye and Robert Woof.

New York, Pierpont Morgan Library and London, Royal Academy of Arts, 1972–73, *English Drawings and Watercolours 1550–1850 in the Collection of Mr. and Mrs. Paul Mellon*, catalogue by John Baskett and Dudley Snelgrove.

Newcastle upon Tyne, Laing Art Gallery, 1962. *Two Centuries of British Water Colour Painting.*

Newcastle upon Tyne, Laing Art Gallery, 1970. *John Martin 1789–1854: Artist – Reformer – Engineer.*

Norwich, *Art Circle*, 1888.

Norwich, Castle Museum, 1955. *A Selection of English Watercolours.*

Norwich, Castle Museum, 1969. *A Decade of English Naturalism 1810–20.*

Norwich, *Society of Artists,* 1807, 1808.

Nottingham, Castle Museum and Art Gallery, 1965. *R. P. Bonington.*

Osaka, Hankyu Department Store, 1991. *The Landscape of the Lakes.*

Oslo, Kunstindustrimuseet, 1966. *Spode Copeland 1765–1965. Englesk Stentoy og Porselen.*

Oxford, Examination Schools, 1906. *Loan Portraits.*

Paris, Galerie Ren Drouin, 1947. *William Blake (1757–1827).*

Paris, Grand Palais, 1983–84. *J. M. W. Turner.*

Paris, Grand Palais, 1991–92. *Géricault,* catalogue by Sylvain Laveissire and Régis Michel.

Paris, Louvre, 1938. *La Peinture Anglaise XVIIIe et XIXe Siècles.*

Paris, Petit Palais, 1972, *La Peinture Romantique Anglaise et les Préraphaélites.*

Pescara, Castello Gizzi, 1983. *Blake e Dante, Casa de Dante in Abruzzo.*

Philadelphia, *International Exhibition*, 1876.

Philadelphia, Philadelphia Museum of Art and Detroit, Detroit Institute of Arts, 1968. *Romantic Art in Britain. Paintings and Drawings 1760–1860,* catalogue by Frederick Cummings and Alan Staley.

Philadelphia, Philadelphia Museum of Art and London, Tate Gallery, 1981–82. *Sir Edwin Landseer*, catalogue by Richard Ormond.

Plymouth, City Art Gallery, 1965–66. *Sir Charles Lock Eastlake P.R.A. 1793–1865*, catalogue by Eugene I. Schuster and A. A. Cumming.

Port Sunlight, Lady Lever Art Gallery, 1948. *Theatrical Exhibition.*

Queensland Art Gallery, Museums and Art Galleries of the Northern Territory, Art Gallery of Western Australia, Art Gallery of New South Wales, Tasmanian Museum and Art Gallery, Cambridge, Fitzwilliam Museum, 1982–83. *Town, Country, Shore and Sea. British Watercolours from Anthony Van Dyck to Paul Nash.*

Richmond, Virginia Museum of Fine Arts, 1963. *Painting in England 1700–1850.*

Rouen, Musée des Beaux-Arts, 1981–82. *Géricault: Tout l'Oeuvre Gravé et Pièces en Rapport,* catalogue by François Bergot.

Sheffield, Graves Art Gallery, 1961. *Samuel Palmer.*

Shrewsbury, Music Hall, 1898. *Loan Exhibition of Shropshire Antiquities.*

Stoke-on-Trent, City Museum and Art Gallery, 1983. *Copeland-Spode 1733–1983. Potters to the Royal Family since 1806.*

Stoke-on-Trent, City Museum and Art Gallery, 1991. *Fantastic Figures.*

Sunderland, Northern Centre for Contemporary Art, 1988. *The Circus Comes to Town*, catalogue by George Speaight and Rosemary Hill.

Sunderland, Sunderland Museum and Art Gallery, 1979. *The Spectacular Career of Clarkson Stanfield 1793–1867: Seaman, Scene Painter, Royal Academician,* catalogue by Pieter van der Merwe and Roger Took.

Swansea, Glynn Vivian Art Gallery, 1953. *David Cox (1783–1859).*

Sydney, 1964. Victoria and Albert Museum Loan Exhibition.

The Hague, Gemeentmuseum, 1978–79. *Turner 1775–1851.*

Tokyo, National Museum of Western Art and Kyoto, National Gallery of Modern Art, 1971. *English Landscape Painting.*

Tokyo, 1987. *British Caricature, Hogarth to Hockney.*

Tokyo, National Museum of Western Art, 1990. *William Blake.*

Toronto, George R. Gardiner Museum of Ceramic Art, 1988. *Painters and the Derby China Works.*

Washington D.C., International Exhibitions Foundation, 1983. *Paintings from the Royal Academy: Two Centuries of British Art.*

Washington D.C., National Gallery of Art, 1963. *Turner Watercolours from the British Museum.*

Washington D.C., National Gallery of Art, 1985. *The Treasure Houses of Britain*, catalogue edited by Gervase Jackson-Stops.

York, National Railway Museum, 1988. *Impressions of a Railway – The London and Birmingham Railway 1838–1988.*